TO RUN THE WORLD

What would it feel like *To Run the World?* The Soviet rulers spent the Cold War trying desperately to find out. In this panoramic new history of the conflict that defined the postwar era, Sergey Radchenko provides an unprecedented deep dive into the psychology of the Kremlin's decision-making. He reveals how the Soviet struggle with the United States and China reflected an irreconcilable contradiction between its ambitions as a self-proclaimed superpower and the leader of global revolution. This tension drove Soviet policies from Stalin's postwar scramble for territory to Khrushchev's reckless overseas adventurism and nuclear brinksmanship, Brezhnev's jockeying for influence in the third world, and Gorbachev's failed attempts to reinvent Moscow's claims to greatness. Perennial insecurities, delusions of grandeur, and desire for recognition propelled Moscow on a headlong quest for global power, with dire consequences and painful legacies that continue to shape our world.

Sergey Radchenko is the Wilson E. Schmidt Distinguished Professor at the Henry A. Kissinger Center for Global Affairs, Johns Hopkins School of Advanced International Studies, based at SAIS-Europe, Bologna. He is a historian of the Cold War, and an expert on Russian and Chinese foreign and security policies. Previous publications include *Two Suns in the Heavens: The Sino-Soviet Struggle for Supremacy* and *Unwanted Visionaries: The Soviet Failure in Asia.*

"The historiography of the Cold War was once too narrowly focused on two super-powers. More recently, it has become blurred by overemphasis on minor players. Sergey Radchenko's *To Run the World* brilliantly reconciles the two literatures. Using hitherto unavailable Russian and Chinese sources, he shows that the Cold War was from the outset a 'three-body problem,' with the Soviets seeking an unattainable parity with the United States, while China alternately attracted and repelled the other two. American policymakers in the 1960s and 1970s sought 'détente' with the Soviets, believing there could be 'linkage' to other issues of mutual interest. This was to underestimate the Soviet imperative to retain leadership of revolutionary forces around the world in a bitter competition with Beijing. This is a model of historical writing: scrupulously researched and elegantly presented, *To Run the World* shows how a volatile interplay of ideological, geopolitical, and psychological forces drove the Cold War on its erratic path."

Niall Ferguson, Milbank Family Senior Fellow, the Hoover Institution, and author of *Kissinger: 1923–1968: The Idealist*

"A tour de force. Based on a plethora of previously unmined Soviet (and Chinese) sources, *To Run the World* is a thought-provoking, comprehensive narrative of the Soviet Union's place and aspirations in the global Cold War."

Kristina Spohr, author of *Post Wall, Post Square: Rebuilding the World after 1989*

"If we are entering a new cold war with China, then we should study the lessons from the last Cold War. Radchenko's *To Run the World* is the place to start. Drawing on new archival material, insightful analysis, and brilliant writing, Radchenko's book will instantly become the go-to source for understanding Soviet behavior during the Cold War. This book sets such a high standard that I wonder if any more books on this subject will ever be written."

Michael McFaul, author of *From Cold War to Hot Peace: An American Ambassador in Putin's Russia*

"Sergey Radchenko has produced what can only be described as an invaluable and 'magisterial' book – the fitting culmination of a ten-year odyssey to plumb the archival depths for new insight into the bases of the Soviet Union's power and global ambitions during the Cold War. Radchenko's incisive analysis, crisp prose, and vivid descriptions make for pleasurable and rewarding reading. His final observations on the USSR's craving for 'greatness before history' and its leaders' assertions of the 'right to exceptionalism,' help explain why Vladimir Putin decided to invade Ukraine and confront the West in 2022. Putin has the same drivers and motivations as his Soviet forebears."

Fiona Hill, author of *There is Nothing for You Here: Finding Opportunity in the 21st Century*

"Enthralling and masterful, *To Run the World* is a tour de force of riveting narrative, fascinating new archival research, fresh analysis and acute portraits of global potentates, that reassesses the big questions of the Cold War from Stalin and Mao to Reagan, Deng, Gorbachev, and on to Putin, and illuminates not only the superpowers but also the global players from Vietnam to Cuba and Angola: magisterial world history at its finest."

Simon Sebag Montefiore, author of *The World: A Family History of Humanity*

TO RUN THE WORLD

THE KREMLIN'S COLD WAR BID FOR GLOBAL POWER

SERGEY RADCHENKO

Shaftesbury Road, Cambridge CB2 8EA, United Kingdom

One Liberty Plaza, 20th Floor, New York, NY 10006, USA

477 Williamstown Road, Port Melbourne, VIC 3207, Australia

314–321, 3rd Floor, Plot 3, Splendor Forum, Jasola District Centre, New Delhi – 110025, India

103 Penang Road, #05–06/07, Visioncrest Commercial, Singapore 238467

Cambridge University Press is part of Cambridge University Press & Assessment, a department of the University of Cambridge.

We share the University's mission to contribute to society through the pursuit of education, learning and research at the highest international levels of excellence.

www.cambridge.org
Information on this title: www.cambridge.org/9781108477352
DOI: 10.1017/9781108769679

© Sergey Radchenko 2024

This publication is in copyright. Subject to statutory exception and to the provisions of relevant collective licensing agreements, no reproduction of any part may take place without the written permission of Cambridge University Press & Assessment.

First published 2024

A catalogue record for this publication is available from the British Library

Library of Congress Cataloging-in-Publication Data
Names: Radchenko, Sergey, author.
Title: To run the world : the Kremlin's Cold War bid for global power / Sergey Radchenko.
Description: Cambridge ; New York, NY : Cambridge University Press, 2024. | Includes bibliographical references and index.
Identifiers: LCCN 2023031411 | ISBN 9781108477352 (hardback) | ISBN 9781108769679 (ebook)
Subjects: LCSH: Soviet Union – Foreign relations – 1945–1991. | Soviet Union – Politics and government – 1945–1991. | Cold War.
Classification: LCC DK268.5 .R33 2024 | DDC 327.47009/045–dc23/eng/20231120
LC record available at https://lccn.loc.gov/2023031411

ISBN 978-1-108-47735-2 Hardback

Cambridge University Press & Assessment has no responsibility for the persistence or accuracy of URLs for external or third-party internet websites referred to in this publication and does not guarantee that any content on such websites is, or will remain, accurate or appropriate.

To Odd Arne Westad
A scholar, a teacher, a friend

Contents

Introduction		*page* 1

PART I AMBITION

1	The Postwar World	17
2	The Parting of Ways	39
3	Stalin in Europe	69
4	Stalin in Asia	111

PART II HUBRIS

5	Love Us as We Are	145
6	The Golden Hoop	171
7	Twin Crises	199
8	Killing Flies	230
9	The Spirit of Camp David	251
10	Berlin	270
11	Cuba	294

PART III DECLINE

12	Vietnam	331
13	Detente	359
14	Yom Kippur	392
15	Decline	427
16	Tensions Mount	452
17	The Final Nail	474

PART IV COLLAPSE

18	Fear	507
19	Hope	539
20	Collapse	560
	Conclusion	589

CONTENTS

Acknowledgments	604
List of Figures	607
Notes	610
Bibliographical Essay	711
Index	713

INTRODUCTION

"In Stalingrad I witnessed an eerie sight," Nikita recalled. "Our people were collecting German corpses across the city ... If the corpses lay around and began decomposing, we could have an epidemic." The Battle of Stalingrad (1942–43) had raged for months. Hardly a building was left standing in some of the most ferocious urban warfare the world had ever seen. Each side's casualties numbered in the hundreds of thousands, but it was the Soviets who ultimately prevailed. The tide had turned on the Third Reich. "We tried to remove the corpses as quickly as possible and burn them ... There were many corpses, thousands of them. The corpses were piled in layers: a layer of corpses and two layers of railway sleepers, and these were set on fire. Huge piles were on fire ... They made a very grim impression ... Napoleon or someone else said that the enemy's corpse has a sweet smell. I don't know about the others but I did not find the smell sweet at all. Nor was it pleasant to behold the sight."[1]

Recollections of horror only deepened the sense of personal grief: in March 1943 Nikita lost his son whose plane was shot down by the Germans in an air duel. His remains were never found.

Several months later, in the autumn of 1943, Lyonya very nearly lost his life. He had been involved in a landing operation, aimed at capturing Novorossiisk, a Russian Black Sea port. The 30-something-year-old Lyonya was not himself doing much fighting – a party official, he spent the early months of war working out the logistics for the retreating Soviet forces – but this time he was close to the action – too close, it turned out. During one of the trips to the bridgehead, his boat hit a mine. He suffered a head injury and was fished out of the sea unconscious. The injury made itself felt years later, when Lyonya's speech began to slur.[2] Few knew about it and, unknowingly, endlessly mocked him for mispronouncing words. He would often recall a conversation with his father, Ilya, who had asked him about the height of the Eiffel tower. Upon learning that it stood 300 meters high, Lyonya's father said that he wanted to build a tower just like the Eiffel tower on top of Mount Everest, hang Hitler and his associates from that

INTRODUCTION

tower, "and then give telescopes to people so everyone could see their fate." "Then," he added, "there would be no wars."[3]

Misha was just a 10-year-old boy when the war began. His father was drafted in August 1941, and miraculously survived through the end, finishing the war on a hospital bed in southern Poland. Misha himself nearly succumbed to famine in 1944, when many in his village starved. He remembered one particularly shocking scene. Once in the spring of 1943, after the snows had melted, he and his fellow boys came across dead Soviet soldiers. "You can hardly describe this," he recalled years later. "Decomposed, gnawed skulls in rusty steel helmets, bleached hand bones protruding from rotten uniforms, grasping rifles ... They were lying there, unburied, in the dirty sludge of trenches and craters, beholding us with black, gaping eye sockets." Who could forget a sight like this? Not Misha, who had this to say of it all: "When the war ended, I was 14. Our generation is the generation of war children. It burned us, leaving an impression on our characters, on our entire worldview."[4]

When the Second World War ended, much of Soviet Europe was ashes and rubble. Some 1,710 cities and over 70,000 villages were completely or partially destroyed. Twenty-five million people were left homeless. Nearly 32,000 industrial enterprises lay demolished, accounting for 60 percent of prewar steel and coal production. Adding to the toll were some 40,000 levelled hospitals, 43,000 libraries, and 84,000 educational institutions. The uncannily exact price tag of the losses stood at 679 billion rubles, which was roughly equivalent to *four times* the entire expenditure of the last prewar national budget. These were just material losses; as horrible as they were, they were dwarfed by the human tragedy. An estimated 25.5 million Soviet citizens perished in the war, and this number does not include another 13.9 million of the dead children (up to and including 4 years old), and the unborn (due to a precipitous decline in birth rates during the war). There was not a family left untouched by the conflict.[5]

When Nikita, Lyonya, and Misha recalled the horrors of war, they were adding their voices to the collective story of suffering to which millions of their countrymen could easily relate. Nikita Khrushchev, Lyonya (Leonid) Brezhnev, and Misha (Mikhail) Gorbachev were deeply traumatized by the Second World War years before they took the reins of power in the Soviet Union. That trauma – their personal trauma, and the collective trauma, and the bitterness, and the humiliation, and the pride at having prevailed despite it all – added to the determination to shape the future in a way that would assure for the Soviet Union its security, and its place of honor among the great and the mighty of this world. The rest, they thought, would take care of itself.

INTRODUCTION

This book retells the story of the making and the breaking of Soviet superpower. The story it tells begins at the end of the Second World War and ends with the Soviet collapse in 1991, overlapping with that bitter, protracted conflict we call the Cold War.

So much has been written about the Cold War that it well near beggars belief that anyone would still attempt to retell the story, traveling down all those roads well traveled by many a brave and brilliant historian. There must be a very good reason to reopen the old debates.

Here is that reason. The book offers a radical new interpretation of the underlying motivations of Soviet foreign policy, focusing on Moscow's narratives of legitimacy, and on how these narratives were negotiated through constant interaction between Soviet ambitions and those who recognized and so legitimized them, or those who refused to recognize them and, through their refusal, also (unexpectedly) legitimized them. While the way Soviet ambitions interacted with external audiences is something that yields itself to reasonable analysis, the sources of these ambitions must, of necessity, remain metaphysical. Why do some people aspire to greatness while others are content with their lives? Why do some states aspire to a special role in history while others pass history in relative obscurity? There is no easy explanation, but if one observation can be made, it is that the sources of Soviet ambitions are not specifically Soviet but both precede and postdate the Soviet Union, overlapping with the Cold War.

And, obviously, the Soviets were not unique in their ambitions. Throughout history, some countries aspired to greatness, while others did not; kingdoms were made and lost; empires rose and fell.

Ambition seems to be as universal a trait as any. The relationship between ambition and recognition has been probed by other scholars, not least Francis Fukuyama in the much-maligned *End of History*. What makes the end of history possible, argues Fukuyama, is that liberal democracy permits the kind of recognition of individual worth as to render further historical development unnecessary. We would all feel legitimated and empowered through a form of mutual recognition. Indeed, the subject of "recognition" is front and center in most of Fukuyama's work. He traces it to Plato's discussion (in his *Republic*) of the "third part of the human soul" (which craves recognition) and spends much time perusing Hegel's commentary on the question, in the part where Hegel (as interpreted by the Russian-French philosopher Alexander Kojeve) talks about the master's desire for recognition as the master.

All of this is very good, the reader will say – only it is not clear what any of this has to do with the Soviet Union's Cold War. Let me explain.

3

INTRODUCTION

There are different ways of thinking about Moscow's foreign policy. One approach is to emphasize ideology – a slippery concept, used unsparingly by historians to describe a variety of phenomena, a catch-all phrase, an intellectual shortcut that often obscures more than it explains. Since ideology plays an important role in this book, too, let me offer the following definition. Ideology is a way of thinking about the world and one's place in it, and a set of prescriptions for either changing them (the world, and the place), or keeping them unchanged. The desire to change the world, and one's place in it, evidently has to do with the degree of satisfaction with the existing order of things, and this is as true for individuals, as it is for states. Satisfaction requires rationalization in status quo terms; the lack of satisfaction – in revolutionary terms. But since satisfaction is a fleeting sentiment that can and does change, ideology, too, changes accordingly. Much Cold War historiography regards the Soviet ideology as something fixed (as, for instance, described in the Marxist-Leninist canon). In reality, Soviet ideology (i.e. the Kremlin's view of the world, and the Soviet place in it, and the associated prescriptions) changed continuously even if the Marxist-Leninist canon remained largely the same.

In other words, Marxism-Leninism itself does not get us very far in understanding Soviet behavior. It was an ill-fitting cloth that never adequately draped the incongruent outlines of Moscow's ambition.

Another important source of Soviet conduct was the quest for security (in the benign version) or outright imperialism (more commonly accepted). Security and ideology are in fact interrelated concepts. One might even describe one as a subset of the other. For example, one's dissatisfaction with one's place in the world may be a result of thinking underpinned by security considerations (threats to one's physical survival), or, relatedly, dissatisfaction with the world itself (if that world is deemed implacably hostile). The resultant prescription may be, for instance, to build up the army to increase one's own security, or to promote subversive revolutionary activities as a way of changing the world into something more palatable. It thus becomes evident that analytically distinguishing security and ideology is an unrewarding and a self-contradictory undertaking. Most historians of the Cold War will be wise to steer well clear of such philosophical observations since probing our very discourse on ideology and security will yield such mind-boggling uncertainties as to frustrate even the most patient reader.

Assuming, for the sake of the argument, that ideology and security are something altogether distinct, it is still possible to fuse them in the way that, for example, historians Vladislav Zubok and Constantine Pleshakov did when they described the Kremlin's policy making in terms

INTRODUCTION

of "the revolutionary-imperial paradigm." In that reading, imperialism, like Communist ideology, could be the prime mover or it could simply rationalize actions taken for other reasons. For example, one could conceive that Moscow wanted an overseas empire for the sake of the empire, or for the sake of Communism. Disentangling these kinds of motivations is often impossible (and most of the time the actors directly involved could not themselves distinguish between them). This is the reason why historians seek refuge in multicausality.

But where does this argument overlap with ambition, which, we know from philosophers, is a key driver of human behavior?

To answer this question, we must try to understand what the Cold War represented. Was it not just another stage in the long story of the rise and fall of great powers, a story that neither began with, nor ended with the Cold War? But surely there was something unique, too. Unlike previous conflicts between great powers, the Cold War was characterized by the struggle over the best method of ordering the human society, a struggle over the paths towards modernity, which historian Odd Arne Westad has so eloquently and convincingly written about. The whole world became involved in this struggle in one way or another. It was a truly global contest between the Soviet Union and the United States for Hegelian recognition as masters, not just in the immediate physical sense (i.e. through a hub-and-spoke system of allied relations) but also in the philosophical sense: as masters of History. Melvyn Leffler has called it a struggle "for the soul of mankind." Mankind was called upon to accept Moscow's and Washington's global ambition; that is to say, to legitimate this ambition through their recognition.

Legitimacy is a famous can of worms, and since it is central to this book, it is a good idea to consider what it means. The usual definition encompasses notions like legality and justice (or morality).[6] Thus, the Soviet leaders were invariably concerned about legality and justice of their and their country's position in the global hierarchy (and they perceived the world as being hierarchically organized). The emphasis was more often on justice than on legality, the premise being that the Soviet Union for one reason or another *deserved* its high perch in the global order. Being *recognized* by others as legitimately occupying this perch was a central preoccupation of Soviet foreign policy from Stalin to Gorbachev. It was always a challenge, for, as Henry Kissinger had once put it, it entailed a process of reconciliation of a nation's vision of itself with its vision by other powers.[7]

Risking a dangerous analogy, one might say that the process was not unlike that experienced by individuals who perceive one another in time and space. Each should have an understanding of the other that broadly aligns with that other's understanding of him or herself. As the Scottish psychiatrist R.D. Laing argued, "if there are discrepancies of a sufficiently radical kind remaining after attempts to align them have failed, there is no alternative but that one of [them] must be insane."[8] No one would of course accuse the Soviet leaders of being insane but it is nonetheless interesting that what the Soviets saw as their "legitimate" interests were often not seen as particularly "legitimate" by anybody else, leading to a kind of ontological insecurity on the Soviet part that was compensated for by hubris and aggression.

But was the Soviet ambition merely in changing Moscow's standing in the world, or changing the world itself? This does not have to be an either/or question, since by changing the world, the Soviets could *ipso facto* improve their standing in the world, for presumably the rearrangement would be to their benefit. By the same token, by changing their position in the world, they could change the world, since a world that allowed Moscow an ever higher perch would be a very different world from the one that did not. Both scenarios, however, could satisfy the Soviet craving for greatness, which is why this book is concerned above all with Soviet ambition and not Soviet ideology.

Legitimacy has internal, and not just external, sources. This is where the subject of the Soviet revolutionary ideology returns to reclaim the lost turf. For the Soviet leaders were apt at rationalizing their actions in Marxist-Leninist terms even when these actions were clearly driven by security concerns or the need for external recognition. That rationalization was in fact a form of legitimation. By draping their foreign policy moves in Marxist-Leninist rhetoric, the Soviets claimed that whatever place of honor they claimed for themselves in the global order, theirs was a legitimate claim. But such ideological self-legitimation could never replace external validation and recognition. Indeed, it became ever more difficult to legitimize the Soviet position in the world by appeals to Marxism-Leninism as the limitations and brutalities of the Soviet system became more and more manifest. The value of external recognition correspondingly increased.

There is, however, a certain complexity to the subject of recognition that goes beyond the simple assertion that the Soviets wanted their perch to be recognized as legally and justly theirs. What did Soviet Union strive to be recognized as? One obvious possibility is being recognized as a superpower on a par with the other superpower, the United States. Such recognition could only be bestowed by the United States, hence the Soviet obsession with equality or, rather, American recognition of this equality – and invariable resentment at having been denied such recognition. But this is not

INTRODUCTION

the end of the story because in addition to being recognized as a superpower, the Soviets also sought recognition as the leader of the international Communist movement. Such recognition was bestowed by Soviet clients and allies, first and foremost China (until the two powers split up in the 1960s). But even after the Sino-Soviet split, the Soviets remained preoccupied with the Chinese challenge, and spared no effort to rebuff Chinese criticism that they had in fact betrayed the revolution.

These two identities – as a superpower and as the center of world revolution – often did not work well together. Certainly the Americans at times attempted to entice the Soviets to moderate their behavior through recognition of their global importance. This policy was called "linkage," and it never worked, simply because the Soviet leaders proved either unwilling or unable to reconcile their two identities. Perhaps they did not even see the need to reconcile them, because what made the Soviets true "equals" of America was that they represented an ideological pole as leaders of the "revolutionary" world, just as the Americans represented an ideological pole as the leaders of the "reactionary" world.

This led to a paradox that could never be adequately resolved: legitimation was attainable through recognition *either* as a partner *or* as an adversary. It makes sense: American recognition of the USSR as its major adversary supported the notion that the Soviet Union was the leader of the revolutionary forces, while a Soviet–American partnership exposed the Soviets to criticism from at least some of their clients (especially China) that they were not in fact as revolutionary as they claimed. The Soviet answer to the question of whether they were, in fact, America's partners or enemies, could thus be: Why could they not be both?

There was an interesting element in Moscow's striving for equality with the United States in that at some level the Soviets felt very insecure about whether or not they really *were* America's equals, hence, their pathological tendency to fall back on what has since become known as "whataboutism" (i.e. citing US transgressions and ambitions to justify their own). This, as we shall see, sometimes resulted in aggressive and reckless foreign adventures, which could have perhaps been avoided if the Soviets were a little bit more realistic about their own capabilities. The Soviet leaders pursued greatness in the sense Rodion Raskolnikov pursued greatness when he killed the pawnbroker lady and her sister in Dostoevsky's *Crime and Punishment.* "Am I a trembling creature or do I have the right?" muttered the Soviet Raskolnikovs while aggressively planting their flags on remote shores, without, perhaps, recognizing that even by putting forward this question, they showed that they were out of their depth.

INTRODUCTION

That desire for recognition – how did it tally against other desires, for example, the desire for security? This is not an idle question. Historians and policy makers have long linked Moscow's aggressiveness to its insecurity, not in the ontological sense, as in R.D. Laing, but in a very real physical sense. One need not invoke George F. Kennan's musings about Russia's historic fear of the "fierce nomadic people" and the "more competent, more powerful" West: Other countries have been invaded and overrun without developing bizarre fixations, and why should Russia be any different? But there is something to be said for security concerns – especially in the wake of the calamity of the Second World War, when the German invasion was beaten back, but only just barely, and at a monstrous price. This experience, as Stalin knew only too well, and that Nikita, Lyonya, and Misha of our narrative could relate to, created baseline perceptions in relation to national security that often underpinned policy decisions. However, these perceptions varied widely over time, partly in response to the changing security environment in Europe and Asia, and in part because of the nuclear revolution, which changed the meaning of what it meant to be secure.

Indeed, it may be argued that the nuclear revolution ended History in the way that Fukuyama never expected. The ability to destroy the world as we know it that the United States and the Soviet Union developed in the 1950s made it unlikely that either one or the other would ever again share Stalin's despair in the grim weeks after the German invasion, when he told his comrades dejectedly: "Lenin left us a great inheritance and we, his heirs, have fucked it all up." Great powers could and would lose wars on the periphery – from Vietnam to Afghanistan – but they could be reasonably secure of their continued existence. The logic of the Hegelian struggle between the self and the other, where the other submitted on pain of death and thus became slave to master, was hereby broken. Nuclear superpowers would continue to exist unless they decayed internally and fell apart (as, to be sure, the Soviet Union did in the end). But a direct conflict between the superpowers became downright unthinkable, leading logically to the possibility of an unending Cold War: a Cold War after a Cold War after a Cold War. In retrospect, it seems naive that we did not perceive this basic reality of the global order in 1989.

In evaluating how the desire for recognition holds up against basic security concerns, it is best to draw on yet another dangerous analogy – that of A.H. Maslow's hierarchy of needs.[9] In this reading, security needs (broadly understood as not just the need to protect oneself against a foreign invasion but also the need for internal security, i.e. regime stability), serve as a prerequisite for higher needs (i.e. the desire for esteem and

INTRODUCTION

self-actualization). "Esteem" encompasses, per Maslow "the desire for reputation or prestige ..., recognition, attention, importance or appreciation." We are thus back with Fukuyama and, more ambitiously, Hegel and Plato, except, of course, that for Maslow, basic security would precede these other needs. The hierarchy, however, is not rigidly fixed. As we shall see, the Soviet leaders were often willing to trade some basic needs for other basic needs, and would compromise security for the attainment of recognition and through recognition, legitimation.

One may object, correctly, here that states are not people, and people's hierarchy of needs and motivations cannot be compared to that of any state. That is true at one level, but it is also true that states are led by people, and foreign policy decisions are subject to fears, delusions, and, yes, needs of specific individuals. The Austro-British philosopher Karl Popper considered such reductionism preposterous and even dangerous, and unkindly called it "psychologism."[10] No good deed goes unpunished. So it is with this book, so deeply focused on individual psychological traits of Soviet leaders, at the expense of their social environment. In the end, it does not have to be one or the other. The Soviet leaders were able to shape their social environment, while being in their turn shaped by it. Theorizing how this process worked is beyond the abilities of any philosopher, let alone historian. In any case, the Soviet Union was not unique in this respect, though it does provide an excellent case study because of the remarkable concentration of foreign policy decision-making in the hands of just a handful of people. There is an old critique to the effect that a focus on "great men" detracts from the understanding of broader historical patterns, which can pass for a reasonable argument until one comes face-to-face with the painful proposition that fates of entire nations are directly tied to decisions made by specific individuals in their specific circumstances.

The notion that states pursue recognition (sometimes also described as "prestige" or "status") is familiar to theorists of International Relations and to political scientists; so much so that, as Jonathan Renshon argues, "this wide-ranging consensus crosses disciplinary and epistemological boundaries, and might truly be said to be one of the few facts on which world leaders and political scientists agree."[11] Books have even been written identifying Russia and China – the two main protagonists of this story – as particularly conscious of their international status.[12] The Cold War scholarship has not kept up, partly because historians are on the whole poor theorists. At best, they regard theory with suspicion because it ruthlessly simplifies the world, and at worst, they do not read theory at all, since it invariably induces deathly boredom. To disappoint some readers (but delight others), this

INTRODUCTION

book is dangerously thin on theory, and in this regard it treads in the footsteps of other historians of the Cold War, only perhaps with a wistful glance in the direction of the theoretical canon rising to unassailable heights far in the murky distance.

Yet there is also something to be had from thinking about the Soviet Union's Cold War experience in broader theoretical terms, for then we begin to see that it was not *all that* unique, and that there were in fact continuities that predate and, most certainly, postdate the Cold War. The year 1989 becomes less of a watershed moment than we supposed it to be in our immediate post-Cold War euphoria. Some of the underlying motivations of Moscow's foreign policy in a sense remained unchanged. Many of the key Soviet-era institutions survived (including the military and the intelligence services). Toxic nationalism replaced Communism as an overarching narrative of self-legitimation but the need for external legitimation through recognition as a great power or a great adversary remained unchanged. Only, Moscow no longer had the same capabilities as it once did. Another power – China – came forth to play an ever greater role in the global order.

China joins the Soviet Union and United States in this book as one of the three main actors of the story. This, in a sense, is a challenge to the existing Cold War historiography. In recent years we have seen a shift away from the "center" towards the "periphery" of the Cold War, a trend most convincingly represented by the superb scholarship of Lorenz Lüthi.[13] I, too, have taken part in this de-centering of Cold War narratives by writing about the bit players like Mongolia and North Korea. It is a rewarding exercise, to be sure, but it is ultimately unsatisfying, because many of the key decisions that shaped the latter half of the twentieth century were made in Moscow and Washington. And, yes, these decisions affected millions in what we now call the Global South, and, yes, historian Paul Chamberlin is right to argue that it is the Global South that paid the highest prices for the Cold War.[14] Of course, these decisions were not taken in vacuum, and what policy makers in London, Paris, Beijing, New Delhi, Cairo, Havana, and Hanoi thought of Cold War narratives, how they saw themselves in the context of these Cold War narratives, matters a great deal to understanding how and why the Cold War unfolded. However, these regional and local contexts – important though they are – cannot be profitably disconnected from the overarching narrative that infused them with meanings they would not have otherwise. We should not commit the error of rejecting the rich, textured historiography that de-centers the Cold War but nor should we allow this historiography to distract from the broader picture. Enriched by the knowledge of individual trees, we should stand back and enjoy the view

INTRODUCTION

of the forest. And so it is now a good time to re-center the Cold War, to go back to the basics and pose questions about the underlying motivations of the key powers – in the case of this book, mainly the Soviet Union.

There is an important technical reason for why such an examination may be warranted. After a hiatus of nearly twenty years, the Russian archives have now declassified troves of Cold War era documents. Where in the past Cold War historians struggled to divine Soviet foreign policy from a meager trickle of disconnected documentation, there is now a flood – a full-blown deluge – of records, including personal papers of the key decision-makers. Such a cornucopia permits for the first time to turn quantity into quality in reassessing personal motivations in decision-making. Scrolling through hundreds, nay, many thousands of pages of conversations, speeches, and memoranda, one gets to know the Soviet leaders at a very personal level. It is like being a psychological counselor in a session with a client who tells the same stories over and over again to reveal the underlying passions and fears. The book adopts the same close-and-personal approach to the Chinese leaders, for while working on this book I have had the fortune of access to a remarkable treasure-trove of top-level Chinese materials, most of which were never in the public domain. My interest in the psychology of the US decision-making is not as pronounced, mainly because generations of American historians have already mined the field. I am indebted to their efforts.

This is a very long book that recounts the Cold War, mainly from the Soviet perspective, from the mid-1940s to 1991. In doing so, it covers some of the well-known ground – all the major "crimes, follies, and misfortunes of mankind" one would expect in a history of the Cold War. Part I explores the early Cold War, a cold, dark place, when the world, awakening from the horrors of the Second World War, eyed the very real possibility of yet another cataclysm. It was difficult to understand what Stalin wanted but it was clear – as it remains clear today – that his various pathological obsessions and insecurities played a major role in the outbreak of the conflict. But Stalin craved not just security but also recognition. He pinned his postwar hopes on the prospect of a great-power concert, something not unlike the great-power concert of 1815, when Russia stood tall and proud among nations of Europe. In this sense, the Cold War was not just undesirable but also quite unexpected – even for Stalin. Nor was it inevitable – until it happened. To understand why it did happen, the Stalin chapters strip away layers of propaganda to expose the inner workings of the dictator's mind, in particular how he reacted to America's real or perceived atomic blackmail.

INTRODUCTION

Part II brings us face to face with a very different, very boisterous, but also highly insecure personality of Nikita Khrushchev. He has a deserved reputation in the historiography for being something of a romantic figure – perhaps the last revolutionary romantic among Soviet leaders. But, as this book shows, it was Khrushchev who most convincingly demonstrated Raskolnikov's obsession with proving himself to himself: "Am I a trembling creature or do I have the right?" For Khrushchev, asserting this right meant pushing the world to the brink of war over Berlin and sending nuclear missiles to Cuba, precipitating some of the most dangerous moments of the Cold War. Did Khrushchev understand what dangerous games he was playing? This book is a deep dive into his motivations, and his perceptions of risk. It shows, too, how his own memories of the Second World War shaped Khrushchev's view of his choices and his constraints. Those early experiences on the front lines raised questions in his mind about the limits of human rationality, creating a healthy sense of uncertainty and precluding him from pushing his gambler's luck too far.

The book draws on a wealth of new evidence to investigate Khrushchev's relations with US presidents Dwight D. Eisenhower and John F. Kennedy on the one hand and Chinese leader Mao Zedong on the other. Khrushchev's sense of inferiority vis-à-vis the Americans translated into a policy that combined elements of resentment and pleading. He was anxious to win American recognition of his own role as the leader of a rival superpower, even though his claims to equality rested on a flimsy foundation. Khrushchev put his faith in future economic breakthroughs that never materialized. But he also delighted in that the Soviet Union was a nuclear power; that, for all its backwardness, the Soviet Union had the means to destroy the West in a suicidal orgy of fire. Khrushchev envied America for its wealth and power, and resented it for its insufferable arrogance, and yet he was desperate for American acceptance so that, when thus accepted, he could spit America in its face.

Meanwhile, Khrushchev's sense of superiority vis-à-vis the Chinese led to arrogance and bouts of anger when Mao refused to toe the line. The twists and turns of the Sino-Soviet relationship become especially significant here because whatever Khrushchev did in his dealings with the United States, he kept an eye on Mao's opinion. Mao put himself in the position to legitimize Khrushchev's policies or to reject and ridicule them. The Sino-Soviet struggle for leadership is thus one of the central themes of this book.

Part III explores Brezhnev's impact on Soviet foreign policy making. His period in leadership overlapped with a relative decrease in Cold War tensions. After tribulations of the 1950s and the 1960s, detente set in. Brezhnev

INTRODUCTION

had wanted it badly. He envisioned it as stemming from America's recognition of the Soviet Union's equality, and the imagined readiness to share the world in the context of a Soviet–American condominium. Like other Soviet leaders, Brezhnev half-suspected, though he did not fully grasp, that there was no real material basis for any such equality. Indeed, the Soviet decline has already set in. The Soviet economic miracle – at least conceivable in the 1950s in view of breakthroughs in the space race – was proving a flop by the late 1960s. The more apparent it became that the Soviet Union was not in fact a superpower that it claimed to be, the more anxious the Soviet leaders were to prove that it was.

Brezhnev was the most anxious of all. Like Khrushchev before him, Brezhnev put a lot of premium on the might of the Soviet nuclear arsenal. Here was the great equalizer! He sought solace in external gestures of respect and put much faith into his relationship with Richard Nixon, hoping that personal chemistry would help him take the sharp edge off the Soviet–American relationship. Brezhnev, who feared and despised Mao Zedong, counted on American willingness to close ranks with the USSR on a quasi-civilizational basis, as "Europeans."

In the end, the Soviet–American condominium, if there was ever such a thing, proved rather unstable, and this instability goes to the heart of the Soviet leaders' conception of themselves. For, even as they craved America's recognition as "equals," they often opportunistically sought to undercut American influence in the so-called "third world."[15] The same logic applied to Washington, which, too, treasured its detente with the Soviet Union until it saw opportunities for undercutting the Soviets. The nature of this relationship was fundamentally competitive *despite* detente.

Still, in retrospect, the early 1970s were good for the Soviet–American relationship precisely because Brezhnev's personal relationship with Richard Nixon provided the kind of assurance and recognition that mitigated against sharp moves to undermine the global order. Of course, Brezhnev still had to be responsive to the demands of his revolutionary audiences, especially the Vietnamese and the Cubans, who jealously watched his pirouettes with Nixon to see that Brezhnev did not sell out their interests. The Soviet leader's mental decline from late 1974, and Nixon's resignation that same year, severed that personal connection, and made for an increasingly testy, unpredictable relationship towards the end of the decade.

Part IV recounts the last decade of Soviet foreign policy. The most salient aspect of this period was the decay of the domestic narrative of legitimation. Marxism-Leninism, long a dead creed, was largely dispensed with as a new generation of Soviet leaders sought to reframe Moscow's pretensions

INTRODUCTION

in more acceptable terms. Gorbachev's New Thinking, with its emphasis on nuclear arms control and nonintervention, was an effort to do just that. Yet Gorbachev's effort to reinvent the basis for Moscow's global leadership failed, as did his ever greater investment in courting Western recognition as the prophet of the new age, even when he traded away what his predecessors would have deemed to be basic security interests in Eastern Europe for the promise of post-Cold War camaraderie. He had no choice. The Soviet Empire was badly overextended even as Moscow faced growing economic challenges at home. The stark reality – that the USSR was not the superpower that it was claiming to be – had finally caught up with policy. But even though the Soviet Union collapsed under its own weight, its successor, Russia, still eyed a position of prominence in the global order, looking for America's recognition of its claim to a high perch as a partner or, failing this, as an adversary.

On what grounds? Only on the strength of the conviction that Russia deserved special consideration, because it was not a "trembling creature" but had the "right"; that it could stand up to the West because, in the past, it had, even if it meant going to the brink of war. Only, the past generations that had witnessed the horrors of war had largely passed away, leaving their successors their ambition but, alas, not their wisdom.

PART I

AMBITION

PART I

AMBITION

1

THE POSTWAR WORLD

When at the end of the Second World War Soviet policy makers surveyed the world, they saw truly unprecedented opportunities for asserting their influence. Soviet victories against Germany, and the proud knowledge that it was they – the long-shunned lepers of Europe – who brought the Nazis to their knees, engendered a sense of entitlement, a sense that the Soviet Union had every right to reshape Europe in ways that would assure its security and elevate its status as the continent's sole great power.

This chapter revisits internal Soviet debates about the postwar world, finding a basic agreement among wartime planners in Moscow. They took it for granted that the Soviet Union would be Europe's preponderant power, even if Great Britain retained its position as the major offshore competitor. The United States was deemed remote. No one expected the Americans to stay in Europe. The world that was shaping up in 1945 was not all that different, in Moscow's plans, from earlier postwar settlements: it was an explicitly imperial world but also a world where contradictions between great powers could be settled on the basis of mutual acceptance of spheres of influence. The Soviet Union's position in this world ultimately rested on its impressive military power but it also depended on the acknowledgment by Great Britain and especially the United States.

It seemed at first that Stalin would achieve his aims. From his discussions with Churchill in Moscow in October 1944 (which led to the infamous percentages agreement) to the Yalta summit in February 1945, he initially seemed to be getting traction for a great-power concert, not unlike what Europe witnessed at the end of the Napoleonic wars. He was willing to make some concessions in the horse bargaining over the fate of Poland, Germany, and especially China, moderating his appetites in return for Western – especially American – indulgence.

THE POSTWAR PLANNERS

"The USSR must become so powerful," wrote Ivan Maisky in January 1944, "that it would not fear any aggression in Europe or in Asia; more than that – that no one power or a combination of powers in Europe or Asia would ever think up an intention like that."[1] Maisky had been Stalin's ambassador to the Court of St. James between 1932 until 1943, when he was recalled to Moscow and put in charge of the reparations commission. The mustachioed, affable survivor of Joseph Stalin's purges, Maisky had a well-deserved reputation of an Anglophile, which he shared with his long-time patron and former foreign minister, Maksim Litvinov.[2] Both Maisky and Litvinov were closely associated with interwar proposals for collective security, and both believed in the importance of postwar collaboration between the Big Three. But, as Maisky's comments suggest, any such collaboration required that the other two of the Big Three recognize the Soviet Union as Europe's greatest land power.

"What's most favorable for us," argued Maisky in a memorandum he sent to the senior leadership, "is a situation where postwar Europe has only one mighty land power – the USSR, and only one mighty sea power – England." The Soviet Union, he thought, should strive to obtain military bases in Bulgaria and Romania (which would then allow it to reign supreme in the Black Sea), and keep Poland, Hungary, and Turkey weak. The British would pragmatically embrace these changes. After all, Britain would be so weakened by war and so preoccupied with beating off the challenge of American imperialism that it would have every reason to seek accommodation with Moscow. Maisky believed that the British had more to fear from the United States (especially in the colonies) than from the Soviet Union.[3]

Litvinov concurred. In November 1944, in a bid to justify the need for postwar allied collaboration, Litvinov composed a whole treatise on Soviet–British relations, which, he hoped, Stalin would read. He went as far back as the eighteenth century, discussing in great depth what historians have come to call the "Great Game" – the imperial competition between Tsarist Russia and the British Empire. To what end? To argue that although the British and the Russians had long been engaged in rivalry – not least in Central Asia and the Near East – they were also able on occasion to moderate their differences through gentlemen's agreements. There was no reason something like that could not work again. London and Moscow could agree to respect each other's spheres of influence. The Soviet sphere, Litvinov opined, would include Finland, Poland, Czechoslovakia, Hungary, the Slavic countries of the Balkans, Romania, and even – oh, the appetites! – Sweden and Turkey.[4] The British sphere would extend to the Netherlands, Belgium, France, Portugal, and Greece. Litvinov also envisioned a "neutral sphere" in Europe, which would include Norway, Denmark, Germany, Austria, and Italy.

CHAPTER 1 THE POSTWAR WORLD

Litvinov, like Maisky, was recalled from an ambassadorial posting (his had been to Washington) to help plan for the postwar world. His Commission – aptly named the Commission on Peace Treaties and the Postwar Order – churned out memos that were then sent up the food chain to Litvinov's successor at the Foreign Ministry, Vyacheslav Molotov, and further up to Stalin. A lot has been made of the contrast between Litvinov and Molotov, one the proverbial Anglophile who kept President Roosevelt's photo on his desk and evaded arrest and death only thanks to Stalin's bizarre indulgence, the other – the dour Mr. No of Soviet foreign policy who had shaken hands with Hitler and whose signature graced the infamous Molotov–Ribbentrop Pact that carved up Eastern Europe and led directly to the outbreak of the Second World War. Their personal relationship was atrocious. But whether Litvinov represented an entirely different policy than Molotov and, indeed, Stalin is another question.

It is tempting to read too much into subsequent lamentations by Litvinov who was sidelined by 1945 and ousted in 1946 (Maisky fared no better: he was arrested and escaped death only because Stalin went first). People like Litvinov and Maisky, who had called for cooperation with the British and the Americans in 1945, were bound to be disappointed when the wartime alliance crashed. Litvinov blamed the ideologues and the rapacious land-grabbers like Stalin and Molotov, a view not unpopular among historians. As Jonathan Haslam put it, "the option of genuine inter-Allied collaboration had been dashed against the rocks of Kremlin paranoia. The only cooperation Stalin and Molotov envisaged was that which permitted the Soviet Union to grab all the territory that it sought ..."[5]

Yet a close reading of Litvinov's and Maisky's memoranda reveals that their vision for the postwar world was every bit as exacting as Stalin's and probably reflected an elite consensus in Moscow.[6] Consider Litvinov's treatment of Germany. His general idea was to destroy Germany as a political unit by breaking it up into multiple pieces, and giving some away (to Poland, Czechoslovakia, Denmark, and the USSR itself) and setting up others as independent states. Some may complain, Litvinov allowed in one of his lengthy memoranda on the subject, that by cannibalizing Germany the postwar planners would merely repeat the mistakes of the Versailles settlement, feeding Berlin's bitterness and irredentism. But the problem with the settlement was not that it was too harsh on Germany but that it was too lenient, Litvinov wrote, arguing for "absolute necessity of weakening Germany in order to prevent a new aggression on its part." (This passage was highlighted in Molotov's copy).[7]

Why was Litvinov so keen on dividing Germany instead of keeping it united but under Allied control? It was because he worried that Western powers would eventually allow for Germany's rearmament and reindustrialization, overruling Soviet objections.[8] An outright division seemed far more reliable.

Maisky highlighted similar concerns, tempering his hopeful prognosis for an Anglo-Soviet gentlemen's agreement with realist warnings that in the longer term the Americans could create "serious difficulties" for the USSR by building up Germany and Japan, by "hammering together an anti-Soviet bloc in Europe" or, indeed, by forming an anti-Soviet alliance with China.[9] Both Litvinov and Maisky appeared much more in favor of dividing Germany that Stalin himself ultimately was.[10]

There were contradictions in Litvinov's treatment of other European states. He repeatedly argued that the Soviets had to make sure that postwar Poland would have a "government friendly towards us."[11] But, given the history of anti-Russian and anti-Soviet sentiments in Poland, how could it ever have a "friendly" government except one that would be subservient to the USSR? Litvinov argued for assuring Soviet control of the Black Sea and the Turkish Straits but doubted that this could be achieved in partnership with Turkey except "in case of close friendly relations between the two countries." Assuming that such closeness would be out of reach, he suggested that control be handed over to an international control commission made up of Black Sea states but only "under the condition of sufficient strengthening of our influence in Romania and Bulgaria." "In this case," he argued, "we would control three-quarters of the votes in the control commission" (with Turkey always outvoted).[12] During a discussion on Romania in his commission, Litvinov sided with some of his more militant colleagues in arguing for its partition (by setting up Transylvania as an independent state) because this would make Romania "dependent" on the USSR.[13]

As for the parts of Europe that were unlikely to come under direct Soviet military control – for example, France and Italy – there were serious debates between Litvinov and his critics, but these were not debates between the realists and the ideologues but, rather, between different kinds of realists. The idea – by no means an original one, for the British had long followed a similar policy in relation to Continental powers – was to prevent either France or Italy from gaining enough power to challenge the Soviet position in Europe. The key question here was whether restoring these to European prominence was in Soviet interest. Some (for example, Deputy Foreign Minister Solomon Lozovsky) thought so, citing the need to play a stronger France and Italy against Britain and the United States. Others

CHAPTER 1 THE POSTWAR WORLD

deemed such a plan unrealistic: Who could guarantee that these would be open to such manipulation, instead of siding with the British and the Americans against the Soviet Union?[14]

Litvinov was among the skeptics. He foresaw that the French, in particular, would be too dependent on their Western allies in the postwar world to offer an opening to the USSR. "One can foresee with great probability," he wrote to Molotov, "that France will play the role of a vassal of England or of the Anglo-American coalition." They had to "speak out against the return of France into the ranks of great powers." Echoing Maisky's views about the importance of keeping the Soviet Union as the sole great power of Europe, Litvinov warned Molotov: "We must not give anything away to France, especially nothing that we cannot [later] take back. Let her into the 'directorate' [this was a reference to the wartime 'Big Three'] and you won't be able to kick it out ... We must treasure the advantageous position, which has come to us, that is: the position of the sole great continental power of Europe, and we must not voluntarily share this position with anyone else."[15]

Even as they called for Anglo-American–Soviet cooperation in the postwar world, the "anglophiles" were clear-eyed about the need to preserve Soviet control in Europe – whether through dismemberment, or through the establishment of "friendly" governments, or by preventing possible contenders from ever challenging Moscow's political preponderance. If this was the so-called "Litvinov alternative" to the Cold War, then it was not much of an alternative at all. Litvinov and Maisky preferred straightforward imperialism – for example, establishment of bases – as a means of assuring control. Nowhere did they call for communization of Eastern Europe. But neither did Stalin foresee the creation of Communist governments as the Second World War drew to a close. His preference was for assuring Soviet domination by propping up pliable, weak, but not necessarily Communist governments across Eastern Europe with a quiet British and American acquiescence. It was only upon discovering that such acquiescence would not be forthcoming that Stalin changed his tactics but that was not yet in the cards in 1944–45. The "Litvinov alternative" was everyone's preferred alternative.

These views were a part of a policy consensus, and it was a consensus that was based both on the lessons of the last two world wars and, more broadly, Russia's historical experience as a European and an imperial power. This experience was steeped in the good old tradition of land-grabbing, nation carving, and power balancing.

This is not to say that the ideological trope did not matter – of course it did. But the arguments that Litvinov and Maisky were the "realists"

PART I AMBITION

whose efforts were ultimately derailed by the "ideologues" does not stand up to scrutiny. The former were equally skilled in the deployment of the ideological turns of phrase. Maisky, for example, argued that within fifty years – two generations – all of Europe could have undergone socialist revolutions, which would render his balancing prescriptions obsolete. Litvinov made the same point repeatedly, not least about France and Germany: if either of these had Communist revolutions in the foreseeable future, the entire Soviet postwar calculus would have to be revisited.[16] And here is what Maisky once had to say about the relationship between ideology and realism in Soviet foreign policy: "The Soviet government has never pursued and does not pursue *Gefühlspolitik* [emotional politics]. The Soviet government is utterly realistic in its foreign policy. When state interests and feelings collide, state interests always win."[17]

These wartime debates by Soviet diplomats highlight Moscow's core concerns in 1945. The cornerstone was Soviet security. This was understandable. The Soviet Union was emerging from an existential struggle with a powerful adversary. Partitions, annexations, control of straits and sea lanes, the establishment of military bases: all these pointed at attaining security in the sense that the entire foreign policy establishment – from Stalin and Molotov and down – understood security (i.e. territorial control). But there was also an implicit expectation that Soviet control over much of Continental Europe would be accepted if not welcomed by Great Britain and the United States. Such acceptance – recognition – of Soviet primacy would provide a legitimating aspect to exercise of raw power, and it was thus that security and legitimacy went hand-in-hand. Security was already there: the Soviets were already in control or about to gain control over large swathes of the European landmass. But what about legitimacy? As peace dawned, external legitimation was not yet a given but, as we shall now see, it seemed quite within grasp.

PERCENTAGES

There is a well-known story, recounted by Milovan Djilas, about Stalin's assessment of his allies near the war's end. "Churchill," Stalin allegedly said, "is the kind who, if you don't watch him, will slip a kopeck out of your pocket. Yes, a kopeck out of your pocket! By God, a kopeck out of your pocket! And Roosevelt? Roosevelt is not like that. He dips in his hand only for bigger coins."[18] Stalin, whose CV included armed bank robberies, was the least well placed of the Big Three to peddle moralistic takes. If anything, in the matter of slipping kopecks out of his allies' pockets, Stalin was

22

CHAPTER 1 THE POSTWAR WORLD

without equal. But even a company of pickpockets can agree to share the spoils and abide by the rules they set themselves. This willingness to compromise and to recognize that the other side had legitimate interests underpinned the famous encounter between Stalin and Churchill in October 1944, the encounter that resulted in what has become known to history as the "percentages agreement."

Churchill arrived in Moscow with the hope of delineating British and Soviet interests in Southeastern Europe. The prime minister's priorities were clear: maintaining British influence in Greece. He of course keenly realized that given the military success of the Communist-led Greek National Liberation Front (known as ELAS/EAM), and the potential Soviet support for the Greek Communists, the only thing that could prevent a Communist revolution in Greece was Stalin's voluntary abstinence. For this, Churchill was willing to give away a lot. To show just how much, he drew up what he called a "fairly dirty and crude document," a table, in fact, which spelled out percentages of Soviet and British influence in different Balkan states.[19]

The table purported to give the Soviet Union 90% of influence over Romania (with 10% reserved for "the others." The percentages were reversed in Greece (where, Britain "in accord with the USA" would keep a 90% stake). Yugoslavia and Hungary were split evenly, while the Soviet Union received 75% in Bulgaria (to the others' 25%). By the prime minister's later admission, he had simply forgotten about Albania. Churchill recounts what happened next: "There was a slight pause. Then he took his blue pencil and made a large tick upon it, and passed it back to us." Churchill continues: "After this there was a long silence. The penciled paper lay in the centre of the table. At length I said, 'Might it not be thought rather cynical if it seemed we had disposed of these issues, so fateful to millions of people, in such an offhand manner? Let us burn the paper.' 'No, you keep it,' said Stalin."[20]

The haggling over the percentages continued for the next two days between Molotov and the British foreign secretary, Anthony Eden, who had followed Churchill to Moscow. Molotov pressed for better terms in Bulgaria (90 to 10 in Soviet favor), and in Hungary (75 to 25). He also initially pressed for a slight advantage in Yugoslavia (60 to 40).[21] It seems that on the third day they settled on 80 to 20 for Bulgaria and Hungary and returned to an even split for Yugoslavia.[22]

How significant was this bizarre discussion in Moscow? It does provide a good example of brutal, cynical imperialism that Stalin and Churchill freely engaged in, but that Roosevelt would have found jarring and unacceptable (this is of course the reason why the Americans were deliberately kept out of the loop). It is at least possible that by striking a deal with Stalin, Churchill allowed Greece – the one place that really mattered to him in the Balkans – to be saved from Communism.[23] Meanwhile, historian Geoffrey Roberts argues that the percentages agreement was not all that important after all. Stalin had never intended to support the Greek Communists, his argument goes. He realized that the country was of particular interest to the British and was willing to allow them the upper hand there in line with the envisioned division of Europe into Soviet and British spheres of influence.[24]

It is true that Stalin – siding with his own postwar planners who regarded Greece as lying well outside the Soviet sphere – had already resigned to yielding it to the British. There is even evidence that there were pragmatic military reasons for his reluctance to meddle in Greece: Stalin apparently thought that the Soviet Navy was too weak to attempt a take-over.[25] But even if Stalin gave up on Greece because he never intended to go there in the first place, he tried to present his reluctance as a concession, for which he sought a reciprocal British concession: a promise not to meddle in the Balkans. Stalin valued Churchill's recognition of Soviet gains because such a recognition conferred a sense of legitimacy to these gains, which they would not otherwise have had.

Yes, it was a secret, underhand deal with someone Stalin knew would slip a kopeck out of his pocket. Yes, it did not have American blessing (though Stalin had every reason to believe the Americans would resign themselves to the arrangement: neither he nor Churchill thought they would stay in Europe postwar). But it was an agreement, a quid pro quo, something Stalin valued, not because he could not act without one (he could) but because any gains obtained by force alone meant less to him than gains legitimized by the other great powers. In return, he was willing to recognize and accept their gains. It was this spirit of give-and-take that guided Stalin's thinking at the all-important conference of the Big Three that convened in Yalta, Crimea, in February 1945.

THE YALTA FRAMEWORK: GERMANY

The Allied conference at Yalta was the second time Stalin found himself in the merry company of Winston Churchill and President Franklin D. Roosevelt. The last time the three had met was in November–December 1943 in Tehran. On that earlier occasion Stalin was squarely focused on pressing the Allies to open the second front in Europe. The outlines of the postwar world were as yet fuzzy and uncertain. Some of that fog was dispersed by Yalta. The Soviet Army had captured Warsaw. A vicious battle

CHAPTER 1 THE POSTWAR WORLD

was underway in Budapest; the Germans had dug in, but the outcome was hardly in doubt. By late January, the Soviets were already inside Germany proper, moving westward at breakneck speed. Meanwhile, beating back the Ardennes counteroffensive (Berlin's last major effort to change the course of the war in the West), the Allies now pressed the Germans along the entire Western Front. The Third Reich was on its last legs. It was under these highly auspicious circumstances that Stalin hosted Churchill and Roosevelt in the war-ravaged Crimea: auspicious because, as the key architect of the Allied victory, he knew that he could drive a hard bargain.

"There is a universally-known rule," Stalin postulated not long before he set off for Yalta: "if you cannot advance, then resort to defense, but once you have accumulated your strength, go on the offensive ... In his time, Lenin did not dream of the correlation of forces that we have attained as a result of this war ... Lenin never thought that you could be allied with one wing of the bourgeoisie and fight the other [wing]. We managed it." He added, echoing Maisky: "We are not guided by emotions but by reason, analysis, and calculation."[26]

Like Maisky (who followed Stalin to Crimea), the Soviet leader imagined a postwar Europe where the Soviet Union would play the predominant role. But in this he would not rely on force alone. Equally important was the Allied recognition of Soviet gains, because only such recognition would afford the Soviets a degree of legitimacy that Stalin so badly wanted. The purpose of Yalta was to give the Soviet leader exactly that: British and American recognition of the new postwar realities. Yalta would provide a durable framework that would ratify the underhand deal he and Churchill made in Moscow, a framework that Stalin hoped would allow him to make the Soviet Union both more secure and more legitimate as a world power second only to the United States in power and glory. As with Churchill the previous October, now, too, he was willing to make concessions – in fact, much greater concessions than required in view of the Soviet military preponderance in Europe – but Stalin also had red lines. The most important of these were Germany and Poland.

"I hate the Germans," Stalin once said. "But hate should not prevent us from evaluating the Germans objectively. The Germans are a great people ... One cannot annihilate the Germans; they will remain." If they remained, then surely they would again pose a threat to Europe. When? In fifteen, twenty, twenty-five – at most thirty – years; that was Stalin's estimate. Some might say that it showed how the Soviet dictator was entrapped by ideological preconceptions. War was inevitable because capitalism made it so.[27] Yet it hardly required Marxism-Leninism to see Germany as a threat. A brief

Figure 1 Stalin and Molotov confer at Yalta, February 1945.
Source: Universal Images Group/Getty Images.

overview of recent European history would have sufficed. So, following the consensus of Soviet postwar planners and his own gut instincts, Stalin initially wanted Germany partitioned. This was a key item on his Yalta agenda, and he did not expect great difficulties. Who could speak up for Germany? Even Roosevelt was in a vengeful mood, telling Stalin at Yalta that he had become much more "bloodthirsty" towards the Germans, having witnessed their barbarity first-hand in war-torn Crimea. Earlier, in Tehran, Roosevelt had seemed determined to partition Germany. Stalin had good reasons to think that he and the president were on the same page.[28]

Yet Stalin found in Yalta that Roosevelt and Churchill were less keen to dismember Germany than he first expected.[29] The dismemberment can was kicked down the road. The matter was handed down to a London commission, which mulled the issue for weeks, before shelving it altogether. It is not entirely clear why Stalin – who had been so determined to carve up Germany into little fiefdoms – backed away from this goal in the spring of 1945. The likely rationale was his fear that most of these mini-Germanies would come under Western domination, whereas a larger Germany, where the Soviet Union, as one of the occupying powers, had a say, could have been maneuvered into some form of neutrality. This was a reversal of Litvinov's logic who, as we have seen feared the opposite: that a united Germany would inevitably come under Western domination.

The question of what Stalin wanted to do with Germany is important. Getting the answer right would go a long way towards pinning down the degree of his responsibility for the Cold War. But the evidence is sparse and contradictory.[30] Stalin's *later actions* (as we shall see in Chapter 3) do point to a misplaced expectation that he would eventually extend Soviet influence throughout all of Germany, relying on the Communists as a Trojan horse in a left-leaning coalition government.[31] But he was enough of a realist to know that a positive outcome could not be guaranteed. At least he hoped to exercise such a degree of influence that could prevent Germany from posing a threat to Soviet hegemony in Europe.[32] He also wanted to strip Germany bare of assets: it would pay, and pay dearly, and that, too, required that German unity be maintained, giving Moscow access to Germany's wealthier Western regions.

A united Germany was important for Soviet security. It was important for Soviet economic recovery. And it was important for anchoring the Soviet Union in the heart of Europe with tacit acceptance of the Allies.

THE YALTA FRAMEWORK: POLAND

There was also uncertainty in Stalin's approach to Poland. The overall goal was clear enough: to make sure that Poland would never again serve as a "corridor" for foreign invasion. But getting there was not straightforward. Stalin was determined to keep his ill-gotten gains from the 1939 Molotov–Ribbentrop Pact: eastern areas of Poland would stay Soviet; the Poles would have to be compensated in the West, at Germany's expense. That was not negotiable. Where Stalin did allow some haggling was the shape of the future government of independent Poland.

The issue had caused a lot of friction between him and the Allies, and the differences between Stalin on the one hand, and Churchill and Roosevelt on the other, became an early pointer to the Cold War. Stalin had good cards in his hands. In the fall of 1944, the Nazis brutally suppressed the Warsaw Uprising, led by the Home Army and coordinated by the London Poles. The Soviet forces were within a striking distance of Warsaw but did not enter the fray even as the Germans destroyed the Polish resistance. Stalin had no interest in recognizing the "London Poles" – the

Polish government-in-exile in London. He had his own Polish government, which was called the Polish Committee for National Liberation, but that Committee was unacceptable to Churchill and Roosevelt who, not unreasonably, viewed it as a product of Stalin's puppetry.

The question of the future composition of the Polish government was the thorniest issue in Stalin's relations with the Allies in the run-up to Yalta. The Soviet leader was willing to make at least notional concessions by striking a deal with the prime minister of the government-in-exile Stanisław Mikołajczyk. There was no love lost between Stalin and Mikołajczyk, especially not after the explosive (and accurate) allegations that the Soviets had massacred thousands of Polish officers in the Katyń forest had come to light. Nevertheless, with Churchill's prodding, Mikołajczyk travelled to Moscow in the summer of 1944, and then again later that fall, to negotiate with the Soviet Poles, and with the Soviets themselves, about the outlines of the future Polish government and Poland's frontiers.

The Soviet Poles offered Mikołajczyk the position of prime minister in a reconstituted government, and another three (of seventeen) ministerial posts, an offer he deemed too meagre to accept.[33] Instead, he asked Stalin to agree to a government based mostly on the one that already existed in London, with the addition of the Communists. Stalin was unsympathetic, and threatened that if his terms were refused, he would just carry on with the Communist government, and the London Poles would be left out of the loop. He also refused Mikołajczyk's plea to return parts of Poland the USSR had annexed in 1939, hinting darkly that if the Poles did not give up dreams of returning lost lands in the East, he may yield to the pressures of Russian nationalists who thought that all of Poland should belong to Russia as in the old days. "According to the Leninist ideology, all nations are equal," Stalin said, before cynically explaining to Mikołajczyk how moving Poland to the West helped resolve the national question for the Ukrainians and the Belorussians. It was a lesson in brutal *realpolitik* draped in the ideological guise.[34]

But there was a silver lining for Mikołajczyk. When on August 9, just before his departure, he wondered in passing whether Germany may become Communist after the war, Stalin set him straight: "Communism suits Germany about as much as a saddle suits a cow."[35] If Germany did not need Communism, perhaps Poland too would be spared the joy. This was not propaganda or deception. As the Soviet forces crossed over to Eastern Europe, Moscow issued instructions to the fronts: the existing economic and political systems were to be preserved; no sovietization was allowed.[36]

CHAPTER 1 THE POSTWAR WORLD

Only, there was a problem with the arrangement. Although there is no reason to believe that Stalin lied to Mikołajczyk when he promised that Poland be spared Communism, the Soviet dictator was dead set to keep that country under his control. That required excluding all manner of "reactionaries" from the Polish government, which could only be guaranteed if Stalin had the ultimate say. That excluded any sort of a genuine democracy for Poland. Stalin needed Mikołajczyk for window-dressing; more specifically, to legitimize that new government in the Western eyes. This was because Soviet control was made more secure through British and American recognition. If this meant courting Mikołajczyk, Stalin was willing to do that so long as he did not have to give the people he did not trust and could not control any real levers of power.

Mikołajczyk returned to Moscow in October 1944, just as Churchill was also there, negotiating spheres of influence with Stalin. Churchill helped arm-twist the Polish prime minister into acceding to Soviet territorial demands in the East. But the talks with the Soviet Poles once again ran aground over Mikołajczyk's unwillingness to accept the Committee as the preponderant force in postwar Poland.[37] Stalin was prepared to give Mikołajczyk one-third of government portfolios (including that of the prime minister) but the latter insisted on having one-half.[38] He missed the bus. Time was not on the side of the government-in-exile. On December 28, the Committee proclaimed a new provisional government of Poland. The Soviet Union recognized that government on January 5, 1945. "The Soviet government acted simply with Poland," Stalin boasted four days later. "It recognized the provisional government, without regard for England and America. Churchill swallowed this pill, but Roosevelt became despondent and is still sulking."[39]

By Yalta, then, the situation in Poland favored the Soviets. Yet Churchill and Roosevelt came prepared to defend their preference for postwar Poland, which would include a government where Mikołajczyk and other non-Communists were to play the leading roles. This was, Churchill told Stalin at Yalta, "a matter of honour for Great Britain." "For the Russians," Stalin retorted, "the question of Poland is not just a question of honour but also a question of security."[40] The Soviet dictator, knowing that he held all the cards, resisted all formulations that would take control from the hands of the Soviet-supported government. He ultimately agreed to have that government "reorganized" based on the one that already existed by including a few non-Communist personalities. His other major "concession" was to agree to hold "free and unfettered elections as soon as possible." Just how soon remained unclear. Stalin hinted to Roosevelt that it might happen in a month's time (in reality, it took almost two years, and the elections were a complete fraud).

The wording on Poland is probably the most important reason why some historians have been so critical of the Yalta agreement. The Polish-American historian Jan Karski, for example, argued that "at Yalta, the Western leaders not only failed to secure Poland's rights, rightly or wrongly feeling unable to so, but they also indirectly, though not less effectively, sanctioned the Soviet position in Poland."[41] Largely because of Poland, Yalta has come to be regarded as a sell-out, which enabled Stalin to consolidate his sphere of influence in Eastern Europe behind the veneer of legitimacy. What makes Roosevelt's and Churchill's "sins" appear even more prominent in retrospect is the clear evidence that they both realized that there was no practical way of holding Stalin to account. The elections that he promised could never have been "free and unfettered," and the notion that a Soviet-friendly Poland could be anything but a Soviet-controlled Poland was just wishful thinking.

This understanding of Yalta is misguided. Of course, Stalin was going to impose his control on Poland. Not even the "anglophiles" like Litvinov and Maisky could have advised him otherwise. But that does not mean that he was determined to communize Poland. That came later, already when the raging Cold War rendered fence-sitting scenarios increasingly improbable. As historian Norman Naimark has convincingly demonstrated, Stalin never had any blueprints for "communizing" Europe. What he had was an understanding that friendly sentiments were not worth much without a measure of direct control.[42] How much direct control was possible without turning a country like Poland into an outright Soviet puppet? Stalin's calculations in the fall of 1944 indicate that he was willing to give Mikołajczyk a 30 percent stake in the government. His generosity diminished considerably in the following months, simply because he realized that he held all the winning cards.

But here is an interesting question: Why did Stalin even require the façade of a coalition government in Poland – or indeed elsewhere in Eastern Europe? Why did he try so hard at Yalta to have Roosevelt and Churchill "sanction," to use Karski's unkind word, his position in Poland? The reason is that he valued legitimacy as much as security. For him, lesser gains with greater legitimacy often trumped greater gains with lesser legitimacy. Even in Poland, where security was paramount, Stalin was at least making face-saving concessions, if only out of deference to the sensibilities (and the domestic difficulties) of his postwar partners. The broader Yalta framework was about delivering what Litvinov and Maisky had urged upon

CHAPTER 1 THE POSTWAR WORLD

Stalin, and what Churchill had seemed willing to grant in the percentages agreement: a stable and secure Soviet sphere of influence in Europe that benefited from being recognized as such by the powers that mattered the most, Great Britain and the United States. For this, Stalin was willing to make important concessions. But understanding this requires looking beyond Poland, Germany, or indeed even the entirety of Eastern Europe. The most telling example of the Yalta framework in action was Stalin's approach to China.

THE YALTA FRAMEWORK: CHINA

On November 7, 1944 – the twenty-seventh anniversary of the Soviet Revolution – a rebel force, fighting under the green banners of Islam, attacked the sleepy town of Ghulja (also known as Yining) in northwestern Xinjiang, China. The town's Chinese defenders were overwhelmed. On November 12, the rebel leader and the chief mullah of Ghulja, Ali Khan Töre proclaimed the establishment of a new government of the East Turkestan Republic: "Praise be to Allah for his manifold blessings!" thundered Ali Khan Töre's declaration. "Allah be praised! The aid of Allah has given us the heroism to overthrow the government of the oppressor Chinese."[43] Allah's help was of course important but even more important was the Soviet role in what became known as the Three Districts Revolution, a nationalist uprising of, predominantly, ethnic Uighurs and Kazakhs against the Chinese rule. The entire uprising, though certainly reflective of very real anti-Chinese sentiments of the local population, was nevertheless inspired, armed, and coordinated from Moscow.

Supporting the Uighurs and the Kazakhs against the Chinese was a new point of departure for Soviet policy. Until then, they had been doing the exact opposite. In fact, when in 1931–34 Xinjiang erupted in an ethnic anti-Chinese rebellion, the Soviets supported the Chinese government with weapons and instructors. That support helped Xinjiang's brutal overlord Sheng Shicai consolidate his control over the province. Sheng tirelessly tried to prove his loyalty to Moscow, so much so that he asked to join the Soviet Communist Party, proposed to sovietize Xinjiang, and at one point (in early 1941) he even pleaded with Stalin to annex the province outright.[44]

Stalin turned down these entreaties, although he could have supported the sovietization of Xinjiang, and could well have gotten away with the annexation, seeing that around the same time he annexed swathes of new territories in Eastern Europe, including parts of Poland and the Baltic trio. The fact that he did not do so despite Xinjiang's strategic and economic

PART I AMBITION

importance shows that he was perfectly content with a more limited Soviet role, so long as Governor Sheng retained his "friendly" disposition. (As a special favor, Stalin agreed in the end to give Sheng Shicai his membership in the Soviet Communist Party, thus strengthening Soviet control while maintaining the appearance of respecting China's sovereignty).

Xinjiang was only one but not *the* only one method of Stalin's imperial control in Inner Asia. Stalin's annexation of Tuva in 1944 showed that he was not averse to annexation if circumstances were right. He kept Outer Mongolia (then still *de jure* a part of China) under Soviet control but nominally independent. It was, however, thoroughly sovietized. Xinjiang was yet another model: China's sovereignty was respected on paper. The actual Soviet control on the ground was pervasive. But Xinjiang did not become Communist. There was one more model – that of the Chinese Communist Party (CCP), based in the remote hills of Yan'an. Here Stalin exercised ideological influence (CCP was subordinated to Moscow through the Communist International – Comintern), and this influence he could on occasion translate into outright pressure (as when in 1936 he pressured Mao Zedong into a united front with Chiang Kai-shek's Guomindang). But overall Stalin's footprint in Yan'an was modest. Such a diverse portfolio of approaches allowed him to guarantee Soviet security (for example, by maintaining a military force in Mongolia), obtain access to important resources (for example, oil, tin, and tungsten in Xinjiang) and keep China fighting in the war against Japan. In some ways this nuanced strategy was a precursor to the wide variety of policies Stalin later tried in Europe.

Sheng Shicai upset Stalin's strategy by turning against him after the German attack on the USSR. He evidently counted on Moscow's imminent collapse and sought to rebuild bridges to Chiang Kai-shek by putting pressure on the Soviets. Stalin retaliated. On May 4, 1943, barely three months after Stalingrad, the Soviet Politburo secretly resolved to "provide support to non-Chinese nationalities of Xinjiang" in their "struggle against [Sheng Shicai's] and Xinjiang government's colonial-oppressive policy."[45] This support included weapons, even airplanes, as well as personnel. On December 5, 1944, the powerful People's Commissariat of Internal Affairs (NKVD), established a special operations department responsible for the general coordination of the Xinjiang uprising.[46] By the time of Yalta, the Soviet-directed rebels captured control across much of the Yili district (surrounding the town of Ghulja), and their offensive continued in the following months. China's loss of entire Xinjiang, and the establishment here of an ethnic state controlled by Moscow now seemed like a distinct possibility.

32

CHAPTER 1 THE POSTWAR WORLD

But Yalta introduced a change of plans. Roosevelt had come to the summit determined to convince Stalin to join the war against Japan. Unbeknownst to the American president, Stalin himself was itching to join the action despite the existence of a neutrality pact between the USSR and Japan. But that did not prevent him from attaching a hefty price tag to his participation. Stalin wanted territorial adjustments in the Far East (annexation of Southern Sakhalin and the Kurile islands, which would effectively turn the Okhotsk Sea into a Soviet lake). He proposed a "status quo" for Mongolia, which sounded innocuous enough, though what Stalin really meant was formalizing Mongolia's independence from China. He also wanted his "priority interests" in Manchuria to be guaranteed. These included a naval base at Lüshun, known to Russians as Port Arthur (at the tip of the Liaodong peninsula), the nearby large trade port of Dalian, and Soviet control of a railroad that cut across Manchuria, connecting Liaodong to the USSR.

All these things Roosevelt was willing to give away without much of a fuss. It was "just language," he told the US ambassador in Moscow, W. Averell Harriman, who questioned some of Stalin's formulations.[47] As many of the issues discussed and decided at Yalta directly concerned China (which was not represented), Roosevelt cynically agreed to "take measures" to assure Chiang Kai-shek's agreement. Churchill (who was not present at the private talk conversation between Stalin and Roosevelt) pragmatically endorsed their secret deal.[48]

The secret agreement included a clause about a treaty of alliance between China and the USSR (it would ratify all the gains that Stalin had been promised at Yalta). Chiang Kai-shek was outraged. "I did not recognize the Yalta [decisions]," he fumed in his diary. "I did not participate. I have no responsibility [for the decisions]. Why should I carry [them] out? They [the Allies] really see China as their vassal."[49] But Chiang swallowed his pride and sent the head of the Executive Yuan, T.V. Soong (Song Ziwen), alongside his own son, Chiang Ching-kuo, to Moscow to negotiate the treaty. Stalin laid down his conditions in his very first meeting with Soong and the younger Chiang. Mongolia had to be let go of, he said, because it was strategically important to the Soviet Union. Stalin's privileges in Manchuria were to last for forty to forty-five years. All of Stalin's demands were humiliating but it was the Mongolian issue that proved most painful for the Chinese. Soong resisted but Stalin's pressure was relentless. At one point he even threatened the Chinese with Mongolian irredentism. It was not an idle threat: the Mongolian leader Khorloogiin Choibalsan was aware of the opportunities offered by the Second World

33

PART I AMBITION

War endgame in northern China, and he was quietly lobbying Stalin to allow him to extend Mongolia all the way to the Great Wall and the Pacific seaboard![50]

Stalin dangled a carrot, too: China's unity. Already in May 1945 he claimed (in a conversation with the Americans) that he would "help China gather its lands" and that in his opinion Chiang Kai-shek was "China's best leader."[51] Now he promised political support to the Guomindang and told Soong that he did not believe in the success of the Communist project in China. "Good patriots," he said, speaking of the Chinese Communist Party, adding: "as to communists, question mark."[52] The Chinese premier begged for a delay, contacting Chiang Kai-shek for instructions. Chiang was in a bind. An armed insurrection raged in Xinjiang with Soviet support. Who could tell what would happen in Manchuria after the Soviets joined the war and sent their forces pouring across the border? And then there was the deeply distressing problem of the Chinese Communist Party, a "disease of the heart," as Chiang had once memorably referred to it: if Stalin sided with Mao, all bets were off. As against this, relinquishing Mongolia, as painful as it was, was a price worth paying. As Chiang wrote in his diary on July 5, "If [I] do not satisfy this demand of [Stalin's], it will be completely impossible to negotiate about any [Chinese] administration in Manchuria and Xinjiang; the question of the Communist Party is even more difficult to resolve. Moreover, Outer Mongolia has already been occupied by the Russians; courting true misfortunes for the sake of undeserved glory is not at all the way of statesmanship."[53]

Chiang's concession paved the way to a deal. On August 14, after more than a month of negotiating (with a break in the middle, when Stalin left Moscow for the Big Three summit in Potsdam), China and the Soviet Union concluded their Treaty of Alliance. Stalin got Mongolia, as well as his Manchurian railroad, his naval base, and his port after what was one of the most humiliating diplomatic negotiations in China's modern history. But he also reciprocated Chiang's concessions with a written (albeit secret) commitment to only support the national government (not the Chinese Communist Party), to respect China's sovereignty in Manchuria (and withdraw Soviet forces at most three months after Japan's capitulation), and not to meddle in Xinjiang.[54] At Soong's insistence, he even agreed to delete the wording about supporting China's democratization (i.e. the idea that the Guomindang should relax its iron grip by allowing others, in particular, the Communists, a role in politics). "Probably, the Chinese Communists will scold the Soviet government," he grumbled, "for agreeing to aforementioned points."[55]

CHAPTER 1 THE POSTWAR WORLD

Were Stalin's concessions worth the paper they were written on? Yes, and this is exemplified by his approach to the Chinese Communist Party. Needless to say, Mao Zedong and his comrades in Yan'an were not consulted during the treaty negotiations. Unlike Mongolia's Marshal Choibalsan who was at least called to Moscow while Stalin discussed the fate of his country with T.V. Soong, Mao remained in Yan'an, unaware of the promises Stalin was making. In April 1945, the CCP opened its Seventh Party Congress, where Mao delivered a report, promising the abolition of the Guomindang "one-party dictatorship" and the establishment of the "New Democracy."[56] Mao's immediate plans included rapid expansion of the "liberated areas," in effect, a civil war. But just a few days after the Sino-Soviet Treaty was signed, and even before it was published in the newspapers, Stalin sent a cable to Mao, demanding that he travel to China's wartime capital, Chongqing, to meet Chiang Kai-shek and "come to terms with him."[57] "You must do everything possible," the Soviets urged Mao in a cable sent on August 19, "to avoid a civil war, to try to find an acceptable platform for cooperation with Chiang Kai-shek's government."[58]

Mao discussed the situation during a meeting of the Politburo Standing Committee on August 23. "The Soviet Union is not a position to assist us," he said. Therefore, instead of going on a broad offensive, the order of the day was to talk peace. "We will continue to try to wash Chiang Kai-shek's face," Mao explained in his usual proverbial way – "but not to cut off his head."[59] Under pressure from Stalin, on August 28, Mao departed Yan'an for talks with Chiang. He feared for his life, and asked for guarantees. US Ambassador Patrick J. Hurley even flew to Yan'an to escort Mao who worried that Chiang might order his plane shot down. Mao's wife, Jiang Qing, is said to have sobbed at the sight of his departure. Indeed, Mao himself looked "as if he was going to his execution."[60]

Even though he obliged Stalin by going to Chongqing to speak with Chiang, Mao arranged for a fallback option: he ordered Chinese Communist troops to infiltrate Soviet-held Manchuria as soon as possible to preempt Chiang's move in the same direction. His hope was that the Soviets – although in principle committed to handing over Manchuria to the Guomindang – would turn a blind eye to Communist presence. Later in the year, these Communist forces caused the Soviets a serious headache when they clashed with Chiang's armies moving north into Manchuria. Chiang suspected Stalin of covertly aiding the Communists and even sent his son, Chiang Ching-kuo, to persuade the Soviet dictator to back off and stick to the Sino-Soviet agreement. In meetings with the younger Chiang Stalin professed his innocence, claiming the CCP were just doing their own

PART I AMBITION

thing, ignoring his well-meaning advice. The Soviet government, he told Chiang, "is not happy with their [the CCP's] behavior."[61]

Knowing what we do of Stalin, it is easy to dismiss such comments as duplicity but in this case his protests may well have been mostly genuine. We know that from his reaction to reports that suggested that the Communist forces were trying to take over Manchurian towns, including the all-important stronghold of Changchun. In a telegram to the Soviet military command in Manchuria on November 16, 1945, Stalin ordered that "when so-called Communist detachments approach to capture Changchun, Mukden [Shenyang] and other localities, chase them away by force, do not allow them into these localities." He added the reason, too: "Keep in mind that these detachments want to drag us into a conflict with the U.S., which must not be allowed."[62] A few days prior to that he ordered Soviet communications officers and other staff out of the CCP holdout in Yan'an and other areas controlled by "Mao-Ze-Du" (Stalin's misspelling). He gave his reasons: "The civil war in China is taking on a serious character and I am worried that our people in these areas – who are not in charge of anything – will then be declared by our enemies to be the organizers of a civil war in China."[63]

Meanwhile, keeping his promise to Chiang not to meddle in Xinjiang, Stalin effectively pulled the plug on the ethnic insurgency, which he had supported for months. On September 15, 1945 – a month after the Sino-Soviet Treaty – the Soviet Politburo resolved to "mediate" between the insurgents and the Chinese government. The Soviet ambassador in China, Apollon Petrov, was instructed to tell the Chinese that the Soviets had been approached by some Muslims "who call themselves representatives of rebels in Xinjiang." These people "hinted" at the desirability of peace talks with the Chinese government.[64]

This was a completely made-up pretext. There were no such "representatives." In fact, the government of the self-proclaimed East Turkestan Republic was determined to keep fighting. In a letter to "kind," "people-loving," "his serene highness" Stalin, in October 1945 the chairman of that government Ali Khan Töre pleaded for continued Soviet support. The Chinese, he said, had treated Uighurs "like animals." "We the peoples of East Turkestan," the letter went on, "separated [from China] in such a way like water cannot be merged with fire, and how a sheep cannot live together with a wolf. We people of East Turkestan swore before God not to lay down our weapons until we reclaim our motherland and obtain full rights."[65] Before long, the Soviets withdrew all their forces (nearly 3,000 men) from the ranks of the rebels, and largely disarmed them.[66] They even tampered with the rebels' airplanes rendering them unusable.[67] Ali Khan

36

CHAPTER 1 THE POSTWAR WORLD

Töre was sidelined and more pliable representatives of the rebel force were ordered to proceed to Urumqi for peace talks, leading to an agreement (signed on January 2, 1946) that ended all aspirations for independence of the short-lived East Turkestan Republic.[68]

In other words, Stalin was flexible in pursuit of his interests, and his interests were not confined to mindless grabbing of territory. His drawn-out, painful negotiations with T.V. Soong demonstrated Stalin's remarkable attention to legal detail. He wanted his gains in China to be ratified and recognized, and not just by the Chinese but, via the comforting framework of the Yalta agreement, by the British and, most important of all, the Americans. For this, he was willing to make concessions, going even as far as abandoning certain gains he already had (e.g. in Xinjiang) or betraying ideological allies (e.g. the Chinese Communist Party).

CONCLUSION

Since its heyday in the 1960s and 1970s, Cold War revisionism – that blames the United States for the conflict – has fallen into disrepute. This was partly a result of the opening of the former Communist-bloc archives in the early 1990s. The new evidence showed that Stalin was as brutal as many have suspected he was, and more; that he was a master of deceit and manipulation; most importantly, that he was dead set on keeping his gains in Eastern Europe, even when that entailed breaking promises he had given Roosevelt and Churchill at Yalta. In short, the Cold War was inevitable because Stalin made it so. This was, in part, a question of ideology: it was not just that the Soviets were power-hungry but they were also guided by a set of principles – the Marxist-Leninist faith – that, in the long term, made coexistence with the West impossible. It was either us or them. The world would either fall to Communist domination or be saved through brave pursuit of containment. Stalin's two natures – imperialist and Marxist – fused in imperceptible and occasionally contradictory ways, leaving little scope to doubt his personal contribution to the Cold War. These historical narratives are a part of the broader public discourse on responsibility best summarized by Jeffrey Lewis: "there were three causes of the Cold War: Stalin, Stalin, and Stalin."[69]

On the other hand, there is also a substantial body of evidence, also explored in the recent historiography, that highlights Stalin's hopes for postwar great-power cooperation or at the very least suggests that Stalin had no plans for communization of Europe; that he was playing by ear; that, in other words, the Cold War was not inevitable.[70]

PART I AMBITION

This chapter supports the view that Stalin was looking for a great bargain as the war neared its end. His vision was in Russia's *realpolitik* tradition and owed at least as much to the nineteenth-century's Concert of Europe as it did to Marxism-Leninism. Although the details of Stalin's vision are not particularly clear and are often obscured by his diplomatic guile and relatively sparse evidence reflective of his own thinking at this crucial historical turning point, the broader outlines can be discerned, especially in view of the extensive studies conducted by Litvinov's and Maisky's commissions in 1944–45. Of course, neither Litvinov nor Maisky spoke for the Soviet dictator, but they did write for him, and, to adopt Ian Kershaw's favorite phrase, *worked towards*, Stalin. It is indeed remarkable just how close their pronouncements collate with the occasional dark musings of the master of the Kremlin.

Stalin was a believer in power, but he knew that power alone would not suffice. That is why Yalta became so important. He knew that the Americans could endorse or reject his postwar claims. Even if he knew that his position in Europe and Asia rested, first and foremost, on Soviet military power, he wanted more than just power. He wanted legitimacy. In Crimea, he worked hard to achieve it, with Roosevelt's blessing. He could not have known that his treasured Yalta framework would prove so short-lived in the end.

38

2

THE PARTING OF WAYS

On April 25, 1945, Soviet and American forces linked up on River Elbe in Germany. The occasion was immortalized two days later at a little town of Torgau, near a bombed-out bridge: Soviet and American soldiers shook hands in a special performance for a cameraman. The performance was staged. The camaraderie was yet real. But tensions were lurking just under the surface. Far away from the banks of the Elbe Stalin schemed to impose Soviet political control on Poland and Romania. He expected to have his way. Germany's future was also up for grabs; soon the Allies would spar at a conference in Potsdam to decide on its new borders, reparations, and political arrangements. The war in the Pacific still raged. The Soviet dictator expected to take part in the division of spoils there as well. Roosevelt had promised him. He also eyed new colonies in North Africa, though it was not clear that the Americans would give him what he thought he deserved. Secretly, Stalin knew, his American allies were working on a powerful new weapon. It was yet unclear whether they would succeed, and what it would mean for the postwar world, and the Soviet Union's place in it. He found out soon enough.

This chapter explores Stalin's journey from Yalta to Potsdam to London. Attentive historians will perk up at the thought of Stalin visiting London in 1945, and, to be sure he did not. But a remarkable record survives: that of correspondence between Stalin and his foreign minister, Vyacheslav Molotov, who attended the difficult, protracted negotiations of the first postwar Council of Foreign Ministers in London. These records reveal Stalin's fears and delusions. They help us understand how the Soviet leader thought about American power, and why he chose the path of confrontation that, in short order, would lead the Soviet Union into the depths of the Cold War.

THE ROAD TO POTSDAM

In the weeks after Yalta, Stalin moved rapidly to eliminate all threats to Soviet hegemony in Poland. He kidnapped key non-Communist politicians in late March and threw them into prison in Moscow.[1] Soviet–British–US

PART I AMBITION

talks on the composition of the Polish government made little progress. The British and the Americans demanded the inclusion of Mikołajczyk and other "pro-Western" Poles. Stalin and Molotov resisted, closely scrutinizing biographies of every proposed Polish politician for evidence of "reactionary" (i.e. anti-Soviet) views.[2] There was frustration in Moscow with what seemed like unwarranted and unfair Western meddling in Polish affairs and just plain hypocrisy. "Poland – a big deal!" Molotov fumed. "But how to organize governments in Belgium, France, Greece, etc. We don't know. We were not asked, although we do not say that we like this or that government. We did not intervene because this is the area of activities of Anglo-American forces."[3]

Stalin's determination to impose spheres of influence (worked out with Churchill in Moscow and – so he thought – confirmed in the Yalta agreement) contrasted sharply with Roosevelt's postwar vision, which in theory projected American interests to all corners of the globe. In practice, of course, the extent of the US interest was affected by how prominently this or that issue figured in domestic politics. Poland was a particularly problematic issue. This was also the case in London, which still hosted the doomed Polish government-in-exile. As British Ambassador Archibald Kerr tried to explain to the Soviets in April 1945, Churchill and Eden "understood" that the Polish government would be dominated by pro-Soviet elements, but they had to "sell" this government to Parliament by "creating the impression" that it would be an entirely new government, not the one installed by the Soviet occupying forces. But few in Moscow were impressed with this line of argument.[4]

On April 1, just days before his death, Roosevelt sent a personal letter to Stalin, noting that he was "frankly puzzled" by the lack of progress, and that if the Soviets maintained their positions, this "would cause the people of the United States to regard the Yalta agreement as having failed."[5] "We are at a breaking point," Averell Harriman cabled from Moscow on April 3.[6] His British colleague Archibald Kerr remarked gloomily the next day that he was thinking of resigning his post because he was so depressed about the state of Soviet–British relations. "You know," Kerr told Ivan Maisky, "Churchill is a very emotional man ... He is very irritated and discouraged. I fear some unexpected explosion."[7]

Meanwhile, at the end of February – just a fortnight after Yalta – the Soviets imposed their preferred government on Romania. Deputy Foreign Affairs Commissar Andrei Vyshinsky, the infamous prosecutor in Stalin's show trials, presented Romania's King Michael with a two-hour deadline to fire Prime Minister Nicolae Rădescu, whom the Soviets suspected of

CHAPTER 2 THE PARTING OF WAYS

"pro-fascist" leanings. On his way out from his audience with the young Romanian king, Vyshinsky is said to have slammed the door so hard, it cracked the plaster on the wall. He succeeded in making his point: Rădescu's government was dismissed, replaced with a pro-Communist National Democratic Front, headed by Petru Groza.[8] The Allies were scandalized but their angry notes to the Soviet government were stonewalled. Molotov brusquely informed Averell Harriman that the "government of concentrated democratic forces" that the Soviets set up in Romania provided for the security of the Soviet rear communications, and that there was nothing to be done about the change. He also noted that the British and the Americans never consulted with the Soviets about their actions in Italy, implying that they were just being paid in their own coin in Bucharest.[9] These tense exchanges on Poland and Romania between the Soviets and their wartime allies were a pointer to the coming conflict that Roosevelt, for all his diplomatic skills, would have struggled to contain.

As it happened, he did not get the chance. On March 29, the president travelled to the Little White House in Warm Spring, Georgia, to rest before the upcoming United Nations founding conference at San Francisco. On April 12 he complained of a terrible headache. Roosevelt died later that day, aged just 63.

The new president was the former senator from Missouri Harry S. Truman who had little of Roosevelt's diplomatic skills, or of his predecessor's worldliness. The Soviets knew little of Truman, and what they did know they did not like – for instance, his infamous suggestion, in June 1941, that the United States should help Germany against Russia and Russia against Germany, so as to "let them kill as many as possible."[10] In July 1944 the then-Soviet ambassador in the United States, Andrei Gromyko, filed an unenthusiastic report on Truman's selection as Roosevelt's running mate: Truman was seen as a "conservative," a far cry from "progressive" Henry Wallace, Roosevelt's previous vice president. But at least, Gromyko noted, Truman "always supported Roosevelt on foreign policy."[11] But if Gromyko and other Soviet observers did not quite know what to make of Truman, their learning curve was steep.

On April 20, barely a week into his presidency, Truman called Ambassador Harriman to the White House to discuss the state of Soviet–American relations. For some time now, Harriman had felt himself to be something of a canary in a coalmine. Observing Soviet policies at close range – on Poland, Romania, and a host of other issues – he tried to warn Washington that the Soviets were intent on establishing "totalitarianism, ending personal liberty and democracy as we know and respect it."[12] He shared his apprehension with Ivan Maisky in early April. "Recently Soviet–American relations have suffered from ... a series of misunderstandings," Harriman told Maisky. "The President is very upset and disappointed." Pointing to growing "irritation" in the United States with Soviet actions in Europe, Harriman predicted that any further, even minor, "incidents" could lead to a "storm." "Our public," he added, "is prone to hysteria."[13] What the ambassador did not say was that Roosevelt – whether he was really as upset and disappointed as Harriman claimed – had not heeded his warnings and did not take up his suggestion of using economic power to pressure the Soviets into compliance.

Truman, by contrast, appeared open to Harriman's prognostications, and, in particular, to the idea of using economic aid as a lever to assure better Soviet behavior. Truman said that "he was not in any sense afraid of the Russians and that he intended to be firm but fair since in his opinion the Soviet Union needed us more than we needed them." He then explained to Harriman that although he did not rule out concessions, he expected to get his way 85 percent of the time.[14]

Truman soon had an opportunity to test his negotiating stance: Stalin decided to send Molotov to the United States, both to feel out the new president and, while he was at it, to attend the UN conference in San Francisco. Molotov's arrival was preceded by another unpleasant development in Allied relations: the Soviets announced that they were about to conclude a treaty of friendship and mutual assistance with 'their' Polish government, without waiting for the establishment of a government that would be recognized by London and Washington. Vyshinsky reported with glee that after he told Harriman on April 16 that "people of Poland were demanding a treaty with the Soviet Union," the latter was "obviously taken aback" and "did not know how to react."[15] In Washington, though, Molotov faced a pushback from the British and the Americans who accused him of violating the Yalta provisions on Poland. Truman had a showdown with Molotov on April 23, telling him "with great firmness" (according to the US transcript) that "an agreement had been reached on Poland and that it only remained for Marshal Stalin to carry it out in accordance with his word."[16] Truman recalled that Molotov was surprised by the president's tone. "I have never been talked to like that in my life," he supposedly said. "Carry out your agreements and you won't get talked to like that," Truman recalled responding (though he probably made it up).[17]

Truman's get-tough policies raised some eyebrows even inside his own administration. Secretary of War Henry Stimson told the president in a meeting on April 23 that just twenty-five years prior much of Poland was

CHAPTER 2 THE PARTING OF WAYS

Russia's anyway, and that the Americans had to understand that Poland was important for Soviet security, or else – if they just kept pressing Stalin – they could end up in "very dangerous water." The Russians, he added, "were being more realistic than we were in regard to their own security." General George Marshall – Truman's future secretary of state – also urged Truman to tread cautiously.[18] Meanwhile, Stalin warned Molotov to resist pressure on Poland. The Soviet despot took comfort from the fact that his armies were relentlessly advancing on Berlin. "Things are going well on approaches to Berlin," he cabled Molotov. "As for the Allies, one can see that they have got stuck on the Elbe."[19]

The Polish issue was superficially resolved in June 1945. It took a trip to Moscow by Roosevelt's former confidant Harry Hopkins who had helped forge the wartime Soviet–American alliance. Sickly Hopkins, who got off his deathbed to parley with Stalin during the last week of May, told the Soviet leader of Truman's "sense of bewilderment at our inability to solve the Polish question."[20] Stalin launched into a litany of complaints about Soviet mistreatment by the United States, which included efforts to "humiliate" and "pressure" Moscow through, for example, abrupt cessation of Lend-Lease aid.[21] As for Poland, Stalin said, US and British demands marked a departure from the Yalta agreement. "There is a popular opinion in the West," Stalin told Hopkins, "that the Russians are fools, that all Russians are blind. But this is incorrect. The Russians can see as well as anyone else." He added: "If the Russians were treated as equals ... you can get a lot out of them. But they are subjected to pressure, the results will be exactly opposite."[22]

Still, Stalin ultimately gave a green light to several Poles from the Anglo-American list (including the previously blacklisted Mikołajczyk) to come to Moscow for consultations. But in talks with Harriman and Kerr, Molotov made it clear that whatever the result of these consultations, the Communists would remain in control.[23] The consultations ended with a large reception on June 23, which included the bizarre sight of the assembled Polish delegates singing "a traditional Polish drinking song in comrade Stalin's honor."[24] One of the singers, the soon-to-be deputy prime minister in the new Polish government, Mikołajczyk, asked Molotov on June 27 to give him his "utmost trust," promising in turn to "work in the most loyal manner."[25] Mikołajczyk remained in Poland for more than two years, fleeing finally in October 1947, not long after rigged elections entrenched the Communists in power.

The British and the Americans recognized the reconstituted Polish government on July 5, 1945, just in time for the Big Three conference at Potsdam. There was little doubt that the consultations had been a fig

PART I AMBITION

leaf. The new government was clearly subservient to the USSR. Given this unfortunate reality, a historian would have to ask whether Truman overplayed his hand by taking a stand over Poland in the first place. What did this do – except for making Stalin feel "humiliated" and so perhaps less prone to compromise where compromise was in fact possible? One answer to this critique would be to say that such toughness signaled to Stalin America's determination to push back against his postwar ambitions and that in itself had a deterrent effect in other areas of the difficult relationship. This debate cannot be profitably resolved. What is clear, though, is that for all his interest in the American recognition of his postwar gains, Stalin could – and did – discard legitimacy for basic security, when he could not have both, and pushed for his desired outcomes irrespective of whether Truman agreed to offer his blessing. This was not always the case, but it certainly was the case with Poland. Meanwhile, for all of Truman's determination to show the Soviets their proper place, he was not quite ready for a break with Moscow, even over as hot an issue as Poland. His willingness to confront the Soviets was for the time-being offset by the desire to maintain amity, not least for the purposes of the Soviet involvement in the war against Japan.

POTSDAM

By the time of the Allied conference at Potsdam (July 17–August 2, 1945), wartime camaraderie had already dissipated but Cold War tensions had not quite set in. Stalin's first meeting with Truman, on July 17, had none of the friendly banter of his earlier conversations with Roosevelt. Truman professed readiness to be Stalin's "friend," though we know from his diary entries on the same day that he was taken aback by the dictator's postwar appetites.[26] Just the previous day Truman learned that the United States had successfully tested the first atomic device at Alamogordo, New Mexico. That knowledge imbued Truman with a sense of confidence for the postwar world. "I can deal with Stalin," he jotted down. "He's honest – but smart as hell."[27]

At Potsdam, Stalin pushed hard on the Allies – quite a bit harder than at Yalta. His forces had taken Berlin, and he had already imposed his preferred governments on Eastern Europe. An agreement with China was also in sight. The extent of his ambition showed when Stalin announced his claims to a military base in the Turkish Straits and testily reminded Churchill and Truman that the privileges the Soviets wanted were not all that different from what the British already had in Egypt, with the Suez Canal. He

44

CHAPTER 2 THE PARTING OF WAYS

also suddenly brought up Italy's former colonies in North Africa (where Stalin thought he was owed a share.) Churchill pushed back, claiming that Italian colonies were captured by the British through a valiant effort and at tremendous cost, to which Stalin said: "And the Soviet Army captured Berlin."[28] This not-so-subtle reference to double standards was one that the Soviets would frequently use in deflecting Western criticism, though it goes without saying that Stalin's "whataboutism" did not make much of a dent in the British and American resolve in keeping from Stalin what he could not or would not take by force.

But perhaps the most difficult conversations at Potsdam centered on Germany's reparations. At Yalta, Maisky – who oversaw the question on the Soviet side – floated a number: $10 billion for the USSR. As the Soviet forces moved into Germany, the asset-stripping began: whole factories were dismantled and shipped back to the USSR (there was also widespread looting of private property). This was still happening in Berlin even as the Big Three clashed at Potsdam, which was one reason that the NKVD (the precursor to the KGB) tried to obstruct movement of American personnel in and around the German capital, lest they inadvertently witnessed the breathtaking scale of the Soviet effort.[29] Still, Stalin thought that what he had in "his" part of Germany was not nearly enough, especially because a large section of the eventual Soviet zone was sliced off and given over to the Poles in compensation for the land taken from them in the East. That concern about having access to a bigger share of Germany's assets was an important reason for Stalin's U-turn on the dismemberment of Germany. Eventually – after days of bickering – the Western allies agreed to surrender to Stalin 10% of the strippable assets in their zones of occupation while exchanging a further 15% for supplies of foodstuff from the East. These disagreements over reparations were to broaden into disagreements over economic and financial policies that would soon tear Germany apart.

There was another element of the conference at Potsdam that in retrospect appears very significant: Stalin's resolute albeit futile effort to secure American and British diplomatic recognition of governments in his "sphere," especially Bulgaria, Romania, and Hungary. He pressed Truman and Churchill relentlessly to recognize these regimes but was told that they were not democratic and that in any case the Americans and the British did not know what was happening on the ground, as the Soviet authorities had been hampering access. "Fairy tales!" Stalin exclaimed, though he knew the allegations were true.[30] He complained about double standards, highlighting especially the fact that Italy, too, had not had an elected government, and yet it enjoyed the West's diplomatic recognition. None of these

PART I AMBITION

Figure 2 Churchill, Truman, and Stalin at Potsdam, July 1945.
Source: Ullstein Bild/Getty Images.

arguments made much of a difference for the time-being, leaving Stalin disappointed. He did manage to extract an important concession, though. The United States and Britain renounced all rights to German assets in Bulgaria, Finland, Hungary, Romania, and the eastern part of Austria, which amounted to indirect acceptance of the reality of Soviet control of Eastern Europe. The Potsdam decisions, Molotov concluded on August 6, "are to our advantage. In effect, this sphere of influence has been recognized as ours."[31]

THE BOMB

After a tense meeting on July 24, where Stalin and his former wartime partners argued about the merits of recognizing Soviet gains in Eastern Europe, Truman walked up to Stalin and told him about a new weapon of immense destructive capacity. "The Russian Premier showed no special interest," Truman recalled. "All he said was that he was glad to hear it and hoped we would make 'good use of it against the Japanese.'"[32] Churchill, standing at a distance, was carefully watching Stalin's expression. "I was sure," the British prime minister later recalled, "that he had no idea of the significance of

CHAPTER 2 THE PARTING OF WAYS

what he was being told. Evidently in his intense toils and stresses the atomic bomb played no part."[33]

Truman and Churchill could not have been more wrong. The Soviet leadership had taken a keen interest in the Manhattan Project. Stalin knew a great deal because of the extensive Soviet espionage network in the United States. Soviet intelligence became interested in atomic fission as early as January 1941 (when the NKVD instructed their New York station to gather materials on this "apparently feasible problem").[34] By 1942 the NKVD's foreign intelligence directorate and its military partner, the GRU, received hundreds of pages of intelligence on British and US atomic efforts. On September 28, 1942 the Soviet State Defense Committee approved a resolution "on organizing uranium work," which effectively launched the Soviet atomic project.[35] There were limits to this "work," imposed by the war itself: Stalingrad and Kursk still lay ahead. But efforts intensified as the Germans were rolled back: on December 3, 1944 the Soviet leader entrusted the project to his brutal henchman and the head of the NKVD, Lavrenty Beria: a clear sign that he understood the importance of the effort.[36]

The Soviet dictator was a good actor. At Potsdam, he fooled both the president and the prime minister. He later told Molotov about Truman's demarche. "They are raising the price," Molotov replied. "Let them," Stalin said.[37]

The first A-bomb fell on Hiroshima on August 6, 1945, killing tens of thousands, demolishing an entire city in a flash. The bombing of Nagasaki on August 9 was nearly as devastating. Truman knew that he no longer needed Stalin's "help" in defeating Japan, a rationale for Roosevelt's concessions at Yalta. But Stalin was determined to pursue his promised gains. On August 8 – a week before the date Stalin had given Truman at Potsdam – the Soviet Union declared a war on Japan. The Soviet forces presently poured across the border into Manchuria and Korea and launched an assault on the Japanese in South Sakhalin and along the Kurile chain. The fact that Emperor Hirohito made his famous surrender broadcast on August 15 made no difference to Stalin: he pressed relentlessly along the entire front to capture as much territory as possible in the final days of war.[38]

That final push included an episode that has not attracted much attention from historians, although it is of some significance for understanding Stalin's postwar strategy. As the Soviet offensive in the Far East unfolded, Stalin pondered the possibility of invading Hokkaido, Japan's second largest island. It made strategic sense: control of Hokkaido would turn the Sea of Okhotsk into a Soviet lake, protecting newly acquired Sakhalin and the Kurile islands. Hokkaido could also become Stalin's trump card in guaranteeing a serious Soviet role in the postwar governance of defeated Japan. Military plans were duly prepared, with August 24 designated as the landing date.[39] All that remained was obtaining Truman's agreement to this operation. On August 16, Stalin sent Truman a missive, asking that the Soviets be allowed to occupy the northern half of Hokkaido. This, Stalin cynically claimed, was important for the Soviet "public opinion," ending the letter with a plea or perhaps a threat: "I would very much like for my modest requests to meet with no objections."[40]

Truman fired back on August 18, rejecting Stalin's "proposal" about occupying north Hokkaido outright and, indeed, pushing back on Stalin by asking in his turn for the right to establish an American airbase on the Kurile islands, which Yalta had granted to the USSR. Stalin was so scandalized by this message that he crossed out the word "President" in front of Truman, as if suggesting that the upstart in the White House did not deserve such a high title![41] In his response to Truman, probably the most hostile in tone since their correspondence began the previous April, Stalin noted about Hokkaido: "I must say that I and my colleagues did not expect such an answer from you." As for the US airbase in the Kuriles, Stalin's reply read: "such demands are usually made of a defeated state or of such an allied state which is not capable of defending this or that part of its own territory." Stalin also reminded Truman that neither Yalta nor Potsdam allowed for any such airbases.[42] In later correspondence, the Soviet leader relented and agreed mockingly to provide the US with an airbase if the Americans in their turn allowed him to set up a base on the Aleutian Islands. The matter was allowed to quietly fall by the wayside.

Meanwhile, Stalin called off the operation against Hokkaido, precluding the kind of division of Japan that marked the end of war in Germany and in Korea. Although tensions in Soviet–American relations were already quite evident, he was determined to avert a direct clash with the United States. Was that because he feared the Bomb? This is an attractive explanation. We know that although he repeatedly downplayed the Bomb's significance – "not atomic bombs, but armies decide the war," Stalin famously claimed – in reality, he attached great significance to the new weapon, and fully appreciated its power to intimidate.[43] This is a case of paying attention to what Stalin did, not to what he said. Sure enough, on August 20, 1945 – in fact, in the middle of the spat with Truman over Hokkaido and airbase rights – Stalin approved the establishment of the Special Committee (headed by Beria) to marshal all state resources to the accomplishment of what soon became known simply as "Project Number One" – the development of the atomic bomb.[44]

CHAPTER 2 THE PARTING OF WAYS

But while Stalin worried about a confrontation with the United States, there was much more to his policy in the Far East. He was very concerned about keeping the Yalta framework intact because it legitimized his very substantial gains. Stalin was not averse to testing the limits of the agreement when he could get away with it. The attempted operation in Hokkaido was precisely one such test. But he backed off at the first display of American resolve because by keeping at it Stalin would have risked Yalta, and that was plainly unacceptable. It is tempting to regard the Soviet leader as someone who only understood the language of force. Stalin, to be sure, perfectly understood the language of force but it was not the only language he understood. He expected Truman to respect Soviet claims on a quid pro quo basis. But in the summer of 1945 this expectation began to fade. Hokkaido was one such case. Another was Stalin's ploy to acquire a colony in Africa. It is to this frustrated ploy that we now turn.

THE ITALIAN COLONIES

"We wanted Libya after the war," Molotov recalled. "Stalin tells [me]: come on, push!"[45] Reflecting on the unrealized Soviet aspirations in the Mediterranean late in his retirement, Molotov felt they were not worth the effort. These aspirations were "difficult to justify." "It was good that we backed off in time, or it could have led to a joint aggression against us."[46] The abortive Soviet attempt to secure a foothold on the African continent could be seen as an example of Stalin's opportunism and boundless ambition. But from his point of view, there was nothing unusual about this attempt. Far from being a bizarre dictatorial whim that it has on occasion appeared to be in retrospect, the Soviet push for a trusteeship in North Africa was a logical component of Moscow's overall approach to the postwar settlement. It was a manifestation of imperialism in an imperial age. It was the American approach that was out of tune with the prevailing European custom. But Stalin did not know that. As with Eastern Europe, what he most wanted was recognition of his gains by the United States. Only, unlike the case of Eastern Europe, the Soviet Union did not have troops in Africa. In Libya's case, Stalin heavily depended on friendly indulgence of his wartime allies.

The question of divvying up the colonies was first broached in Soviet postwar planning. It was not the most important issue discussed by the Litvinov and Maisky commissions but it was not entirely ignored either. Writing to Stalin and Molotov in January 1945, just before the Yalta

Conference, Litvinov noted that the Soviet Union should not oppose the US "open door" policy where it meant the weakening of British, Dutch, or French hold on their colonies. "We could even support these American aspirations," he added.[47] A few weeks later Litvinov sent another note to Molotov, suggesting that the best solution would be to replace the discredited system of awarding individual colonial mandates with genuinely collective mandates, which would allow for joint management of colonies by major powers. This, Litvinov intimated, would preclude any one power from extracting benefits from these colonies, while denying them to others. Litvinov thus argued that decolonization would benefit both the United States and the Soviet Union to the obvious detriment of the existing colonial powers.[48]

The colonial question reemerged in May, when it came up for discussion at the UN founding conference in San Francisco. The Soviets were alarmed by the US formulation (in the draft of the UN Charter) that would have the effect of leaving the existing mandates in the hands of whatever power exercised control on the ground.[49] The Soviet representative in San Francisco, Andrei Gromyko (who would continue to a long, fruitful career as the Soviet foreign minister), pushed hard to delete this formulation, while his superiors in Moscow tried to understand why the Americans would try to indefinitely freeze the colonial status quo that only benefited the traditional imperialist powers like the British and the French.[50] At last, Molotov ordered Gromyko to strike a bargain: the Soviet delegation would drop its objection to the offending formulation on the condition that "in case the Soviet Government should be proposed as the administering authority of some suitable trust territory – though he had no specific territory in mind – the United States Government would support the Soviet Government as eligible for such a post."[51] The Americans with whom Gromyko raised this reservation on June 9 – the chairman of the US delegation (and the departing secretary of state) Edward Stettinius and member of the delegation Harold Stassen – were completely sympathetic. "Entirely reasonable," was how Stettinius put it at the time.[52]

Gromyko made a tactical mistake by not asking for the assignment of a specific mandate there and then. It is understandable – he did not have the authority to. As a member of the US delegation Senator John Connally noted, sympathetically, poor Gromyko "had developed an inferiority complex as a result of having to wait for instructions from Moscow on every issue."[53] It was difficult to issue clear instructions, however, when in reality the Soviets had very limited knowledge of the vast domains of their imperial rivals. They were now spending time on such basic tasks as drawing up lists of colonies, like the one prepared by the prominent legal expert Vsevolod Durdenevsky on June 8. This offered an overview of territories that could be "redistributed" after the war: their geographic location, their economic resources, their population. Most tellingly, Durdenevsky's list included the "likely claimants" to various colonies, including those of the former enemy states. He thought, for instance, that the most likely claimants to former Italian colonies in Africa would be Great Britain and Ethiopia; China would likely claim Taiwan and Korea; various Pacific islands would end up in the US hands. Durdenevsky took it for granted that the colonies that belonged to Britain and France before the war – from Africa, to the Middle East, to Southeast Asia – would return to their imperial owners.[54] He thus outlined a vision of an explicitly imperialistic world. All that remained was to find the Soviet place in it.

This was a task that Litvinov put himself to later that month. By then, the trusteeship provisions of the UN Charter had already been agreed to, raising the possibility that there would be a redistribution of colonies under trusteeship system of the new international organization. The juiciest piece of territory, Litvinov suggested to Stalin and Molotov in a June 22 memorandum, was Palestine, which had a "huge strategic significance" because of its proximity to the Suez Canal and an Iraqi oil pipeline that reached the sea at Haifa. For this very reason, though, Litvinov expected the British to put up an insurmountable resistance to any Soviet moves in the area. Obtaining Palestine, he wrote, was "extremely desirable but probably unrealistic." Much more realistic was bidding for the colonies of former enemy states. There were islands in the Pacific and colonies in Sub-Saharan Africa, which had belonged to Germany, but they were too far away from and so "cannot really be of interest to the Soviet Union." "Why can't they be?" – someone (probably Molotov) wrote ambitiously in the margins – "they can!" Still, in Litvinov's view, the best bet were the Italian colonies in the Mediterranean and in North Africa.[55]

Among these, Litvinov immediately ruled out Somalia and Eritrea. Both, to be sure, were useful as bases linking the Black Sea and the Far East, and as "a means of influence on the nearby Arab countries and Abyssinia." Unfortunately, though, even if the Soviets managed to secure these colonies, they would be "surrounded on all sides by British colonies and naval bases." Litvinov then looked closer to Soviet shores. Most important, he thought, were the Dodecanese, a string of islands spanning the seas between Greece and Turkey. These islands were of immense geopolitical import, because they could be used "as platform for attacking Anatolia [in

Turkey], Greece and Egypt, and as a key point on the way to the Aegean Sea and, further, to the Dardanelles." Even if the Soviets could not get all these islands (in case of strong British resistance), Litvinov proposed to bid for at least a couple, those lying closest to the Turkish Straits. Finally, there was Libya, useless economically, being just a "huge desert space" but important strategically, as it would allow the Soviets "to stand on firm legs in the Mediterranean." Libya in fact consisted of three parts: Tripolitania, Fezzan, and Cyrenaica, and Litvinov thought the last was the best option, if the Soviets could not get all of Libya.[56]

Litvinov was mindful, however, of the American public opinion. For this reason, it was best for the Soviets to push for joint supervision of the Italian colonies – something the British would find hard to oppose – and then, due to "technical difficulties," to propose simply dividing up the spoils. The alternative was to do it the other way around: to ask for an individual mandate, as a fallback position, to agree eventually to joint supervision, which would still allow the Soviets a measure of influence in the Mediterranean.[57]

Such, then, was the background story to Soviet claims in Libya. Litvinov's letters were read by Stalin and Molotov. How much the Soviet leaders shared the views of the former foreign commissar is another matter. The fact that Stalin in the end made a push for a chunk of Libya (though not Cyrenaica, as Litvinov recommended, but Tripolitania) suggests that he was in agreement with the thinking that underpinned Litvinov's memoranda. The idea, as Molotov later explained in a cable to the Italian Communists, was for the Soviet Union to "wedge itself into the Mediterranean" at England's expense. This would allow Moscow to be "helpful" to the "democratic" (i.e. Communist) forces in Italy, while also "helping Tripolitania to quickly embark on the road of independence and democratic development, which is also in the common interest of the democratic countries."[58]

Molotov's framing was thus both geopolitical and ideological, though that was of course directed to an external Communist audience. Internally, by contrast, geopolitical themes were at the forefront. For all the public Soviet insistence on the right of self-determination for colonies, there was hardly a mention of anticolonialism in Litvinov's memoranda. Instead, Litvinov highlighted the strategic benefits of disrupting British pretensions of imperial hegemony. This approach predated Communism – it was, rather, a direct descendant of nineteenth-century geopolitics. Fittingly, Litvinov's analysis concluded with a historical overview of the tsarist efforts to get involved in the nineteenth-century scramble for Africa. "The hopes

CHAPTER 2 THE PARTING OF WAYS

of Tsarist Russia went unfulfilled," lamented Litvinov in his final pronouncement on the subject.[59] Perhaps Stalin's USSR could do better.

By late June 1945 the Soviet leadership had given thought to the question of colonies: not only what they wanted but also how to get there. However, the Soviets were a little too slow in obtaining American support. Gromyko followed his informal probe of June 9 with a more formal letter, which he sent to Stettinius on June 20. Without disclosing the direction of Soviet thinking, he asked for a concrete offer of a colonial mandate. Stettinius replied three days later, sounding a positive note but not committing to any particular course of action. Gromyko knew that the opportunity was slipping away. On July 10 he wrote a letter to Molotov, suggesting that the foreign minister raise the issue of concrete territories with the new secretary of state, James Byrnes. Gromyko, like Litvinov before him, thought that an individual trusteeship was better for the Soviets than collective administration. Among other benefits, according to Gromyko, this would allow the Soviets to demonstrate their moral and political superiority to the British and the French in preparing these territories for independence (whereas the old colonial empires had no intention of doing this). The most important thing was to get the Americans to back Soviet proposals, keeping in mind that the American position was "a lot closer" to the Soviets than the British and the French. Gromyko asked Molotov to raise the issue at Potsdam.[60]

Stalin himself brought up the issue at Potsdam, during his very first meeting with President Truman. The US record of this meeting – just a few notes jotted down by Truman's interpreter Charles Bohlen – make the Soviet leader sound almost apologetic about his claims: "maybe stupid," Stalin said before discussing his hopes for the redistribution of Italy's colonies.[61] (Nothing of the sort appears in the published Russian version). Truman did not give a direct answer, saying merely that he was prepared to discuss any questions.[62] Later that day Truman recounted his impressions of Stalin's demands in his diary: "it is dynamite – but I have some dynamite too which I am not exploding now."[63] He was clearly referring to the news of the A-bomb. It is curious that Truman linked the two issues: he evidently thought that the Bomb would be a trump card that he would play to beat back Stalin's imperialist ambitions.[64] This was rather out of tune with the Soviet expectations that the US would be more concerned with British imperialism and would welcome the Soviets as a counterweight to the British presence. Stalin's postwar vision began to fall apart as soon as it became apparent that it was his ambitions that bothered Truman, and not the supposed US–British disagreements that never materialized. And it became apparent soon enough.

PART I AMBITION

LONDON CONFERENCE OF FOREIGN MINISTERS

The fall of 1945 became a turning point for Allied relations. With Japan's official surrender on September 2, 1945, the Second World War was over at last. Tensions had long been building up between Moscow and Washington. Yet even Potsdam saw signs – however superficial – of the erstwhile camaraderie. That spirit faded by September. The London Conference of Foreign Ministers, convened on September 11 to discuss peace treaties with Italy and the former Axis satellites, almost immediately ground to an unproductive stalemate. The meeting, attended, in addition to Molotov and Byrnes, by British Foreign Secretary Ernest Bevin, French Foreign Minister Georges Bidault, and his Chinese colleague Wang Shijie, became a harbinger of the coming Cold War.

Old photos of James F. Byrnes and Vyacheslav Molotov often show them holding each other by the elbow, as if they were best friends. They had worked well enough through Potsdam, though there they were still in the shadow of their bosses, Truman and Stalin, and the times were not quite as bad. London was their first independent trial of strength. The two made for quite a contrast. Molotov (real name: Skryabin) was born to a relatively well-off Russian family. Like many young men of his age and background, he read Marxist literature and became involved in revolutionary activities. Molotov was present at the creation of the Soviet experiment and stuck with Stalin through thick and thin, avoiding the sad fate of many of his party comrades who fell victim to the dictator's bloody purges. He became foreign minister in 1939, replacing the hapless Litvinov who, as we have seen, was deemed too much of an Anglophile at a time when Stalin pursued rapprochement with Nazi Germany. Molotov's two most pronounced traits were his dogmatism and his slavish subservience to Stalin. He was also known, unflatteringly, as Iron Arse for his well-known ability to outlast interlocutors in diplomatic negotiations.

Eight years older than Molotov, James F. Byrnes was a former judge and politician from South Carolina who became America's new secretary of state in July 1945, replacing Roosevelt's appointee Edward Stettinius. A New Dealer who had served in all three branches of government, Byrnes became known during the war as "assistant president for the home front." He brought a wealth of experience and a degree of expertise in foreign affairs Truman could hardly match (Roosevelt had even brought him to Yalta). Yet, as British Ambassador Lord Halifax described Byrnes, he was "fundamentally unsure of himself, somewhat insecure socially and intellectually."[65] But would he entertain the Kremlin's ambitious postwar claims? The Soviet foreign minister was eager to find out.

54

CHAPTER 2 THE PARTING OF WAYS

The test case, for Molotov, was the American attitude towards Moscow's colonial claims in Tripolitania, a subject, we have seen, Stalin himself probed with Truman in Potsdam. The Soviet Union, Molotov told Byrnes in their first meeting on September 14, wanted to "try its hand at colonial administration." Baiting Byrnes, Molotov said that the United States and Great Britain should also have a share in the administration of Italian colonies: "the only rivalry would be as to which country could prove itself to be the best administrator." Byrnes rejected the idea out of hand as an imperialist ploy. He could not understand, he said, how the Soviet Union with its huge territory could also "rule millions of Arabs." "The Soviet Union wants to show that it can do it better than the Italians," countered Molotov.[66]

On the same day, at the general session of the five ministers, Byrnes presented the US proposal on collective trusteeship for the Italian colonies. In fairness, the American approach was rather out of tune with the traditional imperial methods of the European powers. There was therefore nothing particularly outrageous about the Soviet demands: indeed, they made sense in the context of the familiar milieu of European colonialism. What Molotov and Stalin did not realize, however, was that this milieu was rapidly giving way to a very different, bipolar world. The shift was apparent right there and then, at that meeting. When Molotov brought up his proposal concerning the Soviet trusteeship over Tripolitania, both the British and the French opposed the idea. Bevin proposed to postpone the issue in order not to "shock the conscience of the world."[67] Molotov recalled the episode in more dramatic terms: "Bevin jumped up, screaming: 'This is shocking, shocking! Shocking, shocking! You've never been there!'"[68]

There is something in the record that Molotov very conspicuously failed to report to Stalin. Three days into the conference, Molotov suddenly asked Byrnes if he had an atomic bomb in his side pocket. "You don't know Southerners," Byrnes replied. "We carry our artillery in our hip pocket. If you don't cut out all this stalling and let us get down to work I am going to pull an atomic bomb out of my hip pocket and let you have it." Molotov is recorded as having "laughed" at this blatant atomic blackmail. It is unclear why he never told Stalin. Perhaps he worried that the dictator would see his lieutenant as having weak nerves.[69]

On the night of September 14, Molotov cabled Stalin. "There was a big discussion," he wrote, adding that the Soviet proposal about colonies "caused certain disarray." Molotov recounted the highlights of the ensuing debate, including the two justifications that he made for claiming Tripolitania. The first was that the Soviet Union suffered at Italy's hands in the war and so had a "moral" right to a colony. The second – rather macabre, in view of brutal deportations and ethnic cleansing that became the hallmark of Stalin's nationalities policy – was that Moscow had "considerable experience" in dealing with the "national question." But it was clear even to Molotov that these justifications were shallow, so he suggested to Stalin that he would raise an additional argument: that the Soviets needed presence in the Mediterranean to assure the safety of their shipping.[70]

Late on the night of September 15 Molotov received additional instructions from Stalin who asked that Molotov remind the other participants of the American promise to give the Soviets an individual mandate: "I have in mind the letter from Stettinius. This argument should be put forward saliently." As an ostensible concession to the Allies, Stalin instructed Molotov to promise that the Soviets would not build bases in Tripolitania. Stalin, however, continued to insist on the right of the Soviet Navy to dock in the ports of Tripolitania. At the end, he stressed again that Molotov had to push for individual trusteeship, "because this was the type of trusteeship implied in San Francisco."[71]

Although there was little point in flogging a dead horse, Molotov had to be true to Stalin's instructions. When he saw Byrnes next, on the afternoon of September 16, the Soviet foreign minister broached the issue of colonies one more time. He referred to the exchange between Gromyko and Stettinius, when the latter, "acting on behalf of the American government promised that the American government would support Soviet demands."[72] Molotov, when recounting this conversation in a cable to Stalin, made a point to stress how Byrnes "pretended" that he knew nothing of the letter, and how, when pushed by Molotov, he claimed that the letter did not refer to any specific territory, "having forgotten about his previous statement to the effect that he was not familiar with Stettinius' promise."[73] "I fell on him," cabled Molotov, "[saying] that the Americans are not living up to their promises ... Byrnes equivocated and hedged with general phrases. At the first opportunity I will press on him and on the others."[74]

Molotov never did get his second chance to "press" Byrnes or any of the others. Tripolitania remained out of reach, although on several later occasions Stalin attempted to bring it back into the equation. The dictator would later argue that the Soviet Union was being short-changed by the Allies. "The United Kingdom," he argued, "had India and her possessions in the Indian Ocean ... the United States had China and Japan, but the Soviet[s] had nothing."[75] He would even try to placate the British by supporting their colonial ventures on a quid pro quo basis.[76] It soon became clear, however, that Stalin's colonial aspirations were becoming less of an end in themselves and more of a means to secure Allied concessions on matters that he really cared about. As he would later write to Molotov, revealing his cynical mindset, colonial independence leaders were "by and large up for sale, and don't so much care about the independence of their territories as about maintaining their own privileges ... The time is not yet ripe for us to cross swords and quarrel with the entire world for the sake of these territories ... Therefore, the interests of our country demand that we show certain flexibility in this matter on the condition that the partners for their part compensate us with appropriate concessions in other areas."[77]

Stalin thus walked back from his claims on Tripolitania, which remained under British military control until 1951, when it was incorporated into the newly proclaimed Kingdom of Libya.

THE DEADLOCK

The unpleasant meeting between Byrnes and Molotov that put an end to Soviet aspirations for a trusteeship also marked the beginning of a different quarrel, one that resulted in the failure of the London Conference. On September 16 Byrnes told Molotov that the United States would not sign peace treaties with the governments of Romania and Bulgaria until they were reorganized on a more "representative" basis. What was Byrnes doing here? Perhaps, emboldened by the American monopoly of the A-bomb, Byrnes had now decided to play it tough, trying to pierce the Iron Curtain and roll back some of the Soviet gains in Eastern Europe. Or perhaps Byrnes recognized the limits of American power. He knew that Romania and Bulgaria had been lost by the West, and all he now wanted was a face-saving compromise: inclusion of some non-Communist personalities in the reorganized governments of these two countries in return for American recognition.[78]

Whatever the reason for the US refusal to recognize the Soviet-sponsored governments of Bulgaria and Romania, the news did not go down well with Molotov. Even as he arrived in London, he received instructions from Stalin, ordering him to "stand firm, and not make any concessions" on this question.[79] Things were about to get nasty.

On September 17, when the foreign ministers gathered again, they discussed the fate of the Dodecanese islands, an archipelago in the southeast Aegean Sea, not far from the Turkish coast. The Soviets had earlier decided not to press their claims to the islands: perhaps Stalin and Molotov believed that such claims were simply unrealistic. But now, at the meeting, Molotov suddenly dug in his heels: he announced that he was not against handing the islands over to Greece but that he wanted additional time to explore the question. Byrnes asked why the problem could not be resolved there and then. If they delegated the question to their deputies, he said, the deputies would merely come back split four-against-one, which would hardly be helpful to "his Soviet friend."[80] Byrnes was clearly losing patience. But the "four-against-one" argument hit a raw nerve with Molotov. Moscow's postwar planners assumed that they could exploit contradictions among the Allies. This presumption was increasingly difficult to sustain.

The same four-against-one argument came up again on September 19. Tensions were running high. That morning Molotov practically accused Bevin of anti-Slavic racism, when the latter spoke in favor of giving the city of Trieste to Italy (rather than to Yugoslavia).[81] Later in the afternoon Bevin and Molotov clashed over Italian reparations. Molotov pushed for a figure. Bevin argued that with Italy in desperate straits, this would just shift the burden of reparations to the British taxpayer. Molotov signaled his "extreme dissatisfaction" but proposed to submit the matter to their deputies when Byrnes chimed in, saying that he would agree to this only on the understanding that the deputies then submit a "majority report." Taken aback, Molotov asked for a couple of days to consider Byrnes's proposal: he needed instructions from Stalin.

Stalin was angry. He had become annoyed with how these negotiations were proceeding. He thought that the US unwillingness to recognize Romania and Bulgaria went a step too far. Already on September 18, he upbraided Molotov for being insufficiently tough with Byrnes. "Byrnes is trying to scare us with the threat of stating officially that they will not want to conclude a peace treaty with Groza's government. You have to reply to Byrnes that such a policy is an unacceptable threat and the rudest interference in Romania's internal affairs." In case Byrnes persisted, Molotov could hint that the Soviet Union would in its turn refuse to sign a peace treaty with Italy.[82]

The following day Stalin elaborated these instructions in another cable, telling Molotov to "directly tie" the questions of peace treaties with Romania and Bulgaria, on the one hand, and Italy on the other. Should the Americans make an official statement refusing to sign peace treaties with the Soviet-sponsored governments, Molotov had to do the same, only with respect to Italy, whose government was in any case was "less democratic" than those in Bucharest and Sofia. Stalin ended with a threat that highlighted the limits of his patience. "It may happen that the Allies would conclude a peace treaty with Italy without us. So what? Then we'll have a precedent. We will have the opportunity to conclude treaties with our satellites without the Allies."[83] This must have been one of the

CHAPTER 2 THE PARTING OF WAYS

first times that Stalin used the term "our satellites" when speaking of the countries of Eastern Europe. There was flexibility in Stalin's vision for the postwar world. Only, it did not extend to the part of the world he already considered "his."

But what Stalin was most concerned about was that the London Conference was increasingly turning into a four-against-one standoff. He probably came to this conclusion after reading Molotov's September 19 telegram about the American efforts to "intimidate" the Soviets with the idea that issues could be resolved by the other four in the face of their resistance. Late that night Stalin sent Molotov a cable, in which he said that he "noticed" that the Chinese were taking part in the discussions of the peace treaty with Italy, although they were not directly affected. This ran contrary to the stipulations of the Potsdam Conference. He demanded that the Chinese be kicked out.[84]

Molotov waited a whole day before replying. He may have been thinking how to correct his mistake: after all, it was Molotov who agreed on the very first day, when procedural questions were being discussed, that the French and the Chinese would participate in the council but not vote unless they were directly concerned.[85] At last he came up with a face-saving method. During the sessions on September 20, Molotov proposed to the other delegations that they entrust discussion of peace treaties with Finland and Romania to their deputies, with only those countries participating who had signed the terms of surrender. In Finland's case, this was Britain and the Soviet Union; and in Romania's, the Soviets, the Americans, and the British.

The transcripts show that Bidault and Bevin vocally opposed the idea. On the whole, however, the sessions lacked the tension of the previous meetings. Molotov even agreed to some American proposals on Romania as forming the basis for discussion. Perhaps he hoped that by appearing cooperative he could win his colleagues' support in implementing the letter of Stalin's instructions. Summing up these discussions on September 21, Molotov noted that "his partners" opposed his idea of excluding some of the deputies from discussion of peace treaties but that he "intended to insist."[86] In effect, Molotov attempted to redirect Stalin's attention from the actual council sessions, in which the French and the Chinese continued to participate, to the rather meaningless meetings of the deputies. It was a risky move, because it suggested that Molotov not only attempted to cover up his mistake but that in doing so he was effectively taking the Allies' side. Given Stalin's propensity to see things in the worst light, this is probably how he interpreted his lieutenant's moves.

PART I AMBITION

Hours after receiving Molotov's cable, Stalin sent a reply. There was a drastic change of tone. Instead of friendly "comrade Stalin," the cable came from "the highest authority" [*instantsiya*]; the familiar *ty* – the pronoun used between friends that Stalin used to refer to Molotov in his earlier telegrams – was dropped in favor of a formal *Vy*. Stalin was not joking. He wanted Molotov to "unequivocally" carry out the decisions of the Potsdam Conference, that is, to close the council to all parties not directly involved in the questions discussed – that is, the French and the Chinese. Stalin then explained his concerns: "When the Soviet Union was opposed by the Anglo-Saxon states – the USA and England – none of them raised the question of majority and minority. But now, when, in contravention with the decision of the Berlin Conference and with your connivance, the Anglo-Saxons managed to rope in the Chinese and the French, Byrnes found it possible to raise the question of majority and minority."[87]

Stalin thus revealed the sources of his dissatisfaction. He had been unhappy with the rejection of Soviet claims to Tripolitania and Allied obstruction on other matters, including peace treaties with Romania and Bulgaria. However, there was a bigger problem still: it was Byrnes's attempt to play the four-against-one card that changed the game for Stalin. His cable to Molotov did not even mention Romania and Bulgaria or any other contentious issues of the council meeting. In other words, he was more concerned with the very fact of American pressure than with any specific issue in Allied relations. Issues could be negotiated (with due respect for bottom lines) but pressure could not be tolerated. Stalin, who himself regularly resorted to bullying in foreign policy deeply resented being bullied and blamed his lieutenant for weakness of nerves.

Molotov hastened to reply, his tone subdued and apologetic. "I recognize," he wrote to Stalin on the morning of the September 22, "that I made a serious omission. I will take measures without delay to implement the decisions of the Berlin Conference in accordance with the instructions from the Highest Authority." Molotov then explained that it would mean in effect kicking the Chinese out of the council (since Asia-related matters were not being discussed) and allowing the French to take part in some sessions. "This way will be better, of course," the foreign minister concluded – "although it will be a sharp turn in the affairs of the Council of Ministers."[88] And so it was. Molotov asked to postpone the council session scheduled for that morning. Instead, at 11:45am he told Byrnes and Bevin that the decisions the council made on September 11 – allowing the Chinese and the French to participate in the discussions – had to be reversed. Flabbergasted, Byrnes and Bevin refused to go along. Bevin thought that Molotov's

60

proposal would make the council into a "farce."[89] Obeying Stalin's instructions, Molotov stood fast.

Substantial discussion quickly ground to a halt. An indication of how tense things had become, Bevin told Molotov to his face on September 23 that he saw parallels in Great Britain's relations with the USSR and Hitler's Germany. Whatever Bevin had in mind – he hurried to qualify himself that he was not actually comparing the Soviet Union to Hitler – Molotov pounced on him right away. Hitler, he said, considered the Soviets to be an inferior race, and the Soviet Union "something like a geographic concept." "But what can be done," he continued, "if we do not consider ourselves to be an inferior race but consider the Soviet Union to be a state that has equal rights with other states[?] ..." Molotov then told Bevin that he wanted the Soviet Union to be treated as an "equal" and lamented that now that Germany had been defeated, it was no longer needed as an "equal partner." He warned Bevin against attempts to "isolate the Soviet Union."[90]

This unusually intense presentation from a man who was not known to be easily given to melodrama reflected the deepest Soviet concern: perception of inequality vis-à-vis the West and resentment on the account of Western pressure and the supposed efforts to isolate the USSR. One could object to this – as Bevin immediately did – that it was not the case (Bevin even claimed that he thought it was the British who were treated by the other two great powers as an "inferior race") but the fact remains that this was what the Soviets thought at the time. It was not a diplomatic trick: this was the line that Stalin and Molotov took in their internal correspondence.

THE ALLIES ARE PRESSING ON YOU ...

Stalin was getting tired. He thought that progress would be made on peace treaties with the satellites. He hoped to reach an agreement on the former Italian colonies. But on all fronts Molotov failed to deliver. The Soviet leader then asked his foreign minister to raise one final issue – Japan. We know that the initiative to bring up Japan came from Stalin despite the absence of the relevant cable. Stalin's hand is evident in the abrupt manner Molotov raised the issue on September 24 and 25. Reading from a memorandum, he announced that the situation in Japan "urgently" called for "immediate" establishment of an Allied Control Council, which would allow the Soviet Union – alongside the United States, Britain, and China – to have a say in the Japanese occupation, and even to patrol streets in Tokyo.[91] Byrnes flatly refused even to consider this request.[92]

Stalin was livid. After receiving Molotov's summary of these fruitless discussions, he fired off a sharply worded cable to his lieutenant, accusing the British and the Americans of "insolence" for their unwillingness to take Soviet interests onboard: "This speaks to the fact that they lack the basic sense of respect for their ally," he wrote.

Stalin then let Molotov in on the intelligence that the Americans allegedly got their hands on Japan's gold reserves ($1–2 billion), and that they got the British to cooperate in the effort to cut the Soviets out of their share of the money. "You should hint at that, letting them understand that herein lies the reason why the Americans and the British oppose the creation of an Allied Control Council for Japan."[93] (This Molotov later did, to utter astonishment of the other council members). Stalin's bizarre interpretation of Byrnes's and Bevin's underlying motives should not surprise us: he was merely extrapolating from what he himself would have done. It was highway robbery but, then, Stalin had been a highway robber in his youth. Still, Stalin's disappointment was genuine. The problem was not just that Byrnes and Bevin were opposed to Soviet proposals but that they were now refusing even to discuss them. This was a big blow to Stalin's self-respect. He did not want to put forward any new arguments, and simply asked Molotov when he planned to finish the conference that was clearly not getting anywhere.

On September 27 Stalin cabled Molotov:

> In all probability the Americans will not want to leave the London Conference with empty hands. They will strive to get the Council to make decisions. The Allies are pressing on you to break your will and force you to make concessions. It is clear that you must display complete obduracy.[94]

In response, Molotov recounted to Stalin how during their latest meeting he "attacked" Byrnes, and called him a "dictator" (the US transcripts show nothing of the kind, suggesting that Molotov made it up to please Stalin with his toughness).[95] In reality, the Soviet foreign minister still held out a hope for a deal, and he explicitly contradicted Stalin, suggesting to him that if the Americans agreed to make at least one concession (on Bulgaria/Romania or on Japan) the Soviets could meet them halfway. Unlike Stalin, Molotov did not want to display "complete obduracy." He did not want the conference to fail.

Stalin, though, was concerned with bigger issues. For him, the diplomatic agenda of the Council of Foreign Ministers was not nearly as important as the overall impression that the conference would produce. If concessions were made, questions would be asked about the reasons for these concessions: Was it because the Soviets buckled under pressure? Was it because they were outgunned and isolated? Was it because they were afraid of the atomic bomb? Of course, Stalin did not explicitly spell out his rationale but it comes through clearly nonetheless. The failure of the conference to him was preferable to a negotiated solution that suggested that the Soviet Union was pressured to make concessions.

As for the conference, it was possible that it would end in failure, he wrote. "This gives us no cause to grieve. The failure of the conference will mean Byrnes's failure, and we have nothing to grieve about here."[96] A few days later, when Molotov cabled to him a draft of the Soviet statement that was to be issued at the end of the ill-fated conference, Stalin corrected his foreign minister by erasing the word "fruitful" from the statement. "We will not lose anything," he cabled on October 2 – "Only they will lose."[97] Later, in December, reflecting on the outcome of the conference, Stalin concluded that the Soviet Union "won the struggle" by taking a firm line. It could not be otherwise. "It is obvious," Stalin wrote, "that when you deal with partners such as the USA and Britain, we cannot make any serious gains if we begin giving in to threats, if we waver. To make any gains with this kind of partners, we must adopt the policy of firmness and perseverance."[98]

THE AFTERMATH

In the months after London Stalin remained in a foul mood. For all his insistence that the failure of the London Conference of Foreign Ministers was no big deal – that the West lost more – the Soviet dictator could not have been oblivious to the obvious. The United States still did not recognize the puppet governments of Bulgaria and Romania. The prospect of peace treaties with his satellites remained uncertain, and although Stalin claimed he did not care, he actually did, or else why would he have put so much effort into bringing the Americans around? He cared because US endorsement of these peace treaties would legitimize the Soviet sphere of influence in Eastern Europe, and Stalin's entire strategy since Yalta had been aimed at exactly this.

Meanwhile, the Americans showed no inclination to accommodate Moscow's pretensions in Japan, leaving Stalin grumbling that he had no role to play there, that the Soviets were being treated like "unneeded furniture" to the detriment of their "prestige."[99] "Perhaps America needs satellites, and not allies?" – he complained to US Ambassador Averell Harriman in late October, who visited with Stalin at his summer residence in Sochi. "I must say that the Soviet Union is not suited for this role. In any case, the

PART I AMBITION

Soviet Union has been placed in a situation, which is incompatible with the situation of a self-respecting ally."[100] But the Americans continued to insist that they would call the shots in Japan, even while promising to take Stalin's views into account.

Despite Stalin's pressure on the Chinese Communists to reach a deal with the Nationalists, peace in China seemed extremely fragile – so fragile that in November 1945 he ordered Soviet advisers and liaison officers out of Mao Zedong's quarters for fear of being implicated in the unfolding civil war.[101] When the Chinese Communist forces arrived in Manchuria to fill the political vacuum after the Japanese surrender, Stalin, as we have seen, ordered the Soviet military to prevent them from entering any of the large Manchurian cities. "Keep them out by force," he cabled Soviet commander Rodion Malinovsky.[102] In China, too, the elaborately constructed Yalta framework seemed to be crumbling, and for reasons that were altogether out of Stalin's hands.

To add to these frustrations, the Western media was rife with rumors of Stalin's ill-health, and of a power struggle in the ranks of the Soviet leadership. Stalin, in his paranoia, suspected that Molotov had permitted and, indeed, encouraged such rumors by failing to enforce censorship against foreign journalists in Moscow. On December 6, he fired off a telegram to the troika of Georgy Malenkov, Lavrenty Beria, and Anastas Mikoyan, accusing Molotov of failing to "treasure the interests of our state and the prestige of our government," all for the sake of "gaining popularity among certain foreign circles." "I can no longer consider such a comrade as my first deputy," the dictator snapped.[103] The trio then put these ominous accusations to Molotov, who "tearfully" begged for forgiveness, cabling Stalin that he would "try to deserve your trust through work."[104]

Amid all this bad news, James Byrnes proposed to hold a conference of foreign ministers in Moscow. The proposal – quite out of the blue – did not say anything about either French or Chinese participation (the key point of contention in London), which Stalin interpreted as a hands-down victory. The fact that Byrnes had failed to consult with the British, causing quite a mini-crisis in the US–British relationship, gave the wily dictator every reason to be pleased.[105] "For a time," he wrote to Molotov on December 9 – evidently forgiving him – "you yielded before the US pressure and intimidation, you started to waver, adopted a liberal policy towards foreign correspondents ..., hoping to thus placate the US and England." "It is obvious," he continued, "that when you deal with partners like the US and England, we cannot get anything serious if we yield to intimidation, if we show wavering."[106]

64

CHAPTER 2 THE PARTING OF WAYS

Compared to London, though, Moscow was relatively smooth sailing. Bevin, Byrnes, and Molotov managed to agree on previously intractable questions like the procedure for the drafting of peace treaties with the defeated powers, the set-up for Allied oversight in Japan, and even that most difficult question – what to do about Bulgaria and Romania, which the US still refused to recognize. The Soviets agreed to dilute puppet governments in both countries by adding several figures from the opposition. There were unexpected breakthroughs in relation to Korea (where it was agreed to set up a unified government) and on atomic energy control (the Soviets agreed to the establishment of the UN Atomic Energy Commission). Molotov would not have dared to indulge in such liberalism, but it was Stalin, in his own conversations with Bevin and Byrnes, who adopted a more reasonable position, making concessions here, curbing demands there. He violated his own rule – to display "complete obduracy" – because his complete obduracy would have resulted in the failure of the Moscow council meeting, and Stalin did not want another failure.

In the end, what ground the Americans and the British gave – for example, by conceding to largely cosmetic changes to the Bulgarian and Romanian governments – did not amount to much, and could have been attained at much lower costs to the USSR. Byrnes and Bevin remained steadfast in keeping the Soviets out of Tripolitania, and the promise to consult with the Soviets in the postwar administration of Japan was so vaguely worded that it could hardly count as a concession at all. So, Stalin's diplomatic victory was illusory; he did not get anything in Moscow that he could not have got by adopting a more reasonable negotiating position months earlier at the London fiasco.

CONCLUSION

During the Allied conference at Potsdam, Ambassador Averell Harriman walked up to Stalin to congratulate him on the capture of Berlin. "Czar Alexander got to Paris," Stalin reportedly said.[107] To Harriman and others like him this comment suggested that the dictator's appetites were limitless, and that only the American pushback saved the rest of Europe from Communism. As this chapter demonstrated, Harriman was almost certainly wrong about Stalin's intentions. The dictator harbored no plans for turning the world red. He, much like his postwar planners Litvinov and Maisky, looked forward to a prolonged period of great-power cooperation after the war. To this end, Stalin was often willing to give up opportunities for advancing Soviet influence. Power without legitimacy was insecure power. Legitimacy, though, was unthinkable without external, especially American, recognition.

Stalin had different methods for projecting Soviet influence: in Europe and in Asia, his arsenal included anything from outright annexation to indirect control through weak coalition governments. He could support (and often betray) ethnic insurgencies; he applied brutal pressure through territorial demands; he often relied on the Communist fifth column or he could just play one set of politicians against another: the choice of methods depended on circumstances, and on the strategic importance of any particular locale. Poland loomed large in his calculations, and he was determined to keep the Polish under tight control. That eventually resulted in the communization of Poland. But it took several years to get to this point, which makes some historians, notably Norman Naimark, think that Stalin had no blueprints for Poland: that he played it by ear. If this is the case, one might ask whether there ever was scope for a less brutal form of Communism than what transpired in Eastern Europe. This is a question that can never be answered with certainty – and neither can the related question of whether a softer American policy or, indeed, US withdrawal from Europe in 1945 (as both the Soviets and the British had initially expected) would have led to something less than the Cold War that we all knew.

Yet one could also argue (which Averell Harriman did with Truman in April 1945) that the Soviet Union needed America more than the other way around, and if Stalin really wanted better relations, it was up to him to live up to promises he had made at Yalta, which included the promise to hold free and fair elections in the Soviet-occupied territories. Perhaps it was only because the United States pushed back against Soviet expansionism that Stalin recognized his limits, which, as we have seen, already extended at least as far as the shores of Africa. The problem with this line of reasoning is that it risks ascribing certain outcomes to US deterrence, which could also be ascribed to Stalin's voluntary abstinence. "Better safe than sorry," some would say. "Better the Cold War than Soviet domination" … Only, we know today that Stalin had no plans to take over the world. "Yes, but only because he was deterred."

What we now can say with greater certainty than before is Stalin was remarkably attuned to psychological pressure. He felt this pressure from the Truman Administration, especially on the question of Washington's nonrecognition of the Soviet client regimes in Eastern Europe. He was willing to give the Americans a few face-saving concessions (for example, by inviting Mikołajczyk to join the new Polish government) but Stalin's basic position was that it was up to him to determine the make-up of these

CHAPTER 2 THE PARTING OF WAYS

governments and he resented having this right challenged by Truman. This became especially clear during the London Conference of Foreign Ministers, which in many ways became the first diplomatic battle of the unfolding Cold War.

Stalin was embittered by Byrnes's resistance to the prospect of a Soviet trusteeship in the Mediterranean. Although the Americans had never promised him Tripolitania, he did feel that certain promises had been made, and interpreted the complete lack of sympathy on the part of the United States as a breach of good faith. This is not to say that Stalin's claims were justified. Rather, the importance of this largely neglected episode is that it showed Stalin that he had been wrong about his ability to play the United States against Great Britain, that the gap between the Soviets and the Americans was much wider than it first appeared, and that his postwar vision of give-and-take could not work in practice. We have seen, too, how Molotov tried to play the card of the Dodecanese islands in the expectation of a possible bargain with the West.

But if Stalin was willing to take, was he also willing to give? Is it not reasonable to argue, for example, that, as Stalin was determined to keep his gains in Eastern Europe, what Truman and Byrnes did – or did not do – did not really matter that much? It is difficult to read history backwards and claim that because of what we know happened in the period 1946–48, things were already set in stone in 1945 – because they were not. What is clear is that in 1945 Stalin was looking for a bargain, and was not averse to making concessions, although the A-bomb made it psychologically hard for him to do so. Some of these concessions were insignificant (as in Bulgaria and Romania). Others were more substantial. For instance, Stalin was initially inclined to cooperate with the United States in preventing the Chinese civil war. He was also quite modest in his demands regarding Japan until, late in the game, he raised the issue of the Allied Control Council, which was just another negotiation ploy to remind Byrnes that his demands regarding Bulgaria and Romania had the same basis as the Soviet demands regarding Japan. Byrnes said that he did not see the connection – but Stalin certainly did.

It is most instructive to see why, exactly, the Soviets became so intransigent. Molotov, we have seen, was not averse to compromise in London. In the end, but for Stalin's pressure, he would have found some middle ground with Byrnes. But what derailed the whole exercise was Stalin's perception that Byrnes was trying to bully Molotov by presenting the standoff at the conference as a four-against-one affair. To be precise, it was by and large a four-against-one affair, for even if the British, the French, and the

PART I AMBITION

Chinese had their own ideas about some aspects of the postwar settlement (for instance, regarding the issue of the Italian colonies), it did not take long before they lined themselves up behind the United States. Stalin felt isolated and threatened. This was not what he had expected. The contradictions of the imperialist world – which, according to predictions of people like Litvinov and Maisky, were supposed to make it easy for Moscow to play various powers against one another – were never there. Faced with perceived American pressure, Stalin stood firm. Concessions under pressure implied weakness. And one thing Stalin valued even above his geopolitical gains was the impression of strength.

3

STALIN IN EUROPE

One underappreciated aspect of the early Cold War is that of Stalin's setbacks, maybe because they are offset by his gains in Europe and Asia. Yet for much of 1946 the Soviet Union was withdrawing and retrenching, sometimes because Stalin wanted to do so and sometimes because Western pressure forced him to. Stalin pulled back from Iran and China. He gave up hopes of a foothold in North Africa, and pedaled back from a confrontation with Turkey, which he himself had brought about through sheer display of chutzpah.

At the same time, however, Stalin consolidated his control over parts of Central and Eastern Europe: Poland, Czechoslovakia, Hungary, Bulgaria, and Romania. Communization of Eastern Europe was gradual; for a time, Stalin believed he could exercise control through left-wing coalitions (or "people's fronts"). For a time, he thought that Communism would ènjoy electoral support not just in Eastern but also in Western Europe. By mid-1946 disappointment was beginning to set in. Stalin became increasingly willing to pursue a confrontational policy vis-a-vis the West, something that was immediately obvious in the ramping up of Soviet support for the Communist insurgency in Greece.

Similarly, reacting to what he saw as the US attempt to consolidate its position in Western Europe, in 1947 the dictator hastily hammered together an eastern bloc of "people's democracies" (i.e. Soviet satellites). The high point of this effort was the creation of the Cominform in September 1947, though he soon found himself quarrelling with perhaps the most important satellite of all, Josip Broz Tito's Yugoslavia. The "loss" of Yugoslavia was a severe setback to Stalin's game in the Balkans. Soon he also had to abandon the Greek insurgency. Most consequentially, Stalin gave up on his initial hope for a united Germany in favor of what then became the German Democratic Republic (GDR) or East Germany. Stalin's effort to squeeze the Western powers out of Berlin by cutting off land routes into the city was perhaps the greatest of his policy blunders. This chapter reviews the evolution of Soviet foreign policy between 1946 and 1949, a period much studied by historians, yet which requires a retelling because it marked the division of the European continent and the emergence of the Soviet-led Communist bloc. This was not the result Stalin had counted on in 1945 but he helped bring it about through his own intransigence and insecurity.

This chapter continues the discussion of two key questions. First, was the Cold War inevitable? Second, to what extent was Stalin personally responsible for the Cold War? The answers are far from straightforward. In the long term, Stalin may well have planned for a conflict with the West. He had every ideological and Machiavellian reason to do so. But that long-term vision did not necessarily define his day-to-day foreign policy, which left space for cooperation with the West, as well as for competition in key theaters. The division of Europe was in part a consequence of Stalin's realization that he was being outcompeted by the United States. Maintaining Soviet power required increasingly extensive reliance on intimidation, on brute force. Washington's unwillingness to recognize unfettered Soviet control over Eastern Europe, or to accept Stalin's meddling in the Middle East, indicated to Stalin that Yalta was not working, at least not in the way he had expected it to. But it was not a sudden realization, which was why the Iron Curtain did not descend overnight. The slide into the Cold War was gradual. Communization of Eastern Europe was gradual, and proceeded in fits and starts. Yet in the end, facing a choice between a legitimating dialogue with the United States – which required sustaining and upholding Yalta – and the Cold War, Stalin chose the Cold War. Facing a choice between legitimacy and power, Stalin chose power.

IRAN AND TURKEY

Is it reasonable to say that the Cold War began in Iran and Turkey? The view is not unfounded, because Soviet–American tensions over Stalin's intentions in relation to both seriously contributed to the downward slide in Soviet relations with the West in 1945–46.[1] What Stalin was doing in Iran in 1945 was not very different from what he had been doing in Xinjiang: in both cases he attempted to manipulate a local ethnic insurgency to create a buffer state under Soviet tutelage. But in Xinjiang, Stalin backed away from the plan even as the insurgents, with his support, were scoring decisive victories. The broader settlement with China (legitimized by the Yalta agreement) proved much more important. In Iran, however, Stalin persisted for longer, withdrawing only under pressure. What was he trying to do?

Stalin's approach to Iran was shaped by perceptions of imperial rivalry with Great Britain rooted in the legacy of the nineteenth-century Great

Game. The wartime Anglo-Soviet alliance at first appeared to take the edge off these old rivalries; for a time, Moscow and London seemingly worked together, not at cross-purposes. In 1941 the two powers jointly occupied Iran, ostensibly to preclude it from helping the Nazis. They forced the older shah into exile, replacing him with his youthful son, Mohammad Reza Pahlavi. Iran subsequently served as an important corridor for transporting Lend-Lease aid to the USSR, as well as the site of intense diplomatic negotiations (Churchill, Roosevelt, and Stalin held their historic meeting in Tehran in November 28–December 1, 1943). But there were mounting suspicions behind the façade of amity. The British, reported the Soviet ambassador in Tehran in April 1942, were in fact attempting to take over Iran, which "can create a real threat to the interests of our country if we do not take timely countermeasures." Stalin highlighted such passages with his thick blue pencil.[2]

The Soviet leader figured that the main reason for British (and increasingly) US interest in Iran was oil. In August 1944 Lavrenty Beria prepared a report, recounting the Allies' attempts to impose their control on the world oil market, and proposing an "energetic" Soviet response: pressuring Iran to grant Moscow an oil concession in the northern part of the country.[3] The Foreign Ministry then prepared a sixty-year concession document (a bilateral agreement giving the Soviets exclusive right to pump oil in northern Iran), modeled on the terms of the 1933 British concession, only quite a bit worse for Tehran. Deputy Foreign Minister Sergei Kavtaradze was dispatched to Tehran in the fall of 1944 to make the Iranians an offer they could not refuse. In a letter to Molotov, Kavtaradze proposed simply bribing Iranian officials so they would sign off on the concession.[4] The shah, who presumably could not be bribed, was to be promised Soviet support for his precarious hold on the throne.[5] Unexpectedly, Kavtaradze failed. The Majlis (Iranian parliament) passed a law against awarding oil concessions until the end of the Second World War, leaving Stalin furious.

It was in this context, then, that in the summer of 1945 the Soviets covertly began supporting ethnic separatists in northern Iran.[6] Moscow dispatched instructors and material aid to help with setting up a rival government in Tabriz and the surrounding area, populated predominantly by ethnic Azeris. Soviet clients on the ground – including the head of the new separatist administration, Ja'far Pishevari – were clearly in favor of a complete break with Iran with possible later accession to the USSR to form a united Azeri Soviet republic. What Stalin thought of these plans is not entirely clear. Most likely, given his well-known opportunism, he was

PART I AMBITION

Figure 3 A Soviet map of a proposed oil concession in northern Iran, 1944. The extent is shown by the line running west-to-east with an angular dip at the center.
Source: AVPRF: f. 06, op. 6dop, p. 75, d. 880, l. 15. Agk.mid.ru. With permission of the Archive of Foreign Policy of the Russian Federation.

playing it by ear, helping the Azeris consolidate power while also closely watching Western and Iranian reactions. By early December the Azeris, backed by Soviet military power, were already in control.

Simultaneously with these developments in northern Iran, the Soviets were also upping their game in Turkey. Here, Stalin's key goal was gaining control of the Turkish Straits that connected the Black Sea and the Mediterranean.[7] The straits were controlled by Turkey by the terms of the 1936 Montreux Convention, which, in times of war, could keep anyone from coming into, much as it could keep the Soviets from coming out of, the Black Sea. It was a situation Stalin was anxious to change. In 1940, the Soviet dictator attempted to work out an agreement with the Germans that would see Turkey carved up and the Turks "driven to Asia" (as Stalin explained to the Comintern functionary Georgi Dimitrov). The German invasion of the USSR put an abrupt end to these aspirations for the time-being but in 1944–45 Stalin turned to Turkey once again.[8]

"In his last years," Molotov recalled much later, "Stalin became a little bit arrogant and in foreign policy I had to demand what [former Russian Foreign Minister] Milyukov used to demand – the Dardanelles! Stalin: 'Come on, push! As joint ownership.' I told him: 'They won't give them.' – 'But you must demand!'"[9] Whatever he may have thought of the wisdom of pushing the Turks, Molotov complied with Stalin's wishes. In tense encounters with the Turkish ambassador in Moscow, Selim Sarper, on June 7 and 18, 1945, he not just pressed for joint Soviet–Turkish (but de facto Soviet) control of the Turkish Straits but also outlined Soviet territorial demands to parts of eastern Turkey. The ambassador was predictably terrified and pointed out to Molotov, not unreasonably, that these demands would only cause the Soviets to "lose the sympathy" of public opinion in Turkey.[10]

Stalin argued the Soviet case with the Allies at Potsdam in July, pointing out that it was impermissible for a "little country" like Turkey to "hold a big country by the throat" by controlling the straits. Highlighting a recurrent theme, Stalin alleged that the Soviets were being subjected to unequal treatment and that if Great Britain or the United States faced such restrictions with Gibraltar or the Panama Canal, they would raise "havoc."[11] But, while in theory willing to revise the Montreux Convention, neither the Americans nor the British had in mind anything like giving the Soviets actual control of the straits, never mind chunks of Turkish territory. The matter dragged on, causing a lot of friction in Soviet–Turkish relations and deepening suspicions of Soviet intentions in the West.

Developments in the Middle East were at the center of controversy during the Moscow Conference of Foreign Ministers in December 1945. The Soviets tried to deflect criticism of their actions in Iran by (unsuccessfully) calling for British withdrawal from Greece and US withdrawal from China.[12] In a meeting with British Foreign Secretary Ernest Bevin, Stalin lied that the Soviets kept their troops in northern Iran to prevent hostile elements from infiltrating across the border into Azerbaijan and sabotaging oil installations in Baku. It was an absurd excuse and was seen as such by the British and the Americans. As for Turkey, Stalin told Bevin that it had nothing to fear from the Soviet Union, though he continued to insist on Ankara's surrender of eastern provinces to the USSR and on letting the Soviets set up bases in the straits.[13] It was in the context of Stalin's intransigence on Iran and Turkey that President Truman wrote a letter to Secretary of State Byrnes (which he never sent), in which he complained bitterly of the Soviet behavior in Bulgaria and Romania, in Turkey but, most of all, in Iran, where Moscow had perpetrated an "outrage." "Unless Russia is faced

PART I AMBITION

with an iron fist and strong language," warned Truman starkly, "another war is in the making. Only one language do they understand – 'How many divisions have you?'"[14]

The mood in Washington only darkened further after Stalin's unusually tough-worded public statement. On February 9 the dictator held what counted in the USSR as a campaign rally (Stalin was being "elected" to the Supreme Soviet). He blamed capitalism for starting world wars, praised Soviet achievements and military might, and promised new breakthroughs for the socialist project. The speech raised grave alarm in the United States, both in the policy circles and among the broader concerned public. The prominent journalist Walter Lippmann wrote a gloomy column entitled "Stalin Chooses Military Power."[15] US intelligence compared Stalin's rhetoric with Hitler's.[16] Historian Frank Costigliola argues, rightly, that the US policy community badly exaggerated just how threatening the speech was. It was directed to an internal audience and was merely an effort to "legitimate continued Communist Party rule."[17]

Indeed, far from declaring "World War III," as some of the more hawkish US observers believed at the time,[18] Stalin reiterated continued affinity with the West by referring to the United States and Great Britain as "freedom-loving countries." (In fact, he hand-wrote this reference into a printed version of the speech, perhaps as a last-minute reminder that the wartime ties had not yet been severed.[19]) Crucially, throughout the speech, which he very carefully drafted and scripted (to the last "spontaneous" applause), Stalin spoke about how "everyone recognizes" that the Red Army turned out to be a mighty force – not a colossus on legs of clay as many in the West had thought before the war. Stalin thus used the Western acknowledgment of Soviet power as evidence of that power and therefore the party's, and his own, political legitimacy. The Yalta framework – though battered – remained alive. If the West recognized Soviet power, surely it would also have to recognize Soviet interests, and it was upon such recognition that Stalin pinned his hopes for the postwar international order.

But was the Soviet Union powerful enough to force its preferred solution on the increasingly wary former allies? Stalin's assertiveness was at least in part a response to Hiroshima but there were limits to his bluff, and he knew it. Despite the Soviet atomic project becoming the first order of national importance in August 1945, Moscow was still years away from the Bomb. On January 25, 1946 Stalin told Igor Kurchatov, the scientific head of the atomic project, to "conduct work quickly, in crude basic form." "Every great invention was crude at first," Stalin added. "As it was with the steam locomotive."[20] Stalin's comments were in reaction to views of

CHAPTER 3 STALIN IN EUROPE

Figure 4 Igor Kurchatov, the scientific head of the Soviet atomic project. Ullstein Bild/Getty Images.

the prominent nuclear scientist Petr Kapitsa who had urged to rely less on US intelligence (the Manhattan Project was riddled with Soviet spies) and develop Russia's own road to the Bomb.[21] Stalin did not care for such sentiments. What he wanted was a basic deterrent, to show something to the Americans as proof that he could not be bullied into giving up on his regional ambitions. The problem was that he was still far from having that basic deterrent. All he could do was to bluff.

The US chargé d'affaires in Moscow George F. Kennan accurately discerned Stalin's strategy of bluff. Kennan elaborated on this theme in a cable back to his superiors in the State Department on February 22, 1946. Dubbed the "Long Telegram" for its verbosity (it ran to a bit over 5,000 words), the cable analyzed the sources of Soviet international conduct. The key argument highlighted Soviet opportunism. "Soviet power," Kennan claimed, "is neither schematic nor adventuristic. It does not work by fixed plans. It does not take unnecessary risks. Impervious to logic of reason, it is highly sensitive to logic of force. For this reason, it can easily withdraw – and usually does when strong resistance is encountered at any point."[22] Kennan's views were not wrong, though what he failed to appreciate was that Stalin viewed the United States through a similar lens. In other words, what to Washington seemed to be a reasonable American response to unreasonable Soviet demands seemed to Moscow as intolerable pressure.

But in this game of nerves, it was Stalin who had the weaker hand, especially if he wanted to retain the Yalta framework on which he wagered so much. For example, could the Soviet Union simply have refused to depart from northern Iran contrary to the previous undertaking to leave by early March? Perhaps – but only at the cost of further undermining relations with the Allies. In January 1946 the Iranians took their case to the United Nations, putting the Soviets on the defensive. In February, revelations of Moscow's atomic espionage (linked to the earlier defection of a Soviet cipher clerk in Ottawa, Igor Gouzenko) stirred up public opinion in the West against the Soviet Union.[23] Containment – so aptly advocated by Kennan in his Long Telegram – had already become the accepted wisdom in Washington and commanded considerable public support in the United States and Great Britain.

In the meantime, Stalin continued his scheming in Iran. He presently pinned his hopes on the newly appointed prime minister, Qavam al-Saltaneh. Moscow pulled strings to have the Iranian Majlis approve his candidacy in a close vote. The Soviet Foreign Ministry characterized Qavam as a right-wing politician.[24] However, he had earlier professed commitment to improving Soviet–Iranian ties, which for Stalin meant Tehran's recognition of the autonomy of Soviet-aligned Azeri republic in the north, and, crucially, an oil concession.

But when the new prime minister turned up in Moscow in February 1946 for negotiations, it turned out that he was unwilling to yield on either point. In tense, drawn-out discussions with Stalin and Molotov, Qavam claimed that allowing the Azeris any autonomy would lead to Iran's break-up (because other nationalities would also demand autonomy). As for the oil concession, Qavam said that he was generally in favor but that he could not promise anything until the Soviet Union pulled back from Iran. In a bid to mollify the prime minister, Stalin carefully hinted that the Soviets would not mind – and perhaps even help Qavam – if he tried to overthrow the shah and establish a republic. Stalin said that so long as Soviet forces remained in Iran, the shah would not dare do away with Qavam.[25] The latter insisted, though, that a Soviet withdrawal would help him politically and that – as he argued in a written submission – as soon as the people of Iran saw that the USSR no longer posed a threat, "they will with great eagerness embrace sincere friendship and cooperation with the Soviet people." "Scumbag!" Stalin wrote in the margin.[26]

The talks failed. Soviet forces, which Moscow had promised to withdraw by March 2, remained in place. On top of that, in the days after the deadline the Soviets sent more troops and heavy military equipment across the border into northern Iran. US diplomats on the ground reported on what appeared to be movement of Soviet combat forces out of northern Iran in the general direction of borders with Turkey and Iraq, and towards Tehran. Reviewing this intelligence on March 7, Byrnes noted that "it now seemed clear the USSR was adding military invasion to political subversion in Iran," adding, as he slammed a fist into his hand: "now we'll give it to them with both barrels."[27] What that meant remained unclear, though on the following day Byrnes sent the Soviets a memorandum, demanding to know the purpose of their maneuvers in Iran.[28] On March 19, following Iran's official complaint, UN Secretary General Trygve Lie, placed the question of Soviet actions in the country on the provisional agenda of the Security Council, due to convene in New York.[29]

And then – quite unexpectedly – Stalin stood down. It is not clear when he made his decision to pull out of northern Iran. There are indications that it was as early as March 14. At least this was when Stalin's lieutenant in Soviet Azerbaijan, Mir Jafar Baghirov, first hinted to the separatist leaders that the Soviet forces might have to leave because of what he described as a new international situation.[30] On March 18 the new Soviet ambassador in Iran, Ivan Sadchikov, arrived in Tehran with a mandate to negotiate an oil deal with Qavam. In the end, the Iranian prime minister promised, within seven months, to deliver a fifty-year oil concession in the form of a joint company.[31] Stalin proposed that the Azeris negotiate with the central government. Disheartened Pishevari dismissed the idea as Qavam's artifice.[32] "Qavam is fooling you," he told his Soviet sponsors, predicting that once Moscow pulled its troops, Iran would crush the separatist movement.[33] Unpersuaded, Stalin ordered full withdrawal beginning on March 24, 1946.

Stalin never spoke about his reasons for the about-face, except in his testy letter to Pishevari, where he criticized the separatist leader for his failure to understand Soviet foreign policy. In the letter, which urged Pishevari to cooperate with Qavam, Stalin claimed, somewhat disingenuously, that keeping troops in Iran "undermined the basis of our liberation policy in Europe and Asia." The Americans and the British, he claimed, could draw attention to Soviet occupation of northern Iran to keep their forces at bases around the world. "Therefore," he continued, "we decided to withdraw our forces ... to pull this weapon out of the hands of the British and the Americans, unleash the anticolonial struggle for liberation and thereby make our policy of liberation more reasonable and effective."[34]

PART I AMBITION

Was this a pretext? Perhaps, though not entirely. The dictator was certainly aware of the importance of looking good on the international stage. It is instructive to read Stalin's reprimand to Molotov after he met James Byrnes on April 28 in Paris (they were both in town for another conference of the Council of Foreign Ministers). Byrnes accused the Soviet Union of expansionism in Iran, just as in Eastern Europe, arguing that the notion that the Middle Eastern country posed any threat to the USSR was like that of Ecuador posing a threat to the United States. Molotov defended the Soviet position but only meekly. He claimed there were forces in Iran that wanted to drag the Soviets, the British, and the Americans into a conflict with each other. He also complained that Washington's stern reaction to what was, after all, a Soviet withdrawal-in-progress showed that it was not "treating the Soviet Union like it would an ally."[35] Stalin was completely dissatisfied with such passivity. In an angry cable to his foreign minister, he argued that Molotov should have told Byrnes that the US "thought up the Iranian question ... in order to cover up for the U.S. and British imperialist proclivities." The Americans and the British, Stalin added, kept their forces at bases all over the world, while the Soviets – hardly anywhere. "In view of the above, accusing the USSR of expansionism amounts to hideous slander."[36] Molotov obediently lashed out at Byrnes during their meeting on May 5: "all these conversations about Soviet expansionism," he said, "are meant to distract attention from those who are really carrying out imperialistic expansionist aspirations."[37]

Yet Stalin's concerns about the Soviet image were secondary to his worry about the possibility of a conflict with the United States. True, there is no record of the Soviet leader specifically tying the Soviet withdrawal to any real or imagined American threats. Stalin even showed a certain bravado, telling one visiting Communist delegation in May 1946 that "neither we nor the Anglo-Americans can start a war now. Everyone is sick of war. Moreover, a war would have no point. We have no intention of attacking England and America, and they won't risk it."[38] But such pronouncements must be taken with a grain of salt. Stalin's policy in the Iran crisis pointed exactly in the opposite direction. The threatening tone of US diplomatic notes, the hostile exchanges at the UN were all signs of a deepening Soviet–American confrontation.

Winston Churchill captured the spirit of the time in his fiery speech in Fulton, Missouri on March 5, at the height of the Iranian crisis. "From Stettin in the Baltic to Trieste in the Adriatic, an iron curtain has descended across the Continent," Churchill declared as President Truman looked on, gravely. Churchill called for British–American unity in the face of the

Soviet provocations, adding that "there is nothing they admire so much as strength, and there is nothing for which they have less respect than for weakness, especially military weakness." Stalin dismissed the speech as militant raving. "Churchill's speech is blackmail," he said. "Its purpose is to intimidate us." "They intimidate, and will continue to intimidate," he added. "But if you do not allow yourself to be intimidated, they will make a little noise and calm down."[39] But what if they did not? What if Churchill's Fulton speech represented a newly discovered Western resolve to push back against Soviet adventurism?

On previous occasions Stalin had changed tack when faced with the prospect of a Soviet–American conflict. He had also backed off in Japan and tried to distance himself from the actions of the Chinese Communists, suspecting (probably correctly) that the latter were not averse to a direct Soviet–American clash in China. Stalin's decision-making in Iran reflected the same logic. For all the tensions in the relationship with the United States, he sought to maintain the outlines of the postwar world ironed out at Yalta.

Stalin's other reason for backing off in Iran was to increase Soviet leverage there by offering Qavam his support. Never mind that he thought Qavam a "scumbag"; never mind, too, that Pishevari had warned him against Qavam's trickery. Stalin still thought that he could play the Iranian prime minister. This was because, as he explained in instructions to the Soviet ambassador, Qavam was under pressure from the "Anglophiles," which made him dependent on the Soviet Union. "We must use this conflict, supporting Qavam in the struggle against the Anglophiles," he cabled Sadchikov.[40] Stalin then restated the same argument in his letter to Pishevari. "I think we must use this conflict [between Qavam and the alleged Anglophiles] in order to extract concessions from Qavam, support him, isolate the Anglophiles and thus create a certain basis for further democratization of Iran."[41] The promised oil concession made the medicine go down.

Stalin's reversal in Iran can be (and has often been) described as evidence that containment worked – that is, that American threats, such as they were, sufficed to alter his behavior. As we have seen, there is something to this explanation, but it does not capture the full complexity of the Soviet leader's calculus. Yalta continued to be his guide, and the implied division of the world into spheres of influence – with the Americans recognizing the Soviet sphere on a reciprocal basis – was still very much on Stalin's mind as he planned Soviet steps in Iran. He did not see the latter as falling exclusively into the Soviet sphere. Instead, it was a grey area, where he could both compete and cooperate with the West. If that required making deals with "reactionary" Qavam, whom he never trusted, Stalin was willing to take his chance. His scheme proved to be too clever by half when in October 1947 Qavam failed to deliver on the promised oil concession, even as his government cracked down on the Azeris.

Yet consider this: before the Soviet withdrawal from northern Iran, Stalin physically controlled a potential buffer state, a positive gain from the standpoint of security and economic interests. And yet, just as in China, he traded these benefits for a promise of greater influence in all of Iran down the road. In China, he did it without any threat of American intervention. American pressure was probably a consideration in the Iranian case. But it is still quite remarkable that Stalin opted out of pursuing maximum security (guaranteed by the Soviet military presence on the ground) in favor of an arrangement that seemed less secure but a great deal more legitimate, because it had an implicit recognition of the West. Only, Stalin underestimated his Iranian opponents who ultimately left him out in the cold.

He had even less to show with Turkey for all his pressure and intimidation (in the form of naval maneuvers in the Black Sea and an anti-Turkish press campaign). Both the straits and Eastern Anatolia remained in Ankara's hands. Moscow maintained formal claims until 1953, when they were dropped in a belated bid to win Turkey's friendship. Here, too, Stalin's record was one of complete failure.

YUGOSLAVIA AND GREECE

When in October 1944 Churchill and Stalin reached their informal "percentages agreement," Yugoslavia was divided equally between British and Soviet spheres of influence. But Churchill had few cards to play to keep it so, since he had little leverage with the Yugoslav resistance and its ambitious leader, Josip Broz Tito. Born to a Croat father and a Slovene mother, Tito had fought in the First World War against the Russians, who captured him near Bukovina and put him in a POW camp in the Urals. Despite such inauspicious acquaintance with Russia, Tito became involved in Communist activities, ultimately rising to the leadership of the Yugoslav Communist Party. Compared to many other Communist leaders in Eastern Europe (who came to power on the back of the Red Army and were hardly autonomous actors), Tito was fairly popular in his own country.[42] He had spent the war fighting the Germans at the head of a substantial army. He was emphatically not Stalin's puppet, though he deferred to the Kremlin on questions of global Communist strategy.

CHAPTER 3 STALIN IN EUROPE

Eyeing the postwar political landscape in the Balkans, Tito perceived opportunities for integration. His vision centered on creating what the Russian historian Leonid Gibiansky called a "mini-USSR," with Albania, Bulgaria, and Greece joining the Yugoslav Federation. Such a federation would have allowed Tito to reconcile two ethnic problems that he had on his hands. One had to do with Kosovo, which, though a part of Serbia, had a large ethnic Albanian population that was drawn to nearby Albania. The other had to do with historic Macedonia, parts of which were now with Yugoslavia, Greece, and Bulgaria. Creating a large federation would allow for a seamless redrawing of these ethnic borders within one country. In September 1944 Tito secretly visited Moscow, where he discussed the idea with the former head of the Comintern and soon to be the de facto Bulgarian leader, Georgi Dimitrov. The latter wrote in his diary that he and Tito "set down a line" – an eventual South Slav Federation.[43]

But it was one thing to set the line; it was quite another to work out practical arrangements. The problem that Tito now faced was how to organize this would-be federation. His idea was simply to have Albania, Bulgaria, and Greece join with the same rights as Yugoslavia's existing six constituent units. But this would leave Tito in charge, while diluting the new entrants in the Yugoslav state structures. The Bulgarians resisted this idea, pushing for something akin to a confederation, which would give Sofia and Belgrade equal rights. Meanwhile, the British, having learned through their channels about these discussions, sent a memorandum to Moscow, where they disagreed with the whole idea because such a federation would translate into increased Soviet influence in the Balkans. They were also worried about the prospect of Greece losing its part of Macedonia to a greater Macedonian republic, which would then be incorporated into an enlarged Yugoslavia.[44]

Stalin's position on these issues was very cautious. He probably did not want to cross the British, especially so soon after the percentages agreement. And he was surely suspicious of Tito's intentions. Creating a mini-Soviet Union in the Balkans would undercut Moscow's regional leverage. Stalin therefore soft-pedaled the proposed federation, telling the Yugoslavs on January 9, 1945 that they should not "create an impression that somebody wants to swallow the Bulgarians."[45] He instead supported the principle of dualism (i.e. a system where Bulgaria and Yugoslavia would have equal weight), and he was not even sure how far he wanted to go down that road. At the end of January, Belgrade and Sofia signed a Treaty of Alliance, and that was as far as the matter was allowed to proceed.[46]

In 1946–47, Tito himself pedaled back from a possible confederation with Bulgaria, pursuing instead the idea of incorporating Albania into Yugoslavia. He already had advisers at every level of the Albanian

PART I AMBITION

government and in the armed forces. A formal union would help resolve the problem of Kosovo, which, though a part of Yugoslavia, had a large Albanian population. When Stalin broached the subject during a meeting with Tito on May 27, 1946, the latter seemed confident that the Albanians would endorse accession. Stalin, however, thought the idea was premature, although he did not rule it out in the long term.[47] The available documents do not provide a clear answer to the crucial question: Was Stalin really contemplating Albania's absorption by Yugoslavia at however remote a future date, or was he just lying to Tito, while in reality sabotaging this kind of a political union? Given what we know about Stalin's Machiavellian ways, it is natural to assume the latter, but the question remains open.[48] For the time-being, at least, Belgrade and Tirana continued building closer ties.

Meanwhile, the Greek Communists eyed the prospects of a revolution and hoped for Soviet, Bulgarian, and Yugoslav support. In December 1944, following the resignation of Communists from the coalition government headed by Georgios Papandreou, a Communist uprising broke out in Athens, which the British helped put down.[49] In the midst of the fighting, a Greek Communist Party (KKE) Politburo member Petros Roussos traveled to Bulgaria and from there appealed to the Soviets for help. "Britain's direct military intervention," Roussos pleaded, "has created a very difficult situation for our struggle ... The wide masses are against England. But the struggle requires moral help, weapons, and foodstuff." He asked the Soviets through Dimitrov whether the KKE could expect "active intervention." Molotov forwarded the document to Stalin with a damning one-liner: "I think we should not respond."[50] Dimitrov then instructed his men in Sofia to tell Roussos "personally, carefully, and amicably" that "our party [the Soviet Communist Party] must not get involved in any way in relation to the unfolding internal struggle in Greece."[51]

Left to their own devices, the Greek Communists were thoroughly defeated in Athens. Stalin was quick to blame the "foolish" KKE who, he complained, blundered by quitting Papandreou's government. "They had not asked for our advice," he said. "They have made it easier for Churchill."[52] Yet, given an opportunity to intervene, Stalin decided not to. The most likely reason was his undertaking, in the percentages agreement, to leave Greece to the British. Perhaps he expected the same sort of deference from the Western allies when it came to would-be Soviet clients in the Balkans.

Later, however, Stalin gradually modified his approach to the Greek problem, reflecting a reorientation of Soviet foreign policy towards a confrontation with the West. In January 1946 the Soviets reportedly advised

CHAPTER 3 STALIN IN EUROPE

the KKE to prepare for the possibility of a military struggle.[53] The KKE boycotted the Greek elections of March 31, 1946, though it is unclear whether they did so with the Soviet blessing. Beginning in March–April 1946 the KKE leadership approached the Soviet Union and its satellites with requests for supplies, including military equipment, but it is not clear that these early approaches met with a positive response.[54] In September 1946 the KKE sent Stalin a detailed report on their activities, indicating that they had 4,000 guerrillas in the Greek mountains and intended to increase this number to 15,000 or 20,000. They asked for weapons (including machine guns and mine-throwers) and direct financial aid ($150,000 per month). Stalin read the request, but we do not know what, if anything, he agreed to provide.[55] For the time-being, the task of arming the Greek insurgency fell primarily to Tito (with Stalin's probable blessing).[56] The Soviet leader was still very cautious about getting directly implicated in the Greek civil war.

Indeed, in December 1946 the Soviets briefly considered settling the Greek problem peacefully, through a great-power agreement. This hope was inspired by an appeal by the Greek prime minister, Konstantinos Tsaldaris, to the UN Security Council, calling for an investigation of Albanian, Bulgarian, and Yugoslav aid to the Greek Communists. Bevin brought up this matter with Molotov on December 6 (the latter was in New York for another session of the Council of Foreign Ministers), and proposed to resolve it by striking a deal between the two of them plus Byrnes.[57] Molotov at first wanted to reject this approach but thought better of it and fired off a telegram to Stalin, suggesting a solution that would entail the replacement of Tsaldaris's government with a "coalition" government (inclusive of the Greek Communists), and national elections in two or three months.[58] Stalin agreed, though he instructed Molotov not to raise the question of Tsaldaris's replacement directly because to do so, he said, would be "to court failure."[59] Thus constrained, Molotov called on Byrnes to discuss the subject of a new coalition government without actually talking about it. The matter went nowhere.[60] Fighting in Greece continued.

The widening insurgency galvanized President Truman into action. On March 12, 1947, he asked a joint session of the US Congress to authorize $400 million in aid to Greece and Turkey. The need for such intervention was precipitated by London's inability to carry the burden of supporting these governments. America now had to step into the breach. "The seeds of totalitarian regimes are nurtured by misery and want," Truman proclaimed. "They spread and grow in the evil soil of poverty and strife. They reach their full growth when the hope of a people for a better life had died.

PART I AMBITION

We must keep that hope alive."[61] Thus was born the Truman doctrine that committed the United States to supporting European governments facing potential or actual Communist insurrections.

We do not have Stalin on record discussing the implications of the Truman doctrine but what we do see from late spring of 1947 is the Soviet Union becoming much more directly involved in aiding the Greek insurgency. In May, the KKE's general secretary, Nikos Zachariadis, submitted a report to Stalin, explaining how insurgency had fared since December 1944. The situation favored the Communists, he argued. That was because, for all the government's efforts to suppress the insurgents with the British and now American help, their numbers were growing. "The British failure," the report went, "now forces the Americans to take off their masks and to take up the initiative of carrying out a reactionary policy in Greece" (Stalin highlighted these words with his thick blue pencil).[62]

Zachariadis was optimistic. His report to Stalin contained a copy of a letter he had sent to the leader of the recently formed Democratic Army of Greece (DAG), Markos Vafeiadis, which spelled out an ambitious strategy of turning the guerrilla force into a regular army and then striking Greek Macedonia, which would then constitute a large base area for taking the revolution forward. To this end, Zachariadis asked Stalin to provide enough equipment to increase the size of the insurgent force from 20,000 to 50,000.[63] The two met on May 23, 1947 for a midnight parley.[64] There is no record of what they discussed, though it is clear that Stalin presently agreed to up his stake in the conflict.[65]

The Russian archival files contain the KKE request for weapons, along with highlighting and extensive commenting in what seems like Stalin's hand, indicating the degree of his involvement in the Greek civil war.[66] Unlike just months earlier – when Stalin would have deferred to the Yugoslavs to direct the insurrection – he now signed off on a list of equipment, including 15,000 rifles and carbines, 5,000 light machine guns, 4,000 heavy machine guns, canons, mine-throwers, grenades, revolvers, millions of rounds of ammunition, etc., all of German and Italian makes to disguise the origins of this equipment.[67] All of this was delivered via the Yugoslavs in June–July 1947. Stalin also directed that Zachariadis be provided with $100,000 in cash. "The Greek partisans must be helped," Stalin told Albania's Enver Hoxha in July. "We will also support them."[68] With this influx of weapons and money, the insurgency intensified. In September 1947 DAG prepared a top-secret plan called "Plan Lake," which proclaimed the establishment of "free Greece" in the northern part of the country, including by capturing the capital of Greek Macedonia, the large port city of Thessaloniki.[69]

84

CHAPTER 3 STALIN IN EUROPE

Was Stalin's direct involvement in the Greek civil war a part of his long-term strategy or was it merely a response to the Truman doctrine?[70] There is no easy answer. We have seen that there was a clear shift in the Soviet approach: from keeping out altogether (1945), to mainly relying on Yugoslavia (late 1946), to taking a more direct role in the conflict (1947). This shift coincided with the deepening of Soviet–American antagonism, and with increasing US involvement in the conflict. But the US involvement was itself a result of the intensification of the war in late 1946 – early 1947, which Stalin at the very least gave his blessing to. The dynamic of Soviet involvement was not straightforward, though the overall trajectory was clearly towards confrontation with the "Anglo-Americans." "The Anglo-Americans," he told Hoxha in July 1947, "are of course aggressive, and are trying to impose their domination on the entire world."[71] His task, as Stalin saw it, was to push back where he could.

STALIN'S COALITIONS

Historians writing of Stalin's early post-Cold War strategy like to cite one statement of his, which he allegedly uttered in a conversation with the Yugoslav Communist Milovan Djilas in April 1945. "This war is not as in the past," he said. "Whoever occupies a territory also imposes on it his own social system. Everyone imposes his own system as far as his army has power to do so. It cannot be otherwise."[72] Strikingly, these words seem to prophesy the division of Europe. Those keen to stress Stalin's responsibility for what happened draw attention to this evidence as if to say: see, he planned it all from the start.

But the balance of evidence paints a more contradictory picture. Historian Norman Naimark argues that Stalin's policy must be looked at piecemeal. What he did in countries like Poland, Hungary, Romania, and Bulgaria – which were important to Moscow's security interests – was different from his policies toward countries like Austria and Finland.[73] For a time, Stalin seemed interested in building left-wing political coalitions, and even entertained the possibility of a parliamentary road to Communism for countries that were not under direct Soviet control.

One way to gauge Stalin's approach to "sovietization" is to see how he himself addressed the question in the early postwar years. The governments he had installed in Eastern Europe in 1945 moved rapidly to nationalize large land holdings and industrial enterprises but Stalin insisted that he was not imposing the Soviet model and that the Eastern European regimes could skip the "dictatorship of the proletariat," arriving at socialism via a shortcut,

PART I AMBITION

"without a bloody struggle." To this end, he even foresaw opportunities for a servile opposition. In Poland's case, for instance, the role was given to Stanisław Mikołajczyk, appointed deputy prime minister. Mikołajczyk's purpose, Stalin argued, was to split the ranks of the anti-Communists by providing them with a legal, parliamentary, method of voicing their grievances. All portfolios of importance were in any case in the hands of the Communists, and Stalin was not averse to maintaining a democratic charade – "for now," as he put it.[74] On another occasion he referred to the arrangement as a "convenient mask for the present period."[75]

Similar arrangements were in place in Romania, Hungary, Bulgaria, and Czechoslovakia.[76] It is anyone's guess how long Stalin intended these arrangements to last. Perhaps he genuinely hoped that the Communists would win a popular mandate through elections. If so, the Polish referendum of June 1946 and parliamentary elections of January 1947 sent a warning signal: to deliver the outcome Stalin's desired outcome, both required extensive fraud.

Whereas Stalin could falsify elections in countries under his direct control, he had no such option available to him in Western Europe. But his approach – fostering left-wing coalitions – was broadly similar, at least in terms of the long-term vision. "We, Marxists-Leninists," Stalin told a British Labour Party delegation in August 1946, "do not think that our road [to socialism] is the only possible one ... The difference is that our road is shorter, though it requires more blood; the parliamentary road is slower but with a lesser quantity of blood."[77] One could dismiss such statements as mere propaganda, but they were more than that. Given just how much stock Stalin put on postwar coalition-building in the West, he really thought this was a viable method of asserting Moscow's influence, at least until 1947. This was particularly the case in France and Italy.

At the end of 1945 both countries lay prostrate. In France, some 25 percent of the housing stock had been lost, leaving a million families homeless. Only 18,000 km of railroads (of 40,000) were still in service. Some 7,500 bridges had been destroyed. Industrial production in 1944 was a mere 38 percent of what it had been in 1938, partly due to the shortfalls in coal imports from Germany. France experienced an unprecedented balance of trade deficit, mainly with the United States.[78] Similar conditions prevailed in Italy, brutalized by years of war and occupation. The industry in the north of the country stood idle for the lack of coal.[79] Although industrial production recovered quickly, living standards did not. Italian wholesale prices more than doubled between May 1946 and May 1947. Inflation was even worse in France.[80]

There were terrible food shortages across Europe, aggravated by bad weather: the drought of summer 1946 and the harsh winter of 1946–47, the worst since 1880. Western Europe was perhaps better off than countries like Romania or indeed the USSR, which witnessed outright starvation and cannibalism, but there was hunger even in France and Italy. C.L. Sulzberger of the *New York Times* wrote of seeing "beggars press their noses against restaurant windows, where the rich, foreigners, and black market profiteers devour food that even in normal times the peasant only expects to see in heaven."[81]

Unsurprisingly, such volatile economic conditions created a fertile soil for Communism. The Parti Communiste Français (PCF) and its equivalent, the Italian Communist Party (PCI), came out of the war with robust public support, partly owing to their role in the anti-fascist resistance, and partly because the Soviet Union initially enjoyed great prestige as the "liberator" of Europe. Stalin's postwar policy, realistically, did not foresee Communist-led attempts to seize power in Western Europe. He was more interested in coalition-building, where the Communists exercised power in the context of popular fronts, assuring a broadly leftist (but by no means Communist) orientation of postwar governments. In November 1944 Stalin instructed PCF head Maurice Thorez (who was departing Moscow for recently liberated France) to build a left-leaning bloc of parties by closing ranks with the socialists. "The Communist Party," he urged, "is not so strong as to hit the government in the head. It must build up its strength and seek allies." Eventually, Stalin averred, the Communists could go on the offensive "if the situation turns for better" – but he set no deadlines.[82] His instructions to CPI leader Palmiro Togliatti were broadly the same: to work with the Allied-supported government, not seek to overthrow it.[83]

Receptive to Stalin's counsel, the French and the Italian Communists worked hand-in-hand with the socialists. This was an easier task for the Italians than for the French, where serious contradictions developed between the PCF and its two coalition partners, the socialists and the center-right Popular Republican Movement (MRP). The Communists found themselves struggling to choose between working with the government (where they held ministerial portfolios) and undercutting government policy from without.[84] In Italy, Togliatti and the PCI were at pains to choose between following Soviet preferences on questions like the disposition of Trieste (which Stalin wanted handed over to Yugoslavia) and sticking to their own nationalist instincts.

And what did Stalin think? It was he who had pushed for coalition-building in the first place. Was it just a temporary measure until, as he explained to Thorez, circumstances favored an offensive? Or was he, by contrast, merely finding a reasonable rationalization for selling a strategy he knew would disappoint his trigger-happy Communist allies? The evidence is sparse and contradictory, and yet so much in our understanding of the early Cold War depends on answering it one way or another. The most sensible approach would acknowledge that Stalin – much as Kennan argued in the Long Telegram – had no fixed plans, that he went by ear. He was not ruling out revolution, but he was not willing to pursue revolution at all costs. He continued to hope that exploitable fissures would develop between the United States and Western Europe. And that meant continued coalition-building. Yet worsening East–West tensions made such a strategy increasingly difficult to sustain.

The strategy began to fall apart in the spring of 1947, beginning with France. In December 1946 fighting broke out in Vietnam between the French forces and the Vietnamese resistance under Ho Chi Minh's leadership. The PCF faced a dilemma: supporting their government and its colonial policies or supporting the Communists who fought against them in Vietnam. In March 1947 Communist deputies abstained in the Assembly on the vote on military appropriations for Vietnam, triggering criticism from their coalition partners. When in April 1947 tens of thousands of workers declared a strike at Renault's factories, the PCF supported the strike for fear of alienating their electorate, even though the strike was not their idea. As Thorez later explained in a letter to Stalin, "this became a warning for the Communist Party, that further concessions [to the government] threatened to cause dissatisfaction in the working class, in the ranks of trade unions, and in the party itself."[85] The PCF therefore decided to vote against the government's economic policy in the National Assembly, leading the socialist prime minister, Paul Ramadier, to evict Communist ministers from his government.

Stalin – who had not been consulted – wrote an angry letter to Thorez (sent in the name of his lieutenant, Andrei Zhdanov) and circulated it to other European Communist parties. Stalin–Zhdanov voiced "concern" about the PCF ending up "overboard," and complained about the failure to consult.[86] But the PCF's departure from the French government was a harbinger of things to come. The same month, the PCI and its ally the PSI (Italian Socialist Party, headed by Pietro Nenni) were kicked out of the Italian government of Prime Minister Alcide De Gasperi.[87] De Gasperi understood that having the Communists and their friends around would undermine Italy's chances of winning American financial support that was essential for the struggling Italian government. The Communists helped his resolve by fiercely criticizing the government from without even though they served in De Gasperi's cabinet. Now, though, the PCI was driven out of power. Stalin's united front strategy was crumbling in the face of the widening Cold War.

THE MARSHALL PLAN AND THE COMINFORM

Meanwhile, in January 1947 President Truman appointed a new secretary of state to replace James Byrnes. Truman's choice for the role was the prominent military leader George Marshall who had just returned from a mediating mission to China, where he tried to broker peace between Chiang Kai-shek and his Communist enemies. Marshall's appointment overlapped with what turned out to be a short-lived uptick in Soviet–American relations: that February peace treaties were finally signed with Italy, Romania, Hungary, Bulgaria, and Finland. Yet no agreement was in sight on the most important postwar question: the future of Germany. The matter was debated at length during heated meetings of the March–April 1947 session of the Council of Foreign Ministers that took place in Moscow but there was no movement forward. Marshall got to see Stalin, however, who urged him "to have patience and not to fall into despair."[88]

Some weeks after returning from Moscow, Marshall travelled to Harvard University, where on June 5, 1947, he made the defining speech of his career. Because of Europe's desperate economic situation, which, he said, some unnamed governments were seeking to exploit, Marshall called on European countries to work together and promised "friendly aid" from the United States to this end.[89] The speech led in time to a massive economic support program, dubbed the Marshall Plan that, between 1948 and the end of 1951 transferred some $12.3 billion to Western European economies.[90]

Washington offered the Marshall Plan to the Soviets as well as their clients in Eastern Europe. Excluding Moscow was politically difficult, though planners in Washington very much hoped that Stalin would pass on the opportunity. The Soviet leader – though suspecting a ruse – still decided to send Molotov to Paris in June 1947 to negotiate the outlines of the proposed economic program. There Molotov discovered that the plan was to set up a multinational committee to coordinate the distribution of American aid. The Soviets, by contrast, had counted on individual aid packages. Such coordination was a priori unacceptable to Moscow. Stalin saw it as Washington's attempt to pay its way into the Soviet sphere of influence. In addition, Molotov could not get his counterparts to confirm that the plan would not impede potential payment of German reparations to the USSR. In the end, he simply stormed out of the conference, as the Western policy makers hoped he would.[91]

Having refused to take part in the Marshall Plan, the Soviets put pressure on their Eastern European satellites to make sure they would also reject it. The Polish and the Czechoslovaks hoped to join the program nonetheless. Stalin intimidated them into renouncing all such intentions. His infamous conversation with the Czechoslovak delegation on July 10, 1947, still stands out as one of the most astonishing examples of the dictator's heavy-handed bullying. "Whether you want it or not," he told his visitors, "but you are helping to isolate the Soviet Union ... We and our people will not understand this." He explained that he viewed the Marshall Plan as an attempt to forge "something like a western bloc against the Soviet Union." He continued: "You must rescind your decision, you must refuse to participate in this conference, and the sooner you do it the better." Foreign Minister Jan Masaryk, aware of the economic importance of the Marshall Plan, asked the Soviet leader to reconsider. "You must do it immediately," Stalin snapped.[92]

To sweeten the pill, Stalin promised to conclude a trade agreement with the Czechoslovaks, entrusting his lieutenant, Anastas Mikoyan, with negotiations. The draft agreement stipulated that the Soviets would provide Czechoslovakia with 400,000 tons of grain in return for Czechoslovak pipes. But when this agreement was sent up to Stalin for his sanction, he angrily vetoed it because it required that the Soviet Union supply grain in 1947, while the Czechoslovaks would not be required to pay until 1948. "We must not allow," he cabled, "that in the alliance system between the USSR and Czechoslovakia, the USSR would look like a naive fool, who cannot defend its own interests, and Czechoslovakia – like a skillful and experienced partner, taking the USSR for a ride. Moreover, one must remember, that the USSR is a Soviet country, a country of socialism, whose interests must not be subordinated to the interests of a non-Soviet country, even if an allied one."[93] Stalin lashed out at Mikoyan for attempting to conclude an "antistate" agreement. The Czechoslovaks were thus reminded of the true costs of Soviet "friendship." Their interests were to be subordinated to Moscow's.

In late September 1947 Stalin had the clients gather in Szklarska Poręba, a sleepy town in the Sudeten Mountains that Poland acquired from Germany in 1945. Szklarska Poręba hosted a colorful assembly of Communist dignitaries from across Eastern Europe and the large Western European Communist parties, the PCF and PCI. Stalin's red-faced lieutenant, Andrei Zhdanov, presented the main report. The report entered the annals of Communist history: it was there that Zhdanov announced that the world was now divided into two hostile "camps" – the "democratic" camp led by the Soviet Union and the "imperialist" camp led by the United States. The actual term – "camp" – seems to have been Molotov's, who had proposed to add it to the report.[94] But the overall direction was undoubtedly Stalin's who was now in the process of fundamentally reshaping Soviet foreign policy.

Zhdanov's "two camps" speech is often seen as Stalin's response to the Marshall Plan which was indeed condemned at Szklarska Poręba as part of a US effort to extend its imperialist control over Europe. But Stalin conceived of the meeting even before Marshall made his famous speech, by some accounts as early as the spring of 1946.[95] The dictator broached the subject with the Polish Communist leader Władysław Gomułka on June 4, 1947, asking him to convene a conference of Communist parties.[96] This was just two days after Zhdanov's angry letter to Thorez, widely circulated to other Communist parties, where the Soviets complained of not having been consulted about the PCF's exit from Ramadier's coalition government, and just days after the PCI's ouster. Stalin's concerns about losing positions in France and Italy clearly played into his decision to overhaul Moscow's European strategy. All this also unfolded against the backdrop of the unsuccessful Moscow Conference of Foreign Ministers, which became deadlocked over Germany and Stalin's decision, at the end of May, to begin direct military support of the Greek insurgency. It is probably fair to say that by the time George Marshall unveiled his plan, Stalin had decided on a decisive change of course: from what remained of great-power collaboration to outright confrontation with the West.

The meeting itself became rather raucous when Zhdanov unexpectedly lashed out against the French and the Italians. The Communists' expulsion from the government, Zhdanov claimed, was American blackmail: it was the price the United States demanded for the Marshall Plan. Never mind that the Marshall Plan was first announced after the Communists had already left the ruling coalitions in Paris and Rome; never mind, too, that in the French case, it was the Communists themselves who precipitated their own eviction from the government by their vote of no confidence in the government. They now stood accused of naivety and insufficient vigilance in the face of reactionary plots. Zhdanov overlooked the fact that it was Stalin who had insisted on the Communists joining ruling coalitions in the first place. Now that they had been ousted, he changed his position: the Communists would henceforth have to be in militant opposition to the government. They would have to protest against the Marshall Plan.[97] Stalin, vacationing

PART I AMBITION

in Sochi, secretly pulled the strings in Szklarska Poręba, telling Zhdanov via cable how to criticize the French.[98]

The conference at Szklarska Poręba saw the establishment of a new organization, the Cominform, headquartered in Belgrade, an indication of the important role Stalin assigned to Tito as the viceroy of the Soviet camp.[99] This reincarnation of the long-disbanded Comintern would now impose discipline across Stalin's East European empire and the international Communist movement. The French and the Italians would have to fall in line (they did, of course: there was no scope for an anti-Stalinist rebellion). There would be further tightening of screws across the Soviet camp. There would be proper sovietization in countries under Moscow's direct control. What Stalin had told the British Labour Party just a year earlier about alternative roads to socialism simply no longer held true. There was now only one road – the Soviet road.

This was already happening before Szklarska Poręba. After the fraudulent election of January 1947, Polish Communists concentrated all power in their hands, pursuing policies that in short order turned Poland into a Soviet-style command economy. The opposition ministers from the Polish Peasant Party resigned from the government. Former Deputy Prime Minister Stanisław Mikołajczyk lingered for a few months before fleeing Poland for Britain in October 1947.[100] Similar events unfolded in Bulgaria, where the Communist-dominated government shut down the opposition press between late April and early May 1947. The Communists moved quickly to arrest the key opposition leader Nikola Petkov who was accused of espionage and sentenced to death in August 1947. In September, Bulgaria's Communist leader, Georgi Dimitrov, wrote to Stalin that he would like to have Petkov's sentence commuted to life in prison but because Britain and the United States had raised hell over the death sentence, it now had to be carried out because anything else would look like "capitulation." Stalin indicated his agreement with this logic, and Petkov was shot.[101]

In Romania, too, the Communists had been tightening the screws since blatantly falsifying the November 1946 election. The opposition National Peasants' Party (PNT) was banned in July 1947, after the discovery of an alleged plot by its leaders to flee the country. The party leadership was arrested, framed (with Soviet help) as "Anglo-American spies" in a show trial and sentenced to lengthy prison terms.[102] In November the remaining liberals were ousted from the Communist-dominated government, including Foreign Minister Gheorghe Tătărescu who had served the Communists loyally and who, in an effort to save his skin, had earlier called for "ruthless

CHAPTER 3 STALIN IN EUROPE

retribution" against the opposition.[103] (He was later arrested.) In December 1947 the Romanian Communists forced the hapless King Michael to abdicate. He left the country and settled in Switzerland. Stalin micromanaged the king's exit via his Communist clients in Bucharest.[104]

Something similar happened in Hungary, where in late 1946–early 1947 the Communist-controlled security services began investigating the Smallholder Party for alleged antistate crimes. This party won the (reasonably) free elections in November 1945 and controlled a good half of the government, including the prime minister's position, occupied since February 1946 by Ferenc Nagy who now found himself in the unenviable position of a leader without actual power. Nagy pleaded with the Soviet authorities in Budapest to allow Smallholder Party members to join the police (controlled by the Communists), to no avail. In February, the Soviets arrested the party's general secretary, Béla Kovács, and sent him to the USSR to serve out his sentence. In May, Nagy was driven into exile. New elections were then held in August 1947, with the Communists and their allies coming through with 60 percent of the vote. Hungary's little Stalin, Mátyás Rákosi, resorted to what became known as "salami tactics": to first slice up and then destroy the opposition. As elsewhere across the Soviet bloc, consolidation of Communist control began well before Szklarska Poręba, though of course the formation of Cominform played the role of an important catalyst.

Just three weeks after Szklarska Poręba, Stalin again received a delegation of British Labour Party MPs. The delegation was not at all representative of the Labour Party (which Stalin had condemned for being agents of American imperialism). It included very leftist characters like Konni Zilliacus (who was later expelled from the party for pro-Communist sympathies), Joe Champion, Ben Parkin, and others, all members of the "Keep Left" group, which aimed at steering Britain away from overreliance on the United States at the expense of the Soviet Union and its satellites. But Molotov concluded (after meeting the delegation in Moscow) that their trip to the USSR was "reasonably well coordinated" with the British government, and recommended that Stalin see them, perhaps in the expectation that they could then influence the British government to move away from its close embrace of the United States.[105]

"Some may say," Stalin told the delegation who had gone down to Sochi to see him,

> that if England behaves itself, if it does not get involved with the Eastern European countries, then America will appreciate it, and take pity on it. But it's naive to think this way. It does not happen in modern life. In international

93

> relations, unfortunately, it is not the sense of pity that predominates but the sense of one's own profit. If some country sees that it can conquer and subjugate another country, then it'll do it ... The weak are neither pitied nor respected. Only the strong are taken into account.[106]

Stalin meant to criticize the United States and intimate to the British that America might "eat" their country if they were not careful, but he really was channeling his inner Thucydides. Like the Athenian generals at Melos in 416 BC, the Soviet dictator believed that the strong must exact what they could, and the weak would grant what they must. It was not a fresh realization. Stalin had always been brutally realist in his approach to international politics. But after Szklarska Poręba there was less scope for compromise than at any point since the dictator first articulated his postwar vision.

Before long, this dark vision of his helped complete the division of Europe.

THE COUP IN CZECHOSLOVAKIA

Czechoslovakia was unusual among Soviet clients in Central and Eastern Europe in having, like France and Italy, a genuinely popular Communist Party. Building on a respectable wartime record of underground resistance, the Communist Party of Czechoslovakia (KSČ) won 38 percent in the May 1946 parliamentary election. Its leaders went on to form a coalition government led by the sturdy pipe-smoking Prime Minister Klement Gottwald, who had risen from a carpenter to a senior Communist functionary. Gottwald spent the war years in exile in the Soviet Union, returning to Czechoslovakia in the spring of 1945 to become the chairman of the National Front. The presidency of the republic was restored to the interwar president, Edvard Beneš, whose National Social Party had joined the National Front and later came second after the Communists in the 1946 election.[107]

Meeting Beneš in March 1945, Stalin tried to reassure him that the Soviets would not try to impose Communism on Czechoslovakia. "We want all people to have a system that they deserve," he said, adding that he "wanted the Czechoslovaks to understand that he speaks sincerely and that he says what he thinks."[108] Yet the key government portfolios in the coalition government – including ministers of defense and of the interior – went to the Communists. Stalin was taking no chances.

Stalin's refusal to allow the Czechoslovaks to join the Marshall Plan contributed to a worsening economic situation in the country. By 1947, average daily bread rations in Czechoslovakia were below those of West Germany. Harvest failure worsened the misery of the impoverished populace. If in Western Europe and Greece such misery contributed to fears of a Communist resurgence, the Communists were already in power in Prague, and they justly feared that the economic adversity would result in their defeat in the forthcoming (1948) elections. In November 1947 Gottwald sent a personal plea to Stalin, asking for grain. "The *political* significance of such a measure on the part of the Soviet Union would be enormous for us, particularly at a time when we are expecting increased pressure on Czechoslovakia from foreign reaction aimed at changing the current regime."[109] On this occasion, Stalin relented and promised to deliver a little extra grain, and to allow some flexibility in payments.[110]

Czechoslovakia's deepening economic crisis worried the Communists who hoped to secure 51 percent of the vote in the next elections. Now the party's popularity was in free fall. A power struggle unfolded inside the dysfunctional coalition government, as non-Communist ministers attempted to roll back Communist influence. Matters came to head in early February 1948, after Communist Minister of the Interior Václav Nosek demoted eight non-Communist police officers (replacing them with Communist loyalists). On February 13, overruling Communist objections, the cabinet ordered Nosek to reinstate the officers. A week later, National Socialist, Populist, and Slovak Democratic ministers resigned from the government to protest Nosek's failure to carry out this order. They expected that President Beneš would refuse to accept their resignations, forcing Gottwald to back down or resign himself, leading to an early election.

These hopes were frustrated, however, when Gottwald organized mass demonstrations in Prague, while ordering the police to seize power. On February 25 Beneš caved in under pressure and accepted both the resignation of opposition politicians and the appointment of new, pro-Communist figures. A symbolic turning point came on March 10, 1948, when non-Communist Foreign Minister Jan Masaryk (who had not resigned on February 20 but stayed in post) was found dead under the windows of his bathroom. Less than a year earlier Masaryk timidly questioned Stalin's line about rebuffing the Marshall Plan in the testy discussions in Moscow. Presently, he was out of the way, his death ruled a suicide, though foul play was suspected. Czechoslovakia succumbed to full Communist control.[111]

THE STALIN–TITO SPLIT

When Cominform was formed in September 1947, few could have imagined that one of its first "accomplishments" would be to expel Yugoslavia from the socialist camp – least of all Tito. His relationship with

PART I AMBITION

Stalin was not friction-free but there was a shared sense in Moscow and Belgrade that the Yugoslavs were the second most important players in the emerging socialist camp. At Szklarska Poręba the Yugoslav delegation played the second fiddle to Zhdanov himself, and the fact that Belgrade was chosen as the headquarters for Cominform spoke to Stalin's confidence in his junior partner. When, then, did Stalin begin to suspect Tito of disloyalty, and why?

The main reason for the antagonism was Stalin's growing suspicion of Tito's plans in Albania. As we have seen, he was noncommittal about Albania's incorporation into Yugoslavia (something Tito had lobbied Stalin for), although he also did not exclude the possibility in the long term. Stalin had only a very limited knowledge of Albania, and in fact spent much of his first meeting with its ruthless dictator, Enver Hoxha, quizzing him on basic geographic and linguistic facts about the Balkan country. Albanian–Yugoslav relations were broached only briefly at the meeting, in a way that indicated that Stalin *knew* that Hoxha was not thrilled about Tito's ambitions in Albania. Still, the Soviet dictator spoke well of the Yugoslavs, and said that what aid Moscow would provide would have to come by the way of Belgrade, for "disguise" [*maskirovka*]. "The Yugoslavs are good people," he said. "They will not just transfer our aid to the Albanians but add a few things of their own." Hoxha appeared to agree.[112]

Later that year, however, things began to go wrong. A conflict developed in the ranks of senior Albanian leadership – in particular, between the deputy prime minister and Tito's man in Albania, Koçi Xoxe, who favored closer integration with Yugoslavia, and Minister of Economy and Industry Nako Spiru, who favored extensive economic cooperation with the USSR and maintaining close ties with the Soviet Embassy in Tirana. Xoxe, with Hoxha's approval, led a campaign to discredit Spiru as an anti-Yugoslav element. In November 1947 the latter committed suicide while still under investigation.[113] Tito then instructed the Yugoslav ambassador in Moscow, Vlado Popović, to raise the Albanian question with the Soviets. Popović held two meetings with Zhdanov, emphasizing Belgrade's intention to increase its involvement with Albania and indirectly signaling displeasure with the fact that Spiru had had contacts with the Soviet Embassy in Tirana.[114] In response, Stalin asked that Tito send a "responsible comrade" to Moscow for consultations. "I am ready to carry out all your wishes," he wrote, "but it is necessary that I accurately know all these wishes."[115]

Tito sent Djilas, who met with Stalin on January 17, 1948. Djilas recounted this meeting in his memoir, in particular Stalin's off-putting remarks to the effect that Yugoslavia was trying to "swallow" Albania. "At

CHAPTER 3 STALIN IN EUROPE

this he gathered the fingers of his right hand and, bringing them to his mouth, he made as if to swallow them."[116] But although he came across as a little bizarre, Stalin reassured Djilas that he *approved* of the merger between Yugoslavia and Albania, and criticized Hoxha as a "petty bourgeois, inclined towards nationalism."[117] Djilas cabled Tito after the meeting that his and Stalin's "views were the same. Stalin is well informed."[118] Yet the actor that he was, it is not clear that Stalin supported the policy he purported to support. Perhaps he was merely testing the Yugoslavs.

Stalin's suspicion of Tito was certainly worsened by the latter's unexpected decision to station a Yugoslav army division in Albania – a decision that Stalin was not consulted about and one that, he claimed, would increase the dangers of Western intervention in Albania. This was not the first time Tito pulled surprises on Stalin. In August 1947, for example, the Yugoslavs and the Bulgarians concluded a treaty of friendship, without telling the Soviets, triggering an angry missive from Stalin who warned them about the increased dangers of an "Anglo-American intervention" in Turkey and Greece.[119] On that occasion, the dictator was mollified. But this time, when he was confronted by the Soviet ambassador in Belgrade, Tito responded merely that he would comply with Stalin's "recommendations" if the latter insisted but said that a failure to send Yugoslav troops to guard Albania's borders could bring on a Greek invasion of Albania, adding that if this were the case, Yugoslavia and the Soviet Union would have to jointly "sort out this mess."[120]

All of this left the suspicious Soviet dictator deeply dissatisfied. Adding to his annoyance, Bulgarian Communist leader Georgi Dimitrov had been talking of forming a Balkan federation, which would include Greece. To be sure, Stalin himself had not ruled out such a federation (though he had never mentioned Greece). Yet it was never clear whether his support for the idea was merely rhetorical or whether he really thought it was a plausible undertaking.

Now, however, he decided that Dimitrov was out of his depth.[121] Stalin summoned the Yugoslavs and the Bulgarians to Moscow for a dressing-down. The testy meeting took place in the Kremlin on February 10, 1948. Tito had sent his second-in-command, Edvard Kardelj (Djilas was also in the room). Dimitrov turned up in person. Stalin was uncharacteristically rude and irritated, and made it clear that he was angry with both Tito's decision to send troops to Albania, and with Dimitrov's comments about the Balkan federation. He claimed that he worried about Washington's reaction to these plans. "The reactionaries in America," he complained, "say that in Eastern Europe there is not only a bloc in the making, but [countries] are merging

PART I AMBITION

into common states."[122] He added that sending Yugoslav troops to Albania was also dangerous because the West could intervene. He compared the situation with the Chinese civil war, where "nobody can reproach the USSR," and argued that if the Chinese Communists could fight on their own, then so could the Albanians who "are not worse than the Chinese."[123]

Perhaps the most interesting parts of the heated discussions in Moscow concerned the Greek civil war. Stalin questioned Kardelj about the prospects of a Communist victory in Greece and added that he "had grave doubts about it." He continued: "one should assist Greece [i.e. the guerrillas] if there are hopes of winning, and if not, then we should rethink and terminate the guerrilla movement … It is not for the first time in history that although there are no conditions now, they will appear later."[124] It was a remarkable about-face. Just months earlier Stalin ramped up support for the Greek guerrillas and agreed to deliver unprecedented quantities of military equipment (through Belgrade) but now he was ready to pull the plug! What happened? Perhaps he had figured that he was fighting a losing battle in Greece. Perhaps he feared escalation. Kardelj (according to the KKE's Nikos Zachariadis who later relayed this information back to the Soviets) recalled Stalin saying that "if the Yugoslavs, helping Democratic Greece, get into a war with the Anglo-Americans, the Soviet Union would not provide Yugoslavia with any aid."[125]

Most probably, Stalin simply did not want to be strung along by the Yugoslavs who, he thought, were throwing their weight around in the Balkans. The Greek civil war had always been dearer to Tito's heart than to Stalin's. And so, even as the Greek civil war continued, Stalin's perception of this conflict was shifting decisively.

While the Yugoslavs and the Bulgarians were in Moscow, Stalin forced them to sign a document requiring them to consult with the Soviet Union on matters of foreign policy. He also pressed for an immediate federation between Yugoslavia and Bulgaria, perhaps as a way of bringing the recalcitrant Yugoslav leadership under his control, and perhaps to preclude Belgrade's absorption of Albania. On February 19, the Yugoslav leadership met in a secret session and explicitly rejected the latter demand – the first time Tito refused to obey Stalin's direct order. At the same time Tito, Kardelj, and Djilas met with the Greek Communist leadership, including Zachariadis, and promised that although Stalin was bailing on them, Yugoslavia would continue to support the war effort.[126]

Stalin had plenty of eyes and ears on the ground in Belgrade to report to him about Tito's insubordination. For example, he received a detailed report of the March 1, 1948 meeting of the Politburo of the

CHAPTER 3 STALIN IN EUROPE

Figure 5 Josip Broz Tito's photo in Stalin's archive. Signed: "To Comrade J.V. Stalin."
Source: RGASPI: f. 558, op. 11, d. 1695, doc. 1.

Yugoslav Communist Party, compiled by a "trusted person" (probably by YCP Politburo member Sreten Žujović), where Tito and other Yugoslav leaders accused the Soviets of "great-power chauvinism" and "expansionism," and of attempting an "economic conquest of Yugoslavia." Tito claimed there were "ideological disagreements" between Moscow and Belgrade.[127] Stalin lashed out in response. At the end of March 1948, the Soviets withdrew their civilian and military experts from Yugoslavia and in effect refused to provide further aid. On March 27, 1948, Stalin and Molotov sent a testy letter to Tito, laying out their complaints about "anti-Soviet statements" by "dubious Marxists like Djilas." The letter also outlined an ideological case against Belgrade (insufficient "party democracy," absence of "class struggle," etc.), though it is clear from the chronology of Soviet–Yugoslav relations that ideology served to rationalize a split that opened up for other reasons.

The relationship between Belgrade and Moscow worsened rapidly in the weeks that followed. There was a nasty exchange of letters, each more uncompromising than the last. Tito refused to give in. He pushed back against the Soviets and indeed purged several pro-Soviet figures in the YCP (including Andrija Hebrang and Stalin's informant Sreten Žujović).

When summoned to a meeting of the Cominform in Bucharest in June 1948, a meeting specifically convened to discuss the "Yugoslav question," he refused to send a delegation. On June 23 the Cominform, in a special resolution, accused Belgrade of "departing" from Marxism-Leninism, and succumbing to nationalism and anti-Soviet sentiments. The resolution called on the "healthy forces" in Belgrade to bring the leaders to account, though the available evidence suggests that Stalin did not expect to see Tito overthrown.[128] What Stalin tried to do by effectively excommunicating Tito from the Communist camp was to solidify his control over the remaining ruling parties in Eastern Europe. Alleged "Titoists" were then brought to trial in Poland, Hungary, Czechoslovakia, Bulgaria, and Albania. Some of these (Koçi Xoxe in Albania, Traicho Kostov in Bulgaria, Rudolf Slánský in Czechoslovakia, László Rajk in Hungary) were executed; others (Władysław Gomułka in Poland) managed to survive.

The Bulgarian–Yugoslav federation never happened. Nor was Tito successful in taking over Albania. Hoxha instead became Stalin's most loyal follower in the Balkans. Stalin had thought the Albanians "backward and primitive" but he was impressed by their loyalty. "They can be loyal like dogs – this is a trait of primitive people," he said.[129] In the end, loyalty and complete deference was what he valued above all else. Tito, with his own ambitions in the Balkans and his reasonable suspicion of Soviet intentions, fell far short of Stalin's expectations.

The Soviet–Yugoslav split also occasioned the beginning of the end of the Greek Communist insurgency. Zachariadis was quick on his feet, condemning the Yugoslavs in a letter to Moscow in mid-June 1948.[130] Stalin did not immediately pull the plug on the insurgency, for all the doubts that he had expressed to the Yugoslavs in February 1948. But his conflict with Tito meant that aid was now sent principally via Bulgaria and Albania. Even that was not a given: in July 1948, the Albanians briefly stopped the flow of aid and even expelled 400 wounded Greeks from their hospitals, delivering them to the border with Yugoslavia, and demanding that they go there, or face deportation to Greece.[131] (After Zachariadis pleaded with Moscow, the Albanians relented).[132] Increased US support for Athens also spelled trouble for the faltering insurgency that suffered heavy defeats in the summer of 1948. Amid these troubles the KKE succumbed to conflict between the two key leaders, Zachariadis and the DAG commander Markos Vafeiadis (in passionate letters to the Soviets the latter accused the former of sleeping with his wife).[133]

In a report for the Soviet leadership in October 1948 Markos argued that the Greek insurgency could only be saved if Moscow and its clients

CHAPTER 3 STALIN IN EUROPE

recognized the Communist government and "provided us with direct military aid."[134] Stalin was too cautious for such a risky move. In April 1949 he abandoned the insurgency altogether.[135] Some of the retreating guerrillas sought refuge in Albania; others were simply dispersed. Stalin's Balkan game, such as it was, came to a rather unremarkable end.

Moscow's defeat in Greece coincided with painful setbacks in what was perhaps the Cold War's most important front, Germany.

THE BERLIN BLOCKADE

Stalin's policy towards Germany, like many of his policies, was contradictory and opportunistic. During the war he wanted to dismember Germany, but he backed away from this goal after the end of the war for reasons that are not entirely clear. Perhaps he hoped for a united Germany under Communist control. When Communist parties in Western Europe seemed ascendant, could a leftist coalition (with the Communists in key positions) come to power in all of Germany? This would be a political outcome worth striving for from Moscow's perspective – arguably a much better outcome than having just a truncated portion of Germany under one's control. Perhaps Stalin foresaw and feared the possibility that Western zones of occupation, which contained the bulk of Germany's industrial potential, and on which he drew for reparations, might be turned into an anti-Soviet bulwark in the heart of Europe.

Above all, Stalin was determined that Soviet occupation forces should remain in Germany. It was, undoubtedly, for this reason that he had Molotov reject the so-called Byrnes Plan for the demilitarization of Germany, presented at the Paris meeting of the Council of Foreign Ministers in April 1946.[136] This was during the same stormy sessions, when Byrnes accused the Soviets of expansionism, triggering an angry rebuttal from Stalin. The Foreign Ministry experts analyzed the plan in detail, discovering in it a disguised effort to push the Soviets out of Germany and interdict the $10 billion in reparations Stalin had hoped to extract. In the words of Deputy Foreign Minister Solomon Lozovsky, who sent Stalin a report on this question, "accepting the Byrnes Plan would lead to the abolishment of the occupation zones, to the withdrawal of our forces, to economic and political unification of German and to US economic control over Germany." This would result in "Germany's military recovery, and in a few years – a German-Anglo-American war against the Soviet Union."[137]

This was a dark and a far-fetched interpretation of US foreign policy but (given the propensity of Soviet officials to air views their superiors

PART I AMBITION

wanted to hear) it likely reflected Stalin's own fears. But does this mean that Stalin was determined by 1946 to see Germany divided? Not necessarily. He pursued two parallel tracks. One was maintaining the Soviet military administration in his own occupation zone, where the Soviets presided over far-reaching reforms, including stripping large property owners of their land and expropriating major enterprises. Stalin's hope was that the Germans would embrace these leftist policies to carry through what he called, in a conversation with German Communists, a "bourgeois democratic revolution."[138] These measures, though undoubtedly "socialist" in character, did not yet amount to full-blown sovietization, and paralleled similar piecemeal approaches elsewhere in Soviet-controlled Eastern Europe.

The other side of Stalin's German policy was playing the electoral card. The dictator was deeply involved in occupied Germany's party politics. Understanding the inherent weakness of the Communist Party (KPD), he pushed for its merger with the much more influential Social Democratic Party (SPD), to present a united leftist front to the German electorate. The SPD in the Western zones rejected the forced merger. The measure succeeded only in the Soviet zone, under the watchful eye of the Soviet military administration. It was thus that the Socialist Unity Party of Germany (generally known by its East German acronym SED) came into being in April 1946.[139] In the summer and fall of 1946 the Soviets carefully monitored its performance, which was first tested in local elections in the Soviet zone in September and October. The Soviet authorities on the ground were directed to "take timely measures in regions where a real danger arises of a victory by the bourgeois parties."[140]

Reflecting on these developments, the ever-apt observer of Soviet foreign policy George Kennan argued that the KPD–SPD merger in the Soviet zone was a part of an attempt "to prepare that zone as spring-board for a Communist political offensive elsewhere in the Reich."[141]

Kennan was not wrong. The extent of Stalin's manipulation can be gauged from a very candid late-night discussion he held in the Kremlin in January 1947 with the SED leadership. This was several months after the merger and after the SED had lost the Berlin elections. Stalin remained relatively upbeat. He now stressed the importance of extending SED influence to Western occupation zones in order to undercut the influence of the Social Democrats. He explained himself as follows. The German Communists had a radical program. They had wanted to "destroy everything, to upturn, to establish the dictatorship of the proletariat." "This scares many people," Stalin argued – "including the workers." Would it not be more reasonable to present the left-leaning German voter in the Western zones with the choice of voting for an ostensibly moderate party like SED. "This would be very good," the dictator concluded. "The sooner the better."[142]

SED co-chairman Otto Grotewohl voiced doubts about the plan, arguing that the establishment of such a party in the Western zones would require that the Soviets allow the Social Democrats to operate freely in the East. But Stalin thought the arrangement perfectly sensible, arguing that the SPD would not be able to criticize beyond the "digestible" (presumably by the Soviet military authorities). Therefore, there was nothing to fear. "What, are you afraid of this?" he asked the puzzled SED leadership, adding: "While this group [SPD] is banned, it has an aureole. The moment you allow it, there won't be an aureole [of sainthood]." Stalin appeared to believe that the hassle from oppositional activities under a watchful Soviet eye would be more than compensated by imaginary gains at the polls in the Western zones.[143] Such optimism probably drew on the experience of the French and the Italians, though it most certainly reflected a lack of appreciation on his part that anything that smelled of a Soviet connection, including the suspiciously "moderate" SED, would be a hard sell with the German voter. Grotewohl had a better understanding of the realities on the ground, which was why he cautiously contradicted Stalin's optimistic analysis.[144]

At one point in the conversation Stalin even began advocating for the creation of a Nazi party in the Soviet zone. His rationale was that unless the former Nazis had their own party, they would gravitate towards the West. But there were many Nazis even among the workers, who had to be won over. Even mid-ranking Nazi officials and former leaders could be brought over, Stalin explained. Their party could be given some innocuous-sounding name like "the National Democratic Party." Grotewohl was horrified. What? His party made it a point to condemn fascism, and it would be "impossible" to allow them the veneer of legitimacy of a political party. "Impossible?" Stalin asked. "I thought it would be possible." This way, he went on to argue, "one could corrupt the camp that is gathering around the British and the Americans. Now they are frightening everyone that, allegedly, everyone is in prison in the Soviet zone, and everyone is being destroyed. And we could say: this is incorrect. They even organized their own party!"[145] Whatever Grotewohl and his comrades thought of this advice, the "National Democratic Party of Germany" was promptly founded. Whether it made the prospect of living in the Soviet occupation zone more attractive is much to be doubted.

These manipulations – undermining the SPD in the West, building up a false democratic façade in the East – made sense in the context of a broader struggle for a united Germany, yet this prospect began to fade

PART I AMBITION

by late 1946. There was a growing conviction in Washington that Stalin would not relinquish control of the Soviet zone, and that the best policy was to consolidate the three Western zones, and promote their economic recovery.[146] This became especially clear after the stalemate of the Moscow Conference of Foreign Ministers (March–April 1947). Disagreements centered on two issues. First, the Soviets wanted reparations from current production in the Western sectors of Germany. The Americans and the British resisted the idea. They were desperately trying to promote economic recovery in their zones (which they still heavily subsidized). Second, the Soviets and the Western allies had very different ideas about how to achieve political unity in Germany. Marshall insisted on a federal system, which would give greater decision-making power to the states (or *Länder*). Molotov wanted a stronger centralized government, on the probable assumption that the Soviets could then exercise control over the Western zones without giving up their grip on their own.[147] The Soviet idea was that they could play the card of German nationalism by making the SED its chief advocate.[148]

The abject failure of the London Conference of Foreign Ministers (November–December 1947) to arrive at any compromise at all on the German question, and the implications for occupied Germany of the Soviet-sponsored coup in Prague in February 1948 made German unity a very remote prospect indeed. The same month a conference of the Western allies (plus Belgium, Netherlands, and Luxembourg) agreed on the creation of a common government for West Germany and instructed the constituent assembly to prepare a constitution. The Western zones were incorporated into the Marshall Plan. There followed a currency reform, deemed essential for the economic recovery of West Germany. With Germany effectively divided, Stalin sought to further consolidate his gains in the East. In March 1948 the Soviets walked out from the Allied Control Council for Germany and later withdrew from the Allied Kommandatura in Berlin.[149]

Having despaired at making the Germans vote for the Communists in areas outside immediate Soviet control, Stalin now coached his East German clients to rely on long-term subversion. Why not have a few Communists, he said, "renounce Communism" and enter the ranks of the SPD and "corrupt it from the inside"? He promised Soviet help, including money. Grotewohl and his colleagues were not immediately convinced but Stalin urged them to take to heart the lessons of the Teutons' struggle with the Roman Empire. "The old Teutons went naked against the Romans, but they suffered setbacks ... The German Communists are in this respect somewhat like the Teutons: they are waging a struggle too

CHAPTER 3 STALIN IN EUROPE

directly. But this method requires much sacrifice and does not always reach its aim. One has to disguise oneself [*maskirovat'sya*], for there is an intense struggle underway under very difficult conditions." He even quoted examples from Eastern Europe, including Poland and Hungary, hinting in passing that he had always regarded "people's fronts" as merely a disguise, paving way to the Communists' seizure of power.[150] But the essential difference was that in Eastern Europe, the key levers of power were already in the Soviet hands in 1945, which was never going to be the case in West Germany.

In June 1948, the Soviets introduced their own currency in their zone and severed all transport links between the Western-controlled sectors of Berlin and West Germany. By imposing the Berlin blockade, Stalin hoped to push the Allies out of the divided capital. By then the political division of Germany was already a given, which made the Allied presence so far inside the Soviet zone all the more unacceptable to Stalin. This was something the SED was asking for, too, citing concerns about their performance in the coming elections. "Let's make a joint effort," Stalin told an SED delegation in March 1948 – "maybe we'll oust them."[151] According to German historian Gerhard Wettig, Stalin had a broader goal as well: to inflict a *political* defeat on the Allies, and to show the West Germans that they could not rely on American protection.[152]

Yet, contrary to Stalin's expectations, the Western allies dug in and launched an airlift, which continued for months. Stalin was unwilling to shoot down US and British planes that brought all the essentials into the blockaded city. The gamble failed.

In May 1949, after nearly a year, Stalin finally lifted the Berlin blockade. Faced with US resolve, he backed off, much as Kennan had predicted. West Germany was established on September 21, 1949 as the Federal Republic of Germany, and two weeks later Communist Germany was set up in the East. For years there was a debate among historians as to whether Stalin regarded the division of Germany as permanent, or whether he still eyed a possible reunification (by concluding a peace treaty and securing Germany's neutrality). But archival materials that have since been released make it absolutely clear: there was little prospect for a united, neutral Germany, not since Stalin understood – as he certainly did by 1947 – that the Communists would be defeated at the polls. He of course continued his peace offensive, for example by presenting the famous Stalin Note of March 1952 (calling for a peace treaty) but that was just propaganda, an effort to sow confusion in West Germany, delay its rearmament, and derail its incorporation into the Western bloc.[153]

In April 1952 Stalin explained his view of the situation in Germany to a visiting SED delegation. The Americans, he said, were in Germany to stay. They needed Germany "to hold Western Europe in their hands." He continued: "The demarcation line between West and East Germany must be viewed as a border, and not just any border, but as a dangerous border." He ordered the East Germans to build an army, at least thirty divisions in strength. "They [the West] understand only force. When you have an army, they'll talk differently with you – they will recognize and learn to love you, because everybody loves force." After the Germans signaled that there was, in fact, considerable pacifism in the GDR, the dictator lectured them: "The Germans have never been vegetarians and have suddenly become such. You should stop being vegetarians or you will be eaten in turn. You just build up the militant spirit, and we will help you."[154] East Germany was to play a key role in Stalin's plans for a war with the West. This war, he thought, was just a matter of time.

CONCLUSION

With all that we know today about Stalin, are we any closer to understanding his role in precipitating the Cold War? Was Stalin chiefly responsible for this conflict, or was he just reacting to Western (mainly American) moves? Were both sides responsible, or perhaps the international system as a whole? Answers remain frustratingly elusive. Part of the problem is that assignment of blame obscures the underlying complexity of the question. If we take Soviet control of Eastern Europe as the starting point of the blame game, then undoubtedly Stalin was responsible for imposing this control, and who can reproach the United States for resisting such imposition? If, on the other hand, we take the division of Europe into spheres of influence as a legitimate exercise, then American unwillingness to permit the Soviets their sphere sets the United States up as the culprit. This latter argument was notably once peddled by revisionist historians like William Appleman Williams, and it rests on an idea (which Stalin would have found appealing) that spheres of influence were legitimate (never mind what the Eastern Europeans thought of it). Thus, inadvertently, by poking the question of blame, we have begun probing the complex interplay of power and legitimacy, which should at any rate be at the bottom of any sensible discussion of the origins of the Cold War.

It is extremely difficult to accept that Stalin was entitled to a sphere of influence in Eastern Europe. Did he, on the other hand, have legitimate security interests in the region? Although seemingly a different question, this is in fact another way of asking the same thing. Stalin would have certainly insisted that he did have legitimate security interests, and the bottom line would be what to consider legitimate – and in whose eyes. One possible approach to the tricky question is this: of course, Stalin had legitimate security interests as long as looking after them did not require the imposition of a brutal Stalinist system of control and repression on the unwilling Eastern Europeans. Since Stalin did exactly that, surely he is chiefly responsible for the confrontation that ensued. This is perhaps the most sensible answer that can be given to that inescapable question of blame.

Here is another interesting question: What were the underlying motivations of Stalin's behavior? The first issue to consider is ideology, which played a very tricky role in Stalin's foreign policy. Among those rooting for ideology was George Kennan who, writing in the midst of the events described in this chapter, pointed to the "innate antagonism between capitalism and Socialism" as the reason why no permanent coexistence was possible between Moscow and the West until, that is, "the internal nature of Soviet power is changed." Kennan listed reasons why it might be so, including differences in the production systems between the East and the West, the Soviet belief that capitalism would self-destruct, and that imperialism would inevitably lead to war and revolution.[155] But he failed to show how these various underpinning principles played out in actual policy making. He also failed to consider the possibility that, far from determining the direction of Soviet policy, ideological dogma helped rationalize conflicts that developed for other reasons. For example, this was the case with the Stalin–Tito split, which is difficult to explain with reference to production systems or long-term views of history's progress. In fact, the conflict was obviously underpinned by Stalin's mistrust of Tito's ambitions in the Balkans, and was only later framed in explicitly ideological terms.

True, an advocate of ideology may say, but the problem goes deeper, for clearly both Stalin and Tito operated within an ideological framework, which included a shared commitment to the Communist cause. Ideology formed the basis of a common identity in a world where Stalin and his clients in Eastern Europe belonged to a particular in-group. Thus, Tito was excommunicated from the socialist camp because Stalin suspected him of disloyalty rather than because he betrayed Marxism-Leninism, but any sensible definition of a socialist camp would require at least some discussion of Marxism-Leninism. Then again, the socialist camp was a sphere of influence, and spheres of influence do not depend on Marxism-Leninism for their existence. The circular argument leads us nowhere, which is why the

PART I AMBITION

argument that the Cold War was inevitable because of Stalin's ideological proclivities turns out to be quite useless on closer inspection.

Things are no easier with the accompanying notion, to wit: that Stalin was a realist or, more colorfully, an imperialist. To be sure, there is plenty of evidence, including in this chapter, that Stalin believed that the other side only understood force. There is plenty of evidence to prove that he sought to control Eastern Europe for reasons of security, geopolitically understood. It is clear in this respect that Stalin belonged to a long and esteemed tradition of thinkers that trace their genesis to the Athenian generals at Melos. The conflict between the Soviet Union and the United States thus appears inevitable as a power struggle between two great powers, quite irrespective of their ideologies. But the ideologists will come back through the backdoor to claim that Marxism-Leninism defined who "the other side" was. Again, perceptions of identity and perceptions of power become closely intertwined to the point where they cannot be sensibly untangled.

This debate can be confusing. Because it is easy to see Stalin as a dogmatic ideologue or Machiavellian actor or both, it is easy to project his ambitions and his convictions backwards to argue that there was certain inevitability about his actions, and about the Cold War that ensued. Because we know where Stalin ended up, we tend to assume that he was always going to end up there. We cling to evidence – sparse though it is – that suggests that Stalin masked his real intentions, that his entire postwar strategy of coalition governments was simply a charade that was useful for a time – but only for a time.[156] Stalin himself in retrospect attributed more consistency to his actions than seemed plausible at the time he made his decisions. Yet Stalin was often very inconsistent. Did he plan to sovietize Europe? Did he plan to divide Germany? The evidence suggests that he was playing it by ear, that many of the developments that unfolded in the Soviet "sphere" after 1947 were not properly planned as a part of Stalin's dark vision of ideological struggle but were rather a reaction to deepening contradictions between the Soviet Union and the West.

If there was a turning point here, it was not so much the Marshall Plan as Stalin's realization that his left-leaning coalitions were not electable. Few wanted Communism, and it had to be forced upon the reluctant populace. Of course, the Truman doctrine and the Marshall Plan provided a convenient excuse for Stalin: he could now claim that it was not that people did not *want* Communism, but that the American capital, to keep Europe in a subjugated state, denied them the actual choice. It was already clear by 1947 that Stalin had to extinguish all political opposition in his sphere of

CHAPTER 3 STALIN IN EUROPE

influence, and this he did with the establishment of the Cominform. The Cold War was thus not inevitable until it happened, but it did not happen overnight: it took months and months of deepening tensions before Europe finally succumbed.

The interesting question here is what, in this case, happened to Stalin's desire for international legitimacy through Western (i.e. American) recognition that seemed to underpin his earlier approach to great-power politics. Up until 1945 he foresaw some form of great-power cooperation in Europe. After Hiroshima and Nagasaki, he became more obstinate, rejecting compromise with the United States, which, he feared, would expose the Soviet Union's weakness, and so invite further pressure. But even in 1946, and into early 1947, there were moments when compromise seemed within reach. The conclusion of peace treaties with Italy, Romania, Hungary, Bulgaria, and Finland pointed in that direction. So did the abandoned probe of a settlement in Greece. Soviet withdrawal from Iran could be seen as another example. True, there is always going to be the opposite argument (i.e. that Stalin pulled out of Iran merely because he feared the United States, that he worried about an escalation he could not afford). He did worry about escalation – not just in Iran but, later, in the Balkans and in China. When, in late 1947, some Italian Communists mulled over the prospect of launching military struggle in Italy, Stalin balked.[157] He was too cautious. He also backed off in Berlin, showing that, as Kennan rightly noted, he really was sensitive to the logic of force.

Henry Kissinger had once argued that the immediate postwar years – when the United States still had its nuclear monopoly – was a missed opportunity to force Stalin to back down in Eastern Europe.[158] Instead, Washington dithered, giving the Kremlin time to consolidate its conquests. It is impossible to know. Yes, Stalin backed down in some places. Yet he also stood his ground elsewhere (usually in places he deemed more important to Soviet security interests), reacting to pressure with defiance and hastening the slide into the Cold War. Thus, to be tough with Stalin or to stop "babying the Soviets," in the memorable phrase of Harry S. Truman's unsent letter to James Byrnes, could either have had the effect of getting better terms from him or the opposite effect – of bringing on the Cold War (if not an actual war) all that much faster.[159] What is clear in retrospect is that Stalin had a keen eye for American weakness and judged that for all his fear of war with the United States, the Americans feared war even more.

In any case he initially allowed for a world where some countries belonged to grey zones, where the Soviets and the Americans could at

PART I AMBITION

least tolerate each other's presence, even as they secretly competed for influence. Yalta did not rule out the possibility of such coexistence and competition, and it continued to exercise residual influence on Stalin's approach to international politics. The principal method of competition was left-wing coalition-building. In Iran, for example, Stalin counted precisely on such a coalition, where Qavam (the "scumbag" that he was) would still defer to Stalin's preferences, if not always, then at least in some cases, because doing so would be in his own interest. The same approach underpinned Stalin's thinking about German unity. Building up a left-wing coalition in the Western-controlled parts of Germany appreciably remained Stalin's goal until 1947. His careful probing for a coalition government in Greece in late 1946 was another example of this approach. When Stalin spoke to British Labourites about alternative roads to socialism, this was what he meant: gradually gaining influence through parliamentary means. Perhaps for this reason he was so upset about the French ditching this strategy in the spring of 1947 in favor of criticizing the government "from the outside."

But the promise of Yalta faded by 1948–49. The demise of the coalition government in Czechoslovakia, the expulsion of Yugoslavia from the Cominform, and, finally, the division of Germany spoke to a very different, starker reality. The great-power concert that Stalin had foreseen in 1945 – based both on security and legitimacy – gave way to a zero-sum game, where neither side could afford to make the slightest concession to the other. In this world, security mattered more: control without legitimacy was far better for a paranoid and insecure leader like him than legitimacy without control. So, Stalin doubled down, moving away from coalition governments that afforded a veneer of legitimacy towards outright Communist dictatorships that did not. If there was a pivotal year, it was clearly 1947 for all the different reasons discussed, but, above all, because it was then that Stalin finally understood that the parliamentary road to Communism was no longer an option, and that the United States was in Europe to stay.

By the spring of 1949 Stalin had given up on squeezing the Allies out of Berlin. He had also given up on the Greek insurgency. He retrenched and consolidated his positions, though not before his brinksmanship led the West Europeans to recognize the importance of collective defense through America's continued involvement on the European continent. The unforeseen consequence of this recognition was the signing of the North Atlantic Treaty on April 4, 1949. The European Cold War was on.

4

STALIN IN ASIA

Around noon on December 16, 1949, chairman of the Chinese Communist Party, Mao Zedong, arrived at the Yaroslavsky train station in Moscow.[1] His journey from China took ten days to complete. Mao was fatigued from travels and had a cold but managed a faint, sickly smile before stepping onto the platform. Breathing steam into bitterly cold air, he greeted members of the Soviet Politburo with handshakes and awkward military salutes. Flanked by his Soviet hosts, Mao made his way past the honor guard to a microphone. "Dear comrades and friends," he said in a high-pitched voice so ill-suited for his towering persona. "My visit to the capital of the first socialist country in the world, the Soviet Union, is a happy event of a lifetime."[2] His words rang in stark dissonance to Mao's sour expression and the stone-faced looks of the welcoming party. After a curtailed ceremony – it was too cold to linger – the Chinese delegation was taken to their residence at Stalin's dacha, a two-story country house just outside of Moscow, where Mao would spend the better part of the next two months. In every sense, it was a very frosty reception, an inauspicious opening to a new era of Sino-Soviet solidarity – a geopolitical earthquake of great consequence, which would open a new chapter in the Cold War.

This chapter revisits the origins of the Sino-Soviet alliance with an eye, specifically, to testing Mao Zedong's later claims that his experience of negotiating with Stalin left him bitter and disillusioned, and that the Soviet Union took advantage of China by imposing quasi-imperialist terms on a junior partner. The chapter argues that although tensions were evident during the negotiations, the 1950 Treaty of Alliance was on balance a remarkable success for China and for Mao Zedong personally.

The conclusion of the Sino-Soviet alliance was soon followed by North Korea's invasion of South Korea. These developments were directly related. The chapter recounts how, and with what consequences, Stalin committed one of the greater follies of his final years in power: giving North Korea's Kim Il Sung the green light to invade. This decision spelled the end of the Yalta framework that Stalin envisioned in 1945.

PART I AMBITION

PEACE AT HAND

Mao's road to Moscow was long and painful. As we have seen, Stalin held a fairly dim view of the prospects for Chinese Communist Revolution. In August 1945 he ordered Mao into peace talks with the Guomindang (a civil war in China certainly did not figure in the dictator's plans). The renewal of hostilities in July 1946 was a setback for Soviet foreign policy. For a time, the Communists were on their back foot. In March 1947 Mao had to flee when his long-time base in Yan'an was captured by the advancing Guomindang forces. Chiang Kai-shek's offensive in Shaanxi stalled that summer, and the CCP counterattacked, but the outcome of the civil war was yet far from certain.

In September 1947 Stalin was in Sochi, from where he kept one eye on developments in Szklarska Poręba as Zhdanov proclaimed the establishment of the Cominform. But he was also watching the situation in China, in particular the unusual approach from the prominent Chinese politician T.V. Soong (Song Ziwen) who had negotiated the Sino-Soviet Treaty in Moscow in July–August 1945. Soong's secretary, Guo Zengkai, contacted the Soviet military attaché in China, Nikolai Roshchin, suggesting that Soong was in favor of immediate talks between the CCP and the Guomindang. He wanted to form a coalition government within only a month-and-a-half, and he would bring Chiang Kai-shek around to endorse it but if the generalissimo balked, "then Soong could do without Chiang Kai-shek."[3]

On September 8, Molotov (who was with Stalin in Sochi) cabled back to China that the "authoritative circles" in the Soviet Union found Soong's position "correct" because it would protect the Chinese economy from "external destructive forces," guarantee China against the resurgence of Japanese militarism, unite "all democratic forces of China," and strengthen Sino-Soviet relations. These "circles," Molotov added, thought that the Chinese Communists "would view such a position with sympathy," and asked that T.V. Soong seek out CCP representatives to hold talks.[4] Stalin only informed Mao of these developments on September 24, when he finally sent him a telegram with the "advice not to reject talks with Soong's representatives" (although he also noted that Soong's statements were "for now" only that – statements). In any case, the gist of Stalin's message was that he was not averse to a peaceful resolution of the ongoing war, worried, as he probably was, that the Communist gains were reversible.[5]

The Soviet liaison officer with the CCP forces, Andrei Orlov (known by his codename: "Terebin"), went looking for Mao, catching up with

CHAPTER 4 STALIN IN ASIA

him on September 30 in the dusty little village of Shengquan in northern Shaanxi, a few kilometers to the west of the great Yellow River. Mao had arrived there a week earlier, setting up temporary military headquarters. Presently he told Orlov that things were going well on practically all fronts. While he was not averse to having contacts with Soong's representatives, he had no intention to engage in real peace talks. "This is extremely unprofitable to us," he said. "But GMD, in order to fight again and [fight] better, is in dire need of a breathing spell." He told Stalin's representative that the CCP now had the initiative, and another year of fighting would bring great changes, while capturing power in all of China would take from three to five years.[6]

Stalin responded to this insubordination with a curt cable, expressing "satisfaction" with Mao's explanations.[7] What he really thought is difficult to gauge, though Dimitrov later heard Stalin say that he had "doubted that the Chinese could succeed." "The Chinese proved to be right," he later said, "and we were wrong."[8] It was a rare admission of error.

In the meantime, Mao had been shopping for a pretext to visit Moscow. He may have asked Stalin as early as spring 1947, though the first solid evidence (in the form of a Soviet invitation) is dated June 15, 1947.[9] Mao (codenamed Pugachev, probably in honor of the leader of the eighteenth-century Russian peasant rebellion, Emelian Pugachev), was asked to proceed secretly to Harbin in Manchuria. The ostensible purpose of the trip was to visit the CCP military command in the city. This was to fool the Americans who could be monitoring Mao's movements. In reality, he would be picked up by a Soviet plane and taken to Moscow.[10]

But these ambitious plans were put on hold, reportedly because the military situation required Mao's presence in China.[11] The idea of him going to the Soviet Union was broached again in December, and, again, Stalin seemingly agreed.[12] Mao was thrilled and promised to stay for three months and even for a year but he first wanted to complete operations in the vicinity of the Ping-Sui railway (running northwesterly from Beijing). "We can't give CKS [Chiang Kai-shek] a break now, we have to keep hitting him," Mao told Terebin on December 17.[13] He returned to his plans of visiting Moscow in the spring of 1948 but Stalin, after inviting him, suddenly proposed to postpone the trip because of the difficult military situation. The bizarre cat-and-mouse game continued until early 1949, with Mao voicing readiness to come, then postponing, either due to military contingencies, or because of alleged sickness or, in one case (in mid-July 1948) because Stalin insisted that there would be no one to receive him in Moscow since all the leading comrades were busy with "harvest work."[14]

PART I AMBITION

On that occasion Mao barely hid his frustration with Stalin's duplicity.[15] It is still not clear why the dictator was procrastinating. Perhaps he was waiting for the situation on the battlefields to clear up. Perhaps he still did not trust Mao, especially now that he had a falling out with Tito. Or perhaps he was once again probing for the possibility of peaceful settlement of the civil war, and having Mao in Moscow would have confused his plans.

By mid-1948 China was in a state of economic meltdown. Sprawling corruption, run-away inflation, and the growing burden of taxation undercut support for the Guomindang. In cities, businessmen complained of extortion by party officials and soldiers. The election of Chiang Kai-shek's old rival Li Zongren as vice president in April 1948 suggested that Chiang was beginning to lose his grip on the party and the country. Chiang thereupon moved against his minister of defense, Bai Chongxi, who had been supportive of Li (Bai was relieved of his post in June 1948). Apt at playing his generals against one another, Chiang seemed oblivious to how infighting undermined his – and his generals' – ability to successfully wage war. Meanwhile, the Revolutionary Committee of the Guomindang – a splinter group formed in January 1948 and headed by another of Chiang's rivals, General Li Jishen, out of Hong Kong – plotted the generalissimo's downfall and eyed a coalition government with the CCP.[16] The military situation was looking more and more dire as the Communists made gains in the northeast.[17]

In April the US Congress finally passed the China Aid Act, worth $400 million (with another $125 million for military aid). Neither Truman nor Secretary of State George Marshall were overly enthusiastic about pouring money down that particular drain (Marshall had had his own share of frustrations with China after he unsuccessfully tried to mediate in the Chinese civil war in 1946). But the president faced Republican detractors in an election year, and they were all too ready to blame the loss of China on his weak policies.[18] In any case, this aid would take months to arrive; by then, it was game over for the Guomindang.

US Ambassador John Leighton Stuart, observing Chiang at close quarters in the summer of 1948, was growing desperate: The generalissimo seemed woefully incapable of rising to the occasion but if he fell – then what? Who could replace the old "peanut" (as he was unkindly known to the Americans) and reverse Communist victories? "No Chinese dares to say to him what many even among his closer associates are now thinking and they are looking to me with a pathetic expectancy," Stuart wrote to Washington on June 14. "And yet I feel impotent to accomplish anything that helps to reverse the downward trend."[19]

114

CHAPTER 4 STALIN IN ASIA

In August 1948 Mao sent a detailed cable to Stalin, describing the chaos in the Guomindang ranks and the US position. According to Mao, Ambassador Stuart, while on the one hand supporting Chiang Kai-shek, was on the other hand probing for the possibility of his replacement (this was a broadly correct conclusion). Mao also recounted probes from Stuart directed at the Communists: supposedly he was secretly feeling the ground for a negotiated peace. Mao then said that although they had previously rejected these approaches, he now wanted to go along, but would drag things out, delaying the arrival of Stuart's representative in the Communist-held territory. When the latter did turn up, that representative would only get to meet local CCP cadres, "and the conversation will not have any concrete meaning." This was "in order to create certain illusions in Marshall's and Stuart's minds." Mao concluded that his strategy was "to widen the existing disagreements between Marshall and Stuart on the one hand and CKS [Chiang Kai-shek] on the other. This will benefit the development of the revolutionary war."[20]

In the fall the Communists launched a new round of large-scale operations, rounding up whole armies of demoralized Guomindang troops. On December 30 Mao summed up his successes in a cable for the benefit of "Comrade Main Master," as he lovingly called the Soviet dictator. He explained that the CCP had been more successful than "we had initially expected." Therefore, the schedule for overthrowing the Guomindang had been brought forward from mid-1951 to the end of 1949. "It is already too difficult for the Guomindang to hold on to power," Mao wrote. "It is degenerating and splitting up. The wide masses of the country are turning to us. The liberal bourgeoisie are vacillating and are looking for a way out with us. From day to day, the number of Guomindang's followers is shrinking." The American policy in China was "bankrupt." All of that meant that Mao was once again ready to go to Moscow for consultations with Stalin ahead of calling the Political Consultative Conference in the summer of 1949, which would pave the way to the establishment of the Communist government.[21] On January 9, Mao asked Stalin to send two aircraft to Shijiazhuang (southwest of Beijing) to pick him up.[22]

On the very same day, however, Stalin had an idea that caused serious friction with Mao, contributing to the latter's complaints that the Soviets never believed in China's Communist Revolution.

On January 8, 1949, the Chinese government in Nanjing separately approached Britain, France, the United States, and the Soviet Union for help in the mediation of the Guomindang–CCP conflict.[23] This request, coming so late in the game, when the Chinese government appeared on

115

the verge of a collapse, confounded Western observers. Ambassador Stuart reported to Washington that the Guomindang were probably just playing to gain time, that if they really intended to negotiate with the Communists, they would have approached the CCP directly, and that the USSR would likely sabotage any such mediation. In other words, there was no point.[24] The British and the French appeared to agree. On January 12 Washington cabled Stuart to turn the Chinese down.[25]

Meanwhile, Stalin thought the proposal was worth considering. On January 10 he cabled Mao, explaining that he intended to answer the meditation proposal by suggesting that the Guomindang first seek the CCP's agreement. If they did, Stalin continued, the CCP should reply that they are prepared to enter peace talks but without the involvement of the "war criminals" that are responsible for the civil war in China (this was of course directed at Chiang Kai-shek), and also without the involvement of third powers, notably the United States which was itself "participating in the civil war." (This was a reference to the fact that there were still American Marines in Qingdao, a legacy of the Second World War, though these were being withdrawn – the last would leave in 1949.) Most annoyingly for Mao, Stalin now wanted to postpone his visit to Moscow, because this visit "would be used by the enemy for discrediting the Chinese Communist Party."[26]

The following day, perhaps worried by the impression he made on Mao with his cable, Stalin fired off an additional explanation. His proposal, he said, aimed at undermining the peace talks with the Guomindang, because it was obvious that they would not agree to negotiate without American mediation. (In fact, Stalin wrongly believed the Guomindang's approach was inspired and directed by the Americans.) "This way," he concluded, "the Guomindang's peace maneuver will be ruined, and you will be able to continue the victorious war of liberation."[27]

To understand Stalin's preoccupation with "peace maneuvers," one needs to recall that it was a fixture of his correspondence with Mao for months. On occasion, the Soviet dictator would slap Mao on the wrist for what he believed was the CCP's undue enthusiasm for the communization of China. For example, in April 1948 he cabled Mao his disagreement with the idea (voiced in Mao's earlier report) that after the Communists claim power in China, they should drive all other forces off the political stage. Stalin insisted, by contrast, that the Chinese government would have to be a "revolutionary-democratic" and not a "Communist" government. This was necessary to "isolate the imperialists and their GMD agents." This seemingly obscure theoretical point was of considerable importance to Stalin, and somewhat counterintuitively at that: in Eastern Europe the Soviet

CHAPTER 4 STALIN IN ASIA

dictator was doing precisely the opposite, i.e. effectively destroying coalition governments in favor of the standard Soviet fare. Intriguingly, he was not even willing to put a date on how long the "revolutionary-democratic" phase would last.[28]

He urged Mao to form a coalition government as soon as possible to preempt Chiang Kai-shek who, Stalin argued as late as January 1949, might form a coalition government of his own, pulling the carpet from under the CCP's feet.[29] Mao responded to this pressure by arguing that even if the Guomindang attempted to form a coalition government so late in the game, they would fail. On January 7, in his conversation with Orlov/ Terebin he explained again that Chiang Kai-shek was at the very precipice of failure, that even Guomindang generals like Bai Chongxi were secretly in touch with the CCP and took instructions from them. "The situation is such," he said, "that if we wanted to, and issued relevant instructions, there would be a massive uprising against Chiang Kai-shek by his forces, and their desertion to our side. But this is not profitable for now. For in this case, we'd have too many Guomindang forces, and this is too troublesome."[30]

Given the backdrop of these conversations, Mao was probably annoyed by Stalin's instructions about the latest peace talks offer from the Guomindang. On January 12, he sent a reply, in which he did something quite unthinkable for a Soviet client: he *advised* Stalin what his response to Nanjing's probe should be – to reject mediation out of hand. He then explained that the CCP agreeing to peace talks would cause "great confusion" among the Chinese people and even in the ranks of the CCP, and harm their political position while strengthening that of the Guomindang and its US backers. Mao concluded by saying that the correlation of forces in China was such that the CCP "no longer required diversionary political maneuvers," which, he added, "were more harmful than useful."[31]

Orlov/Terebin sent a few comments on his own. "Mao Zedong spoke more sharply," he cabled to Moscow. "He is against all participation in mediation, against all participation by the CCP in the negotiations." Mao's interpreter Shi Zhe, alluding to Stalin's decision to postpone his client's visit, even threatened that unless Mao were allowed to come to Moscow in January 1949, he would never come at all.[32] Stalin had had his difficult moments with Tito. Now he faced another instance of quite blatant insubordination.

Instead of lashing out against a delinquent client as he might have done, Stalin reasoned with Mao in another, slightly peevish, but still polite cable. He argued that by turning down Guomindang's offer of peace talks, the Communists would merely allow Chiang Kai-shek to grasp the "banner

PART I AMBITION

of peace." Also – and this was undoubtedly what Stalin was really worried about – it would allow the Americans to "organize a military intervention [in China], similar to the intervention, which took place in Russia in the course of four years between 1918 and 1921." In the end, he pointed out that even if the Guomindang miraculously agreed to the CCP's conditions and formed a coalition government, the Communists would dominate it anyway.[33] It was thus more a matter of short-term tactics than of long-term strategy. Mao telegraphed his agreement, and the quarrel ended before it even began, leaving perhaps a tinge of bitterness in the chairman's mouth, not least because Stalin insisted on postponing Mao's trip to Moscow.

MIKOYAN IN XIBAIPO

Instead of allowing Mao to come to Moscow, Stalin sent a trusted lieutenant, Anastas Mikoyan, to China. Mikoyan, an Armenian, joined the senior Soviet leadership under Lenin and had held a variety of senior positions under Stalin. In 1949 he was the Soviet minister for foreign trade. As we have seen, Stalin accused him of pursuing "antistate" policies in making trading deals with Czechoslovakia, but the wily bureaucrat knew how to survive the dictator's wrath, and in fact outlasted not just Stalin, but continued to serve under Khrushchev and even under Brezhnev, becoming the butt of a well-known Soviet joke about his ability of escape dry from a rain shower by walking between the raindrops. Presently, Mikoyan turned up in Xibaipo, a little village just northwest of Shijiazhuang in Hebei Province. It was there, at the CCP's temporary field headquarters, that he and Mao engaged in lengthy, far-ranging conversations for days on end. Mikoyan kept in touch with Stalin by cable, reporting Mao's words and taking instructions. The extensive record of their conversations provides a front-row view of the evolution of the Sino-Soviet relationship.

Mikoyan's notes for the trip include a list of topics, jotted down in pencil, that he intended to discuss with Mao. These were likely composed in Stalin's presence (he saw Stalin on January 19, shortly before departure) and reflect the dictator's concerns. Characteristically, the very first topic on the list was the Guomindang's peace talks proposal. Stalin, who had claimed that the "peace maneuver" was an American ploy, was clearly embarrassed by the American decision not to involve themselves in mediation. He had to explain to Mao that the US refused only because they learned of the secret Soviet strategy to ruin the talks.[34] Therefore, Mikoyan was to ask whether Mao had "blabbermouths" in his midst. Mao rejected these insinuations out of hand.[35] He boasted that it was the CCP that knew of American

118

CHAPTER 4 STALIN IN ASIA

plans in China, since they learned how to intercept and decrypt US and Guomindang radiograms.[36]

There was only one moment of tension in relation to continued Soviet dithering. It was when China's soon-would-be Prime Minister Zhou Enlai challenged Mikoyan to explain why Soviet Ambassador Nikolai Roshchin followed the retreating Guomindang government from the capital, Nanjing, to Guangzhou, in the south of China. He did so even as many Western ambassadors (including America's Stuart) stayed in Nanjing. Stalin had to explain this point in a separate cable to Mikoyan. He claimed that he sent Roshchin south "for intelligence-gathering," to spy on the Guomindang leadership "and their American masters."[37] The Chinese were likely not convinced.

Another item on Mikoyan's list was the 1945 Sino-Soviet Treaty of Alliance, with its various strings and concessions, including Soviet control of a strategic railroad across Manchuria and the right to use the old tsarist naval base at Lüshun, at the tip of the Liaodong peninsula. These provisions had a blatantly colonial character, which Mikoyan was asked to explain away by saying that the Soviets were afraid lest Chiang Kai-shek would allow the Americans to set up shop in Manchuria. "We don't want concessions in Manchuria," Mikoyan was to say. "Our demands to Chiang Kai-shek have become irrelevant because the Communists have come to power."[38]

But when Stalin's envoy broached this point, Mao unexpectedly claimed that the 1945 Treaty had a "patriotic character," and the Communists did not mind it at all – in fact, they wanted to keep the Soviet base in Lüshun. Taken aback, Mikoyan quizzed Mao how he managed to square his support for the Soviet base with his opposition to the American base in Qingdao, to which the latter responded, cunningly, that while the Soviets were in Lüshun to protect, the Americans were in Qingdao to oppress. Mikoyan's explanation to the effect that the Soviets considered the agreement on Lüshun as "unequal" caused "frank astonishment" on Mao's part (though perhaps Mao was acting). In any case, Mao allowed himself to be convinced that once New China became strong, the Soviets could "leave."[39]

Stalin asked Mikoyan to broach the "nationalities" question with Mao. As the former commissar for nationalities, the Soviet dictator had always considered himself to be a great expert on this subject. He had previously played the nationalities card against the Chinese government when he supported the ethnic insurgency in Xinjiang (which he later traded for the 1945 Sino-Soviet Treaty). Now, Stalin instructed Mikoyan to tell Mao that he "should not become too generous in relation to national minorities, so as not to lose any territory after taking power."[40] Mikoyan passed the message and reported Mao's reaction. Mao was "glad to hear this advice but you could tell by his face that he had no intention of giving independence to anybody whatsoever."[41] Far from giving independence to Xinjiang, Mao pushed his luck with Stalin by asking that Mongolia – long pronounced independent by Chiang Kai-shek – be reunited with China. Stalin immediately cabled his opposition to the idea. Comrades or not, Stalin was not about to give away the strategic victory that he had wrestled from Chiang Kai-shek with so much effort.[42]

Another point of considerable interest was the discussion of the prospects for the Eastern Cominform. Stalin and Mao had exchanged several cables on this issue, with Mao keeping the boss informed about what the CCP knew and did not know about revolutionary activities of different Communist groups in Southeast Asia.[43] Now Stalin advised Mao through Mikoyan that although China should not join the Cominform, it should form its own bureau of Asian Communist parties, which would entail a division of responsibilities between Moscow (with its interests in Europe) and China (which would focus on Asia). The parties that Stalin wanted in China's Cominform included the North Koreans and the Japanese, but not the Southeast Asian parties, which was odd given that the CCP had important contacts there, in particular in Indochina.[44] Stalin knew perfectly well that the Chinese Communists were in touch with Ho Chi Minh in Vietnam; in fact, he even encouraged Mao to provide the Vietnamese with the "necessary aid."[45] In October 1948 Mao reported to Stalin via Orlov/Terebin about his decision to provide Ho Chi Minh with $500,000 in funding and, more importantly, that he had informed the Vietnamese that they could make use of the CCP forces operating out of Guangdong.[46]

Mikoyan's instructions provide a part of the answer to the puzzle, indicating that Stalin envisioned directing the Vietnamese through the French Communist Party.[47] It is not clear whether Mikoyan discussed this idea with Mao but what he did tell the Chinese, also on Stalin's instructions, was to be very careful with these Communist parties because, his instructions said, these parties (including the Vietnamese) were riddled with British and American spies.[48] Stalin's attitude towards Ho Chi Minh only really began to change a year later, when he had a chance to read more about Vietnam in general and Ho Chi Minh in particular. (He eventually concluded that Ho was a "firm and sensible Communist, does his thing well, and deserves every support.")[49]

Finally – though this hardly exhausts the extensive lists of subjects Mikoyan and Mao covered in their lengthy meetings – there was a lot of discussion of China's future relationship with the United States. Here Stalin was characteristically cautious. Mikoyan was to tell Mao "not to taunt the American government too much," and adopt a differentiated approach towards US interests in China, by abstaining for the time-being from expropriating American businesses. "After the new government's complete victory," the instructions said, "its policy towards the US may be discussed again, depending on the US behavior."[50]

The question of Stalin's attitude towards US–Chinese relations is extremely interesting in view of the opinion, once prominent among historians, that there had been a "lost chance" in the Sino-American relationship. The question hinges on the contacts that John Leighton Stuart had with the Chinese through the head of the CCP Aliens Affairs Office, Huang Hua. These contacts (in May–June 1949) created an impression (certainly in Stuart's mind) that there was scope for exploiting the differences between the CCP and Moscow, but his covert diplomacy was shut down by Secretary of State Dean Acheson, primarily for domestic reasons (Acheson was worried about the fallout from engaging with the Chinese Communists).[51] What we know today, from Sino-Soviet discussions, was that these contacts with the Americans were conducted with Stalin's blessing. Stalin explained that he was not averse to CCP establishing relations with the Americans as long as the United States renounced its support for the Guomindang. The question was discussed at the CCP Politburo meeting on May 22, to which Mao invited Stalin's representative Ivan Kovalev who then reported back to Moscow that Mao was very critical of Stuart and did not believe American claims to the effect that they were no longer supporting the Guomindang.[52]

Mao's performance was meant to impress Stalin, to make him understand that Communist China would be a reliable partner to the USSR. To this end, Mao told Kovalev during their meeting on May 12, 1949:

> If one were to depict imperialism as a lion, then in the current situation the body and the head of the lion are bound by the strong vices of the revolutionary forces, by the Soviet Union ... We, the Chinese Communists, pinched "the lion's tail and are trying to cut it off. We suppose that the cutting of the tail will in turn weaken the power of the imperialists, concentrated in the head of the lion.[53]

But there was more to Mao's diplomatic game than he made it seem. As we shall see, he was vitally interested in extracting the promise of recognition from the United States in order to use it as a bargaining chip in his discussions with Stalin.

In the meantime, Mao certainly tried to make an impression – on Mikoyan no less than on Kovalev – that he was Stalin's reliable and humble

PART I AMBITION

pupil. China had "fallen far behind Russia," he told Mikoyan during their first meeting on January 30, adding that the Chinese were "weak Marxists." He bent over backwards to thank Stalin for all that he had done for the Chinese Revolution. He was obviously keen to reassure the wary dictator that he was not a Chinese version of Josip Broz Tito who had so openly and so nastily broken up with Moscow.[54] Later Mao would complain repeatedly that, as he put it, "Stalin … did not trust me, considering [me] a Chinese Tito or … at least 'half-Tito.'"[55]

On his return from China, Mikoyan brought presents, including several bottles of soy sauce, chestnut sweets, tofu, and Chinese spices. Instead of sharing these with comrade Stalin over a hearty meal, as he might have done, Mikoyan had the food analyzed with the result that the tofu was found to contain salmonella, while the spices proved too much for the mouse that was fed the serving. "The mouse died," reads the document in a potent reminder of the uncertain road ahead as Stalin and his ambitious Chinese acolyte embarked on their exotic and perilous relationship.[56]

THE CHINESE COMMUNISTS COME TO POWER

The spring and summer of 1949 witnessed epochal changes in China. In April 1949 the People's Liberation Army (PLA) crossed the Yangtze River, taking Nanjing on the 23rd. By late May, Shanghai, too, fell to the advancing Communist forces. Retreating nationalists fled to Taiwan and to the remote southwest, where sporadic and disorganized resistance continued for a while longer. On September 21, Mao recounted these successes in front of the delegates to the Political Consultative Conference, which he convened in Beijing. His speech replete with references to vanquished internal and external oppressors, Mao promised that his victory would be written into the annals of humankind, and these will say: "the Chinese people, who comprise one fourth of the human race, have now stood up!" The Chinese people, Mao said, "have now joined the big family of peace- and freedom-loving nations … Our revolution has already won the sympathy and the welcome of the people of the entire world. We have friends all over the world."[57]

On October 1, 1949, standing atop the Gate of Heavenly Peace in Beijing, Mao announced the establishment of the People's Republic of China (PRC). His was a moment of triumph against all odds, the moment when a former Communist guerrilla became the leader of the world's most populous country. But, though successful in war, the Chinese Communists faced daunting prospects of postwar reconstruction. Mao knew that he had

122

CHAPTER 4 STALIN IN ASIA

Figure 6 Mao Zedong proclaiming the establishment of the People's Republic of China, Oct. 1, 1949. Source: Bettmann/Getty Images

few options but to ask for Soviet help. He needed experts in every field. He needed technologies. Even the fireworks for the display that marked the establishment of the PRC had to be procured from the Soviet military in Dalian (the Soviets obliged).[58]

At the time of Mao's proclamation of the founding of the PRC, Stalin was recuperating at one of his favorite dachas near Sochi, in the Caucasus. There, he pondered the meaning of Mao's victories and what it could mean for Sino-Soviet relations. "There is a difficult side to him," Stalin told a visitor on September 30, referring to the Chinese Communist leader.[59] When Chiang Kai-shek held the reins of power, he squandered the state, losing parts of China to the imperialists. Mao, Stalin said, would seek to rebuild what Chiang had forfeited. For now, he was busy rounding up the Guomindang in southern China but the big question for Stalin was what would happen once all of China came under the Communists' control. Mao had earlier promised Stalin to respect Soviet wartime gains in China, but would he live up to these promises, and what would he ask for in return?

PART I AMBITION

There was also certain awkwardness to the Mao–Stalin relationship from the start. Mao knew that Stalin had been skeptical about the prospects of the Chinese Revolution. He had ignored or contradicted Stalin's demands. Stalin for his part suspected Mao of disloyalty. He knew about Mao much more than Mao knew about him. Suffice it to say that Mao's "Russian doctor," L.I. Mel'nikov, provided very extensive reports to Stalin on what was going on inside Mao's household, including his conflict with his Soviet-educated son Mao Anying (who accused his father of creating a personality cult), and even his wife Jiang Qing's sexual frustrations. When Jiang Qing came to Moscow for medical treatment (in the summer of 1949), her letters to Mao were opened and read by Stalin. Perhaps expecting this, Jiang Qing made sure that her assurances of love for her husband were interspersed with political commentary highly critical of Tito.[60] Still, from his medical perch Mel'nikov submitted that Mao did not care all that much about Marxism-Leninism and that his attitude towards the Soviet Union was generally opportunistic and was shaped by the expectation that the USSR would "help China free of charge."[61]

It was in part to reassure Stalin of his reliability, and in part to secure the promise of much-needed Soviet aid, that in June–July 1949 Mao dispatched his second-in-command, Liu Shaoqi, to Moscow to meet Stalin. Liu presented Stalin with a long list of Chinese requests: for a Soviet credit worth $300 million, for advisers and specialists to help build up the Chinese industry, for certain types of industrial equipment badly needed in Manchuria, and for Soviet aid in upgrading the Chinese Army, Navy, and Air Force. On all these points Stalin was happy to deliver. His biggest concern, however, was the fate of the 1945 Treaty of Alliance. Apart from giving Stalin the right to keep troops in China, the 1945 Treaty made possible the independence of Outer Mongolia and secured Soviet control over the Chinese Eastern Railroad, which cut across Manchuria. Stalin was unsure what line Mao would take, and his response to Liu's question – what to do with the Treaty? – was a noncommittal offer to wait until he and Mao had a chance to talk about it.[62]

On July 4, 1949, Liu Shaoqi sent a lengthy report to Stalin, summarizing different aspects of China's domestic and foreign policies. Stalin went through the report, at least twice, underlining extensively. He did not offer much in the way of commentary, except once, when the report touched on the future of China's foreign relations: whether Beijing was to court recognition by imperialist powers or "wait and not be in a hurry." Stalin commented here that the CCP could use trade as an incentive to win recognition. He was especially sanguine about the United States. A "crisis" there, he wrote, would

124

"force the US to treasure its trade with China." At the same time, he did not think it was wise to rush recognition: "it's better not to hurry," he wrote in the margins.[63] Was he worried about "losing" China to the West? This was unlikely: Stalin himself had encouraged CCP contacts with the West. In any case, Mao hardly needed convincing, for just days earlier he published an editorial in the *People's Daily*, which became an important milestone in China's alignment with the USSR. "We are firmly convinced," read the editorial, "that in order to win victory and consolidate it we must lean to one side." This was, of course, the Soviet side. There was no third way.[64]

The same theme was highlighted in Liu's report, which likened the relationship between the Soviets and China to one between a general staff and a forward command post. "Comrade Mao Zedong and the CCP Central Committee believe," the report went, that "the interests of a part must be subordinate to the interests of the whole. Our CCP obeys the decisions of the Soviet Communist Party ... If disagreements arise between the CCP and the Soviet Communist Party, the CCP will express its point of view but then obey and resolutely implement the decisions of the Soviet Communist Party."[65] (Stalin preemptively wrote in the margins: "No! No!")[66]

Obedience and subordination were woven into the fabric of the nascent Sino-Soviet alliance, and not by anyone but by Mao Zedong himself. But this obedience carried a price tag: a new treaty. The quid pro quo was never made explicit, but the expectation was there from the start. A new treaty was required not so much because Mao wanted to be rid of the Soviet troops in Port Arthur, or reclaim the railroad, or annex Outer Mongolia (on all these matters he was in fact fairly flexible). It was not because China needed Soviet aid, for such aid would come in any case. It was because such a treaty would confer legitimacy to Mao's China and guarantee its admission to the socialist family. It would symbolize Stalin's acceptance of Mao's status as the family's No. 2 who would one day inherit their common revolutionary enterprise.

Yet both Stalin and Mao realized that theirs was not quite the same kind of a revolution, because the Soviet Union and China had very different historical experiences. For all the decadence, decay, political and economic backwardness of pre-revolutionary Russia, it was a great power and a sprawling empire. It was humiliated in the war against Japan in 1904–05, and practically defeated by Germany in 1914–18. But it was never, in modern times, subjected to foreign oppression as China had been. By contrast, it had oppressed, to a varying degree of success, its own neighbors, including China, whose territory Tsarist Russia gobbled up at a rate unmatched by any other imperialist power. To the extent that the Russian people "stood up" in 1917, they did so at the expense of their domestic oppressors. The Russian Revolution was directed against Russia's own ruling class.

Not so for China. In Mao's mind, China's "reactionaries" merely represented a much more powerful force that had reduced the country to semicolonial servitude: global imperialism.[67] "Standing up" meant casting off those shackles and restoring China's international standing, equal among the best, if not the best among equals. And it was on this point that China's very different revolutionary trajectory brought it into potential conflict with the family relationship that Mao and Stalin had set out to cultivate. Membership in the Communist family required an adherence to a hierarchy. Yet "standing up" implied a rejection of the hierarchy and a proud assertion of sovereign equality. There was a contradiction buried somewhere between these two very different revolutionary paradigms; with time, it would give rise to serious problems, helping to bring the Sino-Soviet alliance to ruin.

THE MAKING OF THE SINO-SOVIET ALLIANCE

Shortly after his arrival in Moscow, Mao was ushered in to see Stalin. "Before I met with Stalin," he recalled years later, "I did not have much good feeling about him … He was very different from Lenin: Lenin shared his heart with others as equals whereas Stalin liked to stand above everyone else and order others around."[68] Stalin, as we have seen, had few reasons to trust Mao, whom he also compared unfavorably with Lenin. Lenin had been a true internationalist in the service of the Communist cause, but Mao's credentials and ideological purity were suspect. Stalin had once derisively called him a "cave Marxist," referring to the Chinese leader's decade of isolation in the caves of Yan'an. The fact that the CCP emerged from those caves to capture political power in China greatly surprised Stalin. He was not at all sure that what happened in China qualified as a victory for Communism: an anti-imperialist revolution, yes, but it was far from clear what would follow: "one would have to have a judgment on this in three to four years, depending on the internal and the external situation."[69] On December 16, however, both Mao and Stalin put their doubts aside for the sake of fraternal solidarity, or so recalled the Chinese interpreter at the meeting, Shi Zhe. Stalin, he wrote, firmly shook Mao's hands, and uttered an indirect acknowledgment of his own errors and the lack of faith in the Chinese comrades: "Victors shall not be judged."[70]

Stalin's self-criticism does not appear in the Russian transcript of the conversation, which opens instead with Mao's question: How long will peace last? China, Mao said, needed a "peaceful respite" of three to five years to rebuild its economy ruined by years of conflict. Was he afraid of war, and so sought Stalin's reassurance that he would not be dragged into an apocalyptic confrontation with the United States? This seems unlikely, for Mao had never been distinguished by caution. It was Stalin who had advised Mao for months to account for the possibility of American intervention in the civil war. This time, though, Stalin appeared confident that the United States would not dare to unleash a war and, so, "there is no one to fight with China, not unless [the North Korean leader] Kim Il Sung decides to invade China?"[71] Reporting on Stalin's assessment in a telegram to Beijing on December 18, Mao noted that this was "the same as our estimate."[72]

Mao now wanted to know whether Stalin would be forthcoming on the most important issue: the treaty. Shi Zhe recalled that the chairman wanted something that "looked good and tasted delicious," and that Stalin did not understand the oblique reference.[73] Again, the Russian transcript does not mention Mao's poetic analogy, but it does note that he brought up the treaty right away, only to be turned down. Stalin explained that revising the existing treaty would undermine Yalta and give the United States and Britain legal grounds for challenging the Soviet Union's postwar gains in Asia, such as the Kurile islands and Southern Sakhalin. "We, within our inner circle, have decided not to modify any of the points of the treaty for now," Stalin said.[74]

This was a major blow, one that Mao had not been prepared for. This much is evident from his ambiguous, muddled response. On the one hand, Mao said that he had "not taken into account the American and the English positions regarding the Yalta agreement" and that "it is already becoming clear that the treaty should not be modified at the present time." On the other hand, he noted that "this question merits further consideration" and asked Stalin if Zhou Enlai should be permitted to come to Moscow "in order to decide the treaty question." Stalin's agreement to Zhou joining Mao in Moscow would have left a possibility for the signing of a new treaty, as in Mao's mind these two questions were linked. But Stalin turned down this indirect approach: "This question you must decide for yourselves. Zhou may be needed in regard to other matters," which meant he could come if he wanted to, but he would not be signing a new treaty, because Stalin was not willing to take that step.[75]

Mao's disappointment is evident from his telegram to Beijing two days later, in which he summarized his first talk with Stalin. Accurately reporting on Stalin's objections to a new treaty, Mao then claimed that the Soviet

PART I AMBITION

leader promised to change the treaty in two years' time. As it is unlikely that the Russian transcript would misquote Stalin on a question of such major importance, it may well be that Mao deliberately tried to soften the blow by putting in a two-year schedule for the new treaty, not least to salvage his reputation in China from failing to revise the old treaty which, in his own words, "has lost all significance."[76]

Probably for the same reason, Mao's telegram omitted any reference to Taiwan. Mao first raised the question of the participation of the Soviet Air Force in the attack on Taiwan in his July 25, 1949, cable to Liu Shaoqi, who was then in Moscow, and who then passed it on to Stalin.[77] Stalin, for all we can tell, ignored this request. Yet the issue only gained in importance after the PLA failed in October to capture the Jinmen islands, seen as a platform for invading Taiwan. "These are first major, unacceptable losses we have suffered in the last three-and-a-half years," Mao cabled to Stalin, referring to Jinmen, adding that taking Taiwan was only possible after the PLA built up sufficient air capabilities.[78]

The PLA was very poorly equipped for amphibious warfare and had practically no air cover. The "lesson" of Jinmen weighed heavily on Mao's mind in Moscow, so he returned to the issue when he met Stalin: would the Soviet pilots help China with Taiwan?[79] Stalin made it clear, though, that no such help would be forthcoming: "what is most important here is not to give Americans a pretext to intervene."[80] For all his claims that Washington was afraid of war, the ever-cautious Soviet leader was unwilling to test his luck in what could lead to a direct Soviet–American confrontation over China. Here, too, Mao was made to feel the limits of his emerging alliance with Moscow.

The most ambiguous part of that first conversation between Stalin and Mao Zedong concerned the fate of the Soviet naval base at Port Arthur. Here, the two leaders were engaged in a ceremonial dance; its intricate sidesteps and feigned bows make it very difficult to understand what each of them really thought of this complex issue. Stalin attached great strategic value to the base, even as he realized that the agreement he had wrestled from Chiang Kai-shek was "unequal." But even as cynical as he was, Stalin remained sensitive to the charge that he pursued an imperialist policy in China. What would the Chinese Communists make of the Soviet presence in Port Arthur? Mao had earlier reassured Stalin through Mikoyan that he did not want the Soviet troops to leave. Still, the dictator now felt compelled to offer Mao the possibility of a withdrawal, even as he insisted on the continued legal right to station the troops in Port Arthur. Mao responded – not unexpectedly, given his line at Xibaipo – that the continued Soviet presence at Port Arthur "corresponds well with Chinese interests."[81]

128

CHAPTER 4 STALIN IN ASIA

Exploiting this opening, Stalin appeared to back away from his preparedness to withdraw: "the troops in Port Arthur can remain there for 2, 5, or 10 years, whatever suits China best. Let them [the enemies] not misunderstand that we want to run away from China. We can stay there even for 20 years."[82] Was Stalin in fact contemplating a withdrawal? Or was he testing Mao? Or was he giving with one hand and taking with the other, expecting somehow to keep the base even while committing himself to recalling Soviet troops? All scenarios seem possible. But what Mao reported in his telegram to Beijing suggests that the Chinese leader now believed the Soviet withdrawal would be a good thing, that it would provide the CCP with "political capital," and that the best way forward was to issue a joint statement announcing the withdrawal. Given Stalin's refusal to sign a new treaty, this possibility now seemed like an attractive consolation prize, something that would at least nominally "look good."

Back at Stalin's dacha after this first encounter with Stalin, Mao had second thoughts. He chose to pretend that Stalin's reluctance on December 16 to sign a new treaty was not final and irreversible, and that the question remained on the agenda. Mao also hinted that he tied the question of the treaty to all practical agreements between China and the Soviet Union; that, in effect, without a treaty there would be no trade agreement, no credit agreement, and no air transport agreement. In a conversation with Stalin's representative to the CCP, Ivan Kovalev, on December 20, Mao presented the Soviets with two options, a subtle ultimatum of a kind. The first was a discussion of the treaty and agreements, which Zhou Enlai would come to Moscow to finalize, or no treaty, and no agreements, in which case Zhou would come "some other time." During the same meeting Mao told Kovalev that he wanted to discuss with Stalin Burma's recognition of China. Seemingly insignificant, this passing reference was in fact a reminder that China had "other options" – the capitalist world.[83] A day earlier, Mao cabled Beijing with specific instructions: if and when capitalist countries announced recognition of Communist China, their representatives were to be invited to Beijing for "talks" leaving the initiative "in our hands."[84] This implicit threat of Western recognition gave Mao a degree of leverage against Stalin, or so he thought.

Mao saw Stalin for another meeting on the night of December 24. Held over a long dinner, their discussion lasted into the wee hours of the following day. Stalin spoke about everything but the treaty and Mao did not push the subject.[85] On the very same day, Kovalev submitted a lengthy report to Stalin, in which he bitterly criticized the Chinese leadership (without blaming Mao directly but sparing few others) for ignoring Soviet advice and

PART I AMBITION

pursuing "anti-Soviet" and even "pro-American" domestic and foreign policies.[86] Stalin had the report delivered to Mao, as if saying: Here is what I am being told about you – should I believe this?[87] Mao spent the last few days of 1949 at the dacha. He was in a foul mood and loudly complained about his mistreatment in Moscow to Stalin's lieutenants who continued to check up on him every so often: "You called me to come to Moscow, but [we are] not doing anything – what did I come for, then? Who would have thought that I came here just to eat, to shit and to sleep every day?"[88]

On January 1 Mao resorted to one of his favorite theatrical tricks. When visited by Nikolai Roshchin (who was in the CCP's bad books for having served as Moscow's last ambassador to the Guomindang), the Chinese leader spoke of his bouts of dizziness and insomnia, which required that he leave for home earlier than originally planned and abstain from touring other Soviet cities. As he did with Kovalev ten days earlier, Mao talked about the impending recognition of China by Burma, India, Great Britain, and other countries. He warned that although he was prepared to meet with other members of the Soviet leadership, he would hold "business discussions" with Stalin only, whom he wanted to see again[89]. Shi Zhe, the interpreter, told Roshchin that Mao had "firmly decided" on sitting it out at the dacha; that he would not go anywhere, preferring to "rest" in the kind of proud solitude that would have left Stalin under no illusions: Mao was gravely dissatisfied. As if to reinforce the point, there were now rumors circulating in Moscow's diplomatic community that Stalin had his Chinese visitor placed under arrest.

The breakthrough came later that afternoon. Kovalev came over for a chat, bringing with him a transcript of an interview with Mao Zedong by a TASS correspondent. Mao had not gone near a TASS correspondent, nor had he given out interviews. He was therefore both surprised and delighted when he saw what Stalin had proposed as the Chinese leader's "answer" to the made-up question about Mao's agenda in Moscow: the first on the list was the treaty of friendship and alliance between the Soviet Union and China.[90] The message was unmistakable: Stalin, who had ruled out signing a new treaty just two weeks earlier, had come around to support the idea. Elated, Mao invited Kovalev for dinner, where, knowing that he was speaking into Stalin's ear, he raised toasts to comrade Stalin for his "great help in the creation of the Chinese Communist Party and in the realization of the revolution in China." Stalin's instructions, Mao said, allowed him to eradicate left- and right- deviationism within the party. "The shots of the October revolution brought to China the teachings of Marx-Lenin-Stalin." If there was no Soviet Communist Party, he added, "there would be no Chinese Communist Party, there would be no victory of revolution in China. Long live the teachings of Lenin-Stalin!"[91] When, many years later, Mao recounted his stay in Moscow, he never said as much as a good word about Stalin. Nor did he remember Stalin's contributions to the Chinese revolutionary cause, highlighting instead his multiple mistakes and his lack of faith in Chinese Communism. These records demonstrate that Mao's historical memory was very selective. He chose to remember and to forget as it suited his immediate political agenda.

Stalin, too, was a master of political flexibility. One of the unanswered questions of the turbulent history of Sino-Soviet relations is why he changed his mind about the treaty. There is no clear-cut evidence here, only speculations. Stalin may have taken seriously Mao's threats to leave Moscow empty-handed, with all that could mean for the future of Sino-Soviet relations. Or he may have believed there was substance to Mao's claims of impending recognition of the People's Republic by capitalist powers, which, too, raised uncertain prospects for the future of Soviet influence in China.[92] Stalin would have had even greater reasons to worry had he known – and he may have known through intelligence – that on December 30, 1949 the US National Security Council (NSC) adopted a new policy document, NSC-48, which ruled out Washington's involvement in the Chinese civil war and downplayed American commitment to defend Taiwan. This, too, would have created unwelcome possibilities for Sino-American rapprochement. Was Stalin genuinely worried about "losing" China? Mao certainly thought so. He attributed Stalin's change of heart regarding the treaty to the unhappy prospect of China's rapprochement with the West, and naturally congratulated himself for his success in outfoxing even as astute an operator as Stalin.

The events of early January 1950 deepened Stalin's concerns about China's future direction. In a press conference on January 5, President Truman revealed that he would not provide military aid to Taiwan, nor get embroiled in the Chinese civil war. On the following day, Britain declared its recognition of China and broke relations with the Guomindang. On January 12 Dean Acheson made what proved to be highly misleading remarks about the US "defensive perimeter" excluding mainland East Asia and Taiwan. Now that Stalin seemed in favor of a new treaty with China, Mao wanted to reassure him that China would not jump ships. On January 6, Mao told Kovalev that China would postpone the exchange of missions with capitalist countries that recognized the Communists. This, Mao explained, was because these foreign governments only wanted relations in order to maintain their interests in China, while carrying out subversive work against the new regime. On January 13, Mao told Vyshinsky that he wanted to delay US recognition of China to "win time" and "bring the country into order."[93] Mao had the same message for Molotov. Ignoring secret US probes to begin negotiations with the Communist government, the CCP was working to squeeze American diplomats out of China. All these reassurances squared perfectly well with Mao's deeply held beliefs about "cleaning the house before entertaining guests," the ideological imperative that underpinned his policy of leaning to one side.[94]

Stalin did not leave anything to chance. In order to preempt a possible Sino-American rapprochement, he insisted (through Vyshinsky) that Communist China demand the expulsion of Chiang Kai-shek's representative from the United Nations. What he probably had in mind was to place Mao in direct opposition to the United States, which would have to defend Chiang at the UN. In a conversation with Mao on January 17, Molotov proposed that the Chinese comrades denounce Acheson for claiming that Moscow had imperialist ambitions in northern China. Whatever Mao thought of the substance of these accusations, he could not possibly fail the test of loyalty. To Molotov's probable satisfaction, he decried Acheson's "slander" as a "smokescreen" for invading Taiwan and agreed that China would publish a rebuttal, which it did a few days later, though not in as forceful a form as Stalin could have hoped.[95] But, as historian Dieter Heinzig has argued, it may well be that Mao secretly welcomed Acheson's statement, as it strengthened Chinese bargaining position in treaty negotiations with the USSR.[96] The Soviets now had to work harder to prove that they were not imperialists in brotherly guise.

On January 22, 1950, Mao, alongside Zhou Enlai and several other Chinese officials, finally met with Stalin for formal talks. This time Stalin cut right to the heart of the matter by telling the Chinese delegation that he had decided to sign a new treaty. He had a convenient pretext: the old treaty was directed against Japan and had therefore become anachronistic, something the Soviet leader conspicuously forgot during his first meeting with Mao. The latter reassured Stalin that he would not regret this change of heart. "Previously," he said, "the Guomindang spoke of friendship in words only. Now the situation has changed, with all the conditions for real friendship and cooperation in place." But Mao also expected that this new relationship "take into account the interests of both sides," something that, as Stalin knew only all too well, could not be said of the 1945 agreements.[97]

Understanding that sacrifices had to be made, Stalin presently repeated what he had claimed consistently since early 1949: that the agreement on the stationing of Soviet troops in Port Arthur was "unequal." "We did not

CHAPTER 4 STALIN IN ASIA

know what Chiang Kai-shek may pull off," Stalin said. "We acted under the premise that the presence of our troops in Port Arthur would be in the interests of Soviet Union and democracy in China." Mao responded in an almost patronizing manner to this awkward attempt to explain Soviet imperialism in China: "The matter is clear." There was, however, an undertone of mockery in his reaction to Stalin's apparent readiness to withdraw from Port Arthur: "But changing this agreement goes against the decisions of the Yalta Conference?!" he said, as if reminding him of Stalin's earlier excuse not to sign the treaty. "To hell with it," Stalin replied, handing Mao his little moral victory. "It is true that for us this [revising of treaties] entails certain inconveniences, and we will have to struggle against the Americans. But we are already reconciled to that." As an additional concession, Stalin declared that the Soviet Union had no interest in maintaining any rights in neighboring Dalian, though he also made it clear that he did not want America and Britain exploiting this opening in their interest.[98]

What Stalin expected in return was Mao's help with the problem of the Chinese Eastern Railroad. The Soviets had maintained that the 1945 agreement, which left the position of the general manager of the railroad in the Soviet hands, was not unequal, because it was Russia that had built it in the first place. Now, Stalin wanted to know what doubts Mao had, "as a communist," about this agreement. The Chinese leader summed up his grievances: he wanted China to be in charge of the railroad, even with partial Soviet ownership, and he wanted the duration of the 1945 agreement – thirty years – shortened. The unpleasant discussion continued between Molotov and Zhou Enlai, as Stalin and Mao watched their proxies from the sidelines. Molotov explained that the Soviets were already making a concession by agreeing to alternate railroad management with the Chinese – parity of ownership implied parity of management. Zhou pressed on, asking if China could increase its stake to 51 percent, but Stalin reminded him that the Soviet Union wanted merely what it already had with other socialist allies, including Czechoslovakia and Bulgaria. Evidently dissatisfied, Mao concluded gravely that "the question needs to be further examined, keeping in mind the interests of both sides."[99]

The most important contrast between the December 16 and the January 22 conversations between Mao and Stalin was the change of tone. If during their first meeting, Mao clearly deferred to Stalin, solicited his opinions, strove to prove his loyalty, and in general attempted to come across as a pupil, a revolutionary underling – in a word, a "son" – of the Soviet ruler, this time he put on a more stately appearance, referred (twice!) to China's interests, and, unthinkably, even dared to disagree with Stalin. Of course,

133

Mao was probably frustrated with the way negotiations had dragged on but more likely his confident demeanor reflected the Chinese leader's realization that Stalin did not have many options, and that the negotiating advantage was ultimately on the Chinese side. Stalin's about-face with the treaty, and his apologetic readiness to scrap "unequal" agreements, suggested that Mao held good cards in this game. There was another important difference between December 16 and January 22. This time, Mao performed not just for Stalin and his lieutenants but for the Chinese delegation, which assured that dignity and statesmanship would be projected to the broader party audience at home. Nothing could look better or taste more delicious than the glorious image of Mao standing up to Stalin.

Treaty negotiations continued for several more weeks, though it was Zhou Enlai rather than Mao who bore the brunt of day-to-day discussions with the Soviets. The new treaty was signed on February 14, 1950, heralding the official establishment of the Sino-Soviet alliance. It would not be long before this new alliance would be put to a test in Korea.

TO THE KOREAN WAR

Korea, though strategically important, was a relatively minor blip on Stalin's radar before 1945. The Russians had taken interest in the reclusive country in the late nineteenth–early twentieth century, but Russia's decisive defeat in the war against Japan in 1905 put an end to the Tsar's Korean adventure before it ever properly began. It was only with Japan's surrender that the Soviets returned to Korea, having agreed to occupy the country together with the Americans, with the thirty-eighth parallel serving as the dividing line: the North was taken over by the Soviets; the South – by the Americans. The idea was American, and it left much of the population and the capital under US control. Stalin agreed: in 1945 he was still in a cooperative mood.[100] At first, neither Moscow nor Washington dreamed of creating their own "Koreas" in their respective zones of occupation. Then, as in Germany, the two sides gradually but surely moved towards de facto division as the Cold War began to unfold.

The Soviet man in North Korea was Kim Il Sung, by every measure Stalin's obedient client. Having fought the Japanese in Manchuria with a band of guerrillas in the 1930s, Kim crossed the border to the USSR in 1940, finding refuge in a mosquito-infested camp not far from Khabarovsk. In 1945, presently a major in the Red Army, he rode to Korea with the advancing Soviet forces, and soon consolidated his position by playing hardball against domestic rivals and endearing himself to his Soviet overlords. When

CHAPTER 4 STALIN IN ASIA

the Democratic People's Republic of Korea was established in September 1948, Kim became its first premier at the tender age of thirty-six. But, as Stalin was soon to find out, Kim was not satisfied with his fate as the leader of a truncated state: he yearned to reunify all of Korea under his leadership.

In March 1949 Kim turned up in Moscow to plead with Stalin to allow him to invade South Korea. The dictator turned him down, warning that should he attempt, he could give the Americans a pretext to intervene.[101] His position remained largely unchanged through the rest of the year.[102] Stalin exchanged views with Mao Zedong on the subject and Mao, too, thought that invading South Korea was a bad idea. In May 1949 the Chinese leader informed Stalin that he had told the North Koreans to hold off and "wait for a more advantageous situation" unless there was an attack from the South. In this latter case, the North Koreans could even retreat and lose some territory, Mao explained, in order to counterattack later on. Mao's key concern (probably shared by Stalin) was that the Americans would ship Japanese troops to fight in Korea. He thought, however, that the Northerners could move in early 1950 "if the international situation is favorable." In this case, Mao explained, if the Japanese entered the fray, the Chinese could send their "select" forces and "destroy" the Japanese.[103]

This was in May. By October, despite winning a resounding victory in China, Mao Zedong became even more skeptical about the prospects of a war in Korea. As he explained to Stalin in a cable on October 21, the North Koreans were pursuing rash policies, which had led to the arrest of many of their reliable cadres in the South. The prospect of a popular revolution in the South that seemed within grasp now appeared to fade.[104] Stalin agreed that "now is not the time for offensive operations on the part of North Korea ... this matter cannot yet be deemed to be adequately prepared."[105]

But Kim Il Sung kept pressing his case. On January 17, 1950, Kim – not for the first time – poured out his soul to the Soviet representative. It happened at a dinner hosted by Foreign Minister Pak Hon-yong (whom Kim would later arrest and execute). The North Korean leader, "a little tipsy" in the words of the Soviet Ambassador Terenty Shtykov, launched into a passionate discussion of the need to invade South Korea, pleading for a meeting with Stalin because, he said, he was a "disciplined person," and held Stalin's instructions as law. Shtykov reported these revelations in a cable to Moscow.[106] Stalin, who was just then engaged in protracted treaty negotiations with Mao, responded on January 30. This time, the dictator was optimistic. "As great a task ... as what he plans to undertake," Stalin wrote, "requires great preparation. The matter must be organized so that there is no great risk ... Tell Kim Il Sung that I am ready to help him in this task."[107] Thus encouraged, Kim soon left for Moscow, where Stalin gave him the green light to attack the South.

We still do not know what exactly happened to Stalin between October 26, when he was so sour on an invasion, and the end of January when he evidently changed his mind. The approximate outlines of his reasoning are evident enough. Stalin himself explained the matter when he met Kim. The key factor was the CCP victory in the Chinese civil war, which allowed Mao Zedong to support the North Koreans in the war, including with his own forces. There was a psychological aspect to this as well. As Stalin put it, Mao's victory "has proved the strength of Asian revolutionaries and shown the weakness of Asian reactionaries and their mentors in the West, in America. The Americans left China and did not dare to challenge the new Chinese authorities militarily." Stalin then added that since China and the USSR had signed a treaty of alliance, the Americans would be more cautious still, especially because the Soviets were now in the possession of the A-bomb. Finally, he explained, "according to information coming from the United States, it is really so. The prevailing mood is not to interfere."[108]

What could Stalin be referring to when he mentioned "information coming from the United States"? The obvious answer is US Secretary of State Dean Acheson's rather ill-thought-through public remarks at the National Press Club in Washington, DC, where, on January 12, 1950, he proclaimed that the American "defensive perimeter" excluded mainland Asia, i.e. both China and the Korean peninsula. These remarks must surely rank among the most misleading signals ever sent. Stalin, who was ever so cautious not to accidentally trigger American intervention, could not have needed a better assurance than a statement by Acheson himself. Perhaps Stalin's spies had access to NSC-48, a document that set the parameters of US policy towards Asia, and that, like Acheson's speech, appeared to take a dim view of military intervention against the Communists in the Asian mainland or even Taiwan.[109] Of course, reading a top-secret document was better than reading public remarks. Stalin valued his intelligence. But we cannot confidently claim that he had read NSC-48. If he did, it may well have played into his thinking on Korea and, indeed, as we have seen, into his decision to sign a new treaty with China.

One more tantalizing piece of evidence may be added to the above. In his book *Spymaster*, former CIA official Tennent H. Bagley tells the story of a cypher clerk at the US Embassy in Moscow whom the Soviet intelligence managed to recruit in 1949. This officer, codenamed "Jack," provided

CHAPTER 4 STALIN IN ASIA

his Soviet handlers with bits and pieces of a broken cypher machine and even helped them encode a sample text for comparison. Armed with this information, the Soviets managed for a time to decipher intercepted US messages not just between Washington and Moscow but also between Washington and other US posts abroad. A high-ranking retired KGB officer Sergey Kondrashev who served as Bagley's source for this story recounted how the head of the Ministry of State Security, Viktor Abakumov, personally furnished Stalin with copies of the deciphered cables, which convinced the latter that the Americans would not oppose Soviet moves in Korea. Kondrashev blamed the Korean War on these intercepts.[110]

Revelations by former Soviet intelligence officials must of course be treated with caution, but there is now an unexpected confirmation of Kondrashev's recollections from another, highly reliable, source. In September 1956 – Stalin was long dead – Anatas Mikoyan visited China again for the Eighth CCP Congress. While in Beijing, he had a conversation with Mao, where the Chinese leader asked him: what, in the end, drove Stalin to change his mind about Korea? Mikoyan's answer was unambiguous: "Before the Korean War broke out," he said, "our intelligence deciphered the enemy's cable, which said that [General Douglas] MacArthur argued in a report to Washington that should there be a military clash between North and South Korea, America must not intervene. Only later did we learn that Washington did not agree with MacArthur's views."[111] It is difficult to say with any degree of certainty what Mikoyan was talking about here. But his description of an intelligence intercept appears too precise and too compatible with Kondrashev's story to ignore. We know, too, that General MacArthur, from his lofty perch in Japan, was not particularly interested in Korean matters, certainly not since US forces were withdrawn from the peninsula in June 1949 (a move he strongly supported). He was much more interested in building up Japan as a bulwark against Soviet influence. He had previously defined the American "defensive perimeter" in terms not dissimilar from Acheson's remarks.[112]

The best case that can be made on the basis of the still incomplete evidence is that Stalin was worried about US intervention but concluded, early in 1950, that such intervention was not likely. Intelligence intercepts probably played a major role but anyone's reading of what US statesmen were saying in public could have yielded a similar conclusion. It was not an unreasonable conclusion, and it accurately reflected American preferences at that particular time, preferences rooted above all in Truman's effort to cut back on defense expenditures to save money badly needed at home.

What Stalin probably did not realize was that the mood was rapidly changing in the United States in the direction of ever greater alarm about Soviet growing capabilities and increasingly sinister intentions. The biggest shock here was the successful test of the first Soviet atomic bomb on August 29, 1949, the crowning achievement of years of hard work by Igor Kurchatov and his team, aided by espionage. Stalin had hoped to keep the cat in the bag but the Americans soon found out through air sampling, and Truman made the public announcement of the breakthrough on September 23, 1949.[113] The sentencing of the former US State Department official Alger Hiss in January 1950 for having lied about his Communist connections and the arrest and trial of the nuclear physicist Klaus Fuchs for espionage in February 1950 deepened public apprehensions about the Soviet menace, something that fire-breathing populists like Sen. Joseph McCarthy were only too ready to exploit. China going "red," and the conclusion of the Sino-Soviet alliance naturally added to the sense of doom and gloom in Washington. On January 31,1950, President Truman initiated a review of US policy, which led to the drafting and eventual approval of NSC-68, a pivotal document that reframed the Soviet threat in near apocalyptic terms.[114]

Meanwhile, Stalin, having invited Kim Il Sung to Moscow, gave him a green light to attack South Korea. But he made it conditional on Mao's agreement. Kim Il Sung and Pak Hon-yong turned up in Beijing in May to bring Mao into the loop. Earlier the Chinese leader had himself told the North Korean Ambassador Ri Ju-yon that the only way to unify Korea was by invading the South, and that "one should not be afraid of the Americans" because they "would not enter the third world war for such a small territory."[115] Now, however, he pretended to be taken aback by the idea, and cabled Stalin for instructions (Stalin confirmed that he okayed the war, but added that the Chinese had to agree, and if they did not, the invasion could be postponed).[116] The Chinese leader would later complain about this little trick of Stalin's.[117] To disagree was to disobey Stalin, and so soon after the signing of the Sino-Soviet Treaty. It was a form of entrapment, or at least that was how Mao presented it later. In reality, he was himself moving in the direction of supporting Kim's invasion. What he resented was having been presented with a *fait accompli.*

CONCLUSION

The Korean War began on June 25, 1950, with a North Korean attack across the thirty-eighth parallel. The South Koreans retreated in disarray. Within days the North Koreans captured Seoul and continued to push south in a

CHAPTER 4 STALIN IN ASIA

swift offensive. But Stalin's key calculation – that the Americans would stay out of the war – proved incorrect when President Truman authorized a military intervention (under the UN auspices) to defend South Korea. This intervention reversed Kim's fortunes and he was bailed out only at the last moment by the Chinese who joined the war. Meanwhile, Truman's deployment of the Seventh Fleet to the Taiwan Strait – itself a consequence of Kim Il Sung's invasion of South Korea – put an end to whatever ambition Mao may have had for capturing Taiwan and unifying the country. After months of fighting, and uncounted deaths (mainly among Korean civilians) the battlelines returned to the vicinity of the thirty-eighth parallel. Korea was reduced to rubble.

It was thus that Stalin, who encouraged Mao to send troops to prevent North Korea's collapse, found himself supporting China and North Korea in a bloody proxy war against the United States. The Soviets, apart from providing some air cover and sending China a large quantity of weapons, remained relatively uninvolved. "I don't think you need to expedite the war in Korea," Stalin cabled Mao in June 1951. "A protracted war, first of all, is allowing the Chinese troops to perfect modern fighting skills on the battlefield, and, secondly, is shaking Truman's regime in America and is undermining the prestige of Anglo-American forces."[118] It took another two years of intermittent fighting before the parties agreed to a ceasefire.

Having the Americans stuck in the Korean quagmire had an important benefit for Stalin's global strategy, for it postponed the possibility of a conflict in Europe, something he was much worried about. As he put it at a Soviet-bloc conference in January 1951, "An opinion arose in recent times that the United States is an invincible power and is prepared to initiate the third world war ... As it turns out, however, not only is the US unprepared to initiate the third world war, but it is unable even to cope with a small war such as the one in Korea." But Stalin was not sanguine about the future. At that same conference, he told his European allies to prepare to field 3 million men in the coming conflict with the West, giving them three years to get ready. Ready for what – an offensive or a defensive war? There is not enough evidence still to answer this question with confidence.[119]

One rationale for a protracted war in Korea that Stalin did not mention to Mao – but which must have surely crossed his mind – was that China at war with America tied the Chinese ever more firmly to the Soviet camp. The Sino-Soviet alliance was tested in the Korean War, and it worked. Mao, whatever private grudges he may have held, was willing to defer to "Comrade Main Master" while the old Georgian was still alive. He would later describe their relationship as that between a father and a son. It was

PART I AMBITION

an odd description given that Mao's relationship with his own father had been very difficult, even hostile. Mao claimed that the socialist camp was a "family" but his explanation of what that meant is revealing in itself: "If one spoke of the relationship between a father and a son, then one ought to bear in mind that it is not a European but an Asian family with its feudal despotism and the supremacy of the father in the family."[120] Needless to say, it was only after Stalin's death that Mao remembered Stalin as a despotic "father." By then, the Sino-Soviet alliance, which the two brought into being, was already beginning to crack.

Indeed, hailed in the propaganda of both countries as unbreakable and eternal, the Sino-Soviet alliance survived for barely a decade falling apart acrimoniously in the early 1960s. That led many historians to conclude, retrospectively, that it never could last, that it was a clay colossus, that it was so ridden by internal tensions and contradictions that it was a miracle to see it hold out for so long. It is even possible to read Mao's misadventures in Moscow in December 1949–February 1950 as a taster of the sort of problems that would ultimately bring this relationship to ruin.

This rings particularly true in view of the kind of issues that caused friction during the negotiations. One was Zhou Enlai's insistence on including a provision to transport Chinese troops from Manchuria in China's northeast to Xinjiang in the northwest through Siberia. This proposal was a reaction to Moscow's demand for rights to transport Soviet troops across the Chinese Eastern Railroad, and it reflected the Chinese leader's sensitivity to anything that appeared like imposition of foreign control. Unable to challenge the Soviets directly on the point, Zhou wanted reciprocal provisions for the transfer of Chinese troops across the USSR, even though, as Mikoyan reminded him, it was hard to imagine a scenario that would require transport of Chinese troops from Manchuria to Xinjiang by such circuitous means, or, indeed, for any reason at all. But what Mikoyan failed to recognize was that Zhou – and by extension Mao – wanted a face-saving concession that would make China stand tall and proud. The fact that they were unable to obtain such a concession probably contributed to Mao's later complaints about Stalin's imperialistic propensities, what he would call the "bitter fruits" of the Sino-Soviet alliance.

These "bitter fruits" included Stalin's ill-conceived plan to keep Manchuria and Xinjiang as Soviet spheres of influence, something that, Mao justifiably felt, looked very much like imperialist practices of old. A secret agreement required China to keep these regions closed to foreigners. (It was not until 1956, well after Stalin's death, that the agreement was abolished).[121] Then, there were also agreements to establish joint-stock companies: one for extraction of oil, one for extraction of rare and nonferrous metals, and one concerned with civil aviation. These agreements provided for equal financing and equal participation by China and the Soviet Union, a point of considerable resentment by the CCP who sought to maintain control over any such ventures. All three companies were to be initially managed by Soviet-appointed general managers, and the term of the agreements for the oil and metals companies was set at thirty years. The enterprises were a good deal for the Soviets, but certainly nothing exceptional. They got to keep 50% of the output but the other 50% went to the Chinese, which was, by the standards of the day, a very generous arrangement for the host country.[122] In addition, the Chinese gained access to technology and expertise. The "bitter fruit" was perhaps not so bitter as Mao claimed. Still, it was probably unwise for Stalin to touch on raw nerves by imposing these terms on China, as it was wise for the Soviets to give up on these joint-stock companies shortly after Stalin's death. Not for the first time, Stalin allowed opportunism to cloud sound judgment.

A careful assessment suggests that things did not turn out as badly as the more pessimistic historiography would suggest, or, indeed, as Mao would later gleefully recount.[123] Perhaps the most dramatic practical outcome of the difficult summit was the Soviet Union's public pledge to return Port Arthur and Dalian. In doing so, Stalin put his money where his mouth had been ever since Mikoyan had described the 1945 deal on the base as "unequal." But this was not all. In a remarkable turn-around, the Soviet leader agreed to give up the Chinese Eastern Railroad, also by 1952, and with no strings attached. Gone were Stalin's demands for parity, which pitted Molotov against Zhou Enlai on January 22. Stalin decided to pull up the stakes and leave. Declassified Chinese documents show Zhou taking most of the credit for the unexpected victory. In a follow-up meeting (Zhou also saw Stalin on January 23), he argued that seeing that the railroad had already changed hands six times, "the Soviet Union could well give it up, which would facilitate Sino-Soviet unity." Thus pressed, Stalin caved in. It was a singular achievement for the Chinese delegation.[124]

Just like that, the Soviet leader signed off most of the key gains he had secured after protracted and painful negotiations in 1945. In addition, China obtained a much-needed loan of $300 million at an interest rate of just 1 percent, meant for postwar reconstruction and economic development. True, this was not gratis aid: China paid back in exports of food and resources for what the Chinese would later complain was outdated technology. Moreover, the scope of Soviet economic assistance was curbed dramatically by the outbreak of the Korean War, leading to later recriminations

PART I AMBITION

that Stalin, in effect, profited from selling weapons to the Chinese, while they shed blood on his behalf in Korea.

Nevertheless, the Soviet aid program in China was far from a self-serving profit-making scheme. During the decade that followed, the Soviets helped in the construction of 256 industrial projects, including iron and steel factories, coal mines, power plants, railroads, and automobile and tractor factories, with over a hundred projects in China's first five-year plan alone. The Soviet Union received tens of thousands of Chinese students and lent thousands of experts and military advisers, seeing through a massive technology transfer. Yes, those advisers proved expensive, but they were there at a time when China had few places to turn for aid or know-how. Although most of these projects were only initiated after Stalin's death in March 1953, Stalin made every effort to assure Mao that he would fulfil China's economic requests. Indeed, it was Mao who, when questioned by Stalin on the specifics, struggled to explain what sort of aid China would need. On the whole, the record suggests that Mao did obtain something that "tasted delicious."

More importantly still, he obtained something that "looked good." We have seen how Mao drew a sense of legitimacy from having overthrown the Guomindang government. "We, the Chinese people, have stood up," he claimed. But this legitimacy was not enough. He depended on the external recognition of his revolution, and the recognizer here was Stalin himself. That is why Mao was so desperate to secure a new treaty of alliance with the USSR. That is why he was so eager to prove to Stalin that he was a true adherent of the Communist faith. He dangled the promise of Western recognition to help Stalin make up his mind but in the end what Mao desired above all was Stalin's endorsement. Stalin, after a long period of dithering, gave Mao what he so badly wanted.

142

PART II

HUBRIS

5

LOVE US AS WE ARE

Joseph Stalin died on March 5, 1953, leaving no obvious successor. The Kremlin reverted to "collective leadership." But the vague euphemism masked a bitter power struggle that continued until at least 1955, when the relatively unknown Nikita Khrushchev emerged at the top. At first, he was not even seen as a serious contender. True, in September 1953 Khrushchev secured the post of the first secretary of the Communist Party but the real power was thought to be in the hands of the prime minister, Georgy Malenkov. His main rival was his deputy in the Council of Ministers, and Stalin's former henchman, Lavrenty Beria, who now also acquired the influential portfolio of the minister of internal affairs. The third major power broker in the new leadership was Molotov who had served as Stalin's foreign minister until 1949, when he was demoted by the jealous dictator. Molotov would have undoubtedly finished his career with a bullet in his head, but Stalin's death saved him, and he presently reemerged as the mighty helmsman of Soviet foreign policy.

The early two or three years after Stalin's death pose problems for students of Soviet foreign policy. There is a dearth of documents at the highest decision-making level, so it is often unclear who defended what policies and why. At times the Soviet leadership appeared willing to move away from Stalin's confrontational stance, peddling even such unorthodox ideas as, for instance, giving up on socialism in East Germany (1953) or joining NATO (1954). Was this just propaganda, a part of a Soviet plot to befuddle the West? This chapter explores these questions in detail before considering two immensely important developments of Khrushchev's early years in power: the nuclear revolution and Moscow's turn to the third world.

The two were closely related. The nuclear revolution, which saw the United States and the Soviet Union acquire the means of ending civilization as we know it, made a conventional great-power war practically unthinkable. Khrushchev was thrilled by the power he now had in his hands. Possession of nuclear weapons gave him the confidence, however provisional, to speak to the United States on equal terms. Nuclear weapons offered a shortcut

145

to greatness that, Khrushchev knew, the USSR did not yet deserve because it was still far behind the West in economic development. Greatness, in turn, translated into a new ambition to win friends around the world. Decolonization, and the appearance of a multitude of aspiring but desperately needy nations in the so-called third world, led to opportunities that Stalin, with his pragmatic emphasis the Soviet Union's immediate neighborhood, would never have grasped. Khrushchev embraced these opportunities with the ebullience of a man who had boundless faith in himself, his country, and the bright future of Communism. In 1955–56 he reached out to Egypt, becoming Cairo's power patron and a major beneficiary of the Suez Crisis. Playing the nuclear card to his advantage, Khrushchev learned from Suez that brinksmanship paid. It was a fateful takeaway.

By the mid-1950s, the Cold War was becoming global in scope, and it gave Nikita Khrushchev a sense of purpose, and a sense of legitimacy.

THE GERMAN QUESTION

In 1953 the Soviet Union boasted overwhelming military power in Europe. Yet the Kremlin was worried: West Germany clamored to join the recently formed NATO. In Southeastern Europe, Yugoslavia, which Stalin had excommunicated from the socialist camp, presented a political and military challenge. Further south, Turkey, frightened by Stalin's territorial claims, had already joined NATO and now boasted a US military presence. In nearby Iran – once a target of Stalin's aspirations – the CIA and the British intelligence cooperated to oust Prime Minister Mohammad Mossadegh in August 1953, whereupon Iran, led by the pro-American shah, became a firm anti-Soviet bastion in the Middle East and, eventually, a key member of the British-led Baghdad Pact. The Korean War dragged on in the Far East, though the Chinese were doing most of the fighting and the dying. Having failed in 1951 to sign the San Francisco peace treaty, the Soviet Union now also faced a hostile Japan, locked into a military alliance with the United States. With so many enemies, and a sense that they were headed towards a crisis and possibly an all-out war, it is scarcely surprising that the Soviet leaders sought reprieve in unwinding international tensions. But how far were they willing to go?

Moscow's approach to their clients overseas paralleled the direction of the Soviet Union's domestic reforms. The most odious facets of Stalinism were being dismantled: camps were closed, hundreds of thousands of people were set free, bloody repressions generally ceased. Changes were afoot in the economy: the new leaders moved away from overreliance on

CHAPTER 5 LOVE US AS WE ARE

the heavy industry, permitting greater investment in consumer goods to raise the standard of living. The leader cult that reached an absurd extent under late Stalin, was quietly toned down. The same ideas were proffered to Eastern Europe, often in the face of bitter resistance of the local "Stalins" like Mátyás Rákosi in Hungary, Valko Chervenkov in Bulgaria, Enver Hoxha in Albania, and Walter Ulbricht in East Germany.

The latter presided over a fiefdom that seemed to be on the verge of falling apart. The flight of people from East Germany to the West (many via West Berlin) was astonishing. Soviet reports showed that 78,831 refugees left in the second half of 1952, a jump of 57,234 in the first half. Over 84,000 fled the socialist paradise in the first quarter of 1953, almost 2,000 of whom were Socialist Unity Party of Germany (SED) members. Beria submitted these statistics in a report to the Presidium on May 6, 1953, though the report did not foresee any radical measures to address the problem and recommended simply improving the police force and strengthening state propaganda.[1] Ulbricht himself seemed oblivious, pressing on with hardline policies like collectivization and socialization of the private sector. On May 5, 1953, in a speech, he proclaimed that the German Democratic Republic (GDR) regime was a dictatorship of the proletariat. The Soviets were unimpressed and asked their client to tone down his rhetoric.[2]

In April 1953 the Soviet Foreign Ministry began working on a draft document that foresaw the creation of an all-German government and downplayed the idea of incorporating the GDR into the Soviet bloc. The German question was debated at the Council of Ministers on May 27, with two points of view emerging. Some, including Beria, evidently insisted on giving up on socialism in the GDR; others (possibly Molotov) argued against "expedited" construction of socialism. On June 2, the Council of Ministers adopted a resolution that was closer to that latter point of view: the East German leaders were asked to abandon some of their more radical measures and focus on propaganda of German unity.[3] The same day, the East Germans – Walter Ulbricht and Otto Grotewohl – turned up in Moscow for difficult talks. The East Germans were told that they had made "mistakes," according to Grotewohl's handwritten notes.

We also have what appears to be Malenkov's draft remarks at the meeting. These are astonishing in their criticism of the GDR. Concerned that East Germany was headed for a "catastrophe," Malenkov was to warn the Germans against trying to build socialism. His notes even referred to the interwar Weimar Republic as the model for the "bourgeois-democratic" Germany the Soviets wanted to see. Never mind socialism. The main Soviet priority, the notes explained, was avoiding West Germany's militarization, which would precipitate another war.[4] Unfortunately, it is not clear what Malenkov said in the meeting. Some of the far-reaching criticism is crossed out in the draft and, indeed, Grotewohl's record goes only so far as to have Malenkov say that "it was necessary to change the current conditions in the GDR."[5]

If Malenkov was capable of changing his positions on such key issues, so could the others. What mattered was the political expediency of one's political position. Giving up on socialism in the GDR seemed expedient, until it no longer was. In fact, soon it became politically dangerous to proffer such heresies. This was for two reasons. First, hardly a fortnight after Ulbricht returned from his Moscow summons, a full-fledged rebellion broke out across the GDR in protest against the recently increased work quotas. With the local Communist authorities nearing a state of paralysis, East Germany briefly teetered on the brink of the "catastrophe" Malenkov had so feared – before Soviet tanks moved in to crush the demonstrators. There was no question of speedy reforms after the bloody crackdown: maintaining stability in East Germany became the order of the day.[6] Historian John Lewis Gaddis even argues that Ulbricht deliberately "sabotaged" Soviet recommendations, perhaps fearing that going easy on socialism would undermine his grip on power.[7]

The other reason was Beria's downfall. As much as Stalin's successors distrusted each other, their shared dread of Beria was enough to make members of the Presidium work together in hatching a plot to rid their midst of such a venomous competitor. Khrushchev claimed to have recruited Georgy Zhukov to their cause, and the faithful general helped arrest the unsuspecting Beria in the Kremlin during the Presidium meeting on June 26, 1953.[8] Interrogation revealed his involvement in kidnappings, torture, and murder, but Soviet political culture was such that these horrible crimes were not deemed sufficient to condemn him. It was important to have some foreign involvement. The questioning of Beria's associates provided snippets of useful information, such as his alleged comments that he would return the Kurile islands to the Japanese, Königsberg to the Germans, and parts of Karelia to the Finns, all to help ease tensions with these neighboring countries.[9] It is hardly surprising, then, that Beria was also blamed for the crisis in East Germany, and for supposedly plotting to surrender Germany to the imperialists. The fact that the new German policy was a collective product, endorsed by Malenkov and Molotov, did not really matter.

On July 2, during a party plenum convened for the purpose of "unmasking" Beria's crimes, Khrushchev led the attack on his former colleague. "Where he [Beria] showed himself most clearly as a provocateur, not as a

CHAPTER 5 LOVE US AS WE ARE

Communist, was on the German question, when he raised the question that one must renounce the construction of socialism, that one must make concessions to the West." Khrushchev continued: "How can there be a neutral, democratic Germany between us and America? ... Beria says that we'll conclude a treaty. A treaty has its power if it's backed up by cannons. If a treaty is not backed up, it's worth nothing. If we talk about a treaty, they'll laugh at us, they'll consider us naive." Later on, Molotov (who had been among the key advocates of the new German policy) added to Khrushchev's charges with his own rambling stream of invective: "We stared at him [Beria]: what kind of a peace-loving bourgeois Germany can there be – a bourgeois Germany that unleashed the first world war, a bourgeois Germany that unleashed the second world war? ... Who, among Marxists, close to socialism or Soviet power, can in general soberly judge, can think of some kind of a bourgeois Germany, which will be peace-loving?"[10]

And so, rather unexpectedly, the German question became closely bound up with the Kremlin power struggle. Under these circumstances, endorsement of the previous policy consensus carried tremendous risks: at the very least, it suggested dangerous naivety or, more ominously, treacherous collusion with foreign enemies.[11] The opportunity for achieving German unity as a part of some grand bargain with the West that would bolster the Soviets' domestic and international legitimacy was missed. Beria was executed in December 1953 as an imperialist spy, a charge a fabricated as any that he himself had fabricated during his lengthy tenure as the chief of Stalin's terror machine.

COLLECTIVE SECURITY

Beria's ouster did not end Moscow's effort to tone down – if not altogether end – the Cold War. The crux of the issue was the resolution of the German question on acceptable terms. The brutal suppression of the June 1953 uprising stabilized the situation in the short term but in the longer term the Soviets were not sure of their ability to sustain Ulbricht's dysfunctional regime. There were new complications in the form of the proposal for the "European Defense Community" (EDC), which would include a Western European army. A treaty to this end was concluded in May 1952, and in 1954 the debate on the ratification raged in the French National Assembly. The Soviets were hostile, fearing that the EDC would open West Germany's way to rearmament as a part of the Western bloc. Even without the EDC, an increasingly polarized Europe – in particular, the threat posed by NATO – added to the Kremlin's sense of isolation and encirclement. What Moscow offered instead was the concept of European collective security, an idea that would loom large in the minds of Soviet decision-makers for the next twenty years, when it was finally realized in the conclusion of the Helsinki Final Act.

Put forward by Molotov at the Berlin Conference of Foreign Ministers in February 1954, "collective security" was scorned by his Western counterparts. Molotov miscalculated by trying to exclude the United States, and confining it, alongside Communist China, to mere observers. To demonstrate the seriousness of their intentions, the Soviets went a step further in March 1954, proposing to join NATO, something the West (correctly) dismissed as a propaganda trick. When on March 26 Molotov first forwarded his proposals concerning NATO to the Soviet leadership, he made it clear enough that the prospect of their acceptance by NATO was minimal. It is significant, however, that he did not rule it out altogether, arguing that "the USSR joining the North Atlantic Pact under certain conditions would radically change the character of the pact."[12] In effect, Soviet participation would turn NATO into exactly what Moscow wanted – a pan-European security organization that would include the Soviet Union rather than be directed against it. This inclusion was, and remained, Moscow's consistent priority because it entailed acceptance by the United States on equal terms. The Soviet probe was rejected out of hand.

This rejection was, in itself, an act of humiliation, as Molotov had half-expected when he warned of the fallout for the Soviet "prestige" if Moscow failed to join. It gave the Soviet leaders a good reason to pout. "We know that NATO was created as a military organization," smarted Khrushchev. "Therefore, NATO is not a sports organization; it was not created to prepare for athletic competitions, nor for football games. It is well-known that [Supreme Allied Commander Europe Alfred] Gruenther is not a football coach. Everyone knows him as a general who is training a 'team' for war ... It is impossible not to notice this."[13]

In May 1955 Moscow came up with a response to this challenge – the Warsaw Pact, formalizing its effective control of Eastern European militaries in an actual alliance. The Warsaw Pact planners spent the rest of the 1950s devising scenarios for an atomic blitzkrieg against the West, even though Khrushchev himself neither wanted a war, nor, indeed, believed that anyone would be so reckless as to launch one in the nuclear age.[14]

Rather than the Soviet Union being accepted into NATO, it was West Germany that became a member in 1955. The news was expected in Moscow, and yet it was received with considerable trepidation. The German question began to assume more ominous overtones. In 1953 the prospect of a bourgeois, nonaligned Germany was still deemed realistic but post-1955 unification would necessarily mean expanded Germany's membership in an anti-Soviet bloc. This was something Khrushchev simply could not accept. "To proceed to unification of Germany now," Khrushchev explained late that spring, "would mean to arm the enemy camp with 18 million inhabitants of East Germany." The Soviet Union could agree to such a scenario, he elaborated, only if unified Germany had an "independent government" and "its own place in Europe." But that was not on the cards anymore. Agree to a united Germany that was a part of NATO? "I think it would be stupid for our side."[15]

It was not that Khrushchev could not make concessions. He could and did make concessions that Stalin, had he been alive, would have found decidedly unpalatable. In 1954, in a bid to court Mao Zedong, whose sympathy and support he badly wanted, Khrushchev gave up Stalin's quasi-imperialist assets in China, including a naval base at Port Arthur and the rights to a major strategic railroad in Manchuria, which Stalin had promised to give up but never did because the Korean War intervened. In 1955 the Soviet Union withdrew military forces from Austria and Finland on the condition that the two countries maintain neutrality – a daring move for someone who supposedly only believed in treaties if, as he had claimed, they were "backed up by cannons." In 1956 Khrushchev promised to return some of the islands of the Kurile chain to the Japanese, even if, in the end, he never did. Khrushchev was not averse to bargaining but giving up East Germany went a step too far, because of its symbolic and strategic significance, which, in Khrushchev's take, only the naive and the stupid did not grasp. If surrendering Germany was the price of acceptance, there could be no bargain.

Khrushchev's initial effort to make a deal with the United States foundered on that very question. In July 1955 he had his first face-to-face meeting with President Dwight D. Eisenhower, known to the loving US public simply as "Ike." The meeting took place in Geneva, much in the face of Washington's reluctance. Ike's secretary of state, John Foster Dulles, was unwilling to hand the Soviets a "propaganda victory" by letting the president interact with the Communists but there was considerable pressure from the American allies, the British and the French. The four-power summit came in the wake of important changes in the Kremlin: Malenkov had been ousted in January 1955, replaced as prime minister by the former minister of defense, Nikolai Bulganin. Khrushchev's stature rose perceptibly. For a time – including in Geneva – he and Bulganin did a double act, confusing observers as to who between these two was the actual boss.

PART II HUBRIS

The transcripts of the meetings make for painful reading. The Soviets did not budge from their insistence on collective security as a prerequisite to any discussion on German unity; the other three were equally adamant. The half-hearted British attempt to find a middle ground by having the Western powers offer guarantees on Soviet security went up in smoke. "Humiliating," Khrushchev remembered months later: it was "as if Soviet security depended on the other powers."[16] Eisenhower's effort to interest Khrushchev and Bulganin in his "Open Skies" proposal – the idea that the Soviet Union and the United States would open their airspace to each other to allow aerial inspection of military facilities – also went nowhere. Khrushchev ridiculed the concept as a cover for American espionage, arguing that when the Soviet Union was surrounded by hostile NATO bases, agreeing to any kind of inspection would be "stupid."[17]

Failing agreement, the first postwar summit was really about the atmospherics. The Soviet delegation, in Ike's words, appeared anxious "to be treated as equals and welcomed."[18] For them, the four-power meeting was a symbolic occasion to demonstrate that the post-Stalin leaders were up to the task of holding the fate of the world in their hands. It was also an attempt to feel the ground to see if there was some personal chemistry that would allow to overcome seemingly intractable problems. In the end, Khrushchev could be, and often was, swayed by personal impressions. So far as that went, he found Eisenhower agreeable, believing that the US president, like himself, wanted peace above all else. Of Dulles he was not so sure, complaining bitterly after the summit that "it required great efforts to make him even dine with us."[19] Who knew that acceptance came at such a price?

Yet when Bulganin proposed to "end the Cold War" in Geneva, the opportunity for doing so was as good as gone. The Soviet leaders still wanted better relations with the West, but important developments made such improvement even less likely than it was in early 1953, when Stalin's successors cautiously probed their way forward on the global stage. First, the stage had become incomparably larger because of the ongoing dismantling of colonial empires. This created new opportunities for Soviet diplomacy, quite unrelated to the stalling fortunes of the East–West detente. Second, the Soviet leaders were learning to love the Bomb.

THE NUCLEAR REVOLUTION

For Stalin, the A-bomb was not just a weapon – primarily not even a weapon. It was an attribute of a great power. The late dictator understood the psychological advantages conferred by the Bomb. Its very existence

CHAPTER 5 LOVE US AS WE ARE

was a threat to which Stalin responded with bluff and bravado. Soviet assertiveness in postwar negotiations with Washington aimed at countering this implicit but real threat with a display of obduracy. Even a minor compromise could give impression of yielding before nuclear threats. However, Stalin did not become any more agreeable when the Soviets obtained their Bomb. He decided that he could pursue an even more ambitious foreign policy on the assumption that American willingness to risk a war with the USSR would decrease even further in view of Moscow's nuclear capability.

It took time before the Soviet military embraced the atomic bomb as the weapon of choice. First steps in this direction were made on November 18, 1949, when the Kremlin ordered the plutonium bomb into serial production. Before the year was out, two more bombs were constructed, and another nine were added to the arsenal in 1950. By early 1951 the Soviet Air Force had reequipped seven TU-4 bombers to carry atomic payloads and had crews trained in their use.[20] At that point the United States had more than thirty of their own for every one of the Soviet bombs. The Soviet military establishment was still primarily concerned with conventional warfare and Stalin himself was reportedly unsure of the bomb's actual – rather than symbolic – usefulness. "One has to have an atomic bomb," he would say, "but that does not mean that we will use it."[21]

It was only after Stalin's death that Soviets really embraced the nuclear age. A key turning point was the August 12, 1953 detonation of a boosted fission weapon of Andrei Sakharov's layer-cake design, which was at the time billed by the Soviets as a successful test of a thermonuclear device. One of the observers of the test, Lieutenant-General S.E. Rozhdestvensky, expressed the views of many of those involved when he wrote, days after the detonation, of the feeling of "exhilaration and pride" at the invention: "It is a great fortune for us that we did not allow the Americans to remain monopolists of this means for a long time."[22] Then-Prime Minister Georgy Malenkov immediately inquired with the officials responsible for the production of nuclear weapons whether it was possible to make five of these new bombs by the end of the year, and was assured that it was.

New capabilities inspired new doctrines. The shroud of secrecy that covered the Soviet atomic project under Stalin and Beria was gradually lifted, giving the military a chance to think about how these weapons might be used in battle. In September 1953, the Council of Ministers agreed to train servicemen for atomic combat. In the autumn of 1953, the Soviets conducted a military exercise in the Carpathian Military District, which included the notion that the enemy would use nuclear weapons on the

153

PART II HUBRIS

battlefield. The first Soviet military exercise with the use of a live atomic weapon took place on September 14, 1954 near the village of Totskoe in southern Russia. The Americans had already carried out several comparable exercises. An atomic war between the superpowers was rapidly becoming a realistic prospect, and some in the Kremlin were beginning to wonder what it would mean. Malenkov was among the first to grasp the simple truth. A nuclear war, he said in a widely publicized speech on March 12, 1954, could mean the "destruction of world civilization."[23]

Malenkov's speech was not well-received in the Soviet leadership. Georgy Zhukov was incensed. As then-deputy minister of defense (he did not succeed Nikolai Bulganin to the top military post until February 1955), Zhukov enthusiastically oversaw the introduction of nuclear weapons in the Soviet armed forces. He ran the 1954 Totskoe exercise. He could not take kindly to the prime minister's rhetoric. That much he told Nikita Khrushchev, who privately agreed that it was not the right thing to say. Khrushchev then called his old acquaintance Vyacheslav Malyshev, the man in charge of atomic work, to ask whether what Malenkov said was true. Malyshev reportedly offered an equivocal response but promised to send Khrushchev an article prepared by Kurchatov and some of his colleagues, which touched on nuclear use.

Kurchatov's article showed little patience for ideological axioms. "Keeping in mind," he argued, "that modern military technology gives the country that possesses atomic weapons the ability to strike locations thousands of kilometers from its borders, and given that it is practically impossible to protect oneself against such atomic weapons, it becomes clear the massive use of these weapons will lead to the annihilation of the warring states."[24] Khrushchev was unsettled by these revelations. Indeed, Kurchatov warned him that the article underestimated the dangers of a nuclear exchange.[25] "I couldn't sleep for several days," Khrushchev later recalled, referring to the article. "Then I became convinced that we could never possibly use these weapons, and when I realized that, I was able to sleep again."[26]

But instead of embracing Malenkov's thesis, Khrushchev used it in the power struggle against his rival, much as he used the German question to frame Beria. When Malenkov was ousted in January 1955, one of his supposed errors was that he did not grasp the Marxist-Leninist perspective on war. At a party plenum called to criticize Malenkov, his former comrade-in-leadership Vyacheslav Molotov announced that the reckless comment had disoriented the world Communist movement: "A hundred years ago Marx wrote the Communist Manifesto. He said that things are heading towards the collapse of capitalism and towards the victory of

Communism ... If we are now saying that some kind of a war can allegedly lead to ... the end of the entire civilization, this means we'd be talking out of our backsides."[27]

But it took only months before Malenkov's views were fully adopted by the rest of the Presidium. This was already evident enough in July in Geneva, where the Soviet delegates appeared fully cognizant of the threat posed by nuclear weapons. Even General Zhukov, whom Khrushchev and Bulganin brought along (primarily as a walking reminder of the heyday of Soviet–American wartime camaraderie), expressed abhorrence at the thought of a nuclear apocalypse. "One can imagine what would happen to the atmosphere," Zhukov told Eisenhower, "if during the first days of war the US dropped 300–400 bombs on the USSR, and the Soviet Union, for its part, dropped the same number of bombs on the US."[28] (On a later occasion the general upped his estimate, claiming that it would take at least 10,000 atomic bombs to level Russia).[29] But whether Zhukov abhorred atomic bombs, or planned to use them, or both, there is no doubt that by the end of 1955 the Soviet leadership came to believe that, whatever the doctrine said, war was no longer inevitable. It was unthinkable. The sentiment was aptly summed up by the Soviet head of state, Kliment Voroshilov, in an off-the-cuff comment on the reality of the nuclear age: "We'll all die in a few generations."[30]

The seamless move from "capitalists will die" to "we'll all die" – that is, from thinking about nuclear war in conventional political terms to seeing it as a global catastrophe – roughly coincided with the November 22, 1955 test of the first proper Soviet hydrogen bomb. It was a tremendous triumph for Soviet science. But it had jaw-dropping implications, as it now appeared that there was no upper limit on the potential power of a nuclear bomb. The test report described utter obliteration within 5 km of the epicenter of the explosion, and some damage even as far as 300–400 km away and indicated that the scientists reduced the power of the blast deliberately, fearing unexpected consequences.[31]

Now that he had the H-bomb, Khrushchev set out to proclaim peaceful coexistence. The idea was spelled out in his report at the Twentieth Party Congress on February 14, 1956. He argued that nuclear weapons gave the socialist camp the means to defend itself against any possible attack, and that made war avoidable. The thesis was discussed at a meeting of the leadership on January 30, 1956, a year after Malenkov's fall. The only person who objected at all to what was, just a year earlier, condemned as defeatist and a politically erroneous stand on nuclear war was Lazar' Kaganovich, a hardline Stalinist and, by now, a relatively insignificant figure in the leadership.

PART II HUBRIS

Kaganovich pointed to "objective laws" – that is, the notion that the nature of imperialism was such that war was inevitable no matter what. Several people spoke up against Kaganovich's "petrified Marxism" and strongly supported the thesis that war was no longer inevitable. Even Molotov registered no objections, conveniently forgetting his own anecdote about "talking out of his backside."[32] As earlier with the German question, the upper echelons of Soviet leaders proved astonishingly apt at adapting their ideological proclivities to political contingencies.

Khrushchev's proclamation of peaceful coexistence is often seen as a concession of a kind, as if he bowed to the inevitable by accepting that the laws of nuclear physics invalidated a key tenet of Marxism-Leninism. Its real significance was not in the limits it imposed on Soviet foreign policy but in the limits it imposed on the West. In Khrushchev's perception, at least, peaceful coexistence meant that the United States was *forced* to respect the Soviet Union as an equal. The Soviet leadership had aspired to acceptance. Now they were getting a grudging recognition as something of an existential menace. A god-like ability to rain atomic destruction on the West bolstered Khrushchev's claims to legitimacy and made him less likely to consider concessions as a means of reducing international tensions. As he put it in 1955 not long before his trip to Geneva, the Americans "are putting pressure where they can. But one should say that the Soviet Union is a kind of country that has never taken off, nor will ever take off its hat before American capitalism."[33] Not, he could have added, while his finger was on the button.

For Stalin, the A-bomb was a ticket to an exclusive club. His successors "weaponized" the bomb but, much like Stalin, they did not have the slightest intention of ever using it. It remained a symbol of power and prestige, and an attribute of global leadership. The Soviet leader still aspired to some grand bargain to end the Cold War with the West – only he felt that it would have to be on his, not Western terms. Or, as Khrushchev told Anthony Eden when he, together with sidekick Bulganin, toured the United Kingdom, he wanted the West "to love them as they were."[34] Or at least to fear.

KHRUSHCHEV AND THE THIRD WORLD

Since the mid-1950s the Soviets increasingly turned their attention from their immediate neighbors, as in Stalin's days, to a wider audience of impoverished nations, some only recently let loose, others still waging violent struggles for independence: the proverbial third world. Stalin would not have bothered about such far-away places. He felt that the Soviet

156

Union lacked the capability to contend with other players for control over colonies. The one time he tried – in Libya – he did not get anywhere. The best he could do was to proffer free advice to far-flung revolutionaries. The essence of this advice was to forget about Communist revolutions and attend to "national liberation." The Indonesians were to focus on the Dutch, and the Indians on the British. The Latin Americans were best off joining their efforts in forming a federation to overthrow the supposed Anglo-American economic yoke. "The Anglo-Saxons," Stalin would say, "like to sit on other people's backs. One has to put an end to this."[35] But he would not say how, nor open the Soviet coffers to help. These anti-imperialists, whom he anyway suspected of being imperialist stooges, were at best accidental co-travelers, and the Cold War was none of their business.[36] Their struggles were for him just a sideshow in the unfolding drama of the Soviet–American confrontation.

Khrushchev had a different view, sensing opportunities that decolonization presented to the Soviet Union. It did not matter how far a colony was from Soviet shores. Nor did it matter to Khrushchev, as it did to Stalin, that such colonies were often not territorially contiguous with the USSR. Khrushchev was beginning to think of the Soviet Union as a truly global power, unconstrained by geographic realities. Unlike Stalin, Khrushchev was willing to go out and explore these faraway places in person. Some of his earliest foreign trips were to Afghanistan, India, and Burma. Before too long Khrushchev made his way as far south as Indonesia. In turn, third world leaders were invited to the USSR, wined and dined in the Kremlin, and sent on tours across the country, including, often, to Central Asia, presented as a model of what backward nations can accomplish under the enlightened Soviet rule.

What did Khrushchev want and what did he have to offer? In one sense, his aims were remarkably similar to Stalin's. Like Stalin, Khrushchev sought to weaken the bonds between the third world and the colonial metropole. Differently from Stalin, he was quite willing to rely on third world nationalists who, in his view, were not necessarily imperialist stooges but, rather, effectively Soviet allies.[37] When he had to choose between supporting national leaders – like India's Jawaharlal Nehru, Indonesia's Sukarno, or Egypt's Gamal Abdel Nasser – over backing various Communist factions and jungle revolutionaries, Khrushchev pragmatically embraced the former and, for the most part, ignored the latter. He invariably faced the suspicion that the Soviets were covertly funding Communist struggles, and he tried to dispel this impression by disclaiming any such links.[38]

PART II HUBRIS

Khrushchev's willingness to tone down Soviet support for Communist revolutionaries was a sign of pragmatism. What mattered in the end was not whether New Delhi, Jakarta, or Cairo embraced Communist doctrine but that in general they leant more to the Soviet side in the Cold War. Here Khrushchev departed from Stalin's legacy. He saw the anticolonial struggles in the third world as not just – indeed, not even primarily – struggles against the old European empires, but rather as battlefronts in the global competition for power and influence between the Soviet Union and the United States.

Unsurprisingly, the main Soviet vehicle for winning influence in the third world was economic assistance. For instance, the Soviet Union supplied credits for specific prestige projects like the massive Bhilai steel plant in India. The agreement to build this factory was signed in February 1955. The Soviet Union extended a twelve-year credit worth some $132 million at the very low interest rate of 2.5 percent. The terms were quite generous – so generous that the Soviet Union had little to gain economically. "The USSR cannot and does not want to earn anything from this venture," Khrushchev commented. "We just want to show how the principle of selfless aid is used in practice ..."[39] To show was to gain recognition across the developing world. And it was quickly forthcoming: not just from Nehru (who diplomatically admitted to being "almost overwhelmed" by Soviet generosity) but, crucially, from Mao Zedong, whose approval was extremely important to Khrushchev's sense of self-righteousness.[40] The Bhilai steel plant agreement, Mao offered, made a "huge impression on Burma, Indonesia, and other Asian countries." This was because, according to Mao, the Soviet Union did not attach any political conditions to these economic projects, unlike the imperialists.[41]

In time, the Chinese leader would change his view of the Soviet intentions and bitterly criticize Khrushchev for pursuing colonial policies in an anticolonial guise. But in the mid-1950s, the USSR and China worked hand-in-hand in the third world to raise the standing of the socialist world.

There was a hint of competition between the two – just a hint. The obvious fact was that the Soviet Union was a European and China an Asian power. For all the fresh glitter of Tashkent and Ashgabat, the Soviets' Asian identity had a hint of artificiality about it. The Chinese, by contrast, were authentic. Already in 1946, three years before he triumphed in the civil war in China, Mao set up a theoretical basis for his leadership in the developing world. He spoke about the existence of a vast region that separated the United States from the Soviet Union and included nations, colonies, and semi-colonies of Europe, Asia, and Africa. To defeat the Soviet Union,

CHAPTER 5 LOVE US AS WE ARE

Figure 7 Burmese Defense Minister U Bashwe (center) instructs Khrushchev (right) in the art of drumming, during Khrushchev's and Bulganin's (left) trip to Rangoon, December 1955. Source: Bettmann/Getty Images.

Mao claimed, the United States would first need to control this "intermediate zone."[42] So now he both supported Khrushchev's turn to the East and, implicitly, contested it by also reaching out to countries like India, Indonesia, and Burma.

DISCOVERING NASSER

On the night of July 22, 1952, a group of Egyptian army officers surrounded government buildings and the Royal Palace in Cairo and deposed King Farouk in a bloodless coup d'état. The nominal leader of the "Free Officers," as they called themselves, was General Mohammed Naguib but he was soon eclipsed by the 34-year-old Colonel Gamal Abdel Nasser.[43] Nasser's key political aspiration was to rid Egypt of the influence of the British who "made us feel like second-class citizens in our own country."[44] A populist and a skilled orator, he rode the wave of public anger and anticolonial sentiment. In a region that was still largely under the thumb of former colonial powers, his brand of nationalism reached beyond Egypt's shores, setting off tremors across the Arab world.

PART II HUBRIS

The Soviets were at first unimpressed by what looked like just another reactionary military coup. The Soviet ambassador in Cairo, Daniil Solod, reported in February 1954 that although "in a typical Oriental style" Egyptian leadership claimed to profess the warmest of sentiments for the Soviet Union, in reality they "in all things copy German and Italian fascism."[45] Then, suddenly, the ice cracked. Khrushchev discovered Nasser.

It happened around 1955 and thus became part and parcel of Khrushchev's broader outreach to the third world. Tito played the role of a match-maker. When Khrushchev visited Yugoslavia that May to repair ties broken in Stalin's days, Tito urged him to take note of Nasser, a "man of statesman-like abilities" who could "play a significant role in the Middle East and among Asian countries." Khrushchev said he "did not know much about Nasser" but was ready to help him.[46] In July 1955 he sent the editor-in-chief of the party daily *Pravda*, Dmitry Shepilov, to Egypt to meet with Nasser. Shepilov returned to Moscow full of enthusiasm for building closer ties with Cairo (he would soon become foreign minister and play a key role in the Soviet–Egyptian rapprochement). Courting Nasser required ignoring his anti-Communism, which Khrushchev was only too willing to do. The Egyptians were promised "that the Soviet Union is not a crocodile that can suddenly open its jaws and swallow Egypt."[47]

Moscow became more receptive to Nasser's requests for arms. Nasser, and even Naguib before him, had been asking for heavy weapons for years but the Soviets turned a deaf ear to these entreaties, suspecting that the Egyptians were just haggling for a better price with the Americans.[48] No more. In May 1955 Nasser launched talks with the Soviets on the supply of weapons: these were carried out in Prague in utmost secrecy, and the agreement, when it was signed on September 12, 1955, became known as the "Czechoslovak" arms deal.[49]

Khrushchev tried to build on this success by probing for possibilities of selling weapons to other countries in the Middle East, including Syria and Saudi Arabia, the soon-to-be independent Sudan and Yemen. This tentative engagement did not represent an effort to dominate the Middle East or gain access to the rich oil deposits of the Persian Gulf. Sure, denying oil to the West was an implied strategic rationale for Soviet involvement – then and later. But there was something else too. The Kremlin wanted to be seen as a major player in the Middle East, being seen – by friend and foe alike – as a power capable of challenging the West on its own turf. Only such recognition afforded the Soviet leaders the mantle of glory of a sprawling superpower.

Khrushchev liked to recall how in April 1956, when he and Bulganin toured Britain in the company of Foreign Secretary Selwyn Lloyd, the latter,

160

in a tongue-in-cheek sort of way, told him that "a little bird had whispered to him" that the Soviets were supplying arms to Yemen. But, Khrushchev returned, "a big bird had told him, not in a whisper but very loudly, that Britain had created the Baghdad Pact on the southern borders of the Soviet Union, and this was an unmistakably anti-Soviet act."[50] The story appealed to Khrushchev because in it explained the rationale for the Soviet involvement in the Middle East. The British were already there. Why, then, could not the Soviets try their hand at winning friends in the region?

THE ASWAN DAM

Nothing fired up the imagination of Egyptian economic planners as much as the prospect of building a massive dam across the Nile at a place called Aswan, not far from the border with Sudan. The great river had nourished the Egyptian civilization, but its frequent flooding brought misery and devastation. Taming the Nile would not only allow for flood protection but also boost the agricultural output through irrigation and contribute to Egypt's industrial growth by offering a cheap source of electric power. But building the massive dam – which, when completed, reached 111 meters in height, measuring nearly 4,000 meters across – required a herculean commitment of labor and capital. Nasser at first turned to the Americans and the British in the hope of soliciting the needed funds.

Yet even as he negotiated with the West about Aswan, Nasser pursued policies that deeply frustrated London and Washington. The biggest problem for Prime Minister Eden was that Nasser tried to subvert the Baghdad Pact and otherwise undermine British influence in the region. The Americans, meanwhile, wanted to see Egypt and Israel work out a peace settlement. Another important goal was to keep Nasser out of the Communist orbit. On both counts, Egypt was not doing as well as expected. Nasser was unwilling to mend fences with Israel: not unless the Israelis agreed to take back Palestinian refugees and make territorial concessions. Anything less than this would tarnish Nasser's prestige in the Arab world. However much he wanted to win American support, the image-conscious Egyptian was not willing to pay such a price.

Things looked even worse on the Soviet front. Not only was Nasser buying Soviet weapons, but he was engaged in a political dialogue with the Communist bloc. He was already asking for Soviet advisers to help Egypt develop a five-year plan and even asked probing questions about collectivization.[51] Part of that was no doubt to impress the youthful Dmitry Shepilov who was becoming something of an Egypt advocate in the Soviet leadership.

Shepilov enthusiastically reported back to Khrushchev that Nasser was letting out political prisoners (i.e. Communists) and even advertising Soviet-inspired economic ideas in his public rhetoric.[52] How much of this was known to the Americans is unclear but evidently enough to make them want to reappraise or, to use one word that was frequently employed by both the Americans and the British, to "deflate" Nasser. To this end, at the end of March 1956, John Foster Dulles submitted a special memorandum to Eisenhower (known as the "Omega memorandum"), advising to stall on the Aswan Dam and generally keep the Egyptian in cold water.[53]

The final straw for Washington was Nasser's decision, on May 16, 1956, to recognize Mao's China. Nasser struck an early rapport with Zhou Enlai when they first met in Rangoon before the April 1955 Bandung Conference. The Chinese premier scored points in the Arab world when he addressed the plight of the Palestinian refugees in his conference. In August 1955 Beijing and Cairo signed a cotton-for-steel trade deal, and the Chinese opened their doors to a growing number of Egyptian visitors – mainly journalists who were taken on propaganda tours to impress them with China's anti-imperialist and Muslim credentials.[54]

And Mao himself pandered to the Egyptian sense of self-importance, telling Egyptian visitors in 1956: "Egypt united 80 million Arabs, and formed a strong front against imperialism. Egypt has put itself at the forefront of this battle ... If you cave in, it will be difficult for us." He also promised weapons, free of charge of course but – because "Egypt is a country with nationalistic pride" – on credit, too, and "you can repay us 100 years later."[55] What he did not promise the Egyptians (but privately considered) was to send Chinese troops to Egypt to fight the imperialists, should it come to war.[56] For Mao, Egypt presented endless possibilities for extending China's influence in the "intermediate zone" between the East and the West.

For Nasser the prospect of getting more weapons was one of the reasons, but clearly not the only reason, for building bridges to China. Other factors were in play, including his desire to be seen as something of the Arabs' Mao: not in the sense of building a Communist society (Nasser had no patience for Communism) but in the sense of standing tall and proud as the man who freed the Middle East from imperialist shackles. This recognition was enormously important to the Egyptian leader. But it clearly stood in the way of some of his other objectives, including the idea of borrowing money from the West to build the Aswan Dam. The contradiction was made painfully clear when, not long after Egypt's recognition of China, the Americans went back on their promises and withdrew their offer of funding.

CHAPTER 5 LOVE US AS WE ARE

The news reached Nasser when he was on a plane with Nehru: they were flying back to Cairo from the Yugoslav island of Brioni, where they met with Tito for one of their nonaligned get-togethers. "There is no end to their [American] arrogance!" offered Nehru.[57] Nasser's reaction is not recorded. Speaking to the Soviet ambassador in Cairo shortly after his return, Nasser appeared "calm" and even said that "Egypt had lived without the Aswan Dam for 5,000 years, it can do without it for 5,005 or 5,010 years, and then we'll see."[58] Yet according to his biographer Mohammed Heikal, Nasser already made up his mind to repay Washington for this "insult."[59] On July 26, in a rambling speech in Alexandria's Manchia Square, he announced the nationalization of the Suez Canal. The fees from the Canal traffic would be used to finance the building the of the dam.

Nasser was not driven solely by economic concerns. What he wanted was to make a statement of defiance of the West. As Miles Copeland, who had spent many hours with Nasser, notes in this connection, "to a frustrated people the satisfactions of pride are more important than even food and shelter."[60] Nasser's prestige in the Arab world soared with this one action. But Britain and France, the dispossessed shareholders of the Canal, were determined to reverse his gains. For both countries, the imperative of "deflating" Nasser became all the more urgent. The British feared giving Nasser a stranglehold on their shipping at a time when London was increasingly dependent on the oil from the Middle East. Perhaps a bigger issue still for the British and the French was their self-perception as great powers, and the misconstrued lessons of history that suggested that appeasing Nasser would only whet his appetites.

The historian-in-chief for the British was Anthony Eden who liked comparing Nasser to dictators of the past. In his increasingly frustrated letters to Eisenhower post-nationalization, Eden called his Egyptian foe a "Muslim Mussolini," an "Arab Napoleon," likened him to Hitler before Munich, and famously lamented that "it would be an ignoble end to our long history if we tamely accepted to perish by degrees."[61] Military preparations began right away in London and Paris to invade Egypt in order to force a change of government.

In August, a result of American pressure on the UK, the British hosted a conference on the future of the Suez Canal. Twenty-two countries sent representatives though not Egypt. The Soviets, after a little wavering on the account of Nasser's opposition, sent Shepilov in the end, "in order to use the platform of the conference to expose the true aims and the colonial nature of the conference."[62] The real reason was to present

163

the Soviet Union in its new global role as the self-appointed advocate of world peace and decolonization. The Soviet leaders were willing to look after Nasser's agenda as long as it served this bigger purpose. Khrushchev resented the Egyptian's "quarrelsome" proclamations and tried to distance himself from Nasser by stressing that the Soviets, "no less than the British," wanted freedom of passage through the Canal. Bulganin summed up the sentiment on August 11, when he and others joined Khrushchev to discuss Shepilov's London directives: "at the conference, we have to play the role of a great power."[63]

Shepilov lived up to these expectations of statesmanship. Even Dulles, never the first to fall for Soviet charm, was impressed with the new face of Communist diplomacy, a refreshing improvement on stale, imperturbable Molotov.[64] The Soviet position was that while they supported nationalization as Egypt's sovereign right, they also recognized that Nasser had responsibilities, such as charging reasonable fees for the use of the Canal. Shepilov evidently enjoyed his new role of a respected mediator, and even ignored Khrushchev's last-minute instructions to "smack the imperialists in the face."[65] Khrushchev was never quite able to resolve the inherent conflict between his craving for respectability and the propensity to resort to bullying. Shepilov, though, did not want to spoil the good impression, for which he was later brutally told off at the Presidium.[66]

THE SUEZ CRISIS

In the end, neither mediation nor American pressure, nor even Nasser's seeming willingness to find a negotiated settlement to the crisis prevented the outbreak of war. Following secret talks in the Parisian suburb of Sèvres, the British and the French conspired with Israel to invade Egypt. The Israelis launched the attack on October 29 and, following a prearranged script, London and Paris issued Israel and Egypt with an ultimatum to stop the fighting or face intervention. Bombing raids followed, and November 5, 1956, first British and French paratroopers were dropped inside Egypt, near Port Said.

The Soviet leaders found themselves in a tight spot. As was the case with just about everyone else, except for the culprits, the war took them by surprise. Khrushchev was in the middle of trying to decide whether or not to crush the anti-Communist rebellion in Budapest – events described in the next chapter. The news from Suez strengthened his resolve: he could not let the "imperialists" (the British, the French, and the Americans) pocket Hungary in addition to their gains in the Middle East.[67] No one

CHAPTER 5 LOVE US AS WE ARE

in Moscow had any doubt that the whole situation was cooked up by the White House or, as Khrushchev said, "with silent American agreement."[68] Dismissive of the obvious American discomfort with the actions of their allies, the Soviets believed that it was just a ruse to deceive the world and domestic opinion. "They will demand their piece of the pie," was how Shepilov put it – "they will demand that England and France make way for the U.S. The lessons of Indochina and Iran ... show that the U.S. squeezes others out to take their place."[69]

The reality was vastly more complicated than the Soviets imagined. Eisenhower was livid, writing on November 2: "I don't see the point of getting into a fight to which there can be no satisfactory end; and in which the whole world believes you are playing the part of the bully ..." And though, as historian Keith Kyle would later write, there was "a sneaking feeling among many that it would be splendid if, despite everything, the 'bullies' were to carry it off," it was not the feeling that came through in Eisenhower's stern letters to Eden, nor in Dulles's tough talk at the UN General Assembly, nor in the harassment of the invading force by the US Sixth Fleet.[70]

The Soviet leaders happened to be in talks with a Syrian government delegation when they heard of the unexpected war in Egypt. In Mohamed Heikal's colorful description, Syrian President Shukri al-Quwatli immediately asked the Soviets to come to Egypt's defense. Zhukov then unfolded a map before al-Quwatli, asking: "President, here is the map, look at it, how can we interfere?" Supposedly al-Quwatli "leapt from his chair and cried: Marshal Zhukov, Marshal Zhukov, Marshal Zhukov, do you want me a poor civilian to tell you, the star of World War Two, how to interfere? You must interfere!"[71]

This anecdote cannot yet be corroborated (the Russian account of this encounter has not been declassified). But it rings true. In fact, on the same day as this dramatic meeting (November 2), Syrian Foreign Minister Salah al-Din al-Bitar asked Shepilov to send planes (with Egyptian markings) to fight off the British and the French.[72] Shepilov was noncommittal.

Two days earlier, Nasser's lieutenant, Ali Sabri, requested the Soviets to send their navy to Egypt's shores. The Soviets waited for four days before giving a reply: it was a "no." Shepilov's explanation was that sending the Soviet Navy would only "complicate" the situation.[73] Instead, Shepilov promised that the Soviet government would consider dispatching "volunteers," recruited from Central Asia (why, surely, no one would be able to tell them apart from the Egyptians).[74] On November 6, in a meeting with the Soviet ambassador, a "not very lively" Ali Sabri reminded the Soviets about volunteers and asked about sending submarines to help sink the Anglo-French

PART II HUBRIS

force that was already landing troops in Port Said. "One could make it look like the submarines were bought by Egypt, and are being taken to Egypt with Egyptian crews."[75]

But instead of intervening directly – something they were clearly unwilling to do for fear of a general war – the Soviets pulled off an unexpected coup. On November 5, Bulganin (as the head of government) sent out three public letters to the British, the French, and the Americans. The first two called on Britain and France to back off or risk an attack from "a more powerful state which possess all means of modern destructive weapons."[76] The third, to Eisenhower, proposed to undertake a *joint* Soviet–American intervention in the Middle East.[77] This unorthodox idea was torpedoed by Washington, which responded that the Kremlin should mind its own business.

Did these Soviet ultimatums to Eden and Mollet play any role in their decision to declare ceasefire on November 7? Shepilov (who called in the British, the French, and the Israeli ambassadors in the middle of the night, for effect, to present them with the ultimatum) recalled that one factor clearly working in the Soviets' favor was Krushchev's impulsiveness: "Devil knows what he might pull."[78] Sure enough, there was some fear and apprehension in both London and in Paris, especially the latter, which did not then enjoy the benefit of a nuclear deterrent. The French immediately asked for US assurances that they would be covered by the US nuclear umbrella in a war with the Soviet Union.

But the general feeling was that the Soviets were bluffing. Khrushchev would not risk a general war for Nasser's sake. A potentially more important factor was the fact the rapidly depleting stock of British foreign reserves and Washington's unwillingness to cooperate in a bail-out. In addition to international condemnation, Eden faced a divided Parliament, which made it all the more difficult to go on with the war. With London calling it quits, neither could the French continue. The crisis was over.

In the end, the collapse of the Anglo-French effort could not be ascribed to any one factor; clearly, different forces were in play, the Soviet ultimatum being one of them, and certainly not the most important. Still, the sudden end of the crisis boosted Moscow's stock, especially in the Arab world. Nasser claimed to be impressed, telling the Soviet ambassador on November 6 that he thought Bulganin's threats were "decisive" in bringing out the ceasefire. "The people of Egypt," he said with his usual pathos, "saw once again who their true and genuine friend is. England and France lost the Middle East forever. The Arabs will never forget these days and recount them from generation to generation." He

CHAPTER 5 LOVE US AS WE ARE

was less generous in his comments on Eisenhower's performance who, he repeated, knew of the whole nefarious business before it even started. "I am confident that the Americans will surrender on the first day of war, if a bomb falls on their country, even if it is not an atomic bomb – that's the kind of warriors they are."[79]

CONCLUSION

Nikita Khrushchev was an opportunist par excellence, and the Suez Crisis presented him with an opportunity for the sort of global projection of power that he deemed essential for recognition of the Soviet Union as an equal of the United States. Fiery ultimatums and unclear Soviet noises about sending volunteers to Egypt were a bluff. But Suez taught the Soviet leader that bluster was a remarkably effective tool of foreign policy, and he would resort to it time and again. A year after Suez, Khrushchev rattled missiles in a bid to dissuade Turkey (and its perceived sponsor, the United States) from invading Syria. When some weeks later the crisis over Syria subsided, Khrushchev congratulated himself on such deft diplomacy, telling a visiting Egyptian delegation that the Americans and their allies were defeated and that the Soviet Union "won the battle without going to war." "This is good," he said, "and we should strive to do the same thing in the future."[80]

And he did. As we shall see in Chapter 7, Khrushchev played the same card in Iraq in July 1958, in an effort to prop up what he thought was a pro-Communist regime. Most infamously, perhaps, he played that same card when in 1958–61 he attempted to force the Americans out of Berlin.

Growing Soviet involvement with Egypt – much as with India, Indonesia, Burma, among increasing number of decolonizing states – raises a key question. What did Khrushchev want in the third world? The Soviet Union was an industrial power, however deficient. It was eager to sell its produce to new markets, bartering equipment for bananas (figuratively speaking). But there were only limited opportunities for such trade, and most of the time the Soviet Union had to provide goods on credit, which fledgling regimes had trouble repaying, sinking further and further into debt. There was no great profit to be had from building factories in India, or damming the Nile in Egypt, or in buying rice in Burma, or sugar in Cuba. The Soviet Union was certainly no trading nation, although its ability to keep allies in line in part depended on supplying cheap energy.

Security issues were certainly relevant. One might argue at first that Khrushchev did not have any security concerns in Indonesia, half a world away, or in Africa, one of the key testing areas for his third world diplomacy. Stalin might have argued that. On the other hand, globalization of the Cold War – its extension beyond Moscow's immediate neighborhood in Europe and Asia – implied also globalization of Soviet security interests. Thus, speaking of Africa (though the same logic could be applied to any area of the third world), Khrushchev highlighted its "great strategic importance ... The national liberation movement that is unfolding there," he claimed, "is exposing the flanks of capitalist Western Europe, and the imperialists' military bases have been partially liquidated."[81] Undermining the "imperialists" in Africa, Southeast Asia, or in the Middle East, or perhaps even in Latin America weakened the West generally, something that did have security implications for the Soviet defense posture. On its own terms, however, the security argument is insufficient.

The ideological argument too adds something to our understanding of the Kremlin's motives. This is because Khrushchev himself professed to understand the third world in ideological terms. In this black-and-white world, the Soviet Union represented the forces of progress and socialism; the United States, the darkness of exploitation and capitalism. You were either with the one or the other. What Khrushchev wanted was to ultimately win Indonesia, India, Burma, Egypt, and others to socialism. He did not want to spread the revolution by force of arms. He only wanted the third world to recognize that the Soviet system was better than that on offer from the capitalists who, he warned, will "continue to provide so-called 'aid' ... and they'll manage to fool a few people, but nothing can change the irreversible course of history."[82] And he delighted when these developing countries appeared to jump on history's bandwagon, proclaiming their socialist "orientation."

Khrushchev would not have succeeded in the third world unless he had ideas to inspire others. These did not have to be complicated. By contrast, they were as simple and yet as appealing as freedom, justice, and prosperity. By promising liberation (from imperialism), greater social justice, and economic progress, Khrushchev both asserted his leadership and acquired a following. Most people in the third world had only a very vague idea of who their new Soviet friends in cheap suits really were. Nehru explained why: "the Soviet Union," he wrote shortly after hosting Khrushchev and Bulganin, "has the great advantage of not coming into conflict over any issue of the old colonial type and, therefore, can denounce colonialism without any injury to itself."[83] But by serving as a champion of anticolonial struggle, the Soviet Union acquired recognition and, through recognition, legitimacy. The third world may have had little to contribute to Soviet wealth or security but as a vast, appreciating audience, it had a lot to contribute to the Soviet image of itself as a superpower.

The Soviet leaders not just wanted the third world to accept their leadership, they equally sought Western recognition of this acceptance. The idea that the Soviet leaders would voluntarily abstain from "exporting revolution" to the developing world in exchange for better relations with the West was a nonstarter because Moscow's relationship with the third world was part and parcel of the Soviet Union's image of itself as a superpower with global interests, a nonnegotiable element that Khrushchev and his successors brought to the negotiating table with the West. "Love us as we are!"

But by presenting the Soviet Union as both a superpower, matched only by the United States, and at the same time as a champion of third world causes, Khrushchev was running with both the hounds and with the hares. The contradiction was not yet obvious in the mid-1950s, but it became much more obvious in later years, especially as the Chinese asserted their own leadership in the third world. Mao's credentials were much better. A philosopher-king, clawing his way to victory in the face of impossible odds, he presented a more convincing role model to jungle revolutionaries than the Soviets. But Mao was not invited to Geneva to schmooze with Eisenhower. Nor did he hold that all-important ticket to the exclusive club of superpowers – the Bomb. He vented rage, threatened the United States from afar, promising to "wipe American cities off the face of the earth," knowing all the while that he was powerless to do so.[84] He dismissed the atomic bomb as a "paper tiger," even as he privately pleaded with Khrushchev to share nuclear technologies with China.[85] His defiance of the West was born of weakness. But he was already beginning to see himself as something of a strategist-in-chief for the socialist camp, helping direct Soviet power in order to intensify the Cold War, not end it.

Stalin's death in March 1953 presented opportunities for reducing international tensions. But the fleeting prospect of "ending" the Cold War faded by the mid-1950s. Was this failure inevitable? There are good reasons to argue that it was. Moscow and Washington adhered to ideologically irreconcilable positions. One wanted to build Communism, the other pursued Capitalism. Moreover, both were given to messianic visions and sought converts to their system around the world. One or the other had to give in, in what effectively was a zero-sum game. Yet, on closer inspection, it was not necessarily always a zero-sum game. Seemingly unthinkable options – like allowing a neutral, capitalist Germany – were not just considered by the Soviets but considered very seriously. When ideological tenets got in the way of common sense – as happened with the notion of the "inevitability of war" – then these tenets were unceremoniously dumped for fresher perspectives. There was nothing immutable about the Soviet doctrine that made the conflict inevitable. It was not that the doctrine was unimportant. But rather than serving as the foundation for policies, it was used to rationalize policies. Policies themselves aimed at securing the new leadership what they most desired for themselves and their troubled country: security and legitimacy.

Prospects of German neutrality faded after West Germany joined NATO in 1955. This meant that there was also no prospect for German reunification on terms Moscow would find acceptable. The fallout from the domestic power struggle added another complication: after Beria's purge, concessions on Germany would not just be self-defeating but potentially treacherous. Meanwhile, the Soviet offer to join NATO was rebuffed on the reasonable ground that Moscow was attempting to wreck the alliance. Of course, it was. But the only way to end the Cold War with NATO intact was to defeat the USSR. To Khrushchev, at least, this did not seem like a plausible option.

The development of thermonuclear weapons and missiles made him feel that the Soviet Union could speak from a position of strength. Concessions were unnecessary, especially when such concessions were being closely scrutinized by Soviet allies and the growing audience in the third world. China's approbation was particularly important. The Soviet Union's effort to end the Cold War would not go anywhere while the Chinese continued to wage it, and they would continue to wage it until China, too, acquired what its ambitious leaders regarded as its rightful position in the hierarchy of nations. Thus, requirements of detente contradicted requirements of revolution. But despite the obvious contradiction, Khrushchev continued running with the hounds and with the hares, pursuing seemingly irreconcilable policies that become understandable only if one allows that the Soviet Union was a status quo power and a revolutionary power at the same time. By the mid-1950s, the Cold War became a permanent fixture of international politics. Military alliances solidified. Decolonization opened up new theaters for conflict, as Khrushchev, looking further and wider afield than Stalin ever did, proclaimed "peaceful" – but in reality, not so peaceful – coexistence between the East and the West.

6

THE GOLDEN HOOP

On February 25, 1956, the final day of the Twentieth Congress of the Soviet Communist Party, Congress delegates were called in for a closed session (foreign visitors were not allowed to sit in). Nikita Khrushchev spoke for nearly four hours. He told the stunned assembly that Stalin was personally responsible for the bloodbath of repressions; that he failed to recognize the danger of the German invasion in 1941 and committed criminal blunders throughout the war; that he sent entire nations into exile; that he ruined the Soviet agriculture; and that he had a mania of greatness and consciously built up his own personality cult. There was a "deathly silence" in the hall. Many of the things Khrushchev said were well known to those present but the scale of Stalin's crimes proved difficult to stomach. There was no transcript of the proceedings but in the following weeks an edited copy of Khrushchev's speech was read out to party members and nonparty activists around the country. This meant, in practice, millions of people.[1]

The Soviet people had learned to live with fear of the state. Traumatized by the brutalities of Stalinist terror, suspicious of friends and neighbors, they had learned to believe in the Communist idols. Khrushchev's denunciation of the chief idol had a shell-shock effect on the population. It also had the effect of suddenly releasing a wound-up spring, of opening the floodgates to expression of emotions: anger, hatred, disappointment, and hope.

Many people simply refused to believe Khrushchev and opposed de-Stalinization. Stalin's indignant defenders wrote to party journals and newspapers, questioning Khrushchev's rationale in criticizing the cult of personality. "One should say," wrote one anonymous author in a letter that was widely circulated among the Soviet leadership, "that the common people often take criticism of Stalin as surrender of the ideological positions we have already won."[2] Some people even took their frustrations and grievances overseas, like one secondary school teacher, Anatoly Danilevsky, who wrote to Mao Zedong alleging unfair criticism of Stalin by "different upstarts and

PART II HUBRIS

wheeler-dealers" with their "ideology of timeserving and careerism, bias and false testimony, hypocrisy and betrayal."[3]

But things got much worse than anonymous letters by disgruntled Stalinists. Shortly after the news of the "secret report" leaked out to the public, Stalin's native Georgia witnessed unrest and rioting as the youths and students took to the streets of Tbilisi, the republican capital, to commemorate the third anniversary of Stalin's death. Chanting "Dideba did Stalins!" "Dideba belads Stalins!" (Long Live Great Stalin! Long Live Our Leader Stalin!), the students converged on the central square. For several days, the square was packed solid with protesters, as one speaker after another addressed the electrified crowd. "The Georgian people," argued one speaker, "will not forgive those who decided to soil the sacred memory of Stalin." "We will not allow criticism of Stalin, our leader. Revision of Stalin is revision of Marxism. They will pay for Stalin with their blood!" The party authorities cracked down on the demonstrators on March 9, leaving scores dead. The square was cleared with tanks.[4]

Even if Stalin remained popular in many quarters, not least in the military and among the ranks of the party conservatives, he was also widely denounced. The fallen demigod was vilified at party meetings and in the street, often by the same people who had earlier worshipped him with slavish devotion. Not all went to the length of engineer L.A. Zolotov who axed the head off a Stalin statue in the front yard of his factory in the city of Cheboksary or the hammer-wielding hooligans in Brest who attacked a bust of Stalin installed in the city library. But portraits of Stalin were coming down in public places and in private apartments. Stalin's works – only recently the must-haves of any library and bookstore – were disappearing off the shelves. And the Central Committee received repeated requests from the disenchanted public to take Stalin out of the Mausoleum where his mummified remains still lay next to Lenin's mummy. "He should be taken somewhere and dumped outside the Soviet borders" read one such proposal.[5]

Why did Khrushchev pull Stalin off his pedestal? Was it a question of morality (to right the wrongs of Stalinism and close the page on past brutalities) or a cynical calculation (to strengthen Khrushchev's standing in the power struggle with Stalinist stalwarts)? In the end, no one can tell for certain. What is certain, however, is that Khrushchev was focused on the home front. He did not really worry about the effect his speech would have around the world. The most important representatives of foreign Communist parties were briefed in Moscow, and some were even provided with the transcript of the speech. Khrushchev hoped to keep the issue

CHAPTER 6 THE GOLDEN HOOP

under wraps. This was not to be. Within weeks a copy of the "secret report" found its way to the streets of Warsaw, from there to the CIA and the US State Department, and by June to the front page of the *New York Times*.[6] "Dead Dictator Painted as Savage, Half-Mad and Power-Crazed," screamed the headlines. The world was stunned. Khrushchev had not taken into account just how central Stalin had been to the international Communist movement. By pulling him down, he very nearly brought down the house. This chapter tells the story of that remarkable year, 1956, and what it meant for the international Communist movement.

THE DEATH OF AN IDEA

Tremors were felt far and wide. Communists and their sympathizers around the world were thrown into turmoil. Those who had fervently believed in the socialist utopia, who closed their eyes and ears to the unspeakable brutalities of the Soviet regime, were now ridiculed as slavish followers of a vile personality cult. Western Communist parties were particularly badly hit. Communists had not been a viable political force except in Italy and France, where they still managed to carry more than 20 percent of the vote in the national legislative elections. But though marginalized in places, they had been well-organized, with a formal membership, central committee structures, party newspapers, and, on occasion, paid-for holidays in the Soviet paradise. It was these, smaller, parties that took some of the heaviest blows post-February 1956, especially because their leaders, seasoned Communists with considerable Soviet connections, were not even informed of Khrushchev's "secret report" until well after the news was announced in the "bourgeois" newspapers.

This lack of information, never mind consultation, deeply troubled Aksel Larsen, the long-time head of the Danish Communist Party who was in Moscow at the time of the Twentieth Party Congress but did not learn of Khrushchev's denunciation of Stalin until Reuters broke the story on March 16, 1956.[7] Back in Copenhagen, Larsen faced confused and bitter questioning by members of his own party. Some – like Larsen himself – were simply shell-shocked. When, on April 5–6, he read the "secret report" at the Soviet Embassy, Larsen could not hide his emotion, exclaiming at one point: "Why wasn't he [Stalin] executed?"[8] Other Danish Communists were less impressed. Readers of *Land og Folk*, the party mouthpiece, sent in angry letters asking where Khrushchev and others had been while Stalin perpetrated these crimes. "The cult of personality, which existed in relation to Stalin, is the responsibility of those who presently want to censure him,"

173

PART II HUBRIS

argued one E. Kjeldgård in what was a typical take. "This is their mistake, which they are now trying to dump on the deceased leader of the international communist movement."[9]

These were desperate times for Larsen's party. Membership declined. Party meetings passed in bickering and recrimination. Larsen himself was under relentless pressure and was soon complaining of headaches and heart problems. "Larsen is very concerned about the state of his health, and the prospects of his future life," commented the Soviet ambassador in a dispatch to Moscow.[10] As he should have been. The prospects of Danish Communism never seemed so bleak. The situation was far from unique.

The Norwegian Communist Party went through the same process of soul-searching, angry questioning, and decline in membership. If anything, their difficulties were even worse. Just Lippe, one of the party leaders, was in Moscow for the Twentieth Congress but, like Larsen, did not learn of the "secret report" until much later. He was furious and let his anger show. At a breakfast hosted by the Soviet Embassy in Oslo in early May, Lippe lashed out at Khrushchev with a familiar set of accusations. "Where were comrades Khrushchev, Bulganin, Kaganovich, Mikoyan, and other Politburo members when Stalin allowed despotism? Why didn't they speak up against Stalin and prevent the abuse of socialist justice?" The Soviets offered a response "in the spirit of comrade Khrushchev's report" but, unsurprisingly, "it did not satisfy Lippe" who now questioned whether the Soviet Union was even a socialist society. "What socialism can you be talking about when tens of thousands of innocent people were sentenced in the USSR?" This commendable, if belated, insight did not endear Lippe to Soviet diplomats, not least because he seemed to think that many of those innocents still had not been let out.[11]

Lippe was not alone in his doubts. The Norwegian Communist Party newspaper *Friheten* published articles calling the Soviet Union a "bureaucratic" state, where "it is not the people who rule but a group of party and state functionaries." For a time, there was some discussion inside the party about dropping the Communist agenda altogether and embracing social democracy instead, an idea the Soviets blamed on Lippe's subversion.[12] At least Lippe remained a Communist, which was more than what could be said for Larsen who soon parted ways with Communism and started his own, Socialist People's Party, further fracturing Denmark's struggling Left.

Before he did, Larsen made a memorable trip in Moscow – memorable for the remarkable document that he submitted to the Soviet authorities: a list of recommendations for improving life in the Soviet Union. These included general ideas like training Soviet dentists (by sending

CHAPTER 6 THE GOLDEN HOOP

them to dental schools in Copenhagen) and Soviet builders (by inviting Danish builders to provide training on-site) to the incredibly specific. For instance, Larsen took issue with the unhygienic mats in Soviet bathrooms, arguing in favor of tiles. He did not like the way the water drained from bathtubs. He was also unhappy with the quality of heating radiators and thought that the Soviets had a lot to learn from Danish and Swedish furniture makers. Soviet banknotes were too large, and a waste of valuable paper, and Soviet-made writing utensils too impractical and expensive. And what was the point of loudspeakers on every corner? "They [loud-speakers] should only be used when there are special reasons or special desire [to use them]. One should take people's nerves into account. One should not think that if you have a loudspeaker, then it should be in constant use."[13]

These and other suggestions went all the way up to Khrushchev who received Larsen and thanked him for his concern. After all, Khrushchev and Larsen shared the belief that socialism was just around the corner, if only you could tinker a bit here and there – maybe replace the bathroom mats and fix the radiators. Khrushchev never gave up on his tinkering. Larsen, by contrast, became so disappointed with the promise of socialism that he signed up as an informer for Western intelligence services.[14]

Ripples from the "secret report" reached across the Atlantic, wreaking havoc in the ranks of one of the oldest Communist parties, CPUSA. Discussions began in mid-March on the pages of the Communist mouthpiece, the *Daily Worker*. The editor, the former leader of the Young Communist League, John Gates, printed critical editorials and letters from readers, and, then the "secret report" itself (which was released by the US State Department in early June). All of this was accompanied by unflattering editorial commentary about the "monstrous perversion of socialist principles under Stalin's brutal rule."[15] The party leadership was paralyzed. The old-time labor organizer and now the head of the party's National Committee, William Z. Foster, was "literally morally crushed by comrade N.S. Khrushchev's report on Stalin." Another senior leader, Eugene Dennis, retreated into his shell, complaining of heart problems. By June 1956 CPUSA was in the deepest crisis since its founding. In the assessment of one insider, the party existed "on paper only." One idea floated at the time was to do away with the party altogether, replacing it with a "Marxist Center" but it just was not clear where to find Marxists to run it.[16]

Khrushchev's "secret report" inadvertently did something that Khrushchev never intended. It undermined the Soviet moral standing in the world. This was of enormous significance. Assertion of leadership

175

requires moral standing, for power is never in itself compelling enough to command a global following. Moscow's "soft power" – to apply a term that was not yet in use – rested on its claim to a superior social system bolstered by the myth of Stalin's infallibility. All these years Stalin had served as a guarantor of justice and freedom for beguiled Communists in the West. But now Khrushchev disclosed that he had been a monster and a tyrant. What Khrushchev did on February 25, 1956, was extremely brave. But it also proved fatal to the Communist project and severely handicapped Moscow's search for international leadership. If it could not deliver on the promise of ideas, then where could it deliver – surely not in daily conveniences? For, on close inspection, the socialist paradise turned out to be a stale, bureaucratic regime, where people went about their daily lives ignoring the blaring loudspeakers, sleeping on uncomfortable sofas, and struggling with bathroom drainage. How, then, were they supposed to lead globally?

THE CHINESE REACT

Unlike the Danes, the Norwegians, and the Americans, the Chinese knew it all right away. A large Chinese delegation, which included the legendary commander of the Red Army Zhu De and the feisty and up-and-coming general secretary of the Communist Party Deng Xiaoping, were in Moscow for the "secret report." They were not allowed to sit in on the closed session but on the next day Deng was called in to the Central Committee and given a summary. Zhu De was seen by Khrushchev personally on February 27.[17] When the Chinese discussed the question among themselves, Zhu De's first impulse was to see the whole thing as "their [the Soviets'] business" – "we are guests here." Deng was not nearly as complacent: "Stalin is an international figure," he argued. "To treat him like this is to mess around [*hulai*]! You cannot treat a revolutionary leader, Stalin, in this way."[18]

On March 2, Deng Xiaoping returned to Beijing, where he briefed Mao.[19] On the evening of March 17 the chairman called together a meeting of the Secretariat to discuss China's response.[20] When all the participants assembled at the Yinian Hall in Zhongnanhai, adjacent to Mao's living quarters, the chairman announced his verdict. Khrushchev did two things, Mao said: one, he "removed the lid"; two, he "made a blunder."[21] By removing the lid Mao meant that the Soviet leader, by showing that even Stalin had made mistakes, opened the way to each party to act in accordance with its own circumstances, freeing itself from "superstitions."[22] The chairman returned to this theme at the extended Politburo meeting on March 24, saying that Khrushchev had broken the "incantation of the golden hoop," a reference to the golden hoop worn by the Monkey King of the Chinese literary classic, *Journey to the West*. The purpose of this magical hoop was to control the Monkey King, as, on the orders of the Tang monk, it shrank on Monkey's head, causing excruciating pain. Mao Zedong, who admired and identified with the Monkey King, was no doubt content to be freed from the Stalinist hoop, and from the attendant "superstitions."[23]

This talk of "superstitions" was not at all a random thought on Mao's part. For some weeks now, the chairman had been thinking about China's economic development. After his return from Hangzhou in mid-January 1956 he heard that Liu Shaoqi had been auditing work reports from different ministries in preparation for the Eighth Congress of the CCP. Mao also decided to listen to the reports to offer broader guidelines on socialist construction in China. For Mao, this work began on February 14 and lasted for the better part of the next two months, overlapping with discussions of the "secret report" by the top leadership.[24] It was in this context that Mao first talked about the avoidance of "superstitions." The superstition that Mao had in mind was China's reliance on the Soviet economic model. China was then in the middle of its first five-year plan, which not only closely followed Soviet planning experience but depended on the Soviet transfer of technologies and know-how, and on the advice of the Soviet experts who commanded considerable influence and prestige among the local Chinese cadres. Yet Mao was not happy.

On February 25, just as Khrushchev battled Stalin's ghost in the Kremlin, Mao passed judgments on the report of the Ministry of Industry. "Can our country's construction surpass the speed of the Soviet Union's first few five-year plans? I think it can catch up, and the industry can surpass." This was because China was both "poor" and had a "clean slate" like the United States under George Washington. So, like the United States, China could storm ahead, especially given that its domestic and foreign circumstances were better than the Soviet Union's had been. In Mao's view, China could take a "shortcut" to modernity.[25]

This was even before the Chinese had learned anything of the "secret report," but there were indications of the Soviet reassessment of Stalin as the Twentieth Congress began with Khrushchev's report on February 15. Both he, and especially Anastas Mikoyan on the following day, and later Mikhail Suslov and several other delegates, touched on the harmfulness of the cult of personality in their speeches at the open sessions of the Congress. Furthermore, Soviet economic de-Stalinization began much earlier than 1956 – in fact, shortly after the dictator's death, with the redistribution of

PART II HUBRIS

state investment to benefit consumer industries. The trend was confirmed by the Twentieth Congress. It was this issue in particular that drew the eager attention of the Chinese delegates, their report dwelling at some length on various Soviet economic shortcomings as elaborated at the Congress, including low productivity of labor, poor management, technological backwardness, and unwillingness to learn from abroad.[26]

But if the Soviets had to learn from abroad, what was it that China could learn from the Soviet Union? This question was highly relevant to Mao's investigation of the state of the country's socialist construction. Mao, like Khrushchev, realized the importance of new technologies. At a Central Committee meeting on January 20, he even characterized the present state of China's revolution as a "technological revolution" and "cultural revolution" – not in the notorious sense it later acquired but in the sense of "grasping science" and "changing the life of stupidity and ignorance."[27] In this scheme of things, the Soviet experience had a role to play but not everywhere. China would not learn from the USSR in matters like land reform, finance, or policy towards capitalists. It was the top leaders' business to decide what and how China would learn from the USSR henceforth, which was one reason that in July 1956 the State Council issued a special set of directions for Chinese organizations employing Soviet experts, directing that contracts not be extended without the center's permission.[28]

Technology was a different matter. As Mao put it, "in any case, [we should] copy everything, whether it is relatively good, or we basically don't know. Having learned, we will see."[29] This applied as much to the USSR as it did to the West. Indeed, when he and Zhou discussed this question on February 25, the chairman spoke in favor of sending students to the capitalist West to "study technology." Mao said that it did not matter whether it was America or France, Switzerland or Norway, the main thing was that if they were "willing to take our students – then we'll send them."[30] If there is a suitable expression to characterize this policy, it is "it does not matter what color the cat is, as long as it catches mice." Mao was often capable of showing a remarkable degree of pragmatism, shying away from ideological "superstitions" in order that "in a few decades [we] overcome the backward circumstances of our economy and science and culture, and quickly achieve advanced rank in the world."[31] In this context, Khrushchev's removal of the "lid" in February 1956 levelled the playing field for Mao, opening the way for experimentation, which would soon lead China to the radicalism of the Great Leap Forward.

If, in the sense of breaking the "golden hoop," Khrushchev's de-Stalinization was a good thing, in which sense was it a "blunder"? The latter term did not figure in Mao's pronouncements until that very first Secretariat meeting on March 17. It was too early to see the full picture of chaos that would soon shake the ranks of the international Communist movement but Mao would have had a good sense of the direction things were going simply by scanning Western press reports, regularly supplied in Chinese translation in the secret (leadership only) Chinese news digest *Neibu Cankao*.[32] It is also likely that Mao would have by then received a report from Zhu De about the latter's dramatic experiences in Georgia, where a public upheaval erupted in the first week of March, as the news of Khrushchev's criticism of Stalin trickled out to the population. Zhu De, who had the indiscretion to turn up in Tbilisi after the Congress, was besieged at a government dacha by angry demonstrators, and had to address the crowd twice – "to prevent possible severe consequences," in the words of a Soviet postmortem – and even to send two representatives to follow the protesters to a Stalin monument in Tbilisi to pay respects.[33] These kinds of experiences did little to bolster Khrushchev's credibility in the eyes of the Chinese leaders.

Khrushchev "made a blunder," Mao explained, by failing to consult with other Communist parties, and so causing them – and the Soviet party – difficulties, for they were not "morally prepared" for his "sudden attack."[34] Mao did not address the issue of what moral difficulties Khrushchev may have caused for the CCP, and most of his colleagues had enough discretion not to raise the issue. Only Deng Xiaoping, with his unsurpassed talent for walking the edge without falling over, spoke of parallels with China, but in a way that portrayed Chairman Mao as the main opponent of the practice of personality cult in China. "A cult of personality is a bad thing. I remember we talked about this question during the Yan'an rectification. When Chairman Mao talked about the leadership style, he especially emphasized the mass line, that is – opposed the cult of personality." Recounting how Khrushchev had mentioned in the "secret report" that those around Stalin were afraid to express opinions different from his, Deng wondered how that could be: "A Communist must insist on truth; if he does not insist on truth, sucks up to his superiors, what kind of Communist is he?"[35] We have no record of any response to Deng's comments. Nor could any record truly reflect what those present in the room were thinking.

For the most part, Mao was successful in steering the conversation away from that sensitive subject towards a more agreeable issue – in this case, Soviet "chauvinism." At the meeting on March 17, old Russia hands Wang Jiaxiang and Zhang Wentian emphasized how difficult it was to change the Soviet attitude of "great-power chauvinism," as demonstrated in their failure to consult. "From Peter the Great, traditions of great-power mentality have had a deep influence on the minds of the Russian people."[36] The same theme came up during the subsequent discussions of the "secret report." Zhang argued that Chinese diplomats who had worked with the Soviets found little in common with them: "they are the same as the English, the French, and the Americans: they all attach extreme importance to European questions. They put Europe first, see themselves as a great power ... and look down on Asia and Africa."[37] Although Zhang probably exaggerated, there was some truth to his allegations about Soviet chauvinism. In any case, the fact that such sentiments were currency among the senior Chinese leaders at the very height of the Sino-Soviet alliance, helps point towards reasons for its ultimate failure.

As for the substance of Khrushchev's "secret report," Mao's first reaction was that it was "chaotic," and during the discussions on May 19 and 24 some of those present pointed to its unsystematic nature, arguing that it was wrong to blame everything on Stalin, as Khrushchev had done. Liu Shaoqi, for instance, questioned how, if Stalin had no military skills (Khrushchev had referred to him having directed the war effort using a globe), the Soviet Union ever managed to win. Liu also recalled that Stalin was not above self-criticism, as he had admitted to the Chinese in 1949 that he had been wrong about the Chinese Revolution. The question for the Chinese was how to find the right ratio of Stalin's mistakes to his achievements.

It was on this issue that Mao Zedong, having let others speak first, announced the principle, which would henceforth guide the Chinese assessment of Stalin – that his achievements made up 70%, while his mistakes accounted for only 30% of his legacy. Mistakes were those that he had committed with respect to the Chinese Revolution, and Mao Zedong personally: bad advice, support of the wrong side in the intraparty struggles, and, worst of all, lack of trust for the Chinese leader whom Stalin had regarded as "half-a-Tito," at least until the Chinese troops proved otherwise in the Korean War. By establishing this kind of a ratio, Mao was, on the one hand, seeking to protect himself against allegations that he, like Stalin, had erred (it was fine to make mistakes, he said, as long as these were not "big" mistakes). On the other hand, Mao was aiming to elevate himself above Khrushchev as a Marxist theoretician and claim the moral leadership of the international Communist movement, while bailing out the hapless de-Stalinizer. It was with these goals in mind that at the Politburo meeting on March 24, the chairman asked his long-time associate Chen Boda to draft what would become a *Renmin Ribao* editorial, "On the historical experiences of the proletariat."[38]

CHAPTER 6 THE GOLDEN HOOP

The main theme of the article, published on April 5, was that it was perfectly alright to make mistakes in the process of socialist construction. It was natural that Stalin made mistakes. "We should view Stalin from an historical standpoint," went the article (which was written with Mao's extensive input), "make a proper and all-round analysis to see where he was right and where he was wrong, and draw useful lessons therefrom."[39] As for the lessons to be drawn, the theme of selective learning from Soviet mistakes was present throughout. Mao put the matter much more bluntly at the CCP Secretariat meeting on the day before, when he listed "independence" as the first of China's "lessons" learned from Khrushchev's de-Stalinization.[40]

After the article was published, the Chinese Foreign Ministry instructed Chinese embassies throughout the world to collect comments. The feedback was very flattering, with the Chinese Embassy in Moscow especially highlighting the "deep impression" the article made on the Soviet people. A report sent, among others, to Mao, pointed out that "not a few Soviet comrades believe that this article's significance exceeded China's sphere, and not only has great educational significance for the Soviet party members and the Soviet people, but also for the fraternal parties and for the people of the world ..."[41] Mao now towered above Khrushchev as the philosopher of the revolution, a true heir to the legacy of Marxism-Leninism. Only a few years earlier the chairman had gone out of his way to emphasize how he was Stalin's loyal pupil, that he was not like the Yugoslavs who had broken free from Moscow's control. Now, in 1956, he was telling the Yugoslavs: "Liberty, equality, and fraternity are slogans of the bourgeoisie, but now we have to fight for them ... Now there is, in a sense, the atmosphere of anti-feudalism: a father-and-son relationship is giving way to a brotherly relationship, and a patriarchal system is being toppled."[42] But who was the younger, and who was the elder brother in this Communist family? Now that Mao claimed a share of the Stalinist legacy discarded by Khrushchev, there was no straightforward answer – not for Mao, not for Khrushchev, not for the millions of Communists and their sympathizers in the socialist bloc and in the wider world.

NORTH KOREA

In the three years since the signing of the 1953 armistice agreement, North Korea made impressive strides in economic recovery. Kim Il Sung skillfully played on his allies' sense of duty to procure aid from Beijing and Moscow, and from countries like East Germany, which rebuilt an entire city for the North Koreans, completely free of charge, even as living standards in the

PART II HUBRIS

German Democratic Republic (GDR) remained dismally low.[43] But an even more impressive feat was Kim's consolidation of personal power. In 1953 he purged Pak Hon-yong, a representative of home-grown Communists, and Kim's rival in the Korean Workers' Party. In a true Stalinist fashion, he later had Pak sentenced to death as an "American spy," ignoring both the Soviet and the Chinese advice to leave him alone.[44] In December 1955 Kim moved against the so-called "Soviet" faction in his party, targeting senior leaders with Soviet connections, in particular the head of the State Planning Committee, Pak Chang-ok, and the head of the Party Propaganda Department, Pak Yon-bing, who were purged in January 1956 after being accused of factionalism, adherence to bourgeois ideology, and links to the "American spy" Pak Hon-yong.[45] Shortly before that, Kim managed to oust and imprison the most prominent representative of the "Chinese" faction in the party, Pak Il-u, known as "Mao's man in Korea" for his allegedly close relations with the Chinese leader.[46] His whole family was sent to the mines.[47] The Chinese thought that Pak Il-u was a "good comrade" and Mao personally complained that he had been "arrested for no reason."[48] For Kim, though, Pak's Chinese connection was reason enough: he targeted anyone who had foreign ties or an independent base in the party, and promoted his cronies from his guerrilla days in Manchuria.

Kim also facilitated the creation of his own personality cult, which by 1956 exceeded anything hitherto seen in the Communist world. Korea's history was rewritten to portray Kim as the country's sole savior and liberator. His images were omnipresent. Composers devoted songs to his bravery. Writers celebrated his heroism and wisdom. Anything remotely connected to Kim's real or imaginary exploits was glorified. He was himself worshipped like a demigod with shouts of "*manse!*" ("ten thousand years!"). The senior party officials competed in paying obeisance to the "beloved leader." Anyone questioning Kim's cult risked losing their job and could end up in prison or worse.[49]

Ironically, Kim's deification played out in a country that had some of the worst living standards in the socialist camp. In 1956, grain production was still below prewar figures. Forced collectivization resulted in the widespread slaughter of cattle. In early 1956 the minimum *monthly* wage stood at 600 won, enough to buy 1 liter of soybean oil or forty eggs or, if one was lucky, 2 kg of meat. State provision differed depending on the worker category: some received as little as two bars of soap and three pairs of socks *per year*.[50] Few of these wonders of North Korean socialism reached the outside, though there were worrying signals, like glimpses of starving peasants. "The scene of people bloated from hunger made a dark impression," recounted a senior Bulgarian diplomat upon witnessing the horror in the countryside, adding

CHAPTER 6 THE GOLDEN HOOP

that "he was surprised why they [the North Koreans] did not tell the truth about this."[51] The real surprise is that he even found it surprising.

The food situation was so desperate that the Chinese People's Volunteers – stationed in North Korea since the war – took it upon themselves to feed the local population by sharing the Chinese soldiers' daily rations with those who needed them most. Commanders were held responsible when the locals in their area died from malnutrition.

No other country was less prepared for the shock of Khrushchev's "secret report" than North Korea. Kim Il Sung took evasive action. In March, at a specially convened party plenum, and in April, at a party congress, Kim argued that Stalinist perversions were not applicable to North Korea, which had always had genuine collective leadership. To the extent that there was any cult of personality to speak of, it was the cult of the "American spy" Pak Hon-yong, now safely purged from the ranks of leadership. Unwilling to allow criticism of his disastrous economic policies in any form, Kim claimed that "only the blind cannot see [North Korea's] great successes."[52] Meanwhile, he took the precaution of instructing the propaganda officials to tone down some of the most odious manifestations of his personality cult. The cosmetic changes were picked up by the Soviet Embassy, which noted in reporting that the North Korean press dropped the ever-present epithet "our beloved leader" for a more neutral-sounding "comrade."[53] These measures did not really fool anyone, least of all the socialist diplomats in Pyongyang who joked: Of course, there is collective leadership in North Korea. All decisions are made by Kim, Il, and Sung.[54]

The Soviet leadership dispatched a delegation to the North Korean party congress: it was headed by the future Soviet general secretary, Leonid Brezhnev, who, in time, would develop his own personality cult, passing his old age in senile self-satisfaction in the company of toadies and yes-men. Unaware that he was, in many ways, writing of his own future, Brezhnev authored an exceptionally brusque report, criticizing Kim Il Sung for his arrogance and for surrounding himself with "immature, incapable sycophants." In a meeting with Brezhnev on April 30 Kim readily admitted to his sins but once the Soviet comrades departed, he went on as before, hoping that the storm would blow over.[55]

On June 1, 1956, Kim Il Sung left North Korea on a lengthy tour of the Soviet Union and Eastern Europe, pleading for economic aid. In July he met with Khrushchev who told him in no uncertain terms that he had to mend his ways. He returned to Pyongyang on July 20 to find the entire leadership in turmoil. Inspired by what seemed like Moscow's support of their actions, Kim's opponents tried to build a case against his personality

PART II HUBRIS

cult. Until then, the dictator managed to play the Soviet faction against the Chinese faction and vice versa. Not this time. He faced a united opposition, which included important Soviet Koreans led by weakened but still prominent Deputy Premier Pak Chang-ok and leaders of the Chinese (or Yan'an) faction, in particular Choe Chang-ik. Pak and Choe were formerly bitter rivals but now they acted together to cut Kim to size.

Instead of conspiring in secret, as they should have done, Kim's challengers raised their concerns with him directly. Kim played it smart, promising improvements here, making threats there. At the eleventh hour he also managed to send away one of his opponents, Kim Sung-hwa, to study in the Soviet Union. When push came to shove, Kim Il Sung outmaneuvered his detractors. The moment of truth came on August 30–31, when Kim convened a special party plenum to discuss the results of his trip to Moscow. The "Great Leader" allowed just a minor acknowledgment of his cult of personality, falling far short of what Khrushchev and his party critics had expected of him.

The opening shot was fired by a "Chinese" Korean Yun Kong-hum. He unleashed a torrent of criticism against Kim and his cronies, including his second-in-command Choe Yong-gon, but he was not allowed to finish. A commotion broke out, with Kim's supporters shouting and swinging their fists at Yun. Choe, calling Yun a "dog," tried to hit him but, in the words of a sympathetic observer, "did not dare." The de facto leader of the Chinese Koreans, Choe Chang-ik, "shaking from fear," mumbled something in Yun's defense. He was cut short. In later proceedings, Pak Chang-ok, a Soviet Korean, made a feeble attempt to complain of mistreatment at Kim's hands: he, too, was shouted down. Kim's opponents returned home in the evening only to discover that their telephone lines had already been cut. Sensing where things were heading, Yun and three more "Chinese" Koreans made a dash for the border and crossed over to China that night. Those who were less decisive – including the old rivals, but now fellow travelers, Choe Chang-ik and Pak Chang-ok – found themselves under arrest. Later, one ended up on a pig farm. The other was sent away to fell trees. The whole group was accused of factionalism, expelled from leadership posts and from the party.

The plenum was a sorry and scary spectacle. Of the 150 or so functionaries present, only 20 took an active part in hounding Kim's critics. The rest, paralyzed by fear, sat in uneasy silence. Some of these passive onlookers had been viciously critical of the "Great Leader" in private. But at the hour of truth, they stayed silent, easing Kim's path to murderous dictatorship.

Among those who wisely chose to put themselves beyond Kim's fatal reach was Yi Sang-jo, North Korea's ambassador to Moscow. Yi was one

CHAPTER 6 THE GOLDEN HOOP

of the early critics, having tried to debunk Kim's personality cult at the Third Party Congress in April (he was ignored but not forgotten). After he learned of the extent of the purge in Pyongyang, Yi refused to return, and instead asked for Soviet and Chinese intervention.[56]

Alerted by Yi's disturbing account, the Soviets belatedly realized they had to do something about Kim. By a fortuitous coincidence, Anastas Mikoyan was in China in September, attending the Eighth Congress of the Chinese Communist Party. He discussed the situation with Mao. "It is difficult to understand Kim Il Sung," Mikoyan said. "The North Korean Party is in a grave crisis. If it goes on like this, the party will collapse." Mao agreed that the situation was "very dangerous." "Kim Il Sung," he said – the pot calling the kettle black – "still does the Stalin thing." "He brooks no word of disagreement and kills all who tries to oppose him."[57] Mao warned, though, that they should not simply "overthrow" Kim, hinting at Moscow's tendency to order others about. "You cannot do the 'I live you die' sort of thing. What's the good of doing that? Today I rise to overthrow you, tomorrow you rise to overthrow me. That's no good. Even the capitalists have a two-party system. When Eisenhower came into office, Truman was not locked up!" Mikoyan deferred to Mao's advice, although just weeks earlier he had arranged for the forced retirement of Hungary's "Stalin," Mátyás Rákosi. In Asia, he had to act with greater circumspection and adjust to Mao's preferences.[58] The latter had good reasons for his apprehension: who knew, he could one day end up on the receiving end of the Soviet practice of overthrowing recalcitrant tyrants.

The North Korean leader, reneging on an earlier promise, skipped the Chinese party congress in Beijing (he called in "sick"). Something had to be done to bring him to senses. It was hard because Kim refused to listen. There followed perhaps the clearest expression of the limitations of Beijing's and Moscow's leverage over North Korea:

CHAIRMAN MAO: "This time we have to mainly rely on you. They won't listen to China!"

MIKOYAN: "I don't know whether they will listen or not. They can listen alright but whether they'll do anything is another matter."

CHAIRMAN MAO: "They won't listen to China a 100% of the time. They won't listen to you 70% of the time."

MIKOYAN: "I really don't understand them."

CHAIRMAN MAO: "He is afraid that our two parties are digging under his wall."

MIKOYAN: "We have to talk to him frankly this time."

CHAIRMAN MAO: "To be honest, if he doesn't mend his ways, he'll fall over even if we don't dig under him."[59]

PART II HUBRIS

In the end, Mikoyan and Mao decided to send a joint delegation to Pyongyang: to corner Kim, hear both sides of the story, and find a "two-party" solution to the problem, which would undo some of the harm but still allow the "Great Leader" to save face. Mikoyan volunteered himself for the task. From the Chinese side, Mao dispatched the former commander of the Chinese People's Volunteers, Peng Dehuai. The trouble-shooters arrived in Pyongyang on September 19.

Mao had worried that Kim would simply disappear to one of his sprawling villas, hiding from the unwanted visitors. No such thing happened. The "Great Leader" received Mikoyan and Peng who assured Kim that they did not want to see him overthrown. Mikoyan spoke at length about the importance of developing "party democracy," and doing away with "fear and repressions." "You have enormous rights," he said. "You can expel from the party, arrest a person, shoot him. No capitalist seat of power has such rights, not, for example, President Eisenhower, nor anyone else." Peng echoed Mikoyan's criticism and cited Mao's benevolence towards his political foes as an example for Kim to follow.

Kim wisely admitted to his wrongdoings. No, it was not that his critics had been blameless: he would not budge on this point. But it was that "we" (Kim used the royal pronoun to dilute responsibility) "succumbed to a temporary mood, succumbed to a sentiment instead of patiently and carefully sorting this matter out." Henceforth, Kim promised, "we" would exercise patience and show greater generosity.[60] In a private meeting with Mikoyan two days later Kim went even further. In a conversation that lasted until two in the morning, he practically begged for forgiveness, saying that he "understood [his] responsibility for the situation and will never again make the same mistakes." When Mikoyan asked Kim what message he should take back to Moscow, the latter replied that he would always listen to the advice of the Soviet Communist Party, which, for him, remained an "undisputed authority."[61] The following day, Kim convened a party plenum, restoring Pak Chang-ok and Choe Chang-ik to their positions in the Central Committee, and the four escapees – to their party membership. He also promised Mikoyan and Peng Dehuai to publish the results of the plenum, though he never did.

On September 23, Mikoyan and Peng returned to Beijing and briefed Mao on their talks with Kim. The Chinese leader was struck by Kim's irreverence. "He is like a seedling," Mao grumbled: "You planted him. The Americans pulled him out. Then we planted him again in the same place. Now he is assuming airs, saying that he is a hundred percent correct." Mikoyan thought that he had made progress but Mao remained

186

CHAPTER 6 THE GOLDEN HOOP

concerned, uttering cryptically: "This is not the end of the problem. It is just the beginning."[62]

Mao's estimate proved right in retrospect. Kim Il Sung did not change. No sooner had Mikoyan and Peng left Pyongyang than things returned to normal: brutality, tyranny, and worship of the "Great Leader." It was an ironic situation. Kim, a Sino-Soviet creation, a "seedling," as Mao called him, successfully defied his creators. If he had tried to do this with Stalin, he would not have lasted. His trip to Moscow would have been his last. By renouncing Stalin's legacy, the Soviet leadership relinquished their leverage on unrepentant Stalinists like Kim Il Sung. Released from the constraints of his own "golden hoop," Kim set out to build his very personal kingdom. It proved more long-lasting than either Khrushchev or Mao would have ever imagined.

There was also another factor in play. The Soviets could not order Kim about without China's agreement. The Sino-Soviet intervention was unprecedented. It showed Mao's growing stature as the strategist of the socialist camp. Khrushchev increasingly deferred to the Chinese leader, especially on questions pertaining to Asia. Stalin, for all his talk about the division of labor, would never have done that. He casually presented Mao with *faits accomplis*. But Stalin was taken off his pedestal in February 1956. Mao then had his chance at the steering wheel. This helped save Kim, for Mao clearly preferred to keep the North Korean leader in place. The chairman's oblique references to Yugoslavia's troubles with Stalin shows that he resented Moscow's bullying much more than Kim's insubordination.

There was something else. Both Mao and Khrushchev may have resented Kim's capriciousness, but the North Korean leader still acknowledged his place as a younger member of the socialist family. He did not try to break out of the Sino-Soviet orbit or question the premises of Communism.

Others did.

POLAND

In 1956 workers of the Polish city of Poznań grew increasingly frustrated with their dismally low living standards. In the relatively more open atmosphere of the spring of 1956, when the people of Poland, much like their neighbors in the East, reflected on the disclosures of Khrushchev's "secret report," it became easier to speak up about the wrongdoings of the past, and the miseries of the present. Poznań, like the rest of Poland, was restless with pent-up anger and anticipation of change. Tensions boiled over when

PART II HUBRIS

on June 28, 1956, employees at the Stalin Metal Works and at enterprises across Poznań stopped work and marched through the streets, demanding better pay and lower production quotas. Political demands were also advanced alongside calls for better living conditions. It was not just "We want bread!" but "We want freedom!"; not only a question of "Down with the exploitation of the workers!" but also that of "Down with Bolshevism!" What began like a peaceful demonstration soon became a full-fledged uprising. The local party and government authorities were briefly paralyzed. The protesters captured the headquarters of the Provincial Committee of the Polish United Workers' Party (PUWP, Poland's ruling Communist party), and besieged the Public Security Office. The uprising was violently put down with the help of the armed forces and the Internal Security Corps, commanded by Soviet generals. At least seventy-three people were killed, mainly the protesters.[63]

Poznań exposed the shallow roots of Poland's Communism. There was not much to show for more than ten years of progressive communization and sovietization, for all the repression of public enemies, for all the propaganda of friendship with the USSR and common interests of the socialist bloc. No sooner did the ruling regime relax controls than it found itself under siege by the people, many of whom may not have known what it was exactly that they wanted but they did know what they did not want: the Soviet connection. Opposition to Communism fed into the traditional anti-Russian sentiments of the Polish public. Poznań articulated this longing for independence from Moscow, highlighting at the same time the continued appeal of the West, as many Westerners (who were in town for the Poznań International Fair) found out first-hand, when they were welcomed and cheered by the demonstrators. The Russians, by contrast, were accused of looting the Polish economy: taking all that was valuable (in particular, coal) and paying next to nothing for it. One could also hear calls to return the Polish lands which the Russians had taken in 1939 by a secret agreement with Germany, including Lvov and Vilnius, and had kept after the war.

But if Poznań showed that the Poles had no great love for either the Reds or the Russians, subsequent developments made it clear that, given the choice between the two, the people preferred Communism over dependence on the USSR. Communism could even be tolerable if it was rid of its ugliest Stalinist facets, and if was sufficiently "national" in orientation. The Polish case was unique in that, at this crucial point in time, the PUWP experienced a vacuum of leadership, occasioned by the helpful death of Poland's "little Stalin," Bolesław Bierut, who had succumbed to

CHAPTER 6 THE GOLDEN HOOP

a heart attack in Moscow shortly after the Twentieth Congress. Factional struggles inside the ruling elite allowed for the unexpected reemergence of Władisław Gomułka, a one-time leader of the Polish Communists who fell into Stalin's disfavor in 1948 for advocating a Polish road to socialism at a time when such ideas were a dangerous heresy. Gomułka subsequently languished in jail (a humane treatment by the standard of the day) until he was quietly let out in February 1955. Growing unrest propelled Gomułka to the forefront of national politics. Although a Communist, he had strong nationalist credentials, and enjoyed a degree of popularity as a leader who would resist Soviet encroachment on Poland's sovereignty. Within the PUWP leadership, Gomułka's conservative opponents were outnumbered by his supporters who saw his return as the one opportunity to reverse the party's plummeting fortunes. On October 21, 1956 Gomułka was put back in charge as the party's first secretary.

Two days before that, on October 19, a Soviet delegation led by Nikita Khrushchev himself turned up, uninvited, in the Polish capital of Warsaw. For some months now the Soviets had been receiving worrisome reports from their embassy in Poland, and from their allies in the ranks of the Polish leadership, about the deepening crisis of the ruling regime, and the flare-up of anti-Communist and anti-Russian sentiments across the country.[64] The same sentiments were evident from reading the increasingly critical Polish press that briefly evaded state censorship. Khrushchev worried about the fate of staunch Soviet supporters, especially of Konstantin Rokossovsky, the Soviet-installed Polish minister of defense, and a Soviet national, who was about to lose his job. Khrushchev's eleventh-hour appearance in Warsaw aimed at preventing a major political reshuffle, which would clearly weaken the Soviet ability to exercise control over Poland. This could blow a huge hole in the Soviet military strategy in Eastern Europe (Khrushchev was particularly worried about the fate of Soviet troops in Germany), as well as have potentially devastating consequences for Moscow's credibility in the socialist camp.[65] Khrushchev was determined to bring the Poles to heel. Ever the bully, he got off the plane in Warsaw showing his fist to the dazzled Polish leaders, threatening Gomułka that "you will not pull this one off."[66]

Even as Khrushchev opened talks with the Poles, Soviet forces in northern and western Poland were redeployed menacingly towards Warsaw in what the Soviets claimed was a routine exercise. It was not difficult for Gomułka to imagine the consequences. Yet he held his ground in the face of Khrushchev's bullying, reassuring him though that Poland would remain steadfast on the road to socialism, and would not leave the Soviet bloc.[67]

PART II HUBRIS

Khrushchev was ostensibly calmed by such promises. He recalled some years later: "although he [Gomułka] spoke about this in a tense manner, he did it in a way that it was difficult not to believe him. And I believed him, telling my comrades: 'I think we have no reasons not to believe Gomułka.'"[68] Mikoyan, who joined Khrushchev on the Warsaw expedition, recalled Gomułka telling the Soviets: "You are afraid we'll go over to the West. We are Communists and won't go over to the West." "He was frank," added Mikoyan. "This frankness made a good impression on us."[69]

The movement of troops towards Warsaw was halted on Khrushchev's orders. But the situation hung in a precarious balance. "Let's sleep on it," Khrushchev decreed upon returning to Moscow on October 20. "Let's take a bath, rest well, and meet tomorrow," Khrushchev told Mikoyan. But no sooner did Mikoyan get home and into his bathtub that he got a phone call from General Ivan Serov, the head of the KGB, demanding his presence at a meeting that Khrushchev convened near his home. "What an outrage," Mikoyan thought – "we agreed to sleep on it." But he still went to the meeting. The mood was ugly. "They were saying that we must take military measures, that things are going badly in Poland. It's not clear how things will turn out."[70] Khrushchev was seemingly in favor of "finishing off" the Poles.[71] But the decision was postponed, and the Soviet invasion of Poland was ultimately averted. It is very likely that what really saved Gomułka from Soviet tanks was the anti-Soviet and anti-Communist uprising in Hungary, which made the Poles look loyal by comparison.

HUNGARY

In June 1953, just months after Stalin's death, Moscow appointed a new prime minister for Hungary, Imre Nagy. A one-time informer for the Soviet secret police, Nagy had spent many years in Moscow before coming back to Budapest after the war to take charge of agricultural questions in the new government. His agricultural expertise, as well as the Soviet connection, served him well in 1953 when the new Soviet leaders decided to curb the excessive powers of Hungary's "little Stalin," Mátyás Rákosi, who had presided over years of bloody repressions and a brutal collectivization campaign. Nagy was charged with steering a "New Course" for Hungary: retrenchment of collectivization and encouragement of consumption in the economic sphere, and reduction of the repressive powers of the police state. Rákosi, who had stayed on as the party secretary of the Hungarian Workers' Party (HWP) – a distinct sign of the Kremlin's ambiguity about Nagy's program – worked hard to undermine the New Course, and his

CHAPTER 6 THE GOLDEN HOOP

rival, too. The demise of Nagy's key supporters in Moscow, Beria and Malenkov, made the task easier: by April 1955 the reformist prime minister was out, replaced by András Hegedüs who deferred to the unreformed Stalinist Rákosi.[72]

The end of Hungary's New Course and Nagy's downfall merely exacerbated subsurface tensions and popular dissatisfaction with the ruling regime, and its personification, Rákosi. As in the USSR, discontent was especially widespread in the Hungarian intellectual circles, and among the youth. As Rákosi, disoriented by the "secret report," hesitated at the helm of a divided party, voices of dissent grew louder, amplified in the heated discussions of the Petőfi Circle, a talking club for the intellectuals and the youth that was sponsored in late 1955 by the ruling regime itself to channel the growing intellectual discontent away from the dangerous shores of anti-Communism. Unfortunately for Rákosi, discussions of the Petőfi Circle quickly went from subtle dissent to outright calls for freedom. Packed halls attracted people from all walks of life. Budapest's factories sent workers' delegations, so the ideas of dissent were propagated far and wide. Many participants of the Petőfi Circle put their faith in Imre Nagy who, though out of power, retained considerable influence. Many, like Nagy himself, remained committed to the idea of a socialist future in Hungary. But this commitment was tested and eroded by the open-ended calls for freedom. "Two half-truths do not make one full truth," thundered the writer Tibor Meray to the 6,000 people that assembled for the Petőfi Circle discussion on June 27, 1956: "We want the full truth. Only the full truth will satisfy us. But you can have truth only where there is freedom. And therefore, first and foremost, we demand freedom!"[73]

That tumultuous session of the Petőfi Circle – the most heated to date – ended on 4:00am, June 28, just two hours before workers took to the streets in Poznań. Using the Polish events as his excuse, Rákosi clamped down on dissent, shutting down the Petőfi Circle. But he was ruling on borrowed time. The Soviets blamed "that idiot" Rákosi for the build-up of discontent in Hungary, forcing him to resign in July.[74] Yet the appointment of Ernő Gerő, one of Rákosi's associates, as the first secretary, was not enough to appease the opposition. Tensions continued to mount and on October 23, 1956, students and workers poured into the streets: Hungary was in the state of a revolution. The protesters called for sweeping reforms: introduction of elections, better terms of trade with the USSR, the public trial of Rákosi and his henchmen, the withdrawal of the Soviet forces from Hungary, and, symbolically, the removal of the Stalin statue in central Budapest.[75] That last demand proved the easiest to realize: that very night a crowd toppled

PART II HUBRIS

the big statue of Stalin next to the City Park, though (in another symbolic twist), leaving his boots standing. The statue was dragged through the streets before being smashed to pieces. Seeing control slipping from their hands, the HWP Political Committee called upon Nagy to rejoin the leadership as prime minister. Yet this belated gesture, which may have sufficed in July, fell far short of the demands now put forward by the radicalized protesters, many of whom were now armed.

As these events unfolded in Hungary, the Soviet leadership discussed their options. Khrushchev's first reaction was to order Soviet forces to Budapest to help disperse the protesters. The decision to this effect was approved by the Presidium late at night on October 23, with only Mikoyan arguing against.[76] By dawn of October 24, Soviet tanks were in the Hungarian capital, occupying parts of the city in the face of occasionally fierce resistance. The Soviets did not have a sufficient force at their disposal to establish effective control. An uneasy stalemate ensued. Khrushchev dispatched Mikoyan and the ideologue Mikhail Suslov to Budapest so that they would meet with the Hungarian leaders to resolve the crisis. The Soviet envoys lent support to Nagy's government, despite what they described as the new premier's "opportunistic" streak.[77] Khrushchev, too, appeared sympathetic. On October 30–31, Soviet forces pulled back from the streets of Budapest. But the respite proved painfully short.

MAO GETS INVOLVED

Faced with a deepening crisis in Eastern Europe, the first secretary decided to consult his allies: he sent invitations to East Germany, Bulgaria, and Czechoslovakia. Reflecting Beijing's rising stature in Khrushchev's world, the Chinese were also asked to send a delegation. Mao dispatched his second-in-command, Liu Shaoqi. From the outset, it was clear that it was Liu – not the other Communist visitors – who really mattered to the Soviet leader. On October 23, Khrushchev personally escorted Mao's envoy from the airport to his residence. This was before the worst of the storm erupted in Hungary and Khrushchev, just back from Warsaw, had his mind on Poland. He asked Liu for China's support and – if Liu's Russian interpreter is to be believed – did what no Soviet leader had ever done before: requested Chinese mediation in the conflict with Poland: "The Soviet Union cannot have a good conversation with Poland. China can have a good conversation. The Polish comrades trust you. They are well-inclined towards you. I hope China can persuade them."[78] Liu reportedly voiced equivocal support and was invited to the Presidium the following day.

On October 24 there were in fact two separate Presidium meetings: the first, involving Soviet allies in Eastern Europe (the East Germans, the Czechoslovaks and the Bulgarians). The second was just for Liu Shaoqi. During the meeting Liu reportedly launched into a two-hour lecture, castigating the Soviets for mishandling relations with their allies, for "great-power chauvinism," and for "imposing views on others." Khrushchev, according to Liu's interpreter, "sat with his head down." The other Presidium members also listened to Liu's charges with strained fortitude. Only Yekaterina Furtseva, the sole woman in the Soviet leadership, felt scandalized, and nearly got up to leave. Khrushchev threw her a heavy glance – she sat back down.[79] In the end, Liu's interpreter recalled, Khrushchev meekly accepted Chinese criticism.[80]

On October 27, Mao Zedong told the Polish ambassador, Stanisław Kiryluk, that China, in effect, saved Poland from Soviet intervention. Mao spoke disparagingly of the remnants of "Great Russian chauvinism," and blamed Moscow for using "methods and forms of action, which should be eliminated from relations within the socialist camp." He told Kiryluk about Liu's sojourn in Moscow, adding that the Soviet leadership ultimately accepted China's views on nonintervention. His one concern was what to do about the Soviet forces: their withdrawal could generate similar demands to withdraw them from other countries, like, for instance, East Germany. That would be dangerous for the socialist camp. (The Poles later assured him that they had no intention to demand the withdrawal of Soviet forces.)[81]

There was something remarkable here. Mao, not so long ago a guerrilla leader battling for survival in the depths of China, Stalin's "pupil," who had humbly submitted to "Comrade Main Master's" advice, was now speaking like the strategist-in-chief for the entire socialist camp. Now that he appointed himself to this position of leadership, he had to take into account the common interests of the Soviet bloc and that meant, perhaps, that the Soviet forces in Poland had to stay where they were.

Or maybe not. For just two days after his conversation with Kiryluk, Mao abruptly changed his position and cabled Liu Shaoqi to remind the Soviet leaders of the need to treat others "equally," and that meant withdrawing Soviet forces from countries that did not welcome them. Liu was just then having one of his lengthy parleys with Khrushchev and his lieutenants. Khrushchev was more combative this time, bitterly disputing the charge that Soviet relations with other socialist countries were "unequal." They had been in the past, he reportedly said, but this was no longer the case, except in the sense that the Soviet Union was the one being economically exploited by its numerous allies. Liu insisted that, to clear the air, the Soviets issue a special statement on equality, which would apply the principles of "peaceful

PART II HUBRIS

coexistence" to relations between socialist countries. Khrushchev agreed.[82] The statement, some of it repeating the very wording of Liu's advice, was approved at the Presidium on October 30, and broadcast on the radio the same night. It contained an astonishing admission of past mistakes that led to inequality in the Soviet Union's relations with its allies and claimed that these inequalities were put right by the Twentieth Congress. More remarkably still, the statement spelled out Moscow's readiness to conduct consultations about the withdrawal of Soviet forces from Eastern Europe (with the exception of East Germany, which was carefully omitted).[83]

By October 30 the Polish problem was superseded by the more urgent problem of Hungary. Earlier that day Mikoyan and Suslov sent a disturbing report from Budapest, which suggested that the situation was growing worse by the hour. The "counterrevolutionaries" were shooting Communists in the street, the party was in the state of collapse.[84] The report was also passed to Liu who immediately requested Mao Zedong's instructions. Mao, who had hours earlier called for the Soviet withdrawal, was no longer sure that was the right thing to do. He said he was personally leaning towards military intervention. This is the message that Liu Shaoqi brought to the Presidium meeting. Deng Xiaoping, who also attended, was even more blunt. The future butcher of Beijing (the nickname Deng acquired after his brutal suppression of student protests in 1989) pressed the Soviets to "protect the people's power" lest it falls into the enemy's hands.[85]

Khrushchev reportedly disagreed. According to Shi Zhe (who interpreted at the meeting), he told Liu that intervention meant occupation of Hungary: "this way, we'll become the conqueror."[86] Just the previous day he went out of his way to prove to Liu that the Soviet Union no longer suffered from "chauvinism." It was done away with just like that after the Twentieth Congress. He had just agreed to issue a statement that promised to negotiate force withdrawal from parts of Eastern Europe, including Hungary. How could he so blatantly contradict himself? It would look bad. It would look like the Soviet Union was merely another imperialist power, not that different from Britain and France, who were just then about to invade Egypt. "I hope we won't end up in the same company," Khrushchev had earlier told his Presidium colleagues.[87] He was worried about his prestige. Bloodletting in Budapest was not the sort of thing that would earn global accolades. He decided not to intervene for the time-being.

But just hours later Khrushchev changed his mind. Several factors probably played a role. On October 30 Nagy announced that Hungary would see the restoration of a multiparty system, ending the political monopoly of the Hungarian Workers' Party, which, in any case, had already fallen apart. The very future of Hungary's socialism seemed in question. Khrushchev was taken aback by reports of Communists in Budapest (often members of the despised State Security, the ÁVH, which Nagy had just abolished) being dragged through the streets and hanged from lampposts. Discussions in the Presidium highlighted additional worries, including the possibility that Czechoslovakia might follow Hungary's example.[88]

Khrushchev was aware of another development: the beginning of the British, French, and Israeli attack on Egypt on October 29–31, the Suez Crisis. The brief war, preceded by Egypt's Gamal Abdel Nasser's nationalization of the Suez Canal, split the West, with the United States being adamantly opposed to what President Eisenhower perceived as outright imperialism on the part of the British and the French, and as something that would likely send Nasser fleeing into the Soviet embrace. The war in the Middle East provided a suitable distraction for the Soviet invasion of Hungary. True, Khrushchev did not want to end up "in the same company" with the British and the French (i.e. as an imperialist oppressor) but, on the other hand, he also felt that unless the Soviet Union intervened, Hungary, like Egypt, would fall prey to the "offensive" of the West. The imperialists would be "encouraged" by the Soviet retreat. "They will understand it as our weakness and continue attacking. We will then show the weakness of our positions." "Our party will not understand us," he summed up – "we have no other choice."[89]

Khrushchev was convinced that he could get away with a full-blown intervention. The Soviets already controlled Hungarian airports and borders. In fact, even as some forces were pulled back from Budapest, more were arriving in the country. Having studied military positions of the two sides, Marshal Zhukov offered his verdict: "We have no reason to leave. If they [the Hungarians] throw up a fuss, we'll smash their faces, and they'll calm down."[90] There was also no prospect of American counterintervention. President Eisenhower had other problems on his mind (presidential election was only a week away). "There will be no big war," the Soviet leader predicted at the Presidium.[91]

On the same day – October 31 – Khrushchev caught up with Liu Shaoqi at the airport. Liu was about to fly back to Beijing. Khrushchev spoke with even greater candor. "If we abandon Hungary, and let the counterrevolutionaries win, all of the world's revolutionaries, all of the Communists will curse us, and say that we are fools."[92] Khrushchev's credibility was on the line. Intervention looked bad but failure to intervene looked even worse: in the eyes of the Soviet Communist Party, in the eyes

PART II HUBRIS

of the socialist camp (including Mao, who had pressed for intervention), and the entire revolutionary world. It was bad to be a butcher. But even worse to be taken for a fool.

CONCLUSION

On October 31, the Soviet leader authorized a massive military intervention in Hungary. By November 4, Soviet forces were again in Budapest. A few days and about 2,500 deaths later, the Hungarian Revolution was finally strangled. Nagy preemptively declared Hungary's exit from the Warsaw Pact and appealed to the United Nations for help. It was all in vain. He then fled to the Yugoslav Embassy (he was ultimately handed over to the Hungarians, tried and executed). János Kádár, a reformist Communist, and a member of Nagy's government (before he defected to the Soviets) was enthroned as the new ruler of Hungary. He promised a milder form of Communism, and implemented gradual reforms, which helped to keep the regime afloat for more than thirty years. The Hungarian Revolution of 1956 ended in failure.

The shock of the intervention deepened the crisis in the ranks of the international Communist movement. The Danes, the Norwegians, the Americans – those who had been reeling from the pains of de-Stalinization – were dealt a new and an even more devastating blow. Party membership dwindled further. Apathy set in. Those in the West who had committed to Communism because they had seen Moscow's support for the struggling republic during the Spanish civil war, or because they had cheered for Communist victories over Nazism, now watched in disbelief as the Soviet military machine crushed defenseless little Hungary. The Soviet Union had made a bid for global leadership. Its leadership was based on an adherence to a particular set of ideas – among them, freedom and justice; but what Khrushchev did in Hungary was neither free nor just. Instead, it was a bloodbath. The intervention spelled the moral bankruptcy of the Soviet leadership. For, if the Communist system could not be sustained without reliance on tanks, this system had no future. In many ways, Hungary was a harbinger of Communism's demise.

In retrospect, one of the most interesting questions about Hungary is why it ended in a crackdown, while North Korea and Poland never did. Events in Pyongyang and Warsaw threatened Soviet control to no lesser extent than the chaos in Hungary. In one case, Kim Il Sung unleashed a party purge that dramatically lessened Beijing's and Moscow's ability to exercise influence on North Korea. In the other case, Gomułka's rise resulted

CHAPTER 6 THE GOLDEN HOOP

Figure 8 The aftermath of the Soviet invasion of Hungary, November 1956.
Source: Hulton-Deutsch Collection/Corbis/Getty Images.

in a similar loss of Soviet leverage over their Polish ally. For all his frustration with Kim and Gomułka, Khrushchev let them both be. Neither was in danger of abandoning the socialist camp, and that made all the difference. Disobedience could be tolerated but the humiliation of losing a country to the West could not. Soviet credibility would be irreparably damaged. The new environment provided considerable leeway for countries of the Soviet bloc. Kim Il Sung learned how to play the Soviet Union against China while keeping a distance from both. Countries like Poland and Romania acquired a previously unthinkable degree of autonomy from Moscow, while Albania broke away completely, eventually finding an ally in China.

Another remarkable aspect of the situation was just how indecisive Khrushchev was at key moments. He came close to intervening in Poland before he changed his mind. He decided to pull back in Hungary, only to turn around the next day and order the intervention. The patchy documentation gives us just enough to hint at his reasoning. He would weigh arguments for and against. At times there was something like a real debate at the Presidium, where the decision would hang in balance. Like few other moments in the history of Soviet foreign policy, 1956 reflects its contingency. Nothing was inevitable until the axe came down and the tanks rolled.

What role did Mao play in the Hungarian intervention? Did Khrushchev act on China's advice or out of conviction? The record suggests that the Soviets acted on their own, and Mao's advice (which coincided with

PART II HUBRIS

Khrushchev's thinking) was hardly essential. In the end, it is not so important whether the Chinese played a role. It is much more important that they *thought* they did. The standard Chinese narrative that emerged from the tribulations of 1956 was that Mao saved Poland from Soviet chauvinism by opposing intervention and saved Hungary from counterrevolution by encouraging Khrushchev to intervene.[93] Until then, China had only "saved" North Korea and North Vietnam: Beijing's scope for action further afield was circumscribed. The year 1956 changed all that. The golden hoop on the head of the Monkey King was finally broken. The hoop had been there to keep him from using his great powers in a reckless fashion. But newly acquired freedom did not translate to bouts of recklessness: the Monkey King had learned to behave. So it was with Mao: the breaking of the Stalinist hoop, and the rise in China's status did not mean that he would immediately challenge the Soviets at every turn. By contrast, he exercised caution and proclaimed adherence to Soviet leadership. But by emphasizing the Soviet leadership in the socialist camp he was implicitly asserting China's.

China's new role was especially evident in the theoretical realm, in Mao's effort to define Stalin's legacy. Khrushchev exposed Stalin's crimes. Mao was more interested in a philosophical assessment. Stalin had his problems. But he was a great Marxist-Leninist. Stalin was a sword and giving up that sword was a folly. Chaos in the international Communist movement in the aftermath of the Twentieth Congress offered a degree of support to Mao's views. He now towered above Khrushchev as the strategist for the socialist camp, an arbiter of disputes and a philosopher of revolution. Chinese diplomatic posts overseas hastened to report on foreign countries' deference to Mao's wisdom. Khrushchev's own apparent deference, evident in his decision to enlist China in joint action to bring Kim Il Sung to his senses, and later in Liu Shaoqi's unprecedented involvement in the deliberations of the Soviet Presidium, added to Mao's sense of self-importance. When the dust settled over Poland and Hungary, Mikoyan emphasized China had played a "big role" and had "great influence" in working out a solution.[94] His words were promptly reported to Mao. This kind of recognition only bolstered China's growing self-perception of importance in world politics.

7

TWIN CRISES

"Beep – beep – beep … Beep – beep – beep …" This was how the world knew. Eyes on the sky, telescopes, binoculars, amateur radio equipment – all to catch the glimpse of a tiny shiny speck passing in the untold vastness above, and to hear its triumphant, promising, and ominous staccato, the opening of a new symphony of the space age. The Soviet launch of the first man-made satellite – Sputnik-1 – on October 4, 1957 enthused and shocked audiences around the world. It was a moment of pride for the Soviet Union, a moment to celebrate the tremendous breakthroughs of Soviet science. Yes, the Americans were closing in. But the Soviets got there first. The political symbolism of this development could not be overstated. The socialist bloc still lagged far behind the West in economic terms (they would never catch up), and the standard of living there was much lower. But Sputnik promised a different future. Every beep was a reminder that the correlation of forces was changing – and changing fast. Every beep enhanced the Soviets' global prestige and, by the same token, diminished America's. The satellite went on to circle the world 1,440 times before it finally burned up in the atmosphere on January 4, 1958. But its political impact was felt for much longer than that.

The Soviet advance in the fields of science and technology created unrealistic expectations of economic growth. The Soviet leadership indulged in fantasies of general prosperity and publicized a priori unrealizable plans of overtaking the West. This was important domestically, to maintain the regime's legitimacy, and internationally, because these achievements, real but often oversold, allowed the Soviets to project their global leadership and defend their position at the head of the socialist camp. Sputnik helped the Soviet Union bounce back from the shock of the Hungarian intervention. It also created jealousies – nowhere more so than in China, where Mao Zedong, himself a great Sputnik fan, tried to beat the Soviets in the pace of economic development and, by doing so, build up his domestic legitimacy and assert China's leadership overseas. In 1958 he launched an unprecedented and ultimately tragic bid to reinvent China as an industrial superpower.

PART II HUBRIS

That same year the world went to the brink of war – twice! An upheaval in the Middle East and a conflagration in East Asia raised the specter of an all-out conflict between the East and the West. Though the two crises unfolded in geographically disparate regions and were not directly related to one another, they became interlinked in the suddenly shrunk post-Sputnik world. In key respects, they were enabled by Sputnik: by the hopes it fed, by the fears it engendered, and by the imperative of sustaining the political momentum of the global Soviet advance. This chapter looks at the Sputnik-era economic craze in the socialist bloc before considering the causes and the consequences of the twin crises of 1958.

KHRUSHCHEV AND MAO

There was one man who flew higher than the Sputnik in 1957: Nikita Sergeyevich Khrushchev. In June 1957 the first secretary was very nearly deposed by his Presidium rivals. Some of his detractors – notably Vyacheslav Molotov and Lazar' Kaganovich – differed with Khrushchev on what one may call questions of principle. But most felt like former Prime Minister Georgy Malenkov: they were not so much opposed to Khrushchev's policies as to his habits of leadership – incessant bullying of colleagues, self-aggrandizement, unpredictability, and failure to consult. When the Presidium assembled to discuss Khrushchev's shortcomings on June 18, Khrushchev was hopelessly outnumbered. Yet his opponents lacked the nerve to oust him right away, and as deliberations dragged on, Khrushchev deftly mobilized his supporters, some of whom had to be flown in from across the USSR. Crucially, as in the case with Beria four years earlier, he was backed by the minister of defense, Georgy Zhukov. Over a period of a few days, Khrushchev was able to turn the situation around and snatch victory from the jaws of seemingly certain defeat. A Central Committee plenum session, called by Khrushchev, condemned the "antiparty group of Malenkov, Molotov, and Kaganovich." Foreign Minister Dmitry Shepilov, Khrushchev's protégé and Nasser's friend, unwisely joined the plot at the last moment, so he, too, was rolled over by resurgent Khrushchev.[1]

The final showdown was between Khrushchev and Marshal Zhukov. Jealous of Zhukov's standing in the party and, much more disturbingly, in the army, Khrushchev repaid the marshal for his support by accusing him of a Napoleonic drive for power.[2] In October 1957 Zhukov was replaced as minister of defense by Khrushchev's crony, Rodion Malinovsky. From now on Khrushchev was alone at the top.

CHAPTER 7 TWIN CRISES

But if Khrushchev was flying higher than ever, so was Chairman Mao. Shortly after ousting the "antiparty group," Khrushchev asked Anastas Mikoyan to travel to China to brief Mao on these developments and, with luck, obtain his support and endorsement. Mao, who admitted to being "shocked" by the news, nevertheless offered his backing for Khrushchev.[3] Later, in October, Mao was prompt to back Khrushchev in the purge of Zhukov.[4] Still, he cautioned the Soviets to tone down the criticism of Molotov, in particular – not because he liked Molotov (in any case, Mao said, he "did not treat us any better than Stalin") but because raising the ruckus about the antiparty group would needlessly compromise the Soviet standing in the socialist camp. Encouraged by Khrushchev's seeming deference to his judgment in the 1956 crises in Poland and Hungary, and now by the Soviet leader's obvious need for endorsement in the domestic political struggle, Mao was positioning himself as the strategist-in-chief for the socialist camp: he was there to give advice to the less experienced Khrushchev, to defend Soviet leadership of the socialist camp, and by doing so, assert his own. But would Khrushchev, rid of domestic challengers, tolerate standing in Mao's long shadow? Their contradictions played out spectacularly in November 1957, when Mao made his second – and last – visit to Moscow to participate in a big conference of Communist and workers' parties.

The idea to call the conference was China's. One would think the Chinese would be the last to want a big Communist gathering that looked suspiciously like a throwback to the age of the Comintern, which Mao, most of all, deeply resented for its meddling in China's affairs; or to the recently defunct Cominform, which Stalin had put to good use to ostracize the Yugoslavs.[5] Mao delighted in recounting his humiliation by Stalin: how he treated him as a cat would treat a mouse, or a feudal, despotic father, his son. "Stalin hated me," he would say.[6] But now that Stalin was dead, the socialist camp could very well be reorganized on a new and more equal basis, and even the Yugoslavs (to whom Stalin – in Mao's opinion – had been just "rude") could be brought back onboard.[7] For a time, in fact, China not just approved of Khrushchev's efforts to improve relations with Tito but was itself actively involved in winning the Yugoslavs back to socialist camp. Mao's original idea was in fact for Beijing and Belgrade to jointly sponsor the next big Communist conference, representing, as they did, the two sides that suffered the most from Stalin's meddling and bullying.[8] But that idea did not go anywhere: Tito was not keen on taking too active a role in the conference business for fear of compromising his nonaligned credentials. And so, when the conference was finally held in Moscow – in

November 1957 – Tito refused to go in person, sending his lieutenants. By contrast, Mao not just went – he was positively the star of the whole show.

Khrushchev went out of his way to honor Mao. Unlike other delegations, the Chinese were put up at the Kremlin, with Mao assigned the "best room" at the gold-gilded palace of the Russian tsars. He was wined and dined and treated to displays of respect and admiration. Mao still found plenty to complain about: for instance, he was not happy with the European-style toilet (he preferred his own chamber pot). Nor was he satisfied with the cuisine, discarding his daily feast of Russian delicacies in favor of spicy Hunanese dishes prepared by his own chef. But, on the whole, he must have felt the contrast with the pains of his 1949 visit. "Look at how differently they are treating us now," Mao told his personal doctor, Li Zhisui, who was taken aback by his patient's deliberately overbearing attitude. "Even in this communist land, they know who is powerful and who is weak. What snobs!"[9] Once during a banquet he rudely cut off infamously loquacious Khrushchev who was just then recounting his memories of war against Germany. "Comrade Khrushchev," Mao said. "I have already finished eating, but have you finished the history of the Southwest front?"[10]

As much as Mao relished humiliating Khrushchev in his rather subtle but nonetheless clearly discernable ways, he was in Moscow on business: it was an occasion to decisively assert China's leadership in the Communist movement. The Chinese had been closely involved in the editing of the final document of the conference, introducing about 100 amendments to the Soviet text, including some significant changes, such as militant anti-imperialist pronouncements and the notion that the road to Communism was not necessarily peaceful (as Khrushchev tended to think since proclaiming "peaceful coexistence" in 1956) but could in fact require a violent revolution. But it would be a mistake to think, as many historians have, that the Moscow Conference became the first real clash between a more "peaceful" Soviet ideology and the more "militant" Chinese. The essence of this supposed ideological divergence was less important than the fact that Mao successfully challenged Soviet positions. What mattered most to Mao was to have the Communist world recognize China's experience of war and revolution as globally applicable and so put himself and China at least on the same plane as Khrushchev.[11]

The fact that it was Mao, of all the Communist leaders, who in Moscow called for the Soviet Union to be recognized as the "head" of the socialist camp makes China's bid for leadership not less but more obvious. The idea of having a "head" was bitterly opposed by some Communist parties, for instance the Polish, who preferred to be rid of Soviet supervision for

CHAPTER 7 TWIN CRISES

good.[12] Even Khrushchev was publicly reluctant to claim such a role for himself, as much as he hoped that Sputnik would beam the obvious without any need for words. Unexpectedly, Mao came forward as the foremost advocate of Soviet leadership, arguing, in his colorful turn of phrase that "even a snake needs a head to crawl."[13]

Khrushchev later claimed that Mao had ulterior motives to call for Soviet leadership: this way, he would have something to contend for. This is a reasonable argument, but surely this is just part of the story. There is no reason not to take Mao at his word, when he explained the Soviet Union was the natural choice because it was, by far, the most advanced country, whereas China "did not launch even half-a-Sputnik."[14] But there was also something else. By taking up the role of defending Khrushchev's title to leadership in the face of obvious and considerable resistance, Mao put himself above Khrushchev. The Soviet first secretary could be the pope of the Communist movement but Mao would be the god, or at the very least the strategist-in-chief, surveying the landscape from unreachable heights of intellectual sophistication. It was from this high position that on November 18, 1957, Chairman Mao made perhaps the most famous pronouncement of his political career: "the East Wind is prevailing over the West Wind."[15]

ILLUSIONS OF GREATNESS

In later years Khrushchev would comment disparagingly on this Maoist thesis about the "East Wind," seeing it as something rather evocative of Chinggis Khan's conquests. In reality, the sentiment lined up perfectly with Khrushchev's own buoyant mood. Inspired by impressive economic growth in the mid-1950s, and by uplifting scientific breakthroughs, he was already beginning to imagine the bright future of fairytale-like socialist abundance with people having so much to eat that they would have to be "careful not to overwork their stomachs," and (with robots doing all the work) spending just one or two hours at their workplace and devoting the rest of the day to rest and study.[16] But this utopian future still being some ways off in 1957, Khrushchev set his mind on more pressing tasks. Thus, his (in)famous pledge to catch up and overtake the United States.

Khrushchev was completely obsessed with America. What bothered him the most was not even that America was rich – there were other rich countries in the world. It was that "everyone feared and flattered" America. "Everyone walks on tiptoes before it lest they cause offense." Not the Soviet Union. "We have always stood proud," Khrushchev announced in a landmark speech on May 22, 1957. "We have [never] recognized its greatness and superiority. By contrast, we thought we have every reason to behold the greatness and superiority of our country." (The note-taker recorded "warm, passionate applause" after these words).[17] But there had to be something to go with that greatness and superiority, and Khrushchev nailed it down: it was meat, milk, and butter. If only the Soviet Union could overtake the United States in the production of these important goods, the entire world, especially the anticolonial world, would see that the Soviet system held the greater promise.

The question was how long it would take to achieve this feat, given that, for instance, his (possibly inflated) estimates indicated that Soviet meat production was only 31 percent of America's in 1957. Here, too, Khrushchev had an answer. Disregarding advice from his own economists who timidly predicted that the targets could be reached by 1975, Khrushchev confidently declared that the Soviets would catch up with the United States by 1960 (i.e. in only three years), which meant that meat production would need to be increased by more than three times – an astounding projection. But Khrushchev brushed skepticism aside. Very much in a Maoist sort of way, he put faith in the human factor, in socialist enthusiasm. "Once we declare this … everyone's fists will be itching to join the fight, and everyone will want to do something to help a kolkhoz, to help a socialist farm, to help a region, to help their oblast or their republic [and] the whole country to solve this task, to solve it once and for all."[18] The outrageous projection was published in the party mouthpiece, *Pravda*. Without thinking too much about it, Khrushchev set himself up with a promise that would prove impossible to keep.

Then, on November 6, 1957, Khrushchev publicly announced a slightly less pressing but in some ways even more ambitious target: to overtake US overall economic production in fifteen years. Never had a Soviet leader promised to accomplish so much with so little in such a short time. But he knew what was at stake. "In the end, questions will not be solved by cannons and hydrogen bombs, but by butter, bread, clothes, shoes, housing, and culture. Those who provide more for the people stand to win. This weapon is more powerful than hydrogen weapons because it concerns people's minds."[19] In a sense, the Soviet leader proved remarkably prescient – just not in the way he had hoped.

At the time, not everyone took Khrushchev seriously. Some of his colleagues were wary of his off-the-wall economics. His domestic standing – for all the enthusiastic applause – failed to keep up with the grand vistas of his rambling speeches. And even in his own memoirs Khrushchev claimed – in a spectacular display of selective historical amnesia – that he did not

CHAPTER 7 TWIN CRISES

"specify particular timeframes."[20] But there was one person who took note of the signals coming from Moscow: Mao Zedong.

In the mid-1950s Mao's China handsomely benefited from Soviet aid and expertise. Thousands of Soviet specialists were employed in different sectors of the Chinese economy. The Soviet Union helped build up China's industrial base, setting up entire factories. Khrushchev tried to satisfy insatiable appetites of the Chinese "brothers-in-arms" even if his own Presidium colleagues questioned the wisdom of helping Beijing when there were so many pressing needs back home. Khrushchev brushed them off: Mao's political support was worth every ruble spent on paving China's way to industrial prowess. But by 1956–57, it was Mao himself who was beginning to question the Soviet model of development. Moscow's economic advice, he felt, was far too conservative. Much as Khrushchev railed against Soviet scientists for failure to understand the latent potential of the masses, so Mao complained that the Soviets underrated the power of the human spirit. True, China exceeded the targets of the first, Soviet-directed, five-year plan. But it could do better, oh so much better. Already in 1956 Mao criticized some of his colleagues for putting too much faith in the Soviet experience: "Farts can be fragrant and foul. You can't say all Soviet farts are fragrant."[21]

Chairman Mao had a very primitive understanding of economy. He looked for simple indicators: for instance, the production of steel. Where Khrushchev measured success of the Soviet project with reference to meat, milk, and butter, Mao thought in terms of tons of steel. Like Khrushchev, he measured China's success by comparing output figures with those of the United States. Initially he had a reasonably modest view of just when China would overtake the Americans. In 1955, for instance, he thought it may take fifty to seventy-five years. Even in November 1957, in Moscow, he thought it may take up to ten five-year plans (fifty years) for China to catch up with the United States.[22] At the same time, evidently inspired by Sputnik, Mao felt the need to set up a target: in fifteen years, he famously declared on November 18, China should be able to match Great Britain's economic production.[23]

Soon after he returned from Moscow, Mao set out to rally the whole country to his vision of a dramatic breakthrough in economic growth. At a party conference in Nanning in January 1958 he bitterly criticized Zhou Enlai for his long-standing opposition to "rash advance" (i.e. the policy of overheated economic development).[24] The problem was political, and not economic, Mao said. "In the end, what's the main thing – successes or mistakes? [Should we] protect enthusiasm, encourage vigor, ride the wind and brave the waves, or pour cold water and let out the air?"[25] To Mao, at least, the answer was clear.

In March 1958 he took his campaign against caution to a whole new level, calling for achievement of "greater, faster, better, and more economical" results. He argued that China could leapfrog the Soviet Union in economic development: what took the Soviets forty years, would take China a mere thirteen.[26] This was because "we have more people, and our political conditions are not the same. [We have] more vitality. We have more Leninism. And they [the Soviets] have partly discarded their Leninism. They are lifeless."[27] China, then, would have to make a leap – a great leap.

The launch of the Great Leap Forward – for this was the name given to the second five-year plan, adopted in 1958 – upturned all previous projections of "catch up and overtake." Already in April, Mao claimed that "it might be possible for China to catch up with advanced capitalist countries ... in a period shorter than what had been previously predicted." He thought that China may be able to catch up with Britain in just ten years, and with the United States in another ten.[28] By May, though, that was old news. The party was succumbing to euphoria. Production figures were arbitrarily revised upwards again and again, driven by pure faith in the power of the human spirit. The Soviet leader would know the feeling. Yet, the chairman's ambition put even Khrushchev's empty boasting to shame. On May 18 Mao indicated that China could catch up with the United Kingdom in just seven years, and with the United States in another eight to ten. In June, he upped the ante again: it would not take seven years to overtake the United Kingdom but only three – "or basically we'll be there by next year." By 1967 China would catch up with the USSR and "approach" America. And in ten years (i.e. by 1968) America, too, would be left behind. And by then "we'll have a missile industry and maybe the atomic bomb."[29]

Liu Shaoqi, the slightly stooping, grey-haired veteran of the Chinese Revolution, who was now Mao's second-in-command but would later become his most prominent political victim, embraced the chairman's radical vision with passion of a true believer. "Some people criticize us for delusions of grandeur, and for being eager for quick success and instant benefit. They're right! How can we not desire greatness for our 600 million people, and boast of the accomplishments of socialism? Are we supposed to prefer smallness and failure, labor for no reward, be content with backwardness and govern by inaction?"[30]

There it was, then: grandeur – the common denominator of the Sino-Soviet friendship *cum* rivalry. Both the Soviet and Chinese Communists

CHAPTER 7 TWIN CRISES

pinned their legitimacy to the prospect of overtaking the United States and unwisely pledged themselves to outperforming the Americans in the general output of material goods.

Thankfully, Khrushchev, in his never-ending search for quick fixes, resorted to relatively harmless methods of bureaucratic restructuring. For example, in January 1957 he decided to abolish several ministries and pass their functions to hastily created regional economic councils: decentralization, in his opinion, would cut the bureaucracy and streamline production. (Not surprisingly, the dissolution of 141 ministries at different levels and their replacement with 105 regional economic councils only resulted in breathtaking administrative chaos.)[31] In February 1958 Khrushchev called a party plenum to discuss how to give the peasants on collective farms better incentives to increase agricultural production. The magic fix: rather than letting the farms rent tractors from so-called machine-tractor stations, to let them buy tractors instead.[32] This was classic Khrushchev. He may have believed in the power of enthusiasm but when push came to shove, his methods of harnessing popular enthusiasm were rooted in earthly common sense of a Russian peasant: less red tape, more incentives, a tractor here, a cow there, and, voilà, behold the dawn of Communism.

Not Mao. For Mao, the Great Leap first and foremost entailed reinventing society itself. The central element of this vision was the "people's commune," a gigantic amalgamation of agricultural cooperatives, collectivization on steroids. These communes would not only allow for unprecedented agricultural breakthroughs but also for the creation of industry, for erasing the border between the city and the countryside. Large communal halls would provide free food. Kids would be looked after in collective kindergartens, freeing women for labor in the field. The family – for centuries the basic unit of the Chinese society – would become something of an anachronism. Workforce would be mobilized on unheard-of scale to dig canals and erect dams, transforming the landscape. And everyone would make steel – in their own backyards.

Steel, that shiny symbol of modernity. Steel, that symbol of power. Steel, the currency of recognition. "I don't think it bad that we are not recognized [by the Americans]," Mao would say. "Rather, it is a good thing, urging us to make more steel, say an output of 600 or 700 million tons, and then they will have to recognize us. At that point they could still feel free not to do so, but what difference would their nonrecognition make by then?"[33]

Where Khrushchev spoke of tractors, Mao hailed the impending arrival of a brave new world. He was inspired by the vision of the turn-of-the-century Chinese philosopher and reformer Kang Youwei who had

PART II HUBRIS

authored a book called "Great Harmony" about a future society. What would the Maoist version of "Great Harmony" look like? We know from his acolytes, people like the mayor of Shanghai, Ke Qingshi, who at the May 1958 party painted the following picture of the near future: "Everyone is literate and well-informed, everyone can read *Das Kapital* and is proficient in calculus. Flies, mosquitoes, bedbugs, rats, sparrows, and other pests are all long extinct, and every work team is blessed with its own [famous poet, writer, and composer] Li Bai, Lu Xun, and Nie Er."[34]

Leaders dreamed up visions. Lieutenants set out to foist these visions on the unsuspecting peasants. On April 20, 1958, several towns in Henan Province were brought under the roof of the aptly named "Chayashan Sputnik People's Commune." The Soviets were launching sputniks into space. But the Chinese would launch a utopia. Those who resisted faced the full wrath of the state. Even the Soviet KGB, by no means a liberal institution, was surprised by the extent of the Chinese repressions. Its head, Ivan Serov, even proposed to Khrushchev that he reach out to his Chinese colleagues to warn them that they should not repeat Stalin's mistakes. "Don't mess with them," Khrushchev noted, adding with a tinge of irritation: "To hell with them. The worse they have it, the better for us."[35]

Aiming high, Khrushchev and Mao sought to overtake the United States. They needed to prove to themselves, to their people, and to the entire world that they truly were global leaders, in a position to shape history and the fate of humankind. This was nothing new. Throughout history there have been leaders who aspired to vaguely defined greatness for themselves and their nations, and sought recognition in conquest or formal or perhaps informal empires. If, for instance, in the nineteenth century, greatness was measured in the extent of annexed territory, then, why should we be surprised that in the twentieth century greatness was sometimes measured in gallons of milk or in tons of steel? These numbers offered a starting point for any educated discussion of national grandeur. Khrushchev and Mao, neither of whom was much of an economist, delighted in such comparisons. Numbers were important to the way these two leaders perceived one another. Thus, no longer content with being on the mouse end of the cat-and-mouse relationship, Mao staked out a claim to catdom. Khrushchev's primary frame of reference was his standing in Washington. But he was closely watching China's progress, eying his rivals in Beijing with growing irritation and suspicion.

Crucially to our story, theirs was a very public rivalry. Each worried about how he looked on the global stage. In the late 1950s Moscow and Beijing were becoming rival meccas of revolution, drawing countless pilgrims from

THE IRAQI REVOLUTION

Between July and August 1958 the Middle East and the Far East witnessed a succession of remarkable events, which, though they were not directly related, cannot be understood in isolation. These events brought the world to the brink of war, very much against the expectations of the key protagonists.

The opening act of the drama took place in Baghdad where on July 14, 1958 a group of army officers led by 'Abd al-Karim Qasim and 'Abd al-Salam 'Arif, launched a coup d'état, killing King Faisal II and his whole family. Nuri al-Said, the prime minister of Western-allied Iraq, attempted to flee, disguised as a woman, but he was apprehended, killed, buried, disinterred, and dragged by the mob through the streets of Baghdad. No one expected this – not the Soviets, not the Americans, not even Nasser in Egypt. Iraq had been the bastion of the Baghdad Pact, a bulwark against both Communist penetration and Arab nationalism. And suddenly, overnight, all of that was gone. Qasim's government swiftly established diplomatic relations with the USSR and embraced Nasser, the great foe of many an Arab king. A fortnight later an Iraqi emissary visited the Egyptian leader with a gruesome gift – Nuri al-Said's finger, wrapped in cotton.[36] Khrushchev was fortunately spared such obeisance.

The coup was bad news for Washington.[37] The Americans had long been concerned about the decline of their prestige in the Middle East, and the concomitant increase of Soviet influence.[38] There was a sense that the Soviets had somehow managed to hitch a ride on Nasser's brand of radical nationalism, and were using him, whether or not he realized it, to make gains at the expense of the West. Whether Eisenhower believed that the Soviets were behind the events in Iraq is another matter. The intelligence community played down the Communist factor and pointed to Arab nationalism as the real source of American troubles. One way or another, though, the coup could not go unanswered. It was not even because other countries could follow Iraq's example (though the local kings and rulers, from Jordan to Saudi Arabia to Kuwait were certainly alive to this disturbing possibility). For Washington the issue was much bigger. Eisenhower's inaction would make people think that the Americans were "afraid" of the Soviet Union and that would translate into loss of America's credibility "from Morocco to Indochina."[39] Something had to be done to "prevent our friends from losing faith in us."[40]

PART II HUBRIS

The American response came one day after the coup – in Lebanon. On July 15, the first US marines waded ashore in Beirut, a part of the eventual force of 14,000. The Lebanese intervention was requested by the country's embattled pro-Western president, Camille Chamoun, who was just then fighting his own civil war against pro-Nasser forces. Two days later, the British airlifted two battalions to Jordan after a plea from King Hussein who belatedly realized that having his regime propped by the imperialists was perhaps not as bad a prospect as sharing the poignant fate of his Iraqi cousin King Faisal II. It all looked very bad, and Eisenhower knew it. He felt he had no choice. The United States, he thought, could not afford to lose any more allies in the Middle East. And if this meant resorting to something as suspect as a quasi-imperialist intervention – something that he so opposed at Suez two years earlier – well, that seemed like an acceptable price.

The decision-making in Washington would have likely taken a different course if at any point Eisenhower concluded that the Soviets would go to war to reverse the American intervention. The collective wisdom of the intelligence community held that it was not going to happen. They were not wrong: Khrushchev never really thought seriously about starting the third world war over the Middle East. Still, just like Eisenhower, he was exceptionally sensitive to questions of credibility, all the more so after taking so much unnecessary credit for the peaceful ending of the Suez Crisis. The American intervention put his credibility to a severe test.

On the happy day that the US marines saved Beirut's beach-goers from the perils of Communism, Khrushchev had his mind on China. In October 1957 the Soviet Union and China had signed a new agreement on defense cooperation, containing a Soviet promise to give the Chinese a prototype nuclear bomb. Historians Shen Zhihua and Xia Yafeng argued that this was Khrushchev's way of thanking Mao for his political support in the ouster of Molotov, Malenkov, and Kaganovich.[41] This was an important commitment – all the more remarkable given that Khrushchev has previously resisted Mao's requests to share the Bomb, and he readily rebuffed other supplicants, not least Nasser, who came asking for nuclear-tipped missiles in April 1958. With China, things were different. As much as he saw Mao as something of a rival, Khrushchev believed that the Sino-Soviet relationship was the bedrock of the socialist camp. This was a relationship that required pushing the limits of what was deemed acceptable. It required going out on a limb for the sake of an ally. So he did.

The 1957 agreement went beyond the Bomb, foreseeing other forms of defense cooperation. Soon, the Chinese were asking for Soviet help in

210

CHAPTER 7 TWIN CRISES

the development of nuclear submarines. Zhou Enlai sent a letter to the Soviet leadership on June 28, 1958, and it was this issue that was discussed at a meeting on the Soviet Presidium on July 15, just as things were heating up in the Middle East. The records of this discussion are rather fragmentary, but the results were clear enough: they were conveyed by the Soviet ambassador, Pavel Yudin, personally to Mao on July 21. Moscow, Yudin explained, wanted to discuss with China the prospects for establishing a joint fleet.[42] This innocuous proposition caused a storm of fury in Beijing, in the longer run helping to sink the unsteady ship of the Sino-Soviet alliance. In the short term, the issue proved to be a serious distraction from Khrushchev's not-so-skillful handling of upheaval in the Middle East.

KHRUSHCHEV'S BRINKSMANSHIP

Nasser heard the news of the coup in Iraq and the Anglo-American intervention while visiting with Tito at his fabled retreat on the island of Brioni in the northern Adriatic. Thinking that it was not altogether improbable that the Americans would ambush his yacht, *Al Honreya*, Nasser opted to return to Egypt in a Soviet-supplied TU-104. Instead of flying directly to Cairo, though, he first turned up in Moscow for an unscheduled parley with Nikita Khrushchev, arriving in the wee hours of July 17. The transcripts of their eight-hour long conversation are yet to surface. But it is possible to piece together the main points of the discussion.[43] The Egyptian leader sought to extract Khrushchev's promise that should the West invade Iraq or perhaps Syria, Moscow would join the melee on Nasser's side. Khrushchev flatly turned him down. All he could do, he said, was to hold a military exercise at the border with Turkey. "Please, Mr. President," he told Nasser on parting. "Keep it in your mind that it is nothing more than maneuvers."[44]

Later, already when the winds of war blew over, Khrushchev wrote a letter to Nasser, in which he tried to explain why he could not offer any guarantees. "Knowing your short-temperedness, we were worried that our unlimited support of your militant sentiments could prompt you to unleash military actions, which we considered and still consider undesirable." Nasser, then, knew very well where his Soviet friends stood. He delighted, in a grim sort of way, in the Soviet interpreter's mistake in translating Khrushchev's "maneuver" as a "game" but ending up saying "a toy." On July 18, in Damascus, Nasser made a rousing speech, promising to defend the Arabs' "honor and dignity," and, among other things, indicating that he had Moscow's support.[45] "You know, that was very strong," a confidant told him as the president emerged from the balcony. "It would have been stronger if it had not been a toy," was Nasser's sardonic reply.[46]

Khrushchev faced a perilous situation. It was not just Nasser who was asking for Soviet guarantees; the Iraqis were making similar enquiries through their intelligence channels. The Soviet military intelligence, meanwhile, estimated that it was "quite possible" that the Americans and the British would intervene in Iraq.[47] Khrushchev believed that the Turks, the Iranians, and the Pakistanis were pleading with Washington to invade and, though the Americans were stalling for now, they could very well take the fatal step in the end. "It is hard to predict," he pondered on July 21, "what Dulles and [British Prime Minister Harold] Macmillan will do." (He continued to think that Dulles, not Eisenhower, ran the show in Washington). "Recently they have committed so many incredible stupidities that there is no guarantee that they will not commit this one final stupidity by invading Iraq." Khrushchev set the chance of their invasion at a whopping 40 percent.[48] These were not very good odds, and they gave rise to not such a far-fetched question: Would the Soviet Union simply stand by and allow the Americans to puncture the grand bubble of Soviet influence in the Middle East?

On July 19, 1958, four days after the American landing in Lebanon, the Soviet leadership formally discussed the matter at a meeting of the Presidium. Khrushchev came up with a great idea: Why not write a public letter to Eisenhower, threatening nuclear war? "In a word, do it like this: 'Mr. President, we are now living through the most responsible moment in history; we have approached a catastrophe and even the slightest rash step, and the war will begin in the Middle East, and having begun in one place, the war, with good wind, will flare up and turn into a world conflagration.'" In the subsequent discussion there was a lot from Khrushchev on the "mountains of the enemy's corpses," on hydrogen bombs that both sides have in their arsenals, and, of course, on Hitler's fatal missteps. "I would not mention Hitler," Mikoyan offered – "it will drive Eisenhower crazy." "I won't insist," conceded Khrushchev. The point of the letter was to propose a great-power summit in some neutral country or even in Washington, "so as to meet and solve all the questions."[49] The British (as the co-culprit in the Middle East) and the French and the Indians (presumably, as "great powers") were sent similar letters.

The most heated moment in the discussion came when the old soldier Kliment Voroshilov questioned Khrushchev's inflammatory language. Voroshilov, once Stalin's brutal commissar of defense, had more recently mellowed into something of a sentimental old man. Although he was the titular head of the Soviet state, he had no real power, and was not infrequently a subject of ridicule by his colleagues, as, for instance, in November 1956, when he mistakenly replied to a letter from the Belgian queen by writing to Queen Elizabeth II of Great Britain.[50] But on this occasion, the old man displayed a remarkable grasp of the fundamental problem with Khrushchev's brinksmanship. If they call your bluff, what then?

The Soviet government could not resort to "threats," Voroshilov began, because if it did, and the Americans refused to back off, Moscow would have to get involved. *That* it simply could not do: "we must not fight a war."

"We are not talking about declaring a war," Khrushchev returned irritably – "only about a letter. What, then, are we supposed to tell them? We ask you [not to invade] but if you swallow the Arabs, be careful not to scratch your throat? This is what it would look like. In this case, it's better not to write the letter."

"They must be afraid of us," echoed Mikoyan.

"I think we should not repeat it so many times," Voroshilov pressed.

"We'll have to repeat it, because they [the Americans] will climb onto our backs if we remain silent," countered Khrushchev.[51]

Voroshilov's proved a lonely voice. The letters were published a day later, and they bristled with menace. Eisenhower was unmoved, calling them a "propaganda stunt." And they were. Khrushchev, like Voroshilov, had no intention of fighting a war in the Middle East or anywhere else. But there was the painful issue of credibility. Bullying the regional players – Iran, Turkey, and Pakistan – was easy enough. Bullying Britain and France was permissible. Now the Soviets had to stick to their guns in a potential standoff with the United States. Anything else would be seen as a "retreat" and would only serve to encourage the Americans. Mikhail Suslov, Khrushchev's dour-faced ideologue who was always ready to deploy this or that quotation from Marx and Lenin, this time came up with a wholly unideological explanation for Moscow's tough posture: to sound weak, he said, "is to humiliate ourselves."[52] This Khrushchev, ever sensitive to his global image, was simply unwilling to do.

Holding a summit to "solve all the questions" – the main point of Khrushchev's proposal – was not, in and of itself, a new idea. The Soviets had peddled it for months. It was floated in December 1957, when then-Prime Minister Bulganin proposed to hold a summit to discuss ways to build trust among great powers. An indication of the direction of Soviet thinking, Bulganin outlined a number of possible steps, including prohibition of atomic testing, withholding atomic weapons from West and East Germany, refraining from the use of force in the Middle East, and even conclusion of a nonaggression treaty between NATO and the Warsaw Pact.[53] The Americans resisted these entreaties, even though this entailed putting pressure on their British allies who, as usual, were a great deal more willing to talk to the Soviets. The British privately protested the "angry" and "threatening" signals but went along for fear of endangering the Anglo-American unity, so fragile since Suez.[54]

Still, Khrushchev's renewed call for a summit in July 1958 caused a new round of the tug-of-war between Washington and London, with the British once again much more open to the idea, and the Americans initially implacably hostile. Eisenhower thought that the Soviets would use any summit to portray the United States as the aggressor in the Middle East, that America's lesser allies would "rebel" at the idea of being excluded and that, when all is said and done, "the men in the Kremlin are serving only their own selfish purposes. They are not trying to do anything decent for any other portion of humanity."[55] There was also another reason for stalling. Khrushchev made it quite clear in his letter that what he really wanted was to find the kind of settlement for the Middle East, which would "take into account the interests of all states, connected to countries of this region."[56] Translated from Soviet-speak, this meant a settlement that would acknowledge the Soviet Union's role and interests in the Middle East. This idea, though, was very much at odds with the National Security Council (NSC) document on America's long-term goals in the Middle East (NSC-5801/1), which specifically prescribed to "resist Soviet proposals for agreements designed to obtain explicit and formal acknowledgment of the Soviet presence and interests in the area."[57] What was there to talk about, then?

Nevertheless, there were also factors in favor of talking to Khrushchev. One was Macmillan's position who, on this occasion, preempted Eisenhower by his announcement that he was ready for a meeting. And, then, there was Eisenhower himself who, then and later, felt that meeting the Soviet leader was just morally the right thing to do. It was an act of statesmanship, and Eisenhower was a statesman. So, on August 1, quite unexpectedly, he announced that he was ready to meet Khrushchev on the condition that the summit take place on the sidelines of a Security Council meeting at the United Nations. This would narrow the agenda to a host of very specific issues directly connected to the Middle East. And so now the summit, which Khrushchev so desperately wanted, appeared within grasp. Yes, there were obvious limitations but also an opportunity for personal diplomacy, for the sort of limelight that he so relished, for being seen as a big-time player on the grand international stage. But an even bigger question that Khrushchev

CHAPTER 7 TWIN CRISES

was now beginning to ask himself was this: Assuming he went up to that stage, what, then, would he say that would count as victory at home, among Moscow's friends in the Middle East and, last but not least, in China, in Mao's unforgiving eyes?

THE SWIMMING POOL PARLEY

On the evening of July 22, Khrushchev, accompanied by his large coterie, showed up at the Polish ambassador's, who threw a party for the diplomatic community to mark Poland's "resurrection day." Towards the end of the evening, Khrushchev and then Mikoyan – "who was close to being drunk" – made their way to the American ambassador, Llewellyn E. "Tommy" Thompson. Thompson, keenly aware of the prying ears, tried to avoid any substantive discussion by strategically sitting his wife between himself and Khrushchev. The first secretary was undeterred. He put on the friendliest performance, which included a shower of inoffensive toasts, a call to end mutual propaganda, and a personal invitation to Thompson and his family to visit him in Crimea in August, where they would "spend our vacation together" and do "some good hunting." Khrushchev's point was all too transparent – to ease Soviet–American tensions, brought to a boiling point by the crisis in the Middle East. "Whole performance," Thompson cabled in the morning, "was an eerie one, perhaps best expressed by fact that throughout evening gramophone was playing number of American jazz songs including repeated renderings of 'Why Must You Be Mean To Me?'"[58]

While at the Polish Embassy, Khrushchev delivered one of his usual rambling speeches. Much of it dwelt on the Middle East but he also touched on wider matters. "Speaking of the state of affairs in the socialist camp," he proclaimed with characteristic ebullience, "our affairs are going well. Better than ever before!"[59] He could not be more wrong.

For on that day, July 22, Mao Zedong called in Soviet Ambassador Yudin for an absolutely unprecedented dressing-down. A day earlier Yudin presented Mao with new Soviet proposal for a "joint navy." Mao was suspicious but did not clearly say yes or no. Now he called the ambassador for another conversation in the presence of his most senior Politburo colleagues. It lasted for the better part of the day.

"I was unable to sleep after you left yesterday," Mao told the ambassador. "Nor did I eat anything. I have invited you for a conversation today, to serve as a doctor, in order that I may be able to eat and sleep in the afternoon." After this inauspicious opening, Mao launched into a lengthy discussion of the Soviet Union's misdeeds in China. He slammed Stalin for

215

PART II HUBRIS

his lack of faith in the Chinese Revolution and his quasi-imperialist policies, and criticized the Soviets for their overbearing attitudes, both among advisers and the high-flying envoys like Mikoyan who, he said, was "haughty and arrogant" when talking to the Chinese. And here was the bottom line: the Chinese would never agree to a "joint navy" or to any other "cooperatives," as Mao sarcastically called them, because they violated China's sovereignty and reminded one of the indignities of the colonial past.

"You don't trust the Chinese," Mao said testily, with barely disguised disdain – "only the Russians."

> The Russians are superior, while the Chinese are inferior, clumsy, hence the question of joint operation. Speaking of that, how about putting everything under joint operation: the army, navy, and air force, industry, agriculture, culture and education? Shall we hand over to you our coastline of over 10,000 kilometers, while we ourselves engage solely in organizing guerrilla forces? You have had some success with atomic energy, so you want to control others, to enjoy the right of lease.[60]

Mao's fiery monologue caused shock and incomprehension in Moscow. "What happened to Mao Zedong?" Khrushchev wondered "excitedly" in a conversation with the downhearted ambassador over a high-frequency telephone line, shortly after Yudin had seen Mao.[61] "How could you [the Chinese] think this up?" Khrushchev pressed at a Presidium meeting on the 24th. "We objected to concessions when Stalin was around." Yudin had suggested that the two leaders meet and talk. "We are for a meeting," Khrushchev said. "But the situation does not allow it."[62] Given the tension in the Middle East and the Soviet proposal for a summit with Eisenhower, which Khrushchev planned for July 28, Mao's flare-up could hardly have come at a worse time. Yudin was asked to tell the Chinese that Khrushchev would not be coming.[63] In the meantime, though, Eisenhower rebuffed the Soviet call for an early summit.[64] Khrushchev fired off another missive to Washington, accusing the Americans of stalling, and then called Yudin to tell the Chinese that he would be coming after all.[65] On July 31 he flew to Beijing for an unscheduled, secret meeting with his difficult ally.

The encounter is mainly remembered for its unusual venue – in Mao's swimming pool. In fact, the meetings began, respectably enough, in Zhongnanhai's Huairen Hall, the place where Mao usually received visitors. Yudin was not there, having fallen ill, no doubt from sheer stress, on July 30. Khrushchev conveniently blamed the whole "joint navy" incident on the ambassador's misunderstanding of his instructions, and assured Mao that he never contemplated infringing on China's sovereignty: "What, do

CHAPTER 7 TWIN CRISES

Figure 9 Mao and Khrushchev during their July–August 1958 talks in Beijing. Some of the discussions took place inside the Zhongnanhai swimming pool. Source: Sovfoto/Universal Images Group/Getty Images.

you take us for red imperialists?". Placated, Mao seemed content to let the matter rest: "All the black clouds have dispersed."[66]

On the following morning, Mao, citing the hot weather, moved the whole discussion to the side of his personal swimming pool. "If you want to swim," he told Khrushchev, "you may."[67] Donning swimming trunks, Khrushchev and Mao headed to the pool, an experience historians have described as Mao's deliberate effort to humiliate his Soviet guest. Khrushchev was sensitive to slight but by all indications he was not put off by Mao's gesture. Perhaps he took it as a sign of Chinese hospitality, an indication that the tensions of the previous days had finally blown over.

The poolside discussions turned on the events in the Middle East. Khrushchev shared with Mao his understanding of what happened in Iraq and where it was headed. He had an optimistic take. Qasim, Khrushchev said, had been known to the Soviets, for he had maintained contact with the Iraqi Communists. There were also three Communists in his cabinet. The coup came as a surprise to Moscow but Khrushchev qualified it as a "victory" for the forces of socialism, to Mao's evident approval. "We can congratulate each other," said Khrushchev. "That's why we gathered here," agreed Mao. True, Iraq was not socialist by any stretch of imagination, and

PART II HUBRIS

Khrushchev realized that Nasser wanted the Iraqis to travel his road. That was fine. But "we can't surrender, either. We must not allow the unification of Iraq with [Nasser's] UAR, the way they did it with Syria." The best-case scenario, Khrushchev continued, would be to keep Iraq "democratic," that is – with the Communists operating freely on the political scene. "We currently have a covert struggle with Nasser, but this is not the main thing ... The main thing is to hold on to Iraq. In either case, the situation will be in our favor."[68]

Mao appeared satisfied with these explanations. What happened in Iraq seemed to confirm his views, which he had so passionately defended in Moscow months earlier: the East Wind was prevailing over the West Wind. "I said in Moscow," Mao recalled, "that both sides are afraid." "That's right," echoed Khrushchev. "But who is afraid of whom more?" asked Mao. "I've considered this question for a few years. Every time something happened, I would test this point of mine. Sometimes it seemed untrue – it looked as if we were more afraid of them. But sometimes it was true – they were more afraid of us. When I spoke to Gromyko, he told me that some of these bastards only appear cocky but in fact they are extremely worried."[69] (In fact, it was Mao, in a conversation with Khrushchev's new foreign minister, Andrei Gromyko, in November 1957, who claimed that the Americans "are really afraid of death ... that's why they don't dare to attack us.")[70]

The probability of the American invasion of Iraq, Mao guessed, was something like 10% (Khrushchev settled on 25%). The Americans were hopelessly overstretched, and, moreover, their troops, as Mao put it, sit around in trenches "eating chocolate candies and drinking milk." ("They are eating ice cream!" added Liu Shaoqi, who had until then politely deferred to the boss to do the talking). Of course, Mao said, one must not underestimate America but it was clear, in his opinion, that they suffered a grave blow: "We definitely won in the Middle East, the enemy is in retreat."[71] Khrushchev agreed that the "victory in the Middle East could have very great consequences."[72]

Before too long the conversation deteriorated into a boisterous exchange about the coming of Communism; how the Soviet Union and China would jointly build public lavatories with pure gold, and how the UN would be "blown up" and replaced with a floating city in the middle of the ocean with all nations sending their representatives (Mao promised to go in person). Meanwhile, in response to Mao's comment that Lenin's ghost was already floating in the Mediterranean, over the Sixth Fleet, Khrushchev promised to augment the Soviet naval presence in the Adriatic with additional nuclear forces. "Then we will see what the American Sixth Fleet will

CHAPTER 7 TWIN CRISES

do." It was a far cry from the alarmed discussions at the Soviet Presidium. In talks with Mao, Khrushchev put on a braver face than he, down below, was really comfortable with.[73]

Meanwhile, Eisenhower wrote to Khrushchev, agreeing to talk on the sidelines of a UN Security Council meeting. Khrushchev, still in China, dictated his reply on August 2. He drew inspiration from a seventeenth-century letter allegedly sent by the Zaporozhian Cossacks to the Ottomans. This letter was their response to the Sultan's demand to surrender. It is famous in folklore, for it consists of the foulest insults and ends with the undiplomatic recommendation that the Sultan "kiss us in the ass." Khrushchev pointed Chairman Mao's attention to the Cossacks' churlish rejoinder. "You should ask Eisenhower to do the same," Mao advised.[74]

However, there was an important difference between Khrushchev and the legendary Zaporozhian Cossacks whom he so sought to emulate: it was the Soviet leader who initiated the exchange of letters. He wanted something from the Americans – not the other way around. But now that the promise of a summit with the world's rich and powerful seemed within grasp, Khrushchev was starting to get cold feet. He told Mao that he was not sure whether the summit would take place at all, adding: "We are interested in the process of the struggle for a meeting, not the meeting itself. I agree with you that we do not need to get downhearted on the account of [international] tensions." Mao's militant attitude was infectious. Khrushchev tried to match it with his gung-ho enthusiasm for a fight: not just in the Middle East but in Southeast Asia and in Latin America, too. What, then, was the point of meeting with Eisenhower?[75]

On his return to Moscow, Khrushchev aired these doubts at the Presidium. By then, the situation in the Middle East had begun to stabilize. The new Iraqi government was recognized by regional players, and by the West, too: the risk of a military operation to topple Qasim seemed minimal. Camille Chamoun, Lebanon's beleaguered president who had requested US intervention, agreed to step aside, and the Americans seemed intent on an early withdrawal. Khrushchev counted these developments as Soviet victories, achieved at very little cost. As he explained to his obliging colleagues on August 4, what he most wanted in the Middle East was to maintain Soviet prestige. "The smashing of Iraq [would be] a blow to our policy from the point of view of our country's prestige." Now that the danger receded, Khrushchev felt that he would only lose by turning up at the Security Council. He suddenly developed a bizarre complex about shaking hands with Eisenhower: who would extend his hand first. What if he did and Eisenhower did not? And then, Chiang Kai-shek would likely be there as well, representing China; surely, that would not go down well with Mao! "So, we come to a meeting. But there is nothing. Why are we going? To determine that he [Eisenhower] is a son of a bitch? We know this [already], and there is nothing else. The basis for calling [the meeting] is narrow, just to quarrel."[76]

Khrushchev's original idea was to somehow force the Americans to recognize the Soviet Union's legitimate interests in the Middle East. He now understood that it was easier said than done. It was not even clear what the Soviet legitimate interests were. Meeting Eisenhower was, after a fashion, a victory but leaving such an important meeting empty-handed could not be construed as anything other than a defeat: it would make Khrushchev look weak, something he found hard to stomach, all the more after his poolside bragging contest in Beijing. Yet to Adlai Stevenson (who was badly beaten by Eisenhower in the 1956 presidential election and now occupied himself with diplomatic tourism, which included a meeting with Khrushchev on August 5), the Soviet leader still appeared very much interested in a summit, just of a different kind. His major concerns, Stevenson revealed in an article in the *New York Times* on September 28, were recognition of the Soviet "equality," and the avoidance of war. "Perhaps," he added, "it is time to make a gesture, difficult though it may be, a gesture that rejects the Communist system but accepts the chance of decreasing the tensions." This meant inviting Khrushchev to the United States for his one-on-one summit with the American president.[77]

Adlai Stevenson was both right and wrong. For, in the end, there were two Khrushchevs: one, who sought to engage Eisenhower in a dialogue of equals for the sake of world peace, and the other, who wanted Eisenhower to "kiss us in the ass." These two Khrushchevs – the bully and the peacemaker – were in a constant tug-of-war with one another, which goes a long way towards explaining the apparent reversals of Soviet foreign policy.

TROUBLE IN THE TAIWAN STRAIT

By August tensions were waning in the Middle East. With the summit falling through, the problem of the Anglo-American intervention was handed down to the General Assembly. The venerable gathering voted on August 21 to kick the can over to the UN secretary general, Dag Hammarskjöld, asking him to make "practical arrangements" to uphold the purposes of the UN Charter in the Middle East, and to "facilitate" an early withdrawal of the US and British forces from Lebanon and Jordan.[78] The fear of World War III that gripped the world since mid-July, finally receded. The

CHAPTER 7 TWIN CRISES

calm lasted for two days. On August 23 the world learned that a war already started – only halfway around the globe. The Chinese People's Liberation Army (PLA) began shelling the Jinmen and the Mazu islands.[79]

The Jinmens and the Mazus are a scattering of minor islands, just off the coast of the Chinese province of Fujian. When Chiang Kai-shek's forces fled to Taiwan a decade earlier, they held on to these sleepy little islands, which, as a consequence, acquired some strategic significance as forward posts in a potential reinvasion of the Chinese mainland, as well as in propaganda, intelligence-gathering, and harassment of Communist coastal shipping. The PLA was naturally keen to push their rivals out into the sea, having done just that in 1954–55 with another string of minor islands off the coast of Zhejiang, just north of Fujian. In March 1958 Minister of Defense Peng Dehuai reported to Mao on the preparations, then underway, to bombard the islands. Preparations took several months and were carried out in utmost secrecy. The sudden escalation in the Middle East was a complicating factor in the Chinese calculation but it did not derail the long-planned operation. By contrast, the coincidence was extremely auspicious.[80]

The attack on the islands was scheduled for July 27, 1958 but Mao was worried. What would the Americans do? And what about the Soviet allies? It was not yet clear how the Middle East crisis would play out. So, after a long, sleepless night, Mao wrote to Peng with a request to postpone the operation: "Let us uphold the principle of not fighting battles we don't know how to handle," he said.[81] The next few days were crucial for the learning process. First, the situation in the Middle East began to show signs of returning to normality, confirming Mao's view that the Americans were unwilling to go to war. Second, Khrushchev's unexpected trip to China was symbolically useful: whatever Mao decided to do now, the Americans would get the impression that the action had been coordinated with the Russians, so they would have to think twice before retaliating.[82] Only, there was a difficulty. Khrushchev's visit was secret, and if Eisenhower did not know anything about it, how could he be deterred? So, Mao came up with a tricky plan: he asked Khrushchev to publish a joint communiqué on his visit. The Soviet leader was taken aback but agreed nonetheless.[83] He had no clue of Mao's intentions: the chairman did not utter as much as a word about shelling any islands while he and Khrushchev floated in the swimming pool.

Why would Mao would do something as audacious as launch a military operation that could very well end in World War III? This question lends itself to a variety of interpretations, one of which is the obvious connection to the events in the Middle East. The connection worked as follows. Mao held that every time the United States became embroiled in a foreign conflict, it put itself in a "steel noose," handing the end of the rope to the "people" who could then yank it and tighten it as they saw fit. Taiwan, and the offshore islands, were one such noose, and the Middle East was another. With the Arabs pulling on one rope, and the Chinese on the other, the Americans would become fatally overextended – a happy thought for many a revolutionary movement around the world. In other words, shelling Jinmen and Mazu to "help" the Arabs was not at all propaganda. It was a part of how Mao conceived the world.

Then, there was the question of tension. Mao loved it. Tension was good to steel the spirit and encourage the people to give all they have got to the task of economic construction. And China faced a huge task. It was, after all, the high tide of the Great Leap Forward.[84]

And then, finally, there was the question of leadership. The shelling of the islands put China front and center of international politics, and Mao – at the forefront of leading the global struggle against the United States. Here was a chance to prove that the East Wind originated not in the deserts of Iraq, or, perhaps, in the slums of Latin America, never mind the stately halls of the Kremlin, but right there, in China, in the azure waters off the coast of Fujian. Here was a chance to prove in action what Mao had already proclaimed in words: that "we" (the revolutionary forces) were not as afraid of "them" (the imperialists) as they of us, and in doing so to align theory and practice in a way that would put Mao at the helm. Yes, Khrushchev had Sputnik and all the industrial might of a modern superpower. But he, Mao, had the revolutionary vision, and a sense of moral superiority. Mao's doctor memorably recalled him saying that he wanted to "stick a needle up his [Khrushchev's] ass."[85]

How did Khrushchev react to this session of acupuncture? To say the least, he was not pleased. Mao had failed to consult. It was, in spirit, as well as in letter a violation of the Treaty of Alliance, for the Chinese were in effect committing their Soviet ally to a possible war with the United States, and Khrushchev knew absolutely nothing of their intentions. The Soviet leader made it very clear in Beijing that when Nasser, days earlier, asked him for carte blanche in a potential war in the Middle East, he refused. True, Mao was not Nasser, but he must have known that he could not ask for unqualified Soviet support – he would not get it! This could be the reason why the chairman decided not to reveal his hand ahead of time. But Mao's nasty surprise put Khrushchev in a tight spot. The unexpected provocation was much bigger than Iraq, and a lot, a lot more dangerous.

CHAPTER 7 TWIN CRISES

True, it was not entirely unexpected. The PLA had been amassing forces in Fujian for weeks. These movements were picked up by both the Americans and the Chinese Nationalists who made certain preparations. But the sheer scale of the assault was still striking. Forty thousand rounds were fired at Jinmen alone on the very first day of bombardment. Hundreds of civilians and Guomindang servicemen were killed, including several generals. The Americans had long warned Chiang not to commit his forces to these indefensible islands. They were purportedly excluded from the terms of America's defense treaty with Taiwan. Chiang ignored these warnings. But now that his ally was under attack, Eisenhower faced a difficult choice: protect Chiang and risk being drawn into a shooting war with the Mainland or stand back and watch the Communists overwhelm their offshore islands, if this is what Mao in fact wanted to do. In the heat of August, few had an idea of what he wanted to do. Mao himself was perhaps not entirely sure, even as the battle got underway.

But there was one group of people who had an answer to Mao's every stratagem: the US military command. These were the people who had plans in place for fighting the "ChiComs" (in the not entirely friendly parlance of the time). These included extensive use of atomic bombs from the earliest stages of a conflict. The idea, as General Nathan D. Twining, chairman of the Joint Chiefs of Staff, explained it, was that once the Americans were drawn in, they would employ 10–15 kiloton atomic bombs against the Chinese. In mid-August, the Strategic Air Command put five B-47 bombers on alert. In the event of hostilities, these were to fly from Guam to dump their lethal cargo on Chinese airfields in Fujian and as far out as Shanghai, Nanjing, and Guangzhou.[86] From the military standpoint, this was completely reasonable. The Americans had a shortage of "iron bombs." Nukes were the only reliable method of wiping out the shore batteries and stopping the Communist landing on Jinmen.[87]

And what if such an operation led to World War III? This was a risk certainly worth taking, because, as Chief of Naval Operations Admiral Arleigh Burke explained at a meeting with John Foster Dulles, the loss of Jinmen would "probably result in the later loss of Taiwan and other free countries one by one." "We must stand and hold firm," he continued, "by conventional weapons as long as this was possible but, if the enemy persisted, with nuclear weapons. Otherwise we faced the prospect of losing the whole world in ten years."[88] So, when on August 25 Eisenhower suddenly vetoed the use of atomic bombs without his explicit authorization, the reaction from his commanders in the field and at the Pentagon was that of incomprehension and resentment. General Laurence S. Kuter of the Pacific Air Forces was

223

later heard complaining that "the military had failed to convince civilian authorities that American forces had to be free to use nuclear bombs at the outset of any conflict."[89]

Unlike his generals, Eisenhower, himself of course a general, was decidedly less upbeat about the virtues of atomic combat. His key concern was diffusing the Far Eastern powder keg without losing face in the process. The problem, as in the Middle East, was that of credibility. Already reports were coming in from America's allies in the region that should the islands be lost to the Communists, "confidence in the United States would be shaken, the entire psychological alignment in Asia would alter in favor of Communism, and [Beijing's] prestige would reach new heights."[90] Dulles, always attuned to vaguely defined concepts like "prestige," lamented that Khrushchev's easy propaganda victories – from Suez in 1956, to Syria in 1957, to Iraq, just weeks earlier – could "give the world the impression that we were afraid of the Communists and were falling back in the face of their threats."[91] But, like Eisenhower, he struggled with the idea of going all the way at the slightest provocation. And they both keenly realized that few American allies – even in Asia – would back a plunge into World War III for the sake of saving someone's face. And, as Eisenhower and Dulles thought, the Soviets pre-approved Mao's actions, it was hard to see how they would stand to the side with folded arms if the Americans launched a nuclear strike on their ally.

Far from pre-approving the Chinese attack on the offshore islands, Khrushchev was at pains to understand what exactly was going on, and, more importantly, where it was all going. So, he dispatched his foreign minister, Andrei Gromyko, to China on a secret mission to probe Beijing's intentions. What Gromyko heard from Zhou Enlai was nothing if not disturbing. "When inflicting blows on the offshore island," the prime minister explained on September 7, "the PRC [People's Republic of China] has taken into consideration the possibility of the outbreak in this region of a local war of the United States against the PRC, and it is now ready to take all the hard blows, including the atomic bombs and the destruction of [its] cities." Should the nukes start falling, Zhou intimated, the Soviet Union should stay out of it, and only if the war expanded should Moscow become involved by making a nuclear strike of its own.[92] It all sounded terrible, but it must be remembered that Mao did not think the Americans would cross the red line. Not only that, he himself was unwilling to cross the red line, and on that very day, instructed his man in the field, General Ye Fei, to be careful not to fire on the Americans involved in the resupply of Jinmen.[93] As with Khrushchev, there was a huge gap between Mao's militant rhetoric and his rather more circumscribed actions.

CHAPTER 7 TWIN CRISES

On September 7 Nikita Khrushchev sent one of his long letters to Eisenhower, after asking Gromyko to clear it with Mao.[94] It was one of his toughest yet, much tougher than his threats in response to the US landing in Lebanon. Indeed, besides the familiar references to the Soviet Union's atomic prowess, the letter contained an unambiguous promise to stand by China, which, Khrushchev said, is "not alone; it has true friends ready to go to its aid at any moment in case of aggression against China, since the interests of the security of People's China are inseparable from the interests of the security of the Soviet Union."[95] What historians have never quite been able to pin down is whether Khrushchev offered this guarantee only because a day earlier Zhou Enlai made a public statement signaling China's willingness to seek peaceful solution to the crisis and proposing the resumption of the Sino-American ambassadorial talks.[96] In this rather cynical view, Khrushchev procrastinated for a whole two weeks, firing his cannons only when it became clear that tensions were beginning to abate. This is not impossible, but it is more likely that the tough language was already in Khrushchev's first draft, the one that Gromyko showed to Mao. As weeks earlier in the case of Iraq, the Soviet leader's fear of war paled before his fear of losing credibility.

A few days later, after pondering Zhou's bizarre request that the Soviet Union not get involved in a nuclear war against China as long as it remained a limited war, Khrushchev addressed the subject in a note to his Presidium colleagues. It was clear, he said, that what Zhou was really doing with that remark was testing the Soviet Union's credibility as an ally. It was necessary to respond to such a probe with a letter to Mao. Khrushchev dictated a draft of this letter to his note-taker. "We cannot allow a situation," he said, "and create some kind of an illusion among our enemies that if the PRC is attacked from America or Japan or anyone else ... the Soviet Union will remain on the sidelines, as an observer." And then, the ultimate expression of the logic of credibility: "If the enemy learned about it or even as much as suspected it, this would create a very dangerous situation."[97] The letter was sent to Mao a week later.[98] Whether he was reassured by Khrushchev's readiness to fight a nuclear war on China's behalf is another matter. He probably had his doubts, much as Chiang had doubts that when push came to shove, Eisenhower would go all the way for his recalcitrant ally.

This missive from Khrushchev, apart from showing that he had a remarkably competent grasp of the workings of nuclear deterrence, highlighted the complexities of preserving credibility. After all, the purpose of his letter to the Chinese was not so much to highlight the importance of appearing credible to the United States and its allies but to defend his credibility as an ally in Mao's eyes! Fortunately, Mao did not push his luck. On October 6, the Chinese announced a halt to bombardment, ostensibly for "humanitarian" reasons and then, on October 25, came the announcement that the islands would only be shelled on odd-numbered days, allowing their resupply on even-numbered days without any harassment from the PLA batteries. Shells continued falling on Jinmen for two decades but in a rather regularized and predictable fashion. The crisis was over.

CONCLUSION

In the space of just a few short weeks in July–September 1958 the world found itself, twice, teetering on what seemed like the verge of another world war. On the one hand, the unexpected coup in Iraq set in motion a train of events that brought American marines to the beaches of Beirut, and the Soviets to the promise of a nuclear retaliation. Events in Baghdad, though of regional significance, really had no wider meaning either for the Americans or the Soviets. Whose heads rolled and at whose behest, whose fingers were being passed around wrapped in cotton – all of this would really not have been all that important but for the fact that both Eisenhower and Khrushchev interpreted the Iraqi situation in the light of their concern for their, and their countries', global prestige. In the White House, Qasim's victory was interpreted as a blow to America's regional standing, and a Soviet victory, and this is exactly how Khrushchev saw this as well, despite the fact that both sides knew that Qasim was hardly a Communist. So, Eisenhower resorted to what he knew was going to be an extremely unpopular step – sending his military forces to the Middle East. And Khrushchev responded by threatening a war that he was both unwilling and unable to fight. Both acted to safeguard their prestige and credibility as global leaders.

On the other hand, Mao, unable to meddle in the Middle East directly, unleashed another crisis nearer to China's shores. The connection to the Middle East was mostly accidental but the general policy direction was not an accident. It was a logical consequence of Mao's famous proclamation, post-Sputnik, that the East Wind was prevailing over the West Wind. Convinced that the Americans were more afraid of war than he was, Mao pushed the world to the brink. In a sense, his estimates were not that different from Khrushchev's. The Soviet leader made similar calculations about the likelihood of war. Both gambled with the lives of millions but it was only in the latter crisis that the threat of a war was particularly acute. If the Americans invaded Iraq in July 1958, it is unlikely that Khrushchev

CHAPTER 7 TWIN CRISES

would actually have gone to war. If, on the other hand, they dropped A-bombs on China (and there was, indeed, a distinct possibility of this!), he very well could have. In the first case, he would have suffered a certain loss of prestige – in the second case, he would have lost all credibility as an ally. Of course, the big question that can never be answered is this: If it came to it, would Eisenhower and Khrushchev go to war? Neither wanted to think of this horrible possibility just yet. Mao's timely move to back out of the mess of his own making allowed all the majors to escape with their feathers generally intact.

Mao saw himself as the clear winner of the hot summer of 1958. For one thing, he brought the Americans to the negotiating table. "If you don't shoot," he said at the height of the crisis, "they won't talk. You have to tighten this noose a bit. When it starts hurting, they will say: OK, OK, we'll come talk!"[99] The resumption of the Sino-American ambassadorial talks did not result in any breakthroughs, but these talks were symbolically important because they put the Americans and the Chinese on an equal plane. The dialogue with the United States was less about the results and more about the process. Mao continued to think that the only way to extract real recognition from the United States was to make a great leap to industrial prowess. The steel fever of 1958 made him think he was well on his way to meeting this challenge. In the meantime, he could keep the Americans in a "noose" off the Chinese coast while wearing them down in the talks in Warsaw. Almost as importantly, he wanted to keep the Soviets out of the whole process. Khrushchev's idea to call a summit on the question of the Taiwan (bringing himself, Eisenhower, Mao, and a few non-aligned leaders) fell on deaf ears in Beijing.[100] The last thing that Mao wanted was Soviet mediation.

The crisis also allowed Mao to project China's global leadership. It was for this reason that he quite explicitly tied the shelling of the islands to the fortuitously timed coup in Iraq. It was for this reason, too, that, at the height of the crisis – even before he explained himself to his Soviet ally – Mao reached out to audiences in the third world, people like Murilo Marrequin and Maria Graca Dutra, Brazilian journalists who saw Mao on September 2. Marrequin left a remarkable account of that meeting. Here, we have Mao, with the world map unfolded before him, pontificating on the combined might of China and Brazil, and how they surrounded America from two sides, and how "we are not afraid of them [though] they always wanted to strangle us, from our very childhood." And, then, the most significant admission of all: "There are still people who say that they, the 'Western world,' are more advanced, that they are superior, and that we are the ones who are more backward and inferior ... I stress once again that from the point of view of strategy, we must look down on them."[101] "We" here referred to the countries of Asia, Africa, and Latin America, where China was the natural leader, or so Mao thought. As for "they," here Mao was clearly referring to the United States but it is perhaps not altogether surprising that just weeks earlier he used those very same terms to decry the arrogance of his Soviet allies.

Khrushchev's performance in the twin crises was something of a mixed bag. The coup in Iraq heralded the death of the Eisenhower doctrine, and the de facto crash of the Baghdad Pact. Khrushchev claimed credit for these gifts of the gods. He was reassured by the fact that Qasim's second-in-command and Nasser's key asset in Iraq, 'Abd al-Salam 'Arif, lost out in the power struggle that ensued after the coup. With Iraq presently leaning to Moscow, relations between Cairo and Baghdad went into a tailspin. Meanwhile, Nasser unleashed a crackdown on the Communists in Syria and Egypt, warning against the international Communist conspiracy. The American policy makers, encouraged by this rather welcome, if unanticipated development, moved swiftly to mend fences with the man whom they just months earlier compared to Hitler. The new enthusiasm for Nasser showed in Washington's willingness to supply him with surplus wheat on credit, to the tune of $153 million, during Ike's last two years in office. The ultimate sell-out, Khrushchev thought: "the UAR wants to play the anti-Communist fiddle for the Western powers. The West likes these melodies, and pays for them."[102]

Matters came to head in March 1959 when, with Washington's tacit encouragement, Nasser helped launched a coup attempt in the Iraqi city of Mosul. The effort was crushed by pro-government paramilitaries, leaving the Egyptian to lick his wounds and seek comfort in the exercise of anti-Communist vitriol. Khrushchev paid back in the same coin, publicly lashing out against Nasser's efforts to stymie revolution in Iraq and elsewhere. These efforts, he said in a widely reported statement, "are doomed to failure," adding that the Soviet sympathies were now with Baghdad, not Cairo. With sympathies came weapons, experts, and economic aid. Khrushchev was already beginning to draw rosy pictures of a "paradise" that could be built in Iraq with Moscow's help. "We would like for the Iraqi Republic, in a short time, to shine like a diamond among Arab countries," he told Iraqi visitors at the end of February, urging them to travel to the Soviet Central Asia to see what good life was all about. As for Nasser, well, "we'll live and see," Khrushchev said, "who will be the leader of the Arab peoples, and whether they will even need one person as a leader. It's unwise

CHAPTER 7 TWIN CRISES

to claim leadership and guide oneself by personal ambition."[103] Here was a piece of disingenuous advice from the Soviet first secretary, who was not particularly well known for modesty or lack of ambition.

In the end, Khrushchev's dreams of a Communist paradise in the Iraqi desert were left unfulfilled. Qasim was not a Communist and had no intention of becoming a Soviet puppet. Khrushchev soon mended fences with Nasser, recognizing him for a better long-term partner and placating his difficult friend with weapons and economic aid. Meanwhile, Moscow's involvement in the Middle East acquired a momentum of its own, bringing with it more commitments to more clients, more concerns about prestige, and the ever-present fear of losing credibility.

The other crisis, off the Chinese coast, proved equally problematic. Here, Khrushchev was in effect forced to make a commitment to defend an unpredictable ally in a nuclear war with the United States. It was not a commitment that came lightly. When he played with fire – as he did at Suez, with Syria, and later with Iraq, threatening to rain atomic destruction on foe near and far – Khrushchev felt that he was making a calculated gamble. He thought he could pull back from the brink, as long as he made the key decisions. Mao's hijacking of this decision-making power came as a rude awakening. Khrushchev's faith in an ally was fatally undermined: never again did he repeat his assurances of nuclear protection that he extended to Mao on the spur of the moment in September 1958. Instead, in 1959, Khrushchev cancelled the agreement to supply China with a prototype nuclear bomb. This repentance came a bit too late to be helpful in restraining Mao's nuclear ambitions but just in time to make the Chinese think that, just as the chairman claimed in his stormy meetings with the Soviet ambassador, Moscow wanted to keep the Chinese under quasi-imperial control. The Sino-Soviet alliance survived the tribulations of the summer of 1958 – but not for long. Instead, the twin crises revealed that in some respects Beijing and Moscow were rivals: in the socialist camp, in the third world, and in their separate but closely related quests for America's recognition.

8

KILLING FLIES

There was something remarkably reckless about Mao's decision to open fire on the Jinmens and the Mazus. The lore has it that the Soviets, confused by the Chinese leader's seemingly inexplicable behavior, made inquiries with their people in Beijing concerning Mao's sanity.[1] Crazy is as crazy does. Khrushchev was himself not averse to "crazy" rhetoric, as he proved repeatedly since Suez. Thankfully, he did not think about acting on his threats by ordering a nuclear strike on any of the countries that lay within the range of Soviet missiles. Dismiss as he may the Chinese methodology as reckless or outright crazy, Khrushchev at the same time had to be mindful that Mao represented an alternative pillar of authority in the revolutionary world. As long as the chairman's actions, however bizarre, appeared successful, Khrushchev had to up the ante by being ever more resolute, ever tougher, ever willing to challenge American imperialism. Not that he would not have done that otherwise. But China's presence clearly added to the pressure: the Sino-Soviet struggle for leadership in the socialist bloc and the third world was well underway.

Understanding this helps make sense of one of Khrushchev's most infamous moves, one that brought the world to the brink of a nuclear conflict: the Berlin ultimatum. What happened in the Taiwan Strait did not directly inspire the Berlin Crisis – at least, not that we know of – but it would also be a fallacy to view these events as disconnected. Even when the Soviet leader pondered the fate of Germany, the Chinese were never far from his mind, and the other way around. Above and beyond the issues of Germany and China loomed the larger question: Where did the Soviet Union fit in the global order? Did it accept this order, or seek its overthrow? And what sort of a relationship with the United States satisfied the Soviet quest for recognition? China, Germany – all these were variables in an equation that Khrushchev was trying to solve in his mind, and in 1958–59 it seemed as if he was getting there, that he could work with Eisenhower to unwind the Cold War.

In a related development, the Sino-Soviet alliance began to fracture. The "black clouds" that seemingly dispersed in 1958 returned to the

CHAPTER 8 KILLING FLIES

uncertain skies, and this time neither Mao nor Khrushchev felt they could
or even would want to clear the atmosphere.

THE BERLIN ULTIMATUM

After brutally squashing unrest with the help of Soviet tanks in June 1953,
East Germany proceeded on its glorious march to Communism. In practice,
this meant that more and more East Germans bid *auf Wiedersehen* to their
Marxist homeland. The introduction of the passport system in December
1957 made escape more difficult, though not in Berlin, where parting with
the wonders of socialism was still as easy as walking across the street or taking
the U-bahn or S-bahn across town. And many did. In 1957 alone some
250,000 people left for West Germany, many of them highly qualified workers. In a letter he sent Khrushchev in May 1958, a tearful Ulbricht lamented
the continued discrepancies in the quality of life between East Germany and
its prosperous Western cousin, and pleaded for at least 2 billion rubles in aid
to help make the country "a shop-window of socialism vis-à-vis the West."[2]

Historians have pointed to the staggering deficiencies of the East
German regime to explain why the status quo was simply unacceptable to
Khrushchev. The big hole of Berlin had to be plugged or else people would
continue fleeing socialism, embarrassing Khrushchev and forcing the Soviet
Union to commit ever greater funds to maintaining its dysfunctional East
German ally. There is merit to the argument: Berlin was, in Khrushchev's
parlance, a rotten tooth that needed to be pulled. But the problem was
less obvious in 1958 than what it may appear to be in retrospect. Yes, the
German Democratic Republic (GDR) was not exactly competitive with West
Germany, but then it certainly was doing much better than it did just a few
years earlier, when Beria, Malenkov, and Molotov considered giving up on
German socialism altogether. Khrushchev was optimistic that things would
change for better – not just in East Germany but across the socialist camp.
Had he not just pledged to overtake the United States in meat, milk, and
butter, and were the Chinese not leapfrogging their way to economic prosperity? There were problems, of course, but they looked manageable.

The issue was broader than economic problems alone. Nearly a decade
since the creation of East Germany as a separate state, it remained largely
unrecognized internationally: an illegitimate, ugly twin of the real Germany
in the West. Even its capital city, Berlin, was partially occupied by foreign
forces. East Germany was therefore not just an economic problem but
a political one as well, an ever-present reminder of the Soviet inability to
have its postwar gains recognized by the West. "We cannot forever tolerate

PART II HUBRIS

the situation that currently exists in West Berlin," Khrushchev would later explain. "This touches on our prestige ..."[3] By contrast, pushing the Allies out of West Berlin would help increase his – and the Soviet Union's prestige – and thus not just bring economic but, more importantly, political benefits. In the final analysis, resolving the Berlin problem would undermine NATO. As Khrushchev confided to Ulbricht, "if we claw the peace treaty out of them, we will have torn NATO asunder, because the German question cements NATO."[4]

Indeed, he fantasized that West Germany, under Chancellor Konrad Adenauer or his successor, would leave NATO and choose instead to develop closer relations with the USSR because, in Khrushchev's estimate, West Germany and the USSR were not economic competitors, whereas West Germany and other Western powers – the United States, Great Britain, France, and Italy – were. The West Germans needed Soviet resources, and the Soviet Union needed West Germany's manufactured goods. "Capitalism of the FRG [Federal Republic of Germany] is attracted to us," he claimed. "The West understands this and reasonably believes that if the German question is resolved in the way that the Soviet Union has decided, NATO will lose its significance, and the people [of West Germany] will lose faith in it."[5] In other words, Ulbricht's economic difficulties were an issue but there is little doubt that Khrushchev set his sights higher than helping his difficult client. At stake were the future of West Germany, NATO, and the European order itself.

Khrushchev was convinced that he could pull off this gamble. He had nuclear-tipped missiles! If these could be used to dissuade Great Britain and France from fighting Egypt or the United States from attacking China, then, surely, they would also suffice to force concessions on the German question. The situation fundamentally changed from just five years prior, Khrushchev told the Polish leader Władysław Gomułka on November 10, 1958. "Then, we did not have the hydrogen bomb; now, the balance of forces is different. Then, we could not reach the USA. The USA built its policies upon the bases surrounding us. Today, America has moved closer to us – our missiles can hit them directly."[6] Since the Americans had no other choice but to peacefully coexist with the USSR – for the alternative would be war – then, the logic went, why not force them to sign a peace treaty with East Germany, end their military presence in Berlin, and so dispel all that impotence and humiliation that continued to spoil the Soviet game in Germany.

On the very day that he explained his concerns to Gomułka, Khrushchev made his move. In a rally speech he announced that the Soviet Union

CHAPTER 8 KILLING FLIES

intended to unilaterally end the Allies' rights in Berlin by scrapping the Potsdam Agreement. The three powers (the United States, Britain, and France) would then have to negotiate directly with East Germany if they were concerned about their position in Berlin, and if they decided to resort to force to maintain their rights, well, then "we shall sacredly honor our obligations as an ally of the German Democratic Republic."[7]

On November 27, Khrushchev framed his ideas in a note to the Allied powers. They had exactly six months to come to terms with the East Germans, and if they did not, the Soviet Union would sign a separate peace treaty with the GDR, giving Walter Ulbricht the right to decide the fate of the Western presence in Berlin. Ulbricht's inclinations in this respect being rather well known, there seemed little doubt that Khrushchev set the fuse for a standoff leading to a shoot-out leading to a suicidal nuclear war. The unfortunate sequence of events appeared so clear that there was no room for a compromise: either one or the other side would have to capitulate. Khrushchev was confident that the West would be the first to blink. The Americans had not gone to war to undo the Iraqi Revolution. Nor did they do much about Mao's bombardment of the Jinmens and the Mazus. Surely, they would not be so crazy as to go to war for the sake of Berlin?

KHRUSHCHEV SEEKS GLORY

The shock of the Berlin ultimatum rattled the West. The Kremlin yes-men praised the leader's strategic genius. He did better than his predecessors, even Stalin. He had the guts. He would wrestle West Berlin from the United States. How could the Americans risk a war that would kill hundreds of millions over an outpost deep in the Soviet-controlled territory that was anyway impossible to defend? But for all of that, Khrushchev had his doubts. What if they did? Could there be a war over Berlin?

He decided to send his confidante Mikoyan to see what the Americans were really thinking. The Armenian was not happy: "You started it, you go yourself." "No, I can't. I am the first person in the state," Khrushchev said.[8] In January 1959 Mikoyan went to America "on holiday" but, in reality, in Ambassador Llewellyn Thompson's words, "to take our temperature on the Berlin question."[9] Mikoyan had previously opposed Khrushchev's gamble, the only one to do so in the otherwise sycophantic Presidium. Now he defended the first secretary's actions before the vilified personification of American imperialism, John Foster Dulles. Dulles, who was dying of cancer, played it tough: the Soviet leadership should be left in no doubt, he said, that America would resist Khrushchev's plans for Berlin.

PART II HUBRIS

Mikoyan backpedaled the ultimatum. It was not so much an ultimatum, he said, but rather an invitation to hold negotiations.[10] He told President Eisenhower on January 17 that what Khrushchev really wanted was to "end the Cold War."[11]

Khrushchev was satisfied with Mikoyan's probe and concluded that the result was "in our favor."[12] The Soviet Foreign Ministry prepared a report on Mikoyan's trip, painstakingly emphasizing that it was the Americans who raised Germany in conversations with Mikoyan, held on their own (rather than the Soviet) initiative. The idea here was to avoid the impression that Mikoyan hurried to Washington to talk peace because the Soviets were afraid of war, or that they were keen to negotiate with the West to find a solution to what was becoming to look like a serious miscalculation.[13]

Without seeming too eager, Khrushchev nevertheless seized every opportunity to keep the discussions going. In February he hosted the British prime minister.[14] Harold Macmillan braved the Russian winter with Eisenhower's reluctant acquiescence. Macmillan sought the laurels of a peacemaker. "My only wish … is to do good for the world," he told Mikoyan during one of their private exchanges. (The Soviet note-taker registered "passion" in Macmillan's voice). "I believe in this … as firmly as I believe in God himself."[15]

The talks got off to a good start: Khrushchev lifted the ultimatum. It could be May 27 or June 27 or August 27 "or the West could name a date." It was the principle that mattered. The situation in Berlin was abnormal. The Soviet Union would sign a treaty with the GDR and transfer access rights to Ulbricht.[16] Unfortunately, what began like a promising discussion ran aground when Khrushchev reneged on his earlier promise to accompany Macmillan around the country, saying he had a bad toothache. The British thought that the affront had something to do with the way the prime minister defended the Persian shah and Konrad Adenauer against Khrushchev's verbal barrage.[17]

In fact, the change of atmosphere had a far simpler explanation. Khrushchev became upset when, while he was talking, Macmillan (oh, horror!) started conversing with his foreign secretary, Selwyn Lloyd. Khrushchev took this as a deliberate insult and even considered walking out of the meeting.[18] The prime minister concluded that the Russians were "like children. They like to have the last word in an argument, and they have fits of sulking."[19] Fortunately, he did not say as much to Khrushchev's face. One can only imagine his rage at being thought of as a petulant child.

Khrushchev wanted meetings, summits, negotiations, where he would have his chance to shine as an adult among adults, to impress the world, his

234

CHAPTER 8 KILLING FLIES

allies, the public back at home, and, of course, his Presidium colleagues, to hear them praise the wisdom and foresight of "dear Nikita Sergeyevich."

Macmillan's trip to Moscow ticked some of the boxes. Khrushchev was even more pleased when former US ambassador in the USSR and Democratic Party heavyweight W. Averell Harriman paid him a visit in June. Although Khrushchev took an even harder line with Harriman than he did with Macmillan, promising a rain of nuclear destruction on West Germany, Europe, and the United States, and threatening to kick the Americans out of West Berlin, he also went out of his way to appear genial, "smiling incessantly, proposing toasts frequently – chiefly in cognac which he drank liberally – and constantly flattering Mr. Harriman as a great capitalist."

He took Harriman to his dacha outside of Moscow. Their conversation continued well into the night, as Khrushchev, the self-proclaimed miner, competed in self-depreciation with Mikoyan "the plumber"; Khrushchev's heir-apparent Froz Kozlov, "the homeless waif"; and Andrei Gromyko, "the son of a beggar." Khrushchev joked that when he died and capitalists came to his grave, he would turn over. But if Harriman came, he would not. "We would like to deal with you because you have authority. You are a master, not a lackey."[20]

It was a telling snapshot of Khrushchev's emotional make-up. He wanted recognition – but not any kind of recognition. He was, for instance, still recognized as the leader of the socialist camp. But when one of the camp's most prominent personalities, the indefatigable Ho Chi Minh, paid a call on him just days after Harriman's departure, Khrushchev came across as cool and remote. He certainly did not entertain Uncle Ho, nor ply him with cognac. Ho may have been a revolutionary but from Khrushchev's perspective he really was just another functionary of the Communist bloc, not a "master" like Harriman.[21]

If Khrushchev's discussions with Harriman were revealing, his encounter with Vice President Richard Nixon was downright bizarre. The staunch red-baiter Nixon turned up in late July 1959, spending eleven days in the USSR. The trip offered an occasion for schmoozing with Khrushchev and his colleagues. There were exchanges on Berlin (with Khrushchev predictably putting emphasis on the need to avoid injuring anyone's (i.e. his own) "prestige," some scaremongering about the prospect of China receiving Soviet rockets if it came under US attack, complaints about American bases encircling the USSR, and, of course, Khrushchev's incessant boasting about the power and the reach of the Soviet intercontinental ballistic missiles, of which one had just overshot its target by 2,000 km and, according to the Soviet leader, nearly landed in Alaska. "Fortunately, it fell into the ocean."[22]

But the real highlight of Nixon's trip, and the reason why it will forever stay in the annals of ridiculous Cold War encounters, was his and Khrushchev's attendance at the opening of the American National Exhibition in Moscow: the infamous "kitchen debate." The Exhibition showcased the latest achievements of the US consumer culture, including the technological marvel of a modern kitchen (hence, the name). Khrushchev was dissatisfied with the kitchen, telling Nixon that it was no good that all the equipment was made of steel and aluminum rather than plastic: "better and cheaper." He dismissed Nixon's claim that the Americans took care of housewives' needs: "we respect women more than you do in capitalist countries." "You have some things," Khrushchev allowed, "but we also have some things, and better than yours ... So don't talk about diktat and ultimatums. Let's not pull a dead cat by his tail." "I like the way you talk," Nixon said.[23]

After they reviewed some of the stands, Khrushchev and Nixon were brought before television cameras. Responding to Khrushchev's comments that the Soviet Union would soon overtake the United States, Nixon said: "There are some instances where you may be ahead of us – for example, in the development of your ... of the thrust of your rockets for the investigation of the outer space. There may be some instances – for example, color television – where we are ahead of you. But in order for both of us ..." Here, Khrushchev, not letting Nixon finish, waived his hand energetically: "No, no, never!" He went on to say that the Americans were "smart people." But, he said to general laughter, "we also do not kill flies with our nostrils."[24]

Nixon, smiling unfailingly, mouthed a muffled "what?!" as the interpreter struggled to explain Khrushchev's colorful language. What the first secretary was really saying was that the Soviet Union was not given to lazy leisure. By contrast, it was steaming ahead. The "correlation of forces" had changed but it was only just the beginning. Every passing day shrank America's space for maneuver, including in Berlin.

Meanwhile, the original deadline of the Berlin ultimatum, May 27, expired with hardly a whimper (Khrushchev postponed the Armageddon, extending the deadline by six months). Since March, foreign ministers of the four powers had been talking in Geneva: it had been the West's idea to draw the Soviets into what Khrushchev complained were endless negotiations without so much as a hint of a compromise on either side. Yet in June Khrushchev told East Germany's Ulbricht that they should not be trying to "push the West to the wall" over the peace treaty. He thought it was best to postpone the issue by a year or year-and-a-half. By then the standards of

CHAPTER 8 KILLING FLIES

living in East Germany would exceed West Germany's. "This will be a bomb for them. Therefore, our position is to gain time."[25] What mattered for now was to avoid a showdown over Berlin. He wanted to continue talking to the "masters" of the West. What he wanted most, though, was a four-power summit, where, Khrushchev naively believed, he could cut the various Gordian knots, which he himself had tied, and achieve a solution on the problems of Germany, disarmament, and European security.[26]

THE SPIRIT OF CAMP DAVID

Ike knew that Khrushchev was angling for an invitation. He was not in a hurry to extend it. The idea of inviting Khrushchev to the United States when he threatened to kick the Americans out of West Berlin looked like buckling under pressure. It looked like appeasement. John Foster Dulles took time off his deathbed to warn Eisenhower that inviting Khrushchev would enhance the Soviet prestige – and who would want to do that?[27] But then, again, there was the good old "what if." What if talking to Khrushchev made him lift the ultimatum: Was it not part of Eisenhower's grave responsibility to strive to avoid a devastating war? In March 1959 the president secretly instructed the State Department to consider the possibility of Khrushchev's visit. In the end he decided that it was a risk worth taking but he wanted to tie the invitation to progress at Geneva, where foreign ministers were just then practicing fruitless posturing. The bear could be admitted to the table but only if he promised to behave.

The opportunity to dangle the carrot soon presented itself: in July Frol Kozlov came to America to open the Soviet exhibition in New York. Ike instructed Undersecretary of State Robert Murphy to pass an invitation to Khrushchev through Kozlov, strings attached. But the strings were lost on delivery: Murphy somehow bungled it up and issued an unqualified invitation.[28] Eisenhower was a bit annoyed but then, again, here was an opportunity to feel the man; to try, as he said, "to get behind each other's facial expressions" to see what the other guy was thinking.[29] When the stakes were as high as war and peace, who would not give it his best? Not Ike.

"I have to admit I did not even believe it at first," Khrushchev later recalled. "It seemed completely improbable! But the fact was that Eisenhower invited a government delegation, and I headed it. It was unexpected but gratifying."[30] He was proud, Khrushchev explained, that he finally "forced" the United States to recognize the necessity of a direct dialogue. He approached this visit with a degree of trepidation. Khrushchev was a globe-trotter. His was a familiar face in China and Eastern Europe.

237

PART II HUBRIS

He had seen the squalor and the promise of Burma and India. He had been wined and dined in London and Geneva. But America was something altogether special. It was the mightiest of them all, the bastion of imperialism. Going to the United States meant being recognized by the one country whose recognition Khrushchev craved: it meant more than the sycophantic praise of his Presidium colleagues, or the flattering murmurs of approval of Khrushchev's socialist allies, or the gratitude of the savvy political operators of the third world for all the aid and advice he so generously bestowed. It was a proof that Khrushchev had one-upped Stalin who had warned that the imperialists would strangle them after his death. Strangle? How about spread out the red carpet? For once even Mao had to admit – grudgingly, no doubt – that Khrushchev had scored a coup. "The United States is so afraid of the USSR that it had to invite Comrade Khrushchev to the United States," Mao said. "This indicates a major change in the balance of power in the world."[31]

The Soviet leader prepared for his meetings with Eisenhower as he would for an important test. He started early, dictating memoranda to his stenographer, attempting to straighten out the key questions in his mind before he put them across to Ike. It was a bit like talking to a mirror: he imagined how he would reason with the president, how Ike would reject his arguments at first but then yield to the logic of what Khrushchev was saying. Take the question of Germany. Khrushchev was a realist enough to admit (at least to himself) that the Americans would never agree to sign a peace treaty with East Germany: "this would mean capitulation for them." But was there not a way to work out a compromise where we (the Soviets) would gain nothing and you (the Americans) would lose nothing? Of course, there was: hence, the free city of West Berlin. "No one will infringe on West Berlin." "But we want you to understand correctly," Khrushchev continued, speaking to imaginary Eisenhower: "we will sign a treaty with the GDR." This could "raise the temperature" but "you, Mr. President, as a former military commander and a participant in a war, understand that war is unacceptable."[32]

There was the question of disarmament. Khrushchev spoke about American bases along the Soviet periphery. "We were thinking, why do you need these bases?" The reason was obviously to exhaust the Soviet Union economically. But – and here was an argument that the imaginary Eisenhower would surely buy – nuclear technologies changed all that. Things changed because the Soviet Union no longer needed to keep large armies; all it had to do was to stockpile missiles – not too many, just a limited number. "It used to be that we would make a plane and when it became

CHAPTER 8 KILLING FLIES

old, we replaced it. But now, if we make a missile, and it is meant to fly 2,000 [km], then it will fly its 2,000 [km] in a year or two years. The atomic charge also does not get old. It will lie and wait." Clearly, Ike would understand this and embrace step-by-step disarmament, including bases and all.[33]

What else? There was trade, "not so much for trade's sake but for the sake of equality and good will." There was China. Here, Khrushchev's imaginary Eisenhower was asked to understand that America's support for Chiang Kai-shek in Taiwan was simply unreasonable. "He is dead. Why are you, Americans, hanging on to a corpse? It just poisons the air ... Therefore, would it not be better, as they did it in the old days, to kindly say farewell and bury him as deeply as possible?"

Then, there was Iran: "the more Americans there are in Iran, the sooner the Shah's dynasty will be finished, and we need nothing [there]." There was the third world, where the key thing was to avoid intervention, for it would lead to war.[34] And so on. The line-up was clear. Khrushchev hoped that his imaginary interlocutor would see the Soviet point of view on these global issues, recognize and accommodate Soviet interests, understand that the Soviets had the means to back up their interests (missiles, missiles!), realize that further conflict could only lead to the end of civilization, and so, end the Cold War. This, argued a front-page editorial in the Communist Party mouthpiece *Pravda*, was the "ardent dream" of the entire world.[35]

The difficulty of speaking to imaginary opponents is that we unconsciously make them say what we want them to say. So it was with Khrushchev. He simply did not think what would happen if Eisenhower resisted his logic, as he was bound to. How high would the temperature be allowed to rise? For now, the Soviet leader put these worrying thoughts out of mind. Thinking long-term was not one of his stronger character traits.

Khrushchev arrived at Andrews Air Force Base just past midday on September 15. He flew nonstop from Moscow in a four-engine turboprop, TU-114. The newly built plane had not yet been properly tested but Khrushchev brushed off safety concerns. He wanted to impress the Americans with a plane so huge that when Kozlov pioneered the flight in June 1959, the hosts did not have a ramp high enough to allow him to disembark.[36] Eisenhower was at the airfield to greet him. Together they walked past the honor guard, heard American and Soviet anthems, and a twenty-one-gun salute. Khrushchev was elated: "It gave us special satisfaction to receive these honors. It was not because I was being greeted like this but because a representative of a great socialist country was being greeted like this." Yet it was not exactly a warm welcome. The curious

239

PART II HUBRIS

observers who lined the streets of Washington stared at the Soviet leader with uncharacteristic reserve and even Ike kept back his trademark broad grin. "It was a model of how to be nice without actually being rude," wrote the *New York Times*.[37]

Wherever Khrushchev went – and he spent nearly two weeks in the United States, flying coast-to-coast – he remained exceptionally sensitive to anything that smacked of disrespect. He was enraged by protests, such as one involving a woman dressed in black, who stood at a crosswalk waving a black flag and holding a sign: "Death to Khrushchev, the butcher of Hungary." It took considerable effort to convince him that the woman was not planted there personally by President Eisenhower.[38] He flared up at dinners and press conferences every time his hosts made even concealed criticism of the Soviet system. Some of that was surely theater but on one occasion, after what he took to be a particularly insolent speech by the Los Angeles mayor, Norris Poulson, Khrushchev worked himself up to such a state of fury that Foreign Minister Gromyko's wife tried to give him tranquilizers.[39] Some Americans, he told a stunned audience, wanted to "rub him in your [American] sauce" and show him the might of the United States so that he had become "a little shaky in his knees." Well, he could fly back home any minute.[40]

In the end the Soviet leader calmed down. He later held cordial talks with Eisenhower, even though he was initially very suspicious of why he was being taken to some place called Camp David. "What is Camp David?" he inquired. "Maybe it is the place where they take untrustworthy people? Some sort of a quarantine institution?"[41] He was relieved to learn that it was the president's dacha, and that to be invited there was in fact an honor, not an insult.[42] "See, we were afraid we'd be humiliated," he recalled years later with evident embarrassment.[43]

There were no breakthroughs – not on Berlin, not on disarmament, not on China, not on any of the other issues that divided Khrushchev and Ike. The real Eisenhower, unsurprisingly, proved to be a more formidable opponent than Khrushchev had imagined. Still, there was an unexpected degree of mutual rapport. Somehow, they were able to peel away layers of ideologically clad rhetoric to see each other's humanity. They shared war memories and chocolates. Khrushchev learned to say "my friend" in English. Ike practiced the Russian equivalent – "moi drug." The president took his guest for a walk in the woods, and Khrushchev pinned red stars on Eisenhower's grandchildren. Khrushchev would later recall his fondness for Ike. "He really does represent the interests of imperialist circles. But at the same time, he has many good human traits."[44]

CHAPTER 8 KILLING FLIES

It was a start. Eisenhower agreed to a four-power summit (something Khrushchev had long wanted). He also promised to visit the Soviet Union in his turn.

This was a high point in the postwar Soviet–American relationship, a brief era animated by "the spirit of Camp David." This amity was unfortunately built on rather fragile foundations. It very much depended on Khrushchev's willingness to retreat from his militancy on Berlin in return for recognition, which, he thought, he obtained precisely for being tough. Eisenhower faced a similar challenge. Inviting Khrushchev was like paying a blackmailer. He would come for more – and would make who knows what new demands. Yet, while fragile and short-lived, "the spirit of Camp David" bolstered Khrushchev's legitimacy as a statesman and a leader of a super-power. In the two years that passed since 1957, the Soviet leader had not just fought off his domestic challengers but also reclaimed leadership in the socialist camp that had been encroached by the Chinese. Now he stood shoulder-to-shoulder with Ike, and what did Mao have to show for all his boasting?

THE GREAT LEAP FORWARD

Mao was worried: the Great Leap Forward was going off the rails. Ramshackle backyard furnaces dotted the landscape: there was even one inside the Chinese leadership compound at Zhongnanhai.[45] Millions of people fanned flames or scoured the countryside in search of fuel. But the metal born of this orgy of fire and smoke was of a dismally low quality, much of it completely unusable. Most backyard furnaces stood abandoned by spring of 1959. Production targets fell far short of the initial euphoria. The promise of 30 million tons announced in August 1958 was revised down to 20 million tons in November and to 13 million in May 1959 (the actual production, including the low-quality junk, stood at 4.3 million tons on June 1).[46]

Things were hardly better in agriculture. With the workforce conscripted in the building of dams and reservoirs, the fields were left unattended. Close planting and deep plowing – Mao's infamous innovations – resulted in reduced yields. Free kitchens – the pinnacle of the Communist craze – led to colossal waste of food as peasants ate like there was no tomorrow, emptying annual supplies of grain in weeks. But the real killer was state procurement. Encouraged by fake reports of bumper crops from the localities, the center imposed impossibly onerous procurement quotas, and brutally enforced them, leaving peasants starving. By

PART II HUBRIS

early 1959 people were dying in their hundreds of thousands. China was in the grip of a massive man-made famine.

It took time before these tragic developments made a dent in the Chinese leaders' bloated egos. In October 1958 Mao still brimmed with confidence, telling socialist visitors that China's main problem was not meeting production targets but in coming up with targets that would keep up with the soaring production. "Imperialism will come to ruin, and we are moving forward," Mao proclaimed. "Perhaps someone here does not agree with me?" His words were greeted with laughter and cheers.[47] As late as March 1959 – when he certainly knew better – Deng Xiaoping insisted to a party audience that the Great Leap Forward was a "great success" and a "great victory." "It is a big shock to the entire world, including America," professed Deng, highlighting again who he thought China was out to impress. "America says that the Great Leap is definitely going to fail. But then again, even if we cut the declared production by half, it would still be great."[48] In an effort to keep the magnitude of the disaster hidden, the Chinese stopped providing the Soviet Embassy with copies of the internal news digest.[49] It was only in the summer of 1959 that officials like Zhou Enlai began to speak a little more candidly about their "difficulties," conspicuously avoiding any mention of the dreaded term "famine."

What mattered to people like Mao and Zhou was not that millions of people were dying but whether or not China could maintain its prestige. In a callous effort to keep face, China continued to export foodstuff and goods to the socialist camp and the rest of the world, including, ironically, the East Germans who pressed the Chinese to deliver on the promised numbers to help the GDR catch up with West Germany's living standards.[50] Exports of essential products like rice, grain, and edible oil increased dramatically in 1959 even as the countryside starved.[51] Already in November 1958 Zhou stated: "I would rather that we don't eat or eat less and consume less, as long as we honor contracts signed with foreigners."[52] Mao hammered the point in March: "We can't relax. We have to save on food and clothing and protect exports. We'll eat a little less and use fewer things … Old Yu does not eat meat, and he is already 83 years old. Horses and cows do not eat meat to plow the field. We have to exhibit Old Yu's spirit."[53] In the same spirit, Beijing refused foreign aid, including that offered by the Red Cross.[54] For to accept aid meant a colossal loss of face, something Mao and his lieutenants simply could not countenance.

But the Chinese leaders certainly toned down some of the boasting. In January 1959 Zhou Enlai – in Moscow for the Twenty-First Soviet Party Congress – respectfully insisted to Khrushchev to maintain the formulation

242

CHAPTER 8 KILLING FLIES

"the socialist camp *headed by the Soviet Union*" in the bloc propaganda: abandoning the term would "give the enemy a knife, and they would come after us."[55] In February the Chinese Central Committee circulated a letter asking the localities to avoid "arrogant" behavior with foreigners; Mao, who edited the instructions, personally scribbled an injunction to "learn from the Soviet Union and other fraternal parties."[56] Elaborating this point to party officials in March, Deng said: "In the last year some comrades exhibited a cold attitude towards the socialist fraternal countries and towards Afro-Asian countries: they disrespected them; they looked down on them. We just have 10.7 million tons of steel, and a lot of backyard furnaces, and we stick our tail so high."[57] In June Mao grudgingly admitted defeat, asking the seasoned planner Chen Yun to steer the Chinese economy. "The biggest victory," he proclaimed, "are these defeats."[58]

Khrushchev had mixed feelings about China's setbacks. At one level, he was of course worried about the terrible travails of the Soviet Union's most important ally. These came as Khrushchev faced mounting difficulties in delivering on his own 1957 promise to catch up and overtake the United States. Even as the propaganda machine trumpeted the achievements of the seven-year plan, launched with fanfare in January 1959, Khrushchev received reports of how there was only 52 grams of milk per person per month in Baku, and how construction workers at a metal factory in Karaganda lived in tents amid flies and rats, with little water or food, and how wheat stood abandoned in the virgin lands because of poor organization of harvest work. At one point in August 1959 an actual rebellion broke out in the city of Temir-Tau (in Kazakhstan), with workers demanding shorter workdays and higher salaries. After three days of rioting, the army was called in: sixteen rioters were killed.[59] This socialist paradise could not of course compete with China's but there were disturbing similarities.

Then, there were incessant requests for aid. A rare party-government delegation arrived in Moscow without a begging list. East Germany's Ulbricht was among the most audacious: in June 1959 he asked Khrushchev for a 700 million ruble credit and for other forms of "help," which, he emphasized the Soviets had to consider, because the issue was obviously political, not economic. Annoyed, Khrushchev told him that "we began the competition with capitalism naked and with bare feet. The people believed us not only due to the promises of sausage and beer, but also due to the teachings of Marx and Lenin."[60] Yet he also knew that it was sausage and beer that really mattered. In January 1959 Khrushchev approved the construction of a large highway in Afghanistan, waiving most of the costs; in February he promised to help India with building pharmaceutical factories, to lessen its

243

dependence on expensive Western drugs; in June the North Vietnamese asked for help in implementing their new five-year plan.

In August, a delegation from newly independent Guinea surprised Khrushchev by asking for Soviet assistance in setting up collective farms. True to form, the Soviet leader promised help, encouraging his African guests to grow more coffee, bananas, and pineapples. In the Guineans' wake came the Ghanaians who, citing Ghana's determination to "build socialism," requested Soviet help in setting up an air force base and strengthening armed forces. Khrushchev inquired who they planned on going to war with and learned that these were strictly for defense, to hold off an imperialist attack "until the Soviet Union sends its help." Khrushchev was sympathetic: "We have had and still have many white [younger] brothers, and now we'll have black brothers as well."[61]

Then, there were the Mongolian brothers. When Mongolia's leader Yumjaagiin Tsedenbal turned up in Khrushchev's office asking for aid, the latter reportedly greeted the visitor by turning out his pockets: "See, I have nothing! You can take my watch!"[62]

Even the Chinese, for all the boasting of the Great Leap, managed to score a new agreement with the USSR in February 1959, by which the Soviets undertook to build yet another seventy-eight enterprises in China.[63] These showed, Deng Xiaoping explained, that all the talk in the United States, Britain, and Japan that there were disagreements between China and the USSR was just that – empty talk. "We are now a big socialist family."[64] But it was a poor family, made only poorer by the heart-breaking devastation of the Great Leap. This was worrying.

Then, again, Mao's setbacks helped Khrushchev regain his confidence. He was no longer under such tremendous pressure to prove himself a better Marxist as he had been since Mao thundered about the advance of the East Wind. He could temporarily rest on his laurels as the indisputable leader of global Communism. Khrushchev was now increasingly willing to ridicule China – something he would have not dared before the Great Leap. In July he told of his frustration to Ho Chi Minh. "The Chinese comrades have become arrogant and made big mistakes. Their mistakes are a warning for all of us."[65] A few weeks later, while touring Poland, Khrushchev openly criticized communes organized by people "who did not know what Communism was, and how to build it." Although he did not mention China it was all too clear who he meant.[66] These comments were enough to make Mao blow hot. But there was one additional complication that turned Khrushchev's moment of supreme confidence into a major new milestone on the road to the Sino-Soviet split.

CHAPTER 8 KILLING FLIES

The problem was that in by mid-1959 Mao faced serious criticism from his domestic detractors. The most important among them was Minister of Defense Peng Dehuai, Mao's comrade-in-arms from the dark early days of the Communist revolution, and later the able commander of the Chinese forces in Korean War. Old Peng had a penchant for speaking truth to power. On July 14, 1959, disgusted with the misery in the countryside that he had personally witnessed, he wrote a private letter to Mao, in which he condemned the Great Leap.[67] Mao used this indiscretion to lash out against Peng and a few others, accusing them of plotting to seize power. The defense minister was purged and placed under house arrest.[68] "Peng Dehuai had great personal ambition," Mao later recalled, citing a cracking smoking-gun piece of evidence: "His original name was Peng Dehua [Peng gains China]!"[69] In a ferocious party speech on August 11 Mao likened Peng to his old foe Wang Ming who had schemed against him while supposedly drawing on Moscow's support. Until the end of his life Mao believed, or at least claimed, that the Soviets "colluded with defense minister Peng Dehuai to topple the regime, but did not succeed."[70] Never mind that it was not true. In Mao's view, Khrushchev's ridicule of the Great Leap dangerously dovetailed with Peng's accusations. It was a case of *waiyou neihuan* – "external worries and internal troubles" – which had historically marked critical points for Chinese rulers. Sino-Soviet relations were about to take a decisive turn for worse.

THE CLASH IN BEIJING

Khrushchev just barely returned to Moscow from his maiden American trip when he flew off again – this time, to China. Beijing was celebrating the tenth anniversary of the establishment of the People's Republic of China. The city was unrecognizable. Much of the old town was gone: its exquisiteness and charm replaced by mammoth grey façades and wind-swept concrete throughways of ugly modernity. The Soviet leader got there a little later than politeness would require. It was something of a snub, too, that he came to China right after he had toured the United States, symbolically relegating his ally to secondary importance. It did not help that in his public speeches Khrushchev boasted of his conversations with Eisenhower and harped on the theme of relaxation of international tensions.[71] Mao treated his guest with visible coldness, even disdain. "He was quite arrogant," Mao later recalled, speaking of Khrushchev, "because he had seen General Eisenhower ... and he attained the so-called 'spirit of Camp David.' And he boasted to me in Peking that he got to know the President and the two English words concerning President Eisenhower were that he was 'my friend.'"[72]

245

PART II HUBRIS

But Camp David was not the only thing that bothered Mao. An even worse problem was Khrushchev's take on China's relations with India. These were in a tailspin after the March 1959 rebellion in Tibet. The PLA brutally suppressed the unrest, but the Dalai Lama escaped to India. For Mao, the issue was bigger than Tibet alone. The rebellion showed that class struggle inevitably leads to the final showdown between the forces of revolution and reaction. "It is for this reason that I always repeat to foreigners to prepare morally for the fight, because without having this fight one cannot take power," Mao concluded in April, after crushing the rebels.[73] The Chinese bore a grudge against India for sheltering the Dalai Lama, and the situation was made worse by increasing border tensions in the Himalayas. The Chinese were spotted building strategic roads in poorly accessible areas India considered hers. On August 25 there was a skirmish at a place called Longju on the McMahon line that divides China from India. The conflict claimed its first victim, an Indian.

The Chinese blamed the Indians; the Indians, the Chinese. Nehru could not understand why the Chinese, who had not brought up border issues before, suddenly became so assertive. He wanted Beijing's official recognition of the McMahon line, which the Chinese dismissed as an imperialist imposition, even while promising not to go beyond the line. These were just technicalities. The bottom line was national prestige: neither side wanted to yield for fear of being regarded as weak. As Nehru put it, "friendship cannot exist between the weak and strong, between a country that is trying to bully and the other who accepts to be bullied." So India, he declared, would henceforth resist Chinese encroachments born of "pride and arrogance," resist their efforts "to show us our place."[74] The feeling was perfectly reciprocated by the Chinese. "In the past the imperialist countries had bullied both India and China," Marshal Chen Yi told the Indians when he and Zhou Enlai journeyed to New Delhi in what turned out to be a futile bid to settle the differences. "China today could not be bullied by the imperialists but when our Indian friends want to bully us, then we do not know what to do."[75] In time, they worked out exactly what to do: go to war, what else? Here was the beginning of a long and bitter conflict.

The flare-up in the Himalayas caught Khrushchev off-balance. He had been thinking about the big issues: Germany, disarmament, the future of Soviet–American relations. The last thing he wanted to worry about was the Chinese and the Indians shooting at each other at some obscure spot in the Himalayas that few could find on the map. Not sure who to believe, Khrushchev embraced cautious neutrality. In September the Soviet news

CHAPTER 8 KILLING FLIES

agency, TASS, issued a statement of "regret," calling on China and India to work it out amicably. The statement was printed on September 10 in the corner of page 3 in the same issue of *Pravda* that trumpeted the Soviets' "ardent dream" to end the Cold War. TASS blamed reactionary Western circles for seizing on the incident to sabotage this dream.[76] Privately, Khrushchev blamed the Chinese.

All these problems blew up in a spectacular fashion at Khrushchev's meeting with Mao Zedong and his lieutenants on October 2, 1959. The Soviet leader began by criticizing China's handling of Taiwan. Why were the Chinese keeping their Soviet comrades in the dark about their intentions? Then, too, there was the question of five US citizens held in Chinese prisons (the Americans had mentioned this at Camp David, and Khrushchev knew nothing about it). Why was he not being told about things like this? The Chinese should release their American prisoners right away. Then, finally, there was India. The Chinese were in the wrong. They should not have fought India. Tibet was their fault. The Dalai Lama's escape was their fault. The border conflict was their fault. They were undermining Nehru. Why did they not learn from the Soviet handling of border disputes? Why did they have to kill an Indian border guard?

Zhou Enlai intervened: "It follows from your reasoning that, if burglars break into your house and you beat them up, then you are guilty."[77]

Khrushchev went on with his harangue.

Why were the Chinese not listening to their "big brother"? Why were they so arrogant, rejecting Soviet objections to their mistaken policies? On and on he went in such an overbearing manner: one could think he was the party boss out to discipline a local functionary, quite literally humiliating Mao in front of the other Chinese.

Mao kept his cool, though his face registered "clear displeasure." He had long got used to the thought that he was the strategist-in-chief of the socialist camp, and here he was being told off by an upstart. Chen Yi rose to the chairman's defense, disputing Khrushchev's allegations and, in his turn, accusing him of "unprincipled accommodation."[78]

At this point, Khrushchev just lost it:

> "I just pointed to some mistakes of yours, and did not put forward principled accusations, and you have put forward a principled accusation. And if you believe us to be accommodationists, comrade Chen Yi, do not give me your hand, I will not accept it."
>
> "I won't either," Chen Yi retorted. "I must say I do not fear your wrath."
>
> "Do not spit at us from the marshal's height," raved Khrushchev. "You do not have enough spit."

247

Figure 10 Khrushchev, Mao, and Ho Chi Minh, at a dinner in Beijing, September 1959. This was Khrushchev's last, most tumultuous, visit to Beijing.
Source: Underwood & Underwood/Corbis/Getty Images.

Mao offered some conciliatory remarks – just in time, it seemed, as the meeting was not far from ending in a brawl. Shortly Khrushchev left China. He never came back.[79]

What accounts for Khrushchev's bizarre outburst? It was in part his boisterous personality: he really relished a fight, as Nixon and many others had learned. But there was clearly something else. He returned from Camp David in glory. Here he was, deciding the fate of the world with Eisenhower. It had not been but two weeks since Ike told Khrushchev he "had an opportunity to become the greatest political figure in history." He did not say that about Mao. And who was Mao, anyway, and what did he have to show for all his pomp except for the miserable failure of the Great Leap? "They wanted to show us how to build Communism," smarted Khrushchev. "Well, all they got was a stink, nothing else."[80]

Mao had a different take on things. Not only did Khrushchev resort to bullying but in doing so he joined ranks with other perceived bullies: the Americans and the Indians. Khrushchev carried messages for Eisenhower: release the imprisoned Americans! But the Chinese had had their own channels to the bedrooms of the rich: they had been talking to the Americans since 1955. Khrushchev distanced himself from the Sino-Indian quarrel.

CHAPTER 8 KILLING FLIES

This was a violation of his obligations as an ally. So, it is entirely possible to see why the Chinese would interpret Khrushchev's recent performance as not just bullying but betrayal.

CONCLUSION

On the way back from his disastrous trip to China, Khrushchev stopped off in the Far Eastern city of Vladivostok. On October 6 he made one of those rambling speeches that he was so well known for. Khrushchev boasted at length about his reception in America and his talks with Eisenhower, and offered some curt and dishonest observations about the wonderful state of friendship with China. But there was one thing he said, though, that was immediately picked up by the Chinese – and it was not taken lightly. "It is unreasonable," Khrushchev argued, "to strive for war like a rooster spoiling for a fight."[81] The turn of phrase did not directly refer to Beijing but was interpreted as such by the slight-sensitive Chinese leaders. Mao circulated the report on the speech to his comrades-in-leadership, asking that they "think it over."[82] Years later, he would still remember Khrushchev's rooster gaffe. "Well, then, we the Chinese fight like roosters," he would tell the Soviets – "and you, like hens, perhaps?"[83]

Mao was not entirely fair. If anything, in 1958–59 Khrushchev acted every bit the rooster spoiling for a fight. The biggest fight that he picked, without thinking through the consequences, was the ill-conceived idea to force the Allies out of Berlin. Coming in the wake of Mao's militant action in the Taiwan Strait, the Berlin ultimatum was in one sense Khrushchev's answer to the Chinese challenge. It was also a product of a similar calculation of the risks of war. Just as Mao felt that bombarding the Jinmens and the Mazus would not trigger an American military response (though, as we saw in the last chapter, he came dangerously close to being wrong about that), so Khrushchev figured that as the Soviet Union had overwhelming superiority in conventional forces, never mind the nuclear deterrent, the United States would simply have to accept his demands. If the gamble worked, the Soviet leader's self-esteem would soar to the sky. But he knew almost from the start that he miscalculated.

He knew that carrying out his threats would face Eisenhower with a choice: capitulate or resort to military measures to maintain access to Berlin. Now, everything – experience, logic, the balance of forces, the Sputnik in the skies – suggested that Eisenhower would choose capitulation over war. But there was no absolute certainty. And, given the incalculable costs of

249

PART II HUBRIS

war, would Khrushchev be willing to run the risk? Mao did, and got away with it but now the stakes were so much higher.

So, instead of sticking to his deadline, Khrushchev sought to engage the West in a dialogue. It worked: his talks with Eisenhower proved that the American president was just as eager to avoid a suicidal war. The Soviet leader acquired the recognition and respect that he badly craved. In the end, it seemed that playing the part of a bellicose rooster could have an upside. But there could also be a downside. By putting his head in the Berlin noose Khrushchev tied the long-term fortunes of the Soviet–American detente to the resolution of this thorny issue. Further postponement could undercut Moscow's credibility. Khrushchev had to act to prove to the Americans, the Chinese, and most of all his own people that in Berlin, as elsewhere, he was not in the business of killing flies with his nostrils.

9

THE SPIRIT OF CAMP DAVID

As the dangerous 1950s yielded to the turbulent 1960s, the world was in flux. On the positive side, a nuclear apocalypse had fortunately been avoided. The scenario foreseen by the popular writer Neville Shute in his 1957 novel *On the Beach* (where the whole world gradually perished from radioactive poisoning) did not come to pass. All things considered, that was in itself an important achievement. Moreover, it briefly seemed as if the worst of the Cold War was already over. True, Khrushchev had made ultimatums: the status of West Berlin was yet undecided, contributing to jittery uncertainty. But his deadlines came and went, and nothing happened. Instead, the Soviet leader seemingly exchanged his aspirations in Berlin for the prospect of Soviet–American detente, epitomized by the spirit of Camp David. Berlin was important but the relationship between resolving this problem on his – Khrushchev's – terms and his view of himself as the leader of a mighty superpower was not straightforward. Of course, it would be great if Eisenhower capitulated and let him have Berlin but if he did not (and he did not), Khrushchev was still very keen to engage in a dialogue of equals with the American president since that, too, legitimized Soviet claims to greatness.

Indeed, lifted by the spirit of Camp David, Khrushchev was taking measures that just years earlier he would have himself dismissed as naive or stupid, such as drastically, and unilaterally, cutting the Soviet armed forces. The rationale was famously articulated in his December 8, 1959 memorandum to the Soviet Presidium. "How can a country, or a group of countries in Europe, attack us if we can literally wipe these countries off the face of the earth with our atomic and hydrogen weapons ... ?"[1] And if this was the case, there was no need for a large army. Cutting troops would free up badly needed funds for the economy and bring international recognition to the Soviet Union as a peace-loving nation. And if the West refused to reciprocate, they would just be doing themselves disservice by keeping their large armies. The Presidium rubber-stamped Khrushchev's proposals. In January he announced the cuts in public: the military would lose 1.2 million servicemen. In February, Khrushchev came up with an even better idea: scrapping all missiles and all

PART II HUBRIS

means of delivery of nuclear payloads. And, unlike some other Soviet proposals that were little more than propaganda tricks, this one was the real thing. As he explained it to his colleagues, the idea was to rule out "accidents." He went on: "Even if a madman came to power ... while he starts to sharpen his knife, the others will see that he is a madman, and tie him down."[2]

There it was, then: the world of responsible statesmen, not madmen.

But all was not well. For even as he indulged in fantasies of ending the Cold War, Khrushchev faced big unanswered questions, some of which threatened to spill over into the realm of superpower relations, poisoning the weak sprouts of detente. One very substantial question concerned anti-colonial struggles around the world. The late 1950s marked the high tide of decolonization. In 1960 alone, seventeen new countries joined the United Nations, all but one of them African. Anticolonial struggles continued in places, notably Algeria, where the French were embroiled in a bloody, hopeless war. A revolution shook Cuba in January 1959, as Fidel Castro ousted the US-supported dictator Fulgencio Batista. It was a jolt to the Americans and sheer joy to the Soviets, making them, famously, "feel like boys again."[3] And things were beginning to look grimmer and grimmer for the Western-backed regime of Ngo Dinh Diem in South Vietnam as the North Vietnamese launched their military struggle south of the seventeenth parallel.

What did these matter to Khrushchev in his quest for international recognition? They mattered because they brought into focus the practically irresolvable contradiction between Khrushchev's two roles: as a statesman and a leader of a superpower, and as a revolutionary and the head of the international Communist movement. On the one hand, Khrushchev wanted acceptance by the West as an equal. On other hand, he also sought recognition by the third world and his allies for his opposition to the West, as a revolutionary and an anti-imperialist. Catering to multiple audiences in practice meant running afoul of all. And then there was Mao Zedong actively seeking to exploit Khrushchev's inconsistencies in order to assert his own moral leadership of the international Communist movement, which the Soviet leader was simply unwilling to give up.

All of that made for a highly volatile mix that ultimately sank the spirit of Camp David. This is the story of this chapter.

KHRUSHCHEV AND MAO EYE THE WEST

In the spring of 1960, Khrushchev and his Chinese critics were seemingly on very different trajectories. The first secretary basked in his post-Camp David glory and awed the world with his far-reaching disarmament

252

CHAPTER 9 THE SPIRIT OF CAMP DAVID

proposals. This set up a fine stage for the much-anticipated four-power summit of France, Great Britain, the Soviet Union, and the United States, scheduled to take place in Paris in May 1960. In March Khrushchev had an advance preview of the place, when General de Gaulle invited him to visit France. It was glorious. Khrushchev partied his way across the country, toured the Champs-Élysées, the Louvres, and the Versailles, and even on one particularly proletarian occasion slept in the bed of Napoleon III.[4]

He knew which button to press with the French president. Unlike "some other countries," he would say, the Soviet Union respected France's claims to greatness – not just respected but positively supported. But, Khrushchev added, "no matter how great France becomes ... our greatness would always be worthy of France's greatness." He tried to sound understanding on subjects like Algeria, Africa, and decolonization, and repeatedly told de Gaulle that he did not mind if these various countries, of which he knew nothing anyway, remained a part of the French Union, if this helped the cause of French greatness. "Our épées don't cross anywhere," Khrushchev assured his host, an image he must have borrowed from *The Three Musketeers*.[5]

Perhaps the most telling episode of Khrushchev's visit was the deal with the devil he briefly entertained before his departure for Paris. De Gaulle invited Khrushchev to visit Sahara (in Algeria) to see the oil production. It was an outrageous ploy of course, for if Khrushchev went there, he would have been seen, in effect, as endorsing France's sovereignty over Algeria, not exactly something the Algerian revolutionaries would love him for. But – the horror! – Khrushchev considered selling out Algeria if only de Gaulle could be prevailed upon to take the Soviet position on Berlin.[6] (The General could not, for all of Khrushchev's cajoling and the hypocritical praise of France's greatness.)

Nonetheless, the tour of France left Khrushchev with the feeling, in the words of his son-in-law, that he had "completely and brilliantly risen to world recognition."[7]

How could China, in the midst of the catastrophe of the Great Leap Forward, match Khrushchev's achievements?

Not long after his disastrous October 1959 trip to China, Khrushchev instructed Suslov to prepare an internal report on the state of Sino-Soviet relations. Suslov produced a scathing account of Chinese transgressions, which he read out at a party plenum in December 1959. The Chinese were given to "pomposity," "arrogance," and "empty boasting." Above all, they suffered from "leftist puerility." A lot of this was Mao's fault. Mao, propped up by a burgeoning personality cult, "believed in his own infallibility."[8] But,

PART II HUBRIS

Suslov concluded, the Chinese appeared to heed the Soviet advice in the end, and showed signs of mending their erroneous ways. He could not have been further from the mark!

Mao's response to Soviet criticism was defiance. In a world where "Eisenhower is the father, Khrushchev is the son, and we are the grandson," China was on the receiving end of abuse, Mao said.[9] Everyone was cursing China. That was fine. "The more I am attacked … the more I am content, because I know then that I am on the right road."[10]

He redoubled his efforts to build a bloc of sympathizing countries and movements. Encouraged by developments like the Cuban Revolution and the ongoing anticolonial war in Algeria, Mao was optimistic that his militancy would trump Khrushchev's peaceful coexistence. While Khrushchev courted de Gaulle, contemplating neat arrangements of the Sahara-for-Berlin type, Mao discussed the coming defeat of France with the Algerian revolutionaries – and gave them weapons: "We can give you good guns. They are not atomic bombs, but they are still very efficient."[11] Even as Khrushchev made arrangements to roll out the red carpet for Eisenhower, Mao met the Cubans to discuss revolutionary prospects for Latin America – and gave them weapons. "The Americans fear you," he told the Cuban Communist Party leader Blas Roca. "They bully the weak and fear the strong."[12]

Then came a nasty surprise in the form of the April 16 editorial in the CCP Journal *Red Flag*," called "Long Live Leninism!" The article, which Mao personally edited several times, did not attack Khrushchev directly but it was not difficult to decipher what stood behind the reference to "the modern revisionists represented by the Tito clique" who went about praising "the chieftain of U.S. imperialism Eisenhower" and even dared to think that it was possible to end the Cold War and establish lasting peace. True Marxists-Leninists knew that some wars simply had to be fought.[13] Khrushchev was stunned by the unexpected Chinese ambush.[14] "Long Live Leninism!" was a huge blow to his credibility as the leader of the socialist camp. Coming only days after his summit with de Gaulle, where, Khrushchev realized all too well, he failed to reach agreements on any of the issues that mattered, this pointed criticism from Beijing made it even more difficult for the Soviet leader to claim that he was not being duped by the hypocritical Western leaders into disarming before a formidable enemy. "The West simply does not want disarmament," Khrushchev told a visitor on April 20, after recounting all the Soviet proposals that seem to have gone unanswered. "If people don't want to disarm, you can talk for 100 years, but it would all be pointless."[15]

The four-power summit was less than a month away.

254

CHAPTER 9 THE SPIRIT OF CAMP DAVID

THE GARY POWERS INCIDENT

At 6:26 on the morning of May 1, 1960 an unmarked airplane soared into the crispy skies over Peshawar in northern Pakistan. Reaching the altitude of 60,000 feet, it crossed into the Soviet airspace over Tajikistan. The 30-year-old pilot, Francis Gary Powers, was on a mission to fly across the Soviet Union; his destination, an airbase in the Norwegian town of Bodø, was 6,096 km away. This was no ordinary expedition. The single-engine ultra-high-altitude plane, codenamed U-2 (and affectionately known as the "Dragon Lady"), was one of several in the service of the US Central Intelligence Agency. It was crammed full of equipment: films, lenses, cameras – all that was needed to take high-resolution photos of Soviet military installations. About halfway into his flight, just as neared the industrial hub of Sverdlovsk in the Ural mountains, Powers was blown out of the sky by Soviet anti-aircraft batteries. Cheating death, he climbed out from the plane as it fell apart, and deployed his parachute. Minutes later Powers landed in a field, startling the unsuspecting farmers. Among his possessions were a custom-made .22 caliber pistol, a silver dollar with a shellfish toxin pin, a stack of rubles and gold coins, and a silk banner, reading "I am an American and do not speak your language. I need food, shelter, assistance. I will not harm you. I bear no malice toward your people. If you help me, you will be rewarded."[16]

U-2s had been flying over the Soviet Union since July 1956. The Soviets protested the violations at first, but protests were nearly as humiliating as being repeatedly overflown: they showed helplessness in the face of a more technologically advanced enemy. So, Moscow took it in its stride, quietly working on anti-aircraft defense. For his part, Eisenhower hesitated to send these planes over hostile territory. He had been assured by the head of the CIA Allen Dulles that there was no chance on earth one of these would be shot down, but what if it was? He was especially concerned about the possible fallout from these flights for the seemingly improving Soviet–American relationship. There were long periods of hiatus between flights. Yet, Ike was under pressure from the intelligence community. Khrushchev was boasting of producing missiles like sausages. Sputnik gave these pronouncements an air of credibility. But where did the sausages go? U-2s were designed to answer this question, providing hard evidence to test rampant speculations that America was falling behind in the arms race. So, in the spring of 1960 Eisenhower reluctantly approved two more flights. The first, on April 9, returned successfully. The second, on May 1 – the Soviet Labor Day – was downed. The unexpected downing of the U-2 came just two weeks before the four-power summit, an opportunity, some hoped, to end the Cold War.

The news was broken to Khrushchev as he stood atop the Lenin Mausoleum in the Red Square, reviewing the May Day parade. The plane was shot down, but the pilot was alive and in the care of the KGB. For the Soviet leader this was a moment of immense satisfaction. He had been humiliated again and again by the Soviet inability to do anything about these planes. Just three weeks earlier he raved at the military's failure to shoot down a U-2 flight. Now, at last, Khrushchev stood in triumph. Within days he had it all: the wreckage of the plane, rolls of film showing secret Soviet installations, the rubles and the toxic pin, and, most importantly, the pilot's confession. But at first Khrushchev did not reveal his cards: on purpose, it turned out. He hoped the Americans would "get completely bogged down in lies" – then, he would show the pilot and claim moral victory.[17] He certainly was delighted in a malicious kind of way when Washington took the bait and issued a ridiculous cover story about a NASA weather plane that accidentally strayed into the Soviet airspace. "The Americans fell for it like a fly for sticky paper," Khrushchev smarted.[18]

Then the truth was out. But the Soviet leader misjudged Eisenhower. He hoped that the president would disclaim responsibility, blaming the whole incident on rogues in the chain of command. This is what Khrushchev would have done: Did he not do exactly that in July 1958, when he blamed Ambassador Yudin for making a joint fleet proposal to Mao Zedong? But Ike was a different kind of a man. He took the blame. On May 9 Secretary of State Christian Herter issued a statement, acknowledging that the United States had engaged in intelligence-gathering and would do so again because "it is unacceptable that the Soviet political system should be given an opportunity to make secret preparations to face the free world with the choice of abject surrender or nuclear destruction."[19] Two days later Eisenhower made a brief statement confirming that it was he who had authorized the flights.[20]

Khrushchev was livid. "Insolence! Insolence!" he raved at an impromptu meeting with the press at the hastily assembled Moscow exhibition of the downed plane. In what was almost a word-for-word repetition of Zhou Enlai's justification for fighting India (which Khrushchev had so peremptorily brushed aside), he now blamed the Americans for having "a burglar's philosophy": a burglar was caught in his house, and he was being blamed for putting a lock! He was no longer sure, Khrushchev added, that Eisenhower would be welcome in Moscow. The Russian approach was: "if you party, you party all the way; if you fight, you fight all the way!"[21] Three days later, the Soviet leader flew to Paris for the four-power summit.

256

CHAPTER 9 THE SPIRIT OF CAMP DAVID

One way of looking at Khrushchev's theatrics is to say that he was deeply outraged by the U-2 incident but that he was determined to keep the spirit of Camp David alive. He was desperate to de-escalate and was just looking for a way to save the fruits of detente without losing face. "This U-2 thing has put me in a terrible spot. You have to get me off it," he reportedly told the American ambassador days after the shooting down.[22] But Eisenhower missed the boat and instead chose to deliberately humiliate Khrushchev by claiming responsibility for these flights. The first secretary's son Sergei Khrushchev supported this interpretation. His father, he recalled, continued to believe until the very last moment that the summit could be saved. But Khrushchev was an emotional man, and he simply "boiled over" when he learned of the American response.[23]

There is virtue to this interpretation. For one thing, Khrushchev was indisputably an emotional man. But there is another, less benign, take – the one advanced by one of the Soviet leader's foreign policy aides Oleg Troyanovsky. Khrushchev, in Troyanovsky's account, realized by the spring of 1960 that he really could not count on a breakthrough at the summit, neither on Berlin nor on the question of disarmament.[24] The U-2 incident was an opportunity to blame the Americans for the failure of the spirit of Camp David that was anyhow already failing of its own accord. Ambassador Thompson shared this view in a cable to Washington. It could well be that "Khrushchev realizes ... that he cannot make progress at the Summit and ... therefore could be exploiting this incident to prepare public opinion for an eventual crisis."[25]

In retrospect, it is clear that Thompson and Troyanovsky were closer to the mark. Sergei Khrushchev overstated his father's enthusiasm for the spirit of Camp David. The elder Khrushchev explained his views at the party plenum, which convened just days after the shooting down. "If the summit is ruined, then, we think, it would not be a loss for us; it would even be profitable, because the situation now is weak for solving any questions at the meeting." He continued: "There are no losses. In fact, we achieved what we wanted. We had meetings in America, in France, in England. And what we achieved actually works, and we defended our reputation before the peoples ..."

Why were the Americans sending these planes to spy on the USSR? To this, too, Khrushchev had an answer. This was an effort, he said (revealing complete ignorance of Ike's actual motivations), to apply "moral pressure" on him while he met with Eisenhower in Paris. "[I] will be speaking with Eisenhower, and Eisenhower will think: here you, see, we are flying, and you can't do anything to us. Such pressure deserves attention." Now, though, it

PART II HUBRIS

was different. Now, if and when they met, "we can be barrel-chested: don't trespass on our farming plot. So the situation has much improved in our favor."[26] Khrushchev's trusted lieutenant, Anastas Mikoyan, echoed the sentiment: "The Soviet Union is a peace-loving country but it will never allow anyone to sit on its head. If you [the Americans] consider this a threat, then it really is a threat, although in reality it's just an elementary demand to treat us with respect."[27]

Meanwhile, Khrushchev still decided to go to Paris, not least because he relished the opportunity to "bust the Americans' faces," something, he incorrectly surmised, the French and the British would privately enjoy.[28]

Khrushchev had been wined and dined in London, Paris, and Washington. He had been given the podium to lecture the West about the Soviet might and the bright prospects of Communism. But for all that he remained an enemy of the West, one to be countered at every turn. His threats were resisted. His concessions were pocketed without anything like the reciprocity he had hoped for. So what substance was there, in the end, to the famed spirit of Camp David? Khrushchev was likely pondering these questions in the days before his departure for the four-power summit. But even before he boarded that plane on May 14 he made up his mind: he would go to Paris not to end the Cold War but to wage it.[29]

THE FIASCO

On May 15, the day after his arrival in Paris, Khrushchev met with the host, President de Gaulle, and delivered an ultimatum: Eisenhower would have to apologize for the U-2 incident and promise that there would be no further flights. If he did not, the summit was off. Anything less would mean Soviet capitulation, Khrushchev said, adding: "No one will force us to bow our head. No one will bring us to our knees!"[30]

Then, it was Macmillan's turn to get an earful of Khrushchev's angry tirades. The Soviet Union, bellowed the first secretary, was a great power that could stand up for its honor. The Soviet people would never accept such insults. The Americans suffered from a mania of greatness: "it seems that they think that they can do anything because they have plenty of dollars." And then – missiles, missiles, missiles. And bitterness. "My friend … He [Eisenhower] called me *moi drug* in Russian. And now this "friend" is sending his military planes to the Soviet Union for reconnaissance … God, rid me of friends like this, and I will rid myself of my enemies." Khrushchev's spiel reached such a feverish pitch that Macmillan told him, perhaps only half-jokingly, that "when you speak, I seem to understand Russian. You

CHAPTER 9 THE SPIRIT OF CAMP DAVID

speak with such an expression, and so clearly manifest what you have in your heart that I understand your thoughts even before what you say is translated into English."[31]

Privately, Macmillan was dismayed. He had looked forward to this summit, and he was heartbroken to see that it was on the verge of failure. De Gaulle was annoyed but resigned to the worst. The American camp was in confusion, bitterness and "considerable disarray," though, as Macmillan learned, they remained hopeful that problems would resolve themselves in the end, and that Khrushchev's outburst was "largely bluster." But as it turned out, it was just the opening shot.

On May 16 all four delegations assembled at the Palais de l'Elysée. Khrushchev was the first to speak. He spoke for forty-five minutes, his hands trembling, reading from a prepared text, pausing occasionally for water.[32] He went on about American aggression, and insults, and not standing on his knees – on and on, nearly shouting.[33] The highlight of the speech was the humiliating dis-invitation to Eisenhower: he would no longer be welcome in Moscow. Ike, his bald head turning a shade of red, "could scarcely contain himself, but he did."[34] De Gaulle "assumed a pained but patient expression."[35] Macmillan thought it was a "most unpleasant performance."[36] He wrote in his diary that the meeting "has blown up, like a volcano! It is ignominious; it is tragic; it is almost incredible."[37] But there it was. Eisenhower went so far as to promise that there would be no more flights, but he steadfastly refused to apologize. Macmillan thought that maybe he should have but, seeing Ike's anger at Khrushchev – "a real son of a bitch" – figured it was better not to mention it.[38] But it was an apology that Khrushchev demanded, and a public one at that. Humiliated, he sought to humiliate. The summit – never properly beginning – ended in tatters.

Back in Moscow, Khrushchev forwarded copies of his meetings with de Gaulle, Macmillan, and Eisenhower to Soviet allies in the socialist bloc, including the Chinese. He wanted them to know that he refused to be bullied and stood up for Soviet honor. Beijing's reaction was ostensibly quite favorable. On May 17, Deng Xiaoping told the Soviet ambassador that Khrushchev did the right thing by going to Paris, where he "exposed Eisenhower's – and the imperialists' – real faces." The trip had a "deep educational" significance. Deng likened it to Zhou Enlai's fruitless talks in India earlier that spring: they showed the true nature of American imperialism (in Khrushchev's case) and Indian reaction (in Zhou's case). Here was ground for Sino-Soviet unity on the basis of "common ideas and common aims."[39]

PART II HUBRIS

Privately, Mao Zedong was less enthusiastic. "It's hard to follow his [Khrushchev's] baton," he told to Kim Il Sung sarcastically when they met on May 21. "First he said: welcome Eisenhower. Now, he says don't welcome him. He is infatuated [with the US president]. On May 1 they shot down an American plane, and captured the pilot alive. On the second [sic] Eisenhower said that he had sent the U-2, and said that he would send more of them. This left the elder brother [Khrushchev] without ground to retreat to, and he made up his mind at last. He went to Paris not to meet but to expose."[40]

KHRUSHCHEV QUARRELS WITH CHINA AND ALBANIA

The Paris fiasco emboldened Mao Zedong.[41] It also created a unique moment of opportunity to bring Khrushchev around to endorse Chinese positions on war and peace. If the Soviet leader as much as admitted that he had been wrong, Mao's prestige as the strategist-in-chief for world Communism would soar to new highs. On May 22 he set out his hopes while speaking to his colleagues at the side of a swimming pool at his villa in Hangzhou. "There are some common points between the two parties," Mao said. "We can use this moment to pull Khrushchev over." Of course, this would not be easy. Khrushchev, Mao said, was not just "unpredictable" but also "stupid," and "does not think about his next move." "He came back from Camp David boasting so much. He did not think the Americans could change [their attitude]."

Sensing the first secretary's weakness, Mao sought to assert his own leadership in the world Communist movement. But he would not attack the Soviets directly. The idea, rather, was to "curse the locust tree while pointing to the mulberry tree," that is – to criticize "revisionism" without saying that it was Khrushchev who was the main "revisionist." Those in the know would get the message.[42]

The opportunity to go on the offensive presented itself soon enough. In early June the World Federation of Trade Unions – a Communist-dominated organization – held a conference in Beijing. The Chinese hosts used every opportunity to advertise their views to foreign delegations, and hoped to have these views included in the final conference statement. Only very few delegations, including the Indonesians, the North Koreans, and the North Vietnamese, cautiously supported criticism of "revisionism." The Soviets, represented by the high-ranking trade union functionary Viktor Grishin, lodged a protest with the Chinese, and at one point even demonstratively walked out of a conference session. The meeting ended in some disarray on June 9, the Chinese having learned that imposing their

CHAPTER 9 THE SPIRIT OF CAMP DAVID

views on the wary majority was more difficult than it might have seemed.[43] Undeterred, Mao insisted days later that "the majority of the people are our friends, or can become our friends," while the reactionaries and the opportunities were destined to lose out sooner or later because they ignored the "objective laws" of nature. "Is there any doubt about this? There is absolutely no doubt! The entire world's victories are ours."[44]

There was at least one man who positively doubted Mao's claims – Khrushchev. After hearing from trade union delegations returning through Moscow from the scandalous meeting in Beijing, he decided to retaliate. His retaliation was an example of tasteless bullying that had become a hallmark of Khrushchev's foreign policy. It came in the form of a sixty-eight-page letter from the Soviet Central Committee to Moscow's allies (except for the Chinese) that criticized China and asserted the correctness of the Soviet positions. Khrushchev then personally lashed out against China when he visited Bucharest in June to represent the Soviet Union at a Romanian party congress. He also got other delegations to condemn Chinese "factionalism." All but, unexpectedly, the Albanians, toed the line. Peng Zhen, the mayor of Beijing and the Chinese representative at the meeting, found himself under a concerted attack and in the end had to sign a joint communiqué, reflecting the Soviet views, or else take the blame for splitting the Communist movement. He signed, if grudgingly, later becoming one of the fiercest critics of Soviet "revisionism" in the Chinese leadership. Ironically, some years later Mao labelled Peng a pro-Soviet revisionist and had him purged.[45]

Meanwhile, shortly after he returned from Bucharest, Khrushchev called a party meeting where his presumed successor Frol Kozlov delivered a lengthy and complex report on Beijing's ideological transgressions. For Khrushchev, though, the issue was simpler. He was not even particularly convinced that the Chinese were as militant as their proclamations made it sound. He tried to criticize Mao's ideological conceptions – including the famous claim that "the East Wind was prevailing over the West Wind" but in doing so he only revealed that he had no real understanding of what Mao had meant. But what came through very clearly in Khrushchev's rambling remarks was the depth of his resentment of Mao's challenge to his leadership. "Mao Zedong is very difficult," he said. "When I speak to him, I look at Mao Zedong, and just see Stalin – an exact copy. The difference was that Stalin stood higher. Not taller – he was shorter [than Mao], but higher in terms of his intelligence, and he was more educated."[46] This was Khrushchev in a nutshell. Here he was, launching rockets into space, and Mao was trying to teach him how to interpret Marxist theory – what an outrage!

PART II HUBRIS

Determined to show the Chinese their place, Khrushchev ratcheted up the pressure. On July 18, 1960 the Soviets presented the Chinese with a note that they would be withdrawing some 1,400 experts from China. Given that these experts had been deeply involved in China's industrialization effort, their sudden recall was akin to economic sanctions. The sole precedent was the withdrawal of Soviet experts from Yugoslavia, when it was ostracized from the socialist camp in 1948. The Chinese picked up on the similarity but projected a demeanor of utter defiance: "We are not Yugoslavia ... If you treat us like Yugoslavia, then we will not accept it."[47] What Khrushchev had not thought of, though, was that he merely gave Mao Zedong an opportunity to blame the failures of the Great Leap Forward on Soviet sabotage.

Khrushchev subjected China's few real and potential allies to a stick-and-carrot strategy. The one to fare the worst was a little country in the corner of Southeastern Europe, Albania. China and Albania were by far the most absurd nexus of the entire Cold War. But there was logic here, at least in Khrushchev's mind.

For one thing, Albania stepped out of line in Bucharest. But that was just the tip of the iceberg. Down below the surface, Khrushchev knew, the Albanians and the Chinese were already closing ranks in challenging his policies. He learned that much from pro-Soviet players in the Albanian leadership, including one Liri Belishova who leaked the content of the Sino-Albanian discussions to Khrushchev. Albania's dictator Enver Hoxha had Belishova purged from power and expelled from the party, which hardly endeared him to Khrushchev. The Soviet leader resorted to economic pressure, refusing to provide Albania with emergency grain supplies. Hoxha accused Moscow of attempting to subvert the Albanian military.[48] By late 1960, Soviet–Albanian relations were in free fall.

Khrushchev had the Albanians over in Moscow in November 1960. The discussions did not go well. "You have no respect for me," thundered Khrushchev. "I respect you and you should also respect me," countered Hoxha. "You lose your temper. It is impossible to have a conversation with you," pressed Khrushchev. He threatened to pull the Soviet submarine base from Albania, amid growing tensions between Soviet and Albanian servicemen. "If you remove the base, you would be making a big mistake. We have fought without bread, without shoes and ...," Hoxha said but Khrushchev interrupted: "We also fought ... The submarines are ours."

HOXHA: "Yours and ours. We fight for you."
KHRUSHCHEV: "But you spit on me."

CHAPTER 9 THE SPIRIT OF CAMP DAVID

On and on it went until Khrushchev had the indiscretion to compare what he thought was Hoxha's disrespectful attitude with the way Harold Macmillan had talked to him in February 1959. Hoxha's colleagues Mehmet Shehu and Hysni Kapo jumped to the Albanian's defense: "Comrade Enver is not Macmillan, so you should take back that statement."

KHRUSHCHEV: "And where should I put it?"
MEHMET SHEHU: "Put it in your pocket."[49]

Unsurprisingly, the heated encounter ended with the Albanians storming out of the room. In the following months Khrushchev continued to squabble with Tirana over the submarine base, eventually demanding that the Albanians vacate this joint base altogether and let the Soviets run it. With Hoxha refusing to give in, Khrushchev did not just pull the plug on the base but withdrew all Soviet experts and cut off economic aid. In 1962 Albania was effectively expelled from the Warsaw Pact. Hoxha sought support in China, and got it, too. Beijing offered its only European ally an unprecedented aid program, even though millions were just then starving in a horrible famine induced by Mao's Great Leap Forward. Mao played on Hoxha's defiance in the face of Khrushchev's bullying to win friends in the socialist camp. Albania was not exactly an influential friend, but it was better than having none. Mao's bid for recognition of his leadership in the international Communist movement was producing first results.

As for Khrushchev, his hatred of the Albanian leadership assumed an almost pathological character. In August 1961 the North Vietnamese leader Ho Chi Minh – who was something of a self-styled peacemaker in the socialist camp – appealed to Khrushchev to magnanimously forgive Hoxha's transgressions. Khrushchev recounted Hoxha's many sins and announced that his tactic was like a robber's. "But," he added, "a robber must always be stronger than the one he is robbing. This is the correlation of forces in this case: a cat cannot eat a tiger." Ho Chi Minh suggested that Khrushchev would not lose out from being the first to seek reconciliation: "If the tiger forgives the cat, he will only become more glorious." Khrushchev did not buy the argument and declared that he did not want to "breathe the same air" with the people who, he said, "shit where they eat."[50]

What accounts for these outbursts? The main problem with Albania was not its strategic or economic significance to the Soviet Union. It was the fact that the Albanians posed a challenge to Khrushchev's leadership of the socialist camp. It was one thing to have to compete for leadership with the Chinese – but the Albanians? It was humiliating. Khrushchev only knew one response to humiliation: to humiliate in his turn. The Soviet–Albanian

PART II HUBRIS

spat that appeared like thunder in the clear skies in 1960 lasted for decades – a reminder of the difficulty of resolving intractable conflicts tied up in fuzzy but powerful sentiments of "respect" and "disrespect."

KHRUSHCHEV AT THE UN

Khrushchev's deepening divergences with China and the quarrel with Albania were but a sideshow to the great unravelling of the spirit of Camp David. In September 1960 – just a year after his triumphant tour of the United States, Khrushchev went back – this time, uninvited. "Khrushchev's character," recalled his foreign policy aide, "had something mischievous. Judging by some of the things he said, he got the irresistible urge to turn up as an uninvited guest at the court of the 'Prince of Darkness' [Eisenhower], and so to humiliate him."[51] The reason for the visit was the meeting of the UN General Assembly. He decided to attend this forum in person both to condemn the United States and to defend his revolutionary credentials against encroachment by the unsympathetic Chinese. This time Khrushchev took a slow boat to America, the *Baltika*. He arrived in the New York harbor on September 19 after a transatlantic voyage lasting ten days.[52]

The first secretary spent his time on the high seas pondering what he would say at the UN and dictating notes to aides. This time, as in 1959, Eisenhower was not far from his thoughts. But, unlike Khrushchev's musings a year earlier, he showed absolutely no interest in engaging the American president in the kind of earnest debate that he and Ike had had on occasion. A reflection of his post-Paris and post-Bucharest combative mood, Khrushchev resolved to "hit [Eisenhower] in the teeth." "I did not want to do it," he dictated. "But understand my situation: I had to do it because you showed your teeth."[53] This was all figurative combat, of course. He did not have any one-to-one meetings with his erstwhile friend while at the UN. For one thing, the Americans dared not give Khrushchev any more "standing" by arranging such a meeting.[54] But they need not have worried: he did not want to meet. His aim, rather, was to appeal to a wider international audience, to exchange the tainted spirit of Camp David for a new spirit of revolutionary struggle centered on the third world.

Khrushchev's thoughts returned to Africa, which he aimed to make the centerpiece of his UN performance. While he braved seasickness on the decks of the *Baltika*, the world's attention was turning to the jungles of the Congo. The new-born country – a witness, in its day, to some of the most brutal practices of imperial rule – proclaimed independence from Belgium on June 30. Days later, the Congo's richest province, Katanga, declared succession, leading to a bitter conflict between the central government in Leopoldville and the Katanga warlord Moïse Tshombe. The Belgians intervened by sending paratroopers to occupy parts of the country, including Katanga, where they had key economic interests. The Congo's prime minister, Patrice Lumumba, sought UN help in dealing with the situation. The UN secretary general, Dag Hammarskjöld, promptly moved in with troops to assert control in the abiding chaos. Lumumba protested that the UN, instead of strengthening his rule, were helping the Belgians in retaining their presence in the former colony.

The young, charismatic, and fiercely anticolonial Patrice Lumumba, like many African leaders of his day, tried to play both sides of the Cold War. He would tell the Americans that he was not a Communist, pleading for aid, and at the same time sought – and obtained – support from the Soviet bloc.[55] The Americans were wary, suspecting that Lumumba was under Communist influence, "a Castro or worse."[56] With Ghana and Guinea veering off to the left, the prospect of losing the Congo to Moscow was more than the Eisenhower Administration was willing to countenance. The president himself reportedly ordered that Lumumba be got rid of. In September a CIA chemist Sidney Gottlieb, codenamed "Joe from Paris," travelled to the Congo carrying vials of poisons and a syringe for injecting it into the prime minister's food or toothpaste.[57]

The ingenious effort proved superfluous. On September 5, Lumumba was dismissed on the orders of the Congo's president, Joseph Kasavubu. Lumumba initially refused to step down but on September 14 he was arrested by the army chief, Joseph-Désiré Mobutu, in a coup d'état that enjoyed tacit US support and covert CIA funding. Mobutu made it immediately clear whose side he stood on by ordering the Soviet and Czechoslovak specialists out of the country. Three days later Khrushchev, still in his Atlantic crossing, fumed: "They have ousted a legal government and the parliament. And this is done with the support of countries which call themselves the free world." But for all his anger, he did not feel the Soviet Union could intervene militarily to change the balance of forces on the ground. He would instead complain from afar, directing his verbal fury against the imperialists and their supposed representative, Dag Hammarskjöld, whom Khrushchev took to calling "Ham" (Russian for "boor").[58]

This anger gave birth to one of Khrushchev's most bizarre international proposals: to reform the United Nations by scrapping the general secretary and replacing the post with a troika representing the capitalist, the socialist, and the nonaligned worlds. Khrushchev brought up this idea at the UN session and on many later occasions. "The Americans," he would say, "would like to keep the UN as a branch of the State Department ... But we cannot have a situation where each General Secretary in essence does America's bidding ... Now the Americans don't want a situation of equality. On our part, we are no longer willing to accept a situation of inequality."[59] The Soviet Union, he would argue, wanted "equal rights" in managing the United Nations. "We have grown out of being children. We don't wear shorts but long trousers, and we demand for ourselves equal conditions and equal opportunities."[60] Equality, equality, equality. As so many times in the past, Khrushchev's real concern was that he was not getting the recognition he deserved. And where? At the United Nations that was supposed to represent the entire world! He would take the UN by the storm.

Khrushchev made several appearances at the UN, stunning the international audience with some of his most memorable performances. Memorable not in terms of the content: here, he predictably sought to name and shame the United States as an international aggressor and advertise his solidarity with the struggling people of Africa, especially the Congolese. Even his "declaration of war against the UN" (as the Americans privately called the troika proposal) was soon enough forgotten.[61] What was unprecedented though was the decree of boorishness, and that is saying a lot for a man of Khrushchev's character and proclivities. He shouted, slammed his fists on the table and, in one infamous instance, took off his shoe and started banging it on the desk to protest the speech of the Philippine delegate Lorenzo Sumulong who likened the Soviet control of Eastern Europe to colonialism.[62] Later, at a press conference, Khrushchev brandished his pocket knife, and wondered if he could "puncture such a sack as [the US delegate] James J. Wadsworth."[63]

The Soviet leader was evidently satisfied with his performance. It was not some sort of an emotional outburst but more of a carefully calculated ploy to "gain weight in the eyes of all the African and Asian peoples." His speech, Khrushchev said a day after his first appearance, must have greatly offended the imperialists. "But that's OK, let them get used to it." His rash methods, Khrushchev told Nasser, whom he was now again courting after a period of coolness, was a way of countering the imperialists' "bandit philosophy." "When they see that they can strangle someone ... they will definitely strangle him. But if they see that they don't have enough strength to do it, they will begin to respect him."[64]

Figure 11 Khrushchev and Soviet Foreign Minister Andrei Gromyko misbehaving at the UN, October 13, 1960. Source: PhotoQuest/Getty Images.

Whether Khrushchev managed to win respect by such unorthodox methods as shoe-banging is another question. His sycophantic colleagues, as expected, praised his performance to the sky. "It raised the USSR's authority." "It resonated around the world." "It was a colossal victory."[65] Khrushchev himself in retrospect regretted his outbursts. He recalled how much he was being ridiculed by friends and foes alike.[66] Macmillan, who, too, had quarreled with his Soviet counterpart at the UN, confided to Ike that Khrushchev "has begun to bore the so-called uncommitted countries."[67] An "astonished" Nehru politely offered that perhaps Mr. K "shouldn't have behaved that way."[68] Eisenhower commented sardonically that "he [Khrushchev] seemed to be trying to find out how many new countries he could alienate."[69] In China, Mao did not seem to care at all – neither for Khrushchev's antics nor for the UN. China, he said, was itself like the United Nations, with millions of people and fifty-four nationalities.[70]

Khrushchev set out to humiliate the Prince of Darkness but, unsurprisingly perhaps, humiliated only himself.

PART II HUBRIS

CONCLUSION

Here is the big question. Could the Cold War have ended before the shoe hit the desk? If our answer to this question is yes, then we would be likely to take issue with Eisenhower's malice or short-sightedness, or both: surely he did not have to okay something that he himself recognized as provocative and dangerous – sending U-2s into the Soviet airspace. Perhaps if Khrushchev did not feel as insulted, he would have been a better sport in Paris: he would have toned down his demands, including plans to force the Allies out of West Berlin. Khrushchev and Eisenhower would have met again in the Soviet Union in June and, embracing the spirit of Camp David, built a firm foundation for the Soviet–American relations. This would have given him the political legitimacy to stand tall in the face of Chinese criticism, without having to worry about Chinese criticism. All of this would have happened years before Richard Nixon finally made the journey in 1972. By then, America was not the same, and the Soviet Union was not the same, and Khrushchev and Eisenhower were both dead and deaf to passions and fears that divided them – but somehow, too, brought them together. So, a chance squandered, then?

The skeptics will say that this is just not the case. The form of Soviet–American relations could have changed for better, but the substance remained the same. Khrushchev believed – and there is no doubt about this – in building Communism and, given the basic incompatibility between the two social systems, their long-term coexistence was impossible. Berlin would continue to be a strain in the relationship and Khrushchev would have to do something about Berlin one way or another, because of the economic consequences of open borders. No spirit abiding at Camp David or at Khrushchev's dacha would have plugged that hole.

And then there was disarmament. Khrushchev may have even been a sincere believer in reducing arms but there were serious limitations on what both sides could plausibly commit to. Ike would have found it nearly impossible to disarm in the face of the domestic uproar over the "missile gap," while Khrushchev faced similar pressures from his military – not to mention the Chinese – even before Gary Powers fell from the skies over Sverdlovsk. And even if Khrushchev overcame these pressures and disarmed or, for instance, pulled out Soviet troops from Eastern Europe, which he considered doing on a reciprocal basis – would he not immediately send them back the moment there was another anti-Communist rebellion somewhere in the socialist bloc? And was he going to give up aiding the third world just for the sake of better relations with the United States? Khrushchev's

CHAPTER 9 THE SPIRIT OF CAMP DAVID

willingness to end the Cold War rested on the premise – and it was quite a premise – that Communism was on the winning side. Now we know it was not. It was never going to be.

The key actors of the drama of 1959–60 catered to multiple audiences. They deeply cared about issues like prestige and their relative standing in the global pecking order. Mao Zedong's words about the relationship between Eisenhower, Khrushchev, and himself were telling: Eisenhower was the father, Khrushchev was the son, and Mao was the rebellious grandson. It was jest of course – but not all of it: it revealed deeply held aspirations and his resentment at the hierarchy that was heavily stacked against China.

Khrushchev sought legitimation through recognition, something the four-power summit was supposed to deliver. And yet signs of external recognition by the greats of this world was never enough for him. Would he ever be satisfied with the prestige of the Soviet–American detente – sufficiently satisfied, that is, as to shy away from provocations like his Berlin ultimatum? Would it be enough to keep the Soviets out of the jungles of the Congo or away from Cuba's beaches? This is a difficult question, because being seen in the jungles and on the beaches – fighting against imperialism and building socialism – was another way of legitimation, and it led in the direction directly opposite to that of the first. Was the Soviet Union a satisfied superpower, seeking to preserve its position in the world, or was it the center of the world revolution, seeking to overthrow this order? How did Khrushchev decide which one it was? What roads were not taken in 1960 that would have made all the difference? We will never know for certain. What we do know is that the Soviet leader realized in the spring of 1960 that he had gone out on a limb for the sake of his "friend" Eisenhower. And he reversed course, to smirks in Beijing and sighs in Washington. The Cold War was about to heat up.

10

BERLIN

On November 9, 1960, the Soviet public learned that the United States had just had a presidential election. The short announcement was squeezed on the last page of the party daily *Pravda*, between a short article proclaiming the Soviet Union "the lighthouse of humankind" and a photo of young children feeding pigeons in Red Square. The official take was unenthusiastic. Not only were the Democrats and Republicans described as running on the same platform, but the election was supposedly rigged, with millions of people denied their right to vote.[1] Did it even matter who was at the helm in Washington? Well, it did.

Public posturing notwithstanding, the Soviets privately greeted the election of the young Massachusetts senator, John F. Kennedy, as US president with considerable optimism. True, Kennedy had taken a hawkish line on the USSR and, in his campaign, made much of the imaginary missile gap (where the United States was allegedly falling behind the Soviets in the number of missiles). But Khrushchev was willing to overlook some of that rhetoric as electoral tricks. Kennedy was certainly a better alternative to the Republicans. His relationship with Eisenhower poisoned after the failed summit in Paris, Khrushchev now described his old American "friend" as a "nonentity." Meanwhile, the Republican presidential contender, Richard Nixon, was, for Khrushchev "a very unbalanced person," "a careerist," "a time-server," and even "an empty suit" [*pustoe mesto*].[2] Kennedy, on the other hand, was as yet untested. While describing Kennedy to a Warsaw Pact audience, Khrushchev noted that "each president can have a different approach to various issues, a different perception of ongoing events. This is why we cannot put all of them in the same bag solely on the basis of the fact that they are all representatives of monopolistic capitalism." He vowed to attempt to return Soviet–American relations to where they had been under Roosevelt.[3]

In a goodwill gesture, the first secretary ordered the release of US airmen from the downed reconnaissance plane, RB-47H (the Soviets had shot down the plane on July 1, 1960), though not Gary Powers who had been

270

CHAPTER 10 BERLIN

sent to prison for ten years as a spy. (He would be exchanged in 1962.) "The American imperialists received a blow," Khrushchev boasted. They "disgraced themselves in front of the whole world, and now they will be less arrogant in their deeds."[4] Khrushchev later mentioned to Kennedy that by releasing these airmen after the election, the Soviets in effect "voted" for him, as an early release would have contributed to Nixon's standing. The Soviet leader then did something altogether unprecedented: he ordered the publication of Kennedy's entire, unedited inauguration address. Unaccustomed Soviet readers, flipping nonchalantly through the pages of the party mouthpiece, *Pravda*, would have learned, from page five of the January 22 issue, that the American president was determined "to pay any price" and "bear any burden ... to assure the survival and success of liberty."[5] Never mind: if this was what it took to win Kennedy's cooperation, Khrushchev was willing to pay the price. In his latter recollection, "when he [Kennedy] arrived in the White House, we wanted to establish contact with him and to try to reach an agreement on a sensible basis. We, too, were afraid of war, because only a fool is not afraid of war."[6]

Nothing mattered to Khrushchev quite as much as arriving at a resolution of the Berlin problem. More than two years had now passed since his first ultimatum. He never got anywhere with Eisenhower. He hoped Kennedy would be more amenable to a solution. The urgency of the problem had only increased with time as the economic fortunes of the German Democratic Republic (GDR) declined and more and more people voted with their feet. But the problem was bigger than that. Khrushchev had staked his reputation on driving the Allies out of Berlin. He had little to show for it. His credibility as a leader of a great power was on the line.

Berlin was a big headache for Khrushchev. It was not the only one. The other persistent pain was China. The nasty quarrel in Bucharest and the withdrawal of Soviet experts in the summer of 1960 brought the alliance to the brink of a rupture. In the latter half of 1960 Khrushchev pulled back from the brink, though it mattered that the Chinese, too, seemingly chose to pursue a more moderate line, humbled no doubt by the unfolding catastrophe of the Great Leap Forward. Yet tensions were simmering just below the surface.

In the meantime, Khrushchev had a new preoccupation. A revolution that brought Fidel Castro to power in January 1959 commanded a greater and greater share of his attention. Cuba was an unlikely place for a socialist revolution, so Castro's unexpected victory became both a blessing and a nagging concern: Would he survive in dangerous proximity to American power? Would he embrace the Soviet leadership or would the

Chinese win him over to their cause? The overlapping problems of Cuba, China, and Berlin befuddled Khrushchev throughout 1961 as he juggled his growing foreign commitments. The many trials of that difficult year would expose Khrushchev's deep insecurity behind the brave façade of revolutionary hubris and remind him that true statesmanship lay not so much in the pursuit of boundless greatness but in knowing where and how to stop.

THE MOSCOW CONFERENCE

No sooner had Khrushchev returned from his rabble-rousing trip to New York that he had a new and, in many ways, more challenging task: playing the host to a conference of ruling and major nonruling Communist parties in Moscow. The last such conference took place in November 1957, when Mao stole Khrushchev's thunder by proclaiming, to an astonished audience of dignitaries, that the East Wind was prevailing over the West Wind. This time around Mao did not turn up. He sent his lieutenants, including the combative general secretary Deng Xiaoping and Politburo member Peng Zhen, who had quarreled with Khrushchev in Bucharest earlier that year. Before the delegation's departure for Moscow, Deng handed the Soviet ambassador in Beijing, Stepan Chervonenko, a 143-page letter listing various Soviet transgressions against Marxism-Leninism. "Marxists do not fear debates," Deng proclaimed on delivering the letter, "or they'd have to be thrown away in the garbage bin."[7]

The Sino-Soviet talks began in Moscow on September 17 and continued for five days in a decidedly acrimonious atmosphere. The task of arm-twisting the Chinese fell to the Soviet ideologue-in-chief, Mikhail Suslov, whose growing portfolio included doctrinal debates with Beijing. The idea was to bring the two sides closer together ahead of the conference of Communist parties, so they showed a united front at the conference itself, and thus avoided giving the impression that the international Communist movement was falling apart. Instead, the discussion merely accentuated the growing gap between the USSR and its recalcitrant ally. Deng and Peng brought up a long list of grievances, ranging from Soviet softness vis-à-vis the United States, to Moscow's neutrality in the Sino-Indian border dispute, to mistreatment of China by Stalin and, later, Khrushchev. Deng complained testily about the lack of "equality" between China and the Soviet Union. Suslov defended Khrushchev as someone with "an enormous and deserved authority in our party, country, and the entire world."[8] Khrushchev, at the UN, was slamming the shoe.

CHAPTER 10 BERLIN

Talks presently continued in Moscow in a broader format: twenty-six Communist parties sent their delegations to take part in an editorial commission, tasked with working out a draft document that the big conference would then approve. The going proved difficult in view of the Chinese resistance. Deng criticized the draft for saying that wars were no longer inevitable, for advertising peaceful transition from capitalism to socialism, for trumpeting disarmament, and for opposing personality cult. (He thought, not unreasonably, that Soviet criticism of personality cult was aimed not so much at Stalin, long dead, as at Mao.) Deng was unhappy that the draft included a prohibition of "factional activities," which he justifiably concluded was directed against China. He opposed including any mention of Soviet party congresses and claimed that relations between Soviet and other Communist parties were like those between a father and his sons. Suslov accused the Chinese of duplicity and concluded that what Deng was really trying to do was to win freedom of action for China in the international Communist movement while at the same time undermining the Soviet authority.[9]

Khrushchev, now back in Moscow, received the delegates on October 22. In characteristically rambling remarks, he did not criticize the Chinese by name, but he did criticize Chinese positions on war and peace, arguing that no one could accuse him of "bending down before imperialists" but that if it took a war to reach Communism, then he would quit the Communist Party. "Of course, we cannot compete in who shouts louder," he added, hinting at Deng Xiaoping who was in attendance.[10]

Khrushchev then revealed his dilemma – indeed, the core contradiction of Soviet foreign policy: the different requirements of being a statesman and of being a revolutionary. On the one hand, imperatives of class struggle would preclude engagement with imperialist statesmen like Eisenhower, Macmillan, or de Gaulle. On the other hand, he also could not avoid this engagement. "When I meet with Eisenhower," he said (reflecting of course on the Chinese criticism of the spirit of Camp David), "if he extends his hand to me, I can't spit into his hand." Khrushchev reconciled this "duality" (as he termed it) by invoking Jesus Christ's injunction to give to Caesar what is Caesar's and to God what is God's. "So we, Communists, give one thing to the working class and the other thing to Devil but we have contacts both with Devil and with God. So, comrades, this should not be a question of disagreement."[11]

But disagreements could no longer be papered over, and the editorial commission failed to agree a document, precipitating clashes at the conference of Communist parties, which began in Moscow on November 10.

273

This was Khrushchev's big show. Here he was on home turf, not like at the UN, where he looked like something of a bear in a cage. Here he was the king and expected deference. Some 262 representatives of eighty-one Communist parties assembled in the Kremlin's majestic St. George's Hall, built for Tsar Nicholas I, to hear the first secretary deliver his opening remarks, which he did to "roaring applause" (in Suslov's recollection). Visiting delegates jumped to their feet. Only the Chinese, Suslov added, "remained seated in tense poses," while the Albanians were "in confusion."[12]

Before the official proceedings began, the Soviets circulated a 127-page letter to the Chinese, which they billed as a response to the earlier Chinese letter. It was an effort to frame the debate and have the Chinese delegates toe the line at the conference. On November 14 Deng Xiaoping made a four-hour speech, rebutting the Soviet letter and criticizing Khrushchev. But only the Albanians supported his position. Enver Hoxha accused the USSR of great-power chauvinism, and of treating Albania "unequally." He was roundly and viciously condemned by the pro-Soviet delegates.[13]

Mao and his lieutenants followed this drama from Beijing with unceasing interest, and issued detailed instructions to Deng, and to Liu Shaoqi – who had now joined him – on how to carry themselves. One such cable, from Zhou Enlai (but approved by Mao), advised Liu, Deng, and Peng that they should not sign the final conference statement unless the Chinese objections were addressed. "We insist on the equal position of each brotherly party," Zhou's cable read. "No party has the right to impose opinions on others. In this struggle, we must be prepared for worst."[14]

Yet in the end, at the last moment, the Chinese caved in to pressure. The conference adopted a declaration that by and large ignored Beijing's objections. It was a clear victory for Khrushchev. What happened? The most obvious explanation is that the Chinese delegation realized that they were badly outnumbered. It was good to have the Albanians' backing, and it was also encouraging that some Asian Communists (notably, the Vietnamese and the Indonesians) showed signs of wavering (they generally favored China's militant rhetoric), but it just was not enough to tilt the balance. Should the Chinese have dug in their heels, they would have stood accused of wrecking the international Communist movement, and that was yet a step too far.

Mao himself adopted a philosophical position. On December 3, in the presence of Ho Chi Minh and another senior Vietnamese official, Le Duan, who stopped over in Beijing on their way back to Vietnam from the Moscow meeting, Mao explained himself thus: "In the great socialist family, one must surely unite. Inevitably there are quarrels, but the result must be unity and

CHAPTER 10 BERLIN

reconciliation. First reconcile, then quarrel, and after quarrelling, reconcile again. After reconciliation, quarrel again. After quarrelling, reconcile again." He added that Sino-Soviet unity was not just in the two sides' interest, but it was also the hope of all parties, and all people, and a requirement of struggle against imperialism.[15] Uncle Ho, who spent the better part of the year mediating between Moscow and Beijing, could not have agreed more.

There was also another, a less immediately obvious reason for Mao's unexpected docility. The Great Leap Forward was going off the rails. On November 3, 1960, the Chinese Central Committee sent around a circular effectively bringing the atrocious experiment to a halt. People's communes were suspended. Private plots returned.[16] On November 28 – just two days before the Chinese delegation in Moscow affixed their signature to the conference statement – Mao circulated an unexpected self-criticism, taking (partial) responsibility for the unrealistic expectations of the Great Leap, arguing that "he shares the same fate and breathes in concert with all those comrades who are willing to correct their errors" because "he had committed errors ... and definitely needed to correct them."[17] In a conversation with Ambassador Chervonenko on December 26, Mao sounded a tame note, noting China's "lack of experience" in socialist construction. Ever the actor, Mao spared no praise for Khrushchev (who had just sent him birthday greetings). Chervonenko noted in his report that the Chinese leader was "deeply moved, and did not hold back his feelings." Mao claimed, too, that he was very old and practically already in retirement if not on the brink of death.[18]

In late November 1960, Mao corrected a congratulatory telegram that Zhou Enlai had prepared for him, which was to be sent to the South African Communist Party, and which reiterated that the East Wind was prevailing over the West Wind. Mao deleted the offending formulation, replacing it with a much more modest "The forces of world revolution have an advantage."[19]

The revolutionary wind had seemingly gone out of his sails. But it was not for long. For all his setbacks Mao continued to believe that history would prove him right, not just in China but around the world: Asia, Africa, and Latin America, where imperialism was under pressure from revolutionary forces. The struggle was only just beginning. Cuba was a case in point.

THE CUBAN REVOLUTION

It was remarkable how quickly Cuba became a central preoccupation of the Communist world. Until the turn of the 1960s the poor Latin American country – indeed its entire neighborhood – were too far away to matter for the Soviet Union, never mind China. It was moreover in the US backyard, for most intents and purposes out of the Communists' reach. There were, of course, Communist parties operating in the Western hemisphere, not least in Cuba, where the Communist Party was known as Partido Socialista Popular (PSP). There was, to be a sure, a degree of fraternal feeling for the like-minded, but little else. When Castro and his band of *barbudos* (bearded ones) triumphantly marched into Havana on January 8, 1959, the Soviets and the Chinese were as surprised as anyone else.

The Soviets were better positioned than the Chinese to help the struggling Cuban Revolution, but they were not in any great hurry. In February 1959 Mikhail Suslov held a preliminary exchange of views on where things were heading in Cuba with PSP functionary Severo Aguirre del Cristo who was in Moscow for the Twenty-First Party Congress. Aguirre advised Suslov that the Communists were secretly in touch with Castro through his brother Raúl and Ernesto "Che" Guevara. He also asked for a long-term Soviet loan and a trade agreement between Cuba and the USSR (Suslov indicated that doing this might be "very difficult").[20] Later that year, the Soviet Union did purchase 500,000 tons of Cuban sugar, raising hopes in Havana that Moscow was coming around to offer a helping hand. In April 1959, following a request from Raúl, the Soviet Presidium resolved to send two Moscow-trained Spanish military officers to Cuba. But they were careful not to overcommit. They knew too little about Castro who spent April 1959 touring the United States and even meeting American officials. Who was he? A comrade-in-arms? Or simply another strongman who would succumb to America's charm and keep the Soviets at bay?[21]

In November 1959 Suslov and Boris Ponomarev of the Central Committee received another Cuban, one of the PSP leaders, Anibal Escalante. This time, there was already a notable change in the undertone of the discussion. Escalante spoke with great urgency about the threat of a US military intervention in Cuba and asked for Soviet advice about how to deal with such a scenario (he imagined a protracted guerrilla war). Fidel, he explained, was practically a Communist – at least he constantly consulted with the PSP. Escalante even reported that Castro had criticized Yugoslavia's road to socialism (as in Mao's case ten years earlier, one's position on Yugoslavia was still deemed a sign of deference – or otherwise – to Moscow's authority).

Presumably to remind the Soviets of the high stakes involved, Escalante painted bright prospects of a coming revolutionary upheaval across Latin America, including, most immediately, in Nicaragua, the Dominican Republic, and Paraguay (where the Cubans were already "in talks" with the

CHAPTER 10 BERLIN

local Communists about launching an armed struggle). Escalante hinted at the need for weapons and told Suslov and Ponomarev that he was planning to ask the Czechoslovaks to build the Cubans a "sewing factory," which would be of a kind that could be easily converted to produce guns instead. Escalante said that Castro intended to establish diplomatic ties with the Communists world, including the USSR and China and indicated that the Cuban leaders wanted their economy completely reoriented to "break" the US stranglehold on Cuban trade.[22] The Soviet functionaries made general sympathetic noises. They were beginning to pay more attention.

The Soviets moved in decisively from early 1960. Khrushchev's indefatigable sidekick Mikoyan travelled to Havana in February bearing gifts: a readiness to purchase 1 million tons of sugar annually (later increased to 2.7 million tons), and a twelve-year $100 million credit agreement for economic development.[23] That summer a Cuban economic mission toured the Soviet bloc, coming back with a promise of construction of thirty factories.[24] Moscow also began shipping oil to Cuba from the Black Sea and, by September 1960, weapons. By then, Eisenhower had already approved a CIA-run "program" for Cuba that would soon lead, among other things, to an attempted invasion of the island.[25] In the meantime, the US effort to strangle Castro's revolution through imposition of economic sanctions, including an oil embargo (June 1960), reduction of Cuba's sugar quota (July 1960), a general trade embargo (October 1960), and the severance of US–Cuban diplomatic relations (January 1961), surely facilitated Havana's drift in the Soviet direction.

In September 1960 Khrushchev took time off his fist-swinging at the UN to pay a visit to Castro, also in New York for the annual UN General Assembly session. Castro was staying at a run-down hotel in Harlem, where he moved after a nasty row at his prebooked hotel in mid-town Manhattan. By visiting him there, amid all the squalor, Khrushchev wanted to show his solidarity not just with the Cubans but also, as he recalled, with African Americans. The stunt succeeded, and the international media were treated to a juicy spectacle of Castro embracing Khrushchev in a bear hug.[26] In their first private conversation, on September 20, Khrushchev boasted that imperialism could no longer "dictate its terms" to the socialist world, and that the USSR had both superior ideas, and, increasingly, better technology and a better economy that the West. Castro appeared impressed.[27]

The New York encounter between Khrushchev and Castro became notable for another reason. On September 26, during his vitriolic speech at the UN mainly directed at America's colonial domination of Cuba, Castro took a swipe at Admiral Arleigh Burke (Ike's chief of naval operations) for implying that if the United States attacked Cuba, the Soviet Union would dare not respond with its missiles for fear of being itself destroyed. "Let us imagine that Admiral Burke, although an Admiral, is wrong," Castro said. "If he is wrong, he is playing irresponsibly with the strongest thing in the world." At this point, Khrushchev brandished his fist, while yelling something in Russian, which was not immediately translated. It later transpired that he shouted: "he [Burke] is mistaken!"[28]

Khrushchev's ebullient promises to protect Cuba notwithstanding, the Cuban revolutionaries were deeply worried. At the end of October, a Cuban delegation, including one of the leaders of the People's Socialist Party of Cuba, Anibal Escalante, and the cigar-chomping head of the National Bank, Che Guevara, turned up in Moscow to press the Soviets for more aid: not just economic aid (purchase of Cuban sugar) but military aid (Soviet instructors). Escalante warned that the Americans were training Cuban paramilitaries in Florida and Guatemala ahead of an attempted invasion that, in Havana's estimate, would take place between November 1960 and February 1961, perhaps in the dying days of the Eisenhower presidency, when the Pentagon could supposedly act unsupervised. Escalante added that "it was clear to everybody … that Cuba has now become a dangerous hotbed where a new world war may break out."[29] It is difficult to judge what the Soviets made of these predictions. In any case, they promised the Cubans to buy more sugar.

The Cuban delegation then proceeded to China, where on November 19 they met Mao Zedong who was just then preoccupied with the disastrous meltdown of the Great Leap Forward and the ongoing standoff with the Soviets in Moscow at the protracted Communist party conference. Mao did not show any concern about his flailing fortunes. He reminded the Cubans of China's revolutionary road, seeing parallels to what he saw unfolding in Cuba. And he urged vigilance against the imperialists: "Be firm to the end," he said, "… and imperialism will find itself in greater difficulty. But waver and compromise, and imperialism will find it easier [to deal with you]." Che, for his part, professed admiration for Mao, whom, he said, he and his comrade "venerated" in their struggle.[30]

Che Guevara discovered, to his probable satisfaction, that the Chinese, regardless of their domestic difficulties, were also willing to help by buying Cuban sugar. In talks with the Cubans, Zhou Enlai offered a barter of sorts: China would buy sugar and pay for it with Chinese rice. "We could help you just by each person having one less bite of rice," he told Che in a rather callous comment, considering that millions of Chinese peasants were just then starving in the countryside. Zhou, like Mao, drew parallels between the Chinese and Cuban revolutions, and compared Chiang Kaishek to Batista. "We drove away a representative of the US imperialists; you, too, drove away another," he said. "Without the military [approach], they wouldn't have left; without the military [approach], both of us wouldn't have been able to meet each other today."[31]

It was, of course, an implied criticism of Khrushchev's idea of peaceful transition to Communism and peaceful coexistence between the East and the West. Before too long, this criticism would become much more explicit as Cuba drifted to the center of the Sino-Soviet rivalry.

THE BAY OF PIGS

Meanwhile, Khrushchev held out a hope for building a new and different relationship with the Kennedy Administration. There were serious irritants. Three days before Kennedy's inauguration, Patrice Lumumba and two of his associates were shot dead in the state of Katanga in Congo. Khrushchev was furious, blaming the deaths on UN Secretary General Dag Hammarskjöld and his assumed backers, "American imperialists," who were acting through local proxies but whose agenda – colonialism and subjugation of the third world – remained much the same as before.[32] Laos was another sore point. A tripartite civil war was raging in the country, with the two superpowers becoming increasingly involved in the supplies of weapons to the rival parties. But Khrushchev could – and did – blame both Congo and Laos on the Eisenhower Administration. Moreover, Congo was already water under the bridge, while Laos could, and did soon become, a subject of a high-powered diplomatic conference in Geneva.

In March 1961 Gromyko visited the United States and talked with Kennedy who appeared generally upbeat about the direction of Soviet–American relations. An internal Soviet assessment concluded that talks had been "friendly," and that "American government leaders were clearly trying to create the impression that there is a fresh wind blowing from Washington."[33]

The good times did not last. On April 17, 1961, much as feared and predicted by the Cubans, CIA-trained paramilitaries launched their botched Bay of Pigs invasion of the island. The forces, anti-Castro Cuban exiles, were transported by the Americans from Nicaragua and Guatemala but, crucially, the US Navy did not intervene even as the landing force encountered vicious resistance on shore. The landing was a complete disaster for the paramilitaries and a huge embarrassment for Kennedy who signed off on the hare-brained plan he inherited from the Eisenhower Administration.[34]

PART II HUBRIS

The Bay of Pigs invasion generated some of the sharpest exchanges between Kennedy who was then still feeling his ground, and his Soviet nemesis. Their relationship, which seemingly began on a promising note only months earlier, now seemed under threat. Khrushchev promised Kennedy a "chain reaction in all parts of the globe."[35] Not to be outdone, the president asked that Khrushchev not try to use Cuba as a pretext "to inflame other areas of the world."[36]

In response, the Soviet leader dictated a long missive to Kennedy on April 21. Calling the attempted invasion of Cuba a "crime which has sickened the entire world," Khrushchev raved against what he saw American duplicity and aggressive imperialism. He was struck, in particular, by Kennedy's claim that the United States had the right "to protect this [i.e. Western] hemisphere against external aggression."[37] "This is the morality of the colonialists, of robbers, who once carried out such policies," he testily dictated. "But now, in the second half of the twentieth century, one must not be guided by such robber morality of the colonialists."[38] He thought the idea that the Soviet Union could not have a base in Cuba while the United States could have bases all along the Soviet periphery was plainly unfair. "We note the following as a fact, and not as a speculation," he said, "there are unreasonable governments in countries bordering the Soviet Union by land and by sea, which have treaties with you, and you have your bases there." What would prevent Moscow, he continued, from launching an invasion of these countries *à la* the Bay of Pigs? The parallel was clearly there. "Is it fair," asked Khrushchev, harping on his favorite theme, that the United States had such a "right" whereas others did not?

In the same letter, Khrushchev assured Kennedy that he did not intend to establish bases in Cuba and anyone who believed otherwise was a "simpleton."[39] Yet, clearly the idea that he may one day change his mind was right there, between the lines: it was a matter of making things "fair" in the Soviet–American relationship; it was a matter of having a "right."

On the following day, the Soviet ambassador in Cuba, Sergei Kudryavtsev, passed a copy of Khrushchev's letter to Kennedy to the Cuban leadership. Castro heaped praise on Khrushchev for the "remarkable" document, "strong and convincing," as well as "calm and confident." "I am confident," Fidel said with his characteristic pomposity, "that this new message ... will raise the prestige of the Soviet Union by an enormous degree and will be evaluated by all peoples as a document of peace."[40] This was what Khrushchev liked to hear, concerned, then as ever, that his prestige might be seriously tarnished by the loss of the "island of freedom" to the

CHAPTER 10 BERLIN

Americans. Should that have happened, it would have vindicated Mao's militancy and Beijing's long-running opposition to peaceful coexistence.

Although the Bay of Pigs fiasco proved a moral victory for Khrushchev, it also alerted him to the possibility that the young American president, driven by God knows what motives, might do something dangerous and unpredictable. "If we judge Kennedy by his actions in relation to Cuba," he mused, "you could expect anything from him."[41] The biggest worry of all was Berlin.

A ROTTEN TOOTH

In late 1960–early 1961, the situation in the GDR went rapidly from bad to worse. The refugee flow intensified. Over 182,000 people left East Germany in 1960, many of them qualified cadres on whom Walter Ulbricht depended to build his socialist paradise.[42] Ulbricht went to Moscow in November 1960 pleading for Soviet aid. He warned Khrushchev that East Germany was simply unable to match the salaries in the Federal Republic of Germany (FRG), and even if it tried, there was nothing to spend them on. The Soviet leader sounded a sympathetic note, though he was clearly annoyed by Ulbricht's demands for 68 tons of Soviet gold: "Inconceivable!"[43] Ulbricht pressed Khrushchev on the long-promised peace treaty, which would allow East Germany to fully close its border with the FRG and plug the exodus hole in West Berlin. Khrushchev promised to deliver the treaty in 1961 because otherwise, "our prestige will have been dealt a blow." But what if the Americans refused the imposition? "They will not start a war," he reassured Ulbricht. "Of course, in signing a peace treaty, we will have to put our rockets on military alert. But, luckily, our adversaries still haven't gone crazy; they still think and their nerves still aren't bad."[44]

In late March 1961 Khrushchev hosted a meeting of the Warsaw Pact in Moscow. Ulbricht spoke, with the undertone of urgency, about the ongoing crisis in Berlin, about the "systematic poaching" of skilled workers by West Germany through what he described as a "big hole in the middle of our republic" – West Berlin.[45] But Khrushchev seemed to dither. In any case, he argued against setting a concrete date for the peace treaty. Instead of focusing on this key issue, he drifted to the discussion of Laos, Congo, and the Albanians. The latter he spent much time maligning for their "lack of respect" for the USSR, and for claiming that he, Khrushchev, did not enjoy the confidence of the Soviet people. "Just go mingle with the masses, tell this to the masses," he bawled at the Albanian minister of defense, Beqir

Balluku, "and you will die from being spat at. You will be spat at in the Soviet Union and you will drown in spit!"[46]

Khrushchev knew that Balluku had mocked his lack of resolve on the Berlin question, and that he had told Soviet generals that their commander-in-chief was dragging his feet because he was a "coward." He ascribed such insinuations to Albanian "stupidity." He argued that he needed the extra time to extract the rotten tooth, like a good dentist, by first shaking it loose. "Comrades, this patience, which we have shown, is patience of intelligence and not of cowardice," he told the assembled party leaders of the socialist camp.[47]

Ulbricht, though he heartily endorsed Khrushchev's outbursts against Albania, was himself growing rather impatient with the dental operation. When they saw each other on March 31, Ulbricht again pressed for a German peace treaty before September 17 (the date of West German elections). Again, the Soviet leader responded with deliberate vagueness, pushing the decision to November at the earliest, after the Soviet Union had held its Twenty-Second Party Congress (scheduled for October). He told Ulbricht that it was yet "too early" to develop a concrete plan for what he would do in the probable scenario that the West rejected Khrushchev's demands regarding Berlin. In the meantime, he warned Ulbricht against trying to change the existing access rules single-handedly. "It's better not to taunt the wasps," he advised. East Germany had better "prepare itself" economically by overhauling its industry. To Ulbricht's plea that the GDR was "losing a lot" through the hole of West Berlin, Khrushchev just shrugged: "Did you find out just now that you are losing there?... If you look at your losses and your achievements, the GDR is winning, and Adenauer is losing. So, don't show false modesty!" One can well imagine Ulbricht grinding his teeth at this remark.

With Ulbricht, as in the general meeting of the Warsaw Pact, the Soviet leader appeared to be kicking the can down the road. He announced that he had just agreed with Kennedy to hold a summit meeting (it would take place in Vienna in June), and that the Berlin question could wait until then.[48]

As his summit with Kennedy neared, Khrushchev continued to obsess over the Berlin problem. He had proposed that the four occupying powers reach an interim agreement to end occupation, leaving it to the two Germanies to work things out among themselves within a six-month period (which of course they would not). This, Khrushchev imagined, would allow America to save face rather than risk a showdown with the USSR. Then, after the occupying powers left, West Berlin would be left to its own devices, as a "free city" (with its independence assured by the much-disdained UN).

CHAPTER 10 BERLIN

He even allowed for the possibility that the four powers would maintain a token presence in this free city. The key issue in his mind was to force the United States to negotiate with East Germany for access to West Berlin (and thus recognize its existence). Why would they not do it, he wondered in frustration? If the Soviets needed access anywhere, they always negotiated with whoever they had to negotiate with, whether they liked them or not. Washington's failure to do the same "could only be explained by [America's] mania of greatness."[49]

Would Kennedy overcome this "mania" and buy Khrushchev's arrangement, or would he go to war, if this meant a nuclear exchange with the USSR? "I assure you, there won't be a war," the Soviet leader offered to West German Ambassador Hans Kroll when he saw him on April 24. "The British and the Americans are not such idiots as to sacrifice 400 million for the sake of 2 million [of West Berliners]. No matter how blinded they are by their hatred of Communism, they are looking after their own skin." Kroll contradicted Khrushchev and talked about very clear assurances that the Americans had given West Germany. "Put them in your pocket," smarted Khrushchev, his confidence improved by the striking feat of Yuri Gagarin's maiden space flight a fortnight earlier. "The time has passed when one could frighten [us]. And if they want war, they'll get it."[50]

A month later, in a conversation with the Indian ambassador in Moscow, K.P.S. Menon, Khrushchev echoed his conviction that there would be no war. "We think that an idiot who would start a war over this has not yet been born," he said. "They talk about prestige but can you start a war over prestige?"[51] This was quite improbable, he thought, telling the ambassador that once the "malignant tumor" – West Berlin – had been removed, Germany's division will be made "permanent," which would remove all ground for conflict in Europe.[52]

On May 26, the Presidium held an extensive discussion that went to the heart of Khrushchev's concerns with his own "prestige," with Berlin, and with questions of war and peace. The purpose of the meeting was to prepare for the Soviet leader's forthcoming meeting with Kennedy in Vienna. Khrushchev wanted his colleagues to endorse his position. He rehashed some of the same arguments that he made in the previous months in his various conversations with foreign visitors, although this time he was just slightly less convinced by his own logic. The biggest unknown was America – "the most dangerous," as he put it. This was because the United States had no firm policy, according to Khrushchev. Decisions were made by different influential actors who could bend Kennedy this way or that. "One cannot vouch for America," he reiterated.[53]

283

PART II HUBRIS

Then he made the following estimate. The chances of war over Berlin, he said, were 5%. Khrushchev was 95% sure that there would be no war. If he were a gambler in a casino, a 95% chance of winning would have made for excellent odds. But he gambled with the fate of civilization. And therein was the problem.

We do not have a full record of what the other Presidium members thought. Only Mikoyan, it seems, disagreed with Khrushchev's estimates, if only partially. The cautious Armenian predicted that the West could resort to military actions short of a nuclear strike. Foreign Minister Gromyko noted that he "almost completely" ruled out the possibility of war over Berlin. That "almost" stuck out like a big red flag. Khrushchev, though, convinced himself that he had no other choice but to steam ahead, concluding that "we must be firm if we want for our policy to be recognized, respected, and feared."[54]

THE VIENNA SUMMIT

On June 3–4, 1961 Khrushchev and Kennedy met face to face in Vienna. This meeting, brokered by the Austrians, offered opportunities for each side to feel the other out. Plump and bald Khrushchev and his wife, your kindly grandma Nina Petrovna, made for a stark contrast with the young wealthy Bostonian and glamorous Jacqueline, when the quartet appeared in public. In private, Khrushchev played the part of the wise old man instructing a youngster. He spoke about America's "mania of greatness." He asked why Washington felt that it had a right to interfere in foreign countries. He compared the US policy to Rome's distribution of indulgences (appealing to Kennedy's Catholic background perhaps?) And he talked about equal rights. "Does the United States really consider itself to be such a rich and powerful country that it will not recognize any rights on the part of other nations, that it pretends to be exceptional? We won't reconcile ourselves to such a situation!"[55]

The difficult discussions between Khrushchev and Kennedy shifted back and forth between subjects like Laos (Kennedy sought an agreement with the USSR to disengage from the civil war), to Taiwan (Khrushchev demanded that the US abandon the island and grant Mao Zedong's China diplomatic recognition), finally to Cuba (the Soviet leader warned Kennedy, belatedly, that he risked turning Castro into a Communist by pursuing hostile policies). Kennedy pleaded with Khrushchev to respect America's strategic interests, which the latter refused to do, arguing that the United States might want to "invade Crimea" if it really wanted to improve its strategic positions – "But how would the other side look at it?"[56]

Figure 12 Kennedy and Khrushchev during their famous encounter in Vienna, June 1961.
Source: Central Press/Hulton Archive/Getty Images.

Some of the discussions had a prophetic character (as, for instance, when Khrushchev predicted the shah's eventual overthrow in Iran by the dissatisfied masses). There were downright bizarre moments, as when Khrushchev and Kennedy argued which system – American or Polish – was more democratic. But perhaps the most heated and ultimately fruitless exchanges concerned the subject of divided Berlin. The Soviet leader again spelled out his rationale: sixteen years have passed since the Second World War ended; the existence of two German states was an undeniable reality; it was abnormal that there was no peace treaty with Germany. Moscow would therefore conclude its own treaty with the GDR, which would unilaterally terminate Allied rights in West Berlin. "I would like to ask you," Kennedy queried, "whether your words mean that in the case of [your] peace treaty is signed, our access to West Berlin will be barred." "You understood correctly, Mr. President," Khrushchev snapped.[57]

Kennedy rejected such pressure, citing concerns over American credibility. If the United States were pushed out of Berlin this way, who would ever take the United States seriously? "You are trying to humiliate us," countered Khrushchev. "You speak about your prestige but do take our prestige into account." Kennedy was unmoved, prompting Khrushchev's menacing comment: "Let the war happen now rather than later, when there will be even more horrible types of weapons."[58] He promised to sign a peace treaty with the GDR before the year was out. "Looks like it will be a cold winter this year," Kennedy said dejectedly. "We will not go back on our decision," Khrushchev replied.[59]

Back in April, when he lectured the president about the Bay of Pigs in their exchange of letters, Khrushchev asked the Foreign Ministry to use moderate language in order to (in his own words) "spank [Kennedy] without lowering his pants." "Let's not tear down, let's not burn bridges, ... by contrast, one should facilitate better mutual understanding, build bridges, so to speak."[60] But Khrushchev did not build bridges in Vienna even if, in all fairness, there were not that many left to burn. The encounter left him feeling on the gloomy side. "If the Western powers want us to capitulate before West Germany," he concluded not long after Vienna – "if they want to bring us down to our knees, then they can be sure that it will never happen. This will never be."[61]

Upon his return from Vienna, Khrushchev ordered full transcripts of his conversations with Kennedy to be sent to all Soviet allies, including China and Cuba (but excluding Albania: Hoxha, despised as ever, would receive only an oral briefing). Detailed information on the talks was also provided to friendly governments in the third world. As so often, Khrushchev sought recognition for the USSR – not just from the United States, as a great power, but from the non-Western world, as a great *revolutionary* power on a mission to push back against American imperialism.

THE WALL

In the days and weeks after Khrushchev's meeting with Kennedy, Ulbricht tried to press his case. He was concerned, no doubt, that the refugee flow continued unabated and, if anything, intensified. But Ulbricht may well have deliberately inflated public fears of the impending closure of access to West Berlin by claiming, at a press conference on June 15, 1961, that "no one has any intention of building a wall."[62] If, frightened by such denials, more panicky East Berliners made for the exit, perhaps Khrushchev would be forced to deal with the problem once and for all.

A few days later Ulbricht wrote to Khrushchev asking for a Warsaw Pact meeting to discuss practical steps ahead of the signing of the peace treaty. The Soviet leader agreed, setting the meeting for August 3.[63] Perhaps to

CHAPTER 10 BERLIN

cover all his bases and exert additional pressure on Khrushchev, Ulbricht also reached out to Mao Zedong, inviting him, unsuccessfully, to come to Moscow (it is not clear whether he had consulted with Khrushchev).[64] East German diplomats reporting from Beijing indicated that the Chinese were more cautious than Khrushchev and Ulbricht would have liked, and were not enthused by Khrushchev's renewal of the Berlin ultimatum during his meeting with Kennedy in Vienna.[65]

The Sino-Soviet relationship was just then going through a period of detente, following China's retreat at the Moscow Conference of Communist parties. The two sides worked well together at the Geneva Conference on Laos, which opened in May 1961. The Chinese delegation was headed by Foreign Minister Chen Yi, with whom Khrushchev famously quarreled in Beijing two years prior. In July 1961, Chen Yi stopped over in Moscow and had a long conversation with the Soviet leader on the 5th. Khrushchev went out of his way to curry favor with his visitor. He professed readiness to defer to the Chinese on the question of Laos, which, he said, the Chinese and the Vietnamese understood much better than he did. He announced that the Soviet Union would soon be resuming nuclear testing because he did not want to be considered a "pacifist." He badmouthed the Indians, claiming that they were effectively taking orders from Kennedy. He recycled Mao's militant language, calling the A-bomb a "paper tiger," and he even offered the Chinese (albeit jokingly) the position of the "elder brother" in the Sino-Soviet alliance (Chen Yi anxiously rejected any such ambition on China's part).

It was, in many ways, a remarkable performance from a man who had previously claimed that he would not so much as shake Chen Yi's hand. Khrushchev understood very well that, given that he had painted himself into a corner in Berlin, he desperately needed China's backing. The German question was indeed discussed at length. Khrushchev recounted the dire economic conditions in the GDR and rehashed his various arguments in favor of a peace treaty that he planned to sign by the end of that year. War was unlikely, he said, citing his earlier 5 percent estimate. Chen Yi did not contradict him. Khrushchev slipped into his customary boasting, declaring that if the West chose war, "we could blow up Europe in one day and in one strike. There will be nothing left of England, West Germany, and France." He added that he recognized that atomic bombs would also fall on the USSR, and that war would result on enormous losses, which was why it was important to do everything to avoid. "We'll see whose nerves are stronger," he told Chen Yi. The foreign minister conceded that he simply "could not imagine what an atomic war would look like."

Khrushchev's overall outlook remained bullish and determined. "We cannot cajole our enemies to give up anything," he told Chen Yi. "We can only take it by force." "Correct, good," nodded the Chinese marshal.[66]

This renewed militancy on Khrushchev's part impressed Mao who noted that the Soviet leader had made "a big positive turn," which made him "very happy." He was especially keen about Moscow's apparent retreat from advocacy of disarmament (Khrushchev announced in a public speech on July 8 that he would increase the Soviet military budget by about 25 percent). "How can the bourgeoisie, the imperialists throw their weapons into the sea?" he wondered, telling North Korea's Kim Il Sung – who visited with Chairman Mao at one of the latter's villas in Hangzhou in mid-July – that if the Chinese Communists ever decided to shed their army, "our heads would all be cut off." Nuclear disarmament was also a myth, he told Kim, though it was useful to talk about it for propaganda purposes. China, though poor and backward, was determined to manufacture several dozen or several hundred atomic bombs, no less. "Several dozen, to nuke Japan, would do just fine," Chen Yi – just back from Moscow – helpfully offered.[67]

Meanwhile, Khrushchev was running out of time. Communist representatives were gathering in Moscow, called by Ulbricht – and still he had no clear plan. Above all, his doubts about Kennedy continued to mount. One remark of Kennedy's that reached Khrushchev's ear made an impression. In late June Khrushchev's son-in-law and editor-in-chief of the Soviet daily *Izvestiya*, Aleksei Adzhubei, travelled to the United States. The purpose of the trip – arranged on the sidelines of the Vienna Summit – was for Adzhubei and a colleague from the Soviet Foreign Ministry, Mikhail Kharlamov, to debate with White House Press Secretary Pierre Salinger and Harrison Salisbury of the *New York Times*.[68] The taped debate on the NBC was inconsequential but Salinger also organized a secret meeting between Kennedy and the two Soviet officials. In Khrushchev's later account, Kennedy asked them: "What should I do? If I attempt what Khrushchev proposes, I will be arrested [impeached?] by senators."[69]

This remark – whether accurately reported or not – confirmed to Khrushchev what he already suspected: that Kennedy was, supposedly, a political lightweight, and his ability to compromise on as important an issue as the Berlin question was severely circumscribed. He made much of the fact that Kennedy was elected with a very small margin, barely defeating Nixon in the popular vote by just over 100,000 votes.[70] It is significant that during these tense weeks and months, the Soviet leader repeatedly compared Kennedy to late Secretary of State John Foster Dulles (who died in

May 1959). According to Khrushchev, Dulles, though a dyed-in-the-wool anti-Communist, nevertheless knew where to stop in his anti-Soviet policies, and, moreover, he could afford to stop, because no one could accuse him of being soft on Communism. Kennedy, in the meantime, "could be accused of being a coward." Kennedy was "an unknown quantity in politics; he is too lightweight for both the Democrats and Republicans."[71]

Did Khrushchev really believe his theory or was he using departed Dulles as a strawman to convince himself that if it were only Dulles who was still in charge of US foreign policy, things would be much different? For the real problem was not the relative merits of Dulles or Kennedy but the profound uncertainty borne of one's inability to know what the other would do in a given situation. Never did the old Russian proverb – that another's soul is a dark place – ring more true. This uncertainty weighed heavily on Khrushchev, confounding his plans and reducing his "5 percent" estimate to the rank of a preposterous and irresponsible conjecture.

The first secretary made a last-ditch effort to appeal to Kennedy when John McCloy, Kennedy's disarmament adviser, visited Khrushchev at the latter's dacha in Pitsunda, on the Black Sea, in late July. On this occasion, he practically pleaded with McCloy to understand his situation because, as he put it, he had already publicly declared that he would sign a peace treaty, and now he could not back out, because it would look like retreat under Western pressure. "We are not Guatemala, but the great Soviet Union," he reminded his visitor, revealing once gain his deep sense of insecurity vis-à-vis the West. McCloy, for his part, also spoke about US credibility and that "begging" Ulbricht for access to West Berlin would be simply "intolerable" for the United States.[72] There was no breakthrough.

After McCloy's departure, Khrushchev, too, headed back to Moscow. He opted for the slow route, taking a train north that took him to Kuban and onwards to Ukraine. He visited fields of corn and beetroot and spoke to kolkhoz farmers, to whom he offered unsolicited advice on how to improve the effectiveness of farming implements.[73] But his thoughts could not have wandered too far from the biggest question at hand: Berlin. On August 1, he dictated rambling remarks on the subject, making some of the points he had so frequently made on earlier occasions but also recounting a remarkable story that goes a long way to explaining his subsequent actions.

It happened in the first days of Hitler's invasion of the USSR, in late June 1941, when the Soviet forces, surprised and disorganized, retreated chaotically before the raw power of the Wehrmacht. After the Red Army suffered a calamitous defeat in the Battle of Brody, losing thousands of

PART II HUBRIS

tanks, an army corps commissar, Nikolai Vashugin, sought out Khrushchev who was then a member of the Kiev Special Military District. Khrushchev recalled Vashugin's appearance: the commissar was in shock, he looked terribly distressed. He told Khrushchev that he had given his subordinates the wrong order, contradicting instructions that he had received from his command, and that he did not want to live. "I told him," Khrushchev recalled, "You are crazy. Get a grip." But Vashugin pulled out his handgun and blew out his brains right in front of Khrushchev. "What was it?" the Soviet leader wondered. "What do you call this? Heroism?"[74]

It was odd that Khrushchev would recall a twenty-year-old episode, tragic as it was, in a dictation on Berlin. But he was trying to make a point: the Americans were like Vashugin. They had cornered themselves in Berlin, and were now threatening a suicidal nuclear war. But the parallel did not quite hold. The parallel that held was Khrushchev's own blunder. It was *he* who was Vashugin, who, having misjudged his adversary, made a bad call, and was now threatening to blow his brains out if the Americans did not accommodate his wishes.

When on August 1 Khrushchev met Ulbricht in Moscow, he had already made up his mind. Instead of planning for the impending conclusion of a peace treaty, he decided that he would solve the pressing problem – the exodus of people into West Berlin – by building a barrier in the city. He presented his ideas to Ulbricht who not just eagerly endorsed them but was clearly prepared for exactly this development. Ulbricht told Khrushchev that he had already stored barbed wire nearby and that he had a plan to move quickly to cut off West Berlin: he just needed two weeks' lead time. Khrushchev told him to go ahead, promising Soviet backing for these measures. Yet he remained vague about his earlier promise to push through a peace treaty. In any case, he failed to mention a deadline. The moment of truth was being postponed to uncertain future.

The Warsaw Pact meeting, called in Moscow on Ulbricht's request to deal with the German question, turned out to be a contentious affair but not for reasons one would have thought. The Albanians, in the spirit of their ongoing quarrel with the USSR, sent a delegation at a lower level than Khrushchev had expected (party secretaries). The Albanian delegate was duly expelled, but his case was taken up by the Chinese representative and ambassador in Moscow, Liu Xiao, who condemned the move. Khrushchev and Liu Xiao traded barbs while the other party secretaries lined up behind the Soviet leader. It was a reminder of the deepening rift between China and the USSR that had been superficially patched up at the November 1960 conference.

CHAPTER 10 BERLIN

Figure 13 A scene in Berlin after the construction of the Wall, October 1961. Source: Ron Burton/Mirrorpix/Getty Images.

One thing that the Warsaw Pact meeting failed to do was to agree on a date for concluding the supposedly imminent peace treaty. The date was not even discussed. A week after the summit ended, on August 13, the East Germans, acting with the Soviet help, erected a barbed-wire fence around West Berlin. Before too long, the fence was upgraded to a concrete wall. The hole was plugged. The world beheld a divided city, a telling symbol of the Cold War, and a reminder of Khrushchev's failures, but also of his sanity. He was no Vashugin.

CONCLUSION

On October 17–31, 1961 Khrushchev presided over the great gala of the Twenty-Second Party Congress. Thousands of delegates assembled in the Kremlin's gigantic Congress Hall, built for the occasion. The Congress would adopt the new party program that highlighted well-known Soviet positions on peaceful coexistence and peaceful transition to Communism and, infamously, proclaimed that in the Soviet Union the Communist society would be largely attained by 1980. Mao, who read a copy of the program, likened it to "the foot binding bandages of Wang's wife, not just

PART II HUBRIS

long but also stinking."[75] The Congress became notable for another reason: it was there that Khrushchev decided to take Stalin's body out of the Mausoleum in Red Square, where the dictator lay in coffin, next to Lenin, since 1953. Stalin was unobtrusively reburied near the Kremlin wall under a truck-load of concrete, presumably so that no one would attempt to steal his body.[76] It was a symbolic moment in Khrushchev's long-running struggle with Stalin's legacy and a signal to the Chinese.

Zhou Enlai, representing China, was in Moscow for the Congress, though he left early after a spat with Khrushchev occasioned by the latter's criticism of the Albanians. Khrushchev told him that China's opinion no longer "carried weight" for him.[77] "The Chinese comrades," he commented some days after Zhou's departure, "have not yet taken the road of establishing truly friendly relations ... Evidently, they are too infected by nationalism." Recycling an earlier epithet that he had used to describe Kennedy, Khrushchev claimed that "they [the Chinese] are haunted restlessly by the mania of greatness."[78]

The Berlin question unexpectedly flared up just as the Congress was drawing to a close. On October 22, an American diplomat in West Berlin, Alan Lightner, decided to test the new realities by visiting a theater in the East without showing his documents, but he was stopped by the GDR border guards, a part of a long-standing East German effort to harass Western representatives in Berlin. Before too long, the Soviets got involved and soon there were Soviet and American tanks facing off at Checkpoint Charlie (a border crossing that connected East and West Berlin). The unhappy incident was fortunately settled at the eleventh hour through back-channel diplomacy, involving the president's brother Robert Kennedy and GRU operative Georgy Bolshakov. On October 28, the two sides pulled back their tanks. The status quo in Berlin would never again be challenged by force.

The standoff at Checkpoint Charlie could have led to a shooting war in Berlin, a war in which the 11,000 allied troops would have been almost certainly annihilated by the powerful Soviet force within a striking distance of the city. And what then? Khrushchev had been mulling this question over for months and months. He knew that Kennedy was afraid. But so, too, was he. He knew that a nuclear war should not have been fought over anyone's prestige, but could he be sure that it would not be? Again and again, the image of Vashugin blowing his brains out crept into his mind. "When one person does it, it's his right," he would say. "But if, by killing himself, this person brings deaths to millions of people, this must not be allowed."[79] And so he did not. He backed off, withdrawing the end-of-the-year ultimatum he had given Kennedy that June. Never mind his

CHAPTER 10 BERLIN

"5 percent" theory, never mind the risk of being accused of cowardice by those who, like the Albanians and the Chinese, seemed unwilling to understand the consequences of a face-to-face encounter with the "paper tiger." Kennedy, too, walked back from the brink. The cold winter that he envisioned at Vienna was thankfully postponed.

On October 30, 1961, the Soviet Union carried out a major new thermonuclear test at a testing range in Novaya Zemlya, in the Artic. At more than 50 megatons (or over 3,300 Hiroshimas), it became the most powerful explosion ever set off by man. The flash of light was seen as far away as a 1,000 km while the thermal effect from the blast was felt at a distance of 270 km. The monstrous cloud from the explosion reached the mesosphere. "The ground surface of the island has been levelled, swept and licked so that it looks like a skating rink," a witness later reported from ground zero. "There is not a trace of unevenness in the ground … Everything in this area has been swept clean, scoured, melted and blown away."[80] The world beheld the Tsar Bomb.

Khrushchev's decision to unilaterally resume nuclear testing earlier that fall was closely linked to the German problem. It was, as he put it to Chen Yi in July, "an effort to solve the German question. This will be a good method of putting pressure on the West."[81] When India's prime minister, Jawaharlal Nehru, complained to him about the move, indicating that it would cost Moscow international support, the Soviet leader brushed him off, telling the Indian that he was "a Bolshevik, not a pacifist."[82] Yet his retreat in Germany spelled the limits of Soviet leverage. He could brandish the stick – and he did – but would he dare to use it against his enemies? The absurd destructiveness of the Tsar Bomb made its actual use utterly unthinkable.

Khrushchev had not yet given up on the idea of signing a peace treaty with East Germany. He continued fantasizing about doing it, but he was very careful not to set up any more deadlines he knew he would not be able to keep. Ulbricht, who saw Khrushchev again on November 2, still had his hopes up but Khrushchev told him to cool it. He said that discussing the peace treaty now had merely a "propagandistic" significance. "Then it's all clear," Ulbricht allowed with evident resignation. And it was. But it did not matter as much as before. The Berlin Wall – that hideous structure that would now divide the city – took the urgency out of the question of the German peace treaty. With time, he assured Ulbricht, West Berlin would die out. It would not survive economically. Then the mean East German would get what he wanted but without the risk of a global nuclear war.[83]

293

11

CUBA

Nikita Sergeyevich Khrushchev had two outsized personality traits. The first was his hypersensitivity to real or perceived slights. His self-perception as a great leader of a great power brooked no contradiction, and where situations arose that suggested that, as a leader, he was not so great, or perhaps that his country was not as great as he claimed, he became defensive, apprehensive, and resentful. Unsurprisingly, he worried still more about any challenge to his authority from his underlings, not so much in the Kremlin (where he could rely on sycophantic deference from all but the occasional contrarian Mikoyan) but in the world Communist movement. His outbursts of rage directed at the Albanians in 1961 showed that side of his personality but it was not the Albanians that he worried about most. It was the Chinese. Nothing stung quite as much as Mao's sarcastic commentary on the questionable accomplishments of the great Marxist-Leninist in Moscow.

The second personality trait was Khrushchev's propensity for quick fixes. He rarely had any patience for deep thinking or complex strategies. On too many occasions he acted precipitously, only coming to regret his actions afterwards. His ebullience and hubris, and a belief that he could outfox all his opponents, translated into a foreign policy that could, and often did, lead towards crises that the Soviet leader never expected. No sooner would he extricate himself from one than he would plunge himself into another, riding, as he did, a rollercoaster of crisis and opportunity, half-frightened, half-expectant that his enemies were perhaps even more frightened than he was, and so, with luck, would let him score a victory at their expense. The more he rode the rollercoaster the more confident he became that it was a game he was very good at, the more dismissive he became of the risks involved, and the more he came to believe in his own intuition and infallibility.

In October 1962, intuition failed Khrushchev. His plan to ship nuclear-tipped missiles to Cuba misfired in a spectacular fashion. At the last moment, he jumped off that deathly rollercoaster, but not before bringing his country – and the world – to the brink of a nuclear war. This is the story of this chapter.

CHAPTER 11 CUBA

MISSILES AND BASES

Historians have disagreed over the key questions of just how, when, and why Nikita Khrushchev came to the fateful decision to send nuclear missiles to Cuba. The idea is said to have occurred to him as early as April 1962 when, during a conversation with Zhukov's replacement as defense minister, Rodion Malinovsky, he suddenly asked what the minister thought of "throwing our hedgehog in the Americans' pants."[1] It is not uncommon to point to this snippet of evidence to suggest that what Khrushchev was really after was changing the strategic equation. He knew only all too well that, for all his boasting, the Soviet Union's nuclear forces were simply no match for America's. Enter Cuba, the unsinkable carrier.[2]

There is a lot to this interpretation, but it gets more complicated. It is absolutely true that Khrushchev's boasting that he was "holding America by the throat" had no real basis in fact.[3] The main problem was geographic: successfully threatening America's key population centers required a reliable intercontinental ballistic missile (ICBM). The first Soviet ICBM – the R7 – was tested successfully in August 1957 (a variant delivered Sputnik into space). But the missile was plagued by problems from the start. One test in May 1959 saw the R7 overshoot its target by nearly 2,000 km; another, that July, overshot by more than 2,000 km.[4] It was not until September 1960 that the first (modified) R7As were deployed at a launching pad in the Soviet northwest.[5] These (liquid-propelled) missiles proved vulnerable to attack, very difficult to operate, and expensive to maintain, and were decommissioned in 1968.

At the turn of the 1960s, the Soviets were better endowed with intermediate and medium-range missiles: the R-12 (range: about 2,000 km), which was first deployed in March 1959 and was already being mass-produced, and the newer R-14 (range: up to 4,500 km), which just entered service around the time of the Bay of Pigs. Neither of these was terribly accurate (flight tests regularly showed deviation from the target by 1 or 2 km, often more) but this handicap was compensated by the presence of powerful thermonuclear warheads.[6] It was these weapons that allowed Khrushchev to claim, credibly, that he was holding Great Britain, France, West Germany, and Italy as "hostages": it was these countries, not the United States, that would see the worst of a Soviet nuclear strike. America, though no longer invulnerable, remained at a safer distance. Khrushchev knew this, and the Americans knew that he knew this. Indeed, several days before the Soviet test of the Tsar Bomb, US Deputy Secretary of Defense Roswell Gilpatric publicly confirmed that the missile gap – if there was one – favored the United States.

295

This lopsided strategic equation bothered Khrushchev, pointing to Soviet vulnerabilities. He had worried about the presence of American bases along the Soviet periphery. For one thing, these bases in countries like Pakistan, Turkey, Norway, and Japan (among others) were used for espionage against targets in the USSR (for example, for sending U-2s on aerial photography missions). Also, some of the bases hosted US nuclear bombers and missiles. The problem with these bases was not just that they posed a security threat (although that aspect was very important) but also their symbolism: they were a nagging reminder of Moscow's inability to weaken America's alliances and of the reality of the hostile encirclement.

For several years Khrushchev tried (to no avail) to exchange the prospect of a Soviet military withdrawal from Eastern Europe for America giving up on its bases. "What does it mean to get rid of the bases?" – he asked his colleagues back in February 1960, when, in the afterglow of Camp David, Khrushchev still appeared optimistic on this score. "This means the demise of NATO, SEATO, CENTO. And this is what we want. This is our ardent dream."[7] Khrushchev's comments came in the wake of the US decision – long in coming – to base intermediate-range ballistic missiles (IRBMs) in Italy and Turkey. These "Jupiter" missiles were largely obsolete at the time of their deployment (Kennedy's secretary of state, Dean Rusk, recalled joking "about which way the missiles would fly if they were fired").[8] But their deployment deeply upset Khrushchev, and he rained vitriol, promising nuclear retaliation against countries hosting American bases.

Khrushchev was briefly encouraged by a military coup in Turkey in May 1960, which brought General Cemal Gürsel to power. In October that year he advised the Turkish foreign minister, Selim Sarper, to do away with US bases and proclaim neutrality, promising, for his part, to bring down Soviet troop levels at the Soviet–Turkey border and even to decommission his Black Sea fleet, turning the Black Sea into "a sea of peace."[9] The example Khrushchev had in mind was that of Afghanistan, with which Moscow "never had – and one can hope will never have – any misunderstandings."[10] But the Turks were not buying it, and the "Jupiter" deployment proceeded apace, beginning in the fall of 1961. The Italians, too, ignored Soviet complaints, seeing American IRMBs, deployed in 1960, as an important card in raising Rome's "prestige."[11] These "Jupiters" would yet play an important role in the Cuban drama.

SAVING CUBA

There is little doubt that Khrushchev's deep insecurity, as well as his desire to redress what he perceived as an unfair situation, contributed to his resolve, as he put it, "to give the Americans a little of their own medicine."[12] But there was something else. Sergo Mikoyan, son of Khrushchev's famous lieutenant, Anastas Mikoyan, and himself a historian of the Cuban Missile Crisis, has drawn attention to Khrushchev's fears of an American invasion of Cuba.[13] Mikoyan Jr. became perhaps the most prominent advocate of the notion that Khrushchev sent missiles to Cuba not because he wanted to fix the strategic imbalance but, first and foremost, because he was a revolutionary romantic acting out of sense of responsibility to fellow Communists. There is something to this interpretation, though this, too, gets more complicated.

There is scarcely any doubt that Khrushchev was worried about Kennedy invading Cuba, both in the run-up and, even more, in the aftermath of the Bay of Pigs misadventure. He spoke about this very issue at the Presidium meeting on May 21, 1962, which rubber-stamped his decision to send missiles to Cuba. "How to help Cuba so that it holds on," reads the section title to the discussion (the details of the discussion itself are unfortunately missing).[14] He was probably aware of US planning for a possible invasion of Cuba, including the well-publicized military maneuvers in April–May 1962, which entailed landing an invasion force on a Caribbean island.[15] One did not have to suffer from paranoia to suspect that the exercises were a preparation for an actual landing aimed at invading Cuba and toppling Castro. Indeed, Khrushchev returned to this question on October 22, 1962, at the height of the crisis, in order to convince his comrades (and himself) that he had done the right thing by sending missiles to the island.

There are two versions of what he said on October 22: one, notes jotted down by the head of the General Department of the Central Committee, Vladimir Malin, have Khrushchev say: "we wanted to frighten them a bit, deter the USA in relation to Cuba."[16] The other, notes by the head of the first sector of the same department, Aleksei Serov, differ only slightly: "Our whole operation," Khrushchev said, according to Serov, "was to deter the USA so they don't attack Cuba." However, at this point Khrushchev added, pivoting back to bases: "In their time, the USA did the same thing, having encircled our country with missile bases. This deterred us."[17] In other words, the two issues – protection of Cuba and redressing the strategic imbalance were intricately linked in Khrushchev's mind.

There is a broader question here. Why was Khrushchev so concerned about losing Cuba to an American invasion? A simple explanation would be to highlight the excitement in the Kremlin with Cuba's revolution, which (according to Mikoyan) "made us [the Soviet leaders] feel like boys again."[18] But things are never that simple. The question bothered Khrushchev because he knew that, just as in Berlin, he had oversold Soviet power and, were his bluff to be called – that is, if the Americans simply moved in and toppled a Soviet client – his credibility would be in tatters. Soviet clients and rivals around the world watched Khrushchev, none more closely than the Chinese who hardly needed a pretext to accuse him of caving in before American imperialism.

This is exactly what Khrushchev pointed out in his memoirs. "I was going up and down Bulgaria," he reminisced, recalling his trip to the country between May 14–20, 1962, "but there was a nagging thought in my brain: 'What will happen to Cuba? We will lose Cuba!' This would be a huge blow to the Marxist-Leninist teaching, and this would push us back from Latin American countries [and] lower our prestige. How will they look at us then? The Soviet Union is such a mighty power, and could not do anything other than empty statements, other than protests and discussing the question at the UN."[19] By contrast, "doing something" about Cuba would bolster the Soviet prestige and credibility not just in Latin America but, indeed, worldwide. "He said," wrote Ivan Serov, then head of the Soviet military intelligence (GRU) of a meeting with Khrushchev in early 1962, "that this step (deployment of missiles) would take us to negotiations with the Americans with a stronger position. All the others – England, France, and Germany – would speak up for the recognition of the interests of the USSR around the world."[20] Khrushchev's explanation to the Soviet ambassador in Cuba, Aleksandr Alekseev, was broadly the same: "Installing missiles in Cuba will restore parity between the US and the USSR and we will be able to speak to the Americans as equal partners."[21]

It is perhaps unsurprising that even as he considered sending missiles to Cuba, Khrushchev again returned to the idea of forcing the Americans out of West Berlin. He even discussed the two issues – Cuba and Berlin – in the same meeting of the Presidium on July 1, 1962, though there is no evidence that he ever linked one to the other directly. But the implication was clear: missiles in Cuba would objectively strengthen Khrushchev's hand in resolving the Berlin problem to his satisfaction.[22]

The dice fell on May 21, 1962. It was then that Khrushchev proposed to his Presidium – a gathering of yes-men – to ship medium- and intermediate-range ballistic missiles to Cuba, provided Castro agreed.

"WE WILL WIN THIS OPERATION"

Who opposed Khrushchev's idea? It does not take much to be wise in hindsight. Later claims should be taken with a pinch of salt. Among those who claimed to have warned Khrushchev that the move was going to backfire on him are his close confidante Anastas Mikoyan, Foreign Minister Andrei

CHAPTER 11 CUBA

Gromyko, and his foreign policy aide Oleg Troyanovsky. The latter recalled that the Soviet leader politely heard him out but pointed out in the end that he was not doing to the United States anything that the United States was not already doing to him. Castro himself was also among the skeptics. He received the proposal from the candidate member of the Presidium, Sharif Rashidov, and the head of the nuclear forces, Sergei Biryuzov, who left for Cuba on a top secret mission on May 31. Castro's reservations were understandable: his own reputation was on the line. Accepting Soviet missiles would cast him in the role of Moscow's puppet: not the sort of thing that sold well with the revolutionary audiences of Latin America. He would be turning Cuba into a Soviet base even as he protested against the American base in Guantanamo! But Castro, according to his later recollections, accepted the missiles because he felt it was his socialist duty.[23] They were willing, he told Biryuzov, to take a thousand missiles if this helped in the defense of the social-ist camp.[24] Castro's associate, Che Guevara, echoed this view. "We felt guilty," he recalled in December 1962, "given the fact that such a radical proposal might actually drag them [the Soviet Union] into war whereas we remained undecided on whether we should provide them with missile bases."[25]

On May 24, 1962 the Presidium gathered to discuss the operation. A remarkable document survives from that meeting: a seven-page letter from Rodion Malinovsky and Chief of General Staff Matvei Zakharov to "Chairman of the Council on Defense" Nikita Khrushchev – so secret that it was hand-written rather than typed – that outlined the details of the proposed deployment. The Soviets were to send, in utmost secrecy, twenty-four R-12 missile systems and sixteen R-14 systems, for a total of forty (the number of missiles and warheads was in fact sixty: some extra missiles would be brought along). But the missiles were just the tip of the iceberg. To protect them, and also to protect Cuba from invasion, the Soviet military planned to deploy: two anti-aircraft divisions (including forty MiG-21-f13s fighter jets); "Sopka" coastal defense units, armed with missiles capable of striking ships at an 80 km range; twelve missile boats; two FKR cruise missile regiments (armed with eighty conventional and eighty nuclear warheads, and capable of striking targets at the distance of 180 km; thirty-three Il-28 bombers; and about 44,000 servicemen and 1,800 support staff.[26] Later the plan was amended with the addition of "Luna" rockets with nuclear warheads.[27]

What was being proposed was not just missile deployment but a military operation that would turn Cuba – sitting just 145 km (90 miles) off the US coast – into a formidable Soviet military base or, to cite the words Malinovsky and Zakharov used in one of their instructions, "into an impregnable fortress."[28]

PART II HUBRIS

There are no details of what transpired at the May 24 Presidium meeting (the protocol reads simply: "to agree with the proposal of com[rade] Khrushchev N.S on Cuba" and "accept the plan." The final decision was evidently taken after Rashidov came back from his trip to Cuba and reported to the Presidium (on June 10).

In the intervening days Khrushchev was preoccupied with an unexpected matter. As a result of his decision to raise food prices, protests and riots broke out in the southern city of Novocherkassk on June 1–3, 1962. Police, army, and the KGB were brought in to crack down on the protesters. More than twenty people were killed. These events cast a dark shadow on Khrushchev's plans to build Communism in twenty years and highlighted growing public dissatisfaction with the sobering Soviet reality. On June 10, before dealing with Cuba, Khrushchev heard Frol Kozlov recount events in Novocherkassk at the Presidium. His conclusion was simply that "we had no other choice." He also decreed to "strengthen the work of the KGB." Yet

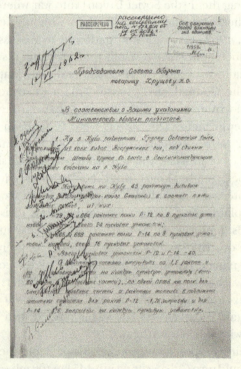

Figure 14 Proposal from Rodion Malinovsky and Matvei Zakharov about dispatching nuclear missiles to Cuba. Signed by Khrushchev (at the top) and other senior leaders, June 1962.
Source: CWIHP/DA.

CHAPTER 11 CUBA

despite the setbacks of Communist construction in the USSR, the Soviet leader seemed optimistic in relation to Cuba. "I think we will win this operation," he proclaimed, after hearing Rashidov's report.[29]

Before the meeting adjourned, Khrushchev had all those present sign their name on Malinovsky's and Zakharov's May 24 letter, indicating their approval of the operation. At the top was Khrushchev's signature: "In favor," followed by Suslov, Brezhnev, Mikoyan, and other top leaders, in all sixteen people, including Khrushchev.[30]

In July 1962 Fidel's brother Raúl was in Moscow to discuss the details of the missile deployment. Fidel recalled that before Raúl's departure he asked him to query the Soviets about what would happen if the Americans discovered the operation while the missiles were being shipped. Khrushchev's answer, according to Raúl, was: "Don't worry, I am going to grab Kennedy by the testicles and he will just have to come and talk it over because, after all, they have our country surrounded by bases, in Turkey, here, there, everywhere." According to Raúl, Khrushchev promised to send the Baltic Fleet in case things got out of hand.[31] In late August Khrushchev repeated the same absurd promise to Emilio Aragonés and Che Guevara who had come to Moscow to finalize the secret agreement on missile deployment.[32] "At the time," Che recalled with some bitterness, "we believed their words were true."[33]

OPERATION "ANADYR"

"Operation Anadyr" – so named after a river in the Arctic wilderness – began in July 1962. On the 10th – merely a month after Khrushchev approved the operation – sixty generals and senior officers led by the grizzled 60-year-old Red Army veteran Issa Pliev departed for Cuba on a flight that supposedly inaugurated the opening of the Moscow–Havana air route. Before departure, the military brass were told that they were "specialists in civilian aviation," though before the plane landed the story was changed, and they became "specialists in agriculture." No one bothered to tell them of their new profession, and in fact no one – not even the Soviet Embassy – had been forewarned of their arrival, so that the officers poked around the Havana airport for three hours before finally being whisked away to take up accommodation in the lodgings for specialists in air defense.

These officers were followed, a week later, by reconnaissance groups tasked with finding suitable places for missile deployment. In the following weeks, the freshly minted agriculturalists, wearing Cuban army uniforms and accompanied by Castro's personal bodyguards for protection, crisscrossed the island and identified ten sites for deployment.

PART II HUBRIS

Major General Igor Statsenko, who arrived in Cuba with the first group of officers and who was later charged with preparing a postmortem on the operation, noted in his report that the Soviet lacked even basic knowledge of the conditions in Cuba. Thus, it immediately transpired that the original plan – which was to house the arriving troops in dugouts to hide their presence on the island – could not be carried out, partly because the Cuban soil proved rocky and resistant to digging, and partly due to unceasing rains and high humidity. They had to be housed in tents instead, which made them all too visible to enemy reconnaissance. Tropical rainstorms also delayed work at missile sites, a situation that, remarkably, no one in Moscow had foreseen. There were language problems (officers were tasked with learning Spanish but it was a tall order on such a short notice). And it transpired that the Cuban electrical system operated on the US standard of 60 Hz, which made it incompatible with the Soviet equipment (50 Hz). "This should have been known before the reconnaissance work started," Statsenko reported with an undertone of irritation.[34]

The main part of the deployed force began to ship out in mid-July. Only forty-two (of the intended sixty) missiles arrived before the crisis flared up, of which six were intended for training only. Only thirty-six (of the intended sixty) nuclear warheads ever made it. Missiles were off-loaded in utmost secrecy, between 12:00am and 5:00am. Statsenko reported that the Soviet personnel involved in this process were dressed in Cuban army uniforms and ordered to use a few memorized Spanish phrases. Speaking Russian was "categorically forbidden" (someone wrote in the margin of the report: "this should have been prepared beforehand" but that someone clearly did not understand Khrushchev's modus operandi). The Cubans then staged "car accidents" along the deployment route (complete with the evacuation of "victims") in order to confuse the local population and close off the roads for the passage of missiles. Three hundred Cuban soldiers and even some "specially tested and selected fishermen" were charged with protecting the ports of disembarkation. Yet by October 22 only fifteen Cubans, including Fidel Castro, were told what the operation was about.[35]

The most preposterous idea that originated, evidently, with Marshal Sergei Biryuzov, and which Khrushchev wholly embraced, was that the missiles could be hidden in the Cuban forests, under the palm trees. Relevant instructions (to hide the missiles "under the foliage") were signed by the deputy head of the general staff of the missile forces, Aleksei Butsky.[36] But when this was attempted, it transpired that the palm trees in the alleged forests stood apart from each other at a distance of 12–15 meters and provided no cover whatsoever for hiding anything, least of all missiles.

302

CHAPTER 11 CUBA

When the command decided to use camouflage nets to camouflage their equipment, it turned out that the coloring of these nets was in line with the foliage of a moderate climate and stood out sharply against the Cuban landscape.[37]

"The whole operation," Statsenko reported testily, "should have been preceded by at least a minimum acquaintance with, and the study of the economic capabilities of, the local physical geography, and the military-political situation of the country by those who were charged with practically implementing this task."[38] Given the challenges of the shambolic operation, it was a miracle that it was even completed in such a short time without being uncovered by the Americans.

The possibility that the Soviets might just be installing missiles on Cuba was certainly in the humid tropical air. Cuban exiles heard rumors of unusual activity in ports. These were fed through dubious channels to anyone who might believe them, including Senator Kenneth Keating (R-NY) who claimed as early as August 31 that the Soviets had set up a missile base in Cuba.[39] In September the CIA repeatedly reported on the upgrade of Cuba's air defense capabilities and on the appearance of the MiG-21s.[40] It did not take much imagination to fathom what it was that the Soviets were so keen to protect. Yet the idea that someone in Moscow would take the fatal step of sending nuclear missiles to Cuba appeared so wild, so out of tune with the Soviet practice, that on the whole the American intelligence community remained skeptical.[41] By contrast, the West German intelligence (Bundesnachrichtendienst or BND), embraced the obvious; one BND report (dated September 21, 1962 and evidently shared with the Americans) not just stated plainly that the Soviets were building a missile base in Cuba but that the work would be complete by the end of November.[42] This information, too, was brushed aside as unverifiable speculation.

The only way to know for sure what was happening in Cuba was to send U-2s over the island. But the White House hesitated. On August 30, a Strategic Air Command U-2 accidentally violated Soviet airspace, prompting a protest from Moscow. On September 9, another U-2 (piloted by a Taiwanese officer) was lost over China. The discovery that the Soviets had shipped surface-to-air batteries to Cuba made Kennedy especially apprehensive of authorizing these missions. If a U-2 were shot down over Cuba, he would have found himself under tremendous pressure to do something about Castro in the run-up to the November congressional elections. For these reasons, and because of poor weather in the Caribbean, no U-2s were sent over western Cuba (the site of previously reported suspicious activities)

303

until October 14, when finally a mission brought back high-resolution photos of what on inspection turned out to be Soviet nuclear missiles.[43] The crisis was about to begin.

THE EXCOMM DEBATES

Late Tuesday morning, October 16, Kennedy called an off-the-record meeting at the White House to discuss the latest developments. The participants included Kennedy's trusted confidantes and senior administration officials, including his brother, Attorney General Robert Kennedy, Secretary of Defense Robert McNamara, Secretary of State Dean Rusk, National Security Adviser McGeorge "Mac" Bundy, and the new head of the Joint Chiefs of Staff, Maxwell Taylor. These men became the core of the Executive Committee of the National Security Council, known simply as ExComm, charged with advising Kennedy on the course of action in Cuba. The president secretly taped many of these deliberations, providing historians with a rare opportunity (unfortunately lacking in the Soviet case) to truly understand how the key decisions were made.[44]

One interesting angle illuminated by the tapes is just how Kennedy and his advisers interpreted Khrushchev's motivations in placing missiles in Cuba. Here, the prize for critical thinking goes to Dean Rusk. The secretary's puffy face, receding hairline, and large-rimmed eyeglasses, which he seemed to chew as often as he wore them, made for a passing resemblance to the recently appointed Soviet ambassador, Anatoly Dobrynin. Rusk and Dobrynin shared another trait: they would both stay put for years: Dobrynin well into the 1980s, outlasting every other Soviet ambassador, and Rusk through both the Kennedy and the Johnson administrations, or longer than all secretaries of state but Cordell Hull. But Rusk had no special insights into Soviet behavior, nor a direct telephone line into the inner crevasses of Khrushchev's consciousness. And yet during that very first off-the-record meeting on Cuba he ticked many of Khrushchev's boxes when he explained Khrushchev's actions thus: "he [Khrushchev] also knows that we don't really live under fear of his nuclear weapons to the extent that, uh, he has to live under fear of ours. Also we have nuclear weapons nearby, in Turkey and places like that."[45]

It was the first time that the Turkish "Jupiters" featured in the discussion but they would creep back repeatedly: it did not take a genius to draw the parallels between the missiles in Turkey and those in Cuba.[46] The focus of analysis then drifted to strategic rationalization: perhaps, it was Khrushchev's gambit to make up for the inferiority of the Soviet ICBMs, or

CHAPTER 11 CUBA

even a carefully calculated gamble to trade Cuba for West Berlin. Looked at from these angles, it was almost as if Khrushchev was a cold calculating machine: here are the inputs; here are the outputs; the journey from A to B is as straightforward as punching numbers into a calculator. Later, as noted, historians moved away from seeing Khrushchev as a machine to seeing him as a romantic; they created an imaginary system of coordinates, complete with revolutionary passions and visions of a Communist world. But there was something missing in this picture, something that Rusk perhaps only inadvertently touched upon: strategic considerations aside, why should Khrushchev accept a situation that the Americans, were they in his position, would never have agreed to accept?

The next reasonable question, then, is why Kennedy felt that Soviet missiles in Cuba were unacceptable and had to be removed. The evidence here is quite clear. It was not the military aspect of the Soviet presence that worried Kennedy. After all, the Soviets had their ICBMs, which covered the entire territory of the United States. True, these were few and unreliable but, unless one thought in terms of winning a nuclear war, the ostensible missile gap did not really make a huge difference: just one nuclear blast over a major city would produce unacceptable casualties. The real importance of the Cuban missiles, then, was summed up in two words: political and psychological.[47] There was bound to be a huge domestic backlash if Kennedy swallowed these missiles before the important mid-term congressional elections on November 6: he would be seen as a weak, spineless leader appeasing a bully. Washington's international credibility would also suffer, particularly in Latin America, and, of course, in Berlin.

But if prestige and credibility mattered most to the American president, what reason is there to suppose that Khrushchev was not swayed by similar considerations? Eventually, Kennedy recognized that there would have to be some give-and-take that would allow his nemesis to salvage his reputation. But not before things nearly came to nuclear war.

Kennedy's first impulse, after he received incontrovertible evidence of the Soviet missiles in Cuba, was to order an airstrike against the Soviet installations – in the military parlance, to "take them out." The option was strongly favored by the Chiefs of Staff and their spokesman on the ExComm, General Taylor. But there were certain drawbacks. First, there was the problem of the world public opinion (what would it look like if the Americans attacked Cuba out of the blue, even if missiles were an obvious provocation)? There were problems with America's allies: would they go along, especially when they could end up on the receiving end of the Soviet retaliation? (Berlin was the most obvious target). Most importantly, perhaps, there was small print attached to Taylor's every prescription: Military action? Sure. A 100 percent guarantee that all the missiles would be taken out? No one could give such guarantees. Yet even one missile, if launched successfully, had the capacity to kill hundreds of thousands, if not millions, of people, a price that Kennedy most definitely did not want to pay.

Another possibility considered was that of an outright invasion of Cuba to finish the job that the Cuban paramilitaries proved so incapable of doing. This raised a whole array of new issues, including possible American casualties, and the question of the endgame: invade, and what then?

It was just as well that the idea was never attempted. Many years later we learned what Kennedy and his advisers did not realize in October 1962: that the Soviet military units on Cuba were armed with tactical nuclear weapons and that their commander General Issa Pliev may have had pre-delegated authority to use them. The question whether he did or not befuddled a generation of historians.[48] The case that he did rests on oral history from witnesses long dead, and there are indications that the question was at least seriously considered by Soviet Defense Minister Rodion Malinovsky, though he ultimately decided against signing off on specific instructions to this effect.[49]

THE SINO-INDIAN WAR

As Soviet ships unloaded their deadly cargo, as soldiers, missiles, and material were whisked away to hastily constructed bases in the cleared jungle, as Kennedy and his advisers secretly pondered their response to Moscow's latest move, Khrushchev's attention was elsewhere. He was worried, as usual, about his difficult relationship with China, which was now entering a new phase due to a brooding conflict in the Himalayas. It so happened that the Cuban Missile Crisis, dangerous as it was, looms much larger in our historical memory but the big question Khrushchev faced in mid-October 1962 was not whether he would soon be in a nuclear war with the United States but whether he would have to take sides in China's war with India. The crisis in the Caribbean and the Sino-Indian War of 1962 became intertwined in strange ways and both ultimately had a significant impact on the direction of Moscow's rivalry with Beijing.

The war between China and India began on October 20 but the clouds had been gathering for months. Zhou Enlai's tense talks with Nehru in April 1960 were the last serious attempt to resolve the border problem. The failure of this attempt meant that Beijing and New Delhi were on a collision course. This was not immediately obvious. China was for a time preoccupied with internal problems: millions were starving. At the enlarged Central Committee working meeting in Beijing (known as the "Seven Thousand Cadre Conference") in January–February 1962, Liu Shaoqi admitted the party's responsibility for the disasters of the preceding years, and even Mao made a half-hearted self-criticism. Faced with a domestic crisis of such gargantuan proportions, Beijing seemed ill-prepared to tackle major international problems. This was perhaps the reason why in February 1962 one of China's top diplomats, Wang Jiaxiang, famously offered to adjust foreign policy goals in the direction of lessening tensions with the "imperialists" (the United States), the "revisionists" (the Soviet Union), and the "reactionaries" (India), while also reducing support for overseas revolutionary struggles. Mao mockingly termed Wang's proposals "three reconciliations and one reduction" but they in fact reflected a certain consensus in the party stemming from the chairman's own temporary caution.

There was another reason to seek conflict-avoidance with India – brewing conflicts with other immediate neighbors. China's sorry state in 1960–62 bolstered Chiang Kai-shek's hopes that he may yet be in a position to recapture the mainland. Already in November 1961 Chiang considered approaching the United States with a request to hold "talks at the highest level to discuss U.S. interests in Asia" – that is to say, to obtain American support for a possible "counteroffensive" against the mainland.[50] The generalissimo also intensified military preparations, sharply increasing his military budget and ordering mobilization of reservists.[51] In February 1962 he pleaded with the Americans to allow him to "save people now in commie slavery" and promised that he would not drag the United States into a general war.[52] Kennedy disabused Chiang of any prospect of American support for their trigger-happy ally's plans, plunging Chaing, in the words of a CIA report, into the "trough of despair."[53]

Still, Mao Zedong had every reason to worry that "Chiang's bandit army" would jump on the chance to reverse the verdict of 1949. The Central Committee even issued special instructions on June 10 to prepare for repelling an attack on China's eastern seaboard.[54] Tensions ebbed a bit in late June, and only after an emphatic reassurance from the US ambassador in Warsaw, John M. Cabot, to his Chinese colleague, Wang Bingnan, that the United States would not support Chiang's invasion of the mainland.[55] Ironically, improvement in the security situation in the east made it possible for the Chinese forces to concentrate on the western neighbor, India.

Just as in the case with Khrushchev's decision to send missiles to Cuba, historians have debated endlessly as to why China went to war with India.

PART II HUBRIS

There are two prevailing explanations. One centers on what one might call ideological reasons.[56] Specifically, in August–September 1962, at a leadership conference in the resort town of Beidaihe and later at the Tenth Party Plenum, Mao Zedong pushed back against right-wing proclivities in the party (represented by Liu Shaoqi's self-criticism at the Seven Thousand Cadre Conference). Mao stressed the continued relevance of "class struggle" and spoke ominously of "Chinese revisionists" taking China towards a possible restoration of capitalism.[57] In this context, Wang Jiaxiang's policy of "three reconciliations and one reduction" began to look rather like selling out to foreign enemies.[58] As the argument goes, the defeat of Wang's conception led directly to a more militant Chinese foreign policy, of which India became the first case.

This explanation is plausible and, as it is neither supported nor contradicted by overwhelming evidence, it will continue to appear in the scholarly accounts of the war as a curious example of the interrelationship between China's domestic and foreign policies.

The other popular explanation highlights China's security concerns. The usual focus here is on Tibet, and how, ever since the 1959 uprising, Mao and his colleagues feared India's quiet subversion. They were also deeply suspicious of Nehru's controversial "forward policy," which entailed sending out forward patrols and establishment of border posts in the disputed territory in order to preempt its occupation by the Chinese.[59] The policy, conceived in 1960 but implemented in earnest from late 1961, was advertised by the Indians as a defensive measure but it is not hard to see why it would have been interpreted as encroachment in Beijing. The evidence for this line of argument is extensive, for the Chinese policy makers rarely missed an opportunity to question Nehru's activities in Tibet and along the entire extent of the Sino-Indian border, or to accuse him of "inheriting the British imperial legacy."[60] Of course, this still leaves the question of separating these pronouncements from propaganda: naturally, the Chinese would claim self-defense; otherwise, how would they ever be able to justify invading India before the world – surely, not by invoking principles of class struggle?

For what they are worth, the few available internal Chinese assessments of the Indian security threat are in complete alignment with the propaganda façade. One Chinese Foreign Ministry Report, produced in July 1962, is replete with references to the construction of Indian "bases" aimed against China, and especially highlights the dangers posed by the Soviet Union's sale of helicopters, transport planes, and modern fighter MiG-21 fighter jets to India.[61] The latter complaint would figure high on the list

CHAPTER 11 CUBA

of Chinese grievances with their Soviet ally. The Soviets claimed, in their turn, that their few planes did not change the balance of power between China and India, but the argument was a hard sell in Beijing. This example of Soviet duplicity nicely dovetailed with perceived Soviet meddling in Xinjiang in May 1962. In that latter case, thousands of ethnic Uighurs fled China across the border to the relative safety and prosperity of the Soviet Union. The Chinese blamed the Soviets for subversion. The Soviets, just as in the case with the Indian planes, claimed that they were surprised by the allegation.[62] Their surprise was probably genuine but that does not detract from the fact the Chinese also genuinely believed that they were being subverted on all sides.

In short, China security concerns were very real. But there was something else. The Chinese leaders were very sensitive about making the impression of yielding under pressure. The year 1962 here was an especially difficult time. The catastrophe of the Great Leap Forward was already public knowledge, though perhaps not yet the extent of the devastation in the Chinese countryside. Historically, the Chinese have associated internal turmoil (*neiyou*) with external threats (*waihuan*). Beijing faced plenty of *waihuan* in the first half of 1962: from Taiwan, to potential Soviet pressure, to India with its relentless "forward policy." Between Kennedy (and his alleged frontman Chiang Kai-shek), Khrushchev, and Nehru, the last particularly stood out as a brazen challenger. If China could not resist India's encroachment, how could it resist anyone else's?

In talking about foreign policy in 1962, the Chinese leaders emphasized a very familiar theme: bullying. As before, China was being "bullied" by different countries. The entire international situation could be explained with reference to a web of relationships between bullies and their victims. Chen Yi described this "bully bullies bully" world in a speech in mid-April 1962, just around the time Khrushchev pondered his own response to perceived American bullying in Turkey. "Now in the world," Chen Yi said,

> big countries bully big countries, as in America bullying China (hint: India is also bullying us); big countries bully small countries, as in America bullying lots of small countries; small countries bully small countries, as in Thailand bullying Cambodia; there are also small countries bullying big countries ... China is the most bullied country. It is bullied by big countries, and it is also bullied by small countries.[63]

The same refrain was later deployed specifically to criticize Jawaharlal Nehru's "bullying" of India's neighbors. In September 1962, just weeks before China's attack, Liu Shaoqi explained to Pakistani Ambassador

N.A.M. Raza that the Chinese formerly believed that only the imperialist countries, like the United States and Great Britain, suffered from "great-power chauvinism." "Now, we find that India too has great-power chauvinism ... India has adopted an attitude of great-power chauvinism toward China, and believes erroneously that China is easily bullied." Raza, as a Pakistani, did not need to be persuaded of the reality of India's "bullying."[64] So, when on October 20 the Chinese attacked in force across the Himalayas, their aim was, more than anything, simply to take Nehru down a notch, and to deliver a message to domestic and global audiences: that China will not put up with "bullying."

Meanwhile, somewhat unexpectedly, Khrushchev took China's side in the dispute with India. His decision came in the wake of a hare-brained Indian attempt to dislodge the Chinese from a remote mountain pass not far from the junction of India's, China's, and Bhutan's borders. India's claims to the area in question were demonstrably flimsy, even by New Delhi's maps, yet somehow Nehru lulled himself into believing that he was in the right and that the Chinese would in any case back down when confronted. This was not to be. A border clash on October 10 left scores dead on both sides.[65] On October 13 Khrushchev reassured Ambassador Liu Xiao, who was leaving for China, that he thought the Chinese take on the border was "reasonable," and that the borderline itself, a legacy of "British imperialism," disadvantaged China. He told Liu Xiao that the Soviet Union could not be "neutral" towards China. "If anyone invaded China and we declared neutrality, it would be betrayal. If the enemy fights, he will fight both of us. He will never be able to fight us separately, and you separately."[66] On the next day, October 14, Khrushchev confirmed his pro-China leaning at a Presidium meeting, ordering that Nehru be told that the Soviets were "disappointed" with his behavior, and that the shipment of MiG-21 planes to India be placed on hold.[67]

This was of course the very same day that an American U-2, flying over Cuba, obtained incontrovertible evidence of the presence of Soviet missiles in Cuba. True, Khrushchev did not yet know that his clever scheme had been uncovered. But historians have asked whether his sudden love for China was a sign that he was getting anxious about the Cuban situation: Would he not need Mao by his side if his missile gamble misfired?

We may never know what exactly Khrushchev had in mind. But his two-hour conversation with the Chinese ambassador offers a good vantage point for gauging the Soviet leader's worldview just days before the most dangerous moment in modern history. In a nutshell, it was remarkably "Maoist," which is to say, Khrushchev was full of optimism about the

CHAPTER 11 CUBA

ongoing "offensive" against the West but fully cognizant of the fact that "imperialism can impose war on us at any time." This was not at all different from Mao Zedong's views of international affairs. Was Khrushchev simply telling the Chinese what they wanted to hear? Hardly. In reality, the difference between Khrushchev's and Mao's views of the international situation was never as great as each side would later claim. The key issue was not the largely nonexistent ideological divergence but leadership, which is why Khrushchev went out of his way to impress skeptical Liu Xiao of the importance of Soviet involvement in various "revolutionary" theaters: from Laos to Indonesia, from Algeria to Yemen. And, most important of all, Cuba.

Just a day earlier, unbeknownst to Khrushchev, the Chinese ambassador in Havana, Shen Jian, brought up Moscow's international behavior in a conversation with Che Guevara's close friend Emilio Aragonés. Shen spoke derisively of the Soviet revolutionary credentials, highlighting the projected sale of MiG-21s to India as an example of Khrushchev's failure to "conform to proletarian internationalism." Aragonés appeared sympathetic to China's complaints but also quite pragmatic: "We never gave up our principles, but we have a realist mind. Cuba would perish in a few hours if we lost the support from Soviet Union."[68] Having just come back from Moscow where he and Che negotiated all the last-minute details of the Soviet missile deployment, Aragonés kept this knowledge to himself, giving the Chinese no inkling of what was about to unfold.

Nor did Khrushchev spill the beans to Liu Xiao, preferring instead to speak about Soviet military and economic aid to Cuba in opaque terms.[69] "The Americans," he boasted, "have no choice but to swallow it." Of course, he continued, they were interdicting Soviet shipments and conducting "provocative" actions. "But the Americans are very afraid." "Cuba," he said, was like a "sword stuck in America's body." Protecting it was therefore imperative, and not just for Cuba's sake alone. The issue at stake was much larger. "By protecting Cuba one can revolutionize all of the Latin American countries ... This costs us a lot but it is advantageous for the international revolutionary forces." He concluded with what sounded rather like a citation from Kennedy's inaugural address: "For this goal, we shall pay any price."[70]

Khrushchev's reference to Latin America's revolutionary struggles in the context of a discussion, it must be remembered, with the Chinese ambassador, highlighted an important dimension of Soviet policy. As Mao made a bid for global revolutionary leadership, the Chinese were publicly and privately questioning Moscow's credibility and reliability.

Khrushchev had to win back the lost ground and especially avoid "losing" Cuba to an American invasion that, he thought, would come sooner or later, and perhaps sooner rather than later. The big question was: Would Khrushchev really "pay any price" to protect his credibility as the leader of the socialist world?

QUARANTINE

On October 20, 1962, the day that saw a massive Chinese assault on Indian positions in the Himalayas, Kennedy at last decided against an immediate air strike on Cuba, opting, to the chagrin of the hawks, for a naval blockade called, following Rusk's suggestion, a "quarantine." On Monday, October 22, at 7:00pm, Kennedy announced his decision in a televised broadcast to the American people. For the next six days the world held its breath as Washington and Moscow balanced on the edge of a precipice.

The first secretary called a meeting of the Presidium immediately upon hearing of Kennedy's planned broadcast. The meeting began at 10:00pm, Moscow time, on October 22, with Khrushchev's announcement that he had learned that Kennedy "is preparing some speech."[71] There was little doubt in his mind that the speech would be about Cuba. He could see this from Gromyko's cables; the foreign minister was in the United States for the UN General Assembly meeting and had seen both Rusk and Kennedy. Rusk, Khrushchev said, "got drunk at a reception, talked about Berlin and insistently hinted at Cuba," while Kennedy also spoke about Cuba, though in more careful, reserved tones. Khrushchev later returned to Rusk's indiscretion, highlighting that the secretary of state had compared Cuba to Hungary, thus drawing a parallel between Soviet unwillingness to tolerate a hostile Hungary to America's unwillingness to allow a hostile Cuba. The fact that Rusk was supposedly "drunk" while making these remarks evidently gave them additional weight in Khrushchev's mind. "The tragic thing," he said, "is that they can attack, and we'll respond. This could turn into a big war."[72]

He then outlined Soviet options. The first was to publicly announce that the Soviet Union and Cuba had concluded a defense agreement. The Americans could react in three ways, Khrushchev reasoned: to declare a blockade of Cuba; to capture Soviet ships in route to Cuba; and to say that they had no intention of invading the island. The second option – if the US invaded Cuba – was for Cuba to declare war on the northern neighbor, and for the Soviet Union to announce that the Cubans would use tactical – but not strategic – nuclear weapons. He then announced a recess of five to ten minutes, asking his comrades to ponder these scenarios.

CHAPTER 11 CUBA

After the recess, Malinovsky produced a draft cable with instructions for Pliev. What happened at this point is not entirely clear. According to Mikoyan's later recollection, Malinovsky's original instruction mentioned repelling the Americans with all available means. It was Khrushchev supposedly who noticed the glaring problem: "if [you say] by all available means without reservations, this means with the missiles as well – that is, to begin a thermonuclear war. How can you do this?" "Malinovsky," recalled Anastas Mikoyan, "could not say anything in response because this was an extreme lack of caution on his part."[73]

Serov's contemporaneous notes are more ambiguous. Evidently reacting to wording about "all available means," Khrushchev said: "it should say: with all means but at first, not to use nuclear weapons. Use tactical weapons when they land [on Cuba]; as for strategic, they will receive special instructions." After further discussion of the situation in the Caribbean (which indicated increased concentration of US forces), the participants (or at least Suslov and Mikoyan) seemingly concluded at first that the United States had decided to invade. At this point, Malinovsky returned to his instructions, noting that if Pliev's forces used tactical nuclear weapons to repel the US invasion, then they could stand accused of having resorted to nukes first. "But if we don't use atomic weapons," Khrushchev retorted, "they could capture Cuba." Malinovsky argued, however, that the forces that the United States then had in the Caribbean were insufficient to capture Cuba, evidently downplaying this scenario. Khrushchev, for his part, "ruled out" that the Americans might use nuclear weapons to strike Cuba.

At last, the participants agreed to instruct Pliev to repel the US invasion, if it ever came, with all forces at his disposal, "excluding the use of Statsenko's means (i.e. atomic weapons) and Beloborodov's (strategic)." Malinovsky read out the cable again. It was approved, and carried off to the general staff for transmission. The final cable, sent at 11:30 at night, read: "In connection with the possible landing of Americans participating in the maneuvers in the Caribbean Sea on Cuba, undertake urgent measures to increase combat readiness, and to repel the enemy by joint efforts of the Cuban Army and all units of the Soviet troops, excluding the weapons of Statsenko's and of all of Beloborodov's cargo."[74] The use of tactical – never mind strategic – nuclear weapons was thus explicitly ruled out.

But could the Soviet forces have used these weapons if they had the permission to? Statsenko's postmortem on the operation contains valuable clues. The general staff, realizing perhaps that they were about to be uncovered, issued an instruction on September 8 to expedite site preparation. The task was made more difficult by the fact that some key equipment had

313

PART II HUBRIS

failed to turn up by October 22 (including the powerful R-14 missiles and their warheads, which the Soviets ordered turned around in mid-Atlantic in the early hours of October 23). One site with R-12 missiles (commanded by Ivan Sidorov) was operational by October 20, and two more (commanded, respectively, by Nikolai Bandilovsky and Yury Solov'yov) were made operational by October 25, although that involved sharing fueling equipment and cannibalizing regiments originally intended for the R-14s. Finally, by the nightfall of October 27, all twenty-four launchers, eight per regiment, were (almost) ready to launch on order. "Almost" – because the storage facility for R-12 warheads was located at a considerable distance from missile sites: 110 km from Solov'yov's regiment, 150 km from Bandilovsky's regiment, and 480 km from Sidorov's regiment.

This – and the shortage of fueling equipment – meant that after receiving an order from Moscow, the Soviet command in Cuba would have needed a full twenty-four hours to prepare and launch missiles from Sidorov's regiment (the only one in service on October 22), and fourteen to sixteen hours to prepare and launch from the other two regiments. Understanding that the lead time was too long, Statsenko ordered some of the warheads moved closer to Sidorov's regiment, but this only happened in the wee hours of October 27. When it did, the lead time for Sidorov was reduced to ten hours.[75] US intelligence accurately picked up on the readiness of all twenty-four launchers by the morning of October 28, though it consistently underestimated how long it would take to fire the missiles (six to eight hours, according to an estimate on October 28, where in fact it was ten to sixteen, depending on the site).[76] Be that as it may, on October 22, as Khrushchev and his comrades debated what to do ahead of Kennedy's expected address, "only" eight R-12 could fire, albeit at a twenty-four-hour notice, and not before warheads were delivered across nearly 500 km of treacherous terrain. From Khrushchev's later dictations, we know that he was deeply worried about these vulnerabilities, understanding that once the Americans discovered where the missiles were, they could easily take them out, even with conventional strikes.[77]

ON THE BRINK

Khrushchev and his comrades stayed late into the night of the 22nd, until early in the morning on the 23rd, debating, strategizing. The first secretary briefly speculated that Kennedy's speech was just a "bluff" ahead of the mid-term elections (scheduled for November 6). "Kennedy wants to show his firmness," he guessed. But these hopes were dispelled when, at·

CHAPTER 11 CUBA

1:15am – forty-five minutes before the president's television appearance – Deputy Foreign Minister Vasily Kuznetsov read out Kennedy's personal letter to Khrushchev that had just been delivered to the Foreign Ministry by the US Embassy. In the letter, Kennedy stated that he had been "most concerned" since Vienna that "your Government would not correctly understand the will and determination of the United States." Noting that, despite this, the Soviet Union constructed missile bases in Cuba, Kennedy expressed his resolve to remove "this threat to the security of this hemisphere." The action threatened was the "minimum necessary."[78] "This is not a war against Cuba," Khrushchev offered, with evident relief. "It's an ultimatum of some kind."

Much of the discussion that followed was omitted in the fragmentary notes by the two note-takers. Serov recorded Khrushchev's lengthy rant about American "piracy" and Cuba's right to defend itself against imperialism. "Let the crazy men know," he exclaimed with untimely pathos, "that we have always been faithful to the UN Charter." At the same meeting, Khrushchev approved a militant letter to Castro, endorsing Cuba's right of self-defense, and informing the Cuban leader that the Soviet forces on the island were being placed on high alert. He also decided that while he would order the surface ships carrying troops and weapons to Cuba to be turned around, four nuclear-armed submarines would be allowed to proceed on their way.[79] On the following day, Khrushchev dictated his first reaction to Kennedy's letter. "Think of what you are saying!" he raved. "You want to convince me to agree to this and submit myself!? This would not be submission to reason, but submission to insolence."[80] (His words were just slightly toned down in the letter sent to the president).[81]

However, on the next day, October 25, with tensions over Cuba building up, Khrushchev backed away from some of his more militant pronouncements. In a rambling dictation that was a little too bizarre even by the first secretary's standards, he claimed that what the Soviets were shipping to Cuba were "ordinary potatoes." (This was not completely random: one of the ships – the Swedish freighter Coolangatta – was indeed en route to Cuba with a cargo of potatoes from Leningrad.)[82] Khrushchev then tried to shame Kennedy: "If you realize your threats and stop our ships ... you will see [that they are carrying potatoes] and, in this case, I think you will feel ashamed. If I were in your shoes, I'd be shocked." But in the same dictation, Khrushchev offered a deal to Kennedy: he would withdraw missiles from Cuba if the United States publicly declared that it would not invade the island. In the end, Khrushchev rendered a verdict on what, in his opinion, Kennedy was doing: "He himself is looking for a way out."[83]

PART II HUBRIS

Having finished his dictation, Khrushchev summoned a meeting of the Presidium to have it approved. If Kennedy had had an inkling of what transpired at this meeting, he would have breathed an immediate sigh of relief, for, three days after Kennedy's quarantine speech, Khrushchev "blinked": he was ready to back out of Cuba. "The Americans are saying that the missile installations should be dismantled," Khrushchev began. "Maybe it should be done." He went on to explain that this was not at all "capitulation" on the Soviet part because the Americans, too, were afraid. He even attempted to crack a joke: "Kennedy slept with a wooden knife." The reference fell flat. "Why wooden?" asked Mikoyan, prompting Khrushchev belabored explanation to the effect that when a man goes on a bear hunt the first time, he must bring along a wooden knife, which makes it easier to clean his soiled underpants.

But it was a good question at that point whether it was Kennedy who had slept with a wooden knife – or whether Khrushchev did. Deputy Foreign Minister Kuznetsov, who was present at these meetings, was later heard saying that Khrushchev had "shitted his pants" after he was told that on October 24 the United States had moved the status of nuclear readiness – Defcon – to Defcon-2, one short of nuclear war.[84]

"This is not cowardice," Khrushchev continued at the Presidium, telling his comrades that the situation must not be allowed to reach a boiling point and adding (unconvincingly) that, in any case, the Soviets could "defeat" the United States by simply ordering a strike from the Soviet territory. "We must not make the situation any more tense but conduct a reasonable policy. This way, we will strengthen Cuba and save it for 2–3 years," at which point it could become so strong that the United States would find it even more difficult to do away with it. "The future depends on our country, not on Cuba," he said. "Is this correct?" he asked. Everyone in the room echoed Khrushchev's words.[85]

It remained only to "inform" Castro. "It half-worked, half-didn't," Khrushchev said, explaining what he would tell the Cuban leader. "It's unsubstantial for Cuba, and substantial for the USA … Time will pass, and we can send them [missiles?] again if need be."[86]

The Presidium meeting approved Khrushchev's missive to Kennedy, but it took until late afternoon of the following day to rework his lengthy ramblings into an actual letter. The reference to potatoes was dropped, and the message about Khrushchev's capitulation was worded more cautiously. If the United States made a pledge not to invade Cuba, the letter read, "the necessity for the presence of our military specialists in Cuba would disappear." Khrushchev explained in his dictation that it was

CHAPTER 11 CUBA

best not to explicitly mention the withdrawal of missiles. Kennedy would understand "that if there are no specialists, there will be no missiles."[87] More painful hours passed before the long message was translated and finally delivered to Kennedy. It was not even properly discussed at the ExComm meeting until the morning of Saturday, October 27, more than two days after Khrushchev – upset about the deepening crisis – dictated it to his stenographer.[88]

Meanwhile, another probe, confirming Khrushchev's proposal about the US non-invasion pledge, arrived from an unexpected source. The matter was broached on October 26 in a lunchtime meeting at the Occidental Restaurant, in Washington, between the KGB resident, Aleksandr Feklisov (alias Fomin), and an ABC News correspondent, John A. Scali. Just what exactly transpired at this meeting – whether the proposal was articulated by Feklisov or Scali – has been the subject of a fierce debate among historians. Scali, in any case, presented this proposal as coming from Feklisov. In the end, it did not matter. The idea was already on Khrushchev's mind more than a day earlier, when he first dictated his letter to Kennedy.[89]

It is difficult to gauge what went on inside Khrushchev's head as he awaited Kennedy's response to his letter. There was certainly a fair dose of resentment at his unequal position relative to the United States. On October 26, Khrushchev touched on this subject in a conversation with Iran's deputy foreign minister, Mahmoud Foroughi, comparing America to a "general who had aged and retired but still continues to think that he commands a division." "USA still wants to order other countries about," Khrushchev said. "But they [the Americans] are not being recognized. This is dangerous. America wants to run things. But this can prompt a rebuff ... We say in Russia, 'cut your coat according to your cloth.' If the forces are equal, then the opportunities are equal."[90]

But while talking to a visiting Indian politician, Keshav Dev Malviya, on the same day, Khrushchev demonstrated a degree of anxiety. A strange encounter it was. The Sino-Indian War had now raged for a week. Khrushchev used the opportunity to encourage the Indians to talk to the Chinese (whom, as we have seen, he now supported). In fact, the entire encounter was evidently organized to allow Khrushchev to convince the Chinese that he was on their side (to this end, an edited version of his conversation with Malviya was promptly dispatched to Beijing).

In the conversation, Khrushchev drew on the Soviet experience of overcoming disputes through negotiations and compromise without getting mired in considerations of "prestige." But Khrushchev's discussion of

317

PART II HUBRIS

the Sino-Indian conflict reflected on the dilemma that he himself faced that very week. "From the experience of my life, I know," Khrushchev said, "that war is like a card game, though I myself never played and do not play cards, because I think it's a waste of time." He continued: "If one follows this dangerous road, then the border conflict will not just continue but it can escalate into a large war. One should not rule out that the time will come when the two sides will claim that territory in itself does not play any role in this conflict, and that the main thing is in the prestige and the blood that has been shed."

And then, a great insight, from someone who had sleepwalked to the precipice of a nuclear war: "History tells us that in order to stop a conflict one should begin not from exploring reasons why it happened but from a ceasefire. When people are shooting at each other, sometimes it is difficult to determine who started. [But] the main thing is not in the crying for the dead or in avenging them, but in saving those who can die if the conflict continues."[91]

In the meantime, seeing that the United States had not yet invaded Cuba, Khrushchev decided to up the ante. He had been getting drips of information that suggested that Kennedy might just consider a swap of missiles: those in Cuba for those in Turkey. This information may have come from the GRU or perhaps even from Walter Lippman, who on October 25 penned the now famous column suggesting a Cuba-for-Turkey trade. Lippman's article was translated for Khrushchev's benefit and – perhaps – inspired him to change the terms of the proposed deal.[92] A non-invasion pledge would not be enough: the United States would have to remove the Jupiters. Khrushchev then dictated another letter to Kennedy, which was openly broadcast on October 27, before the American president responded to the first, from October 25/26.

The ExComm was briefly confused and even worried that the second letter was the product of some militant forces in the Kremlin that opposed Khrushchev's readiness to compromise. In the end Kennedy decided to respond positively to the first letter while mostly ignoring the second. At the same time, his brother Bobby Kennedy reassured Ambassador Dobrynin privately on Saturday night, October 27, that the "Jupiters" would go in four to five months – but this was the extent of the US willingness to compromise. Dobrynin was also told that unless Khrushchev accepted Kennedy's conditions, the United States would have to act in the immediate future. Earlier that day, the Americans lost a U-2 over Cuba: it was shot down by Soviet anti-aircraft defense; the pilot was killed. Things were beginning to spin out of control.

CHAPTER 11 CUBA

Figure 15 A Soviet military map of Cuba with the location of missile bases, November 1962. Source: CWIHP/DA.

Khrushchev was increasingly worried about Castro's state of mind. On that very day he received a missive from Castro, in which the latter proposed to nuke the Americans if they invaded Cuba. Historians have long known that this message was one key reason for Khrushchev's rapid move to de-escalate the crisis by announcing the withdrawal of Soviet missiles. The new evidence suggests that it was even more important than we realized. "He [Castro] sent us a proposal ... to begin a nuclear war," Khrushchev mused aloud on October 30. "What is it – a temporary madness or the absence of brains?"[93] On the same day, in a conversation with the visiting Czechoslovak party leader Antonín Novotný, he went further:

> Fidel Castro proposed that we ourselves should be the first to start an atomic war. Do you know what that would mean? That probably cannot even be expressed at all ... What would we gain if we ourselves started a war? After all, millions of people would die, in our country too. Can we even contemplate a thing like that? Could we allow ourselves to threaten the world of socialism which was hard won by the working class? Only a person who has no idea what nuclear war means, or who has been so blinded, for instance, like Castro, by revolutionary passion, can talk like that.[94]

Fearing imminent war, Khrushchev backed down. His decision to pull missiles out of Cuba was broadcast over Radio Moscow on October 28 (to save time). Dobrynin was in the meantime instructed to meet with Robert Kennedy to tell him that Khrushchev counted on the United States to keep its promise to remove missiles from Turkey.[95] Dobrynin cabled back on October 28, noting that the younger Kennedy impressed on him that

PART II HUBRIS

the "agreement" was to be completely secret. The word "agreement" in Dobrynin's cable encouraged Khrushchev who immediately instructed his ambassador to meet with Robert Kennedy again to stress that the Soviet Union would "view this agreement as strictly secret."[96]

Why did Khrushchev attach so much importance to what after all was a secret deal, and one that had no real practical significance? The reason for his excitement is that it allowed him to cover up a shameful retreat from his Cuban misadventure, which he browbeat his colleague to endorse amid so much hubris. He lost and now looked like a fool. But there was something else, too. Khrushchev's decision to send missiles to Cuba was, as we have seen, at least in part a reaction to the seeming unfairness of the US presence in Turkey. This presence, even if it did not matter all that much militarily, mattered a great deal psychologically. Khrushchev now sought to convince his colleagues and, above all, himself, that he wrestled a concession from the American president. All that remained was to convince the Cubans, who were not even consulted.

THE CRISIS AFTER THE CRISIS

Castro was livid. Khrushchev sent him a short missive on October 28, "recommending" him "not to yield to ... emotions, to show restraint."[97] He followed with another, longer, letter on October 30, explaining that there was no time for close consultations because he feared that the US attack on Cuba was imminent. He also chastised Castro for his proposal to nuke America first.[98] The letter was at least reasonably polite. Privately, though, the Soviet leader was incensed, comparing Castro to a peasant who, on having been saved by another fellow from being mauled by a bear, complains that his savior spoiled the bear's skin by piercing him through.[99]

Even before Castro's reply reached Khrushchev, he composed yet another letter, twenty-five pages long. "Allow me to congratulate you on a great victory," the letter began. "We repeat, precisely a great victory, dear friends." He then went on to explain why he considered his withdrawal from Cuba a great victory: sending missiles there was merely an expedient to stave off an imminent American invasion. Now that Kennedy pledged that America would not invade, mission was accomplished. "They [the Americans] understood that Cuba is a steel hedgehog, which cannot be swallowed and on which they cannot sit without piercing those parts of the body that are needed for sitting."

"It would be preposterous to think," he continued, "that we agreed to remove the missiles from Cuba to please imperialism. No, we took this step because the missiles have played their role, without being launched." He said that he merely "showed a fist" to the Americans, and they immediately recognized Cuba's right to independence. "Is this a defeat? No, dear friends! Of course, the imperialists will claim the opposite in their newspapers. But this is merely so that they can save their face." He sweetened the pill by claiming that the Cuban armed forces were now much stronger than before, that they had the means to repel an invasion with tactical missiles and coastal batteries. However, the passage was crossed out, perhaps when Khrushchev realized that some of those batteries had nuclear ammunition.

In a sign that Khrushchev was still upset over Castro's apparent suggestion to nuke the United States, he argued – in a passage that the Cuban leader would not have taken kindly – that "only know-nothings in the field of Marxism-Leninism can act recklessly, in line with the principle that if one has to die, then better die beautifully. This is suicidal psychology."[100]

Whether he ever sent this long letter is unclear. But, evidently concluding that letters alone were not enough, he asked Mikoyan to fly to Havana to explain the situation to Castro in person. "He [Castro] doesn't understand that we saved them from invasion," Khrushchev told Mikoyan. "We saved [them,] and he doesn't understand."[101] The Armenian, whom Khrushchev jokingly called "a Cuban" for his experience of dealing with Castro, would spend most of November in and around Havana in difficult talks with the Cuban leadership.

Castro was deeply insulted by the way he had been treated. It was not just that he was not consulted about the decision to withdraw the missiles: that, at least, could be (and was) explained away as a necessary measure to avoid an imminent war. But how could one explain Khrushchev's outrageous public proposal of a Turkey-for-Cuba swap: did that mean that Cuba was just a trading chip? And how could Castro accept the American demand, now seemingly backed by the Soviets, to allow teams of inspectors in Cuba to verify that the weapons were gone? And how could he permit American U-2 planes to crisscross the Cuban skies unmolested? Even years later Castro would still brood over how Khrushchev had treated him like "a favorite naughty child," whereas what he really wanted was "equality" – he wanted to be treated like a statesman.[102]

Castro spoke in a language Khrushchev could understand: the language of prestige. Although in no sense an elected politician, the Cuban leader was acutely aware that his domestic standing would suffer if he was seen caving to American demands. Moreover, his international standing – in Latin America and even as far afield as Algeria – would not easily recover from such humiliation. The presence of Soviet missiles gave the Cubans a sense of "psychological power," Castro told Mikoyan. "Our people were proudly conscious of their role as the protectors of the interests of socialist countries. The anti-aircraft troops and all soldiers who protected the areas of missile deployment, were full of enthusiasm and were prepared to defend them with their very lives ... And suddenly – concessions." Moscow's unexpected retreat "dealt a moral blow" to the Cuban Revolution. "We always remember about the prestige of our revolution," Castro revealed. "The people were worried that our prestige in Latin America would be undermined."[103] In a later conversation, after he learned that the Soviets were not just taking out the missiles but also the tactical nukes, Castro exclaimed with desperation: "What are we? A nonentity! A dirty rag!"[104]

Mikoyan reassured the Cubans repeatedly that they were better off now that Kennedy made his non-invasion pledge. As revolutionaries they had to learn to "maneuver." There was no point in "dying beautifully." And, in any case, as a result of the missile crisis, "Cuba's prestige undoubtedly increased." It is unlikely that Castro and the rest were particularly convinced.[105]

As Khrushchev and Mikoyan worked tirelessly to put a positive spin on the Soviet withdrawal, the Chinese sensed their opportunity. The Chinese propaganda machine went into high gear, likening Khrushchev's retreat to Chamberlain's appeasement of Hitler's Germany in 1938. Cuba was another Munich! Five million Chinese took to the streets in the first week of November, condemning Washington's "piratical crimes." The Cuban Embassy became a pilgrimage site for tens of thousands of protesters, carrying Castro's portraits and messages of support. Before long, these messages were piled several feet high outside the embassy gates. Even the motley crew of American Communists living in Beijing paid their respects, marching in the street, shouting: "Go, Go, Go, Guantanamo!"[106] Chinese embassy workers in Havana went to the hospital to donate blood. The aim of the propaganda offensive was to advertise the Chinese as "the most reliable and loyal comrades-in-arms of the Cuban people [who] will forever share their weal and woe."[107]

This kind of propaganda fell on fertile soil, nowhere more so than in Cuba. China's best friend in Cuba was Che Guevara. On December 1, 1962, Che, over at the Chinese Embassy for dinner, grimly told Ambassador Shen Jian that Cuba's "international prestige" has suffered a blow. "Now they [the Soviets] have left. Though they promised to continue their support, only the naive would keep buying their empty words." Shen Jian exploited the opening. It was good, he said, that the Soviets had now

CHAPTER 11 CUBA

shown their true nature. Here was an opportunity for the "Leftists" to "act and raise their distinct flag."[108]

China had just victoriously concluded its month-long war with India over their shared border: the Chinese triumph over the Indians made for a sharp contrast with the Soviet retreat from the Caribbean. After the battering of the Great Leap, it seemed that Mao, once again, was back on his feet, towering over hapless Khrushchev and leading the world revolution.

The Soviet leader was acutely aware of the blow to his global prestige. He was furious with people like Che Guevara who questioned Moscow's willingness to risk it all for its allies, far and near. He sent angry tirades to Mikoyan, asking him to tell Castro that if the Cubans continued to be difficult, the Soviets would pull up the stakes and leave: then, he will see who will come to their rescue. He cursed himself for "getting entangled with [these] immature people."[109] Most of all, he fumed at China for taking advantage of his predicament. "Some know-it-alls say that imperialism must not be trusted," he railed at a party plenum in late November. "What wisdom! Well, then what, stab it to death? Stab it, then! These know-it-alls, who teach the others so well, have gotten used to capitalist shit and tolerate Macao on their territory."

Khrushchev often pointed to Macao, controlled by the Portuguese, as a proof that the Chinese were not as militant as their propaganda claimed because, in reality, Mao, too, was afraid of war "like the Devil of holy water."[110] Failure to make concessions in Cuba, meanwhile, would have meant a nuclear war. This would be, Khrushchev explained, recalling one of his favorite parables, like that tsarist army officer who accidentally broke wind while dancing at a ball. He was so embarrassed that he blew his brains out! "This is a tragedy," he said, "but a tragedy for one person. But if the government does it, it is a tragedy for the people. I apologize for such a rude comparison but it makes sense."[111]

In the same breath Khrushchev, forgetting his earlier endorsement of Beijing's position in the border dispute with India, lashed out against China's war in the Himalayas. "Who needs this war? What are they shedding blood for? ... It is bad that this war is being fought by Communists. Who started the shooting? It's always hard to figure it out. But you can see who is doing the fighting."[112] Khrushchev's words met with "thunderous applause" of the party faithful. They did not need to be convinced. Now, the first secretary just needed to convince the revolutionary world that he, not Mao, was the true leader of the struggle against the dark forces of imperialism. In particular, he had to convince the petulant Cubans.

In December Khrushchev tried his charm on the Cuban Communist official Carlos Rafael Rodriguez, who visited Moscow for talks with the senior Soviet leadership. His frustration showed through though. He called the Cubans "fighting roosters," the same epithet he previously used to describe the Chinese, and complained that they had criticized the Soviets "using the words of the Albanians and the Chinese." Rodriguez downplayed Cuba's pro-Chinese drift, claiming that Beijing's solidarity came "too late" and, oddly enough, was not sufficiently enthusiastic. He tried to explain to Khrushchev that the problem was not with the Chinese: the problem was with the way the Soviets had handled the crisis, which "threatened the influence and prestige of the Cuban revolution." Khrushchev understood that sort of language: "You have Spanish blood," he told Rodriguez. "You are proud, you speak of principles. Maybe you think that we Russians have a different temperament, and maybe you do not appreciate this about us, but we too are proud." The bottom line – as he pressed to Rodriguez – was that despite all appearances the Soviets had won: it was imperialism that had to retreat in Cuba by giving the non-invasion pledge (he of course did not divulge any hint of the agreement on the Turkish Jupiters).[113]

A month later, in mid-January 1963, Khrushchev turned up in Berlin for an East German Communist Party Congress. It did not go well. The Chinese delegate, Wu Xiuquan, raised a ruckus, indirectly but viciously attacking Khrushchev for Cuba and a host of other sins. He was helpfully booed, and Khrushchev himself skipped the occasion by opting to tour an East Berlin television factory, but the embarrassment was real. On January 16 the Soviet leader met with a delegation of Cuban Communists, also in town for the Congress. He tried hard to persuade them that he was a committed revolutionary, citing his favorite examples of Soviet largesse: Indonesia and Yemen. The Soviet Union supplied weapons, even men, to fight these remote wars: a true example of Communist solidarity. Latin American revolutionaries were no exception. "We are ready to support them in every way," he claimed, "including by giving them weapons if they opt for an armed insurrection."[114] After his well-known promises to send in the Baltic Fleet to help Cuba, these new commitments sounded a little hollow: his credibility was at a low point.

A few days later, the first secretary boarded a train back to the Soviet Union. As it ploughed its way across the snow-draped winterscapes of rural Belorussia, Khrushchev dictated another twenty-seven-page letter to Castro. He wound his memories back to the beginning of the Cuban Missile Crisis, recounting again how the Americans were determined to crush Cuba,

CHAPTER 11 CUBA

and how the Soviets were prepared to save it, and how their readiness to help showed a commitment to support revolution. And he hammered the Chinese. Again and again he returned to Mao's perfidy, reminding Castro how the Chinese did nothing during the crisis to help Cuba, except for cursing the imperialists. "You can curse imperialism all you want but it won't lose any weight, it won't weaken, and its insolence will not lessen. Imperialism takes into account only real force. It does not recognize anything else." "So," he continued, "you can call imperialism a paper tiger, shit, or whatever," – it will not help unless one is prepared to stand up to the Americans the way the Soviets had done in Cuba. "So, those who think that we are begging for peace are either deliberately perverting our position, or they just don't know what they're talking about."[115]

Maybe it was the logic of Khrushchev's argument or, more likely, the promise of Soviet economic aid that Cuba still desperately needed but Fidel Castro at last heeded his call for reconciliation. In April–June 1963 he toured the length of the Soviet Union, visiting factories, speaking at massive rallies, signing autographs for Soviet children, exploring the wild expanse of Siberia. Khrushchev engaged the Cuban in extensive and intense conversations, including on China. "He asked me," Khrushchev recalled "'what are [our] differences with China?' I said: that's exactly what I am asking: what are the differences? ... I said: '[It's] a question of nationalism, a question of egotism. This is the main thing. They want to play the first fiddle.'" And then:

> But this is not decided by vote. This is determined by one's status and by the others' recognition. Even among friends: 5–10 people are friends, and one of them is the leader. They don't elect him. They just *recognize him for certain qualities*. This is how it is, and how it will be in the future. People won't all be black or red-haired. There will be different colors, and different temperaments, and different mental capabilities among people. There will be inequality, like elsewhere in nature.[116]

Never did Nikita Khrushchev come so close to uncovering the psychological undercurrents of his political behavior. It was an exceptionally revealing statement – one that went to the very core of Soviet beliefs about the world, and about the Cold War.

CONCLUSION

Khrushchev finally knew: his problems with China were not about ideological divergences. Simply, they wanted to play "the first fiddle." If he were a little more reflective, he would have perhaps realized that the same was equally true of himself: *he* wanted to play the first fiddle. *He* wanted to be recognized for certain qualities. Being seen as the "leader" of the so-called revolutionary world was the central element of Khrushchev's quest for political legitimacy, and a major part of his long-standing effort to win recognition from the United States. This is why Cuba was so important to the first secretary. A missile base in Cuba addressed two of Khrushchev's major problems: first, it bolstered his self-perception as an equal of the United States. Addressing Soviet strategic vulnerability was probably a concern, though perhaps a lesser concern than the symbolic satisfaction of acquiring a missile base under America's nose. That is why the parallel between the Turkish "Jupiters" and the Cuban missiles was a big part of the picture: both in facilitating the Soviet decision to deploy missiles and, later, in guiding Moscow's exit strategy.

Second, there is of course no denial that Khrushchev was deeply worried about the possibility of an American invasion of Cuba. We are used to seeing his commitment in ideological terms, as if the prospect of Cuba's failure was something that the Soviet leader, as a true Marxist-Leninist, simply could not countenance. In reality, Khrushchev was not so much concerned with the peculiarities of the Marxist-Leninist dogma (of which in any case he had a rather vague understanding), as he was with the idea that his reputation was tied to Cuba's fortunes. If Cuba were invaded, if Castro were overthrown, Khrushchev's credibility would come into question, the Soviet Union's image as an "equal" of the United States could no longer be sustained. Cuba's survival was indeed one of the important reasons for Khrushchev's decision to launch Operation Anadyr. Having become, in his own words, "entangled" with the Cubans, he was willing to go to extraordinary lengths to protect his reputation. Just not to the point of a nuclear war.

In the end he backed down, with considerable loss of face, which the Chinese immediately sought to exploit. Khrushchev could not understand why anyone would choose China's leadership over his: the Soviet Union, after all, had "certain qualities": it was more industrially developed. It had launched the Sputnik and Gagarin into orbit. It had missiles. Yet, surely, there was more to leadership than these physical assets. Leadership was about moral authority, and it was that authority that he had so hopelessly squandered in Cuba, giving Mao the much-needed opening. Khrushchev was exasperated by the absurdity of the Chinese war with India over remote wilderness in the Himalayas but for Mao the

CHAPTER 11 CUBA

Indian adventure was rather similar to what Cuba was for Khrushchev – an effort to show China's grandeur, a way to resist perceived "bullying," and claim leadership in the third world. The outcome of the short but intense conflict was more favorable to Mao than the Cuban adventure had been to Khrushchev: China's crushing defeat of India, followed by a magnanimous offer to negotiate, stood in stark contrast with what the Chinese called Moscow's "capitulationism" in Cuba.

In the public memory, the Cuban Missile Crisis was an extremely dangerous point in the Soviet–American relationship when Khrushchev and Kennedy came "eyeball to eyeball," and Khrushchev "blinked first." This real sense of drama tends to obscure some bigger themes. More than anything, the crisis was about the Soviet challenge to America's right to play the "first fiddle." Kennedy understood the gravity of this challenge: allowing Khrushchev to have his way would undermine Washington's credibility as much as it would strengthen Moscow's. Soviet missiles in Cuba were unacceptable not just because they posed a security threat to the United States, though they did, but because their presence would indicate Kennedy's weakness in the face of Soviet bullying. But Kennedy recognized that Khrushchev's resentment was not without cause, which is why he secretly agreed to dismantle the Turkish "Jupiters." Historians have wondered whether this promise might have been made public if only Khrushchev stuck to his guns. Possibly. Though unwilling to admit it publicly, he knew that what the Americans had in Turkey was not all that different from what he refused to allow the Soviets in Cuba.

Fortunately, Khrushchev decided against pushing his luck. Recognition was important but it was better to live in humiliation than to be recognized in death. There would be more opportunities to fight back. Khrushchev thought that time was on his side. The crisis brought him closer to Kennedy, and he looked forward to picking up the strands of dialogue and perhaps rebuilding some of the spirit of Camp David. There were inherent limitations to the enterprise: as in 1960, the Chinese stood ready to jump at Khrushchev for betraying Marxism-Leninism, and defending himself against the Chinese accusations would necessarily impose constraints on the depth of his engagement with Kennedy. Still, the conclusion of the Partial Nuclear Test Ban Treaty in August 1963 pointed to real possibilities of compromise. There would be no more Tsar Bombs, and that in itself was an impressive achievement.

But Kennedy was shot dead in Dallas in November 1963, and then Khrushchev himself fell prey to his colleagues' scheming. In October 1964 the Soviet leader was ousted from power, replaced by the triumvirate of

PART II HUBRIS

Leonid Brezhnev, Aleksei Kosygin, and Nikolai Podgorny. Mao rejoiced at the demise of his nemesis. Yet the new Soviet leaders proved to be as concerned as Khrushchev had been about their political legitimacy. They were just as attentive to their standing in the world, and their credibility in the eyes of the West and the world Communist movement. They, too, sought recognition of their global leadership. They were just as keen to play the "first fiddle." Before long, the fears and ambitions of the Americans, the Soviets, and the Chinese would come to clash in the jungles of Vietnam.

PART III

DECLINE

12

VIETNAM

When he committed the United States to a bloody conflict in Vietnam, President Lyndon B. Johnson seriously overstated the consequences of a Communist takeover. What we know today of the relationship between North Vietnam (or the Democratic Republic of Vietnam, DRV) and its two key allies and sponsors, China and the Soviet Union, puts to rest uncritical assumptions about a global, Moscow-directed, conspiracy, aimed at turning all of Southeast Asia into a sea of red. Finding itself at odds with the Chinese and the Russians, the Vietnamese Communist leaders worked to preserve their freedom of maneuver while assuring the continuation of political support, and the supply of economic and military aid from both. Hanoi kept its eyes on the prize: national unification and the defeat of the United States on the battlefield, a task only possible with support from its difficult allies. Moscow and Beijing recognized the importance of this goal, but their prize was Vietnam itself – that is to say, its loyalties in the unfolding Sino-Soviet split.

What was it about Vietnam that proved so important to its Communist allies? There was a range of issues, from the geopolitical and security rationales to ideological zeal and the fates of world revolution. Historians have explored these questions in depth.[1] Acknowledging the importance of their contributions, this chapter makes the case for interpreting the Chinese and Soviet policies in light of their need to be recognized as credible allies, which had a legitimizing aspect for both the Chinese and the Soviet leaders. Credibility was central to the Chinese and Soviet bids for leadership in the socialist camp and the third world, while the notion of leadership was closely related to perceptions of legitimacy of the ruling elites. Their costly, long-lasting commitment to Vietnam was, in a sense, not so much about Vietnam as it was about the Sino-Soviet rivalry for leadership in the third world and the international Communist movement.

In the end, Moscow won the contest. Its victory was as much a function of the Soviet material commitment to Hanoi's war effort as it was a consequence of China's domestic meltdown. But it was a very costly victory.

331

PART III DECLINE

The Soviets became a party to a distant war that they could neither adequately control nor even fully understand.

HANOI CHANGES COURSE

At the turn of the 1960s, Nikita Khrushchev and Mao Zedong were on parallel trajectories in Southeast Asia: both wanted to avoid conflict. In the late 1950s Khrushchev had his hands full with other problems. In 1958–61 he was preoccupied with the Berlin Crisis, which he himself had started but was desperate to end, and with the unrest in the Middle East, which he did not start, but hoped to turn to his advantage. The spirit of Camp David that followed Khrushchev's talks with Eisenhower in September 1959 imbued the Soviet leader with hope that the Cold War itself could be quietly wound down, if only the Americans recognized Moscow's legitimate interests. These did not include Southeast Asia in any meaningful way. By contrast, the Chinese were very interested in what transpired south of the border but primarily from the standpoint of national security rather than revolutionary strategy. China's domestic difficulties – the failure of the Great Leap Forward – called for a cautious posture in foreign policy.

In the early 1960s North Vietnam drifted perceptibly in China's direction. Those were the years of the Sino-Soviet polemics, when China openly challenged Moscow's leadership in the international Communist movement. Mao accused Khrushchev of betraying Marxism and colluding with the United States to sell out revolutionary movements around the world. This charge appeared all the more credible after Khrushchev's capitulation in the Cuban Missile Crisis. If Khrushchev sold out Cuba, would he not sell out Vietnam as well? Those were questions that the Chinese were now raising with the Vietnamese leaders hoping to win their support.

Ho Chi Minh was cautious. As we have seen, when Sino-Soviet relations came under strain because of Khrushchev's falling out with Albania, he pleaded with the Soviet leader to forgive the Albanians. Ho was genuinely worried that the fracturing of the socialist camp would undercut Vietnam's war in the south. Mao was unhappy. "Ho Chi Minh," he surmised in June 1962, "is afraid that, if N. Khrushchev expelled Albania today, he may tomorrow expel Vietnam too." He went on: "In a meeting that Ho Chi Minh had with me, I asked him, why are you afraid? In our country, in China, the grass is growing just fine even though N. Khrushchev is attacking and fighting us. If you do not believe this, go have a stroll around our mountains and see with your own eyes."[2]

332

CHAPTER 12 VIETNAM

Two months later, Mao proclaimed the return to class struggle in China's foreign policy. Because of this new militant posture and a growing concern about the increased American presence in South Vietnam, China upped its political and military commitment to Hanoi.[3] Meanwhile, North Vietnamese requests for Soviet aid and cash went largely unanswered.[4]

Mao and other Chinese leaders repeatedly assured the Vietnamese that they would back them in the conflict with the United States, even as the Soviets carefully probed for the possibility of a peaceful settlement. Unsurprisingly, by late 1963 the ranks of "pro-Soviet" Vietnamese leaders grew thinner, while the Chinese gained influence by the day. For a time, Ho kept up the pretense of friendship with the USSR, blaming rumors of Hanoi's anti-Soviet tilt on "hooligans and reactionary elements."[5] But the Soviets knew that Ho himself was "swimming between the currents" while others, including the Vietnamese Workers' Party general secretary, Le Duan, already "stood on the Chinese bank."[6] "Pro-Soviet" players in the Vietnamese leadership reported the feeling of "complete isolation."[7]

The North Vietnamese faced a dilemma. They wanted to take advantage of the deteriorating political situation in the South through an armed uprising. They needed political support and weapons, which the Chinese were happy to provide, even as Khrushchev, his eyes on better relations with the West, continued to procrastinate. Under these circumstances, Hanoi's turn to China was a tactical move in the absence of better options. Khrushchev himself precipitated this shift by ignoring his client's needs. But, characteristically blind to his own policy failures, he blamed his loss of North Vietnam on the imaginary machinations of "Chinese half-breeds" in the Vietnamese party leadership.[8] For Khrushchev, the problem of Vietnam was only an aspect of his broader struggle with China, and a rather peripheral aspect at that. The Chinese worried about Vietnam much more for strategic and historical reasons.

On August 2, 1964 an American destroyer USS *Maddox* on patrol in the Tonkin Gulf was fired on by Vietnamese torpedo boats. The minor incident had far-reaching consequences. Apprehensive of the Communist menace in Vietnam, President Lyndon B. Johnson asked for, and was given by the Congress, the authority to fight an undeclared war. In March 1965, not long after a Viet Cong attack on a US army base near Pleiku in South Vietnam, the US Air Force began bombing targets in the North. US Marines arrived that same month; the American ground presence then increased exponentially. Washington's direct involvement in the Vietnam War, which Mao and Khrushchev had so hoped to avert in the late 1950s, was now a brutal reality.

PART III DECLINE

KHRUSHCHEV'S FALL

The Tonkin Gulf incident barely registered on Khrushchev's mental map: he had bigger problems. Perhaps the biggest of all was a new, unexpected turn in the Sino-Soviet relationship: Mao was laying claims to Soviet territory. The shocking revelation came in the form of comments Mao made to a visiting Japanese socialist delegation, on July 10, 1964. He lamented that the Soviet Union had robbed China of Mongolia, and occupied "too many places" both in Europe (at German, Polish, Romanian, and Finnish expense) and in Asia, where it annexed territories "east of Lake Baikal, including Khabarovsk, Vladivostok, and the Kamchatka Peninsula." "We have yet to settle this bill with them," he added ominously.[9]

These comments – which Mao later claimed were just "idle talk" – were promptly published in Japan and caused an outrage in Moscow.[10] "Have you read the hideous document about the border? ...," Khrushchev asked his colleagues on August 19. "I read it yesterday and became indignant." He went on to talk about how the Chinese were "evil, hypocritical, crafty and cunning," citing no less of an authority than the famous nineteenth-century Russian explorer and spy, Nikolai Przhevalsky, who had left many a racist reflection on China in his voluminous writings.[11]

What really got under Khrushchev's skin was that Mao was evidently feeding the "bacillus" of nationalism, knowing full well that borders in the socialist world did not coincide with ethnic groups: not just the Soviets but the Polish, the Hungarians, the Romanians, the Yugoslavs – they all had these historical legacies. But so did the Chinese! The Chinese emperors, Khrushchev thought, had also conquered territories and enslaved peoples. Out of desperation he even thought of an idea: why not ask the Chinese to let the Uighurs and the Kazakhs living on both sides of the border to form an independent country – see what the Chinese say to that! (Predictably, the improvisation was a nonstarter.) "This is criminal," Khrushchev fumed, referring to Chinese claims. "It leads to butchery between peoples. And when this happens between states, this already creates wars. There is a danger of a war. We must struggle against this."[12]

The future of this relationship bothered Khrushchev deeply. He incessantly talked about it in the late summer and early autumn of 1964, defending the Soviet position, trying to understand what drove Mao. Was he mad? What else could explain his outrageous claims? "Mao lives in the Middle Ages," Khrushchev told Indian President Sarvepalli Radhakrishnan on September 12, 1964. "It is completely evident that this is a person who has lost his mind. And we feel it very well, because recently we ourselves

CHAPTER 12 VIETNAM

got rid of a similar 'genius.' We were constrained by such a genius, Stalin; it was impossible with him to develop policy that would be to the people's benefit."[13] What made it worse was that the Chinese were on the verge of developing the A-bomb, something the Soviets had generously contributed to. Khrushchev's only solace was that the Chinese economy was too weak to allow it to join the nuclear arms race. "They'll need decades to produce enough atomic weapons to become dangerous. But even then, they won't be able to catch up with the others, because the others won't remain in place."[14] A few days later, in a conversation with another visitor, Khrushchev likened Mao to Chinggis Khan.[15]

It was with such sad and disturbing thoughts that Khrushchev departed on his autumn vacation. He went to his sprawling dacha in Pitsunda, on the Black Sea. While Khrushchev was away, his party comrades plotted his overthrow. The leading plotter was Khrushchev's long-time protégé, Leonid Brezhnev, a 57-year-old party apparatchik who had risen through the ranks after stints in Ukraine, Moldavia, and Kazakhstan. On the evening of October 13, Khrushchev was urgently summoned back to Moscow, and on the following day the Presidium voted to have him "voluntarily" removed from power. The list of his sins was long and, on the whole, had little to do with foreign policy. It was Khrushchev's "style of leadership" – his bureaucratic reorganizations, his failure to consult with his colleagues, his "mania of greatness" (in the words of the party ideologue Mikhail Suslov who was tasked with detailing Khrushchev's misdeeds at a party plenum).[16] Another party functionary, Dmitry Polyansky, prepared a lengthy report listing a few of Khrushchev's foreign policy misadventures, including the Berlin Crisis and the Cuban Missile Crisis, which "dealt a serious blow to the country's authority and prestige." Polyansky also noted that Khrushchev had demonstrated "arrogance" in dealing with socialist allies, and had even called Mao Zedong "an old shoe."[17]

Khrushchev was replaced by Leonid Brezhnev as the new first secretary of the party (later becoming the general secretary) while Aleksei Kosygin, a capable economic manager, became the prime minister, thus separating the two key posts Khrushchev had appropriated for himself.

Mao knew very little of any of this. There was hope in Beijing, however fleeting, that Khrushchev was overthrown because, as the Chinese propaganda had long insisted, he had betrayed the revolution. The news of Khrushchev's fall coincided with the successful test of the first Chinese A-bomb (on October 16), giving Mao plenty to celebrate.

To see what the new Soviet leaders were up to, he sent a delegation to Moscow in early November, which included Zhou Enlai and Marshal

335

PART III DECLINE

Figure 16 A Soviet instructor training a North Vietnamese pilot, September 1966. Source: Sovfoto/Universal Images Group/Getty Images.

He Long. The idea was to feel the ground for possible rapprochement, if it turned out that the Soviets were prepared to accept that they had been wrong all along, and that the Chinese had been right. However, before the talks could properly begin, they were derailed by a bizarre diplomatic incident when, at the Kremlin banquet on November 7, Soviet Defense Minister Rodion Malinovsky made drunken comments to the Chinese delegation to the effect that "the Soviet and the Chinese people want happiness, and we will not allow any Maos or Khrushchevs to put obstacles in our way." The Chinese stormed out. The talks, when they finally began, mainly came down to Brezhnev attempting to persuade Zhou Enlai that Malinovsky was simply drunk and did not know what he was saying. Zhou insisted that the defense minister revealed his true feelings. The Sino-Soviet rapprochement ended at this, never having begun.[18]

THE WAR ESCALATES

All these dramatic events overlapped with the escalation in Vietnam, which soon became the core concern of China's foreign policy, becoming entangled imperceptibly with a very different struggle that unfolded in China

CHAPTER 12 VIETNAM

itself. The Soviets half-suspected that the Tonkin Gulf incident was a secret Chinese ploy to prod Vietnam towards an open war with the United States and so instill their allegiance to, and dependence on, China.[19] There is no evidence of such devious plotting on Mao's part. But when the war began in earnest, he embraced it with relish. As Mao famously advised the North Vietnamese in October 1964:

> If the Americans are determined to invade the inner land, you may allow them to do so ... You must not engage your main force in a head-to-head confrontation with them, and must well maintain your main force. My opinion is that so long as the green mountain is there, how can you ever lack firewood?[20]

He preferred to keep the war to South Vietnam. But if it expanded to the North, that was fine, too, because the Americans would then find themselves embroiled in a quagmire.

Three considerations underpinned Beijing's approach to the deepening conflict. First, the Chinese believed that for all the dangerous escalation, the chances of a broader regional (never mind global) conflagration were minimal. America was already badly overextended. The more overextended it became, the less chance it had of winning. Speaking in the immediate aftermath of Tonkin Gulf, Chinese Premier Zhou Enlai outlined the stratagem in nearly poetic terms:

> If there were just a few more Congos in Africa, a few more Vietnams in Asia, a few more Cubas in Latin America, then America would have to spread 10 fingers to 10 different places, spreading its power very thin ... If we make America extend its 10 fingers to 10 different places, then we can chop them off one by one."[21]

It did not matter how long the struggle would take – a hundred years or more, perhaps – but it would end in victory. It was imperative that the United States leave Indochina – indeed, not just leave, but, as Mao put it, "leave in shame."[22] Mao valued the Vietnam War for the chance to "humiliate" the Americans, and so undermine their global influence.

Second, the struggle helped mobilize the "people" – not just the Vietnamese but also the Chinese. The Vietnam War intersected with the trajectory of Chinese domestic politics. Mao's leftward turn in domestic politics in mid-1962 stemmed from his dissatisfaction with the pace of his country's revolutionary transformation. Mao now saw an opportunity to drum up support for more radical policies by invoking the threat of war. As he explained shortly after the Tonkin Gulf incident, "though the Americans cannot win in Vietnam, it is useful to have them there because 'imperialism' is necessary to unify revolutionary forces, and excesses of 'imperialism' are necessary to prove that socialism is the way of the future."[23]

Millions of Chinese took to the streets in August 1964 to "angrily denounce U.S. imperialist aggression." The DRV Embassy in Beijing became a pilgrimage site for expressing officially sanctioned outrage, and for handing in thousands of letters of support, including one by a "78-year-old professor with a long silvery beard" and by a "12-year-old Young Pioneer who, in his summer vacation, had collected signatures to a pledge of support from 11 classmates."[24] This outpouring of support was far from spontaneous. The massive demonstrations were organized by the CCP Central Committee to "raise vigilance among the army and the people," and to "educate [the people] about the concepts of national defense." The instructions even included the slogans for the demonstrators' banners: "Resolutely oppose!" "Resolutely support," and, of course, "Long Live World Peace!"[25]

Third, the war gave Mao an opportunity to assert leadership in the international Communist movement amid the deepening conflict with the Soviet Union. The worse the fighting, the better ground to claim that the Soviets got it wrong: one could not have peaceful coexistence with the United States. By attempting to build bridges with the United States, the Soviets betrayed Vietnam's hopes and the hopes of the entire revolutionary world. That was the message that the Chinese were now selling in Southeast Asia and further afield, and with some success. That said, the Chinese themselves were very careful to keep the war within certain bounds and signaled to the United States that as long as the Americans did not directly attack China, Beijing would not intervene. As Zhou Enlai put it in August 1964, "We do not provoke, but answer America's provocation. As America takes one step, the people of China follow in taking one step ... If America wants to expand the war, we will certainly resist."[26] The message was reiterated through multiple channels, and it gave China's policy greater nuance than one could extract from loud proclamations of solidarity.

Meanwhile, Moscow's approach began to change after Khrushchev was overthrown. Brezhnev and Kosygin made an effort to prove that they were truly committed to supporting an ally in need. In late 1964, the duo reached out to the Vietnamese leaders with an offer to rebuild bridges. Prime Minister Pham Van Dong visited the Soviet Union in November and was promised help. In February 1965 Kosygin travelled to Hanoi, just as the Americans began their bombing campaign. This only served to increase the Soviet resolve in aiding Vietnam. The underlying rationale for Moscow's

CHAPTER 12 VIETNAM

increased interest was that the Soviet leadership faced a deficit of political legitimacy. Aiding Vietnam in a war against "imperialism" helped them in being recognized – by their people, their clients and allies, and the broader world – as the legitimate heirs to the leadership of the socialist camp. An effort to improve relations with China also served the same purpose.

Mao, however, was not inclined to reciprocate. This became clear during Kosygin's February 1965 trip to Beijing, where he stopped on the way to and from Vietnam. Kosygin spoke of the need for "united action" to help Hanoi's war effort. Zhou Enlai initially appeared sympathetic, even enthusiastic. During their meeting on February 10, 1965, Zhou readily agreed that the US bombing campaign gave Moscow and Beijing the freedom to offer the Vietnamese the unconditional support they needed. When Kosygin spoke of sending artillery, tanks, and surface-to-air missiles to North Vietnam, Zhou urged him to supply the equipment more quickly, and promised China's cooperation in transporting these weapons by railroad.[27] If Zhou were in charge of Chinese foreign policy, he and Kosygin could well have worked out a joint approach to North Vietnam, which was what the Vietnamese desperately wanted.

This was not to be. On February 11, 1965, Mao, responding to Soviet pleas with hostile sarcasm, told Kosygin that the Sino-Soviet struggle would last for 10,000 years. "The US and the USSR are now deciding the world's destiny," Mao said acidly. "Well, go ahead and decide. But within the next 10–15 years you will not be able to decide the world's destiny. It is in the hands of the nations of the world, and not in the hands of the imperialists, exploiters, or revisionists." Mao appeared unconcerned by the new round of escalation in Vietnam – "So what? What is horrible about the fact that some number of people died?" – and countered Kosygin's worries about the deepening conflict with optimistic calls for a "revolutionary war."[28] Kosygin left Beijing disheartened and empty-handed. The tentative move towards Sino-Soviet rapprochement, of which Kosygin was a foremost advocate in the Soviet leadership, was peremptorily aborted.

The malaise in Sino-Soviet relations made it more difficult for Moscow to supply North Vietnam with military aid. The Chinese flatly refused to establish air corridors for deliveries and rejected the Soviet proposal to cover the Sino-Vietnamese border against US air incursions as a heinous plot to put China under military control.[29] Beijing accepted the transit of Soviet military equipment by train but the shipments were often delayed, and occasionally looted. The Vietnamese approached the Chinese with a proposal to jointly inspect the transit of shipments through the Chinese territory but (according to Soviet information) were told in response: you

339

PART III DECLINE

must trust us, nothing can disappear in China.[30] "I think no country in the world would tolerate such humiliation," Brezhnev later complained. "Only we tolerate it. We don't even know what they deliver to the Vietnamese."[31]

Still, Chinese obstructionism helped the Soviet standing in Vietnam, because it made it easier to accuse Beijing of hypocrisy: on the one hand, the Chinese propaganda hammered the Soviets for "selling out" Vietnam; on the other, the Chinese were demonstrably obstructing the delivery of vital supplies to an ally on absurd pretexts. Brezhnev used every opportunity to alert the Vietnamese to this discrepancy between Beijing's words and actions. "Don't think that I am trying to cause a quarrel between you and the Chinese," he told the North Vietnamese deputy prime minister and Politburo member, Le Thanh Nghi, when the latter turned up in Moscow in June 1965. "We are surprised and saddened that the Chinese leaders are willing to pay this price to achieve some kind of selfish aims."[32]

The Chinese did their best to downplay the extent and the quality of the Soviet aid. "The Soviet leaders are not sincere or serious about providing help to Vietnam," Zhou Enlai told Le Thanh Nghi. Zhou reasoned that the Soviets had given Egypt, India, and Indonesia more than they were now giving Vietnam, and this was allegedly "so that Vietnam will not be able to fight big battles, so that it will not be able to start a war."[33] The Soviet leaders were angered by such insinuations, and did not tire of pointing out that not only were they supplying modern military equipment – including surface-to-air missiles and jet aircraft – but were even allegedly willing to send volunteers to fight in the war, if the Vietnamese would only take them. Some of these promises were undoubtedly propagandistic because when in 1965 the Vietnamese requested that Moscow supply Soviet officers to pilot MiGs in the air war, Brezhnev demurred.[34] There was a fine line between being an enthusiastic supporter of the Vietnamese struggle and fighting the war on their behalf, which was fraught with a direct Soviet–US clash. "What are we supposed to do," Brezhnev complained in July 1965, with evident exaggeration – "resort to atomic weapons? Is this what peoples of the world would want? … This would not be aid to Vietnam but an assured war. We cannot allow this."[35]

Around the same time, the Soviet leadership even reportedly considered breaking off diplomatic relations with the United States over Vietnam but – according to Brezhnev – walked away from such a "decisive measure," having concluded that it would not in any case compel the Americans to stop bombing North Vietnam.[36] In any case, Brezhnev had a good ground to claim that (unlike Khrushchev) he went out on a limb for the sake of a fraternal ally.

340

CHAPTER 12 VIETNAM

Figure 17 Zhou Enlai in Moscow atop the Mausoleum, flanked by Anastas Mikoyan (left) and Nikolai Podgorny (right), Nov. 7, 1964. Source: AFP/Getty Images.

As Moscow increased the quantity and the quality of their military aid, providing equipment that China did not have and could not match, the Vietnamese began to move away slowly from their pro-Chinese orientation that characterized Hanoi's policy in the early 1960s. It was a significant victory for Soviet foreign policy, and a reminder that Vietnam's friendship could be bought if the price was right. Khrushchev had been unwilling to pay but his successors understood that the brutal war unfolding in Southeast Asia was a test of their credibility as the leaders of the socialist world.

TOWARDS THE PEACE TALKS

The war continued to escalate. The US ground troops carried out combat missions against Communist units in South Vietnam, with mounting casualties (with over 6,000 dead in 1966, the American losses were more than three times greater than the previous year). Meanwhile, with brief respites in May and December 1965/January 1966, bombs continued to fall on North Vietnam. Operation "Rolling Thunder" aimed at dissuading Hanoi from supplying their war effort in the South. But it did not work, not even when, in the summer of 1966, the Americans expanded the list of targets by bombing petroleum, oil, and lubricants (POL) facilities. The POL campaign came to an end in September, after a CIA study concluded that it did not significantly diminish Hanoi's ability to fight. The US president faced a divided counsel: Defense Secretary Robert McNamara had lost faith in the war by

PART III DECLINE

late 1966. Others, including, prominently, National Security Adviser Walt Rostow, were upbeat about the prospects. "My feeling is that the pressures on the regime may be greater than most of us realize," Rostow told President Johnson in September.[37] Yet, two years after Tonkin Gulf, Johnson was beginning to waver, looking for a way out.

In public, Hanoi presented an impregnable façade of resolve. Summed up in Pham Van Dong's "Four Points" of April 8, 1965, this position called for the unconditional US withdrawal from Vietnam, followed by the country's unification on Communist terms. Continued escalation was spun as evidence of America's growing difficulties, not just in public but also internally, for the benefit of the war-weary audiences in the socialist camp. Records of North Vietnamese discussions with the Soviet leadership often read like propaganda: so many airplanes downed, so many enemies destroyed, and not a word of one's own losses. Thus, Le Thanh Nghi (in a conversation with Brezhnev in December 1965): "The American imperialists are suffering new defeats ... As the latest fighting, and our observations show, American soldiers are afraid of dying in Vietnam. They cannot stand the difficulties and the losses and cannot spend more than 3–4 days in the swampy areas, in the jungles."[38]

Careful Soviet probes about potential peace talks met with stubborn rebuffs, presented in terms of: yes, we are in favor of peace talks but not now. This was the argument Pham Van Dong cited to Brezhnev in October 1965 (Brezhnev was amused that the argument was made through the interpreter who read from a prepared text). "The Americans cannot be trusted," Dong said. "We don't want to end up in a trap."[39] He did not decipher this reference to a "trap" but, given Hanoi's bitter experience at the 1954 Geneva Conference, where the North Vietnamese were arm-twisted by their allies into dividing the country along the seventeenth parallel, it is not surprising that they would be more suspicious the second time around. "An old story," Brezhnev noted in his diary with evident resignation.[40]

Brezhnev was frustrated with Hanoi's stonewalling, especially because the Vietnamese had promised him "flexible" tactics. But when pushed on what that "flexibility" meant for them, it turned out that it was merely in the "fact of maintaining contact with the other side." He was, for example, annoyed that the Vietnamese leaders torpedoed the Canadian diplomat Chester A. Ronning's missions (Ronning had tried mediating between Washington and Hanoi, making two trips to Vietnam, in March and June 1966).[41] "When he [Ronning] started recounting to the Vietnamese representatives the American point of view on the conditions of settlement," Brezhnev later complained, "they just told him: you are an American agent and we received you in vain. And this is what they call flexible tactics!"[42] This kind of attitude, Brezhnev thought, prevented the Vietnamese from "snatching the banner of peace from Johnson, which he deceitfully uses to turn the world public opinion in his favor."[43]

This sort of rigidness on Hanoi's part, for which Brezhnev blamed mainly the Chinese – it was the Chinese, he thought, who were opposed to peace talks – was fraught with further escalation of conflict. No one could tell where this might lead, and Brezhnev personally did not rule out the possibility of a big Sino-Vietnamese-American war. "The Chinese could easily send one or two million people there," he noted grimly. "But this will be a difficult war for America. They won't find it easy to fight on land on a large scale."[44]

Economic losses from ongoing US bombing were partly made up for by a steady stream of economic aid from the socialist camp, especially the Soviet Union. But there was no making up for the tens of thousands of the dead, the maimed, and the deprived. Recalled Janusz Lewandowski, Poland's representative at the International Control Commission and (at one point) a crucial interloper in a failed US–North Vietnamese peace probe: "Population was starved, the rations were very limited, you know, the people gathered grass, herbs, finding the crickets ... For every American, I think, there were a hundred Vietnamese killed."[45] Although an exaggeration, the claim accentuates the brutal reality of war and helps us understand why, from late 1966, the North Vietnamese began sending signals of interest in peace talks. However, the signals were too weak and too equivocal to provide sufficient impetus for sustained negotiation. That would have to wait for another two years of carnage and casualties, two years of internal deliberation centered in no small part on the question of China.

The Chinese persisted in their opposition to peace talks. They were at first quite successful. The Sino-Vietnamese relationship seemed to grow ever closer as the war intensified. The DRV leaders were frequent visitors in Beijing, informing, listening, consulting. "At present all the world is depending on you to defeat imperialism," Foreign Minister Chen Yi told Ho in June 1965, while Zhou Enlai and Deng Xiaoping warned him that Moscow would sell out Vietnam. Ho played along but there was a perennial concern in Beijing that the Vietnamese may one day tilt the other way: towards the Soviets, and towards peace talks. This helps explain why the Chinese obstructed the shipment of Soviet aid and why they warned Hanoi against accepting this aid. "Their help is not sincere," Zhou cautioned Pham Van Dong in October 1965. "The US likes this very much. I want to tell you my opinion. It will be better without the Soviet aid."[46]

PART III DECLINE

Dong went on to Moscow, where, in talks with Brezhnev, he did exactly what Zhou hoped he would not – asked for aid – but also showed his loyalty by claiming commonality of views with the Chinese: "they have long been helping us."[47]

The DRV's dependence on Chinese aid – light weapons, ammunition, and daily necessities – could partly explain North Vietnam's opposition to peace talks. This was the preferred Soviet interpretation: Brezhnev and Kosygin were ever prone to see the Chinese hand behind the Vietnamese recalcitrance. "They are just petrified," Brezhnev commented in 1966, explaining that if the Chinese stopped transit of goods to Vietnam through their territory, "Vietnam would be finished. They will have neither bread, nor fuel, nor weapons."[48] Brezhnev told Pham Van Dong quite frankly at one of their meetings in 1966 that he thought that the reason for the Vietnamese resistance to peace talks was China. In response (according to Mikhail Suslov, who was present at the exchange) Dong simply "got up and kissed Brezhnev" – an action that spoke louder than words.[49]

Yet the Chinese pressure was not the whole story. Hanoi's struggle lined up with Mao's theory of the "people's war." When the Vietnamese leaders spoke in well-rehearsed catchphrases that sounded like Chinese propaganda, it was because they believed that propaganda, and were open to Chinese methods of guerrilla warfare. "Fighting a war," Mao instructed Pham Van Dong in April 1967, "is like eating: you eat a bite at a time. It is not hard to understand."[50] The Vietnamese thanked Mao profusely for China's help, and were invariably thanked in return: you are on the front lines, Mao would say. You are waging the struggle against American imperialism.

In June 1966 Mao proposed to Ho – half in jest, perhaps – that he would not mind heading down the Ho Chi Minh trail to carry on with the struggle. "We wouldn't be able to vouch [for your safety]," Ho replied in bemusement. Mao pressed on: "Isn't this the same thing to die and to be buried in China as to die and be buried in Vietnam? It would be good to be killed by the Americans."[51] Mao never went to Vietnam but hundreds of thousands of Chinese did. Between June 1965 and March 1968 a total of some 320,000 railroad, engineering, and minesweeping troops served in North Vietnam (the peak year was 1967, when the number reached 170,000).[52] One could say that the Vietnam War was organically linked to China in ways that it was not, and never could be, linked to the USSR. Even after the Vietnamese and the Chinese began to develop disagreements, it took years before they proved sufficiently serious to give the Soviets an opening in Vietnam.

Divergences did eventually spring up between Beijing and Hanoi, for two reasons. The first was China's slide into the chaos of the Cultural

CHAPTER 12 VIETNAM

Revolution. Begun in earnest in mid-1966, this campaign thrust China into radical violence. Senior leaders were purged. Those in "position of authority" were beaten and tortured by radicalized youngsters. Convulsing in a bacchanalia of rallies and struggle sessions, China turned inwards. All but one ambassador were recalled from overseas and diplomacy was downgraded to revolutionary propaganda. The chaos decreased Beijing's credibility as the DRV's protector. Disorder bordering on a civil war, especially in the southern provinces, disrupted the flow of weapons and supplies to Vietnam. Most importantly, Hanoi resented China's efforts to "export" the Cultural Revolution, especially by relying on the local Chinese community and the railroad troops. There was, as Le Duan put it in 1967, a "crisis of trust" between yesterday's comrades-in-arms. In an even more telling assessment by deputy Politburo member Nguyen Van Vinh, "as paradoxical as it sounds, we (the Vietnamese) do not fear the Americans but fear the Chinese comrades."[53]

The second reason was Hanoi's decision to begin peace talks with the United States in Paris. Discussions began on May 14, 1968, following an inconclusive round of fighting in South Vietnam, the infamous Tet Offensive. A brainchild of General Secretary Le Duan, the general offensive aimed at overwhelming the South Vietnamese in a series of powerful conventional strikes against cities. The idea did not go down well in Beijing or in Moscow, but for different reasons. The Chinese were upset that their preference for protracted guerrilla warfare had been ditched in favor of large-scale battles.[54] The Soviets had long sought a negotiated solution to the war and did not like further escalation. But the failure of the Tet Offensive eventually prodded Hanoi towards the negotiating table. The Soviets were relieved, and the Chinese – outraged.

CHINA AND VIETNAM PART WAYS

The DRV presently showed a little flexibility, eventually agreeing, for instance, to Saigon's representation at the peace talks. This was in line with Moscow's preferences. More by innuendo than by diktat, the Soviets continued to encourage their allies to make concessions, and they were annoyed by Hanoi's stubborn insistence on an all-or-nothing, take-it-or-leave-it approach. Brezhnev was most annoyed that the North Vietnamese leaders seemed incapable of understanding the twists and turns of American politics that could open but also close the doors to peace. He was worried by the prospect of Richard Nixon in the White House. "We've known Nixon for a long time," Brezhnev told Pham Van Dong in November 1968, days after the Republican presidential nominee clinched victory. "This does not

345

mean that we are afraid of him. But one must take into account that in a situation when no solution has been reached, he will have only one policy – to continue the war."[55]

What Brezhnev probably did not know was that Nixon was quite possibly working behind the scenes to torpedo peace talks by encouraging the South Vietnamese president, Nguyen Van Thieu, to resist President Johnson's pressure for compromise. These dealings have attracted historians' attention: it is tempting to think in terms of the thousands of lives that could have been saved if only the talks had succeeded earlier.[56] But the Soviet–Vietnamese discussions make painfully clear that there was little scope in 1968 for a breakthrough. As much as the Soviet leaders wanted a peaceful solution to the war, they had only limited leverage over Hanoi, given the complex dynamics of the Sino-Soviet-Vietnamese triangle and Soviet concerns with their credibility. In the words of the Soviet ambassador in Washington, Anatoly Dobrynin, "The Soviet Union could not afford to ... find itself accused of having undermined a fellow Socialist country."[57]

There was even a hidden blessing in dragging out the conflict. The rationale was, rather cynically, spelled out by Foreign Minister Andrei Gromyko in a report to the Politburo on April 13, 1969. The quagmire in Vietnam, Gromyko argued, "restrain[ed]" the United States in other parts of the world, served as a "source of tension" between the United States and China, and pegged down the Chinese forces in the south, away from Soviet borders. In the circumstances, Gromyko added, Moscow's aim was to strive to "rule out the possibility of cutting the Soviet Union out of a political settlement [of the Vietnam War], which is what the Chinese are driving at."[58]

Meanwhile, the North Vietnamese were not in any great hurry. They interpreted Johnson's October 31 announcement of ending the bombing of North Vietnam as a momentous victory for the Communist forces. "This new victory of ours," Dong told Brezhnev in November, "bred the spirit of confusion and decay in the ranks of the enemy, the American and the Saigon armies." The initiative was in the Vietnamese hands. They had to press on.[59]

Hanoi's optimism came through in the Vietnamese Workers' Party Politburo discussions. The records demonstrate that six months into the Nixon Administration, the North Vietnamese remained upbeat about the near-term prospects of the ongoing war. This was due to the perceived weakness of South Vietnam's armed forces, which were supposedly "falling apart," with three out of four top military commanders secretly supportive of the Viet Cong. These included, for instance, the head of the First

CHAPTER 12 VIETNAM

Corps, General Hoang Xuan Lam, who had already written a letter to the Liberation Front, claiming that he had decided to "take the road of the people." According to the Communist Party of Vietnam (VWP) Central Committee secretary, Le Van Luong (who reported on these developments to the Politburo in early July), Hanoi's problem was not so much in beating the "puppet" army as in working out what to do with them once they defected: how to feed them, and how to sort the good from the bad.[60] Not long after this, Nixon announced his policy of "Vietnamization" of the war: a phase-out of the US military presence accompanied by a considerable strengthening of the South Vietnamese forces. Hanoi was implacably opposed to the move but remained confident of victory just around the corner.[61] In August–September 1969 alone, Luong reported to the Politburo, the Viet Cong killed some 30,000 Americans. This was a preposterous overstatement, but these kinds of overstatement underpinned a rosy vision of the future. Time was working for the DRV, Pham Van Dong declared in April 1969, arguing that Nixon would not be reelected if the war continued.[62]

The North Vietnamese thought in wider terms than Vietnam alone. In April 1968 the Politburo adopted a special directive linking the success of the Vietnam War to the broader revolutionary struggle in Indochina, which Vietnam was historically entitled to lead.[63] The focus of this struggle was on Laos and Cambodia, both important strategic theaters for the Vietnam War. But it says something of Hanoi's ambition that it was looking beyond its immediate neighbors, actively planning to spread the war to Thailand. There were several meetings between Le Duan and the Thai Communists – one in January 1969, and another in September. The plan was to boost the Thai Communist force by deploying some 7,000 Vietnamese troops and providing weapons and food. By May 1970 the haphazard Thai guerrilla army was to be transformed into a regular army, with Vietnamese advisers. "This is an urgent question. These forces can be created from Vietnamese migrants living in Thailand," Le Van Luong noted in one of his reports to the Politburo in September 1969. Why these plans were not realized remains unclear; perhaps the US incursion into Cambodia beginning in late April 1970, and the intensification of fighting in Laos in 1971 focused Le Duan's mind on more immediate needs.[64]

As the 1970s dawned, the end of war was finally in sight. Much of Indochina was in ruins but the North Vietnamese leaders looked forward to their long-sought victory, which would herald Hanoi's rise to ranks of the leader of, and the socialist bridgehead to, the third world. "We would like to carry on this mission together with the Soviet Union, because no one can do it without the Soviet Union," argued General Vo Nguyen

347

PART III DECLINE

Giap in a December 1971 meeting with Brezhnev and Kosygin, outlining mouth-watering prospects of a "region of peace and neutrality" in Southeast and South Asia that would, down the line, include countries like Thailand, Malaysia, Burma, and India. Then the Soviet Navy would call at ports in South Vietnam, including in Cam Ranh Bay, where the tsar's navy had once called in 1905 (ironically, on the way to being annihilated by the Japanese at Tsushima). "This will be after the victory?" Kosygin inquired with hope. "Yes," said Giap. "Undoubtedly, after the victory. This is not an illusion."[65]

These ambitions were compatible with being a Soviet client. As a mid-size power, the DRV desired deference even as it itself deferred to the Kremlin for overall guidance. Vietnam continued to rely heavily on Moscow's economic and military aid. Fiercely independent Hanoi accepted this dependence on the Soviet largesse, partly because the Vietnamese had little choice, and in part because the Soviets were not competitors for Vietnam's regional hegemony. Nor, ironically, were the Americans. With the United States on the way out and the Soviets detached in advice if generous in contributions, the politics of Southeast Asia were gradually reverting to more ancient rivalries.

Unhealthy tendencies in Sino-Vietnamese relations, present during the early years of the Cultural Revolution, continued to worsen. The feeling in Hanoi was that the Chinese "support our revolution only to the extent to which we support the Cultural Revolution." Zhou, who turned up in the Vietnamese capital in September 1969 to attend Ho Chi Minh's funeral, was apologetic, blaming the difficult political situation inside China. "The situation inside our party is very complicated," he confidentially told the Vietnamese. "These difficulties have reached such a degree that they cannot be resolved at present."[66] He might have added that externally China was also facing an unprecedented crisis. In March 1969 the long-simmering tensions along the Sino-Soviet border erupted in a major skirmish. Scores were killed. It seemed that the Soviet Union would invade any moment. Shortly after Hanoi, Zhou Enlai met with Kosygin to try to bring tensions down a notch. The frosty meeting in Beijing airport did not resolve any problems, though it arrested the slide towards war. The jolt of the Sino-Soviet confrontation forced Beijing to reassess its foreign policy priorities. This reassessment would soon bring a sea change to Beijing's relations with Vietnam.

Meanwhile, the Vietnamese were unhappy: not just with the collapse of Chinese aid (that was at least ascribable to the chaos of the Cultural Revolution), not just with meddling in Vietnam's domestic politics (this

348

the Chinese conveniently blamed on the exploits of their Ambassador in Hanoi, whom Mao accused of being a Guomindang spy), but with Beijing's fundamental unwillingness to recognize the global importance of the Vietnamese Revolution. For instance, Hanoi was unhappy with the Chinese message of condolences on the occasion of Ho's death, because, it was felt, the wording of the message did not recognize Ho's standing as one of the great leaders of the international Communist movement. The reason for the slight was supposedly Beijing's fear that "with the recognition of Ho Chi Minh's role in the international communist movement, Mao Zedong's role would be necessarily diminished." Yet, "the Chinese comrades claim that comrade Mao Zedong is the second greatest leader in the international communist movement after Lenin."[67]

This all may sound like hair-splitting but it was not. China had long presented itself as the role model for revolutionary war. Mao instructed visiting revolutionaries – the Vietnamese among them – in the art of guerrilla warfare. The Chinese claimed leadership in the third world partly by the right of their experience in the revolution and then the war with Korea, where China fought the Americans to a standstill. Well, now, the Vietnamese were more than fighting the Americans to a standstill, emerging as yet another role model in Asia, another leader.

This rivalry was checked by continued Vietnamese obeisance and the decline of Chinese radicalism. In May 1970 Le Duan found Mao more accepting of Hanoi's conduct of the war and the peace talks in Paris. "You may negotiate," he told Le Duan. "I am not saying that you cannot negotiate." "But," Mao added, "your main energy should be put on fighting." This was one of the last meetings between the Chinese and the Vietnamese leaders, when they still spoke from the same script. Mao was at his militant best: still berating the Americans and the Soviets, still upbeat about the prospects of the global revolution, still full of praise for the Vietnamese war effort. "Who fears whom? Is it you, the Vietnamese, Cambodians, and the people in Southeast Asia, who fear the U.S. imperialists? Or is it the U.S. imperialists who fear you? ... It is a great power which fears a small country – when the grass bends as the wind blows, the great power will be in panic." Le Duan responded with deference, and even requested "Chairman Mao's instructions."[68] Yet even as he encouraged the Vietnamese to continue fighting, the Chinese leader was also carefully exploring the idea of rapprochement with the United States. Beijing was spooked by Nixon's decision to escalate the war in Cambodia in the spring of 1970 but probes soon resumed, leading in July 1971 to US National Security Adviser Henry

Kissinger's bombshell China visit, and the announcement that Nixon himself would soon come to Beijing.

This development was in part the result of China's changing strategic environment: the Soviet military build-up in the North and gradual American retrenchment in Indochina. It was also a consequence of Mao's disappointment with the fortunes of his revolution. The Cultural Revolution, which, he acknowledged, even the Vietnamese did not understand, had been extremely chaotic. Mao thrived on chaos. But it was hard to see how the motley crews of foreign radicals that looked to Beijing for weapons, money, and inspiration, would ever succeed in taking political power, or help restore China's global standing. Rapprochement with the United States served as a stepping stone to China's reintegration in the community of nations, especially in Asia, where it was shunned and feared. Mao's reorientation was half-hearted, for the Chinese continued to aid Communist insurrection across Southeast Asia. Mao the statesman never quite replaced Mao the revolutionary. Nevertheless, China's about-face was a geopolitical tremor that occasioned tectonic shifts across the region, first and foremost in Vietnam.

Hanoi was flabbergasted. The Chinese had not consulted them before Kissinger's trip, and Zhou's reassurances about how Nixon's visit to China would be of great benefit to Vietnam, and Beijing's readiness to increase the aid flow, could hardly compensate for the injury, and the insult, of such mistreatment. It was clear that Beijing and Washington had been talking, noted Hanoi's chief peace negotiator, Le Duc Tho, days after Kissinger's visit. "But the Chinese invitation to Nixon to visit Beijing was completely unexpected for us." In November 1971 Pham Van Dong visited Beijing in a bid to persuade the Chinese to uninvite Nixon.[69] The detailed records are still inaccessible, but the attempt was unsuccessful. In any case, in the words of General Vo Nguyen Giap, who briefed Brezhnev and Kosygin on the visit several days later, Dong "concluded that the general strategy of the Chinese leaders is a compromise with American imperialism." "At whose expense will this compromise be reached?" interjected Kosygin. "It's hard to say," uttered Giap. "I think you and I can guess at whose expense."[70]

THE ENDGAME

Giap was in Moscow on a very special mission. Spurred by the imminence of the Sino-American rapprochement and rightly suspecting that it would blow a big hole in Hanoi's negotiating strategy, the Vietnamese resolved to seize the initiative on the battlefield. The idea, Giap told Brezhnev, was

CHAPTER 12 VIETNAM

to "achieve military success in order to break the stalemate in the political struggle." Hanoi would try to achieve a military victory in 1972, banking on the fact that Nixon – facing a reelection campaign – would not dare to reengage. These would be very large conventional operations, Giap explained, that would draw on the Soviet experience in the Second World War. Moscow's support was essential to protect the DRV's supply lines. As Giap laid out the maps and spoke about the details of the planned operations, Brezhnev sounded a sympathetic note. It was unusual for the Vietnamese to be so open with the Soviets about their military plans: this in itself suggested a shift in Hanoi's loyalties. Brezhnev was also reassured by Giap's emphasis that the fruits of victory would be shared. It would be a "victory of the Vietnamese human resources combined with the Soviet technology."[71] The Soviet leader expected that Hanoi's Spring (Easter) Offensive would "allow to turn the Paris talks to a fruitful channel and encourage the Americans to turn to a political settlement."[72]

As Brezhnev later explained, "he [Giap] hinted [at the time] that they would start the offensive just as Nixon arrived in Beijing. We did not ask for this promise. He said it himself." This would then look like a coordinated Soviet–Vietnamese answer to the Sino-American rapprochement. But the Soviets were in for a disappointment. "Nixon comes to Beijing," Brezhnev recounted. "But there is no offensive. We don't ask anything. The Vietnamese are keeping quiet."[73] In fact, the offensive did not start until the end of March (i.e. just weeks before Nixon's planned visit to Moscow). The Vietnamese blamed the wrong season. Brezhnev suspected double-dealing.

The so-called Easter Offensive led to the resumption of large-scale US bombing of North Vietnam, an escalation unseen since the end of Operation Rolling Thunder in 1968. At one level, Brezhnev was appalled. "I am telling them [the Americans]," he raged at a meeting with his top military commanders in April 1972, "I just can't figure it out: have the Americans become so stupid that they can't understand that bombs will not solve the Vietnamese problem?"[74] On the other hand (and despite being in the know about some of the military planning), he also thought that the North Vietnamese had overplayed their hand by so brazenly crossing the dividing line between North and South Vietnam. "This led to counteraction by the Americans," he acknowledged. "They began massive bombardment and started a real slaughter." All of this could have been avoided if only the North Vietnamese were a little more "flexible" in their approach to the peace talks.[75] Now there was a risk that "this madman Nixon" would obliterate North Vietnam through massive bombardment – and what then?[76]

351

Kissinger, too, could not understand what the Vietnamese had been thinking. "Hanoi could have achieved almost all of its objectives if it had agreed to wait a little," he told Soviet Ambassador Anatoly Dobrynin on April 3. "But that is not enough for the DRV leadership; it wants to publicly humiliate the U.S. and to humiliate President Nixon."[77] The US president, then, faced the choice between humiliation – an electoral nightmare – and the unpalatable alternative of escalation at the cost of a possible cancellation of the upcoming Moscow summit with its broad agenda of arms limitation and superpower detente. Nixon and his national security adviser calculated, though, that after the shock of the Sino-American rapprochement, Brezhnev was even more interested in detente, and that he would swallow the obvious affront.[78]

Their reading of the situation was about right. Explaining his decision to go ahead with the summit despite Vietnam, Brezhnev pointed to the importance of his broader agenda. It was centered on European and global matters: the planned security conference, inviolability of postwar borders, strengthening East Germany, and curbing the arms race. Better Soviet–American relations would serve Soviet goals in the Middle East and Latin America by constraining the scope for American meddling. More importantly still, Brezhnev reasoned, "the ruin of the Moscow summit would certainly lead to Sino-American rapprochement on a clearly anti-Soviet basis. It's hardly necessary to say how unfavorable that would be from the point of view of our national interests." There it was, then – "national interests," which, Brezhnev, in a somewhat cynical and not wholly original fashion, equated with the interests of "world socialism."[79] The bottom line was that the Soviet Union had multiple interlocking agendas, of which the Vietnam War was only one.

Nevertheless, there was nuance to the Soviet position. Not all in the Soviet leadership liked the idea of feting Nixon in Moscow while the United States was bombing the living daylights out of North Vietnam. "There were voices in the Soviet leadership," recalled Brezhnev's foreign policy aide A.M. Aleksandrov-Agentov, "that demanded to refuse to receive Nixon as a response to the American attack on the DRV, to 'smack them in the face,' to strengthen the prestige of the Soviet Union ..."[80] The possible cancellation of the summit was debated at the Politburo several times before being resolved, at last, in Brezhnev's favor.[81] Brezhnev's detractors included as senior a figure as Aleksei Kosygin who called Brezhnev on the phone one day in March to tell the general secretary that Nixon had become so "insolent" that it was best to postpone his visit. "Are you kidding?" Brezhnev said. "Why not! This would be the right kind of a bomb,"

Kosygin replied. "It'll be a bomb alright," Brezhnev commented, "but who will it affect more!?"[82] Later recounting to Kissinger the internal opposition that he had to overcome to make the summit happen, Brezhnev said that "he always decisively defended his views, without being afraid to quarrel with my friends on occasion because of this ... You cannot look at all these things primitively."[83]

The Soviet leader was personally invested in the success of the summit. It was, in the final analysis, a question of his personal prestige. So he pressed on – "a ball of nerves" in his aide's apt phrase – spending days in anxious expectation, chain-smoking, prepping himself for what was meant to become a turning point in the Soviet–American relationship, the moment of Moscow's graduation to a true superpower status, and the symbol of Brezhnev's own emergence as a global statesman.[84] But what Nixon and Kissinger did not quite appreciate was that Vietnam was an important element of Brezhnev's bid for global leadership. Soviet support for Hanoi was what made the Soviet Union a true superpower, and America's equal. That is why the idea of "linkage" – that is, the notion that Moscow would be willing to curb support for its global clientele in return for improved Soviet–American relations – was fundamentally misconstrued. Brezhnev was unwilling to do this. Nor did he think that there was any contradiction between these two facets of Soviet foreign policy.

The Moscow summit (May 22–30, 1972) demonstrated both facets. Brezhnev was hospitality himself. He showered Nixon with lavish praise, engaged in warm banter, and personally drove the president around in a display of camaraderie. But all of that did not prevent Brezhnev from lashing out at Nixon in most uncompromising terms when the two discussed Vietnam on May 24. The president recalled being taken aback when Brezhnev, "who had just been laughing and slapping me on the back, started shouting angrily."[85] For Brezhnev, though, the point was to prove to his colleagues – who were there by his side – that he was tough on imperialism. This was a point he later emphasized at a party plenum, when he assured the assembled high-ranking functionaries of his "radical sharpness" in raising the question with Nixon. "Did our approach affect the American administration? Yes, comrades, it did," boasted the general secretary. "It was exactly after the Moscow summit that the US returned to the table of negotiations in Paris."[86] As he later put it, "you must have the courage to say: your hands are bloody, you are a murderer ..."[87]

This was also the point Brezhnev tried to sell to the North Vietnamese. He asked Soviet "President" Nikolai Podgorny to deliver the message (and the transcript of the conversation with Nixon), which the latter did in

June. As Podgorny himself recalled days after returning from Vietnam, he shared the transcript with Le Duan and another Politburo member, Truong Chinh, who, "having read it, were very moved. They got up and began to hug and kiss me."[88] Brezhnev also shared the transcript with another revolutionary whose approval he craved – Fidel Castro. "Having read it," Brezhnev boasted, "F. Castro understood how intense the arguing had been, and he jumped up and down like a child."[89]

Brezhnev would return to this feat of his in conversations with the Vietnamese leaders long after the fact. "In the more than twenty years of my work in the Central Committee and the Politburo," he assured Le Duan and Pham Van Dong in July 1973, "I don't remember that I or my comrades ever had to speak to anyone so sharply and so harshly as we spoke to Nixon about Vietnam."[90] "We can show the record of this conversation to the entire world," Brezhnev announced.[91] (Of course, he could: the whole point of the conversation was to make sure that he could.) "The Vietnamese," Brezhnev would later say, "did not immediately understand our game with America. But then, when they read the transcript of conversation with Nixon ... they understood the crux of the matter."[92] Unsurprisingly, the Russian record of that conversation – the one that the Vietnamese and other Soviet allies got to see – omitted the references to "light banter" between the angry outbursts, or to the subsequent friendly dinner, "where the conversation was devoted entirely to nonsubstantive matters."[93] Nor were the Vietnamese informed that Brezhnev, in a later meeting with Nixon, asked the president to *forgive* him for his tough talk that night.[94]

Soon after Nixon's departure from Moscow, Kissinger and Le Duc Tho resumed their meetings in Paris, leading, in January 1973, to the signing of peace accords, a development Brezhnev attributed to his patient coaching of the Vietnamese and Moscow's pressure on the White House. The war continued for another two years, ending in April 1975 with the fall of Saigon. As the conflict began to wind down, Soviet–Vietnamese relations were in a better shape than at any time since the early 1960s. In talks with Brezhnev in July 1973, Le Duan and Pham Van Dong restated the idea that Giap had formulated two years earlier that Vietnam and the Soviet Union, not China or India, were leading the Asian, and therefore world revolution – "and this makes us feel justifiably proud." Le Duan went out of his way to praise Moscow's support throughout the war, telling Brezhnev that, were it not for this aid, "we would of course not be able to achieve victory."[95] This was music to the Soviet leader's ears. America's defeat translated into hefty political dividends as Brezhnev basked in the reflection of Vietnam's glory.

CHAPTER 12 VIETNAM

By 1973, as the Vietnamese leaders whetted Brezhnev's appetites by invoking the bright prospects of a Soviet–Vietnamese revolutionary partnership in Asia, Hanoi's relationship with Beijing was on a steep downward trajectory. The differences were still carefully papered over, not just in public but also, for the time-being, in private. Mao, looking (in Le Duan's words) "old and very sick," praised the Vietnamese leaders in a mawkish sort of way when they met in June 1973. "The people of the world, including the Chinese people and the Chinese party have you to thank," he said. "You've defeated the United States." He even went so far as to thank the Vietnamese for the Sino-American rapprochement: "Think about it, why did Nixon come to Beijing? If you hadn't won the war, he wouldn't have come."[96] What struck Le Duan was that this time there was no discussion of the Soviet Union, no scaremongering about the Soviet threat, no pressure to combat "revisionism." This was a sign of a broader shift in Chinese foreign policy – away from ideology towards *realpolitik*. But what role would Vietnam play in this overtly geopolitical game?

A few weeks later Le Duan and Pham Van Dong discussed Mao's intentions with Brezhnev. They were worried about China's growing ambition in Southeast Asia. Le Duan confided to Brezhnev that since the mid-1960s he had been concerned about the concentration of Chinese troops in the five provinces of southern China. This measure, in theory aimed at securing the DRV's rear, was, in Le Duan's reading, but a part of Mao's plan "to invade all of Indochina and Southeast Asia if the circumstances were right."[97] He then pleaded with Brezhnev to help strengthen Vietnam's defenses against China.[98]

Meanwhile, Mao, for all his superficial nods of support for Hanoi's victory, could hardly be blind to the obvious: it knocked China off the pedestal of the uncontested leader of global revolution. The Vietnamese managed to do what China did not do in Korea twenty years earlier: defeat the United States. For years Mao delighted in instructing jungle revolutionaries. But this position of the strategist-in-chief of world revolution was now challenged by the Vietnamese who showed less and less deference to the chairman's wisdom. The seeds of the coming Sino-Vietnamese conflict were already beginning to sprout.

CONCLUSION

None of that was yet foreseen in the early 1960s, when Vietnam was lodged firmly in the Chinese embrace. Moscow's involvement with Vietnam was Brezhnev's project. Had Khrushchev not been ousted in October 1964, it is unlikely that the Soviet commitment would have been as strong or as lasting as it later became. Although Khrushchev pioneered the Soviet pivot to the third world, he was in the end quite unconcerned about Vietnam. He even resented his Vietnamese allies. Hanoi's decision to turn to armed struggle was an irritant in Soviet–American relations at a time when the Soviet leader sought rapprochement with Washington. But that was not the main problem. The spirit of "peaceful coexistence" did not prevent Khrushchev from aiding national liberation movements and revolutions around the world. What made the Vietnamese theater so problematic for Khrushchev was that Hanoi's militancy served China's interests. He did not think of Vietnam as an East–West problem so much as a Sino-Soviet problem, suspecting the Vietnamese of pro-Chinese leanings. "Winning" Vietnam in this case required him to tone down his disagreements with China and making a massive commitment to Hanoi's war effort. Khrushchev was not willing to do that, before or after Tonkin.

Brezhnev and his comrades-in-leadership were an altogether different lot. They faced a deficit of political legitimacy, and the related imperative of securing leadership in the socialist camp. Vietnam offered an opportunity to demonstrate one's revolutionary colors. Supporting Vietnam became a test of leadership that the Soviets were determined not to fail. Moscow's shift resulted in the DRV's return to something of an equidistance between its two powerful patrons. This was an important early achievement of Moscow's post-Khrushchev diplomacy that the Soviet leaders continued to build on as the war escalated in the late 1960s. This did not mean that the Soviets were prepared to back Vietnam to the hilt. The new Soviet leadership, like Khrushchev, had a broader agenda, which included the East–West detente. Brezhnev and Kosygin used every opportunity to prod their allies towards negotiations with the United States. But they were careful all the same not to overdo the prodding for fear of losing Vietnam to Chinese influence.

Supporting Vietnam's war effort served two related purposes: the first was to advertise Soviet credibility to global revolutionary audiences, in particular would-be clients in the third world. "Credibility" is an all-too-familiar notion to historians of America's war in Vietnam. It helps explain not just Washington's decision to "go in" but also why it took so painfully long to leave. Abandoning South Vietnam was unacceptable, because doing so undermined trust in Washington's reliability as an ally, undercut America's global standing, and entailed a domestic backlash. Yet the notion of credibility was equally dear to the hearts of the Soviet decision-makers who came to regard Vietnam as a test of their reliability in the face of Chinese

CHAPTER 12 VIETNAM

accusations of betrayal. Moscow's (and for this matter, Beijing's) involvement in the Vietnam War are therefore best understood not in ideological but in psychological terms, in terms of a struggle for leadership, and not just an East–West struggle but also an East–East struggle.

Second, for the Soviet Union, the Vietnam War was closely tied to being recognized as America's equal. Recognition was at the center of Brezhnev's approach to detente. But better relations with the United States did not at all entail curbing Soviet support for revolutionary wars – rather, the opposite! Superpower equality, from the Soviet perspective, required a clientele. Clients were what made the Soviet Union a superpower. The same logic worked for China as well. The Chinese were not quite in the same category of "superpowers." Even so, China's relationship with Vietnam strengthened Mao's hand when it came to mending fences with the United States. Mao was stating the obvious when he said the America's defeat in Vietnam was what forced Nixon to come to Beijing. Yet the decision-makers in Washington were often under the false impression that recognizing a foe (be it the Soviet Union, China, or anyone else) would prompt the other side to be more "cooperative." The term itself – "recognition" – entails a follow-up question: recognition as what? Recognition as an equal often precluded cooperation of the kind that Washington expected.

As the war escalated, commitment by both Beijing and Moscow grew. In the end, this tug-of-war for the DRV's loyalty was won by the Soviets. But Moscow's effort to court Vietnam would not have been nearly as successful were it not for China's self-defeating policies. Mao Zedong's insistence on military struggle was not in itself objectionable, certainly not from Le Duan's perspective. Like Mao, Le Duan was bitterly opposed to peace talks with the enemy until a decisive victory had been achieved. Where they differed was in their assessment of how long that victory would take, and by what means it was to be achieved, which was why the Tet Offensive of 1968 upset Beijing. The Chinese preferred protracted warfare. Disagreements over military tactics aside, there was frustration in Hanoi with the absurdities of the Cultural Revolution, and fears that it might spill over to Vietnam, causing chaos and undermining the war effort. The Vietnamese leaders' mounting unease about the political loyalties of the large ethnic Chinese minority were a pointer to deep-seated fears that would poison Sino-Vietnamese relations in the 1970s. But the biggest blow to this relationship of "lips and teeth" was Beijing's decision to mend fences with the United States, a clear-cut case of "betrayal" that the Soviets tried their best to turn to their advantage, but they did not even have to try all that hard.

PART III DECLINE

The end of America's war in Vietnam not just occasioned Washington's but also Beijing's defeat. Moscow, by contrast, emerged as a clear winner. Yet it was a Pyrrhic victory. Once the fighting stopped, reconstruction began, and Brezhnev, having invested so much in Vietnam, had to continue investing. Le Duan and Pham Van Dong were quite straightforward with him about Hanoi's expectations: a massive Soviet aid effort to help "industrialize" Vietnam to show Southeast Asia the practical benefits of socialist orientation. "We have nothing," Le Duan told Brezhnev in July 1973, suggesting that everything would have to come from the Soviet bloc, at least for the next ten to fifteen years.[99] Brezhnev agreed to cancel all of Hanoi's debts (at that point, over 1.3 billion rubles), in part because he had been advised that the Chinese, in an effort to "boost their influence" in Southeast Asia, had been supplying Vietnam with gratis aid.[100] Credits kept coming, and by 1990 Vietnam received 16.4 billion rubles in aid, most of which was never repaid. In addition, Soviet military aid to Vietnam just in the 1980s came to over 4 billion rubles.[101] Subsidizing Vietnam became an immense burden on the Soviet economy in the 1980s, contributing to Moscow's financial insolvency. Such were the long-term fruits of the Soviet–Vietnamese victory in the war.

13

DETENTE

By the early 1970s, having sidelined his internal rivals, Brezhnev emerged as the undisputed leader of a superpower. He was 67, and still in relatively good health (Brezhnev's rapid decline began in 1974, when he suffered a breakdown). The Soviet leader had a privileged lifestyle, spending time between his dacha in Moscow and the hunting lodge in Zavidovo, taking time off on the Black Sea every summer. He indulged in luxury, and developed expensive interests in cars and jewelry. Brezhnev surrounded himself with yes-men and sycophants, and ultimately enabled a cult of his own personality. But he wanted more than just the admiration of his insincere colleagues: he wanted to do great things, even if it meant overworking to the point of utter exhaustion. "I become unwell at [Politburo] meetings," he complained in March 1973. "I am not a man who works [just] on paper ... This is what I live for."[1] In the early 1970s, the general secretary set out to transform the Soviet Union's position in the world through detente with the West.

For a time, it seemed he would succeed. He ordered the invasion of Czechoslovakia in 1968, but he also reached out to the West Europeans, in particular to France and West Germany. In 1972 he welcomed Richard Nixon to Moscow, and, in 1973, toured the United States. He kept the Chinese at bay. The early 1970s really did seem like the dawn of a different age for Soviet foreign relations. "We are happy that now the Cold War is finally over," Brezhnev declared in early 1973 – a bit prematurely, as it soon turned out.[2] This chapter explores Brezhnev's road to detente. What was it that he set out to accomplish? And what does his striving for detente tell us about Brezhnev's view of the Soviet position in global politics, and his own role in history?

THE CRUSHING OF THE PRAGUE SPRING

In January 1968 the deeply unpopular first secretary of the Czechoslovak Communist Party, Antonín Novotný, relinquished his post under pressure of party reformers. The new party secretary, Alexander Dubček, initially enjoyed Soviet support. The message sent back to Moscow – that Novotný was like Khrushchev, only more stupid – found a receptive audience in the Kremlin, even though Brezhnev and others were a bit worried by the overly "revisionist" leanings of Novotný's critics. Dubček, in any case, seemed moderate enough and ostensibly loyal to the Soviets. But in the months that followed Novotný's ouster Brezhnev's cautious endorsement gradually turned to alarm and then to dismay as Dubček steered Czechoslovakia in the direction of greater openness. As state censorship weakened, voices of political dissent grew more audible by the day. The Prague Spring of 1968 heralded hopes of change, of "socialism with a human face."[3]

Brezhnev had seen it all before. He was merely Khrushchev's yes-man in 1956, and had, as yet, no real input into policy making but he was present at the crucial Presidium meetings that October when his predecessor agonized over Hungary. The Prague Spring, he feared, was a rerun of the Budapest autumn. "It is quite probable," Brezhnev predicted in April 1968, "that they will start hanging Communists there [in Czechoslovakia], as they did in Hungary in 1956. Everything is going in accordance with the plan developed by the forces of counterrevolution."

– "In accordance with the Hungarian recipe," echoed Podgorny.
– "Taking into account the Hungarian events of 1956," added Kosygin.[4]

That spring the Soviet leaders were still hopeful – though increasingly skeptical – that Dubček would keep the situation within the bounds of what Moscow called "healthy" party criticism. But the lid was off: in the following months the assertive press came to question the very nature of Czechoslovakia's political system, with occasional encouragement and endorsement of party functionaries.

By mid-August 1968 Brezhnev concluded that the situation had reached the point of no return, and that if he waited on Dubček to curb reforms, he could well lose Czechoslovakia. What did "losing" Czechoslovakia entail? In discussing the problem Brezhnev and other Soviet leaders invoked ideological tropes, not just publicly but privately as well. One way of looking at the situation was to interpret the Prague Spring as (in Brezhnev's words) "an ideological sabotage to restore capitalism in Czechoslovakia."[5] On other occasions, Brezhnev's language was starkly geopolitical. Czechoslovakia was a key link in the Warsaw Pact; to "lose" it meant to allow a "large and unfavorable change of the military and political situation not just in Europe but in the entire world."[6] Even more ominously Brezhnev proclaimed that "if we did not put an end to counterrevolutionary plans in Czechoslovakia, NATO's forces would soon end up directly at our western frontiers."[7]

CHAPTER 13 DETENTE

Then, too, the general secretary sounded a pompously philosophical note, as when he spoke about his "responsibility before history." "A question will be asked: where was the Soviet Union ... and the other socialist countries, what did they do to save the situation in Czechoslovakia?"[8]

History is a friend of multicausality. When on August 21, 1968, Soviet and other Warsaw Pact forces (minus Romania) moved in to crush the Prague Spring in line with what was presently christened the "Brezhnev doctrine of limited sovereignty," the Soviet leader could deploy all the above arguments and more. In this sense, he was hardly any different from Khrushchev who, too, had justified the Soviet invasion of Hungary in a variety of ways. Both understood the implications of "losing" an ally for their credibility and their domestic and international political legitimacy. "Losing" Czechoslovakia that was "won" with so much sacrifice in the Second World War, projected the kind of weakness that Brezhnev, for all his friendly sentiment for "Sasha" Dubček, was unwilling to contemplate.

The international reaction to the Soviet invasion of Czechoslovakia was relatively mild, which reassured Brezhnev who gloated that the West's response was confined to measures of "formal, propagandistic character," and that "imperialists" shied away from economic sanctions, never mind a military response.[9] "The Soviet Union," Brezhnev told the North Vietnamese leaders not long after the invasion, "can protect the revolution in deeds, not words, and to rebuff imperialism and counterrevolution. This was well demonstrated in Czechoslovakia." As always, the audience mattered: in this case, the Vietnamese, who had their own doubts about Moscow's credibility. It was in this roundabout way that the crushing of the Prague Spring echoed in the jungles of Vietnam. Added Brezhnev: "Imperialism, when it conducts its policies, is compelled to take into account the power, authority, and the military might of the Soviet Union."[10]

The Vietnamese liked the message and endorsed the invasion. By contrast, many Western European Communist parties, including the influential French and Italian Communist parties, were far from thrilled by the Soviet intervention. The rift between Moscow and the so-called "Eurocommunists" proved too wide to heal, and this further undermined the Soviet authority in the once uniform international Communist movement. And then, there was China.

The echoes of the Soviet invasion of Prague reverberated in Beijing. Oddly, the Chinese, who had until then claimed that the Soviet "revisionists" were aiming at a "capitalist restoration," now became the foremost critics of Brezhnev's attempt to prevent a "capitalist restoration" in Czechoslovakia. The reason was all too obvious. If the Soviets could "save" socialism in the

PART III DECLINE

Czechoslovak case, why not also in the case of China? How difficult would it be for Soviet tanks to roll across the border and "liberate" the Chinese from unhealthy perversions of Maoism? Perhaps, they could be dissuaded from attacking by a show of force. This, in any case, must have been the Chinese military's calculation for what followed.

BREZHNEV THE EUROPEAN

During the turbulent spring of 1969 an islet lying close to the Chinese bank of the Ussuri River – called Damansky in Russian and Zhenbao Dao in Chinese – became the unhappy stage for a game-changing encounter. It was there that on March 2 the Chinese set up an ambush, killing thirty-one Soviet border guards. The fighting died down but renewed two weeks later. The Soviets deployed tanks and resorted to massive bombardment of the Chinese positions with new BM-21 "Grad" rockets, killing (in their estimate) up to 1,000 Chinese troops. After several months of uneasy quiet, punctuated by occasional exchanges of fire, another skirmish broke out on August 13, this time along the Western section of the heavily militarized Sino-Soviet frontier. Twenty-one Chinese and two Soviets lost their lives.[11] After a decade of deepening hostility, China and the Soviet Union found themselves teetering on the brink of an all-out war.

Thus, five years after Brezhnev assumed the reins of leadership in the USSR, he faced two adversaries: one in the West and the other in the East. The imperialists, at least, were willing to talk. There was regular contact, for instance, between the Soviet ambassador in Washington, Anatoly Dobrynin, and Presidents Johnson and Nixon. Kosygin had enjoyed Johnson's hospitality at Glassboro in June 1967. But between 1967 and 1970, there was no Soviet ambassador in Beijing, and the diplomats who remained on the ground in China feared for their lives. Talking to the Chinese proved difficult. When, after the border skirmish broke out, Kosygin tried to call his opposite number in Beijing Zhou Enlai via the emergency phone line, he was told off by a youthful radical telephone operator in Beijing who refused to connect the call.

In March and April 1969 the Soviet Politburo returned to China again and again. On April 13, Foreign Minister Gromyko submitted an extensive report detailing potential Soviet countermeasures: ideas like stirring up trouble inside China (by covertly playing the ethnic card, especially in the Chinese northwest and in Tibet), "isolating" China on the international stage, and fostering better relations with China's Asian neighbors, including Taiwan. In the worst-case scenario, Gromyko foresaw the

CHAPTER 13 DETENTE

Figure 18 A scene on the Sino-Soviet border in the run-up to the deadly clashes of March 1969. Source: Sovfoto/Universal Images Group/Getty Images.

need to annex Mongolia to save it from the Chinese invasion. As for the Chinese themselves, if they dared invade the USSR, the recommendation was not just to repulse the Chinese attack but to "smash" China, achieving a complete victory.[12]

Yet the prospect of an all-out war with China was deeply disturbing. It would be an existential war, a war of national survival. For all the Soviet military power and technological superiority, a smashing victory was anything but assured. Brezhnev joked: "For me they [the Chinese] have ordained an honorable death. They plan to shoot me. Mr. Kosygin they plan to hang, and Mr. Mikoyan they will boil alive. At least, I have an honorable fate, not like Mikoyan, like those who will be boiled alive."[13] Brezhnev's "joke" betrayed a deep-seated anxiety about the future of Sino-Soviet relations.

Brezhnev's fear of China highlights an interesting aspect of his identity. He very often called himself a "European." What did this mean for a Soviet apparatchik of a working-class background? Brezhnev, a son of the Russo-Ukrainian borderlands, was not particularly cultured, nor spoke foreign languages, nor boasted the refined manners of the old tsarist aristocracy.[14] He first saw Europe during the Second World War, which took

PART III DECLINE

him to Prague in 1945. "I really miss the Motherland, mama," Brezhnev recalled writing to his mother at the end of war. "When I get to Paris, I will climb the Eiffel Tower, and spit from it at all of Europe!"[15] (He did not get to Paris until much later in his life.) Brezhnev identified himself with Europe in a vague cultural sense, and usually in contrast to something that he felt he was not (i.e. an "Asian"). Such crude and unhelpful categories as "European" and "Asian" would not get us very far in contemporary social science but Brezhnev was not a social scientist. His understanding of these categories was strongly colored by conceptions borrowed from Russia's nineteenth-century experience with the so-called "Orient." Brezhnev internalized these conceptions, and he certainly was not unique in this respect: the question of Russia's identity was, and remains, one of the central elements of the national political discourse.

Thanks to the ample documentary record, it is possible, in Brezhnev's case, to go beyond generalizations and pinpoint the exact source where the general secretary picked up his ideas about Asia in general and China in particular. It was from the writings of someone called Aleksandr Maksimov, a Russian traveler and ethnographer. In 1894 Maksimov published a pamphlet, *Our Tasks in the Pacific*, which recounted the history of Russia's relations with Beijing and reflected on the Chinese in brutally racist terms: "insolent," "dishonorable," "vicious," "immoral," unwilling to stick to agreements or abide by European diplomatic practices. Moreover, in a passage that was sure to impress Brezhnev, Maksimov predicted China's rise as a military power and the coming conflict between China and the West. "The Chinese race will come to clash with the white population of Europe and America concerning the main question of civilization, and this inevitable clash will slow down the progress of humanity for a more or less prolonged period of time."[16] The extent of Brezhnev's fascination with this particular writer is evident from how often he quoted from him in meetings with foreign leaders, including Nixon and Kissinger.[17]

Following Maksimov, Brezhnev's depictions of China and the Chinese were shockingly racist, exceeding even the starkest of Khrushchev's pronouncements. The Chinese, Brezhnev would say, were characterized by "brutality, perfidy, and hypocrisy."[18] They were "treacherous and spiteful," "not honorable," "exceptionally sly and perfidious."[19] "Try telling the Chinese: 'this is red' – and they'll immediately declare that it's white," Brezhnev complained. "Tell them that it's white – and they'll immediately declare that it's red." Worst of all was Mao himself – "you cannot agree on anything with Mao." "What kind of person is he? Who is he? Is he a communist or a fascist? Or, perchance, he is the new Chinese emperor?"[20]

CHAPTER 13 DETENTE

Why is this important? In the late 1960s Soviet relations with the West reached a degree of equilibrium. The successful Soviet invasion of Czechoslovakia in August 1968 met with a very muted reaction in the West. This was a pointer to Western acceptance of the Soviet sphere of influence in East-Central Europe. For all the ostensible ideological differences between the Soviet Union and the West, there was also a common ground and a shared interest in the avoidance of conflict. This was not at all the case in the East. There was no equilibrium with China, very little common ground, and a lot of mistrust. Ironically, though, China and the USSR were still broadly on the same page in ideological terms. Both in theory proclaimed adherence to Marxism-Leninism. Both were concerned about the "restoration of capitalism." Like Khrushchev before him, Brezhnev had trouble understanding the nature of the Sino-Soviet ideological differences. "If you ask me: what is the nature of these differences, I would not be able to answer this question," he told one visitor in 1971.[21] With the ideological affinities as fuzzy as this, it was the cultural affinities that mattered more. These affinities underpinned Brezhnev's approach to both Europe and to the United States: it was the basis for the Soviet quest for detente.

THE ORIGINS OF EUROPEAN DETENTE

In the late 1960s there were new opportunities for Soviet engagement with Western Europe. The most important reason was America's domestic scene. Already in the summer of 1968 the Soviet policy makers noted opportunities for using the "long-term positive trends" in the United States (i.e. the antiwar movement) to "limit their global pretensions."[22] Getting America out of Vietnam was one thing. Undermining the US presence in Europe was a more difficult proposition. But here, too, there were positive developments like, for instance, President Charles de Gaulle's idea of building a Europe "from the Atlantic to the Urals." The Soviet take on this inspirational idea was cynically utilitarian: "it undermines the existing organization of the Western camp, and objectively leads to the weakening of our main imperialist adversary, the United States."[23] In any case, Brezhnev encouraged de Gaulle's view of France as the third force in global politics when he hosted him in Moscow in June 1966. Brezhnev told de Gaulle quite frankly that he wanted to "weaken US influence in Europe and then squeeze the US out of Europe."[24] The Soviet leader came away from the talks feeling that "the so-called Atlantic solidarity ... is showing cracks."[25] "Many facts demonstrate," he proclaimed in 1966, "that our work was not in vain, and that NATO is becoming increasingly obsolete."[26]

365

PART III DECLINE

There was something ironic in Brezhnev's enthusiasm for de Gaulle. When the latter had just ascended the presidency of the Fifth Republic, the Soviet attitude was generally hostile. De Gaulle was a representative of the "bourgeoisie," someone who was seen taking France on the road towards a right-wing dictatorship. How times change. By the time of his departure, in 1969, he had become Moscow's closest partner in Western Europe, seemingly on the same page on issues dear to Brezhnev's heart: criticism of the US involvement in Vietnam and the need to contain Germany, and in particular, bar its access to nuclear weapons. Soviet diplomatic reports glittered with joy over perceived rivalries between France, on the one hand, and the United States and West Germany on the other. And nothing endeared de Gaulle to the Soviet leaders more than his decision to withdraw from NATO's military structures in 1966: just the sort of move that, for Brezhnev, heralded a new European age. Detente began as a Franco-Soviet project.

By contrast, Soviet views of West Germany seemed exceedingly bleak. Even though diplomatic relations were normalized in 1955, deep divisions remained between Moscow and Bonn on subjects like Germany's postwar borders and the (non)recognition of the German Democratic Republic (GDR). Brezhnev incessantly raised the alarm about the supposed imminent return of Nazism to West Germany, made worse by Bonn's alleged effort to obtain nuclear weapons (which, the Soviet leader believed, the Americans quietly encouraged). "Circumstances will tell which measures will be needed," Brezhnev told de Gaulle in June 1966, "but we are prepared to take any measures to prevent this [i.e. West Germany's access to nuclear weapons]."[27] There was little there that would suggest Soviet interest in trying to reset relations with Bonn.

This Soviet position stayed basically unchanged for the remainder of the decade even though the political situation in West Germany was undergoing an important transformation with the emergence, in December 1966, of the grand coalition government of Kurt Georg Kiesenger and Willy Brandt. The latter, the fierce anti-Nazi and a Social Democrat who had previously served as the mayor of West Berlin, began to formulate a new policy of engagement with the socialist bloc, dubbed New *Ostpolitik*. The Soviets were suspicious: it seemed as if what Brandt was really trying to do was to use West Germany's growing economic clout to tempt the Soviet Union's European satellites away from Moscow; the Soviet-speak for this sort of activity was "subversion," and it was not something to be taken lightly. "Let's not fool ourselves," Brezhnev told Nicolae Ceaușescu of Romania, who pioneered closer ties with the West Germans and had

CHAPTER 13 DETENTE

been urging Moscow to follow suit. "What changed was just the packaging but not the content of the revanchist policy."[28]

But events took an unexpected turn in September 1969, when Brandt and the Social Democrats won the West German elections, forming a coalition with the Free Democratic Party. As the new federal chancellor, Willy Brandt, redoubled his effort to engage with the East. Brezhnev, for his part, began to warm to the idea of an improved relationship. This was for a series of interconnected reasons. He realized that Brandt was trying "to free [West Germany] from its increasing dependence on America."[29] Improving relations with Bonn thus served a similar aim as engagement with France – the idea was to weaken the Western alliance.

There were also economic reasons – and this was the case as much with West Germany as it was with France. The question here was in no small part about gaining access to advanced technologies and capital (that became enormously important in subsequent years, particularly when the Soviets turned to Western Europe for supply of pipes for their gas pipeline from Siberia). Brezhnev put a lot of faith in the extraction of Siberian gas and, like the good salesman that he was, tried to get the West Germans, the French, the Japanese, and of course the Americans to buy into the promise of a gas bonanza. Still, the Soviet reporting emphasized how selling energy to the West brought not just economic but also political dividends for the Soviet Union.[30]

Brandt, meanwhile, dangled the carrot of West German investments in developing Kursk iron-ore deposits and even suggested that Bonn would build nuclear power plants in the USSR, and pay for them by exporting electricity back to West Germany.[31] The French contributed through Renault's participation in the Soviet automotive industry.[32] Brezhnev, for his part, worked hard to access European markets, spending much time on convincing the French, among others, to buy Soviet metal processing and nuclear technologies. In short, detente for the Soviet leader was substantially about breaking down barriers to trade and investment with Western Europe in a way that benefited the Soviet Union economically and politically.

Interestingly, Brezhnev, like indeed Khrushchev before him, was a determined opponent of the European Economic Community (EEC). The Soviet leader tried to convince both the French and the West Germans that the best way to advance economic ties between the USSR and Western Europe was on the bilateral basis and seemed very sensitive about Brussels playing much of a role at all in this story. The Soviets were undoubtedly worried about the EEC's growing economic clout, made even more obvious when Great Britain joined the bloc in 1973. But what really worried the

PART III DECLINE

Soviet leader was the prospect of a political rival emerging in Europe, especially if this rival were in fact dominated by West Germany. Unsurprisingly, he played up the latter theme in dealing with the French, telling President Georges Pompidou at one point that if, as some predicted the EEC turned into a "united Western Europe without borders ... many nations of Western Europe would have to eventually [learn to] speak German and forget their native language."[33]

Brezhnev thus not just hoped to weaken the transatlantic ties but also to undermine moves towards Western European political integration.

In the same spirit of good old realism, the Soviets looked to detente with the West as a part of the solution to their growing problems in the East. Indeed, Sino-Soviet relations reached their lowest point ever in 1969. With an all-out war in the East a distinct possibility, even the West German "revanchists" did not seem so bad after all. Brandt's aide Egon Bahr, who played the key role in the secret discussions between Bonn and Moscow, pointed to Moscow's paranoia in a letter he penned to Brandt in March 1970, during one of his trips to the USSR. The Soviets, he wrote, were "absolutely convinced that the Chinese want war."[34]

The Soviet leaders certainly made the connection between the East and the West and hoped to "actively use" improved relations with the West Europeans to counter a rising threat from China.[35] Things were so tense with Beijing by August 1969 that the Soviets hinted at a preemptive strike against Chinese nuclear facilities. On September 11, 1969 Aleksei Kosygin stopped in Beijing on his way back from Ho Chi Minh's funeral. Zhou Enlai agreed to talks. As an indication of the tense atmosphere, Kosygin was not even invited into town: the two premiers met in the airport. Kosygin did his best to convince Zhou that the Soviet Union was not thinking of starting a war. But Zhou did not believe him, nor were his own assurances about China's peaceful intentions particularly convincing. The talks at least paved the way to the resumption of the Sino-Soviet border negotiations. These served little purpose except as an outlet for hot air. The Chinese negotiators accused their Soviet counterparts of "suspending the atomic bomb over the negotiating table."[36]

Brezhnev knew that the Chinese leaders schemed to undermine European detente, comparing it (as Mao Zedong did) to another Munich (with China as the victim this time, and Brezhnev as the new Hitler).[37] Chairman Mao's prescription for dealing with Brezhnev was deterrence rather than appeasement and he lamented the short-sightedness of European politicians who were simply whetting Moscow's appetite through engagement. This profound, almost irrational, lack of trust in the former

CHAPTER 13 DETENTE

ally's intentions was perfectly mirrored in Brezhnev. "These are people who can craftily conceal their real aims," he would say. "I am not proposing anything, but any student of China feels the same way."[38] But for all these sentiments, and the unclear threats of Gromyko's report to the Politburo, there is no reason to think the Soviets were at any point seriously considering going to war against China. Even in the darkest hours of 1969 the name of the game was restraint. Brezhnev was, however, much worried about the Chinese lashing out and warned the West Europeans against undue *schadenfreude*. "Even if one allows that a Chinese invasion overwhelms the Soviet Union, then Western Europe, too, will not be left unpunished. Chinggis Khan's hordes did not stop with the Russian lands – they reached Western Europe," he claimed.[39]

OSTPOLITIK

A secret back channel between Moscow and Bonn was established in November 1969.[40] In January–February 1970 Brandt's state secretary, Egon Bahr, travelled to Moscow for talks with Foreign Minister Andrei Gromyko. The East Germans unsuccessfully tried to derail his trip for fear that Bahr may reach a deal with the Soviet leadership behind the GDR's back.[41] The negotiations proved very difficult. Gromyko wanted the West Germans to recognize all of Europe's post-Second World War borders, including, crucially, East Germany's. Bahr, citing the West German constitution, refused to renounce the goal of German reunification. "You have to understand," he told Gromyko, "that the feelings of Munich residents for the residents of Dresden are not the same as, say, the feelings of Munich residents for the residents of Milan. This is also reality." The Soviets found Bahr "evasive," Gromyko telling him that "unless we can agree with you on the question of borders, we would probably not be able to agree with you at all."[42]

But the talks moved along, with Bahr shuttling back and forth between Bonn and Moscow. Then, in August 1970, Brandt travelled to the Soviet Union to sign the breakthrough Moscow Treaty, one that ticked an important box for Brezhnev: it guaranteed the frontiers between West Germany and the GDR, on the one hand, and between East Germany and Poland on the other. It was a bitter-sweet victory for the Soviets. It was important to guarantee frontiers but the fact that Brandt was doing this on East Germany's behalf somehow devalued the long-term Soviet goal of having the GDR recognized, not least by its nemesis in the West, as an equal, sovereign state. The West Germans followed the signature of the treaty with a letter, which pointed out that Bonn would not renounce its long-term agenda of German unification. (Brezhnev ignored the letter: "We did not even acknowledge its receipt.")[43] However, since until then the Soviets actively opposed any such insinuations, passive acceptance of the West German letter was in itself an important breakthrough for Bonn.[44]

Brezhnev was thrilled. He proudly announced that he managed to accomplish something that had eluded previous Soviet leaders for some twenty years. The treaty, in Brezhnev's opinion, weakened links between West Germany and the United States, serving the long-standing Soviet goal of undermining NATO. "Of course, the Bonn–Washington axis still exists. But it is showing clear cracks," concluded the general secretary.[45] "After this [the treaty], there will be this quiet process of the NATO bloc's erosion in Europe," he said. "All sides want this erosion, but they hope that the Soviet Union will not resort to some dangerous escalation later on."[46] Guaranteeing GDR's frontiers was also a victory, which the Soviet leader characterized as a kind of policy of "Lebensraum" in reverse. "If prewar Hitlerite Germany wanted to obtain more Lebensraum at our expense," he said, "we in response 'chopped off' a third of Germany in favor of socialism."[47]

Geopolitics aside, the importance of the treaty was also in the political legitimacy that Brezhnev derived from it. Meetings with Brandt – for whom Brezhnev developed a great liking – translated into his increased personal prestige among the party elites at the expense of real and potential rivals like Prime Minister Aleksei Kosygin.[48] Unsurprisingly, his internal assessment centered on the all-too-familiar themes of prestige and recognition. "We have the right," he said, "to view this action [the signature of the Moscow Treaty] as not just something major but as an action of world significance. One can confidently say that it will play a huge positive role in the further increase of the Soviet role and of the influence of the socialist commonwealth in European and world politics."[49]

In September 1971, Brezhnev invited Brandt to visit him at his summer resort in Crimea. During their extensive discussions, Brezhnev let the chancellor know that he was very worried about the delay in the ratification of the 1970 Moscow Treaty. "I do not want us to gallop," he said, "but promenading is also boring." He added that it would be a "real tragedy" if the Bundestag failed to ratify the Moscow Treaty. "Progress in relations between the USSR and the FRG [Federal Republic of Germany]," he told Brandt, "would completely change the political climate of Europe, undermine positions of the reactionary forces in the FRG, and also some of the so-called allies who give these forces all the help that they can."[50] But although the meetings highlighted Brezhnev's frustrations (he made

CHAPTER 13 DETENTE

sure that the records were shown to the GDR's Erich Honecker and his other East European allies), the very fact of Brandt visiting with the Soviet general secretary in Crimea spoke volumes about the changing nature of Moscow's relationship with Bonn.[51]

So central was this relationship to Brezhnev's sense of what he personally stood for in international politics that he pulled all stops in "helping" Brandt in having the Treaty ratified, including by putting pressure on the East Germans to negotiate their own detente with Bonn, and by making concessions in the four-power negotiations over Berlin, which led (no small thanks to Moscow's constructive attitude) to the conclusion of the September 1971 Berlin Agreement, which provided Soviet guarantees for Western access to West Berlin, something that Khrushchev, in his time, went to the brink of war to deny. He even went so far as to hint, in a speech in March 1972, that he would recognize the much-reviled EEC – a move now viewed to have been a part of Brezhnev's effort to help Brandt with the ratification process (the Treaty was at last successfully ratified in May 1972).[52]

So keen was Brezhnev on his relationship with Brandt and the Social Democratic Party (SPD) that he was even willing to completely overlook the long-time Communist aversion to social democracy. This was something that the East Germans were very worried about: they even fed internal SPD documents to the Soviet ambassador in Berlin that showed how the Social Democrats remained deeply anti-Communist.[53] Even Brezhnev's own foreign policy adviser, the supposedly "liberal" A.A. Aleksandrov-Agentov, drew the boss's attention to the "dangerous role of the social democratic ideology," which could be used to "undermine the foundations of certain socialist countries."[54] To no avail. Brezhnev broached the issue in a speech to the top military brass in 1972. "We do everything to help this government of Brandt's, with whom I would not shake hands under different circumstances ... we are now doing everything to help this government. After all, this is the best thing that exists in West Germany."[55] Yes, he said at another meeting, highlighting the underlying realism of Soviet foreign policy, ideologically, the SPD and Communism were still incompatible, but he had to "take into account our common interests along government lines."[56]

Brezhnev was bound by certain rules of political correctness, at least in official speeches to party functionaries. These rules did not apply to the private musings of one of these functionaries, Anatoly Chernyaev (who later became Mikhail Gorbachev's top foreign policy aide): "Brandt knows very well that our ideology is for internal consumption only ... We are not such fools as to engage in ideological exercises in business, state-to-state relations with those who can easily tell us to f*** off."[57]

PART III DECLINE

One remarkable encounter in October 1972 between Brezhnev and Egon Bahr demonstrates the strange demotion of ideology as a factor in Soviet–West German relations. This was in the run-up to the federal election of 1972. Brezhnev asked Bahr what he thought Moscow should do to make sure that the Social Democrats remain in power. Bahr noted that the SPD had to emphasize the distance between social democracy and Communism (lest the opposition accuse Brandt of yielding too much ground to the Soviet bloc). Brezhnev then offered to criticize the SPD in Soviet propaganda, to which Bahr replied: "this would be very helpful." He added that whenever Brandt spoke critically about Communists, the Soviets were to understand this as strictly a matter of domestic politics, and not as something directed against the Soviet Union or East Berlin.[58] A few days later, Brezhnev instructed his foreign policy aide to do exactly that: to criticize the West German Social Democrats in the Soviet media, "only smartly," because "this will help Brandt."[59]

The realists would say that it was a case of national interests trumping ideological proclivities, or indeed, a case of a blatantly cynical use of ideology in the service of national interests. Brezhnev and Brandt of course thought in terms of national interests. As politicians, they also had an eye for the imagery that would reflect on their unsurpassed qualities as statesmen. Working hand-in-hand to save Europe from war sent the perfect message.[60] Willy Brandt got the Nobel Peace Prize for his efforts. Brezhnev was reportedly gutted that he was bypassed by the selection committee.[61]

Forging personal links with de Gaulle (and later his successor Georges Pompidou) and now with Willy Brandt was a part of Brezhnev's vision for Europe: it was here that his European identity, such that it was, became wedded to policy. "Europe is closer to us," Brezhnev would say. "We are Europeans ... Peace in Europe and a system of security would evidently change the general climate of world politics. Because this is where we have the most civilized society, this is the most densely populated territory on earth, economically it has the greatest potential."[62] Those were some remarkable (if not altogether accurate) views. Brezhnev the European was seeking to engage with Europe on loosely civilizational terms, and not just to engage but to lead. But given that he wanted to undermine the transatlantic solidarity, that he played West Germany and France against one another, that he tried to prevent the rise of the EEC, and that the Soviet Union continued to dominate Eastern Europe – is it really all that surprising that Brezhnev's leadership was a hard sell with the Europeans? Probably not.

There was a serious contradiction between Brezhnev's pan-European vision and the brutal geopolitics of the Brezhnev doctrine, a contradiction

372

CHAPTER 13 DETENTE

that was not resolved in his lifetime. It was only with Mikhail Gorbachev's rise to power that the Soviet Union's European project was placed on a more realistic, albeit very shaky and sadly impermanent, footing.

TRIANGULAR DIPLOMACY

The Soviet leadership had a generally negative view of Richard Nixon before he won the 1968 presidential election. His well-known record as a red-baiter and an anti-Communist, and his July 1959 visit to Moscow as Eisenhower's vice president, when he sparred with Khrushchev in the infamous "kitchen debate," gave little cause for an optimistic assessment. Moscow's favorite presidential candidate was the Democrat and John Kennedy's younger brother, Robert F. Kennedy, who was assassinated by a Palestinian militant on June 5, 1968. (Brezhnev did not believe the Palestinian connection and thought it was a set-up involving – who else? – US intelligence).[63]

Unsurprisingly, the general secretary's initial take on Nixon was that he was "the biggest demagogue of all American presidents" who was driven by domestic political imperatives rather than some grand strategy.[64] For this reason, it would be difficult to conclude lasting agreements with Washington. "Nixon," Brezhnev explained in November 1968, "is distinguished by extremely pronounced self-love, and great irritability ..."[65] Presiding over a rotting society, Nixon was a "living corpse, albeit unfortunately still a strong one."[66] Moreover, he was an evil man. "Nixon's hands," Brezhnev said, "are stained with blood; he has the deaths and suffering of millions of people on his conscience. I am surprised by those states that grovel before the Americans, before Nixon. What do they want? What favor are they hoping to obtain from him?"[67]

On one occasion (in 1971) Brezhnev even cautioned a fellow statesman (Yugoslavia's Josip Broz Tito) against seeking a meeting with Nixon because, in his view, one could count on little more than "demagoguery" from the American president.[68] As for his own summit with Nixon, the Soviet leader was not at first in any great hurry. It was not that he was completely averse to the idea: only, recalling perhaps Khrushchev's futile summitry with Eisenhower, Brezhnev wanted concrete results. Just meeting and talking, even recreating the "spirit of Camp David," simply would not do.

Progress on the concrete results proved very slow. The problem was with the differences in the basic approaches to outstanding issues. Brezhnev wanted to advance in several areas. One was arms control. The unquestionable motivation here was to curb the spending on nuclear weapons.

373

PART III DECLINE

By the late 1960s both the Soviet Union and the United States had enough nuclear-tipped missiles to destroy the world many times over. The build-up was incredibly wasteful. The appearance of new technologies – more powerful missiles, multiple independently targetable (MIRVed) warheads, and anti-ballistic missile systems – promised to make the race even more costly and irrational. The Soviets were also deeply concerned about the possibility of a first strike by the United States, and especially about the American forward-based systems (such as nuclear forces stationed in Western Europe) that could obliterate the Soviet command and control at a moment's notice. Talks on limiting strategic arms (SALT) got off to a difficult start in October 1969, and dragged on in Helsinki and Vienna.

Another issue was trade. Brezhnev sought to attract Western investments and technologies, and to make up for the growing shortfall in foodstuff and consumer goods. West Germany, unsurprisingly, took an early lead, showing that *Ostpolitik* could have practical benefits: in 1970 Bonn agreed to supply the Soviet Union with large-diameter pipe and related technology for the construction of a gas pipeline (in return for long-term supplies of natural gas).[69] Austria, Italy, and France concluded similar agreements. In the late 1960s the Soviets reached out to Italy's Fiat in a $1.5 US billion bid to modernize Soviet car production. The idea was to have the new production lines in the city of Togliatti opened by April 1970, coinciding (most ironically) with Lenin's 100th birthday. There was extensive Western involvement in building another megaplant, the Kamaz truck production factory. The Soviets imported, reverse-engineered, or stole Western technologies to improve labor productivity: these piecemeal efforts often failed due to problems inherent in the Soviet state planning system. Brezhnev wanted more: large-scale investments in turnkey factories built on US government credit. In an ironic twist for a country that claimed to have a superior economic system, the Soviet leader also sought long-term contracts for the purchase of US wheat. He wanted to boost Soviet–American trade on "equal" terms, which meant removal of export control and other US restrictions.

Then, there were also regional issues: Vietnam, most prominently, but also the Middle East. Soviet options with Vietnam, as we have seen in the previous chapter, were very limited. The desirable results – a full US withdrawal – was for the time-being unachievable. The main Soviet concern here was that Nixon would do something drastic like escalate the war, for any such escalation would put Moscow's credibility to the test, one that Brezhnev was not sure he could pass. Similar problems befuddled the Soviet approach to the Middle East. Here, the Soviets continued to rebuild

CHAPTER 13 DETENTE

the militaries of their Arab clients, battered in the 1967 war against Israel, while fearing all the same that another showdown could yet lead to a new defeat, with all that meant for Soviet prestige and credibility as a superpower patron. The goal was therefore to bring the United States around towards a political settlement where the Americans would pressure the Israelis to withdraw from the territories occupied during the Six Day War.

By 1971, neither Vietnam nor the Middle East had delivered enough progress to justify a summit, and there were only meagre accomplishments in the SALT negotiations. Talks over Berlin were making only very modest progress. Brezhnev seemed in no hurry to court the United States, which he still called a "gluttonous vulture," "unwilling to part with dreams of world domination."[70] And yet internally, in the corridors of Soviet power, there gradually emerged an impression, and then a conviction, that it was in the Soviet interest to actively push for an improvement of relations with the United States.

The direction of Soviet thinking can be gleaned from a remarkable document prepared in the depths of the Foreign Ministry and the KGB. The top-secret document, signed by Andrei Gromyko and Yury Andropov, argued in favor of detente with the United States on the rather cynical basis that it would "weaken the US role in world affairs, including in the West's political and military alliances" and, inevitably, "deepen the contradictions between the US and its allies." Gromyko and Andropov felt that the moment was "clearly auspicious" for "discrediting the United States, their internal and external policies, thus undermining the US position as the leader of the bourgeois world." This they proposed to do by widely advertising the failures of the American social model (highlighting US crime rates and drug addiction, and capitalizing on America's racial tensions). They also wanted Moscow to take a more active role in the third world in order to facilitate "the dispersal and the weakening of the forces of American imperialism."

But there was something else. In the conclusion to the lengthy paper, Gromyko and Andropov argued that it was in Moscow's interest to create the impression not just in Washington but everywhere in the world that the Soviet Union was an indispensable power, and that "it was only by reaching a mutual understanding with the USSR that one could solve those international questions, which the United States is interested in settling, and that there was no other way." It was through Soviet–American detente, then, that Soviet greatness could meet with appropriate acknowledgement of the entire world and, in particular, the United States. At the same time, Gromyko and Andropov recognized that neither could Washington be

375

PART III DECLINE

bypassed in solving key international problems that mattered to the Soviet Union, whether in Europe or elsewhere in the world.[71]

The paper was meant for a Politburo discussion in January 1971. It is unclear what transpired at that meeting. Yet a breakthrough in relations with the United States was becoming more urgent by the day. Lunching with Kissinger on April 23, 1971, Soviet ambassador in Washington, Anatoly Dobrynin, still tried to link the prospects of a Brezhnev–Nixon summit (which the Americans had been pressing for months) with concrete progress in the talks on access to Berlin. He encountered a "very sharp" response to the effect that Nixon would never buckle under pressure.[72] The Soviets were then told that Nixon would not propose a summit again. Writing to Brezhnev on May 2, his foreign policy aide Aleksandrov-Agentov blamed Dobrynin for "clumsiness" and argued that dragging out the summit was not in Moscow's interest, given, in particular "Nixon's demonstrative flirt with Beijing." By contrast, having a summit announcement would "strengthen our position in discussions with China."

In general – and this is also visible from Aleksandrov-Agentov's memorandum (which he co-authored with senior colleagues in the Central Committee and the Foreign Ministry) – there was a fear in Moscow that, after making good headway in the late 1960s in the East and in the West, it could see its gains reversed. "One has to recognize that our main adversaries on the international stage – above all, the Americans and the Chinese – found means to block our actions and obstruct us in the achievement of the foreign policy aims, which we had set." Reversing these setbacks required engagement across the board: with the West Germans, with the Americans, with the French (to put the Americans and the West Germans on notice), and even with the Chinese.[73]

Just weeks after Aleksandrov-Agentov's memorandum to Brezhnev, something happened that summer that highlighted the unacceptable costs of complacency. In July 1971 Henry Kissinger secretly travelled to China. The visit was followed by a bombshell announcement: Nixon himself would soon go to Beijing.

The Soviets were suspicious this might happen one day. Already in the mid-1960s Soviet intelligence saw signs of China's coming rapprochement with the West. As early as June 1966 the head of the GRU, Pyotr Ivashutin, argued in a top-secret memorandum to the Central Committee that there had been a change of tone in Johnson's handling of China and that the Americans were feeling out Beijing for the possibility of improving relations, which the Chinese leaders might just reciprocate "in order to raise their prestige and further slander Soviet foreign policy." The Americans, Ivashutin argued, were making all the necessary effort "to deepen the split between China and the Soviet Union."[74]

In 1967 Moscow instructed its diplomats overseas to watch for signs of China's rapprochement with the West.[75] Nixon's early months in power coincided with the outbreak of hostilities on the Sino-Soviet border. The Americans attempted to reassure Moscow (using the newly established back channel between Kissinger and Ambassador Dobrynin) that they would not exploit these hostilities but at times these assurances sounded more like taunting. "What exactly are you up to? Are you trying to annoy the Soviet Union?" wondered Dobrynin in one of his tête-à-têtes with Kissinger. The latter of course reassured him that "needling the Soviet Union was an unhistoric and not worthwhile effort."[76] In April 1969 Gromyko predicted that Beijing might reach out to the United States, West Germany, and even Japan, and argued in favor of "improving relations with the United States and other big imperialist powers" as a countermeasure. His was proven right – and sooner than anyone expected.[77]

US rethinking of China accelerated when in August 1969, with tensions on the Sino-Soviet border running high, the Soviets began droppings hints of a possible preemptive strike against China's nuclear facilities.[78]

Kissinger played a key role in bringing about the Sino-American rapprochement. But all his efforts would have fallen flat were it not for the fact that Mao Zedong, for reasons of his own, sought out Nixon whose visit to China in February 1972 ushered in a new chapter in the Cold War.[79] Mao who had so viciously condemned the Soviet sell-out to imperialism, who had so bitterly quarreled with Nikita Khrushchev over the appropriateness of "peaceful coexistence" with the United States, suddenly threw his former reservations to the wind. His change of heart was already in evidence in 1970. "A good fellow! Nixon is a good fellow!" Mao told the US journalist Edgar Snow that December. "The No. 1 good fellow in the world."[80] He evidently expected Snow to pass on these observations to the White House. Mao also had the transcript of his talk with Snow circulated to lower party organizations (for discussion and debate). The record of these discussions showed that even the Chinese party faithful were dumbfounded by the chairman's stand, with many wondering why Mao would call "reactionary" Nixon "the No. 1 good fellow in the world," and why, if the Americans were so good, could China not mend fences with the USSR as well.[81]

The answer is at least in part connected with the state of affairs on the Sino-Soviet border. With a Soviet invasion within the realm of the possible, Mao opted to improve relations with the United States to deter a more

PART III DECLINE

dangerous enemy to the north.[82] It is also possible to view Mao's actions through the prism of his resentment of the unequal nature of Sino-Soviet relations. That was why Mao angrily dismissed suggestions that he should try to improve relations with Moscow: "You [the Soviet Union] piss on my head and I should respect you? ... No matter who tries to persuade us [to mend fences], we won't move. The more they talk the worse relations will become."[83] Nixon, by contrast, did not "piss" on China's head. He showed respect. He himself wanted to come. That, at least, was Mao's spin.

Nixon's visit to Beijing was a colossal setback for the Soviet Union in strategic terms, and also a personal affront to Brezhnev who felt sidelined from being at the front and center of global politics. One little thing that annoyed him the most was the remark that Nixon made in a toast to Zhou Enlai (after consuming an inordinate quantity of *maotai*, according to Kissinger's later embarrassed explanation): that the United States and China "hold the future of the world in our hands."[84] Months later, Brezhnev still brooded over the slight. "This remark circled the world. It gave us concern."[85] The whole thing was "quite inappropriate and unworthy," Brezhnev said.[86]

The Soviet–American summit that was scheduled to take place that May was intended to put things back into their proper perspective. Yet, as we saw in the previous chapter, the historic occasion was nearly cancelled because of the deteriorating situation in Southeast Asia. It took Brezhnev's personal commitment, and a willingness to confront his skeptical colleagues, not to rescind the invitation to Nixon after the US resumed large-scale bombardment of North Vietnam and mined the Haiphong Harbor in the spring of 1972.

In April 1972 Brezhnev hosted Henry Kissinger who secretly visited Moscow in an unsuccessful bid to prod Brezhnev to deliver on Vietnam before the summit. Brezhnev was hospitality himself (despite the ongoing bombardment of North Vietnam). He plied Kissinger with pie and chocolate-covered plums, appeared nonconfrontational and even jovial, and, indeed, joked gregariously in a way that the North Vietnamese (and perhaps some of his own colleagues) would have found most inappropriate (which was why, perhaps, his jokes were only recorded in the American transcripts).

Speaking of Brezhnev's colleagues, none (other than Gromyko, the foreign minister) joined the lengthy sessions: the general secretary appropriated big issues of foreign policy – like Soviet–American relations – for himself. Nevertheless, records of the meetings make clear that Brezhnev had to "sell" his accomplishments with Kissinger to colleagues who, in

CHAPTER 13 DETENTE

some cases, were not particularly sanguine about Nixon's envoy, or about the whole idea of Soviet–American summitry.[87] Brezhnev also felt bound to justify his meeting with Kissinger before the broader audience of the party faithful, at a party plenum, which Brezhnev did by citing selectively from the record of his conversations with Kissinger – that is, from the place where he spoke most angrily about the US bombardment of North Vietnam and even suggested that the forthcoming summit with Nixon would have to be cancelled. (Brezhnev of course conveniently omitted the part where he "reaffirmed again and again" Soviet interest in the summit.)[88]

Kissinger, for his part, read the situation correctly. "Brezhnev's performance suggests," he reported to Nixon after his talks in Moscow, "that he has much riding on the summit ... [H]e sees his relationship with you as legitimizing and strengthening his own position at home. We may have an election in November; he acts as if he has one next week and every week thereafter." Brezhnev, in Kissinger's words, was "tough, brutal, insecure, cunning and very pragmatic."[89] Which of course made Brezhnev and Nixon two peas in a pod.

THE SUMMIT

The Moscow summit (May 22–29, 1972) was a highlight of Brezhnev's career, the moment he shone on the international stage as the leader of a superpower, a global statesman. It was a historic occasion: the first time a sitting American president visited the Soviet Union since Roosevelt's parley with Stalin in wartime Yalta. (Nixon massaged Brezhnev's bottomless ego by proposing, in their first meeting, that the two of them have a relationship similar to that which Roosevelt and Stalin had in their time). For Brezhnev, sitting across the table from an American president, engaging him in serious conversation and trivial banter, sharing caviar and exchanging toasts meant basking in glory, rising head and shoulders above his Kremlin colleagues, and winning for the Soviet Union that international recognition as America's equal that the Soviet leaders craved above all else. "There is an old saying," Brezhnev said, explaining his approach to the United States, that "he who sups with the devil should have a long spoon." This meant speaking from strength, because "force is the language the American imperialists understand best." But whether Brezhnev had a long spoon to show for it, he certainly was not going to miss the supper.[90]

The summit occasioned the signing of different agreements, including the hard-bargained Strategic Arms Limitation Treaty (SALT-I), and the Anti-Ballistic Missile (ABM) Treaty. Aimed at curbing the nuclear arms race,

PART III DECLINE

these agreements were major breakthroughs that took years of painstaking effort to negotiate. Brezhnev justified both treaties internally by saying that they would benefit the Soviet Union. The ABM Treaty would prevent the United States from protecting itself against the Soviet intercontinental ballistic missiles, while the restrictions on the build-up of offensive armaments would help save money badly needed for economic development. Most importantly, as Brezhnev told the party leaders "in strict confidence," the arms limitation agreements "would in any case not obstruct in any way the implementation of the previously envisioned measures to strengthen our country's defense."[91] In Brezhnev's assessment, the Soviet Union benefited from the agreements more than the United States did, which was how he was able to sell them to the reluctant military.

But to say that Brezhnev pursued arms control agreements for military advantage is to entirely misconstrue what he was trying to do. True to his heartfelt commitment to world peace, Brezhnev proclaimed that his goal was nothing short of saving civilization itself or, to be more precise, European civilization. As he put it in candidly racist terms, "Our countries have a great quantity of weapons. As President Nixon once said, you can destroy us seven times over, and we can destroy you seven times over. I told him in response that after this happens, the whites will be gone, only the blacks and the yellows will remain."[92]

On the subject of China, Brezhnev was quite tight-lipped, although Gromyko had supplied him with a three-page litany of complaints. For example, Brezhnev did not use his opportunity to chastise Nixon once again for his inappropriate toast about the United States and China holding the world's destiny in their hands, which (his talking points claimed) had a "political coloring" suggestive of "some special role of the two countries, China and the US."[93] The general secretary probably concluded that such reproachments would have made him appear rather desperate, which of course they would have.

Economic issues were front and center of discussions in Moscow. Brezhnev eyed US investments in the extraction of Soviet natural resources, in particular Siberian gas. Not only would Moscow thereby acquire badly needed technologies, but the long-term nature of these "compensation agreements" (at least twenty to thirty, if not fifty, years) would secure an economic foundation for a stable political relationship between the two superpowers. "President Nixon," Brezhnev explained, characteristically downplaying the role of ideology in superpower relations, "likes his system, and we like ours. Our countries have more than a few divergences and contradictions. But what do they have to do, say, with cooperation on gas? Nothing."[94]

CHAPTER 13 DETENTE

The prospects of trade relations heavily depended on Washington's willingness to grant the Soviet Union the so-called "Most Favored Nation" (MFN) status, which would bring down tariffs on Soviet products. The Soviets were stripped of their MFN privileges in 1951, a very different time in the Soviet–American relationship. For Brezhnev, the lack of MFN status had not just economic but political ramifications, which he interpreted squarely in terms of Soviet prestige: "you people keep humiliating us."[95] Nixon was broadly supportive and promised to deliver. The Soviets, for their part, after much handwringing (it took days of painful negotiations with Kissinger in September 1972), agreed to pay back their Second World War Lend-Lease loans – but only if Nixon came through with MFN status.

Among all these important agreements, the one that Brezhnev valued most was the rather vaguely worded proclamation of the "basic principles" of Soviet–American relations. These committed the two countries to develop their relations on the basis of "sovereignty, equality, noninterference in internal affairs and mutual advantage." Brezhnev made a big deal of this document in internal deliberations, praising it as an "important political document," which would create a "solid basis" for developing Soviet–American relations and "improve the entire international atmosphere."[96] The bottom line here was that such a document showed, so far as the Soviet leaders were concerned, that Washington and Moscow were equal partners bound together by the necessity of preventing a nuclear war, and that in this sense they – and not the Chinese – held the fate of the world in their hands.

On the day after Nixon's departure, the prominent Soviet journalist and political insider Yury Zhukov wrote Brezhnev a letter. "Let me, the old, battered wolf, who has witnessed a quarter of a century-worth of the most important international meetings, say to you: bravo!" Citing his conversations with the visiting US press corps, Zhukov said that no one expected such a performance from Brezhnev. They believed in a "caricature" and yet encountered a "living person who skillfully and confidently, and with an understanding of his strengths, defends his country's interests and at the same time humanely draws the interlocutor towards himself." Zhukov concluded that although Nixon may yet "behave hysterically and make zigzags ... what is done is done and, in any case, you have documents with his signature (first and foremost, the 'basic principles!'), which we can always use to substantially obstruct, if not paralyze, his maneuvers." The letter was phrased to raise the general secretary above his colleagues. The head of Brezhnev's Secretariat, Konstantin

PART III DECLINE

Figure 19 Brezhnev and Nixon in Moscow, following the signing of the SALT-I accords, May 26, 1972. Source: Bettmann/Getty Images.

Chernenko, circulated it to the Politburo, so that no one would have doubts about the authorship of the "big victory."[97]

CONDOMINIUM

In the run-up to the Moscow summit, Brezhnev came up with an idea that he would relentlessly pursue for months on end in the face of American resistance: an agreement between the two superpowers renouncing the use of nuclear weapons against one another.[98] He returned to this issue again and again during his private meetings with the American duo, in an almost conspiratorial fashion. Why was this so important to the Soviet leader? It was in part a reflection of what historian Vladislav Zubok describes as Brezhnev's personal commitment to preventing war.[99] There is no doubt that it was a genuine commitment, but it also had a legitimating quality for the Soviet leader unlike any other idea. "Every leading statesman," he would say, "enters history differently. Some enter it as brutal, blood-thirsty, horrible, heartless power-seekers; others – as humane, peace-loving, democratic politicians."[100] There is no doubt as to what historic role Brezhnev assigned to himself. There is a lot here that harkens back to Khrushchev who in

CHAPTER 13 DETENTE

1962 stepped away from the brink, and much that foreshadows Gorbachev: the common thread here is what Gorbachev later identified as a universal human value: survival through peace. "If the United States and the Soviet Union went to war over Europe, Brezhnev warned, "European civilization would be destroyed, and someone else would come in its stead."[101] That "someone else" was of course China.

Nixon and Kissinger were decidedly sour on what later became known as the prevention of nuclear war agreement. The basic reason was that by outlawing the possibility of nuking the USSR, the Americans in effect tied their own hands in case the Soviets decided to invade Western Europe or – much more likely – China. But since Brezhnev continued to insist, they agreed reluctantly to a seriously watered-down declaration that then became the centerpiece of the general secretary's reciprocal visit to the United States in June 1973. The Americans were somewhat puzzled by this stubborn advocacy of what in the end was bound to prove about as successful at outlawing war as the ill-fated 1928 Kellogg–Briand Pact. As usual, there was a tendency to see a deeply buried strategic rationale in Brezhnev's proposal – namely, to "cast doubt on our Allied commitments" and to "give the impression of a freer Soviet hand against China."[102] There is some evidence, to be sure, that motives of this kind formed the basis for Brezhnev's calculations. But there is also evidence for motives of a different kind. In Brezhnev's own words, signing the agreement would be a "great exploit." "None of us in this world is eternal," he told Kissinger in May 1973, "but history is eternal ... This will raise the prestige of our governments to an all-time high. Nothing in history can compare with this."[103]

The original Soviet draft of the agreement contained a provision for joint Soviet–American intervention to stop conflicts between other states.[104] This would be something like a mini-UN Security Council, with only two members, the two that mattered. There was a clear anti-Chinese angle to this condominium, and Brezhnev was increasingly willing to put it in those terms. When Kissinger turned up in Moscow in September 1972, Brezhnev – departing from his previous reserve – launched into quite an anti-Chinese spiel. He accused Beijing of misrepresenting contacts between the two superpowers as "collusion," and of trying to bring a head-on clash between them. He shared with Kissinger sensitive intelligence about the death of Mao's heir-apparent Lin Biao who had fled China in September 1971 aboard a military plane, which then crashed in Mongolia. Soviet experts, Brezhnev told Kissinger in confidence, had gone down to Mongolia to excavate the bodies (presumably removing their heads) to compare these with the dental records held in Moscow. The conclusion – according

PART III DECLINE

to Brezhnev – was that the corpse was really Lin Biao's, and that his defection clearly indicated China's political instability.[105]

For his part, Kissinger deceptively claimed that he did not discuss the Soviet Union in his conversations in Beijing and harped on this favorite theory about China one day joining hands with Japan on "racial" grounds as the real long-term threat to the world. (Brezhnev readily signed up to this theory).[106]

The Chinese theme returned with a vengeance in May 1973, when Kissinger again travelled to the Soviet Union to iron out the details of the prevention of nuclear war agreement. "One cannot allow any kind of a play involving the Chinese aspect," Brezhnev warned the secretary of state. He was of course speaking about the fear in Moscow that it was precisely what the Americans were doing with their "triangular diplomacy." Kissinger disclaimed any such effort. Brezhnev went on: "In principle, of course, the Chinese aspect is not connected to any serious danger right this moment. In this sense, we, and our children, can live peacefully. But we must think of future generations, in whose lifetimes the situation can substantially change."[107]

Kissinger's May 1973 trip to the USSR had an unusual aspect: whereas normally he would have been feted in Moscow, meeting with Brezhnev amid the grandeur of the Kremlin halls, this time – to inject the talks with special intimacy – the general secretary invited Kissinger to his dacha in Zavidovo, a hunting lodge about two hours' drive from the capital. On May 6, he took Kissinger out hunting. There, in the privacy of the hunting tower, with only the Soviet interpreter Viktor Sukhodrev at their side, Brezhnev tried a heart-to-heart approach. He reproached the Americans for trumpeting foreign policy from the "position of strength." He understood that this was done in part to reassure American allies, but this was not the main thing. The Soviet Union and the United States, acting hand-in-hand, could bring peace to any corner of the world, including particularly the Middle East. True, in public statements, the Soviet Union would still have to criticize Israel and its American sponsor but that did not preclude a private understanding. The same approach applied to China, whose "great-power chauvinism and hegemonism" presented a long-term problem. "We have to think about this together."[108]

The bottom line was clear enough. As Kissinger later summed up for Nixon's benefit, the general secretary put it in the following simple and brutal terms: "Look, I want to talk to you privately – nobody else, no notes ... Look, you will be our partners, you and we are going to run the world."[109]

CHAPTER 13 DETENTE

Figure 20 Brezhnev and Nixon on the White House portico, June 21, 1973.
Source: Dirck Halstead/Getty Images.

The June 1973 Soviet–American summit offered the Soviet leader an opportunity to take his idea of a condominium to a new level. To this end, he was willing to invest himself even more deeply in the personal relationship with the American president. The record of his first, private, meeting with Nixon in the Oval Office on June 18, is extraordinary for Brezhnev's effort to relate to the US president on human terms. He spoke at length about his wife, his son, and his grandchildren, and was overjoyed to hear that Nixon would invite his relatives to come to the US as his "special guests." He clearly delighted in Nixon's flattery and flattered in his turn. Most of all, Brezhnev savored the historical opportunity to speak to Nixon on equal terms, as the leader of a superpower to the leader of another superpower. "There are some people who keep throwing in this idea of there being two superpowers. What are the superpowers? What, do they want the Soviet Union to become Guinea or some other little country?"[110]

It quickly became apparent just how much stock Brezhnev put in the idea of trust – personal trust between him and the leader of another superpower. He returned to the theme again and again to highlight how the Cold War had infused the Soviet–American relationship with mistrust and

PART III DECLINE

how that was already becoming a thing of the past.[111] Now Brezhnev wanted to restore trust by trusting Nixon, whom he unironically now called "my dear friend" – being trusted in his turn.[112] "Without trust," Brezhnev told Nixon at Camp David on June 20, "it would have been impossible to achieve all that you and I began last year; the current visit would have been impossible, too. At the same time, I must state with satisfaction that, as I think, personal trust between us is growing from day to day."[113] What this meant in practice was that the Soviet leader was willing to conclude "gentlemen's agreements" with Nixon on sensitive issues like European security, the Middle East or, indeed, China.

Brezhnev brought up China in a conversation he had with Richard Nixon on June 21, 1973, at Camp David. It was after Kissinger had left for Washington, leaving the Soviet leader one-on-one with the president, bar the interpreter. Brezhnev complained how difficult the Chinese have been, rejecting every reasonable proposal the Soviets had put on the table, including a nonaggression treaty. This was because "they don't see a peaceful solution as profitable. Their aims are completely different." Brezhnev predicted that Beijing would slander the prevention of nuclear war agreement and asked Nixon to privately consult with the Soviets on their policy towards China before undertaking any moves in relations with Beijing (Brezhnev later revealed that he was worried about Nixon compensating the Chinese for the nuclear war agreement with a similar agreement directed against the USSR).[114] This sort of management of China through a Soviet–American gentlemen's agreement was a nonstarter with the American president but Brezhnev did not know that. He approached the problem from the civilizational angle, telling the president: "You and I can understand one another better and easier than either of us can understand the Chinese."[115] According to Brezhnev's later self-assessment, his revelations on China "made a definite impression" on the American president.[116]

After Washington and Camp David, Brezhnev followed Nixon to the West Coast. The president hosted him at his so-called Western White House, La Casa Pacifica, in San Clemente, CA – an honor intended to convey the intimacy and the importance of their relationship. It was there, too, that on June 24, at a one-on-one dinner with Nixon, Brezhnev heard the American president utter the words that he had so wanted to hear. "The future of the world," Nixon said, raising a glass, "is in our hands. And while you and I lead our countries, this future is in good hands."[117] Of course, Nixon's private toast did not have the international resonance of that other toast, which had so upset Brezhnev, about the United

States and China holding the future of the world in their hands. This time, Nixon's revelations were quite literally classified "top secret" (in a memorandum prepared by Brezhnev's interpreter). It did not matter. What mattered was that Nixon said what he said, and Brezhnev heard him say it. Was this not a good basis for an implicit Soviet–American understanding?

What this really meant, in Brezhnev's interpretation, was mutual accommodation. He was encouraged to hear Nixon say (uncharacteristically he even wrote this down in his personal notes) that the United States did not intend to "push the Soviet Union out of the Middle East." For his part, Brezhnev even told Nixon "in strict confidence" (as the two shared a helicopter ride from San Clemente) that the Soviet Union "did not mind the presence of US forces in Europe."[118] Assuming Brezhnev meant it, his comments show that he was perhaps more concerned about the potential rise of Europe (especially of course West Germany) than he was about the United States, and that he looked to the United States as a partner in managing Europe and, indeed, the rest of the world.

What would Karl Marx have said had he joined Brezhnev in shooting boars with Kissinger or shared that helicopter ride with the American president? After all, that business about running the world had un-Marxist connotations. It did not square with the ideological premises of the whole Soviet project. The idea was to oppose American imperialism, not to join forces with it in "running the world." But this was not the first time that the Soviet leaders sacrificed ideology for glory. Brezhnev, much like Khrushchev and Stalin, valued recognition of his greatness at least on a par with his loyalty to the Marxist dogma. Such recognition bolstered his claim to political legitimacy, and his sense of belonging to an exclusive old boys' club (of just two). At a time when the Soviet economy (as Brezhnev knew) faced mounting challenges, when the prospect of overtaking the United States in production – something Khrushchev looked forward to in his time – seemed ever more remote, this notional equality with Nixon became all the more important. This is the reason why there is precious little discussion of ideology in the annals of Soviet–American relations of the early 1970s: little ideology but plenty of greatness and glory.

The same was true, as we have seen, of Soviet relations with France and West Germany. Why did Brezhnev so patiently court the Western leaders in his single-minded pursuit of detente? Here is his answer, in his own words: "if Brandt, Pompidou and Nixon have to speak to the Soviet Union and the Soviet Communist Party, it means that the USSR and the Soviet Communist Party are such a political and social force, without which one cannot solve any important international questions."[119] Brezhnev's search for detente was underpinned by a well-known adage: "Show me your friends and I will tell you who you are."

CONCLUSION

Nixon was not interested in running the world together with Brezhnev. He was suspicious of the Soviet moves in Europe and only reluctantly endorsed Soviet rapprochement with West Germany. He was unwilling – despite Brezhnev's relentless prodding – to jointly force Israel off the occupied territories and so help strengthen the Soviet standing in the Middle East. Most of all, he was not going to embrace Brezhnev's conceptions of China as inherently treacherous and dangerous. Nixon continued to court both Moscow and Beijing, leaning often closer to Beijing than to Moscow. It was a delicate balancing act. The Chinese eyed the Soviet–American detente with suspicion. As Nixon and Kissinger had feared, Mao concluded that the real purpose behind improved Soviet–American relations was to free Moscow's hands for dealing with China.

Running the world together with the United States or, at least, alongside the United States, meant playing down the ideological divide between the East and the West. By embracing Brandt's *Ostpolitik* in the late 1960s Brezhnev already made clear that ideological disagreements with long-reviled social democracy were less important to him than the prestige and the practical benefits of an improved relationship with Bonn. Defying Cold War divisions, he sought to foster cultural affinities between the Soviet Union and Western Europe and later the United States. The idea that he was a European was evidently more important to the Soviet leader than class-based distinctions between the East and the West. His approach to Nixon was also underpinned by the notion that as two Europeans (the American president was also in this sense a "European") they could relate to each other, learn to respect each other, and build a peaceful future for the world.

Not long after his return from talks with Nixon, he was approached by the head of the Russian Orthodox Church, Patriarch Pimen. "We, comrade Brezhnev," Pimen said, "held a service in churches in your honor, to recognize your achievements in the struggle for peace."[120] Things were clearly going well for comrade Brezhnev if even the Russian Orthodox Church recognized his achievements in securing peace for the world. But where did this leave Marxism-Leninism? Brezhnev tried to square ideology and policy like one might square a circle: simply by ignoring the obvious

CHAPTER 13 DETENTE

contradictions of his worldview. "Sometimes I think about the following," he told Walter J. Stoessel, Nixon's newly appointed ambassador, in March 1974. "Ideologically you and we defend completely different positions. Each one 'prays to his god.' But this does not mean that relations between the USSR and the US cannot be normal and kind ... In the final account, who are we, you and us – civilized people or savages? If civilized people, then we should act accordingly."[121]

But can you be "kind" and still pursue a relentless class struggle? Anatoly Chernyaev, the ever-perceptive insider, noted the obvious in his diary: "no one believes in our 'revolutionary example' anymore. But our country must by its nature maintain an ideological character, including for the external world, including for the Communists. Therefore, it must have a universalist mission. Peace is that mission."[122] And elsewhere: "The main idea of Brezhnev's life is the idea of peace. It is for this that he wants to be remembered by mankind. He will give preference to practical achievements in this sphere over any ideology."[123]

Practical achievements, however, were less impressive than Brezhnev had expected. The key area where Soviet–US detente was not delivering was the economic relationship. There were some breakthroughs, to be sure. For example, Nixon's confidante and PepsiCo executive Donald Kendall managed to conclude a deal on setting up a Pepsi bottling plant in the USSR, which in some ways symbolized detente for the average Soviet consumer. Moscow also managed to attract about $1.3 billion (including $500 million from US firms) for the gigantic truck manufacturer Kamaz.[124] But, on the whole, the Soviet market proved less attractive to American companies than Brezhnev had imagined. The great Siberian gas deals with America fell through. Trade turnover grew dramatically (from 183 million rubles in 1971 to 538 million rubles in 1972) but most of this was just Soviet import of US goods, in particular American wheat.[125] Meanwhile Soviet access to the US market was still barred by the absence of MFN status. Nixon, for all his promises, failed to deliver on this front, partly because he was bogged down by domestic difficulties, and had trouble bringing Congress around to endorsing his foreign policy agenda.

Indeed, Brezhnev's quest for detente with the United States overlapped with Nixon's political downfall. In June 1972 there was a break-in at the office of the Democratic National Committee in the Watergate Hotel – an effort, it turned out, to eavesdrop on Nixon's political opponents. On June 25, 1973 – the same Monday that Brezhnev left the United States after his week-long tour – a special investigative committee of the US Senate began hearing the testimony of Nixon's former

PART III DECLINE

counsel, John W. Dean III. Dean not just disclosed that Nixon knew of the Watergate cover-up for months but hinted that he also tape-recorded at least some of his conversations in the Oval Office.[126] The existence of a secret tape-recording system was confirmed weeks later. These tapes would sink Nixon's presidency.

The Soviet leadership were slow to recognize the gravity of the situation. What they did recognize had a characteristic conspiratorial spin that saw Watergate as a "carefully planned" attempt by the enemies of detente to undermine Nixon's foreign policy. Brezhnev's foreign policy alter ego, Aleksandrov-Agentov, argued in May 1973 that whereas in 1963 the "reactionary" opponents of detente simply killed President Kennedy, this time "they [were making] an attempt to destroy Nixon morally, force him to leave the presidency and so put an end to the serious rapprochement between the US and the USSR, which had already begun." KGB head Yury Andropov promised to try to dig up *kompromat* on Nixon's fiercest critics as the Soviets pondered whether or how to approach Kissinger in order to find out from him what Moscow could do to help Nixon. "Probably, we can't do too much here," Aleksandrov-Agentov wrote to Brezhnev, "but some things, perhaps, we can."[127]

But Moscow's leverage proved limited. The scandal grew rapidly, and soon engulfed the White House. By early August 1974 the architect of the Beijing and Moscow summits was at the end of his rope. Just then, Brezhnev wrote a very personal letter to the US president, where he spoke of their friendship, and all those great things they had managed to achieve. "We see," the letter went, "how tendentiously and how shamelessly some of your opponents manipulate the assessments of this or that side of your work and the work of your Administration, just in order to harm your position." He concluded with a touch of sadness: "I cannot say it all. I think you will understand everything the way I want you to understand it."[128] On August 8 Nixon announced his resignation. Brezhnev's sympathetic letter was never sent.

The winds had long been blowing in that direction and yet Brezhnev was still flabbergasted. He had thought until the end that Nixon would "wiggle his way out" of the situation because, after all, he had Kissinger: "a smart, cunning guy [who] will help him."[129] When Nixon failed to "wiggle his way out," the general secretary concluded: "the American society is an astonishing society. I don't even know how to characterize it."[130] He lamented the demise of an American president whom he himself had accused of "demagoguery" not too long before. Nixon may have once been an evil man with blood stains on his hands but that was before he became

CHAPTER 13 DETENTE

Brezhnev's friend. "I wouldn't want to hide the fact that there was personal affinity between me and Mr. Nixon," Brezhnev told his successor Gerald Ford in 1974, during their summit in Vladivostok.[131]

The Soviet propaganda machine still spewed out propaganda about the sins of imperialism. The struggle against imperialism was a must-mention in public speeches of the Soviet leaders, Brezhnev included. But the general secretary was unimpressed. "Imperialism, imperialism," he grumbled privately. "The times have changed! Imperialism looks differently depending on who leads it."[132]

14

YOM KIPPUR

There is a popular theory (that Richard Nixon wholeheartedly embraced) that Soviet interest in the Middle East was but a desperate scramble for warm-water ports and oil.[1] It was not. Of course, the military appreciated the region's geopolitical importance – not because they necessarily needed access to its oil and ice-free ports but because they wanted to deny the region to the Americans and the British. Given the region's "exceptional importance" for the West, argued Defense Minister Andrei Grechko in June 1973, "the Ministry of Defense deems it appropriate not to decrease our presence in the Indian Ocean and in the Persian Gulf, to continue visits by Soviet naval vessels to Iraqi and Indian ports, and to strengthen contacts between the Soviet Navy and the navies of India, Iraq, and the People's Democratic Republic of Yemen."[2] Brezhnev often talked about the "strategic" significance of the Middle East, both because of its oil reserves and because of its proximity to the Soviet Union's southern borders (a concern of a defensive, not offensive, character).[3] If we ever had to look for "geopolitical" reasons for Moscow's involvement in the Middle East, there is certainly evidence to back up the claim.

Another way of thinking about the Soviet involvement in the Middle East is to reference Marxism-Leninism. Now, it is true that most Soviet clients in the region were not remotely Marxist. There was a sense in Moscow that perhaps one day "Arab socialism" of Nasser's variety would evolve into something more Soviet-like but, as we have seen, the Soviet leaders were quite accepting of the anti-Communist policies of their clients for as long as they continued to defer to Moscow's preferences. Soviet policies in the region were often rationalized in Marxist terms – for example, as aiding revolutionary regimes in their struggle against world imperialism, and such a framing obviously reinforced the military's strategic preoccupation with denying the Middle East to Western powers.

But there was something else, too, to look after: the prestige of a superpower. One might think of the Middle East as a stage, where the Soviet leaders asserted their greatness against the claims of rival powers (first and

CHAPTER 14 YOM KIPPUR

foremost the United States). They built up clients, supplied weapons, provided economic aid, weighed in on questions of war and peace – in other words, stayed relevant, seeking recognition as an indispensable player, on a par with the Americans. This was a policy Nikita Khrushchev had pursued since the 1950s, and once Khrushchev was dethroned, Brezhnev stepped into his shoes, inheriting commitments to willful, often unreliable, clients. Such commitments carried with them the danger of entrapment. Crises could spin out of control, endangering detente, potentially even bringing the two superpowers to the brink of war. This is precisely what happened in October 1973. This chapter recounts the dramatic Soviet–American confrontation that grew out of a conflict fought mainly between Egypt and Syria, on the one hand, and Israel, on the other. This confrontation was all the more remarkable given that 1973 was the high point of detente that Brezhnev and Nixon had so tirelessly worked to bring about. Was there something peculiar about the Soviet–American relationship that made it particularly unstable? Was it perhaps prone to violent crises even despite the best intentions of policy makers in Moscow and Washington? The chapter helps to answer this question.

BREZHNEV AND SADAT

The Soviet standing in the Middle East – relatively solid since Khrushchev's infamous saber-rattling in the Suez Crisis – was badly damaged in 1967, when Egypt and Syria lost to Israel in the Six Day War. Gamal Abdel Nasser's Soviet-equipped forces were obliterated in Israel's preemptive strike, and the Israelis then went on to occupy the Gaza strip, the Sinai Peninsula, the Golan Heights, and the West Bank of the Jordan River (including, most importantly, East Jerusalem). Nasser never quite recovered from the humiliation. But nor did he turn back on his ally. Instead, he called on Moscow to help rebuild Egypt's battered army. He tempted the Kremlin with the offer to permit Soviet military bases on the Egyptian territory, which (according to Cairo's calculations) would help the Soviets project power into the Mediterranean. For his part, Brezhnev understood Nasser's needs and, in late 1969, agreed to supply new anti-aircraft systems to Egypt. These included the S-125s (SA-3s in NATO classification): the first time such a system was being deployed anywhere outside Soviet borders. The beginning of the deployment in March 1970 and the related build-up of Soviet combat personnel and advisers in Egypt (their number soon reached 10,000) caused a brief crisis in Soviet–American relations but Brezhnev proved willing to probe the limits of Washington's forbearance. At the same time, he pleaded with the Egyptians to stop provocative rhetoric and focus on

PART III DECLINE

peace talks with Israel. "You must have resilience and patience," he warned the Egyptians, "and [you must be] active in political, economic and other spheres. This is very important! Very important!"[4]

The last time Nasser and Brezhnev met in person was in July 1970. The Soviet leader stressed the need for political dialogue. "We have been waiting for four years," Nasser said, adding: "I don't believe the Americans." He died two months later, never having regained the territories lost to Israel in the Six Day War.[5]

Brezhnev's relationship with Nasser's successor Anwar Sadat was from the start characterized by a degree of mutual wariness. Sadat, like his contemporary Nasser, was twelve years Brezhnev's junior. Born in a small village in the Nile Delta, he studied at the Royal Military Academy in Cairo, and later served in Sudan, where he linked up with Nasser and joined the Free Officers. He remained in Nasser's shadow and his succession to the presidency was anything but preordained. In the unflattering characterization of the Soviet ambassador, Vladimir Vinogradov, Sadat was "receptive to flattery" and "vain," but also a "believer in power." "He was mortally afraid of Marxism, and anything connected with it," Vinogradov recalled.[6] Once in power, Sadat moved quickly against his rivals, including Vice President Ali Sabri, Minister of Interior Sharawy Gomaa, Defense Minister Mohamed Fawzi, and Minister for Presidential Affairs Sami Sharaf who were widely regarded as pro-Soviet politicians. The purge unsettled Brezhnev, especially because Sadat tried to implicate the Soviets (including Ambassador Vinogradov) in plotting a coup against him. The latter denied any connection to the alleged plotters.[7]

Brezhnev's cautious response to Sadat's insinuations was at odds with some of the advice he was receiving at the time from regional experts, not least 42-year-old former *Pravda* correspondent Evgeny Primakov, who in July 1971 sent a memorandum to Brezhnev where he argued that the Soviets suffered from the "inferiority complex" of noninterventionism in the internal affairs of Arab states. "They'll take us into account more if we behave with greater assertiveness and firmness – the Arab world respects you for this."[8] But instead of putting pressure on Sadat, Brezhnev tried to institutionalize the relationship by concluding a Treaty of Friendship and Cooperation with Egypt in May 1971, a significant upgrade to the relationship, at least on paper.[9]

The treaty was an effort to appease Sadat who had aired persistent complaints about insufficient military and political support from Moscow (at one point, Sadat even seemingly asked for atomic weapons so that he could successfully "deter" Israel – he was rebuffed).[10] "He narrows

CHAPTER 14 YOM KIPPUR

the whole issue and all conversations down to us giving him bombers," Brezhnev complained testily after meeting the Egyptian president in March 1971 – "which would be completely under his control and would fly in any direction on his orders."[11] Given that Sadat proclaimed 1971 as the "Year of Decision" and made other militant statements in relation to Israel, Brezhnev had good reasons to worry what he might be up to. He pressed Sadat on his plans in relation to Israel during their meeting in October 1971. The Egyptian leader proclaimed that he planned only limited military action, just to prod the Israelis towards a political settlement. However, the fact that at the same time he asked for Soviet-made missiles to enable him to strike deep inside Israel's territory, was far from reassuring and fed Brezhnev's worries that Sadat might inadvertently start a "big war" in the Middle East.[12] It did not help that Sadat told Brezhnev that "we alone [i.e. Egypt] will make the decision to start the battle and we alone will bear the responsibility for it."[13]

What bothered Brezhnev the most was this unpredictability. "Sadat," Brezhnev noted paternalistically in June 1973, "is an emotional man, he is not always mentally balanced. Every so often he declares that a war will start tomorrow, that he is creating a Defense Committee, and introduces martial law. And he does it without consultations with us."[14] What the Soviet leader was worried about was that Sadat would do what he had repeatedly promised to do – unleash another war in the Middle East – and then would lose (as he might despite the unending flow of Soviet equipment). "This will bring us all to political ruin," lamented Brezhnev.[15] Or, as he put it on another occasion, "We discuss the Middle Eastern problem almost at every meeting of the CC CPSU [Central Committee of the Communist Party of the Soviet Union] Politburo. We are fully cognizant of the fact that by their unthoughtful actions the Arabs could do themselves irreparable damage and deal a blow to our prestige, and we must not allow this."[16] But what Brezhnev did not fully appreciate was that doing nothing was also not an option – not for Sadat. As one insider had put it, "by 1973 Egypt had almost become the laughingstock of the Arab world ... Each day that passed was a day of humiliation for Egypt."[17]

Of course, humiliation from doing nothing could only be exceeded by humiliation of doing something – and being crushed while doing it. So, at least, the Soviets thought. From their perspective, avoiding a war in the Middle East was not just something to strive towards for its own sake. Brezhnev's real concern here was not even war as such: it was more the question of the consequences of war: the all-too-likely Arab defeat and the loss of credibility that this entailed for Sadat's Soviet friends. "I speak

395

frankly," Brezhnev told the Egyptian foreign minister after hearing him spell out plans for an imminent war. "If you begin, you must succeed – so that you begin so as to win. You can't allow a situation where you decide to scare Israel and then you yourselves have to retreat. I show great caution in this matter, for here one must take into account the interests of our peoples and considerations of international nature."[18]

Given his difficulties with Sadat, it is not surprising that Brezhnev hoped to tackle the problem from the other end: to achieve a lasting settlement involving great power guarantees, whereby the United States would put pressure on Israel to make concessions to the Arabs. He was annoyed that Nixon showed little inclination to do so. As was the case with Vietnam, both superpowers were engaged in a strange pirouette with their intractable allies, and the scope for a breakthrough was extremely limited. Even more annoying (from the Soviet perspective) was the US effort "to claim for themselves the role of allegedly impartial middleman between the Arabs and Israel, and to convince the Arabs that the key to solving the Middle Eastern conflict is in Washington's hands."[19]

The problem for Brezhnev was not just that Sadat might lash out against Israel and lose yet again, undercutting the Soviet prestige in the Middle East, but that he could well flip to the United States, and that, too, would leave the Soviets in the cold. "Of course, you can get millions [of dollars] from them," he warned the Egyptians in 1971, "but later the Americans will eat you together with these millions ..."[20] The prospect of Sadat's defection became more realistic in the summer of 1972, when he expelled more than 10,000 Soviet military advisers to signal to the United States that he wanted a closer relationship with the West.[21]

The Soviet leaders had themselves considered a withdrawal but only in the context of a superpower settlement in the Middle East, which had not yet materialized.[22] They were blindsided by Sadat's move and angered by this slap in the face. Soviet advisers, Brezhnev lamented, had been a "trump card," which the Egyptian president had foolishly discarded.[23] Internally, the Soviets concluded that Sadat acted the way he did under pressure from the "reactionary" political elites, as a way to consolidate his personal power.[24] Brezhnev circulated his thoughts to the Politburo on July 24, 1972: it was important to evaluate Sadat's actions "in cold blood" and adopt suitable "tactical measures."[25] The main idea here was not to overreact. Egypt remained economically and militarily dependent on the Soviet Union. It made sense to continue patiently working with the Egyptians to "counterattack US efforts to weaken the Soviet influence in the Middle East."[26]

CHAPTER 14 YOM KIPPUR

Meanwhile, the Soviets tried shopping around by probing the Israelis.[27] Moscow broke off diplomatic ties with Israel during the June 1967 war. As is often the case, breaking relations proved easier than repairing them.[28] Sadat, in the meantime, had second thoughts about quarrelling with the Russians and soon tried to mend fences.[29] The Soviet leader obliged, noting privately: "I know he is sorry for that. Unfortunately ambition and prestige do not allow him to say it publicly."[30] In February 1973 Sadat sent first his national security adviser and, later, his defense minister to Moscow for talks.[31] The latter, Ahmed Ismail, told Brezhnev that Egypt and Syria would go to war against Israel in April 1973.[32] April came and went. Brezhnev even thought that Sadat's saber-rattling was merely a ploy to put Israel under "psychological pressure." But, he added, he simply could not rule out that Sadat would start a war.[33] The KGB suspected that he might even do so at the time of the superpower summit, in June 1973, and secretly approached the CIA station in Cairo to inform their rivals that the Soviet Union was by no means interested in a new conflict.

But while on the one hand Brezhnev clearly was not thrilled by the prospect of a war in the Middle East, on the other hand he continued to satisfy Sadat's demands for weapons, which made such a war much more likely. One example of this was the story behind the Soviet decision to supply Sadat with surface-to-surface Scud missiles. "I don't remember when we promised this [to him]," Brezhnev wrote testily to the Politburo on February 7, 1973. "But this is not even the main thing. The main thing is what it will mean for Egypt; after all, the US will also provide Israel with such missiles, and no one knows where this could end up."[34] But for all these concerns, Brezhnev ultimately signed off on the Scuds. Evidently, he thought that Sadat's friendship was worth the price. Andropov later proposed to withhold the shipment of missiles to Egypt until *after* the Soviet leader returned from the United States lest the trigger-happy sometime-ally started a war and derailed the fruit of Brezhnev's labor, his dearly loved detente.[35] According to US intelligence sources, the Scuds arrived in July.[36]

Brezhnev's June 1973 visit to the United States became the glorious highlight of his political career. He was wined and dined in Washington and visited with Nixon at Camp David and at the president's spacious home in San Clemente, CA. Thirteen years after Khrushchev last banged his fists at the United Nations, Brezhnev's dignified appearance carried a promise of a different, friendlier relationship between the superpowers.

But even as Brezhnev embraced the relationship with his new friend Richard Nixon, he was mindful of the smoking powder keg in the Middle

PART III DECLINE

East and tried to use his negotiations in the United States to deliver a breakthrough. Using a moment of Kissinger's absence (Brezhnev wanted to cut him out of the conversation), the Soviet leader broached the subject with Nixon in a one-to-one at Camp David.[37] Warning that but for Soviet efforts, the Arabs would have long started another war, Brezhnev probed the ground for a superpower agreement that would pave the way to Israel's withdrawal behind the borders of 1967. But Nixon, citing his problems with difficult clients, merely referred the general secretary back to Kissinger. Brezhnev waited for another two days and then quite literally imposed the Middle East on the unsuspecting president in a bizarre meeting in San Clemente, which illustrates the intensity of Brezhnev's concern with and the urgency of the problem.

At 10:00pm on June 23, Kissinger got a phone call from the Secret Service: Brezhnev wanted an urgent meeting with the president. "It was a gross breach of protocol," the secretary of state later recalled. "For a foreign guest late at night to ask for an unscheduled meeting with the President on an unspecified subject on the last evening of a State visit was then, and has remained, unparalleled. It was also a transparent ploy to catch Nixon off guard and with luck to separate him from his advisers."[38] (This remark was probably on target.) Nixon, bizarrely, called the midnight session "a reminder of the unchanging and unrelenting Communist motivations beneath the diplomatic veneer of detente."[39]

It may have been that Brezhnev's supposed pushiness was a result of work-related stress. Brezhnev's doctor, Evgeny Chazov (who followed the general secretary to San Clemente), recalled that Brezhnev already exhibited signs of asthenia (a nervous system disorder), a combined effect of fatigue and powerful sedatives. Chazov noted that he managed to keep the condition under control and the Americans did not seem to notice that anything was amiss. Upon his return to Moscow, Chazov sought out the KGB head, Yury Andropov, with a warning: somehow they had to keep Brezhnev off his sleeping pills and restrict his access to his nurse (the suspected source).[40] Could it be that Brezhnev was not quite himself? Nixon seems to have thought so. The president (who met Chazov in November 1973) jokingly told Brezhnev's doctor that he should "look after the General Secretary's health and makes sure that he, after all, rests more." That meeting in San Clemente, Nixon recalled, was so intense that it took him (the president) two days to recover.[41]

During the meeting, Brezhnev pleaded for a superpower understanding on the Middle East. Moscow would press the Arabs to tone down their hostility; Washington would press the Israelis to withdraw from the territories they conquered in the June 1967 war.[42] The alternative, Brezhnev warned,

CHAPTER 14 YOM KIPPUR

was war. The president fought off this late-hour onslaught the best he could. The last thing he wanted was a Soviet-inspired peace in the Middle East. As Nixon once quipped, "We want Peace. They want the Middle East."[43] Or, as Kissinger put it, "We were not willing to pay for detente in the coin of our geopolitical position."[44] Brezhnev pressed on, and Nixon had to cut him short in the end: "we have to break up now." "He was screwing with me," Brezhnev conceded a few days later. "But ... I read him the riot act ... I said that the Middle East is a powder keg, and I can't predict now what will happen if the war breaks outs."[45]

The Israelis thought they knew, smugly believing that the Arab soldier was a good-for-nothing, and any future conflict would be won hands-down by Israel, which was in itself a good reason to do nothing. "The Israelis," reported KGB chief Yury Andropov at the end of August 1973, "do not rule out the possibility that Egypt may launch limited military action; however, in this case they plan to deliver a powerful blow to the Egyptian Army, and, having inflicted a new defeat on the Egyptians, to guarantee the indefinite maintenance of the status quo."[46] Unbeknownst to the Israelis, the Egyptians and the Syrians were finalizing plans for putting this confidence to a test.

THE WAR

At 2:00pm on October 6, 1973, taking advantage of Yom Kippur, the holiest day in Judaism, Egypt and Syria at last launched a coordinated attack across the Suez Canal (piercing the touted Bar-Lev Line) and the Golan Heights. Few in the Israeli high command or among the intelligence officials believed that the Arabs – so badly beaten in 1967 – would nevertheless do something quite so audacious. Now, caught off guard, the Israeli Defense Force struggled to contain the onslaught, losing territory and suffering heavy casualties on both fronts in the first few days of bitter fighting. It was a moment of long-awaited glory for Anwar Sadat and his Syrian "brother," President Hafez al-Assad. Nothing helped restore the Arab prestige quite as well as the sight of the mighty Israelis being pushed back from their seemingly impregnable positions in the Golan Heights and the Sinai Peninsula.[47] On the evening of October 8 Sadat rang Ambassador Vinogradov with the good news: "Yes, yes. Magnificent! Magnificent! Tell Comrade Brezhnev I feel thankful to him from the bottom of my heart." When his old acquaintance Mohamed Heikal asked Sadat what he thought the Soviet game really was, the president said that "this was their chance to regain most or all of their lost prestige in the Middle East," adding: "I don't think they'll miss this chance."[48]

PART III DECLINE

On October 6 Kissinger phoned Ambassador Dobrynin at 6:40am, Washington time, just hours before the outbreak of hostilities, to tell him that a war in the Middle East would have highly detrimental consequences for the Soviet–American relationship. "Syrians and who?" Dobrynin replied over what he claimed was a bad phone connection. "If this keeps up the way this is going – there is going to be a war before you understand my message," Kissinger said.[49] Later that day, the Soviets sent a vaguely worded cable to the US leadership, claiming that they were as surprised by the war as anyone else.[50] In fact, they knew perfectly well that a war would break out, and even began to evacuate their civilians from the region two days before hostilities began: in this respect they were ahead of the United States intelligence that slept through the opening stage of the conflict.[51]

The Soviet leaders received their advance notice on September 30. Assad confidentially informed the Soviet ambassador that the Syrians and the Egyptians, acting jointly, would launch an attack on Israel in just a few days.[52] Sadat confirmed that much on October 4.[53] Brezhnev's reaction was an unenthusiastic, cautious approval. On October 3, the Politburo resolved to tell Assad that it was his business whether to start the war, because "only leaders can make decisions about their countries' military actions, and only they shoulder the full burden of responsibility before their people and before history for the consequences of such decisions." At the same time, though, Assad was warned that he had to take into account the readiness of the Syrian forces, and the possibility that Egypt might drop out of the war.[54] Sadat was told that although the Arabs "had the right to resort to any forms of struggle" in liberating their lands, it was important to take into account the state of military readiness because another defeat would result in a serious blow for the prospects of a peace settlement in the Middle East.[55]

The Soviet assessment was that neither the Egyptians nor the Syrians were ready to go to war against a "well-prepared adversary like Israel."[56] Just two weeks prior, on September 13, the Syrians lost planes in a dogfight with the Israelis – that did not bode well. Egypt, too, reported Soviet Ambassador Vinogradov, was "poorly prepared and failed to maintain any secrecy at all."[57] The Soviet leaders had to show the Arabs that they stood by them by supplying advanced weapons.[58] Yet they were also mortified by the prospect of the Arabs using these weapons to launch a war they were going to lose. They squared the circle by sending military personnel to Cairo and Damascus to instruct their clients on how to put these weapons to the best possible use while hoping that they would not test these skills in real battle. When the Arabs resolved to go to war nonetheless, Brezhnev ordered the evacuation of Soviet civilians in a deliberately orchestrated

400

effort to distance himself from his quasi-allies. It was a very messy policy, which aimed at maintaining Moscow's influence in the Arab world without being dragged along, against its will, into a conflict it ultimately cared little about.

The Americans were also in an awkward situation. The opening of the Yom Kippur War (or, as it was otherwise known, the October War or the Ramadan War) coincided with a political meltdown in Washington. On October 10, Spiro Agnew, Nixon's vice president, resigned after being investigated for criminal conspiracy, bribery, extortion, and tax evasion. This was bad news for the embattled president, already fatally weakened by Watergate, and fighting in court to stop the Special Prosecutor Archibald Cox from gaining control over secretly recorded White House tapes. Kissinger (in a conversation with Dobrynin) claimed that Agnew's resignation "would in no way decrease but probably, by contrast, increase, the President's effectiveness in foreign policy."[59] What he probably meant was that with Nixon struggling to contain this domestic emergency, it was his secretary of state (a title Kissinger had just added to his portfolio as Nixon's national security adviser) who would now take charge of the US response to the new round of fighting in the Middle East.

The Israelis were pressing the United States for political support and for an urgent resupply of weapons, especially to compensate for the heavy losses they incurred fighting the Egyptians in Sinai. But US support for Tel Aviv would cause an uproar among the Arabs, endangering American relationships across the region and potentially triggering an oil embargo. The United States itself would hold out but the West Europeans and Japan (who were overreliant on the Middle Eastern oil) would take a hit. Under these circumstances, the best outcome for Washington was to seek refuge in neutrality, brokering a ceasefire with a subsequent withdrawal to the lines of October 6. If the Soviets joined in the effort – great. But if, as Kissinger suspected, they were supporting the Arabs despite the pretense of "surprise," the Americans would have to back the Israelis for fear of a domestic backlash (from the pro-Israel lobby), and to maintain credibility as a superpower patron.[60] But that would lead to countless problems for the American position in the Middle East. "My nightmare is a victory for either side," Kissinger would argue in terms that, on this occasion, seemed not too far from the truth.[61] It was much better, then, to bring the Soviets on board on the premise that detente was more important to Brezhnev than the confidence of his trigger-happy Arab allies. That linkage never seemed to work before: Would it work now? Or, as the recently appointed head of the CIA, William Colby, put it on the first day of fighting: "Is there an argument with the Soviets that their real interest lies with us and not with the crazy Arabs?"[62]

Ever worried about the fallout from another Arab defeat, Brezhnev had never liked Sadat's belligerent policies. But once the fighting started, the Soviets had even less space for maneuver than the Americans. As Dobrynin quite candidly told Kissinger on October 6, if the Soviets told the Arabs to stop, "it would look like we are trying to sell them out."[63] On the same day, the Soviet ambassador passed on Moscow's decision: the Soviet Union would be against convening the Security Council. Brezhnev was playing for time. Kissinger concluded on the evening of October 7, 1973 that "They [the Soviets] are leaning over backward not to get involved and to make it clear to us that they're not getting involved."[64] But why? Why would the Soviets, as Kissinger put it in a "quite an emotional" conversation with Dobrynin, "sacrifice even [their] relations with the US President in the name of dubious friendship with the Arab leaders who are willing to betray each and everyone?"[65]

Kissinger did not know this, but the Soviets were in fact more than happy to get involved in joint Soviet–American action – only, they were not sure that Sadat would come along. The problem was discussed at the Politburo meeting on the evening of October 6, the very first day of the conflict.[66] The prevailing view was that a ceasefire – as a Soviet–American initiative – would be the best outcome. As one Soviet diplomat privy to some of these discussions, later recalled: "They assumed that a Soviet peace initiative at the United Nations would consolidate the success of the Arabs and elevate the Soviet Union's international standing and prestige."[67] The problem: how to sell the idea to the Arabs while they were winning on the ground. What if, say, Sadat resisted, exposing Moscow's political impotence? What if – and this was the worst-case scenario – the Chinese vetoed the Soviet–American ceasefire proposal? Argued Vasily Kuznetsov (who, as deputy foreign minister, stayed abreast of the conflict from the start): "Do you want the Chinese to become leaders of the national liberation, anti-imperialist forces?"[68]

The Chinese angle kept cropping up during the Politburo discussions on the Middle East. "Dread of China's potential influence in the region sometimes overshadowed other concerns of the Soviet leaders," recalled Viktor Israelyan, a senior Soviet diplomat involved in the policy discussions. "Washington did not have this problem in planning and carrying out its policy in the Middle East."[69] Israelyan's comment points to a long-standing Soviet fear of appearing less revolutionary than China, something, we have seen, that underpinned Nikita Khrushchev's policy during the Cuban Missile Crisis. Here was a different crisis, and a different man in

CHAPTER 14 YOM KIPPUR

the Kremlin, and the Sino-Soviet polemical exchanges of the early 1960s were already a distant memory but China continued to play a role in the Soviet policy making because it offered a potential pole of attraction for the third world audiences that mattered a great deal to the Soviets in their bid for global leadership.

As they had on so many occasions in the past, Brezhnev and his comrades had difficulties reconciling their desire for global recognition as a superpower, on a par with the United States, with the imperative of being recognized as the leader of the "anti-imperialist forces." The premise behind "linkage" (as seen by Nixon and Kissinger) was for the Soviet leaders to abandon one in favor of the other: to prioritize detente over the third world. But that was not how it worked in practice. The Soviets catered to different audiences. Maintaining leadership in the third world (in the face of encroachment by the Chinese and others) was a precondition for being a superpower, for who ever heard of a superpower without a third world clientele?

In any case, the order of the day was to bring the fighting to an end as quickly as possible, and before Israel had a chance to obliterate their Arab neighbors or before the Americans got the chance to cut the Soviets out of a potential settlement. Already on October 6, Dobrynin highlighted both prospects after his talks with Kissinger. Noting that it was all too possible that the Israelis would quickly turn the tide, the ambassador advised his superiors in Moscow that "it is not in our interests for the possible settlement to be linked just to the Americans, who are already directly contacting the Egyptians ..., leaving us on the sidelines."[70]

Brezhnev was certainly in tune with this logic. On the morning of October 8, he approved instructions for Ambassador Dobrynin: tell Kissinger that the Soviets were keen to "act jointly" with the Americans in the Middle East. They had already contacted the Arabs about a ceasefire and were waiting for their reply. In the meantime, the message stated, could Nixon make sure that the Israelis "don't lose their head?"[71] The latter was a reference to the likely forceful counterattack from the Israelis that the Soviets so feared. After weighing the wording, Brezhnev had the reference to the Israelis "losing their head" taken out of the message.[72] This was so that Nixon and Kissinger did not get the impression that the Soviet leaders were pessimistic about the prospects of their Arab friends.

True to his word, that same day Brezhnev turned to Sadat with a proposal for an immediate ceasefire in situ. "Dear friend and brother, President Sadat," Brezhnev's letter began. "We in the Soviet Union express deep satisfaction on the account of the successes attained by your military forces." The letter – or, rather, the draft concocted in the depths of the Foreign Ministry – continued thus: "That which you have achieved has already overturned the myth of Israel's military might, which the aggressors and their sponsors have worked hard to create. Of course, we would welcome further gains at the front …" Brezhnev did not like these last two sentences. Perhaps he did not want to remind Sadat of the humiliation of 1967. It was also unwise to say that the USSR welcomed further military gains, encouraging Cairo to continue the war just when Brezhnev felt it had to be brought to a speedy conclusion. The passage was excised; the letter continued: "We would like to ask you strictly confidentially whether you could tell us, your friends, what concrete plans you have about the near future."

That the Soviet leaders were in the dark about Sadat's intentions is unsurprising: this was how the Egyptian president operated, which infuriated Brezhnev. He had all the liabilities of supporting Egypt against a powerful adversary with very little control. In any case, the Soviet leader ventured to offer an opinion: Was it not time to have ceasefire in situ to clinch the gains? If so, the Soviet Union would move without delay to sponsor a resolution to this end at the UN Security Council. The struggle would then move to the political sphere, with a humiliated Israel now more agreeable to a full withdrawal from the occupied territories.[73] The Soviets already prepared instructions to this end for their representative at the UN Security Council, Yakov Malik. (The instructions were held up pending Sadat's reply.) But Sadat frustrated the Soviets by turning down the Soviet feeler. His troops had done well on the Sinai battlefields. Perhaps they could do better still.

On October 10, Brezhnev tried again, sending his "brother and friend" another missive about a ceasefire. This time Brezhnev's letter spelled out Moscow's reasoning. The Syrians were running into trouble on their front, Brezhnev explained. If the Israelis prevailed and Damascus were knocked out of the war, Egypt would face the full onslaught of the Israeli Defense Force in Sinai, with unpredictable consequences. For now, he continued, the Soviets had managed to drag out discussions at the UN Security Council, but it was inevitable that someone would soon try to sponsor a simple ceasefire resolution. If they did, the Soviet Union would have to go along. Otherwise – if the Soviet representative opted to veto a simple ceasefire – what would happen if the tables turned and Israel regained the initiative on the battlefield? The earlier Soviet rejection of a ceasefire would then give the Americans a reason to veto a resolution aimed at stopping Israel in its tracks. The final point was this: the Americans will do everything

CHAPTER 14 YOM KIPPUR

to prevent Israel's defeat. "They have all the capabilities in this region to furnish Israel with help."[74]

The latter was a reference both to the US ability to resupply Israel, and to America's regional assets – namely, the powerful Sixth Fleet that closely monitored the Soviet movements in the Mediterranean. The Soviets had sizable assets of their own. On the eve of the war, the Fifth Eskadra (Fleet) had some fifty-two ships in the Mediterranean, including eleven submarines. (The number soon increased to eighty-eight).[75] This formidable force was reportedly capable of launching at least forty surface-to-surface missiles in the opening salvo of a strike against the US fleet.[76] The first strike was also the only one that mattered, since whoever was battered by such a strike would hardly be capable of retaliating, which put both the US and Soviet ships in the area at each other's mercy. Testing these awesome capabilities in battle was the last thing the general secretary had in mind as the war continued.

Despite his evident frustration with Sadat's unwillingness to countenance an early ceasefire, Brezhnev had to do what he had to do as the leader of a superpower: keep his clients afloat. On October 9, the Soviets began a massive resupply effort, shipping equipment, spare parts, and ammunition over sea and by air to Cairo and Damascus. Meanwhile, on the same day, the US intelligence picked up reports of the Soviet ambassadors in Jordan and Algeria telling the leaders of those countries that they should "enter the battle."[77] Kissinger, "in great agitation," called up Dobrynin to tell him that "if it turns out that you fooled us [by claiming interest in peaceful resolution of the crisis], you are going to pay a heavy price in your relationship with us."[78] Dobrynin seemed genuinely surprised by the claim. "It's an unbelievable story, I should say," he told Kissinger.[79]

His cable back home that night showed that he probably knew more than he let Kissinger believe, but that he was not thrilled by the whole idea of prodding the Arab world to join the war. He reported that Kissinger's comments showed how he and the president were "clearly nervous, because they understand the complexity of the situation." Dobrynin further predicted that if Israel's situation worsened, "one has to assume that there would be a real possibility of direct US intervention." Soviet–American relations would take a hit, the ambassador predicted, and everything had to be done to contain the damage, especially because (and here his "triangular" mentality came through with particular clarity) the Chinese would benefit from any deterioration of Soviet–American relations over the Middle East. The Chinese, for all the loud noises in support of the Arabs, had very little capability to influence events on the ground, and the Americans knew that.[80]

PART III DECLINE

But what was Brezhnev thinking? The record shows that the US reports were indeed not all that far from the truth, even if some aspects of Soviet discussions with the Arabs were dramatized or misunderstood. The instructions to the Soviet ambassador in Algiers, for instance (in an October 8 letter from Brezhnev) called on that country to "use all opportunities and take the necessary measures" to help Egypt and Syria (without, however, explicitly spelling out that it would mean joining the fight). King Hussein of Jordan was asked to do the same thing "without the slightest delay or wavering."[81]

It seems incredible that Brezhnev would secretly prod the Arabs to join the melee even as he encouraged Sadat to agree to a ceasefire and protested to Nixon that he had the most peaceful intentions in the Middle East. Was he not worried that his double-dealing would become known to the Americans? (King Hussein, for instance, almost immediately passed the news of the Soviet approach to the US ambassador, while the Algerians leaked the news of the Soviet approach to the Arab press). Brezhnev reportedly became "furious" after he learned of the publication of his secret messages.[82] If so, it was a case of incompetence so astonishing that one almost wants to find some secret ploy behind it, like Brezhnev deliberately trying to stir the pot to make the Americans more amenable to putting Israel under pressure to compromise on disadvantageous terms. Alas, incompetence is usually the better explanation.

The Kremlin responded to Kissinger's complaints with disingenuous self-righteousness: we have never made secret of our support for the Arab cause, and anyhow look at yourselves: you are supporting Israel's aggression![83]

Meanwhile, Kissinger faced a major unknown: the prospect of a direct Soviet involvement in the war. In a sense, the Soviets were fighting already (their pilots and anti-aircraft experts were in action on both fronts).[84] But could they deploy actual ground troops? There was danger of inadvertent escalation, and a reminder of that came on October 9, when Israeli planes raided Damascus, accidentally hitting the Soviet cultural center in the capital, and prompting fears of Moscow's retaliation. In a separate incident, Israel sank a Soviet merchant ship off the Syrian coast. Apologies were duly offered but the Kremlin remained jittery. At a "testy" luncheon with Kissinger on October 12, Dobrynin threatened that "matters might get out of hand."[85] He warned Kissinger that the other side also had the capability of striking Israel's cities (this was an oblique reference to the Soviet-controlled Scud missiles in Egypt).[86]

Just at that very time the Americans learned of the Soviet decision to alert three airborne divisions.[87] "I warned," Kissinger recalled, "that any Soviet military intervention would be resisted and wreck the entire fabric of

US-Soviet relations."[88] The warning, as Dobrynin reported it to Moscow, was this: the United States had no plans to get militarily involved in the Middle East, except in case "the Arab armies seriously advanced into the Israeli territory" and the survival of Israel itself was at stake. That, he added, was not a likely scenario.[89] Dobrynin countered by citing the recent movements of the US Sixth Fleet and the allegation that the United States had already dispatched 150 aircraft pilots to Israel (Kissinger strenuously denied this). "This can't help but cause apprehension in the Soviet Union, especially because [these] actions are taking place in the immediate vicinity of our borders, and the US is thousands of miles away from them," the ambassador noted. Dobrynin reported that these comments caused "apprehension" on Kissinger's part, and he kept returning to the subject again and again, highlighting that the United States would not intervene except if the Soviet Union intervened first, in which case the United States would "definitely" get involved.[90]

On the following day, President Nixon himself made a plea for moderation. At a reception at the White House for new Vice President Gerald Ford, Nixon pulled Dobrynin aside to tell him that Brezhnev and he were being provoked on all sides by those who wanted to undermine detente. "We cannot yield to these provocations," Nixon said, "because too much depends on this for the fate of our countries." "Tell the General Secretary that ... I will not yield to this pressure," Nixon added. He expected Brezhnev to stick by his side of the bargain.[91]

Heavy fighting continued on both fronts. The Israelis had taken unexpected losses in aircraft and tanks and pleaded for American supplies (Prime Minister Golda Meir even secretly proposed to make an incognito visit to the United States to make the case to Nixon in person. Kissinger ruled this out: he was unenthusiastic about arms deliveries, fearing that this would "drive the Arabs wild").[92] He had been hoping for the tides to turn quickly but the Arabs were holding up remarkably well. King Hussein of Jordan was under tremendous pressure to join the fight; the Iraqis and the Moroccans were sending forces to fight for the Arab cause.[93] Despite Israeli progress in the Golan Heights against the Syrians, their quick victory in the war no longer seemed so certain as Kissinger predicted on the first day of fighting. To cite Kissinger, "they [the Israelis] fucked it up."[94] Delaying the US airlift was no longer a viable option. On October 13, the United States began a massive effort to resupply their struggling client.

Until then it seemed that a solution to the conflict was just within reach. On October 10 Brezhnev sent a missive to Nixon, suggesting that the Soviet Union would not veto a simple ceasefire resolution, if it were

PART III DECLINE

brought forward at the Security Council.[95] The idea was to get the British to introduce the resolution, at which point the Soviets would abstain, permitting hostilities to end. But the plan hit a snag when it transpired that Sadat himself would oppose a ceasefire. The Soviets now informed Washington that they could only agree to such a resolution if it were accompanied by Israel's pledge to withdraw to the 1967 borders. Kissinger was scandalized. "You have to ask a question," he told Dobrynin: "What, in this case, is the role of the Soviet Union as a great power ... if it submissively yields to all of Sadat's demands?" The secretary of state added that he could not understand why the Soviet leaders seemed willing to "sacrifice a lot" in Soviet–American relations "for the sake of a momentary success on the part of Sadat who is a very unreliable and changeable man."[96]

Some of Kissinger's rage was probably theatrics (and an effort to justify the US military supply to Israel) though Dobrynin noticed a trace of genuine hope that the Soviets would somehow help the United States out of its predicament, which support for the Israelis would inevitably entail. Kissinger, Dobrynin reported, is "not unintelligent" but somehow he "harbored illusions" that Moscow "could be convinced" to put pressure on the Arabs in the name of better Soviet–American relations – not because the Soviets cared for Washington's standing in the Arab world (of course they did not) but because detente was supposed to be a higher goal than Moscow's prestige with the Arabs. It is interesting that Dobrynin dismissed this linkage as an "illusion," even though the ambassador had invested in detente like no one else. Perhaps he understood that detente was simply unthinkable except in the context of an assertive Soviet strategy in the third world.[97]

After a further few days of fighting, the tides of war began to turn. On October 14 the Israelis repelled an Egyptian offensive in the Sinai desert, and then exploited their success in a forceful counteroffensive that split Egypt's Second and Third Armies. After brutal fighting on October 16–17, the Israelis began crossing the Suez Canal north of the Great Bitter Lake. As these events unfolded Soviet Prime Minister Aleksei Kosygin turned up in Egypt for talks with Sadat, staying until the 19th. "Remind him," Brezhnev reportedly told the prime minister the night before his departure, "that Cairo is not far away from the Canal." He also told Kosygin to make it absolutely clear to Sadat that the Soviet Union had no plans of getting involved in the fighting.[98] Kosygin and Sadat spent several days in fruitless discussions. The Egyptian president was simply not ready for an immediate ceasefire, even though the battlefield situation was worsening by the hour. Even the Soviet imagery of the Israeli troop concentrations on the west bank of

CHAPTER 14 YOM KIPPUR

the Suez Canal, which Kosygin shared with Sadat, failed to impress. Sadat, who, according to Vinogradov, was smoking hashish incessantly during his sessions with Kosygin, claimed that someone was "trying to snatch victory from under his nose, in a word, carried himself like there was no Israeli breakthrough, and the Egyptian forces stood at Jerusalem's gates."[99] The Soviet prime minister left empty-handed.[100]

Despite Kosygin's failure, the Soviets pressed on with the ceasefire. Dobrynin called Kissinger on October 18, offering a ceasefire in situ with Israel's subsequent withdrawal from the occupied territories in line with the impossibly imprecise UN Security Council Resolution 242.[101] But Kissinger was stalling in the hope that the Israelis would exploit their battlefield victories, putting the United States into a favorable negotiating position vis-a-vis the Kremlin and the Arabs. "The fact of the matter is, Kissinger told General Brent Scowcroft late on the evening of October 18, "when all is said and done, it is a Soviet defeat ... that should make them [the Arab states] realize they better get on our side." "It couldn't have been better," echoed Scowcroft.[102] The logic was not lost on the Soviets. On the morning of October 19, Washington time, Dobrynin called Kissinger with an urgent missive from Brezhnev. Warning that the situation "could take [an] even more dangerous turn," Brezhnev requested that Kissinger go to Moscow for urgent talks on finding a way out of the crisis.

KISSINGER IN MOSCOW

The invitation was Dobrynin's idea. He cabled his superiors after seeing Kissinger on October 18, explaining the reasons: inviting Kissinger would "undoubtedly stroke his ego." More importantly – and highlighting the ever-present concern of Soviet policy makers – "the Secretary of State's visit to Moscow would stress the special role of the Soviet Union in resolving world problems." As a bonus, Kissinger's visit to Moscow would force him to postpone his planned trip to China, "which would not be bad." Dobrynin, ever the card player, was always looking for ways to show that the Soviets – not the Chinese – were the ones Washington turned to deal with the pressing issues of global politics.[103]

Brezhnev's invitation came just as another crisis was unfolding in Washington. President Nixon had been subpoenaed by Congress to hand over the Watergate tapes, which he at first refused to do. On October 19 he proposed a compromise: he would hand over the tapes to Democratic Senator John C. Stennis who would listen to the tapes and summarize them for the

409

PART III DECLINE

benefit of the Special Prosecutor Archibald Cox's Office. Cox rejected the idea that night, prompting Nixon to fire him the next day. Attorney General Elliott Richardson and Deputy Attorney General William Ruckelshaus chose to resign rather than to carry out their president's order. (The third in line at the Justice Department, Robert Bork, at last complied and fired Cox.) The "Saturday Night Massacre" (as it instantly became known) was a political earthquake of unprecedented magnitude, and the beginning of the end for Nixon. On October 22, the House launched its impeachment proceedings. It was under these inauspicious circumstances that, on October 20, Kissinger flew to Moscow.

Hours before he left, Kissinger telephoned the Israeli ambassador in Washington, Simcha Dinitz, to remind him of the one thing that mattered for Nixon: "it is important for your sake that the President look good and is not accused of selling anybody out … praise him for his statesmanlike achievements."[104] As so often during the Cold War, nothing mattered quite as much as the prestige of a superpower and its leaders. The same, of course, was equally true of the Soviet side, as Nixon and Kissinger understood like no others.

With Kissinger already on his way to Moscow, Nixon – who was then in the epicenter of a political maelstrom – sent a set of instructions for his secretary of state that reflected just how much hope the president now pinned on Brezhnev in helping him secure a foreign policy success at a time of an acute domestic crisis. "If he and I together can be reasonable and achieve a Middle East settlement it will without question be one of the brightest stars in which we hope will be a galaxy for peace stemming from the Nixon–Brezhnev relationship."[105] Kissinger pragmatically ignored these strange instructions from his boss: the subject of a peace galaxy was never broached in Moscow.[106]

The most remarkable thing about Kissinger's talks with the Soviet leaders was just how they ever managed to agree to anything in such a short time. The credit in part goes to Nixon who undermined his secretary of state's negotiating positions by cabling Brezhnev ahead of time that Kissinger spoke with full authority. Kissinger privately lambasted his boss for "poor judgment" and made an unconvincing attempt to persuade Brezhnev that it would "very dangerous" if he really had the authority to make decisions on Nixon's behalf.[107] But, it seems, Brezhnev did not really exploit this negotiating advantage: he was too desperate for a breakthrough.

Negotiations began at 9:15pm on October 20, and went until 11:30pm, when Brezhnev and Kissinger had a private dinner at the Kremlin until 12.45am, "featuring only an abbreviated version of the normal cascade of

CHAPTER 14 YOM KIPPUR

Brezhnev anecdotes."[108] Kissinger emphasized just how difficult it was for the administration to plough ahead with detente in the face of "serious opposition" and therefore how important it was to achieve an agreement in Moscow in order to disarm Nixon's critics. Brezhnev retorted that such an agreement would also undermine the Chinese: "I'd say that if we manage to silence the guns, we will simultaneously silence all these slanderers."[109] Reporting on this first round to Nixon in the middle of the night, Moscow time, Kissinger gave the prospect of agreement "an even chance."[110] The big question was just how insistent Brezhnev would be on Israel's withdrawal to the 1967 borders.

Meanwhile, Brezhnev was having a very sleepless night. After Kissinger left for his guest house, the Soviet leader had another session at the Kremlin, strategizing with his comrades. He left at 1:25am. But if Brezhnev had any rest, it was not for long, because at 4:00am he had to take a call from Cairo. A desperate Sadat (through Ambassador Vinogradov) now pleaded with the Soviet leader to arrange for an immediate ceasefire without further strings attached.[111] The Israelis had set up a bridgehead on the western bank of the Suez Canal and now pushed forward rapidly. All morning Brezhnev conferred with subordinates and with Cairo by phone.[112] He then went back to the Kremlin just past 8:00am for another strategizing session, followed by a Politburo meeting until 11:35am. By the time he met Kissinger again – for the second round of their talks – Brezhnev would have been working practically nonstop for more than twenty-four hours.[113] This tiredness, and a sense of urgency, translated into a most agreeable negotiating position. "To our amazement," Kissinger recalled, "Brezhnev and Gromyko accepted our text with only the most minor editorial changes ... After only four hours of negotiation, the text of the ceasefire resolution was agreed ... This was extraordinary speed for any negotiation but particularly for one with the Soviet leaders."[114]

But the stress took its toll on the general secretary. He had to cancel his final meeting with Kissinger on the evening of October 21, citing his doctor's instructions.[115] It was left to Gromyko to see off the American delegation amid toasts to Nixon and to Brezhnev, and to "affection" in Soviet–American relations.[116]

For their part, the Soviet leaders claimed (in their explanations to their Arab allies) that the negotiations with Kissinger had been "far from easy," and that they had to "commit great effort" to make the Americans accept the ceasefire proposal. It was a "serious defeat of Israel's political line, and international Zionism as a whole," achieved by the "will and decisiveness" of the Arab people "in combination with the efforts to provide them with enormous support in terms of both weapons and political means."[117]

411

PART III DECLINE

On the same day the Politburo approved a letter to some of Moscow's socialist allies, explaining the Soviet take on the situation in the Middle East. "[We] have extinguished insinuations that in the conditions of detente, the national liberation movement can allegedly no longer count on the help of world socialism. The authority of the socialist commonwealth in the 'third world' has unquestionably increased."[118] In other words, just when Nixon and Kissinger were dangling the carrot of detente in the hope Brezhnev and his comrades desist from meddling in the third world, the Soviet leaders were doing just that to bolster their "authority" and to translate this authority into a more equal relationship with the United States. The same logic underpinned the Soviet approach to many other problems of international politics, most notably (as we have seen) Vietnam.

In the Middle East, the key aim of Soviet policy making was to demonstrate to their clients that the Soviet Union had the means to force the United States to tame the Israelis, while reminding the Americans that only Moscow could bring the Arabs to the negotiating table. This was the meaning of the Soviet–American condominium in the Middle East that Brezhnev had long been seeking to inaugurate – from his perspective, one of the key outcomes of detente. What mattered the most, perhaps, was to finally have the Americans buy into this arrangement, and the sense of legitimacy that such buy-in engendered for Brezhnev. As he put it at the Politburo meeting on October 21, "Nixon feels a deep respect for all Soviet leaders and for me personally."[119] He privately boasted that whereas Kosygin was unable to get anything done after three days of negotiating with Sadat, Brezhnev achieved a breakthrough only after a few hours of talks with Kissinger.[120]

On the evening of October 21, the Soviet–American ceasefire proposal was introduced to the UN Security Council, where it was approved just past midnight as Resolution 338.[121] In addition to the ceasefire, the resolution called for Arab–Israeli negotiations "under appropriate auspices," a vague reference to Brezhnev's hope of "commanding" the Arabs and the Israelis in the context of the Soviet–American condominium.[122] But even as the Soviets celebrated the seeming triumph of their crisis diplomacy, the conflict in the Middle East took an unexpected turn.

DEFCON 3

The ceasefire was to go into effect twelve hours after the adoption of Resolution 338 but the Israelis (who, under pressure from Kissinger, accepted the Soviet–American intervention) felt they could push their

412

luck a little further. Commanders in the field, like General Avraham Adan, whose division had crossed west of the Suez Canal and was wreaking havoc in the Egyptian rear, were loath to accept a ceasefire just at the point of smashing the adversary. Tel Aviv preferred to look the other way. On the 23rd, Adan's forces continued to press forward south of the Great Bitter Lake in a last-minute effort to cut off Egypt's Third Army, one of two that had crossed the canal into Sinai. The plan worked. The Egyptians' supply lines were severed. Suddenly, Sadat faced the prospect of a military catastrophe.[123]

The day before, on October 22, an exhausted Brezhnev left Moscow for Zavidovo, his hunting lodge two hours northwest of Moscow. He had every reason to be pleased with himself: hard work and sleepless nights had paid off. He had saved a client in need from obliteration. He had acted in concert with the United States to sort out a messy situation in the Middle East. He was in for a nasty surprise. That night he received a report from Soviet Chief of General Staff Viktor Kulikov, an update on the situation on the fronts. We do not know what he learned from that report but it could not have been particularly reassuring because the next we hear of Brezhnev, he is on the phone to the Kremlin and the Central Committee at 2:00am. History has left no record of whom he was looking for, and whether he even found anyone at their desks at such an hour. On the 23rd Brezhnev's secretaries recorded that documents were being sent to Zavidovo as the general secretary continued to hand-steer the crisis from his hunting lodge.[124]

Meanwhile in Moscow the Politburo gathered for an extraordinary session (Mikhail Suslov presided in Brezhnev's absence). The gathering heard reports from Gromyko and Kulikov, and approved a personal message from Brezhnev to Nixon, professing "shock" at the Israeli "treachery" and calling for speedy action to fulfil Resolution 338.[125] The meeting also confirmed instructions for Dobrynin to protest with Kissinger against the Israelis' "flagrant deceit," and to ask for a new resolution that would order the two sides to withdraw to positions they occupied when 338 went into effect. Dobrynin was out of town when these instructions reached Washington; his deputy, Yuly Vorontsov, phoned Kissinger to hear him say that the renewed fighting in the Middle East was a total surprise (this was not true: while in Israel, after his talks with Brezhnev, Kissinger privately told Golda Meir that the Israelis could keep going until at least noon on the 23rd without "violent protests" from Washington).[126] Later that night the secretary of state reassured Dobrynin: "You have known me long enough. I will not trick Brezhnev. That is the stupidist [sic] thing I could do. Even if

PART III DECLINE

we win this one we could never have a trusting relationship again."[127] On the same day the UN Security Council adopted a follow-up resolution (No. 339), confirming a ceasefire in the position the two sides occupied when it first went into effect, and providing for the dispatch of UN observers to the front lines.

Brezhnev, meanwhile, worked in Zavidovo all through October 24. What this "work" entailed remains unclear. Usually, his secretaries would record the ins and outs – his meetings and telephone conversations. On that day, no such conversations were recorded, and that is all the more interesting, because it was the day when the situation in the Middle East became absolutely critical.[128]

The bad news from Sadat came via Ambassador Vladimir Vinogradov: that morning Israeli forces attacked the little port town of Adabiya on the western bank of the Gulf of Suez, while continuing their operations against Egypt's Third Army, stranded on the eastern bank of the canal. (The KGB separately confirmed the same.) The situation was desperate, and Sadat pleaded with the Soviets to talk to Nixon so that he would press the Israelis to stop their offensive. The Soviet response was to draft Brezhnev's letter to Nixon (which Dobrynin read out to Kissinger on the morning of October 24, Washington time). Brezhnev was consulted in the drafting of the letter. It was he who insisted on including the following passage: "So what is happening? Hardly have we reached an understanding and received from you very solemn assurances concerning its implementation, when gross defiance occurs of both this understanding of ours and of decisions of the Security Council."[129]

There was a sense of betrayal here, a feeling of having been tricked by the Americans. True, the Soviets were not themselves averse to tricking the Americans when the circumstances allowed. (Encouraging other Arab states to join the fighting while professing interest in a peaceful settlement was but one recent example). But the Soviet leaders had a much greater sensitivity to being mistreated by others than a sense of self-awareness in mistreating others. Senior Soviet Foreign Ministry official Viktor Israelyan (who had been one of the drafters of some of these instructions and letters at the height of the crisis) recalled a widespread sense of anger and disillusionment among senior Soviet policy makers after what many interpreted as Kissinger's deceit. "One cannot trust the imperialists," "The Americans will never give up their support of Israel and international Zionism," "We should force the Americans to carry out their commitments."[130]

At 1:00pm, Washington time (8:00pm in Moscow), on October 24, the Soviet Embassy received Nixon's reply to Brezhnev; the letter said that the

CHAPTER 14 YOM KIPPUR

Israelis had already ceased fighting. It was late evening in Moscow when the Soviets began working on their response. The Soviet sources indicated that the Israelis continued their military offensive against the Third Army and were trying to capture the city of Suez. With Sadat screaming murder, and the military situation teetering on the brink of a catastrophe, the drafters of Brezhnev's response (a group of six, including Andropov and Gromyko) played the one card that had not up to now been deployed: the threat of a Soviet military intervention.[131] "Let us together, the Soviet Union and the United States," the letter said, "urgently dispatch to Egypt Soviet and American military contingents, with their mission the implementation of the decision of the Security Council." If the Americans refused to do that, the letter continued, "we should be faced with the necessity urgently to consider the question of taking appropriate steps unilaterally."[132] The letter was finished at 1:00am and voted on by those Politburo members who could be gotten out of bed. At 1:30am, the head of the General Department, Konstantin Chernenko, forwarded the letter to a sleepless Brezhnev at Zavidovo who signed off on the ultimatum. It was received in Washington, DC at 10:00pm local time (5:00am in Moscow).[133]

Fifteen minutes after receiving Brezhnev's ultimatum, a clearly stressed Kissinger phoned Dobrynin to tell him that any Soviet unilateral measures in the Middle East would have "very serious" consequences. "Don't you pressure us. I want to repeat again, don't pressure us!"[134]

When Brezhnev's message arrived, President Nixon was reportedly asleep (possibly drunk[135]); Kissinger and White House Chief of Staff Alexander Haig decided not to wake him up. Instead, Kissinger called together a meeting of principals to discuss the reasons for the ultimatum, and to consider America's response. Why would Brezhnev do something like this? Haig thought that it was because the Soviets realized that they were losing: "the question was whether or not this was a rational plan or a move of desperation as the Soviets watched their influence in the Middle East go down the drain." This was an opportunity to take advantage of a president in distress. Added Kissinger: "Now the Soviets see that he [Nixon] is, in their mind, non-functional."[136] Admiral Thomas Moorer, who authored the only contemporaneous record of this meeting of principals, noted that "during the discussions we kept coming back to the $64.00 question: 'If the Soviets put in 10,000 troops into Egypt what do we do?'"[137] The principals dispersed at 3:30am, having formulated the American response: to raise the US nuclear alert level to DEFCON 3, the highest since the Cuban Missile Crisis. The Soviets were also sent a letter "from Nixon" (who was soundly

415

asleep) – a response to Brezhnev's October 24 ultimatum.[138] The response, without mentioning DEFCON 3, made it clear that the United States "could in no event accept unilateral action," and that any Soviet intervention in the Middle East would have "incalculable consequences."[139]

The letter from Nixon to Brezhnev was delivered via Ambassador Dobrynin. Kissinger's deputy, Brent Scowcroft, called him at 5:40am, warning that the letter would be hand-carried by courier. Dobrynin already knew that things were going off the rails. The embassy monitored US radio broadcasts, which were presently running reports of the US nuclear forces being placed on alert. What angered Dobrynin was that these reports preceded any effort to work out the problem through the back channel to Moscow. This "drama," the ambassador reported, was just a way of "distracting attention" from America's cover-up of Israel's treachery, and from Nixon's domestic woes caused by Watergate. The ambassador's advice was to remain firm, criticize the White House for its "nuclear psychosis" but also downplay any prospect of a unilateral Soviet intervention. "It seems important not to leave the impression – neither in the US nor among the Arab countries – that we retreated under US pressure."[140]

On the morning of October 25, after three tense days at Zavidovo, Brezhnev went back to Moscow, arriving at 12:30pm. He immediately received Grechko, Gromyko, and Chernenko and then presided over a Politburo meeting for another three hours. Only Grechko appeared willing to respond to DEFCON 3 by sending troops to the Middle East.[141] (The defense minister later circulated a memorandum to the Politburo, arguing that the Americans were "intimidating" and "pressuring" the Soviets in what he described as a "faith-breaking act.")[142] But Grechko's hawkishness inspired no enthusiasm among his colleagues. Kosygin thought it was "not reasonable to become engaged in a war with the United States because of Egypt and Syria" while Gromyko pondered: "Where is the brink, the line between peace and a new, nuclear war?"[143] It was Brezhnev who formulated Moscow's response: there would be no response. The nuclear alert would just be ignored.[144]

Dobrynin called Kissinger at 2:40pm, dictating Brezhnev's reply. Although some of the details were lost in the twisted incoherence of the ambassador's English, the main point was clear enough: the Soviets were not sending a force to the Middle East. Instead, they would be sending ceasefire observers – seventy in number – while undertaking other *political measures* and [sic] corresponding to [the] decision of the Security Council and … to the understanding in Moscow."[145] According to Dobrynin,

CHAPTER 14 YOM KIPPUR

Kissinger appeared gratified, saying that he had "hoped" for this kind of reaction, although he was "not fully confident of it."[146]

Kissinger did not know it, but the letter had gone through some rigorous editing, following the discussion at the Politburo. The original draft response still contained an unspecified threat: "You and we cannot limit ourselves to such measures as sending observers ... This is clearly insufficient if the violations on Israel's part are not brought to an end." However, the threat was carefully crossed out, replaced with a passage about *political measures*. A note in the file shows that the letter was dictated and corrected by Brezhnev himself and approved at the Politburo meeting. The general secretary has come too close to conflict for comfort: he needed to de-escalate and could not allow any ambiguity on this score.[147]

Brezhnev's caution was evident in the instructions for the Soviet ambassador in Damascus, adopted at the same Politburo meeting. Ambassador Nuridin Mukhitdinov had earlier met with Syrian Foreign Minister Abdul Halim Khaddam who asked whether Syria should restart military actions against Israel (as a way of helping the Egyptians). The Soviet recommendation was unequivocal: do not do it. "It would hardly be justifiable to give an excuse to Israel to renew military actions against Syria."[148] At the same time, the Soviets pleaded with the Iraqis to keep their forces in Syria to deter the Israelis from restarting the war in the north (the Iraqis withdrew nonetheless).[149] This was a remarkable reversal: having just threatened the Americans with a military intervention in the Middle East (which would dramatically escalate the level of hostilities), the Soviets not just climbed down in no time but even advised their clients in the region to keep it cool even at the cost of leaving Egypt to its unenviable fate. "Mr. President, you have won again," Kissinger triumphantly announced to Nixon on October 25. "You think so?" Nixon asked.[150]

But, as is often the case with history, great victories only appear great in retrospect. The threat of intervention was almost certainly a bluff but there was internal logic to the escalation. With nerves at the breaking point, with Brezhnev working through consecutive nights, probably on sleeping pills, and possibly on the verge of a mental breakdown, and with the Soviet Navy facing off against the Americans in the eastern Mediterranean, it was not easy to discern where the red lines were, and whether someone might accidentally overstep them, leading to a conflagration.[151] This much is clear from Anatoly Chernyaev's diary. Writing soon after the events, Chernyaev recounted that at the height of the crisis, Brezhnev sent a memorandum from Zavidovo, asking the Politburo to do "something" – anything – to save

417

PART III DECLINE

Sadat. The proposed measures included a show of Soviet naval power off Tel Aviv, and giving the Egyptians permission to strike Israel with the Soviet-supplied Scud missiles.[152]

Sure enough, on October 22, Egypt launched up to three missiles against Israeli positions, killing seven. It was not so much the death toll that mattered as the display of might: the same missiles could easily be launched against Tel Aviv or Jerusalem.[153] (The move reportedly caused a sharp disagreement between Gromyko – who thought it reckless – and Grechko, who had authorized it.[154]) The CIA reported, perhaps erroneously, that a Soviet ship "probably carrying nuclear weapons" arrived in Egypt on October 24.[155] Seven airborne divisions (tens of thousands of troops) were put on alert. There are also indications that the Soviets were preparing to land forces in Egypt. Thousands of "volunteers" reportedly signed up to fight the Israelis.[156] Soviet naval ships converged just off Egypt's coast on October 25 (but dispersed two days later).[157] It was perhaps this military maneuver that Chernenko very mysteriously referred to in his October 25, 1:30am, missive to Brezhnev: "The military received the instructions you have conveyed through comrades Kirilenko and Gromyko."[158] It is true that, as the decisions of the October 25 Politburo meeting show, collective decision-making was conducive to de-escalation. However, the chaos of the preceding days, the desperate pleas from Sadat, and the midnight drafting sessions highlighted the dangers of an inadvertent war.

The full record of the Soviet deliberations is yet to be declassified but one document gives an idea of the underlying problem. On October 29, Andropov sent a personal letter to Brezhnev. The head of the KGB (who already knew from Chazov of Brezhnev's addiction to sleeping pills and his erratic work schedule) warned the Soviet leader that the Americans and Sadat had conspired (!) to overwork him by constantly keeping him engaged in difficult decision-making. This was "sabotage," Andropov argued, pure and simple. They (the Americans and the Egyptians) were trying to "keep us focused on the Arab–Israeli conflict, creating overstrain for all, and especially for you." He continued: "Such a situation, in my opinion, is frankly dangerous, because human capacity is not limitless." Andropov concluded by advising taking a slow, distant approach to the Middle East, so that no one gets overly exhausted. "By this, first, and foremost, I mean you, Leonid Ilyich – your extreme over-exhaustion and your nearly round-the-clock activity."[159] Translated from Soviet-speak: a stressed, sleep-deprived general secretary could inadvertently do something reckless, like start a world war on the Arabs' behalf.

Figure 21 Israeli tanks crossing the Suez Canal, October 25, 1973.
Source: Ilan Ron/GPO/Getty Images.

THE ENDGAME

Tensions began to dissipate from the afternoon of October 25. The United Nations – following Sadat's request – agreed to send ceasefire observers to the area, drawing on personnel from neutral and nonaligned states. The encircled Egyptian Third Army received vital nonmilitary supplies with UN convoys. On October 28 the Israelis and the Egyptians militaries began direct negotiations (for the first time in history). Two days earlier Brezhnev sent another letter to Nixon, much calmer than his messages of the previous few days. He criticized Israel for undermining global peace to the detriment of Soviet and American "prestige" but did not threaten anything and barely even reacted to DEFCON 3, except to deny that it was "the result of any kind of actions by the Soviet Union."[160] Interestingly, an earlier draft of the same letter indicated that the Soviets, too, had brought their forces on heightened alert, adding that the measure "is in no sense directed against the United States and its allies."[161] The passage was crossed out, perhaps because Brezhnev did not want to do anything that could potentially make an already tense situation even worse.

PART III DECLINE

Instead, the Soviet leader bent over backwards to show that detente was still operational; that it had not been derailed by the events in the Middle East. His opportunity to do so came during his speech at the World Congress of Peace-loving Forces, on October 26. It was ironic and disconcerting for Brezhnev that this Congress – which was supposed to highlight the benefits of detente and Brezhnev's contribution to it – overlapped with the Arab–Israeli war. In his long speech, Brezhnev shied away from direct criticism of the United States. The CIA called it "a ringing endorsement of detente." "He clearly was out to demonstrate that the USSR wants good relations with the US to continue."[162] Brezhnev had personally been "excited and inspired" by his own speech, and, in all fairness, it was well received by the thousands of assembled delegates in the hall.[163] That was the kind of recognition the general secretary had always craved. Few delegates had any idea of what he had gone through in the days prior to the Congress, although his tiredness showed: Brezhnev slurred a little, and stammered on the word "peace-loving."

If Brezhnev had to appear statesmanlike and supportive of detente (something, he knew, helped his legitimacy as a leader of a superpower), Nixon catered to a somewhat different audience. For internal domestic reasons, first and foremost Watergate, he had to show his toughness in the face of the supposed Soviet threat. He did this during a lengthy press conference on October 26, when "remarkably calm and lucid" (in the words of James Reston of the *New York Times*) he spoke of his "very firm" response to Brezhnev's message, and how further escalation was avoided because Brezhnev understood "the power of the United States" and knew that the American president "would do what was right." Nixon compared the situation to the Cuban Missile Crisis but claimed that "because we had had our initiative with the Soviet Union, because I had a basis of communication with Mr. Brezhnev, we not only avoided a confrontation, but we moved a great step forward toward real peace in the Mideast."[164]

Nixon's bravado upset Kissinger who feared a blowback from Moscow. "The crazy bastard really made a mess with the Russians," he told Haig, asking him to seek out Dobrynin to calm him down.[165] Haig told the ambassador that all Nixon meant to say was that he had "unique" relations with Brezhnev, which allowed them to resolve even the most dangerous crises. Dobrynin complained bitterly about the scaremongering, and especially about comparisons with the Cuban Missile Crisis, which created a "false impression" that Soviet–American relations had reached a nadir. "The crisis," he told Haig, "did not arise because suddenly the security and national interests of the United States became engaged but was in fact artificially created by the American side." The ambassador claimed that the real reason for the crisis was the US leader's effort to gain "internal political capital" and cover up for Israel's ongoing aggression. "The Soviet Union cannot be intimidated," concluded Dobrynin (at least according to the report he filed that day), "and if Moscow still shows restraint, it's not because of weakness but because of the sense of responsibility for the fate of the world."

Haig seemed unwilling to argue and merely noted that not everyone agreed with the idea of declaring DEFCON 3 (and he hinted that he himself had not been in favor). On this basis, the ambassador reported to Moscow that there were internal disagreements in Nixon's circle, and that Haig was among the more reasonable players because he was "not a Jew but an Anglo-Saxon."[166]

Over the next few days and weeks both Nixon and Kissinger privately made every effort to reassure Dobrynin and, through him, Brezhnev, that everything was fine, that detente was still on track. Nixon complained incessantly about Israel, presumably to persuade the Soviets what a difficult client it was. Several times he promised to put Israel under "brutal pressure" to bring about a peace settlement. One of his statements – to the effect that the Israelis "wanted war" – was too radical even for Brezhnev who instructed Dobrynin to tell the president that "it was not the people of Israel who wanted war but the people who currently determine its policy." "I fully understand," Nixon concluded, "that I must 'deliver' Israel to the final point of a peace settlement, despite all the difficulties and obstacles ... I have come to the firm conviction that one must not lose the current opportunity." This, he said, would prevent Soviet–American relations from being derailed by the "egoistic" actions of the Israelis and the Arabs.[167]

On October 30, Nixon invited Dobrynin to Camp David for a lengthy talk. Dobrynin again complained about the completely unnecessary escalation to DEFCON 3. The president, he later reported to Moscow, "justified this action with reference to different motives but he did not do it particularly convincingly or energetically." But the real heart-to-heart moment happened after the conversation when Nixon, taking leave of Haig and Kissinger, walked Dobrynin outside. Suddenly, he said: "Tell the General Secretary that while I am alive and remain President, I will never allow a real confrontation with the Soviet Union. Perhaps we (the US) got a little rash but (not to justify myself) I will say that I am currently under constant and brutal siege by all of my adversaries who have united on the pretext of 'Watergate' and use every opportunity to bite me in this or that way and undermine my authority even further." Nixon added: "Thank

PART III DECLINE

God, this is unknown to the Soviet leaders but, speaking as humans, it's very difficult for me sometimes."[168]

The besieged president tried to stoke Brezhnev's ego by telling him (through Dobrynin) how much he appreciated the fact that the Soviet Union and the United States were now "equals" – that there was no longer any place for an "inferiority complex" in their relationship. He disclosed in this connection that he was not fond of Franklin D. Roosevelt who, Nixon said, was too "idealistic" for his liking. Churchill and Stalin were much better, he added. They – not Roosevelt – were his "heroes."[169]

Kissinger wisely agreed with everything the president said to the Soviet ambassador but, when left alone with Dobrynin, he blamed the crisis on Nixon. In a conversation with Dobrynin that he is unlikely to have reported to his boss, Kissinger (ignoring his own central role in the DEFCON decision) recounted how the White House made a "serious mistake," when it "hastily raised the [nuclear] readiness." It would have been better, he said, if the president contacted Brezhnev beforehand. Kissinger explained that "these few weeks and even months the President has been under considerable pressure. This, of course, cannot excuse the haste, especially as against the background of the patience demonstrated at that moment by the General Secretary and other Soviet leaders." "The General Secretary's nerves," Kissinger added, "turned out to be stronger than the President's."[170]

Brezhnev reluctantly bought this explanation, blaming the crisis on the pressures of the Watergate investigation. "He [Nixon] is acting bravely," the Soviet leader concluded after the dust settled. "But all bravery has its limits. After this limit, one's nerves start to act up. In such situations, in search for a solution, one makes mistakes. President Nixon also made a couple of mistakes in this case. I magnanimously forgave him, seeing that he does not go back on the principles of relations between the USSR and the US, which we agreed on. Therefore, I forgave the mistakes, which he had made."[171]

The Soviet leader was less forgiving of the Arabs. The war scare in Moscow had been real enough, and it had a sobering effect on Brezhnev. The general secretary was still fuming days after the worst had passed. The biggest lesson for him was that the Soviet Union had to stand on two legs in the Middle East. Having severed relations with Israel in 1967, the Soviets found themselves unable to "deliver" the Israelis and hoped that Kissinger might do it for them. In the aftermath of the Yom Kippur War, Brezhnev considered (not for the first time) the necessity of restoring relations with Israel. He even considered the idea of allowing US businessman Armand Hammer to serve as a secret go-between who could arrange a meeting between himself and Golda Meir.[172] He mentioned the idea to Gromyko,

422

CHAPTER 14 YOM KIPPUR

who thought the Arabs would take offence. "Fuck them!" Brezhnev reportedly countered. "We've been offering them a reasonable way all these years. But, no, they wanted to have a fight! ... And what then? They were screwed again. And they screamed that we save them ... No, we won't fight for them. The people will not understand us. Nor, in particular, will we start a world war on their behalf."[173]

CONCLUSION

In the event, the Soviets did not restore diplomatic relations with Israel until 1991. One could argue that it took so long because of what Chernyaev called "an inertia of proletarian internationalism." The term is evocative of the ideological underpinnings of Soviet foreign policy but only superficially so. "Proletarian internationalism" had no real meaning, except insofar as it was an instrumental rationalization for the Soviet involvement in the Middle East, a region of great strategic importance but very few "proletarians." Historically, the Soviet Union developed a clientele among the Arab states (mostly a result of opportunistic action that was rationalized as support for so-called "progressive" – or "anti-imperialist" – regimes). But now that it had regional clients and allies, Moscow's credibility was fully engaged, and it was that credibility, and the need to maintain it, that gave rise to a degree of inertia. There were real risks involved in reaching out to Israel: this could mean greater political leverage but also possibly damaged relations with the Arabs, a prospect unfathomable to the military and to the career third-worldists in the Central Committee. Brezhnev could have broken the logjam but his rapid decline into ill-health from 1974 severely constrained the general secretary's ability to influence policy.[174]

In the end, Brezhnev's vision of a Middle Eastern condominium ran aground. The Soviet policy, Brezhnev proclaimed in the war's aftermath, was to "participate in the talks, insistently and everywhere. We have the right and the responsibility to do so."[175] But for all the money spent on bolstering Egypt, Brezhnev had little leverage with Sadat. Already during the war, to considerable Soviet annoyance, Sadat maintained back-channel communication with Washington (the Soviets had no such facility with Tel Aviv). After the war, the Soviet role as a mediator weakened further still, as Sadat realized that it was the United States, not the Soviet Union, that could deliver peace with Israel. Brezhnev was deeply annoyed that the Soviets were entirely bypassed in the Israeli–Egyptian talks at the 101st kilometer (so called for their location along the Suez–Cairo road), which led to the January 1974 disengagement agreement.

"I think in cases like this you have to consult with your friends," Brezhnev complained to Egyptian Foreign Minister Ismail Fahmi. "This is what principles of friendship demand."[176] Privately, he grumbled: "Looks like they are playing some dirty game."[177]

The general secretary tried to bring pressure on Sadat by withholding new weapons shipments, but the ploy backfired, especially in view of Washington's ongoing military shipments to Israel. "I think any person in President Sadat's shoes would also feel dissatisfied," Fahmi told Brezhnev in October 1974. "In a short time, the Americans gave Israel more weapons than it lost during the entire October war. But in a year [since October 1973], Egypt received just three shipments with ammunition and spare parts." Brezhnev in response peddled platitudes about the Americans' "venal aims" in contrast to Soviet "internationalism."[178]

In memoirs penned in 1975, Ambassador Vinogradov (on whose watch Sadat changed sides in the Cold War) accused the Egyptian president of opportunism and of failing to distinguish between the United States and the Soviet Union, whose reasons for engagement in the Middle East were supposedly fundamentally different.[179] Yet, in retrospect, it is difficult to blame Sadat for seeking to play one superpower against the other. Sadat wanted to stand tall and glorious, and if that meant stabbing the Soviets in the back, then stab he did. The Soviet leaders were themselves hardly amateurs when it came to back-stabbing.

The Americans were equally skilled, judging by Kissinger's postwar shuttle diplomacy, which effectively cut the Soviets out of key decisions in the Middle East. After becoming president in January 1977, Jimmy Carter briefly tried to overhaul the Middle Eastern problem by proposing a comprehensive settlement.[180] On October 1, 1977 the United States and the Soviet Union issued a joint communiqué to this end, briefly reviving the spirit of the long-dead "condominium." But both the Israelis and Sadat were bitterly opposed to a comprehensive approach. They were already engaged in secret talks that led to Sadat's dramatic, unexpected trip to Israel in November 1977. Carter was annoyed at first but then duly changed tack, cutting the Soviets loose.[181] The result of this shocking realignment was the Camp David Accords of September 1978, followed by a separate peace treaty between Israel and Egypt in March 1979. The Soviets and their remaining Arab friends in what was now called the "rejection front" were scandalized by the apparent betrayal: hopes for a "comprehensive" settlement in the Middle East (never great) faded into oblivion. Yet, even having lost Egypt, the Soviets continued to seek clients in the Middle East, strengthening relations with Syria and Iraq. The Soviet game

CHAPTER 14 YOM KIPPUR

in the region was to try to stay relevant: by engaging in the Middle East (minus Egypt), the aging, sclerotic Kremlin leadership maintained their myth of global importance: if not as a partner of the United States, then, at least, as a rival.

But there was an unexpected blessing in what by all other measures was a long-term Soviet defeat: the Yom Kippur War prompted oil-producers to work together to cut production (an embargo was also imposed). This led to a sharp increase in the price of oil. The Soviet Union, a major oil-exporting country, benefited from this bonanza. As the West reeled from an oil-induced recession, the Soviets earned hard currency on the world market, which helped sustain their sluggish living standards, including by purchasing increasing volumes of grain from the West, and to finance quasi-imperial ventures overseas. Within just a few years, Moscow found itself embroiled in protracted wars in Africa. By then, detente was going down the drain.

What would have happened if Watergate had not torpedoed the Nixon presidency or if Brezhnev remained in good health? Would their personal chemistry have saved detente? Or would the logic of superpower confrontation have derailed it regardless of who was at the helm? We could well wonder the same about the U-2 incident of 1960 that helped derail the spirit of Camp David, or the premature physical and political demises of Kennedy and Khrushchev in 1963 and 1964. Or we could project forward to see how having the right people in the right places (i.e. Ronald Reagan and Mikhail Gorbachev) made it possible to mend fences even at the height of Cold War antagonism. Counterfactuals only go so far. But there are also underlying conditions that eat away even at the best intentions, no matter who is at the helm. In truth, it is important to have both: the right people, and the right conditions, or at least overlapping visions.

Now, to the visions. Let us bring ideology into the picture. The argument would go something like this: yes, detente failed, but that was because the Soviet leaders never gave up their hopes of a world revolution. Detente for them was just a means of getting there. The aim – spelled out in the Marxist-Leninist canon – remained the same. This is a compelling argument, but it does not capture the essence of the problem. Even though the Soviet propaganda rationalized Moscow's foreign policy in Marxist-Leninist terms, there were clearly other issues at stake. Detente was not about achieving a world revolution. It was about attaining recognition by the United States as a superpower, a co-ruler of the world. It was about rearranging the pecking order of the world in a way that would place the Soviet Union on an equal footing with the United States.

425

PART III DECLINE

Yet despite detente, the Soviet–American relationship remained essentially competitive. This competition could be rationalized in ideological terms (i.e. a competition of two rival political and social systems or two visions of modernity) or it could be rationalized in great-power terms. No one in Moscow made this distinction and did not have to. For the very fact of a competition made for a very fragile equilibrium, where any side's gains were invariably interpreted in zero-sum terms. The Yom Kippur War demonstrated this fragility. It showed both the Soviets and the Americans acting opportunistically to undermine each other even as each in turn pretended to be interested in cooperative solutions. It does not mean that the actors of this drama were disingenuous. Both sides were clearly interested in detente, but they were subjected to competing pressures and had to cater to diverse audiences, which created real constraints on cooperative action, especially when great-power credibility was engaged.

The Yom Kippur War demonstrated the limits of detente. It served as a reminder that the Cold War, which Brezhnev proclaimed dead and buried, continued to play out in its different ways, presently in the Middle East, and soon – in Africa. The Soviets craved American recognition, but they demanded the right of equal access to a clientele. Moscow's imperial overextension – the curse of the 1970s – was the consequence of a search for attributes of a superpower. The Soviet leaders needed clients to feel imperial. Their mistake was to think that they could do this hand-in-hand, rather than in competition, with the United States.

426

15

DECLINE

"I am deeply worried about our position in the world resulting from Angola. It is opening the Vietnam wounds again."[1] Henry Kissinger, a survivor of the cratered Nixon presidency, was in the Oval Office, just back from what was probably his least reassuring trip to Moscow. He was now recounting the results of his talks to Nixon's successor, President Gerald Ford. The results were not great. There was some marginal progress on nuclear arms control – SALT-II negotiations were gradually edging forward – but there was one issue where Kissinger, a genius of diplomatic negotiation, simply failed to make any headway at all: Angola. A full-blown war was raging in the former Portuguese colony. The Americans were backing one faction – the Soviets, another. And now, in January 1976, the Soviets were poised to win. Not quite a year since the fall of Saigon to Communist forces, another country on another continent was about to go red. Once again, America's credibility was on the line.

There was one thing Kissinger could not quite understand. Why would Leonid Brezhnev, who had invested so much in improving relations with the United States, would now throw his caution to the wind and commit to fighting a war in Africa, knowing full well – as he had to – that he would be putting detente on the chopping block? For irrespective of what Ford thought of the problem (and, in fact, he thought the whole problem was "useless"), the Soviet intervention in Angola was bound to have political repercussions in Washington.[2] Ford's congressional detractors would hold him accountable for weakness in the face of Communist pressure, never a pleasant prospect, and especially not in an election year. Kissinger tried to make this point to Brezhnev and Gromyko but his pleas were rebuffed with uncharacteristic irritability. "Don't mention that word to me," Brezhnev said, referring to Angola. "We have nothing to do with that country. I cannot talk about that country."[3]

The Soviet–American bickering over Angola provided a fitting post-scriptum to two years of unfulfilled expectations. Detente was not delivering. In Washington, Ford and Kissinger were fending off critics who accused the administration of turning a blind eye to Soviet adventurism in the third world. In Moscow, Brezhnev, debilitated by mounting health problems, fumed over Ford's failure to deliver on the long-promised Most Favored Nation (MFN) status, and over his unwillingness to consider Soviet interests in the 1974 Cyprus crisis. He was also annoyed by relentless American criticism of the Soviet human rights record, which was only temporarily offset by the satisfaction of having signed the 1975 Helsinki Accords, the crowning achievement of years of Soviet diplomacy that, alas, ended up as more of a liability than an asset to Moscow. Looked at from the Soviet perspective, opportunistic involvement in Angola was a fair deal. When did the Americans consider *Soviet* interests? In the Middle East? In Cyprus perhaps?

This chapter, offering a snapshot of detente in downward flight, shows just how fragile it proved to be in the end, how susceptible to the logic of superpower rivalry, and how utterly dependent on domestic variables – especially in the United States.

CYPRUS

The very day that Gerald Ford assumed presidency from the hands of his humiliated predecessor, he wrote Brezhnev a letter, pledging to truthfully follow the course laid out by Nixon.[4] He was just as committed to detente, Ford claimed, as the former president had been. Brezhnev was not so sure. Of course, even Nixon had failed to come through in the way that the Soviet leader had expected (e.g. in the Middle East). But Brezhnev had that personal connection to Nixon that allowed him to overlook some of the setbacks in Soviet–American relations, or at least blame these setbacks on the malicious plotting of Nixon's domestic critics. But he had not 'clicked' with Ford in the same way. Ford was distant and unknown. Could he really deliver for detente? It did not take long before a sense of disappointment began to set in.

The first real "trial" in this respect was the crisis in Cyprus in July–August 1974. Nixon was still in power when, on July 15 the president of Cyprus, Archbishop Makarios III, was ousted in a coup d'état that was immediately traced back to the Greek military junta. Makarios, initially feared dead, just barely escaped from his palace with his life, and was spirited away from the island by the British. The Greek-supported coup triggered a Turkish intervention on July 20, which eventually led to a de facto partition of Cyprus into two ethnic communities – the Greeks and the Turks – and pushed their respective backers in Athens and Ankara to the brink of an all-out

CHAPTER 15 DECLINE

war. The British, who maintained a sizable presence on the island – also narrowly averted being drawn into the fighting. Nixon (on his way out) and Ford (on his way in) were hardly in a position to deal with the unfolding crisis, signing it off to Kissinger. The secretary of state had one key concern: how to keep the Soviets out of the honeypot. A related aim was to prevent tensions between Greece and Turkey from exploding. Both, after all, were members of NATO.[5]

The Soviets were upset by the coup. They had maintained a decent relationship with Makarios (although he never became the "Castro of the Mediterranean" that he was sometimes depicted as). Moscow also exercised a degree of influence with the Cypriot Communist Party (AKEL). The coup and the subsequent Turkish invasion – which raised the prospect of the island's partition between Greece and Turkey (called "double enosis") – were in this sense not at all in Moscow's interest. Therefore, the initial Soviet position was to restore Makarios to power, while preserving Cyprus's independence. The big question was what they were willing to do to achieve this aim. The first worrying signal came via the British. The British high commissioner to Cyprus, Stephen Olver, was approached by the Soviet counsellor, Vladimir Belyaev, asking: How would the British government react if the Soviet Union sent troops to undo the coup?[6]

Within hours Kissinger had Ambassador Dobrynin on the phone. Could it be true, he asked, that the Soviets were contemplating such a move? Dobrynin disclaimed any knowledge of this.[7] No evidence has surfaced yet to explain what this probe really was. It seems unlikely that after the fiasco of their October 1973 proposal to intervene in the Arab–Israeli war, anyone in Moscow would seriously entertain the idea of inserting themselves uninvited into another conflict, even if the political crisis in the US offered such an opportunity. Instead, the Soviets attempted to resurrect the idea of a superpower condominium – and work with the US to impose a political settlement from above. But this effort did not get very far, because behind the scenes Kissinger was doing everything in his power to keep Moscow at arm's length, and stubbornly resisted all suggestions of joint action or superpower guarantees.

In late August – already after the Turks imposed a de facto partition of the island – the Soviets tried to breathe new life into their diplomatic effort. Partly this was because the new democratic government in Greece (the old one, the junta, collapsed in the wake of the Turkish invasion of Cyprus) showed interest in Soviet mediation. Another reason was that the Soviets assumed that Gerald Ford would want to start his presidency by engaging with the USSR to resolve a regional dispute.[8] To this end, on August 23

429

PART III DECLINE

Moscow called for an international conference on Cyprus, to be held under the UN auspices, an idea that Kissinger privately described to the British as "decidedly unhelpful" because by inserting the Soviets into the peace process, it would "undermine further our basic security interests in the eastern Mediterranean."[9] Yet the expectation in Moscow was that because the proposal was "constructive," the Americans would have no choice but to go along. When Kissinger enquired on what basis the Soviets thought one could "solve" the Cyprus problem, that very question was interpreted in Moscow as evidence that "America is already being drawn into a dialogue with the Soviet Union ... This is already a serious political victory for us."[10]

These hopes were dashed, however, and the Soviets were outplayed on most points. Although Makarios was eventually able to return to Cyprus, his preferred solution to the problem – which would avoid a de facto partition – ran aground. The island remained divided, while Moscow's role in the diplomatic negotiations remained negligible. Anatoly Chernyaev, the ever-astute observer of Soviet foreign policy, wrote in his diary: "the NATO imperialists (the British and the Americans) have prevented a war between Turkey and Greece, overthrew the fascist putschists ... in Cyprus and are liquidating a fascist regime in Greece!!"[11] All of that, it might be said, without much Soviet help.

Brezhnev, in the meanwhile, felt very unhappy about the situation. Combined with Ford's occasional anti-Soviet pronouncements, the reality of Moscow's marginalization in the Cyprus conflict suggested to him that the new US administration was, in reality, departing from the promise of detente. In late August, Brezhnev penned a letter to Ambassador Dobrynin, which he never sent, but which highlights his state of mind. "Don't you think," he wrote, "that under such conditions, we must not only demonstrate our goodwill and readiness to develop relations with the US but also in some form let [the Americans] understand that we are not prepared to patiently stomach all unfriendly manifestations of US policy?"[12]

This new Soviet testiness soon became more apparent in view of the Soviet–US exchanges on Jewish emigration.

JACKSON–VANIK

The 1974 mid-term elections saw the Republicans lose control of Congress. Ford was under fire from the left and from the right for appeasing the Soviet Union and overlooking Moscow's unsavory human rights record. Foremost among Ford's critics was Democratic Senator Henry M. "Scoop" Jackson, a man of presidential ambitions and anti-Soviet sentiments. Jackson hit

430

CHAPTER 15 DECLINE

out against restrictions on Jewish emigration from the USSR and tried to link the issue of emigration and trade with the United States (already in October 1972 he introduced legislation denying trade advantages – MFN status – to countries that do not allow free emigration).[13]

The Soviet leaders were outraged by Jackson's obstructionism, condemning the senator as a "shouter" who lacked "elementary decency" (as Gromyko did in a conversation with Nixon in September 1973).[14] Brezhnev bent over backwards to claim that the Soviet Union had no "Jewish problem," and that anyone who wanted to leave could do so if they so wished. "I have many friends and good acquaintances among the Jews," Brezhnev explained, not very convincingly. "Many Jews lived in the town where I was born. I studied together with them, and played soccer with them ... There is no ground for blabbering about alleged hardships, suffered by the Jews in the Soviet Union."[15] He even drew comparisons with Northern Ireland, complaining that no one in the US has ever raised their voice on the account of "murders and outrage" perpetrated by British authorities, and yet "every time some Jew in the Soviet Union says something, a whole campaign begins in America, one hears desperate cries in defense Soviet Jews."[16]

Brezhnev's annoyance in part stemmed from the knowledge of the actual statistics, which showed that approximately 70,000 Jewish emigrants left the USSR for Israel between 1945 and 1973 – of whom 60,000 left since 1969. For the period from January 1, 1969 to June 15, 1973, 97.8% of the 61,500 emigrant petitions were approved, with the remaining 2.2% being denied for reasons like access to classified information – something, Brezhnev labored to point out, that all countries did.[17] Meanwhile, between 1972 and June 1973 as many as 300 former Soviet citizens who had emigrated to Israel had requested to return to the USSR.[18] The prohibitive emigration tax, set up in August 1972 (causing an outrage in the West) was, in practice, not levied by the Soviet authorities – though that was probably as much a consequence of Western pressure as anything else.[19] Meanwhile, the pressure continued all the same, and the Soviets were regularly presented with lists of would-be Jewish emigrants who were barred from leaving. Moscow was denied its much-wanted MFN status.

The MFN issue was both symbolically and economically important to the Soviets. Detente was not for prestige alone: it promised economic dividends in the form of highly anticipated trade deals with the United States. Whether these trade deals would materialize even if MFN were approved is another issue; now that it was not approved, the Soviets knew

PART III DECLINE

whom to blame for the unrealized promise of a trade bonanza. Brezhnev grew increasingly frustrated with the intractably anti-Soviet American public opinion and blamed it all on the average America's dimness and laziness. "Many laymen [in America]," Brezhnev lamented in early 1974, "know very little about the Soviet Union. They have succumbed to internal propaganda and have become so lazy that they do not even want to read anything. They only watch TV, and that only if the programs are interesting."[20]

In December 1973 Ford – then still vice president – was optimistic (or at least so he appeared to Ambassador Dobrynin) that he would be able to "split" the anti-Soviet faction in Congress, undercut the "demagogue" Jackson, and to "shepherd though all the necessary laws."[21] It did not work out. Instead, it was a politically weakened Ford who had to sign off on what became known as the Jackson–Vanik amendment a year later.

Jackson became a figure of hate in Moscow, demonized as an ideologically hardened hawk who brought down detente for the sake of his presidential ambitions. "What does he want," Brezhnev raged. "What alternative does he offer? Doesn't he understand that for 56 years the Soviet Union did fine without Jackson, and we can do fine without him going forward?"[22] When in June–July 1974 Nixon travelled to Moscow to shore up the eroding edifice of detente, "Scoop" headed to China to be feted by the Kremlin's bitterest enemies. The *New York Times* summed up his views: "He sees only the dark riddle of Moscow, and puts his trust in missiles."[23] The democratic senator was offended by these insinuations. In June 1975, over a lengthy breakfast with Dobrynin, held at Jackson's modest home, the senator claimed that there was practically no difference between his views and those of Nixon, Ford, and Kissinger. "Ideological considerations do not weigh me down so much that I would stubbornly cling to some dogmatic position when the real situation requires a different approach," he told Dobrynin. "I am for a practical, pragmatic approach."

Noting casually that he did not feel any special love for the Chinese, for "you can't trust them," he hastened to add: "I am a realist and an American who first and foremost wishes well for his own country … You and China are our adversaries. But the USSR is significantly more powerful and mightier than China." "Therefore," he continued, "we, the US, must play the game, use the Sino-Soviet contradictions. Perhaps in 10–20 years China will become so strong and aggressive that we'll have to draw a lot closer to the USSR than we are today." Dobrynin cynically concluded in his own report to Moscow that "Scoop's" revelations indicated that the Kremlin's nemesis was quietly shopping for an invitation to visit the USSR to bolster his credentials in the run-up to the 1976 presidential elections. Dobrynin proposed not to extend it, in order not to reward Jackson for his outlandish anti-Soviet behavior.[24]

Kissinger was scandalized by Jackson's machinations, which, he argued, were "humiliating to the Soviets."[25] "I have no interest in the survival of Brezhnev as a person. But he has made a major political commitment to improved relations with the U.S." In conversations with Dobrynin he was blunt in his criticism of the congressional action as "irresponsible" and the Jackson–Vanik amendment as "contrary to the national interests of the United States and needlessly discriminatory."[26]

ARMS CONTROL

Despite the setbacks with the Jackson–Vanik amendment, both the White House and the Kremlin tried to maintain detente's momentum. The key tracks for making headway were the arms-control negotiations – what became known as SALT-II – and the "Helsinki process" that would lead in the summer of 1975 to the conclusion of the Helsinki Accords. The big question for Brezhnev was whether Ford could deliver on these grand themes – that is, whether he could still "run the world" with Ford much as he had expected to run it with Nixon before the Watergate debacle.

One of Brezhnev's obsessive ideas – and one of his last before his irreversible mental decline – was that of a quasi-alliance between the Soviet Union and the United States, whereby if one were attacked, the other would come to its aid. He first broached the idea in his conversation with Nixon during the president's swansong visit to the Soviet Union in June–July 1974. It was a private conversation in the depth of a "grotto" cut out of the seaside cliffs at Brezhnev's dacha in Oreanda, Crimea.[27] Unusually, even Kissinger was excluded. But the secretary of state heard a restatement of the same proposal during his visit to Moscow in October, already after Nixon's resignation. The idea, Brezhnev said, was that "each side, in the interests of keeping the peace, would use military power in support of the other."[28] While introducing this proposal, Brezhnev fiddled with a toy artillery piece, aiming it now at Kissinger, now at Kissinger's aide Helmut Sonnenfeldt, something that the secretary found particularly "bizarre" when he recounted the whole episode to Ford. Needless to say, the idea of a de facto alliance did not fly.[29]

It was, however, an astonishing idea, once again highlighting, as it did, the strange transmutation of Soviet foreign policy. How could such

Figure 22 Kissinger and Brezhnev, Moscow, June 1974.
Source: Bernard Charlon/Gamma-Rapho/Getty Images.

alignments as what Brezhnev proposed be even explained from the Marxist-Leninist perspective? Just as Mao did in the late 1960s–early 1970s, Brezhnev instrumentally dispensed with ideology when doing so suited his interests. At least Mao did so in the expectation of what he thought was a likely Soviet invasion. For Brezhnev, China was also a big concern. This was unquestionably a major pragmatic reason for seeking a pact with the United States. But there was something else – the greatness of keeping world peace hand-in-hand with the Americans. "Such an agreement," Brezhnev explained, "could generate conditions to warn anyone that no one has the right to attack anyone so all nations should live at peace with each other."[30] It would be a *Pax Sovietica-Americana*.

Kissinger deliberately encouraged this kind of thinking by China-baiting the Soviets on every suitable occasion. His take held that China's vast population, empowered by Japan's industrial might, would make for a tremendous challenge to the West. "The Japanese," Kissinger told Dobrynin on November 16, 1974, "are like ants: as individuals, they don't make any impression on you ... They are all flat and narrow." But they had hidden nationalistic ambitions and, together with China, could build a "superpower" bloc. "If the ants come together in an anthill," Kissinger continued,

CHAPTER 15 DECLINE

"they can do a lot of things, and the picture that emerges is an impressive one."[31] The same day, he warned Ford of the prospects of the Sino-Japanese alliance, adding: "If we decline in world power, we will lose the Japanese."[32]

Just a few days later Ford and Kissinger ventured out to the Soviet far eastern city of Vladivostok for another summit with Brezhnev. This time there was remarkably little discussion of China even though Vladivostok was just a short distance away from the Sino-Soviet – the world's most militarized – border. Instead, the discussions focused on the arms control negotiations, as Ford and Brezhnev worked out the basis for what later became the SALT-II agreement. At an appropriate moment, Brezhnev returned to his proposal of a de facto Soviet–American alliance to prevent the outbreak of a nuclear war.[33] Ford seemed noncommittal, and this time Brezhnev, too, downplayed its importance. It came across as an unnecessary afterthought. Brezhnev put up an impressive show of hospitality, presenting Ford with a set of smoking pipes, and the president's portrait made of inlaid wood.[34] There was a lot of chit-chat and joking about Kissinger getting fat on the Russian pirozhki but the kind of intimacy that characterized the earlier Brezhnev–Nixon encounters was just not there.

Upon his return from Vladivostok, Ford faced a domestic outcry spearheaded by "Scoop" Jackson who accused the president of helping legitimize "the massive continuation of Soviet arms expenditures."[35] Brezhnev did not have to deal with the same sort of domestic constraints but he had another problem – ill-health. In fact, it was during the train journey after his talks in Vladivostok that – according to Brezhnev's doctor – the general secretary suffered a breakdown from which he would never recover.[36] After Vladivostok, Brezhnev's mental capabilities declined rapidly, and he lost the grip on policy making. Detente, steered by a weak president and a frail general secretary, was still alive on paper. But it was coming to a standstill.

Further troubles were in the offing. In the spring of 1975 detente took a hit from dramatic events in Southeast Asia. In April 1975, the North Vietnamese moved rapidly on the South. On April 30 the city of Saigon fell to the Communists. The images of an Air America helicopter taking out evacuees from the rooftop of the US Embassy symbolized the defeat of American policy in Southeast Asia, a policy that Kissinger helped craft and execute. This was a moment of political vulnerability for the secretary of state, which his Soviet interlocutors did not seem to fully appreciate. Or, if they appreciated it, they did not care. America lost. The Soviets won. "The world," a prominent third world apparatchik in the Central Committee famously concluded, "was going our way."[37]

435

PART III DECLINE

HELSINKI

So, detente was under considerable stress already when in July 1975 President Ford headed out to Finland for what turned out to be his very last summit with Brezhnev. The occasion was the signing of the Helsinki Final Act, the last act of the multilateral Conference on Security and Cooperation in Europe (CSCE) that had dragged on since November 1972 between Helsinki and Geneva. This was a Soviet idea, pursued since 1954.[38] More than that, it was Brezhnev's personal prestige project, the celebratory culmination of detente.[39] A successful conference, he told his East German counterpart Eric Honecker, "will have not just a general political impact but we will also win powerful allies in the form of the peoples."[40] Its failure, by contrast, would mean that "we would lose prestige and influence." Historian Michael Morgan argues that the CSCE was "the capstone on Brezhnev's strategy to rebuild the legitimacy of the Soviet system."[41] That legitimacy was to be arrived at through collective recognition of the Soviet Union's rightful place in Europe, much as the Concert of Europe inaugurated Russia's centrality to the nineteenth-century European order.

Brezhnev's vision ran against serious obstacles. His core idea, "inviolability" of postwar borders – which he thought would become the central element of the conference declaration – ran into opposition from the West Germans who saw in it an attempt to deny the possibility of a peaceful reunification of Germany. Bonn insisted on inserting an additional clause permitting "peaceful" changing of borders. The wrangling went on for months, frustrating Soviet diplomacy. Hopes that Kissinger would intervene to bring a difficult ally into line proved largely misplaced. In the end, the Soviets agreed to a compromise that allowed for borders to change "in accordance with international law, by peaceful means and by agreement." Such a compromise became necessary for the CSCE to be brought to a conclusion, but it went a long way towards undercutting the whole idea of "inviolability" – and was seen as such by Moscow's wary East German allies.

But perhaps the biggest Soviet concession was the inclusion of "human rights" as a free-standing principle in the Helsinki Final Act. This idea was reflective of the Western interpretation of "peace" as a consequence of an open society, and it was at odds with the Soviet preference for sovereignty and noninterference in internal affairs. Problematically for Brezhnev, it was once again the Western Europeans – especially the French – who now relentlessly pressed for the inclusion of the human rights agenda, including a range of principles for facilitating exchange of people and information across the Iron Curtain (something that became known as the "third

CHAPTER 15 DECLINE

basket"). The Soviets complained that what the Western Europeans were trying to do by talking about human rights was to impose their own, bourgeois, values on the socialist bloc. That was unacceptable. The key was to maintain "respect" for each country's laws. "Indeed," Brezhnev explained to French Prime Minister Jacques Chirac in March 1975, "if you in France do not allow people to go into the street naked, a visitor must at the very least don his underwear – otherwise, he'll be picked up by the police. By the same token, if our laws require one to wear pants, then please be so kind as not to go into our streets without."[42]

Behind the Soviet leader's awkward jokes was his sense of insecurity at the thought of yielding to the Western European conception of "peace" with its open borders, its freedoms, and its political pluralism. It had been but a few years since he had sent tanks to crush the Prague spring with its promise of socialism with a human face, and now he was being asked to endorse those very values that the Soviets helped strangle in Czechoslovakia. Brezhnev therefore railed bitterly against "certain bureaucrats in Geneva who were rummaging through the 'third basket' like through garbage, piling one obstacle upon another, just in order to drag out the conference."[43] "Can we allow the garbage from the 'third basket' to clog up the mechanism of deciding upon vital questions of peace and security?" he would ask.[44] The answer was evidently "yes": having invested so much energy and face into the deadlocked conference, Brezhnev was simply in no position to resist Western European demands. In the final months of the conference, he went a long way to "show flexibility" in the negotiations, hoping only that Moscow's gains on noninterference would mitigate his concessions on human rights. Brezhnev even decided to cancel the May 9, 1975 Victory Day parade because, as he put it, "there is no need to rattle the tanks and the missiles along the square during the period of the intensive struggle for peace."[45]

The fact that it was Moscow that made most concessions to get to the finishing line in Helsinki was lost on some observers, certainly in the United States, where President Ford's detractors – Ronald Reagan (on one side) and "Scoop" Jackson (on the other) – accused him of giving away too much ground to the Soviets by going to Helsinki to sign off on the hard-negotiated Accords. Jackson proclaimed that "there are times in international diplomacy when the President of the United States ought to stay home."[46]

Even members of Ford's own administration seemed to be undercutting the president's foreign policy. Secretary of Defense James R. Schlesinger, for example, not only criticized detente publicly but also, in May 1975, called for the use of tactical nuclear weapons to stop a conventional attack

PART III DECLINE

by the Warsaw Pact.[47] Brezhnev, not at all amused by being thus threatened before the grand summit that symbolized detente itself, sent an oral warning to Ford: "We are puzzled by this fact, Mr. President. And of course it would be good to introduce clarity about the real meaning of these statements and the purpose they serve."[48] He even touched on Schlesinger's misdeeds in a rare entry in his diary, though he only managed to write "Shlisi" for Schlesinger's name (probably not out of spite: simply, Brezhnev at this stage, was beginning to lose it mentally, and had trouble remembering complex names).[49]

Brezhnev had intended for Helsinki to be the crowning achievement of detente, and a milestone on the road to ever closer US–Soviet relations. But in his meetings with Ford the general secretary clearly struggled with the complexities of arms control and other pressing international issues. The awkward pauses as Brezhnev shuffled through his talking points became longer and more and more embarrassing.[50] Even his complaints concerning Schlesinger had to be read from notes, and Brezhnev also relied on notes in a private tête-à-tête with Ford, when he reassured the president that the Soviets hoped for his victory in the upcoming elections and would "do everything we can to make that happen."[51] The notes of this secret promise were left in Brezhnev's ashtray in Findlandia's Hall, from where they were rescued by a National Security Council staffer and preserved for posterity – a reminder as much of the Soviet leader's mental decline as of his hopes for a positive relationship with Ford.

What many contemporary commentators did not quite grasp was that the agreement was a long-term defeat for the Soviets. Who would have thought that the general secretary would affix his signature to a document that required the Soviet Union to "respect human rights and fundamental freedoms, including the freedom of thought, conscience, religion or belief?"[52] This commitment unexpectedly strengthened the dissident movement in the USSR, and in some ways contributed to the Soviet demise because it created a vast gap between Soviet realities and the claims of the Communist Party leadership, further undercutting its legitimacy.[53] As Richard Davy, a former journalist and later historian of the Helsinki Final Act justly put it, "Brezhnev's vanity and insecurity drove him on to a conference that brought him little but trouble."[54]

Two weeks before Helsinki, on July 17, 1975 Soviet and American spacecraft made history, docking in space. The Apollo–Soyuz mission was not just a technological feat. It aimed at symbolically overcoming Cold War divisions between the East and the West and opening the new era of Soviet–American cooperation. That, of course, was what Brezhnev had wanted to

CHAPTER 15 DECLINE

see, for detente elevated his – and his country's – prestige to the skies. Yet the glorious era proved remarkably short, for even as the astronauts and the cosmonauts shook hands in space, the edifice of detente was beginning to crumble under the weight of superpower rivalry in the third world, first and foremost in Angola.

THE ANGOLAN CAULDRON

There is one fairly obvious explanation for the rapid escalation of Soviet involvement in African conflicts. They did it because they could. The Soviet military now had the wherewithal to carry out logistical feats that had previously been beyond their means. The Soviet Union had become a global superpower and acted like one. But such a deterministic explanation runs up against an obvious defect: capabilities do not necessarily equate with intentions. Having the power to invade someone does not make invasion inevitable. But what if an opportunity presented itself? George F. Kennan had long argued that the Soviet Union was an "opportunistic" but cautious power that would seek expansion unless faced with superior force. America's global retrenchment post-Vietnam offered that opportunity, and Moscow eagerly seized it. Angola, with its wonderful strip of South Atlantic coastline, offered the Soviet clear geopolitical advantages. From that perspective, too, getting a toehold was a no-brainer. In fact, in later years Luanda hosted the headquarters of the Soviet Navy's Thirtieth Operational Squadron, with eleven patrol ships and first-rate communications facilities. If geopolitical advantage was what the Soviets were after, then going into Angola made sense.

But this is the same as saying that Moscow supported Vietnam because the Soviet leaders wanted a base in Cam Ranh Bay, or that they supported Egypt and Syria because they wanted access to the Mediterranean. Yes, they wanted bases – in Vietnam and in the Mediterranean, no less than in Angola – but in Vietnam, as we have seen, Soviet decision-making was vastly more complicated than that and often hinged on issues like prestige, recognition, and credibility. Why, then, should Angola have been any different?

Another approach to the problem, one that would not have gained much traction with Kissinger the realist but that has been subsequently embraced by historians as a valuable explanation for Soviet behavior, is ideology. By this measure, Moscow's support for the People's Movement for the Liberation of Angola (MPLA) – Angola's Marxists – stemmed directly from the latter's pro-Communist leanings. In the words of a leading scholar of the subject, Odd Arne Westad, "as the Angolan group came under

439

PART III DECLINE

pressure from its enemies, many Soviet officials used opportunity, capability, and strategic interest as rationalizations of a desire to uphold a regime willing to link up to the Soviet experience."[55]

There is logic here. The MPLA, and its leader Agostinho Neto, were not just some random guerrillas; the movement had a long history of struggle against Portugal's colonial rule, and a relationship with the Soviet Union that went back to the early 1960s, nearly fifteen years before Angola acquired independence. Neto, a philosopher and a poet who would have certainly rejected the appellation of a Soviet "client," had long proclaimed adherence to Marxism. But there are also complexities in store. Soviet support for the MPLA, recalls Karen Brutents, the first deputy head of the International Department of the Soviet Communist Party, "was not dictated, as is often believed, by ideological but by pragmatic considerations: it seemed to be the only nationwide movement ... which carried on a real struggle against the colonizers."[56] Yet the very term "colonizers," which Brutents so lightly used to highlight the supposedly nonideological nature of Soviet support for Angola, can (perhaps, should) be understood in ideological terms, highlighting the complex relationship between the Marxist-Leninist trope (that the Soviets could – and did – use to rationalize great-power struggles) and the geopolitical trope (that the Soviets could – and did – use to identify their great-power competitors in any particular theater).

One way to reconcile these complexities is to think about the Soviet desire to sponsor regimes willing to "link up" to their experience in terms of a shared identity. Moscow craved recognition by clients far and wide: this was what made the Soviet Union a superpower. Recognizing Soviet leadership required that these clients embrace the Soviet experience and, indeed, adopt the Soviet terminology: only then could they be deemed to have chosen sides. The act of embracing the Soviet experience was thus the ultimate expression of the recognition of – and submission to – Soviet leadership.

The uprising against Portuguese rule in Angola broke out in 1961, and it was from the start characterized by intense rivalry between would-be revolutionaries: the MPLA (itself hopelessly faction-ridden), its main competitor FNLA (the National Liberation Front for Liberation of Angola), and later yet another movement, UNITA (the National Union for the Total Independence of Angola). The leaders of all three movements – MPLA's Neto, FNLA's Holden Roberto, and UNITA's Jonas Savimbi – met in Alvor, Portugal in January 1975 to sign an agreement that would grant Angola its independence. As the Portuguese readied to pull the stakes (the transition would take place on November 11), the three contenders for power in

440

CHAPTER 15 DECLINE

post-independence Angola were primed for battle. Moscow's sympathies were clearly with the MPLA, though very late in the game – until early November 1975 – the Soviets pushed for unity between the three movements. Yet they were also covertly supplying the MPLA with weapons. The decision to do so was taken in December 1974, though the first Soviet weapons did not arrive until May of the following year.[57] By November 5, 1975, the Soviet Union had provided the MPLA with 30 million rubles' worth of goods and equipment, including weapons and ammunition to arm 5,000 soldiers.[58] The MPLA described this aid as "paltry, given the enormity of the need."[59]

Meanwhile, the United States lined up support behind FNLA. On January 22, 1975, the "40 Committee" (a special group for the oversight of covert operations) approved $300,000 for Holden Roberto (a long-term recepient of CIA funding). Arrangements were made for arming the FNLA from neighboring Zaire, whose deeply corrupt and authoritarian leader, Mobutu Sese Seko, held Roberto for a friend. That spring fighting flared up in Luanda between the MPLA and the FNLA in defiance of the half-hearted efforts of the Portuguese caretakers to keep up the pretense of normality. In July the MPLA managed to consolidate their control over the capital. The FNLA, with Zaire's involvement, continued to pose a threat in the north, even as UNITA challenged the MPLA in the south. Backed from South Africa, brutal but charismatic Savimbi steadily expanded influence in the countryside. For a good measure, the Chinese also sent arms and instructors to support the FNLA.

China's involvement with Africa's liberation movements went back to the mid-1950s. A platform for advertising the achievements of Chinese Communism, and an object of bitter rivalry in the Sino-Soviet struggle for leadership, Africa had been firmly embedded in Beijing's foreign policy since the early 1960s. The high tide of China's revolutionary zeal in the postcolonial world was reached in 1964–65. But the debacle of the pro-Chinese Indonesian Communist Party (PKI) in September 1965, and the failure to convene the Second "Bandung" Conference – which would have offered China a podium for projecting leadership among the "Afro-Asian peoples" – tarnished Beijing's credentials. The Cultural Revolution further undermined China's global standing, and it was only after the chaos subsided that the Chinese tried to reassert themselves in Africa, presently in the context of Mao Zedong's theory of the "three worlds," which the Chinese leader spelled out to Zambian President Kenneth Kaunda in February 1974.

PART III DECLINE

By then, Mao was on a rapid downhill slope. Thirteen years Brezhnev's senior, the ailing revolutionary suffered from heart disease and poor eyesight. He also developed symptoms of a rare degenerative disorder, amyotrophic lateral sclerosis, which led to gradual paralysis (and ultimately, in September 1976, his death). Mao's revelations to Kaunda can therefore be read as something of a final testament of this self-proclaimed strategist of global socialism. "The way I see it," Mao said, "the United States and the Soviet Union belong to the First World. Those in the middle, such as Japan, Europe and Canada belong to the Second World, and we are of the third world." Kaunda signaled his understanding. Mao continued: "The United States and the Soviet Union have many atomic bombs and are richer. Europe, Japan, Australia and Canada of the Second World do not possess as many atomic bombs and are not as rich, but they are richer than the third world countries." Under these circumstances, China's duty was to help the third world. "If we don't, we will be betraying Marxism."[60]

But help who, exactly? In Africa, the staging ground for superpower conflict, "helping" entailed a choice of a client. What sorts of "Marxist" considerations did the Chinese apply in backing what often were avowedly reactionary regimes and factions? The answer is simple: hard-nosed pragmatism. China had tried to support various leftist factions, Mao told Zaire's Mobutu, but found that these simply could not deliver. "It's not that we don't want them to revolt, but they were a disappointment. What can I do if they can't defeat you?"[61] It was, then, through Mobutu that the Chinese became invested in supporting Angola's FNLA, sending instructors to train Roberto's troops. In time, the Chinese came to back UNITA as well. It was not because Roberto or Savimbi were "progressive" – in fact, they were anything but. Simply, they were anti-Soviet, and so aligned with China's aim of undercutting the Soviet Union where it could. Although the Chinese still attempted to distinguish their activities in Angola from the struggle of the two "hegemons," the United States and the USSR, they found themselves, objectively, allied with the former against the latter.

All of that was gravely disconcerting to those in the Soviet Union whose job it was to look after Moscow's clients in Angola, for example, to the head of the African section of the Communist Party's International Department, Petr Manchkha, who grimly and prematurely commented in early June 1975 on the distinct possibility that "all ours [Soviet friends in Angola] will be beaten."[62] Manchkha was a mid-level functionary, and in other circumstances his views would not have mattered all that much. But these were no ordinary circumstances. Physical decline and mental paralysis at the highest levels of leadership meant that policy

442

CHAPTER 15 DECLINE

recommendations thought up at the lower levels of the party hierarchy suddenly turned into policy by virtue of bureaucratic inertia.

Indeed, where was Brezhnev while the likes of Manchkha rang alarm bells about the MPLA's prospects? He certainly was not strategizing over the maps, plotting Communist revolutions, or naval bases along the Atlantic coast of Africa. Brezhnev generally split his time between his suburban dacha and the party clinic on Granovsky street. He still attended to government business and even, on occasion, presided over Politburo meetings but his impact on policy was not nearly what it once had been. He was becoming something of a figurehead. After the Helsinki Conference, Brezhnev went to Crimea, where he recuperated for a whole month, returning at the end of August 1975, but not the office – only to the dacha.

"Brezhnev's incapacity is more and more noticeable," Chernyaev noted on September 13. "He returned from vacation on August 29 but has not appeared anywhere, and his presence is not felt at the C[entral] C[ommittee]. And since everything more or less significant depends on him, things have stalled."[63] The Politburo records confirm Chernyaev's observations. The general secretary was simply not doing much in the fall of 1975, leaving it to his aides – mostly Andrei Aleksandrov-Agentov and Anatoly Blatov – to sign off on the voting slips for Politburo resolutions. While Brezhnev recuperated, the Angolan cauldron heated up. In July 1975 Ford authorized a covert operation to bolster the anti-MPLA forces, code-named IAFEATURE. In arguing in favor of forceful involvement, Kissinger made it clear what was at stake: "If all the surrounding countries see Angola go Communist, they will assume that the U.S. has no will."[64] But even buoyed by aid, weapons, and troops from Zaire, the uneasy coalition between the FNLA and UNITA faced a hard time defeating the better-motivated MPLA. It took the South African invasion of Angola in mid-October to turn the tables on the self-proclaimed Marxists.

On October 14, 1975, the day the South African column, Zulu, crossed the border into Angola, Brezhnev hosted French President Giscard d'Estaing. In years past, he carefully cultivated relations with the French leaders, first de Gaulle, and then Pompidou, hoping, as he did, to weaken their ties to the United States and West Germany. That was a different age, and a different Brezhnev. Brezhnev of 1975 was so exhausted by his two-hour meeting with d'Estaing that he had to take two days off to recuperate at his dacha, leaving his distinguished guest sightseeing in embarrassment. "The situation in the upper echelons of the party and the country is almost at a dead end," noted Chernyaev. "Brezhnev's illness and mental degradation is becoming evident to everyone ... In the meantime, the leadership of the country is effectively paralyzed."[65]

It was this Brezhnev – a mere shadow of his former self – who committed to Angola in late October 1975. So, to return to that question that perplexed Kissinger: why did he do it? It certainly was not because he lost faith in detente or realized Angola's revolutionary significance. It was because, for the purposes of Soviet foreign policy, he *was* detente. Now that he was losing it, mentally and physically, policy making succumbed to bureaucratic interests.

Consider, for example, the role played by the International Department of the Central Committee, long known to have been a key player in Moscow's interventions in the third world. Here we find people whose job description included support for third world revolutionaries, people who (unlike Brezhnev) knew Neto personally, and who had followed his struggle with the Portuguese much closer than they had followed the ups and downs of detente.[66] Detente had its advocates, mainly in the Foreign Ministry, but Gromyko was too cautious to go out on a limb while his boss preoccupied himself with his long list of ailments. That is why, his deputy, Georgy Kornienko, remembered, Gromyko signed off on a memorandum prepared by the International Department, that approved of the Soviet supplies of weapons to Angola. He did so only after "certain wavering" and because he "did not want to have conflicts with his colleagues."[67]

Whether or not Gromyko privately disagreed with the Soviet involvement in Angola, his signature, alongside that of his counterpart in the International Department, Boris Ponomarev, appears on the key relevant documents, including the October 28, 1975 recommendation for the Politburo to recognize the MPLA as the sole government of independent Angola. The one-pager says nothing at all about detente. Instead, Gromyko and Ponomarev referred to the Soviet Union's long-standing support for the MPLA. The MPLA had been a Soviet client for so many years. Now that they were on the verge of capturing power, why would Moscow *not* continue helping the ostensible Marxists?[68] A letter to the allies spelled out another rationale (which the Politburo did not have to be reminded of, probably because everyone took it for granted): recognition of the MPLA would allow the Soviet bloc to "strengthen political positions in Angola and in other African states."[69]

There was logic to this position even before the military had anything to say. But the military did have a lot to say. Not only was Grechko overly trigger-happy (just recall that he alone advocated a military intervention in the Middle East in 1973) but as the minister of defense, he like no one else

CHAPTER 15 DECLINE

eyed Angola from the strategic perspective, somewhere he could challenge the United States, which he so distrusted. The Americans "threaten us," Brezhnev reportedly lamented in December 1975 – "either because of our fleet, or because of Angola, or they think up something else altogether. Grechko comes to me. They [the Americans] have added here, he says; they threaten to increase there. Give me more money, he says ... What am I supposed to tell him? I am the head of the country's Military Council. I am responsible for its safety. The Minister of Defense tells me that if I don't give it to him, he will renounce all responsibility. So, I give, again and again."[70]

The bureaucratic consensus, then, favored intervention in Angola. Would Brezhnev have made a difference had he been in a better shape? It is possible of course, since for the Soviet leader detente had been a very personal project. On the other hand, years before Angola Brezhnev already committed to third world adventures by backing militant clients in Southeast Asia and the Middle East. Indeed, it was on his watch that the Soviets became secretly involved with the MPLA and a host of other liberation movements in Africa. As much as he treasured detente, he also treasured the Soviet status as a global superpower; in his mind, the two issues were two sides of the same coin. Even a healthier Brezhnev would have found it difficult to resist the Angolan adventure. A sick Brezhnev found it practically impossible.

But there was one more factor that contributed, perhaps decisively, to the Soviet decision to help the MPLA – Fidel Castro's position. The Cubans had helped other liberation movements in Africa, and had fought in Guinea-Bissau, and Congo-Brazzaville. They had a long-standing relationship with Neto, and, following the MPLA's request, had sent a number of military advisers to Angola (who were in place by August 1975). But why? The leading historian of Cuba's involvement Piero Gleijeses narrows Castro's motivations to his sense of a "revolutionary duty."[71] "Of course, there was ego – but above all there was ... mission."[72] This makes sense, but here is a question. *Why* was Castro so preoccupied with Cuba's "revolutionary duty" if not for the sense of glory and accomplishment – that is, *recognition* that came with pushing far above one's weight in great struggles against mighty adversities? Revolutionary missions and glory are after all not just compatible, but one is a way of attaining the other. We have seen how revolutionary prestige played into foreign policies of other actors in this story, not least the Chinese and the Soviets. There was a difference, however, in the sense that Beijing and Moscow did not just seek revolutionary legitimacy but legitimacy through recognition as great powers. But Castro's greatness had no other platform except for revolutionary exploits in the jungles of Africa.

PART III DECLINE

The South African intervention in October 1975 created an entirely new situation in Angola. No one in Moscow believed that the South Africans, never mind Zaire, acted on their own behalf. "It is clear," Gromyko and Ponomarev reported to the Politburo on November 10, one day before the MPLA proclaimed Angola's independence, "that behind all of this stand certain imperialist circles, for it is hard to imagine that the R[epublic] of S[outh] A[frica], and Zaire, would send their military force to Angola without the sanction of the large Western powers."[73] In other words, a civil war in far-off Angola, where the Soviets hardly had any tangible interests, was reinterpreted as a Cold War theater, which required Soviet involvement not because of its own worth but because loss in any theater would resonate for Moscow's global standing. The same logic applied fully to the United States.

Meanwhile, Castro decided to dispatch Cuban combat troops to stave off what seemed like the MPLA's imminent defeat. This decision was made without consulting the Soviets, but Cuba's involvement was a godsend. As long as the Cubans deferred to the "elder brothers" (as they did), the Soviets not just defended their credibility but also highlighted their status as a global power, an equal of the United States. There was a contradiction between these aspects of Moscow's third world policy, and detente, but the same contradictions were in place earlier on, with Vietnam, and Brezhnev squared that circle. Whether he could square such circles in his dim world of 1975 is a good question. Whatever his mental weakness, he knew one thing: he was the leader of a superpower, and if he was asked to do something to uphold this superpower's credentials – by Grechko, Neto, or Castro – he had to "give, again and again."

Castro's involvement made the Angolan problem much worse for Washington: Cuba was a red cloth for many a militant Congressman, much more so than the Soviet Union itself. Democratic Senator Ted Kennedy tried, jokingly, to bring this point across to Ambassador Dobrynin. "US attitude towards the Cubans headed by F[idel] Castro is still rather emotional, not rational." He added that if, instead, it was the Uzbeks or Kyrgyz who fought in Angola, "the Americans would pay less attention to it."[74] Kissinger, too, dwelt on the Cuban role, telling Dobrynin that Castro "is deeply mistaken if [he] thinks that [Cuba] will go unpunished and the US will not act" in the future, adding that its current apparent "nonaction" was just a result of temporary domestic difficulties.[75] (This was a reference to Ford's political weakness and a hostile Congress.)

Months later, when the Cuban victory in Angola was already a done deal, Kissinger would still beat that dead horse in meetings with Dobrynin, telling him again and again how the Cuban intervention was the key factor in worsening Soviet–American relations. After the defeat in Vietnam, "a painful blow at the national prestige," the United States suffered another defeat in Angola. "Especially humiliating for the US is the fact that the Soviets defeated the Americans with Cuban hands," Kissinger explained, adding that this in itself introduced a "major emotional aspect" into the situation.[76] Most emotional of all was Kissinger himself: it was, after all, his policy that was now collapsing.

It is hardly surprising, then, that the secretary of state obsessively warned Dobrynin that Angola would undermine detente and that he probed the Soviets regarding the possibility of a secret Soviet–American discussion to settle the crisis. The ambassador stonewalled these approaches, instructed by Gromyko that there would be little "real benefit" to any such discussion but that the very fact of talks would undoubtedly be leaked and be used against the Soviet Union by the Chinese and various reactionary African leaders.[77] It is instructive that even ostensibly private communications from the Soviet leadership to Kissinger on the Angolan question were composed with an eye to their possible publication (and so the tone was uncharacteristically propagandistic).[78] This was something that Kissinger – who was used to backroom dealings with the Soviets – found difficult to accept.

Nevertheless – and this is an important reservation – the Soviets carefully calibrated their response to events in Angola and pushed the brakes when it looked like the cauldron might be overheating. For instance, this happened in late November 1975, when the Soviet ambassador in Conakry picked up rumors that the Cubans were about to deploy a full regular division (5,000–6,000 men) to Angola at Neto's request. It says something about the nature of Soviet–Cuban relations that the Politburo had to instruct their ambassador in Havana to speak to Castro to find out if the planned deployment was true and if (as suspected) it was, to dissuade the fiery Cuban from doing this for fear of prompting "provocations from Western countries, including the USA, and not necessarily just in relation to Angola."[79]

An even more interesting development was the Soviet initiative – in early December 1975 – to shift the Angolan question from the realm of military struggle to that of political negotiation. Worried that – for all the military support afforded to the MPLA – the Soviet clients might yet be unable to clinch victory or that the whole crisis could "put in question the main policies of international detente," the Soviets opted to encourage Neto to talk to his rivals, the FNLA and UNITA, to see if they could be split or won over to a political settlement. Interestingly, this idea was presented to the

PART III DECLINE

Politburo in a joint memorandum by Andrei Gromyko, Boris Ponomarev, Yury Andropov, and Andrei Grechko.[80] Barring Gromyko, these were not known to be great lovers of detente, and the institutions that they represented (the International Department, the KGB, and the Ministry of Defense) had hawkish reputations when it came to third world adventures. Even with Brezhnev increasingly incapacitated, there was enough collective understanding at the Politburo that detente was something worth defending for its own sake, even if that meant a degree of self-restraint in places like Angola.

A key Soviet concern in early 1976 was that the Cubans, inspired by their success in Angola, would attempt to invade neighboring countries, in particular Namibia. Castro tried to reassure Moscow that he had no such plans. On March 23, 1976 he told Soviet Ambassador Nikita Tolubeev that "the Soviet Union should not worry in this regard. Cuba will never make any steps in Africa or some other place without taking the Soviet opinion into account." He promised to act in Angola "in accordance with what the Soviet Union tells us" and not to help Neto even if he decided to invade Namibia.[81]

But the Soviets were not fully convinced because a week later they wrote a letter to Fidel Castro (sent in Brezhnev's name), which, despite all the congratulatory noise about defeating the forces of "imperialism, racism, and Maoism," contained a clear warning to the Cubans not to get involved in further fighting and proposed the beginning of a phased withdrawal of the Cuban forces from Angola. "We are expressing all these thoughts, dear Fidel," the letter went, "being guided by the best intentions – the desire to solidify the victory of the Angolan people and at the same time not to give the imperialist forces a pretext to harm fraternal Cuba."[82] Castro was taken aback by the Soviet pressure, and argued in turn that "if the forces are withdrawn today, tomorrow the situation inside and around Angola could become worse." He disclaimed any intention to invade any other African countries: "we are not even thinking about it."[83] Moscow, however, remained somewhat wary of their trigger-happy ally. In May 1976 Brezhnev personally advised Castro's brother Raúl to act cautiously in order not to needlessly provoke the United States. "You must view the situation in the world realistically. If you do not view it in this way, you'll end up paying."[84] But by then the Cubans had already accepted a phased withdrawal. Raúl was in fact in Angola just days earlier, where he sold the Soviet idea to the (likely) reluctant Neto.[85]

Realism was called for but, in any case, by early 1976 the Soviets – and their allies – had essentially won on the ground. The South Africans were beaten back by the Cubans and the MPLA, armed with Soviet

448

CHAPTER 15 DECLINE

weapons. A hostile Congress prevented Ford from helping America's allies. China, too, called it quits. Neto did not have to compromise with Roberto or Savimbi as his Soviet patrons worried that he might have had to. The Soviet leadership had a reason to stand tall and proud. The Soviets derived political legitimacy not just from being recognized by the United States as equals but also from being recognized around the world as Washington's powerful adversary and as a defender of "revolution." "Detente," argued Boris Ponomarev in December 1975, "cannot mean freedom of action for reactionaries and aggressors, for colonizers and racists who rudely violate the freedom and independence of the Angolan people." Ponomarev's rationalization was packaged in a set of instructions to Soviet ambassadors across Africa and the Middle East, for passing on to the leaders of actual or potential Soviet allies: this was how the Soviets wanted to be seen in the third world.[86]

But there is a broader question that begs addressing. Was there a point of equilibrium in Africa for Soviet and American interests? In the early 1970s Brezhnev was shopping for a Soviet–American condominium in the Middle East. It did not materialize because when the United States had a choice between working hand-in-hand with the Soviets and scoring unilateral gains, the second option turned out to be by far preferable. In 1974 Brezhnev hoped for a Soviet role in achieving a settlement in Cyprus – only Kissinger kept him well away. The situation in Angola was broadly analogous, only now the Soviets had the upper hand. They simply had no interest in finding a place for the Americans.

CONCLUSION

There is an interesting document that captures the spirit of the Soviet policy towards Africa in 1975. That December the chief Soviet ideologue, Mikhail Suslov, travelled to Cuba where he met with Fidel Castro. The record of their conversation is missing but what we do have is a detailed rundown of Soviet positions on key international issues in the form of Suslov's talking points. "Detente helped create a new climate in international relations," Suslov's notes said. "[It] opens additional opportunities for struggle against imperialism, for social progress." American defeat in Vietnam, Communist revolutions in Laos and Cambodia, the fall of "fascist regimes" in Greece and Portugal, widening international recognition of East Germany, victories in Angola and Cuba's growing "prestige" – these unfolding against the background of an economic crisis in the West – all pointed to a changing "correlation of forces." The reactionaries "see that things are not going in

PART III DECLINE

their direction and try their best to prevent this." But – and here Suslov supplemented his talking points with notes scribbled in the margins – "we know who we are dealing with." The notes continued: "We do not overdramatize the situation. On the whole, the initiative is in our hands, and the question is merely in energetically repulsing the reactionaries' attempts at a counterattack."[87]

In a true condominium, the Soviets would have taken US concerns in Angola on board, forcing their client to participate in peace talks, perhaps even a coalition government. This was what Kissinger might have expected, even though his own record of undercutting the Soviets in the Middle East and in Cyprus gave him little ground to stand on. The problem with the condominium idea was that it was inherently unstable. Each power continued to undercut the other despite detente. The temptation to win clients and to shift that correlation of forces a little further in one's own favor seemed overpowering. Angola was a prominent example. It must be remembered, too, that above all the Soviet leaders were realists. In their world, detente itself was enabled by Soviet strength. Whatever contributed to Soviet strength therefore contributed to detente itself: where was the problem?

Yet, there was also something the Soviets never quite grasped. America's defeat in Vietnam, followed within months by serious setbacks in Angola, undermined Kissinger who now looked weak and helpless in the face of Soviet pressure. "You could see," reported Ambassador Dobrynin in February 1976, "that his [Kissinger's] self-esteem was seriously hurt by the failure of his Angolan adventure and [became] a new serious blow to his personal prestige, and he is just not willing to reconcile himself to this."[88] "The emperor has no clothes," Kissinger's aide told the US journalist Elizabeth Drew. "He's down to his underwear in terms of what he has in backing."[89] But Kissinger had been one of the faces of detente. His declining stock and growing resentment at the Soviet unwillingness to wheel and deal in Angola meant that the secretary of state was no longer as committed to detente as he claimed in meetings with Dobrynin.

His boss in the White House, Gerald Ford, had even less at stake. As the electoral contest heated up, Ford proved only too willing to trump up the Soviet threat if that helped him ward off potential challengers like former California governor Ronald Reagan. Ford's national security adviser, Brent Scowcroft, privately pleaded with Dobrynin not to take the campaign rhetoric seriously: all the anti-Soviet excitement was just Ford's "pre-electoral tactical maneuvering."[90] Kissinger observed in May 1976 that Ford was "close to panic" on the account of Reagan's challenge. "His fear of losing [primaries] determines all of his actions."[91] The same fear cast

CHAPTER 15 DECLINE

its long shadow over Kissinger himself. Reagan castigated Kissinger for a foreign policy that had led to "the loss of American military supremacy ... All I can see is what other nations the world over see: the collapse of the American will and the retreat of American power." Detente, Reagan and his like claimed, had been a "one way street" that gave America little more than "the right to sell Pepsi-Cola in Siberia."[92] The challenge from the right put pressure on Kissinger to make detente work at a time the Soviets appeared least willing to go along.

The toughening of American public discourse had real consequences for Soviet–American relations. Having outperformed the Americans in Angola, the Kremlin presently had to contend with the increasingly vocal advocates of get-tough policies. Detente was rapidly withering on the vine. Being recognized as a powerful enemy inevitably goes with being treated like one. Whether Brezhnev in the dimness of his asthenia realized this is an altogether different story.

16

TENSIONS MOUNT

In 1812, at the height of Napoleon's war with Russia, a Frenchman named Charles Louis Lesur published a book, in which he infamously summarized what he claimed to be the Last Testament of the Russian czar Peter the Great. In that Testament, Peter supposedly counselled his successors to seek world domination by stirring up quarrels in Europe and extending Russia's power southward, towards the Middle East.[1] Long exposed as a hoax – it is one of the most well-known episodes in the history of political forgeries – the fake Testament looked convincing enough to the Chinese leaders to use it as a rough guide to Moscow's intentions.[2] It was advertised in Chinese propaganda, and was even brought up by senior policy makers in conversations with foreign counterparts. As the 1970s yielded to the 1980s, the Chinese leaders, from Deng Xiaoping down, conjured memories of the distant past, arguing that "that Soviet imperialism started with Peter the Great" and that it followed a certain clear, immutable logic.[3]

Deng Xiaoping had a special theory to explain Moscow's foreign policy – the "barbell" theory. According to this theory, the Soviet Union drove southward at two points. One side of the barbell was Southeast Asia and the Pacific; the other – the Middle East and India. The connecting point – the bar of the barbell – was the Strait of Malacca, which, should it ever come under the Soviet control, would give the Kremlin a stranglehold on global commerce, in particular oil shipments. The West would then have to either surrender or fight a world war. In words reminiscent of George Kennan's Long Telegram, Deng argued that "wherever there is vacuum in the world, the Soviet Union gets in there."[4] Their ultimate goal: "control the strategic resources of the entire Middle East."[5] At the other end, acting through Vietnam, they would invade Thailand.[6]

These stark predictions were in no sense original. The notion that the Kremlin was determined to acquire ice-free ports because its existing ports were allegedly frozen for most of the year was a common claim for all manner of experts in geopolitics. President Carter's national security adviser, Zbigniew Brzezinski, coined the term "the arc of crises" to

452

CHAPTER 16 TENSIONS MOUNT

describe the secret Soviet strategy of subversion of disparate states spread out along the Indian Ocean coast. "A strange theory ... an absolute fairytale," commented Brezhnev.[7] "We don't need the Persian Gulf. All of this is made up, it's lies."[8] Few believed him. Whether or not he followed the fake Testament of Peter the Great, Brezhnev appeared to preside over a remarkable Soviet expansion into the third world. From Angola to the Horn of Africa, to Afghanistan, to Southeast Asia, the Soviets went from one gain to the next. Even the 1978 Islamic revolution in Iran (which was in no sense a Soviet plot) appeared from Washington like a part of some global Moscow-directed conspiracy.

Could one say, in retrospect, that Brzezinski confused Soviet capabilities with Soviet intentions? This would not be entirely accurate: he did not confuse them, he deliberately conflated them. "In the past," he wrote to President Carter in 1979, "we could discount Soviet intentions because Soviet capabilities were limited; today, even benign Soviet intentions are becoming increasingly suspect because of the implications of Soviet capabilities."[9] It did not matter what the Soviets actually did: their power was an unacceptable threat on its own terms. Such perceptions helped erode whatever support there remained in Washington for detente with the USSR. By the late 1970s the Cold War was back with a vengeance. Why did this happen, and why did the Soviet leaders, who treasured detente as the key accomplishment of the Brezhnev era, not moderate their appetites for the sake of developing their partnership with the United States or addressing Beijing's worries? Would it have mattered if they did, given how their capabilities alone seemed to imply an intention to dominate the world? This is the story of this chapter.

SOVIET–AMERICAN RELATIONS DURING THE CARTER YEARS

The 1976 American presidential election campaign left the Soviet leadership in a state of utter exasperation. Gerald Ford, for all his brave promises, failed to steer detente in the desired direction, while the hostile anti-Soviet rhetoric of his campaign raised questions about the president's true priorities. Ford was under pressure to fend off critics from the left and from the right, especially from the fellow Republican candidate Ronald Reagan who, in a testy run for the nomination, accused Ford of neglecting US national interests in his pursuit of agreements with Moscow. Meanwhile, Democratic nominee Jimmy Carter annoyed the Soviets by ramping up human rights rhetoric and by slamming the 1975 Helsinki Final Act for supposedly ceding Eastern Europe to the USSR.[10] "We have been turned into some kind

PART III DECLINE

of a scarecrow," Brezhnev grumbled just days before the American election. "Everywhere you hear: 'The Russians are arming themselves, the Russians could invade America,' and so on."[11]

Given how badly things turned out under Ford, his departure was not mourned in Moscow. In fact, Brezhnev was willing to give Carter the benefit of a doubt, especially since two respectable envoys, the old-time Soviet hand Averell Harriman and the businessman Armand Hammer, turned up in the USSR before the election to advertise him to the Soviet leaders. Hammer was especially blunt, telling Brezhnev that Carter's rhetoric was just that – rhetoric, and that "after the election much of what is being said now, will be forgotten." Carter, Hammer said, was a "realistic politician." "He will face real problems and real responsibility as the leader of the country."[12]

Whether or not Brezhnev was reassured, he decided, in his words, to "show goodwill" to the president-elect; this he did in a speech on January 18, 1977. Carter responded with a goodwill letter of his own, highlighting his continued interest in arms control but also reiterating one theme that would soon be causing a lot of friction in Soviet–American relations: "we cannot be indifferent to the fate of freedom and individual human rights."[13] "I had made it clear in the campaign," Carter later recalled, "that I was not going to ignore Soviet abuse of human rights, as I believed some previous administrations had done."[14]

To drive the point home, Carter replied to a letter authored by the Soviet physicist and dissident Andrei Sakharov (in the letter – one of his many to candidate and then President Carter – Sakharov decried the "unbearable situation" with human rights in the Soviet Union and Eastern Europe).[15] In his response to Sakharov, Carter reiterated that human rights would be "a central concern of my Administration."[16] The dissident showed this letter to foreign reports at his Moscow apartment, from where it went straight to the pages of the *New York Times*.[17]

The Soviets were scandalized. Brezhnev's foreign policy alter-ego Andrei Aleksandrov-Agentov penned a note for the general secretary, calling Carter's letter an "idiotic move."[18] He was encouraged, however, by the criticism of this move in the international media. He forwarded Brezhnev a TASS selection of Western media comments on this story. These pointed out that criticizing the Soviet human rights record too loudly would be counterproductive because the Soviets might then crack down on the dissident movement or create problems in other areas, such as nuclear arms control. "Although the President denies that his support for human rights is a slap in Russia's face," one of the translated

CHAPTER 16 TENSIONS MOUNT

commentaries went, "the Russians seemingly consider it precisely a slap in the face and may now conclude that he went too far." Brezhnev underlined the words "he went too far."[19]

Aleksandrov-Agentov's view was that Moscow could not let the matter rest. He recommended that his boss think about a tough response "in order not to create the impression that you can treat the Soviet Union any way you want."[20] Accordingly, Brezhnev – and by then it was increasingly a collective appellation, which usually included Defense Minister Dmitry Ustinov, Yury Andropov (for the KGB), Andrei Gromyko (for the Foreign Ministry), and Boris Ponomarev (for the Central Committee) – sent Carter a lengthy response on February 25. "This is our position of principle," the letter went. "We do not intend to impose upon your country or upon other countries our rules but neither shall we allow interference in our internal affairs whatever pseudo-humanitarian slogans are used to present it."[21]

The Politburo also approved instructions for Ambassador Dobrynin who was to tell Carter's new secretary of state, Cyrus Vance, that America, too, had its problems with human rights and that, "by the way" (a classic iteration of what later would become known as "whataboutism"), Washington was happily supporting all kinds of "dictatorial, anti-democratic regimes," without worrying all that much about their dismal human rights record.[22] Carter was undeterred and just days after receiving this letter, hosted in the White House another prominent dissident, Vladimir Bukovsky, whom the Soviet authorities had previously expelled in return for the release of the Chilean Communist leader Luis Corvalán. "He [Bukovsky] is a through-and-through conman," Brezhnev complained days later. "Is this the President's business [to receive him]? How can we react to this?"[23]

The Soviet propaganda machine in its turn began to criticize Carter. When the latter complained of being thus mistreated, Brezhnev had this to say: "If we had normal relations, we would not treat him badly. Carter's predecessors were not gold either, but Nixon met us halfway and we met him halfway. We had a meeting. Ford also met us halfway and we also met him halfway. Honestly, I don't understand what Carter wants."[24]

The human rights agenda loomed large in Soviet–American relations throughout the Carter presidency, and it was a constant irritant for Moscow.[25] The Republicans had proven to be difficult partners but at least, as Kissinger put it in a conversation with Dobrynin (whom he continued to see regularly after leaving office), they had never been attached to such "silly things" as human rights.[26] But Carter's emphasis on the problem drove the Soviet leaders to the point of exasperation. Carter's national

PART III DECLINE

security adviser Zbigniew Brzezinski thought he knew why: "The reason that Brezhnev et al are reacting so strongly to your insistence on human rights," he wrote to Carter on April 1, 1977, "is not because they fear that we will make human rights a condition for our relations with them; they fear this insistence because they know that human rights is a compelling idea, and that associating America with this idea not only strengthens us, but it also generates pressures from within their own system."[27]

But Brzezinski did not fully grasp the problem. The Soviet leaders were overreacting for the same reason that the Chinese overreacted, in the late 1950s–early 1960s, to Soviet lecturing about the correct revolutionary path. In both cases, the problem was that on paper these were "equal" relationships. In practice, however, the Chinese in their time, and the Soviets now, felt that they were being forced into a humiliating position of delinquents, being presently taught by someone who (in all truth) was also not beyond reproach. This resentment of moral hierarchy, which placed the Soviet leaders in an inferior position, undercutting their legitimacy, was the main reason why Carter's intervention on behalf of alleged "renegades" and "criminals" like Sakharov and Bukovsky (and a few others) caused so much consternation in the Kremlin.[28]

This was the unpleasant backdrop to the first major Soviet–American engagement of the Carter years – Cyrus Vance's March 1977 trip to Moscow. Vance brought ambitious arms control proposals that went well beyond the SALT-II thresholds agreed at Vladivostok (proposing, for instance, to cut overall limits of strategic missiles to 1,800–2,000 in place of the previously agreed 2,400, and pushing the Soviets on the "Backfire" bomber in exchange for proposed American concessions on the cruise missile, which, the Soviets thought, the Americans had already given away in 1974).[29]

Brezhnev used the first meeting with Vance (on March 28, 1977) to read out a litany of complaints about Carter's interference in the Soviet Union's domestic affairs. The Americans, Brezhnev said, should look into violations of human rights in their own country, with its gender and racial inequalities and the lack of social care. Reading out from a dossier prepared by his aides, he went even so far as to cite US unemployment and literacy statistics to argue that the US had huge unresolved problems of its own and was therefore in no position to tell others how to protect human rights.[30] Brezhnev even read out translated bits from a letter by the US novelist James Baldwin to Jimmy Carter (which was published in the *New York Times* in January), in which Baldwin called on Carter to address racial injustice in the United States, and to which Carter – as Brezhnev was careful to stress – had not yet responded.[31] The message

CHAPTER 16 TENSIONS MOUNT

was clear enough: the US president had no business writing letters to Soviet dissidents if he was not engaging with his domestic critics. Anatoly Chernyaev, who received a copy of the record, noted in his diary that he thought Brezhnev and Gromyko were "fairly rude" with Vance but it is telling that even as an astute observer as Chernyaev (who was himself a closet dissident) found Carter's human rights agenda quite over the top. "Carter ... does not understand," he wrote, "that he looks like a petty provocateur in the eyes of serious Soviet people."[32]

Brezhnev and Vance met again two days later but the discussion on arms control went nowhere, with Brezhnev accusing Vance of reneging on the Vladivostok understanding, and generally attempting to secure unilateral gains at Soviet expense. "Do you think that we are naive simpletons," he charged, "that we'll agree to this?"[33] Even Chernyaev, after reading about Vance's arms control proposals, concluded that the Americans were out to "dupe" the Soviets: their limits, while looking good on paper, in fact maximized Washington's technological advantage. "Do they really think that we cannot do without their capital and technologies (which we pay for with gold, and which for years rust in the open under the snow)?! Do they really, like we do, believe in nuclear blackmail, and want to use it to push us out from world politics?!"[34] Brezhnev's rejection was unsurprising. An early effort to relaunch detente prematurely ran aground.[35]

"When I learned ... what package Vance proposed in Moscow, I told Vance that he should not have entered negotiations with proposals like this in order to save his reputation in the eyes of the Soviet leadership."[36] This was Kissinger's reaction to the failure of his successor at the State Department, a failure the former secretary of state clearly "delighted in" (according to Dobrynin at least). The problem with Carter, Kissinger explained, was that he was "trapped in his own propagandistic illusions" and that there was not a single "influential" person in his circle (here he was obviously referring to himself) who could tell the president what the Soviet Union may and may not accept.

CHINA

The spat over human rights and the failure of Vance's mission to Moscow derailed early hopes for the revival of detente and weakened those who – like Vance – were invested in improving the climate of Soviet–American relations. The main beneficiary of this in the White House was Brzezinski who was widely seen as a Russia hawk. Born in 1928, Brzezinski was five years Kissinger's junior. He was born in Warsaw, but his father (a Polish diplomat)

PART III DECLINE

took him in tow to France, Germany, the Soviet Union, and finally Canada. After the Second World War, he studied and then worked at Harvard alongside Kissinger. Brzezinski then continued his academic career at Columbia, moving in and out of policy and politics. In the early 1970s he headed the Trilateral Commission, a forum founded by the financier and philanthropist David Rockefeller to facilitate closer relations between the United States, Western Europe, and Japan. (It was in this context that Zbig – as he was known to friends – became something of a foreign policy tutor to Georgia's young governor, Jimmy Carter.)

Still, his selection as the national security adviser raised eyebrows. As prominent a Democrat as Averell Harriman (himself a leading expert on Soviet affairs and, in the early days of the Cold War, a prominent "hawk") called it an "irony of fate" that the "ambitious Polish, traditionally anti-Russian Jesuit" was put in charge of looking after relations with the Soviet Union.[37] "Appointing Brzezinski, a Pole, to the role of the main adviser on Russian affairs," Harriman said, "is like appointing an Irishman the President's adviser on England."[38] Nor did Kissinger hide his competitive disdain for his successor. Brzezinski, he told Dobrynin, is a "theoretician of Communism" who "knows nothing" of strategic questions because "unlike Kissinger, he never studied them" and who "dominates in the White House over the President and his closest circle with his knowledge of quotes from Marx and Lenin." It was Brzezinski who was prodding Carter on the path of an ideological struggle with the USSR.[39]

These unflattering comments were carefully recorded by the Soviet ambassador, and forwarded to Moscow, adding to a sense of frustration with the unfulfilled promises of detente.

Meanwhile, Brzezinski pressed Carter to let him take the lead on an issue of major strategic importance: normalization of America's relations with Communist China. The latter's human rights record made the Soviets look decidedly reasonable but that did not deter Brzezinski who acted on the premise that the enemy of my enemy is my friend. The turn to China came as a result of what one astute observer called an "all-out civil war within the Carter Administration."[40] Cyrus Vance – reflecting the interests of the Democratic establishment (the likes of Harriman) – wanted to soft-pedal China and focus on the relationship with the USSR, or at least to take an even-handed approach. But Brzezinski, undercutting his rival in the State Department, prioritized Beijing.

In May 1978 Brzezinski travelled to China to jumpstart the normalization process. He told Deng Xiaoping that he shared his apprehension of the Soviet Union: "we face the same challenge from the polar bear." But

458

CHAPTER 16 TENSIONS MOUNT

the Chinese leader remained unimpressed, accusing the United States of softness and encouraging Soviet aggression.[41] Human rights never came up.

Brzezinski had many detractors but he brushed them aside for their inability to understand his strategy. One example was the bizarre conversation in the Oval Office on June 4, 1980 between then-US ambassador in Moscow, Thomas J. Watson, and Jimmy Carter. Watson – who privately worried about Carter's policy – attempted to convince the president that it was best for the United States to steer a neutral course between China and the USSR: "I think we should keep in mind the basic nature of the Chinese and what they believe in." By not leaning overly in China's direction, the United States would not antagonize the Soviets who, the ambassador felt, had a "paranoid fear of China." Moreover, the Chinese, Watson continued, "have a tendency to jump around from bed to bed. And I think we ought to make sure they are lashed down to our bed before we undertake actions, which we might regret later on." Brzezinski (who walked in on the conversation) retorted at this point: "You have to remember that we are very sexy people."[42]

Nine years later, to the day, Deng buried these hopeful expectations when he unleashed the army to crack down on unarmed student protesters in Tiananmen Square.

The future "butcher of Beijing," Deng Xiaoping recovered his position as China's leader after a brief power struggle that followed Mao's death in 1976. Diminutive in stature but intense in demeanor, Deng was well known to the world. He was best known to the Soviet leadership who had the singular displeasure of hosting him in 1963 for the last-ditch effort to avert the crash of the Sino-Soviet alliance. Deng rained vitriol: the Soviets were behaving like "gods" and "fathers," daily betraying Marxism-Leninism, and colluding with the United States to rule the world. "The United States is an imperialist country, the Soviet Union is a socialist country," Deng charged indignantly. "How can in this case anyone imagine ... that the United States and the Soviet Union can coexist harmoniously? This is perfectly unthinkable, and one must not allow any illusions in this regard."[43]

But the passage of fifteen years, which included the harrowing experience of being purged and exiled during the Cultural Revolution, cleared Deng's vision. Once he assumed full power, Deng moved rapidly to do what he had accused the Soviet leaders of doing: embrace the United States. Sino-American relations were normalized in January 1979.

On January 28 Deng arrived in Washington. It was his second visit to the bastion of imperialism. The first time he came was in April 1974, to criticize the hegemony of the two superpowers from the UN podium. On that earlier occasion, Deng articulated Mao's theory of the three worlds, by which China was firmly entrenched in the third world. But five years later, the West (including Japan) ranked on Deng's list of priorities far above the third world, with its revolutionary poverty and desolation. Even some of the terminology was beginning to change: the third world was now sometimes referred to as the "lower-rung world" (*dilan shijie*).[44] Deng was determined to climb up the ladder. "If we do not develop ourselves," he said, betraying concerns that had been central to China's foreign policy since 1949, "people will look down on us and even bully us."[45]

Save for sporadic demonstrations by American Maoists who, with foresight, condemned Deng for betraying the revolution in angry outbursts complete with the waving of Mao's Little Red Book, and uneventful protests by a handful of pro-Taiwanese activists, Deng – now the Man of the Year, according to the Time magazine – met with a very warm welcome in Washington, DC and in other places on his itinerary. An indication of his priorities, this itinerary included visits to the Johnson Space Center in Houston, a Ford automobile plant in Atlanta, and a Boeing assembly plant in Seattle. The Chinese leader nailed deals on the purchase of a Landsat mapping satellite, a communications satellite for color television, and a 50-billion volt nuclear particle accelerator. Reportedly, in the airplane on the way back to China, Deng, very much satisfied with the visit, told his assistants: "If we look back, we find that all of those [third world countries] that were on the side of the United States have been successful [in their modernization drive], whereas all of those that were against the United States have not been successful. We shall be on the side of the United States."[46]

Although Carter went out of his way to reassure Moscow that normalization with China did not target third countries, the Soviet leaders watched Deng's visit with fatalistic anticipation. If they had read the transcripts of Carter's meetings with Deng, most of their worries would have been confirmed. Deng and Carter discussed military cooperation against the USSR, including the US proposal to install an intelligence-gathering station in Xinjiang to monitor Soviet strategic communications in Central Asia. In 1958 Mao angrily condemned a similar proposal by the Soviets as an impossible violation of China's sovereignty. The row over that proposal had played an important role in the chain of events that led to the breakdown of the Sino-Soviet alliance. For Deng, too, it was a major step to approve of something like this. Negotiations over the US monitoring station continued into the summer of 1979, with Deng's condition being the sale of US weapons to China (in particular, he wanted a squadron of

CHAPTER 16 TENSIONS MOUNT

fighters, F-14s, F-15s, or even F-16s). But, facing Washington's resistance to the idea, Deng gave up his conditions by August, and the monitoring station was installed after all.

All of that was a matter of great concern to the aging Soviet leaders who returned to Sino-American military cooperation again and again at Politburo meetings, alternately blaming the Americans for instigating a Sino-Soviet war, and the Chinese for attempting to provoke a thermonuclear conflict of superpowers in order the rule the world – or whatever is left of it – in the aftermath. "A 'strong' China would ... begin swallowing neighboring countries, occupy regions of vital importance to the entire world, and will certainly not serve as an instrument in the hands of the USA or some other country."[47] So, at least, the Soviet Politburo wanted everyone to believe, approving special instructions in 1980 to persuade the international public opinion that China was the real danger to world peace. Brezhnev, who was still rolled out on occasion for various summits and conferences, read out angry denunciations of the Chinese perfidy.[48] Foreign Minister Gromyko complained about the inadequate American reaction to Deng's anti-Soviet rhetoric. "You (i.e. the West) may be in a euphoric mood now about China," he said, "but the time will come when you will be shedding [tears]."[49]

Brzezinski was not going to be swayed by such scaremongering. Recounting the details of Deng's visit to Dobrynin, the National Security Adviser claimed that he understood that the Chinese were "playing a game" but that closer US relations with China were in the interest of international stability. Dobrynin reported that Brzezinski saw a "guarantee" of a lasting Sino-American friendship even after China becomes strong, in ten to fifteen years, in that "the Chinese have traditionally treated the Russians with suspicion, but they have [never] held unfriendly sentiments towards the Americans."[50]

Of course, Brzezinski's views were far from universally shared in the American policy community. Worried predictions of Ambassador Watson have already been noted upon. His boss Cyrus Vance sounded a note of gloom in his own conversations with Dobrynin, whom he told that, in his opinion, by the end of the century the USSR and the United States "would have to unite against the Chinese threat."[51]

A similar lack of consensus was observable in Moscow around the same time. There were those like Oleg Rakhmanin, the famously anti-Chinese apparatchik in the Central Committee who was deeply opposed to any rapprochement with Beijing and lambasted the Chinese for their suspected hegemonic designs and expansionism. But there were others, for instance, the Foreign Ministry's China hands, who held more nuanced views.

PART III DECLINE

Thus, the head of the Foreign Ministry's South Asia Department, Nikolai Sudarikov (who had watched the Sino-Soviet split unfold from the Soviet Embassy in Beijing), skeptically noted in February 1979 that Deng "seems to have reached the conclusion that in the U.S.A. China has a suitable partner who can help China as a donor to get out of the rut that it is in." However, Sudarikov continued, "it would not be in the interest of the U.S.A. to see China grow very strong nor would it be in China's interest to be a horse in a troika pulling the American cart. China would not want to play the role of a junior partner."[52]

Similarly, the ministry's leading China hand Mikhail Kapitsa recognized China's anti-Soviet stance for what it was: an effort to secure Western support in China's modernization. "China has nothing to lose from anti-Soviet views," he explained in 1982. "They pay with these views for the Western capital." The good news, though, was that the Chinese "never befriended anyone for long."[53] Kapitsa even looked forward to the time – ten to fifteen years hence – when the Chinese might "open their eyes" and adopt a position of equidistance between the Soviet Union and the West.[54] Yet as the 1980s dawned, as Soviet–American relations reached new lows, and as Beijing bravely advertised itself as America's most reliable friend in Asia, such optimistic prospects appeared very, very dim.

Meanwhile, despite the setback to Sino-American relations in the form of the Taiwan Relations Act, passed by Congress in March 1979 against bitter Chinese protests, and despite the failure of China's efforts to obtain US weapons, Deng had every reason to think that his gamble on normalization – when he made certain last-minute concessions to the United States on Taiwan – had paid off. What made this work was Deng Xiaoping's temporary willingness to find for himself – and for China – a role in the American-led world order. There was no hope for true equality in his calculations, nor any claims of a condominium. Understanding that modernization of China trumped all other concerns, Deng scaled down immediate ambitions in favor of the long game.[55]

This was not a relationship that could last, just as the Sino-Soviet alliance was not a relationship that could last. Stable relationships are those that combine shared values with the two parties' recognition of their respective places in the relationship hierarchy. China and the USSR shared values but Mao was unwilling to find a place for China in the Soviet-led order. Deng did not share America's values, but he was temporarily willing to defer to American leadership until such time that it was no longer necessary. The more perceptive thinkers in both the United States and the Soviet Union recognized that the time would come: the question was not whether but when.

462

CHAPTER 16 TENSIONS MOUNT

THE SANDS OF OGADEN

Brzezinski was less interested in the long-term prospects of China's rise and more in the immediate imperatives of the struggle against a common adversary. He was particularly worried about the Soviet penetration of Africa, even when they acted through proxies. Thus, during their meeting in Beijing in May 1978, Brzezinski pressed Deng to do more "to expose the role of Cuba as a Soviet agent" in Africa, where Cuban troops, Brzezinski averred, were fighting on the Soviet Union's behalf.[56] Deng appeared receptive but what could China really do? The demands of economic reform at home took the wind out of Beijing's adventures in the third world: China was losing interest in Africa, at least for the time-being. But China's graceful exit did little to lessen Cold War tensions on the continent. Before the decade was out, the Americans found themselves at odds with the Soviets and the Cubans in a bizarre conflict on the African Horn. Brzezinski famously claimed that their struggle there "buried" detente. He probably exaggerated, though of course the conflict contributed to rising superpower tensions.

Cuba's victories in Angola in 1975–76 helped Fidel Castro's self-esteem and bolstered his political legitimacy. By the late 1970s he emerged as something of an unsolicited strategist for the socialist bloc, a position once also sought by Mao Zedong in the wake of China's victories in the Korean War. History goes in circles. But Castro's challenge was of incomparably lesser magnitude for the Soviet leaders than Mao's had been. Cuba was a small country, economically and militarily dependent on the USSR. Castro made no claims to theoretical sophistication of the universally applicable kind that undercut and enraged the Soviet leaders in the late 1950s–early 1960s. For the most part, he deferred to the Soviets. But in places that mattered relatively little to Moscow – for example, Africa – the comandante could and did help shape the Soviet policy, especially at a time when Brezhnev's decline left the Soviet Union without anything resembling a coherent strategy. Emboldened by Angola, he now looked for new opportunities to leave his mark.

An opportunity presented itself soon enough. On March 16, 1977 Castro took part in what was perhaps one of the most surreal encounters in the history of African "socialism." The occasion was a meeting between Somali dictator Mohamed Siad Barre and up-and-coming Ethiopian tyrant Mengistu Haile Mariam. Two things must be noted about Siad Barre and Mengistu. First, they considered themselves – and their countries – "Marxist-Leninist." Second, they deeply loathed each other. Presently the two met

463

in Aden, in a Cuban-sponsored effort to resolve their seemingly intractable territorial conflict. Castro was there to mediate. But very quickly he found himself siding with Ethiopia against Somalia.

There was a good reason to feel frustrated with Siad Barre. His territorial claim on the Somali-populated Ogaden – an integral and very substantial part of Ethiopia – irritated most of Somalia's neighbors, most of Africa, and indeed most reasonable observers around the world. Somalia's long-time superpower sponsor, the Soviet Union, was not amused (given Moscow's obsession with maintaining the inviolability of postwar frontiers and the lingering territorial dispute with China, it could hardly be otherwise). Siad Barre's argument – that Ethiopia was an "empire" and that it had to be "decolonized" in accordance with Leninist principles of self-determination – found little traction with Lenin's successors in the Kremlin.

But for Castro, there was something else, too. The problem was Siad Barre's unbearable arrogance. That came across all too clear in the Aden meeting. A short while later the comandante had this to report: "I have made up my mind about Siad Barre, he is above all a chauvinist. Chauvinism is the most important factor in him. Socialism is just an outer shell that is supposed to make him more attractive … The party is there only to support his personal power." Siad Barre tried to sound like "the great Socialist, the great Marxist."[57] For Castro, who no doubt considered *himself* to be a great socialist and a great Marxist, such behavior by an unaccomplished former general of the gendarmerie – who had little to his record except for staging a military coup in his country and then running it ineffectively on Soviet credit – was really too much to countenance. Castro reported on his observations to Moscow.[58] The Soviets had to think hard.

Only a few years earlier Somalia seemed poised to become Moscow's outpost in East Africa.[59] A year after coming to power in October 1969 Siad Barre proclaimed adherence to "scientific socialism." One could take this proclamation as an interesting example of how third world countries chose one "modernity" (socialism) or the other (capitalism), a salient characteristic of the Cold War. This may, however, needlessly complicate the issue. "Building socialism" in a largely premodern, religiously conservative, tribal society was less about choosing a particular path towards modernity and more about bolstering Somalia's standing in African politics, and Siad Barre's own legitimacy. It is hardly surprising, then, that in an internal directive, issued in November 1970, he insisted that "by proclaiming socialism … we increased [Somalia's] international prestige." The same directive, however, was predictably thin,

CHAPTER 16 TENSIONS MOUNT

when it came to defining what "socialism" would mean for Somalia, other than stating that it would end "exploitation of man by man," and lead to "social fairness" and "overarching progress."

In June 1976 Siad Barre established the Somalian Revolutionary Socialist Party, thus earning the sought-after appellation of "comrade Siad" from Brezhnev – and renewed promises of military aid.[60] Moscow provided the usual mix of credits, equipment, specialists, and weapons. Why? Certainly not because anyone seriously thought that Somalia was ready for socialism; in fact, the Soviet diplomats in Mogadishu argued with Siad Barre that rather than pursuing "socialism," he should opt for the less ambitious task of "noncapitalist development." (Siad rejected such moderation, suggesting that noncapitalist development was a hard concept to explain, whereas socialism was understood by everyone, and, indeed, compatible with the Holy Koran).

Was it because Somalia was strategically positioned on the Horn of Africa, and offered a promise of naval bases? To some extent. It is true that some of the Soviet reporting on Somalia specifically referred to the country's "strategic importance" – but Soviet interest in inserting themselves into the Horn of Africa fell far short of Siad Barre's expectations. He repeatedly called for increasing the Soviet military presence in the Horn as a means of "deterrence" (his term) against internal and external enemies. He not only pushed for bigger Soviet bases but also offered himself as a conduit for further Soviet advances on the African continent. Moscow took the bait, eventually establishing a base in Berbera in the Gulf of Aden (though not, despite Siad Barre's prodding, in Mogadishu), but it was less a case of actively pursuing an imperialist venture than being dragged into one by an overly eager client.

Finally, there was, as was often the case, the Chinese angle to the Soviet involvement. Soviet reporting from Mogadishu consistently zeroed in on the threat of Beijing's subversion, and blamed the Somali leadership for trying to play the Chinese card in order to "prod the Soviet Union to provide more effective aid."[61] (The threat was widely overblown: the Chinese were already on their way out of Africa.) There were echoes here of the Sino-Soviet struggle for global revolutionary mantle. The struggle was moot in the early 1970s but a sense of inertia remained.

In short, the Soviets became involved in Somalia for a combination of strategic and reputational reasons. The relationship was of course rationalized in ideological terms but not because anyone in Moscow really had any hope of turning Somalia into a socialist country but because adherence to "scientific socialism" really meant deference to the Soviet Union's global leadership. Siad Barre knew how to play that game, endorsing Moscow's international initiatives (in particular in the Middle East) and recognizing, when needed, that the Soviets played a "leading role" in beating back imperialist ploys.[62] The Somali leaders referred to Marx and Lenin on every suitable occasion, and impressed the Soviets by requesting Marxist literature for Somali libraries.[63] That, too, was a part of the ritual of implicit and explicit recognition that underpinned Soviet–Somali relations at the height of the Cold War. Such requests were promptly reported to Moscow, impressing the Africa hands in the Communist Party of the Soviet Union (CPSU) International Department. Meanwhile, a leading official of the same International Department, Anatoly Chernyaev, ruefully confided to his diary that "the main leaders of the CPSU have not touched a book by Lenin (never mind Marx) in decades," nor, he added, their advisers. "And they do not feel the need to."[64]

The 1974 revolution in Ethiopia, the emergence of another "socialist," Mengistu, and the quarrel between Mengistu and Siad Barre, presented the Soviets with a dilemma. Mengistu was doing what Siad Barre had done just a few years earlier: proclaiming deference to Moscow's global leadership, committing his country to the "world revolutionary process," and spicing up his rhetoric with references to Marx and Lenin. The cooling of Ethiopia's relations with the United States – the country's former superpower patron – offered additional proof that Mengistu was for real, even while Siad Barre's flirting with the United States and the region's conservative Arab states seemed to prove Castro's point about the Somali leader's treachery. In December 1976 Ethiopia signed its first arms deal with the USSR, and in May 1977 Mengistu was invited to Moscow to hold counsel with Brezhnev. Mengistu, like Siad Barre earlier, bent over backwards to pledge loyalty to the Soviet Union, promising to "make every sacrifice for revolution" and even citing from Lenin. Brezhnev urged him to build up a Marxist party – "the soul of the revolution" – and promised more weapons.[65] A Soviet postmortem on the visit concluded that Mengistu "gave the impression of a serious figure who firmly believes in his cause, although he still lacks political and state experience."[66]

Given their relatively good relations with both Siad Barre and Mengistu, the last thing the Soviet leadership wanted to do was to get involved in their territorial dispute but the worsening situation left them with few alternatives. The key was to work on the Somalis to see whether they could be brought about to moderate their irredentist policies. Somalia and Ethiopia, Brezhnev told Somalia's vice president, Ali Samatar, in June 1977, reading from notes, were "bones that were stuck in the imperialists' throats ... One should not gladden the imperialists." Samatar, for his

CHAPTER 16 TENSIONS MOUNT

part, promised the Soviets that Somalia would not be the first to start a war. He also begged for economic aid, however, implicitly linking good behavior with Soviet willingness or otherwise to subsidize Somalia's modernization. "We are waiting for the proof of the Soviet Union's political and economic support." Brezhnev mumbled a vague commitment in response but warned the Somalis not to think that they could get a better deal somewhere else, for example in America or the "reactionary" Arab world. "Do not believe those who today are promising you mountains of gold but tomorrow will be prepared to strangle your regime and liquidate Somalia's independence."[67]

In July 1977, the Soviets sponsored a last-ditch effort to resolve the issue at a round of talks between their two clients in Moscow. "We are deeply convinced," read Brezhnev's letter to Siad Barre, "that there are no questions that cannot be resolved if one has good will, if they are approached with an open heart, and without bias."[68] But these pleas fell on deaf ears. Perhaps, too, Siad Barre sensed an opportunity, for Mengistu was busy dealing with a separatist albeit also "Marxist-Leninist" movement in Eritrea, in the north of the country. In any case, on July 23, Somalia invaded Ethiopia in the east and moved rapidly to extend control deep into Ogaden.

All of that happened when Brezhnev was on his annual vacation in Crimea. The Soviet leader's understanding of these events was limited, not just because of their inherent complexity but because of his mental decay. Back in May, "upset" Brezhnev wondered whether he should speak to the ambassadors of the two countries; Boris Ponomarev (the head of the International Department) advised him to "stay out of this mess."[69] At the time of Somalia's invasion, Brezhnev – judging by his diary entries – spent most of his time weighing himself (clothed *and* naked), or playing the dominoes, and just bathing in the sea. Surprisingly, he still participated in occasional meetings with high-profile foreigners, and – in a particularly embarrassing episode in June 1977 – even toured France. His French hosts were surprised to discover that the Soviet leader read out his statements as if seeing them for the first time, that he "seemed bewildered about the facts," and that "he acted as though he had never heard of Djibouti."[70] In view of his rapidly declining mental faculties, who knows – perhaps this was not an act!

The Soviet leader registered an awareness of Mengistu's plight in his diary entries, although he repeatedly misspelled the client's name (on one occasion calling him "mongoose").[71] On August 9, while in Crimea, he told Bulgaria's leader Todor Zhivkov that Somalia had veered too far to the "right," and that he empathized with Ethiopia, which was under pressure

Figure 23 Leonid Brezhnev on holiday in the late 1970s.
Source: Laski Diffusion/Getty Images.

on several fronts. "If the progressive regimes," Brezhnev told Zhivkov, "are unable to ... give a joint, collective rebuff [to the imperialists], the task of Africa's socialist orientation may be thrown back by many years." It should be added perhaps that he did not so much "tell" Zhivkov as read out notes, prepared for him by his aide Anatoly Blatov. When Zhivkov attempted to engage the Soviet leader on one of the issues raised in the notes, Brezhnev, instead of responding, requested "comrade Blatov" to make corrections to his notes.[72] This was not the sort of mental state that allowed for deep engagement with the underlying issues.

"Comrade Blatov" could well have been a collective entity, serving as he did as a compilation point for inputs from the vast foreign policy bureaucracy, including the Foreign Ministry, the Defense Ministry, KGB, the International Department and, for the purposes of the Somali–Ethiopian conflict, Fidel Castro, who played an important role in the shift of Soviet sympathies in the Horn. Castro was not in the room on August 11 when the Soviet Politburo voted to lean to Ethiopia's side but he was – and would be – intimately involved in the decision-making. In the following months Castro took the lead in supplying troops (12,000 Cubans took part) to fight back the Somali onslaught in Ogaden. Unlike the Angolan operation, where Castro went out on a limb, in Ethiopia he closely coordinated with the Soviets who sent weapons and instructors.

Siad Barre was reluctant to burn bridges to Moscow, if for no other reason than to have access to weapons. He visited the USSR at the end of August for brief talks with Kosygin, Suslov, and Gromyko (Brezhnev was in Crimea). As Kosygin recounted several weeks later, the Somalian leader played up the threat from Ethiopia. "We got the impression that the Somalians are afraid of the Ethiopian Army," he told Mengistu in October, "and Siad Barre himself is not very confident in the success of his army."[73] It is unclear what, if anything, he managed to procure from the Soviets, but Siad Barre's visits to Egypt and Saudi Arabia in the fall of 1977 (where he was reportedly promised millions of dollars in aid) did not increase his credibility in the Kremlin's eyes.[74]

In November 1977 Siad Barre abrogated the Soviet–Somali friendship treaty (signed only three years earlier) and kicked out his Soviet advisers. Even before then he tried to actively reengage with the United States, seeking economic and military aid from the recently elected Jimmy Carter. To do so, the "Great Marxist" jettisoned Marxist terminology in favor of Carter's terminology of human rights. There was almost a ritual quality to the way Brzezinski pressed the Somalis to issue public declarations in support of President Carter's human rights pronouncements – as if this could change Siad Barre's dismal human rights record.[75] Somali ambassador in Washington Abdullahi Addou – "a gifted diplomat and a superb liar" – played it smart and told Carter what the president wanted to hear: "now we see in you, Mr. President, hope and inspiration. We hope your human rights drive encourages other people."[76] It did not really matter, though, whether the Somalis were Marxists or democrats. What mattered was whose side they were on, whose global authority they recognized.

In February 1978 the Ethiopians (bolstered by Cuban troops and Soviet advisers) turned the tides on the Somalis. Seeing where the wind was blowing, Siad Barre instructed Ambassador Addou to seek out Dobrynin and see about a reconciliation. Their meeting in Washington on February 23 brought Somalia's foreign policy to a whole new level of absurd. Addou, who only recently pinned on Carter the hopes of humankind, now asked Dobrynin for Soviet help in creating a federation of Somalia and Ethiopia (an idea previously supported and indeed actively encouraged by Moscow but torpedoed by Siad Barre). "Unlike the Americans," Addou told

Figure 24 Ethnic Somalis enlisted to fight in the Ogaden War, September 1977.
Source: Jean-Claude Francolon/Gamma-Rapho/Getty Images.

Dobrynin, "the Soviet Union does not seek for itself some special advantages in Somalia or Ethiopia." "We are convinced," he added, "that American policy is in no sense dictated by sincere concerns about helping Somalia, and merely comes down to the expression of their general effort to undermine the USSR in all regions of the world, including in Africa."[77]

Dobrynin faithfully recorded these revelations but of course the Soviets were not about to reopen a relationship that had gone so badly wrong: too much water under the bridge. As Brezhnev put it around this time, "we don't trust Siad, he behaves himself dishonestly. Entering into contact with us, simultaneously he continues to actively flirt with the US and the Arab reactionaries, probably counting to win time and build up strength for new provocations in this region."[78]

By the spring of 1978 Mengistu recovered Ogaden. The uprising in Eritrea was soon suppressed as well. The Soviets and the Cubans helped one "Marxist-Leninist" to defeat the neighboring "Marxist-Leninists." Ethiopia became firmly lodged in the Soviet camp. Moscow ostensibly "won" this latest episode of proxy warfare, though the long-term costs of this victory – the burden of supporting a brutal regime thousands of miles from Moscow – outweighed the perceived gains. The Ethiopia hand on the National Security Council, Paul B. Henze, was quite right to argue at the time that the Soviets were "winning neither love nor respect" and that "in the longer run, their adventures in the Horn are not likely to increase their prestige or attractiveness elsewhere in Africa."[79] If Henze was a bit more self-critical, he could well say the same of his own government's efforts in the Horn. This conflict was truly the apotheosis of the Cold War. Not since the dramatic crash of the Sino-Soviet alliance a decade before had ideology been so cynically and blatantly manipulated to serve the ends of brutal *realpolitik*.

CONCLUSION

The late 1970s present a remarkable series of case studies for understanding the Cold War. Perhaps the biggest story was China's transformation, as Deng Xiaoping abandoned revolution in favor of development. In truth, these two directions were not mutually exclusive. What was Mao's revolution if not an effort to rebuild the country so that it returned to centrality on the global stage? This vision motivated Mao Zedong as he sought to break free from Soviet tutelage in the late 1950s but it later transpired that Mao's ideas about economic development suffered from a distinct lack of realism. The aim – having China stand tall and proud – was worth pursuing but, as Deng Xiaoping knew only too well, the means of getting there had to change. Thus, he looked to modernize China by leaning to one side – this time, America's side. The Soviets were right to suspect that it was a tactical choice. The United States, however, embraced the opportunity by reaching out to Beijing, in part because a closer Sino-American relationship helped contain the Soviet threat. This de facto alignment did not rest on shared values – merely on tactical choices. But there was an underlying expectation in Washington: if China turned capitalist, would it also not eventually embrace a democratic form of governance? The nervous Soviet leaders were naturally worried about the direction of the Sino-American relationship, even if the most insightful of them had a hunch – based undoubtedly on their checkered experience with the Chinese – that Beijing would never become America's ally.

The Horn of Africa became another stage for Soviet–American competition, with Moscow and Washington backing rival regimes. Historian Odd Arne Westad rightly argues that superpower involvement "helped put a number of third world countries in a state of semipermanent civil war."[80] He draws on Joseph Conrad to highlight the importance of *ideas* – "something you can set up, and bow down before, and offer a

PART III DECLINE

sacrifice to" – as a key factor, not just for Soviet and American interventionism, but also for the local elites who embraced these ideas and sought to rearrange their societies in line with prescriptions from their sponsors overseas. Ideas have a legitimating aspect. Bowing before an idea thus in practices means bowing before the carrier of this idea. In *Heart of Darkness*, it was not Kurtz's idea but Kurtz himself who was worshipped by the natives *because* he was legitimated by an idea. Ideas establish and reinforce patterns of authority in a hierarchical relationship. Both the Americans and the Soviets were keen that their clients embrace specific legitimating discourses, whether human rights or Marxism-Leninism. Why was it so important to them?

One way of thinking about this question is reconceptualizing superpower rivalry in the third world in quasi-Maslow terms. There were basic security reasons for superpower engagement in the third world. A strategist tracing a finger on a world map could perhaps conclude that there was something about the Horn of Africa, for instance, that was relevant to the security of the Western alliance or, alternatively, the socialist bloc. The region lay in proximity to shipping arteries, a striking distance from important sources of oil. We have seen that these kinds of considerations entered the minds of Soviet policy makers, especially the military, though they probably did not dominate their thinking quite to the extent Brzezinski or Deng Xiaoping liked to imagine. Preempting the Soviets was undoubtedly an important consideration for American involvement in the third world. But security concerns alone fall short of offering a viable explanation, because it was possible to reconceptualize security in ways that would exclude much of the third world. Stalin did this. He was much more interested in areas directly adjacent to the USSR, his abortive quest for an African colony notwithstanding.

But once security needs, however defined, have been met, there remains the need for recognition and self-actualization as a superpower – that is, for setting up patterns of deference and recognition and, through recognition, legitimation. Moreover, it was not just the superpower patrons who were legitimated through recognition by clients; the relationship obviously worked the other way too. By being recognized as a Soviet or, alternatively, an American client, regimes like Siad Barre's or Mengistu's could then draw on their respective sponsor's support in the form of economic aid and weapons – naturally – but also, crucially, political legitimation.

This chapter has focused on the Soviet decision-making, but similar logic underpinned US and Chinese involvement in Africa. By the late 1970s, the Chinese concluded that the game was not worth it, and

CHAPTER 16 TENSIONS MOUNT

retrenched. The Soviets, by contrast, ploughed on, despite the tremendous costs that such overseas adventures entailed. A part of the explanation was that Moscow suffered from "an inertia of proletarian internationalism," which prompted involvement in faraway struggles simply as a consequence of a long-standing Soviet desire to be recognized as the leader of revolutionary forces. As we have seen, such involvement undermined detente but the contradiction between having a positive relationship with the United States and supporting third world revolutions was often lost on the Soviets who believed that detente itself rested on America's recognition of their equal right to meddle.

And in any case, detente was already on life support, partly because of the growing Soviet frustration with what they perceived as America's hypocritical peddling of the human rights agenda. It was infuriating to be "taught" by people like Carter – not because it mattered for the Soviets domestically (the regime was stable enough) but because such a teacher–student relationship was fundamentally incompatible with the Soviet sense of self-importance.

In the mid-1940s the Soviet Union eyed colonies in Africa, as we have seen, for reasons that had to do with geopolitics but also with prestige. But Stalin's plans ran aground: he simply did not have the capabilities to project Soviet power so far from the Soviet shores. By the late 1970s the Soviets developed such capabilities. But was Brzezinski right in thinking that Soviet capabilities were in themselves sufficiently threatening – never mind what Moscow actually intended? As we have seen, the dynamic was more complicated. There simply was no Soviet plan for southward expansion, no Testament of Peter the Great to draw upon. The Soviets were often engaged in opportunistic behavior. The third world offered such opportunities in a way that Europe and much of Asia did not. The Soviets embraced them because they believed they could thus grow rich with clients and so not just improve their geopolitical position but also raise their global prestige, an issue that was closely connected with the political legitimacy of the entire Soviet project.

They soon found those who were willing to defer to Moscow for a reasonable price, at least until the Americans came along with a better offer. The greatest irony of the Cold War in the third world was just how shallow commitments to alternative modernities proved in practice. What did tyrants like Siad Barre and Mengistu really believe in, in the end? Did it even matter? What mattered above all was their ability to maintain their brutal hold on power, whether in the name of God, Marx, or Milton Friedman.

17

THE FINAL NAIL

The 1970s were a turbulent decade, punctuated by wars, revolutions, coups, economic stagnation, and a nuclear arms race. Political crises shook the United States, where a president was forced to resign, and China, where a long-time revolutionary leader finally died, which led to an immediate and very brutal power struggle. The Soviet Union, by contrast, remained relatively stable – perhaps too stable. Brezhnev's long reign entered its most decadent years. The old party leadership grew even older. Reforms were postponed. Exports of oil and gas kept the country afloat. Purchases of foreign wheat plugged the hole left by the deflated promise of a Communist bonanza. The Soviets even managed to have Moscow selected as the site of the 1980 Summer Olympics. Brezhnev, in a rare moment of mental alertness, once attempted to back out of the Games because he feared they might prove too costly and would create too many reputational problems for the USSR.[1] But in the end, he stayed the course. The rusting ship of the Soviet state, leaking oil and taking water, continued to drift.

But as the decade drew to a close, troubles multiplied. An Islamic revolution shook Iran. Communists came to power in Afghanistan. On the other side of the world, Vietnam invaded Cambodia, and was in its turn invaded by China. The Soviet leaders were mostly passive observers of these breathtaking developments. They pragmatically tried to take advantage of the revolutionary chaos in Iran to advance their interests at America's expense but did not get very far. They embraced the Afghan Communists, only to discover that their clients were afflicted by lethal internal rivalries even while they pursued radical policies that enjoyed very little support among the Afghans. The Sino-Vietnamese-Cambodian triangle had its own dynamic that had very little to do with the Soviet vision for Southeast Asia, but Moscow could hardly remain on the sidelines as tensions mounted: it was too closely bound up with the actions of its ambitious Vietnamese ally. These confusing events overlapped with the final demise of detente. The fruit of Brezhnev's labor withered and finally collapsed. The general secretary was powerless to avert the return to confrontation. The Soviet

474

CHAPTER 17 THE FINAL NAIL

invasion of Afghanistan hammered the final nail in the coffin of the still-born Soviet–American condominium of Brezhnev's healthier years. The Cold War returned with a vengeance. That is the story of this chapter.

AFGHANISTAN

The highest point of Soviet interventionism in the third world was the invasion of Afghanistan in December 1979. "Why did the Soviets invade Afghanistan? They decided to begin with the first letter of the alphabet," went a dissident joke. There was something to it. At the time the decision was made, Brezhnev was in no position to understand the implications of what he was doing and, indeed, his role was fairly limited: others made the key decisions and had him sign off on them. The invasion proved a very costly undertaking and one that further contributed to the Soviet Union's isolation on the international stage. Like previous Soviet interventions, it seriously undercut Moscow's claims to global leadership and, indeed, the legitimacy of the socialist project itself. But there was very little strategy in the venture. Contrary to views expressed by Brzezinski and Deng Xiaoping who immediately perceived the invasion as a part of a grand design, a step in the Soviet push towards ice-free ports and (from there) towards world domination, this was a case of foreign policy sent adrift, with no direction nor destination.

The invasion of Afghanistan came a quarter-century after the Soviet leaders first turned their attention to this very poor but strategically important Islamic nation. Afghanistan was on Khrushchev's and Bulganin's whistle-stop tour in 1955, as a part of a broader third world outreach. At the time when Iran and Pakistan were firmly lodged in the American embrace, Afghanistan raised the banners of neutrality, which, in reality, entailed a close association with the Soviet Union. (It became one of the few countries that managed to combine the office of king and the institution of the five-year plan.) The Soviet Union did what it did in many parts of the third world: it sent experts, built roads, supplied weapons, and, when called upon, imported Afghan produce. In other words, it used Afghanistan as a testing ground for socialist modernization. Between 1954 and 1977, it provided Afghanistan with about 1 billion rubles' worth of economic aid (not including the substantial military supplies).[2]

There was a nonstop pilgrimage of Afghan VIPs to Moscow, including even the king himself (whom Khrushchev took deer-hunting in Crimea just weeks before the Cuban Missile Crisis) and his cousin and reformist prime minister, Mohammed Daoud Khan. Khrushchev told the latter in 1959: "We

PART III DECLINE

are Communists, but we think that if a child is born prematurely, he dies. Communism is a historical regularity. This depends on how history unfolds. We are against surgical intervention."[3]

But – and this was a part of prenatal treatment – the Soviet intelligence worked hard on developing Afghan assets, especially among the intellectuals. Two of these – the journalist Nur Muhammad Taraki (codename: Nur) and a translator turned political activist Babrak Karmal (codename: Marid) – were to play the key roles in the lead-up to the Soviet intervention.[4] In 1965 Taraki and Karmal joined forces in establishing the People's Democratic Party of Afghanistan (PDPA) – the Communist Party. The party was from the beginning ridden by the bitter rivalry between Taraki's faction, Khalq ("the masses"), and Karmal's Parcham ("the banner"). The KGB resident in Kabul reported to Moscow that the difference between the two "is not of a principled political, or ideological, character, but comes down to the struggle for leadership and for their recognition by the Soviet Union."[5] In this, the Khalqists and the Parchamists were hardly unique: the same could well be said of many other rivalries of the Cold War. For their part, the Soviets encouraged reconciliation for the common good and kept the party afloat through generous subsidies.[6]

Why did the Soviet Union need a Communist Party in a state that for most intents and purposes was already their client? The answer is that this was just how the Soviets operated. The KGB relied on various leftists as informants and political saboteurs, and Afghanistan was no exception. For example, in 1967 Taraki, the leader of the PDPA, was tasked by the KGB with organizing anti-Chinese demonstrations in Kabul and calling the Chinese Embassy on behalf of the "workers" of Afghanistan to protest their anti-Soviet actions. He also wrote letters in Persian, criticizing the Chinese, which were then thrown over the embassy wall.[7] But neither the KGB nor the Soviet leadership could have foreseen that within just a few years, agent Nur would take power in a Communist coup d'état.

In 1973 former Prime Minister Mohammed Daoud Khan deposed King Zahir Shah and proclaimed himself president. Daoud Khan was a modernizer and an advocate of a close relationship with the Soviet Union, which he continued to rely on for substantial economic and military aid. Brezhnev saw the events in Afghanistan as a "revolution," and was prompt to label Daoud Khan a "comrade." In September 1973 Brezhnev tutored Daoud's brother Mohammad Naim in the mechanics of the revolution and pointed to the example of Chile's Salvador Allende (deposed in a military coup) as one the Afghans had to be wary of repeating. "The experience of our revolution and revolutions in many other countries teaches that one must

CHAPTER 17 THE FINAL NAIL

be ruthless with the enemies of the revolution ... It is dangerous to try to get along with the opposition by compromising ... Let the struggle be brutal – later it will justify itself."[8] Brezhnev also advised the new Afghan government to create a strong political party – in short (in Mohammad Naim's later recollection), he received Naim "as though I were an emissary of a state which was establishing communism."[9]

To be fair, though, Daoud Khan himself went out of his way to create this impression. Repeatedly – including in talks with Brezhnev – he empha-sized that Afghanistan had taken the socialist path. "I and my friends," Daoud Khan told Brezhnev in June 1974, "took power in our hands in order to gradually take Afghanistan down the road we call socialist." But it would have to be a gradual move, he emphasized, simply because "the great majority of our people still live by a medieval understanding of the world, having been brought up in the spirit of religious fanaticism."[10] Brezhnev did not contradict the Afghan president; if anything, he thought that such a "gradual" socialization of Afghanistan was exactly the right thing to do. The Soviet position was that "one should act with care, without getting ahead of oneself, thoroughly preparing the planned reforms but at the same time not delaying them without due cause." It was important that the people "not lose their orientation."[11]

The elephant in the room was the PDPA, whose prominence in Afghan politics only increased after 1973. Daoud Khan was wary of the PDPA, with its growing influence in the military. In 1974 he pulled Brezhnev's ear about the "lack of discipline" among the Afghan military cadres who had under-gone training in the USSR.[12] In January 1977, Mohammad Naim again drew Brezhnev's attention to Daoud Khan's detractors who claimed they enjoyed Soviet support. "Who cares what people say," Brezhnev retorted.[13] In April 1977 Daoud Khan turned up in Moscow again, holding extensive talks with the entire Soviet leadership. There is little in these records to suggest Soviet frustration with their neutralist client. Daoud Khan went out of his way to stress the depth of Soviet–Afghan relations and readily accepted Soviet proposals for deepening economic cooperation. The Soviets were evidently satisfied with the state of military ties. Soviet military supplies between 1975 and 1977 neared half a billion rubles. Over 200 Soviet military personnel (including some sixty advisers) were already working in the country.[14]

The Soviets feared US and Chinese penetration of South Asia more broadly and Afghanistan in particular. The Soviet leaders pressed Daoud Khan to explain the nature of both Chinese and US aid to his country. "The Americans will not leave Asia alone," Gromyko warned, adding: "The same could also be said of China, which conducts a real great power, chauvinist policy." "One could of course stay on the sidelines, sit in the boat and wait to see where the current carries you," Gromyko lectured Daoud Khan. "But this is a passive policy. It entails a great risk."[15] There is some evidence to suggest that Moscow was worried about Daoud Khan's overly cautious effort to steer a neutral course in the Cold War, which was only natural, given their previous bitter experience with Anwar Sadat. But this is not the same as to say that the Soviets had given up on Daoud Khan's "socialist path."

Expressions of Soviet support may have helped convince Daoud Khan that he could move against the Communists with impunity. His opportunity was the assassination of one of the leaders of the PDPA, Mir Akbar Khyber, on April 17, 1978. The Soviets, in their internal reporting, blamed the Muslim Brotherhood and even the CIA for the plot, though the story remains shrouded in mystery.[16] Whatever the case, Daoud Khan decided to take advantage of the assassination – and the public protests that followed – to arrest the PDPA leadership. But the belated measure backfired. On April 27–28, the PDPA-aligned military launched a coup, killing Daoud Khan and his family. It is unclear how much the Soviets knew of the coup. They certainly knew that it was possible, since the eventual Communist prime minister, Hafizullah Amin, kept them in the loop by submitting regular written reports to the effect that the PDPA were "prepared to take power into their own hands."[17] On the other hand, much circumstantial evidence suggests that the PDPA and the military acted on the spur of the moment, and the April revolution was as much of a surprise to the Soviets as it was to everyone else. In any case, the socialist world presently welcomed its newest member state, one that was singularly unprepared to undertake the brave march to Communism.

Taraki (like so many other Soviet clients in the third world) knew how to please Moscow. Meeting the Soviet leaders in December 1978, he generously peppered his spiel with references to "scientific socialism," drawing parallels between the PDPA coup and the 1917 Bolshevik Revolution in Russia. "In us, you have acquired a new brother who has neither clothes nor home nor bread," Taraki told Brezhnev. "You, as the elder brother, must take this into account. We pin all our hopes on you, as our elder brother. The April revolution is an example for the region, and we want for our country to be an example for other countries." Such obeisance did not come free of charge, of course: Taraki presented demands for aid amounting to 1.5 billion rubles (exceeding Soviet aid extended over the previous five years by a whopping factor of ten).[18] The Afghan leaders also tried to press Moscow to cancel all of Afghanistan's previous debts – "in a comradely fashion," as Amin put it.[19]

CHAPTER 17 THE FINAL NAIL

The Afghan leadership skillfully played on the Soviet fear of China. Taraki and Amin would almost inadvertently raise the subject, suggesting that Beijing (and Islamabad for good measure) were probing the ground for rapprochement but that, no, Afghanistan would never betray the Soviet comrades, and that they "understood China's policy very well."[20] These revelations were expeditiously reported to Moscow. Taraki and Amin also told the Soviets about their dealings with the Americans, not least the visit by Deputy US Secretary of State David Newsom (July 13–14, 1978). The purpose of such explanations was to show to the Soviets that they could trust their Afghan comrades to staunchly defend Moscow's record in Afghanistan.[21]

In the meantime, the PDPA launched radical reforms in the countryside. Expropriations, land redistribution, and similar modernist policies (pursued with unsparing brutality) helped turn the Afghan population against the party. In July 1978 Taraki recounted to the Soviet ambassador what was probably one of the first counterinsurgency operations against "terrorists" in the Afghanistan–Pakistan border area. He proudly noted that the Afghan armed forces razed a village to the ground, though later apparently distributed aid to women and children and allowed them (!) to rebuild on

Figure 25 The Afghan Mujahideen navigating a river, April 1979.
Source: Alain Mingam/Gamma-Rapho/Getty Images.

PART III DECLINE

the same site. The ambassador was abhorred and tried to "tactfully" persuade Taraki that razing entire villages was probably not the best way of winning hearts and minds.[22]

The PDPA increasingly turned against itself. The Khalqists, under the leadership of General Secretary Taraki and Foreign Minister (and later Prime Minister) Hafizullah Amin unleashed violent repressions against the Parchamists, compete with mass imprisonment, torture, and executions. The leading Parchamist (and theoretically the second man in the hierarchy), Babrak Karmal, complained to the Soviet ambassador (as the enraged Taraki looked on) that thousands of Communists were being subjected to "terror," and that he himself felt like he was being held in a "golden cage," without any power or influence.[23] Karmal was eventually appointed Afghanistan's ambassador to Czechoslovakia, where he licked his wounds while his faction faced the prospect of complete annihilation (he was eventually purged and expelled from the party). The Soviets looked on with concern and advised their Afghan allies to ease off on the bloodletting. Taraki was undeterred, telling the Soviet ambassador to his face that those who opposed the revolution would be "flattened with an iron roller."[24] Taraki and Amin spared no effort to convince the Soviets that the Parchamists, working hand-in-hand with Pakistan, Iran, and the CIA, had attempted to stage an antigovernment plot, and that their purge and prosecution were justified. The Soviet diplomats were likely unconvinced but tried to keep their distance from the purge, even when they were secretly approached by some of the surviving Parchamists and asked to do something.[25]

For all these brutalities, and certainly in part because of them by March 1979 the PDPA faced a full-fledged rebellion. Insurgents – helped by mutineers from a government army – captured the city of Herat in western Afghanistan, prompting Taraki's and Amin's pleas for Soviet intervention. The Politburo considered their response on March 17–18. One thing everyone seemed to agree on was that they could not afford to "lose" Afghanistan to the "bandits," many of whom the Soviets believed hailed from Pakistan and Iran but who were trained and supported by the United States and China. On the other hand, an outright Soviet intervention was also not an option. If they went in, argued Andropov and Gromyko, they would be labeled an aggressor.

Gromyko made perhaps the most eloquent case against intervention that, had Kissinger heard him speak, would have made the latter think that linkage worked after all. "Who will [the Soviet Army] fight against?" asked the foreign minister and went on to answer his own question: "Against the Afghan people first and foremost, and they'll have to be fired on ... Everything that

CHAPTER 17 THE FINAL NAIL

we created in recent years in terms of detente, arms control, and many other things – all of that will be thrown back. Of course, it will be a good present for China. All the nonaligned countries will be against us."[26] The Soviet leaders seemed to understand that as much as they feared "losing" Afghanistan, reputational losses from an invasion were unacceptable: the Soviet "international authority" – in the third world, and in the realm of superpower relations – would be badly compromised.[27] It was therefore decided that the Soviet Union would not intervene. Brezhnev himself informed Taraki of this decision, reading out a prepared Soviet position in their meeting on March 20.[28] The matter seemed closed. The recapture of Herat by the government forces (with many thousands of casualties) postponed the prospect of the Communists' collapse.

VIETNAM

While the Soviet Communists debated whether to accept an invitation to intervene, the Vietnamese Communists intervened uninvited. In December 1978 Vietnam invaded and occupied Cambodia, setting off a train of events that redefined Southeast Asia's political landscape. Advertised at the time as a humanitarian intervention to save the people of Cambodia from genocide at the hands of Pol Pot and his followers, Hanoi's action was in fact an attempt to reassert Vietnam's regional preponderance. Vietnam – still riding the euphoria of having defeated the world's mightiest power – expected others to defer to their leadership. Mongolian party officials visiting Hanoi in December 1979 were surprised that the Vietnamese leaders objected to having their country officially referred to as a "forward platform of peace and socialism in Southeast Asia." It was not because they were overly shy. It turned out that it was because "the Vietnamese comrades themselves assess the role and influence of Vietnam on a wider scale, i.e. they include South Asia into their sphere of influence."[29]

But Hanoi's great ambitions did not translate into the sort of recognition that they desired, neither broadly in Asia, nor even in Vietnam's own neighborhood. This was especially the case in Cambodia, where Pol Pot, having secured Mao's political and military support, brazenly defied his long-time benefactors across the border, much as the Vietnamese chose to defy China. The story that Hanoi sold the Soviets was that Cambodia – or Democratic Kampuchea as it was then called – turned itself over to the Chinese who were using Pol Pot to "realize their expansionist plans in Southeast Asia."[30] These far-reaching plans, Moscow was told, included, in the long term, "annexation of Vietnam, Laos, and Cambodia." "The Chinese

PART III DECLINE

expansionists and hegemonists want to become masters in Southeast Asia in order to rule the world later on."[31]

This was a story the China-obsessed Kremlin elders were only too willing to buy. In November 1978 Moscow and Hanoi concluded a treaty of friendship and cooperation, one of distinctly anti-Chinese connotations. Both Le Duan and Pham Van Dong journeyed to Moscow for the signing. It is still unclear whether they used that occasion to tell Brezhnev – or his aides – of Vietnam's impending invasion of Cambodia. The Soviet report on the visit noted that the Vietnamese considered it their "duty" to provide "help and support to the Kampuchean revolutionaries" but that they would also avoid any impression of "interfering in Kampuchea's internal affairs."[32] A month later, the Vietnamese invaded Cambodia.

Did anyone seriously consider the possibility that China may try to bail out its Cambodian ally, Pol Pot, by in turn invading Vietnam? The prospect was discussed in Moscow, but Le Duan and Pham Van Dong did not think they would do it. The Chinese, they said, know of the Soviet military support and "have to take this into account."[33] It was a bad miscalculation.

Deng Xiaoping responded with a show of force: on February 17, 1979, the Chinese Army launched an attack on Vietnam in what became one of the most bizarre conflicts of the Cold War. Facing determined resistance of the battle-tried Vietnamese troops, the Chinese made slow advances, capturing a few towns along the border. After inconclusive but bloody battles, the People's Liberation Army (PLA) declared victory on March 5 and began to withdraw towards the border, claiming to have taught the Vietnamese "a lesson." "In reality," smarted Vietnamese Prime Minister Pham Van Dong later that year, "it was not they who gave us a 'lesson,' but it was us who gave them a 'lesson.'"[34]

It may be difficult to understand why one ostensibly Communist country (China) would invade another ostensibly Communist country (Vietnam), especially after the two had fought shoulder-to-shoulder, first to expel the French from Indochina, and then to defeat the Americans. It was one of those conflicts that devalue the meaning of ideological tropes and bring to the fore recollections of ancient hatreds and age-old grievances. But cultural explanations also fall short: If the Chinese and the Vietnamese so hated each other, how could they have worked so closely together for so long? Only by reconceptualizing the conflict in terms of rival claims to regional leadership can we begin to understand what Deng had meant by teaching Vietnam a "lesson."

Deng laid it all out for Jimmy Carter when they met in Washington in January 1979, just days before China's invasion of Vietnam. Recalling

482

CHAPTER 17 THE FINAL NAIL

his visits to Singapore, Thailand, and Malaysia in November 1978 – an ice-breaker tour that heralded Beijing's embrace of non-Communist Southeast Asia – Deng said that all three had wanted the Chinese "to do something." "Some friends," he said, "even criticized China for being too soft." The Vietnamese, Deng continued, "are extremely arrogant." "They now claim to be even the third most powerful military nation in the world, after the United States and the Soviet Union." If they were allowed to continue unopposed, they would soon be threatening the rest of Southeast Asia and China itself. And so, Deng summed up, the time had come for China to put an end to Hanoi's "rampant ambitions." He asked Carter for "moral" support.[35]

The US president was taken aback by these revelations. He was at a loss for words for a moment but later drafted a written response, in which he called the Chinese leader's idea of invading Vietnam a "serious mistake."[36] (That said, he certainly was not going to try too hard to prevent Deng from doing what he had already decided to do, something Brezhnev later picked up on and complained about incessantly: "they kept quiet but in fact they approved!")[37]

Reminding Vietnam who was the "boss" in Southeast Asia was not Deng Xiaoping's only consideration. Historians have pointed to multiple agendas, from asserting control over the bloated and faction-ridden military (and, through the military, over the levers of political power in China), to testing the effectiveness of the PLA, which had not seen major engagement since the Korean War nearly thirty years earlier, in modern warfare.[38] Still more importantly, the war was a result of Deng's strategic calculus: it mattered for China's relationship with the United States and with the USSR. By ordering an attack on Vietnam, Deng wanted to frustrate Soviet efforts to "encircle" China, and to signal to the United States where China's global priorities truly lay. And signal he did. What more evidence could Carter ask for to prove that China was really on America's side in the Cold War than going to war against Washington's most bitter adversary?

All these developments looked extremely worrying to Moscow. Much as Brzezinski worried about "the arc of crises," so did the Soviets eye with grave suspicion what seemed like Sino-American coordination over China's invasion of Vietnam. Brezhnev accused Carter of complicity in angry letters.[39] On top of that, the conclusion of the Camp David Accords the previous September left Moscow out in the cold in the Middle East: Carter had won big as Moscow's former client Anwar Sadat opted for an American-sponsored peace with Israel, putting to rest whatever delusions the Soviets may have entertained about the Soviet–American condominium. The Soviets rained

483

vitriol, Brezhnev telling Carter in a letter that "the position of the USSR in the world cannot be changed at someone's wish." But it could be, and it was, and it hurt.[40] Add to this Carter's human rights agenda, selectively applied to the USSR, and there we have it: all the necessary ingredients in place for fostering a siege mentality. Hence the irony: at the very moment when the world was supposed to be going "their way," with more allies they had ever had all over the world, the Soviets found themselves in a state of deep insecurity and mounting anxiety bordering on outright paranoia.

THE IRANIAN REVOLUTION

The Sino-American normalization and the Chinese invasion of Vietnam overlapped in time with momentous developments in Iran. In January 1979, Mohammad Reza Pahlavi, the Shah of Iran, fled the country, never to return. The shah inherited his throne in 1941, after his father's abdication and consolidated his personal power after the US- and British-supported coup against Mosaddegh in 1953, turning more and more authoritarian and more and more brutal towards his political opponents, some of whom, like the prominent cleric Ruhollah Khomeini, were forced into exile, while others languished in prison in Iran. Since the 1960s the shah pursued policies of modernization – which he called the "White Revolution" – which spurred economic growth but also contributed to inequality. This fed resentment on the part of the religious establishment that decried the supposedly corrosive effects of Westernization (especially equal rights for women) and the deepening rot of corruption.

In Iran, the Soviets perceived an opportunity. They had resented Tehran's pro-Western tilt and its membership in the Central Treaty Organization (CENTO, also previously known as the Baghdad Pact), and worked hard to bring the shah around to some form of nonalignment. Khrushchev tried to conclude a nonaggression pact with the shah in 1959, but the latter pulled the plug on the idea at the last moment, prompting Soviet ire.[41] Brezhnev renewed the offer in 1965, proposing a pact for a 100 – even 200 – years, with "solid guarantees."[42] The shah, a fierce anti-Communist, who never quite forgot about Moscow's sponsorship of a breakaway republic in northern Iran, was not taking the bait.

He was, however, interested in economic cooperation, which grew substantially from the mid-1960s. The Soviets built a gigantic metallurgical complex in Isfahan, a machinery plant in Arak, a series of hydropower dams, a railroad, and, perhaps most importantly, a gas pipeline that entered service in 1970 and allowed Iran to supply gas to the Soviet Union across their shared border.[43] The Soviet leaders did their best to court the shah and his family, inviting them on extended visits to the USSR. The shah himself turned up on multiple occasions beginning in 1956, getting to know Khrushchev and later Brezhnev. His twin sister, Princess Ashraf Pahlavi, enjoyed Brezhnev's company on occasion. His half-brother, Abdul Reza Pahlavi, made several hunting trips to the USSR, once bringing Ashraf's son, Shahriar Shafiq, along to Siberia to hunt Yakut bears.[44]

But for all this positive engagement, the Soviet leaders were not happy with the state of their relations with Iran and in fact grew increasingly disillusioned with the shah because of his perceived closeness to the United States. This closeness became all too obvious in the first half of the 1970s when Iran made a bid for regional leadership as America's most reliable ally in the Persian Gulf. Richard Nixon was only too happy to defer: "I like him," he said of the shah. "I like him, and I like the country. And some of those other bastards out there I don't like."[45] In that spirit, the US president authorized the sale of billions of dollars' worth of weapons to Iran, helping cement its claim to regional preponderance.

The Soviets were puzzled at first – then upset.[46] Brezhnev repeatedly upbraided the Iranians for the purchase of inordinate quantities of American weapons. He was worried that Iran was fueling a regional arms race, which the Soviet Union was inadvertently also contributing to by arming Iran's regional rival, Iraq. There was a familiar Cold War logic to this rivalry, one that the general secretary did not want to unfold but felt helpless to avert. Brezhnev was told in response that Iran had a right to a mighty military, and that in any case no one was asking Britain, France, or West Germany about their military expenditures – why, then, about Iran's?[47] The shah's long-serving prime minister, Amir-Abbas Hoveyda, told Brezhnev in August 1973 that Tehran had learned from Egypt's bad example: its defeat at the hands of Israel in the Six Day War showed that by the time the UN gets around to passing a resolution, you could see your country overrun: And then what? "The last two decades have shown that the weak pay for their weakness."[48]

Hoveyda promised the Soviets on the shah's behalf that the substantial American presence in Iran was just "temporary" – that the Americans were training the Iranian military in the use of weapons, and once that was done, they would go back home, and Iran would stand tall, strong, and independent.[49] The Kremlin remained unconvinced.

It was perhaps this uncertainty about Iran's trajectory that persuaded the Politburo to adopt a resolution on September 1, 1975 that instructed the KGB to "destabilize" the shah's regime with an eye to having it replaced

PART III DECLINE

with something "progressive-democratic."[50] The shah had good reasons to worry about an insurrection, especially after the overthrow of Zahir Shah in neighboring Afghanistan, and even more after the murder of his successor Daoud Khan. "How can we not be worried," he probed Soviet Ambassador Vladimir Vinogradov, "when your army has merely 400 kilometers to go before it reaches the warm seas?" (At one point the shah predictably cited Peter the Great's Last Testament. He was assured that it was fake but, like the Chinese and the Americans, he probably suspected that the Soviets had expansionist aims, whatever Peter the Great had willed.)[51]

Demonstrations against the shah intensified in the summer and autumn of 1978, with crippling strikes and street protests amid frequent and worsening bloodshed. The chief of the Soviet intelligence station in Tehran, Leonid Shebarshin, claimed in retrospect that by August–September 1978 the KGB had already concluded that the shah's days were numbered.[52] It is difficult to verify such claims. As likely as not, the Soviets were just as puzzled as anyone else, unsure about where events were heading but quietly worried about possible US intervention at the eleventh hour to rescue the faltering regime. "The Americans will not shy away from anything to keep the Shah in power," Brezhnev lamented in December 1978. Just in case, he sent a personal message to Jimmy Carter warning that any US intervention in Iran would "touch on Soviet security interests" – that is, possibly lead to a Soviet counterintervention.[53] In mid-January the tired, sickly general secretary established a special Politburo commission to follow events in Iran and counter US moves. "The Americans are doing everything to keep their influence in this region," he observed in a Politburo memorandum. "If necessary, [we] have to take appropriate measures."[54]

Thus, when a few days later the shah fled, the Soviet leaders were moderately optimistic. Moscow was quick to extend recognition to the new revolutionary government headed by Mehdi Bazargan. Beyond Bazargan, Moscow sought out the ostensible real power in Iran, Ayatollah Khomeini, who had returned from exile about two weeks after the shah's departure. The Soviet-backed Tudeh (the closest Iran had to a Communist party) proclaimed support for Khomeini despite the latter's anti-Soviet pronouncements and in fact worked to undermine the moderate provisional government in the hope that its downfall would bring about a leftward shift in the revolutionary dynamic.[55] Of course, in the early weeks and months of the revolution, it was very hard to discern what direction it might take: it was only in retrospect that it became clear that Moscow's (and Tudeh's) hopes of harnessing Islamic fundamentalism proved somewhat premature.[56]

CHAPTER 17 THE FINAL NAIL

Historian Jeremy Friedman has argued that Moscow's pragmatic embrace of Khomeini was a consequence of a lesson learned in 1973 in Chile – in particular, the fear of a US-backed military coup.[57] Another, perhaps even a bigger, lesson was the one Moscow learned in Iran itself, in 1953, when the Soviets allowed their suspicions of Mossadegh's political game to cloud their appreciation of his nationalism.[58] Ayatollah Khomeini had an important selling point: for all his anti-Soviet rhetoric, he directed his ire mainly against the United States. His revolution, whatever else it was, was most certainly anti-American, and in this sense, he seemed like a good fellow traveler, especially since few in Moscow believed in the long-term prospects of an Islamic government in Iran.[59]

Soviet contacts with Khomeini yielded promising results. Ambassador Vladimir Vinogradov met him first on February 24, 1979. Vinogradov tried to draw parallels between the Iranian Revolution and the Bolshevik Revolution in 1917 and talked about the need for closer Soviet–Iranian relations. Khomeini made the right noises in response.[60] "Khomeini," the Soviet ambassador recalled, "perceived many things fairly realistically; he also took into account concrete circumstances, he was reasonable." When presented with complaints about this or that anti-Soviet act, he adopted a conciliatory tone and promised things would improve once the Iranian youths vented their frustrations with years of imperialist oppression.[61]

In April 1979, Brezhnev sent a congratulatory telegram to Khomeini on the occasion of the referendum that established the Islamic Republic, calling it "a big historic victory for the Iranian people." He assured him that Soviet policy towards Iran was based on "sincere friendship and good neighborliness."[62] In a different telegram to Khomeini, in August, Brezhnev again highlighted Soviet commitment to nonintervention on economic, political, or ideological pretexts but also warned of the need "to show vigilance in the face of any efforts on the part of the imperialist forces to obstruct successful development of good-neighborly Soviet–Iranian relations, to rebuff aspirations by these forces to plant poisonous seeds of mistrust and suspicion between the peoples of the two countries."[63]

That latter reference to imperialist forces spoke to Soviet fears that Bazargan's "bourgeois" government secretly schemed to repair relations with the United States. This was true to a certain extent: Prime Minister Bazargan, Foreign Minister Ebrahim Yazdi, and other "moderates" were not averse to playing the US card in the domestic power struggle against Khomeini and the clerics. They reportedly tried to develop contacts with the US government, including the CIA, evidently "to get the Agency on their side in the event of a clear break with Khomeini," and reached out

487

PART III DECLINE

to Brzezinski, meeting him in Algiers on November 1.[64] Soviet concerns about the possibility of a Chilean-style turn of events were thus not without some foundation, although there is no evidence that the United States ever tried to organize a coup of some kind.[65] What there is ample evidence of is that the United States attempted to restore intelligence-sharing with the Bazargan government, and, in particular, to regain access to the Tacksman electronic surveillance site in northeast Iran, which helped gather intelligence on Soviet missile tests.[66]

In any case, the Soviet leaders were quietly preparing for a possible civil war in Iran and tried to strengthen their most reliable client, Tudeh. On August 30, 1979, the Central Committee Secretariat instructed the KGB and the Ministry of Defense to furnish Tudeh with non-Soviet weaponry. However, this never came to pass, ostensibly due to Tudeh's inability to guarantee a secure transfer.[67]

Meanwhile, matters took an unexpected turn on November 4, when radicalized students, demanding the extradition of the shah from the United States, stormed the American Embassy in Tehran, taking sixty-six diplomats hostage.[68] Khomeini seized the opportunity to undermine both the moderate Islamists and Tudeh and other leftists.[69] Bazargan's government fell. The Islamic revolution entered a new, radical stage. The crisis would last for 444 days, and it would not only dramatically change the US–Iranian relationship but also fatally undermine Carter's reelection bid. But this American loss was hardly a Soviet gain. Soviet relations with Iran also went from bad to worse, mainly, though not entirely, because of what was about to unfold in neighboring Afghanistan.

CONCERNING THE SITUATION IN 'A'

As the Afghan forces mopped up after the massacre in Herat and the Chinese plodded back across the border with Vietnam after their inconclusive "lesson," Cyrus Vance called Ambassador Dobrynin for what he called an "unofficial" talk. Three months had passed since Brzezinski famously outlined his "arc of crises" theory that required robust American action to counteract Soviet expansionism. Relations went from bad to worse amid tensions in Southeast Asia and the Middle East. Afghanistan seethed with unrest. The US ambassador in Kabul, Adolph Dubs, was killed in Kabul, ostensibly by militants although no one really could tell. The Soviets were at least in part suspect. Cuba was becoming an irritant (again!) as US defense officials worried (improbably) that Castro was developing a capability to threaten America's southern flank even as he continued to undercut

488

American interests in Africa and elsewhere in the third world.[70] Detente was on life support, and though for people like Brzezinski this was not necessarily a bad thing, Vance was very worried, and told Dobrynin as much.

That morning, Vance said, he had a completely private conversation with President Carter. The president told Vance that he was often thinking of American–Soviet relations – "even during the night." He then went on to say that Washington and Moscow should not, in his opinion, see every third world conflict as an arena for Soviet–American confrontation, and that there could be "parallel interests" in some of these areas. The president was determined, Vance said, to discuss these matters with Brezhnev in a candid conversation, "without undue emotions." That was because he was no good at writing letters. "He believes more in personal interaction, in a personal meeting."[71]

Dobrynin thought – and so reported to Moscow – that the real reason Vance so looked forward to a Carter–Brezhnev summit was that Carter was under Brzezinski's influence and perhaps Brezhnev could help dispel the president's "erroneous views" about the Soviet Union. Vance singled out Brzezinski and his "arc of crises" for particular criticism. "I don't personally believe," he told Dobrynin, "that the Kremlin has such a 'general plan' ... However, the theory of Soviet encirclement of the Middle East sounds nice and convincing to many. Even the President is partly is under its influence."[72]

President Carter and Leonid Brezhnev met that summer in Vienna. But Vance's hopes for a dialogue between the two leaders proved completely misplaced. Already in the spring of 1979 rumors swirled in Moscow about Brezhnev's worsening health. He was so poorly that his March meeting with French President Valery Giscard d'Estaing had to be postponed by nearly a month, and when it was finally held, the French came away shocked at the "extreme Soviet rudeness." Brezhnev "talked loudly with his colleagues while Giscard was speaking in French and while his own remarks were being translated into French." But it was not because Brezhnev was so insensitive; it was because he was losing it. There was no dialogue as the Soviet leader read prepared positions from cards, "asking Gromyko how he had done on completion."[73] The French reported that "Brezhnev's speech was slow and heavily slurred, his attention span was good for only about ninety minutes per session, and that he at times seemed disoriented." Also – that he was so weak physically that during the state dinner, he could "only use a spoon for his food."[74]

Such was Brezhnev's state when in June 1979 he set out for Vienna for his first, and last, meeting with Jimmy Carter. The highlight of the summit

PART III DECLINE

was the signing of the long-delayed SALT-II agreement, a breakthrough in arms control. Less than five years before, when he met Ford in Vladivostok, Brezhnev could still grapple with the complexities of throw-weights and missile diameters. All he could do now was to read out his prepared remarks, and even that – "haltingly and laboriously."[75] Brezhnev and Carter had one private meeting – with only the interpreters present – but there was no dialogue. Every time Carter raised a subject, Brezhnev's interpreter Viktor Sukhodrev would hand Brezhnev a set of notes to read a response from, having crossed out anything that seemed irrelevant. Sukhodrev recalled that at one point the Soviet leader, having read out the first part of his "response," turned to Sukhodrev and loudly asked: "What, should I not read out the second part?" To this the interpreter answered, also loudly (because Brezhnev was going deaf): "No need, Leonid Ilyich."[76]

Perhaps the most memorable moment of the summit was the signing of the SALT-II agreement. After a prolonged handshake, Carter hesitantly embraced the Soviet leader, only to have Brezhnev kiss him on both cheeks. "He leaned forward and put his cheek against mine for a more intimate embrace," Carter wrote in his diary. "We were both somewhat emotional."[77]

Meanwhile, the situation in Afghanistan went from bad to worse. After exterminating or exiling their Parcham opponents, the Khalqist leaders turned on one another. "A bunch of scorpions biting each other to death" was how the US chargé d'affaires in Kabul, J. Bruce Amstutz, described the politics of the place to the State Department.[78] The Soviets were worried about the situation and advised Taraki (who was in Moscow on September 10, en route from Cuba to Kabul) to prevent Amin from consolidating power in his hands. "This could have unfortunate consequences," Brezhnev said. (Brezhnev himself read out this advice – it was prepared by the KGB and approved by the powerful trio of Andropov, Gromyko, and Ustinov).[79] Taraki, who claimed to be surprised by these warnings, declared that there was unity in the PDPA ranks but promised to keep an eye on the situation: "Now I will carefully watch what is happening behind my back."[80]

There is some evidence to the effect that the KGB may have tried to kill or at least abduct Amin to preempt the latter from ousting Taraki and his supporters.[81] If so, they failed. Other evidence indicates that the Soviets were hopeful of a reconciliation between Taraki and Amin and mediated between the two after Taraki returned to Kabul.

On September 14, 1979 the Soviet ambassador in Afghanistan, Aleksandr Puzanov, and his three colleagues turned up at Taraki's residence in another ostensible bid to heal the rift between the two PDPA leaders. Taraki phoned Amin, who agreed to come over. When Amin arrived, Taraki's aide Sayed Daoud Tarun (who was likely spying for Amin) went to greet him, but he was gunned down by Amin's bodyguards. It was never made clear whether it was an ambush that failed, or perhaps Amin's provocation. In any case, Amin took advantage of the situation to move against Taraki, who was purged from leadership and imprisoned.[82]

The Soviets were appalled but appeared to have pragmatically reconciled themselves to this challenge. On September 20, 1979, Brezhnev addressed himself to the problem in a Politburo meeting. After Taraki's return from Havana, the general secretary noted, Amin made an all-out bid for power. "Despite our determined calls to both sides to act in unison, and not to exacerbate the situation, neither one nor the other side took measures to restore unity." The Soviets had their problems with Amin, Brezhnev continued; in particular, they did not like his "exceptional lust for power, his brutality in relation to yesterday's colleagues, his propensity for intrigues and the willfulness of his assessments." But there was no choice but to work with Amin, "considering the actual situation."[83]

Not all was lost, Brezhnev further explained. For a start, there were honest "Marxists-Leninists" in Amin's circle (people who had received education in the USSR). Amin kept up the right talk about friendship with the Soviets. Most importantly, perhaps, Afghanistan would remain utterly dependent on Soviet economic and military aid, which meant that Amin would have nowhere else to turn to, that he would opt for accommodation.[84]

Or would he? Brezhnev had held out the hope that Taraki would be spared; instead, he was strangled in prison (apparently smothered with pillows) on October 8. When Andropov informed Brezhnev of what happened, the general secretary vented his anger, fondly speaking of Taraki as a national poet and a wonderful person.[85] Worse still, after killing Taraki, the Afghan leader unleashed a brutal purge of other potential opponents. In a rare diary entry, the Soviet leader noted that Amin was "executing many cadres," presumably the "honest Marxist-Leninists" the Soviets had hoped to rely on.[86] Brutality aside, could Amin be another Sadat? He regularly expressed his loyalty to the Soviet Union, but he was far from a pliable client. Having just recently lost Egypt to the Americans, could Moscow afford to lose another country to American influence?

The prospect of Amin's betrayal loomed large in the minds of the Soviet policy makers. Amin's background – in his younger years he had studied in the United States – was suspicious enough. The KGB received bits and pieces of intelligence from Amin's circle indicating that he made derisive comments about the USSR while his brother claimed that it was "expedient" for Afghanistan to follow Egypt's path, and "act with regard to the Russians like President Sadat did."[87] Most problematically, Amin was reported as having repeatedly met with various shady Americans and, in particular, with the US chargé d'affaires, Archer K. Blood.[88]

Oddly enough, reports of these suspicious discussions were largely off-the-mark. In the autumn of 1979 the Carter Administration was still mostly exploring ways of funneling arms and money to insurgents on the ground and encouraging the Saudis and the Pakistanis to do the same.[89] US diplomats in Kabul were reporting that Amin, although by no means a "Soviet toady," was in no rush to embrace the United States because, after all, "our political ideology is so different from his."[90] It is true, however, that Blood was asked to approach Amin to size him up.[91] This he did on October 27, 1979, cabling to Washington that the man was "impressive" and that he emphasized "his personal desire for an improvement of US–Afghan relations."[92] That "desire" alone would have alarmed the KGB had they read Archer's cable. What made things look ever more suspicious from Moscow's perspective was that Amin preferred to keep quiet about the nature of his discussions with American diplomats.[93]

The Soviets were thus not at all confused by the fact that Amin's "political ideology" differed from Washington's. They understood that for people like Amin, ideology was just a set of convenient tropes that could be dispensed with as soon as an opportunity presented itself. It was a cynical take, to be sure, but if anyone, the Soviet leaders knew how to be cynical. Especially knowledgeable in this regard was the head of the KGB, Yury Andropov, who was emerging as one of the key players on the Soviet side of the Afghan equation.

In early December 1979 Andropov sent Brezhnev a handwritten memorandum, arguing that Amin had made a mess of Afghanistan's government and that he may defect. "Now there is no guarantee that Amin, in order to secure his personal power, would not turn over to the West."[94] The prospect of Amin's betrayal – whether realistic or not – formed the background for the deliberations in Brezhnev's office on December 8, 1979. The arguments in favor of intervention were generally of a "strategic" character: that the Americans would place their intermediate-range nuclear missiles in Afghanistan, from where they could threaten vital Soviet military sites; including the Baikonur cosmodrome in Kazakhstan.[95] Later Andropov identified at least two more important factors. One was his fear that Amin would turn Afghanistan over to the Americans to install their signal intelligence there (to spy on the USSR). The other, intriguingly enough, was a concern that with American support, Amin would

CHAPTER 17 THE FINAL NAIL

embrace Islamic fundamentalism and help export it to Soviet Central Asia. "This," he said, "would be a highly dangerous abscess for us."[96]

Although the discussions took place in Brezhnev's office, the general secretary's voice is decidedly absent: his illness was such that he was in no position to counter the united front presented by people like Andropov, Ustinov, and Gromyko (the latter, reportedly, only hesitantly). And once Brezhnev gave his blessing, there was nothing to stop the invasion. On December 12, the decision was formalized in the infamous Politburo resolution: "Concerning the situation in 'A'."[97] The Soviets invaded on Christmas Day. On December 27 special forces stormed Amin's palace (Amin was preemptively poisoned by the KGB, only to be resuscitated by his Soviet doctor, only to be gunned down, along with his 5-year-old son).[98] Babrak Karmal, rescued from exile in Czechoslovakia, was presently installed as the puppet ruler of Afghanistan. Thus began the biggest Soviet misadventure of the Cold War.

Historians have endlessly debated the subject of Soviet intervention in Afghanistan. It is unlikely that this debate will ever result in anything approaching a consensus. There are essentially two lines of arguments: that it was an effort to save the Afghan Revolution, and that it was a strategic move to preempt the "loss" of Afghanistan to various hostile forces. These divergent interpretations were starkly highlighted in the exchange that took place at the September 1995 oral history conference in Lysebu, Norway. Among the Russians attending were some of the most knowledgeable insiders: Ambassador Dobrynin and the deputy head of the Central Committee International Department, Karen Brutents. Neither was involved in the shenanigans in Brezhnev's office, but they were close enough to the center of power to know at least the general direction of policy. It is then all the more surprising to see them offer diametrically opposing explanations.

"I think ideology was the key factor," argued Dobrynin. "[T]he driving factor was ideological … So without proclaiming that ideology was the priority, we acted in a way that was consistent with that interpretation."[99] There was something odd in that Dobrynin – an ambassador and a member of a vast bureaucracy that had always been at the forefront of defending Soviet national interests – argued the ideological case. But it was perhaps odder still that Karen Brutents of the Central Committee International Department (the department that helped promote Communist revolution in the third world) embraced the strategic rationale. "I am absolutely convinced," decreed Brutents, "that by that time – and for a long time before that – ideological considerations did not play any major role whatsoever in our policy. State interests, as they were then understood, were the main consideration."[100] And elsewhere: "security interests were predominant here; nothing else mattered."[101]

One could square this circle by claiming, simply, that strategy and ideology overlapped. Yes, the Soviet leaders worried about the enemy's inroads into Afghanistan, but the enemy (for instance, American imperialism) was ideologically defined. By the same token, the Soviets may have wanted to promote revolution in Afghanistan because it was only by keeping the latter Communist that they could secure be assured that their strategic position in the country would remain secure. Separating strategy from ideology in this sense is a pointless exercise: as on many other occasions during the Cold War, they were closely intertwined.

There is another issue to consider. Whether the Soviets were afraid to lose Afghanistan for ideological or strategic reasons, their very fear was a motivation to act. It was the act of losing that was unacceptable for reasons of superpower prestige. The Soviet Union had taken losses before. For example, it "lost" China in the 1960s. It "lost" Chile in 1973. But it could not do much about China, and even less about Chile. It could do something about Afghanistan. Moreover, given its capabilities, and Afghanistan's proximity, it had to. The same logic that led America into Vietnam led the Soviets into Afghanistan. Both may have defined these adventures in ideological or strategic terms, but the bottom line was the question of superpower credibility. Even Brezhnev, in his dim world of 1979, recognized that the problem of Afghanistan (as historian Odd Arne Westad had put it) was "closely tied to his personal status on the world stage."[102]

Superpowers are easily taunted. That is because their status in the world depends not just on their material capabilities but on the others' recognition of their resolve. Afghanistan provides a very good illustration of this thesis. There was an ironic moment at Lysebu in 1995 when General Valentin Varennikov, who commanded the ground forces in Afghanistan, threw the following accusation at the American participants: "If you were guided by your interest in peace in the world, then you had to prevent the Soviet Union from taking that misstep. Why did you not prevent us?"[103] It speaks volumes of America's standing in the world that its implacable foes thought it had the leverage and perhaps the responsibility to stop them from doing something so shortsighted as invading Afghanistan.

THE HOSTAGE CRISIS AND THE IRAN–IRAQ WAR

The invasion of Afghanistan had far-reaching consequences for the Soviet position in the region, mostly in the negative sense. The effort that went into courting Khomeini largely went to waste. Angry protesters stormed the Soviet Embassy in Tehran and burned the flag. Ambassador Vinogradov surmised that the protesters' plan was to capture hostages, as with the US Embassy. But, Vinogradov later learned, Khomeini allegedly turned down the idea, having concluded, not unreasonably, that it was quite enough to have quarreled with one superpower. It was better to keep the other at bay.[104]

When Vinogradov informed Khomeini of the invasion of Afghanistan on December 27, the Imam, while disapproving of the move, said that he hoped that the Soviets would quickly finish what it was that they came for, and return home. He also raised an unexpected and unrelated issue that suggested that, after all, even Khomeini was not averse to quid pro quos. He asked the Soviets to prevent the UN Security Council's approval of economic sanctions against Iran – something the Americans tried to push through in retaliation against the hostage-taking. Vinogradov, without even asking Moscow for instructions, promised to deliver.

There was a degree of duplicity in the Soviet position in relation to US hostages. At one level, this was hardly something to rejoice over. There were also Soviet diplomats in Iran (as well as various experts working in the field), and none had forgotten the unhappy precedent of Aleksandr Griboyedov, the Russian playwright and envoy to Persia who was killed by an angry mob in 1829 alongside other members of the Russian mission. Maybe for this reason, on December 4 the Soviet Embassy in Washington passed an oral message from Brezhnev to Carter, noting that the Soviets had asked Iran to release the hostages, though also warning against precipitous US retaliation. "This is b.s.," Carter wrote at the top of the message – and he was not wrong.[105] For, sure enough, in public, the Soviets took a more ambiguous line, suggesting that the United States brought it upon themselves. Nevertheless, when on December 31 the United States sought UN Security Council's condemnation of the hostage-taking, the Soviets oddly abstained. The resolution foresaw the imposition of economic sanctions on Iran if the hostages were not released soon (but that would require a separate resolution).[106]

Back in Moscow, the subject of sanctions was discussed at the Politburo. The internal Soviet deliberations show remarkable realism (or, put crudely, cynicism) in how they approached the hostage crisis. On January 3 – probably in reaction to angry crowds breaking into the Soviet Embassy in Tehran – the Politburo held a meeting, which moved in the direction of an abstention at the UN. But after the meeting, the powerful trio of Brezhnev's aides, Andrei Aleksandrov-Agentov, Anatoly Blatov, and Evgeny Samoteikin, sent the general secretary a lengthy memorandum, where they argued that the only reasonable course open to the USSR was to veto the American sanctions resolution.

They gave several reasons. Rather cynically (but characteristically) they did not think that economic sanctions had anything to do with the hostages per se: they were merely a way "to punish Iran for the fact that after the revolution the country pursued an openly anti-imperialist and first and foremost anti-American policy." But the Soviet Union was the "recognized flag-carrier of the anti-imperialist struggle"; therefore, it had no business being seen endorsing American actions, even by abstention. That notion of being seen as a "recognized flag-carrier" linked up to the Soviet legitimacy narrative: legitimacy attained by being *recognized* as a leader – in this case, by the "progressive" world.

Sure enough, the memorandum went, allowing the sanctions resolution to pass would harm Moscow's reputation in the third world, "among the progressive revolutionary countries, which in the last few days have shown understanding and support in relation to our actions in Afghanistan." Moreover, Iran which had shown "certain caution" on the issue of Afghanistan, "clearly trying to avoid any real aggravation of relations with the Soviet Union", would accuse Moscow of a "collusion" with the United States. The outburst of "fanatical hate" against Moscow would not just endanger Soviet diplomats but, crucially, undermine Soviet economic talks with Iran, especially on the supply of gas.

Even if the Soviet Union abstained on the sanctions resolution, Brezhnev's aides argued, it would have to abide by its terms. "This would mean, the Soviet Union would have to participate in the blockade of Iran, imposed by America! Even if it did not mean much for us in practice, in principle the situation would be strange, mildly put." And if the Soviets decided to violate economic sanctions and continue trading with Iran, well, they would then be violating a resolution that they allowed to pass in the first place: "For some reason, no one had thought about it during the [Politburo] discussion." Finally, addressing the concern that by vetoing the US resolution, the Soviets would further aggravate relations with the United States at a time when Moscow was already under fire for invading Afghanistan, Brezhnev's aides noted that relations were already so bad, they could not possibly get any worse. "In any case, one should not expect gratitude from the US government for our support of its position in the Security Council."[107]

Brezhnev wrote "urgent" at top of the memorandum and forwarded it to the mighty troika of Gromyko, Andropov, and Ustinov who were evidently persuaded by the argumentation because on January 13 the Soviet Union duly vetoed the US sanctions resolution on Iran.

CHAPTER 17 THE FINAL NAIL

This granular analysis reveals a great deal about how policy was made in the Kremlin, as well as its underlying motivations. There is a lot to unpack here, a bewildering complexity of factors that fed into the decision-making process. Ambassador Dobrynin later explained that the Soviet decision to veto the sanctions resolution was merely a quid pro quo for the Carter Administration's anti-Soviet actions post-Afghanistan.[108] In reality, it was one of many factors, certainly not even the most decisive one. The more fundamental problem was about the Soviet view of themselves. Could they have approached Iran in the spirit of a Soviet–American condominium of 1972–73? If they did, then working with the United States to rein in the Iranians would have been the right policy choice. But, in reality, that condominium was never destined to last. When an opportunity came up to profit (geopolitically or just economically) at US expense, as in Iran, the temptation was considerable. Add to this the idea, articulated in the memorandum above, that being seen acting together with the United States would undermine Soviet reputation in the third world – and there we have it: the Soviet standing as America's great rival won over the idea of the Soviet Union as America's great partner that Brezhnev had once entertained.

Of course, the very fact that Brezhnev was already on his last legs helped steer policy towards this conservative outcome. Brezhnev had been personally invested in detente, much more so than Aleksandrov-Agentov, Blatov, and Samoteikin – but he had no choice but to defer to their expertise now that his own physical and mental faculties noticeably declined.

Interestingly, the Soviets continued to court Iran, even when it became patently clear that the radical regime in Tehran had no intention of replacing the American "Satan" with the lesser Soviet one – and even in the face of obvious Iranian involvement in the conflict in Afghanistan through its support for the anti-Soviet mujahideen. So careful was Moscow not to antagonize their neighbor that when in September 1980 the Soviet client Iraq invaded Iran, the Soviets went out of their way to appear neutral, even to the point of greatly annoying Iraqi dictator Saddam Hussein by failing to supply ammunition and spare parts for his vast store of Soviet military equipment. "These actions, comrades," Saddam Hussein complained in a letter to Brezhnev in October 1980, "leave a bitter residue in one's soul ... We are most worried that this bitterness will penetrate the hearts of all Iraqis when they learn of all these lamentable facts."[109] Brezhnev brushed him off, telling him that the war served no purpose, and that it only benefited the Americans in that it was forcing Iran to abandon its anti-American position.[110] As he would later explain to Jordan's King Hussein, who, oddly enough, in May 1981 pleaded with the Soviets to lean to Iraq's side: "Iran is our neighbor, and we

497

PART III DECLINE

are interested in maintaining, as far as possible, good relations with it. One can't overlook the fact that the Iranian Revolution delivered a serious blow to imperialism, and that Iraq's war against Iran is pushing the latter back into the embrace of the Western powers."[111]

Even when in December 1980 raging crowds broke into the Soviet Embassy in Tehran and vandalized the old building, the site of the 1943 Allied Conference, the Soviets kept their protests to a bare minimum. Even when Tudeh – the Soviets' client in Iran – was effectively strangled by the regime, Moscow did not burn bridges, and at the earliest opportunity, in the late 1980s, sought to rebuild relations with Tehran. Pragmatic? Of course, it was. The Soviets got burned in Iran so many times – they had learned at last how to keep their fingers out of the fire.

THE CHINESE ANGLE

How did the Chinese fit into this story? For a time, they actively cooperated with the United States in undercutting the Soviet influence in the third world. China played a very active role in Afghanistan by supplying and training the anti-Soviet insurgents. As Deng Xiaoping told Carter's secretary of defense, Harold Brown, "We [China and the United States] must turn Afghanistan into a quagmire in which the Soviet Union is bogged down for a long time in guerrilla warfare." "That is what we intend to do," Dr. Brown dutifully replied, adding: "But we must keep our intentions confidential."[112] The United States and China were on parallel tracks in Southeast Asia. Carter saw Pol Pot as an abomination but his ouster by the Vietnamese fed fears of a growing Soviet influence in Indochina, so in this sense, Deng Xiaoping's war against Vietnam was objectively in America's interest. This was how Deng understood it, and that was a major reason for why he did it.

Were the Chinese leaders really as worried about the Soviet menace as they made it sound in conversations with their Western counterparts? It is now possible to answer this question based on internal documents of the Chinese Foreign Ministry. In February 1980 the Party Central Committee circulated the Foreign Ministry's views on the international situation and policy guidelines. The document is generally in tune with what Deng Xiaoping repeatedly emphasized: that the Soviet Union was driving at world domination, "crazily" expanding in the third world, seeking to control waterways and seize oil. The documents illustrate China's concern about the potential Vietnamese invasion of Thailand (and as well as its resolve to come to Thailand's aid should such a scenario transpire). Lastly, they confirm China's determination to get the Soviets "mired" in Afghanistan.

498

CHAPTER 17 THE FINAL NAIL

But there is nuance. In his dialogue with the Americans, Deng never tired of emphasizing that opposing the Soviet Union was more important for the United States than for China, which, in any case, could weather a long (nuclear) war, and even Soviet occupation. But the internal documentation highlights that Beijing's real fear was in "the US playing China as a card" and in "us [China] serving someone else's [America's] strategic interests." To avoid such an unfavorable situation, China was to assert its "leading role" in the global Sino-US-European-third world anti-Soviet front. This included maintaining a tentative dialogue with the USSR (but without showing too much enthusiasm), discouraging Moscow's Eastern European satellites from one-sided reliance on the USSR, improving relations with India (though not to the extent that would impair Sino-Pakistani ties), encouraging the Arab states to tone down their anti-American and anti-Israeli rhetoric in order to focus on the Soviet threat, and putting China's support of third world revolution "in the service of our grand strategy of opposition to the USSR." The latter provision meant "properly managing" the revolutionary struggles of Southeast Asia, which had long drawn on Beijing's support. "Properly managing" was just a euphemism for winding them down – something that was already quietly happening since Mao's death.

Indeed, the only Southeast Asian country that the Chinese still appeared determined to subvert was their old ally Vietnam, to which end the Foreign Ministry spoke of the need to sponsor internal dissent against the indefatigable Le Duan.[113]

What is striking about these guidelines is just how nuanced, sophisticated, and strategic the Chinese leaders had become in managing their relations with the two superpowers. The only term to describe this cold, calculating policy is *realpolitik* in the Kissingerian sense.

Of course, this policy was fully in place a decade before, at the very start of the Sino-American rapprochement, when Kissinger first crossed the seas and met Mao and Zhou who more than matched him in diplomatic guile. As one prominent Chinese policy maker, General Geng Biao, explained in 1975, the essence of the Sino-American relationship was in "using [Soviet–American] contradictions to attack the Soviet revisionists and weaken the American imperialists." "The American imperialists," he added, "also [try to] use our contradictions with the Soviet revisionists ... only they can't use [these contradictions]. We [by contrast] can use them [the Americans]."[114]

Yet there was a perceptible difference between Mao's and Deng's eras. "We agreed to Nixon's visit to China," Geng Biao argued in 1975, not long before Mao's death, "not because we have a warm feeling towards the

United States, and certainly not because we want to obtain something from them." But five years later, the same Geng Biao – now raised in status to vice premier – was sent on massive procurement trips to the United States, where, tirelessly repeating the mantra of czarist expansionism, he bought, and bought, and bought. By the turn of the decade, Deng's China clearly wanted something from the West: technologies, capital, and the know-how to make China the sort of great power that it never could have become under Mao. That was the great difference between *realpolitik* à la Mao and *realpolitik* à la Deng.

In one sense, though, Chinese foreign policy did not change from Mao to Deng. As Geng Biao put it, there never was any "warm feeling" for America: the attitude throughout was purely transactional. This was not how things appeared from Washington; there was a genuine hope that China may gradually gravitate towards the United States by embracing its values. The American policy makers failed to distinguish between the Chinese leaders' short-term tactics and their long-term strategy.

By contrast, the Soviets picked up on the difference. In the early 1980s – as the Soviet operation in Afghanistan turned into a quagmire – the Soviet leaders began cautiously probing for the possibilities of a rapprochement with China. The complete collapse of detente encouraged creative thinking in Moscow about ways of overcoming international isolation. The result of internal policy deliberation was Brezhnev's March 1982 speech in Tashkent, where he announced his readiness to mend fences with China. Brezhnev was barely aware of what he was reading when he made the landmark speech. It did not matter: it represented a new departure for Soviet foreign policy, and a victory for voices of reason among the ailing Soviet leaders. Deng noticed the signal: he, too, was beginning to understand that his alignment with America constrained China in ways he had not anticipated.[115] Perhaps by answering Brezhnev's probe, he could gain a greater room for policy maneuver. The Cold War entered the endgame.

CONCLUSION

Several days before the Soviet leaders made their fateful decision to intervene in Afghanistan, Henry Kissinger called on his old friend Anatoly Dobrynin. The Soviets were disappointed with the former national security adviser. Far from being an advocate of detente as he promised he would be, Kissinger had been calling for a tougher stand against the Soviet Union, not least on issues of arms control. "From the conversation with Kissinger," Dobrynin cabled Moscow, "you could see that he is still an unprincipled politician, and a political chameleon who only cares about staying visible in the US public life and returning to power."[116] But despite this very unflattering characterization, Dobrynin approvingly reported on one important thesis that Kissinger put forward. "Without worrying about being called a cynic," Kissinger told Dobrynin, he was "in favor of some kind of a division of the spheres of influence between the USSR and the USA ... For this, one needs a confidential dialogue between the two, which, in his opinion, is absent."[117]

Kissinger's thinking was thus in line with what Churchill's must have been when he presented Stalin with a scrap of paper bearing percentages for the British and Soviet spheres of influence in the post-World War II world. Churchill's ill-fated percentages agreement lacked any mention of Afghanistan or, for this matter, much of the rest of the third world. Dividing Europe was difficult enough. Agreeing on the division of the world was an impossible proposition. Kissinger knew this better than most because it was he who, after all, did so much to undercut the Soviet influence in the Middle East. The American and Soviet leaders had different perceptions of what was "theirs," and what was not, which helps explain why they found themselves at loggerheads over places like Angola, the Horn of Africa, Iran, or Afghanistan. There was also the temptation to undercut the other's positions and extend one's own definition of "legitimate" interests to cover far-flung areas that challenge most reasonable meanings of "legitimacy."

When Somalia invaded Ogaden, superpower detente was on life support; by the time of Afghanistan, it was as good as dead. The decline was attributable to multiple factors but one that has gained most traction with historians is that it was a function of the Soviet insatiable appetites in the third world. In this reading, Richard Nixon and Henry Kissinger share the blame for mistakenly believing that "linkage" would dissuade the Soviets from exporting revolution to the third world in return for better Soviet–American relations. This did not happen – not in Vietnam nor in the Middle East, nor, indeed in Africa or Afghanistan.

The basic problem with linkage was that it did not fit with what the Soviet leaders sought to accomplish. They would not "behave" in the third world for the sake of a better relationship with the United States. Their behavior in the third world was in itself an indicator of a relationship that they wanted. This meant, for instance, being involved in the Middle East for the sake of being involved (and not necessarily to obtain ice-free ports, as Brzezinski believed, never mind spread world revolution). Acquiring overseas bases or ideological allies were of course acceptable means to being recognized as a true equal of the United States. This is where what Odd Arne Westad

PART III DECLINE

called the willingness "to link up to the Soviet experience" had an important role to play: Moscow's position in the world was recognized through the ritual of adherence to "Marxism-Leninism" (much as the US position in the world was recognized through the ritual of adherence to "democracy" and "human rights"). Such lip service was an important though sometimes dispensable prerequisite to obtaining external support, and a game the would-be clients – Egypt, Angola, Ethiopia, Somalia, Afghanistan, and many others in the third world – played remarkably well, even though the price of participation was death and destruction, a fact that the very term – the "Cold War" – does much too little to acknowledge.

This is not to say, however, that the Soviets were hell-bent on undermining the Americans everywhere they could. There *was* an understanding in Moscow that certain Soviet actions would work against detente, and since detente was a key achievement of Brezhnev's foreign policy, moderation *was* advisable in certain cases. Such moderation was most effectively on display in March 1979 when the Soviets decided against helping Taraki and Amin suppress the rebellion in Herat. In fact, even as late as September 1979 the Soviets appeared determined to resist the idea of sending troops into Afghanistan because doing so would "would have extremely negative consequences" for both Afghanistan and the general international situation.[118] But Brezhnev's physical and mental decline left detente without a powerful supporter. Moreover, detente was under severe strain for years. This was partly – perhaps mainly – a function of US domestic politics, as the Democrats and the Republicans competed in the show of resolve in the face of the overinflated Soviet menace.

In the fall of 1979, for instance, the American public opinion was agitated by the news that the Soviets had stationed a "brigade" of up to 3,000 military personnel in Cuba, even though the US intelligence had kept track of this presence for years.[119] Bickering about this "brigade" – which unarguably posed no threat to the United States – seriously undercut the Soviet–American dialogue after the Carter–Brezhnev summit in Vienna.[120] Another irritant (from the Kremlin's perspective) was the US intention to station intermediate-range nuclear missiles (Pershing-IIs) and the ground-launched cruise missiles (Gryphons) in Europe (the final decision to this end was made on December 12, 1979). By December 1979 it was already doubtful that the US Senate would ratify the SALT-II Treaty – at least that was how Dobrynin presented the situation in reports to Moscow after feeling out Brzezinski's views on this score.[121] When the Soviets went into Afghanistan in December 1979, they did not have to worry about killing detente. Detente was already dead.

CHAPTER 17 THE FINAL NAIL

After the Soviet invasion of Afghanistan, the Soviet–American relationship entered a deep freeze. In January 1980 Carter asked the US Senate to delay debating the SALT-II agreement (the treaty would have most certainly failed). He also declared a grain embargo against the Soviet Union and ordered a boycott of the summer Olympic Games in Moscow. To say that Brezhnev was annoyed is to understate the degree of his perplexity. He seemed almost bewildered that things deteriorated as rapidly as they did; just half a year after Vienna, detente seemed like a very distant memory. The Cold War was raging with renewed force.

Addressing himself to these events in a meeting with his old-time acquaintance, the US businessman Armand Hammer, Brezhnev professed ignorance of what Carter was doing and, more importantly, why. Hammer – whose own business interests were threatened by the downturn – sounded a sympathetic note. He ferociously attacked Zbig Brzezinski, the "spiteful Pole who hates the Soviet Union." Carter was "naive," Hammer said – he was still learning how to be president. "Unfortunately," Brezhnev retorted, "if Carter is learning anything, he is learning just the bad things ... How many follies has Carter committed as of late!" He was unequivocal in his general assessment: "we cannot be intimidated by this, and we cannot be forced to our knees."[122]

Brezhnev had once imagined a different world, one co-managed by the Soviet Union and the United States who would respect one another as "equals." Little was left of that sentiment now, or, indeed, of that younger and more hopeful version of Brezhnev. The Soviet leader, reduced by old age and sclerosis, presently faced a much more uncertain and hostile world than at any time since he replaced Khrushchev at the helm.

The year 1980 was an election year in the United States. As in 1976, the political discourse was fiercely anti-Soviet across the board. Four years earlier, at least, there had been the hope that it was a temporary condition, a consequence of Ford's post-Watergate weakness; that passions would die down, and that Carter (as Hammer had promised) would prove more "realistic" than his election pronouncements allowed. There was no hope of this in 1980. The Republican candidate – former California governor Ronald Reagan whom Brezhnev had met in passing in San Clemente in 1973 – was militantly anti-Soviet. So worried was Brezhnev about Reagan's candidacy that he privately voiced his support for Carter, saying that although Carter had of course "made mistakes" and had even "lost his head on occasion," he was still better than Reagan who represented the "most reactionary ideology."[123]

PART IV

COLLAPSE

18

FEAR

The early 1980s were a period of almost unprecedented tension in Soviet–US relations. The contrast with the early 1970s could not be starker: gone were the days of fraternizing; detente lay in ruins. President Ronald Reagan's anti-Communist rhetoric – well summed up by his promise to leave Marxism-Leninism in the ash heap of history – was a million miles apart from Nixon's polite deference. The Soviets were scandalized. A relationship that was already extremely bad at the time Carter left office – no small thanks to the ongoing invasion of Afghanistan – was presently in a downward slide towards an abyss. Brezhnev – himself in terminal physical decline – was unwilling and unable to reverse this slide. Judging by his diary, Brezhnev's key preoccupation in those twilight years was measuring his weight, which he meticulously recorded from day to day.[1] Actual policy making passed into the hands of Foreign Minister Andrei Gromyko, KGB Chairman Yury Andropov, and Minister of Defense Dmitry Ustinov, whose collective judgment tended towards toughing it out with the United States.

The war in Afghanistan dragged on year in, year out. The Soviets were looking for a way out but could not bring themselves to face the probable consequence of an early withdrawal – the collapse of their client regime in Kabul. Meanwhile, in Europe, they faced the worst crisis since the Prague Spring: Poland was in an economic and political meltdown. Facing the threat of a Soviet military intervention, the Polish authorities introduced martial law. But the Polish crisis brought tensions in Soviet–US relations to a new level. The Reagan Administration imposed new sanctions. The Soviets responded with vitriol.

November 1982 brought a change of guard: Brezhnev died. He was replaced at the helm by Yury Andropov, an aging apparatchik with the weight of KGB experience on his shoulders, and bad kidneys to match. There was no perceptible impact on the Soviet–American relationship, nor could there have been since Andropov had been the key architect of Soviet foreign policy in Brezhnev's final years. Tensions continued to

PART IV COLLAPSE

build up, coming to head in the fall of 1983, with the Soviet shooting down of the South Korean airliner, KAL 007, the planned deployment of US intermediate-range Pershing-IIs and cruise missiles in Western Europe, and especially NATO's command-and-control exercise, Able Archer, which quite possibly spooked the nervous Soviet leadership. The Soviet Union found itself in a state of growing international isolation: a sprawling empire, feared, despised, burdened with expensive and demanding clients, and ultimately at a loss when it came to formulating a coherent grand strategy. There was, however, an early effort to escape this isolation through a reengagement with China. After a quarter of a century of bitterness and confrontation, the early 1980s thus marked the beginning of the Sino-Soviet rapprochement, which was to have dramatic geopolitical consequences for the future.

POLAND

The 1980–81 crisis in Poland had its origins, quite simply, in the deep, systemic failure of socialist economic management that was symptomatic of the broader malaise of Soviet-style socialism and indeed a precursor of the economic meltdown later experienced across Eastern Europe and in the USSR itself. The lack of incentives kept labor productivity low. Agricultural output stagnated. Poland was not producing enough to feed itself and resorted to heavy borrowing from the West, which meant a steady build-up of debt. Polish workers were restive, unwilling to appreciate the wonders of socialism, reacting angrily to the government's attempts to raise consumer prices to balance the books. On two occasions in the previous decade, the authorities resorted to force and intimidation to stifle protests. Dozens were killed in the December 1970 crackdown against worker protests in Gdańsk, Gdynia, Elbląg, and Szczecin, a crisis that also led to the replacement of the authoritarian long-timer Władysław Gomułka with the ostensible reformist Edward Gierek. But protests erupted again in 1976 after another hike in prices; this time, the government backed down, revealing both economic incompetence and apparent weakness in the face of popular discontent.[2]

Oppositional activities in Poland grew with the establishment of the Workers' Defense Committee (KOR in its Polish abbreviation), an association of intellectuals who rallied in support of detained workers and their families. KOR was a harbinger of other grassroots associations that fed into the protest culture of the late 1970s, which, as in the USSR (but to a much larger extent), was energized by the signing of the Helsinki Final

CHAPTER 18 FEAR

Act. Uncensored publications proliferated. The influence of the Catholic Church, always strong, became even greater when in October 1978 the College of Cardinals in Rome elected Cardinal Wojtyła of Kraków as Pope John Paul II. The "Polish" pope's pilgrimage to his home country in June 1979 – where he was met by adulating multitudes – became a shocking reminder of the precariousness of Communist rule in the still deeply religious country.[3]

The Soviets watched this slow-motion trainwreck with growing apprehension and proffered advice, most of it exceptionally bad. For example, Brezhnev encouraged the Polish comrades to hasten collectivization of agriculture, complaining that the government's attempts to give more latitude to private farming and retail sales – in itself a response to the deepening economic crisis – could empower the private sector and so undermine the regime in the long term. Brezhnev also called for deeper party involvement in economic management: "any difficulties can be overcome if the party is united and the Communists actively support the leadership's line."[4] The general secretary railed about the dangers of borrowing from the West and warned against trying to join the International Monetary Fund in the hope of attracting more credits. "The capitalists," Brezhnev lectured, reading from printed notes, "give credits precisely because they want to use them at the right moment in order to extract various concessions, and sometimes for blackmail, including political blackmail."[5] Gierek was generally receptive to such criticism, blaming the state of affairs in agriculture on his predecessor Gomułka. He also made the right noises about trying to curb borrowing in the West. But he made it clear that his room for maneuver was limited. "They are holding us by the throat," he told Brezhnev.[6]

Where Gierek disagreed with Brezhnev was in the attitude towards the political opposition. The Soviet leader stood for tougher measures than the Polish authorities were willing to allow. He complained about the growth in the influence of the Catholic Church, and the proliferation of nationalist (i.e. anti-Soviet) sentiments. Gierek downplayed these dangers, explaining, "this [the opposition] is a small group of people and it would cost us nothing to throw them all behind bars in one blow. But we don't see great danger in their activities." Later the Soviet leadership would cite these views to argue that Gierek did not heed their advice until it was too late. But for all these discussions, Poland's economic performance continued to worsen. Despite promises to curb borrowing, the debts piled up, going up from $14 billion in early 1978 to some $22 billion by 1980.[7] That happened even as the Soviet Union extended aid, including billions of dollars' worth of subsidized oil, to their Polish comrades.

PART IV COLLAPSE

By mid-1980, the situation was rapidly spiraling out of control. In July Brezhnev called Gierek to Yalta, his summer retreat, for another heart-to-heart. Their meeting took place several weeks after the Provincial Committee of the Polish United Workers' Party (PUWP) made the fateful decision to raise food prices (again!), which predictably caused an uproar of public dissatisfaction, leading to widespread strikes. What really worried the Soviets was that, just as so many times before, some of that dissatisfaction found expression in anti-Soviet sentiments. For instance, someone desecrated tombs of Soviet soldiers in Świnoujście, and there was an unsuccessful attempt to blow up Lenin's monument in Kraków. These were of course reported to Brezhnev. He told Gierek to come down hard against "nationalism," telling him to mind the "very thin line" that existed between "healthy" patriotism and anti-Soviet nationalism.[8]

Once again Brezhnev pressed Gierek to play hardball with the opposition, by which he meant arresting them: "sometimes this is inevitable."[9] Gierek, though, pushed back on this idea, saying that if the authorities were to arrest these dissidents, "they [the opposition] will depict themselves as victims of the Communist regime, which could make the Polish public pity them." He then tried to reassure Brezhnev that he "had a realistic appraisal of the political situation" and simply did not want to escalate matters towards a head-on collision.[10] He promised Brezhnev to persevere with fiscal tightening and pleaded for economic aid (the Soviet leader promised to entertain new requests, even though the Soviet economic situation was hardly anything to boast about).

But Gierek was already losing control. Merely two weeks later, a massive strike erupted at the Lenin Shipyard in Gdańsk, bringing the political situation in Poland to boiling point. Faced with a near-uprising in the country on the one hand, and relentless Soviet pressure on the other, the PUWP Politburo vacillated between repressions and dialogue. It was the latter course that won the day when, on August 29, the Communist leadership approved a compromise with the strikers. The so-called Gdańsk Agreement, concluded two days later, contained guarantees for the freedom of speech and several generous social provisions. Crucially, it recognized workers' right to form self-governing trade unions.[11] "If we waited for another 2–3 days," the deputy prime minister of Poland, Mieczysław Jagielski, explained to Brezhnev two weeks later, "Poland would end up with a general strike with all the attendant consequences. By taking this step, we practically averted the possibility of a great national catastrophe."[12] The trade union – Solidarność (Solidarity) – rapidly acquired a massive following, propelling its leader, the charismatic former electrician Lech Wałęsa, to national prominence.

510

The Soviets were deeply alarmed by these concessions and accused Gierek of ignoring Moscow's advice (i.e. curbing foreign lending and taking hardline measures against the opposition).[13] "He was repeatedly asked the question about growing indebtedness to the capitalists," Mikhail Suslov – who headed the powerful Politburo Commission on Poland – noted testily in a conversation with one of Gierek's colleagues, "but Gierek would obfuscate and not tell the truth. We warned him many times that one must not guzzle away the national income." As for Gierek's optimistic take on the opposition, Suslov added with a hint of menace, "perhaps he did it [minimized this problem] unintentionally – was he just not well informed?"[14] Having lost Soviet support, Gierek had to fall on his sword. He resigned in September 1980, handing over to a fellow party apparatchik Stanisław Kania.

Worried about spill-over effects, the Kremlin moved to curb tourist travel and the exchange of periodicals with Poland.[15] The KGB located and expelled "Solidarity activists" who were allegedly instigating strikes in the USSR.[16] The parallels between the dire economic situation in Poland and that in the USSR were much too close for comfort. "Our food situation is very bad," Anatoly Chernyaev noted in his diary on September 19, 1980." This became especially obvious after the enormous expense of the Moscow Olympics (July 19–August 3). There were shopping queues everywhere but "there are no potatoes, nor cabbage, nor onions, nor carrots, nor cheese." There was already labor unrest and even strikes at factories across the USSR – something almost unheard of! "And we have no real means of ending strikes," Chernyaev noted ruefully from his perch in the Central Committee: "for we have no meat, nor order, nor justice." The Soviet Union itself was a potential Poland – only on a much larger scale. Only the Soviet leaders buried their heads deeper and deeper in the sand. "Our moral-ideological prestige is lower than anyone could imagine. And it keeps falling because we lie: we lie to our people, to ourselves, to all other peoples and parties. And everything that does not accord with these lies we call anti-Sovietism, enemy ploys, or revisionism."[17]

Chernyaev was flabbergasted by the Soviet response to the events in Poland – and perhaps there were many like him, sitting high up in the offices of Soviet power. Only not high enough. The mood was very different at the very top. "In general, comrades," Brezhnev declared at the Politburo on September 18, "we are dealing with a new type of an offensive against socialism by the class enemy: different than it was in Hungary or in Czechoslovakia, in many ways more nuanced and dangerous." He added: "the influence of the events in Poland will have a long-term impact, far from Poland's borders."[18] Moscow's advice for fixing the Polish problem predictably centered on strengthening the party "ideationally" and "organizationally." Another piece of advice Brezhnev proffered, drawing on his own experience in power, was to avoid rotation among the leading party cadres in Poland to assure stability.[19] Coming from the ailing wreck of a general secretary who was barely able to stray from his talking points (carefully prepared by his aides in large font for the ease of reading), this advice struck a tone of irony but Brezhnev, as the rest of the Soviet leadership, was beyond irony at this point.

On October 21, the Soviet Communist Party held a plenum to consider Soviet economic and social development plan for 1981. Brezhnev's veteran speechwriters Georgy Arbatov, Nikolai Inozemtsev, and Aleksandr Bovin prepared a draft speech for him, criticizing the state of the Soviet economy and in particular the worsening food situation. They were taken by surprise when the draft was "categorically rejected." The speech, according to Bovin, was written "under the impression [of events in] Poland and the almost desperate situation in the [Soviet] economy." But the senior leadership would have none of it. Brezhnev was reportedly "annoyed," and sent the draft out to his Politburo colleagues, many of whom also provided negative comments, in particular Suslov who methodically cut out all the critical bits – in Arbatov's words, "sliced off the balls." "Mikhail Andreevich [Suslov] always knows where the balls are," Arbatov complained to Chernyaev during the plenum, "no matter how you hide them, how you wrap them, he'll immediately see them and – bam, he slices them off." Bovin, for his part, complained about Andropov who "knows everything." "Does he not understand where this is going?! Unthinkable!"[20] In the end, Brezhnev's speech just only hinted at the deep problems below the surface – perhaps because no one knew what to do. One thing the plenum did accomplish – which was of great later significance – was that it elevated the Central Committee secretary responsible for agriculture, the young and promising Mikhail Gorbachev, to full membership of the aging Politburo.[21]

While turning a blind eye to the unfolding disaster at home, the Soviet comrades pondered the ever-worsening situation in Poland. It did not take long for them to narrow down the options to the one thing that would surely work: martial law. Kania's visit to Moscow at the end of October 1980 offered an opportunity to prod him in this direction. Before his arrival, on October 29, the Politburo gathered to strategize. Brezhnev criticized the Poles' apparent inability to crack down on "the enemies of the people." Andropov, Ustinov, and Gromyko echoed his words, calling for the imposition of martial law to rein in the "anti-socialist elements ... who

CHAPTER 18 FEAR

want to take power away from workers."[22] Ustinov, as minister of defense, helpfully pointed out that the "northern group of forces is in the state of complete battle readiness." Gromyko added that the Soviet Union simply "could not lose Poland" as it had lost 600,000 lives in the Second World War "liberating" it.[23]

But when Kania and the Polish prime minister, Józef Pińkowski, turned up in Moscow, they showed, in Brezhnev's words, a "distinct hesitation" in following the Soviet advice in unleashing brute force. This was despite the internal Polish military planning – then ongoing – for exactly this contingency.[24] According to Kania, Warsaw was beholden to the West for credits, and a crackdown could lead to the rejection of Polish requests for more money. Remarkably – given the tough talk at the Politburo – the Soviets backed off for now. Brezhnev chose to trust Kania. Reporting on his talks to the Politburo, the Soviet leader noted that for their lack of decisiveness Kania and Pińkowski "made a good impression." They would do the right thing, he thought, if push came to shove, in stark contrast to Amin in Afghanistan just a year earlier. Of course, the stakes in Poland were also that much higher. For the time-being, there was little choice, Brezhnev said, but to try to bail the Poles out by providing aid "no matter how burdensome it will be for us." But, he added, "we must remain on guard because the situation in Poland is still dangerously explosive."[25]

What happened in Poland in November only confirmed the Soviet leaders in their worst fears. First, the Polish authorities backed down after Solidarity refused to accept their insistence on including a provision about the Communist Party's leading role in the trade union's statutes. The Supreme Court overturned this requirement, and although this was a rubber-stamp decision (the compromise was ironed out behind the scenes between Wałęsa and the party authorities), it did appear like a triumph for the rule of law, which by all accounts was an alien idea in the socialist world. As Erich Honecker, who nervously watched these events unfold from neighboring East Germany, put it: "Honestly, I would never have been able to come up with such an idea: the party becomes an appendix to the statute."[26] The second development was the Narożniak–Sapeło affair, when Solidarity sympathizers leaked documents that showed plans to harass trade union activists. Those responsible, including Jan Narożniak and Piotr Sapeło, were arrested only to be released, suggesting the party's weakness in the face of Solidarity blackmail. How could such a state of affairs be tolerated?

The leaders of the Warsaw Pact therefore assembled in Moscow on December 5 to hear Kania present his case and to criticize him for

PART IV COLLAPSE

his weak-kneed response.[27] By then it seemed likely – not least to the Poles themselves – that the Soviets would intervene, using military exercises as a cover. President Carter thought that they might (the key US intelligence asset in Warsaw, Ryszard Kukliński, had seen the plans and forewarned the United States), so the White House issued a statement, warning Moscow against any such precipitous move.[28] The Soviets were ostensibly prepared to invade, having already in August approved the mobilization of some 100,000 reservists to provide "military assistance" to Poland in case it was needed.[29]

Whether they intended to do so or not is another matter. As so often the case, there was probably a disagreement among the ailing seniors about the course of action, confounded by tiredness and growing desperation. Brezhnev's former comrade-in-leadership Aleksei Kosygin died after a prolonged illness on December 18, and his passing marked the beginning of the end for that leadership cohort. Not that they showed any particular awareness. On the very day Kosygin died, Politburo members assembled in the Kremlin to present Brezhnev with an award – the Order of the October Revolution. Frail Suslov read out a eulogy, claiming that "many millions of people in our country and abroad turn to you with words of love and affection." Brezhnev mumbled thanks, and promised that "he would give all his strength" to the task of building Communism.[30] It was all too much for Chernyaev who swore at the TV showing the ordeal. "I get the impression that our leaders have firmly decided: 'Fuck them all, let them say what they want but they won't be fucking able to do anything to us!'"[31]

It was that cohort of leaders that had to decide whether to intervene in Poland. In the end the Soviets did not intervene – neither in December 1980, nor again in March–April 1981, when it seemed that they were on the verge of doing just that under the cover of military exercises. Instead, they put pressure on the Polish leaders to declare martial law on their own account, lambasting them in private for making political concessions to Solidarity.[32] These political concessions (in the Soviet interpretation) included: effective surrender of the mass media to Solidarity; inability to tighten border controls to prevent "imperialist agencies" from infiltrating Poland; unwillingness to ban strikes; and, most importantly, the registration of the farmers' Solidarity as an independent trade union. The Polish leaders were also not doing enough to curb nationalist sentiments, allowing "anti-Soviet" elements to slander the Soviet–Polish friendship.[33]

All of that deeply worried Brezhnev who was increasingly suspicious of Kania. "The [Polish] friends listen, agree to our recommendations, but do nothing in practice," he complained at the Politburo on April 2. Andropov spoke of the need to "apply greater pressure" on the Poles. Gromyko noted that neither Kania nor his new prime minister and long-time defense minister, Wojciech Jaruzelski, were "in a good shape," and the latter was particularly "dejected." Ustinov argued that there was still time to save the situation because the army, the state security, and the police could still act in unity but this would not last. "I think that bloodshed is inevitable," he added menacingly, "it will happen."[34] The Politburo resolved to send Andropov and Ustinov to the border town of Brest for another meeting with the Polish leaders. The meeting took place on the night of April 3–4, 1981. Andropov and Ustinov tried to pressure the Polish duo to sign off on plans to implement martial law: to no avail.[35]

Later in April Mikhail Suslov was dispatched to Warsaw with a broadly similar mandate. Suslov, for all his involvement in Polish affairs since the previous August, did not want to go. "What can I do there?" he reportedly complained. "Everything, it seems, has been said, everything is clear, what else can you achieve?!"[36] Still, he went, presenting the Poles with the one argument that was sure to fall flat. "If the worst were to pass," he told the Polish leaders, "if the anti-socialist forces came to power, if, in other words, Poland fell out of the socialist commonwealth, the imperialists would immediately outstretch their greedy hands towards it. And who, in this case, would guarantee the independence, sovereignty, and borders of Poland as a state?"[37]

Meanwhile – and despite the sorry state of the Soviet economy – Moscow offered substantial economic aid, which, between 1980 and mid-1981 added up to $4 billion, including $1.5 billion in cash.[38] This entailed cutting subsidized supplies of oil to other Warsaw Pact allies, which no one liked, but which particularly upset East Germany's Honecker. This may be one reason why he was so critical of Kania, pressing the Soviets to replace him with a hardliner. That Brezhnev did not – that he went along with Kania for so long, imploring him, threatening him, but not trying to dislodge him – shows just how few options Moscow had in view of Solidarity's clout and the growing disarray in the ranks of the Polish Communists.[39] Kania was finally replaced as the party leader in October 1981: not by any of the hardliners on Honecker's list but by General Wojciech Jaruzelski who had served as the prime minister. It was Jaruzelski who finally did what the Soviets had long called for: imposed martial law on December 12–13, 1981.[40]

To say that he did so under duress is to tell half the truth. Yes, Moscow put Jaruzelski under a lot of pressure. But the notion that the prospect of Soviet military intervention hung over Poland like the sword of Damocles is not fully borne out by the historical evidence – much to the contrary. In fact,

PART IV COLLAPSE

it was Jaruzelski who, in the weeks and days prior to the crackdown, begged Moscow to send forces, and was repeatedly and quite unceremoniously rebuffed.[41] Already in July Brezhnev told Romania's Nicolae Ceauşescu when the two overlapped in Crimea on their vacations that he never had any intention to send forces to Poland.[42] He sidestepped the question of intervention in his talks with Honecker,[43] and reportedly also with Bulgaria's Todor Zhivkov, Hungary's Janos Kadar, and Czechoslovakia's Gustáv Husák who, in particular, was pressing on Brezhnev to intervene. Chernyaev, who had read all the transcripts, found himself in rare agreement with the general secretary. "The approach proposed by Brezhnev is the only wise one. He said, after all, that we cannot adopt Poland as our dependent."[44] That same rationale would later underpin Gorbachev's thinking about Soviet nonintervention in Eastern Europe: it was simply something Moscow could no longer economically afford.

When the matter came up for discussion at the Politburo meeting on December 10, not one person supported the idea of sending Soviet troops – and that included Minister of Defense Ustinov (who had previously made militant noises), Foreign Minister Gromyko, and KGB Chairman Andropov, the trio that prodded Brezhnev to endorse the invasion of Afghanistan two years earlier. There was to be no repetition. As Gromyko put it, "we must try to somehow pour cold water on the sentiments of Jaruzelski and other Polish leaders concerning the introduction of [Soviet] forces. There can be no introduction of forces into Poland whatsoever."[45]

It is difficult to imagine a more unequivocal statement, but it begs a question: Why was it that the Soviet leaders were so determined to avoid the very scenario they had resorted to in 1953, 1956, 1968 and, indeed, only two years earlier, in Afghanistan? It is tempting to conclude that it was because they feared a bloodbath if the Poles put up strong resistance. If the Afghanistan experience was anything to go by, Soviet efforts to help fraternal Poland could well become a protracted affair. Kania claimed in retrospect that it was this fear of a quagmire that forced Brezhnev to cancel the planned invasion of December 1980, and to act cautiously in the months that followed.[46] However, if present, this particular rationale was hardly ever broached at the Politburo, and – as the evidence above suggests – one might even argue that the Soviets never intended to invade to begin with – only to intimidate.[47]

What *was* repeatedly raised was the fallout for the Soviet Union's international standing, and in particular the likely negative Western reaction to the Soviet intervention. For example, during a Politburo meeting at the end of October 1981, Brezhnev spoke of his worry that any Soviet

CHAPTER 18 FEAR

intervention would lead to a cancellation of his visit to Bonn (scheduled for November), where he would raise issues of nuclear arms control and, as was the Soviet habit, try to drive a wedge between West Germany and the United States. Although European detente – as detente in general – was by then as good as dead, Brezhnev was clearly worried about things getting even worse.[48] Suslov echoed this sentiment when he argued that the Soviet intervention would undercut Moscow's global credentials as a champion of peace. "The international public opinion will not understand us," he said.[49]

One report prepared in the Soviet Central Committee (and then distributed to socialist allies) alluded to concerns about Soviet "isolation" on the international stage, and pointed to a potential escalation that could lead to a military conflict. Another argument put forward was that the Soviet intervention could then be used to justify Western intervention in other countries.[50] What this referred to is not entirely clear, although one tantalizing piece of evidence from Soviet talks with Jaruzelski in December 1981 suggests that Moscow was concerned about a potential US retaliation in Cuba.[51] Andropov had earlier voiced worries about "potential [US] provocations" against Cuba: "Indirectly, this is related to the situation in Poland," he argued in internal counsels.[52] (Given that moving against Cuba was at least discussed by the Reagan Administration in 1981 – Secretary of State Alexander Haig had allegedly promised to turn the island into a "fucking parking lot" – such concerns were certainly not unfounded.)[53]

But in the list of reasons not to intervene militarily, the one that probably had the greatest resonance with Soviet policy makers was the fear of Western sanctions. Yury Andropov spelled out the problem for the Politburo on December 10. "We cannot take the risk," he argued. "We do not intend to send forces to Poland ... I don't know how things will turn out with Poland, but even if Poland were to come under Solidarity's rule, this would be one thing. But if the capitalist countries come down against the Soviet Union – and they already have an appropriate agreement on various economic and political sanctions – this will be very difficult for us. We must take care of our country, of strengthening the Soviet Union. This is our main policy."[54] This was an expression of profound realism from a key architect of the Soviet intervention in Afghanistan that had since turned into a quagmire. As Andropov reportedly told an associate around this time, "the quota of our foreign interventions has been exhausted."[55]

This leaves one question unanswered: What would have happened if Jaruzelski ultimately failed to deliver, if he continued to stall and did not declare martial law? Would the Soviets have intervened when faced with the

PART IV COLLAPSE

prospect of a complete meltdown of Communist rule and Solidarity's triumph? The evidence is patchy. Brezhnev, during his often difficult discussions with Kania, expressed concerns about Poland being ruled by Solidarity as in this case "who will guarantee the inviolability of the commonwealth's vital lines of communication that pass through the PPR [Polish Workers' Party], including strategic lines of communication?"[56] On the other hand, the same Brezhnev – in conversations with Ceaușescu and others – implied that a "capitalist" Poland was within the realm of possibility and even warned Kania that should Poland become capitalist, it could no longer count on the generous Soviet aid.[57] Andropov – judging by his comments at the Politburo – also seems to have at least theoretically accepted the possibility of Solidarity coming to power in some of his pronouncements.[58] And yet in other pronouncements, he appears to have voiced determination to "fight for Poland," telling his East German colleague Erich Mielke that "Poland must remain a member of the Warsaw Pact."[59]

If Solidarity did come to power and if Lech Wałęsa did not at the same time demand Poland's withdrawal from the Warsaw Pact or question the Soviet right to keep troops in Poland, then it is conceivable that Moscow would have put up with him. But what if he did try to pull out from the Soviet orbit altogether? Then, they would have to think hard and perhaps choose between crippling Western sanctions and international isolation and a meltdown of the Warsaw Pact. A difficult choice it would have been.[60] Fortunately, General Wojciech Jaruzelski spared the Soviets the agony by helpfully bringing down the fist.

DEALING WITH REAGAN

Leonid Brezhnev met Ronald Reagan only once, when the general secretary visited with Nixon in California in June 1973 (Reagan was the governor of the state at the time). Little did he know then that the former actor and a long-time Republican right-winger would carry the American vote in November 1980. What Reagan said during his election about the Soviet Union certainly did not endear him to listeners in Moscow. Unlike Carter, he did not particularly dwell on human rights, though to the extent that he touched on the subject, he was fiercely critical. The Soviet Union, Reagan said, had "no human rights at all."[61] But what he did talk about at length was the urgent need to reverse what he described as the US lag in strategic defense. The Soviet Union, he argued, was a hostile power, with which peace was possible but – lest it become peace of Czechoslovakia or peace of Afghanistan – it had to be peace through strength. If the

518

CHAPTER 18 FEAR

United States only built up its "margin of safety," it could then renegotiate nuclear arms control agreements with the Soviets, in particular, the long-suffering SALT-II.[62] To add insult to injury, Reagan also accused the Soviets of sponsoring international terrorists. It was little wonder, then, that the Soviet leaders dreaded Reagan's presidency, even if Carter had not turned out well either.

Nevertheless, Reagan's entry into the White House provided Moscow with an opportunity to test his intentions on the premise that perhaps his rhetoric was only just rhetoric, and that he would not mind building bridges to the Soviet Union, beginning with nuclear arms control. Their immediate effort was directed towards a rehabilitation of SALT-II – though that was rebuffed early on (the Soviets were stiffly reminded that they were still in Afghanistan).[63] On January 20, 1981 Brezhnev sent good wishes to Reagan on his inauguration, expressing a vague hope of "constructive cooperation" to resolve international problems.[64] But in his first press conference nine days later Reagan decried detente as a "one-way street" and implied that the actual goal of the Soviet leadership was "world revolution," and the construction of a "one-world Socialist or Communist state."[65] In his first letter to Gromyko upon assuming the duties of the secretary of state, the tough-talking General Alexander Haig criticized the Soviets for their misdeeds in Afghanistan and for trying to profit off the American misery in Iran. But the toughest rhetoric was reserved for the subject of the possible Soviet intervention in Poland, which, he said "would fundamentally alter the entire international situation, and the US with its allies would be compelled to act in a manner which the gravity of the situation would require."[66]

In late February 1981 the Soviet Communist Party held its Twenty-Sixth Congress – a grandiose affair that was attended, apart from a small army of Soviet party functionaries, by Communist leaders from world over, including by besieged Kania, fire-breathing Castro in his military tunic, and aging Le Duan in a grey suit and tie. Brezhnev's 25,000-word report, which he clearly struggled through, lambasted imperialism but professed continued interest in giving detente a "new lease on life." Among his ideas for doing so was a moratorium on the deployment of intermediate-range nuclear forces in Europe (including US Gryphon cruise missiles and Pershing-II missiles), and various confidence-building measures. The moratorium idea, in particular, was Brezhnev's favorite, which he supposedly advanced against the advice of his own military.[67]

"Outrageous," Haig commented on hearing Ambassador Dobrynin spell out Brezhnev's initiative at the end of March.[68] The Americans could not possibly agree to any such moratoriums after the Soviet deployment of

PART IV COLLAPSE

the powerful intermediate-range SS-20 missiles, which triggered NATO's double-track decision in the first place.[69] Dobrynin for his part mentioned that the Soviet leaders were "nervous and unhappy" over the administration's rhetoric and "tried to portray Brezhnev as [a] good and experienced leader who has urged his colleagues to remain calm and has thus far prevented a harsh Soviet response."[70] Brezhnev felt generous enough to send Reagan a personal letter with well-wishes for his prompt recovery following the president's attempted assassination on March 30. The attacker, John Hinckley Jr., was mentally deranged. "We decisively condemn this criminal act," Brezhnev's letter read.[71] But even as Reagan was recovering on his hospital bed, he sent Brezhnev a stern warning about Poland, saying that a Soviet intervention would force the United States to respond and that "prospects for renewed progress to reduce strategic and other arms would be dealt a serious and lasting blow."[72]

The Soviet response, composed by Gromyko and Ustinov but sent in Brezhnev's name, predictably accused the United States of interference in Polish affairs and rejected the linkage between Poland and arms control.[73]

As these long-range exchanges continued, the Soviet leadership appeared increasingly confused about Reagan's intentions and desperate for contact – any contact. Used to the give-and-take of diplomacy, they were perplexed not just by the tough rhetoric from the Reagan Administration – that was to be expected – but by the fact that this rhetoric apparently represented what the administration thought. The Soviets tried – almost desperately, it seemed at times – to establish back channels to the White House, or, better yet, directly to Reagan.

One such attempt led to some bemusement in Washington. It involved the young managing editor of the prominent journal *International Security*, Derek Leebaert. He travelled to Moscow in April 1981 for a talk at the USA and Canada Institute, which was headed by Brezhnev's self-proclaimed confidante Georgy Arbatov. The magisterial director had Leebaert over for a meeting, where he unburdened himself. "All channels have been cut off," Arbatov lamented, noting that "he had never seen such a low intellectual level in Washington. There is an obvious understanding that U.S. leaders have to pay off political debts by giving people positions but this was going too far ..." He lambasted Reagan's national security adviser, Richard Allen; the Russia expert at the National Security Council (NSC) (and prominent historian), Richard Pipes; and Secretary of Defense Caspar Weinberger, and sought direct contacts with Reagan. Pipes, to whom Leebaert showed the record of this talk, noted acidly that Arbatov was simply trying to undercut his rival, Ambassador Dobrynin, but that in any case this approach to a

CHAPTER 18 FEAR

young man without any obvious connections to the Reagan Administration "suggests the degree of nervousness in Moscow over the refusal of this Administration to negotiate for the sake of negotiating."[74]

This was only one attempt – there were more. There was an apparent KGB effort, through someone called Sitnikov, to set up a back channel with the US chargé d'affaires in Moscow, Jack Matlock. This Sitnikov told Matlock at a dinner party where the two met that "the Soviets now are very eager to start talking to us about major issues and that everything is negotiable."[75] He proposed a channel through the KGB or Arbatov. Although approved by the Americans, this channel was for some reason dropped. Arbatov, however, met with Matlock separately to voice his growing worries about the absence of communications. "If a Yom Kippur war occurred today," he averred, "I'm not sure a serious confrontation could be avoided."[76] Then there was Dobrynin himself who scurried around Washington, trying to break through to those who would listen with a message: the Soviets did not understand what the Americans wanted, and they were extremely worried. He was rebuffed: there first had to be progress on Afghanistan, and, of course, no invasion of Poland. "If the Soviets were to go in," Haig told him on July 2, "everything in Soviet–American relations would go by the board."[77] And that was saying something – because there really was not all that much left to that relationship.

However, there was one positive development that spring, when Reagan lifted the grain embargo against the USSR (much against the counsel of his advisers). He wrote a personal letter to Brezhnev, announcing this decision, which was not just moderate in tone but in some ways rather emotional. Reagan wrote that should the United States have wanted to dominate the world (as the Soviet propaganda incessantly claimed), they could have done so in 1945, when they had the atomic monopoly. But they did not. "May I say there is absolutely no substance to charges that the United States is guilty of imperialism or attempts to impose its will on other countries by use of force."[78] Brezhnev reciprocated nearly a month later with a personal letter of his own, which, though drafted by aides, included some of his own interventions. He asked, for example, to include a paragraph, blaming the collapse of Soviet–US relations on the Carter Administration, and tentatively suggesting that the two of them meet and talk.[79] "The major impression I get from the letter," Haig wrote to Reagan, "is a sense of substantial Soviet nervousness and concern."[80] He was not wrong.

That Soviet nervousness, however, had two effects. First was their caution in Poland – as we have seen above. The second was their effort, however tentative, to begin a search for a way out of Afghanistan.

521

An ailing Brezhnev continued to keep the latter problem in the center of his attention. He saw Babrak Karmal briefly at the end of February (the Afghan Communist leader was in Moscow for the Twenty-Sixth Party Congress). Brezhnev encouraged Karmal to do more to secure Afghanistan's borders against insurgents but, first and foremost, to focus on building up the party. What he was alluding to, of course, was the continued factionalism between Parcham and Khalq, though now the Parchamists were in charge, and were going after their rivals the Khalqists. Karmal sang praises to the Soviets and claimed that everything was wonderful inside the People's Democratic Party of Afghanistan (PDPA). "Every day our people turn to the party more and more," Karmal claimed, "believe its policy more and more, unite around it. The situation inside the party has also improved considerably, and the process of strengthening the principled Leninist unity of its ranks is in the stage of completion."

Eager to demonstrate just how much the Afghans loved the Soviet troops, Karmal told Brezhnev that "the population of even remote rural areas asks that Soviet military detachments are sent to them for protection against bandit attacks." Brezhnev, clearly unenthused, mumbled in response that it was time to start improving the quality of Afghan own forces.[81]

Some two weeks later Reagan made it publicly known that his administration considered arming the anti-Soviet insurgents.[82] Moscow projected outward defiance. Inside, though, the Soviets were thinking hard. Troubling news was coming through from the military commanders in Afghanistan. In a wide-ranging report sent to Ustinov on May 1981 Soviet military advisers with the Afghan Army – General Aleksandr Mayorov, Lieutenant-General Viktor Samoilenko, and Lieutenant-General Vladimir Cheremnykh – lambasted Karmal for taking a much greater interest in settling personal scores with the Khalqists than in establishing party authority in the rural areas. Karmal, the advisers argued, was trying to set himself up as a dictator in Afghanistan even as he failed to tackle pressing social and economic problems.[83] The Politburo trio of Andropov, Gromyko, and Ustinov met with Karmal to persuade him to end factionalism in the party and put more effort into building up Afghanistan's home-grown military and administrative capacity. "We stressed in the talks," Gromyko noted at the Politburo on June 4, "that [the] Afghanistan question is now blocking many other points in our politics, and it should be solved as soon as possible."[84]

The Soviets began to send out tentative feelers about a possible Soviet withdrawal just months after their misadventure.[85] Dobrynin hinted at the prospect in his conversation with Haig on March 24, 1981 – but (according to Haig) "in very vague terms."[86] Brezhnev himself in a carefully scripted

CHAPTER 18 FEAR

performance in the Soviet republic of Georgia on May 22 floated the idea of a Soviet stage-by-stage withdrawal – but only after a political settlement that would include guarantees of nonintervention by Afghanistan's neighbors, especially Pakistan.[87] However, when later that summer the European Economic Community (EEC) tried to get Moscow interested in an international conference on Afghanistan, which would include permanent members of the UN Security Council as well as Iran and Pakistan, they were rebuffed because the proposed conference would not include the Soviet-installed government of Afghanistan.[88] "They [the West] would like to sow doubts about the stability of revolutionary Afghanistan," Brezhnev told Babrak Karmal in Yalta in July 1981, painfully reading from speaking notes. They want to "create an impression that there are 'options' in that which concerns the existing regime."[89]

But although he rejected the EEC plan, Brezhnev also pressed Karmal to get his act together: stop rife factionalism inside the PDPA and take over a greater share of responsibility for military operations. This would leave the Soviets with the task of tackling border protection to prevent insurgents from infiltrating from Iran and Pakistan. Crucially, Brezhnev asked Karmal to stop claiming that the Soviet forces had come to Afghanistan to stay. "This is harmful," added the general secretary. Karmal sounded a note of agreement though he was also clearly frustrated by what Moscow had been hearing about him from their men on the ground. "Trust my judgment," he told the Soviet leader. "If we see that comrade Babrak Karmal is making a mistake," Brezhnev retorted, "we will not be shy to point it out."[90]

Later that fall, there was, so it seems, one half-baked Soviet effort to engage the Americans in a dialogue on Afghanistan. This followed a meeting between Alexander Haig and Gromyko in New York, in which the secretary of state inadvertently signaled to the Soviets that cross-border infiltration of insurgents could stop even before a complete Soviet withdrawal from Afghanistan (until then the Soviet withdrawal had been a precondition for any such arrangement).[91] It took a month for the Soviets to process the meaning of these words but on October 31 Dobrynin delivered a demarche, proposing Soviet–American expert talks on Afghanistan "in a business-like manner, in the spirit of realism, and without unnecessary polemics."[92] This, however, did not go anywhere partly because of the skepticism on the US side (especially among Haig's critics on the NSC) about Moscow's actual intentions, and partly because of the declaration of martial law in Poland that December, which torpedoed any hopes for an early return to dialogue in Soviet–American relations.[93]

523

PART IV COLLAPSE

On Christmas Eve, 1981, Reagan announced wide-ranging economic sanctions against Poland, including the suspension of credits, and restrictions on technology exports and government-to-government shipment of food aid. He also threatened sanctions against the Soviet Union for its role in the crackdown.[94] On December 23, Reagan sent a letter to Brezhnev in which he pointed to Soviet violation of the provisions of the Helsinki Final Act and threatened retribution should the violence in Poland continue.[95] "Reagan's letter is boorish in form and in substance," Gromyko commented in a note to Brezhnev the morning the letter was received. He informed the Soviet leader that the Foreign and Defense Ministries and the KGB would prepare a reply. "Agree," Brezhnev scribbled on the note.[96] The reply came in the form of a lengthy tongue-lashing letter, where "Brezhnev" lambasted Reagan for interfering in Poland's affairs.[97]

A few days later, Reagan approved a series of tough economic sanctions against Moscow, including a suspension of licenses for oil and gas equipment (designed to derail the planned Siberian gas pipeline to Europe). "Looks like Washington doesn't know our country and our leadership that well," Gromyko told US Ambassador Arthur Hartman when the latter handed over the list of sanctions. "They don't know our character."[98]

Declaring sanctions against the Soviet Union was not an uncontroversial decision for the Reagan Administration, with Alexander Haig arguing for a softer approach, much against the hawks like Defense Secretary Caspar Weinberger and Reagan's UN ambassador, Jeane Kirkpatrick. Poland itself was not even the key issue here – it was more of a pretext. At stake were broader considerations of policy: how to lessen Western Europe's reliance on Soviet energy imports, and how to make life difficult for Moscow by denying them export earnings. As Reagan himself later acknowledged, "Poland gave us a reason to act."[99]

Haig argued, however, that pushing for sanctions against the USSR would alienate America's NATO allies, in particular Britain, France, Italy, and West Germany that all had extensive business dealings with Moscow and had a huge stake in the construction of the Siberian gas pipeline. Reagan was annoyed to no end by the West Germans and other waverers, calling them "chicken littles" in an NSC meeting on December 22; ultimately, he overruled Haig. But, as it turned out, the secretary of state was right: sanctions did create a crisis in US–Europe relations, which took months to patch up.[100] In fact, things got so bad by June 1982 (when Reagan further expanded the pipeline sanctions) that French Foreign Minister Claude Cheysson declared the possible "beginning of the end of the Atlantic Alliance."[101]

CHAPTER 18 FEAR

Undeterred, Reagan kept up the pressure on the Soviets; by mid-1982 the relationship reached lows unseen since the coldest depths of the Cold War. The general East–West malaise was made worse by the unrelated flare-ups in the South Atlantic, where Great Britain fought to recapture the Falklands from Argentina, which had invaded the disputed islands in April 1982; and by the Israeli invasion of southern Lebanon on June 6, 1982, to dislodge the Syrian forces and the PLO guerillas from their positions in the war-torn country. The war in Lebanon was particularly worrying for the Soviets. While the Falklands were far away, in an area of marginal strategic importance, the Middle East was ever in the focus of Moscow's strategic ambitions. A cross-border foray by the Israelis aimed at altering the strategic equation in Lebanon at the expense of Soviet clients was a serious affront to the Kremlin, particularly because it became immediately obvious that the Israeli action was not a limited incursion but a full-fledged operation aimed at capturing Lebanon's capital, Beirut. The Israeli siege of West Beirut continued until the end of September 1982.[102]

Brezhnev blamed both the Falklands and Lebanon on the United States, which, he claimed, covertly, or even overtly, backed the aggressive policies of their clients.[103] "The [Margaret] Thatcher government," he wrongly argued, "would not have dared to act in the South Atlantic in a way similar to colonial raids, but for the fact that the US backs it directly." "Could Israel have acted so insolently but that it has an American accomplice?"[104]

On June 9 the general secretary sent a letter to Reagan about the Israeli operations, hinting that the Soviet Union would not stand aside while the interests of its friends, and its own interests, were threatened by the Israelis.[105] (Reagan replied on June 13 disclaiming, truthfully, any foreknowledge of the conflict and explaining that he had restrained Israeli Prime Minister Menachem Begin from pressing his advantage.) The Soviets did not believe such assurances, especially because the Americans did not evidence any interest in working with the USSR to diffuse the crisis in the Middle East. The American president was just then drumming up support for more sanctions against the USSR, pressing the European allies to fall into line. In early June he toured Western Europe for the first time since becoming president, and although some of Reagan's remarks hinted at a desire to negotiate, not least on nuclear arms control, he also subjected Moscow to a fair dose of verbal abuse, most memorably perhaps in his speech to the British House of Commons where Reagan talked about "the march of freedom and democracy which will leave Marxism-Leninism on the ash-heap of history."[106]

PART IV COLLAPSE

Such rhetoric did not go unnoticed in Moscow. "Reagan exponentially increased the worst of what we had under Carter," Brezhnev grumbled after hearing of his speeches in London, Bonn, and West Berlin. "Washington's aim is to unleash the 'Cold War' on all fronts, including ideology and trade. That's at the very least. But the final aim of the current US cabinet strategists is to squeeze socialism out and to establish America's world hegemony. Of course, it is a crazy, chimerical aim. But this is all very, very dangerous."[107] Even the beginning of the US–Soviet strategic arms reduction talks in Geneva in June 1982 did not dilute the Soviet leader's somber, pessimistic mood. The Reagan Administration only agreed to these talks, he claimed, to distract the public attention from its military build-up.[108] In August, the revelation that the Pentagon had worked out a strategy for winning a nuclear war against the USSR added to the Kremlin neurotic view of the American leadership.[109] In September 1982 Brezhnev called the strategy "a monstrous and, let me be frank, a crazy doctrine, dangerous for the entire humankind."[110] He was in the final few weeks of his life.

TASHKENT

In March 1982 Leonid Brezhnev travelled to Uzbekistan to present the republic with the Order of Lenin. On March 23 he toured an aviation factory in Tashkent. Hundreds of workers climbed the scaffolding to catch a glimpse of the general secretary as he plodded on down below. At one point the scaffolding gave way, burying Brezhnev and his entourage. He narrowly escaped death, breaking his collarbone.[111] It was in this sorry and anesthetized state – barely standing on his feet – that the Soviet leader delivered his March 24 speech, famous for its unexpectedly soft language on China. "We remember well the time when the Soviet Union and People's China were united by bonds of friendship and comradely cooperation," Brezhnev said, reading from his notes. "We are prepared to come to terms, without any preliminary conditions."[112]

It is clear in retrospect that the "Tashkent line" – which would later lead to full normalization of Sino-Soviet relations – was not universally embraced in the Soviet leadership and foreign policy elite. In particular, Oleg Rakhmanin, who managed the China portfolio at the Central Committee, was vehemently against rapprochement with Beijing and tried to derail it both in the run-up to, and even after, Brezhnev's Tashkent speech. As it was often the case in the Soviet corridors of powers, he did so less for ideological than for personal reasons: as the Communist Party's China czar, he had

526

CHAPTER 18 FEAR

shaped and implemented Moscow's policy as it then was: implacably hostile, and basically unwilling to acknowledge the sea change that China was witnessing after Mao's death. Reversing this policy would have undermined his position and reputation.[113]

But – as Tashkent was to prove – there was a growing consensus *elsewhere* in the Soviet policy community that the hostile relationship with China was abnormal, especially at a time of a deep freeze with the West. As we have seen, some experts, including the Foreign Ministry's Asia hand, Mikhail Kapitsa, thought that China's supposed pro-Western orientation was just a temporary aberration. Anatoly Chernyaev at the Central Committee adopted a similar position and successfully worked to prevent his colleague Rakhmanin from sabotaging the move towards rapprochement.[114] Crucially, Brezhnev's aide Viktor Golikov became personally involved in trying to change policy, drafting a memorandum for Brezhnev (which the latter forwarded to Andropov), arguing that as "our main enemy is US imperialism ... the main strike should be made in that direction."[115]

In August 1982 Moscow and Beijing agreed to hold bilateral consultations aimed at repairing their relationship; these began in October in the Chinese capital and continued for several years. Progress was slow because the Chinese insisted on preconditions for normalization, the removal of "three obstacles" – that is, the presence of a mighty Soviet military force along the Sino-Soviet border and in Mongolia; Soviet ally Vietnam's control of neighboring Cambodia; and the Soviet invasion of Afghanistan. But the process was underway by the autumn of 1982, with Brezhnev's blessing. As he put it at a Politburo meeting in September, "we have to treat them [the Chinese] seriously, on a grand scale, and in a balanced manner, without forgetting, of course, about our state interests."[116]

As the Chinese saying goes, it takes two hands to clap, which is why it is very important to understand why Beijing reciprocated Soviet feelers. The key issue here was undoubtedly Deng Xiaoping's growing frustration with the United States, which, he thought, was not delivering the sort of partnership that he had expected when in January 1979 China and the US normalized relations.

The biggest problem was Taiwan. Reagan set off alarm bells in Beijing during his presidential campaign with his vague promises to restore "official" ties with Taiwan.[117] His running mate, George H.W. Bush, even travelled to China in August 1980 to smooth the roughened feathers by suggesting that Reagan's statements were mainly just campaign rhetoric. The appointment of Alexander Haig – Kissinger's protégé – as secretary of state seemed to suggest that the Americans would continue to invest

PART IV COLLAPSE

political capital in the relationship with China as a strategic counterweight to the Soviet Union. In fact, this was exactly what Haig intended to do: he wanted an alliance with China in all but name, becoming a key advocate in the administration for lifting restrictions on the transfer of sensitive technologies to the Chinese, and for selling weapons. On June 4, 1981, Reagan made the decision to this effect – allowing for arms transfers on a case-by-case basis – and although the decision was secret, Haig soon publicly advertised it, causing visible apprehension in Moscow but clear delight in Beijing.[118] "We are pretty happy," Deng told Haig on June 16, 1981, referring to the general direction of the relationship. Haig seemingly reassured Deng by promising to handle the issue of Taiwan "with the greatest care ... in no way conduct[ing] ourselves in a way which conflicts with the fundamental understandings of the normalization communiqué."[119]

What Haig clearly hoped for was that the promise of a closer military partnership between the United States and China would somehow reconcile the Chinese to continued US arms transfers to Taiwan, foreseen by the 1979 Taiwan Relations Act. The litmus test of this idea was Beijing's reaction to the planned sale of the new FX aircraft to Taiwan. Long mulled over by the Reagan Administration, the sale was bitterly opposed by the Chinese leadership who accused the United States of undermining prospects for peaceful reunification. The rhetoric in Beijing suggested that, should the sale go through, the Chinese would go so far as to downgrade the relationship. In October 1981, Beijing upped the ante by demanding that the United States set a date for ending all military transfers to Taiwan.

Deng vented growing frustration with Reagan in conversations with former officials of the Carter Administration, whom he continued to receive in Beijing in what became something of a snub to the Republicans. Former Assistant Secretary of State Richard Holbrooke got an earful on May 5. "We know there is an opinion in the US," Deng said, "that as long as the US is firm towards the Soviet Union, American can do anything, and the Chinese people will swallow it. This is impossible."[120] On August 27, he repeated the warning to President Carter himself, threatening a downgrade of relations if the issue of weapons sales to Taiwan was not resolved.[121] Former Vice President Walter Mondale heard the same message in November: "on the question of US weapons sales to Taiwan, China has no alternatives. In China, we have the feelings of one billion people. And if on this question, the leaders go against the will of the people, then at least we should step down from our posts."[122]

In February 1981 Beijing downgraded relations with the Netherlands after the Dutch – ignoring angry warnings – sold Taiwan two submarines.

CHAPTER 18 FEAR

The tough move was meant as a warning to the United States and was in fact understood as such by the US intelligence community.[123] By October Deng seemed ready to carry out his threats. "By dealing with the Dutch question," he announced at a Politburo meeting on October 16, "we gave America a warning. Because what America is doing with Taiwan is actually hegemonism." Having thus described the United States with the bad word normally reserved for the Soviets, the Chinese supremo laid out his big-picture view. "We look at the Sino-American relationship from the strategic angle. The two sides should not be playing card games ... If you play cards, the cards can change any time, and can also be discarded at any time."[124]

Frustrations over the question of the FX sale to Taiwan were compounded by the feeling in Beijing that despite the June 4 decision on technology transfers, the United States continued to drag its feet, refusing to grant export licenses for some of the items China had requested. This was, as Chinese Foreign Minister Huang Hua put it, a case of "loud thunder with little raindrops."[125] To this one might add a gradual realization in Beijing that perhaps the Soviet threat, as bad as it had been, was overblown. The Soviets did not invade Poland and, far from building on their invasion of Afghanistan to continue southward expansion, they were obviously stuck in a quagmire.[126] In view of this changing strategic situation, and even despite the fact that Reagan cancelled the FX sale in January 1982, Beijing began to drift away from the kind of quasi-alliance with the United States that Deng had tried to develop just a few years earlier. The beginning of the Sino-Soviet rapprochement – however tentative – was a sign of a tectonic shift in Chinese foreign policy.

NUCLEAR FEARS

Leonid Brezhnev died in his sleep on November 10, 1982. By then the general secretary was much more of a secretary than a general: he aired policy decisions arrived at in murky, bureaucratic wrangles between his aides and his comrades-in-leadership. One of the latter, former KGB head Yury Andropov, took over the reins of leadership upon Brezhnev's death. Sixty-eight years old, Andropov was three-and-half years younger than Ronald Reagan and ten years younger than Deng Xiaoping but he was much more frail than either of them. He had long suffered from a kidney disease, a condition that would rapidly deteriorate in 1983 and lead to his death in February 1984. These months saw Soviet–US tensions escalate amid a sense of approaching nuclear doom.

One puzzling and, as yet, unresolved question about Yury Andropov is just what he thought of the dangers of war and the prospects for peace.

PART IV COLLAPSE

In May 1981, when he was still the head of the KGB, Andropov famously authorized Project RYaN, a large KGB effort to spot Western preparation for a nuclear war. Historian Nate Jones traces the origins of this operation to Soviet fears of a decapitating nuclear strike, spurred in part by the decision to deploy US nuclear-tipped cruise missiles and Pershing-IIs to Western Europe.[127] Worried that they would not have the time to react if and when the United States decided to begin their preemptive strike (which would leave them only minutes for retaliation), the Soviets resolved to keep an eye on a variety of indicators that could be pointers to a coming war, including odd movement of key officials, emergency meetings of Western leaders, and even parking patterns around the White House. These observations continued for some years, even after tensions began to subside.[128]

But did Andropov really worry that Reagan would go off the rails and order a nuclear strike on the USSR? The evidence is mixed. Soviet Ambassador Anatoly Dobrynin recalled a private conversation with Andropov, where the latter claimed that Reagan was just unpredictable and that "you should expect anything from him."[129] But on some occasions in 1981–82, he seemed to downplay the danger of an actual military clash. In July 1981, with tensions mounting over Poland and with the impending deployment of Pershing-IIs and cruise missiles keeping the Soviets on the edge, Andropov still felt that although "the US is preparing for war … it is not willing to start a war." "They are not building the factories and palaces in order to destroy them," he told Erich Mielke of the East German Stasi. What, then, were the Americans doing? "They strive for military superiority in order to 'check' us and then declare 'checkmate' against us without starting a war."[130]

Andropov was encouraged by Reagan's November 13, 1982 decision to lift the Siberian pipeline sanctions, imposed after the Polish events. This decision was largely a consequence of Reagan's effort to patch up strained relations with his West European allies.[131] But it also suggested at least a possibility of a return to a dialogue with Moscow. When Brezhnev died, Reagan visited the Soviet Embassy in Washington and signed the book of condolences, where he wished for "our two peoples live in peace in the world together."[132] These were just minor signs, but they were positive signs.

Andropov was cautiously optimistic after meeting with Vice President George H.W. Bush and new US Secretary of State George Shultz at Brezhnev's funeral in Moscow. The Americans, he said, spoke "in a more accommodating or externally well-wishing tone than they had done until recently." Bush, according to Andropov, "stressed his desire to improve the atmosphere of our relations, as well as [our] contacts, and to strive towards

CHAPTER 18 FEAR

agreements." "We had to confirm," Andropov reported to the Politburo, "that we take such American statements into consideration, and that we would be ready to respond to their positive steps in the same spirit."[133] Contrary to perceptions that the Soviets felt completely besieged and isolated – a consequence of the post-Afghanistan sanctions – Andropov saw in the fact that so many VIPs (including the Americans) turned up for Brezhnev's funeral "the weight and authority of our country on the international stage."[134]

It is important to stress here that these were Andropov's thoughts as expressed to his own Politburo colleagues, which sharply reduced the need for posturing and propagandistic bombast. On the other hand, there are other pieces of evidence that need to be taken into account: for example, his speech at the Warsaw Pact summit in Prague on January 4, 1983, where the Soviet leader sounded rather apprehensive about what he described as a recent US move from nuclear deterrence to the idea of a winnable nuclear war. "It is difficult to say," he added, "where we have blackmail, and where an actual preparedness for the fatal step."[135] If he was worried then, he surely would have had more reason come spring 1983, which was marked both by Reagan's over-the-top rhetoric about the "Evil Empire" (in a March 8 speech to evangelical Christians), and by his announcement of the Strategic Defense Initiative (SDI) later that month. SDI, popularly dubbed "Star Wars," was a far-fetched bid to protect the United States against Soviet missiles by setting up interceptors in space. To the Soviets this could only mean one thing: America was attempting to construct a shield to protect itself against a retaliatory nuclear strike. And why would they need that?

The Kremlin reacted with measured fury. On March 27 the party daily *Pravda* published an interview with Andropov where he decried Reagan's attempt to "sever" the link between offensive and defensive weapons. "The present Administration," he said, "is continuing to tread an extremely dangerous path. The issues of war and peace must not be treated so flippantly."[136] But he did not yet evidence any willingness to negotiate his way out of the unfolding crisis by reversing the deployment of SS-20s. That, he thought, would only be a sign of weakness.

In the months before he became general secretary, Andropov, alongside Defense Minister Dmitry Ustinov and Foreign Minister Gromyko, torpedoed accommodating arms control proposals that originated with Brezhnev's entourage. One such proposal had come from Brezhnev's foreign policy aide, Aleksandrov-Agentov, who was in turn inspired by George Kennan. On May 18, 1981 the author of containment, on receiving the Albert Einstein Peace Prize, made a sweeping proposal: the superpowers,

PART IV COLLAPSE

he said, should halve their strategic arsenals across the board. Deterrence, he argued, could be achieved with just 20 percent of the existing nuclear stocks. Several weeks later the former director of the US National Security Agency, Noel Gayler, made a similar proposal in a piece in the *Washington Post*.[137] These brave statements drew only limited attention in the West, but they were picked up in Moscow, with Aleksandrov-Agentov urging Brezhnev to back the idea. This would "make a huge impression on the world," he argued. "This would arouse public opinion in the United States itself, strengthening those who already criticize Reagan's policy as a road towards unleashing a new world war." Brezhnev supported the idea, writing to the troika (Andropov, Ustinov, and Gromyko) that backing Kennan's and Gayler's proposals would be a "step of great political significance." "There is nothing unacceptable here, in my opinion," he added. "But we could squeeze Reagan quite well."[138]

It is interesting to see how the troika reacted. They were strongly against, making the following arguments. First, they noted, the 50 percent cut would not impinge on British, French, and Chinese nuclear forces – "and they are US allies." Proliferation in countries like Israel, South Africa, and Pakistan – all of them more or less supportive of the United States – would further erode the Soviet nuclear advantage. Second, such deep cuts would benefit the United States much more because of its better geographic position, and its ability to threaten the Soviets from bases in Europe and Asia. Third, across-the-board cuts would entail cutting tactical nuclear weapons, and so inspections would be called for – something the Soviet Union could not agree to. Fourth, if, after making such cuts, the need arose to build up arms once again, the United States would be better positioned to do so because of their better "industrial-technical base." Finally, coming up with such an "unrealistic" proposal would undermine SALT-II, which the Soviets were still desperate to see enter into force. Brezhnev's idea was vetoed – a remarkable thing in itself, which shows that he had little policy leverage in his final months in power – although it is interesting to reflect that it was later picked up by Mikhail Gorbachev as one of his first major arms control initiatives.

The exchange highlights how Andropov, Ustinov, and Gromyko – the real crafters, it turns out, of Soviet policy – perceived the nuclear arms race in the early 1980s. The most obvious element here is their concern about the precariousness of nuclear balance, and their understanding that, given the realities of alliance politics (even China was seen as a "US ally"!) and America's much more advanced economic and technological capabilities, the Soviets simply could not afford deep cuts. Nor

CHAPTER 18 FEAR

could they afford the continuation of the arms race. Therefore, the only viable option that seemed open was to press for cuts in areas where the US had an advantage, for example cruise missiles. These were the kinds of ideas the Soviets were now putting forward in the slow-burning START talks in Geneva – and even these ideas were conditioned on the United States foregoing the deployment of Pershing-IIs and cruise missiles to Western Europe.[139]

To say that these were not very revolutionary ideas is to allow a serious understatement but Andropov found himself between a rock and a hard place. As he put it to the Kremlin doctor, Evgeny Chazov, reacting to Chazov's comments about the desirability of a breakthrough on the disarmament front: "Why don't the Americans try disarmament? Why do we have to begin it? Keep in mind ... they only speak to the ones who are strong." To demonstrate his point, Andropov recalled a scene from Sergey Eisenstein's 1944 film, *Ivan the Terrible*, which (at the start of the film) shows a conversation between foreign ambassadors present at Ivan's coronation as the Tsar. "Europe will not recognize him as the Tsar," says one. "If he is strong, they will recognize him," says another. "This is a principle that both we and the Americans adhere to," Andropov said. "And neither of us wants to become weaker."[140] The connection between military strength and Moscow's standing as a superpower, on the one hand, and the realization that the Soviet Union simply could not compete with the more powerful United States on the other, were the x and y axes of Andropov's strategic outlook, and he trudged along, uncertain that there was any light at the end of the tunnel, especially Reagan, evidently sensing his strength, was now upping the ante.

A sense of exasperation pervaded the Politburo meeting on May 31, 1983, which followed a G7 in Williamsburg, VA – one where US allies (including this time Japan) confirmed the decision to deploy US Pershing-IIs and cruise missiles to Western Europe. "An anti-Soviet coalition is being formed out there," Andropov told his colleagues, before proposing measures to improve relations with China and Japan to weaken this "coalition." He called for more anti-American propaganda, but for very utilitarian reasons: Andropov hoped to use what patriotic sentiments could be summoned to mobilize workers and so arrest the slide of the stagnating Soviet economy. Gromyko was the only one of those present who explicitly referred to the prospect of a nuclear war but he appeared fairly upbeat: "I think that they [the Americans] wouldn't dare to use nuclear missiles without sufficient reason." No one contradicted Gromyko, not even Andropov's protégé Gorbachev who was beginning to assume a more

PART IV COLLAPSE

prominent political role. On this occasion, Gorbachev mostly kept quiet, noting only that the United States was "moving to Europe" and therefore "we can't wait. We have to act."[141]

Andropov registered a growing sense of alarm during his meeting with the 91-year-old patriarch of Soviet–American relations, W. Averell Harriman, when the former New York governor turned up in Moscow. The War, he told Harriman on June 2, "may perhaps not occur through evil intent, but could happen through miscalculation. Then nothing could save mankind." Harriman commented after the meeting: "the principal point which the General Secretary appeared to be trying to get across ... was a genuine concern over the state of US–Soviet relations and his desire to see them at least 'normalized,' if not improved. He seemed to have a real worry that we could come into conflict through miscalculation."[142] But how "real" was that "real" – and how much of it was simply a restatement of Andropov's long-articulated apprehension that the Soviet Union was being outbid by the United States and would eventually be checkmated if things continued as they did?

The Soviet leader's health continued to worsen that summer, so much so that the KGB proposed to install an escalator to Lenin's Mausoleum to allow Andropov to ascend the structure for his parade appearances. But he never got to use it. He was hospitalized in the fall, and spent several months on an artificial kidney before he died in February. It was in that interim – when frail Andropov was clinging to his life – that a series of unfortunate developments worsened the already volatile atmosphere of Soviet–American relations.

On September 1, 1983 the Soviets shot down a Korean Air Boeing-747 over the island of Sakhalin, killing all 269 onboard. The civilian airliner had accidentally intruded into the Soviet airspace. As mangled body parts washed up on the beaches of the Sea of Japan, the world demanded answers. Reagan led the denunciations, calling the shooting down "an act of barbarism born of a society which wantonly disregards individual rights and the value of human life and seeks constantly to expand and dominate other nations."[143] The Kremlin sheltered behind denials, blaming the "provocation" on the United States. In the months prior, the United States had repeatedly probed the responsiveness of Soviet air defense by sending military aircraft on so-called "psy-op" missions along the Soviet borders, so the Soviets had some reason to be worried (not that it justified the trigger-happy response).

Another shocking incident – straight out of the nuclear apocalypse fiction – took place just past midnight on September 26, 1983. A Soviet early

CHAPTER 18 FEAR

Figure 26 South Koreans burning the Soviet flag after the shooting down of KAL 007, September 1983. Source: Allan Tannenbaum/Getty Images.

warning station in Serpukhovo, near Moscow, registered what appeared to be five nuclear missile launches from a base in the United States. The officer on duty wisely concluded that the system had malfunctioned, informing his superiors that there had been a false alarm. The well-documented mishap had a happy ending but it points to multiple imponderables: how would the Soviet leadership have reacted should there have been someone more prone to panic in the chain of command?[144] Two unrelated developments added to the general climate of uncertainty and apprehension: the bombing of US Marine barracks in Lebanon on October 23, 1983, and the US invasion of Grenada two days later. The planned deployment of Pershing-IIs and cruise missiles (which would begin in November) was another big question mark: How would the Soviets react to what Gorbachev later called a "gun to our head"?[145]

Then, on November 2, NATO began its annual Able Archer command-post exercise, which practiced transition to nuclear weapons in a conflict situation. Historians have long debated what exactly happened during this

PART IV COLLAPSE

seemingly routine exercise. Did the nervous Soviet leadership really confuse it with Washington's preparation for a nuclear first strike? Did the world really teeter on the brink of an abyss? There are disparate pieces of evidence, including that of Soviet forces in Poland and East Germany going on a heightened state of alert (to a greater degree than warranted by the exercise). There are even indications that some units of the Soviet Air Force were readying actual nuclear bombs for action. In 1990 the President's Foreign Intelligence Advisory Board (PFIAB) – a group charged with advising the US president on intelligence matters – authored an alarming report, indicating that "there was in fact a genuine belief among key members of the Soviet leadership that the United States had embarked on a program of achieving decisive military superiority that might prompt a sudden nuclear missile attack on the USSR."[146]

But the evidence is far from unequivocal. Yes, the Soviets were worried. Yes, Andropov personally feared a war through miscalculation – though what he feared even more was the Soviet Union being "checkmated" in the longer term. Yet it is still impossible to know for certain how close we came to nuclear war in November 1983.[147]

CONCLUSION

Yury Andropov died in February 1984, and was replaced by his old rival and Brezhnev's protégé, Konstantin Chernenko, a 72-year-old bureaucrat who suffered from life-threatening asthma and a serious lack of new ideas. Vice President George H.W. Bush, who made the habit of attending Soviet funerals, had a positive impression from meeting the frail new general secretary on February 14. The atmosphere was "positive and quite upbeat," US diplomats reported from Moscow. The Soviets – including Chernenko and the irreplaceable Aleksandrov-Agentov – went out of their way to emphasize their interest in peaceful coexistence.[148] After the wild ride of the previous several years, there was a real sense of fatigue in Moscow. Foreign policy was in shambles. Chernenko needed breathing room.

It is remarkable to think just how much changed in the Soviet global posture between the early 1970s and the early 1980s. In the early 1970s Brezhnev dreamed of a world which he would co-manage with the United States. The two countries would put their disagreements aside and cooperate as partners-in-greatness. There was nothing left of these hopes a decade later. Tensions were mounting before 1979 but Soviet–US relations really went off the rails when the Soviet Union invaded Afghanistan. The error became apparent almost immediately. The war turned into a

CHAPTER 18 FEAR

Figure 27 Reagan signs the book of condolences at the Soviet Embassy after Yury Andropov's death. February 1984. Source: Jean-Louis Atlan/Sygma/Getty Images.

quagmire. Brezhnev implored Babrak Kamral to rely on his own forces in tackling the "counterrevolution," all to no avail. But Afghanistan was a lesser problem than the unfolding disaster in Poland, where it seemed like the Communist government might fall any day. Poland was a black hole, to which Moscow committed more and more economic aid, apprehensive that the malaise might spread across Eastern Europe: And then what? No one could tell for sure. There is sufficient evidence to conclude that, after Afghanistan, the Kremlin was simply unwilling to militarily intervene beyond Soviet borders. It may well be that their hesitation at least in part resulted from the fear of Western sanctions.

Reagan imposed the sanctions anyway, bringing Soviet–US relations to a new low. His vitriolic rhetoric and apparent unwillingness to scale back the nuclear build-up added to Soviet apprehensions about being "checkmated" in the longer term. It was this rhetoric and the growing sense of Soviet isolation that contributed to a very significant turn in Soviet foreign policy – the beginning of a rapprochement with China. The Chinese, whom Brezhnev had feared and dreaded in the better days of Soviet–US "frenemyship," were now looked to with certain anticipation: could they really be worse than Reagan?

PART IV COLLAPSE

Fundamentally, however, the Kremlin leaders were at a loss. Their long-time vision of a partnership-through-recognition was on the rocks. The American leadership did not want to accept the Soviets as their equals, and instead evidently banked on winning the Cold War. What the Soviets realized all too keenly, especially with dim Brezhnev out of the way, was that they were, in fact, losing, simply because their over-bureaucratized, over-militarized economy was not coping with the demands of the modern age. Poland, in this sense, was a wake-up call. Did the Soviet leaders get the message? Andropov, who had long warned Brezhnev about the deep economic problems the USSR faced, now had the opportunity to apply himself directly to solving these problems. Records of his discussions with fellow party officials show clearly that he simply did not know what to do. He was tinkering around the margins with his anticorruption campaigns and his calls for strengthening worker discipline. The writing was already on the wall.

What remained was the bloated Soviet military-industrial complex with thousands of nuclear warheads that could render the Earth unlivable in minutes. That, in the early 1980s, was the backbone of the Soviet claim to greatness. "If he is strong, they will recognize him," said one European ambassador of Ivan the Terrible in the Eisenstein film – and Andropov agreed. The problem was that he knew that neither he nor, indeed, his country, were in fact as strong as he made them out to be.

538

19

HOPE

Some revolutions bubble up from below. Some are imposed from above. Gorbachev's revolution was of the latter type. He came to power in March 1985, and immediately launched into extensive economic and political reforms. This restructuring – *perestroika* in Russian – often met with incomprehension and outright hostility among the party faithful. Defying resistance, Gorbachev pressed on. Six years later the Soviet Union was restructured out of existence. The Cold War as we knew it seemed over. Gorbachev's dramatic appearance at the helm of Soviet power, and his even more dramatic disappearance into the annals of history is the subject of the next two chapters. It is not a detailed account of the Soviet reform experience, nor even of Gorbachev's foreign policy. I aim, rather, at pinpointing the Soviet leader's key concerns as he unleashed forces that promptly engulfed the party, the state, and Gorbachev himself.

Gorbachev looms larger than life in every story of the end of the Cold War – and rightly so. His personal contribution to ending the arms race and Soviet interventionism are beyond any doubt. Yet as this chapter demonstrates, there were important continuities between Gorbachev's policies and those pursued by his predecessors. One continuity that has to some extent eluded histories of the Gorbachev era is that of the importance that the Soviet leader attached to global leadership, and to recognition of this leadership by domestic and international audiences. Gorbachev understood leadership in moral terms. Greatness was not a matter of having multiple clients, or in rattling missiles. Greatness was in projecting new ideas, and showing a good example to the world by doing things others would deem naive, or even dangerous: a genuine commitment to arms control, and a genuine willingness to pull back from quasi-imperialistic foreign ventures.

The strategy proved remarkably effective, at least in the short term. In 1987–88, the Soviet Union enjoyed a moment of international glory. Gorbachev himself became something of a global superstar and a prophet of peace. For all the drabness of stagnant socialism, Moscow briefly shone as a city on the hill, showing the way to a brave new world.

PART IV COLLAPSE

PERESTROIKA

Senior Soviet apparatchiks had an important privilege denied to most ordinary Soviet citizens: travel in the West. These were often highly controlled occasions, but they did offer opportunities (to those who cared and dared) to transcend Soviet propaganda and get a sense of what life in the West was really like. Stalin's only post-Second World War visit to the West was to the ruins of Berlin but, even had he been taken to Hollywood instead, it is hard to imagine that he would have been enchanted. Khrushchev did go to Hollywood and was (allegedly) appalled by the depravities he witnessed there. Brezhnev had visited West Germany, France, and the United States but had very little to say of these places in his personal diary: despite his claim that he was "European," he was never particularly curious about what the West actually looked like. Gorbachev was. Even before he became the general secretary, Gorbachev travelled extensively across Western Europe, visiting Italy, Belgium, the Netherlands, West Germany, the United Kingdom (where Margaret Thatcher famously discerned his hidden promise), and – perhaps his favorite destination – France, which he toured by car in the company of his wife Raisa.[1] Gorbachev openly identified himself with Europe: like Brezhnev, he claimed that he was a "European."[2] Differently from Brezhnev, he knew what Europe was like.

The Soviet propaganda painted the West in grim colors, contrasting the opulence of the few with the poverty and misery of the many. Although Gorbachev's first-hand observations sometimes aligned with these distorted claims, on the whole he found life in the West to be more plentiful, more relaxed, and freer than the self-proclaimed workers' paradise he called his home. These contrasts were there before. Khrushchev would not have agreed to build the Berlin Wall if he were not worried about the contrasts between the East and the West. But in the 1950s and the 1960s Soviet society was still in a euphoric postwar construction phase. Deprivation was widespread but there was also enthusiasm about the not-so-distant future when the Soviet Union would surpass the United States, and the rest of the West, in delivering on the quality of life. That was supposed to have happened by 1980, when, according to Khrushchev's infamous promise, Soviet society was to have reached Communism.

Instead, the politically incorrect Soviet joke went, it was decided to hold the 1980 Moscow Olympics. The event was boycotted by most Western countries and China (all a part of the Soviet post-Afghanistan isolation). But even the third world delegations that did participate gave their Soviet hosts constant headaches, complaining about the poor quality of the food,

CHAPTER 19 HOPE

problems with accommodation, bad service, and unreliable public transport. Some foreign athletes disassembled fire alarms and radio sets in their rooms, looking for KGB bugs (the KGB dutifully reported on the futility of these efforts).[3] Foreign athletes saw the best of what was to be seen. Life of a rank-and-file Soviet citizen was incomparably drabber. The queues were long. The shelves were empty. The goods were defective. The service was nonexistent. The KGB did not have bugs in every radio set. But there was a stifling, pervasive air of unfreedom, reflected in another Soviet joke: Brezhnev asks the pope: "Why do people believe in the Christian paradise but refuse to believe in the Communist paradise?" Says the pope: "That's because we do not show them our paradise."

To Gorbachev, this was no laughing matter. Having inherited a dysfunctional superpower with claims to global preeminence, the general secretary knew that he had to move fast to improve the domestic conditions for fear of being exposed as a naked emperor. But move how? His predecessors had tried and failed to deliver economic prosperity. Khrushchev attempted to improve the country's performance through incoherent bureaucratic restructuring that bred chaos and contributed to his downfall. Kosygin spearheaded reforms that aimed at improving individual incentives in the production process, but these abortive reforms drowned in the bureaucratic morass. As early as 1968 the head of the KGB Yury Andropov sent Brezhnev a prophetic memorandum criticizing low labor efficiency, wastefulness, oversupply of money, and, especially, the inability to keep up with the United States in research and development, education, and the use of computers. "We are talking here about the factors that will determine the face of the world in 15–20 years, and it is therefore important here not to overlook something substantial," pleaded Andropov. Brezhnev locked the memorandum in his desk (where it was discovered after his death in 1982).[4]

After he became the general secretary in 1982, Andropov could and did try to address the mammoth challenges the country faced – many of the same challenges he correctly identified fifteen years earlier, only much worse. But he faced serious problems. The external environment was just not what it used to be in the 1970s. Oil prices began their slide from historic heights (before collapsing outright in early 1986). This limited Moscow's ability to earn hard currency. In July 1983 Andropov extolled his lieutenants, including Mikhail Gorbachev, "to look for a way out of this situation" by selling more TVs and cars on the world market – only, no one was buying them. His next idea was to sell more lumber, or maybe more gold. The cash was running short, but the answers simply did not add up.[5]

PART IV COLLAPSE

The ailing general secretary (Andropov had a fatal kidney condition) tried to resuscitate the stagnating economy with KGB-style methods. Proclaiming discipline to be order of the day, he cracked down on slackers, imposing sharp penalties for unauthorized absence from work. He also launched an anticorruption campaign, targeting some of Brezhnev's cronies.[6] He died before these measures had a chance to really get off the ground, in February 1984. But there was one thing of consequence Andropov managed to accomplish: he empowered Gorbachev, opening the door to the latter's eventual ascent to leadership.

One thing Gorbachev understood extremely well was that economic performance and political legitimacy were intimately related: you could not get one without the other. Technology and labor productivity were two things that, Gorbachev believed, sank the "leftist" (i.e. Communist) project in the United States and Western Europe. Without technology and productivity, "we cannot hold on to the third world." Without technology and productivity, "we cannot hold on to the socialist countries." In other words, without technology and productivity the Soviet Union could not possibly hope to remain a superpower, whatever ideology it publicly espoused. "Life beats any ideology," Gorbachev said in 1986, as he unveiled new ambitious economic initiatives.[7]

The Soviet leader drew inspiration from the legacy of stillborn reform initiatives and hare-brained schemes peddled by his predecessors. He also looked to earlier economic experiments of the Bolshevik regime, namely, Lenin's New Economic Policy (NEP) that allowed a degree of private enterprise in the 1920s. Gorbachev's early economic initiatives – giving enterprises greater autonomy in day-to-day management (khozrasshchet), permitting start-ups ("cooperatives") – did have a tinge of NEP pragmatism but even these modest initiatives met with bureaucratic resistance and accusations of backtracking from "socialism." Gorbachev beat back these accusations with one of the most astonishing definitions of "socialism" to have ever fallen from the lips of a Communist Party leader: "Socialism," he said, "is when the people feel good."[8]

Inadvertently, then, Gorbachev discovered something that approximated Deng Xiaoping's famous maxim: "It does not matter what color the cat is, as long as it catches mice." By 1985–86, when Gorbachev launched perestroika in the USSR, the Chinese economic reforms were in full swing. Between 1979 and 1984 substantial coastal areas in China were opened up to foreign investment as so-called "Special Economic Zones." Small private workshops popped up in villages and towns. China was abuzz with entrepreneurial activity.

CHAPTER 19 HOPE

Among the early Soviet witnesses of the Chinese economic miracle was Georgy Arbatov, the head of the USA and Canada Institute. Arbatov had been close to Brezhnev (he was an important member of the general secretary's speech-writing team) but he was also a reformer and fed political unorthodoxies into Gorbachev's ear whenever the latter was willing to listen. Having toured China in October 1985, Arbatov sent Gorbachev a report on all the remarkable things he encountered, including the wide availability of quality consumer goods and even computers – most of them Chinese-produced – in regular stores. Arbatov cited astonishing statistics of industrial growth – in double-digits – and recounted a problem Gorbachev wished he had: the pace of economic expansion was too fast, and the Chinese were working hard to apply the brakes. Of course, not all was well in China (Arbatov pointed, for instance, to the young people's problematic "indulgence in sexual literature and video recordings") but, on the whole, there were some lessons here to ponder if only Gorbachev cared to look China's way.[9]

Eventually, Soviet reformers would come to pay more and more attention to the Chinese experience of reforms, though it was not until the late 1980s that there was any real effort at emulation. This, as historian Chris Miller notes, was in part a question of the suitability of the Soviet conditions (unlike China, with its oversupply of cheap, uneducated workers, the Soviets faced the daunting challenge of promoting export-led growth with an educated, and so expensive, workforce).[10] He notes, too, that by the time the Soviets came around to trying to emulate the Chinese experience, the USSR was already falling apart. But a question remains: Why did it take so long for Gorbachev to accept the viability of Chinese reforms? This, simply put, was because he conceived of perestroika as an event of international significance that would refocus the world's attention on the Soviet Union's achievements and allow it once again to project global leadership. By that very fact, then, perestroika had to carry the label: "Made in the USSR." It could not be rooted in someone else's experience.

The point was put across in rather crude terms by one of Gorbachev's foreign policy advisers, Georgy Shakhnazarov:

> The question of priority is being raised. One should say that some people are already raising these questions and even consciously try to prove [their] priority. One can hear insinuations of this kind in the Chinese press ... Let's say the Chinese started several years ago, the Hungarians started their own reforms even earlier, the Polish had them, and so on. If we leave these disagreements aside, I think everyone will agree that perestroika in

the Soviet Union has, of course, the decisive significance. It has it because the Soviet Union is the leading state of the socialist system ... this is one of the greatest powers or superpowers of the modern day, upon which depends the fate of the world more than on anyone else.[11]

Such hair-splitting may appear odd, but it is important to understand where Gorbachev was coming from. He inherited a troubled superpower that was muddling through on the road to nowhere, looking for direction. Perestroika was that bright idea that was supposed not just to reverse the Soviet Union's fortunes but also raise Gorbachev's status, and his historical importance. A Central Committee functionary, Karen Brutents (who himself had for years overseen projection of Soviet leadership in the third world), left the following unkind but perhaps not entirely unreasonable assessment: "What moved Gorbachev in his attitude towards China and Chinese politics? Perhaps I am mistaken but I think it was first and foremost his personal ambition, [his] jealous view of China as a competitor in his messianic path-breaking pretensions, a certain arrogance, which prevented [him] from correctly appraising anything that is done *differently from us*."[12]

To be fair, it was not just the Chinese who annoyed Gorbachev with their reformist pretensions. He was equally annoyed with his Eastern European allies, including East Germany's Erich Honecker, who claimed that he had personally seen empty store shelves in the USSR, and Bulgaria's Todor Zhivkov, who pretended that his predominantly agricultural fiefdom was a mini-Japan in the making.[13] "All of them (the socialist countries) claim that they started perestroika before us," Gorbachev grumbled in an exchange with his Politburo colleagues in July 1987.[14]

The most annoying by far was Romania's dictator Nicolae Ceaușescu who, far from heeding Gorbachev's advice, had the sheer insolence to "teach us." "To hell with him," Gorbachev concluded. "We are talking here about the fate of humankind!"[15]

As for the Chinese, Gorbachev's main concern was that Deng Xiaoping was unwilling to carry out political liberalization. Keen to curb poisonous Western influences, the Chinese leader instead unleashed a campaign against "bourgeois liberalization," to which he sacrificed even his own protégé, General Secretary Hu Yaobang (Hu was purged in January 1987 in the wake of student protests). Deng equated democracy with chaos. Meanwhile, Gorbachev resolved to thoroughly democratize the Soviet society. "What, are we afraid of our people?" he thundered at a discussion with aides on November 19, 1986. "Then this is not socialism. Socialism is first and foremost a society of the people and in the name

CHAPTER 19 HOPE

of the people," he added, unwittingly paraphrasing Abraham Lincoln.[16] "Democratization" and "glasnost" (openness) henceforth became Gorbachev's rallying cries. By putting the economy first, Gorbachev held, the Chinese had "disturbed the dialectic between the base and the super-structure, and that created difficulties."[17]

What would have been Deng's answer, should have he heard Gorbachev's pronouncements? We know that he was generally unsympathetic. "Gorbachev is an idiot," Deng reportedly said: "he won't have the power to fix the economic problems and the people will remove him."[18]

There was another important difference between Deng Xiaoping's and Gorbachev's approaches to reform. Deng was famously gradualist: he preferred, to cite one of his favorite Chinese proverbs, "to cross the river by feeling for the stones." Not so Gorbachev. Once in 1987, at the Politburo, while discussing the failure of Kosygin's abortive reforms, Gorbachev put his finger on the problem. "Why didn't [they] succeed? Because ... if you carry out reforms, you have to do it quickly and deeply."[19] And so he did. From launching economic "acceleration" in 1985, to proclaiming "glasnost" in 1986, to permitting private enterprise and substantially curbing central planning in 1987, to implementing deep political reforms in 1988, to holding first competitive elections in 1989: it took Gorbachev just four years to change the Soviet Union beyond recognition. Far from crossing the river by feeling for the stones, Gorbachev's reform experiment was more akin to jumping off a cliff into a raging sea in order to learn how to swim.

NEW THINKING

Domestic reforms were for Gorbachev a matter of necessity. His frequent refrain was simply: "there is no alternative."[20] But could the same be said of the Soviet foreign policy? One might say, for instance, that Gorbachev's foreign policy was but an extension of his domestic reforms: one is seen as abandoning ideological dogma in economic policy; the other, in international affairs. As noted above, Gorbachev understood that unless his domestic reforms succeeded, it would be very difficult for him personally – and for his country – to claim global leadership. "The key to success in our foreign policy," he averred at the Politburo on July 1, 1987, "is our internal perestroika." "The main thing in foreign policy is to influence the world with our perestroika, democratization, glasnost, with our transformation."[21] However, Gorbachev's foreign policy should also be understood on its own terms: as an effort to project leadership regardless of what happened or failed to happen at home. Enter "New Thinking."

PART IV COLLAPSE

In August–September 1987 the Soviet leader went to Crimea on vacation. There, by the seaside, in the company of his foreign policy aide, Anatoly Chernyaev, Gorbachev edited what turned out to be his most well-known book, *Perestroika and New Thinking for Our Country and the World.* Largely recycling Gorbachev's own verbose pronouncements at Politburo discussions (strung together by Chernyaev), the book is a good starting point for understanding the fundamentals of "New Thinking" in his foreign policy. It is also a good point for misunderstanding it. For example, it is commonplace to think of Gorbachev as the Soviet leader who abandoned ideology in foreign policy, replacing it with "universal human values." "Universal human values" do in fact come up in the book. Gorbachev also talks about "de-ideologization" of international relations. But the context makes it clear that Gorbachev's take was essentially a restatement of Nikita Khrushchev's views on peaceful coexistence and peaceful competition.

"The core of new thinking," Gorbachev argued, "is the recognition of the priority of universal human values, and to be more precise – the survival of humankind."[22] He returned to this basic idea time and again: that the world was a dangerous place; that nuclear arsenals made a big war suicidal; that it was therefore crucial to achieve a perestroika of international relations, by which Gorbachev meant Washington's embrace of Soviet disarmament initiatives. None of these ideas were qualitatively different from Khrushchev's or Brezhnev's approach to international relations: both, in fact, repeatedly spoke of the inadmissibility of war in a nuclear age, and were, in this sense, as much adherents of "universal human values" as Gorbachev.[23]

The novelty of "New Thinking" was not so much in its content as in the spin. Gorbachev placed peaceful coexistence at the very center of his pursuit of global leadership. Ideas are indispensable for leadership (raw power in and of itself cannot legitimize). But the stale Marxist dogmas that Gorbachev inherited from his predecessors failed to inspire. The Soviet Union's attractiveness as an "ideological power," to use Chernyaev's apt term, had irretrievably waned. This was in part a function of the Soviet economic malaise – but only in part. The worst blows were political, not economic: the Soviet invasions of Hungary, Czechoslovakia, and Afghanistan probably did more damage to the Soviets' global standing than the empty shelves and the famously atrocious service. But if Marxism-Leninism was hard to sell, peace, dialogue, and disarmament remained as relevant as ever. Capitalizing on these ideas offered a sure path to reasserting Soviet leadership. To recall the subtitle of Gorbachev's book, New Thinking was not just "for our country" – it was "for the world."

Gorbachev was certain that the strategy was paying off on the world stage. "A lot is expected of our perestroika around the world," he wrote.

546

CHAPTER 19 HOPE

"They anticipate that it will positively impact on the development of the entire world, on international relations in general." And more: "the entire world needs perestroika." And then: "a serious perestroika of Soviet–American relations is long overdue." (Now, what could *that* possibly mean? Gorbachev explains, with reference to the United States: "one has to get rid of the habit of ordering others about.")[24] Was there anything else to the idea? Yes, there was the promise of joint action. In a few places in the book, Gorbachev highlighted the need for the Soviet Union and the United States to do things together: to pool their technologies and resources in offering solutions to the world, and to address the disparities between the developed and the developing countries. His key point was that these two countries "have a special, increased responsibility for the fate of the world."[25]

How different was this to Brezhnev's aspiration for a Soviet–US global condominium? It was not dramatically different. Collective memories of Gorbachev, especially in the West, are so decisively defined by the events of 1989 that scarcely anyone remembers these continuities between different generations of Soviet leaders. The main continuity was, of course, the desire for recognition by the West as a worthy partner in leading the world to a brighter future.

One may object to this analysis: if there were many similarities, surely there were also considerable differences between Gorbachev and his predecessors. It was on Khrushchev's watch that the Soviet Union invaded Hungary; and, on Brezhnev's watch, Czechoslovakia and Afghanistan. But Gorbachev did not order invasions of other countries, and, indeed, at last brought the Afghan adventure to an end. By the same token, Khrushchev and Brezhnev pursued arms control but were ultimately unable to rein in the arms race. Gorbachev and his American counterparts, Ronald Reagan and George H.W. Bush, oversaw dramatic leaps in the disarmament dialogue. Soviet leaders had always eagerly promoted "peace" but Gorbachev was the first to put his money where his mouth was. Understanding these changes is important for explaining the end of the Cold War. Gorbachev's nonintervention in Eastern Europe is the subject of the next chapter. This chapter reviews the Soviet–American disarmament dialogue, and the Soviet withdrawal from Afghanistan.

ARMS CONTROL

The years between the Soviet invasion of Afghanistan (December 1979) and Gorbachev's ascent to power (March 1985) was an anxious time for the Soviet leadership. Some of the problems were of the Soviets' own

PART IV COLLAPSE

making: for example, the not so bright idea to deploy the RSD-10 Pioneer (NATO's name: SS-20). This highly advanced, three-warhead, mobile missile was supposed to replace some of the badly outdated medium- and intermediate-range missile systems that had been in service since the late 1950s–early 1960s. There was no intention to drastically alter the strategic balance.[26] Yet because the SS-20 was so effective against targets in Western Europe, its deployment set off alarm bells across NATO. As we have seen, NATO responded to this ostensible Soviet provocation by upgrading US nuclear missiles in Western Europe. The arrival of new American missiles in November 1983 added dramatically to Soviet insecurity: their command-and-control posts could now be obliterated with little to no warning.

We have seen how tense the Soviets were during 1983, especially during Able Archer. By then, Andropov was already on his deathbed. Gorbachev chaired Politburo meetings in his absence. He shared Andropov's views about the dangers of the international situation and, like Andropov, he blamed Reagan for ratcheting up nuclear tensions. There is no doubt that he worried about the Pershings – at the Politburo, he called them "a gun to our head."[27] Five to seven minutes was, in Gorbachev's gloomy assessment, how long it would take for these missiles, once launched, to reach the Soviet territory.[28] Even if the Soviets managed to retaliate, in what sort of a world would they be living after a nuclear exchange?

Gorbachev was treated to a preview in April 1986. On April 26, engineers at the Chernobyl nuclear power plant in Ukraine attempted to carry out an emergency power shut-down test on reactor No. 4. The test did not go as planned: the reactor exploded, sending plumes of radioactive smoke into the atmosphere. Tens of thousands of people had to be evacuated from the vicinity of the plant; scores died from radiation poisoning. Apart from further tarnishing the Soviet image as a global power, the Chernobyl disaster reminded Gorbachev of the terrible consequences of a nuclear conflict. "Look at the Chernobyl accident," he argued at the Politburo just days after the meltdown. "We felt the breath of a nuclear war."[29] Why are these statements important? Because they show that Gorbachev's push for nuclear disarmament was at least in part based on his genuine fear of war, and his very sensible conclusion that not just the Soviet Union but the entire world was better off with fewer nukes. This was hardly a revolutionary insight. As Gorbachev admitted to his aides: "Everybody understands that 100 missiles would suffice to fuck up Europe and the greater part of the Soviet Union ... What, are we planning to fight a war?"[30]

548

CHAPTER 19 HOPE

Unsurprisingly, though, Gorbachev's motivations were more complicated than his peace-loving talk allowed. One important issue was the escalating costs of the arms race. Is it true, for example, that the United States bankrupted the Soviets: Gorbachev had to sue for peace, because he could not keep up with the arms race? The view is not without basis, though it highlights only one of Gorbachev's many concerns. Gorbachev repeatedly spoke about the spiraling costs of the arms race. For example, he was deeply concerned about Reagan's "Star Wars," and feared that competing with the United States in space would be prohibitively expensive.[31] If the Soviet Union did not end the arms race, Gorbachev claimed at the Politburo in October 1986, "there will be unthinkable pressure on our economy." "We'll be dragged into an impossible race," he explained, "and we'll lose it, for we are at the limit of our abilities." This was exactly what the Americans wanted to do, according to Gorbachev. "The United States are interested in the negotiations spinning in the neutral gear, while the arms race overloads our economy." He was right. The Reagan Administration, sensing the Soviet weakness, was at this point resolved to push the Soviets into making concessions that would benefit Washington's strategic posture.[32] In the words of the Secretary of State George Shultz, "Our interest is to keep the Russians well behind us but not so far behind that they become desperate and dangerous."[33]

As Gorbachev prepared for his meetings with Reagan, first in Geneva, in November 1985, and then in Reykjavik, in October 1986, there was a curious contradiction that underpinned his approach to the American president. Even as he prepared to unleash major new disarmament initiatives, Gorbachev doubted that he would get very far with Reagan, whom he dismissed as a political dinosaur, "a product of certain forces … installed and paid by them." The idea that US presidents were just puppets of the military-industrial complex was, of course, hardly original. Reagan just seemed to be a particularly difficult case. In Geneva, Gorbachev recalled, he "at first saw vacant, uncomprehending eyes of the President who mumbled banalities from a script." Only with difficulty was Gorbachev able to finally have a "human conversation."[34] It was not an auspicious opening.

But Gorbachev pressed on. Ahead of Reykjavik he developed a package of proposals that would see the strategic nuclear arsenals of the two powers cut by 50 percent, an idea that harkened back to Brezhnev's (in fact, Aleksandrov-Agentov's) proposal, in 1981, to "squeeze Reagan quite well." On that earlier occasion, as we have seen, the idea of deep cuts was vetoed by the troika of Andropov, Ustinov, and Gromyko. But Gorbachev

PART IV COLLAPSE

Figure 28 Reagan and Gorbachev at Reykjavik, October 1986.
Source: Dirck Halstead/Getty Images.

had more space for maneuver. Indeed, this time, the Soviets would also agree to dismantle all their SS-20s in Europe (leaving some for Asia). In response, Gorbachev wanted the United States to remove Pershing-IIs and cruise missiles from Europe, and to refrain from testing the "Star Wars" by committing not to withdraw from the Anti-Ballistic Missile (ABM) Treaty for ten years. The aim was to preserve strategic stability as the Soviet Union and the United States drastically cut their nuclear arsenals. (The more cynical idea – one that comes through only in the Soviet preparatory papers for Reykjavik – was that ten years was as long as it would take for the Soviets to develop their response to Reagan's "Star Wars").[35] Earlier in the year, Gorbachev also reversed Soviet policy concerning on-site inspections.

The "package" seemed so ambitious that before he went to Reykjavik, Gorbachev was very doubtful of success. One thing that, he thought, might compel Reagan to compromise was his "personal ambition" – after all, he wanted to go down in history as a "peace president."[36] But if – as was likely – Reagan simply intended to have a meeting for the sake of a meeting, the Soviets would still win in the eyes of the international public opinion by

CHAPTER 19 HOPE

unfurling the banners of peace. Hence, the third important reason for Gorbachev's pursuit of disarmament: projection of global leadership.

It was an important part of Gorbachev's peace offensive from the start. Soviet foreign policy, he claimed at the Politburo in late November 1985, "is gaining understanding and support of the people, and of the realistic politicians in the West. Reagan is maneuvering. They have nowhere to retreat."[37] In January 1986 he unveiled an ambition to rid the world of nuclear weapons by the year 2000. That ambition was reportedly developed with approval – and, indeed, active involvement – of the Soviet military who saw it as a useful propaganda stunt (which, to be fair, was largely how it was perceived in the West at the time).[38] Gorbachev's Reykjavik package was a way of showing that deep nuclear cuts were not just empty talk. As he put it at the Politburo shortly before his trip to Iceland: "Reykjavik will allow us to improve the image of our foreign policy. It will highlight its constructive nature, our desire to untie the knots ..."[39]

But then something quite unexpected happened. On October 12, in the course of a long, fractious, confusing discussion in Reykjavik of what it was that the Soviets were proposing to cut, Reagan suddenly proposed to forgo the difficult terminology and say that the United States and the Soviet Union would agree to eliminate nuclear weapons in ten years. "We could say that, list all those weapons," Gorbachev said.[40] Did he improvise? Did he understand the implications of what was being proposed? Was he afraid that by pushing the brakes there and then he would have blinked first, yielding the initiative to Reagan? It is difficult to tell. But if either the Soviet leader or the American president dropped their conditions (abandoning the SDI in Reagan's case, or relaxing his stand on the ABM in Gorbachev's case), they would have committed their countries to a deal that neither side could deliver. Conditions stayed, and Reykjavik fell through.

Reagan's advisers were shocked by the turn of events. Not long after the president returned from Iceland, his national security adviser, John Poindexter, drafted a memo pleading with the president not to talk about complete nuclear disarmament as an actual possibility: the US military could not take it, and the US allies could not take it, and it would in any case lead to a build-up of conventional armaments.[41] We do not have anything of this nature on the Soviet side: no one at the Politburo asked Gorbachev whether he really was planning on giving away the Soviet nuclear shield as the summit transcripts suggested. But what the Soviet internal deliberations do point at is the notion that the Americans themselves would never allow something like this to happen. In the words of Vitaly Kataev – a senior official in the Central Committee's Defense Department – "neither the internal

551

forces nor [America's] allies would have allowed Reagan to realize the idea of destroying all [nuclear weapons]."[42] He was right of course but that also meant that the Soviets risked relatively little by their one-upmanship: by advancing bold initiatives, they put Reagan on the defensive and won global recognition. As Gorbachev summed up at the Politburo: "Reykjavik is the new beginning of our massive peace offensive."[43]

This emphasis on the world's *perception* of Moscow's foreign policy moves became even more important the following year, which ended with the conclusion of the Intermediate-Range Nuclear Forces (INF) Treaty – the most important breakthrough in arms control up to that date. The prospect of war faded significantly post-Reykjavik, and although the costs of the arms race were still a serious concern – indeed even more so than before, due to the Soviet Union's worsening economic woes – the fear of being bankrupted by having to outcompete the Americans in space was mitigated somewhat by the growing realization in Gorbachev's circle that Reagan's "Star Wars" was more a PR trick than an actual threat.[44] But one concern that did not fade was that of projecting leadership by taking the "peace offensive" to a new level.

The latter concern underpinned Aleksandr Yakovlev's memorandum to Gorbachev dated February 25, 1987 – a document that played an important role in untying the "Reykjavik package" by pursuing separate negotiations on the INF. Yakovlev entered the annals of history as the "ideologue" of perestroika: a key Gorbachev ally who helped turn the conservative tide in favor of openness. His contribution to breaking the disarmament deadlock cannot be overstated. But it is instructive to look closely at his reasoning, because here we discover the same preoccupation with leadership-centered narratives that informed Gorbachev's New Thinking.

In his memorandum, Yakovlev characterized Reykjavik as "an *extremely important and effective beachhead* for our offensive against Reagan." "Today," he continued, "we should expand it, turn it into a beachhead for an offensive against the positions of the forces of the far right and of the active proponents of the arms race in general, while at the same time ensuring opportunities *for cooperation in this sphere with moderately conservative and liberal groups* in the US and Europe." Yakovlev added that by focusing on the INF, the Soviets would not just remove a "serious threat," but "boost our reputation in Europe." Reputation – to Yakovlev and, indeed, to Gorbachev – was more important than the military's arguments about nuclear superiority. Fighting a nuclear war in Europe was a nonstarter but fighting the war for the hearts and minds of the Western public – in Yakovlev's words, "responding positively to the aspirations of the masses" – was a serious proposition.[45]

CHAPTER 19 HOPE

A few days before Yakovlev's memorandum, a crowd of foreign guests descended on Moscow – artists, scientists, doctors, and politicians. They were in town for a large forum on nuclear disarmament, Gorbachev's brainchild. In an effort to show the changing nature of the Soviet Union, Gorbachev allowed a prominent dissident and nuclear physicist, Andrei Sakharov, to speak at the forum. But it was Gorbachev himself who delivered the keynote speech, claiming that the USSR was "a part of the world community." "The worries of humankind are our worries. Its pains are our pains. Its hopes are our hopes," Gorbachev said.[46] It was a great success. Recounting the event at the Politburo, Gorbachev noted how "the world saw what great respect our work enjoys among the cultural figures, scientists, writers, and businessmen ... One can already see a serious change in the perception of the USSR by world public opinion."[47]

World public opinion! The notion was never far from the minds of Soviet policy makers, even before Gorbachev. But none could match him in the sheer power to charm and to make sense. Where his predecessors rattled missiles and sought to intimidate, Gorbachev relied on the appeal of soft power, to misuse a concept introduced by the Harvard political scientist Joseph Nye at the turn of the 1990s. Nye, too, was invited to the disarmament forum but, understanding what Gorbachev was after, declined to attend: the role of the guests, he said, was "going to be like the role of extras in a grand opera – and it was a long way to go to be an extra."[48]

But that grand opera had a finale unlike any other propaganda stunt in recent memory. Gorbachev not just agreed to decouple the INF from his package, but he made further concessions, giving up, in addition to the infamous SS-20s, the very capable shorter range "Oka" SS-23 missile. The Soviet military were scandalized by the move.[49] Gorbachev pressed on. His point was that the projection of leadership required matching words with deeds. If not, he told the Politburo, "we will undermine the credibility of our political decisions. Now the world is following us. But if we don't change our behavior in practice, they'll tell us: guys, were you bluffing?"[50] In a remarkable twist, then, Gorbachev took credibility to a whole new level. The proof was in the pudding. And the pudding was the unprecedented INF Treaty, concluded to much acclaim during Gorbachev's maiden trip to Washington, DC in December 1987.

"Comrades, an actual revolution is taking place," the Soviet leader proclaimed upon his return from America. "We must not be afraid. Before the entire world we must look the part of a people who are prepared to go to the end in their revolutionary perestroika."[51]

PART IV COLLAPSE

THE BLEEDING WOUND

The Soviet withdrawal from Afghanistan entered public memory as a foremost example of Gorbachev's New Thinking. The image of Soviet armored personnel carriers rolling back across the Hairatan bridge on February 15, 1989, has come to symbolize Moscow's global retrenchment, the end of interventionism, in many ways the end of the Cold War. Gorbachev's singular achievement of ending the quagmire sets him apart from his predecessors, so much so that it is easy to forget just how long it took before the last Soviet soldiers left: almost four years of this ten-year war were fought with Gorbachev at the helm. Gorbachev bid goodbye to this fateful adventure but it truly was, as historian Artemy Kalinovsky calls it, "a long goodbye." Gorbachev's approach to Afghanistan reveals a deep contradiction at the heart of his foreign policy and allows us to understand both the oft-neglected continuities between the earlier generation of Soviet policy makers and Gorbachev, but also certain differences that help account for the peaceful end of the Cold War.

Withdrawing from Afghanistan was one of Gorbachev's early political priorities. The idea was by no means revolutionary. A wide segment of the Soviet political elites – including people like Anatoly Chernyaev who was soon drawn into the new general secretary's close circle of advisers – despised the war. As we have seen, the intervention itself had been a subject of considerable contestation: it was ultimately forced on an ailing Brezhnev by the troika of Yury Andropov, Dmitry Ustinov, and Andrei Gromyko. Yet it did not take long for Ustinov – and the military that he represented – to grow disillusioned with the war, while Brezhnev and Andropov – both tried (but failed) to find a political settlement. If it were not for the fact that, as Reagan quipped, the general secretaries kept dying on him, it is not inconceivable that a solution would have been found even without Gorbachev. The latter's desire to find a way out of the quagmire – Gorbachev called the war a "bleeding wound" – was among the least controversial ideas that he brought to the policy table in March 1985.

The Western historiography of the war is replete with dubious claims to the effect that Afghanistan bankrupted the USSR (Reagan and the CIA are usually given the credit for wisely supporting the mujahideen in their jihad against the Soviet invaders). There is no evidence to support this argument. Soviet spending on the war was substantial – about $7.5 billion between 1984 and 1987 alone – but that number was but a drop in the bucket compared to the annual Soviet military budget (roughly $128 billion).[52] And although more than 13,000 Soviet troops perished in the war between 1979 and 1989, the party's control of the press assured that the public knew little of the true extent of the casualties. It is hardly surprising, then, that when he discussed the need to withdraw from Afghanistan early on in his tenure, Gorbachev did not seem particularly concerned about the economic or the social consequences of the war.[53]

What he *was* concerned about was what that war was doing to the Soviet global image. "What, are we going to sit there forever?" Gorbachev fumed at the Politburo in November 1986. "Or should we be ending this war? Otherwise, we'll disgrace ourselves in every respect ... We have to get out of there now. We have to get out of there!"[54] At that meeting, Gorbachev set himself a deadline: leave within two years.

The situation on the ground was not getting any better. Reagan used every opportunity to slam the Soviets for committing unspeakable atrocities in Afghanistan. The United Nations General Assembly passed resolution after resolution condemning the invasion, including one just a week before Gorbachev's comment, at the Politburo, that the USSR was disgracing itself in the war. In January 1987 Soviet Foreign Minister Eduard Shevardnadze paid a visit to Afghanistan. "There is little left of the friendly feelings towards the Soviet people, which were in place in Afghanistan for decades," he glumly told the Politburo upon his return. "A lot of people died, and not all of them were bandits." The bottom line, according to Shevardnadze, was that "all that we did and continue to do in Afghanistan, is incompatible with the moral image of our country."[55]

Gorbachev and his "liberal" foreign minister (Shevardnadze had replaced Gromyko, the notable hardliner, in July 1985) were thus on the same page about the war in Afghanistan: it was a horrible blot on Moscow's reputation. Even as the entire world, to recall Gorbachev's words, was allegedly turning towards perestroika, the ongoing conflict was a very painful reminder of the gap between Gorbachev's words and his deeds. By framing Afghanistan in moral (as opposed to ideological or geopolitical terms), the Soviet leader portrayed the war as an impediment to his broader effort to reclaim the mantle of global leadership. He and Shevardnadze both realized that nothing quite helped tarnish the image of national renewal as much as fighting a protracted war in a foreign country.

Realize it they did – but why did it take so long to translate this realization into practice? The answer, ironically, is once again the Soviet image. Gorbachev was very worried about the kind of message that a defeat in Afghanistan would send to Moscow's allies around the world, particularly in the third world. "The situation is complicated," Gorbachev argued at the Politburo in early 1987, discussing the prospects of a withdrawal. "We could leave quickly, without thinking about anything, and refer to the previous leadership, which started the whole thing. But we can't do it this way. India is worried. They are worried in Africa. They think it will be a blow to the authority of the Soviet Union in the national liberation movement. And they say: if you run away from Afghanistan, imperialism will go on the offensive."[56]

Other Politburo members voiced very similar concerns. Soviet Prime Minister Nikolai Ryzhkov worried that "giving everything up" would "scare many countries away from us." His solution was a mercenary army. "What stops desertions? Good money. They don't believe in slogans." Yegor Ligachev, a Gorbachev ally who eventually came to lead the conservative backlash against perestroika, felt that diplomacy was the only way out but "to leave like the Americans did from Vietnam – no, we aren't 'ripe' for that, as they say."[57]

An even more candid discussion took place in May 1987. Candid, because by then there was a general consensus in the Soviet leadership – including in the military – that the war could never be won. Of course, the Soviets could – and did – win practically every individual engagement, simply because the mujahideen could never match their conventional capabilities. But winning battles was not the same as holding territory: the moment the Soviet troops left, the opposition would reoccupy the lost ground, a pattern that repeated itself from place to place, from year to year. In a bid to give the struggling regime in Kabul a veneer of legitimacy, Gorbachev had tried, since early 1987, to achieve a "national reconciliation." The program aimed at backpedalling socialism, embracing Islam, and opening the government to serious participation by the opposition. Nothing seemed to be working, even after the Soviets replaced the ineffective Babrak Karmal with Mohammad Najib, nicknamed "the ox." The "ox" sabotaged Moscow's efforts to broaden the social base of his shaky regime and managed to win support even from ostensible liberals like Eduard Shevardnadze who now dreaded the prospect of cutting him loose.

Gorbachev summed up the prevailing sentiment: "If we do not work with Najib, who, then, do we work with? If we turn away entirely – let it all go to hell – they'll say: the Soviet Union betrayed [us]."[58]

There was a problem here. Staying was impossible but leaving was fraught with the loss of credibility, the charges of betrayal, ultimately the loss of Soviet prestige in the third world as a country that could be depended upon to defend its allies. And there was the domestic angle to consider, now that glasnost was taking hold: if the Soviets dropped everything and pulled out, how could the government explain the sacrifice of so much blood and

CHAPTER 19 HOPE

treasure? The situation was anything but unique. The United States faced some of the same dilemmas in Vietnam, which points to the similarities of the underlying logic of policy making in Moscow and Washington during the Cold War.

Gorbachev's concerns were also remarkably similar to those of his predecessors in the Kremlin. Like Gorbachev, Brezhnev and Khrushchev had in their time craved international recognition of Soviet leadership. They were aware of the benefit of standing up for "moral" causes, in particular global peace. But, like Gorbachev, they were committed to clients worldwide, and were worried about losing credibility. But Khrushchev and Brezhnev did not see a contradiction between being recognized as "great" by the West and as a superpower patron by numerous clients in the third world – indeed, they perceived these two forms of recognition as mutually reinforcing.

Not so Gorbachev. Maybe it was a result of his growing frustration with the third world: the escalating costs of maintaining clients, and their seeming deafness to Soviet advice. "Everyone wants us to work for them," Gorbachev grumbled. "And now they want us to fight for them. Adventurists who claim to be great strategists ..."[59] There was a growing realization in the Kremlin that these various quasi-revolutionary regimes with their self-proclaimed Marxist-Leninist petty dictators, were the wrong crowd to mingle with, that the real greatness was elsewhere: in Geneva, Reykjavik, Washington, in working with Reagan to solve global problems, including the problems of the third world. Reagan's willingness to deal with Gorbachev – to grant him that badly needed recognition and the international legitimacy that stemmed from such recognition – made it easier for the Soviet leader to renege on some of the third world commitments that he deemed problematic in the first place. It was this trade-off that allowed Gorbachev to agree to a diplomatic solution to the Afghan conflict, a solution that was far more disadvantageous to Moscow than what the Soviet negotiators had hoped for. "Having lost in Afghanistan," Gorbachev said after the signing of the 1988 Geneva Accords that marked the settlement of the conflict, "we have to win in the world."[60]

CONCLUSION

On May 31, 1988, Mikhail Gorbachev and Ronald Reagan, followed by a small crowd of advisers and photographers, strolled out of the great gates of the Kremlin's Spasskaya Tower and into the Red Square. With Gorbachev leading the way, the pair stopped in places to chat to bemused Soviet citizens and, at one point, even a frightened toddler. "That which has been happening in recent years in relations between our two countries agrees with the sentiments of our peoples," Gorbachev said. "I think so. Isn't it so?" "Yes, yes," shouted people in the crowd. Reagan echoed Gorbachev's words. Only five years earlier he declared the Soviet Union an "Evil Empire." Presently the American president found himself in the heart of that empire, with the Communist Party general secretary as his tour guide. Truly, the world had changed. For Gorbachev, too, this was a remarkable moment. His domestic reforms were running aground. He faced bitter resistance from the conservatives. Political power was already beginning to slip from his hands. But here was a foreign policy triumph. Here was proof that New Thinking was delivering practical results.

This chapter attempted to uncover the origins of New Thinking. At the basic level, it really was not all that new. The focus on peaceful coexistence (because nuclear weapons made war impossible) was something Gorbachev shared with his predecessors. There is no doubt, however, that he was willing to go further than the Kremlin's previous occupants, including by making unilateral concessions. The conclusion of the INF – the key breakthrough of the Gorbachev era – was only made possible because of substantial Soviet concessions (e.g. the decision to discount the British and the French nuclear arsenals). The Soviet military resented some of these giveaways but Gorbachev had enough political weight to override the powerful military lobby. For him, the main issue was not the numbers (the Soviets could and did end up cutting more than the Americans). The main issue was the principle. Gorbachev was keen to show that he was willing to commit to disarmament, as well as to intrusive inspections – that he was not just "bluffing."

There were gains to be had from such an open and honest policy. The main gain was that Gorbachev's international stock soared dramatically. Whereas Khrushchev and Brezhnev both understood the importance of "peaceful offensives," they could not quite commit to one wholeheartedly, and inevitably faced accusations of duplicity and hypocrisy. This time, as Chernyaev put it, there would be no "fooling around" – talking peaceful coexistence while privately seeking ways to outdo one's opponent.[61] Gorbachev did the real thing, and gained praise and recognition of his moral leadership, the kind of moral leadership that the Soviet Union of the 1950s–1970s – with its pathetic record of faux arms control initiatives and foreign interventions – could never have had. Gorbachev discovered a simple truth about global leadership: there had to be a moral basis for it, and genuine commitment to disarmament provided that moral basis. And so did nonintervention.

CHAPTER 19 HOPE

With the INF, Gorbachev's fallback position – to beat back criticism from the military and his conservative opponents – was that no one was planning to fight a nuclear war to begin with. Stockpiling missiles was madness. Disarmament would not just save money and lessen the dangers of war – it would raise Moscow's global standing. Matters were more complicated with foreign commitments, especially with the quagmire of Afghanistan. Few in Moscow opposed a withdrawal: it was necessary, and it was overdue. But the moral liabilities of fighting a foreign war had to be weighed against considerations of prestige and credibility. The issue was not Afghanistan. The issue was the Soviet standing in the third world. That is why it took Gorbachev so long to bring this conflict to an end.

He did in the end, primarily because he did not value the Soviet standing in the third world quite as much as his predecessors. Khrushchev and Brezhnev, for instance, both derived legitimacy from being recognized as revolutionary leaders. They also thought in terms of strategic platforms that far-off clients afforded to the Soviet Union. Gorbachev inherited the strategic vision of his predecessors. He, too, spoke of countries like Vietnam and Mongolia – among others – as "platforms." He reminded his Politburo comrades that it was important to preserve good relations with the likes of Ethiopia, Angola, and Mozambique. The rapid Soviet retrenchment from the third world in the late 1980s was not so much a conscious choice as a consequence of the Kremlin's bankruptcy.

And yet Gorbachev was clearly not as interested in maintaining Moscow's reputation as a revolutionary leader of the third world, and that was simply because he understood that "revolution," which the Soviets had been hard-selling to the third world, led into a cul-de-sac. The Soviet Union was itself trying desperately to reform, to escape its poverty and backwardness. What, then, could it teach the third world? He may have written in his famous book that he wanted to work hand-in-hand with the United States to help the developing world but in the privacy of the Politburo sessions, Gorbachev admitted that the Soviet Union itself was in dire need of development. Therefore, Gorbachev sought recognition as a revolutionary center of a different kind – one that stood for a new type of international relations, for overcoming the divides of the Cold War. And, as was the case with nuclear disarmament, he understood that he had to square his words and his deeds. By quitting Afghanistan, the Soviet Union would lose credibility as a superpower patron but gain credibility as a force for good in the world.

20

COLLAPSE

In the space of just a year or two the empire that Stalin had built up in Eastern and Central Europe, and that his successors had labored to maintain by periodic invasions and economic subsidies, crumbled to dust. Soviet satellites abandoned their plans for building a socialist paradise and transitioned to democracy, mostly peacefully. Mikhail Gorbachev looked on, refusing to intervene. Why? This chapter explores Gorbachev's decision-making as the familiar socialist world unraveled. It is commonly argued that Gorbachev had an "aversion to violence."[1] There is a lot in this explanation. But there were many other reasons for his nonaction: some based on hard-nosed acceptance that the Soviets simply could no longer maintain their overseas clients; others that had to do with Gorbachev self-perception as a prophet of reformed socialism who would bridge the divides of the Cold War by sheer magic of a powerful vision.

It was this vision that Gorbachev sought to sell to US President George H.W. Bush, but without success. Bush perceived an opportunity in Gorbachev's weakness and pursued a fairly robust strategy aimed at locking in the gains of American victory in the Cold War. This became particularly clear in the months after the fall of the Berlin Wall, in the lead up to Germany's reunification. The Soviet leader maneuvered to keep a united Germany out of NATO, offering a variety of alternative proposals, none of which found any buyers. Gorbachev's effort to repurpose the USSR for a brave new world of his imagination world fell flat. The Soviet Union, fatally weakened by internal political strife and ethnic separatism, began to come undone. The brave new world refused to be born.

THE UNRAVELLING

In 1989 the Soviet world fell apart. Within a few months Moscow's Eastern European clients – the formidable Communist and workers' parties that had clung to power for over forty years – embraced democratic change. The popular revolutions that swept across Eastern and Central Europe in 1989 were

CHAPTER 20 COLLAPSE

a reaction to decades of political repressions and economic misman- agement. In a bid to maintain a moderately acceptable standard of liv- ing in their fiefdoms, Communist authorities in countries like Poland, Hungary, and Czechoslovakia had resorted to heavy external borrowing. In the 1980s, the debt burden grew, and the quality of life stagnated. Authoritarian practices fatally eroded whatever internal legitimacy these regimes may have had (and they never had much). There was, moreo- ver, no political will, nor ability, among the party stalwarts to pursue fun- damental reform even as perestroika unfolded in the USSR. Gorbachev was privately frustrated by this failure to emulate the Soviet example but resolved not to interfere, telling his Politburo comrades in January 1987: "we do not want to be blamed for what's happening there, or for what may happen."[2]

In 1988 things began to unravel in Hungary. The long-time leader of the Hungarian Socialist Workers' Party János Kádár resigned in May as the country faced mounting economic difficulties and bubbling discontent at the grassroots. In February 1989, the new party leadership – inept and divided – opted for a dialogue with the as yet amorphous political oppo- sition, a process that led to a new constitution and free elections, won hands-down by the center-right. Meanwhile, the leader of the Polish United Workers' Party Wojciech Jaruzelski, also pressed by economic necessity and the rumblings of political dissent, entered negotiations with the long- banned Solidarity, agreeing rapidly to hold semi-free elections, which he evidently hoped would give the opposition a stake in the political status quo without overly undermining the government. Jaruzelski badly miscal- culated: on June 4, 1989 Solidarity trounced the Communists in all but one electoral contest, leading to the appointment of Tadeusz Mazowiecki – the first non-Communist prime minister in Poland since 1946.[3]

The power transition did not always go smoothly. The Communist rul- ers of Czechoslovakia had no interest in emulating the experience of their reformist neighbors. Czechoslovakia's living standards were higher than in Poland or Hungary but it, too, experienced stagnating standards of living, resorting to increasing borrowing in the 1980s to fill up the shelves. If you only supply \$1–2 billion a year's worth of imported goods to the internal market, reasoned the Communist hardliner Vasiľ Biľak, "the people will stay quiet."[4] He misjudged the situation. In January 1989 political dissidents held a demonstration in Prague to honor Jan Palach, the young man who committed an act of self-immolation in 1969 in protest against the Soviet invasion of Czechoslovakia. The police brutally dispersed the gathering, arresting some of the activists, including the playwright Václav Havel.

PART IV COLLAPSE

The general secretary of the Czechoslovak Communist Party, Miloš Jakeš, was a hardliner who had paid lip service to perestroika – but just that. "This whole hideous lot [*kodla*] viciously hate our perestroika," wrote Anatoly Chernyaev two weeks into the year, referring to Jakeš and his colleagues. "They predict we'll end with chaos and failure."[5] Jakeš was not wrong but that did not save his regime: in November 1989, vast crowds filled Prague's public spaces as more and more people headed to the streets. Unable to resist the upheaval, the Communist authorities quietly gave in. Václav Havel, not long out of jail, became the new president of post-Communist Czechoslovakia.

The Bulgarian leadership was equally, if not more, resistant to change. Todor Zhivkov had ruled Bulgaria since 1954 as a personal fiefdom. Zhivkov's nepotism and corruption fed public discontent. The Bulgarian leader also pursued hard-headed national minority policies (in the mid-1980s he unleashed measures to force Bulgarian Turks into adopting Slavic names, triggering widespread protests). Concerns about Bulgaria's worsening economic and environmental conditions stirred grassroot activism. Zhivkov promised to crush the budding opposition: "We'll force them to shut their mouths," he raved in February 1989. "We must force them into their rat holes."[6] This information was passed on to the Soviets who are rumored to have had a hand in Zhivkov's downfall. He was sent into quiet retirement on November 10, 1989.

A much more violent scenario unfolded in nearby Romania, whose long-time ruler and Gorbachev critic, Nicolae Ceaușescu, resisted change to the bitter end. Unable to cope with the swell of public protests, he fled the capital city of Bucharest, was eventually apprehended, tried by a kangaroo court, and executed on Christmas Day, 1989, together with his wife Elena.

With the exception of the dramatic events in Bucharest, the collapse of socialism in Eastern Europe was remarkably peaceful and swift, taking observers by surprise. Gorbachev did not intervene to save his clients from losing power. To intervene meant to use force but Gorbachev was personally averse to using force. But the problem was not even just that. The problem was: to intervene – and then what? The regimes racked up massive debts to keep up the standards of living. "Some people accuse us now: where is the Soviet Union looking, why is it letting Poland and Hungary 'drift' to the West," Gorbachev explained. But we cannot underwrite Poland ... Poland already paid out 49 billion dollars, and still has to pay out almost another 50 billion." The same problems, he added, applied to Hungary.[7]

There was a further reason for Gorbachev not to resort to force. His credibility as a world leader depended on him not doing it, for if he did,

CHAPTER 20 COLLAPSE

how could have he ever claimed that he stood for different values than his interventionist predecessors? Gorbachev knew that he was losing clients, but he hoped that he was gaining the world. "There are fundamental changes happening here," he concluded in the final days of November 1989. "They are happening so fast that if one did not look at them from a certain political, philosophical perspective, but reacted immediately, one could even succumb to panic." And then: "I've already been accused of all sins: that everything is falling apart inside and out. Yes, it's falling apart. That which had to be destroyed, and that which outlived itself. And it's good that we've begun this process ourselves, and have a plan of action ..."[8]

THE BREACH OF THE WALL

Things did not go according to plan.[9] On the evening of November 9, 1989, Günter Schabowski, the unremarkable bureaucrat responsible for press relations of the Socialist Unity Party of Germany (SED), announced new travel regulations for East German citizens. The changes were not particularly encouraging (applications for travel still entailed significant bureaucratic hurdles) but Schabowski's rambling, incoherent announcement at the end of a lengthy, otherwise uneventful press conference, inadvertently made it sound like the borders between East and West Berlin were already open. Having picked up the news from television broadcasts, many East Berliners decided to see for themselves and headed for the checkpoints, where it was business as usual. Harald Jäger, the commanding officer at the Bornholmer Straße checkpoint, called to check with his superiors: he was told nothing had changed. But the crowds outside the checkpoint continued to swell. Facing a raucous multitude, lacking clear instructions, and unwilling to resort to lethal force, Jäger gave the order to open the gates. Jubilant thousands poured through the breach.[10]

The end was sudden, but it was not completely unexpected. The East German state had been teetering on the brink of insolvency. Berlin accumulated massive debts, and by 1989, some 62 percent of the exports of the German Democratic Republic (GDR) exports – $4.5 billion's worth – paid for the interest on loans. A dire economic situation was enormously complicated by the mass exodus of East Germans: thousands headed for Hungary, which had opened borders with Austria. Thousands camped out in Prague in the hope of obtaining permission to emigrate to West Germany. Eventually permission was obtained and in early October 1989 the refugees were safely transported to West Germany in what became a colossal embarrassment for Erich Honecker's regime. Even more embarrassing was Gorbachev's visit

PART IV COLLAPSE

to the GDR (to celebrate the fortieth anniversary of its establishment). At public rallies, where Honecker and Gorbachev appeared side-by-side, the crowds chanted Gorbachev's name – "Gorby! Gorby!" – pleading for Soviet support against their own ruler.

In private conversations with Honecker, Gorbachev made it clear: "When we are late, we are punished by life."[11] Honecker ignored Gorbachev's warnings and instead launched into a discussion of Karl Marx's "Critique of the Gotha Program," dated 1875. Weeks later, already after Honecker was forced out by his party comrades (Egon Krenz succeeded him as general secretary), Gorbachev recalled that he had "decent relations with Honecker but as of late he [Honecker] had become sort of blind."[12] That is what he told Krenz. Among his close comrades, Gorbachev was more forthcoming, calling Honecker a "dickhead."[13] Now Honecker was out of the picture. Egon Krenz had privately told Gorbachev on November 1 that he would impose martial law if the crowds stormed the Wall but did not do so on November 9, or in the days that followed. And that could only mean one thing: German reunification was inevitable. This was the message that the Soviet ambassador in West Germany, Yuly Kvitsinsky, tried to convey to Moscow in the immediate aftermath of the fall of the Wall. "I almost physically felt," he recalled, "that the reunification will happen, that the GDR is finished, that there is no return to the past."[14]

Gorbachev was not so sure. It was psychologically difficult and politically perilous to accept the loss of the most important Soviet ally in Western Europe. Gorbachev knew that he had important cards in his hand, including the fact that Soviet forces – over 300,000 troops – were stationed in East Germany, giving Moscow serious leverage in the "German question." Here was an opportunity, Gorbachev suggested on November 17 to British Ambassador Rodric Braithwaite, to forge a new kind of Europe, one with places for both Germanies. But, he warned, it was important that no one should try to use the unprecedented developments to further their "egotistical" agendas. "Not by an axe, and not by a bulldozer," Gorbachev summed up, referring to post-Cold War diplomacy in Europe. "Otherwise, we'll just scare each other."[15]

ON THE ROAD TO MALTA

Two weeks later Gorbachev went to Malta for his first summit with President George H.W. Bush. It was long in coming. After assuming the presidency in January 1989, Bush at first put Soviet–American relations on ice, initiating a "strategic review" that would take months to complete.

564

CHAPTER 20 COLLAPSE

Some historians think that Bush was too slow in embracing Gorbachev, that he should have acted with greater decisiveness instead of listening to the opinion of a few trusted advisors – people like Brent Scowcroft (his national security advisor), Scowcroft's deputy (and later the CIA chief) Robert Gates, and even Richard Nixon – who believed that "perestroika was a giant hoax."[16]

Part of the delay was due to the fact that he was quite busy with China. Having served in Beijing in the 1970s as head of the US Liaison Office, he saw himself (and was perceived by the Chinese) as something of a China hand. Bush was worried that the Chinese leaders who had been trying for some time now to improve relations with Moscow would finally mend fences, leaving the Americans out in the cold. In February 1989 Bush flew to Beijing and met with Deng Xiaoping, telling Deng that he was not concerned about the prospects of the Sino-Soviet rapprochement, though of course he was. Deng reassured his guest that China was not about to forget or forgive the Russians for their many trespasses. In his eagerness to engage China, Bush overlooked Beijing's appalling human rights record. The Chinese were, broadly speaking, on the right historical path: they were turning more and more capitalistic and so perhaps they would eventually also embrace freedom.

Such expectations proved premature. In April 1989, following the death of a reformist-minded former general secretary of the Chinese Communist Party, Hu Yaobang, thousands of students headed into the Tiananmen Square in Beijing to mourn his passing and demand change. The demonstration swelled in the following days as the Chinese leaders debated the course of action. A supporter of dialogue and "China's Gorbachev," General Secretary Zhao Ziyang, was ultimately sidelined as the hardliners pushed for the introduction of martial law. Deng favored a harsh response. On June 4 – the day that Poland held its first semi-democratic elections that resulted in Solidarity's remarkable victory – the army moved in, massacring thousands of demonstrators. The "Beijing spring" was over.

The Tiananmen crackdown was condemned around the world – but not in Moscow. Gorbachev distanced himself from these events although in a twist of fate, he was himself in Beijing just weeks before the massacre to meet with Deng Xiaoping and normalize Sino-Soviet relations after thirty years of conflict. That normalization was a major achievement of his years in power, and he was not about to squander the capital he earned on students who naively appealed to Gorbachev to take their side

Figure 29 Gorbachev and Deng Xiaoping sharing a meal in Beijing, May 1989.
Source: Forrest Anderson/Getty Images.

in the dispute with the Chinese authorities. So, when presented with the evidence that the army massacred 3,000 students in Beijing, Gorbachev privately remarked: "We must be realists. They, like us, have to hold on. Three thousand ... So what?"[17]

But Gorbachev himself was only a reluctant realist. He did nothing as his clients were toppled in Eastern Europe one at a time. His options were limited, true. But he was also convinced that he was helping bring into being a new Europe. It was not a defeat – it was a transformation. Gorbachev had a very particular, if blurry, vision of Europe post-Cold War, something he called "the Common European Home." He first articulated it in 1984, even before he became the general secretary. The idea was to reconcile security interests of all nations of Europe. Three years into perestroika, Gorbachev made it the centerpiece of his European strategy, elaborating on it in Prague (April 1987), Belgrade (March 1988), and finally Strasbourg (July 1989). He saw East and West Europe moving closer to each other in the years ahead, with the two alliances, NATO and the Warsaw Pact, gradually shedding their military character and becoming more political. There would be cross-integration between the European market and the Soviet-sponsored Comecon. There would be disarmament.

CHAPTER 20 COLLAPSE

This process would lead to the creation of a new Europe, of which the Soviet Union would be an integral part.[18]

But unlike the leaders who would "hold on" by massacring student demonstrators, Gorbachev proposed to hold on by letting go. In effect, he put himself forward as the moral leader of a new Europe and hoped to obtain Washington's endorsement of this vision. It was only after the Tiananmen tragedy that the American president – frustrated in his efforts to build up a dynamic relationship with Deng Xiaoping – turned to Gorbachev and expressed a readiness to meet. The summit would be held in Malta, on December 2–3, 1989, and alternate between the American cruiser *USS Belknap* and the Soviet liner *Maxim Gorky.*

Gorbachev arrived in Malta after a month of dramatic changes in Eastern Europe, and these changes did not strengthen his hand. On paper he still headed a mighty superpower, supposedly an equal of the United States. But in reality he faced mounting economic difficulties at home and a near-complete meltdown of Soviet influence in Eastern Europe. Gorbachev was fond of recalling his very first meeting with Ronald Reagan in Geneva – how Reagan shuffled his little cards and read out a litany of complaints against the Kremlin's behavior, and how Gorbachev valiantly told him: "You are not a teacher and I am not a student. You are not a prosecutor and I am not a defendant." Supposedly Reagan recognized that "if we want to talk about politics, ... then we have to do it as equals," and the two got off to a good start.[19] Now Gorbachev expected Bush to recognize that Gorbachev was not a defendant, nor a student: that he would not be accused nor taught. And yet he worried that that would be precisely what Bush might do and now – differently from 1985 – he would have to take what he was given because he was too weak to demand anything else.

Gorbachev repeatedly voiced these concerns in the days before Malta, for instance in a conversation with Canadian Prime Minister Brian Mulroney. "The Americans are having a hard time comprehending the new world, new values. They still have strong pretensions to be a world gendarme, aspirations to impose their opinion onto others, attempts to dictate." "The Americans," he continued, "have an itch: to give instructions to everyone as to how they should live. This American illness is like AIDS – a cure has not been found yet."[20] A few days later Gorbachev reiterated the same to Italian Prime Minister Giulio Andreotti: the Americans "remain in the past." "They are trying to convince their public opinion that the US won the 'Cold War,' [and] that therefore their policy was correct. This concerns us most of all."[21]

567

He was even more forthcoming with a group of Italian Communists, explaining how he thought that it was not just Eastern Europe that had to change but Western Europe as well. "The fact that the Americans are bidding on overcoming Europe's division on the basis of 'Western values' is very dangerous. Every nation has a right to choose – the right, as they say, to pray to their own god."[22] Finally, one day before he met Bush, Gorbachev broached the question of values in a conversation with the pope. "One must not claim to have the absolute truth and to try to impose it on others," he said. "This is no way to treat nations, their history, traditions, and identities ... It reminds me of the religious wars of the past." Surprisingly (given John Paul II's anti-Communist credentials), the pope agreed: "It would be wrong for someone to claim that changes in Europe and the world should follow the Western model. This goes against my deep convictions. Europe, as a participant in world history, should breathe with two lungs."[23]

THE MALTA SUMMIT

This was the sort of mood that Gorbachev brought to him to that first summit with George H.W. Bush. The weather over Malta was atrocious: the worst storm in recent memory.[24] Gorbachev and Bush faced each other across a narrow table, flanked by aides. "It's so narrow," Gorbachev quipped, "that if we don't have enough arguments, we'll kick each other."[25] The meetings lasted for two days, alternating between plenary and restricted sessions, and covering a lot of ground: disarmament, the third world, changes in Europe, and the future of Soviet–US relations.[26] Malta entered history as a turning point – the moment the Cold War ended. But what neither Bush nor Gorbachev yet fully realized was that they were talking past each other on the key issues; that their philosophical divergence that came through very clearly in their lengthy exchange pointed in opposite directions of travel for their countries; that the end of the Cold War would not bring lasting peace because the two sides were at odds over what the end of the Cold War actually meant.[27]

The first key divergence became manifest in Bush's and Gorbachev's approach to the problem of Latin America. Here, Bush pressed Gorbachev to stop helping Cuba and Nicaragua, both of which, he claimed, were trying to export revolution and undermined "fledgling democracies" in the Western hemisphere. Gorbachev for his part complained to Bush about what he saw as Washington's propensity to judge others by a higher standard than it applied to itself. Pointing to a recent example – the Philippines – where the United States intervened to help an ally, Corazon Aquino, to fight

CHAPTER 20 COLLAPSE

off an attempted coup, Gorbachev wondered why the Soviet Union could not intervene if any of its allies in Eastern Europe were in danger of being overthrown. He was also concerned about the situation in Panama, and the prospect that the Americans would intervene there as well to overthrow an inconvenient ruler, Manuel Noriega. "In the Soviet Union," Gorbachev said, "people ask: the fact that these are sovereign countries – is this not a barrier for the United States? Why does the U.S. arrange a trial, reach a verdict, and carry it out by itself?" Behind these comments was that same nagging sense of unfairness that bothered Khrushchev in his time: Why is it that *we* are not allowed what America does all the time?

Bush did not seem to grasp what Gorbachev was on about. After all, the situation in the Philippines was radically different from Eastern Europe and Latin America: Aquino had been democratically elected – a friend asking for help. "It never occurred to me that this would cause problems in the Soviet Union," Bush said, adding: "though I probably would have done it anyway." As for Noriega, he was a drug lord, and there were US indictments against him and "I can't stop the indictments" (Bush would move to overthrow Noriega before Christmas). To Gorbachev, though, all of that looked like US duplicity. "Some are beginning to say that the 'Bush doctrine' is replacing the 'Brezhnev doctrine.'" "I simply cannot understand this," Bush retorted. "He was embarrassed by this [question]," Gorbachev recalled a few days later, suggesting that Bush did understand – only pretended that he did not.[28]

Gorbachev made nonintervention the central pillar of his foreign policy and an integral part of his New Thinking that he now sought to inspire the world with. "Cold War methods and confrontations have suffered defeat," Gorbachev told Bush. The key message that Gorbachev was trying to carry across – the one that Bush seemed unwilling to understand – was that it was not that the Soviet Union had been "defeated" but the Cold War itself had been "defeated," and, with it, America's attempts to tell the world how to live. Recalling his conversations with Bush days after Malta, Gorbachev wondered how one could claim "that socialism failed and that the West had won." "What sort of logic is this – is this new thinking? ... What will this lead to?"[29]

The conversation shifted to the question of values, with Gorbachev reiterating his concerns about the tendency to present the end of the Cold War as a triumph for Western values. Imposing values "for the purpose of satisfying certain unilateral interests" was unacceptable. He added darkly: "If someone is making a claim to the ultimate truth, they can expect disaster." "Yes," the president agreed (according to the US

PART IV COLLAPSE

transcript) – "absolutely right" (in the Russian version). But Bush's seeming agreement with Gorbachev obscured a very deep divergence between the two. For Bush the matter was clear-cut. America stood for freedom. Freedom won. Therefore, America won the Cold War. And he was genuinely perplexed why Gorbachev seemed unable or unwilling to recognize this basic fact. Gorbachev was willing to embrace freedom, just not the American leadership that had attached itself to the concept.

Recounting this conversation to the French president, François Mitterrand, whom he suspected of sharing his resentment of American haughtiness, Gorbachev recalled telling Bush: "Freedom turns out to be a US monopoly. Market also turns out to be a US monopoly. But aren't there universal human values, which appeared even before America was discovered? Let's build our relations on that basis."[30]

It is tempting to see the Malta summit as a symbolic end of the Cold War. It crowned Gorbachev's quiet acceptance of the collapse of Soviet influence in Eastern Europe, the death of the Warsaw Pact, and German reunification.[31] This is partly true, but it is also true that the summit highlighted Gorbachev's pronounced concerns with the post-Cold War. He came to Malta hoping that he could convince Bush to abandon triumphalism. Bush, for his part, promised not to "jump up and down" on the Berlin Wall.[32] They parted with a different understanding of what transpired in the Soviet–American relationship: Bush thinking that the US had won the Cold War but crediting himself with not rubbing it in; Gorbachev hoping that it was the New Thinking that had won but still uncertain as to the president's willingness to acknowledge that common victory and even less certain that Bush would sign up to the imperative of solving the world's problems in consultation and working hand-in-hand with the USSR. The weeks and months that followed showed that there were good reasons for Gorbachev's doubts.

THE TEN POINTS

On November 28, 1989, speaking to the West German Bundestag, Chancellor Helmut Kohl outlined his vision for German reunification. The "Ten-Point-Program" called for a German confederation, an idea that seemed radical at the time. Kohl just barely informed the Americans of the bombshell and he kept his other allies, never mind the Soviets, entirely in the dark. But two days after he came back from Malta, the Soviet leader lashed out at Foreign Minister Hans-Dietrich Genscher who, to be fair, had nothing at all to do with the Ten Points, hailing from a different party than his chancellor. This

570

CHAPTER 20 COLLAPSE

was one of Gorbachev's most undiplomatic performances (he may have deliberately put on a show of indignation to shock Genscher – and if that was his purpose, he handsomely succeeded).

Why did Kohl not consult before issuing his declaration? – raved Gorbachev. "He is probably thinking that his music is playing – a march melody – and he has already started to march." What will happen to a united Germany, he continued: Will it join NATO or the Warsaw Pact, or become neutral? The chancellor's statement, Gorbachev concluded, was a "political mistake." "If you want to cooperate with us, we are ready. But if not – we'll draw political conclusions. I ask you that you treat the aforesaid with utmost seriousness."[33]

But what could Gorbachev really do? As 1989 drew to a close, he faced an increasingly dire situation at home. The economic crisis intensified. Miners' strikes spread across the country. Shelves stood empty. But the problem that consumed Gorbachev's attention was centrifugal nationalism that now threatened the very survival of the USSR. Tensions mounted in the Baltics. In December the Lithuanian Communist Party proclaimed independence from the center. Gorbachev tried to force the genie of nationalism back into the bottle, claiming that it was unthinkable for the Lithuanians who lived side-by-side with Russia "for two hundred years" to now walk out on the new and reformed USSR. "Today, in these halls of the Kremlin, the fate of the world is being decided – what it will look like – because what we are doing is too great."[34] But the Lithuanians, like their Latvian and Estonian comrades, no longer wanted to be a party to this "greatness." They wanted out.

"I consider it to be my main task to take the country through perestroika without a civil war," Gorbachev told a close circle of advisers on January 3, 1990. "Victims are inevitable. Some people are being killed here and there, can't get away from it. But it's not the same as repressing with force, with weapons. They won't get me to do it."[35] But only ten days later, Gorbachev's resolve was put to a test, as ethnic riots broke out in Baku, Azerbaijan. Scores of Armenians were massacred by the Azeris. Troops were deployed to stop the killing, resulting in more deaths. It was a scenario that Gorbachev had dreaded, and though uneasy calm returned to the streets of Baku, no one could predict where the lid might blow off: the whole country was staring into an abyss.

As the domestic pressures multiplied, Gorbachev had little time to take the lead on Eastern Europe. Despite his forceful intervention with Genscher, the Soviet leader continued to drift on the question of Germany – the biggest of questions for post-Cold War Europe. Gorbachev continued

571

PART IV COLLAPSE

to peddle his vision of the Common European Home. But though grand, it remained rather blurry. At the core of that vision was the idea of gradual dismantlement of the military blocs, with NATO and the Warsaw Pact shedding their military structures. De-fanged, the blocs would meet halfway under the great roof of a pan-European process, something like "Helsinki-2," a successor to the original Helsinki Conference, inaugurated by the Soviet–American detente in the 1970s. As in the 1970s, Moscow and Washington would steer the process. Gorbachev repeatedly emphasized a role for the United States, stressing how he would never seek to expel it from Europe, as doing so would be "unrealistic." His concern for the United States betrayed a hidden fear that it was the Soviet Union that would be expelled from Europe as the Iron Curtain finally lifted.

As the Soviet Union teetered on the brink of collapse, Gorbachev looked forward to a united Europe from the Atlantic to the Urals. "When I first used that term [a Common European Home], I was told that it was utopia …" Gorbachev told the prominent Japanese politician Shintaro Abe. "Some time passed, and now they say that we need to create a confederation or perhaps a federation in Europe. What's important for me is the direction of thinking, people's thoughts. That Europe that will take years, decades to create, will have an environment that will resolve the problems that have piled up over decades: ethnic, geopolitical, and demographic. And we, the Europeans, have agreed on this. We have a mutual understanding."[36]

But there was no real "mutual understanding," certainly not on the question of Germany. Gorbachev had hoped that other European players – notably, the French and the British – would side with the Soviet Union on the need to prevent German reunification. Britain's Prime Minister Margaret Thatcher told him that much in September 1989. Forewarning that she did not want her remarks to be recorded (Chernyaev had to restore them from memory), Thatcher claimed that Britain and Western Europe were "not interested in the unification of Germany." "The words written in the NATO communiqué may be different, but disregard them," she said, reiterating: "We do not want the unification of Germany. It would lead to changes in the post-war borders, and we cannot allow that because such a development would undermine the stability of the entire international situation and could lead to threats to our security."[37]

François Mitterrand, speaking to Gorbachev in Kiev on December 6, 1989, chose his language a bit more carefully, yet he too made it clear that he expected German reunification to lag behind the broader process of European integration. "Kohl's speech – his ten points – turned everything upside down," Mitterrand said. "He mixed up all the factors, he is in a

572

CHAPTER 20 COLLAPSE

hurry. I told Genscher about it, and he did not really object to my conclusions."[38] Gorbachev and Mitterrand agreed that it was a big problem that Kohl had forgotten to mention Germany's borders in his statement, stoking fears that a united Germany may turn irredentist and eye the lost territories of the former Third Reich. Both also agreed that the American position was unclear and contained elements of duplicity. Unfortunately for Gorbachev, Mitterrand's position also contained elements of duplicity. Meeting President Bush just a few days after his conversation with the Soviet leader, Mitterrand struck a highly triumphalist note: "the West is winning hands down."[39] Mitterrand's key concern was not building a Europe from the Atlantic to the Urals (as he seemed to suggest to Gorbachev) but increasing the pace of integration in Western Europe, making sure that Germany, united or not, remained firmly anchored to the European Community. "Otherwise, the whole thing will end up in the ditch."[40]

Meanwhile, it was East Germany that found itself in the ditch. Once the Wall fell and it became possible to freely cross the frontier between the GDR and West Germany, many voted with their feet, putting the survival of East Germany in limbo. Honecker's successor Egon Krenz (who had just weeks earlier promised martial law for East Germany) resigned on December 3, as Gorbachev and Bush met in Malta. The SED changed its name to the Party of Democratic Socialism but that hardly helped: having for most intents relinquished its hold on power, it left the caretaker Premier Hans Modrow to steer the sinking ship of state. Modrow turned up in Moscow in late January, and what he told Gorbachev was deeply alarming. The government was falling apart. The economy was in a meltdown and required infusions of cash from West Germany to remain afloat. Fifty thousand people left the GDR in January alone, mainly the young and the educated.

"Volcanologists continue to work even as ash falls on their heads," Gorbachev told Hans Modrow. As the GDR edged closer to doom, the Soviet leader was frantically searching for a dignified exit for the Warsaw Pact's crown jewel. On January 26, 1990, he held a meeting with senior officials and close advisers to brainstorm the German problem. It was a much bigger problem, he said, than Moscow's relations with other countries of Eastern Europe. Bulgaria, Czechoslovakia, and Hungary depended on the USSR. "The [anti-Soviet] illness will run its course but they won't able to get away." East Germany, by contrast, very much could "get away" by integrating into Western Europe. Indeed, it was probably inevitable. "The main thing," he said, "is to drag out the process, whatever the final result (reunification). What we need is for the Germans, Europe, and the USSR to

573

PART IV COLLAPSE

get used to this idea." But there was a darker undertone to some of his comments: "There was the Brest-Litovsk Treaty No. 1," he said, referring to the punitive terms of the 1918 treaty between Russia and the German Empire and its allies, which forced the Bolsheviks to surrender vast territories to the Central Powers. "Now we are in a situation of a Brest-Litovsk Treaty No. 2. If we don't succeed, we face the prospect that they [the West] will once again bite off half the country. It is very important to understand this."

The Soviet Union, Gorbachev acknowledged, had an important card – the presence of the Soviet forces in the GDR. "This is a real fact, which stems from the legal consequences of the war, which were determined by the winners." "The main thing," he said, "is that no one should count on a united Germany entering NATO. The presence of our forces will not allow this. And we can withdraw them only if the Americans withdraw their troops. And they will not do it for a long time." The (inevitable) merger between the two Germanies would take several years, and that afforded the Soviets an opportunity for some kind of pan-European settlement. Gorbachev's liberal ally Aleksandr Yakovlev formulated the core idea as follows: the Soviets would support German reunification in return for Germany's neutralization and demilitarization. The West Europeans (allegedly worried about Germany) would oppose this solution, the Americans would not know what to do, and the Soviets could thus stir a conflict between Germany and its allies, while "sitting on the mountain and watching a fight."[41]

"You can see that the Americans will try to restore their leadership in the world. An opportunity has opened up for them ...," Gorbachev later said. "But one must not idealize relations between the capitalist countries. There are cracks there as well, which can be widened."[42] The idea of "widening cracks" in the West was of course nothing new to Soviet foreign policy: Stalin had been an enthusiastic proponent, and so were Khrushchev and Brezhnev, all with meagre results.[43] Gorbachev's results in this regard were even less impressive.

Indeed, there was no fight in the West over the future of Germany. Instead, the NATO allies were lining up behind the necessity of German reunification and a united Germany's membership in NATO. The only real question was how to bring the Soviet Union to recognize these new realities. Foreign Minister Genscher thought he knew how. On January 31, he proposed a formula that would help set the terms of the debate for the immediate future. Germany would reunite and stay in NATO. But the alliance's jurisdiction would not extend to the territory of the former GDR or (as Genscher soon made clear privately) anywhere else in Eastern Europe.[44] This "Tutzing formula" (named so after the town where Genscher made his speech) hinged on a reconceptualization of NATO as a political organization to the point of its eventual disapparence within the broader security architecture of a new Europe. Genscher shared his ideas with US Secretary of State James Baker who seemingly embraced the Tutzing formula as it pertained to East Germany without perhaps understanding the full implications of Genscher's thinking about the future of NATO.

NOT ONE INCH?

In any case, it was a version of the Tutzing formula that James Baker brought to Moscow where he turned up for meetings with Eduard Shevardnadze and Mikhail Gorbachev on February 9, 1990. His assurances to the Soviets have been at the center of a rather acrimonious debate: What did he and what did he not promise?[45] Did he, for example, promise that NATO would not expand to the East? (In which case, its subsequent enlargement was a broken promise.) The record itself is straightforward. NATO was touched upon in Baker's conversations with both Shevardnadze and Gorbachev. With both, the secretary of state consistently maintained that a united Germany had to remain in NATO but the alliance would become something of a political rather than a military organization. The GDR would in any case be left out of NATO's military structures. As he told Gorbachev, "We understand the need for assurances to the countries in the East. If we maintain a presence in a Germany that is a part of NATO, there would be no extension of NATO's jurisdiction for forces of NATO one inch to the East."[46] To this Gorbachev said: "it is a given that the extension of NATO's zone is unacceptable."[47] Baker promptly agreed.

Significantly, on the same day, that same "sound proposal" of NATO's nonexpansion into East Germany was broached by the deputy national security adviser, Robert Gates, when he met with the head of the KGB, Vladimir Kryuchkov.[48] Political scientist Joshua Shifrinson argues that the significance of Gates's approach was that Baker's was not a random thought but a part of broader agreed position that the White House was putting across to the Soviet leadership.[49] The proposal was reiterated by Kohl and Genscher to, respectively, Gorbachev and Shevardnadze on the following day. The Soviet agreement to negotiate in the 2+4 format (the two Germanies plus Great Britain, France, the United States, and the Soviet Union) could be construed as acceptance of this informal offer. To Shifrinson, to say that Baker was merely airing a negotiating position belittles the importance of the quid pro quo.

PART IV COLLAPSE

Baker's embrace of the Tutzing formula proved short-lived (he received instructions from Bush to adopt more obscure language regarding the status of East Germany in NATO). Bush understood that he held all the cards. National Security Council (NSC) policy papers reveal a determination to affect a "fundamental shift in the strategic balance" in Europe by facilitating the Soviet pullback from the region. Condoleezza Rice, then on the NSC staff and, years later, the national security adviser, summed up the prevailing sentiment. The Soviets, she wrote, were in no position to resist German reunification, nor threaten the Germans. "Within six months, if events continue as they are going, no one would believe them anyway."[50]

President Bush presently became preoccupied with winning Helmut Kohl's commitment to a united Germany's continued membership in NATO, where all of its territory (including the GDR) would be protected by Article 5. Bush worried that Kohl was so eager to reunify that he was in fact considering concessions to the USSR, at least along the lines of the Tutzing formula, if not something more generous.[51] The president was adamant: "What worries me is talk that Germany must not stay in NATO. To hell with that. We prevailed and they didn't. We can't let the Soviets clutch victory from the jaws of defeat." Kohl eventually agreed, venturing an opinion that perhaps Gorbachev's cooperation could be bought. "You've got deep pockets," replied the American president.[52]

There is, however, a danger in going too far in blaming the United States for selfishly looking after their interests while exonerating Gorbachev. The Soviet leader was far from naive. He understood which way the wind was blowing, and that he had very little leverage in a highly untenable situation. His vision of the brave new post-Cold War world changed depending on whom he was speaking to. With President Bush, he invariably highlighted the danger from the emerging alternative centers of power. The Japanese, he told Bush in May 1990, are "creating their empire," while the Europeans are also working on building up a "center of power and economic might." Look at China, India, Latin America, he told Bush. Was not it about time the United States realized that it could not lead the world alone, and "doesn't the question arise in these circumstances about cooperation of our two countries?"[53]

But in Europe, he would say something else altogether, highlighting American fears of the Soviet–European or Soviet–West German rapprochement and how a strong Europe (in his opinion) would counterbalance the US–Japanese alliance (that is why the Americans were so afraid!).[54]

Meanwhile, he told Chinese Prime Minister Li Peng in April 1990 that what the Americans feared most was the "Sino-Soviet embrace." Promising to adhere to the socialist path, Gorbachev called Deng Xiaoping and Li Peng "comrades" (both were infamously responsible for the massacre in Tiananmen) and conspicuously omitted the subject of the massacre itself. That was because he did not want to upset the chances of building up what he called a "triangle" involving the Soviet Union, China, and India (naturally, with the Soviet Union in the position of leadership). As he told Indian Prime Minister Rajiv Gandhi weeks after the crackdown in Tiananmen, "They [the Chinese] were grateful for our measured response, and, perhaps, now they will value more their relations with us and with you ... Do you remember how we talked about a 'triangle'? ... We made a good forecast. Perhaps now is that exact moment."[55]

Gorbachev was far from naive. On the one hand, he was offering a brave new vision of the world and of Europe that would include both the Soviet Union and (as he made a point of stressing) the United States. On the other hand, he was shopping around for the best deal to increase Moscow's leverage, whether it meant cooperating with the United States to contain the aspirations of other centers of power, or cooperating with other centers of power to contain America's bid for global hegemony. The latter was more often than not the case. He repeatedly warned (non-American) interlocutors not to trust the United States. "Do not take everything [the Americans say] at face value," he told Czechoslovakia's new president, Václav Havel, just days after hearing Baker talk about NATO's nonexpansion to the East.[56] "The West can set traps," he warned the Polish non-Communist Prime Minister Tadeusz Mazowiecki, before meeting Bush in Malta.[57] He assured Li Peng that the Soviet leaders "realistically assess American policy, see all of its aspects, very carefully watch their efforts to attain superiority."[58]

The clearest indication that Gorbachev had not accepted the deal offered by Baker and Kohl but was holding out for better terms comes from the Soviet leader's own comments at an internal meeting on February 13, 1990, just four days after his talks with Baker. Pointing to what he called a "collusion" between the Americans and the West Germans, he argued that the Soviet Union would have to hold firm on matters affecting security, so as "not to upset the European and international balance."[59] Days later Gorbachev spoke to Bush by phone, explaining what he meant by "balance." "If there is no threat, if the balance will not be upset, then why are the Western countries so keen to integrate Germany in one military-political organization? Won't this change the balance? If we come to the conclusion

PART IV COLLAPSE

that this will impair the security of the Soviet Union and its allies, we'll have to seriously think about this."[60]

On March 6, Gorbachev explained in a public interview that East Germany's accession to NATO was not acceptable to the Soviet Union.[61] He reiterated the same in his very first speech as president of the USSR (Gorbachev was elected to the newly created post on March 15, 1990).[62] Throughout that spring – even as negotiations began on the future of Germany – the Soviet leader remained steadfast in his opposition to German membership in NATO, ostensibly rejecting the Tutzing formula (which was not even on offer any more). On April 2, for example, the Politburo approved instructions ahead of Shevardnadze's talks with Baker and Bush that asked him to inform the American leaders that the USSR would not "put up with an effective Anschluss of the GDR," nor with a united Germany's membership in NATO.[63]

Gorbachev became more and more frustrated with the United States, condemning Washington's duplicity in much stronger terms than he had in the run-up to the summit in Malta. America, Gorbachev argued in a conversation with Senator Ted Kennedy, oddly referring to himself in the third person, "takes it upon itself to encourage Gorbachev, to punish Gorbachev, to censure Gorbachev, to praise him or to condemn him. That's not good. It will be difficult for us to get on if you do not understand in the US that our perestroika is equally important for America, and also for the entire world."[64]

Far from being a naive victim of American trickery, Gorbachev was angered by what he perceived as the White House effort to dominate the post-Cold War world. But the bigger question is this: What would he have done if he were in President Bush's shoes; if it were not Moscow but Washington that was about to lose its empire in Europe; if it were not the Soviet Union but the United States that teetered on the brink of collapse? Would he not have pushed his advantage to the utmost? Bush spoke on occasion about his responsible handling of the situation, assuring Gorbachev that he was not "jumping up and down on the Berlin Wall." In a way, he was, and this emerging triumphalism deeply bothered the Soviet leader. But would Gorbachev not have done the same had the tables turned? The Soviet Union had never been known for its particular kindness to former enemies, so Moscow's later lamentations of having been brutalized in a brutal world are somewhat misplaced.

But there was another issue at stake. Gorbachev had sought to change the basis for Soviet influence in Eastern Europe, replacing a system of brutal oppression with one of voluntary deference to Moscow's leadership. He

578

CHAPTER 20 COLLAPSE

sought to overhaul Europe's security architecture, lessen the level of confrontation, and bring the Soviet Union into Europe in a way that his predecessors in the Kremlin never deemed possible. There was a degree of path dependency in this vision: once he embarked upon the path, Gorbachev found it difficult to retrace his steps. The traditional Soviet method of maintaining influence in Europe – brute force – was in theory still available but any resort to force would have backfired, completely undermining Gorbachev's international legitimacy and probably leading to his downfall. For this reason, the Soviet leader tried the best he could to sell his vision for a "Common European Home," even as he increasingly realized that there were no buyers. He pleaded with his Western partners to respect the "balance of interests." But without a balance of power, could there ever have been a balance of interests?

GORBACHEV FOLDS

On March 18, 1990, East Germany held its first democratic election. The Party of Democratic Socialism – the successor to the Communists – landed with a thud in the third place. But that was not surprising. More unexpected was the resounding victory of the Christian Democratic Union (CDU) who pushed their main opponent, the Social Democratic Party (SPD), into the second place. The CDU's triumph dramatically narrowed Gorbachev's space for maneuver. Until then, he hoped that he would be able to play on Kohl's worries over a possible SPD victory to extract concessions from the chancellor. "We have to invite Kohl," Gorbachev pondered aloud on January 26, "and [we have to] tell him: Look what's happening. You are also playing this game, and can well lose. The Social Democrats have better chances in the GDR than you have ... So, therefore, dear Helmut, we are proposing that you, too, adopt the European [read: Gorbachev's] point of view on German matters."[65] The Soviet leader proved inept at electoral forecasts. The CDU's victory immeasurably strengthened Kohl's hand and opened the door to a rapid reunification, leaving Gorbachev, and his pan-European process, in the dust.

On April 18, the head of the Communist Party's International Department and an old-time Germany hand, Valentin Falin, sent Gorbachev a frank memorandum, arguing that the Americans had been "spoiled by the Soviet side's flexibility, good faith, and agreeability" on the German question. "The West is outplaying us," lamented Falin, "when it promises to respect the USSR's interests, while in practice, step by step, shutting our country out of 'traditional Europe.'" He continued, with hard-nosed insight: "Drawing an interim conclusion to the last six months, one must

579

state that the 'common European home' is turning from a concrete task ... into a mirage." Falin pointed out that the Western position on Germany's NATO membership was "hardening from week to week" (the promise of NATO non-expansion into the GDR, for instance, was no longer on the table). His solution was to play hardball in response, pushing for a peace treaty with Germany, something, he knew, the Americans bitterly opposed. So what? The Soviets had leverage. "The Soviet forces," noted Falin, "could stay in the current territory of the GDR for as long as the USSR would deem it necessary in the presence of foreign military forces in the current territory of the FRG and the absence of a pan-European security structure."[66]

For a time, the Soviet leader went along with the gist of these recommendations and remained adamantly opposed to Germany's membership in NATO. At the end of April, for instance, he told East Germany's Lothar de Maizière (who had replaced Hans Modrow as prime minister after the elections) that he was not buying the assurances, offered by the West, that Germany's NATO membership would in no way threaten the USSR. "They don't need to talk us into it; this is not a kindergarten, and we are not talking about toys, but about such a serious matter as security." He concluded by restating that "we cannot conceive of a united Germany fully integrated in NATO," and by promising that the Soviet troops would stay in the GDR for the foreseeable future.[67]

But Gorbachev was running out of options. His threat to keep the Soviet troops in East Germany fell on deaf ears: Who would pay for them, and how could they remain if the Germans ordered them out? His threat to retaliate in other areas – for example, by freezing the conventional forces talks in Vienna – were also not being taken seriously. He tried floating imaginative scenarios – for instance, the notion that a united Germany would join *both* NATO and the Warsaw Pact but these were dismissed out of hand by Gorbachev's opposite numbers in the West. In desperation, Gorbachev even floated the prospect of the Soviet Union joining NATO. "What is NATO for? It was created in a different situation – what do we need it for?" Gorbachev pleaded with James Baker on May 18. And then: "You say NATO is not directed against us, that it's just a defense structure. So, we'll propose to join NATO ... I think in the current situation you should not leave us in solitude. This is a very responsible moment, and in this case we can take completely unexpected steps." He pressed his point: "Our joining NATO is not such a crazy fantasy. There was a big coalition at one time [during the Second World War], why would it be impossible now?"[68] Baker did not respond but noted, in his own readout of the meeting: "Germany definitely overloads his [Gorbachev's] circuits right now."[69]

CHAPTER 20 COLLAPSE

A few days later, Gorbachev flew to the United States and put the same proposal to President Bush directly. It was obviously not a spontaneous improvisation. In 1954 the Soviet leaders had already proposed that the USSR join NATO. They were rebuffed. *That* approach was clearly a ploy to weaken, perhaps destroy NATO by paralyzing the organization. By contrast, Gorbachev's knocking on NATO's door had no such malign undertones. Not so much a studied policy, it was a sign of the general secretary's growing desperation. Unable to build his own Common European Home, he now sought admittance to someone else's home for fear of losing the roof over his head.

Gorbachev was receiving conflicting advice. On May 4, his most open-minded adviser, Anatoly Chernyaev, sent him a memorandum that sharply diverged from Falin's earlier obstinate recommendations. There was no point, Chernyaev argued, in flogging the dead horse of German neutrality. Germany will be in NATO, and the sooner the Soviets recognized that, the better it would be because, if they procrastinated, their eventual agreement would later look like a major concession. By acting now, Chernyaev proposed a few months too late, it was possible to constrain the inevitable with all kinds of strings beneficial to the USSR. And then Chernyaev ventured an opinion that would have struck the Soviet military brass as unacceptable, even crazy. It was not a big deal, he noted, if Germany and even Poland joined NATO. These concerns, he wrote, "are from the past; this is the strategy of the Second World War and 'Cold War.'" It did not matter, argued Chernyaev, a Second World War veteran, where the West placed their conventional arms, whether it was along the Elbe (the river that separated the two Germanies) or the Oder (the river that separated Germany from Poland) because "the situation is defined by the nuclear balance between the USSR and the USA." "The real security of the Soviet Union," he concluded, "did not depend on the amount of forces in the West and in the East, and their armaments." That was because no one would dare to start a war with a nuclear power.[70]

What Chernyaev was suggesting was that nuclear arms allowed the Soviet Union to peacefully wind down its presence in Eastern Europe, and let the Americans in: the security concerns that were at the bottom of Stalin's quest for a sphere of influence in the region were rendered obsolete by the evolution of military technology. Did Gorbachev subscribe to the same argument? Possibly. During an internal meeting on May 19, the Soviet leader wondered aloud whether the "line of strategic balance" was along the Elbe or the Oder, reflecting that he and Chernyaev were likely already on the same page.[71] Given that within weeks of receiving this memorandum, Gorbachev abandoned his hard-fought position on NATO

581

PART IV COLLAPSE

membership also indicates that his and Chernyaev's thinking was on parallel tracks. For months he had proclaimed that he would not agree to a united Germany's membership in NATO for security reasons. Now Gorbachev was coming around to accept the unacceptable while he could still hope to get at least something in return for this concession.

But even if Chernyaev were not there to provide a strategic rationale for concessions on Germany, Gorbachev was hardly in a position to play for time. The spring of 1990 was a turning point on the downward political spiral in the Soviet Union. On March 11, Lithuania proclaimed its independence. Gorbachev had tried for months to rein in the Lithuanians. It was now clear that his strategy was not working; Vilnius and, for a good measure, Riga and Tallinn, were breaking away. But the news from the Baltics, as disturbing as it was, faded in significance before a much greater problem: the emergence of Russia as a separate (and increasingly separatist) entity at the center of the Soviet political landscape. The first Congress of People's Deputies of Russia opened in Moscow on May 16. Gorbachev tried to co-opt the budding narrative of Russia's national sovereignty. In his speech at the Congress on May 23, he warned those present that "without Russia, the Soviet Union itself is unthinkable." "We have a thousand years behind us," he pleaded. "The Russian people sacrificed a lot in order to unite many nations across vast distances, allowing them to emerge upon the stage with the help of a mighty state."[72]

"We should not run around now," Gorbachev told his aides on May 17, "we should not allow any panic. Everything is under control." But "control" was slipping through the president's fingers. One of his aides, Georgy Shakhnazarov, wrote in amazement: "During such moments, [Gorbachev] more and more reminds me of a daredevil desperately convinced of his own correctness, stubbornly breaking through to his objective across all the obstacles in the face of hostile fury."[73]

Gorbachev's other big problem was the deepening economic crisis, which weakened his political position even further. What he now needed was a full-fledged bail-out. The theme of credits began to appear prominently in Gorbachev's interactions with his Western counterparts from April 1990. The Americans proved very reluctant. Gorbachev even charged James Baker with blatant obstructionism of Soviet efforts to secure credits.[74] The Americans, Gorbachev complained to Helmut Kohl's foreign policy aide Horst Teltschik, were "narrow-minded pragmatists who think in old categories, from one election to the next."[75] Teltschik, as the man closest to Kohl's "deep pockets," also got an earful. Gorbachev wanted low-interest credits, telling Teltschik that the Germans had to see whom they were dealing with. "Who is in front of you – Poland, Bulgaria, India, or a great power like the Soviet Union?"[76] Meanwhile, the "great power" was turning even to China for commodity loans. "We were taken aback when they first raised this," Chinese Foreign Minister Qian Qichen recalled, adding: "We have agreed to extend some money to them."[77] On June 4, 1990, Gorbachev agreed to meet with the South Korean president, Roh Tae-woo, despite vitriolic protest in Pyongyang (the Soviets had promised Kim Il-sung to never recognize South Korea). That was after Chernyaev pragmatically informed his boss that by snubbing Roh he would be "letting billions slip out of hand."[78]

Gorbachev spent his last two weeks before the summit with Bush desperately drumming up support for a compromise solution on Germany and lambasting the United States in the harshest of terms. "We tell the Americans that we see everything," Gorbachev confided to Egyptian strongman Hosni Mubarak on May 15. "We are not simpletons. We are for cooperation as equals but we will not allow ourselves to be ordered about. They have difficulties understanding this …"[79] "We won't allow [them] to outmaneuver us," he warned a week prior to the summit. "We won't be simpletons."[80]

On May 25 Gorbachev had one final go at François Mitterrand whom he had hoped to enlist in his plans for the Common European Home. Now he pressed the French president to support the notion of Germany's dual membership (in NATO and the Warsaw Pact). Mitterrand demurred, calling the idea "a little bizarre."[81] "Not the slightest chance," he said, adding that he wanted Gorbachev to understand one thing: France could not afford to end up on the margins of NATO by advocating imaginative solutions that no one else found acceptable. This was *realpolitik*, Mitterrand-style. It left Gorbachev with little but to lament the behavior of Bush and Kohl "who are trying to squeeze the maximum for themselves out of the situation … All of that does not raise these leaders' prestige in my eyes."[82]

Just as Gorbachev left for the United States, he received one final blow. His long-time nemesis Boris Yeltsin was elected chairman of the Supreme Soviet of Russia, narrowly defeating Gorbachev's candidate. The road was now open to Russia's "independence" from the USSR, which would imply the latter's demise and Gorbachev's political death. Two days later Gorbachev held his talks with President Bush. He told Bush how he "could not be allowed to lose," and how much the success of perestroika depended on America's help. And then, at the end of a long discussion, he made the one concession that the American president had long waited

PART IV COLLAPSE

for: he would let the Germans decide what alliance to join. After spending weeks and months talking about how he was not a simpleton, and how he would never allow himself to be outmaneuvered by the United States, Gorbachev simply folded.

Soviet officials attending the summit, including Falin, military aide Sergei Akhromeev, and Minister of Defense Dmitry Yazov were reportedly aghast at hearing the Soviet leader concede on Germany. Bush himself was "astonished."[83] But, as historian Vladislav Zubok writes, Gorbachev's sudden concession was not "a slip of the tongue."[84] It was already becoming clear that Germany would reunify within months. And then what? "After Germany attains full sovereignty," Mitterrand told Gorbachev just a few days before the fateful summit in Washington, "we won't be able to say to them anything at all. The Germans will say: 'We have the same right as the others to control our destiny.'" "Looks like you are right," Gorbachev replied. This was more or less in line with what Chernyaev had been saying for weeks, and that was the argument that Gorbachev accepted: there was simply nothing to be done. By making a concession there and then, the Soviet leader was hoping to build "trust" with the American president, something he badly needed as he desperately tried to hold together the rapidly unravelling USSR.[85]

Gorbachev's detractors, in particular Valentin Falin, later alleged that the Soviet leader committed a tremendous blunder by making this unexpected concession. Others – for instance, Gorbachev's interpreter, Pavel Palazhchenko – argued that no one else had any better ideas at the time. Falin himself, Palazhchenko argued, had not offered any practical solutions short of preventing German reunification by force – and that would have meant war.[86] His views were echoed by many others in later recollections, for instance by the head of the KGB's Foreign Intelligence Directorate, Leonid Shebarshin: "Only a lunatic, detached from reality, could have suggested to resort to military force."[87]

Who is right? To say that Falin did not offer alternatives short of war is not entirely accurate. In fact, on June 1, 1990, one day after Gorbachev's astonishing concession, he sent his boss a short memorandum on German reunification. Falin dismissed the idea of Germany's membership in NATO, arguing presciently that it would "solidify the separation of European security," and that it would "give impetus ... to NATO's advance to the Soviet Union's borders along the entire frontline." Falin then outlined possible alternatives, most of which Gorbachev had peddled in one form or another during the preceding weeks, including: turning NATO and the Warsaw Pact into strictly political (not military) organizations; dual membership

584

CHAPTER 20 COLLAPSE

of Germany in NATO and the Warsaw Pact (which would hasten the creation of a pan-European security architecture); NATO's reform to allow anyone's (read: Moscow's) membership; and, ultimately, concluding a general peace treaty, which would guarantee Soviet interests and address timeless questions like European borders. In the meantime, Falin noted, the Soviet Union was best off insisting on keeping its forces in East Germany.

Falin was not the only canary in the coal mine. The CPSU Central Committee received letters and outside advice lambasting Gorbachev's European policy. For example, Eduard Gams, a People's Congress deputy of military background, argued in a letter that reached Yakovlev and Falin that Gorbachev's hasty agreement to withdraw Soviet forces from Czechoslovakia and Hungary under "humiliating" conditions not just "seriously undermine[d] the USSR's international prestige" but led to Moscow's surrender of "a most important trump card" in the 2+4 negotiations on Germany. Gams contrasted this with the United States, which, when it negotiates base rights, "is not inclined to take anyone's interests into account, save its own." "The US uses the entire arsenal of available means of pressure – political, economic, and military," Gams argued, concluding that the Soviet concessions had an element of "criminal, frivolous sell-out of the vitally important interests of our state."[88]

The reaction of people like Gams – and there were many more like him among Gorbachev's detractors – is understandable. In fact, views like these were not confined to the Soviet hardliners and the military brass. For example, a prominent West German politician, Egon Bahr, floated similar concerns. "I never thought," Bahr told a Soviet official in late June, "that in the twilight of my life, I would be thinking about the Soviet Union's interests more than its own representatives do." Bahr continued: "Moscow's concessions strengthen the influence of those circles in NATO that have no burning desire to take the road of all-European cooperation and of ending the confrontation." The current road, he predicted, "doomed the USSR to international isolation."[89] Interestingly, these were not the views of a marginal German left-winger but of one of the most influential mainstream voices in Bonn, and a founding father of West Germany's *Ostpolitik*. "Astonishment" was Bush's term for what he heard from Gorbachev on May 31, 1990. It is fair to say that the Soviet leader astonished both his friends and his critics. It did not take long before the critics (in particular, among the hardliners) began attacking Gorbachev, equating his concessions on Germany with high treason.

Gorbachev hesitated for a few more weeks. It was typical of him: he had not yet publicly committed to anything, and all the options were on

PART IV COLLAPSE

the table. On June 7, speaking at a meeting of the Warsaw Pact (which was rapidly falling apart), Gorbachev again refloated his proposal for Germany to be anchored in two blocs. He highlighted the price of error: "If we make a mistake ... it will be impossible to correct later." He criticized the Americans for "forgetting" about the Soviet interests in Europe and expressed his worries that "some people" were trying to drag his Eastern European allies into NATO at the expense of the Common European Home. "This, obviously, is not new thinking, but an effort to attain the same aims that were set during the Cold War by using the current situation and, maybe, elements of instability and the weak position of certain countries."[90]

The final act of this remarkable drama played out in July between Gorbachev and Kohl. The German chancellor met the Soviet leader in Moscow and then followed Gorbachev to Arkhyz, a picturesque mountain resort in the Caucasus, where the two ironed out the outline of the settlement. None of Gorbachev's grand schemes made the cut. What it came down to was Kohl's agreement to provide financial inducements in return for the Soviet military withdrawal from East Germany. The price of the deal was agreed in September 1990 after some further bargaining over the phone between Kohl and Gorbachev: 12 billion deutschmarks plus an interest-free credit to the tune of another 3 billion.[91] It was thus that as Roberts Gates would later say, the Soviet Union was, quite literally, "bribed out" of Europe.[92]

CONCLUSION

Germany reunified on October 3, 1990, forty-five years after it was carved up by the Allies in the opening chapter of the Cold War. Its reunification was a point of symbolic closure for the Germans. But not for the Soviet Union. Gorbachev set out to transform Europe. His idea – the Common European Home – checked out on multiple fronts. It promised the end of confrontation, which in the early 1980s had brought Europe to the brink of a nuclear war. It promised to return the Soviet Union to Europe, something that Gorbachev – as a self-identified "European" to the core – felt he was well placed to do. It was the best way to reform the dysfunctional web of relationships in Eastern Europe that made no economic or strategic sense. Finally, Gorbachev's European project allowed him to stake a claim to leadership in Europe and the world. Understanding that the Soviet project was failing, he sought to redefine Moscow's global mission as creation of a brave new post-Cold War, post-hegemonic world. Gorbachev

586

loved philosophy. One of his favorite Greek philosophers was Heraclitus, whose well-known adage, "everything flows, everything changes" the Soviet leader often fondly recalled. He wanted to flow with, but also to direct change, to be recognized not just as the leader of a superpower but as the world's strategist-in-chief for change: it was his mission, his historical role, and his claim to legitimacy.

Of course, Gorbachev also wanted to maintain the Soviet Union's influence in Europe and in the world. Depending on the context, he either envisioned working side-by-side with the United States in leading the world, or leading Europe, or, indeed, joining forces with the up-and-coming players like China, India, and even Brazil, in midwifing a truly multipolar world that would somehow still defer to his intellectual leadership. But maintaining "influence" sometimes required measures that went right against the philosophical underpinnings of a new world order that Gorbachev sought to bring into being. It quickly transpired, for instance, that the Soviet Union simply was not able to maintain its influence in Eastern Europe without the threat of force, and that as soon as Moscow's clients sensed that they could get away from under the Soviet tutelage, they made the dash for the West, leaving Gorbachev in the cold. They wanted no part of a Soviet-led Europe when there was another, prosperous, democratic Europe right at their doorstep.

The Soviet leader pleaded with President Bush to respect the Soviet Union's legitimate interests. It quickly transpired that he would not, probably because Bush had a different conception than Gorbachev of what was "legitimate." Gorbachev knew that he would not, and yet he still made concession after concession in the hope of sustaining the momentum of change that would somehow work out well for the Soviet Union in the end, securing Gorbachev's legacy as the prophet of a new world order. This hope ultimately explains why Gorbachev gave his blessing to Germany's reunification and its membership in NATO. Yes, he was desperate. Yes, he held few cards. But he could have held out for longer. But there were dangers in waiting. The Soviet economy was in a tailspin. He faced grave political uncertainties at home. Amid all these failures, the end of the Cold War was one notable achievement. By waiting, Gorbachev risked damaging Soviet–American relations that he worked so hard to build up, and undermining his legacy as the man who brought peace to Europe. So, he cashed in, winning Bush's goodwill, taking Kohl's money, and pulling back.

The money in the end proved insufficient: it did not save the Soviet Union, and it did not save Gorbachev. The collapse of Soviet influence in Eastern Europe in 1989–90 was but a prelude to the meltdown of

PART IV COLLAPSE

the Soviet Union itself. Gorbachev had been fatally weakened and found himself under pressure from the hardliners. It briefly seemed in early 1991 that he would succumb to this pressure and resort to a major crackdown to avoid collapse. In the end, the hardliners moved first, attempting a coup in August 1991. The coup failed but Gorbachev never recovered his authority. Boris Yeltsin had by then emerged as the most powerful player in Moscow. He swiftly moved to take away whatever vestiges of power the hapless Soviet leader still enjoyed. Gorbachev resigned in December 1991, and the Soviet Union degenerated into a motley assembly of sovereign republics plagued by a deepening economic crisis.

Mikhail Gorbachev was unable to accomplish what he had set out to do. The Soviet Union had relied on the threat of force to stay in Europe. As this threat diminished, the Soviets were politely asked to leave. The brave new world Gorbachev wanted to lead to a brighter future did not require nor desire his leadership.

CONCLUSION

November 1997 marked the tenth anniversary of the publication of Mikhail Gorbachev's visionary pamphlet, *Perestroika and New Thinking for Our Country and the World*. In the ten intervening years the country Gorbachev had once presided over was transformed almost beyond recognition, losing nearly a quarter of its territory and a half of its population. More than anything, it lost a sense of direction, a core idea. Gorbachev himself epitomized this loss. At the end of November, he infamously starred in a Pizza Hut commercial: why, to keep afloat of course. He had a foundation to sustain, and salaries to pay. At the end of the commercial, a small crowd of Muscovites is seen toasting Gorbachev with slices of their pizza: "Hail to Gorbachev!" One elderly lady explains: "Because of him we have many things ... like Pizza Hut!"[1]

The commercial was filmed for an international audience where the former Soviet leader still enjoyed popularity. There *was* a Pizza Hut in Moscow, but few Russians found Gorbachev an appealing advertiser. Most were actively hostile, blaming him for Soviet collapse, and Russia's concomitant loss of global stature. Pizza was not enough to compensate for the deep sense of resentment. In the 1996 Russian presidential elections Gorbachev garnered a paltry half of 1 percent of the national vote. His old nemesis Boris Yeltsin won the second term, but only just. If it were a fair election (it was not), Yeltsin may well have been defeated by the Stalinist Gennady Zyuganov.

Yeltsin, by then a wreck of a man, plagued by alcoholism and heart problems, presided over Russia's tumultuous transition from bankrupted socialism to a new and yet undefined modernity. It was a very painful process. The economy was in a deep recession. Between 1991 and 1999 Russia lost an estimated 40 percent of its GDP, an astonishing figure by almost any measure. The country also went through a period of hyperinflation that wiped out savings, impoverishing millions. Some turned to cross-border trading, shuttling back and forth between China or Turkey and the sprawling Russian markets, their checkered polypropylene bags stuffed full of cheap clothing and plastic toys. Others found solace in drink, or scoured around garbage bins, looking for discarded old shoes or slices of half-eaten pizza.

And there was a new caste of entrepreneurs or, in any case, what passed for them: slick multimillionaires who had made a fortune from looting the broken state, and clean-shaven gorillas in Adidas pants and Snickers to match, fighting over this or that street market. Private banking emerged. Money-laundering became an art. Absurd Ponzi schemes proliferated. A tiny circle of powerful insiders helped finance Yeltsin's reelection campaign and were rewarded with shares of major state enterprises at knockdown prices. Behold, Russia was entering the age of the oligarchs. It was very much the best and the worst of times, full of opportunities for the few and untold miseries for the many. But it lacked something – an *idea* perhaps? In the words of a protagonist of Svetlana Alexievich's classic *The Second Hand Time*, "No one is even trying to explain what country we are living in. What idea do we have, besides salami?"[2]

To be fair to the 1990s, there was not one idea but a proliferation of ideas. Political parties emerged in great numbers, peddling all kinds of ideologies: from militant Stalinism to fascism to neoliberalism. Russia was being pulled in different directions and seemed, on occasion, to teeter on the brink of an outright civil war. In October 1993 a long-running conflict between President Yeltsin and the Russian legislature ended in tragedy when Yeltsin ordered an attack on his parliamentary detractors. These were hardly champions of democracy. Their number included unrepentant Communists and blood-and-soil nationalists who, if given an opportunity, would have happily seen Yeltsin hang. But the shock of the assault on the Parliament was nevertheless severe. Could Russia's democratic future be built on a foundation of political violence? The first Duma elections, held in December 1993, produced a shock result: Vladimir Zhirinovsky's far-right nationalists obtained the highest number of votes, with the Communists in third place. This militant "red-brown opposition" would continue to pose a formidable challenge to Yeltsin's political authority for much of the rest of the turbulent decade.

Then, in December 1994, Yeltsin ordered the invasion of the breakaway republic of Chechnya. The brutal assault on the republican capital Grozny left much of the city in ruins: tens of thousands were killed, mainly civilians. The attackers, too, suffered serious casualties in grueling, urban fighting. Barely six years had passed since the last Soviet troops withdrew from the meaningless quagmire of Afghanistan. Here they were at it again. Yeltsin explained his reasoning in a televised speech. "The Russians have

CONCLUSION

long and justly reproached us, and me as President," he declared, "for indecisiveness, for the lack of political will, and unwillingness to restore order to the territory of the Chechen republic."[3] But the war became another quagmire. It dragged on and on, sapping Yeltsin's domestic popularity amid an international uproar over Russian barbarity and unrepentant imperialism. The war ended in August 1996 with the signing of the Khasavyurt Accords, which marked Russia's humiliating defeat.

President Bill Clinton had made Russia one of his foreign policy priorities, offering economic aid and political support even as Yeltsin cracked down on the opposition and waged a brutal war in Chechnya. As historian Mary Elise Sarotte writes, he sensed that "Yeltsin drunk was better for the United States than most other Russian leaders sober."[4] Yeltsin for his part looked for Clinton's recognition of his leadership. It would have had a legitimating aspect for Yeltsin. For the same reason he also wanted Russia to join NATO. As he told Clinton in January 1994, "There should be a kind of cartel of the US, Russia, and the Europeans to help to ensure and improve world security."[5] Yeltsin's Western-oriented foreign minister, Andrei Kozyrev, put the argument in even starker terms at a meeting of senior Russian diplomats: "The most important thing," he argued, "is the partnership with the U.S. Furthermore, one has to be [America's] primary partner; otherwise, nothing will remain from [our] great-power status."[6]

Yeltsin's and Kozyrev's expectations proved misplaced. The United States moved quickly to enlarge NATO into what was once Warsaw Pact territory. The decision to admit Poland, Hungary, and the Czech Republic was formally taken in 1997, and it was based in part on concerns about letting these countries drift without a security anchor in their historically volatile region, and in part on hedging against Russia. It was not yet clear in the mid-1990s where Russia was going but if the war in Chechnya was a pointer in any direction, it certainly did not point to liberal democracy. The Central and Eastern Europeans pleaded to be accepted. The first such enlargement was of course just the beginning: there were others in the queue, including the Baltics. Ukraine sat uncomfortably in the grey zone of assumed Russian influence and wanted to get out. Yeltsin was indignant about NATO's eastward enlargement, telling Clinton when he saw him in Moscow in May 1995 that it was "nothing but humiliation for Russia."[7]

Clinton turned up in Moscow for the fiftieth anniversary of the Soviet Victory Day, a controversial move, given Russia's ongoing war in Chechnya and Washington's complaints about Russia's sale of nuclear technologies to Iran. He decided to go, to advertise his support for Yeltsin and to help reenergize the Russian–American relationship, which was beginning to

PART IV COLLAPSE

show signs of strain. He came to the parade as well, a relatively low-key affair, which on that occasion still featured some 6,000 Soviet veterans of the Second World War. They marched across the Red Square against the backdrop of a large banner showing a Soviet soldier and an American soldier in a friendly embrace. "I just can't get over the faces," Clinton later said. "The faces are incredible."[8] Who knows what he read in those faces? But one of the marching veterans, retired colonel Viktor Gaevsky, probably spoke for many, when he told a reporter: "Yes, we are hurt and humiliated. But let the whole world see for themselves that the veterans have not been broken, and they are ready to stand for themselves, and for their impoverished, insulted nation."[9]

Gaevsky, then a still a teenager, dug antitank trenches on the outskirts of Moscow in 1941, and fought in Karelia and in Eastern Europe. He was wounded in hand-to-hand combat, was nearly burned alive in one hostile engagement, but survived and greeted the end of war in Czechoslovakia.[10] He was of that generation for whom the war was a formative experience, the point of greatest horror but also of greatest pride at having overcome, at having *proven* to the world that they *could*. The war was a legitimating experience, and the victory in that war, at however atrocious a cost, served to confirm the legitimacy of the Soviet project and the Soviet Union's exalted place in the global order. That idea – that the Soviet Union acquired true greatness by waging and winning a war against a mighty enemy – proved so resilient that it outlived the Soviet collapse and the death of Marxism-Leninism. The peculiar Soviet ideology was only a means to greatness but greatness itself – that was for the ages.

But – and this is where the Soviet Cold War experience became so interesting – greatness could not be simply proclaimed. It had to be recognized. Germany's unconditional surrender in the Second World War was a form of recognition – recognition through submission, as Hegel would have had it. But it was not enough. The recognition that Moscow craved had to come from the United States. The underlying premise of the Yalta discussions was that the United States would recognize certain Soviet gains in Europe and Asia, and by recognizing legitimize them. It was strange that Stalin, cynical operator that he was, put so much stock on the legitimacy of Soviet gains. But he did, and, as we have seen, he was even willing to surrender illegitimate gains in exchange for those legitimated by Yalta (this was clear in his approach to China in particular). But it quickly transpired that what Stalin deemed "legitimate" – that is, roughly corresponding to Moscow's new postwar self-perception of greatness – was deemed quite illegitimate by the Americans. Early disagreements over Poland, the US initial failure

CONCLUSION

to recognize the Bulgarian and Romanian governments, and Washington's unwillingness to permit Stalin a colony in North Africa all pointed to a gap in the perception of legitimate entitlements.

The A-bomb played a very interesting role in this early clash. As we have seen, Stalin understood the significance of the new weapon, not as a weapon per se (though this was important) but as a status symbol. America's atomic monopoly invalidated Stalin's claims to great-power equality. Therefore, while the Soviets secretly and urgently pursued their own A-bomb, Stalin played it tough in diplomatic encounters with the Americans, fearing that any, even minor, concessions, would be interpreted by the US leadership as a sign of weakness, as a sign that he had "blinked" in the face of American power and so lead to even more pressure. And yet Stalin blinked again and again: in Iran, where he retreated, betraying a separatist movement that he had brought to power; in Turkey, where he made threats and territorial demands but did little to follow through; in Berlin, when he tried to elbow the Allies out but refused to open fire on the American planes that resupplied the city. He was very cautious in China, leading Mao to suspect, rightly, that Stalin did not believe in the Chinese revolution. What Stalin was worried about above all was inadvertently triggering US intervention in the Chinese civil war, which could upend the regional balance of power and result in the loss of his gains, won after so much toil at Yalta.

Historians have long debated whether the communization of Eastern Europe in the late 1940s was inevitable, and this book sides with those who argue that it was not. Kennan was right to say that Stalin worked by no fixed plans; that, in effect, he was an opportunist. Moreover, he expected Communist parties to do better in elections. Only after it transpired that the Communists could not gain power peacefully did Stalin really give up on the idea of separate roads to socialism. The Marshall Plan contributed to this rethinking, increasing Stalin's paranoia about the American penetration of Europe, though it was only one factor among several. The more important factor was the Communists' declining electoral chances. The way to fix this problem was to falsify elections and to intimidate the opposition – but this option was only available to Stalin in countries under his direct control.

There is still the unresolved question of whether the Soviet Union at the outset of the Cold War was a status quo or a revolutionary power. If it was a status quo power, it was basically satisfied with its place in the global order, and would not seek to disrupt it. Stalin's entire approach at Yalta seems to be pointing in this direction. But here is the problem. If it was true

PART IV COLLAPSE

that Stalin had a long-term vision for worldwide triumph of Communism, then he would never be content with a particular perch, even an exalted one. There would be tempting opportunities to go from gain to gain if he could reasonably get away with it. We could observe this with the Soviet behavior in Greece, the only country that was clearly assigned to the British "sphere" in the percentages agreement and where Stalin first refused to support a Communist insurgency but later came around to cautiously supporting it, until he changed his mind once again. He tested the boundaries of the possible in Iran and in Japan, retreating only when faced with US threats. This does not point in the direction of a stable equilibrium.

Thus, a failure to push back against Stalin's demands could well have resulted in him making ever greater demands. On the other hand, pushing back hard against demands that Stalin deemed legitimate clearly contributed to the erosion of trust and the escalation of tensions, feeding the spiral of conflict. Henry Kissinger was right to argue in his 1957 book that "the powers which represent legitimacy and the status quo cannot 'know' that their antagonist is not amenable to 'reason' until he has demonstrated it. And he will not have demonstrated it until the international system is already overturned."[11] In Stalin's case, we never reached that point, because Truman pushed back. If he had not, would he have discovered that Stalin was, in fact, a reasonable old chap who merely wanted America to be equally reasonable? Maybe. But the price of getting it wrong would have been Soviet conquest. The price of pushing back was "just" the Cold War.

Stalin's (eventual) successor, Nikita Khrushchev, was a revolutionary romantic. He looked beyond the immediate Soviet neighborhood to distant shores of Asia, Africa, and Latin America, where he saw opportunities for forging closer ties with nationalist leaders. Why did he do it? For a start, it was because the world was rapidly changing. Decolonization created opportunities that were simply not there when Stalin was at the helm. But opportunities do not explain choices. One way to explain Khrushchev's turn to the third world is to look at geopolitics (any such relationships could be, and often were, rationalized in military and strategic terms). But this was not how Khrushchev would have described his involvement. He was keen on stressing the ideological component: his revolutionary duty to help the "anti-imperialist struggle." Khrushchev wanted to be recognized for his contributions to the anticolonial and anti-imperialist movements: such recognition translated into legitimacy. He wanted to be seen leading the global revolutionary forces, and this meant forging links with the likes of Nasser, Nehru, and Sukarno, sending weapons and economic aid.

CONCLUSION

The recognizers here were obviously the leaders and the publics of the third world, but not only. China loomed large in Khrushchev's world. He cared enormously about how his policies were understood in Beijing, and craved Mao Zedong's recognition of his revolutionary merit. Many of his foreign policy moves in the late 1950s and the early 1960s reflected this preoccupation. As we have seen, both the dangerous Berlin ultimatum of 1958 and Khrushchev's decisions to send nuclear missiles to Cuba are best understood in the context of his competition with China for leadership in the international Communist movement. After Stalin's death, Mao made a bid to be recognized as the strategist-in-chief for the Soviet bloc and pursued radical domestic and military foreign policies that he expected Moscow to accept and endorse. The sources of the Sino-Soviet split can be traced back to Mao's unwillingness to defer to the Soviet leadership. Interestingly, he was willing to defer to the Soviets when Stalin was still alive, even though Stalin treated China as a semi-colony. But Mao accepted Stalin's authority, recognizing his revolutionary merit. He was not willing to be equally generous to Khrushchev.

Although China loomed large among audiences Khrushchev catered to, he cared even more about American recognition of Soviet greatness. He understood that the Soviet Union was the underdog of the Cold War. It was playing perpetual catch-up with America but as much as Khrushchev promised to overtake the West, he fell short: the Soviet system was simply not delivering the kinds of breakthroughs that would speak to its supposed superiority, the Sputnik moment notwithstanding. There was one important exception: nuclear arms. During the 1950s the Soviets made remarkable strides in building up a thermonuclear capability coupled with increasingly reliable means of intercontinental delivery. Khrushchev possessed the means to obliterate the United States. This enormously increased his self-confidence, translating into a more militant foreign policy. He was no longer the trembling creature of global politics. He had the right to demand respect and deference – above all, from the great nemesis, the United States.

But there was a problem. Although Khrushchev craved American recognition and worked hard to develop a personal relationship with Presidents Eisenhower and Kennedy, he was never quite sure what this kind of recognition would mean in practice. For example, would he be willing to moderate Soviet foreign policy in return for being accepted as America's equal? The proposition never worked because the very fact of being accepted as an equal meant rejecting external constraints on foreign policy behavior. Khrushchev's approach to Cuba was underpinned by considerations of this kind. He could not accept that the United States had a right to maintain bases, even place nuclear missiles, at the Soviet periphery while the Soviets were not allowed the same facility: What sort of equality could one talk about then? Soviet engagement in the third world and, indeed, American acceptance of this engagement were part and parcel of what it meant to be a superpower.

Moreover, Khrushchev needed to keep an eye on the Chinese reaction. Mao was jealously watching the Soviet leader's pirouettes with the Americans and was not shy to point to what looked like Soviet betrayal of principles of revolutionary solidarity. It was not by accident that Soviet–US relations finally began to improve when, after the Cuban Missile Crisis, Sino-Soviet relations went into a tailspin. Khrushchev no longer had to look over his shoulder as he pursued detente with the United States.

There were of course other reasons for Khrushchev's embrace of detente, the terrifying experience of the Cuban Missile Crisis being key. We might argue that Khrushchev blinked and lost the round, but it would be more accurate to say that both Khrushchev and Kennedy blinked. Having come close to the brink, they glimpsed the darkness on the other side and understood that the world had changed forever. Nuclear-armed great powers were simply indestructible from without. Great wars of conquest that once changed the course of history were simply out of the question now. All that remained was perpetual coexistence until one superpower or the other collapsed of its own accord. The nuclear revolution ushered the end of history – and we did not notice.

Khrushchev's ouster in 1964 produced a deficit of legitimacy in the Kremlin. Soviet leaders lacked legitimacy even in the best of times, owing to the unrepresentative nature of the system. How did Leonid Brezhnev become the leader of a superpower? Clearly, it was because Khrushchev liked and promoted him, until his protégé overthrew him in a cloak-and-dagger plot that had no public input whatsoever. One could of course argue that Brezhnev's leadership was legitimized by Marx and Lenin, but it was also important to be recognized externally. It was this desire for recognition that underpinned Soviet reengagement with Vietnam (which more or less fell off Moscow's radar on Khrushchev's watch) and the Soviet leaders' attempted rapprochement with China, which was quite brutally subverted by Mao Zedong. Recognition by the third world and the revolutionary forces was important to Brezhnev and Kosygin for the same reasons it had mattered to Khrushchev. For the same reasons, it was ultimately unsatisfactory. The recognition that the Soviet leadership wanted above all else could only come from the rival superpower, the United States.

CONCLUSION

In the early 1970s Brezhnev pursued recognition by developing a close relationship with President Richard Nixon. It was Brezhnev's personal project, and he invested himself fully, sometimes putting his reputation on the line. The Soviet–American summit of May 1972 raised his personal stature at the expense of Kosygin: one example of how external recognition translated into domestic legitimacy. Unlike Khrushchev, Brezhnev had a fairly concrete idea of what kind of recognition he expected. He aimed at a US–Soviet condominium, a superpower partnership that would allow the Soviet Union and the United States to peacefully coexist while resolving difficult international problems, like Vietnam and the conflict in the Middle East. The biggest problem of all, though, was China, which by then had become one of Brezhnev's obsessions. The Soviet leader's appeal to Nixon to close ranks against China had civilizational undertones. He felt that as a "European," he could trust other "Europeans" (including Nixon) in a way that he could never trust the Chinese.

Brezhnev's condominium was not that different from Stalin's conception at Yalta, and it entailed mutual recognition of the other side's "legitimate" interests. Herein lay its key weakness, because just as Stalin could be tempted to overstep the boundaries of the agreed, Brezhnev, too, could be patting Nixon on the back with one hand while stabbing him with the other. He was an actor, performing for different audiences. Even as he schmoozed with Nixon and Kissinger, Brezhnev tried to position himself as a true revolutionary with Castro and Le Duan. It was a difficult balancing act, fraught with an occasional temptation to profit at America's expense. The same temptation existed for the United States, as Kissinger proved with his able diplomacy in the Middle East that left the Soviets out in the cold. However, there was a sea change from the earlier years of the Cold War, so much so that Brezhnev now spoke of the end of the Cold War. Brezhnev considered detente his singular foreign policy achievement, drawing political legitimacy from being recognized as a peacemaker of sorts.

As we have seen, with Brezhnev's illness and Nixon's resignation, detente withered quickly. Moscow was often perplexed by the twists and turns of US domestic politics, and especially resented efforts to tie the fortunes of detente to emigration policies, or to the Soviet human rights record. The reason – as this book has shown – was that such perceived American interference in Soviet "internal affairs" undercut the idea of superpower equality, denying the Soviets the recognition they so craved. It was not even particularly harmful – just humiliating. The Soviets resented "linkage" between detente and their involvement in the third world, largely because the free right to meddle was a presumed right of a co-equal superpower.

Could Brezhnev and Nixon have made a difference if Brezhnev did not fall into senility and Nixon remained at the helm? Possibly. One could argue all day about irreconcilable differences between the Soviet Union and the United States, but what looks outwardly impossible between states becomes entirely achievable between specific individuals, and it is individuals who ultimately make policy, not abstract states. So much here depends on trust (or the lack of it), on empathy, on personal respect. But when bureaucratic interests take over – as they did for the Soviets from the mid-1970s, or when domestic politics shape the foreign policy agenda (as often happens in the United States), then the scope for breakthroughs becomes much narrower.

Brezhnev was a mere shadow of his former self when the Soviets invaded Afghanistan. The decision was not easy. As we have seen, fears of compromising detente played into Soviet reluctance until the very last moment. Amin's coup was not pretty, but Moscow could live with a brutal dictator. They had lived with other brutal dictators. But there was a lingering doubt about his intentions. The Soviets worried about "losing" Afghanistan, although just years earlier they were perfectly content with a neutral Afghanistan, where they exercised a degree of political and economic influence. But now that the Afghans were "comrades," the temptation to replace an unreliable client with someone more to their liking was simply irresistible. Detente, too, was becoming a distant memory, so the Soviets went in. It was meant to be a brief war. It lasted for ten years. The invasion abruptly terminated what remained of Soviet–American dialogue. The crackdown in Poland in 1981 deepened Soviet isolation. There was nothing left of Brezhnev's treasured condominium. Growing fearful and more desperate, the beleaguered Soviet leadership began to rethink their relationship with China.

The final years of the Soviet Union are still subject to fierce debates. What combination of idealistic proclivities and economic realities prompted Mikhail Gorbachev to launch his New Thinking that in short order transformed Soviet foreign policy in a way his predecessors would never have thought possible? This book has only hinted at possible answers. Maslow was right to argue in favor of multicausality in human behavior. Even Gorbachev would have struggled to untangle his motivations. He had everything in 1985 – an empire, however decrepit; an ideology, however stale; above all, an office and truly awesome bureaucratic power. What he

CONCLUSION

did not have was greatness as he chose to understand it – greatness before History. He pursued that fleeting dream for himself and his country all the way to Pizza Hut.

———————◆———————

In August 1998 Russia suffered a financial meltdown: the value of the ruble collapsed; Russia defaulted on its debt. Economic chaos exacerbated political instability. On December 31, 1999 battered and humiliated Yeltsin bowed out. Vladimir Putin soon became the president of Russia. To many a Russian he stood for something that they longed for: stability, sausages. But also – a renewed promise of greatness. The more perceptive understood that Putin was bad news, very bad news. His reinvasion of Chechnya – to put an end to a festering insurgency – suggested a degree of cynical brutality that did not augur well for the future. But many Russians embraced Putin. They wanted a "strong leader," not a frail drunkard like Yeltsin. Putin knew how to play the gullible electorate and spoke frequently about "raising Russia from its knees."

Putin's relationship with the United States got off to a relatively good start. Putin offered Washington his backing in the "war on terror," drawing parallels between the US invasion of Afghanistan and then Iraq and Russia's own war in Chechnya. Like Khrushchev at Camp David and Brezhnev at San Clemente, Putin enjoyed his moment of American hospitality when President George W. Bush invited him to tour his ranch in Crawford, Texas, where the president went out of his way to praise him and his statesmanship. On another occasion, Bush famously claimed that he had "looked the man in the eye," finding him "very straightforward and trustworthy ... I was able to get a sense of his soul."[12] The honeymoon did not last.

When did Putin turn sour on the idea of a partnership with the United States? It was a gradual process. A noticeable rhetorical shift occurred around 2007. Putin began to speak of America with an undertone of resentment, building up over time to spite and hatred. He began to protest against what he called American "exceptionalism." Perhaps it was the US intention to set up missile interceptors in Poland and the Czech Republic (publicly announced in January 2007). There were also other perceived affronts, including the US agreements with Romania (December 2005) and Bulgaria (April 2006), allowing for the stationing of up to 5,000 US troops in the two countries. Putin's criticism of American exceptionalism overlapped in time with Washington's greater assertiveness, which challenged Russia's conventional position in Europe and potentially (though doubtfully) eroded Moscow's ability to threaten the United States and its allies with nuclear obliteration.

Putin's Munich speech was interesting for another reason. It was there that he complained about the allegedly broken promise of NATO's non-enlargement. "What happened to those assurances that were given by our Western partners after the dissolution of the Warsaw Pact. Where are these declarations? No one even remembers about them."[13] Munich became an early warning sign that Putin was turning the ship of Russian foreign policy towards confrontation. Coming almost twenty years after Gorbachev's *Perestroika and New Thinking*, Putin's Munich speech represented perhaps not so much a return of old thinking as a rethinking anew of those very notions that Gorbachev had once held dear: that the Cold War was an aberration, that true greatness was in overcoming confrontation with the West, in building bridges, in seeing a common purpose.

The build-up of Russian–Western tensions began visibly in early 2007, and led, in short order, to Russia's suspension of its participation in the Treaty on Conventional Forces in Europe (announced in July 2007), resumption of strategic bomber flights (August 2007), and, soon enough, to Russia's war in Georgia (August 2008). The downward slide in Russian–American relations was briefly arrested with the change of guard in the Kremlin. Dmitry Medvedev's presidency was characterized by the renewal of the Russian–American dialogue, even despite the regime's growing obsession with the challenge posed by the domestic opposition.

But with Putin's "return" (to the extent that it can even be called a return, for he had never left) returned also his preoccupation with countering American "exceptionalism." He mentioned the issue in his well-remembered op-ed in the *New York Times* in September 2013, where he called for "caution" in Syria. The op-ed followed President Barack Obama's speech to the US Congress, justifying strikes on Syria in the wake of Bashar al-Assad's use of chemical weapons with reference to American exceptionalism. "It is extremely dangerous to encourage people to see themselves as exceptional, whatever the motivation ... When we ask for the Lord's blessings, we must not forget that God created us equal," Putin wrote in response. In fact, he personally added this passage to the op-ed written largely by his aides, a reminder of his obsession with the American sin of "exceptionalism."

Obama's occasional dismissive remarks about Putin – such as when the American president compared him to "the bored kid at the back of the classroom" – added to the sense of a personal affront. It was not just that the Americans felt they were "exceptional." They also pretended to be teachers. They wanted to teach him – *him*! Stalin, Khrushchev, Brezhnev,

CONCLUSION

and even Gorbachev complained in their time about being "taught" by the Americans. Putin stood in the shadow of an old tradition of resentment.

These emotional underpinnings of Putin's conflict with the West were enormously important, more important perhaps than the perceived harm to Russia's security interests from NATO's eastward enlargement. The issue hinged on Putin's perception of himself as the leader of a great power, one that, although not nearly America's equal by most measures, nevertheless had the means at its disposal to destroy the United States, and so end in one stroke its arrogant exceptionalism, even if this meant also destroying the world. If he had the means, then did he, like Rodion Raskolnikov, also not have the *right?*

Putin's ideas were put to a test in 2014, when Ukrainian President Viktor Yanukovych was overthrown in what Putin described as a "coup" and the Ukrainian protesters called the "revolution of dignity." Putin perceived an opportunity to cannibalize Ukraine and so prove that he could push back against American exceptionalism. "Those who keep talking about their exceptionalism," he proclaimed in the wake of his annexation of Crimea, "do not like Russia's independent foreign policy. Events in Ukraine confirmed this. As they also confirmed that the double-standard model of relations with Russia does not work."[14]

In speaking about "double standards" Putin was alluding to America's wars in the Middle East, beginning with the invasion of Afghanistan in 2001 and Iraq in 2003. The latter invasion was infamous for having benefited from the made-up pretext of ridding Saddam Hussein's regime of the weapons of mass destruction that he evidently did not have. Back in 2003, Putin was careful in his criticism of the Iraq war, and even compared it positively with the Soviet experience in Afghanistan. The Soviets, he argued, had merely tried to "improve" their position in Afghanistan but instead got mired in a war that lasted for ten years. By contrast, the United States attacked a regime that "had been opposed to the international community for a long time" and that "brooked no compromise."[15] As for the US invasion of Afghanistan, that, too, Putin accepted as a necessary measure in the war on terrorism. What doubts he harbored, he kept to himself.

It was only later that Putin would cite Afghanistan and Iraq (and the 1999 bombing Yugoslavia and the 2011 NATO intervention in Libya) as examples of American exceptionalism in action, using them to justify his invasion of Ukraine. "Our Western partners," he complained bitterly on March 18, 2014, "prefer the right of might over international law. They have come to believe in their chosen-ness and exceptionalism."[16] On the same day Russia formally annexed Crimea.

PART IV COLLAPSE

The world looked on in disbelief but there was very little reaction, much as there was little reaction when the Soviets invaded Hungary and Czechoslovakia. The sanctions that were imposed on Russia were of symbolic, superficial character, not so much as a slap on the wrist. It was as if Raskolnikov murdered the old pawnbroker lady in plain sight, and then walked down the street, brandishing the bloodied axe: see, I did it because I could! With Russia promptly annexing a part of Ukraine, and successfully bolstering a defiant tyrant in Syria, it may well be that Putin came to believe in his own Manifest Destiny.

Indeed, Putin had in effect proclaimed Russia's exceptionalism; that is, its ability to intervene in its neighbors' affairs at will, to threaten, to annex. He presented this exceptionalism as a response to American exceptionalism. "Democratization" of international relations, which Russian propaganda has trumpeted for years as a remedy against the US-led unipolar world came down, on closer inspection, to the assertion of Russia's *right* to do as it wanted at the expense of those deemed weaker, the "trembling creatures" of global politics, including Georgia and Ukraine.

As he set his mind on destroying Ukraine, Putin's rhetoric about American exceptionalism became shriller. Unsurprisingly, the term crept into his February 24, 2022 announcement of the Russian invasion of Ukraine. "Why is all of this happening?" he raved. "Where does this insolent manner of speaking from the position of your own exceptionalism, infallibility, and all-permissiveness come from? Wherefrom comes that condescending, arrogant attitude towards our interests and absolutely legitimate demands?"[17] He could well have added, without missing a beat: "Am I a trembling creature, or do I have the *right?*"

Putin's war against Ukraine drew the line under thirty years of post-Cold War efforts to find Russia a place in the Western order, which it would deem legitimate enough to avoid disrupting. This was mainly Russia's failure: it proved unwilling or unable to overcome its toxic resentments and imperialist impulses. But there was another factor in play. Stalin's belligerent foreign policy, whatever his motivations, helped forge the West on an anti-Soviet basis. Throughout the Cold War, the Soviets tried hard to undermine Western unity even as they craved Western recognition. They never managed. Post-Soviet Russia, eyeing jealously the West's formidable power, sought a seat at the table without understanding the price that it would have to pay for admission, if it was ever admitted (and that was arguably not in the cards). Russia would have to change itself, recognize its own flaws, attempt to tackle them. It was just too difficult, perhaps even humiliating. It was that much easier to slam the door and, like Brezhnev

CONCLUSION

once promised in a letter to his mom, to spit on Europe from the top of the Eiffel Tower. This was Putin's chosen course.

At the same time, Putin continued to hope that the West, whose unity he helped reinforce through his brutal and shortsighted policies, would fall apart, and that the West's overall importance in the global pecking order would decline as that of the Global South increased. A more diverse – "multipolar" – world, with many more actors throwing their weight about was, for Putin, vastly preferable to a world run from Washington. This would result in a chaotic situation, sure. But chaos creates opportunities for the daring. Perhaps, with the right combination of chutzpah and good luck, Russia could one day recover its illusive greatness and its unsatiable, self-destructive ambition to run the world.

Acknowledgments

While writing this book – a ten-year-long journey, as it turned out – I incurred an enormous debt to a very, very long list of people. I used to have this list handy somewhere, but then I lost it, and started another. After a while, lists proliferated, and I gave up keeping track. So, today, on this lovely Sunday morning, I plodded down to my neighborhood coffeeshop, Coffee No. 1, down on Wellfield Road, ordered myself a cappuccino, and just felt grateful.

I then tried to recall where I was when I began this book, and I could not even do that. But it seems that I was in China, so let me begin there. Two ancient comrades who guided my work at the early stage are brilliant Cold War historians Shen Zhihua and Chen Jian. Shen Zhihua and I became archival pals of many years, sharing many a wild adventure in more places than historians should be allowed to go. From Chen Jian I plagiarized most good ideas that appear in this book. Thank you both.

A good part of the book was written in Wales, mainly in cafés like Coffee No. 1 that made a real killing off this door-stopper. I enjoyed every moment. I am deeply grateful to my colleagues in Aberystwyth and Cardiff who, at different points, either read parts of the manuscript, or just supplied good ideas and much-needed encouragement: Huw Bennett, Campbell Craig, Gerry Hughes, Jenny Mathers, Len Scott, and especially Urfan Khaliq.

My move to the Johns Hopkins School of Advanced International Studies in the middle of the project brought exciting new opportunities to discuss and debate this book. I did so for hours on end with Frank Gavin and Mary Sarotte, both of whom proved an endless source of valuable advice and inspiration. Frank even organized a book workshop for me at King's College London, where superb scholars – among them, Alexander Bick, Anne Deighton, Lawrence Freedman, Rana Mitter, Maeve Ryan, and Kristina Spohr – subjected my manuscript to relentless scrutiny. I am grateful for their input.

ACKNOWLEDGMENTS

Among other long-time friends, co-authors, and colleagues who made various contributions to this project, or encouraged me to probe further, are Dmitri Alperovitch, Tom Blanton, Hal Brands, Malcolm Byrne, Jeremy Friedman, Mark Gilbert, Nigel Gould-Davies, Jussi Hanhimäki, Hope Harrison, Artemy Kalinovsky, Barak Kushner, Li Danhui, Will Quinn, Michael Kofman, Guy Laron, Julia Lovell, Lorenz Lüthi, Boris Lvin, Joe Maiolo, Vali Nasr, Leopoldo Nuti, Pavel Palazhchenko, Andrew Preston, Mikhail Prozumenshchikov, Thomas Rid, Peter Ruggenthaler, Svetlana Savranskaya, Balasz Szalontai, Natalia Telepneva, Joseph Torigian, Jay Veith, David Wolff, Xia Yafeng, Yamada Kojiro, Philip Zelikow, and Zhang Qian, to name but a few.

I am especially grateful to Jim Hershberg and Mark Kramer, who scrutinized every chapter and at least halved the number of embarrassing errors. Vladislav Zubok, an old friend, whose standard-setting work helped inspire this project, proved a reliable commentator on many a bizarre and provocative idea readers will encounter in the book. Philip Zelikow was an equally thoughtful and critical reader.

I wrote much of the book in Washington, DC, where I held a public policy fellowship at the Wilson Center, benefiting greatly from the generous support of Wilson Center colleagues and friends, first and foremost Christian Ostermann, but also Chuck Kraus and Piet Biersteker.

Michael Watson, at Cambridge University Press, was characteristically patient with me throughout the writing process. I am grateful to him for not giving up on me when the manuscript fell years behind schedule. I am grateful to Rosa Martin, the Press's editorial assistant, as well as Jem Langworthy and Ruth Boyes who helped prepare the book for publication. Jim Diggins created an amazing index that will help readers find their way through the maze this book has become. Last, but not least, I am hugely grateful to my agent Andrew Wylie who guided me through the publication process.

Did I forget to mention someone important in these brief acknowledgments? I probably did. But the coffee has grown cold. Dark clouds are gathering over Cardiff: it will rain soon. And so, I must leave it here, and plod back up the hill. "How did it go," my wife Onon will ask me. "Did you say what you wanted to say?" "Fine," I'll say. "It went just fine." For I have more debts than I can ever repay.

So, therefore, old friends, comrades-in-arms, and random people who extended me a helping hand when I needed it most: thank you for your help. Thank you for your words of wisdom, your criticism, your encouragement, and your skepticism, above all, for your kindness and commitment.

ACKNOWLEDGMENTS

An important final observation. This book would not have been written without the love and generosity of my wife Onon and my children Nikita and Inessa. They patiently put up with me all these years, with all my eccentricities and my penchant for chaotic spontaneity. They deserve all the credit I can give them, and so much more.

This book is dedicated to the great Cold War historian Odd Arne Westad: a scholar, a teacher and, above all, a dear friend.

Cardiff. October 29, 2023.

Figures

1 Stalin and Molotov confer at Yalta, February 1945.
Source: Universal Images Group/Getty Images. *page* 26
2 Churchill, Truman, and Stalin at Potsdam, July 1945.
Source: Ullstein Bild/Getty Images. 46
3 A Soviet map of a proposed oil concession in northern Iran, 1944.
The extent is shown by the line running west-to-east with
an angular dip at the center. Source: AVPRF: f. 06, op. 6dop,
p. 75, d. 880, l. 15. Agk.mid.ru. With permission of the Archive
of Foreign Policy of the Russian Federation. 72
4 Igor Kurchatov, the scientific head of the Soviet atomic project.
Ullstein Bild/Getty Images. 75
5 Josip Broz Tito's photo in Stalin's archive. Signed:
"To Comrade J.V. Stalin." Source: RGASPI: f. 558,
op. 11, d. 1695, doc. 1. 99
6 Mao Zedong proclaiming the establishment of the
People's Republic of China, Oct. 1, 1949.
Source: Bettmann/Getty Images. 123
7 Burmese Defense Minister U Bashwe (center) instructs
Khrushchev (right) in the art of drumming, during
Khrushchev's and Bulganin's (left) trip to Rangoon,
December 1955. Source: Bettmann/Getty Images. 159
8 The aftermath of the Soviet invasion of Hungary, November
1956. Source: Hulton-Deutsch Collection/Corbis/Getty Images. 197
9 Mao and Khrushchev during their July–August 1958 talks
in Beijing. Some of the discussions took place inside the
Zhongnanhai swimming pool. Source: Sovfoto/Universal
Images Group/Getty Images. 217
10 Khrushchev, Mao, and Ho Chi Minh, at a dinner in Beijing,
September 1959. This was Khrushchev's last, most tumultuous,
visit to Beijing. Source: Underwood & Underwood/Corbis/
Getty Images. 248

LIST OF FIGURES

11 Khrushchev and Soviet Foreign Minister Andrei Gromyko misbehaving at the UN, October 13, 1960. Source: PhotoQuest/Getty Images. — 267

12 Kennedy and Khrushchev during their famous encounter in Vienna, June 1961. Source: Central Press/Hulton Archive/Getty Images. — 285

13 A scene in Berlin after the construction of the Wall, October 1961. Source: Ron Burton/Mirrorpix/Getty Images. — 291

14 Proposal from Rodion Malinovsky and Matvei Zakharov about dispatching nuclear missiles to Cuba. Signed by Khrushchev (at the top) and other senior leaders, June 1962. Source: CWIHP/DA. — 300

15 A Soviet military map of Cuba with the location of missile bases, November 1962. Source: CWIHP/DA. — 319

16 A Soviet instructor training a North Vietnamese pilot, September 1966. Source: Sovfoto/Universal Images Group/Getty Images. — 336

17 Zhou Enlai in Moscow atop the Mausoleum, flanked by Anastas Mikoyan (left) and Nikolai Podgorny (right), Nov. 7, 1964. Source: AFP/Getty Images. — 341

18 A scene on the Sino-Soviet border in the run-up to the deadly clashes of March 1969. Source: Sovfoto/Universal Images Group/Getty Images. — 363

19 Brezhnev and Nixon in Moscow, following the signing of the SALT-I accords, May 26, 1972. Source: Bettmann/Getty Images. — 382

20 Brezhnev and Nixon on the White House portico, June 21, 1973. Source: Dirck Halstead/Getty Images. — 385

21 Israeli tanks crossing the Suez Canal, October 25, 1973. Source: Ilan Ron/GPO/Getty Images. — 419

22 Kissinger and Brezhnev, Moscow, June 1974. Source: Bernard Charlon/Gamma-Rapho/Getty Images. — 434

23 Leonid Brezhnev on holiday in the late 1970s. Source: Laski Diffusion/Getty Images. — 468

24 Ethnic Somalis enlisted to fight in the Ogaden War, September 1977. Source: Jean-Claude Francolon/Gamma-Rapho/Getty Images. — 470

25 The Afghan Mujahideen navigating a river, April 1979. Source: Alain Mingam/Gamma-Rapho/Getty Images. — 479

LIST OF FIGURES

26 South Koreans burning the Soviet flag after the shooting
down of KAL 007, September 1983. Source: Allan
Tannenbaum/Getty Images. 535

27 Reagan signs the book of condolences at the Soviet
Embassy after Yury Andropov's death. February 1984.
Source: Jean-Louis Atlan/Sygma/Getty Images. 537

28 Reagan and Gorbachev at Reykjavik, October 1986.
Source: Dirck Halstead/Getty Images. 550

29 Gorbachev and Deng Xiaoping sharing a meal in Beijing,
May 1989. Source: Forrest Anderson/Getty Images. 566

Notes

INTRODUCTION

1 Nikita Khrushchev, *Vospominaniya: vremya, lyudi, vlast'*, Vol. 1 (Moscow: Moskovskie Novosti, 1999), 458.

2 Susanne Schattenberg, *Brezhnev: The Making of a Statesman* (London: Bloomsbury, 2021), 101. Less flatteringly (but doubtfully), the speech defect was a result of "hormone treatment." Vladimir Kuzichkin, *Inside the KGB: Myth and Reality* (London: André Deutsch Ltd, 1990), 101.

3 Douglas E. Selvage and Melissa Jane Taylor (eds.), *Foreign Relations of the United States, 1969–1976*, Vol. 15 (Washington, DC: US Government Printing Office, 2011), Document 43.

4 Mikhail Gorbachev, *Zhizn' i Reformy*, 2 vols., Vol. 1 (Moscow: Novosti, 1995), 50–51.

5 A.E. Surinov et al. (eds.), *Velikaya Otechestennaya voina: yubileinyi statistichesky sbornik* (Moscow: Rosstat, 2015).

6 E.g. Ian Clark, *Legitimacy in International Society* (New York: Oxford University Press, 2005), 3–4.

7 Henry Kissinger, *A World Restored: Metternich, Castlereagh and the problems of peace 1812–22* (Boston, MA: Houghton Mifflin Company, 1957), 144.

8 R.D. Laing, *The Divided Self* (London: Penguin, 1990), 36.

9 A.H. Maslow, "A Theory of Human Motivation," *Psychological Review*, 50(4) (1943), 370–396.

10 See, in particular, ch. 14 in Karl Popper, *The Open Society and Its Enemies*, Vol. 2 (Princeton University Press, 1963), 89–99.

11 Jonathan Renshon, *Fighting for Status* (Princeton University Press, 2017), 5.

12 Deborah Larson and Alexei Shevchenko, *Quest for Status: Chinese and Russian Foreign Policy* (New Haven, CT: Yale University Press, 2019).

13 Lorenz M. Lüthi, *Cold Wars: Asia the Middle East Europe* (Cambridge University Press, 2020).

14 Paul Thomas Chamberlin, *The Cold War's Killing Fields: Rethinking the Long Peace* (New York: Harper, 2019).

15 For the genesis of the term "third world," see Artemy Kalinovsky and Sergey Radchenko (eds.), *The End of the Cold War in the Third World: New Perspectives on Regional Conflict* (London: Taylor and Francis, 2011).

NOTES TO PAGES 18–23

1 THE POSTWAR WORLD

1 Maisky to Stalin and Molotov, Jan. 11, 1944, AVPRF: f. 06, op. 6, p. 14, d. 145, l. 3.

2 The positions were called "polpred" (plenipotentiary representative) and the People's Commissar for Foreign Affairs. I use the terms "ambassador" and "foreign minister" to avoid confusion.

3 Maisky to Stalin and Molotov, Jan. 11, 1944, AVPRF: f. 06, op. 6, p. 14, d. 145, l. 38.

4 Litvinov, Nov. 15, 1944, AVPRF: f. 06, op. 6, p. 14, d. 143, l. 31. See also Vladislav Zubok, *A Failed Empire: The Soviet Union in the Cold War from Stalin to Gorbachev* (Chapel Hill, NC: University of North Carolina Press, 2007), 8.

5 Jonathan Haslam, "Litvinov, Stalin, and the Road Not Taken," in Gabriel Gorodetsky (ed.), *Soviet Foreign Policy, 1917–1919* (London: Routledge, 1994), 59; Geoffrey Roberts, "Litvinov's Lost Peace, 1941–1946," *Journal of Cold War Studies [JCWS]*, 4(2) (Spring 2002), 23–54.

6 Mastny comes to the same conclusion in Vojtech Mastny, *The Cold War and Soviet Insecurity: The Stalin Years* (New York: Oxford University Press, 1996), 18–19.

7 Litvinov to Molotov, Mar. 8, 1944, AVPRF: f. 06, op. 6, p. 14, d. 142, ll. 1–110.

8 Ibid., l. 118.

9 Maisky to Stalin and Molotov, Jan. 11, 1944, AVPRF: f. 06, op. 6, p. 14, d. 145, ll. 39–40.

10 For a discussion of this difference, see Aleksei M. Filitov, "Problems of Post-War Construction in Soviet Foreign Policy Conceptions during World War II," in Francesco Gori and Silvio Ponds (eds.), *The Soviet Union and Europe in the Cold War, 1943–53* (London: Macmillan Press, 1996), 19.

11 Memorandum of a meeting of the Commission on Peace Treaties and the Postwar Order, AVPRF: f. 06, op. 6, p. 14, d. 142, l. 117.

12 Litvinov to Molotov, Nov. 15, 1944, AVPRF: f. 06, op. 6dop, p. 64, d. 869.

13 Memorandum of a meeting of the Commission on Peace Treaties and the Postwar Order, June 8, 1944, AVPRF: f. 06, op. 6, p. 14, d. 141, l. 53.

14 Memorandum of a meeting of the Commission on Peace Treaties and the Postwar Order, Mar. 25, 1944, AVPRF: f. 06, op. 6, p. 14, d. 141, ll. 1–20 and Memorandum of a meeting of the Commission on Peace Treaties and the Postwar Order, Sept. 4, 1944, AVPRF: f. 06, op. 6, p. 14, d. 141, ll. 66–87.

15 Litvinov to Molotov, Mar. 25, 1944, AVPRF: f. 06, op. 6, p. 14, d. 146, ll. 1–29.

16 Maisky to Stalin and Molotov, Jan. 11, 1944, AVPRF: f. 06, op. 6, p. 14, d. 145, l. 3.

17 Gabriel Gorodetsky (ed.), *The Complete Maisky Diaries*, Vol. 3 (New Haven, CT: Yale University Press, 2017), 1177.

18 Milovan Djilas, *Conversations with Stalin* (Harmondsworth: Penguin Books, 1967), 61.

19 O.A. Rzheshevsky, *Stalin i Cherchill'. Vstrechi, besedy, diskussii* (Moscow: Nauka, 2004), 423.

20 Winston Churchill, *The Second World War*, Vol. 6: *Triumph and Tragedy* (London: Reprint Society, 1961), 195. The latter part of the discussion is not reflected in

NOTES TO PAGES 23–29

the otherwise very detailed Russian transcript, suggesting that it was perhaps made up by Churchill.

21 Memcon, Molotov and Eden, Oct. 10, 1944, AVPRF: f. 06, op. 6, p. 2, d. 19, ll. 64–72.

22 Ibid., ll. 77–78.

23 David Carlton, *Churchill and the Soviet Union* (Manchester University Press, 2000), 114.

24 Geoffrey Roberts, "Beware Greek Gifts: The Churchill-Stalin 'Percentages' Agreement of October 1944," unpublished paper cited with the author's permission. Also, Geoffrey Roberts, *Stalin's Wars: From World War to Cold War, 1939–1953* (New Haven, CT: Yale University Press, 2008), 217–225.

25 Memcon, Stalin and a Yugoslav delegation, Jan. 9, 1945, RGASPI: f. 558, op. 11, d. 397, l. 14.

26 Ibid.

27 Roberts, *Stalin's Wars*, 360–1; Silvio Pons, *Stalin and the Inevitable War, 1936–41* (London: Frank Cass, 2002), xiv.

28 Memcon, Stalin and Roosevelt, Feb. 4, 1945, AVPRF: f. 06, op. 7a, d. 7, p. 58, l. 16.

29 Memcon, Churchill, Roosevelt, and Stalin, Feb. 5, 1945, AVPRF: f. 06, op. 7a, d. 7, p. 58, ll. 20–44.

30 Norman Naimark, *The Russians in Germany: A History of the Soviet Zone of Occupation, 1945–49* (Cambridge, MA: Harvard University Press, 1995), 9–11.

31 For a different view – emphasizing Stalin's early resignation to the division of Germany – see Marc Trachtenberg, "The United States and Europe in 1945: A Reassessment," *JCWS*, 10(4) (Spring 2008), 118.

32 Vladimir Pechatnov, "The Soviet Union and the World, 1944–1953," in Melvyn P. Leffler and Odd Arne Westad (eds.), *The Cambridge History of the Cold War* [*CHCW*], Vol. 1 (Cambridge University Press, 2010), 102.

33 This account of Mikołajczyk's July–Aug. 1944 visit to Moscow is partly based on Jan Karski, *The Great Powers and Poland* (Lanham, MD: University Press of America, 1985), 535–539.

34 Tatyana Volokitina (ed.), *Sovetsky faktor v vostochnoi Evrope, 1944–1953*, Vol. 1 (Moscow: Rosspen, 1999), 73.

35 Ibid., 87.

36 Ibid., 53. Similar instructions were given in relation to other Eastern European countries.

37 Christian Ostermann et al. (eds.), *Stalin and the Cold War, 1945–1953*, Document Reader (Washington, DC: CWIHP, 1999). See also Karski, *The Great Powers and Poland*, 544–551.

38 Ostermann et al. (eds.), *Stalin and the Cold War, 1945–1953*.

39 Memcon, Stalin and a Yugoslav delegation, Jan. 9, 1945, AVPRF: f. 06, op. 7, p. 53, d. 872, l. 22.

40 Memcon, Churchill, Roosevelt, and Stalin, Feb. 6, 1945, AVPRF: f. 06, op. 7a, p. 58, d. 7, ll. 59–60.

NOTES TO PAGES 30–35

41 Karski, *The Great Powers and Poland*, 614.

42 Norman Naimark, "The Sovietization of Eastern Europe," in *CHCW*, Vol. 1, 175–197.

43 James Millward, *Eurasian Crossroads: A History of Xinjiang* (New York: Columbia University Press), 216.

44 Molotov to Sheng Shicai, July 3, 1942, RGASPI: f. 558, op. 11, d. 323, ll. 54–57. Obtained by Jamil Hasanli. For background and analysis, see Dzhamil Gasanly, *Sin'tszyan v orbite sovetskoi politiki* (Moscow: Flinta, 2015), chapters 1–3.

45 Politburo Decision, May 4, 1943, RGASPI: f. 17, op. 162, d. 37, l. 76. Obtained by Jamil Hasanli.

46 Gasanly, *Sin'tszyan*, 166.

47 Tsuyoshi Hasegawa, *Racing the Enemy: Stalin, Truman and the Surrender of Japan* (Cambridge, MA: Harvard University Press, 2005), 36; Michael Dobbs, *Six Months in 1945* (New York: Knopf, 2012), 69–70.

48 The Soviet copy of the agreement is in AVPRF: f. 06, op. 7a, p. 59, d. 29, l. 1.

49 Wang Jianlang, "Xinren de liushi: Cong Jiang Jieshi riji kan kangzhan houqi de zhongmei guanxi," *Jindai Shi Yanjiu*, 3 (2009), 62. Also, Sergey Radchenko, "Lost Chance for Peace: The 1945 CCP-Kuomintang Peace Talks Revisited," *JCWS*, 19(2) (2017), 84–114.

50 Sergey Radchenko, "Carving up the Steppes: Borders, Territory and Nationalism in Mongolia, 1943–1949," *Eurasia Border Review*, 3, Special Issue (2012), 11–31.

51 Memcon, Stalin and Harry Hopkins, May 28, 1945, RGASPI: f. 558, op. 11, d. 376, l. 38; Ralph R. Goodwin et al. (eds.), *Foreign Relations of the United States, 1945*, Vol. 7 (Washington, DC: US Government Printing Office, 1969), Document 617.

52 Ostermann et al. (eds.), *Stalin and the Cold War, 1945–1953*, 158. The Russian version (RGASPI: f. 558, op. 11, d. 322, l. 14) omits Stalin's skepticism about the CCP.

53 Jitian Fengzi, "Minguo Zhengfu dui Ya'erta 'Miyue' zhi Yingdui yu Menggu Wenti," in Wu Jingping (ed.), *Song Ziwen Shengping yu Ziliao Wenxian Yanjiu* (Shanghai: Fudan Daxue Chubanshe, 2010), 366.

54 On the Stalin Note, see A.M. Ledovsky, R.A. Mirovitskaya, and V.S. Myasnikov (eds.), *Russko-kitaiskie otnosheniya v XX veke*, Vol. 4-2 (Moscow: Pamyatniki Istoricheskoi Mysli, 2000), 197. Stalin's commitment to withdraw forces within three months is ibid., 195.

55 Memcon, Stalin and T.V. Soong, Aug. 10, 1945, RGASPI: f. 558, op. 11, d. 322, l. 88.

56 *Mao Zedong Selected Works*, Vol. 3 (Beijing: Foreign Languages Press, 1965), 290.

57 Cable, CC CPSU to Mao Zedong, n.d. (late Aug. 1945). A copy was kindly provided Alexander Pantsov. See also Alexander Pantsov and Steven Levine, *Deng: A Revolutionary Life* (New York: Oxford University Press, 2015), 121–122; Sergey Radchenko, "Lost Chance for Peace," 88–89.

58 Draft cable, Stalin to Mao, n.d. (no earlier than Aug. 19, 1945), RGASPI: f. 82, op. 2, d. 1239, l. 110.

613

NOTES TO PAGES 35–41

59 Chen Jian and Zhang Shuguang, *Chinese Communist Foreign Policy and the Cold War in Asia: New Documentary Evidence, 1944–1950* (Chicago, IL: Imprint Publications, 1996), 31–32.

60 Sergey Radchenko, "Lost Chance for Peace," 93–94.

61 Memcon, Stalin and Chiang Ching-kuo, Dec. 30, 1945, RGASPI: f. 558, op. 11, d. 322, l. 105.

62 Stalin to Malinovsky, Nov. 16, 1945, RGASPI: f. 558, op. 11, d. 98, l. 144.

63 Ibid., l. 81.

64 Memorandum on the situation in Xinjiang, Sept. 15, 1945, RGASPI: f. 17, op. 162, d. 36, l. 150; Also, Gasanly, *Sin'tszyan*, 195–201.

65 Yegnarov and Langvang to Beria, Nov. 3, 1945, GARF: f. R9401ss, op. 2, d. 100, ll. 270–272. Obtained by Jamil Hasanli; Gasanly, *Sin'tszyan*, 214–215.

66 Gasanly, *Sin'tszyan*, 209.

67 Ibid., 217.

68 Ibid., 222.

69 Jeffrey Lewis, "The U.S. President who finally went to Hiroshima," *Foreign Policy*, May 26, 2016.

70 Norman Naimark is the most prominent representative of this line of argument.

2 THE PARTING OF WAYS

1 Michael Dobbs, *Six Months in 1945* (New York: Knopf, 2012), 140–141.

2 Information on the Poles, proposed for the provisional Polish government, Apr. 2, 1945, AVPRF: f. 06, op. 7, p. 39, d. 588, ll. 23–36.

3 Note, Molotov, undated (early 1945), AVPRF: f. 06, op. 7, p. 39, d. 588, l. 1.

4 Maisky and Archibald Kerr, Apr. 13, 1945, AVPRF: f. 06, op. 7, p. 5, d. 51, l. 25.

5 Rogers P. Churchill et al. (eds.), *Foreign Relations of the United States [FRUS], 1945*, Vol. 5 (Washington, DC: US Government Printing Office, 1969), Document 161.

6 Ibid., Document 162.

7 Memcon, Maisky and Archibald Kerr, Apr. 4–5, 1945, AVPRF: f. 06, op. 7, p. 5, d. 51, l. 21.

8 Dobbs, *Six Months in 1945*, 120–123. For Soviet concerns about the pro-fascist leanings of the Rădescu government and problem of security in Romania, see Tatyana Volokitina (ed.), *Sovetsky faktor v vostochnoi Evrope, 1944–1953*, Vol. 1 (Moscow: Rosspen, 1999), 156–159. For details of Vyshinsky's visit, see T.V. Volokitina et al. (eds.), *Tri vizita A. Ya. Vyshinskogo v Bukharest. 1944–1946* (Moscow: Rosspen, 1998), esp. 94–117.

9 Draft letter, Molotov to W. Averell Harriman, Mar. 17, 1945, AVPRF: f. 06, op. 7, p. 46, d. 735, ll. 49–50.

10 Turner Catledge, "Our Policy Stated," *New York Times*, June 24, 1945, 7; Vladimir Pechatnov, *Stalin, Ruzvel't, Truman: SSSR i SShA v 1940-kh gg* (Moscow: Terra – Knizhnyi Klub, 2006), 316–317.

11 Gromyko to Molotov, July 24, 1944, AVPRF: f. 0129, op. 28, d. 13, ll. 4–8.

NOTES TO PAGES 41–46

12 *FRUS, 1945*, Vol. 5, Document 622.

13 Memcon, Maisky and W. Averell Harriman, Apr. 5, 1945, AVPRF: f. 0129, op. 29, p. 166, d. 4, ll. 15–16.

14 *FRUS, 1945*, Vol. 5, Document 190.

15 Memcon, Vyshinsky and W. Averell Harriman, Apr. 16, 1945, AVPRF: f. 0129, op. 29, p. 166, d. 4, ll. 21–22.

16 *FRUS, 1945*, Vol. 5, Document 196.

17 Harry S. Truman, *The Year of Decisions* (New York: Signet Books, 1955), 99. This phrase does not appear either in the US or on the Russian transcript of the conversation, or in Molotov's cable to Stalin on the same day. The Russian version is: AVPRF: f. 06, op. 7b, p. 60, d. 1, ll. 11–13. Molotov's cable to Stalin is in AVPRF: f. 06, op. 7, p. 1, d. 8, l. 2.

18 *FRUS, 1945*, Vol. 5, Document 195.

19 Stalin to Molotov, Apr. 19, 1945, RGASPI: f. 558, op. 11, d. 770, ll. 1–2.

20 Velma Hastings Cassidy, Ralph R. Goodwin, and George H. Dengler (eds.), *FRUS, 1945*, Vol. 1 (Washington, DC: US Government Printing Office, 1967), Document 24.

21 Ibid., Document 25.

22 Memcon, Stalin and Harry Hopkins, May 27, 1945, RGASPI: f. 558, op. 11, d. 376, ll. 22–23.

23 Memcon, Molotov, W. Averell Harriman and Archibald Kerr, June 15, 1945, AVPRF: f. 06, op. 7, p. 39, d. 591, l. 8.

24 "Reception at comrade Stalin's," June 23, 1945, AVPRF: f. 06, op. 7, p. 39, d. 594, l. 16.

25 Memcon, Molotov and Stanisław Mikołajczyk, June 27, 1945, AVPRF: f. 06, op. 7, p. 39, d. 585, l. 6.

26 Richardson Dougall et al. (eds.), *FRUS, The Conference of Berlin (The Potsdam Conference), 1945*, Vol. 2 (Washington, DC: US Government Printing Office, 1960), Document 1418.

27 Truman's diary entry for July 17, 1945. https://catalog.archives.gov/OpaAPI /media/976500/content/arcmedia/eyewitness/11875_2005_001_a.jpg.

28 Record of the plenary meeting on July 22, 1945 (the Russian version), in Andrei Gromyko (ed.), *Sovetsky Soyuz na mezhdunarodnykh konferentsiyakh perioda VOV 1945–1945* [*SSnMKPVOV*], Vol. 6 (Moscow: Izdatel'stvo Politicheskoi Literatury, 1984), 132.

29 I. Kharlamov to Vyshinsky, July 24, 1945, AVPRF: f. 0129, op. 29, p. 171, d. 43, l. 27.

30 Plenary meeting, Potsdam Conference, July 24, 1945 (the Russian version), in *SSnMKPVOV*, Vol. 6, 172.

31 Ivo Banac (ed.), *The Diary of Georgi Dimitrov* (New Haven, CT: Yale University Press, 2003), 377.

32 Truman, *The Year of Decisions*, 458. The only contemporaneous Russian account is Aleksandr Khinshtein (ed.), *Ivan Serov: zapiski iz chemodana: tainye dnevniki pervogo predsedatelya KGB* (Moscow: Prosveshchenie, 2016), 311. "He [Truman]

NOTES TO PAGES 47–53

did not say that it [the bomb] was an atomic one. Stalin just listened, and did not ask a single question, and then they parted."

33 Winston Churchill, *The Second World War*, Vol. 6: *Triumph and Tragedy* (London: Reprint Society, 1961), 580.

34 Cited in Campbell Craig and Sergey Radchenko, *The Atomic Bomb and the Origins of the Cold War* (New Haven, CT: Yale University Press, 2008), 44.

35 Ibid., 48–49.

36 Ibid., 53.

37 David Holloway, *Stalin and the Bomb: The Soviet Union and Atomic Energy, 1939–1956* (New Haven, CT: Yale University Press, 2008), 117.

38 The best account is Tsuyoshi Hasegawa, *Racing the Enemy: Stalin, Truman and the Surrender of Japan* (Cambridge, MA: Harvard University Press, 2005).

39 Library of Congress, Manuscript Division, Dmitry Volkogonov papers, 1887–1995, Reel 5, containers 7–9.

40 Stalin to Truman, Aug. 16, 1945, RGASPI: f. 558, op. 11, d. 372, l. 111.

41 Truman to Stalin, Aug. 18, 1945, RGASPI: f. 558, op. 11, d. 372, l. 112.

42 Stalin to Truman, Aug. 22, 1945, RGASPI: f. 558, op. 11, d. 372, l. 116.

43 Andrzej Werblan, "The Conversation between Władysław Gomułka and Joseph Stalin on 14 November 1945," *CWIHP Bulletin*, Issue 11 (Winter 1998), 136.

44 Resolution, State Committee on Defense, Aug. 20, 1945, RGASPI: f. 644, op. 1, d. 458, ll. 27–30.

45 Feliks Chuev, *Sto Sorok Besed s Molotovym* (Moscow: Terra, 1991), 103.

46 Ibid.

47 Litvinov to Molotov, Jan. 10, 1945, AVPRF: f. 06, op. 7, d. 173, l. 50.

48 Litvinov to Molotov, Feb. 23, 1945, AVPRF: f. 06, op. 7, d. 173, l. 134.

49 *FRUS, 1945*, Vol. 1, Document 258.

50 Litvinov to Molotov, June 7, 1945, AVPRF: f. 06, op. 7, d. 174, ll. 49–51.

51 *FRUS, 1945*, Vol. 1, Document 288.

52 Ibid.

53 Ibid., Document 285.

54 Memorandum, Vsevolod Durdenevsky, June 6, 1945, AVPRF: f. 06, op. 7, d. 671, ll. 17–28.

55 Litvinov to Molotov, June 22, 1945, AVPRF: f. 06, op. 7, d. 174, ll. 52–61.

56 Ibid.

57 Litvinov to Molotov, June 28, 1945, AVPRF: f. 06, op. 7, d. 174, ll. 62–68.

58 Molotov to Togliatti, Feb. 5, 1946, RGASPI: f. 558, op. 11, d. 319, ll. 1–2.

59 Litvinov to Molotov, June 28, 1945, AVPRF: f. 06, op. 7, d. 174, l. 68.

60 Gromyko to Molotov, July 10, 1945, AVPRF: f. 0129, op. 29, d. 45, ll. 210–213.

61 *FRUS, 1945*, The Conference of Berlin (The Potsdam Conference), 1945, Vol. 2, Document 710(#5).

62 *SSnMKPVOV*, Vol. 6, 39–41.

63 Harry S. Truman and Robert F. Ferrell, *Off the Record: The Private Papers of Harry S. Truman* (Columbia, MO: First University of Missouri Press, 1997), 53.

NOTES TO PAGES 53–62

64 This argument is not to be confused with the well-known thesis that Truman bombed Hiroshima to intimidate the Soviets, which is not borne out by the evidence.

65 Robert L. Messer, *The End of an Alliance: James F. Byrnes, Truman, and the Origins of the Cold War* (Chapel Hill, NC: University of North Carolina Press, 1982), 6.

66 Memcon, Molotov and Byrnes, Sept. 14, 1945 (15:30), AVPRF: f. 06, op. 7, d. 33, l. 11.

67 N.O. Sappington et al. (eds.), *FRUS, 1945*, Vol. 2 (Washington, DC: US Government Printing Office, 1967), Document 73.

68 Chuev, *Sto Sorok Besed*, 103.

69 Byrnes made this comment on Sept. 13. See Barton J. Bernstein, "Roosevelt, Truman, and the Atomic Bomb, 1941–1945: A Reinterpretation," *Political Science Quarterly*, 90(1) (1975), 64.

70 Molotov to Stalin, Sept. 14, 1945, RGASPI: f. 558, op. 11, d. 770, ll. 22–24.

71 Stalin to Molotov, Sept. 16, 1945, RGASPI: f. 558, op. 11, d. 770, l. 20.

72 Molotov and Byrnes, Sept. 16, 1945 (17:30), AVPRF: f. 06, op. 7, d. 33, l. 25.

73 Molotov to Stalin, Sept. 16, 1945, RGASPI: f. 558, op. 11, d. 770, l. 26.

74 Ibid.

75 *FRUS, 1945*, Vol. 2, Document 260.

76 Ibid.

77 Stalin to Molotov, Nov. 20, 1946, RGASPI: f. 558, op. 11, d. 102, l. 93.

78 For the latter view, see Marc Trachtenberg, "The United States and Europe in 1945: A Reassessment," *JCWS*, 10(4) (Spring 2008).

79 Stalin to Molotov, Sept. 12, 1945, RGASPI: f. 558, op. 11, d. 770, l. 5.

80 *FRUS, 1945*, Vol. 2, Document 82.

81 Ibid., Document 102.

82 Stalin to Molotov, Sept. 18, 1945, RGASPI: f. 558, op. 11, d. 770, l. 34.

83 Stalin to Molotov, Sept. 19, 1945, RGASPI: f. 558, op. 11, d. 770, l. 41.

84 Stalin to Molotov, Sept. 20, 1945, RGASPI: f. 558, op. 11, d. 770, l. 42.

85 Stalin was in fact informed of this on Sept. 11, and his copy of Molotov's telegram highlights the very paragraph where Molotov talks about procedural questions. Molotov to Stalin, Sept. 11, 1945, RGASPI: f. 558, op. 11, d. 770, l. 6.

86 Molotov to Stalin, Sept. 21, 1945, RGASPI: f. 558, op. 11, d. 770, ll. 43–44.

87 Stalin to Molotov, Sept. 21, 1945, RGASPI: f. 558, op. 11, d. 770, l. 45.

88 Molotov to Stalin, Sept. 22, 1945, RGASPI: f. 558, op. 11, d. 770, ll. 46–47.

89 *FRUS, 1945*, Vol. 2, Document 120.

90 Memcon, Molotov and Bevin, Sept. 23, 1945 (15:30), AVPRF: f. 06, op. 7, d. 33, l. 87.

91 *FRUS, 1945*, Vol. 2, Document 139.

92 Ibid., Document 142.

93 Stalin to Molotov, Sept. 26, 1945, RGASPI: f. 558, op. 11, d. 770, ll. 59–60.

94 Stalin to Molotov, Sept. 27, 1945, RGASPI: f. 558, op. 11, d. 770, l. 68.

95 Molotov to Stalin, Sept. 28, 1945, RGASPI: f. 558, op. 11, d. 770, ll. 66–67.

NOTES TO PAGES 63–73

96 Stalin to Molotov, Sept. 27, 1945, RGASPI: f. 558, op. 11, d. 770, l. 68.

97 Stalin to Molotov, Sept. 28, 1945, RGASPI: f. 558, op. 11, d. 770, l. 71.

98 Stalin to Molotov, Dec. 9, 1945, RGASPI: f. 558, op. 11, d. 771, ll. 2–3.

99 Memcon, Stalin and Harriman, Oct. 25, 1945, RGASPI: f. 558, op. 11, d. 378, ll. 66–67.

100 Ibid.

101 Stalin to Molotov, Beria, Mikoyan, Malenkov, Nov. 10, 1945, RGASPI: f. 558, op. 11, d. 98, l. 82.

102 Stalin to Malinovsky, Nov. 16, 1945, RGASPI: f. 558, op. 11, d. 98, l. 144.

103 Stalin to Malenkov, Beria and Mikoyan, Dec. 6, 1945, RGASPI: f. 558, op. 11, d. 771, l. 15.

104 Malenkov, Beria and Mikoyan to Stalin, Dec. 7, 1945, RGASPI: f. 558, op. 11, d. 771, l. 18; Molotov to Stalin, Dec. 7, 1945, RGASPI: f. 558, op. 11, d. 771, l. 17.

105 *FRUS, 1945*, Vol. 2.

106 Stalin to Molotov, Dec. 9, 1945, RGASPI: f. 558, op. 11, d. 771, ll. 2–3.

107 E.g. W. Averell Harriman's statement to the US Congress (Subcommittee on Priorities and Economy in Government), Aug. 9, 1971, *The Economic of National Priorities* (Washington, DC: US Government Printing Office, 1971), 339.

3 STALIN IN EUROPE

1 On Iran see Louise Fawcett, "Revisiting the Iranian Crisis of 1946: How Much More Do We Know," *Iranian Studies*, 47(3) (2014), 379–399. Dzhamil' Gasanly, *SSSR-Iran: azerbaidzhansky krizis i nachalo kholodnoi voiny, 1941–1946 gg* (Moscow: Geroyi Otechestva, 2006); Vladislav Zubok, "Stalin, Soviet Intelligence, and the Struggle for Iran, 1945–53," *Diplomatic History*, 44(1) (2020), 22–46. On Turkey, see Dzhamil' Gasanly, *SSSR-Turtsiya: ot neitraliteta k kholodnoi voine, 1939–1953* (Moscow: Tsentr Propagandy, 2008).

2 Report by A. Smirov, Apr. 14, 1942, RGASPI: f. 558, op. 11, d. 317, l. 6.

3 Report by Lavrenty Beria, Aug. 16, 1944, AVPRF: f. 06, op. 6, d. 461, l. 17; Gasanly, *SSSR-Iran*, 66.

4 Kavtaradze to Molotov, Aug. 16, 1944, AVPRF: f. 06, op. 6, d. 461, l. 29.

5 Instructions for Kavtaradze, Aug. 22, 1944, AVPRF: f. 06, op. 6, d. 461, l. 1.

6 The Azerbaijan State Archive of Political Parties and Social Movements (GAPPOD) AzR, f. 1, op. 89, d. 90, ll. 4–5. Obtained by Jamil Hasanli. Translated for CWIHP by Gary Goldberg. CWIHP DA: http://digitalarchive.wilsoncenter.org/document/112021.

7 Gasanly, *SSSR-Turtsiya*.

8 Ibid., 50–89. For Stalin's comment to Dimitrov, see Ivo Banac (ed.), *The Diary of Georgi Dimitrov, 1933–1949* (New Haven, CT: Yale University Press, 2003), 137.

9 Sergey Radchenko, "Stalin," in Steven Casey, Jonathan Wright (eds.), *Mental Maps in the Early Cold War Era, 1945–1968* (Basingstoke: Palgrave Macmillan, 2011), 23.

618

NOTES TO PAGES 73–77

10 Molotov and Selim Sarper, June 7, 1945, AVPRF: f. 06, op. 7, p. 2, d. 31, l. 7.

11 Stalin's comments at the Seventh Meeting of the Potsdam Conference, July 23, 1945, RGASPI: f. 558, op. 11, d. 236, l. 20.

12 Molotov to Stalin, Dec. 15, 1945, RGASPI: f. 558, op. 11, d. 99, l. 158.

13 Memcon, Stalin and Bevin, Dec. 19, 1945, RGASPI: f. 558, op. 11, d. 285, ll. 1–10.

14 Longhand Draft Letter, Truman to Byrnes, Jan. 5, 1946, www.trumanlibrary .gov/library/truman-papers/longhand-notes-presidential-file-1944-1953/ january-5-1946?documentid=NA&pagenumber=1.

15 Walter Lippmann, "Stalin Chooses Military," *Los Angeles Times*, Feb. 13, 1946, A4.

16 Frank Costigliola, "Creation of Memory and Myth," in Martin Medhurst and H.W. Brands (eds.), *Critical Reflections on the Cold War* (Texas A&M University Press, 2000), 53.

17 Ibid., 46.

18 E.g. James Forrestal, *The Forrestal Diaries* (New York: Viking Press, 1951), 134.

19 *Pravda*, Feb. 10, 1946, 1–2. For Stalin's various drafts, see RGASPI: f. 558, op. 11, d. 1172, ll. 4–72.

20 Igor Kurchatov's notes of his meeting with Stalin, Jan. 25, 1946. Shared with the author by Yury Smirnov.

21 Campbell Craig and Sergey Radchenko, *The Atomic Bomb and the Origins of the Cold War* (New Haven, CT: Yale University Press, 2008), 55–56.

22 Roger P. Churchill and William Slany (eds.), *Foreign Relations of the United States [FRUS], 1946*, Vol. 6 (Washington, DC: US Government Printing Office, 1969), Document 475.

23 Amy Knight, *How the Cold War Began: The Igor Gouzenko Affair and the Hunt for Soviet Spies* (New York: Carroll & Graf Publishers, 2006).

24 Gasanly, *SSSR-Iran*, 254.

25 Memcon, Stalin and Qavam al-Saltaneh, Feb. 21, 1946, RGASPI: f. 558, op. 11, d. 317, ll. 20–28.

26 Qavam al-Saltaneh to the Soviet leadership, Feb. 26, 1946, RGASPI: f. 558, op. 11, d. 317, l. 31.

27 Herbert A. Fine, John G. Reid and John P. Glennon (eds.), *FRUS, 1946*, Vol. 7 (Washington, DC: US Government Printing Office, 1969), Document 254.

28 Ibid.

29 Harold B. Hinton, "Iran Files Pact Charge Violation by Soviet with UNO," *New York Times*, Mar. 20, 1946, 1.

30 Gasanly, *SSSR-Iran*, 285.

31 Ahmad Qavam to Ambassador Sadchikov, Apr. 4, 1946. GAPPOD AzR, f. 1, op. 89, d. 113. Obtained for CWIHP by Jamil Hasanli. Translated for CWIHP by Gary Goldberg.

32 Memorandum by Ashurov, Tehran, Apr. 5, 1946, GAPPOD, f. 1, op. 89, d. 114. Obtained for CWIHP by Jamil Hasanli. Translated for CWIHP by Gary Goldberg.

33 Gasanly, *SSSR-Iran*, 311.

34 Stalin to Pishevari, May 8, 1946, RGASPI: f. 558, op. 1, d. 317, l. 70.

619

NOTES TO PAGES 78–83

35 Molotov and Byrnes, Apr. 28, 1946, RGASPI: f. 558, op. 11, d. 218, ll. 128–133.

36 Stalin to Molotov, Apr. 30, 1946, RGASPI: f. 558, op. 11, d. 218, ll. 126–127.

37 Georgy Kynin and Jochen Laufer (eds.), *SSSR i germansky vopros, 1941–1949*, Vol. 2 (Moscow: Mezhdunarodnye otnosheniya, 1996), 478.

38 Memcon, Stalin and a Polish delegation, May 23, 1946, RGASPI: f. 558, op. 11, d. 355, l. 53.

39 Memcon, Stalin and a Polish delegation, May 23, 1946, RGASPI: f. 558, op. 11, d. 355, l. 53.

40 Stalin to Ivan Sadchikov, May 8, 1946, RGASPI: f. 558, op. 1, d. 317, l. 66.

41 Stalin to Pishevari, May 8, 1946, RGASPI: f. 558, op. 1, d. 317, l. 71.

42 Tito won the Nov. 1945 election by a landslide, though, as so often the case in postwar Eastern Europe, it was hardly a free and fair election.

43 Banac (ed.), *The Diary of Georgi Dimitrov, 1933–1949*, 337.

44 British Embassy in Moscow to Molotov, Jan. 1, 1945, AVPRF: f. 06, op. 7, p. 26, d. 311, ll. 1–2.

45 Memcon, Stalin and a Yugoslav delegation, Jan. 9, 1945, AVPRF: f. 06, op. 7, p. 53, d. 872, l. 22.

46 L. Ya. Gibiansky, "Ideya balkanskogo ob'edineniya i plany ee osushchestvleniya v 40-e gody XX veka," *Voprosy Istorii*, 11–12 (2001), 49.

47 L.A. Velichanskaya (ed.), *Vstrechi i peregovory na vysshem urovne rukovoditelei SSSR i Yugoslavii v 1946–1980 gg*, Vol. 1 (Moscow: Mezhdunarodnyi Fond Demokratiya, 2014), 46.

48 Gibiansky, "Ideya balkanskogo ob'edineniya …," 52.

49 For a discussion of the December uprising, see Andre Gerolymatos, *An International Civil War: Greece, 1943–1949* (New Haven, CT: Yale University Press, 2016), 134–142.

50 Dimitrov to Molotov, Dec. 8, 1944, RGANI: f. 3, op. 3, d. 117, l. 1. Banac (ed.), *The Diary of Georgi Dimitrov, 1933–1949*, 345.

51 Nikos Papadatos, *Akrōs aporrēto: hoi scheseis ESSD-KKE / 1944–1952* (Athens: Ekdoseis KPsM, 2019), 53.

52 Memcon, Stalin and a Yugoslav delegation, Jan. 9, 1945, AVPRF: f. 06, op. 7, p. 53, d. 872, l. 22; Banac (ed.), *The Diary of Georgi Dimitrov, 1933–1949*, 353.

53 Nikos Marantzidis, "The Greek Civil War (1944–1949) and the International Communist System," *JCWS*, 15(4) (Fall 2013), 29.

54 Ibid., 30; Papadatos, *Akrōs aporrēto*, 221.

55 Report from Ioannidis, Sept. 12, 1946, RGANI: f. 3, op. 23, d. 117, ll. 25–39. See also a discussion of this KKE approach in Artiom A. Ulunian, "The Soviet Union and the 'Greek Question', 1946–53: Problems and Appraisals," in Francesca Gori and Silvio Pons (eds.), *The Soviet Union and Europe in the Cold War, 1943–1953* (London: Macmillan Press, 1996), 147.

56 Suslov to Stalin, Oct. 18, 1946, RGANI: f. 3, op. 23, d. 117, ll. 23–24.

57 Molotov to Stalin, Dec. 7, 1946, RGASPI: f. 558, op. 11, d. 104, ll. 15–16.

58 Ibid., ll. 37–38.

59 Stalin to Molotov, Dec. 9, 1946, RGASPI: f. 558, op. 11, d. 104, l. 36.

NOTES TO PAGES 83–87

60 William Slany (ed.), *FRUS, 1946*, Vol. 2 (Washington, DC: US Government Printing Office, 1970), Document 400.

61 Harry Truman, "Address to a joint session of Congress," Mar. 12, 1947, www.trumanlibrary.gov/library/research-files/address-president-congress-recommending-assistance-greece-and-turkey.

62 Nikos Zachariadis to Stalin, May 13, 1947, RGANI: f. 3, op. 23, d. 117, l. 49. Ulunian, "The Soviet Union and the 'Greek Question'," 149–150.

63 Nikos Zachariadis to Markos Vafeiadis, Apr. 17, 1947, RGANI: f. 3, op. 23, d. 117, ll. 50–59.

64 Record of Stalin's visitors, May 23, 1947, RGASPI: f. 558, op. 11, d. 417, l. 19.

65 Ulunian, "The Soviet Union and the 'Greek Question'," 150.

66 Suslov to Stalin, May 27, 1947, RGANI: f. 3, op. 23, d. 117, ll. 62–63.

67 Memorandum by N. Slavin, May 31, 1947, RGANI: f. 3, op. 23, d. 117, ll. 64–65.

68 Memcon, Stalin and Hoxha, July 16, 1947, RGASPI: f. 558, op. 11, d. 249, l. 15.

69 Plan Lake, Sept. 10, 1947, RGANI: f. 3, op. 23, d. 117, ll. 73–77.

70 See e.g. Marantzidis, "The Greek Civil War."

71 Memcon, Stalin and Hoxha, July 16, 1947, RGASPI: f. 558, op. 11, d. 249, l. 15.

72 Milovan Djilas, *Conversations with Stalin* (Harmondsworth: Penguin, 1967), 90.

73 Norman Naimark, *Stalin and the Fate of Europe: The Postwar Struggle for Sovereignty* (Cambridge, MA: The Belknap Press, 2019); Norman Naimark, "The Sovietization of Eastern Europe," in Melvyn P. Leffler and Odd Arne Westad (eds.), *The Cambridge History of the Cold War* [*CHCW*], Vol. 1 (Cambridge University Press, 2010), 175.

74 Memcon, Stalin and a Polish delegation, May 23, 1946, RGASPI: f. 558, op. 11, d. 355, ll. 33–62.

75 Banac (ed.), *The Diary of Georgi Dimitrov, 1933–1949*, 414.

76 Naimark, "The Sovietization of Eastern Europe," 184.

77 Memcon, Stalin and a British Labour Party delegation, Aug. 7, 1946, RGASPI: f. 558, op. 11, d. 286, l. 5.

78 Jean-Pierre Rioux, *La France de la Quatrième République*, Vol. 1 (Paris: Éditions de Seuil, 1980), 32–38.

79 John Harper, *America and the Reconstruction of Italy, 1945–48* (Cambridge University Press, 1986), 44–45.

80 Alessandra Casella and Barry Eichengreen, "Halting Inflation in Italy and France After World War II," NBER Working Paper 3852 (Sept. 1991), 4–5.

81 C.L. Sulzberger, "Vast New Areas of Hunger Appear in Europe," *New York Times*, Feb. 23, 1947, E3.

82 Memcon, Stalin and Thorez, Nov. 20, 1944, RGASPI: f. 558, op. 11, d. 390, l. 88.

83 Banac (ed.), *The Diary of Georgi Dimitrov, 1933–1949*, 303–304. For a detailed discussion of Stalin's policy towards the PCI, see Elena Aga-Rossi and Victor Zaslavsky, "The Soviet Union and the Italian Communist Party, 1944–8," in Francesco Gori and Silvio Ponds (eds.), *The Soviet Union and Europe in the Cold War, 1943–53* (London: Macmillan Press, 1996), 161–184.

NOTES TO PAGES 87–93

84 For a discussion, see W.I. Hitchcock, *The Struggle For Europe: The Turbulent History of a Divided History, 1945 to the Present* (New York: Anchor Books, 2004), 76–77.

85 PCF to CC VKP(b) (All-Union Communist Party (Bolsheviks)), June 9, 1947, RGASPI: f. 558, op. 11, d. 392, l. 72.

86 Zhdanov to Thorez, June 2, 1947, RGASPI: f. 558, op. 11, d. 392, ll. 33–34.

87 John Whittam, "The Reluctant Crusader: De Gasperi and the Crisis of May 1947," *War & Society*, 2(1) (1984), 85–103.

88 Memcon, Stalin and George Marshall, Apr. 15, 1947, RGASPI: f. 558, op. 11, d. 374, l. 158.

89 Speech to Harvard University Alumni, June 5, 1947, https://library .marshallfoundation.org/Portal/Default/en-US/RecordView/Index/15434.

90 For an overview, see William I. Hitchcock, "The Marshall Plan and the Creation of the West," in *CHCW*, Vol. 1, 154–174.

91 For a detailed discussion of the Soviet reaction to the Marshall Plan see Scott Parish, "The Marshall Plan, Soviet–American relations, and the Division of Europe," in Norman Naimark and Leonid Gibiansky (eds.), *The Establishment of Communist Regimes in Eastern Europe, 1944–49* (Westview Press, 1997), 267–290.

92 Memcon, Stalin and a Czechoslovak delegation, July 10, 1947, RGASPI: f. 558, op. 11, d. 393, ll. 101, 105.

93 Stalin to Molotov et al., Oct. 2, 1947, RGASPI: f. 558, op. 11, d. 106, ll. 148–149.

94 L. Ya. Gibiansky, "Dolgii put' k tainam: istoriografiya Kominforma," in G.M. Adibekov et al. (eds.), *Soveshchaniya Kominforma, 1947, 1948, 1949. Dokumenty i materialy* (Moscow: Rosspen, 1998), xxxvii.

95 Csaba Békés, "Soviet Plans to Establish the Cominform in early 1946: New Evidence from the Hungarian Archives," *CWIHP Bulletin*, Issue 10 (Mar. 1998), 135–136.

96 Gibiansky, "Dolgii put' k tainam: istoriografiya Kominforma," xli.

97 For Zhdanov's speech, see Adibekov et al. (eds.), *Soveshchaniya Kominforma, 1947, 1948, 1949*, 152–171, 297–302.

98 Stalin to Molotov, Sept. 24, 1947, RGASPI: f. 558, op. 11, d. 106, l. 117.

99 For a discussion of the Yugoslavs' role at Szklarska Poręba see Silvio Pons, "A Challenge Let Drop: Soviet Foreign Policy, the Cominform and the Italian Communist Party, 1947–8," in Francesco Gori and Silvio Ponds (eds.), *The Soviet Union and Europe in the Cold War, 1943–53* (London: Macmillan Press, 1996), 246–263.

100 Stanisław Mikołajczyk, *The Rape of Poland: Pattern of Soviet Aggression* (Westport, CT: Greewood Publishers, 1972), 243–250.

101 Tatyana Volokitina (ed.), *Sovetsky faktor v vostochnoi Evrope, 1944–1953*, Vol. 1 (Moscow: Rosspen, 1999), 492.

102 Tatyana Volokitina (ed.), *Vostochnaya Evropa v dokumentakh rossiiskikh arkhivov, 1944–1953* [*VEvDRA*], Vol. 1 (Novosibirsk: Sibirsky Khronograf, 1997), 734.

103 Ibid., 683.

104 Molotov to Stalin, Oct. 30, 1947, RGASPI: f. 558, op. 11, d. 107, l. 100.

NOTES TO PAGES 93–100

105 Molotov to Stalin, Oct. 13, 1947, RGASPI: f. 558, op. 11, d. 107, ll. 23–28.

106 Memcon, Stalin and a British Labour delegation, Oct. 14, 1947, RGASPI: f. 558, op. 11, d. 286, l. 37.

107 Victor S. Mamatey and Radomír Luža (eds.), *A History of the Czechoslovak Republic, 1918–1948* (Princeton University Press, 1973), 404.

108 Memcon, Stalin and a Czechoslovak delegation, Mar. 28, 1945, RGASPI: f. 558, op. 11, d. 393, l. 59.

109 Gottwald to Stalin, Nov. 25, 1947, RGASPI: f. 558, op. 11, d. 393, l. 123.

110 Stalin to Gottwald, Nov. 29, 1947, RGASPI: f. 558, op. 11, d. 393, l. 125.

111 Mamatey and Luža (eds.), *A History of the Czechoslovak Republic, 1918–1948*, 412–415.

112 Memcon, Stalin and Enver Hoxha, July 16, 1947, RGASPI: f. 558, op. 11, d. 249, l. 19.

113 *VEvDRA*, Vol. 1, 687–688, 735–737, 786–787.

114 Jeronim Perović, "The Tito–Stalin Split: A Reassessment in Light of New Evidence," *JCWS*, 9(2) (2007), 47; L. Ya. Gibiansky, "The Soviet–Yugoslav Conflict and the Soviet Bloc," in Francesco Gori and Silvio Ponds (eds.), *The Soviet Union and Europe in the Cold War, 1943–53* (London: Macmillan Press, 1996), 232.

115 Stalin to Tito, Dec. 23, 1947, RGASPI: f. 558, op. 11, d. 398, l. 17.

116 Djilas, *Conversations with Stalin*, 111.

117 Ibid., 113.

118 Cited in V.G. Titov and B. Stefanovich (eds.), *Sovetsko-yugoslavskie otnosheniya, 1945–1956* (Novosibirsk: Alfa-Porte, 2010), 210.

119 Stalin to Tito and Dimitrov, Aug. 12, 1947, RGASPI: f. 558, op. 11, d. 398, l. 11.

120 Perović, "The Tito–Stalin Split," 49; L. Ya. Gibiansky, "K istorii sovetsko–yugo-slavskogo konflikta, Part 1," *Sovetskoe Slavyanovedenie*, 3 (1991), 13–14.

121 Gibiansky, "K istorii sovetsko–yugoslavskogo konflikta, Part 1," 15–18.

122 "Report of Milovan Djilas about a Secret Soviet-Bulgarian-Yugoslav Meeting," Feb. 10, 1948. Translated by Vladislav Zubok. CWIHP DA: https://digitalarchive .wilsoncenter.org/document/117100.

123 Ibid.

124 Ibid.

125 Nikos Zachariadis to the Soviet leadership, June 15, 1948, RGANI: f. 3, op. 23, d. 117, l. 83.

126 Perović, "The Tito–Stalin Split," 55–56; Nikos Zachariadis to the Soviet leadership, June 15, 1948, RGANI: f. 3, op. 23, d. 117, l. 83.

127 "Report from a trusted person," undated (Mar. 1948), RGASPI: f. 558, op. 11, d. 393, ll. 19–26. The record of the actual YCP Politburo meeting on Mar. 1, 1948 is in Titov and Stefanovich (eds.), *Sovetsko-yugoslavskie otnosheniya, 1945–1956*, 225–227.

128 The Cominform resolution on Yugoslavia is in *Pravda*, June 29, 1949. On Stalin's expectations see Perović, "The Tito–Stalin Split," 59–62; RGASPI: f. 558, op. 11, d. 319, ll. 21–22.

NOTES TO PAGES 100–104

129 Cited in Titov and Stefanovich (eds.), *Sovetsko-yugoslavskie otnosheniya, 1945–1956*, 156.

130 Nikos Zachariadis to the Soviet leadership, June 15, 1948, RGANI: f. 3, op. 23, d. 117, l. 84.

131 Nikos Zachariadis to the Soviet leadership, July 7, 1948, RGANI: f. 3, op. 23, d. 117, l. 89.

132 Sokolov (Tirana) to Vasilevsky, Sept. 30, 1948, RGANI: f. 3, op. 23, d. 117, ll. 120–121.

133 See e.g. Bulganin and Suslov to Stalin, Sept. 17, 1948, RGANI: f. 3, op. 23, d. 117, ll. 115–117.

134 Vafeiadis to the Soviet leadership, Oct. 15, 1948, RGANI: f. 3, op. 23, d. 23, l. 140.

135 Marantzidis, "The Greek Civil War," 51.

136 Peter Ruggenthaler, *The Concept of Neutrality in Stalin's Foreign Policy, 1945–1953* (London: Lexington Books, 2015), 58–64.

137 Lozovsky to Stalin, May 26, 1946, in Kynin and Laufer (eds.), *SSSR i germansky vopros*, Vol. 2, 523–524.

138 Notes by Wilhelm Pieck on a Consultation with Stalin, Molotov, Zhdanov, June 4, 1945. Translated by Ruud van Dijk. CWIHP DA: http://digitalarchive.wilsoncenter.org/document/123362.

139 Christian F. Ostermann, *Between Containment and Rollback* (Stanford University Press, 2021), 59–66.

140 Directive, V. Sokolovsky and F. Bokov, June 18, 1946, in N.V. Petrov et al. (eds.), *SVAG i nemetskie organy samoupravleniya. 1945–1949* (Moscow: Rosspen, 2006), 159–163.

141 Ostermann, *Between Containment and Rollback*, 64.

142 Memcon, Stalin and an SED delegation, Jan. 31, 1947, RGASPI: f. 558, op. 11, d. 303, l. 15.

143 Gerhard Wettig, *Stalin and the Cold War in Europe. The Emergence and Development of East–West Conflict, 1939–1953* (Lanham, MD: Rowman & Littlefield, 2007), 115–116.

144 Memcon, Stalin and an SED delegation, Jan. 31, 1947, RGASPI: f. 558, op. 11, d. 303, l. 16.

145 Ibid., ll. 8–11. Also, Wettig, *Stalin and the Cold War in Europe*, 114–115.

146 Ostermann, *Between Containment and Rollback*, 76–77.

147 For the records, see William Slany (ed.), *FRUS, 1947*, Vol. 2 (Washington, DC: US Government Printing Office, 1972), https://history.state.gov/historicaldocuments/frus1947v02/ch5.

148 Memcon, Stalin and an SED delegation, Jan. 31, 1947, RGASPI: f. 558, op. 11, d. 303, ll. 2–3. See also Ostermann, *Between Containment and Rollback*, 81–83; Wettig, *Stalin and the Cold War in Europe*, 116–118.

149 Ostermann, *Between Containment and Rollback*, 86–88. Peter Ruggenthaler, "Germany and the Soviet Union During the Cold War Era," in *The Oxford Handbook of German Politics* (Oxford University Press, 2022), 84–85.

624

NOTES TO PAGES 105–113

150 Memcon, Stalin and an SED delegation, Dec. 18, 1948, RGASPI: f. 558, op. 11, d. 303, ll. 84–85, 87.

151 Memcon, Stalin and an SED delegation, Mar. 26, 1948, RGASPI: f. 558, op. 11, d. 303, l. 34.

152 Wettig, *Stalin and the Cold War in Europe*, 166–167.

153 On the Stalin Note, see Peter Ruggenthaler, "The 1952 Stalin Note on German Unification: The Ongoing Debate," *JCWS*, 13(4) (2011), 172–212; for Stalin's fears in relation to West Germany, see David E. Murphy, Sergei A. Kondrashev, and George Bailey, *Battleground Berlin: CIA vs. KGB in the Cold War* (New Haven, CT: Yale University Press, 1999), 142–146.

154 Memcon, Stalin and SED delegations, Apr. 1 and 7, 1952, RGASPI: f. 558, op. 11, d. 303, ll. 167–197.

155 George Kennan, "The Sources of Soviet Conduct," *Foreign Affairs*, July 1947, 566–582.

156 The "masking" quote appears in Banac (ed.), *The Diary of Georgi Dimitrov, 1933–1949*, 414.

157 Pons, "A Challenge Let Drop."

158 Henry Kissinger, *The White House Years* (London: Weidenfeld and Nicolson and Michael Joseph, 1979), 62–63.

159 Longhand Draft Letter, Truman to Byrnes, Jan. 5, 1946, www.trumanlibrary .gov/library/truman-papers/longhand-notes-presidential-file-1944-1953/ january-5-1946?documentid=NA&pagenumber=1.

4 STALIN IN ASIA

1 A portion of this chapter first appeared in Sergey Radchenko, "The Origins of the Sino-Soviet Alliance, 1949–1950," *Rivista Italiana di Storia Internazionale*, 2 (July–Dec. 2019), 189–208. Reproduced with permission.

2 Film of of Mao Zedong's arrival in Moscow, www.youtube.com /watch?v=gFLz2juVbY8.

3 Stalin to Mao Zedong, Sept. 24, 1947, RGASPI: f. 558, op. 11, d. 330, ll. 1–2.

4 Molotov to Roshchin, Sept. 8, 1947, RGASPI: f. 558, op. 11, d. 106, l. 38.

5 Stalin to Mao, Sept. 24, 1947, RGASPI: f. 558, op. 11, d. 330, ll. 1–2.

6 Orlov to F.F. Kuznetsov, Oct. 2, 1947, RGASPI: f. 558, op. 11, d. 330, ll. 10–12.

7 Stalin to Mao, Oct. 4, 1947, RGASPI: f. 82, op. 2, d. 1239, l. 139.

8 See Ivo Banac (ed.), *The Diary of Georgi Dimitrov, 1933–1949* (New Haven, CT: Yale University Press, 2003), 443.

9 Stalin to Mao, June 15, 1947, RGASPI: f. 82, op. 2, d. 1239, l. 135.

10 Ibid.

11 For a discussion of the possible motives for the cancellation of the trip, see David Wolff and Sergey Radchenko, "To the Summit via Proxy-Summits: New Evidence from Soviet and Chinese Archives on Mao's Long March to Moscow, 1949," *CWIHP Bulletin*, Issue 16 (Fall 2007/Winter 2008), 106.

NOTES TO PAGES 113–120

12 Stalin to Mao, Dec. 16, 1947, in A.M. Ledovsky, R.A. Mirovitskaya, and V.A. Myasnikov (eds.), *Sovetsko-kitaiskie otnosheniya* [*SKO*], Vol. 5-2 (Moscow: Pamyatniki Istoricheskoi Mysli, 2005), 378.

13 Terebin to Kuznetsov, Dec. 17, 1947, ibid., 378.

14 Stalin to Mao, July 14, 1948, ibid., 447.

15 Terebin to Stalin, July 14, 1948, ibid., 447–448; Radchenko and Wolff, "To the Summit," 106–107.

16 Ralph R. Goodwin, Francis C. Prescott and Velma Hastings Cassidy (eds.), *Foreign Relations of the United States [FRUS], 1948*, Vol. 7 (Washington, DC: US Government Printing Office, 1973), 337–339.

17 Odd Arne Westad, *Decisive Encounters: The Chinese Civil War, 1946–1950* (Stanford University Press, 2003), 181–188.

18 Ibid., 186.

19 *FRUS, 1948*, Vol. 7, 299–301.

20 Mao to Stalin via Terebin, Aug. 13, 1948, RGASPI: f. 558, op. 11, d. 330, ll. 36–40.

21 Mao to Stalin via Terebin, Dec. 30, 1948, RGASPI: f. 558, op. 11, d. 330, ll. 84–88.

22 Mao to Stalin via Tebebin, Jan. 9, 1949, RGASPI: f. 558, op. 11, d. 330, l. 92.

23 The note sent to the Soviets is in RGASPI: f. 558, op. 11, d. 330, ll. 98–99. Stalin forwarded it to Mao Zedong.

24 Francis C. Prescott et al. (eds.), *FRUS, 1949*, Vol. 8 (Washington, DC: US Government Printing Office, 1978), 26.

25 Ibid., 42–43.

26 Stalin to Mao via Terebin, Jan. 10, 1949, RGASPI: f. 558, op. 11, d. 330, ll. 95–96.

27 Stalin to Mao via Terebin, Jan. 11, 1949, RGASPI: f. 558, op. 11, d. 330, l. 97.

28 Stalin to Mao via Terebin, Apr. 24, 1948, RGASPI: f. 82, op. 2, d. 1239, ll. 140–141.

29 Stalin to Mao via Terebin, Jan. 6, 1949, RGASPI: f. 82, op. 2, d. 1240, l. 33.

30 Terebin to Kuznetsov, Jan. 10, 1949, in *SKO*, Vol. 5-2, 12.

31 Mao to Stalin via Terebin, Jan. 12, 1949, RGASPI: f. 558, op. 11, d. 330, ll. 100–103.

32 Terebin to Kuznetsov, Jan. 13, 1949, in *SKO*, Vol. 5-2, 20.

33 Stalin to Mao, Jan. 14, 1949, RGASPI: f. 558, op. 11, d. 330, ll. 110–113.

34 Mikoyan's notes, undated (Jan. 1949), GARF: f. 5446, op. 120, d. 957, l. 2.

35 Memcon, Mikoyan and Mao, Feb. 3, 1949, in *SKO*, Vol. 5-2, 62–66.

36 Mikoyan to Stalin, Feb. 8, 1949, RGASPI: f. 558, op. 11, d. 344, ll. 112–114.

37 Stalin to Mikoyan, Feb. 2, 1949, RGASPI: f. 558, op. 11, d. 344, ll. 45–46.

38 Mikoyan's notes, undated (Jan. 1949), GARF: f. 5446, op. 120, d. 957, l. 2.

39 Wolff and Radchenko, "To the Summit," 108–109.

40 Mikoyan's notes, undated (Jan. 1949), GARF: f. 5446, op. 120, d. 957, l. 2.

41 Wolff and Radchenko, "To the Summit," 108.

42 Memcon, Mikoyan and Mao, Feb. 6, 1949, in *SKO*, Vol. 5-2, 81–87.

43 See e.g. Mao to Stalin, Aug. 14, 1948, RGASPI: f. 558, op. 11, d. 330, ll. 36–40.

44 Memcon, Mikoyan and Mao, Feb. 3, 1949, in *SKO*, Vol. 5-2, 62–66.

45 Stalin to Mao, Oct. 15, 1948, RGASPI: f. 82, op. 2, d. 1240, l. 9.

NOTES TO PAGES 120–126

46 Terebin to Kuznetsov, Oct. 16, 1948, Oct. 17, 1948, RGASPI: f. 558, op. 11, d. 330, ll. 72–73.

47 Mikoyan's notes, undated (Jan. 1949), GARF: f. 5446, op. 120, d. 957, l. 6.

48 Ibid., l. 4.

49 Stalin to Mao, Jan. 6, 1950, RGASPI: f. 558, op. 11, d. 334, l. 16.

50 Mikoyan's notes, undated (Jan. 1949), GARF: f. 5446, op. 120, d. 957, ll. 2–3.

51 *FRUS, 1949*, Vol. 8, 770. See also Thomas J. Christensen, "A 'Lost Chance' for What? Rethinking the Origins of U.S.–PRC Confrontation," *The Journal of American–East Asian Relations*, 4(3) (Fall 1995), 249–278.

52 Kovalev to Stalin, May 23, 1949, RGASPI: f. 558, op. 11, d. 331, ll. 66–69. The Russian documents seem to confirm the view that Mao's probes in the US direction were a tactical ploy. For a good summary of the debate see Warren I. Cohen, "Introduction: Was There a 'Lost Chance' in China?" *Diplomatic History*, 21(1) (Winter 1997), 71–75. See, especially, articles by Odd Arne Westad and Chen Jian.

53 Wolff and Radchenko, "To the Summit," 110.

54 Memcon, Mikoyan and Mao, Jan. 30, 1949, in *SKO*, Vol. 5-2, 33–37; Memcon, Mikoyan and Mao, Feb. 3, 1949, ibid., 62–66.

55 Memcon, Stepan Chervonenko and Mao, May 2, 1956, AVPRF: f. 0100, op. 49, p. 410, d. 9, l. 129.

56 Sergey Radchenko and David Wolff, "'The Mouse Died ...': New Documents on Mao Zedong and Anastas Mikoyan at Xibaipo," unpublished paper; List of Products Brought Back, n.d. (probably Feb. 1949), GARF: f. 5446, op. 120, d. 957, l. 35.

57 Zhonggong zhongyang wenxian yanjiushi, *Jianguo Yilai Mao Zedong Wengao* [*JGYLMZDWG*], Vol. 1 (Beijing: Zhongyang Wenxian Chubanshe, 1987), 6.

58 Kovalev to Vasilevsky, Sept. 21, 1949, RGASPI: f. 558, op. 11, d. 332, l. 37.

59 Cited in Lkhamsurengiin Bat-Ochir, *Choibalsan* (Ulaanbaatar: Tsomorlig, 1996), 186.

60 Jiang Qing to Mao, RGASPI: f. 82, op. 2, d. 1240, ll. 98–99.

61 Report by L.I. Melnikov, undated (Aug. 1949), RGASPI: f. 82, op. 2, d. 1240, ll. 131–139.

62 *SKO*, Vol. 5-2, 148–151.

63 CCP's report for Stalin, July 4, 1950, RGASPI: f. 558, op. 11, d. 328, l. 46.

64 Mao Zedong, "On the People's Democratic Dictatorship," June 30, 1949, www.marxists.org/reference/archive/mao/selected-works/volume-4/mswv4_65.htm.

65 Zhonggong zhongyang wenxian yanjiushi, *Jianguo Yilai Liu Shaoqi Wengao*, Vol. 1 (Beijing: Zhongyang Wenxian Chubanshe, 2008), 16–17.

66 CCP's report for Stalin, July 4, 1950, RGASPI: f. 558, op. 11, d. 328, l. 50.

67 For the most effective exposition, see Jeremy Friedman, *Shadow Cold War: The Sino-Soviet Competition for the Third World* (Chapel Hill, NC: University of North Carolina Press, 2015).

NOTES TO PAGES 126–131

68 "Minutes, Mao's Conversation with a Yugoslavian Communist Union Delegation, Beijing [undated]," Sept. 1956. Translated and Annotated by Zhang Shu Guang and Chen Jian. CWIHP DA: http://digitalarchive.wilsoncenter.org /document/117035.

69 Mikoyan's notes, undated (Jan. 1949), GARF: f. 5446, op. 120, d. 957, ll. 2–3.

70 Shi Zhe, *Zai Lishi Juren Shenbian*, rev. ed. (Beijing: Zhongyang Wenxian Chubanshe, 1995), 435.

71 Memcon, Stalin and Mao, Dec. 16, 1949, RGASPI: f. 558, op. 11, d. 329, ll. 9–26.

72 Mao to Liu, Dec. 18, 1949. Translation adapted from Shuguang Zhang and Jian Chen, *Chinese Communist Foreign Policy and the Cold War in Asia: New Documentary Evidence, 1944–1950* (Chicago, IL.: Imprint Publications, 1996), 128. CWIHP DA: http://digitalarchive.wilsoncenter.org/document/110393.

73 Shi Zhe, *Zai Lishi Juren Shenbian*, 436.

74 Memcon, Stalin and Mao, Dec. 16, 1949, RGASPI: f. 558, op. 11, d. 329, ll. 9–26.

75 Ibid.

76 Mao to Liu Shaoqi, Dec. 18, 1949, in Pang Xianzhi and Jin Chongji (eds.), *Mao Zedong Zhuan, 1949–1976*, Vol. 1 (Beijing: Zhongyang Wenxian Chubanshe, 2003), 36.

77 *SKO*, Vol. 5-2, 170–172.

78 Mao to Stalin, Nov. 8, 1949, RGASPI: f. 558, op. 11, d. 333, ll. 63–64.

79 *JGYLMZDWG*, Vol. 1, 190.

80 Memcon, Stalin and Mao, Dec. 16, 1949, RGASPI: f. 558, op. 11, d. 329, ll. 9–26.

81 Ibid.

82 Ibid.

83 Kovalev to Stalin, Dec. 20, 1949, RGASPI: f. 82, op. 2, d. 1241, ll. 185–186.

84 Mao to the CCP, Dec. 19, 1949, *JGYLMZWG*, Vol. 1, 193.

85 Pang Xianzhi et al. (eds.), *Mao Zedong Nianpu*, Vol. 1 (Beijing: Zhongyang Wenxian Chubanshe, 2013), 63; Pang Xianzhi and Jin Chongji (eds.), *Mao Zedong Zhuan*, Vol. 1, 39.

86 *SKO*, Vol. 5-2, 234–243.

87 Shi Zhe, *Zai Lishi Juren Shenbian*, 438.

88 Ibid., 437.

89 Memcon, Roshchin and Mao, Jan. 1, 1950. Obtained by Odd Arne Westad. Translated by Daniel Rozas. CWIHP DA: http://digitalarchive.wilsoncenter .org/document/110404.

90 This episode is recounted in detail in Dieter Heinzig, *The Soviet Union and Communist China 1945–1950: The Arduous Road to the Alliance* (New York: Routledge, 2015), 290–291, though Heinzig appears to suggest that it was Mao who initiated the interview.

91 *SKO*, Vol. 5-2, 254.

92 This take is endorsed by Alexander Pantsov and Steven Levine in their biography of Mao. *Mao: The Real Story* (New York: Simon & Schuster, 2012), 371.

NOTES TO PAGES 132–139

93 Mao to Liu, Jan. 13, 1950. Translation from Shuguang Zhang and Jian Chen (eds.), *Chinese Communist Foreign Policy and the Cold War in Asia*, 136–137. CWIHP DA: http://digitalarchive.wilsoncenter.org/document/112674.

94 Chen Jian, *Mao's China and the Cold War* (Chapel Hill, NC: University of North Carolina Press, 2000), 50–53.

95 Memcon, Molotov, Vyshinsky, and Mao, Jan. 17, 1950. Obtained by Odd Arne Westad. Translated by Daniel Rozas. CWIHP DA: http://digitalarchive .wilsoncenter.org/document/112671.

96 Dieter Heinzig, *The Soviet Union and communist China 1945–1950*, 304.

97 Memcon, Stalin and Mao, Jan. 22, 1950. Translated by Danny Rozas. CWIHP DA: http://digitalarchive.wilsoncenter.org/document/111245.

98 Ibid.

99 Ibid.

100 Bruce Cumings, *The Origins of the Korean War*, Vol. 1 (Princeton University Press, 1981), 120–121.

101 Kathryn Weathersby, "'Should We Fear This?': Stalin and the Danger of War with America," CWIHP Working Paper 39 (July 2002), 4.

102 Ibid., 5–8.

103 Kovalev to Stalin, May 18, 1949, RGASPI: f. 558, op. 11, d. 331, ll. 59–61.

104 Mao to Stalin, Oct. 21, 1949, RGASPI: f. 558, op. 11, d. 333, ll. 49–51.

105 Stalin to Mao, Oct. 26, 1949, RGASPI: f. 558, op. 11, d. 333, l. 46.

106 Shtykov to Vyshinsky, Jan. 19, 1950, RGASPI: f. 558, op. 11, d. 346, ll. 64–68.

107 Stalin to Shtykov, Jan. 30, 1950, RGASPI: f. 558, op. 11, d. 346, l. 69.

108 Kathryn Weathersby, "'Should We Fear This?'," 9.

109 Ibid., 11.

110 Tennent H. Bagley, *Spymaster: Startling Cold War Revelations of a Soviet KGB Chief* (New York: Skyhorse Publishing, 2015), 1–15. The author is grateful to David Easter for drawing his attention to Bagley's book.

111 Memcon, Mao and Mikoyan, Sept. 23, 1956. In the author's possession.

112 See e.g. Samuel Wells, *Fearing the Worst: How Korea Transformed the Cold War* (New York: Columbia University Press, 2019), 55, 59, 121.

113 For the backstory, see Craig and Radchenko, *The Atomic Bomb and the Origins of the Cold War*; also Michael S. Goodman, *Spying on the Nuclear Bear: Anglo-American intelligence and the Soviet bomb* (Stanford University Press, 2007).

114 National Security Council Report, NSC-68, 'United States Objectives and Programs for National Security'," Apr. 14, 1950, CWIHP DA: http:// digitalarchive.wilsoncenter.org/document/116191.

115 Shtykov to Vyshinsky, May 12, 1950, CWIHP DA: https://digitalarchive .wilsoncenter.org/document/112980.

116 Vyshinsky to Mao, May 14, 1950, RGASPI: f. 558, op. 11, d. 334, l. 55.

117 Memcon, Mao and Mikoyan, Sept. 23, 1956. In the author's possession.

118 Cable, Stalin to Mao, June 5, 1951, RGASPI: f. 558, op. 11, d. 339, l. 17.

NOTES TO PAGES 139–148

119 Cited in Sergey Radchenko, "Joseph Stalin," in Casey and Wright (eds.), *Mental Maps in the Early Cold War Year, 1945–68*, 24–25.

120 Memcon, Gromyko and Mao, Nov. 19, 1957, AVPRF: 0100, op. 50a, p. 423, d. 1.

121 Heinzig, *The Soviet Union and Communist China 1945–1950*, 348–351.

122 Ibid., 372–376. Texts of these agreements are in Sergei Lavrov and Yang Jiechi (eds.), *Sovetsko-kitaiskie otnosheniya, 1949–1951. Sbornik dokumentov* (Cheboksary: Krona, 2009), 132–152.

123 For the most pessimistic take, see Levine and Pantsov, *Mao: The Real Story*, 372–273. Shen Zhihua, by contrast, gives a more generous assessment to Mao's scorecard. See Shen Zhihua, "Zhongsu tiaoyue tanpan zhongde liyi chongtu jiqi jiejue," *Lishi Yanjiu*, 2 (2002), 39–55.

124 Zhou Enlai to Liu Shaoqi, Feb. 8, 1950, in Lavrov and Yang (eds.), *Sovetsko-kitaiskie otnosheniya, 1949–1951*, 96–101. However, Stalin went back on his promise due to the outbreak of the Korean War.

5 LOVE US AS WE ARE

1 David E. Murphy, Sergei A. Kondrashev, and George Bailey, *Battleground Berlin: CIA vs. KGB in the Cold War* (New Haven, CT: Yale University Press, 1999), 156.

2 A.M. Aleksandr-Agentov, *Ot Kollontai do Gorbacheva* (Moscow: Mezhdunarodnye Otnosheniya, 1994), 90–91.

3 V. Naumov and Yu. Sigachev (eds.), *Lavrenty Beriya. 1953: stenogramma iyul'skogo plenuma TsK KPSS i drugie dokumenty* (Moscow: Mezdunarodnyi Fond Demokratiya, 1999), 55–59.

4 Georgy Malenkov's draft speaking notes, June 1, 1953, RGASPI: f. 83, op. 1, d. 3, ll. 131–136. The author is grateful to Mark Kramer for sharing this document.

5 A.M. Filitov, "SSSR i GDR: god 1953-i," *Voprosy Istorii*, 7 (2000), 127.

6 The most detailed accounts are Hope M. Harrison, *Driving the Soviets Up the Wall: Soviet–East German Relations, 1953–1961* (Princeton University Press, 2011) and Christian F. Ostermann and Malcolm Byrne (eds.), *Uprising in East Germany 1953: The Cold War, the German question, and the First Major Upheaval behind the Iron Curtain* (Budapest: Central European University Press, 2001).

7 John Lewis Gaddis, *We Now Know: Rethinking Cold War History* (New York: Clarendon Press, 1997), 130.

8 Other accounts point to Malenkov's centrality in Beria's downfall. For the best overview see Joseph Torigian, *Prestige, Manipulation, and Coercion: Elite Power Struggles in the Soviet Union and China after Stalin and Mao* (New Haven, CT: Yale University Press, 2022), 19–43.

9 See Beria's interrogation protocol, July 10, 1953 in V.N. Khaustov (ed.), *Delo Beriya: prigovor obzhalovaniyu ne podlezhit* (Moscow: Mezhdunarodnyi Fond Demokratiya, 2012), 46. Such claims must of course be taken with a grain of salt. See Murphy, Kondrashev and Bailey, *Battleground Berlin*, 155–156.

NOTES TO PAGES 149–154

10 Khrushchev's and Molotov's remarks at the July (1953) CC CPSU Plenum, July 2, 1953, in Naumov and Sigachev (eds.), *Lavrenty Beriya. 1953*, 97, 102.

11 Interestingly, Malenkov was very worried about his previous position on Germany, telling Khrushchev that "he feared that the case directed against Beria will be turned against him [Malenkov]." Khrushchev reassured Malenkov that the German question was far less important than the question of purging Beria. See Nikita Khrushchev, *Vospominaniya: vremya, lyudi, vlast'*, Vol. 2 (Moscow: Moskovskie Novosti, 1999), 175.

12 Geoffrey Roberts, "Molotov's Proposal that the USSR Join NATO, March 1954," *CWIHP E-dossier No. 27*. See also Geoffrey Roberts, *Molotov: Stalin's Cold Warrior* (Washington, DC: Potomac Books, 2011).

13 Memcon, Khrushchev and a GDR delegation, Sept. 19, 1955, RGANI: f. 52, op. 1, d. 557, l. 5.

14 For a discussion of Warsaw Pact strategies, see Malcolm Byrne and Vojtech Mastny (eds.), *Cardboard Castle? An Inside History of the Warsaw Pact* (Budapest: Central European University Press, 2005).

15 Memcon, Tito et al. and Khrushchev et al., May 27–28, 1955, Yugoslavia Archive (AJ): KPR 1-3-a/101-4, 10.

16 Memcon, Nehru and Khrushchev, Nov. 19, 1955, Nehru Memorial Library and Museum (NMLM), Subimal Dutt Papers, Subject File #17, 5. For a general overview of the Geneva summit, including the Soviet position, see Günter Bischof and Saki Dockrill (eds.), *Cold War Respite: The Geneva Summit of 1955* (Baton Rouge, LA: Louisiana State University Press, 2000).

17 See e.g. Khrushchev's comments to Harold Macmillan on Feb. 22, 1959, British National Archives: PREM 11/2690.

18 William Slany (ed.), *Foreign Relations of the United States [FRUS], 1955–1957*, Vol. 5 (Washington, DC: US Government Printing Office, 1988), 445.

19 Memcon, Nehru and Khrushchev, Nov. 19, 1955, NMLM, Subimal Dutt Papers, Subject File #17, 2.

20 Beria to Stalin, Mar. 26, 1951, in L.D. Ryabev et al. (ed.), *Atomnyi proekt SSSR [AP SSSR]*, Vol. 2-5 (Sarov: RFYaTs-VNIIEF, 2005), 665–668.

21 Beria attributed the above phrase to Stalin. See V. Makhnev's letter to Malenkov, July 11, 1953, in Khaustov (ed.), *Delo Beriya*, 59.

22 Report, S.E. Rozhdestvensky, Aug. 17, 1953, in *AP SSSR*, Vol. 3-2 (Sarov: RFYaTs-VNIIEF, 2009), 64–65.

23 Harrison Salisbury, "Malenkov Says Both Sides Would Lose in Atomic War," *New York Times*, Mar. 14, 1954, 1.

24 Article by Igor Kurchatov et al. (unpublished), Mar. 1954, in *AP SSSR*, Vol. 3-2, 163–167. See also David Holloway, *Stalin and the Bomb: The Soviet Union and Atomic Energy, 1939–1956* (New Haven, CT: Yale University Press, 2008), 337–338.

25 Sergei Khrushchev, *Nikita Khrushchev: reformator* (Moscow: Vremya, 2010), 167.

NOTES TO PAGES 154–159

26 Quoted in Holloway, *Stalin and the Bomb*, 339.

27 Molotov's remarks at a party plenum, Jan. 31, 1955, RGANI: f. 2, op. 1, d. 127, ll. 112–114. This is a somewhat colloquial rendering. Molotov's actual phrase was: "this means that we have something quite opposite from the head on our shoulders."

28 Memcon, Zhukov and Eisenhower, July 22, 1955, in Aleksandr Yakovlev (ed.), *Georgy Zhukov: stenogramma oktyabr'skogo plenuma (1957 g) TsK KPSS i drugie dokumenty* (Moscow: Mezhdunarodnyi Fond Demokratiya, 2001), 40.

29 Memcon, P. Ratnam and Georgy Zhukov, Mar. 21, 1957, NMLM: S. Dutt papers, subject file 50, 312–314.

30 Memcon, Voroshilov, Khrushchev et al. and an Iranian delegation, Jan. 13, 1956, AVPRF: f. 06, op. 15a, p. 21, d. 8, ll. 12–29.

31 Report on the test of RDS-37, Nov. 23, 1955, in *AP SSSR*, Vol. 3-2, 423–424.

32 For a more detailed account, which partly inspired this section, see Campbell Craig and Sergey Radchenko, "MAD, not Marx: Khrushchev and the Nuclear Revolution," *Journal of Strategic Studies*, 41(1–2) (2017), 1–26.

33 Memcon, Khrushchev and Subandrio, Mar. 22, 1955, RGANI: f. 52, op. 1, d. 565, l. 4.

34 "Visit to the United Kingdom of Bulganin and Khrushchev, 19–27 April 1956," British National Archive: FO 371/122836. The author is grateful to James Vaughan for obtaining this document.

35 Memcon, Stalin and L. Brazo, Feb. 7, 1953. RGASPI: f. 558, op. 11, d. 250, l. 9.

36 See e.g. Memcon, Stalin and a CPI delegation, Feb. 9, 1951, RGASPI: f. 558, op. 11, d. 310, ll. 71–85. The author is grateful to David Wolff for drawing his attention to this document. Also, Stalin's draft letter to Aidit, Jan. 1951, RGASPI: f. 558, op. 11, d. 313, ll. 45–50.

37 It should be noted, however, that Stalin, too, relied on third world revolutionaries on occasion, the most prominent example being his support for the united front between the Chinese Communists and the Guomindang.

38 E.g. Memcon, Khrushchev and the Burmese ambassador, Aug. 1, 1956, RGANI: f. 51, op. 1, d. 549, l. 17.

39 Memcon, Khrushchev and Subandrio, Mar. 22, 1955, RGANI: f. 52, op. 1, d. 565, l. 10.

40 Memcon, Nehru, Bulganin, and Khrushchev, Dec. 13, 1955, NMLM, Subimal Dutt Papers, Subject File No. 17.

41 Memcon, Mao and Nehru, Oct. 26, 1954. Obtained by Chen Jian. Translated by Chen Zhihong. CWIHP DA: https://digitalarchive.wilsoncenter.org/document/117828.

42 On the "intermediate zone," see Chen Jian, "China's Changing Policies toward the Third World and the End of the Global Cold War," in Artemy Kalinovsky and Sergey Radchenko (eds.), *The End of the Cold War in the Third World: New Perspectives on Regional Conflict* (London: Taylor and Francis, 2011), 101–121.

NOTES TO PAGES 159–164

43 James Jankowski, *Nasser's Egypt, Arab Nationalism, and the United Arab Republic* (Boulder, CO: Lynne Rienner Publishers, 2002), 14–25.

44 Miles Copeland, *The Game of Nations: The Amorality of Power Politics* (London: Weidenfeld & Nicolson, 1969), 58.

45 V.V. Naumkin, *Blizhnevostochnyi konflikt, 1947–1967* [*BK*], Vol. 1 (Moscow: Mezhdunarodnyi Fond Demokratiya, 2003), 200.

46 Ibid., 96.

47 Memcon, V. Semenov and Avad Al Kuni, Aug. 27, 1955, RGANI: f. 5, op. 30, d. 123, l. 39.

48 Such requests came as early as 1948. See Memcon, Vyshinsky and Bindari-Pasha, July 1, 1948, in *BK*, Vol. 1, 44 and Cable, S.P. Kozyrev to MFA, Jan. 29, 1953, in *BK*, Vol. 1, 180. Also, Guy Laron, "Cutting the Gordian Knot: The Post-WWII Egyptian Quest for Arms and the 1955 Czechoslovak Arms Deal," CWIHP Working Paper 55 (Feb. 2007).

49 Laron, "Cutting the Gordian Knot"; Laurent Rucker, "L'URSS et la Crise de Suez," *Communisme*, 49/50 (1997), 154–156; Keith Kyle, *Suez* (New York: St. Martin's Press, 1991), 76–78.

50 Visit to the United Kingdom of Bulganin and Khrushchev, Apr. 19–27, 1956, British National Archive: FO 371/122836.

51 Shepilov to Khrushchev, June 19, 1956, in *BK*, Vol. 1, 437.

52 Ibid.

53 Kyle, *Suez*, 99.

54 For an interesting account to date of Sino-Egyptian relations during this period see Kyle Haddad-Fonda, "Revolutionary Allies: Sino-Egyptian and Sino-Algerian Relations in the Bandung Decade," Ph.D thesis, Oxford University, 2013.

55 Memcon, Mao and Hassan Ragab, Sept. 18, 1956. In the author's possession.

56 Mao apparently agreed to do this in Sept. 1956, after a discussion with his lieutenants. As reported in Memcon, Mikoyan and Peng Dehuai, Sept. 19(?), 1956, GARF: f. 5446, op. 98c, d. 718, ll. 7–8.

57 Cited in Kyle, *Suez*, 131.

58 Memcon, Kiselev and Nasser, July 21, 1956 in *BK*, Vol. 1, 454.

59 Mohammad Heikal, *The Cairo Documents: The Inside Story of Nasser and His Relationship with World Leaders, Rebels, and Statesmen* (New York: Doubleday, 1973), 72.

60 Copeland, *The Game of Nations*, 122.

61 Peter G. Boyle (ed.), *The Eden–Eisenhower Correspondence, 1955–1957* (Chapel Hill, NC: University of North Carolina Press, 2005), 167, 183–184.

62 Instructions for the Soviet ambassador in Egypt, Aug. 5, 1956, in *BK*, Vol. 1, 465.

63 A.A. Fursenko (ed.), *Prezidium TsK KPSS, 1954–1964*, Vol. 1 (Moscow: Rosspen, 2003), 156–157.

64 Nina J. Noring (ed.), *FRUS, 1955–1957*, Vol. 16 (Washington, DC: US Government Printing Office, 1990), 210.

NOTES TO PAGES 164–172

65 Feliks Chuev, "V tot den' Shepilov rasskazyval o suetskom krizise, no ne tol'ko …," *Pravda*, Aug. 10, 1996, 4.

66 Fursenko (ed.), *Prezidium TsK KPSS*, Vol. 1, 162–163.

67 Ibid., 191.

68 Memcon, Khrushchev and a GDR/FRG delegation, Nov. 11, 1956, RGANI: f. 51, op. 2, d. 557, l. 29.

69 Memcon, Shepilov and Salah ad-Din al-Bitar, Nov. 2, 1956, in *BK*, Vol. 1, 546.

70 Kyle, *Suez*, 427.

71 Heikal, *The Cairo Documents*, 111.

72 Memcon, Shepilov and Salah al-Din al-Bitar, Nov. 2, 1956, in *BK*, Vol. 1, 544.

73 Cable, Shepilov to E.D. Kiselev, Nov. 3, 1956, in *BK*, Vol. 1, 550.

74 Ibid.

75 E.D. Kiselev to the MFA, Nov. 6, 1956, in *BK*, Vol. 1, 554–555.

76 N.A. Bulganin to Anthony Eden and Guy Mollet, Nov. 5, 1956, *Pravda*, Nov. 6, 1956, 1–2.

77 *FRUS, 1955–1957*, Vol. 16, Document 505.

78 Cited in Evgeny Primakov, *Blizhnii vostok: na stsene i za kulisami* (Moscow: Rossiiskaya Gazeta, 2012), 49.

79 Memcon, E.D. Kiselev and Nasser, Nov. 6, 1956, in *BK*, Vol. 1, 555–557.

80 Memcon, Khrushchev and Amer, Nov. 2, 1957, RGANI: f. 52, op. 1, d. 560, l. 16.

81 Khrushchev's speech at a Warsaw Pact meeting, Mar. 29, 1961, RGANI: f. 10, op. 3, d. 6, ll. 1–84.

82 Memcon, Khrushchev and Sekou Toure, Sept. 9, 1960, RGANI: f. 51, op. 1, d. 556, l. 113.

83 Note by the prime minister, 1955, NMLM, Subimal Dutt Papers, Subject File No. 17.

84 Memcon, Carl-Johan Sundström and Mao, Jan. 28, 1955, National Archive of Finland Min Peking dagbok 13.8.1954–1.3.1955; page 172 carton nr 2. Obtained by Sergey Radchenko. Translated by Riitta Väisänen.

85 On Mao's 1954 effort to obtain the A-bomb technology from Khrushchev, and the latter's unenthusiastic response, see Dmitry Shepilov, *Neprimknuvshii* (Moscow: Vagrius, 2001), 373–386.

6 THE GOLDEN HOOP

1 The best accounts are Kathleen Smith, *Moscow 1956: The Silenced Spring* (Cambridge, MA: Harvard University Press, 2017) and William Taubman, *Khrushchev: The Man and his Era* (New York: W.W. Norton & Co., 2003), 270–299.

2 K. Aimermakher et al. (eds.), *Doklad N.S. Khrushcheva o kul'te lichnosti Stalina na XX s'ezde KPSS: dokumenty* (Moscow: Rosspen, 2002), 591.

3 Anatoly Danilevsky to Mao, Aug. 12, 1957, Chinese Foreign Ministry Archive (CFMA): 109-01098-03, 19.

4 Aimermakher et al. (eds.), *Doklad N.S. Khrushcheva*, 257–264.

NOTES TO PAGES 172-178

5 Ibid., 502, 544, 594–595.

6 "Khrushchev Talk on Stalin Bares Details of Rule Based on Terror …," *New York Times,* June 1, 1956, 1.

7 John Rettie, "The Day Khrushchev Denounced Stalin," Feb. 18, 2006, BBC, http://news.bbc.co.uk/1/hi/programmes/from_our_own_correspondent/4723942.stm.

8 Memcon, N.V. Slavin and Aksel Larsen, Apr. 5–6, 1956, RGANI: f. 5, op. 28, d. 435, ll. 99–100.

9 E. Kjeldgård to the editor-in-chief of *Land og Folk,* undated (before May 9, 1956), RGANI: f. 5, op. 28, d. 435, ll. 142–147.

10 Memcon, N.V. Slavin and Aksel Larsen, June 27, 1956, RGANI: f. 5, op. 28, d. 435, ll. 222–225.

11 Memcon, N.I. Molyakov and Just Lippe, May 4, 1956, RGANI: f. 5, op. 28, d. 436, ll. 48–51.

12 Boris Ponomarev and V. Tereshkin to CC CPSU, Aug. 10, 1956, RGANI: f. 5, op. 28, d. 382, ll. 111–112.

13 Aksel Larsen to CC CPSU, June 5, 1956, RGANI: f. 5, op. 28, d. 382, ll. 54–60.

14 On Larsen's cooperation with Western intelligence, see Dansk Institut for Internationale Studier, *Danmark under den kolde krig: Den sikkerhedspolitiske situation 1945–1991,* Vol. 4 (Copenhagen: DIIS, 2005), 157–178.

15 "The Khrushchev Speech: an editorial," *The Daily Worker,* June 6, 1956, 1.

16 Memcon, S.R. Striganov and Theodore Beer, June 13–15, 1956, RGANI: f. 5, op. 28, d. 439, ll. 215–221.

17 CFMA: 109-00985-01, 165–166.

18 Shi Zhe, *Zai Lishi Juren Shenbian: Shi Zhe Huiyilu,* rev. ed. (Beijing: Zhongyang Wenxian Chubanshe, 1995), 596.

19 Ibid., 598.

20 Wu Lengxi, *Shinian Lunzhan, 1956–1966: Zhongsu Guanxi Huiyilu,* Vol. 1 (Beijing: Zhongyang Wenxian Chubanshe, 1999), 6; Liu Chongwen and Chen Shaoshou (eds.), *Liu Shaoqi Nianpu, 1898–1969,* Vol. 2 (Beijing: Zhongyang Wenxian Chubanshe, 1996), 363.

21 Wu Lengxi, *Shinian Lunzhan,* Vol. 1, 6.

22 Ibid.

23 Ibid., 15.

24 Pang Xianzhi and Jin Chongji (eds.), *Mao Zedong Zhuan, 1949–1976,* Vol. 1 (Beijing: Zhongyang Wenxian Chubanshe, 2003), 471.

25 Ibid., 476.

26 CFMA: 109-00985-01,154.

27 Pang Xianzhi and Jin Chongji (eds.), *Mao Zedong Zhuan,* Vol. 1, 469.

28 CFMA: 122-00017-02,60.

29 Pang Xianzhi and Jin Chongji (eds.), *Mao Zedong Zhuan,* Vol. 1, 474.

30 Ibid., 476.

31 Ibid., 470.

NOTES TO PAGES 179–182

32 On March 18, there was another meeting of the top leadership to discuss specifically Western broadcasts about the Soviet situation. See Liu Chongwen and Chen Shaoshou (eds.), *Liu Shaoqi Nianpu, 1898–1969*, Vol. 2, 364; Chen Yangyong and An Jianshe (eds.), *Zhou Enlai Nianpu, 1898–1976*, Vol. 1 (Beijing: Zhongyang Wenxian Chubanshe, 1997), 1043.

33 A.A. Fursenko (ed.), *Prezidium TsK KPSS, 1954–1964*, Vol. 2 (Postanovleniya, 1954–1958) (Moscow: Rosspen, 2006), 285–286. This episode is also recounted in Vladimir Kozlov and Elaine McClarnand, *Mass Uprisings in the USSR: Protest and Rebellion in the Post-Stalin Years* (Armonk, NY: M.E. Sharpe, 2002, 117–8. Zhu De himself did not come back to Beijing until April 2, after an extended trip across the USSR, to Eastern Europe, and Mongolia. See "Zhu De Nianpu (The Censor's Version)," Vol. 2 (unpublished, 1986), 96–99. For a Chinese memoir account of the incident, see Liu Xiao, *Chushi Sulian Banian* (Beijing: Zhonggong Dangshi Ziliao Chubanshe, 1998), 20–21.

34 Wu Lengxi, *Shinian Lunzhan*, Vol. 1, 6.

35 Ibid., 19.

36 Ibid., 7.

37 Ibid., 9.

38 Ibid., 20.

39 *On the Historical Experience of the Dictatorship of the Proletariat* (Beijing: Foreign Languages Press, 1959), 18.

40 Wu Lengxi, *Shinian Lunzhan*, Vol. 1, 23.

41 Report, Chinese Embassy in Moscow to Beijing, Apr. 11, 1956, CFMA: 109-01615-03, p. 20.

42 Mao Zedong's conversation with a Yugoslav delegation, Sept. 1956, in *CWIHP Bulletin*, Issue 6–7 (Winter 1995/96), 151. On Mao's earlier comments, see Sergey Radchenko and David Wolff, "New Evidence on the Mao–Stalin Relationship in 1947–1949," *CWIHP Bulletin*, Issue 16 (Fall 2007/Winter 2008), 105–182.

43 On the GDR reconstruction of Hamhung, see Rudiger Frank, "Lessons from the Past: The First Wave of Developmental Assistance to North Korea and the German Reconstruction of Hamhung," *Pacific Focus*, 23(1) (Apr. 2008), 46–74.

44 For details see Andrei Lankov, *The Real North Korea: Life and Politics in the Failed Stalinist Utopia* (New York: Oxford University Press, 2015), 15. On Soviet and Chinese advice, see Memcon, Mao Zedong and Mikoyan, Sept. 18, 1956. In the author's possession.

45 Resolution of the CC KWP, Jan. 18, 1956, RGANI: f. 5, op. 28, d. 410, ll. 44–56.

46 Andrei Lankov, *Crisis in North Korea: The Failure of De-Stalinization, 1956* (Honolulu, HI: University of Hawaii Press, 2005), 17. See also "On anti-party, factional activity of Pak Il-u," Dec. 2–3, 1955, GARF: f. 5446, op. 98, d. 721, ll. 205–210.

47 Li San-cho to CC KWP (Sept. 1956), RGANI: f. 5, op. 28, d. 410, l. 273.

48 Memcon, Mao and Mikoyan, Sept. 18, 1956. In the author's possession.

NOTES TO PAGES 182–190

49 "On the cult of personality in the DPRK," Apr. 5, 1956, RGANI: f. 5, op. 28, d. 410, ll. 57–67.

50 "On the situation in the KWP and the DPRK," Dec. 28, 1956, RGANI: f. 2, op. 28, d. 486, l. 8.

51 Memcon, V.I. Ivanov and Grigorov, May 23, 1956, RGANI: f. 5, op. 28, d. 410, l. 186.

52 Report by Leonid Brezhnev on the Third Congress of CC KWP, undated (after Apr. 1956), GARF: f. 5446, op. 98, d. 721, l. 217.

53 Report on the DPRK's coverage of the Twentieth Congress, Mar. 16, 1956, RGANI: f. 5, op. 28, d. 410, ll. 164–170.

54 Diary of V.I. Ivanov, Aug. 20, 1956, RGANI: f. 5, op. 28, d. 410, l. 350.

55 Report by Leonid Brezhnev on the Third Congress of CC KWP, undated (after Apr. 1956), GARF: f. 5446, op. 98, d. 721, ll. 212–219. This and other GARF materials in this section were obtained by Joseph Torigian who kindly shared them with this author.

56 Report on a conversation with Yi Sang-jo, Sept. 10, 1956, RGANI: f. 5, op. 28, d. 410, ll. 230–232.

57 Memcon, Mao and Mikoyan, Sept. 18, 1956. In the author's possession.

58 Ibid.

59 Ibid.

60 Memcon, Mikoyan, Peng Dehuai, and the North Korean leadership, Sept. 20, 1956, GARF: f. 5446, op. 98c, d. 718, ll. 17–34.

61 Mikoyan's note on his conversation with Kim Il Sung, Sept. 22, 1956, GARF: f. 5446, op. 98c, d. 718, l. 6.

62 Memcon, Mikoyan and Mao, Sept. 23, 1956. In the author's possession.

63 One of the best treatments is Pawel Machhewizc, *Rebellious Satellite: Poland 1956* (Washington, DC and Stanford, CA: Woodrow Wilson Center Press and Stanford University Press, 2009). For another treatment, see Mark Kramer, "The Soviet Union and the 1956 Crises in Hungary and Poland: Reassessments and New Findings," *Journal of Contemporary History*, 33(2) (Apr. 1998), 168.

64 Aleksandr Orekhov, *Sovetsky Soyuz i Pol'sha v gody "ottepeli": iz istorii sovetsko-pol'skikh otnoshenii* (Moscow: Indrik, 2005), 170–171.

65 On the danger to Soviet troops in East Germany, see especially Dictation by Anastas Mikoyan, May 28, 1960, RGASPI: f. 84, op. 3, d. 115.

66 Orekhov, *Sovetsky Soyuz i Pol'sha*, 184.

67 L.W. Gluchowski, "Poland, 1956: Khrushchev, Gomulka, and the 'Polish October,'" *CWIHP Bulletin*, Issue 5 (Spring 1995), 1, 38–49. See also Kramer, "The Soviet Union and the 1956 Crises in Hungary and Poland," 169–171.

68 Nikita Khrushchev, *Vospominaniya: vremya, lyudi, vlast'*, Vol. 2 (Moscow: Moskovskie Novosti, 1999), 196.

69 Dictation by Mikoyan, May 28, 1960, RGASPI: f. 84, op. 3, d. 115

70 Ibid. See also Taubman, *Khrushchev: The Man and his Era*, 294.

71 A.A. Fursenko (ed.), *Prezidium TsK KPSS, 1954–1964*, Vol. 1 (Moscow: Rosspen, 2003), 173.

NOTES TO PAGES 191–195

72 Charles Gati, *Failed Illusions: Moscow, Washington, Budapest, and the 1956 Hungarian Revolt* (Washington, DC and Stanford, CA: Woodrow Wilson Center Press and Stanford University Press, 2006).

73 William E. Griffith, "The Petofi Circle: Forum for Ferment in the Hungarian Thaw," *Hungarian Quarterly* (Jan. 1962), 25.

74 Mark Kramer, "New Evidence on Soviet Decision-Making and the 1956 Polish and Hungarian Crises," *CWIHP Bulletin*, Issue 8–9 (Winter 1996/97), 363.

75 Csaba Bekes, Janos M. Rainer, and Malcolm Byrne (eds.), *The 1956 Hungarian Revolution: A History in Documents* (Budapest: Central European University Press, 2003), 188–189.

76 Fursenko (ed.), *Prezidium TsK KPSS*, Vol. 1, 176–177.

77 On the Mikoyan–Suslov mission, see V.K. Volkov et al. (eds.), *Sovetsky Soyuz i vengersky krizis 1956 goda: dokumenty* (Moscow: Rosspen, 1998), 371–375, 385–390, 403–407, 416–418, 467–468.

78 Cited in Shi Zhe, "Boxiong Shijian Yu Liu Shaoqi Fangsu," *Bainian Chao*, 2 (1997), 13.

79 Ibid., 14–15. Shi Zhe's detailed account, written years after the events, coincides with the available Soviet record, a sure sign that he kept notes or otherwise had access to the Chinese version of this meeting. It is likely, however, that Shi Zhe exaggerated the impact of Liu's presentation.

80 Fursenko (ed.), *Prezidium TsK KPSS*, Vol. 1, 188.

81 Stanisław Kiryluk to Gomulka, Oct. 27, 1956. The author is grateful to Andrzej Werblan for publishing the telegram, in Andrzej Werblan, "The Polish October of 1956: Legends and Reality," in Jan Rowiński and Tytus Jaskułowski (eds.), *The Polish October 1956 in World Politics* (Warsaw: Polski Instytut Spraw Międzynarodowych, 2007), 31.

82 Shi Zhe, "Boxiong Shijian Yu Liu Shaoqi Fangsu," 16.

83 For the declaration, see Bekes, Rainer, and Byrne (eds.), *The 1956 Hungarian Revolution*, 188–189. It is worth noting that a certain "declaration" was also discussed at the Presidium meeting on October 28, though it appears to have been Nagy's declaration on the same date. Fursenko (ed.), *Prezidium TsK KPSS*, Vol. 1, 971.

84 Volkov et al. (eds.), *Sovetsky Soyuz i vengersky krizis*, 467–468.

85 Shi Zhe, "Boxiong Shijian Yu Liu Shaoqi Fangsu," 16–17.

86 Ibid., 17. Shi Zhe is the only detailed source for what may have transpired at the meeting. The Presidium transcript does not point to an argument between Liu and Khrushchev. Fursenko (ed.), *Prezidium TsK KPSS*, Vol. 1, 188.

87 Fursenko (ed.), *Prezidium TsK KPSS*, Vol. 1, 186.

88 Ibid., 195.

89 Ibid., 186, 191.

90 Aleksandr Khinshtein (ed.), *Ivan Serov: zapiski iz chemodana: tainye dnevniki pervogo predsedatelya KGB* (Moscow: Prosveshchenie, 2016), 487.

91 Fursenko (ed.), *Prezidium TsK KPSS*, Vol. 1, 192.

NOTES TO PAGES 195–204

92 Shi Zhe, "Boxiong Shijian Yu Liu Shaoqi Fangsu," 17.

93 Memcon, Gomułka and Liu Shaoqi, Nov. 20, 1960. Obtained by Douglas Selvage. Translated by Malgorzata Gnoinska. CWIHP DA: http://digitalarchive .wilsoncenter.org/document/117782.

94 Liu Xiao to Beijing, Nov. 28, 1928, Jilin Provincial Archives: 1-12-1956, 1–4.

7 TWIN CRISES

1 For a good overview, see William Taubman, *Khrushchev: The Man and His Era* (New York: W.W. Norton, 2003), 300–324.

2 For a detailed account see V. Naumov (ed.), *Georgy Zhukov: stenogramma oktiabr'skogo (1957 g.) plenuma TsK KPSS i drugie dokumenty* (Moscow: Mezhdunarodnyi Fond Demokratiya, 2001).

3 Shen Zhihua and Xia Yafeng, *Mao and the Sino-Soviet Partnership, 1945–1959: A New History* (Lanham, MD: Lexington Books, 2015), 190.

4 Memcon, Yudin and Mao, Oct. 29, 1957, *Istochnik*, 4 (1996), 110–113.

5 Cominform was disbanded in 1956, a part of the process of de-Stalinization.

6 Memcon, Gromyko and Mao, Nov. 19, 1957, AVPRF: 0100, op. 50a, p. 423, d. 1, l. 14.

7 Memcon, Yudin and Mao, Apr. 5, 1958, AVPRF: f. 0100, op. 51, p. 432, d. 6, ll. 132–33.

8 Shen and Xia, *Mao and the Sino-Soviet Partnership*, 244–247.

9 Li Zhisui, *The Private Life of Chairman Mao: The Memoirs of Mao's Personal Physician* (New York: Random House, 1994), 221.

10 Cited in Alexander Pantsov and Steven I. Levine, *Mao: The Real Story* (New York: Simon & Schuster, 2012), 445.

11 This argument is eloquently put forward by Shen and Xia, *Mao and the Sino-Soviet Partnership*, 253.

12 Suslov's speech, Dec. 17, 1957, RGANI: f. 2, op. 1, d. 279, ll. 20–21.

13 Mao's speech, Nov. 18, 1957, in N.G. Tomilina (ed.), *Nasledniki Kominterna: mezhdunarodnye soveshchaniya predstavitelei kommunisticheskikh i rabochikh partii v Moskve (noyabr' 1957): dokumenty i materialy* (Moscow: Rosspen, 2013), 374. The citation is to an unedited translation, which I edited for clarity.

14 Mao's speech, Nov. 14, 1957, ibid., 203.

15 Mao's speech, Nov. 18, 1957, ibid., 372.

16 On the need to protect stomachs, see Khrushchev's speech, May 22, 1957, in N.G. Tomilina (ed.), *Nikita Sergeyevich Khrushchev: dva tsveta vremeni*, Vol. 2 (Moscow: Rosspen, 2009), 105. On robots, see Memcon, Khrushchev and the Burmese Deputy Prime Minister, Nov. 30, 1957, RGANI: f. 52, op. 1, d. 549, l. 34.

17 Khrushchev's speech, May 22, 1957, in Tomilina (ed.), *Khrushchev: dva tsveta vremeni*, Vol. 2, 101.

18 Ibid., 102.

NOTES TO PAGES 204–210

19 Memcon, Khrushchev and Finn Mu, Apr. 23, 1958, RGANI: f. 52, op. 1, d. 575, l. 113.

20 Khrushchev, *Vospominaniya: vremya, lyudi, vlast'*, Vol. 3, 447.

21 Mao's speech at the expanded Politburo meeting, Apr. 1956, Chinese Anti-Rightist Campaign Database (1957–).

22 Memcon, Gromyko and Mao, Nov. 19, 1957.

23 Mao's speech, Nov. 18, 1957, in Tomilina (ed.), *Nasledniki Kominterna*, 371.

24 Frank Dikötter, *Mao's Great Famine: The History of China's Most Devastating Catastrophe, 1958–62* (London: Bloomsbury, 2011), 16–18.

25 Mao's speech, Jan. 11, 1958, in *Mao Zedong Sixiang Wansui [MZDSXWS], 1958–1960* (Neibu – internal circulation. No publication information), 6. In the author's possession.

26 Shen and Xia, *Mao and the Sino-Soviet Partnership*, 285.

27 Mao's speech, Mar. 20, 1958, in *MZDSXWS, 1958–1960*, 35.

28 Shen and Xia, *Mao and the Sino-Soviet Partnership*, 286.

29 Mao's remarks at an expanded meeting of Central Military Commission, June 21, 1958, *MZDSXWS, 1958–1960*, 93.

30 Yang Jisheng, *Tombstone: The Untold Story of Mao's Great Famine* (London: Penguin, 2013), 104.

31 Presidium CC CPSU Discussion on Jan. 28, 1957, in A.A. Fursenko (ed.), *Prezidium TsK KPSS, 1954–1964*, Vol. 1 (Moscow: Rosspen, 2003), 221–223, 990.

32 Khrushchev's speech, Feb. 25, 1958, RGANI: f. 2, op. 1, d. 288, ll. 1–112.

33 Mao's speech on the international situation, Sept. 5, 1958, in Ministry of Foreign Affairs, PRC (ed.), *Mao Zedong on Diplomacy* (Beijing: Foreign Languages Press, 2007), 268.

34 Yang, *Tombstone*, 107–108.

35 Aleksandr Khinshtein (ed.), *Ivan Serov: zapiski iz chemodana: tainye dnevniki pervogo predsedatelya KGB* (Moscow: Prosveshchenie, 2016), 475.

36 Mohammad Heikal, *The Cairo Documents: The Inside Story of Nasser and His Relationship with World Leaders, Rebels, and Statesmen* (New York: Doubleday, 1973), 97–98.

37 Douglas Little, "His Finest Hour? Eisenhower, Lebanon, and the 1958 Middle East Crisis," *Diplomatic History*, 20(1) (1996), 27–54; Salim Yaqub, *Containing Arab Nationalism: The Eisenhower Doctrine and the Middle East* (Chapel Hill, NC: University of North Carolina Press, 2004), 205–267.

38 Edward C. Keefer (ed.), *Foreign Relations of the United States [FRUS], 1958–1960*, Vol. 12 (Washington, DC: US Government Printing Office, 1972), Document 5.

39 Louis J. Smith (ed.), *FRUS, 1958–1960*, Vol. 11 (Washington, DC: US Government Printing Office, 1972), Document 27. Also, Yaqub, *Containing Arab Nationalism*, 224.

40 *FRUS, 1958–1960*, Vol. 11, Document 196.

41 Boris Vereshchagin, *V starom i novom Kitae: iz vospominanii diplomata* (Moscow: IDV, 1999), 119–121; Shen and Xia, *Mao and the Sino-Soviet Partnership*, 217–218.

NOTES TO PAGES 211–218

42 Shen and Xia, *Mao and the Sino-Soviet Partnership*, 313.

43 Heikal, *The Cairo Documents*, 130–133; Osgood Caruthers, "Trip Was Secret," *New York Times*, July 19, 1958, 1; Khrushchev to Nasser, Apr. 12, 1959, in V.V. Naumkin, *Blizhnevostochnyi konflikt, 1947–1967*, Vol. 2 (Moscow: Mezhdunarodnyi Fond Demokratiya, 2003), 267–275.

44 Heikal, *The Cairo Documents*, 132. See also the second conversation between Mao Zedong and Nikita Khrushchev, Aug. 1, 1958. In the author's possession.

45 "Nasser Speech Excerpts," *New York Times*, July 19, 1958, 2; Heikal, *The Cairo Documents*, 133.

46 Heikal, *The Cairo Documents*, 133.

47 Khinshtein (ed.), *Ivan Serov: zapiski iz chemodana*, 548.

48 Memcon, Khrushchev and Krishna Menon, July 21, 1958, RGANI: f. 52, op. 1, d. 562, l. 37.

49 Fursenko (ed.), *Prezidium TsK KPSS*, Vol. 1, 318–326.

50 Ibid., 210.

51 Ibid., 318–326.

52 Ibid., 325.

53 Nikolai Bulganin to Eisenhower, Dec. 10, 1957, *Pravda*, Dec. 12, 1957, 1–2.

54 See e.g. "Lord Privy Seal for the Secretary of State," Jan. 30, 1958, British National Archives: FO 371/135789. Also, Ronald D. Landa et al. (eds.), *FRUS, 1958–1960*, Vol. 7, Part 2 (Washington, DC: US Government Printing Office, 1993), Document 336.

55 *FRUS, 1958–1960*, Vol. 11, Document 213.

56 Draft letter, Khrushchev to Eisenhower, July 19, 1958, in A.A. Fursenko (ed.), *Prezidium TsK KPSS, 1954–1964*, Vol. 2 (Postanovleniya, 1954–1958) (Moscow: Rosspen, 2006), 868.

57 *FRUS, 1958–1960*, Vol. 12, Document 5.

58 Ronald D. Landa et al. (eds.), *FRUS, 1958–1960*, Vol. 10, Part 1 (Washington, DC: US Government Printing Office, 1993), Document 49.

59 Khrushchev's speech at the Polish Embassy reception, *Pravda*, July 23, 1958, 2.

60 Memcon, Mao and Yudin, July 22, 1958, in Ministry of Foreign Affairs, PRC (ed.), *Mao Zedong on Diplomacy*, 250–251.

61 Vereshchagin, *V starom i novom Kitae*, 127.

62 Fursenko (ed.), *Prezidium TsK KPSS*, Vol. 1, 326.

63 Vereshchagin, *V starom i novom Kitae*, 129.

64 *FRUS, 1958–1960*, Vol. 11, Document 230.

65 Memcon, Yudin, Zhou Enlai, and Peng Zhen, July 28, 1958, AVPRF: f. 0100, op. 51, d. 6, p. 432, ll. 170–172. The author is grateful to Lorenz M. Lüthi for sharing a copy of this record.

66 Memcon, Khrushchev and Mao, July 31, 1958. In the author's possession.

67 Memcon Mao and Khrushchev, Aug. 1, 1958. In the author's possession.

68 Memcon, Khrushchev and Mao, Aug. 1, 1958. In the author's possession.

69 Ibid.

NOTES TO PAGES 218–225

70 Memcon, Gromyko and Mao, Nov. 19, 1957, AVPRF: 0100, op. 50a, p. 423, d. 1, l. 8.

71 Memcon, Mao and Khrushchev, Aug. 1, 1958. In the author's possession.

72 Memcon, Khrushchev and Mao, Aug. 1, 1958. In the author's possession.

73 Ibid.

74 Memcon, Khrushchev and Mao, Aug. 2, 1958. In the author's possession.

75 Ibid.

76 Fursenko (ed.), *Prezidium TsK KPSS*, Vol. 1, 328–333. On Khrushchev's concern of sitting in the same room with Chiang Kai-shek, see also *FRUS, 1958–1960*, Vol. 10, Part 1, Document 54.

77 Adlai Stevenson, "Khrushchev Stresses Ties to U.S., Stevenson Says," *New York Times*, Aug. 28, 1958, 1, 6.

78 "UN Adopts Arabs' Plan for Hammarskjold Visit; Vote is 80-0; Session Ends," *New York Times*, Aug. 22, 1958, 1–3.

79 Michael Szonyi, *Cold War Island: Quemoy on the Front Line* (Cambridge University Press, 2008), 64–78.

80 Shen and Xia, *Mao and the Sino-Soviet Partnership*, 321–322.

81 Mao to Peng Dehuai, July 27, 1958, in Zhonggong zhongyang wenxian yanjiushi, Zhongguo renmin jiefangjun junshi kexueyuan (eds.), *Jianguo Yilai Mao Zedong Junshi Wengao*, Vol. 2 (Beijing: Junshi Kexue Chubanshe & Zhongyang Wenxian Chubanshe, 2010), 407.

82 Interestingly, this was exactly the American impression, so one has to conclude that Mao's ploy worked. Harriet Dashiell Schwar (ed.), *FRUS, 1958–1960*, Vol. 19 (Washington, DC: US Government Printing Office, 1996), Document 63.

83 Shen and Xia, *Mao and the Sino-Soviet Partnership*, 323.

84 For a thorough exposition of this argument, see Chen Jian, *Mao's China and the Cold War* (Chapel Hill, NC: University of North Carolina Press, 2000).

85 Li, *The Private Life of Chairman Mao*, 261.

86 *FRUS, 1958–1960*, Vol. 19, Document 63.

87 Jacob Van Staaveren, *Air Operations in the Taiwan Crisis of 1958* (USAF Historical Division Liaison Office, 1962). Obtained by the National Security Archive: http://nsarchive.gwu.edu/nukevault/ebb249/doc11.pdf.

88 *FRUS, 1958–1960*, Vol. 19, Document 62.

89 Bernard C. Nalty, *The Air Force Role in Five Crises* (USAF Historical Division Liaison Office, 1968), 19, 24. Obtained by the National Security Archive.

90 *FRUS, 1958–1960*, Vol. 19, Document 69.

91 Ibid., Document 82.

92 Cited in Vladislav Zubok and Konstantin Pleshakov, *Inside the Kremlin's Cold War: From Stalin to Khrushchev* (Cambridge, MA: Harvard University Press, 1996), 225.

93 Pang Xianzhi et al. (eds.), *Mao Zedong Nianpu*, Vol. 3 (Beijing: Zhongyang Wenxian Chubanshe, 2013), 441.

94 Mao saw Gromyko on the night of Sept. 6, and the Chinese submitted their comments on Sept. 7. See ibid., 439–440. For a useful discussion of Gromyko's trip to China see Chen, *Mao's China and the Cold War*, 188–189.

642

NOTES TO PAGES 225–233

95 *FRUS, 1958–1960*, Vol. 19, Document 74.

96 Tillman Durdin, "Shelling of Quemoy is Halted," *New York Times*, Sept. 7, 1958, 1–2.

97 Khrushchev's note, with the draft letter to Mao, Sept. 19, 1958, RGANI: f. 52, op. 1, d. 351, ll. 137–140.

98 Zubok and Pleshakov, *Inside the Kremlin's Cold War*, 225. Also, Vladislav Zubok, "Khrushchev's Nuclear Promise to Beijing during the Crisis," *CWIHP Bulletin*, Issue 6–7 (Winter 1995), 219.

99 Pang et al. (eds.), *Mao Zedong Nianpu*, Vol. 3, 438–439.

100 Khrushchev's dictation, Sept. 19, 1958, RGANI: f. 52, op. 1, d. 351, ll. 145–150.

101 Memcon, Mao, Murilo Marrequin, and Maria Graca Dutra, Sept. 2, 1958. In the author's possession.

102 Memcon, Khrushchev and Mohammed al-Kuni, May 22, 1959, RGANI: f. 52, op. 1, d. 561, l. 29.

103 Memcon, Khrushchev and an Iraqi delegation, Feb. 26, 1959, RGANI: f. 52, op. 1, d. 566, l. 32.

8 KILLING FLIES

1 Odd Arne Westad (ed.), *Brothers in Arms: The Rise and Fall of the Sino-Soviet Alliance, 1945–1963* (Washington, DC and Stanford, CA: Woodrow Wilson Press and Stanford University Press, 1998), 22.

2 CC SED to N.S. Khrushchev, May 13, 1958, in A.A. Fursenko (ed.), *Prezidium TsK KPSS, 1954–1964*, Vol. 2 (Postanovleniya, 1954–1958) (Moscow: Rosspen, 2006), 792–806. See also Hope Harrison, "Ulbricht and the Concrete 'Rose': New Archival Evidence on the Dynamics of Soviet East German Relations and the Berlin Crisis, 1958–61," CWIHP Working Paper 5 (May 1993).

3 Memcon, Khrushchev and Frank Roberts, July 2, 1961, RGANI: f. 52, op. 1, d. 553, ll. 99–115.

4 Memcon, Khrushchev and Ulbricht, Mar. 31, 1961, in M. Yu. Prozumenshchikov et al. (eds.), *Vensky val's kholodnoi voiny: vokrug vstrechi N.S. Khrushcheva i Dzh. F. Kennedi v 1961 godu v Vene* (Moscow: Rosspen, 2011), 143.

5 Memcon, Khrushchev and Nehru, Sept. 9, 1961, RGANI: f. 52, op. 1, d. 563, l. 207.

6 Memcon, Khrushchev and Władysław Gomułka, Nov. 10, 1958 in Douglas Selvage, "Khrushchev's Berlin Ultimatum: New Evidence from the Polish Archives," *CWIHP Bulletin*, Issue 11 (Winter 1998), 200.

7 Khrushchev's speech, Nov. 10, 1958, *Pravda*, Nov. 11, 1958, 2.

8 Anastas Mikoyan, *Tak bylo: razmyshleniya o minuvshem* (Moscow: Vagrius, 1999), ch. 49.

9 Ronald D. Landa et al. (eds.), *Foreign Relations of the United States [FRUS], 1958–1960*, Vol. 10, Part 1 (Washington, DC: US Government Printing Office, 1993), Document 59. For Mikoyan's description of his mission as a "holiday," see Charles

NOTES TO PAGES 234–239

S. Sampson (ed.), *FRUS, 1958–1960*, Vol. 8 (Washington, DC: US Government Printing Office, 1993), Document 121.

10 *FRUS, 1958–1960*, Vol. 8, Document 121.

11 Ibid., Document 137.

12 Presidium discussion, Jan. 24, 1959, in A.A. Fursenko (ed.), *Prezidium TsK KPSS, 1954–1964*, Vol. 1 (Moscow: Rosspen, 2003), 345.

13 Fursenko and Naftali argue there was a difference of opinions on Berlin between Mikoyan and Khrushchev; however, the evidence of such disagreement is scant. See A.A. Fursenko and T. Naftali, *Khrushchev's Cold War: The Inside Story of an American Adversary* (New York: Norton, 2006), 220.

14 For accounts of the visit, see ibid., 218–222; William Taubman, *Khrushchev: The Man and his Era* (New York: W.W. Norton & Co., 2003), 410–412.

15 Memcon, Mikoyan and Macmillan, Mar. 1, 1959, GARF: f. R5446, op. 120, d. 1384, l. 118.

16 Memcon, Macmillan and Khrushchev, Feb. 25, 1959, British National Archive: PREM 11/2690.

17 Memcon, Macmillan and Khrushchev, Feb. 26, 1959, ibid.

18 Memcon, Selwyn Lloyd and Gromyko, Mar. 1, 1959, ibid.

19 Letter, Macmillan to Adenauer, Mar. 2, 1959, ibid.

20 *FRUS, 1958–1960*, Vol. 10, Part 1, Document 75.

21 Memcon, Khrushchev and Ho Chi Minh, July 3, 1959, RGANI: f. 52, op. 1, d. 555, ll. 89–92.

22 *FRUS, 1958–1960*, Vol. 10, Part 1, Document 99.

23 Memcon, Khrushchev and Nixon, July 24, 1959, RGANI: f. 52, op. 1, d. 580, l. 133.

24 Recording of the "Kitchen Debate," July 24, 1959, www.youtube.com /watch?v=-CvQOuNecy4.

25 Memcon, Khrushchev and a GDR delegation, June 9, 1959. Obtained and translated by Hope M. Harrison. CWIHP DA: https://digitalarchive.wilsoncenter .org/document/112000.

26 Khrushchev's speech to voters, Feb. 24, 1959, *Pravda*, Feb. 25, 1959, 2.

27 *FRUS, 1958–1960*, Vol. 10, Part 1, Document 85.

28 Historians diverge on whether Ike deliberately invited Khrushchev or whether Murphy misunderstood his instructions. See Taubman, *Khrushchev*, 415–416.

29 Cited ibid., 415.

30 Nikita Khrushchev, *Vospominaniya: vremya, lyudi, vlast'*, Vol. 2 (Moscow: Moskovskie Novosti, 1999), 294. Also, Taubman, *Khrushchev*, 423–424.

31 Memcon, Antonín Novotný and Mao, Oct. 1, 1959, Czech National Archive: ÚV – KSČ, dílčí fond kancelář Antonína Novotného II – zahraničí ČLR, karton 82. The author is grateful to Oldřich Tůma and his team in Prague for sharing this document.

32 Khrushchev's memorandum for the record, Aug. 10, 1959, RGANI: f. 52, op. 1, d. 598, ll. 51–54.

33 Ibid., ll. 55–60.

NOTES TO PAGES 239–243

34 Ibid.

35 *Pravda*, Sept. 10, 1959, 1.

36 On Kozlov's airplane, Harry Schwartz, "Kozlov Flies to New York From Moscow in 11 Hours," *New York Times*, June 29, 1959, 1.

37 James Reston, "Reserved Reception for Khrushchev Unusual for Demonstrative Capital," *New York Times*, Sept. 16, 1959, 1.

38 Henry Cabot Lodge, *The Storm Has Many Eyes* (New York: W.W. Norton & Co., 1973), 165.

39 Taubman, *Khrushchev*, 432–433.

40 Harrison Salisbury, "Khrushchev Threatens to Return Home," *New York Times*, Sept. 20, 1959, 1.

41 Khrushchev, *Vospominaniya: vremya, lyudi, vlast'*, Vol. 2, 298.

42 Taubman, *Khrushchev*, 421.

43 Khrushchev, *Vospominaniya: vremya, lyudi, vlast'*, Vol. 2, 299.

44 Memcon, Khrushchev and Llewellyn Thompson, Sept. 8, 1960, RGANI: f. 52, op. 1, d. 581, l. 46.

45 Memcon, Liu Shaoqi and S.F. Antonov, Oct. 10, 1958. Kindly shared with the author by Shen Zhihua.

46 Report on the economic situation in the PRC, July 2, 1959, AVPRF: f. 5, op. 49, d. 243, ll. 1–8.

47 Memcon, Six socialist delegations and Mao, Oct. 2, 1958. In the author's possession.

48 Deng Xiaoping's speech, Mar. 20, 1959. Sichuan Provincial Archives: 001-1-1615.

49 Lorenz M. Lüthi, *The Sino-Soviet Split: Cold War in the Communist World* (Princeton University Press, 2008), 109.

50 Frank Dikötter, *Mao's Great Famine: The History of China's Most Devastating Catastrophe, 1958–62* (London: Bloomsbury, 2011), 79.

51 Ibid., 76.

52 Ibid., 80.

53 Mao's comments at a meeting in Shanghai, Mar. 25, 1959, Gansu Provincial Archives: 91-18-5-494, 46.

54 Dikotter, *Mao's Great Famine*, 114–115.

55 Li Ping and Ma Zhisun (eds.), *Zhou Enlai Nianpu, 1949–1976*, Vol. 2 (Beijing: Zhongyang Wenxian Chubanshe, 1997), 203

56 Mao's comments on a CCP instruction, Feb. 13, 1959, Zhonggong zhongyang wenxian yanjiushi, *Jianguo Yilai Mao Zedong Wengao [JGYLMZDWG]*, Vol. 8 (Beijing: Zhongyang Wenxian Chubanshe, 1993), 41.

57 Deng Xiaoping's speech, Mar. 20, 1959. Sichuan Provincial Archives: 001-1-1615.

58 Pang Xianzhi et al. (eds.), *Mao Zedong Nianpu*, Vol. 4 (Beijing: Zhongyang Wenxian Chubanshe, 2013), 71.

59 Fursenko (ed.), *Prezidium TsK KPSS*, Vol. 1, 362; A.A. Fursenko (ed.), *Prezidium TsK KPSS*, Vol. 3 (Postanovleniya, 1959–1964) (Moscow: Rosspen, 2008), 40–54;

NOTES TO PAGES 243–249

N.G. Tomilina (ed.), *Nikita Sergeyevich Khrushchev: dva tsveta vremeni*, Vol. 2 (Moscow: Rosspen, 2009), 150.

60 Memcon, Khrushchev and a GDR delegation, June 9, 1959. Obtained and translated by Hope M. Harrison. CWIHP DA: https://digitalarchive.wilsoncenter.org/document/112000.

61 Memcon, Khrushchev and a Ghanian delegation, Aug. 5, 1960, RGANI: f. 52, op. 1, d. 556, l. 21.

62 The author's interview with D. Molomjamts, Ulaanbaatar, 2003.

63 Li Ping and Ma Zhisun (eds.), *Zhou Enlai Nianpu, 1949–1976*, Vol. 2, 205.

64 Deng Xiaoping's speech, Mar. 20, 1959, Sichuan Provincial Archives: 001-1-1615.

65 Memcon, Khrushchev and Ho Chi Minh, July 3, 1959, RGANI: f. 52, op. 1, d. 555, ll. 89–92.

66 *Pravda*, July 21, 1959, 1.

67 *JGYLMZDWG*, Vol. 8, 358–361.

68 Jun Chang and Jon Halliday, *Mao: The Unknown Story* (New York: Anchor Books, 2006), 432–444.

69 Memcon, Mao and Kim Il Sung, May 21, 1960. In the author's possession.

70 Memcon, Mao and Sirimavo Bandarnaike, June 28, 1972. In the author's possession.

71 *Pravda*, Oct. 1, 1959, 2.

72 David P. Nickles (ed.), *FRUS, 1969–1976*, Vol. 18 (Washington, DC: US Government Printing Office, 2007), Document 58.

73 Memcon, G.C. Pajetta and Mao, Apr. 19, 1959, Fondazione Instituto Gramsci, APC, 1959, Partito, Cina, mf. 464/pp. 2903–2908.

74 Cited in Neville Maxwell, *India's China War* (New York: Pantheon Books, 1970), 120–121.

75 Memcon, Sarvepalli Radhakrishnan and Zhou Enlai et al., Apr. 21, 1960, NMML: P.N. Haksar Papers, Subject file 26.

76 *Pravda*, Sept. 10, 1959, 3.

77 Memcon, Khrushchev and Mao. Translated by Vladislav M. Zubok. CWIHP DA: https://digitalarchive.wilsoncenter.org/document/112088.

78 The Russian term is *prisposoblenchestvo*, which lends itself to several possible translations. My translation – "unprincipled accommodation" – comes from the term Chen Yi used, *qianjiuzhuyi*.

79 Memcon, Khrushchev and Mao. Translated by Vladislav M. Zubok. CWIHP DA: https://digitalarchive.wilsoncenter.org/document/112088.

80 Cited in Sergey Radchenko, *Two Suns in the Heavens: The Sino-Soviet Struggle for Supremacy* (Washington, DC and Stanford, CA: Woodrow Wilson Press and Stanford University Press, 2009), 12.

81 Khrushchev's speech in Vladivostok on Oct. 6, 1959, *Pravda*, Oct. 9, 1959, 1.

82 Shen Zhihua and Xia Yafeng, *Mao and the Sino-Soviet Partnership, 1945–1959: A New History* (Lanham, MD: Lexington Books, 2015), 332.

83 Memcon, Stepan Chervonenko and Mao, Feb. 23, 1963, AVPRF: f. 0100, op. 56, d. 7, ll. 98–121.

NOTES TO PAGES 251–256

9 THE SPIRIT OF CAMP DAVID

1 Khrushchev to the CC CPSU Presidium, Dec. 8, 1959, RGANI: f. 52, op. 1, d. 351, ll. 3–12.
2 A.A. Fursenko (ed.), *Prezidium TsK KPSS, 1954–1964*, Vol. 1 (Moscow: Rosspen, 2003), 425.
3 For a discussion of the use and abuse of Mikoyan's alleged statement to this effect see Sergey Radchenko, "On Hedgehogs and Passions: History, Hearsay, and Hotchpotch in the Writing on the Cuban Missile Crisis," in Len Scott, R. Gerald Hughes (eds.), *Cuban Missile Crisis: A Critical Reappraisal* (London: Routledge, 2015), 189.
4 Nikita Khrushchev, *Vospominaniya: vremya, lyudi, vlast'*, Vol. 2 (Moscow: Moskovskie Novosti, 1999), 380–421.
5 A.D. Chernev, "N.S. Khrushchev i Sharl' de Goll'. Vstrechi v Parizhe. 1960," *Istorichesky Arkhiv*, 1 (1996), 27–40 and 2 (1996), 105–132. The French version (which has two more conversations compared with the Russian) in Commission de Publication des Documents Diplomatiques Français (ed.), *Documents Diplomatiques Français, 1960*, Vol. 17, Tome 1 (Paris: Imprimerie Nationale, 1995), 356–398.
6 Fursenko (ed.), *Prezidium TsK KPSS, 1954–1964*, Vol. 1, 422.
7 Aleksei Adzhubei, *Krushenie illyuzii: vremya v sobytiyakh i litsakh* (Moscow: Interbuk, 1991), 229.
8 Mikhail Suslov's report, RGANI: f. 2, op. 1, d. 133, ll. 92–133.
9 Memcon, Mao and Kim Il Sung, May 21, 1960. In the author's possession.
10 Memcon, Krim Belkachem and Mao, May 17, 1960. A copy of his document (from the Algerian archives) was kindly shared by Matthew Connelly.
11 Ibid.
12 Memcon, Mao and Blas Roca Calderio, Apr. 28, 1960. In the author's possession.
13 "Liening zhuyi wansui – jinian liening dansheng jiushi zhounian," *Hongqi*, Apr. 16, 1960. A reference to Mao's editing of the same is Pang Xianzhi et al. (eds.), *Mao Zedong Nianpu*, Vol. 4 (Beijing: Zhongyang Wenxian Chubanshe, 2013), 376. For detailed discussion see Lorenz M. Lüthi, *The Sino-Soviet Split: Cold War in the Communist World* (Princeton University Press, 2008), 160–163.
14 Ibid., 163.
15 Memcon, Khrushchev and Walter Nash, Apr. 20, 1960, RGANI: f. 52, op. 1, d. 575, ll. 82–99.
16 Michael R. Belschloss, *May-Day: Eisenhower, Khrushchev and the U-2 Affair* (New York: Harper & Row, 1986), 15.
17 Sergei Khrushchev, *Nikita Khrushchev: rozhdenie sverkhderzhavy* (Moscow: Veche, 2019), 311.
18 Memcon, Khrushchev and Koča Popović, July 8, 1961, RGANI: f. 52, op. 1, d. 594, ll. 129–141.
19 Statement by Secretary of State Herter, May 9, 1960, in *Background Documents on Events Incident to Summit Conference* (Washington, DC: US Government Printing Office, 1960), 18.

NOTES TO PAGES 256–262

20 Transcript of President Eisenhower's press conference, May 11, 1960, ibid., 19.

21 M. Yu. Prozumenshchikov et al. (eds.), *Vensky val's kholodnoi voiny: vokrug vstrechi N.S. Khrushcheva i Dzh. F. Kennedi v 1961 godu v Vene* (Moscow: Rosspen, 2011), 30–38.

22 Harrison Evans Salisbury, *Disturber of the Peace: Memoirs of a Foreign Correspondent* (London: Unwin Hyman, 1989), 175.

23 Khrushchev, *Nikita Khrushchev: rozhdenie sverkhderzhavy,* 312.

24 Oleg Troyanovsky, *Cherez gody i rasstoyaniya* (Moscow: Vagrius, 1997), 221.

25 Cited in Belschloss, *May-Day,* 63.

26 Khrushchev's comments at the party plenum, May 4, 1960, RGANI: f. 2, op. 1, d. 451, ll. 21–23.

27 Memcon, Mikoyan and Sen. John S. Cooper, Dec. 10, 1960, GARF: f. R5446, op. 120, d. 1526, l. 24.

28 Khrushchev's comments at the party plenum, May 4, 1960, RGANI: f. 2, op. 1, d. 451, ll. 21–23.

29 Troyanovsky, *Cherez gody i rasstoyaniya,* 225–226.

30 Memcon, Khrushchev and de Gaulle, May 15, 1960, RGANI: f. 52, op. 1, d. 631, ll. 78–82.

31 Memcon, Khrushchev and Macmillan, May 15, 1960, RGANI: f. 52, op. 1, d. 631, ll. 83–85.

32 Belschloss, *May-Day,* 284–285.

33 Prozumenchshikov et al. (eds.), *Vensky val's,* 52–65.

34 Peter Catterall (ed.), *The Macmillan Diaries,* Vol. 2 (London: Pan Books, 2011), 298.

35 Vernon A. Walters, *Silent Missions* (Garden City, NY: Doubleday, 1978), 343.

36 Catterall (ed.), *The Macmillan Diaries,* Vol. 3, 298.

37 Ibid., 297.

38 Ibid., 299.

39 Memcon, Stepan Chervonenko and Deng Xiaoping, May 17, 1960, RGANI: f. 5, op. 49, d. 327, ll. 129–133.

40 Memcon, Mao and Kim Il Sung, May 21, 1960. In the author's possession.

41 Lüthi, *The Sino-Soviet Split,* 165.

42 Pang et al. (eds.), *Mao Zedong Nianpu,* Vol. 4, 399–400; Wu Lengxi, *Shinian Lunzhan, 1956–1966: Zhongsu Guanxi Huiyilu,* Vol. 1 (Beijing: Zhongyang Wenxian Chubanshe, 1999), 270–273.

43 Lüthi, *The Sino-Soviet Split,* 167–168.

44 Mao Zedong's interventions at the Shanghai Party Conference, June 15 and June 18, 1960. In *Mao Zedong Sixiang Wansui, 1958–1960* (Neibu – internal circulation. No publication information), 291–292.

45 Lüthi, *The Sino-Soviet Split,* 169–173.

46 Khrushchev's comments at a party plenum, July 16, 1960, RGANI: f. 2, op. 1, d. 476, l. 231.

47 Memcon, Stepan Chervonenko and Chen Yi, Aug. 4, 1960, AVPRF: f. 0100, op. 53, d. 8, ll. 204–218. Kindly shared with the author by O.A. Westad.

NOTES TO PAGES 262–266

48 Ana Lalaj, Christian F. Ostermann, and Ryan Gage (eds.), "'Albania is not Cuba': Sino-Albanian Summits and the Sino-Soviet Split," *CWIHP Bulletin*, Issue 16 (Fall 2007/Winter 2008), 183.

49 Memcon, Albanian and Soviet delegations, Nov. 12, 1960. Obtained by Ana Lalaj. Translated by Enkel Daljani. CWIHP DA: https://digitalarchive.wilsoncenter.org /document/117494.

50 Memcon, Khrushchev and Ho Chi Minh, Aug. 17, 1961, RGANI: f. 52, op. 1, d. 555, ll. 125–150.

51 Troyanovsky, *Cherez gody*, 229.

52 Taubman, *Khrushchev*, 472–479.

53 Dmitry Volkogonov, *Sem' vozhdei: galereya liderov SSSR*, Vol. 1 (Moscow: Novosti, 1995), 404.

54 Suzanne E. Coffman and Charles S. Sampson (eds.), *Foreign Relations of the United States [FRUS], 1958–1960*, Vol. 2 (Washington, DC: US Government Printing Office, 1991), Document 187.

55 Sergei Mazov, "Soviet Aid to the Gizenga Government in the Former Belgian Congo (1960–61), as Reflected in Russian Archives," *Cold War History*, 7(3) (2007), 425–437.

56 Harriet Dashiell Schwar and Stanley Shaloff (eds.), *FRUS, 1958–1960*, Vol. 14 (Washington, DC: US Government Printing Office, 1992), Document 140.

57 Tim Weiner, *Legacy of Ashes: The History of the CIA* (New York: Doubleday, 2007), 162–163. For an excellent but heavily excised documentary account, see Nina D. Howland, David C. Humphrey, and Harriet D. Schwar (eds.), *FRUS, 1964–1968*, Vol. 23 (Washington, DC: US Government Printing Office, 2013). "Joe from Paris" is from ibid., 36.

58 Khrushchev's reflections on the Congo, Sept. 17, 1960, RGANI: f. 51, op. 1, d. 598, ll. 63–64. On Ham for boor see Taubman, *Khrushchev*, 477.

59 Memcon, Khrushchev and Nasser, Sept. 24, 1960, V.V. Naumkin, *Blizhnevostochnyi konflikt, 1947–1967* [*BK*], Vol. 2 (Moscow: Mezhdunarodnyi Fond Demokratiya, 2003), 335.

60 Memcon, Khrushchev and John McCloy, July 27, 1961, RGANI: f. 52, op. 1, d. 581, ll. 144–150.

61 *FRUS, 1958–1960*, Vol. 2, Document 190.

62 That is, according to the *New York Times* story by Benjamin Welles. William Taubman's research yielded contradictory evidence as to whether the banging took place, though there seems no doubt that the shoe did come off Khrushchev's foot at one point, and ended up on his desk. See William Taubman, "Did He Bang It?: Nikita Khrushchev and the Shoe," *International Herald Tribune*, July 26, 2003.

63 Benjamin Welles, "Khrushchev Bangs His Shoe on Desk," *New York Times*, Oct. 13, 1960, 1, 14.

64 Memcon, Khrushchev and Nasser, Sept. 24, 1960, in V.V. Naumkin, *Blizhnevostochnyi konflikt, 1947–1967*, Vol. 2 (Moscow: Mezhdunarodnyi Fond Demokratiya, 2003), 338.

NOTES TO PAGES 267–275

65 Fursenko (ed.), *Prezidium TsK KPSS, 1954–1964,* Vol. 1, 445.

66 Khrushchev, *Vospominaniya: vremya, lyudi, vlast',* Vol. 3, 269.

67 E. Bruce Geelhoed and Anthony O. Edmonds (eds.), *The Macmillan–Eisenhower Correspondence, 1957–1969* (Houndmills: Palgrave Macmillan, 2005), 385.

68 Khrushchev, *Vospominaniya: vremya, lyudi, vlast',* Vol. 3, 269; *FRUS, 1958–1960,* Vol. 2, Document 191.

69 *FRUS, 1958–1960,* Vol. 2, Document 191.

70 Memcon, Edgar Snow and Mao, Oct. 22, 1960, Edgar Snow papers, University of Kansas: Box 15, Folder 188.

10 BERLIN

1 "Vybory v SShA," *Pravda,* Nov. 9, 1960, 4.

2 Memcon, Khrushchev and Llewellyn Thompson, Oct. 8, 1960, RGANI: f. 52, op. 1, d. 581, l. 47; Memcon, Khrushchev and K.P.S. Menon, May 25, 1961, RGANI: f. 52, op. 1, d. 563, l. 26.

3 Khrushchev's speech at a Meeting of the Warsaw Pact Political Consultative Committee, Mar. 29, 1961, https://phpisn.ethz.ch/lory1.ethz.ch/collections /colltopic9605.html?lng=en&id=17897&navinfo=14465.

4 Ibid.

5 "Rech' prezidenta Dzh. Kennedi," *Pravda,* Jan. 22, 1961, 5.

6 Nikita Khrushchev, *Vospominaniya: vremya, lyudi, vlast',* Vol. 2 (Moscow: Moskovskie Novosti, 1999), 480.

7 Memcon, Stepan Chervonenko and Deng Xiaoping, Sept. 12, 1960. Document kindly shared with the author by Shen Zhihua.

8 Short version of the negotiations between CC CPSU and CC CCP, Sept. 1960, Stiftung Archiv der Parteien- und Massenorganisationen im Bundesarchiv, Berlin: JIV 2/202–280, Bd. 3. Translated by Christian Ostermann; also, Suslov's report, Jan. 12, 1961, RGANI: f. 2, op. 1, d. 495, l. 35.

9 Suslov's report, Jan. 12, 1961, RGANI: f. 2, op. 1, d. 495, l. 40.

10 Khrushchev's remarks at a reception, Oct. 22, 1960, RGANI: f. 52, op. 1, d. 450, ll. 11–12.

11 Ibid., l. 13.

12 Suslov's report, Jan. 12, 1961, RGANI: f. 2, op. 1, d. 495, l. 51.

13 Ibid., ll. 56–57.

14 Pang Xianzhi et al. (eds.), *Mao Zedong Nianpu,* Vol. 4 (Beijing: Zhongyang Wenxian Chubanshe, 2013), 480.

15 Ibid., 492–493.

16 Lorenz M. Lüthi, *The Sino-Soviet Split: Cold War in the Communist World* (Princeton University Press, 2008), 187. Yang Jisheng, *Tombstone: The Untold Story of Mao's Great Famine* (London: Penguin, 2013), 436–437.

17 Yang, *Tombstone,* 436–437; Pang et al. (eds.), *Mao Zedong Nianpu,* Vol. 4, 488–489.

NOTES TO PAGES 275–280

18 Memcon, Stepan Chervonenko and Mao, Dec. 26, 1960, AVPRF: f. 0100, op. 55, p. 454, d. 9, l. 102.

19 Pang et al. (eds.), *Mao Zedong Nianpu*, Vol. 4, 491.

20 Memcon, Suslov and Severo Aguirre del Cristo, Feb. 12, 1959, RGANI: f. 81, op. 1, d. 333, ll. 3–9.

21 A.A. Fursenko and T. Naftali, *"One Hell of a Gamble": Khrushchev, Castro, and Kennedy, 1958–1964* (New York: W.W. Norton & Co., 1997), 5–18.

22 Memcon, Suslov, Ponomarev, and Anibal Escalante, Nov. 8, 1959, RGANI: f. 81, op. 1, d. 333, ll. 25–40.

23 Sino-Soviet Bloc Economic Activities in Underdeveloped Areas [SSBEAUA], January 1–March 30, 1960, www.cia.gov/readingroom/docs/CIA-RDP80 -00006A000100020034-7.pdf. For an interesting first-hand account of Mikoyan's Feb. 1960 visit, see Sergo Mikoyan, *Anatomiya karibskogo krizisa* (Moscow: Akademiya, 2006), 54–84; also, Sergo Mikoyan and Svetlana Savraskaya, *The Soviet Cuban Missile Crisis: Castro, Mikoyan, Kennedy, Khrushchev, and the Missiles of November* (Washington, DC: Woodrow Wilson Center Press, 2012).

24 SSBEAUA, July 18, 1960, www.cia.gov/readingroom/docs/CIA-RDP92B01090 R000700010116-2.pdf.

25 Stephen E. Ambrose, *Eisenhower: The President*, Vol. 2: *1952–1969* (London: George Allen & Unwin, 1984), 557.

26 James G. Hershberg, "New Russian Evidence on Soviet–Cuban Relations, 1960–61 When Nikita Met Fidel, the Bay of Pigs, and Assassination Plotting," CWIHP Working Paper 90 (Feb. 2019).

27 Memcon, Khrushchev and Castro, Sept. 20, 1960, RGANI: f. 52, op. 1, d. 512, ll. 2–5. Obtained by James G. Hershberg. Translated by Svetlana Savranskaya.

28 Charles S. Sampson (ed.), *Foreign Relations of the United States [FRUS], 1961–1963*, Vol. 6 (Washington, DC: US Government Printing Office, 1996), 1074.

29 Memorandum of conversation between Aníbal Escalante, Manuel Lusardo, Ernesto [Che] Guevara, Anastas Mikoyan, Mikhail Suslov, Alexey Kosygin, and Boris Ponomarev, Moscow, Oct. 31, 1960, https://nsarchive.gwu.edu /document/29391-document-1-memorandum-conversation-between-anibal-esc alante-manuel-lusardo-ernesto. Obtained and translated by S. Savranskaya.

30 Memcon, Mao and Che Guevara, Nov. 19, 1960, CMFA: 202-00098-01, 1–14. Obtained by Sergey Radchenko. Translated by Zhang Qian.

31 Memcon, Zhou Enlai and Che Guevara, Nov. 18, 1960, CFMA: 204-00098-02,1–16. Obtained by Sergey Radchenko. Translated by Zhang Qian.

32 Khrushchev's reflections on Congo, Feb. 18, 1961, RGANI: f. 52, op. 1, d. 346, ll. 106–113.

33 Information for Soviet ambassadors, undated (Apr. 1961), RGANI: f. 3, op. 16, d. 468, l. 50.

34 For an overview, see e.g. Serhy Plokhy, *Nuclear Folly* (New York: W.W. Norton, 2021), 12–18.

35 *FRUS, 1961–1963*, Vol. 6, Document 9.

NOTES TO PAGES 280–286

36 Ibid., Document 10.

37 Ibid.

38 Ibid., Document 11. For Khrushchev's dictation, on Apr. 21, 1961, RGANI: f. 52, op. 1, d. 644, ll. 110–116.

39 *FRUS, 1961–1963*, Vol. 6, Document 11.

40 Cited in James G. Hershberg, "New Russian Evidence on Soviet–Cuban Relations, 1960–61," 41.

41 Memcon, Khrushchev and K.P.S. Menon, May 25, 1961, RGANI: f. 52, op. 1, d. 563, l. 27.

42 Hope Harrison, *Driving the Soviets up the Wall: Soviet–East German Relations, 1953–1961* (Princeton University Press, 2003), 158.

43 Ibid., 154.

44 Memcon, Khrushchev and Ulbricht, Nov. 30, 1960. Translated by Hope Harrison. CWIHP DA: https://digitalarchive.wilsoncenter.org/document/record-meeting-comrade-ns-khrushchev-comrade-w-ulbricht. Also, Frederick Kempe, *Berlin 1961: Kennedy, Khruschev, and the Most Dangerous Place on Earth* (London: Penguin, 2012), 46–48.

45 Ulbricht's speech, Mar. 29, 1961, https://phpisn.ethz.ch/kms2.isn.ethz.ch/serviceengine/Files/PHP/17895/ipublicationdocument_singledocument/a835f2a8-accb-4940-a850-470454a60f3a/de/Speech_Ulbricht_1961_3.pdf. Harrison, *Driving the Soviets Up the Wall*, 169–170.

46 Khrushchev's speech at a Warsaw Pact meeting, Mar. 29, 1961, RGANI: f. 10, op. 3, d. 6, ll. 1–84.

47 Ibid.

48 Memcon, Khrushchev and Ulbricht, Mar. 31, 1961, in M. Yu. Prozumenshchikov et al. (eds.), *Vensky val's kholodnoi voiny: vokrug vstrechi N.S. Khrushcheva i Dzh. F. Kennedi v 1961 godu v Vene* (Moscow: Rosspen, 2011), 143.

49 Memcon, Khrushchev and Nehru, Sept. 6, 1961, RGANI: f. 52, op. 1, d. 563, l. 60.

50 Memcon, Khrushchev and Hans Kroll, Apr. 24, 1961, in Prozumenshchikov et al. (eds.), *Vensky Val's*, 175.

51 Memcon, Khrushchev and K.P.S. Menon, May 25, 1961, RGANI: f. 52, op. 1, d. 563, l. 28.

52 Ibid., ll. 19–20.

53 A.A. Fursenko (ed.), *Prezidium TsK KPSS, 1954–1964*, Vol. 1 (Moscow: Rosspen, 2003), 502–503.

54 Ibid.

55 Memcon, Khrushchev and JFK, June 4, 1961 (first conversation), in Prozumenshchikov et al. (eds.), *Vensky val's*, 233. Khrushchev's outburst was in reaction to Kennedy's careful probe for Soviet willingness to put pressure on its clients in Laos to avert a slide towards civil war in that country.

56 Memcon, Khrushchev and JFK, June 3, 1961 (second conversation), ibid., 230.

57 Memcon, Khrushchev and JFK, June 4, 1961 (first conversation), ibid., 245.

58 Ibid., 247–249.

NOTES TO PAGES 286–293

59 Memcon, Khrushchev and JFK, June 4, 1961 (second conversation), ibid., 252.

60 Khrushchev's dictation, Apr. 21, 1961.

61 Memcon, Khrushchev and Frank Roberts, July 2, 1961, in Prozumenshchikov et al. (eds.), *Vensky val's*, 334.

62 Harrison, *Driving the Soviets Up the Wall*, 180.

63 Ibid., 181.

64 Ibid., 293.

65 Ibid., 181.

66 Memcon, Khrushchev and Chen Yi, July 5, 1961, in Prozumenshchikov et al. (eds.), *Vensky val's*, 344–352.

67 Memcon, Mao and Kim Il Sung, July 13, 1961. In the author's possession.

68 "Newsmen Debate 'Cold War' on TV," *New York Times*, June 25, 1961, 7.

69 Khrushchev's speech at the Warsaw Pact meeting, Aug. 4, 1961, RGANI: f. 10, op. 3, d. 12, l. 107.

70 Memcon, Khrushchev and Nehru, Sept. 6, 1961, RGANI: f. 52, op. 1, d. 563, l. 63.

71 Khrushchev's speech at the Warsaw Pact meeting, Aug. 4, 1961, RGANI: f. 10, op. 3, d. 12, l. 95.

72 Memcon, Khrushchev and John McCloy, July 26, 1961, RGANI: f. 52, op. 1, d. 581, ll. 91–143.

73 "Vstrechi i besedy N.S. Khrushcheva s sel'skimi truzhennikami Ukrainy," *Pravda*, July 30, 1961, 10.

74 Vashugin's story is recounted in Khrushchev's dictation on the Berlin question, Aug. 1, 1961, in Prozumenshchikov et al. (eds.), *Vensky val's*, 420–1, and (in a slightly different form) in Khrushchev, *Vospominaniya: vremya, lyudi, vlast'*, Vol. 1, 306–307. The quote is from the archival document.

75 Lüthi, *The Sino-Soviet Split*, 206.

76 Yu. S. Solov'yov, "Ryadom so Stalinym," *Istorichesky Vestnik*, 5 (2013), 182.

77 Lüthi, *The Sino-Soviet Split*, 208.

78 Memcon, Khrushchev and Luís Carlos Prestes, Nov. 9, 1961, RGANI: f. 3, op. 23, d. 102, l. 136.

79 Memcon, Khrushchev and Nehru, Sept. 6, 1961, RGANI: f. 52, op. 1, d. 563, ll. 53–54.

80 Viktor Adamsky and Yuri Smirnov, "Moscow's Biggest Bomb: The 50-Megaton Test of October 1961," *CWIHP Bulletin*, Issue 4 (Fall 1994), 19.

81 Memcon, Khrushchev and Chen Yi, July 5, 1961.

82 Memcon, Khrushchev and Nehru, Sept. 6, 1961, RGANI: f. 52, op. 1, d. 563, l. 68. Khrushchev's resumption of nuclear testing took place in the midst of a nonaligned movement conference in Belgrade, which had sent envoys to Washington and Moscow to urge peace (that is why Nehru was in Moscow that September).

83 Memcon, Khrushchev and Ulbricht, Nov. 2, 1961, in Prozumenshchikov et al. (eds.), *Vensky val's*, 602–613.

NOTES TO PAGES 295–298

11 CUBA

1 The anecdote about the hedgehog originates with Dmitry Volkogonov, *Sem' vozhdei: galereya liderov SSSR*, Vol. 1 (Moscow: Novosti, 1995), 420.

2 For a cogent summary of this argument, see Steven J. Zaloga, *The Kremlin's Nuclear Sword: The Rise and Fall of Russia's Strategic Nuclear Forces, 1945–2000* (Washington, DC: Smithsonian Books, 2002).

3 Memcon, Khrushchev and Mao, July 31, 1958, RGANI: f. 52, op. 1, d. 498, ll. 44–77.

4 For a full list of tests, see V.I. Ivkin and G.A. Sukhina (eds.), *Zadacha osoboi gosudarstvennoi vazhnosti: iz istorii sozdaniya raketnoyadernogo oruzhiya i raketnykh voisk strategicheskogo naznacheniya (1945–1959 gg.). Sbornik dokumentov* (Moscow: ROSSPEN, 2010), 999–1069.

5 Aleksandr Zheleznyakov, *Legendarnaya semerka: raketa Koroleva i Gagarina* (Moscow: Yauza, 2016), 28.

6 Ivkin and Sukhina (eds.), *Zadacha osoboi gosudarstvennoi vazhnosti*, 999–1069.

7 A.A. Fursenko (ed.), *Prezidium TsK KPSS, 1954–1964*, Vol. 1 (Moscow: Rosspen, 2003), 424.

8 Nur Bilge Criss, "Strategic Nuclear Missiles in Turkey: The Jupiter Affair, 1959–1963," *Journal of Strategic Studies*, 20(3) (Sept. 1997), 114.

9 Memcon, Khrushchev and Selim Sarper, Oct. 2, 1960, RGANI: f. 52, op. 1, d. 351, l. 41. It seems doubtful, however, that Khrushchev promised the Turks $500 million per annum in aid if they abrogated NATO membership. For this claim, see Nur Bilge Criss, "Strategic Nuclear Missiles in Turkey: The Jupiter Affair, 1959–1963," *Journal of Strategic Studies*, 20(3) (Sept. 1997), 113.

10 Memcon, Khrushchev and Selim Sarper, Oct. 2, 1960, l. 41.

11 Leopoldo Nuti, "Extended Deterrence and Nuclear Ambitions: Italy's Nuclear Policy, 1955–1962," *Journal of Strategic Studies*, 39(4) (2016), 566.

12 N. Khrushchev, *Khrushchev Remembers* (Boston: Little, Brown & Co., 1970), 494.

13 Revelations about the CIA-run Operation Mongoose (a campaign of covert operations against Castro's regime) give credence to these concerns. Sergo Mikoyan, *Anatomiya karibskogo krizisa* (Moscow: Akademiya, 2006). For a detailed discussion of Operation Mongoose, see James G. Hershberg, "Before 'The Missiles of October': Did Kennedy Plan a Military Strike against Cuba?" *Diplomatic History*, 14(2) (1990), 163–198.

14 Fursenko (ed.), *Prezidium TsK KPSS*, Vol. 1, 556.

15 Hershberg, "Before 'The Missiles of October'," 181.

16 Fursenko (ed.), *Prezidium TsK KPSS*, Vol. 1, 617.

17 Notes of Oct. 22–23, 1962 Presidium meeting (A. Serov), Oct. 23, 1962, RGANI: f. 3, op. 16, d. 164, l. 4.

18 Sergey Radchenko, "The Cuban Missile Crisis: Assessment of New, and Old, Russian Sources," *International Relations*, 26(3) (Sept. 2012), 333.

19 Nikita Khrushchev, *Vospominaniya: vremya, lyudi, vlast'*, Vol. 2 (Moscow: Moskovskie Novosti, 1999), 505.

NOTES TO PAGES 298–303

20 Aleksandr Khinshtein (ed.), *Ivan Serov: zapiski iz chemodana: tainye dnevniki pervogo predsedatelya KGB* (Moscow: Prosveshchenie, 2016), 568.

21 V.E. Yesin (ed.), *Strategicheskaya operatsiya Anadyr': kak eto bylo* (Moscow: MOOVVIK, 2007), 122.

22 Fursenko (ed.), *Prezidium TsK KPSS*, Vol. 1, 569.

23 Ignacio Ramonet, Fidel Castro, *Fidel Castro. My Life: A Spoken Autobiography* (New York: Scribner, 2007), 272. See also Castro's account of his meeting with Biryuzov in Memcon, Brezhnev and Fidel Castro, June 27, 1972, RGANI: f. 80, op. 1, d. 676, ll. 18–19.

24 Philip Brenner and James G. Blight, *Sad and Luminous Days: Cuba's Struggles with the Superpowers after the Missile Crisis* (Lanham, MD: Rowman & Littlefield, 2002), 44.

25 Memcon, Shen Jian and Che Guevara, Dec. 1, 1962, CMFA: 109-03157-01, 1–10. Obtained by Sergey Radchenko. Translated by Zhang Qian.

26 Malinovsky and Zakharov to Khrushchev, May 24, 1962, TsAMO: f. 16a, op. 3657ss, d. 3, ll. 1–7.

27 Malinovsky and Zakharov to Commander of Group of Soviet Forces in Cuba, Sept. 8, 1962, CWIHP DA: https://digitalarchive.wilsoncenter.org /document/111539. Translated by Raymond Garthoff.

28 Ibid.

29 Fursenko (ed.), *Prezidium TsK KPSS*, Vol. 1, 568.

30 Malinovsky and Zakharov to Khrushchev, May 24, 1962, TsAMO: f. 16a, op. 3657ss, d. 3, l. 1.

31 Brenner and Blight, *Sad and Luminous Days*, 43 and James G. Blight, Bruce J. Allyn, and David A. Welch, *Cuba on the Brink* (Rowman & Littlefield, 2002), 83–84.

32 Sergo Mikoyan and Svetlana Savraskaya, *The Soviet Cuban Missile Crisis: Castro, Mikoyan, Kennedy, Khrushchev, and the Missiles of November* (Washington, DC: Woodrow Wilson Center Press, 2012), 109.

33 Memcon, Shen Jian and Che Guevara, Dec. 1, 1962, CMFA: 109-03157-01, 1–10. Also, Memcon, Mikoyan and Rodriguez, Nov. 19, 1962, https://nsarchive2.gwu .edu/rus/text_files/MikoyanCuba/1962.11.19%20Mikoyan%20Rodriguez.PDF

34 Igor Statsenko to Sergei Biryuzov [Statsenko's report], Dec. 18, 1962, TsAMO: f. 1, op. 14041ss, d. 1, ll. 192–224.

35 Ibid.

36 Instruction (by Aleksei Butsky), June 23, 1962, TsAMO: f. 1, op. 14041ss, d. 1, l. 43.

37 Statsenko's report.

38 Ibid.

39 Speech by Senator Keating, "Soviet Activities in Cuba," Aug. 31, 1962, CWIHP DA: https://digitalarchive.wilsoncenter.org/document/134658.

40 Cable to (sanitized) from director re SAMs, Sept. 8, 1962, CIA CREST, Document 0005640612; Report of Soviet medium-range missile and submarine base in Cuba, Sept. 5, 1962, CIA CREST, Document 0001264825;

NOTES TO PAGES 303–307

Central Intelligence Bulletin, Sept. 8, 1962, CIA CREST, Document CIA-RDP79T00975A006600060001-2; Central Intelligence Bulletin, Sept. 18, 1962, CIA CREST, Document CIA-RDP79T00975A006600140001-3.

41 The military build-up in Cuba, Sept. 19, 1962, CIA CREST, Document CIA-RDP80B01676R001800050003-7. CIA's John McCone, however, reported a "hunch" from his honeymoon trip to France that the Soviets were putting missiles in Cuba. Mary S. McAuliffe (ed.), *CIA Documents on the Cuban Missile Crisis* (Washington, DC: CIA, 1992), 51–52.

42 Report from Prague, Sept. 21, 1962, CWIHP DA: https://digitalarchive .wilsoncenter.org/document/134746. Oddly enough, the Soviets, too, had learned that the West German intelligence had discovered the missiles. See Memcon, Khrushchev and Carlos Rafael Rodriguez, Dec. 11, 1962, CWIHP DA: https://digitalarchive.wilsoncenter.org/document/115171.

43 For a detailed discussion of the reasons for the Sept.–Oct. 1962 "photo gap," see David M. Barrett and Max Holland, *Blind Over Cuba: The Photo Gap and the Missile Crisis* (College Station, TX: Texas A&M University Press, 2012), 1–21.

44 For a concise summary, see Ernest May and Philip Zelikow, *The Kennedy Tapes: Inside the White House During the Cuban Missile Crisis, concise edition* (New York: W.W. Norton, 2002).

45 Edward C. Keefer, Charles S. Sampson, and Louis J. Smith (eds.), *Foreign Relations of the United States [FRUS], 1961–1963*, Vol. 11 (Washington, DC: US Government Printing Office, 1996), Document 18.

46 The best account is still Philip Nash, *The Other Missiles of October: Eisenhower, Kennedy, and the Jupiters, 1957–1963* (Chapel Hill, NC: University of North Carolina Press, 1997).

47 These terms were repeatedly used by JFK and McNamara, in discussing why the missiles were not acceptable. See e.g. *FRUS, 1961–1963*, Vol. 11, Document 18 and National Security Council meetings, Oct. 20, 1962, JFK Presidential Library: JFKNSF-313-038-p0001.

48 See the exchange between Mark Kramer and James G. Blight, Bruce J. Allyn, and David A. Welch: Mark Kramer, "Tactical Nuclear Weapons, Soviet Command Authority, and the Cuban Missile Crisis," *CWIHP Bulletin*, Issue 3 (1993), 40, 42–46; and James G. Blight, Bruce J. Allyn, and David A. Welch, "Kramer vs. Kramer, Or, How Can You Have Revisionism in the Absence of Orthodoxy?" *CWIHP Bulletin*, Issue 3 (1993), 41, 47–50. For a recent treatment, see Mikoyan and Savraskaya, *Soviet Cuban Missile Crisis*, 184–185.

49 A. Gribkov, "Karibsky krizis," *Voenno-Istorichesky Zhurnal*, 10 (1992), 44. Mark Kramer, "The 'Lessons' of the Cuban Missile Crisis for Warsaw Pact Nuclear Operations," *CWIHP Bulletin*, Issue 5 (Spring 1995), 110.

50 Chiang Kai-shek's (deleted) views on the advisability of GRC action against the Mainland, Jan. 5, 1962, CIA CREST, Document 0000107415.

51 Central Intelligence Bulletin, Apr. 24, 1962, CIA CREST, Document CIA-RDP79T00975A006300310001-7.

NOTES TO PAGES 307–311

52 Cable to director from Taiwan re meeting with (deleted) and general Chiang, Jan. 6, 1962, CIA CREST, Document 0000608237.

53 Cable from CIA / OCI to the White House Situation Room re China situation, Mar. 4, 1962, CIA CREST, Document 0000608252.

54 Zhonggong Zhongyang Wenxian Yanjiushi (ed.), *Mao Zedong Nianpu*, Vol. 5 (Beijing: Zhongyang Wenxian Chubanshe, 2013), 104–106.

55 Edward C. Keefer, David W. Mabon, and Harriet Dashiell Schwar (eds.), *FRUS, 1961–1963*, Vol. 22 (Washington, DC: US Government Printing Office, 1996), Document 131.

56 For a useful account see Niu Jun, "1962: The Eve of the Left Turn in China's Foreign Policy," CWIHP Working Paper 48 (Oct. 2005).

57 Mao's speech at the Tenth CCP Party Plenum, Sept. 24, 1962, *Mao Zedong Sixiang Wansui, 1961–1968* (Neibu – internal circulation. No publication information), 33–37. In the author's possession.

58 Zhonggong Zhongyang Wenxian Yanjiushi (ed.), *Mao Zedong Nianpu*, Vol. 5, 159.

59 On the evolution of Nehru's border policy, see Neville Maxwell, *India's China War* (Bombay: Jaico Publishing House, 1970), 173–256.

60 Memcon, Zhou Enlai and Raza, Sept. 5, 1962. Obtained by Sulmaan Khan. Translated by Anna Beth Keim. CWIHP DA: https://digitalarchive .wilsoncenter.org/document/112750.

61 Report on Soviet–Indian relations, July 11, 1962, CMFA: 105-01519-03.

62 Li Danhui, "Dui 1962 nian Xinjiang yita shijian qiyin de lishi kaocha – laizi Zhongguo Xinjiang de dang'an cailiao," *Dangshi Yanjiu Ziliao*, 4–5 (1999).

63 Chen Yi's speech at the Political Consultative Conference Session, Apr. 17, 1962, Gansu Provincial Archives: 116–2-1-350, 37–38.

64 Memcon, Liu Shaoqi and Raza, Sept. 1, 1962. Obtained and translated by Christopher Tang. CWIHP DA: https://digitalarchive.wilsoncenter.org /document/121571.

65 Maxwell, *India's China War*, 338–340.

66 Memcon, Liu Xiao and Khrushchev, Oct. 13, 1962, CMFA: 109-03809-06, 17–32.

67 Fursenko (ed.), *Prezidium TsK KPSS*, Vol. 1, 616. Khrushchev's letters to Zhou Enlai and Nehru, telling one of his Marxist-Leninist sympathies, and the other of his disappointment, are in RGANI: f. 3, op. 16, d. 163.

68 Memcon, Shen Jian and Emilio Aragonés, Oct. 12, 1962, CFMA: 111-00361-03, 3–7. Obtained by Dai Chaowu.

69 It was not until Oct. 23 that the Chinese ambassador in Moscow was briefed on the situation in Cuba. See Memcon, Mikoyan and Liu Xiao, Oct. 23, 1962, RGASPI: f. 84, op. 1, d. 143, ll. 92–97. Mikoyan's excuse for not informing Moscow's allies earlier was that they planned to do so after the missiles had been put in place, in early November.

70 Memcon, Liu Xiao and Khrushchev, Oct. 13, 1962, CMFA: 109-03809-06, 17–32.

NOTES TO PAGES 312–320

71 The following account of the Oct. 22, 1962 meeting is based on both the Malin notes and the Serov notes. Malin notes are in RGANI: f. 3, op. 16, d. 947, ll. 36–41. Serov notes are in RGANI: f. 3, op. 16, d. 164, ll. 3–14.

72 Gromyko to Moscow, Oct. 20, 1962, copy courtesy of NSA. Translated by Mark H. Doctoroff. CWIHP DA: https://digitalarchive.wilsoncenter.org /document/111779.

73 Dictation by Mikoyan, Jan. 19, 1963, RGASPI: f. 84, op. 3, d. 115, l. 116. The episode is also recounted in Mikoyan, *Anatomiya karibskogo krizisa*, 251–254.

74 Malinovsky to Pliev, Oct 22, 1962. Translated by Svetlana Savranskaya. CWHP DA: https://digitalarchive.wilsoncenter.org/document/117316.

75 Statsenko's report.

76 McAuliffe (ed.), *CIA Documents on the Cuban Missile Crisis.*

77 Khrushchev's draft letter to Castro, Oct. 31, 1962, RGANI: f. 3, op. 16, d. 169, ll. 77–106.

78 *FRUS, 1961–1963*, Vol. 11, Document 44.

79 Presidium meeting, Oct. 22, 1962, RGANI: f. 3, op. 16, d. 947, ll. 36–41; RGANI: f. 3, op. 16, d. 164, ll. 3–14.

80 Khrushchev's dictation, Oct. 24, 1962, RGANI: f. 3, op. 16, d. 165, l. 131.

81 *FRUS, 1961–1963*, Vol. 11, Document 63.

82 Michael Dobbs, *One Minute to Midnight: Kennedy, Khrushchev, and Castro on the Brink of Nuclear War* (New York: Knopf, 2008), 147–148.

83 Khrushchev's dictation, Oct. 25, 1962, RGANI: f. 3, op. 16, d. 165, l. 63.

84 Georgy Kornienko, *Kholodnaya voina: svidetel'stvo ee uchastnika* (Moscow: Olma-Press, 2001), 129.

85 Presidium meeting (Serov's notes), Oct. 25, 1962, RGANI: f, 3, op. 16, d. 165, l. 72.

86 Fursenko (ed.), *Prezidium TsK KPSS*, Vol. 1, 618.

87 Khrushchev's dictation, Oct. 25, 1962, RGANI: f. 3, op. 16, d. 165, l. 63.

88 ExComm meeting, Oct. 27, 1962, https://catalog.archives.gov/id/193723.

89 Good accounts are T. Naftali, "Using the KGB Documents: The Scali-Feklisov Channel in the Cuban Missile Crisis," *CWIHP Bulletin*, Issue 5 (Spring 1995), 58, and Dobbs, *One Minute to Midnight*, 165–168. See also *FRUS, 1961–1963*, Vol. 11, Document 80.

90 Memcon, Khrushchev and Mahmoud Foroughi, Oct. 26, 1962, RGANI: f. 52, op. 1, d. 567, ll. 113–120.

91 Memcon, Khrushchev and Keshav Dev Malviya, Oct. 26, 1962, RGANI: f. 52, op. 1, d. 564, ll. 1–14.

92 A.A. Fursenko and T. Naftali, *"One Hell of a Gamble": Khrushchev, Castro, and Kennedy, 1958–1964* (New York: W.W. Norton & Co., 1997), 274–275.

93 Khrushchev's dictation, Oct. 30, 1962, RGANI: f. 52, op. 1, d. 600, l. 8.

94 Memcon, Delegations of the CPCz and the CPSU, Oct. 30, 1962, CWIHP DA: https://digitalarchive.wilsoncenter.org/document/115219.

95 Fursenko and Naftali, *"One Hell of a Gamble,"* 286.

96 Instructions for Dobrynin, undated, RGANI: f. 3, op. 16, d. 168, ll. 47–48.

NOTES TO PAGES 320–331

97 Khrushchev to Fidel Castro, Oct. 28, 1962, CWIHP DA: https://digitalarchive .wilsoncenter.org/document/114504.

98 Khrushchev to Castro, Oct. 20, 1962, https://nsarchive2.gwu.edu/nsa/cuba _mis_cri/621030%20Letter%20to%20Castro.pdf.

99 Khrushchev's dictation, Oct. 30, 1962, RGANI: f. 52, op. 1, d. 600, l. 8. The bear story is a reference to Ivan Krylov's 1815 fable, which Khrushchev apparently heard in his youth.

100 Khrushchev to Fidel Castro, Oct. 31, 1962, RGANI: f. 3, op. 16, d. 169, ll. 77–106.

101 Dictation by Mikoyan, Jan. 19, 1963, RGASPI: f. 84, op. 3, d. 119.

102 Memcon, O. Darusenkov and Carlos Rafael Rodríguez, May 31, 1972, RGANI: f. 80, op. 1, d. 677, l. 64.

103 Memcon, Mikoyan and Fidel Castro, Nov. 3, 1962, https://nsarchive2.gwu .edu/rus/text_files/MikoyanCuba/1962.11.03.PDF. Obtained by Svetlana Savranskaya.

104 The actual phrase Castro used was "cero a la izquierda" (or "zero to the left"), translated here as "nonentity." Memcon, Mikoyan and Fidel Castro, Nov. 22, 1962. https://nsarchive2.gwu.edu/rus/text_files/MikoyanCuba/1962.11.22 %20Mikoyan%20in%20Cuba.PDF. Obtained by Svetlana Savranskaya.

105 Memcon, Mikoyan and Fidel Castro et al., Nov. 4, 1962, https://nsarchive2 .gwu.edu/rus/text_files/CMCrisis/39.PDF. Obtained by Svetlana Savranskaya.

106 "We Stand by Cuba," *Peking Review*, Nov. 2, 1962.

107 Ibid.

108 Memcon, Shen Jian and Che Guevara, Dec. 1, 1962, CMFA: 109-03157-01, 1–10. Obtained by Sergey Radchenko. Translated by Zhang Qian.

109 Khrushchev's dictation on Cuba, Nov. 9, 1962, RGANI: f. 52, op. 1, d. 600, l. 14.

110 Cited in Sergey Radchenko, *Two Suns in the Heavens: The Sino-Soviet Struggle for Supremacy* (Washington, DC and Stanford, CA: Woodrow Wilson Press and Stanford University Press, 2009), 36.

111 Khrushchev's speech at a party plenum, Nov. 23, 1962, RGANI: f. 2, op. 1, d. 603, ll. 160–161.

112 Ibid., ll. 161–162.

113 Cuban Mission to the United Nations, Dec. 2, 1962. Translated by Chris Dunlap. CWIHP DA: https://digitalarchive.wilsoncenter.org/document/115170.

114 Memcon, Khrushchev and a Cuban delegation, Jan. 16, 1963, RGANI: f. 52, op. 1, d. 488, l. 27.

115 Khrushchev to Castro, Jan. 31, 1963, National Security Archive, Washington, DC.

116 Fursenko (ed.), *Prezidium TsK KPSS*, Vol. 1, 720. My italics.

12 VIETNAM

1 Ilya Gaiduk, *Confronting Vietnam: Soviet policy toward the Indochina Conflict, 1954–1963* (Washington, DC: Woodrow Wilson Center Press, 2003); Ilya Gaiduk, *The Soviet Union and the Vietnam War* (Chicago, IL.: Dee, 1996); Mari Olsen, *Soviet–Vietnam*

NOTES TO PAGES 332–337

Relations and the Role of China, 1949–64: Changing Alliances (New York: Routledge, 2006); Qiang Zhai, *China and the Vietnam Wars, 1950–1975* (Chapel Hill, NC: University of North Carolina Press, 2000); Chen Jian, *Mao's China and the Cold War* (Chapel Hill, NC: University of North Carolina Press, 2000).

2 Memcon, Mao and Hysni Kapo, June 29, 1962, Central State Archive, Tirana, AQPPSh-MPKK-V.1962, L. 14, D. 7. Obtained by Ana Lalaj. Translated by Enkel Daljani.

3 Chen, *Mao's China and the Cold War*, 207.

4 Olsen, *Soviet–Vietnam Relations*, 127.

5 Memcon, Tovmasyan and Ho Chi Minh, July 20, 1963, AVPRF: f. 079, op. 18, d. 7, l. 66.

6 Memcon, P.I. Privalov and Duong Bat Mai, Oct. 21, 1963, AVPRF: f. 079, op. 18, d. 8, l. 42.

7 Memcon, Tovmasyan and Ung Van Khiem, Oct. 11, 1963, AVPRF: f. 079, op. 18, d. 8, l. 30.

8 Memcon, Khrushchev and Sarvepalli Radhakrishnan, Sept. 12, 1964, RGANI: f. 52, op. 1, d. 564, l. 87.

9 Memcon, Mao and a delegation of Japanese socialists, July 10, 1964. In the author's possession.

10 Lorenz M. Lüthi, *The Sino-Soviet Split: Cold War in the Communist World* (Princeton University Press, 2008), 277.

11 A.A. Fursenko (ed.), *Prezidium TsK KPSS, 1954–1964*, Vol. 1 (Moscow: Rosspen, 2003), 848–849.

12 Khrushchev's comments at a meeting on border issues, Sept. 9, 1964, RGANI: f. 52, op. 1, d. 598, ll. 156–157.

13 Memcon, Khrushchev and Sarvepalli Radhakrishnan, Sept. 12, 1964, RGANI: f. 52, op. 1, d. 564, l. 91.

14 Ibid., l. 92.

15 Memcon, Khrushchev and Sukarno, Sept. 29, 1964, RGANI: f. 52, op. 1, d. 622, ll. 103–106.

16 A.N. Artizov et al. (eds.), *Nikita Khrushchev. 1964: stenogrammy plenuma TsK KPSS i drugie dokumenty* (Moscow: MFD Materik, 2007), 241.

17 Ibid., 197–199.

18 Sergey Radchenko, *Two Suns in the Heavens: The Sino-Soviet Struggle for Supremacy* (Washington, DC and Stanford, CA: Woodrow Wilson Press and Stanford University Press, 2009), 131–137.

19 Note on a conversation by Tarka, Jurgas, and Milc at the Soviet Embassy in Hanoi, Sept. 10, 1964. Translated by Lorenz Lüthi. CWIHP DA: http://digitalarchive.wilsoncenter.org/document/117707.

20 Memcon, Mao, Pham Van Dong, and Hoang Van Hoan, Oct. 5, 1964, in Odd Arne Westad et al. (eds.), "77 Conversations between Chinese and Foreign Leaders on the Wars in Indochina, 1964–77," CWIHP Working Paper 22 (May 1998).

NOTES TO PAGES 337–343

21 Memcon, Zhou Enlai and Mohamed Yala, Aug. 6, 1964, CFMA: 106-01448-02, 98–117. Translated by Jake Tompkins. CWIHP DA: http://digitalarchive.wilsoncenter.org/document/118723.

22 Memcon, Mao and Jacques Duhamel, Sept. 10, 1964. In the author's possession.

23 Ibid.

24 "China Vows: We Stand by Vietnam," *Peking Review*, 33 (Aug. 14, 1964), 7.

25 Instructions from the CC CCP on organizing demonstrations, Aug. 7, 1964, Ningbo City Archive. In the author's possession.

26 Memcon, Zhou Enlai and Mohamed Yala, Aug. 6, 1964, CFMA: 106-01448-02, 98-117. Translated by Jake Tompkins. https://digitalarchive.wilsoncenter.org/document/118723.

27 Memcon, Zhou Enlai and Kosygin, Feb. 10, 1965, CFMA: 109-03957, 121–135. Obtained by Chen Jian.

28 Memcon, Kosygin and Mao, Feb. 11, 1965. Translated by Margolzata Gnoiska. In the author's possession.

29 Suslov's speech at the Mar. 1965 CC CPSU Plenum, RGANI: f. 2, op. 1, d. 782, l. 99.

30 Memcon, Brezhnev and Luigi Longo, Aug. 18, 1966, RGANI: f. 80, op. 1, d. 642, l. 62.

31 Memcon, Brezhnev and Fidel Castro, June 30, 1972, RGANI: f. 80, op. 1, d. 676, l. 93.

32 Memcon, Brezhnev and Le Thanh Nghi, June 9, 1965, RGANI: f. 80, op. 1, d. 517, ll. 27–46.

33 Le Thanh Nghi's report on meetings with party leaders of eight socialist countries, 1965. Obtained by Pierre Asselin. Translated by Merle Pribbenow (with introduction by Pierre Asselin). CWIHP DA: https://digitalarchive.wilsoncenter.org/document/134601.

34 Memcon, Brezhnev and Antonin Novotny, Sept. 14, 1965, RGANI: f. 80, op. 1, d. 877, l. 82. However, thousands of Soviet experts served in Vietnam, including with anti-aircraft batteries and as flight instructors.

35 Memcon, Brezhnev, Ceaușescu and Ion Maurer, July 20, 1965, RGANI: f. 80, op. 1, d. 758, l. 34.

36 Memcon, Brezhnev and Ceaușescu, May 13, 1966, RGANI: f. 80, op. 1, d. 760, l. 143.

37 Cited in James Hershberg, *Marigold: The Lost Chance for Peace in Vietnam* (Stanford University Press, 2012), 200.

38 Memcon, Brezhnev and Le Thanh Nghi, Dec. 22, 1965, RGANI: f. 80, op. 1, d. 519, ll. 1–14.

39 Leonid Brezhnev diary, Oct. 1965. In the author's possession.

40 Ibid.

41 On Ronning's missions, see Hershberg, *Marigold*, 88–89 and 116–117.

42 Memcon, Brezhnev and Luigi Longo, Aug. 18, 1966, RGANI: f. 80, op. 1, d. 642, l. 58.

NOTES TO PAGES 343–349

43 Ibid.

44 Ibid., l. 64.

45 Cited in Hershberg, *Marigold*, 238.

46 Memcon, Zhou Enlai and Pham Van Dong, Oct. 9, 1965, CWIHP DA: https://digitalarchive.wilsoncenter.org/document/113065.

47 Leonid Brezhnev diary, Oct. 1965. In the author's possession.

48 Memcon, Brezhnev and Luigi Longo, Aug. 18, 1966, RGANI: f. 80, op. 1, d. 642, l. 67.

49 Memcon, Suslov and a Bulgarian delegation, Oct. 8, 1966, RGANI: f. 81, op. 1, d. 266, l. 6.

50 Memcon, Mao and Pham Van Dong, Apr. 11, 1967. In the author's possession.

51 Memcon, Mao and Ho Chi Minh, June 10, 1966. In the author's possession.

52 Qiang Zhai, *China and the Vietnam Wars*, 135.

53 On Vietnamese–Chinese relations at the current stage, July 22, 1967, RGANI: f. 5, op. 59, d. 330, ll. 269–277.

54 For a detailed account of Le Duan's strategy and divergences with the Chinese over the Tet Offensive, see Lian-Hang T. Nguyen, *Hanoi's War: An International History* (Chapel Hill, NC: University of North Carolina Press, 2012).

55 Memcon, Brezhnev et al. and Pham Van Dong et al., Nov. 20 1968, RGANI: f. 80, op. 1, d. 525, ll. 5–67.

56 See e.g. John A. Farrell, *Richard Nixon: The Life* (New York: Vintage, 2018). However, there is disagreement as to whether Nixon was in fact guilty of trying to subvert peace talks. For a view that he was not, see Niall Ferguson, *Kissinger, 1923–1968: The Idealist* (New York: Penguin Press, 2015).

57 Memcon, Kissinger and Dobrynin, Apr. 14, 1969. Edward C. Keefer et al. (eds.), *Soviet–American Relations: The Detente Years, 1969–1972* (Washington, DC: US Government Printing Office, 1972), 52.

58 Report, Andrei Gromyko to the Politburo, Apr. 13, 1969, RGANI: f. 3, op. 68, d. 1025, l. 25.

59 Memcon, Brezhnev et al. and Pham Van Dong et al., Nov. 20, 1968, RGANI: f. 80, op. 1, d. 525, ll. 5–67.

60 Le Van Luong's speech at the VWP Politburo, July 5, 1969, RGANI: f. 5, op. 61, d. 462, ll. 1–49.

61 Le Van Luong's speech at the VWP Politburo, Sept. 22, 1969, RGANI: f. 5, op. 61, d. 452, ll. 7–48.

62 KGB Memorandum, Sept. 9, 1969, RGANI: f. 5, op. 61, d. 671, ll. 104–112.

63 GRU report, Aug. 27, 1969, RGANI: f. 5 op. 61, d. 461, ll. 61–69.

64 Le Van Luong's speech at the VWP Politburo, Sept. 22, 1969.

65 Memcon, Brezhnev, Kosygin, and Vo Nguyen Giap, Dec. 1, 1971, RGANI: f. 80, op. 1, d. 526, ll. 67–99.

66 Le Van Luong's speech at the VWP Politburo, Sept. 22, 1969, RGANI: f. 5, op. 61, d. 452, l. 18.

67 Ibid.

NOTES TO PAGES 349–354

68 Memcon, Mao and Le Duan, May 11, 1970. Translated by Chen Jian and Anne Beth Keim. In the author's possession.

69 Xia Yafeng, *Negotiating with the Enemy: U.S.–China Talks during the Cold War, 1949–1972* (Bloomington, IN: Indiana University Press, 2006), 184; Zhonggong Zhongyang Wenxian Yanjiushi (ed.), *Mao Zedong Nianpu*, Vol. 6 (Beijing: Zhongyang Wenxian Chubanshe, 2013), 420.

70 Memcon, Brezhnev, Kosygin, and Vo Nguyen Giap, Dec. 1, 1971.

71 Ibid.

72 Draft of Brezhnev's speech at a party plenum, May 15, 1972. Brezhnev asked for this paragraph to be taken out of the draft, RGANI: f. 80, op. 1, d. 159, l. 3.

73 Memcon, Brezhnev and Fidel Castro, June 30, 1972, RGANI: f. 80, op. 1, d. 676, l. 98.

74 Brezhnev's speech to leading military cadres, Apr. 25, 1972, RGANI: f. 80, op. 1, d. 261.

75 Memcon, Brezhnev and Fidel Castro, June 30, 1972, RGANI: f. 80, op. 1, d. 676, l. 106.

76 Memcon, Brezhnev and Gus Hall, Apr. 25, 1972, RGANI: f. 80, op. 1, d. 826, l. 106.

77 Edward Keefer (ed.), *Soviet–American Relations, Detente Years, 1969–1972* (Washington, DC: United States Department of State, 2007), 639.

78 For a detailed account see Pierre Asselin, *A Bitter Peace: Washington, Hanoi, and the Making of the Paris Agreement* (Chapel Hill, NC: UNC Press, 2002).

79 Brezhnev's speech at a party plenum, May 19, 1972, RGANI: f. 2, op. 1, d. 270, l. 67.

80 A.M. Aleksandr-Agentov, *Ot Kollontai do Gorbacheva* (Moscow: Mezhdunarodnye Otnosheniya, 1994), 224.

81 Memcon, Brezhnev et al. and Le Duan et al., July 11, 1973, RGANI: f. 80, op. 1, d. 528, l. 34.

82 Anatoly Chernyaev, *Sovmestnyi iskhod: dnevnik dvukh epokh* (Moscow: Rosspen, 2008), 8.

83 Memcon, Brezhnev and Kissinger, May 8, 1973, RGANI: f. 80, op. 1, d. 799, l. 90.

84 Aleksandr-Agentov, *Ot Kollontai do Gorbacheva*, 224.

85 Richard Nixon, *RN: The Memoirs of Richard Nixon* (New York: Simon & Schuster, 2013), 613.

86 Brezhnev's speech at a party plenum, Apr. 26, 1973, RGANI: f. 80, op. 1, d. 162, l. 92.

87 Brezhnev's comments at an internal meeting, Mar. 30, 1973, RGANI: f. 80, op. 1, d. 163, l. 2.

88 Memcon, Brezhnev et al. and Fidel Castro et al., June 30, 1972, RGANI: f. 80, op. 1, d. 676, l. 100.

89 Memcon, Brezhnev and Luis Corvalan, Nov. 22, 1972, RGANI: f. 80, op. 1, d. 916, l. 8. For the Brezhnev–Castro discussion on Vietnam, see Memcon, Brezhnev and Fidel Castro, June 30, 1972, RGANI: f. 80, op. 1, d. 676, l. 100.

90 Memcon, Brezhnev et al. and Le Duan et al., July 11, 1973, l. 34.

NOTES TO PAGES 354–360

91 Information on the visit of Josip Broz Tito, June 1972, in L.A. Velichanskaya et al. (eds.), *Vstrechi i peregovory na vysshem urovne rukovoditelei SSSR i Yugoslavii v 1946–1980 gg*, Vol. 2 (Moscow: Mezhdunarodnyi Fond Demokratiya, 2017), 412.

92 Memcon, Brezhnev and Carlos Rafael Rodríguez, Sept. 26, 1973, RGANI: f. 80, op. 1, d. 678, l. 47.

93 Keefer et al. (eds.), *Soviet–American Relations*, 886–904. The references to "light banter" and the dinner only appear in the US record.

94 Douglas E. Selvage and Melissa Jane Taylor (eds.), *Foreign Relations of the United States [FRUS], 1969–1976*, Vol. 15 (Washington, DC: US Government Printing Office, 1996), Document 131.

95 Memcon, Brezhnev et al. and Le Duan et al., July 10, 1973, RGANI: f. 80, op. 1, d. 528, ll. 25–26.

96 Memcon, Mao and Le Duan, June 5, 1973. Translated by Caixia Lu. In the author's possession. On Le Duan's account of his meeting with Mao, see Memcon, Brezhnev and Le Duan, Aug. 4, 1973, RGANI: f. 80, op. 1, d. 528, ll. 129–146.

97 Memcon, Brezhnev and Le Duan, Aug. 4, 1973, l. 141.

98 Memcon, Brezhnev et al. and Le Duan et al., July 10, 1973.

99 Memcon, Brezhnev et al. and Le Duan et al., July 10, 1973.

100 Gromyko and Konstantin Katushev to the Politburo, July 2, 1973, RGANI: f. 3, op. 69, d. 694, l. 148.

101 On the volume of special cooperation and trade and economic cooperation between the USSR and the Socialist Republic of Vietnam, July 15, 1991, both in Gorbachev Foundation Archive: f. 2, Document 8997.

13 DETENTE

1 Brezhnev's comments at an internal meeting, Mar. 30, 1973, RGANI: f. 80, op. 1, d. 163, l. 7.

2 Memcon, Brezhnev and Armand Hammer, Feb. 15, 1973, RGANI: f. 80, op. 1, d. 828, l. 50.

3 There is a vast literature on the Prague Spring, and the Soviet invasion. For a good overview, see Günter Bischof, Stefan Karner, and Peter Ruggenthaler (eds.), *The Prague Spring and the Warsaw Pact Invasion of Czechoslovakia in 1968* (Lanham, MD: Rowman & Littlefield, 2009); Mark Kramer, "New Sources on the 1968 Soviet Invasion of Czechoslovakia," *CWIHP Bulletin*, Issue 2 (1992), 4–13.

4 Memcon, Brezhnev, Kosygin, Podgorny, and Tito, Apr. 29, 1968, in L.A. Velichanskaya et al. (eds.), *Vstrechi i peregovory na vysshem urovne rukovoditelei SSSR i Yugoslavii v 1946–1980 gg*, Vol. 2 (Moscow: Mezhdunarodnyi Fond Demokratiya, 2017), 222.

5 Ibid., 221.

6 Brezhnev's speech at a party plenum, Oct. 1968, RGANI: f. 2, op. 3, d. 146, l. 8.

7 Brezhnev's speech at a party plenum, Dec. 1969, RGANI: f. 2, op. 3, d. 171, l. 118.

NOTES TO PAGES 361–366

8 Memcon, Brezhnev, Kosygin, Podgorny, and Tito, Apr. 29, 1968, in Velichanskaya et al. (eds.), *Vstrechi i peregovory*, Vol. 2, 222.

9 Brezhnev's speech at a party plenum, Oct. 1968, RGANI: f. 2, op. 3, d. 146, l. 23.

10 Memcon, Brezhnev et al. and Pham Van Dong, Nov. 22, 1968, RGANI: f. 80, op. 1, d. 525, l. 21.

11 Andrei Musalov, *Damansky i Zhalanashkol, 1969* (Moscow: Eksprint, 2005) offers an account of both events.

12 Report, Andrei Gromyko to the Politburo, Apr. 13, 1969, RGANI: f. 3, op. 68, d. 1025, ll. 1–71.

13 David C. Geyer, Nina D. Howland, and Kent Sieg (eds.), *Foreign Relations of the United States [FRUS], 1969–1976*, Vol. 14 (Washington, DC: US Government Printing Office, 2006), Document 134.

14 On Brezhnev's early years, see Susanne Schattenberg, *Leonid Breschnew: Staatsmann und Schauspieler im Schatten Stalins* (Cologne: Böhlau Verlag, 2017). On his upbringing in the borderlands, see Andreï Kozovoï, *Brejnev* (Paris: Perrin, 2021), 27–31.

15 Vadim Pechenev, *Vzlet i padenie Gorbacheva: glazami ochevidtsa* (Moscow: Respublika, 1996), 61.

16 Aleksandr Maksimov, *Nashi zadachi na Tikhom Okeane* (St. Petersburg: Tip-Lit K.L. Pentkovskogo, 1901), 24.

17 Douglas E. Selvage and Melissa Jane Taylor (eds.), *FRUS, 1969–1976*, Vol. 15 (Washington, DC: US Government Printing Office, 2011), Document 131. Maksimov is misspelled in the transcript as Semomas.

18 Memcon, Brezhnev and V. Micunovic, Aug. 10, 1971, in Velichanskaya et al. (eds.), *Vstrechi i peregovory*, Vol. 2, 309.

19 *FRUS, 1969–1976*, Vol. 15, Document 131.

20 Memcon, Brezhnev and Fidel Castro, June 30, 1972, RGANI: f. 80, op. 1, d. 676, l. 93.

21 Memcon, Brezhnev and Mirko Tepavac, Feb. 27, 1971, in Velichanskaya et al. (eds.), *Vstrechi i peregovory*, Vol. 2, 298.

22 Draft memorandum (by Yury Andropov) to the Politburo, July 6, 1968, in *General'nyi sekretar' L.I. Brezhnev, 1964–1982*, Special Issue of *Vestnik Arkhiva Prezidenta* (Moscow, 2006), 77.

23 G. Zh. Mullek (ed.), *Ot Atlantiki do Urala: sovetsko-frantsuzkie otnosheniya* (Moscow: Mezhdunarodnyi Fond Demokratiya, 2015), 331.

24 Memcon, Brezhnev and Charles de Gaulle, June 21, 1966, RGANI: f. 80, op. 1, d. 856, l. 28.

25 Brezhnev's speech at a party plenum, Dec. 12, 1966, RGANI: f. 2, op. 3, d. 45, l. 34.

26 Memcon, Brezhnev and Ceaușescu, May 11, 1966, RGANI: f. 80, op. 1, d. 760, l. 48. For a discussion of de Gaulle's reasons for reaching out to Moscow, see Garret Joseph Martin, *General de Gaulle's Cold War* (New York: Berghahn Books, 2013), 61–73, 104–110.

27 Memcon, Brezhnev and de Gaulle, June 22, 1966, RGANI: f. 80, op. 1, d. 856, l. 66.

NOTES TO PAGES 367–370

28 Memcon, Brezhnev and Ceaușescu, Dec. 15, 1967, RGANI: f. 80, op. 1, d. 762, l. 33. "Revanchist" was the Soviets' term describing Bonn's alleged quest for post-Second World War "revenge."

29 Memcon, Brezhnev and Pompidou, Oct. 7, 1980, RGANI: f. 80, op. 1, d. 857, l. 22.

30 Report, Andrei Gromyko to the Politburo, Apr. 13, 1969, RGANI: f. 3, op. 68, d. 1025, l. 43.

31 Memcon, Brezhnev and Edgar Faure, July 24, 1973, RGANI: f. 80, op. 1, d. 863, l. 128.

32 In 1971 Renault signed a contract to supply technologies for the Kamaz factory in the USSR.

33 Memcon, Brezhnev and Pompidou, Mar. 13, 1974, RGANI: f. 80, op. 1, d. 864, ll. 54–55.

34 Cited in Mary Sarotte, *Dealing with the Devil: East Germany, Détente, and Ostpolitik, 1969–1973* (Chapel Hill, NC: University of North Carolina Press, 2001), 41–42.

35 A.A. Aleksandrov-Agentov to Brezhnev, Aug. 6, 1970, RGANI: f. 80, op. 1, d. 331, l. 19.

36 G.V. Kireev, *Rossiya-Kitai: neizvestnye stranitsy pogranichnykh peregovorov* (Moscow: Rosspen, 2006), 126.

37 Memcon, Edward Heath and Mao Zedong, May 25, 1974, British National Archives: FCO 21/1240.

38 *FRUS, 1969–1976*, Vol. 15, Document 131.

39 Memcon, Brezhnev and Edgar Faure, July 24, 1973, RGANI: f. 80, op. 1, d. 863, l. 134.

40 On the establishment of the secret channel between Brezhnev and Brandt (via Egon Bahr and Andropov), see Vyacheslav Kevorkov, *Tainyi kanal* (Moscow: Geya, 1997).

41 Julia Von Dannenberg, *The Making of the Moscow Treaty between West Germany and the USSR* (Oxford University Press, 2008), 52–55.

42 Memcon, Gromyko and Bahr, Jan. 30, 1970, RGANI: f. 5, op. 62, d. 685, ll. 19, 21. The author is grateful to Peter Ruggenthaler for sharing a copy of this document. For an exhaustive treatment of the talks (based on West German sources), see Dannenberg, *The Making of the Moscow Treaty*, 50–62.

43 Brezhnev's speech at a Warsaw Pact meeting, Aug. 20, 1970, www.php.isn .ethz.ch/lory1.ethz.ch/collections/colltopica3f5.html?lng=en&id=18051& navinfo=14465.

44 KGB report on a joint session of the Bundestag and the Bundesrat, Aug. 18, 1970, RGANI: f. 5, op. 62, d. 568, ll. 58–74. The author is grateful to Peter Ruggenthaler for sharing a copy of this document.

45 Brezhnev's speech at a Warsaw Pact meeting, Aug. 20, 1970, www.php.isn.ethz.ch /lory1.ethz.ch/collections/colltopica3f5.html?lng=en&id=18051&navinfo=14465.

46 Brezhnev's speech to leading military cadres, Apr. 25, 1972, RGANI: f. 80, op. 1, d. 261, l. 28.

666

NOTES TO PAGES 370–373

47 Brezhnev's speech to the personnel of the Soviet Embassy in Havana, Feb. 2, 1974, RGANI: f. 80, op. 1, del 679, l. 199.

48 Andrey Edemskiy, "Dealing with Bonn: Leonid Brezhnev and the Soviet Response to West German Ostpolitik," in Carole Fink and Bernd Schaefer (eds.), *Ostpolitik, 1969–1974: European and Global Responses* (Cambridge University Press, 2009), 15–38.

49 Brezhnev's speech at a party plenum, Dec. 7, 1970, RGANI: f. 2, op. 3, d. 217, l. 67.

50 Memcon, Brezhnev and Brandt, Sept. 16–18, 1971, RGANI: f. 3, op. 72, d. 476, ll. 173–206.

51 Heinrich August Winkler, *Germany: The Long Road West*, Vol. 2: *1933–1990* (Oxford University Press, 2007), 271.

52 For a good analysis, see Wolfgang Mueller, "Recognition in Return for Détente? Brezhnev, the EEC, and the Moscow Treaty with West Germany, 1970–1973," *JCWS*, 13(4) (2011), 79–100.

53 P. Abrasimov to P. Demichev, Nov. 18, 1970, RGANI: f. 5, op. 62, d. 574, l. 131. The author is grateful to Peter Ruggenthaler for sharing a copy of this document.

54 A.A. Aleksandrov-Agentov to Brezhnev, Aug. 6, 1970, RGANI: f. 80, op. 1, d. 331, l. 18.

55 Brezhnev's speech to leading military cadres, Apr. 25, 1972, RGANI: f. 80, op. 1, d. 261, l. 26.

56 Brezhnev's speech at a party plenum, Dec. 7, 1970, RGANI: f. 2, op. 3, d. 217, l. 69.

57 Anatoly Chernyaev, *Sovmestnyi iskhod: dnevnik dvukh epokh* (Moscow: Rosspen, 2008), 25.

58 Memcon, Brezhnev and Bahr, Oct. 10, 1972, RGANI: f. 80, op. 1, d. 572, l. 107. The author is grateful to Peter Ruggenthaler for sharing a copy of this document.

59 Brezhnev's comments on a memorandum from Aleksandr-Agentov to Brezhnev, Oct. 20, 1972, RGANI: f. 80, op. 1, d. 331, l. 63.

60 The Soviet Embassy in Bonn highlighted in their reports that Brandt and the SPD leadership continued, for their part, to emphasize the vast gap between social democracy and Communism. See e.g. Soviet Embassy in the FRG to CC CPSU, Dec. 28, 1970, RGANI: f. 5, op. 62, d. 574, ll. 201–222. The author is grateful to Peter Ruggenthaler for sharing a copy of this document.

61 Evgeny Chazov, *Zdorov'ye i vlast': vospominaniya kremlevskogo vracha* (Moscow: Novosti, 1992), 93.

62 Velichanskaya et al. (eds.), *Vstrechi i peregovory*, Vol. 2, 322.

63 Memcon, Brezhnev and Nasser, July 5, 1968, RGANI: f. 80, op. 1, d. 602, l. 90.

64 Velichanskaya et al. (eds.), *Vstrechi i peregovory*, Vol. 2, 296.

65 Memcon, Brezhnev et al. and Pham Van Dong et al., Nov. 20, 1968, RGANI: f. 80, op. 1, d. 525, l. 49.

66 Memcon, Brezhnev and Fidel Castro, June 30, 1972, RGANI: f. 80, op. 1, d. 676, l. 116.

NOTES TO PAGES 373–379

67 Memcon, Brezhnev and Mirko Tepavac, Feb. 27, 1971, in Velichanskaya et al. (eds.), *Vstrechi i peregovory*, Vol. 2, 297.

68 Memcon, Brezhnev and Veljko Mićunović, Feb. 4, 1971, ibid., 290–291.

69 Antony J. Blinken, *Ally versus Ally: America, Europe, and the Siberian Pipeline Crisis* (Westport, CT: Greenwood Press, 1987), 27.

70 Velichanskaya et al. (eds.), *Vstrechi i peregovory*, Vol. 2.

71 Report, Andrei Gromyko and Yury Andropov to the Politburo, Jan. 12, 1971, AVPRF: f. 0129, op. 55, por. 12, p. 412, ll. 1–26.

72 David C. Geyer (ed.), *FRUS, 1969–1976*, Vol. 13 (Washington, DC: US Government Printing Office, 2011), Document 189.

73 Aleksandrov-Agentov to Brezhnev, May 2, 1971, RGANI: f. 80, op. 1, d. 331, ll. 37–50.

74 Report, Pyotr Ivashutin (GRU) to CC CPSU, June 11, 1966, RGANI: fond: 5, op. 58, d. 259, ll. 25–30.

75 Sergey Radchenko, *Two Suns in the Heavens: The Sino-Soviet Struggle for Supremacy* (Washington, DC and Stanford, CA: Woodrow Wilson Press and Stanford University Press, 2009), 198.

76 Edward C. Keefer et al. (eds.), *Soviet–American Relations: The Detente Years, 1969–1972* (Washington, DC: US Government Printing Office, 1972), 106.

77 Report, Andrei Gromyko to the Politburo, Apr. 13, 1969, RGANI: f. 3, op. 68, d. 1025, l. 21.

78 Henry Kissinger, *The White House Years* (London: Weidenfeld and Nicolson and Michael Joseph, 1979), 183. For a detailed discussion of these hints, see William Burr, "Sino-American Relations, 1969: The Sino-Soviet Border War and Steps towards Rapprochement," *Cold War History*, 1(3) (2001), 73–112.

79 See, for example, Margaret Macmillan, *Nixon and Mao: The Week that Changed the World* (New York: Random House, 2007) and Chris Tudda, *A Cold War Turning Point: Nixon and China, 1969–1972* (Baton Rouge, LA: Louisina State University Press, 2012).

80 Memcon, Mao and Snow, Dec. 18, 1970: Folder 197, Edgar Snow Papers, University of Missouri, Kansas City.

81 Shanghai Municipal archives: B250-2-395 and B158-3-935.

82 Yang Kuisong, "The Sino-Soviet Border Clash of 1969: From Zhenbao Island to Sino-American Rapprochement," *Cold War History*, 1(1) (2000), 21–52.

83 Memcon, Mao and Ceaușescu, June 3, 1971. In the author's possession.

84 "Text of Nixon Toast at Shanghai Dinner," *New York Times*, Feb. 28, 1972, 16. On Kissinger's explanation, see e.g. Memcon, Brezhnev and Gus Hall, Apr. 25, 1972, RGANI: f. 80, op. 1, d. 826, l. 110.

85 Keefer et al. (eds.), *Soviet–American Relations*, 726.

86 Memcon, Brezhnev and Abdul Zahir, Mar. 15, 1972, RGANI: f. 82, op. 1, d. 458, l. 54.

87 In his conversation with Kissinger, Brezhnev repeatedly referred to the need to consult with his colleagues.

NOTES TO PAGES 379–384

88 For Brezhnev's selective reading of his transcripts of conversation with Kissinger, see Brezhnev's speech at a party plenum, May 19, 1972, RGANI: f. 2, op. 3, d. 270, ll. 58–59. The actual transcript is in *Soviet–American Relations*, 697–709. For Brezhnev claims that he "firmly pressed" Kissinger on Vietnam, see Memcon, Brezhnev and Gus Hall, Apr. 25, 1972, RGANI: f. 80, op. 1, d. 826, l. 103.

89 Keefer et al. (eds.), *Soviet–American Relations*, 780.

90 Brezhnev's speech at a party plenum, May 19, 1972, RGANI: f. 2, op. 3, d. 270, l. 43.

91 Ibid., l. 52.

92 Memcon, Brezhnev and Walter J. Stoessel, Mar. 5, 1974, RGANI: f. 80, op. 1, d. 807, l. 32.

93 Talking points for Brezhnev's meeting with Nixon (by Gromyko), May 14, 1972, RGANI: f. 80, op. 1, d. 792, l. 67.

94 Memcon, Brezhnev and Peter Peterson, July 30, 1972, RGANI: f. 80, op. 1, d. 795, l. 32.

95 *FRUS, 1969–1976*, Vol. 15, Document 115.

96 Memcon, Brezhnev and Peter Peterson, July 30, 1972, RGANI: f. 80, op. 1, d. 795, ll. 48–49.

97 Letter from Yury Zhukov to Brezhnev, May 31, 1972, RGANI: f. 80, op. 1, d. 794, ll. 131–132.

98 *FRUS, 1969–1976*, Vol. 15, Document 121.

99 Vladislav Zubok, *A Failed Empire: The Soviet Union in the Cold War from Stalin to Gorbachev* (Chapel Hill, NC: University of North Carolina Press, 2007). Other historians dwell on the same theme, e.g. Michael Morgan, *The Final Act: The Helsinki Accords and the Transformation of the Cold War* (Princeton University Press, 2018), 52–53.

100 Memcon, Brezhnev and Peter Peterson, July 30, 1972, RGANI: f. 80, op. 1, d. 795, l. 34.

101 Memcon, Brezhnev and Bahr, Oct. 10, 1972, RGANI: f. 80, op. 1, d. 572, l. 121.

102 *FRUS, 1969–1976*, Vol. 15, Document 77.

103 Ibid., Document 104; also RGANI: f. 80, op. 1, d. 799, l. 22.

104 *FRUS, 1969–1976*, Vol. 15, Document 121.

105 Memcon, Brezhnev and Kissinger, Sept. 13, 1972, RGANI: f. 80, op. 1, d. 796, l. 132. The idea to share information about the Lin Biao investigation was Brezhnev's – he wrote it into his talking points. Evidently, by doing so, he wanted to emphasize the intimacy of Soviet–American consultations.

106 Ibid., l. 130.

107 Memcon, Brezhnev and Kissinger, May 5, 1972, RGANI: f. 80, op. 1, d. 799, l. 25. This discussion of China is not reflected in the US transcript of the same meeting, having taken place immediately after the meeting.

108 Memcon, Brezhnev and Kissinger, May 6, 1972, RGANI: f. 80, op. 1, d. 799, ll. 85–88.

NOTES TO PAGES 384–390

109 As reported by Kissinger: *FRUS, 1969–1976*, Vol. 15, Document 115. When at one point Bahr questioned Brezhnev about prospects for a superpower condominium, the Soviet general secretary disclaimed any interest: "The idea that supposedly there exist superpowers that only care about their own security originates with the Chinese." Memcon, Brezhnev and Bahr, Oct. 10, 1972, RGANI: f. 80, d. 1, d. 572, l. 121.

110 This is my translation of what Brezhnev said, as recorded by the secret Oval Office taping system. The tape: www.nixonlibrary.gov/white-house-tapes/943/conversation-943-008. Sukhodrev's translation is: *FRUS, 1969–1976*, Vol. 15, Document 123.

111 As cited in the Russian version of the record, Memcon, Brezhnev and Nixon, June 18, 1973, RGANI: f. 80, op. 1, d. 805, l. 21.

112 See e.g. Memcon, Brezhnev and Nixon, June 21, 1973, RGANI: f. 80, op. 1, d. 805, l. 146.

113 Memcon, Brezhnev and Nixon, June 20, 1973, RGANI: f. 80, op. 1, d. 805, l. 101.

114 Memcon, Brezhnev and Nixon, June 21, 1973, RGANI: f. 80, op. 1, d. 805, l. 151; Memcon, Brezhnev and the leadership of CPUSA, June 22, 1973, RGANI: f. 80, op. 1, d. 805, ll. 157–158.

115 Memcon, Brezhnev and Nixon, June 21, 1973, RGANI: f. 80, op. 1, d. 805, l. 151.

116 Memcon, Brezhnev and the leadership of the PCF, June 26, 1973, RGANI: f. 80, op. 1, d. 863, l. 91.

117 Nixon's toast at the one-on-one dinner with Brezhnev, June 24, 1973, RGANI: f. 80, op. 1, d. 806, l. 13.

118 Memcon, Brezhnev and Nixon aboard a helicopter, June 24, 1973, RGANI: f. 80, op. 1, d. 804, l. 14; Brezhnev's notes are ibid., l. 17.

119 Memcon, Brezhnev and a Communist Party of India delegation, June 28, 1972, RGANI: f. 80, op. 1, d. 617, l. 132.

120 As described by Brezhnev himself in a conversation with Josip Broz Tito in Yugoslavia, in Velichanskaya et al. (eds.), *Vstrechi i peregovory*, Vol. 2, 443.

121 Memcon, Brezhnev and Walter J. Stoessel, Mar. 5, 1974, RGANI: f. 80, op. 1, d. 807, l. 26. For Stoessel's report, see https://aad.archives.gov/aad/createpdf?rid=43725&dt=2474&dl=1345.

122 Chernyaev, *Sovmestnyi iskhod*, 92.

123 Ibid., 133.

124 According to a CIA report. "Truck production at the Soviet Kama River plant – Western technology in action," CIA CREST, Document CIA-RDP86T00591R000300400003-5.

125 Statistics from Memcon, Brezhnev and Kissinger, May 8, 1972, RGANI: f. 80, op. 1, d. 799, l. 70.

126 James M. Naughton, "Dean Tells Inquiry that Nixon Took Part in Watergate Cover-Up for Eight Months," *New York Times*, June 26, 1973, 1.

NOTES TO PAGES 390–395

127 A.A. Aleksandrov-Agentov to Brezhnev, May 15, 1973, RGANI: f. 80, op. 1, d. 807, ll. 155–156. The archival document incorrectly indicates the date as May 15, 1974; it was misdated when filed.
128 Letter, Brezhnev to Nixon, Aug. 5, 1974 (unsent), RGANI: f. 80, op. 1, d. 811, ll. 5–8.
129 Memcon, Brezhnev and Carlos Rafael Rodríguez, Sept. 26, 1973, RGANI: f. 80, op. 1, d. 678, l. 54.
130 Memcon, Brezhnev and Bahr, Feb. 27, 1974, RGANI: f. 80, op. 1, d. 580, l. 21.
131 David C. Geyer (ed.), *FRUS, 1969–1976*, Vol. 16 (Washington, DC: US Government Printing Office, 2012), Document 90.
132 As reported by Chernyaev in *Sovemstnyi iskhod*, 102.

14 YOM KIPPUR

1 See e.g. Craig A. Daigle, "The Russians Are Going: Sadat, Nixon and the Soviet Presence in Egypt, 1970–1971," *MERIA*, 8(1) (2004).
2 Andrei Grechko to the Politburo, June 27, 1973, RGANI: f. 3, op. 69, d. 693, ll. 26–29.
3 See e.g. Brezhnev's speech at a party plenum, Apr. 26, 1973, RGANI: f. 80, op. 1, d. 162, l. 144.
4 Memcon, Brezhnev et al. and Sadat, Dec. 10, 1969, RGANI: f. 80, op. 1, delo 602, l. 186.
5 Memcon, Brezhnev et al. and Nasser, July 16, 1970, RGANI: f. 80, op. 1, d. 603, ll. 88–89.
6 Vladimir Vinogradov, *Egipet: ot Nasera k oktyabr'skoi voine: iz arkhiva posla* (Moscow: IV RAN, 2012), 87–88, 98.
7 Memcon, Brezhnev and Mahmoud Riad, July 2, 1971, RGANI: f. 80, op. 1, d. 604, l. 35. See also Vinogradov, *Egipet*, 90–91. In a later meeting with Sadat, Brezhnev pleaded for clemency in relation to Ali Sabri and others arrested. Sadat told him that "in the old days, I would have personally shot these people with my handgun." Memcon, Brezhnev and Sadat, Oct. 13, 1971, RGANI: f. 80, op. 1, d. 604, l. 120.
8 Memorandum, Evgeny Primakov to Brezhnev, July 28, 1971, RGANI: f. 80, op. 1, d. 604, l. 53. For background to this memorandum, see Leonid Mlechin, *Evgeny Primakov: chelovek, kotoryi spas razvedku* (Moscow: TD Algoritm, 2015).
9 On the treaty, see Karen Dawisha, *Soviet Foreign Policy towards Egypt* (New York: St. Martin's Press, 1979), 61–63.
10 Vinogradov, *Egipet*, 113. The request came in April 1971 with a letter carried by Sami Sharaf. Memcon, Brezhnev and Sharaf, Apr. 13, 1971, RGANI: f. 80, op. 1, d. 604, l. 23.
11 Memcon, Brezhnev and Aziz Sedky, Mar. 15, 1971, RGANI: f. 80, op. 1, d. 604, ll. 9–10. For more on Sadat's March visit to Moscow, see Mohrez Mahmoud El Hussini, *Soviet–Egyptian Relations, 1945–1985* (New York: Palgrave, 1987), 195.

NOTES TO PAGES 395–397

12 Memcon, Brezhnev and Sadat, Oct. 12, 1971, RGANI: f. 80, op. 1, d. 604, l. 84.

13 Ibid., l. 77.

14 Memcon, Brezhnev and Pompidou, June 24, 1973, RGANI: f. 80, op. 1, d. 863, l. 74.

15 L.A. Velichanskaya et al. (eds.), *Vstrechi i peregovory na vysshem urovne rukovoditelei SSSR i Yugoslavii v 1946–1980 gg*, Vol. 2 (Moscow: Mezhdunarodnyi Fond Demokratiya, 2017), 330.

16 Ibid., 296.

17 Mohamed Heikal, *The Road to Ramadan* (London: William Collins Sons & Co., 1975), 205.

18 Memcon, Brezhnev and Mahmoud Riad, July 2, 1971, RGANI: f. 80, op. 1, d. 604, l. 49.

19 Brezhnev's speech at a party plenum, Nov. 22, 1971, RGANI: f. 2, op. 3, d. 248, l. 35.

20 Memcon, Brezhnev and Sami Sharaf, Apr. 13, 1971, RGANI: f. 80, op. 1, d. 604, l. 21.

21 Daigle, "The Russians Are Going." For a first-hand account by the Soviet ambassador, see Vinogradov, *Egipet*, 44–45. Cairo's side of the story is in Heikal, *The Road to Ramadan*, 165–184. The precise number of Soviet military advisers varies depending on the source. A ballpark figure is in the CIA's Intelligence Report on the Soviet military presence in Egypt, Feb. 1975, CIA CREST, Document CIA-RDP86T00608R000600150002-9, which estimates that by 1971 there were up to 15,000 Soviet advisers in Egypt.

22 This idea is present in Gromyko's memorandum to Brezhnev in the run-up to the May 1972 Moscow summit, May 5, 1972, RGANI: f. 80, op. 1, d. 792, l. 31.

23 Memcons, Brezhnev and Tito, Nov. 12–15, 1973, in Velichanskaya et al. (eds.), *Vstrechi i peregovory*, Vol. 2, 432–443.

24 B. Ponomarev, A. Andropov, A. Gromyko and V. Kulikov to the Politburo, July 26, 1972, RGANI: f. 3, op. 69, d. 408, ll. 75–78.

25 Brezhnev to Kirilenko et al., July 24, 1972, RGANI: f. 3, op. 69, d. 408, l. 91.

26 Ibid.

27 Chernyaev's diary entry for Feb. 6, 1973, in Anatoly Chernyaev, *Sovmestnyi iskhod: dnevnik dvukh epokh* (Moscow: Rosspen, 2008), 37.

28 For a first-hand account of the Soviet–Israeli contacts (which began in 1971), see Evgeny Primakov, *Blizhnii vostok: na stsene i za kulisami* (Moscow: Rossiiskaya Gazeta, 2012), 260–307.

29 Isabella Ginor and Gideon Remez argue (incorrectly) that the expulsion of Soviet advisers was an act of deception to begin with. Isabella Ginor and Gideon Remez, *The Soviet–Israeli War, 1967–1973: The USSR's Military Intervention in the Middle East* (New York: Oxford University Press, 2017), 301–314.

30 Viktor Israelyan, *Inside the Kremlin during the Yom Kippur War* (Penn State Press, 2010), 92.

31 Ginor and Remez, *The Soviet–Israeli War*, 310–312. Sadat was simultaneously trying to set up a back channel to the United States, dispatching his national

NOTES TO PAGES 397–399

security adviser to Washington for talks with Kissinger. These efforts proved fruitless.

32 Brezhnev's diary entry for Feb. 27, 1973, in S.V. Kudryashov, *Leonid Brezhnev: rabochie i dnevnikovye zapisi* [*Brezhnev's Diary*], Vol. 1 (Moscow: IstLit, 2016), 549.

33 Brezhnev's speech at a party plenum, Apr. 26, 1973, RGANI: f. 80, op. 1, d. 162, l. 143.

34 Brezhnev to the Politburo, Feb. 7, 1973, RGANI: f. 80, op. 1, d. 317, l. 11.

35 "About the Middle East. Folder 81. The Chekist Anthology," June 2007, Contributed to CWIHP by Vasili Mitrokhin, CWIHP DA: https://digitalarchive .wilsoncenter.org/document/111894.

36 "DI Memo: Soviet Nuclear Weapons in Egypt?" Oct. 30, 1973, CIA CREST, Document 51112a4b993247d4d8394554.

37 In a handwritten note (presumably) to Sukhodrev, Brezhnev asked how he could skip a detailed discussion on the Middle East until he had a chance to talk to Nixon "in private." RGANI: f. 80, op. 1, d. 805, l. 107. Such an opportunity came up at the end of the meeting he had with Nixon and Kissinger on June 21, when Kissinger left early. See Memcon, Brezhnev and Kissinger, June 21, 1973, RGANI: f. 80, op. 1, d. 805, ll. 152–153.

38 Henry Kissinger, *Years of Upheaval* (New York: Simon & Schuster, 2011), 297.

39 Richard Nixon, *The Memoirs of Richard Nixon* (New York: Grosset and Dunlap, 1978), 885.

40 Evgeny Chazov, *Zdorov'ye i vlast': vospominaniya kremlevskogo vracha* (Moscow: Novosti, 1992), 115.

41 Memcon, Chazov and Nixon, as reported by Anatoly Dobrynin, Nov. 14, 1973, AVPRF: f. 0129, op. 57, p. 431, d. 8, l. 42.

42 Douglas E. Selvage and Melissa Jane Taylor (eds.), *Foreign Relations of the United States [FRUS], 1969–1976*, Vol. 15 (Washington, DC: US Government Printing Office, 2011), Document 132.

43 Daigle, "The Russians Are Going."

44 Kissinger, *Years of Upheaval*, 299. See also Raymond Garthoff, *Detente and Confrontation: American–Soviet Relations from Nixon to Reagan* (Washington, DC: Brookings, 1994), 364–365. Martin Indyk argues, however, that Kissinger was possibly in favor of a military conflict in the Middle East, which would open the road for a US-sponsored diplomatic solution. Martin Indyk, *The Master of the Game: Henry Kissinger and the Art of Middle East Diplomacy* (New York: Alfred A. Knopf, 2021), 112.

45 Brezhnev's comments at a meeting with his aides, June 28, 1973, RGANI: f. 80, op. 1, d. 806, l. 90. A few days after this meeting, Brezhnev explained to Georges Pompidou that he thought Nixon was simply too constrained by Watergate to do much about the Middle East at that juncture. Memcon, Brezhnev and Pompidou, June 24, 1973, RGANI: f. 80, op. 1, d. 863, l. 73.

46 Andropov to CC CPSU, Aug. 30, 1973, RGANI: f. 5, op. 66, d. 1040, l. 114.

NOTES TO PAGES 399–402

47 For a military history of the conflict (told primarily from the Israeli side) see Abraham Rabinovich, *The Yom Kippur War: The Epic Encounter that Transformed the Middle East* (New York: Schocken Books, 2004).

48 Heikal, *The Road to Ramadan*, 214.

49 Nina Howland and Craig Daigle (eds.), *FRUS, 1969–1976*, Vol. 25 (Washington, DC: US Government Printing Office, 2011), Document 100.

50 Ibid., Vol. 25, Document 108. Kissinger reproduces many of these telcons in his book, *Crisis*, but I relied on the *FRUS* version. Henry Kissinger, *Crisis: The Anatomy of Two Major Foreign Policy Crises* (New York: Simon & Schuster, 2003).

51 See e.g. The President's Daily Brief (PDB), Oct. 6, 1973, CIA CREST, Document 0005993950; PDB, Oct. 27, 1973, CIA CREST, Document 0005993968. See also Aleksandr Okorokov, *Sverkhsekretnye voiny SSSR* (Moscow: Yauza Eksmo, 2010), 89–90.

52 For a full discussion, see Israelyan, *Inside the Kremlin during the Yom Kippur War*, 1–19.

53 The Soviet Union also had intelligence information that suggested the conflict would begin on Oct. 6 or 7. Soviet information for select socialist countries, Oct. 6, 1973, RGANI: f. 3, op. 69, d. 804, l. 7. For an early discussion, see Garthoff, *Detente and Confrontation*, 366–377.

54 Instructions for the Soviet ambassador in Damascus, Oct. 3, 1973, RGANI: f. 3, op. 69, d. 795, l. 39.

55 Instructions for Soviet ambassador in Cairo, Oct. 4, 1973, RGANI: f. 3, op. 69, d. 804, ll. 124–125.

56 Gromyko, Grechko, Ponomarev, and Tsvigun to the Politburo, Oct. 3, 1973, RGANI: f. 3, op. 69, d. 795, l. 40.

57 Note (on the basis of a telephone conversation with Vinogradov), undated, RGANI: f. 3, op. 69, d. 795, l. 41.

58 Ginor and Remez, *The Soviet–Israeli War*, 320–346.

59 Memcon, Dobrynin and Kissinger, Oct. 10, 1973, AVPRF: f. 0129, op. 57, p. 431, d. 7, l. 147.

60 On the domestic and international dilemmas, see *FRUS, 1969–1976*, Vol. 25, Document 116.

61 Telcon, Kissinger and Dobrynin, Oct. 18, 1973. William Burr (ed.), "Kissinger told Soviet envoy during 1973 Arab–Israeli War: 'My nightmare is a victory for either side,'" NSA Briefing Book No. 680, Aug. 9, 2019. https://nsarchive.gwu .edu/briefing-book/henry-kissinger/2019-08-09/kissinger-told-soviet-envoy-during-1973-arab-israeli-war-my-nightmare-victory-either-side-soviet.

62 *FRUS, 1969–1976*, Vol. 25, Document 112.

63 Ibid., Document 111.

64 Ibid., Document 121.

65 Memcon, Dobrynin and Kissinger, Oct. 6, 1973, AVPRF: f. 0129, op. 57, p. 431, d. 7, l. 107.

NOTES TO PAGES 402–406

66 The Politburo meeting took place from 9:00pm to 11:00pm, which coincides with the recollections of Viktor Israelyan. *Brezhnev's Diary*, Vol. 2, 615. Israelyan, *Inside the Kremlin during the Yom Kippur War*, 31–32. Israelyan's book was published in 1995. It has now become clear that his "recollections" were generally accurate, and were evidently based on copies of documents now stored at RGANI. However, notable discrepancies remain. Thus, Israelyan incorrectly recounts Brezhnev's presence and comments at an Oct. 24 Politburo meeting, though we now know that Brezhnev was at the hunting resort of Zavidovo at the time.

67 Israelyan, *Inside the Kremlin during the Yom Kippur War*, 32. Of course, there was some distance between the US preference (ceasefire, with withdrawal to the lines of Oct. 6) and the Soviet preference (ceasefire in situ).

68 Ibid., 38.

69 Ibid., 97.

70 Dobrynin's commentary comes at the end of his conversation with Kissinger, Oct. 6, 1973, AVPRF: f. 0129, op. 57, p. 431, d. 7, l. 116.

71 Draft instructions for Dobrynin, Oct. 8, 1973, RGANI: f. 3, op. 69, d. 806, l. 156. The author is grateful to Kojiro Yamada for help in obtaining this document. Dobrynin delivered the message to Kissinger on Oct. 8 at 9:54am. *FRUS, 1969–1976*, Vol. 25, Document 123.

72 Draft instructions for Dobrynin, Oct. 8, 1973, RGANI: f. 3, op. 69, d. 806, l. 156.

73 Brezhnev to Sadat (draft), Oct. 8, 1973, RGANI: f. 3, op. 69, d. 806, ll. 17–18.

74 Brezhnev to Sadat, Oct. 9, 1973, RGANI: f. 3, op. 69, d. 808, ll. 12–15.

75 Lyle J. Goldstein and Yuri M. Zhukov, "A Tale of Two Fleets: A Russian Perspective on the 1973 Naval Standoff in the Mediterranean," *Naval War College Review*, 57(2) (2004), 44, 51.

76 Ibid., 51.

77 *FRUS, 1969–1976*, Vol. 25, Document 135.

78 Telcon, Kissinger and Dobrynin, Oct. 9, 1973, 12:32pm, Nixon Library, Box 28. The author is grateful to Kojiro Yamada for sharing a copy of this document. Dobrynin's version of the conversation is in AVPRF: f. 0129, op. 57, p. 431, d. 7, ll. 138–139.

79 Kissinger, *Crisis*, 149.

80 Memcon, Dobrynin and Kissinger, Oct. 9, 1973 (with Dobrynin's comments), AVPRF: f. 0129, op. 57, p. 431, d. 7, ll. 145–146.

81 Instructions to Soviet ambassadors in Algiers and Amman, Oct. 8, 1973, RGANI: f. 3, op. 69, d. 807, ll. 123–124, 127–128.

82 Israelyan, *Inside the Kremlin during the Yom Kippur War*, 62.

83 Memcon, Dobrynin and Kissinger, Oct. 10, 1973, AVPRF: f. 0129, op. 57, p. 431, d. 7, ll. 148–150.

84 Ginor and Remez, *The Soviet–Israeli War*, 337; Okorokov, *Sverkhsekretnye voiny SSSR*, 97–98.

85 Kissinger, *Crisis*, 194.

NOTES TO PAGES 406–411

86 Memcon, Dobrynin and Kissinger, Oct. 12, 1973, AVPRF: f. 0129, op. 57, p. 431, d. 7, l. 161. See also Martin Indyk, *Master of the Game: Henry Kissinger and the Art of Middle East Diplomacy* (New York: Alfred A. Knopf, 2021), 140.

87 Kissinger, *Crisis*, 200.

88 Ibid., 194.

89 Memcon, Dobrynin and Kissinger, Oct. 12, 1973, AVPRF: f. 0129, op. 57, p. 431, d. 7, l. 168.

90 Ibid., ll. 161, 168.

91 Memcon, Dobrynin and Nixon, Oct. 13, 1973, AVPRF: f. 0129, op. 57, p. 431, d. 7, ll. 176–177.

92 *FRUS, 1969–1976*, Vol. 25, Document 135.

93 Ibid.

94 Kissinger, *Crisis*, 218.

95 *FRUS, 1969–1976*, Vol. 25, Document 149.

96 Memcon, Dobrynin and Kissinger, Oct. 13, 1973, AVPRF: f. 0129, op. 57, p. 431, d. 7, ll. 181–188.

97 Ibid.

98 Israelyan, *Inside the Kremlin during the Yom Kippur War*, 91, 97.

99 Vinogradov, *Egipet*, 141, 151.

100 Ibid., 103–114. Garthoff (drawing on Kissinger) claims that Kosygin was able to secure Sadat's agreement to a ceasefire on Oct. 18. This "agreement," however, still depended on Israel's willingness to withdraw to the borders of 1967, so it does not really count as agreement. Garthoff, *Detente and Confrontation*, 370.

101 *FRUS, 1969–1976*, Vol. 25, Document 202. UN Resolution 242 (adopted by the UN Security Council on November 22, 1967) called for Israel's withdrawal from "territories occupied in the recent conflict" and noted each State's right "to live in peace within secure and recognized boundaries." https://peacemaker.un.org/sites/peacemaker.un.org/files/SCRes242 %281967%29.pdf.

102 Kissinger, *Crisis*, 291.

103 Memcon, Dobrynin and Kissinger, Oct. 18, 1973, AVPRF: f. 0129, op. 57, p. 431, d. 7, l. 210.

104 Kissinger, *Crisis*, 301.

105 *FRUS, 1969–1976*, Vol. 25, Document 218.

106 Garthoff, *Detente and Confrontation*, 371.

107 On "poor judgment," see *FRUS, 1969–1976*, Vol. 25, Document 220. See also Indyk, *The Master of the Game*, 162–163. On the danger of making independent decisions, see Memcon, Brezhnev and Kissinger, Oct. 20, 1973, RGANI: f. 80, op. 1, d. 800, l. 33.

108 Israelyan, *Inside the Kremlin during the Yom Kippur War*, 128.

109 Memcon, Brezhnev and Kissinger, Oct. 20, 1973, RGANI: f. 80, op. 1, d. 800, ll. 35–36.

NOTES TO PAGES 411–415

110 *FRUS, 1969–1976*, Vol. 25, Document 219.

111 Instructions for Soviet ambassadors [no later than Oct. 23, 1973], RGANI: f. 3, op. 72, d. 583 [ll. numbers unknown]. Vinogradov recounts his talks with Sadat in the middle of the night in Vinogradov, *Egipet*, 60–61.

112 Israelyan, *Inside the Kremlin during the Yom Kippur War*, 129–130.

113 *Brezhnev's Diary*, Vol. 2, 619

114 Kissinger, *Crisis*, 305. Memcon, Brezhnev and Kissinger, Oct. 21, 1973, RGANI: f. 80, op. 1, d. 800, ll. 44–58.

115 Telcon, Brezhnev and Kissinger, Oct. 21, 1973, 10:30pm, RGANI: f. 80, op. 1, d. 800, l. 59.

116 *FRUS, 1969–1976*, Vol. 25, Document 229.

117 Instructions for Soviet ambassador in Iraq [no later than Oct. 23, 1973], RGANI: f. 3, op. 72, d. 583.

118 Instructions for Soviet ambassadors [no later than Oct. 23, 1973], RGANI: f. 3, op. 72, d. 583.

119 Israelyan, *Inside the Kremlin during the Yom Kippur War*, 128.

120 Ibid., 148

121 Robert Alden, "Meeting Called after US and Russians Reach Accord," *New York Times*, Oct. 22, 1973, 1.

122 Israelyan, *Inside the Kremlin During the Yom Kippur War*, 134.

123 On Adan's operations see Rabinovich, *The Yom Kippur War*, 452–477.

124 *Brezhnev's Diary*, Vol. 2, 619–621.

125 FRUS, *1969–1976*, Vol. 15, Document 145. The Russian original (and the Politburo protocol) are in RGANI: f. 3, op. 72, d. 583.

126 *FRUS, 1969–1976*, Vol. 25, Document 230. For a discussion of Kissinger's encouragement of the Israelis, see Indyk, *Master of the Game*, 172–174.

127 Telcon, Dobrynin and Kissinger, Oct. 23, 1973, 7:10pm. Nixon Presidential Library, Kissinger telcons, Box 28. The author is grateful to Kojiro Yamada for sharing a copy of this document.

128 *Brezhnev's Diary*, Vol. 2, 620.

129 Brezhnev's draft letter to Nixon, undated (no later than Oct. 24, 1973), RGANI: f. 3, op. 69, d. 821, ll. 152–154.

130 Israelyan, *Inside the Kremlin during the Yom Kippur War*, 160.

131 Soviet intervention was also being requested by Sadat. Vinogradov, *Egipet*, 63. See also Anatoly Dobrynin, *Sugubo doveritel'no: posol v Vashingtone pri shesti prezidentakh SShA* (Moscow: Avtor, 1996), 273.

132 *FRUS, 1969–1976*, Vol. 15, Document 146.

133 Ibid.

134 Telcon, Kissinger and Dobrynin, Oct. 24, 1973, 10:15pm. Nixon Library, Kissinger Telcons, Box 28. The author is grateful to Kojiro Yamada for sharing a copy of this document.

135 See Richard Ned Lebow and Janice Gross Stein, *We All Lost the Cold War* (Princeton University Press, 1995), 470–471 and Indyk, *Master of the Game*, 180,

NOTES TO PAGES 415–418

185 for discussion of the evidence that Nixon was "drunk." See also Garthoff, *Detente and Confrontation*, 378–379.

136 *FRUS, 1969–1976*, Vol. 25, Document 269.

137 Ibid.

138 The US version: *FRUS, 1969–1976*, Vol. 25, Document 274. The Russian translation (and Dobrynin's explanation) is in RGANI: f. 3, op. 69, d. 821, ll. 5–7.

139 Ibid.

140 Addendum to the memorandum of conversation between Dobrynin and Brent Scowcroft, Oct. 25, 1973, AVPRF: f. 0129, op. 57, p. 431, d. 7, ll. 260–263.

141 Israelyan, *Inside the Kremlin during the Yom Kippur War*, 180; Dobrynin, *Sugubo doveritel'no*, 274.

142 A. Grechko to CC CPSU, Oct. 26, 1973, RGANI: f. 3, op. 69, d. 821, ll. 79–81. Israelyan claims that the Soviets became aware of DEFCON 3 "soon" after it happened but it is not clear what "soon" means in this context.

143 Israelyan, *Inside the Kremlin during the Yom Kippur War*, 181.

144 Ibid., 182–183.

145 Telcon, Dobrynin and Kissinger, Oct. 25, 1973, 2:40pm, Nixon Library, Kissinger Telcons, Box 28. The author is grateful to Kojiro Yamada for sharing a copy of this document. The author's italics.

146 Memcon, Dobrynin and Kissinger, Oct. 25, 1973, AVPRF: f. 0129, op. 57, p. 431, d. 7, l. 266. This reaction does not appear in the Kissinger/Dobrynin telcon, which has Kissinger react by saying that he "takes threats very badly" (this phrase, by contrast, did not make it into Dobrynin's report).

147 Draft letter from Brezhnev to Nixon, Oct. 26, 1973, RGANI: f. 3, op. 69, d. 821, ll. 104–106.

148 Instructions for the Soviet ambassador in Damascus, Oct. 25, 1973, RGANI: f. 3, op. 69, d. 821.

149 Ibid.

150 *FRUS, 1969–1976*, Vol. 25, Document 277.

151 I therefore disagree here with Anatoly Dobrynin who claims that there was never a threat of a Soviet–US clash, even as he notes (correctly) that Grechko was pushing for escalation. Dobrynin, *Sugubo doveritel'no*, 276.

152 Chernyaev's diary entry for Dec. 1, 1973 in Chernyaev, *Sovmestnyi iskhod*, 75.

153 Ginor and Remez, *The Soviet–Israeli War*, 351.

154 Israelyan, *Inside the Kremlin during the Yom Kippur War*, 143–145.

155 PDB, Oct. 26, 1973, CIA CREST, Document 0005993967. See also Garthoff, *Detente and Confrontation*, 378. Historians have not arrived at a clear conclusion concerning the meaning of this intelligence. Moreover, in a postmortem, the CIA (?) concluded that the evidence for Soviet nuclear weapons in Egypt was "far from conclusive." https://nsarchive2.gwu.edu/NSAEBB/NSAEBB276/doc03.pdf. The author is grateful to William Burr for pointing his attention to this document.

156 Lyle J. Goldstein and Yuri M. Zhukov, "A Tale of Two Fleets," 50.

678

NOTES TO PAGES 418–424

157 Ginor and Remez, *The Soviet–Israeli War*, 353. Also, PDB, Oct. 27, 1973, CIA CREST, Document 0005993968.

158 Chernenko to Brezhnev, Oct. 25, 1973, RGANI: f. 3, op. 69, d. 821, l. 185.

159 Andropov to Brezhnev, Oct. 29, 1973. Translated by Sergey Radchenko. CWIHP DA: https://digitalarchive.wilsoncenter.org/document/198187.

160 *FRUS, 1969–1976*, Vol. 25, Document 288.

161 The draft is in RGANI: f. 3, op. 69, d. 821.

162 PDB, Oct. 27, 1973, CIA CREST, Document 0005993968.

163 Israelyan, *Inside the Kremlin during the Yom Kippur War*, 207.

164 For transcript of Nixon's press conference on Oct. 26, 1973, see www .presidency.ucsb.edu/documents/the-presidents-news-conference-84. Re "calm and lucid," see James Reston, "Provocative President," *New York Times*, Oct. 27, 1973, 15.

165 Cited in Indyk, *Master of the Game*, 193.

166 Memcon, Dobrynin and Haig, Oct. 26, 1973, AVPRF: f. 0129, op. 57, p. 431, d. 7, l. 285.

167 Memcon, Dobrynin and Nixon, Dec. 13, 1973, AVPRF: f. 0129, op. 57, p. 431, d. 8, ll. 123–132. This conversation remains classified but Brezhnev's subsequent letter to Nixon made references to it. Also: Memcon, Dobrynin, Nixon, and Kissinger, Dec. 26, 1973, AVPRF: f. 0129, op. 57, p. 431, d. 8, ll. 141–159.

168 Memcon, Dobrynin, Nixon, Haig, and Kissinger, Oct. 30, 1973, AVPRF: f. 0129, op. 57, p. 431, d. 7, ll. 294–306.

169 Memcon, Dobrynin, Nixon and Kissinger, Dec. 26, 1973, AVPRF: f. 0129, op. 57, p. 431, d. 8, l. 158.

170 Memcon, Dobrynin and Kissinger, Nov. 4, 1973, AVPRF: f. 0129, op. 57, p. 431, d. 8, l. 17.

171 Memcon, Brezhnev and Armand Hammer, Nov. 16, 1973, RGANI: f. 80, op. 1, d. 828, l. 95.

172 Ibid., l. 102. Hammer promised the mission would be so secret, he would not even tell his own wife.

173 Chernyaev's diary entry for Nov. 4, 1973 in Chernyaev, *Sovmestnyi iskhod*, 74.

174 Primakov claims that in addition to Brezhnev (who "did not mind") restoring relations with Israel, Gromyko and Andropov were generally in favor. "But many were against." Primakov, *Blizhnii vostok*, 287.

175 Ibid.

176 Memcon, Brezhnev and Ismail Fahmi, Oct. 15, 1974, RGANI: f. 80, op. 1, d. 609, l. 54.

177 Memcon, Brezhnev and Castro, Feb. 2, 1974, RGANI: f. 80, op. 1, d. 679, l. 25.

178 Memcon, Brezhnev and Ismail Fahmi, Oct. 15, 1974, RGANI: f. 80, op. 1, d. 609, l. 46.

179 Vinogradov, *Egipet*.

NOTES TO PAGES 424–432

180 Douglas Little, "The Cold War in the Middle East: Suez Crisis to Camp David Accords," in Melvyn P. Leffler and Odd Arne Westad (eds.), *The Cambridge History of the Cold War*, Vol. 2 (Cambridge University Press, 2010), 305–326.

181 On Carter's "comprehensive" approach, see, in particular, Indyk, *Master of the Game*, 282–283.

15 DECLINE

1 David C. Geyer (ed.), *Foreign Relations of the United States [FRUS], 1969–1976*, Vol. 16 (Washington, DC: US Government Printing Office, 2012), Document 259.

2 Ibid., Document 228.

3 Ibid., Document 256.

4 Ford to Brezhnev, Aug. 9, 1974, RGANI: f. 80, op. 1, d. 811, ll. 12–13.

5 For a good overview of US policies (on which this account is partially based), see Jan Asmussen, *Cyprus at War: Diplomacy and Conflict during the 1974 Crisis* (London: Bloomsbury Publishing, 2020).

6 Asmussen, *Cyprus at War*, 28.

7 Laurie Van Hook (ed.), *FRUS, 1969–1976*, Vol. 30 (Washington, DC: US Government Printing Office, 2007), Document 83.

8 Aleksandrov-Agentov and Blatov to Brezhnev, Aug. 22, 1974, RGANI: f. 80, op. 1, d. 331, l. 6.

9 *FRUS, 1969–1976*, Vol. 30, Document 144.

10 Aleksandrov-Agentov to Brezhnev, Aug. 27, 1974, RGANI: f. 80, op. 1, d. 811, l. 23.

11 Anatoly Chernyaev, *Sovmestnyi iskhod: dnevnik dvukh epokh* (Moscow: Rosspen, 2008), 103.

12 Unsent letter from Brezhnev to Dobrynin, Aug. 28, 1974, RGANI: f. 80, op. 1, d. 811, l. 26. The letter was not sent because of Gromyko's visit to the United States (presumably, Gromyko shared these impressions with Dobrynin).

13 Robert G. Kaufman, *Henry M. Jackson: A Life in Politics* (University of Washington Press, 2011), 266.

14 Douglas E. Selvage and Melissa Jane Taylor (eds.), *FRUS, 1969–1976*, Vol. 15 (Washington, DC: US Government Printing Office, 2011), Document 137.

15 Memcon, Brezhnev and Walter J. Stoessel, Mar. 5, 1974, RGANI: f. 80, op. 1, d. 807, l. 36.

16 Memcon, Brezhnev and Gus Hall, Apr. 13, 1972, RGANI: f. 80, op. 1, d. 826, l. 39.

17 Nikolai Shchelokov to Brezhnev, June 15, 1973, RGANI: 80, op. 1, d. 799, l. 156.

18 Ibid., l. 158.

19 Ibid., l. 157.

20 Memcon, Brezhnev and Bahr, Feb. 27, 1974, RGANI: f. 80, op. 1, d. 580, l. 29. This document was kindly shared with the author by Peter Ruggenthaler.

21 Memcon, Dobrynin and Ford, Dec. 11, 1973, AVPRF: f. 0129, op. 57, p. 432, d. 9, l. 165.

NOTES TO PAGES 432–437

22 Memcon, Brezhnev and Walter J. Stoessel, Mar. 5, 1974, RGANI: f. 80, op. 1, d. 807, l. 27.

23 James Reston, "Scoop Goes to Peking," *New York Times*, June 28, 1974, 33.

24 Memcon, Dobrynin and Sen. Henry "Scoop" Jackson, June 26, 1975, AVPRF: f. 0129, op. 59, p. 449, d. 4, ll. 206, 207, 211.

25 *FRUS, 1969–1976*, Vol. 16, Document 102.

26 Memcon, Dobrynin and Kissinger, Jan. 6, 1975, AVPRF: f. 0129, op. 59, p. 449, d. 9, l. 9.

27 Henry Kissinger, *Years of Upheaval* (New York: Simon & Schuster, 2011), 1172–1173.

28 *FRUS, 1969–1976*, Vol. 16, Document 73.

29 Ibid., Document 77.

30 *FRUS, 1969–1976*, Vol. 16, Document 73.

31 Memcon, Dobrynin and Kissinger, Nov. 16, 1974, AVPRF: f. 0129, op. 58, p. 440, d. 8, l. 36.

32 *FRUS, 1969–1976*, Vol. 16, Document 88.

33 Ibid., Document 93.

34 Ibid., Document 92.

35 Cited in Jussi M. Hanhimäki, *The Flawed Architect: Henry Kissinger and American Foreign Policy* (Oxford University Press, 2004), 379.

36 Evgeny Chazov, *Zdorov'ye i vlast': vospominaniya kremlevskogo vracha* (Moscow: Novosti, 1992), 137.

37 The comment is by Karen Brutents, most famously cited in Christopher Andrew and Vasili Mitrokhin, *The World Was Going Our Way: The KGB and the Battle for the Third World: Newly Revealed Secrets from the Mitrokhin Archive* (New York: Basic Books, 2006).

38 For early Soviet thinking on European collective security, see Michael Morgan, *The Final Act: The Helsinki Accords and the Transformation of the Cold War* (Princeton University Press, 2018), 77–78.

39 On the lead-up to Helsinki, see Marie-Pierre Rey, "The USSR and the Helsinki Process, 1969–75," in Andreas Wenger, Vojtech Mastny, and Christian Nuenlist (eds.), *Origins of the European Security System: The Helsinki Process Revisited, 1965–75* (London: Routledge, 2008), 65–81.

40 Quoted in Morgan, *The Final Act*, 122.

41 Ibid.

42 Memcon, Brezhnev and Chirac, Mar. 24, 1975, RGANI: f. 80, op. 1, d. 867, l. 19.

43 Memcon, Brezhnev and Giscard d'Estaing, Dec. 5, 1974, RGANI: f. 80, op. 1, d. 865, l. 6.

44 Memcon, Brezhnev and Chirac, Mar. 24, 1975, RGANI: f. 80, op. 1, d. 867, l. 15.

45 Cited in Svetlana Savranskaya, "Unintended Consequences: Soviet Interests, Expectations, and Reactions to the Helsinki Final Act," in Oliver Bange and Gottfried Niedhart (eds.), *Helsinki 1975 and the Transformation of Europe* (New York: Berghahn Books, 2008), 180–181. The parade was replaced by a "festive

NOTES TO PAGES 437–444

manifestation of the youth." See "Vremya," May 9, 1975, www.youtube.com /watch?v=YZ0c9ow3ABs.

46 Cited in Sarah B. Snyder, "'Jerry, Don't Go': Domestic Opposition to the 1975 Helsinki Final Act," *Journal of American Studies*, 44(1) (2010), 71.

47 *FRUS, 1969–1976*, Vol. 16, Document 150.

48 Brezhnev to Ford, May 31, 1975, RGANI: f. 80, op. 1, d. 814, l. 25.

49 Brezhnev's diary entry for June–Nov. 1975 in S.V. Kudryashov, *Leonid Brezhnev: rabochie i dnevnikovye zapisi [Brezhnev's Diary]*, Vol. 1 (Moscow: IstLit, 2016), 614.

50 *FRUS, 1969–1976*, Vol. 16, Documents 171–174.

51 Ibid, Document 172.

52 Helsinki Final Act, www.osce.org/files/f/documents/5/c/39501.pdf.

53 For a good summary, see Svetlana Savranskaya, "Human Rights Movement in the USSR after the Signing of the Helsinki Final Act, and the Reaction of Soviet Authorities," in Leopoldo Nuti (ed.), *The Crisis of Detente in Europe: From Helsinki to Gorbachev, 1975–1985* (London: Routledge, 2009), 26–40.

54 Richard Davy, "Helsinki Myths: Setting the Record Straight on the Final Act of the CSCE, 1975," *Cold War History*, 9(1) (2009), 1–22.

55 Odd Arne Westad, "Moscow and the Angolan Crisis: A New Pattern of Intervention," *CWIHP Bulletin*, Issue 8–9 (Winter 1996/97), 21.

56 Karen Brutents, *Tridtsat' let na staroi ploshchadi* (Moscow: Mezhdunarodnye Otnosheniya, 1998), 205

57 Odd Arne Westad, "Moscow and the Angolan Crisis," 24.

58 Instructions for the Soviet ambassador in Algeria, Nov. 5, 1975, RGANI: f. 3, op. 69, d. 1863, l. 40.

59 Piero Gleijeses, *Conflicting Missions: Havana, Washington, and Africa; 1959–1976* (Chapel Hill, NC: University of North Carolina Press, 2009), 255.

60 Memcon, Mao and Kenneth Kaunda, Feb. 22, 1974. In the author's possession.

61 Memcon, Mao and Mobutu Sese Seko, Jan. 13, 1973. In the author's possession.

62 Natalia Telepneva, *Cold War Liberation: The Soviet Union and the Collapse of the Portuguese Empire in Africa, 1961–1975* (Chapel Hill, NC: University of North Carolina Press, 2022), 183.

63 Chernyaev's diary entry for Sept. 13, 1975 in Chernyaev, *Sovmestyi iskhod*, 165.

64 Myra F. Burton (ed.), *FRUS, 1969–1976*, Vol. 28 (Washington, DC: US Government Printing Office, 2011), Document 115.

65 Chernyaev's diary entry for Oct. 16, 1975 in Chernyaev, *Sovmestnyi iskhod*, 176; *Brezhnev's Diary*, Vol. 3, 731–2.

66 For a convincing exposition of this argument see Telepneva, *Cold War Liberation*.

67 Georgy Kornienko, *Kholodnaya voina: svidetel'stvo ee uchastnika* (Moscow: Olma-Press, 2001); Kornienko does not explain which memorandum his boss agonized over. There were in fact several. Soviet weapons supplies to the MPLA in the run-up and in the immediate aftermath of independence included: 2 AN-2 airplanes, 21 BM-21 "Grad" surface-to-air systems, 24 "Grad-P" surface-to-air launchers, 120 "Strela-2M" (SA-7) SAM launchers, 76 tanks and armored

NOTES TO PAGES 444–450

personnel carriers, 16,000 guns, and other types of equipment. In relative terms, this was not all that much (Soviet supplies to long-time clients like Egypt or Syria were incomparably greater) but it was a significant force in the Angolan context. See Suslov's talking points for a meeting with Fidel Castro, Dec. 1975, RGANI: f. 81, op. 1, d. 334, ll. 117–118.

68 Gromyko and Ponomarev to the CC CPSU, Oct. 28, 1975, RGANI: f. 3, op. 69, d. 1860, l. 87.

69 Draft instructions for Soviet ambassadors, undated (Oct. 28, 1975), RGANI: f. 3, op. 69, d. 1860, l. 79.

70 Chernyaev, *Sovmestnyi iskhod*, 200.

71 Gleijeses, *Conflicting Missions*, 377.

72 Ibid., 376.

73 Gromyko and Ponomarev to Politburo CC CPSU, Nov. 10, 1975, RGANI: f. 3, op. 69, d. 1867, l. 24.

74 Memcon, Dobrynin and Ted Kennedy, Feb. 2, 1976, AVPRF: f. 0129, op. 60, p. 458, d. 5, l. 69.

75 Memcon, Dobrynin and Kissinger, Feb. 16, 1976, AVPRF: f. 0129, op. 60, p. 458, d. 5, l. 107.

76 Memcon, Dobrynin and Kissinger, May 14, 1976, AVPRF: f. 0129, op. 60, p. 458, d. 5, l. 254.

77 Instructions for the Soviet ambassador in Washington, Nov. 18, 1975, RGANI: f. 3, op. 69, d. 1875, l. 66.

78 Instructions for the Soviet ambassador in Washington, Nov. 27, 1975, RGANI: f. 3, op. 69, d. 1881, l. 84.

79 Instructions for the Soviet ambassador in Havana, Nov. 27, 1975, RGANI: f. 3, op. 69, d. 1883, ll. 127–132.

80 Gromyko, Boris Ponomarev, Andropov, and Grechko to CC CPSU Politburo, Dec. 3, 1975, RGANI: f. 3, op. 69, d. 1892, l. 17.

81 Memcon, Nikita Tolubeev and Fidel Castro, Mar. 23, 1976, RGANI: f. 5, op. 69, d. 2020, l. 6.

82 Brezhnev to Fidel Castro, Mar. 31, 1976, RGANI: f. 80, op. 1, d. 683, l. 5.

83 Memcon, Nikita Tolubeev and Fidel Castro, Apr. 1, 1976, RGANI: f. 5, op. 69, d. 2020, l. 8.

84 Memcon, Brezhnev and Raúl Castro, May 5, 1976, RGANI: f. 80, op. 1, d. 683, l. 8.

85 Memcon, Nikita Tolubeev and Fidel Castro, Apr. 26, 1976, RGANI: f. 5, op. 69, d. 2020, l. 14.

86 Instructions for Soviet ambassadors in Africa and the Middle East, Dec. 15, 1975. Instructions were submitted by Gromyko; the cited passage was added by Pononarev, RGANI: f. 3, op. 69, d. 1909, l. 45.

87 Suslov's talking points for a meeting with Fidel Castro, Dec. 1975, RGANI: f. 81, op. 1, d. 334, ll. 101–103.

88 Memcon, Dobrynin and Kissinger, Feb. 16, 1976, AVPRF: f. 0129, op. 60, p. 458, d. 5, l. 107.

NOTES TO PAGES 450–454

89 Cited in Nancy Mitchell, *Jimmy Carter in Africa: Race and the Cold War* (Stanford University Press, 2018), 38.

90 Memcon, Dobrynin and Scowcroft, Apr. 16, 1976, AVPRF: f. 0129, op. 60, p. 458, d. 5, l. 184.

91 Memcon, Dobrynin and Kissinger, May 14, 1976, AVPRF: f. 0129, op. 60, p. 458, d. 5, l. 254.

92 Cited in Mitchell, *Carter in Africa*, 25.

16 TENSIONS MOUNT

1 For a good summary of the fake Testament, see Albert Resis, "Russophobia and the 'Testament' of Peter the Great, 1812–1980," *Slavic Review*, 44(4) (Winter 1985), 681–693.

2 Hua Guofeng, Deng Xiaoping's rival in power, even brought up the "Testament" in his conversation with US Vice President Walter Mondale, asking him if he had read it. "I confess I have not," Mondale helpfully replied. David P. Nickles (ed.), *Foreign Relations of the United States [FRUS], 1977–1980*, Vol. 13 (Washington, DC: US Government Printing Office, 2013), Document 266.

3 Kristin L. Ahlberg (ed.), *FRUS, 1977–1980*, Vol. 1 (Washington, DC: US Government Printing Office, 2014), Document 52.

4 Deng Xiaoping's comments to an American delegation, Apr. 15, 1980, Shanghai Archives, B1-9-116-10.

5 Ibid.

6 *FRUS, 1977–1980*, Vol. 13, Document 265.

7 Melissa Jane Taylor (ed.), *FRUS, 1977–1980*, Vol. 6 (Washington, DC: US Government Printing Office, 2013), Document 204.

8 Memcon, Brezhnev and Armand Hammer, Oct. 14, 1980, RGANI: f. 80, op. 1, d. 831, l. 56.

9 *FRUS, 1977–1980*, Vol. 6, Document 197.

10 For a good overview, see Sarah B. Snyder, "Through the Looking Glass: The Helsinki Final Act and the 1976 Election for President," *Diplomacy & Statecraft*, 21(1) (2010), 87–106.

11 Memcon, Brezhnev and Armand Hammer, Oct. 20, 1976, RGANI: f. 80, op. 1, d. 830, ll. 7–8.

12 Ibid., l. 7. See also Anatoly Chernyaev, *Sovmestnyi iskhod: dnevnik dvukh epokh* (Moscow: Rosspen, 2008), 245.

13 *FRUS, 1977–1980*, Vol. 6, Document 1.

14 Jimmy Carter, *Keeping Faith: Memoirs of a President* (University of Arkansas Press, 1995), 150.

15 *FRUS, 1977–1980*, Vol. 6, Document 2.

16 Ibid., Document 5.

17 Christopher Wren, "Sakharov Receives Carter Letter Affirming Commitment on Rights," *New York Times*, Feb. 18, 1977, 3.

NOTES TO PAGES 454–458

18 Aleksandrov-Agentov to Brezhnev, Feb. 22, 1977, RGANI: f. 80, op. 1, d. 817, l. 17.

19 TASS Service Bulletin of Foreign Information ("top secret"), No. 73 (Feb. 21, 1977), RGANI: f. 80, op. 1, d. 817, l. 22. The commentary in question was by CBS correspondent Marvin Kalb.

20 Aleksandrov-Agentov to Brezhnev, Feb. 22, 1977, RGANI: f. 80, op. 1, d. 817, l. 18.

21 *FRUS, 1977–1980,* Vol. 6, Document 12. Also RGANI: f. 80, op. 1, d. 817, ll. 25–29.

22 Politburo protocol, Feb. 18, 1977, https://nsarchive.gwu.edu/document/243 69-extract-cc-cpsu-politburo-meeting-about-instructions-soviet-ambassador-washington.

23 Memcon, Brezhnev and Vance, Mar. 28, 1977, RGANI: f. 80, op. 1, d. 817, l. 52.

24 Memcon, Brezhnev and Giscard d'Estaing, June 22, 1977, RGANI: f. 80, op. 1, d. 868, l. 154.

25 For a good overview of Carter's human rights agenda see David F. Schmitz and Vanessa Walker, "Jimmy Carter and the Foreign Policy of Human Rights: The Development of a Post-Cold War Foreign Policy," *Diplomatic History,* 28(1) (Jan. 2004), 113–143.

26 Memcon, Dobrynin and Kissinger, Nov. 23, 1979, AVPRF: f. 0129, op. 63, p. 482, d. 7, l. 152.

27 *FRUS, 1977–1980,* Vol. 1, Document 32.

28 US policy makers were well aware that they opened themselves up to accusations of hypocrisy or "moral arrogance" (in the words of then-Director of Policy Planning Staff Anthony Lake) but apparently thought that the benefits outweighed the risks. See Kristin Ahlberg (ed.), *FRUS, 1977–1980,* Vol. 2 (Washington, DC: US Government Printing Office, 2013), Document 105; and Schmitz and Walker, "Jimmy Carter and the Foreign Policy of Human Rights."

29 Presidential Directive/NSC–7, Mar. 23, 1977, in Erin R. Mahan (ed.), *FRUS, 1969–1976,* Vol. 33 (Washington, DC: US Government Printing Office, 2013), Document 156. For discussion of disagreements see also Barbara Zanchetta, *The Transformation of American International Power in the 1970s* (Cambridge University Press, 2014), 165–168.

30 Memcon, Brezhnev and Vance, Mar. 28, 1977, RGANI: f. 80, op. 1, d. 817, ll. 33–55.

31 James Baldwin, "An Open Letter to Mr. Carter," *New York Times,* Jan. 23, 1977. The excerpted letter is in RGANI: f. 80, op. 1, d. 817, ll. 93–94. Brezhnev underlined the fact that Carter had not responded to the letter.

32 Chernyaev, *Sovmestnyi iskhod,* 265.

33 Memcon, Brezhnev and Vance, Mar. 30, 1977, RGANI: f. 80, op. 1, d. 817, l. 57.

34 Chernyaev, *Sovmestnyi iskhod,* 269.

35 Memcon, Brezhnev and Vance, Mar. 30, 1977, RGANI: f. 80, op. 1, d. 817, ll. 56–63.

36 Memcon, Dobrynin and Kissinger, Apr. 11, 1977, AVPRF: f. 0129, op. 61, p. 467, d. 6, l. 13.

37 Memcon, Dobrynin and Harriman, Mar. 4, 1978, AVPRF: f. 0129, op. 62, p. 474, d. 5, l. 146.

685

NOTES TO PAGES 458–463

38 Memcon, Dobrynin and Harriman, Mar. 14, 1978, AVPRF: f. 0129, op. 62, p. 474, d. 5, l. 183.

39 Memcon, Dobrynin and Kissinger, Apr. 11, 1977, AVPRF: f. 0129, op. 61, p. 467, d. 6, l. 12.

40 Patrick Tyler, *A Great Wall: Six Presidents and China: An Investigative History* (New York: Public Affairs, 1999), 230.

41 *FRUS, 1977–1980*, Vol. 13, Document 110.

42 Memorandum of conversation, June 4, 1980, Carter Presidential Library: Office of Staff Secretary; Series: Presidential Files; Folder: 6/4/80; Container 164. Watson acted cautiously because he worried that prodding Carter too much would "cost him his head." See Memcon, Brezhnev and Armand Hammer, Feb. 27, 1980, RGANI: f. 80, op. 1, d. 831, l. 16.

43 Deng Xiaoping's speech at the July 1963 Sino-Soviet talks, National Security Archive, Russian and East European Archival Documents Database (REEADD), Oct. 26, 1962–1964, 185.

44 Chinese Foreign Ministry, "International Outlook and Outline of Foreign Affairs Work," Feb. 6, 1980, Hubei Provincial Archives: SZ1-8-185.

45 Memcon, Deng Xiaoping and Ramiro Saraiva Guerreiro, Mar. 25, 1982, Shanghai Archives: B1-9-798-105.

46 Chen Jian, "China, the Third World and the End of the Cold War," in Artemy Kalinovsky and Sergey Radchenko (eds.), *The End of the Cold War and the Third World: New Perspectives on Regional Conflict* (London and New York: Routledge, 2011), 112.

47 "On the conduct of additional work," Oct. 2, 1980, RGANI: f. 89, op. 34, d. 10, l. 5.

48 For example, during Brezhnev's meeting with Giscard d'Estaing in Apr. 1979. As reported in Cable from Robert L. Barry to Dr. Shulman, May 11, 1979, Carter Presidential Library (CPL): NLC 13-16-1-1-8.

49 Cable, US Embassy in Moscow to the Department of State, Feb. 16, 1979, CPL: NLC 16-15-2-12-3. The original is missing a word after "shedding": presumably, "tears."

50 Memcon, Dobrynin and Brzezinski, Feb. 9, 1979, AVPRF: f. 0129, op. 63, p. 482, d. 5, l. 94.

51 Memcon, Dobrynin and Vance, Nov. 27, 1978, AVPRF: f. 0129, op. 62, p. 475, d. 7, l. 147.

52 Minutes of meeting between CDA Dr. Teja and Ambassador Sudarikov, Feb. 1, 1979, National Archives of India: MEA wii/104/2/79, Vol. 2.

53 Memcon, D. Yondon and Mikhail Kapitsa, June 9, 1982, Mongolian Foreign Ministry Archive (MFMA): f. 2, dans 1, kh/n 467, khuu 38–39.

54 Report on a meeting with Mikhail Kapitsa, June 21, 1982, MFMA: f. 2, dans 1, kh/n 467.

55 On China's "long game," see Rush Doshi, *The Long Game: China's Grand Strategy to Displace American Order* (New York: Oxford University Press, 2021).

56 *FRUS, 1977–1980*, Vol. 13, Document 110.

NOTES TO PAGES 464–470

57 Transcript of a meeting between East German leader Erich Honecker and Cuban leader Fidel Castro, Apr. 3, 1977, CWIHP DA: https://digitalarchive .wilsoncenter.org/document/111844. Obtained by Christian F. Ostermann. Translated by David Welch (with revisions by Ostermann).

58 The record of Castro's meetings in Moscow in Apr. 1977 is not available but it is unlikely that he would told the Soviets anything different than he reported to Honecker. See also Michael T. Kaufman, "Castro in Ethiopia after Somalia Visit," *New York Times*, Mar. 16, 1977, A11.

59 For an overview, see. L.V. Ivanova, "Rol' SSSR v somaliisko-efiopskom konflikte," in A.S. Balezin, A.B. Davidson, and S.V. Mazov (eds.), *Afrika v sud'be Rossii, Rossiia v sud'be Afriki* (Moscow: Politicheskaya Entsiklopediya, 2019), 318–342.

60 Brezhnev to Siad Barre, Aug. 13, 1976, RGANI: f. 80, op. 1, d. 836, l. 11.

61 On the PRC activities in Somalia (Soviet Embassy in Mogadishu), Nov. 24, 1970, RGANI: f. 5, op. 62, d. 544, l. 235.

62 Memcon, Siad Barre and A.S. Pasyutin, June 18, 1971, RGANI: f. 5, op. 63, d. 590, l. 198.

63 See e.g. Memcon, A.S. Pasyutin and Samantar, Nov. 9, 1970, RGANI: f. 5, op. 63, d. 590, l. 105.

64 Chernyaev, *Sovmestnyi iskhod*, 164.

65 Memcon, Brezhnev and Mengistu, May 6, 1977, RGANI: f. 80, op. 1, d. 922, l. 24.

66 Information on Visit of Mengistu Haile Mariam to Moscow, May 13, 1977. Obtained and translated by Vladislav M. Zubok. CWIHP DA: https:// digitalarchive.wilsoncenter.org/document/111847.

67 Memcon, Brezhnev and Ali Samatar, June 1, 1977, RGANI: f. 80, op. 1, d. 836, ll. 19–25.

68 Letter, Brezhnev to Siad Barre, July 8, 1977, RGANI: f. 80, op. 1, d. 836, l. 37.

69 Chernyaev, *Sovmestnyi iskhod*, 280.

70 *FRUS, 1977–1980*, Vol. 6, Document 33.

71 S.V. Kudryashov, *Leonid Brezhnev: rabochie i dnevnikovye zapisi* [*Brezhnev's Diary*], Vol. 1 (Moscow: IstLit, 2016), 801, 810, 816, 848.

72 Memcon, Brezhnev and Todor Zhivkov, Aug. 9, 1977, Bulgarian State Archive: ChP174B-1-566N. Obtained by Elena Mincheva.

73 Memcon, Brezhnev, Kosygin et al. and Mengistu, Oct. 31, 1977, RGANI: f. 80, op. 1, d. 922, l. 69.

74 Aryeh Yodfat, "The Soviet Union and the Horn of Africa: Part Two of Three Parts," *Northeast African Studies*, 2(1) (Spring 1980), 44–43.

75 Louise P. Woodroofe (ed.), *FRUS, 1977–1980*, Vol. 17, Part 1 (Washington, DC: US Government Publishing Office, 2016), Document 20.

76 Ibid. For the background to this meeting, see Mitchell, *Jimmy Carter in Africa*, 267. For description of Addou, see ibid., 195.

77 Memcon, Dobrynin and Abdullahi Addou, Feb. 23, 1979, AVPRF: f. 0129, op. 62, p. 474, d. 5, l. 113.

NOTES TO PAGES 470–478

78 Memcon, Brezhnev and Edward Gierek, Apr. 18, 1978, RGANI: f. 80, op. 1, d. 744, l. 42.

79 *FRUS, 1977–1980*, Vol. 17, Part 1, Document 29.

80 Odd Arne Westad, *The Global Cold War: Third World Interventions and the Making of Our Times* (Cambridge University Press, 2005), 398.

17 THE FINAL NAIL

1 Brezhnev to Chernenko, Dec. 25, 1975, RGANI: f. 80, op. 1, d. 317, l. 55. For a discussion see also also Andreï Kozovoï, *Brejnev: l'antihéros* (Paris: Perrin), 343–344; Chernyaev's diary entry for Jan. 3, 1976, https://nsarchive.gwu.edu/rus/text_files/Chernyaev/1976.pdf.

2 Preparatory materials for Mohammad Daoud's visit to Moscow, Apr. 1977, RGANI: f. 80, op. 1, d. 460, l. 54.

3 Memcon, Khrushchev and Mohammed Daoud Khan, May 20, 1959, RGANI: f. 52, op. 1, d. 547, l. 52.

4 Vasiliy Mitrokhin, "The KGB in Afghanistan," CWIHP Working Paper 40, Russian Edition (July 2002).

5 Ibid., 5.

6 Ibid., 2.

7 Ibid., 3–4.

8 Memcon, Brezhnev and Mohammad Naim, Sept. 11, 1973, RGANI: f. 80, op. 1, d. 458, l. 74.

9 Paul J. Hibbeln and Peter A. Kraemer (eds.), *Foreign Relations of the United States [FRUS], 1969–1976*, Vol. E–8 (Washington, DC: US Government Printing Office, 2007), Document 24.

10 Memcon, Brezhnev and Muhammed Daoud Khan, June 5, 1974, RGANI: f. 80, op. 1, d. 459, ll. 25–26.

11 Talking points for conversation with Muhammed Daoud Khan, undated (no later than June 5, 1974), RGANI: f. 80, op. 1, d. 459, l. 49.

12 Memcon, Brezhnev and Muhammed Daoud Khan, June 5, 1974, RGANI: f. 80, op. 1, d. 459, ll. 28–29.

13 Memcon, Brezhnev and Mohammad Naim, Jan. 24, 1977, RGANI: f. 80, op. 1, d. 460, l. 3.

14 Preparatory materials for Daoud Khan's visit to Moscow, Apr. 1977, RGANI: f. 80, op. 1, d. 460, l. 54.

15 Memcon, Soviet leaders (Brezhnev, Kosygin, Gromyko, Podgorny) and Mohammad Daoud Khan, Apr. 12–13, 1977, RGANI: f. 80, op. 1, d. 460, l. 39.

16 Political report of the Soviet Embassy in Afghanistan, May 31, 1978, RGANI: f. 5, op. 75, d. 1179, l. 4. For a detailed discussion of Khyber's assassination (which leaves it unclear who was responsible), see Chris Sands and Fazelminallah Qazizai, *Night Letters: Gulbuddin Hekmatyar and the Afghan Islamists Who Changed the World* (London: C. Hurst & Co. Publishers, 2019), 108–111.

NOTES TO PAGES 478–483

17 Memcon, N.N. Simonenko and Hafizullah Amin, May 23, 1978, RGANI: f. 5, op. 75, d. 1181, ll. 5–7.

18 Memcon, Brezhnev and Kosygin and a PDPA delegation led by Nur Muhammad Taraki and Hafizullah Amin, Dec. 4–5, 1978, RGANI: f. 80, op. 1, d. 461, ll. 5–24.

19 Memcon, A.M. Puzanov and Amin, Oct. 22, 1978, RGANI: f. 5, op. 75, d. 1181, ll. 105–108.

20 Memcon, A.M. Puzanov and Taraki, July 1, 1978, RGANI: f. 5, op. 75, d. 1181, ll. 29–33.

21 Memcon, A.M. Puzanov and Taraki, July 18, 1978, RGANI: f. 5, op. 75, d. 1181, ll. 36–40. Memcon, A.M. Puzanov and Amin, July 18, 1978, RGANI: f. 5, op. 75, d. 1181, ll. 41–43.

22 Memcon, A.M. Puzanov and Taraki, July 1, 1978, RGANI: f. 5, op. 75, d. 1181, ll. 29–33.

23 Memcon, A.M. Puzanov, Taraki, and Babrak Karmal, June 18, 1978, RGANI: f. 5, op. 75, d. 1181, l. 26.

24 Ibid., l. 27.

25 Memcon, Yu. Sidel'nikov and Afghan citizens, Nov. 27, 1978, RGANI: f. 5, op. 75, d. 1181, ll. 132–133.

26 Transcript of CPSU CC Politburo Discussions on Afghanistan, Mar. 17, 1979, CWIHP DA: https://digitalarchive.wilsoncenter.org/document/113260.

27 Memo on Protocol #149 of the Politburo, Apr. 1, 1979. Translated by Loren Utkin. CWIHP DA: https://digitalarchive.wilsoncenter.org/document/110060.

28 Memcon, L.I. Brezhnev and N.M. Taraki, Mar. 20, 1979, CWIHP DA: https://digitalarchive.wilsoncenter.org/document/111282.

29 Report on a Mongolian delegation's visit to Vietnam, Dec. 1979, Mongolian Government Archive: f. 1, tov'yog 28, kh/n 20 (1980), khuu 185.

30 On relations between Vietnam and Cambodia, Jan. 20, 1978, Stiftung Archiv der Parteien- und Massenorganisationen im Bundesarchiv, Berlin [SAMPO-BArch], DY 30/13994.

31 Speech of the Vietnamese representative Chan Dong at the Moscow meeting of intelligence agencies, May 1982, Historical Archives of the Hungarian State Security (ÁBTL): NK-VIII-vietnam-1982.

32 On Le Duan's and Pham Van Dong's visit to the USSR, Nov. 14, 1978, SAPMO-BArch, DY 30/13994.

33 Ibid.

34 Memcon, Jambyn Batmunkh and Pham Van Dong, Dec. 1–2, 1979, Mongolian Government Archive: f. 1, tov'yog 28, kh/n 19, khuu 21–55.

35 Memcon, Carter and Deng Xiaoping, Jan. 29, 1979, Carter Presidential Library (CPL), Zbigniew Brzezinski Collection, China, President's Meeting with Deng Xiaoping, Dec. 19, 1978–Mar. 10, 1979.

36 Carter's hand-written note, Jan. 30, 1979, CPL: Zbigniew Brzezinski Collection, China, President's Meeting with Deng Xiaoping, 12/19/1978–10/03/1979.

NOTES TO PAGES 483–486

37 Brzezinski argued in a memorandum to Carter that seriously opposing China's action against Vietnam would have "very negative consequences for the emerging US–Chinese relationship." See Brzezinski to Carter, Feb. 6, 1979, Carter Presidential Library; Sullivan Subject File, Geng Biao Visit, 6/80. On Brezhnev's reaction, see, Memcon, Brezhnev and Armand Hammer, Feb. 27, 1980, RGANI: f. 80, op. 1, d. 831, l. 5.

38 Zhang Xiaoming, *Deng Xiaoping's Long War: The Military Conflict between China and Vietnam, 1979–1991* (Chapel Hill, NC: University of North Carolina Press, 2015).

39 Melissa Jane Taylor (ed.), *FRUS, 1977–1980*, Vol. 6 (Washington, DC: US Government Printing Office, 2013), Document 173.

40 *FRUS, 1977–1980*, Vol. 6, Document 182.

41 The story is recounted in detail in Roham Alvandi, "Flirting with Neutrality: The Shah, Khrushchev, and the Failed 1959 Soviet–Iranian Negotiations," *Iranian Studies*, 43(3) (Feb. 2014), 419–440.

42 Memcon, Brezhnev and the Shah of Iran, June 22, 1965, RGANI: f. 80, op. 1, d. 638, l. 3.

43 For an overview, see V. Ivanenko and Michel Vale, "Twenty Years of Soviet–Iranian Economic and Technical Cooperation," *Soviet and Eastern European Foreign Trade*, 21(1/2/3) (1985), 135–143.

44 Vasiliy Mitrokhin, "Iran," in Churchill College Archives, Cambridge, UK: GBR/0014/MITN, 1/2, Iran-1988, 18.

45 Roham Alvandi, *Nixon, Kissinger, and the Shah* (Oxford University Press, 2014), 58.

46 "Why is the Shah doing it?" asked Brezhnev's aides Andrei Aleksandrov-Agentov and Evgeny Samoteikin in a memorandum to the Soviet leader, undated, RGANI: f. 80, op. 1, d. 331, l. 13.

47 Memcon, Brezhnev and the Shah of Iran, Nov. 18, 1974, RGANI: f. 80, op. 1, d. 638, ll. 111–129.

48 Memcon, Brezhnev and Amir-Abbas Hoveyda, Aug. 7, 1973, RGANI: f. 80, op. 1, d. 638, ll. 78–79.

49 Vladimir Vinogradov, *Diplomatiya: lyudi i sobytiya. Iz zapisok posla* (Moscow: Rosspen, 1998), 397.

50 Vasiliy Mitrokhin, "Iran," in Churchill College Archives, Cambridge, UK: GBR/0014/MITN, 1/2, Iran-1988, 17.

51 Vladimir Vinogradov, *Nash blizhnii vostok. Zapiski sovetskogo posla v Egipte i Irane* (Moscow: Algoritm, 2016) [e-book].

52 Leonid Shebarshin, *Ruka Moskvy: zapiski nachal'nika sovetskoi razvedki* (Moscow: Tsentr-100, 1992).

53 Memcon, Brezhnev and Taraki, Dec. 4–5, 1978, RGANI: f. 80, op. 1, d. 461, l. 9.

54 Memorandum, Brezhnev to the Politburo, Jan. 12, 1979, RGANI: f. 80, op. 1, d. 639, l. 2.

55 For a detailed discussion see Jeremy Friedman, "The Enemy of My Enemy: The Soviet Union, East Germany, and the Iranian Tudeh Party's Support for Ayatollah Khomeini," *JCWS*, 20(2) (2018), 3–37; Mohsen M. Milani, "Harvest

NOTES TO PAGES 486–489

of Shame: Tudeh and the Bazargan Government," *Middle Eastern Studies*, 29(2) (Apr. 1993), 307–320; Maziar Behrooz, *Rebels with a Cause: The Failure of the Left in Iran* (London: I.B. Tauris, 1999). See also Lorenz M. Lüthi, *Cold Wars: Asia the Middle East Europe* (Cambridge University Press, 2020), 505; Dzhamil' Gasanly, *SSSR-Iran: azerbaidzhansky krizis i nachalo kholodnoi voiny, 1941–1946 gg* (Moscow: Geroyi Otechestva, 2006), 488.

56 On Tudeh and the revolution, see, in particular, Mohammad Tabaar, "Causes of the US Hostage Crisis in Iran: The Untold Account of the Communist Threat," *Security Studies*, 26(4) (2017), 665–697.

57 Friedman, "The Enemy of My Enemy."

58 For a full discussion, see Dmitry Asinovsky, "The Soviet Union and the Iranian Revolution," *Russia in Global Affairs*, 16(3) (July–Sept. 2018), 190–208.

59 This view was shared by US experts as well, e.g. Linda Qaimmaqami (ed.), *FRUS, 1977–1980*, Vol. 11, Part 1 (Washington, DC: US Government Publishing Office, 2020), Document 50.

60 Vinogradov, *Nash blizhnii vostok.*

61 Ibid.

62 Draft telegram, Brezhnev to Khomeini, Apr. 3, 1979, RGANI: f. 80, op. 1, d. 639, l. 3.

63 Ibid., ll. 4–6.

64 *FRUS, 1977–1980*, Vol. 11, Part 1, Document 4. See also Zbigniew Brzezinski, *Power and Principle: Memoirs of the National Security Adviser, 1977–1981* (New York: Farrar, Straus, Giroux, 1985), 475–476.

65 See Mark Gasiorowski, "US Covert Operations toward Iran, February–November 1979: Was the CIA Trying to Overthrow the Islamic Regime," *Middle Eastern Studies*, 51(1) (2015), 115–135.

66 Mark Gasiorowski, "US Intelligence Assistance to Iran, May–October 1979," *Middle East Journal*, 66(4) (Autumn 2012), 613–627.

67 Decision of the CC CPSU Secretariat, Aug. 30, 1979, RGANI: f. 89, op. 32, d. 10, l. 11. See also Gasanly, *SSSR-Iran*, 490.

68 The number here is inclusive of the three taken hostage at the Foreign Ministry.

69 It is not entirely clear whether Khomeini merely approved of the attack on the embassy or authorized it. The CIA believed the latter: *FRUS, 1977–1980*, Vol. 11, Part 1, Document 18. On the embassy attack as a way of undermining the Left, see Mohammad Tabaar, "Causes of the US Hostage Crisis."

70 Background Paper Prepared in the Office of the Assistant Secretary of Defense for International Security Affairs, undated, *FRUS, 1977–1980*, Vol. 6, Document 194.

71 Memcon, Dobrynin and Vance, Mar. 29, 1979, AVPRF: f. 0129, op. 63, p. 482, d. 5, ll. 219–221.

72 Ibid.

73 Robert L. Barry to Dr. Shulman, May 11, 1979, CPL: NLC 13-16-1-1-8.

74 Kevin Klose, "Soviet Leader's Lapsing Health Affects Summit," *Washington Post*, May 13, 1979.

NOTES TO PAGES 490–493

75 *FRUS, 1977–1980,* Vol. 6, Document 199.

76 Viktor Sukhodrev, *Yazyk moi – drug moi* (Moscow: ID Tonchu, 2008), 361. The US version of the conversation is *FRUS, 1977–1980,* Vol. 6, Document 206. The Soviet record is in RGANI: f. 80, op. 1, d. 821 (it closely corresponds to *FRUS*).

77 Jimmy Carter, *White House Diary* (New York: Farrar, Straus and Giroux, 2010), 331.

78 David Zierler (ed.), *FRUS, 1977–1980,* Vol. 12 (Washington, DC: US Government Publishing Office, 2018), Document 65.

79 Vasiliy Mitrokhin, "The KGB in Afghanistan," 22.

80 Memcon, Brezhnev and Taraki, Sept. 10, 1979, RGANI: f. 80, op. 1, d. 462, l. 57.

81 Rodric Braithwaite, *Afgantsy: The Russians in Afghanistan 1979–89* (Oxford University Press, 2011), 63–64.

82 Ibid., 66.

83 Brezhnev's notes for the Sept. 20, 1979 Politburo meeting, RGANI: f. 80, op. 1, d. 462, l. 79.

84 Ibid., 81.

85 Vladimir Medvedev, *Chelovek za spinoi* (Moscow: Russlit, 1994), 123.

86 Entry for Nov. 22, 1979, *Brezhnev's Diary,* Vol. 1, 979.

87 Mitrokhin, "The KGB in Afghanistan," 46.

88 Andropov, Gromyko, Ustinov, and Ponomarev, "On events in Afghanistan," Dec. 31, 1979, RGANI: f. 89, op. 42, d. 10. For more on this subject, see Westad, *The Global Cold War,* 316–322.

89 *FRUS, 1977–1980,* Vol. 12, Document 76 and *FRUS, 1977–1980,* Vol. 6, Document 194. Admiral Stanfield Turner claimed that US armed and financial support did not materialize until after the Soviet invasion, which is not correct: relevant decisions were being taken in autumn 1979, weeks before the invasion. For Turner's denial, see Svetlana Savranskaya, David A. Welch and Odd Arne Westad (eds.), *The Intervention in Afghanistan and the Fall of Détente* (transcripts of an oral history conference at Lysebu, Sept. 17–20, 1995 [Lysebu Transcripts]) (Oslo: Norwegian Nobel Institute, 1996), 103.

90 *FRUS, 1977–1980,* Vol. 12, Document 74.

91 Interview with Archer Blood, June 27, 1989, The Association for Diplomatic Studies and Training Foreign Affairs Oral History Project, https://cdn.loc.gov /service/mss/mfdip/2004/2004blo02/2004blo02.pdf.

92 Telegram from the Embassy in Afghanistan to the Department of State, Oct. 28, 1979, *FRUS, 1977–1980,* Vol. 12, Document 78.

93 Mitrokhin, "The KGB in Afghanistan," 49.

94 As cited by Dobrynin in the Lysebu Transcripts, 90–91. The date of the memorandum is unclear.

95 A. A. Lyakhovsky, *Tragediya i doblest' Afgana,* 2nd ed. (Yaroslavl: TF Nord, 2004).

96 Stasi Note on Meeting between Minister Mielke and Andropov, July 11, 1981. Translated CWIHP Bernd Schaefer. CWIHP DA: https://digitalarchive .wilsoncenter.org/document/115717.

692

NOTES TO PAGES 493–502

97 CC CPSU Politburo Resolution # 176/125, Dec. 12, 1979, CWIHP DA: https://digitalarchive.wilsoncenter.org/document/113675.

98 For an account of the storming of Amin's palace, see Gregory Feifer, *The Great Gamble: The Soviet War in Afghanistan* (New York: HarperCollins, 2009), 55–84.

99 Lysebu Transcripts, 13–14.

100 Ibid., 29.

101 Ibid., 98.

102 Odd Arne Westad, "Concerning the Situation in "A": New Russian Evidence on the Soviet Intervention in Afghanistan," *CWIHP Bulletin*, Issue 8–9 (Winter 1996/97), 130.

103 Lysebu Transcripts, 125.

104 Vinogradov, *Nash blizhnii vostok.*

105 *FRUS, 1977–1980*, Vol. 11, Part 1, Document 83.

106 UNSC Resolution 461, Dec. 31, 1979, http://unscr.com/en/resolutions/doc/461.

107 Aleksandrov-Agentov, Blatov, and Samoteikin to Brezhnev, Jan. 3, 1980, RGANI: f. 80, op. 1, d. 639, ll. 13–16.

108 *FRUS, 1977–1980*, Vol. 11, Part 1, Document 147.

109 Saddam Hussein to Brezhnev, Oct. 21, 1980, RGANI: f. 80, op. 1, d. 637, l. 28.

110 Brezhnev to Saddam Hussein, Oct. 24, 1980: RGANI: f. 80, op. 1, d. 637, ll. 45–49.

111 Memcon, Brezhnev and King Hussein, May 27, 1981, RGANI: f. 80, op. 1, d. 633, l. 91. For a broader discussion of the Iran-Iraq War, see Paul Thomas Chamberlin, *The Cold War's Killing Fields: Rethinking the Long Peace* (New York: Harper, 2019), 465–478.

112 *FRUS, 1977–1980*, Vol. 12, Document 150.

113 The guidelines also proposed internal subversion of Kaysone Phomvihane of neighboring Laos. Chinese Foreign Ministry, "International Outlook and Outline of Foreign Affairs Work," Feb. 6, 1980, Hubei Provincial Archives: SZ1-8-185.

114 Geng Biao's speech before an all-country meeting of travel workers, top secret, Mar. 6, 1975. The document has no archival classification. The author obtained it from a secondhand bookshop in China.

115 Sergey Radchenko, *Unwanted Visionaries: The Soviet Failure in Asia at the End of the Cold War* (New York: Oxford University Press, 2014), ch. 1.

116 Memcon, Dobrynin and Kissinger, Nov. 23, 1979, AVPRF: f. 0129, op. 63, p. 482, d. 7, l. 156.

117 Ibid., l. 154.

118 Brezhnev's talking points for his meeting with Taraki on Sept. 10, 1979. This statement was to be made only if Taraki raised the question of sending Soviet troops into the country, which he did not, RGANI: f. 80, op. 1, d. 462, l. 75.

119 David Binder, "Soviet Brigade: How the U.S. Traced It," *New York Times*, Sept. 13, 1979, A16.

NOTES TO PAGES 502–511

120 On the US intelligence assessment of the "brigade," see e.g. "The Soviet Brigade in Cuba," Dec. 1, 1986, CIA CREST, Document CIA-RDP87T00076R000304900001-9.

121 Memcon, Dobrynin and Brzezinski, Dec. 6, 1979, AVPRF: f. 0129, op. 63, p. 482, d. 7, ll. 185–189.

122 Memcon, Brezhnev and Armand Hammer, Feb. 27, 1980, RGANI: f. 80, op. 1, d. 831, ll. 7–11.

123 Memcon, Brezhnev and Armand Hammer, Oct. 14, 1980, RGANI: f. 80, op. 1, d. 831, l. 32. On this point I disagree with authors who argue that the Soviets welcomed Reagan's election because Carter had turned out to be so bad. See e.g. Simon Miles, *Engaging the Evil Empire: Washington, Moscow, and the Beginning of the End of the Cold War* (Ithaca, NY: Cornell University Press, 2020), 22.

18 FEAR

1 E.g. S.V. Kudryashov, *Leonid Brezhnev: rabochie i dnevnikovye zapisi,* Vol. 1 (Moscow: IstLit, 2016), 1066.

2 Garton Ash, *The Polish Revolution: Solidarity,* 3rd ed. (New Haven, CT: Yale University Press, 2002), 15–21.

3 On the pope's visit to Poland, see George Weigel, *Witness to Hope: The Biography of Pope John Paul II, 1920–2005* (New York: HarperCollins, 1999), 291–295.

4 Memcon, Brezhnev and Gierek, Aug. 3, 1978, RGANI: f. 80, op. 1, d. 744, l. 82.

5 Memcon, Brezhnev and Gierek, July 31, 1980, RGANI: f. 80, op. 1, d. 746, l. 34.

6 Memcon, Brezhnev and Gierek, Aug. 3, 1978, RGANI: f. 80, op. 1, d. 744, l. 90.

7 Memcon, Brezhnev and Edward Babiuch, May 6, 1980, RGANI: f. 80, op. 1, d. 746, l. 14.

8 Memcon, Brezhnev and Edward Gierek, July 31, 1980, RGANI: f. 80, op. 1, d. 746, l. 36.

9 Ibid., l. 38.

10 Ibid., ll. 46–47.

11 For a vivid account of how the Gdańsk Agreement was signed, see Ash, *The Polish Revolution: Solidarity,* 41–72.

12 Memcon, Brezhnev and Mieczysław Jagielski, Sept. 11, 1980, RGANI: f. 80, op. 1, d. 747, l. 10.

13 The Soviets warned against the recognition of independent trade unions. See "K voprosu o polozhenii v Pol'she: o nekotorykh sovetakh pol'skim tovarishcham," Aug. 26, 1980, RGANI: f. 81, op. 1, d. 353, ll. 51–52. Kindly shared with the author by Mark Kramer.

14 Memcon, Brezhnev, Mikhail Suslov, and Andrzej Werblan, Sept. 15, 1980, RGANI: f. 80, op. 1, d. 747, l. 35. The Politburo Commission on Poland was set up on Aug. 25, 1980, in response to the deteriorating situation.

15 For a discussion, see e.g. Mark Kramer, "The Soviet Union, the Warsaw Pact, and the Polish Crisis of 1980–1981," in Lee Trepanier, Spasimir Domaradzki, and

NOTES TO PAGES 511–514

Jaclyn Stanke (eds.), *The Solidarity Movement and Perspectives on the Last Decade of the Cold War* (Krakow: Krakow Society for Education, 2010).

16 KGB annual report for 1981, CWIHP DA: https://digitalarchive.wilsoncenter .org/document/112803.

17 Anatoly Chernyaev, *Sovmestnyi iskhod: dnevnik dvukh epokh* (Moscow: Rosspen, 2008), 418.

18 Brezhnev's comments at the Politburo, Sept. 18, 1980, RGANI: f. 80, op. 1, d. 747, l. 52. Curiously, this was exactly the conclusion reached by the US intelligence at around the same time. See Douglas J. MacEachin, *US Intelligence and the Polish Crisis, 1980–1981* (Washington, DC: Center for the Study of Intelligence, 2000), 14–15.

19 Memcon, Brezhnev and Jagielski, Sept. 11, 1980, RGANI: f. 80, op. 1, d. 747, l. 12.

20 Chernyaev, *Sovmestnyi iskhod*, 424.

21 "Informatsionnoe soobshchenie," *Izvestiya*, Oct. 22, 1980, 1.

22 Session of the CPSU CC Politburo, Oct. 29, 1980, CWIHP DA: https:// digitalarchive.wilsoncenter.org/document/113578.

23 Ibid. See also Matthew J. Ouimet, *The Rise and Fall of the Brezhnev Doctrine in Soviet Foreign Policy* (Chapel Hill, NC: University of North Carolina Press, 2003), 144–150.

24 Ryszard Kuklinski, "The Suppression of Solidarity," in Robert Kostrzewa (ed.), *Between East and West: Writings from Kultura* (New York: Hill & Wang, 1990), 80–81; Andrzej Paczkowski and Andrzej Werblan, "On the Decision to Introduce Martial Law in Poland In 1981. Two Historians Report to the Commission on Constitutional Oversight of the Sejm of the Republic of Poland," CWIHP Working Paper 21 (Nov. 1997), 9. Vojtech Mastny, "The Soviet Non-Invasion of Poland in 1980–1981 and the End of the Cold War," *Europe-Asia Studies*, 51(2) (1999), 191–192.

25 Session of the CPSU CC Politburo, Oct. 31, 1980. CWIHP DA: https:// digitalarchive.wilsoncenter.org/document/113580.

26 Stenographic Minutes of the Meeting of Leading Representatives of the Warsaw Pact Countries in Moscow, Dec. 5, 1980, CWIHP DA: https://digitalarchive .wilsoncenter.org/document/111232.

27 Ibid. For an analysis see Ouimet, *The Rise and the Fall of the Brezhnev Doctrine*, 162–167.

28 For Kuklinski's cable, see "Report Warning of Soviet intervention," Dec. 1980, CWIHP DA: https://digitalarchive.wilsoncenter.org/document/111999. Kuklinski's account of the planned invasion is in Ryszard Kuklinski, "The Suppression of Solidarity," in Robert Kostrzewa (ed.), *Between East and West: Writings from Kultura* (New York: Hill & Wang, 1990), 82.

29 Special Dossier on the Polish Crisis of 1980, Aug. 28, 1980. Translated by Malcolm Byrne. CWIHP DA: https://digitalarchive.wilsoncenter.org/document/111230.

30 "Vruchenie tovarishchu L.I. Brezhnevu …," *Izvestiya*, Dec. 19, 1980, 1.

31 Chernyaev, *Sovmestnyi iskhod*, 430.

NOTES TO PAGES 514–517

32 For a detailed discussion, see Vojtech Mastny, "The Soviet Non-Invasion of Poland," 190–200.

33 Suslov's statement to the PUWP Politburo, Apr. 23, 1981, RGANI: f. 81, op. 1, d. 353, l. 54. Kindly shared with the author by Mark Kramer. On increasing Soviet worries about "anti-Soviet" tendencies in Poland see e.g. Kramer, "The Soviet Union, the Warsaw Pact, and the Polish Crisis of 1980–1981," 31.

34 Session of CC CPSU Politburo, Apr. 2, 1981, CWIHP DA: https://digitalarchive .wilsoncenter.org/document/112758. The author's own translation.

35 Ouimet, *The Rise and the Fall of the Brezhnev Doctrine*, 186–193.

36 As reported in Chernyaev's diary, entry for Apr. 25, 1981, https://nsarchive .gwu.edu/rus/text_files/Chernyaev/1981.pdf.

37 Suslov's statement to the PUWP Politburo, Apr. 23, 1981, RGANI: f. 81, op. 1, d. 353, l. 54. Kindly shared with the author by Mark Kramer. On increasing Soviet worries about "anti-Soviet" tendencies in Poland see e.g. Kramer, "The Soviet Union, the Warsaw Pact, and the Polish Crisis of 1980–1981," 31.

38 Nikolai Tikhonov to Suslov, July 23, 1981, RGANI: f. 81, op. 1, d. 353, l. 98. Kindly shared with the author by Mark Kramer.

39 Soviet effort to dislodge Kania in June 1981 apparently failed. See Kramer, "The Soviet Union, the Warsaw Pact, and the Polish Crisis of 1980–1981," 51.

40 On Kania's ouster and the Soviet role, see ibid., 54.

41 On this, see ibid., 56–58 and Mark Kramer, "The Anoshkin Notebook on the Polish Crisis, December 1981," *CWIHP Bulletin*, Issue 11 (Winter 1998), 21.

42 Chernyaev, *Sovmestnyi iskhod*, 469.

43 Memcon, Honecker and Brezhev, Aug. 3, 1981. Translated by Christiaan Hetzner. CWIHP DA: https://digitalarchive.wilsoncenter.org/document/111229.

44 Chernyaev, *Sovmestnyi iskhod*, 459–560.

45 Session of the CPSU CC Politburo, Dec. 10, 1981. Translated by Mark Kramer. CWIHP DA: https://digitalarchive.wilsoncenter.org/document/110482. I used my own translation of the original, which does not fully coincide with Kramer's.

46 Stanisław Kania, *Zatrzymać konfrontacje* (Warsaw: BGW, 1991), 91. For details, see Mastny, "The Soviet Non-Invasion of Poland in 1980–1981 and the End of the Cold War," 195.

47 Ouimet, *The Rise and the Fall of the Brezhnev Doctrine*, 159–162.

48 Session of the CPSU CC Politburo, Oct. 29, 1981, CWIHP DA: https:// digitalarchive.wilsoncenter.org/document/112801.

49 Session of the CPSU CC Politburo, Dec. 10, 1981. Translated by Mark Kramer. CWIHP DA: https://digitalarchive.wilsoncenter.org/document/110482.

50 Information on the Position of the CPSU Regarding the Polish Situation, Oct. 1, 1981, CWIHP DA: https://digitalarchive.wilsoncenter.org/document/111982.

51 Suslov's notes of talks with Wojciech Jaruzelski, Dec. 12, 1981, RGANI: f. 81, op. 1, d. 353, l. 119. The notes are quite jumbled, so the precise context is difficult to decipher. Kindly shared with the author by Mark Kramer.

NOTES TO PAGES 517–520

52 Stasi Note on Meeting between Minister Mielke and Andropov, July 11, 1981. Translated by Bernd Schaefer. CWIHP DA: https://digitalarchive.wilsoncenter .org/document/115717.

53 The possibility that the United States might blockade Cuba in retaliation for the Soviet invasion of Poland was broached at the US National Security Council as early as Feb. 1981: James Graham Wilson (ed.), *Foreign Relations of the United States [FRUS], 1981–1988*, Vol. 3 (Washington, DC: US Government Publishing Office, 2016), Document 15. Alexander Haig broached the subject in a Mar. 1981 meeting: *FRUS, 1981–1988*, Vol. 3, Document 31. For Haig's reported "parking lot" comments see Lou Cannon, *President Reagan: The Role of a Lifetime* (New York: Simon & Schuster, 1991), 196.

54 Session of the CPSU CC Politburo, Dec. 10, 1981. Translated by Mark Kramer. CWIHP DA: https://digitalarchive.wilsoncenter.org/document/110482. Also, Mastny, "The Soviet Non-Invasion of Poland in 1980–1981 and the End of the Cold War," 204; Ouimet, *The Rise and the Fall of the Brezhnev Doctrine*, 168–169.

55 Nikolai Leonov, *Likholet'ye* (Moscow: Mezhdunarodnye Otnosheniya, 1995), 212.

56 Telcon, Brezhnev and Kania, Sept. 15, 1981, CWIHP DA: https://digitalarchive .wilsoncenter.org/document/112799.

57 Chernyaev, *Sovmestnyi iskhod*, 459–460.

58 Session of the CPSU CC Politburo, Dec. 10, 1981. Translated by Mark Kramer.

59 Memcon, Erich Mielke and Andropov, July 11, 1981. Translated by Bernd Schaefer. CWIHP DA: https://digitalarchive.wilsoncenter.org/document/115717.

60 See also Kramer, "The Soviet Union, the Warsaw Pact, and the Polish Crisis of 1980–1981," 61–66, who believes that the Soviets would have intervened to bail out Poland as the last resort. Mastny, by contrast, believes that even a neutral Poland – à la Finland – would have been acceptable. Mastny, "The Soviet Non-Invasion of Poland in 1980–1981 and the End of the Cold War," 206–207.

61 1980 Ronald Reagan and Jimmy Carter Presidential Debate, Oct. 28, 1980, Ronald Reagan Presidential Library: www.reaganlibrary.gov/archives /speech/1980-ronald-reagan-and-jimmy-carter-presidential-debate.

62 See, in particular, Reagan's Aug. 18, 1980 speech, "Peace: Restoring the Margin of Safety," www.reaganlibrary.gov/archives/speech/peace-restoring-margin-safety.

63 *FRUS, 1981–1988*, Vol. 3, Document 3.

64 Brezhnev to Reagan, Jan. 20, 1981 [the draft is dated Jan. 16], RGANI: f. 80, op. 1, d. 825, l. 1.

65 Reagan's press conference, Jan. 29, 1981, https://millercenter.org /the-presidency/presidential-speeches/january-29-1981-first-press-conference.

66 *FRUS, 1981–1988*, Vol. 3, Document 4.

67 Ibid., Document 65.

68 Ibid., Document 35.

69 On the story behind the Soviet deployment of SS-20s, see Dima Adamsky, "The 1983 Nuclear Crisis–Lessons for Deterrence Theory and Practice," *Journal of Strategic Studies*, 36(1) (2013), 4–41.

NOTES TO PAGES 520–524

70 *FRUS, 1981–1988*, Vol. 3, Document 35. On Doby see ibid., Vol. 3, Document 33.

71 Brezhnev to Reagan, Mar. 31, 1981, RGANI: f. 80, op. 1, d. 825, l. 2.

72 *FRUS, 1981–1988*, Vol. 3, Document 39.

73 Ibid., Document 40. Also, RGANI: f. 80, op. 1, d. 825, ll. 6–10.

74 *FRUS, 1981–1988*, Vol. 3, Document 50.

75 Ibid., Document 51.

76 Ibid., Document 61.

77 Ibid., Document 66.

78 Ibid., Document 46.

79 Ibid., Document 58. Brezhnev's instructions on the points to include (May 23, 1981) are in RGANI: f. 80, op. 1, d. 825, l. 19.

80 *FRUS, 1981–1988*, Vol. 3, Document 58.

81 Memcon, Brezhnev and Babrak Karmal, Feb. 27, 1981, RGANI: f. 80, op. 1, d. 464, ll. 6–10.

82 Howell Raines, "Reagan Hinting at Arms for Afghan Rebels," *New York Times*, Mar. 10, 1981, A3.

83 Report of Military Leaders to D.F. Ustinov, May 10, 1981. Translated by Gary Goldberg. CWIHP DA: https://digitalarchive.wilsoncenter.org/document/113138.

84 Transcript of CPSU CC Politburo meeting (excerpt), June 4, 1981, CWIHP DA: https://digitalarchive.wilsoncenter.org/document/112867. For more on Soviet troubles with Karmal see Paul Thomas Chamberlin, *The Cold War's Killing Fields: Rethinking the Long Peace* (New York: Harper, 2019), 457–458.

85 Miles, *Engaging the Evil Empire*, 26.

86 *FRUS, 1981–1988*, Vol. 3, Document 35.

87 "Rech tovarishcha L.I. Brezhneva," *Izvestiya*, May 23, 1981, 1.

88 Joseph Fitchett, "EEC Envoy Sets Trip on Afghan Pullout Plan," *Washington Post*, July 1, 1981, A22.

89 Memcon, Brezhnev and Babrak Karmal, July 17, 1981, RGANI: f. 80, op. 1, d. 464, l. 20.

90 Ibid., l. 27.

91 *FRUS, 1981–1988*, Vol. 3, Document 90. Haig's propensity to say things he was not supposed to was such that after he resigned (in June 1982), his colleagues at the State Department went to extra lengths to edit his records of conversations with Gromyko to make him say things they wanted him to say. See ibid., Document 209.

92 Ibid., Document 109.

93 For a fuller discussion, see Robert B. Rakove, "The Central Front in Reagan's Cold War: The United States and Afghanistan," in Jonathan R. Hunt and Simon Miles (eds.), *America and the World in the 1980s* (Ithaca, NY: Cornell University Press, 2021).

94 Address to the Nation about Christmas and the Situation in Poland, Dec. 23, 1981, Reagan Presidential Library: www.reaganlibrary.gov/archives/speech/address-nation-about-christmas-and-situation-poland.

NOTES TO PAGES 524–527

95 *FRUS, 1981–1988*, Vol. 3, Document 122.

96 Gromyko to Brezhnev, Dec. 24, 1981, RGANI: f. 80, op. 1, d. 825, l. 60.

97 *FRUS, 1981–1988*, Vol. 3, Document 123.

98 Memcon, Gromyko and Arthur Hartman, Dec. 31, 1981, RGANI: f. 80, op. 1, d. 825, l. 75.

99 Minutes of a National Security Council meeting, Sept. 22, 1982, *FRUS, 1981– 1988*, Vol. 3, Document 214.

100 National Security Council meeting, Dec. 22, 1981, www.thereaganfiles .com/19811222-nsc-34.pdf. For a discussion of the pipeline controversy see Antony J. Blinken, *Ally versus Ally: America, Europe, and the Siberian Pipeline Crisis* (Westport, CT: Greenwood Press, 1987); Miles, *Engaging the Evil Empire*, 53–55.

101 Cited in Blinken, *Ally Versus Ally*, 3.

102 For an overview, see Chamberlin, *The Cold War's Killing Fields*, 478–490.

103 Memcon, Brezhnev and Anvaro Cunhal, June 21, 1982, RGANI: f. 80, op. 1, d. 756, l. 85.

104 Brezhnev to Indira Gandhi, July 8, 1982, RGANI: f. 80, op. 1, d. 630, l. 59.

105 Brezhnev to Reagan, June 9, 1982, RGANI: f. 80, op. 1, d. 825, ll. 91–92.

106 Address to Members of the British Parliament, June 8, 1982, www .reaganlibrary.gov/archives/speech/address-members-british-parliament.

107 Memcon, Brezhnev and Anvaro Cunhal, June 21, 1982, RGANI: f. 80, op. 1, d. 756, l. 85.

108 Memcon, Brezhnev and Indira Gandhi, Sept. 20, 1980, RGANI: f. 80, op. 1, d. 631, l. 4.

109 "Pentagon Submits Strategy for Winning Nuclear War," *The Atlanta Constitution*, Aug. 15, 1982, 1A.

110 Memcon, Brezhnev and Indira Gandhi, Sept. 20, 1980, RGANI: f. 80, op. 1, d. 631, l. 3.

111 V.T. Medvedev, *Chelovek za spinoi*, 2nd ed. (Moscow: UP Print, 2010), 167.

112 "Speech at Award Ceremony," Mar. 24, 1982, FBIS Daily Report (FBIS-SOV-82-057).

113 Chernyaev, *Sovmestnyi iskhod*, 486–487.

114 For details see Sergey Radchenko, *Unwanted Visionaries: The Soviet Failure in Asia at the End of the Cold War* (New York: Oxford University Press, 2014), ch. 1.

115 Chernyaev, *Sovmestnyi iskhod*, 498.

116 Minutes of a Politburo meeting, Sept. 9, 1982, Library of Congress: Dmitry Volkogonov Collection, Reel 16, containers 23–24.

117 For earlier accounts of Reagan's China policy in 1981–82 see Patrick Tyler, *A Great Wall: Six Presidents and China: An Investigative History* (New York: Public Affairs, 1999), 289–327; and Jim Mann, *About Face: A History of America's Curious Relationship with China from Nixon to Clinton* (New York: Alfred Knopf, 1999), 115–133; also, Michael Schaller, "Ronald Reagan and the Puzzles of 'So-Called Communist China and Vietnam'," in Bradley Lynn Coleman and Kyle Longley

NOTES TO PAGES 528–532

(eds.), *Reagan and the World: Leadership and National Security, 1981–1989* (Lexington, KY: University Press of Kentucky, 2017), 191–209.

118 Memorandum by Richard V. Allen, June 6, 1981, Digital National Security Archive (DNSA).

119 USDEL Secretary in Beijing to SECSTATE WASHDC, June 16, 1981, DNSA.

120 Wang Zuoling, Leng Rong (eds.), *Deng Xiaoping Nianpu, 1975–1997*, Vol. 2 (Beijing: Zhongyang Wenxian Chubanshe, 2004), 739.

121 Ibid., 765.

122 From AMEMBASSY Beijing to SECSTATE WASH DC, Nov. 23, 1981, Reagan Presidential Library: Douglas Paal Files, China/US meetings/Trips, 5/78-9/82, Binder 6.

123 CIA, "China's View of Relations with the New US Administration," June 2, 1981, DNSA.

124 Wang Zuoling, Leng Rong (eds.), *Deng Xiaoping Nianpu*, Vol. 2, 778.

125 "Summary of Former President Nixon's Report on Trip to China," undated (1982), Reagan Presidential Library: Douglas Paal Files, China/US meetings/ Trips, 5/78-9/82, Binder 7.

126 For a discussion of the changing Chinese assessment of the Soviet threat, see Radchenko, *Unwanted Visionaries*, 31–32.

127 Nate Jones (ed.), *Able Archer 83: The Secret History of the NATO Exercise That Almost Triggered Nuclear War* (New York: The New Press, 2016), 12.

128 See e.g. Indicators to Recognize Adversarial Preparations for a Surprise Nuclear Missile Attack, Nov. 26, 1984. Translated by Bernd Schaefer. CWIHP DA: https://digitalarchive.wilsoncenter.org/document/119338. See also, Christopher M. Andrew and Oleg Gordievsky, *Comrade Kryuchkov's Instructions: Top Secret Files on KGB Foreign Operations, 1975–1985* (Stanford University Press, 1993), 67–89.

129 Anatoly Dobrynin, *Sugubo doveritel'no: posol v Vashingtone pri shesti prezidentakh SShA* (Moscow: Avtor, 1996), 566.

130 Memcon, Erich Mielke and Andropov, July 11, 1981. Translated by Bernd Schaefer. CWIHP DA: https://digitalarchive.wilsoncenter.org /document/115717.

131 Blinken, *Ally Versus Ally*.

132 *FRUS, 1981–1988*, Vol. 3, Document 233.

133 On Andropov's conversations with foreign leaders, Nov. 18, 1982, RGANI: f. 82, op. 1, d. 2, l. 3.

134 Andropov's comments on conversation with foreign leaders at Brezhnev's funeral, Nov. 18, 1982, RGANI: f. 82, op. 1, d. 2, ll. 1–14.

135 Statement by Andropov to the Warsaw Pact Political Consultative Committee, Jan. 4, 1983, National Security Archive: https://nsarchive.gwu.edu /dc.html?doc=5028358-Document-06-Statement-by-Yuri-Andropov-to-the.

136 Excerpts from the interview with Andropov, Reuters, Mar. 27, 1983.

137 Noel Gayler, "A Way Out of the Nuclear Trap," *Washington Post*, June 23, 1981.

NOTES TO PAGES 532–542

138 Brezhnev to Andropov, Gromyko, and Ustinov, June 30, 1981, RGANI: f. 80, op. 1, d. 825, l. 34.

139 James Graham Wilson (ed.), *FRUS, 1981–1988*, Vol. 11 (Washington, DC: US Government Publishing Office, 2021), Document 43.

140 Evgeny Chazov, *Zdorov'ye i vlast': vospominaniya kremlevskogo vracha* (Moscow: Novosti, 1992), 90.

141 Meeting Minutes of the Politburo of the CC CPSU, May 31, 1983, CWIHP DA: https://digitalarchive.wilsoncenter.org/document/115981.

142 Memcon, Averell Harriman and Andropov, June 2, 1983, National Security Archive: https://nsarchive.gwu.edu/document/17311-document-11-memorandum -conversation-between.

143 "Transcript of President Reagan's Address on Downing of Korean Airliner," *New York Times*, Sept. 6, 1983, A15.

144 The most eloquent account in English is David E. Hoffman, *The Dead Hand: Reagan, Gorbachev, and the Untold Story of the Cold War Arms Race* (London; Icon Books, 2011), 6–11.

145 Gorbachev's comments, in Anatoly Chernyaev et al. (eds.), *V Politbyuro TsK KPSS*, 2nd ed. (Moscow: Gorbachev Fond, 2008), 81.

146 "The Soviet 'War Scare,'" Feb. 15, 1990, https://nsarchive2.gwu.edu/nukevault /ebb533-The-Able-Archer-War-Scare-Declassified-PFIAB-Report-Released/2012- 0238-MR.pdf

147 For skeptical views, see Miles, *Engaging the Evil Empire* and Gordon Barrass, "Able Archer 83: What Were the Soviets Thinking?" *Survival*, 58(6) (2016), 7– 30. See also Benjamin B. Fischer, "Scolding Intelligence: The PFIAB Report on the Soviet War Scare," *International Journal of Intelligence and CounterIntelligence*, 31(1) (2018), 102–115.

148 Elizabeth C. Charles (ed.), *FRUS, 1981–1988*, Vol. 4 (Washington, DC: US Government Publishing Office, 2021), Document 176.

19 HOPE

1 William Taubman, *Gorbachev: His Life and Times* (London: Simon & Schuster, 2018), 150–153.

2 Mikhail Gorbachev, *Perestroika i novoe myshlenie dlya nashei strany i dlya vsego mira* (Moscow: Politizdat, 1987), 200.

3 KGB operational information, 09:00, July 2, 1980, RGANI: f. 3, op. 78, d. 161, l. 58.

4 Andropov to Brezhnev, July 6, 1968, RGANI: f. 80, op. 1, d. 314, ll. 70–80.

5 A meeting at Andropov's, July 1, 1983, RGANI: f. 82, op. 1, d. 2, ll. 47–63.

6 Richard Sakwa, *Soviet Politics in Perspective*, 2nd ed. (London: Routledge, 1998), 73–74.

7 Anatoly Chernyaev, *Sovmestnyi iskhod: dnevnik dvukh epokh* (Moscow: Rosspen, 2008), 684–685.

NOTES TO PAGES 542–549

8 Anatoly Chernyaev et al. (eds.), *V Politbyuro TsK KPSS*, 2nd ed. (Moscow: Gorbachev Fond, 2008), 75.

9 Report on the trip to the PRC, undated, Vladimir Lukin's personal archive, kindly provided to the author by Alexander Lukin. The report was signed by Arbatov but Lukin was the actual author.

10 For a thorough exposition of the Soviet debate, see Chris Miller, *The Struggle to Save the Soviet Economy* (Chapter Hill, NC: University of North Carolina Press, 2016), 101–118.

11 Cited in Sergey Radchenko, *Unwanted Visionaries: The Soviet Failure in Asia at the End of the Cold War* (New York: Oxford University Press, 2014), 179.

12 Karen Brutents, *Nesbyvsheesya: neravnodushnye zametki o perestroike* (Moscow: Mezhdunarodnye Otnosheniya, 2005), 230.

13 Ibid., 478.

14 In Chernyaev et al. (eds.), *V Politbyuro TsK KPSS*, 207.

15 Ibid., 45.

16 Ibid., 109.

17 Memcon, Todor Zhivkov and Gorbachev, May 11, 1987, Bulgarian Central State Archives, Sofia (hereafter, BCSA): f. 1b, op. 35, a.e. 387.

18 Ezra Vogel, *Deng Xiaoping and the Transformation of China* (Cambridge, MA: Belknap, 2013), 423.

19 Chernyaev et al. (eds.), *V Politbyuro TsK KPSS*, 191–192.

20 Ibid., 108.

21 Ibid., 199.

22 Mikhail Gorbachev, *Perestroika i novoe myshlenie dlya nashei strany i dlya vsego mira* (Moscow: Politizdat, 1987), 149.

23 Chernyaev, in a diary entry, acknowledged similarities between peaceful coexistence as previously pursued by Soviet authorities and Gorbachev's peaceful coexistence, but argued that the latter was distinguished by its being "genuine," "without fooling around." What Chernyaev failed to acknowledge, however, was that this "genuineness" was itself a consequence of Gorbachev's realization that the Soviet Union was no longer able to "fool around" – it was losing the Cold War. Chernyaev, *Sovmestnyi iskhod*, 655–656.

24 Gorbachev, *Perestroika i novoe myshlenie*, 125, 223

25 Ibid., 237.

26 See Dima Adamsky, "The 1983 Nuclear Crisis–Lessons for Deterrence Theory and Practice," *Journal of Strategic Studies*, 36(1) (2013), 4–41.

27 Chernyaev et al. (eds.), *V Politbyuro TsK KPSS*, 81.

28 Memcon, Gorbachev and Willy Brandt, May 27, 1985, in Mikhail Gorbachev, *Mikhail Sergeyevich Gorbachev: sobranie sochinenii* [*MSG:SS*], Vol. 2 (Mar. 1984–Oct. 1985) (Moscow: Gorbachev Fond, 2008), 287.

29 Chernyaev et al. (eds.), *V Politbyuro TsK KPSS*, 39

30 Ibid., 80.

31 That said, the argument that "SDI became the straw that broke the Communist camel's back" is completely unfounded, as is the notion that SDI prompted

NOTES TO PAGES 549–552

Gorbachev to begin his economic reforms. Gorbachev launched perestroika because the general malaise of the Soviet economy chipped away at the long-term prospects of the socialist project. The arms race (and SDI) contributed to this malaise, but it was a small part of a much bigger problem. For the flawed argument, see Ken Adelman, *Reagan at Reykjavik: Forty-Eight Hours that Ended the Cold War* (New York: Broadside Books, 2014).

32 Joshua R. Itzkowitz Shifrinson, *Rising Titans, Falling Giants* (Ithaca, NY: Cornell University Press, 2018), esp. 119–131.

33 James Graham Wilson (ed.), *Foreign Relations of the United States [FRUS], 1981–1988*, Vol. 6 (Washington, DC: US Government Publishing Office, 2016), Document 94.

34 Chernyaev, *Sovmestnyi iskhod*, 657.

35 Memorandum by Vitaly Kataev, undated (no later than Oct. 1986), Hoover Institution Archive: Kataev Papers, Box 4, Folder 11. The author is grateful to Pieter Biersteker for sharing a copy of this document.

36 Chernyaev's notes from a Politburo session, Oct. 8, 1986, National Security Archive: https://nsarchive2.gwu.edu/NSAEBB/NSAEBB203/Document08 .pdf.

37 Chernyaev et al. (eds.), *V Politbyuro TsK KPSS*, 18.

38 For the origins of Gorbachev's Jan. 1986 proposal, see especially Andrei Grachev, *Gorbachev's Gamble: Soviet Foreign Policy and the End of the Cold War* (Cambridge: Polity, 2008), 68–69. Gorbachev's interpreter Pavel Palazhchenko (whom I quizzed about the proposal), believes that the Soviet leader was fully committed to complete nuclear disarmament; it is, however, more likely that such commitment coexisted in his mind with calculations of political character.

39 Chernyaev's notes from a Politburo session, Oct. 8, 1986, National Security Archive: https://nsarchive2.gwu.edu/NSAEBB/NSAEBB203/Document08.pdf. For a good discussion of the Reykjavik summit, see Archie Brown, *The Human Factor: Gorbachev, Reagan, and Thatcher, and the End of the Cold War* (Oxford University Press, 2020), 167–186.

40 Transcript of Gorbachev–Reagan talks at Reykjavik, Oct. 12, 1986 (the Russian version), FBIS-USR-93–121 (Sept. 20, 1993).

41 John Poindexter to Ronald Reagan, Oct. 16, 1986, Reagan Presidential Library: RAC Box 3 (Alton Keel Files) Reykjavik Briefing.

42 Memorandum by Vitaly Kataev, Dec. 18, 1986, Hoover Institution Archive: Kataev Papers, Box 4, Folder 15. The author is grateful to Pieter Biersteker for sharing a copy of this document.

43 Chernyaev et al. (eds.), *V Politbyuro TsK KPSS*, 85.

44 Svetlana Savranskaya and Thomas Blanton, "The Washington Summit, 1987," in Savranskaya and Blanton, *The Last Superpower Summits: Gorbachev, Reagan and Bush. Conversations that Ended the Cold War* (Budapest: Central European University Press, 2016).

NOTES TO PAGES 552–562

45 Aleksandr Yakovlev to Gorbachev, Feb. 25, 1987. Obtained and translated by Svetlana Savranskaya. National Security Archive: https://nsarchive2 .gwu.edu/NSAEBB/NSAEBB238/russian/Final1987-02-25%20Yakovlev %20memo.pdf.

46 Gorbachev's speech, Feb. 16, 1987, in *MSG:SS*, Vol. 6 (Feb.–May 1987), 26.

47 Chernyaev et al. (eds.), *V Politbyuro TsK KPSS*, 146

48 Dennis Hevesi, "Moscow Convening a Forum on Peace," *New York Times*, Feb. 10, 1987, A8.

49 For a discussion, see e.g. Brown, *The Human Factor*, 214–215.

50 Chernyaev et al. (eds.), *V Politbyuro TsK KPSS*, 36.

51 Ibid., 279

52 Artemy Kalinovsky, *A Long Goodbye: The Soviet Withdrawal from Afghanistan* (Cambridge, MA: Harvard University Press, 2011), 42.

53 Archie Brown, among others, argues that Gorbachev's slow exit from Afghanistan was a consequence of him worrying that "so many young soldiers' lives had been lost in vain." Brown, *The Human Factor*, 143.

54 Chernyaev et al. (eds.), *V Politbyuro TsK KPSS*, 104–105.

55 Ibid., 132.

56 Politburo meeting, Feb. 23, 1987, Archive of the Gorbachev Foundation. Kindly shared with the author by Svetlana Savranskaya.

57 Politburo meeting, Jan. 21–22, 1987. Archive of the Gorbachev Foundation. Kindly shared with the author by Svetlana Savranskaya.

58 Chernyaev et al. (eds.), *V Politbyuro TsK KPSS*, 191.

59 Ibid., 43.

60 Kalinovsky, *A Long Goodbye*, 146.

61 Chernyaev, *Sovmestnyi iskhod*, 655–656.

20 COLLAPSE

1 E.g. Andrei Grachev, *Gorbachev's Gamble Soviet Foreign Policy and the End of the Cold War* (Cambridge: Polity Press, 2018); Vladislav M. Zubok, *Collapse: The Fall of the Soviet Union* (New Haven, CT: Yale University Press, 2021).

2 Anatoly Chernyaev et al. (eds.), *V Politbyuro TsK KPSS*, 2nd ed. (Moscow: Gorbachev Fond, 2008), 136.

3 For an overview, see e.g. Kristina Spohr, *Post Wall, Post Square* (London: William Collins, 2019), 66–127.

4 V.M Shastikov to A.M Yakovlev, "On Jakeš's Visit to Moscow," Apr. 12, 1989, in Mikhail Prozumenshchikov et al. (eds.), *Konets epokhi: SSSR i revolyutsii v stranakh vostochnoi Evropy v 1989–1991 gg* (Moscow: Rosspen, 2015), 663.

5 Anatoly Chernyaev, *Sovmestnyi iskhod: dnevnik dvukh epokh* (Moscow: Rosspen, 2008), 781.

6 Speech by Todor Zhivkov, Feb. 17, 1989, in Mikhail Prozumenshchikov et al. (eds.), *Konets epokhi*, 748.

NOTES TO PAGES 562–568

7 Memcon, Gorbachev and Egon Krenz, Nov. 1, 1989, in Aleksandr Galkin and Anatoly Chernyaev (eds.), *Gorbachev i germansky vopros: sbornik dokumentov, 1986–1991* (Moscow: Ves' Mir, 2006), 239.

8 Memcon, Gorbachev and Giulio Andreotti, Nov. 29, 1989, in *Mikhail Sergeyevich Gorbachev: sobranie sochinenii* [*MSG:SS*], Vol. 17 (Nov.–Dec. 1989) (Moscow: Gorbachev Fond, 2010), 142.

9 One of the best accounts is Mary Sarotte, *1989: The Struggle to Create Post-Cold War Europe* (Princeton University Press, 2014). See also Spohr, *Post Wall, Post Square*, 128–190.

10 Jäger's reluctance to use force stemmed from instructions to this effect that were issued earlier by the SED. See Memcon, Gorbachev and Egon Krenz, Nov. 1, 1989, in Galkin and Chernyaev (eds.), *Gorbachev i germansky vopros*, 240.

11 Memcon, Gorbachev and members of the SED Politburo, Oct. 7, 1989, in Galkin and Chernyaev (eds.), *Gorbachev i germansky vopros*, 211.

12 Memcon, Gorbachev and Egon Krenz, Nov. 1, 1989, in Galkin and Chernyaev (eds.), *Gorbachev i germansky vopros*, 235.

13 Chernyaev, *Sovmestnyi iskhod*, 808.

14 Yuly Kvitsinsky, *Vremya i sluchai: zametki professionala* (Moscow: Olma Press, 1999), 11–12.

15 Memcon, Gorbachev and Rodric Braithwaite, Nov. 17, 1987, in *MSG:SS*, Vol. 17, 54–57.

16 On the pause, see Jeffrey A. Engel, *When the World Seemed New: George H.W. Bush and the End of the Cold War* (New York: Houghton Mifflin, 2017), 86–99.

17 Sergey Radchenko, *Unwanted Visionaries: The Soviet Failure in Asia at the End of the Cold War* (New York: Oxford University Press, 2014), 165.

18 The most thorough exploration of Gorbachev's Common European Home is Marie-Pierre Rey, "'Europe Is Our Common Home': A Study of Gorbachev's Diplomatic Concept," *Cold War History*, 4(2) (2004), 33–65.

19 Recounted, for instance, in Memcon, Gorbachev and Brian Mulroney, Nov. 21, 1989, in *MSG:SS*, Vol. 17, 82 and in Memcon, Gorbachev and John Paul II, Dec. 1, 1989, National Security Archive: https://nsarchive.gwu.edu/document/28344-document-24-transcript-gorbachev-john-paul-ii-meeting-vatican-city-december-1-1989.

20 Memcon, Gorbachev and Brian Mulroney, Nov. 21, 1989, in *MSG:SS*, Vol. 17, 73. See also Engel, *When the World Seemed New*, 293.

21 Memcon, Gorbachev and Giulio Andreotti, Nov. 29, 1989, in *MSG:SS*, Vol. 17, 141.

22 Memcon, Gorbachev and Achille Occhetto, Nov. 30, 1989, in *MSG:SS*, Vol. 17, 159.

23 Memcon, Gorbachev and John Paul II, Dec. 1, 1989, National Security Archive: https://nsarchive.gwu.edu/document/28344-document-24-transcript-gorbachev-john-paul-ii-meeting-vatican-city-december-1-1989. Translated by Anna Melyakova.

24 Engel, *When the World Seemed New*, 292–312.

25 Ibid., 297.

NOTES TO PAGES 568–574

26 I used the US transcripts of the meeting to cite Bush's words, and the Russian version (from the Archive of the Gorbachev Foundation) to cite Gorbachev.

27 For a broad overview, see Svetlana Savranskaya, Thomas Blanton, and Vladislav Zubok (eds.), *Masterpieces of History: The Peaceful end of the Cold War in Europe, 1989* (Budapest: Central European University Press, 2010).

28 Memcon, Gorbachev and François Mitterrand, Dec. 6, 1989, in *MSG:SS*, Vol. 17, 291.

29 Ibid., 292.

30 Ibid., 293.

31 See e.g. Kristina Spohr, *Post Wall, Post Square* (London: William Collins, 2019), 192–200.

32 Up to that point, US policy towards Eastern Europe was characterized by gradualism. Notably, Bush refused to take advantage of the elections in Poland to hasten the Communists' demise. As Shifrinson shows, however, this was simply because the US officials were worried about the prospects of a Soviet intervention triggered by a premature transfer of power. Joshua R. Itzkowitz Shifrinson, *Falling Giants, Rising Titans* (Ithaca, NY: Cornell University Press, 2018), 134–135.

33 Memcon, Gorbachev and Hans-Dietrich Genscher, Dec. 5, 1989, in *MSG:SS*, Vol. 17, 284.

34 *MSG:SS*, Vol. 18 (Dec. 1989–Mar. 1990) (Moscow: Ves' Mir, 2011), 49, 42.

35 Chernyaev et al. (eds.), *V Politbyuro TsK KPSS*, 571.

36 Memcon, Gorbachev and Abe Shintaro, Jan. 15, 1990, in *MSG:SS*, Vol. 18, p. 135. (Abe, characteristically, was less interested in grand visions of Europe than in winning Gorbachev's agreement to resolve their territorial dispute on Japan's terms.)

37 Memcon, Gorbachev and Thatcher, Sept. 23, 1989. Translated for the National Security Archive by Svetlana Savranskaya, CWIHP DA: https://digitalarchive.wil soncenter.org/document/120816.

38 Memcon, Gorbachev and François Mitterrand, Dec. 6, 1989, Archive of the Gorbachev Foundation.

39 Memcon, George H.W. Bush and François Mitterrand, Dec. 16, 1989, George H.W. Bush Presidential Library: https://bush41library.tamu.edu/files/memcons -telcons/1989-12-16–Mitterrand.pdf.

40 Ibid.

41 Chernyaev et al. (eds.), *V Politbyuro TsK KPSS*, 579–581.

42 Memcon, Gorbachev and Hafez al-Assad, Apr. 28, 1990, in *MSG:SS*, Vol. 19 (Mar.–May 1990) (Moscow: Ves' Mir, 2011), 365.

43 Ironically, the Soviets themselves helped reinvigorate NATO just when it seemed to be standing on its last legs – by invading Hungary and Czechoslovakia. See Timothy Sayle, *An Enduring Alliance: A History of NATO* (Ithaca, NY: Cornell University Press, 2019).

44 There used to be a dispute among historians whether Genscher's ideas regarding NATO's nonexpansion to the East only applied to the territory of the GDR. The

706

NOTES TO PAGES 575–577

available record fully clears up the confusion. See Joshua R. Itzkowitz Shifrinson, "'Deal or No Deal?' The End of the Cold War and the US Offer to Limit NATO Expansion," *International Security*, 40(4) (2016), 22. For discussion, see Svetlana Savranskaya and Tom Blanton, "NATO Expansion: What Gorbachev Heard," National Security Archive Briefing Book 613 (Dec. 12, 2017) and Mary Elise Sarotte, *Not One Inch: America, Russia, and the Making of Post-Cold War Stalemate* (New Haven, CT: Yale University Press, 2021).

45 Mary Elise Sarotte, "Not One Inch Eastward? Bush, Baker, Kohl, Genscher, Gorbachev, and the Origin of Russian Resentment toward NATO Enlargement in February 1990," *Diplomatic History*, 34(1) (2010), 119–140; Mark Kramer and Joshua R. Itzkowitz Shifrinson, "NATO Enlargement – Was There a Promise?" *International Security*, 42(1) (2017), 186–192; Marc Trachtenberg, "The United States and the NATO Non-Extension Assurances of 1990: New Light on an Old Problem?" *International Security*, 45(3) (2020), 162–203.

46 Memcon, Gorbachev and James Baker, Feb. 9, 1990, National Security Archive: https://nsarchive2.gwu.edu//dc.html?doc=4325679-Document-05 -Memorandum-of-conversation-between.

47 Russian version in *MSG:SS*, Vol. 18, 269.

48 Memcon, Robert Gates and Vladimir Kryuchkov, Feb. 9, 1990, National Security Archive: https://nsarchive2.gwu.edu//dc.html?doc=4325681-Document-07 -Memorandum-of-conversation-between.

49 Shifrinson, "Deal or No Deal," 24.

50 Joshua R. Itzkowitz Shifrinson, *Rising Titans, Falling Giants*, 140–143.

51 Philip Zelikow and Condoleeza Rice, *Germany Unified and Europe Transformmed: a Study in Statecraft* (Cambridge, MA: Harvard University Press, 1997), 208–217.

52 Memcon, George H.W. Bush and Kohl, Feb. 24, 1990, George H.W. Bush Presidential Library: https://bush41library.tamu.edu/files/memcons-telcons/1990 -02-24–Kohl.pdf.

53 Memcon, Gorbachev and George H.W. Bush, May 31, 1990, in *MSG:SS*, Vol. 20 (May–June 1990) (Moscow: Ves' Mir, 2011), 197.

54 See e.g. Memcon, Gorbachev and Václav Havel, Feb. 26, 1990, in *MSG:SS*, Vol. 18, 337. In this sense, James Baker was not too far off when he argued, in his memoir: "Gorbachev's strategy, I believed, was premised on splitting the alliance and undercutting us [the US] in Western Europe." James Baker, *The Politics of Diplomacy* (New York: Putnam, 1995), 70.

55 Radchenko, *Unwanted Visionaries*, 101.

56 Memcon, Gorbachev and Václav Havel, Feb. 26, 1990, in *MSG:SS*, Vol. 18, 336.

57 Memcon, Gorbachev and Tadeusz Mazowiecki, Nov. 24, 1989, in *MSG:SS*, Vol. 17, 91.

58 Memcon, Gorbachev and Li Peng, Apr. 24, 1990, in *MSG:SS*, Vol. 19, 302.

59 Chernyaev et al. (eds.), *V Politbyuro TsK KPSS*, 593.

NOTES TO PAGES 578–583

60 Telcon, Gorbachev and George H.W. Bush, Feb. 28, 1990, in *MSG:SS*, Vol. 18, 361.

61 "Neobkhodim poetapnyi perekhod," *Pravda*, Mar. 7, 1990, 1.

62 Gorbachev's speech, Mar. 15, 1990, in *MSG:SS*, Vol 19, 64.

63 Vladislav Zubok, "With His Back against the Wall: Gorbachev, Soviet Demise, and German Reunification," *Cold War History*, 14(4) (2014), 635.

64 Memcon, Gorbachev and Edward Kennedy, Mar. 26, 1990, in *MSG:SS*, Vol. 19, 138–139.

65 Gorbachev's comments at a meeting on the German question, Jan. 26, 1990, in *MSG:SS*, Vol. 18, 191.

66 Valentin Falin to Gorbachev, Apr. 18, 1990, in Galkin and Chernyaev (eds.), *Gorbachev i germansky vopros*, 398–408.

67 Memcon, Gorbachev and Lothar de Maizière, Apr. 29, 1990, ibid., 416.

68 Memcon, Gorbachev and James Baker, May 18, 1990, in *MSG:SS*, Vol. 20, 13–22. Gorbachev's push for NATO membership is at odds with some of the claims of the existing historiography, for instance with William H. Hill's argument about the "aversion that he personally and almost all his Soviet colleagues had for the Alliance." See William H. Hill, *No Place for Russia* (New York: Columbia University Press, 2018), 54.

69 James Baker to George H.W. Bush, May 19, 1990, Department of State FOIA release No. 9504381. Mary Elise Sarotte, "Perpetuating US Pre-eminence: The 1990 Deals to 'Bribe the Soviets Out' and Move NATO In," *International Security*, 35(1) (2010), 125.

70 Chernyaev to Gorbachev, May 4, 1990, in Galkin and Chernyaev (eds.), *Gorbachev i germansky vopros*, 424–425.

71 Gorbachev's comments at a meeting in Novo-Ogarevo, May 19, 1990, in *MSG:SS*, Vol. 20, 30.

72 Gorbachev's speech, May 23, 1990, ibid., 95.

73 Radchenko, *Unwanted Visionaries*, 238.

74 Memcon, Gorbachev and James Baker, May 18, 1990, in *MSG:SS*, Vol. 20, 13–22.

75 Memcon, Gorbachev and Horst Teltschik, May 14, 1990, in Galkin and Chernyaev (eds.), *Gorbachev i germansky vopros*, 429.

76 Ibid.

77 Radchenko, *Unwanted Visionaries*, 182. See also Letter from Gorbachev to Jiang Zemin, Dec. 15, 1989, RGANI: f. 84, op. 1, d. 428, l. 120.

78 Radchenko, *Unwanted Visionaries*, 239; Memcon, Gorbachev and Roh Tae-woo, June 4, 1990, in *MSG:SS*, Vol. 20, 293.

79 Memcon, Gorbachev and Hosni Mubarak, May 15, 1990, in *MSG:SS*, Vol. 19, 488.

80 Memcon, Gorbachev and Aleksandar Lilov, May 23, 1990, in *MSG:SS*, Vol. 20, 108.

81 Memcon, Gorbachev and François Mitterrand, May 25, 1990, ibid., 534.

82 Ibid.

NOTES TO PAGES 584–594

83 George H.W. Bush and Brent Scowcroft, *A World Transformed* (New York: Knopf, 1998), 282.

84 Frédéric Bozo et al. (eds.), *German Reunification: A Multinational History* (London: Routledge, 2016).

85 See also Zubok, "With His Back against the Wall," 639.

86 Author's interview with Pavel Palazhchenko, Moscow, Apr. 24, 2019. Palazhchenko recalled that Falin's hardline take on reunification was a part of his strategy for replacing Eduard Shevardnadze (whom he believed to be on the verge of resignation) as foreign minister.

87 Cited in Zubok, "With His Back against the Wall," 625.

88 Mikhail Prozumenshchikov et al. (eds.), *Konets epokhi*, 208–211.

89 Ibid., op. 450.

90 Prozumenshchikov et al. (eds.), *Konets epokhi*, 166–171.

91 Sarotte, *1989*, 191–193.

92 Sarotte, "Perpetuating US Pre-eminence."

CONCLUSION

1 Paul Musgrave, "Mikhail Gorbachev's Pizza Hut Thanksgiving Miracle," *Foreign Policy*, Nov. 28, 2019, https://foreignpolicy.com/2019/11/28/mikhail -gorbachev-pizza-hut-ad-thanksgiving-miracle/.

2 Svetlana Alexievich, *Vremya second-hend* (Moscow: Vremya, 2018), 56.

3 Yeltsin's statement, Dec. 27, 1994, The Yeltsin Center: https://yeltsin.ru /archive/audio/9036/.

4 Mary Elise Sarotte, *Not One Inch: America, Russia, and the Making of Post-Cold War Stalemate* (New Haven, CT: Yale University Press, 2021), 157.

5 "President's Dinner with President Yeltsin," Jan. 14, 1994, Clinton Presidential Library: https://clinton.presidentiallibraries.us/items/show/58577.

6 Anatoly Adamishin, *V raznye gody: vneshnepoliticheskie ocherki* (Moscow: Ves' Mir, 2016), 296.

7 Sergey Radchenko, "'Nothing but Humiliation for Russia': Moscow and NATO's Eastern Enlargement, 1993–1995," *Journal of Strategic Studies*, 43(6–7) (Dec. 2020), 769–816.

8 R.W. Apple, Jr. "V-E Day Plus Fifty; the Overview; Allied Victory in Europe Commemorated in Moscow," *New York Times*, May 10, 1995, A1.

9 "Pobeda rvet gromadu let, shagaya cherez golovy pravitel'stv," *Pravda*, May 11, 1995, 1.

10 Interview with Viktor Gaevsky, *Pervyi Obrazovatel'nyi Kanal*, July 26, 2014, www .youtube.com/watch?v=wQOiBBHR0p4.

11 Henry Kissinger, *A World Restored: Metternich, Castlereagh and the Problems of Peace 1812–22* (Boston, MA: Houghton Mifflin Company, 1957), 14.

NOTES TO PAGES 599–602

12 Press conference by George W. Bush and Vladimir Putin, June 16, 2001, https://georgewbush-whitehouse.archives.gov/news/releases/2001/06/20010618.html.

13 Putin's speech at the Munich Security Conference, Feb. 10, 2007, http://kremlin.ru/events/president/transcripts/24034.

14 Putin's speech, July 1, 2014, http://kremlin.ru/events/president/news/46131.

15 Putin's interview with the New York Times, Oct. 4, 2003, http://kremlin.ru/events/president/transcripts/22145.

16 Putin's speech, Mar. 18, 2014, http://kremlin.ru/events/president/news/20603.

17 Putin's speech, Feb. 24, 2022, http://kremlin.ru/events/president/news/67843.

Bibliographical Essay

Cold War history is a well-mined field. Hundreds of historians have had something useful to say on the subject. Soviet foreign policy, as a subplot of the Cold War, is equally well-covered. Many relevant books appear in the footnotes. They offer a valuable context for my work. Yet, this book relies less on secondary, and much more on primary sources, especially archival documents. Mid-way through this project, the Russian archives suddenly and unexpectedly began to open up troves of classified records. I often became the first researcher to wade through – or rather dip my toes in – what rapidly became a torrent of top-level documentation.

The following Russian archives were extensively relied upon:

AVPRF: Arkhiv Vneshnei Politiki Rossiiskoi Federatsii (The Archive of Foreign Policy of the Russian Federation, Moscow, Russia). I relied mostly on the Molotov files, and on the embassy reports from Washington and Beijing, for the period from 1944 to about 1980.

GARF: Gosudarstvennyi Arkhiv Rossiiskoi Federatsii (The State Archive of the Russian Federation, Moscow, Russia). I used mainly the Mikoyan files; in particular, those pertinent to his travels in Asia in the 1940s and the 1950s.

RGANI: Rossiisky Gosudarstvennyi Arkhiv Noveishei Istorii (The Russian State Archive of Contemporary History, Moscow, Russia). This archive was used widely throughout the book. It holds invaluable collections of party documents, including, most usefully, Nikita Khrushchev's and Leonid Brezhnev's personal files, but also "special dossier" collections on particularly sensitive subjects.

RGASPI: Rossiisky Gosudarstvennyi Arkhiv Sotsial'noi i Politicheskoi Istorii (The Russian State Archive of Social and Political History, Moscow Russia). This archive was used extensively for the earlier chapters. I relied, in particular, on the Stalin and Molotov files.

BIBLIOGRAPHICAL ESSAY

TsAMO: Tsentral'nyi Arkhiv Ministerstva Oborony (The Central Archive of the Ministry of Defense, Podol'sk, Russia). Only a small sample of documents from this archive informed my book (specifically, the section on the Cuban Missile Crisis).

While researching this project, I spent several years living in China, a period that thankfully overlapped with (temporary) openness of the Chinese archives. I worked across China in various provincial archives, collecting documents.

These include:

Gansu Provincial Archives (Lanzhou, China)
Hubei Provincial Archives (Wuhan, China)
Jilin Provincial Archives (Changchun, China)
Ningbo City Archive (Ningbo, China)
Sichuan Provincial Archives (Chengdu, China)
Shanghai Archives (Shanghai, China).

The Archive of the Chinese Foreign Ministry (Beijing, China) was the most important depository. I relied on it extensively for China's diplomatic records before the Chinese authorities curbed all access in 2012–13.

However, this list does not tell the entire story, or even half the story, and careful readers, going through the footnotes, will discover many archival documents, which I declined to fully cite. This is not out of malice, but out of abundance of caution. Readers may be assured that when a document is listed as being "in the author's possession," it does exist. The failure to cite it fully almost always indicates that the document in question comes from the Chinese archives, and that the provenance is too sensitive to permit a full disclosure.

The Russian and the Chinese documents together make up the bulk of primary sources used in this book, though I also relied on additional sources dug up from presidential libraries in the United States, from the British National Archives, and even from as far as Ulaanbaatar in Mongolia or New Delhi in India. I also benefited enormously from the holdings of the Digital Archive of the Cold War International History Project at the Wilson Center, to which I, too, had contributed documents, including those resulting from research for this book. Many of these will eventually be translated, helping other historians make sense of Soviet foreign policy, especially at a time when researching in Moscow is no longer a very attractive proposition.

Index

Abe, Shinzo, 572, 706
Acheson, Dean, 121, 131, 132, 136
Addou, Abdullahi, 469–470
Adenauer, Konrad, 232, 234, 282
Adzhubei, Aleksei, 288
Afghanistan
  American invasion of, 601
  Andropov and, 480, 490–493, 522, 554
  anti-Soviet insurgents in, 522, 523
  Brezhnev and
    Amin and, 478, 491–493
    credibility and, 494
    exit strategy, search for, 522–523
    generally, 475, 547, 554, 598
    reluctance to intervene, 481
    socialism in, 476–477
    unrest and, 490
  Brzezinski and, 475
  Bulganin and, 475
  Chernyaev and, 554
  CIA and, 478, 554
  Deng and, 475, 498
  Dobrynin and, 488, 493–494, 522, 523
  Gorbachev and, 554–557, 559
  Gromyko and, 477–478, 480–481, 490, 493, 522, 554
  Haig and, 523
  Iran and, 522–523
  KGB and, 476, 490–492
  Khalq faction of the PDPA, 476, 490, 522
  Khomeini and, 495
  Khrushchev and, 475–476
  Muslim Brotherhood, 478
  Pakistan and, 522–523
  Parcham faction of the PDPA, 476, 490, 522

  People's Democratic Party of Afghanistan (PDPA), 476–480, 522, 523
  PRC and, 479, 498
  Putin and, 601
  Reagan and, 522, 554, 555
  Soviet expansionism and, 453
  Soviet invasion of
    Afghan Revolution, to save, 493
    as bankrupting USSR, false perception on, 554
    commencement of, 493
    credibility as motivation for, 493–494
    failure of, 536–537
    ideology as motivation for, 493–494
    security as motivation for, 493–494
    strategy as motivation for, 493–494
    unrest leading up to, 478–481, 490–493
    withdrawal from, 554–557
  United States and, 490, 492, 601
  Ustinov and, 490, 493, 522, 554
  Vance and, 488
  Vinogradov and, 495
Africa. *See also specific country*
  Brzezinski and, 463
  Khrushchev and, 167–168
  Mao and, 441–442
  PRC and, 441–442, 472–473
  Soviet expansionism and, 453
  Soviet setback in, 69
  Stalin and, 39, 473
  United States and, 472–473
Agnew, Spiro, 401
Aguirre del Cristo, Severo, 276
Akhromeev, Sergei, 584

713

INDEX

Albania
  Greece and, 100
  Ho Chi Minh and, 332
  Khrushchev and, 262–264, 294
  Moscow Conference and, 274
  percentages agreement and, 23
  PRC and, 197, 261–263
  Stalin and, 100
  Tito and, 81–82, 96–97
  "Titoists" in, 100
  Warsaw Pact in, 263, 290
Aleksandrov-Agentov, A.M.
  arms control and, 531–532
  Brezhnev–Nixon summit and, 352, 376
  Carter and, 454–455
  generally, 443, 536
  Iran Hostage Crisis and, 495–497
  Nixon and, 390
  on social democracy, 371
Alexander I (Russia), 65
Alexievich, Svetlana, 590
Algeria
  decolonization in, 252
  Khrushchev and, 253
  Mao and, 254
  Yom Kippur War and, 405, 406
Allen, Richard, 520–521
Allende, Salvador, 476–477
Ambition
  to change world, 6
  legitimacy, relation to, 3
  recognition, relation to, 3, 5
Amin, Hafizullah
  coup and, 478
  factional violence and, 480,
    490–493
  generally, 513, 598
  Sadat compared, 491–492
  Soviet intervention and, 480, 502
  United States and, 479
Amstutz, J. Bruce, 490
Andreotti, Giulio, 567
Andropov, Yury
  accession to power, 507, 529
  Afghanistan and, 480, 490–493, 522, 554
  Angola and, 447–448
  arms control and, 531–533

Brezhnev and, 398
Bush, George H.W. and, 530
Carter and, 455
Cuba and, 517
death of, 529, 534, 536
Dobrynin and, 530
domestic reforms and, 541–542
Egypt and, 397, 399
failures of, 538
fear of war with United States, 529–530,
  533–534, 536
on food shortages, 512
Harriman and, 534
Iran Hostage Crisis and, 496
Israel and, 399
Japan and, 533
Poland and, 512–518
policy making by, 507
PRC and, 533
Reagan and, 530, 531
on Watergate scandal, 390
Yom Kippur War and, 415, 418
Angola
  Andropov and, 447–448
  Brezhnev and, 427, 443–445, 447–449
  Castro and, 445–447
  Cuba and, 445–449
  Dobrynin and, 446–447
  Ford and, 427, 443, 448–449
  Gorbachev and, 559
  Gromyko and, 427, 444,
    446–448
  ideology as motivation for USSR in,
    439–440
  Kissinger and, 427, 443, 446–447, 450
  National Liberation Front for Liberation
    of Angola (FNLA), 440–443, 447
  National Union for the Total
    Independence of Angola (UNITA),
    440–443, 447
  People's Movement for the Liberation of
    Angola (MPLA), 439–441, 443–449,
    682–683
  Ponomarev and, 444, 446–449
  PRC and, 441, 448–449
  South Africa and, 441, 443, 446, 448–449
  Soviet bases in, desire for, 439

714

INDEX

Soviet expansionism and, 453
Soviet weapons in, 682–683
United States and, 441, 443, 448–449
uprising against Portuguese rule in, 440
Zaire and, 441, 443, 446
Anti-Ballistic Missile (ABM) Treaty (1972),
    379–380, 550, 551
Apollo–Soyuz space mission, 438–439
Aquino, Corazon, 568–569
Aragonés, Emilio, 301, 311
Arbatov, Georgy, 512, 520–521, 543
"arc of crises," 452–453
Argentina, Falklands War and, 525
'Arif, 'Abd al-Salam, 209, 228
arms control
    Aleksandrov-Agentov and, 531–532
    Andropov and, 531–533
    Brezhnev and, 373–374, 379–380,
        531–533, 547
    Bush, George H.W. and, 547
    Eisenhower and, 268
    Gorbachev and
      cost of arms race, 549
      generally, 532, 547
      INF Treaty, 552, 553, 559
      public opinion and, 553
      Reykjavik summit, 549–552
    Gromyko and, 531–533
    Kennan on, 531–532
    Khrushchev and, 238–239, 268–269, 547
    Reagan and, 547
    SALT-I, 379–380
    SALT-II, 433, 435, 489–490, 502, 503, 519
    Ustinov and, 531–533
al-Assad, Bashar, 600
al-Assad, Hafez, 399, 400
Atomic Energy Commission, 65
Austria
    Litvinov and, 18
    renunciation of German interests in, 46
    Stalin and, 85
    trade with USSR, 374
    withdrawal of Soviet troops from, 151
Azerbaijan, riots in, 571

Baghdad Pact, 146, 160–161, 209, 228
Baghirov, Mir Jafar, 77

Bahr, Egon, 368, 369, 372, 585, 670
Bai Chongxi, 114, 117
Baker, James, 575–578, 580, 582, 707
Baldwin, James, 456
Balluku, Beqir, 281–282
Bandilovsky, Nikolai, 314
"Barbell" theory, 452
Batista, Fulgencio, 252, 278–279
Bay of Pigs invasion, 279–281
Bazargan, Mehdi, 486–488
Begin, Menachem, 525
Belgium
    Congo, independence of, 264–265
    Litvinov and, 18
Belishova, Liri, 262
Beloborodov, Nikolai, 313
Belyaev, Vladimir, 429
Beneš, Edvard, 94, 95
Beria, Lavrenty
    after death of Stalin, 145
    downfall of, 148–149, 170
    East Germany and, 147–149, 231
    generally, 64, 200
    Hungary and, 191
    Iran and, 71
    Khrushchev and, 148–149
    nuclear weapons and, 47
    Zhukov and, 148
Berlin blockade, 105, 109, 110
Berlin Crisis (1961)
    Checkpoint Charlie standoff, 292
    generally, 12
    Gromyko and, 284
    Kennedy and, 282–284, 288–289, 292–293
    Khrushchev and
      generally, 268
      Kennedy and, 282–284, 288–289,
        292–293
      Ulbricht and, 293
      ultimatum from, 230–233, 236–237, 249
    Mikoyan and, 233–234, 284
    Ulbricht and, 233, 281, 282, 293
    Vienna Summit and, 285–286
Berlin Wall
    erection of, 286, 290, 291, 293
    fall of, 563–564
    Khrushchev and, 540

INDEX

Bevin, Ernest
Greece and, 83
on Hitler, 61
Iran and, 73
Japan and, 62
at London Conference, 54, 55,
59–62
Molotov and, 58, 60–61
Moscow Foreign Ministers Conference
and, 64–65
on reparations against Italy, 58
Stalin and, 73
Turkey and, 73
Bidault, Georges, 54, 59
Bierut, Bolesław, 188–189
Bil'ak, Vasil', 561
Biryuzov, Sergei, 299, 302
al-Bitar, Salah al-Din, 165
Blatov, Anatoly, 443, 468, 495–497
Blood, Archer K., 492
Bohlen, Charles, 53
Bolshakov, Georgy, 292
Bork, Robert, 409–410
Bovin, Aleksandr, 512
Braithwaite, Rodric, 564
Brandt, Willy
Brezhnev and, 366–368, 387–388
Moscow Treaty and, 369–371
Nobel Peace Prize and, 372
Ostpolitik and, 366, 369–372, 388
Brest-Litovsk Treaty (1918), 574
Brezhnev, Leonid
Afghanistan and
Amin and, 478, 491–493
credibility and, 494
exit strategy, search for, 522–523
generally, 475, 547, 554, 598
reluctance to intervene, 481
socialism in, 476–477
unrest and, 490
Andropov and, 398
Angola and, 427, 443–445, 447–449
arms control and, 373–374, 379–380,
531–533, 547
Berlin and, 371
Brandt and, 366–368, 387–388
Carter and

Chinese invasion of Vietnam and,
483–484
deterioration of relationship, 503
goodwill between, 454
human rights and, 455
Iran and, 486
Soviet troops in Cuba, 502
summit meeting, 489–490
support in reelection bid, 503
Castro and, 354, 597
Chernenko and, 418
Chernyaev and, 389
Chinese invasion of Vietnam and, 483–484
condominium concept, 382–388, 450,
547, 597
counterfactuals regarding, 425
credibility as motivation of, 356–357, 494
CSCE and, 436
cult of personality, 183
Cyprus and, 428, 430
Czechoslovakia and, 547
de facto alliance with United States
proposed, 433–435
de Gaulle and, 365–366, 372, 443
death of, 507, 529
Deng and, 500
detente with West and, 356, 359, 420, 421,
502, 597–598
domestic reforms and, 541
Dong, Pham Van and, 345–346, 354,
355, 358
Duan and, 354, 355, 358, 597
economic issues and, 380, 389
EEC and, 367–368, 371, 372
Ethiopia and, 466–468
as European, 363–364, 540
on food shortages, 512
Ford and
Cyprus and, 428, 430
de facto alliance proposal, 435
generally, 391, 490
Helsinki Final Act and, 433, 436
Schlesinger and, 437–438
foreign policy motivations of, 12–13
France and, 365–366, 387–388
as general secretary, 335
generally, 514

716

INDEX

Gorbachev compared, 382–383, 540, 546, 547

Gromyko and, 489

health of, 398, 435, 443–444, 451, 489–490, 502, 503, 507

Helsinki Final Act and, 428, 433, 436–438

Hungary and, 360

ideology as motivation of, 388–389, 433–434

imperialism and, 391

Iran and, 485, 486

Iran Hostage Crisis and, 495–497

Iran–Iraq War and, 497–498

Israel and, 422–423, 525

Jackson, Henry "Scoop" and, 432

on Jews, 431

Khomeini and, 487

Khrushchev compared, 382–383, 387, 597

Kim Il Sung and, 183

Kissinger and.

  CSCE, 436

  generally, 364, 433, 597

  meetings with, 378–379

  Nixon, summit with, 353

  PRC and, 384

  Yom Kippur War and, 398, 410–412

Kosygin and, 352–353, 370

legitimacy as motivation of, 328, 356, 559, 596–598

Lend-Lease loans and, 381

Mao and, 13, 364, 596

Mengistu and, 466

Middle East and, 374–375, 392, 397–399, 423–424

Mikoyan and, 118

moratorium on missiles proposed, 519–520

Moscow Treaty and, 369–371

Most Favored Nation (MFN) status and, 381, 389, 428, 431–432

Nixon and

  condominium concept and, 385–388

  detente with West, 420, 421

  generally, 13, 364, 388, 597–598

  Middle East, 397–399

  personal relationship, 428

  PRC and, 380, 386, 388, 597

prevention of nuclear war agreement and, 383

summit with, 352–354, 376, 378–382

suspicions of, 345–346, 373, 378

Vietnam War, 345–346, 350–351

Yom Kippur War, 407–408, 419

nuclear weapons and, 13

Olympic Games and, 474, 503

Ostpolitik and, 369–372, 388

ouster of Khrushchev and, 327–328, 335

Pahlavi (Shah) and, 484, 485

peace and, 389

peaceful coexistence and, 558

Poland and

  generally, 598

  martial law, 512–513

  nonintervention, 514–517

  political situation in, 509–512, 518

  Reagan and, 520

Prague Spring, crushing of, 359–361

PRC and

  generally, 362–363, 596, 598

  mistrust of, 368–369, 461

  Nixon and, 380, 386, 388, 597

  preconceived ideas regarding, 364–365

  rapprochement with, 500, 526–527

prevention of nuclear war agreement and, 382–384

Putin compared, 599–601

Reagan and

  animosity between, 526

  first meeting, 518

  Israel, 525

  personal letters, 521

  Poland, 520

  SALT-II, 519

  suspicions of, 503

recognition as motivation of, 328, 357, 387, 393, 557, 596–598

Sadat and, 394–397, 417–418, 424

Second World War and, 1–2

Siad Barre and, 465, 467, 470

Somalia and, 466–468

Stalin compared, 387, 597

Syria and, 417

"Tashkent line," 526

INDEX

Brezhnev, Leonid (cont.)
  third world and, 596
  Tito and, 373
  trade and, 374, 381
  United States and, 340, 375, 381
  Vance and, 456
  Vietnam War and
    generally, 355–357, 374
    Nixon and, 345–346, 350–351
    peace talks, 342–343
    PRC and, 340, 344
    Southeast Asia, outlook for, 347–348
    Soviet military aid, 338
  on Watergate scandal, 389–391, 422
  West Germany and, 366–372, 387–388
  "widening cracks" in West and, 574
  Yom Kippur War and
    ceasefire efforts, 403, 406
    DEFCOM 3 alert level, 416
    evacuation of Soviet civilians,
      400–401
    generally, 401, 418
    Israeli advances in, 413–414
    Kissinger and, 398, 410–412
    Nixon and, 407–408, 419
    Sadat and, 402
    Syria and, 417
    ultimatum from, 414–415
Brown, Archie, 704
Brown, Harold, 498
Brutents, Karen, 440, 493–494, 544
Brzezinski, Zbigniew
  Afghanistan and, 475
  Africa and, 463
  "arc of crises," 452–453
  Cuba and, 463
  Deng and, 458–459, 461, 463
  detente with West and, 489
  Dobrynin and, 458, 461
  Harriman and, 458
  human rights and, 455–456
  Iran and, 487–488
  Kissinger and, 458
  life of, 457–458
  as National Security Adviser, 458
  PRC and, 458–459, 690
  security and, 472

Somalia and, 469
  on Soviet expansionism, 452–453, 473
Bukovsky, Vladimir, 455, 456
Bulganin, Nikolai
  Afghanistan and, 475
  on collective security, 152
  Eisenhower and, 152
  fall of Communism in, 562
  generally, 160–161
  Nasser and, 164
  nuclear weapons and, 155, 156
  as prime minister, 151
  Suez Crisis and, 166
Bulgaria
  Byrnes and, 57
  Greece and, 100
  Litvinov and, 20
  London Conference and, 57–59
  Maisky and, 18
  Molotov and, 57–59
  Moscow Foreign Ministers Conference
    and, 65
  peace treaty with, 89
  percentages agreement and, 23
  renunciation of German interests in, 46
  Soviet hegemony in, 69, 92
  in Soviet sphere of influence, 45
  Stalin and, 58–59, 67, 85, 86
  Tito and, 81, 97–99
  "Titoists" in, 100
  United States and, 63, 599
Bundy, McGeorge "Mac," 304
Burke, Arleigh, 223, 277–278
Burma
  Khrushchev and, 168
  PRC, diplomatic recognition of,
    129, 130
  USSR and, 347–348
Bush, George H.W.
  Andropov and, 530–531
  arms control and, 547
  Chernenko and, 536
  Deng and, 565, 567
  German reunification and, 574–575
  Gorbachev and
    generally, 560
    Germany, 583–585, 587

718

INDEX

Malta summit, 564–565, 567–570
  NATO, 581, 583, 587
  post-Cold War vision, 576
Malta summit, 568–570
NATO and, 576, 578
Nicaragua and, 568–569
Philippines and, 568–569
Poland and, 706
post-Cold War vision of, 578
PRC and, 527, 565
Tiananmen Square massacre and, 567
values and, 569–570
Bush, George W., 599
Butsky, Aleksei, 302
Byrnes, James F.
  Bulgaria and, 57
  Dodecanese islands and, 57–58
  former Italian colonies and, 53–57
  Germany and, 101
  Greece and, 83
  Iran and, 77, 78
  Japan and, 61, 62
  life of, 54
  at London Conference, 54–57, 60–63
  Molotov and, 60–61, 67, 78
  Moscow Foreign Ministers Conference
    and, 64–65
  Romania and, 57
  Stalin and, 58, 60, 62, 67
Byrnes Plan, 101

Cabot, John M., 307
Cambodia
  Communist revolution in, 449
  Dong, Pham Van and, 482
  Duan and, 482
  Nixon and, 349–350
  North Vietnam and, 347
  PRC and, 481–482
  US invasion of, 347, 349–350
  Vietnamese invasion of, 474,
    481–482
Camp David Accords (1978), 424, 483
Camp David Summit (1959), 240–241
Carter, Jimmy
  Aleksandrov-Agentov and, 454–455
  Andropov and, 455

Brezhnev and
  Chinese invasion of Vietnam and,
    483–484
  deterioration of relationship, 503
  goodwill between, 454
  human rights and, 455
  Iran and, 486
  Soviet troops in Cuba, 502
  summit meeting, 489–490
  support in reelection bid, 503
Chinese invasion of Vietnam and, 482–484
Deng and, 460–461, 482–483, 498, 528
generally, 503
Gromyko and, 455
Hammer on, 503
Harriman and, 454
Helsinki Final Act and, 453–454
human rights and, 453–456, 473, 484
Iran and, 486
Iran Hostage Crisis and, 488, 495
Kissinger and, 457
Poland and, 513–514
Ponomarev and, 455
PRC and, 459
Reagan compared, 518–519
Sadat and, 483
Siad Barre and, 469–470
Somalia and, 469–470
Ustinov and, 455
Vance and, 489
Vietnam and, 498
Castro, Fidel
  Angola and, 445–447
  Brezhnev and, 354, 597
  Communist movement and, 276–277
  at Communist Party Congress, 519
  Cuban Missile Crisis and
    Khrushchev and, 316, 319–322, 324–325
    Operation Anadyr, 301, 302
    Soviet missiles in Cuba, 298, 299
    threats to attack United States with
      nuclear weapons, 320–321
  Ethiopia and, 463–464
  generally, 252, 276
  Khrushchev and
    Cuban Missile Crisis, 316, 319–322,
      324–325

719

INDEX

Castro, Fidel (cont.)
  Cuban Revolution, 271–272
  generally, 280, 284
  at UN, 277–278
  Mao compared, 463
  Mengistu and, 463–464
  Mikoyan and, 321–323
  Namibia and, 448
  Nixon–Brezhnev summit and, 354
  Siad Barre and, 463–464, 466
  Somalia and, 463–464
  Somalia–Ethiopia War and, 468–469
  as strategist for socialism, 463
  Suslov and, 449–450
  Turkey and, 321
  United States and, 488–489
  Yugoslavia and, 276
Castro, Raúl, 276, 301, 448
Catholic Church in Poland, 509
CCP. *See* Chinese Communist Party (CCP)
Ceauşescu, Elena, 562
Ceauşescu, Nicolae, 366–367, 516, 544, 562
Central Treaty Organization (CENTO), 484
Chamberlain, Neville, 322
Chamberlin, Paul, 10
Chamoun, Camille, 210, 219
Champion, Joe, 93
Chazov, Evgeny, 398, 418, 533
Chechen war, 590–591
Chen Boda, 180
Chen Yi, 246, 247, 287–288, 293, 309, 343
Chen Yun, 243
Cheremnykh, Vladimir, 522
Chernenko, Konstantin
  accession to power, 536
  Brezhnev and, 418
  Brezhnev–Nixon summit and, 381–382
  Bush, George H.W. and, 536
  peaceful coexistence and, 536
  Yom Kippur War and, 415, 416, 418
Chernobyl nuclear accident, 548
Chernyaev, Anatoly
  Afghanistan and, 554
  Brezhnev and, 389
  Czechoslovakia and, 562
  on food shortages, 511, 512
  generally, 514

Germany and, 584
Gorbachev and, 546
on health of Brezhnev, 443–444
NATO and, 581–582
peaceful coexistence and, 558, 702
Poland and, 511–512, 516
PRC and, 527
Somalia and, 466
South Korea and, 583
Vance and, 457
West Germany and, 371
Yom Kippur War and, 417–418, 423, 430
Chervenkov, Valko, 147, 275
Chervonenko, Stepan, 272
Cheysson, Claude, 524
Chiang Ching-kuo, 33–36
Chiang Kai-shek
  Batista compared, 278–279
  Eisenhower and, 225
  Jinmen and Mazu islands and, 221, 223
  Kennedy and, 307
  Khrushchev and, 219–220, 239
  Mao and, 32, 35–36, 307
  Marshall and, 89
  Mongolia and, 120
  peace efforts in civil war and, 117–118
  political power of, 114
  PRC and, 309
  Roosevelt and, 33
  Sheng Shicai and, 32
  Sino-Indian War and, 307
  Stalin and, 33–34, 112, 117, 123, 128
  UN, expulsion from, 132
  United States and, 119
Chile
  "loss" of by USSR, 494
  US-backed coup in, 487
China (People's Republic of) (PRC)
  Afghanistan and, 479, 498
  Africa and, 441–442, 472–473
  Albania and, 197, 261–263
  American prisoners in, 247
  Andropov and, 533
  Angola and, 441, 448–449
  border clash with USSR, 348, 362
  Brezhnev and
    generally, 362–363, 598

720

INDEX

mistrust of, 368–369, 461
Nixon and, 380, 386, 388, 597
preconceived ideas regarding, 364–365
rapprochement with, 500, 526–527
Brzezinski and, 458–459, 690
"bullying" of, 309–310
Bush, George H.W. and, 527, 565
Cambodia and, 481–482
Carter and, 459
Chernyaev and, 527
Chiang and, 309
Chinese Communist Party (CCP). *See* Chinese Communist Party (CCP)
Cuba and, 278–279
Cuban Missile Crisis, reaction to, 322–323, 402
Cultural Revolution, 344–345, 348, 350, 441
Czechoslovakia and, 361–362
defense cooperation with USSR, 210–211
Duan and, 333
East Germany and, 242
economic reform in, 542–544
emergence as major actor, 10–11
establishment of, 122–123
Foreign Ministry, 498
fracturing of alliance with USSR, 230–231
Gorbachev and, 577, 583
Great Leap Forward, 206, 207, 222, 241–242, 271, 275
Gromyko and, 380, 461
India and, 309
international Communist movement, position in, 7, 202–203
Jackson, Henry "Scoop" and, 432–433
Johnson, Lyndon B. and, 376–377
joint-stock companies in, 140–141
Kennedy and, 309
KGB and, 208
Khrushchev and, 170, 244, 261–262, 271, 294, 309, 595, 596
Kissinger and, 349–350, 376, 384, 434–435
Korean War and, 138–139, 146
Laos and, 481–482
"loss" of by USSR, 494
Macao and, 323
Manchuria, Soviet influence in, 140
Mikoyan and, 198

Moscow Conference and, 274
Nasser and, 162, 222
Nehru and, 246, 308–310
Netherlands and, 528–529
Nixon and
    Brezhnev and, 380, 386, 388, 597
    visit of, 268, 350–351, 376, 378, 499–500
    normalization of relations with United States, 458–459, 462
North Korea and, 187, 198
North Vietnam and
    drift toward, 332, 333
    generally, 198, 332, 333, 355
    move away from, 348–350, 355
nuclear weapons and, 210–211, 229, 335
overtaking US economy, goal of, 203–204
Pakistan and, 499
People's Liberation Army (PLA)
    in civil war, 122
    Jinmen and Mazu islands and, 128, 220–221, 223, 225–226
    Tibet, suppression of, 246
    Vietnam, invasion of, 483
Poland and, 192
Political Consultative Conference, 122
pressure, intent to not be seen as yielding to, 309
propaganda of, 308–309
rapprochement with, 508, 526–527, 537
recognition and, 9
rivalry with USSR, 230
Sino-Indian War. *See* Sino-Indian War
Sino-Soviet relations, impact of Korean War on, 139–140
Somalia and, 465
Soviet aid to, 141–142, 244
Special Economic Zones, 542
Suslov and, 253–254
Taiwan and, 309
"Tashkent line," 526
Thailand and, 498
Tiananmen Square massacre, 459, 565–567
Tibet, suppression of, 246
United States, relations with, 124–125, 458–459, 462, 471, 499–500
USSR and, 308–309, 377

INDEX

China (People's Republic of) (PRC) (cont.)
Vance and, 458, 461
Vienna Summit and, 285–286
Vietnam and
generally, 499
invasion of, 474, 482–484
Vietnam War, 331, 336–340, 343–345
withdrawal of Soviet experts from, 262
Xinjiang, Soviet influence in, 140
Yom Kippur War and, 402–403
China (Republic of)
Chinese Communist Party (CCP) in, 32,
34–37, 64
Churchill and, 33
civil war 113, 115–117
coalition in, 117
deteriorating condition of, 114
Guomindang
downfall of, 114, 115
Mao and, 35, 117
Mikoyan and, 118–119
Stalin and, 34, 35, 112, 116–118
Iran compared, 70, 80
Kazakhs in, 31
Korea and, 51
London Conference, participation in, 59–61
Malinovsky and, 64
Manchuria, Soviet influence in, 32–36, 64
Marshall and, 114, 115
Mikoyan mission to, 118–122
Molotov and, 112
nationalities question, 119–120
peace efforts in civil war, 112–113, 115–119
revolution, 122, 126
Roosevelt and, 33
Soviet withdrawal from, 69, 79
Stalin and, 31–37, 67, 593
Taiwan and, 51
Three Districts Revolution, 31
Truman and, 114
Uighurs in, 31, 36–37
United States, relations with, 114–115,
120–121
US troops in, 116
Xinjiang, Soviet influence in, 31–32, 34,
36–37, 119–120
Yalta Conference and, 31–37

Chinese Communist Party (CCP)
in civil war, 115
international Communist movement
and, 243
Liu and, 177
obedience and subordination to
USSR, 125
peace efforts in civil war and, 112–113,
115–119
in Republic of China, 32, 34–37, 64
Stalin and, 32, 34–37, 64
US–Chinese relations and, 121, 124–125
USSR, relations with, 125
Vietnam War and, 338
Chinese Eastern Railroad, 133, 140, 141
Chinggis Khan, 203, 335, 369
Chinh, Truong, 353–354
Chirac, Jacques, 437
Choe Chang-ik, 184, 186
Choe Yong-gon, 184
Choibalsan, Khorloogiin, 33–35
Churchill, Winston
Germany and, 26
Greece and, 23, 24
"Iron Curtain" speech, 78
Nixon and, 422
nuclear weapons and, 46–47
percentages agreement and, 22–25,
30–31, 501
Poland and, 27–30, 40
at Potsdam Conference, 44–45
Republic of China and, 33
Stalin and, 17, 22–24
Tito and, 80
Truman and, 78
at Yalta Conference, 24, 26, 29–30
Clinton, Bill, 591–592
coalitions
in France, 87–89, 110
generally, 69
in Germany, 110
in Greece, 110
in Iran, 110
in Italy, 87–89
in Republic of China, 117
Stalin and, 86–89, 108–110
Colby, William, 401–402

INDEX

Cold War
  declassification of documents from, 11
  Eisenhower, role of, 268
  generally, 11
  as global struggle for recognition, 5
  Khrushchev, role of, 268
  legitimacy and, 169–170
  Malta summit and, 570
  revisionism, 37
  security and, 169–170
  Stalin, role of, 37–38, 70, 106
  survival of motivations from in Russia, 10
  United States, role of, 106
Cominform
  creation of, 69
  France and, 92
  Gomułka and, 91
  Italy and, 92
  origins of, 92
  Tito and, 92
  Yugoslavia in, 96, 100
  Zhdanov and, 96
Commission on Peace Treaties and the
    Postwar Order, 19
Concert of Europe, 38
Conference on Security and Cooperation in
    Europe (CSCE), 436
Congo
  Angola and (Zaire), 441, 443, 446
  Cuba and, 445
  Eisenhower and, 265
  independence from Belgium, 264–265
  Katanga, secession of, 264–265
  Khrushchev and, 264–265, 279
Connally, John, 50
Conrad, Joseph, 471–472
Containment policy, 79–80
Copeland, Miles, 163
Corvalán, Luis, 455
Costigliola, Frank, 74
Cox, Archibald, 401, 409–410
credibility
  Brezhnev, as motivation of, 356–357, 494
  Gorbachev, as motivation of, 556–557, 559
  Vietnam War, as motivation for United
    States in, 494
Crime and Punishment (Dostoevsky), 7, 12

Crimea, Russian annexation of, 601–602
cruise missiles, 529–530, 533, 535
Cuba
  Andropov and, 517
  Angola and, 445–449
  Bay of Pigs invasion, 279–281
  Brzezinski and, 463
  CIA and, 303
  Congo and, 445
  Eisenhower and, 277, 278
  Guinea-Bissau and, 445
  Haig and, 517
  Khrushchev and
    Cuban Revolution, 271–272
    fears regarding Cuba, 296–298, 326
    generally, 279, 324–325, 595–596
    importance of, 326
    Soviet aid to, 277–278, 311–312
  Mao and, 254, 278–279
  Mikoyan and, 277, 297
  Missile Crisis. *See* Cuban Missile Crisis
    (1962)
  Namibia and, 448
  nuclear weapons in, 306
  Operation Anadyr, 301–304
  Partido Socialista Popular (PSP),
    275–276, 278
  Ponomarev and, 276–277
  PRC and, 278–279
  prestige of, 449
  Reagan and, 517
  revolution in, 252, 275–279
  Soviet missiles in, 295, 298–301
  Soviet troops in, 502
  Suslov and, 276–277
  United States and, 277, 488–489
  Vienna Summit and, 284–286
  Zhou and, 278–279
Cuban Missile Crisis (1962)
  brinksmanship during, 314–320
  Castro and
    Khrushchev and, 316, 319–322, 324–325
    Operation Anadyr, 301, 302
    Soviet missiles in Cuba, 298, 299
    threats to attack United States with
      nuclear weapons, 320–321
  Cuban reaction to, 320–322

INDEX

Cuban Missile Crisis (1962) (cont.)
Dobrynin and, 304, 318–320
"eyeball to eyeball" portrayal, 327
generally, 12, 294
Gromyko and, 312
Guevara and, 299, 301, 311, 322–323
Kennedy and
communications between Khrushchev
and Kennedy during, 314–318
ExComm debates, 304–306
Khrushchev and, 305–306, 314–318, 327
quarantine of Cuba, 312–314
Khrushchev and
American quarantine of Cuba, 312–314
backing down by, 319–320, 326, 327
"blinking first," portrayed as, 316, 327
brinksmanship, 314–320
Castro and, 316, 319, 324–325
communications between Khrushchev
and Kennedy during, 314–318
Cuban reaction to, 320–322
generally, 596
Kennedy and, 305–306, 314–318, 327
PRC and, 402
Soviet missiles in Cuba, 305–306
Malinovsky and, 306, 313
Mikoyan and, 313, 657
nuclear weapons and, 306
Operation Anadyr and, 301–304
PRC reaction to, 322–323, 402
Suslov and, 313
Turkey, linkage with, 304, 318–321,
326, 327
United States and
airstrikes as possible response, 305–306
ExComm debates, 304–306
quarantine of Cuba, 312–314
Soviet missiles in Cuba, 303
U-2 spy planes and, 303–304
West Germany and, 303
Yom Kippur War compared, 420
Cult of personality
Brezhnev, 183
Deng on, 179
Khrushchev on, 177–179
Kim Il Sung, 182–184
Mikoyan on, 177

Stalin, 177–179
Suslov on, 177
Cyprus
Brezhnev and, 428, 430
coup in, 428–429
Cypriot Communist Party (AKEL), 429
Dobrynin and, 429, 430
Ford and, 428–429
Greece and, 428–430
Kissinger and, 428–430
Nixon and, 428–429
partition of, 429–430
Turkey and, 428–430
UK and, 428–429
USSR and, 429
Cyrenaica, Litvinov and, 52
Czech Republic
in NATO, 591
United States and, 599
Czechoslovakia
Brezhnev and, 547
Chernyaev and, 562
Communist Party of Czechoslovakia
(KSČ), 94
coup in, 94–95
debt in, 560–561
fall of Communism in, 561–562
Gorbachev and, 585
lack of reform in, 561
Litvinov and, 18
Marshall Plan and, 90, 94–95
Mikoyan and, 90, 118
National Front, 94
National Social Party, 94
North Vietnam and, 361
Prague Spring, crushing of, 359–362
PRC and, 361–362
Soviet hegemony in, 69
Stalin and, 86
"Titoists" in, 100
trade agreement with, 90
in Warsaw Pact, 360

Dalai Lama, 246, 247
Danilevsky, Anatoly, 171–172
Daoud Khan, Mohammed, 475–478, 486
Davy, Richard, 438

724

INDEX

De Gasperi, Alcide, 88–89
de Gaulle, Charles
  Brezhnev and, 365–366, 372, 443
  Khrushchev and, 252–254, 273
  NATO and, 366
de Maizière, Lothar, 580
Dean, John W. III, 389–390
declassification of documents, 11
decolonization
  in Algeria, 252
  Gromyko and, 50
  Khrushchev and, 146, 252
  Litvinov and, 49–50
  Maisky and, 49–50
Democratic People's Republic of Korea.
    See North Korea
Democratic Republic of Vietnam (DRV).
    See North Vietnam
Deng Xiaoping
  accession to power, 459
  Afghanistan and, 475, 498
  "barbell" theory, 452
  Brezhnev and, 500
  Brzezinski and, 458–459, 461, 463
  Bush, George H.W. and, 565, 567
  Carter and, 460–461, 482–483, 498, 528
  on cult of personality, 179
  on democracy, 544
  on denunciation of Stalin, 176
  economic reform and, 542
  Gorbachev and, 544–545, 577
  as gradualist, 545
  Great Leap Forward and, 242
  Hungary and, 194
  on imperialism, 452
  international Communist movement
      and, 243
  on international situation, 498–499
  Khrushchev and, 259
  Mao compared, 459–460, 471, 499–500
  modernization and, 471
  Moscow Conference and, 272–274
  normalization of relations with United
      States, 458–459, 462
  security and, 472
  Soviet aid and, 244
  on Soviet expansionism, 452

Tiananmen Square massacre and, 459
United States and, 459–460, 462, 483, 527
USSR and, 483
Vietnam, invasion of, 482–484
Vietnam War and, 343
Denmark
  Danish Communist Party, 173–174
  Litvinov and, 18
  Socialist People's Party, 174
Dennis, Eugene, 175
de-Stalinization, 146–147, 171–173, 177–178
detente with West
  Brezhnev and, 356, 359, 420, 421, 502,
      597–598
  Brzezinski and, 489
  demise of, 474–475, 501, 502
  Ford and, 427–428
  generally, 12–13
  ideology and, 425–426
  Khrushchev and, 251
  Kissinger and, 403, 427–428, 501
  Kosygin and, 356
  linkage and, 403, 501–502
  Mao and, 368
  Nixon and, 403, 420, 421, 501
  Yom Kippur War and, 426
Diem, Ngo Dinh, 252
Dimitrov, Georgi, 81, 82, 92, 97–98, 113
Dinitz, Simcha, 410
Djilas, Milovan, 22, 85, 96–99
Dobrynin, Anatoly
  Afghanistan and, 488, 493–494, 522, 523
  Andropov and, 530
  Angola and, 446–447
  Brezhnev–Carter summit and, 489
  Brzezinski and, 458, 461
  Cuban Missile Crisis and, 304, 318–320
  Cyprus and, 429, 430
  generally, 520–521
  Haig and, 420–421, 519, 521, 522
  human rights and, 455
  Iran Hostage Crisis and, 497
  Jackson, Henry "Scoop" and, 432–433
  Johnson, Lyndon B. and, 362
  Kissinger and
    Angola and, 446–447
    Brezhnev–Nixon summit and, 376, 377

INDEX

Dobrynin, Anatoly (cont.)
  ceasefire efforts in Yom Kippur War,
    402, 403, 408, 409
  Cyprus, 429
  "deceit" in Yom Kippur War, 413–414
  direct Soviet involvement, in Yom
    Kippur War, danger of, 406–407
  generally, 450
  human rights, 455
  Soviet observers in Yom Kippur War,
    416–417
  spheres of influence, 500–501
  threats of other nations to enter Yom
    Kippur War and, 405
  Yom Kippur War and, 400, 402, 409,
    415, 422
  Nixon and, 362, 407, 416, 421
  Siad Barre and, 469–470
  Somalia and, 469–470
  Vance and, 455, 461, 488, 489
  Vietnam War and, 346, 352
  Yom Kippur War and
    ceasefire efforts, 402, 403, 408, 409
    direct Soviet involvement, danger of,
      406–407
    generally, 400, 402
    Kissinger and, 400, 402, 409, 415, 422
    Nixon and, 416
    Soviet observers and, 416–417
    threats of other nations
      to enter, 405
Dodecanese islands
  Byrnes and, 57–58
  Litvinov and, 51–52
  London Conference and, 57–58
  Molotov and, 57–58, 67
Dominican Republic, revolutionary activity
  in, 276–277
Dong, Pham Van
  Brezhnev and, 345–346, 354, 355, 358
  Cambodia and, 482
  Nixon and, 350
  Nixon–Brezhnev summit and, 354
  treaty with USSR and, 482
  USSR and, 338
  Vietnam War and, 342
  Zhou and, 343–344

Dostoevsky, Fyodor, 7
Drew, Elizabeth, 450
DRV. *See* North Vietnam
Duan, Le
  Brezhnev and, 354, 355, 358, 597
  Cambodia and, 482
  at Communist Party Congress, 519
  generally, 499
  Mao and, 274–275, 349, 355, 357
  Nixon–Brezhnev summit and, 353–354
  PRC and, 333
  Tet Offensive and, 345
  Thailand and, 347
  treaty with USSR and, 482
Dubček, Alexander, 359–361
Dubs, Adolph, 488
Dulles, John Foster
  Egypt and, 162
  Jinmen and Mazu islands and, 223–224
  Khrushchev and, 151, 152, 212, 237,
    288–289
  Mikoyan and, 233–234
  Suez Crisis and, 165
  U-2 spy planes and, 255
Durdenevsky, Vsevolod, 50–51
Dutra, Maria Graca, 227

East Germany
  after death of Stalin, 145
  Beria and, 147–149, 231
  Berlin Crisis. *See* Berlin Crisis (1961)
  Berlin Wall
    erection of, 286, 290, 291, 293
    fall of, 563–564
    Khrushchev and, 540
  Christian Democrats (CDU), 579
  debt in, 563
  demise of, 573–574
  elections in, 579
  establishment of, 69, 105
  flight of people from, 147, 231, 281, 563
  Gorbachev and, 563–564
  international recognition of, 449
  Khrushchev and, 151
  legitimacy and, 231–232
  living standards in, 181–182, 231
  Malenkov and, 147–148, 231, 631

726

INDEX

Molotov and, 147–149, 231
Party of Democratic Socialism, 573, 579
PRC and, 242
Social Democrats (SPD), 579
Socialist Unity Party of Germany (SED),
    147, 563
Soviet aid to, 243
Soviet troops in, 574
Stalin and, 101–106
uprising in, 149, 231
East Turkestan Republic, 31, 36–37
Eastern Cominform, 120
Eden, Anthony
    Khrushchev and, 156
    Nasser and, 161, 163
    percentages agreement and, 23
    Poland and, 40
    Suez Crisis and, 165, 166
Egypt
    Andropov and, 397, 399
    Aswan Dam, 161–163
    Camp David Accords and, 424
    Dulles and, 162
    Eisenhower and, 162
    Khrushchev and, 146, 167, 168
    nuclear weapons and, 418, 678
    Six Day War, 393
    Soviet military advisers in, 396, 672
    Soviet military aid to, 397, 405
    Suez Canal, 44, 163–164, 195. *See also*
        Suez Crisis (1956)
    treaty with USSR, 394–395
    USSR and, 424–425
    Yom Kippur War. *See* Yom Kippur War
Eisenhower, Dwight D.
    arms control and, 268
    Bulganin and, 152
    Camp David Summit, 240–241
    Chiang and, 225
    Cold War, role in, 268
    Congo and, 265
    Cuba and, 277, 278
    Egypt and, 162
    Hungary and, 195
    Iraq and, 209, 226, 228
    Jinmen and Mazu islands and, 223–224
    Khrushchev and

animosity between, 270
    brinksmanship, 212–213
    Camp David Summit, 237–241, 248–249
    diplomacy and, 273
    four-power summit, 151–152, 259
    generally, 12, 249–250, 264, 267, 373, 595
    proposed summit with, 213–216,
        219–220
Mao and, 169, 245, 260, 269
Middle East and, 210
Mikoyan and, 186, 234
Suez Crisis and, 165–167, 195
U-2 spy planes and, 255–258
Zhukov and, 155
Eisenstein, Sergey, 533, 538
Elizabeth II (UK), 212–213
Eritrea
    Litvinov and, 51
    separatist movement in, 467
Escalante, Anibal, 276–278
Estonia
    Gorbachev and, 582
    independence of, 571, 582
    in NATO, 591
Ethiopia
    Brezhnev and, 466–468
    Castro and, 468–469
    Eritrea, separatist movement in, 467, 470
    Gorbachev and, 559
    Ponomarev and, 467
    revolution in, 466
    Siad Barre and, 464
    Somali invasion of, 467–471
    Soviet interest in, 466, 470–471
European Defense Community (EDC),
    149–150
European Economic Community (EEC),
    367–368, 371, 372, 522–523

Fahmi, Ismail, 424
Faisal II (Iraq), 209, 210
Falin, Valentin, 579–581, 584–585
Falklands War, 525
Farouk (Egypt), 159
Fawzi, Mohamed, 394
Federal Republic of Germany. *See*
    West Germany

727

INDEX

Feklisov, Aleksandr (Fomin), 317
Finland
  Litvinov and, 18
  Molotov and, 59
  peace treaty with, 89
  renunciation of German interests in, 46
  Stalin and, 85
  withdrawal of Soviet troops from, 151
food shortages
  in France, 87
  in Italy, 87
  in North Korea, 182–183
  in USSR, 511, 512
Ford, Gerald
  Angola and, 427, 443, 448–449
  Brezhnev and
    Cyprus and, 428, 430
    de facto alliance proposal, 435
    generally, 391, 490
    Helsinki Final Act and, 433, 436
    Schlesinger and, 437–438
  Cyprus and, 428–429
  detente with West and, 427–428
  generally, 407, 503
  Helsinki Final Act and, 433, 436
  Jackson, Henry "Scoop" and, 430–432, 435, 437
  Kissinger and, 450–451
  Reagan and, 437, 450–451, 453
Foroughi, Mahmoud, 317
Foster, William Z., 175
four-power summit, 253, 258–259
France
  Brezhnev and, 365–366, 387–388
  coalition in, 87–89, 110
  colonies of, 49–50
  Cominform and, 92
  destruction from the Second World War in, 86
  food shortages in, 87
  four-power summit and, 253
  Khrushchev and, 252–253
  Litvinov and, 18, 20–21
  London Conference, participation in, 59–61
  Parti Communiste Français (PCF), 87–91
  peace efforts in Chinese civil war, 115–116
  Popular Republic Movement (MRP), 87

  sanctions against USSR and, 524
  Suez Crisis and, 164, 166–167, 195
  trade with USSR, 374
  Zhdanov and, 91–92
Friedman, Jeremy, 487
Fuchs, Klaus, 138
Fukuyama, Francis, 3, 8, 9
Furtseva, Yekaterina, 638

Gaddis, John Lewis, 148
Gaevsky, Viktor, 592
Gagarin, Yuri, 283
Gams, Eduard, 585
Gandhi, Rajiv, 577
Gates, John, 175
Gates, Robert, 565, 575, 586
Gayler, Noel, 531–532
Geng Biao, 499–500
Genscher, Hans-Dietrich, 570–571, 574–575
Georgia
  pro-Stalin riots in, 172, 179
  Russia, war with, 600
German Democratic Republic (GDR). *See* East Germany
Germany. *See also* East Germany; West Germany
  Allied Control Council, 61–62, 67, 104
  Berlin blockade, 105, 409, 110
  Byrnes Plan, 101
  Chernyaev and, 584
  Churchill and, 26
  coalition in, 110
  Communist Party (KPD), 102
  electoral strategy in, 61–62, 102–103
  Gorbachev and
    NATO, 581–586
    reunification, 570–575
  Kennan and, 102
  Khrushchev and, 150–151, 238
  Litvinov and, 18–20, 27
  London Conference and, 104
  Maisky and, 20
  Marshall and, 104
  Marshall Plan and, 104
  Molotov and, 104
  in NATO, 560, 574–575, 584–587
  partitioning of, 26–27

728

INDEX

recognition and, 592
reparations from, 45, 104
reunification of, 560, 570–575, 586
Roosevelt and, 26
Social Democratic Party (SPD), 61–62, 102
Socialist Unity Party of Germany (SED), 102–105
Soviet occupation of, 101, 103–104
Stalin and, 25–27, 101–106
"Tutzing formula," 574–575, 578
United States and, 101
Yalta Conference and, 25–27
Gerő, Ernő, 191
Ghana
Soviet aid to, 244
USSR and, 265
Giap, Vo Nguyen, 347–348, 350–351, 354
Gierek, Edward, 508–511
Gilpatric, Roswell, 295
Giscard d'Estaing, Valery, 443, 489
glasnost, 544–545
Gleijeses, Piero, 445
Global South, 10
"golden hoop," 176–177, 198
Golikov, Viktor, 527
Gomaa, Sharawy, 394
Gomułka, Władysław
Cominform and, 91
downfall of, 508, 509
Khrushchev and, 189, 190, 196–197, 232
Mikoyan and, 190
reemergence of, 188–189
Gorbachev, Mikhail
Afghanistan and, 554–557, 559
Angola and, 559
arms control and
cost of arms race, 549
generally, 532, 547
INF Treaty, 552, 553, 559
public opinion and, 553
Reykjavik summit, 549–552
Brezhnev compared, 382–383, 540, 546, 547
Bush, George H.W. and
generally, 560
Germany, 583–585, 587
Malta summit, 564–565, 567–570

NATO, 581, 583, 587
post-Cold War vision, 576
Chernobyl nuclear accident and, 548
Chernyaev and, 546
"Common European Home," 372–373, 566–567, 571–572, 578–579, 583, 585–586
continuity in foreign policy, 539
counterfactuals regarding, 425
coup attempt against, 588
credibility as motivation of, 556–557, 559
Czechoslovakia and, 585
demise of USSR and, 539, 560, 587–589
democratization and, 544–545
Deng and, 544–545, 577
domestic reforms and, 541–542
East Germany and, 563–564
Eastern Europe and, 560–563
economic crisis and, 582–583
Estonia and, 582
Ethiopia and, 559
foreign policy motivations of, 13–14
Germany and
NATO, 581–586
reunification, 570–575
glasnost, 544–545
global leadership and, 539
Honecker and, 544
Hungary and, 585
Japan and, 576
Khrushchev compared, 540, 546
Kohl and, 579, 582–583, 586, 587
Latvia and, 582
legitimacy as motivation of, 542, 556, 559, 578–579
Lithuania and, 571, 582
Malta summit, 568–570
Mongolia and, 559
motivations of, 598–599
Mozambique and, 559
NATO and
Bush, George H.W. and, 581, 583, 587
eastward expansion of, 575–582
Germany, 581–586
as political versus military pact, 566
post-Cold War vision, 576–577
"New Thinking," 13–14, 545–547, 558

729

INDEX

Gorbachev, Mikhail (cont.)
Nicaragua and, 568–569
nonintervention and, 516, 569
nuclear weapons and, 533–534
peace offensive, 551, 552
peaceful coexistence and, 558
perestroika
Chinese economic reform compared, 542–544
foreign policy and, 545–547
generally, 539, 553
NEP compared, 542
Nixon on, 565
rapid pace of, 545
Philippines and, 568–569
Pizza Hut commercial, 589
in Politburo, 512
post-Cold War vision of, 576–578
PRC and, 577, 583
on productivity, 542
Putin compared, 600–601
Reagan and, 548, 549, 557–558, 567
recognition as motivation of, 557
resentment against, 589
resignation of, 588
Second World War and, 2
security as motivation of, 578–579
South Korea and, 583
Stalin compared, 540
on technology, 542
third world and, 559
Tiananmen Square massacre and, 565–566
travels of, 540
universal values and, 546
values and, 569–570
Vietnam and, 559
Warsaw Pact and, 566, 584–585
"widening cracks" in West and, 574
Gorbachev, Raisa, 540
Gottlieb, Sidney, 265
Gottwald, Klement, 94, 95
"Great men" theory, 9
Grechko, Andrei, 392, 416, 418, 444–445, 447–448
Greece
Albania and, 100
Bevin and, 83

Bulgaria and, 100
Byrnes and, 83
Churchill and, 23, 24
civil war, 69, 82–84, 98, 100–101
coalition in, 110
Cyprus and, 428–430
Democratic Army of Greece (DAG), 84
fall of regime in, 449
Greek Communist Party (KKE), 82–83, 100–101
Greek National Liberation Front (ELAS/EAM), 23
Litvinov and, 18
Molotov and, 83
percentages agreement and, 23, 24
Stalin and
civil war, 82–85, 98, 100–101
generally, 24, 594
withdrawal from, 109, 110
Tito and, 81
Truman and, 83–84
UK and, 84
United States and, 83–84
Grenada, US invasion of, 535
Griboyedov, Aleksandr, 495
Grishin, Viktor, 260
Gromyko, Andrei
Afghanistan and, 477–478, 480–481, 490, 493, 522, 554
Angola and, 427, 444, 446–448
arms control and, 531–533
Berlin Crisis and, 284
Brezhnev and, 489
Carter and, 455
Cuban Missile Crisis and, 312
decolonization and, 50
former Italian colonies and, 53, 56
Haig and, 519, 523, 698
Harriman and, 235
Iran Hostage Crisis and, 496
Israel and, 422–423
Jinmen and Mazu islands and, 224–225
Kennedy and, 279
Mao and, 218
missiles in Cuba and, 298–299
nuclear weapons and, 533–534
Poland and, 512–516, 520

730

INDEX

policy making by, 507
PRC and, 380, 461
Reagan and, 524
Siad Barre and, 469
Truman and, 41
Vance and, 457
West Germany and, 369
Yom Kippur War and, 411, 413, 415, 416, 418
Grotewohl, Otto, 103, 147
Groza, Petru, 40–41, 58
Gruenther, Alfred, 150
Guevara, Ernesto "Che"
    Cuban Missile Crisis and, 299, 301, 311, 322–323
    USSR and, 276, 278
Guinea
    Soviet aid to, 244
    USSR and, 265
Guinea-Bissau, Cuba and, 445
Gulf of Tonkin incident (1964), 333
Guo Zengkai, 112
Gürsel, Cemal, 296

Haig, Alexander
    Afghanistan and, 523
    criticism of, 523
    Cuba and, 517
    Dobrynin and, 420–421, 519, 521, 522
    generally, 421
    Gromyko and, 519, 523, 698
    on moratorium on missiles, 519
    Poland and, 519, 521
    sanctions against USSR and, 524
    on Soviet nervousness, 521
    Yom Kippur War and, 415, 421
Halifax, Lord, 54
Hammarskjöld, Dag, 220, 265, 279
Hammer, Armand, 422–423, 454, 503
Harriman, W. Averell
    Andropov and, 534
    Brzezinski and, 458
    Carter and, 454
    Gromyko and, 235
    Khrushchev and, 235
    Maisky and, 41–42
    Mikoyan and, 235

Molotov and, 41, 43
Stalin and, 63–65
Truman and, 41–42
Yalta Conference and, 33, 40
Hartman, Arthur, 524
Haslam, Jonathan, 19
Havel, Václav, 561–562, 577
He Long, 335–336
Heart of Darkness (Conrad), 471–472
Hebrang, Andrija, 99
Hegedüs, András, 191
Hegel, G.W.F., 9, 592
Heikal, Mohamed, 163, 165, 399
Helsinki Final Act
    Brezhnev and, 428, 433, 436–438
    Carter and, 453–454
    Ford and, 433, 436
    generally, 150
    Reagan and, 524
Henze, Paul B., 470–471
Heraclitus, 586–587
Herter, Christian, 256
hierarchy of needs, 9
Hill, William H., 708
Hinckley, John Jr., 520
Hirohito, 47
Hiroshima bombing, 47
Hiss, Alger, 138
Hitler, Adolf
    appeasement of, 322
    Bevin on, 61
    generally, 212
    Molotov and, 19
    Stalin compared, 74
Ho Chi Minh
    Albania and, 332
    funeral of, 348–349
    Khrushchev and, 235, 244, 263
    Mao and, 274–275, 332, 344, 349
    PCF and, 88
    Stalin and, 120
    USSR and, 333
    Vietnam War and, 343, 344
Holbrooke, Richard, 528
Honecker, Eric, 436, 513, 515, 516, 544, 563–564
Hopkins, Harry, 43

INDEX

Hoveyda, Amir-Abbas, 485
Hoxha, Enver
    Khrushchev and, 262–263, 285–286
    Mao and, 263
    Moscow Conference and, 274
    Stalin and, 84, 85, 96–97, 100
    as Stalinist, 147
Hu Yaobang, 544, 565
Huang Hua, 529
Hull, Cordell, 304
human rights
    Brzezinski and, 455–456
    Carter and, 453–456, 473, 484
    Dobrynin and, 455
    Helsinki Final Act. *See* Helsinki Final Act
    Kissinger and, 455
    Soviet sensitivity to accusations regarding,
        455–456
Hungary
    Beria and, 191
    Brezhnev and, 360
    debt in, 560–561
    Deng and, 194
    Eisenhower and, 195
    fall of Communism in, 561
    Gorbachev and, 585
    Hungarian Workers' Party (HWP),
        190–192, 194–195
    impact of Soviet intervention in West, 196
    Khrushchev and, 192, 195–197, 361, 547
    Kosygin and, 360
    lack of reform in, 561
    Litvinov and, 18
    Liu and, 194–196
    Maisky and, 18
    Malenkov and, 191
    Mao and, 194, 197–198
    Mikoyan and, 192, 194
    in NATO, 591
    New Course, 190–191
    North Korea compared, 196–197
    peace treaty with, 89
    percentages agreement and, 23
    Petőfi Circle, 191
    Poland compared, 196–197
    renunciation of German interests in, 46
    Smallholder Party, 93

Soviet hegemony in, 69, 93
Soviet military intervention in, 196
in Soviet sphere of influence, 45
Stalin and, 85, 86
Suslov and, 192, 194
"Titoists" in, 100
UN and, 196
uprising in, 191–192
Warsaw Pact in, 196
Zhukov and, 195
Hurley, Patrick J., 35
Husák, Gustáv, 516
Hussein (Jordan), 210, 406, 407, 497–498
Hussein, Saddam, 497, 601
hydrogen bomb, 155

ideology
    Angola, as motivation for USSR in, 439–440
    Brezhnev, as motivation of, 388–389,
        433–434
    detente with West and, 425–426
    as driver of Soviet foreign policy, 3–4
    Khrushchev, as motivation of, 168
    Litvinov and, 21–22
    Maisky and, 21–22
    Mao, as motivation of, 433–434
    Middle East, and Soviet interest in, 392
    Sino-Indian War, as motivation for,
        307–308
    Stalin, as motivation of, 107–108
    third world, and Soviet interest in,
        471–472
imperialism
    Brezhnev and, 391
    Deng on, 452
    as driver of Soviet foreign policy, 4–5
    Litvinov and, 21, 68
    Maisky and, 21, 68
    Peter the Great and, 452
    Stalin, as motivation of, 37, 108
India
    Khrushchev and, 168
    PRC and, 309
    Sino-Indian War. *See* Sino-Indian War
    Soviet aid to, 158
    Soviet Navy and, 392
    USSR and, 347–348

732

INDEX

Indonesia
  Indonesian Communist Party (PKI), 441
  Khrushchev and, 167–168
  Soviet aid to, 324
Indyk, Martin, 673
Inozemtsev, Nikolai, 512
intercontinental ballistic missiles
    (ICBMs), 295
intermediate-range ballistic missiles
    (IRBMs), 296
Intermediate-Range Nuclear Forces (INF)
    Treaty (1987), 552, 553, 559
International Department of the Central
    Committee, 444
International Monetary Fund, 509
International Relations, recognition in, 9–10
Iran
  Afghanistan and, 522–523
  Beria and, 71
  Bevin and, 73
  Brezhnev and, 485, 486
  Brzezinski and, 487–488
  Byrnes and, 77, 78
  Carter and, 486
  CIA and, 487–488
  coalition in, 110
  containment policy and, 79–80
  ethnic separatists, Soviet support for,
    71–72
  hostage crisis. *See* Iran Hostage Crisis
  Iraq, war with, 497–498
  KGB and, 485–486, 488
  Khrushchev and, 239
  Molotov and, 78
  oil and, 71, 76
  Republic of China compared, 70, 80
  revolutionary government in, 486
  Soviet Embassy, storming of, 498
  Soviet expansionism and, 453
  Soviet withdrawal from, 69, 77–78
  Stalin and, 73–74, 76–80, 109, 593, 594
  Truman and, 73–74
  Tudeh, 486, 488, 498
  UK, Russian rivalry with regarding, 70–71
  United States, Russian rivalry with
    regarding, 71
  USSR and, 485

Vienna Summit and, 285
  Western-sponsored coup in, 146
  "White Revolution" in, 484
Iran Hostage Crisis
  Aleksandrov-Agentov and, 495–497
  Andropov and, 496
  Brezhnev and, 495–497
  Carter and, 488, 495
  Dobrynin and, 497
  Gromyko and, 496
  Khomeini and, 488, 691
  storming of US Embassy, 488, 494–495
  UN sanctions proposal, 495–497
  Ustinov and, 496
  Vinogradov and, 488
Iraq
  American invasion of, 601
  coup in, 209
  Eisenhower and, 209, 226, 228
  Iran, war with, 497–498
  Khrushchev and, 167, 212, 217–218, 226,
    228–229
  Liu and, 218
  Mao and, 217–218
  Nasser and, 209, 211–212, 217–218,
    228–229
  Putin and, 601
  Soviet Navy and, 392
  United States and, 209, 601
  USSR and, 424–425
"Iron Curtain" speech, 78
Ismail, Ahmed, 397
Israel
  Andropov and, 399
  Brezhnev and, 422–423, 525
  Camp David Accords and, 424
  Gromyko and, 422–423
  Lebanon, invasion of, 525
  Reagan and, 525
  Six Day War, 393
  Suez Crisis and, 164, 166, 195
  USSR, diplomatic relations with, 423
  Yom Kippur War. *See* Yom Kippur War
Israelyan, Viktor, 402, 414, 675
Italy
  coalition in, 87–89
  Cominform and, 92

733

INDEX

Italy (cont.)
  destruction from the Second World
    War in, 86
  food shortages in, 87
  former colonies of, 44–45, 51–57
  Litvinov and, 18, 20–21
  PCI, 87–91
  peace treaty with, 89
  reparations against, 58
  sanctions against USSR and, 524
  Stalin and, 109
  trade with USSR, 374
  US bases in, 296
  Western recognition of, 45
  Zhdanov and, 91–92
Ivan the Terrible (film), 533, 538
Ivashutin, Pyotr, 376–377

Jackson, Henry M. "Scoop"
  Brezhnev and, 432
  Dobrynin and, 432–433
  Ford and, 430–432, 435, 437
  Kissinger and, 433
  PRC and, 432–433
Jäger, Harald, 563, 705
Jagielski, Mieczysław, 510
Jakeš, Miloš, 562
Japan
  American bases in, 296
  Andropov and, 533
  Bevin and, 62
  Byrnes and, 61, 62
  Eastern Cominform and, 120
  Gorbachev and, 576
  Hiroshima nuclear bombing, 47
  Hokkaido, Soviet designs on, 47–49
  Kissinger and, 434–435
  Korea and, 135
  Kurile islands, 32–33, 47–48, 127, 151
  London Conference and, 61–63
  Molotov and, 61–63
  Moscow Foreign Ministers Conference
    and, 65
  Nagasaki nuclear bombing, 47
  Sakhalin island, 32–33, 47–48, 127
  Soviet entry into war against, 47–49
  Soviet withdrawal from, 79

Stalin and, 32–33, 61–64, 67
  United States and, 146
Jaruzelski, Wojciech, 514–518, 561
Jesus, 273
Jews
  Brezhnev on, 431
  migration from USSR, 431
Jiang Qing, 35, 124
Jinmen and Mazu islands
  Chiang and, 221, 223
  Dulles and, 223–224
  Eisenhower and, 223–224
  Gromyko and, 224–225
  Khrushchev and, 222, 224–227, 229
  Mao and, 221–223, 225–227, 229, 249
  nuclear weapons, threatened use of,
    223–224
  PLA shelling of, 220–221, 223, 225–226
  United States and, 223–224
  Zhou and, 224–225
John Paul II (Pope), 509, 568
Johnson, Lyndon B.
  authorization of Vietnam War, 333
  Dobrynin and, 362
  generally, 304
  Kosygin and, 362
  PRC and, 376–377
  Vietnam War and, 331, 341–343, 346
Jones, Nate, 530
Jordan
  UK and, 210, 220
  Yom Kippur War and, 405, 406
Jupiter missiles, 296, 304, 318, 326, 327

Kádár, János, 196, 516, 561
Kaganovich, Lazar', 155–156, 200
Kalinovsky, Artemy, 554
Kamaz, 374, 389
Kang Youwei, 207–208
Kania, Stanisław, 511–516, 518, 519
Kapitsa, Mikhail, 462, 527
Kapitsa, Petr, 74–75
Kapo, Hysni, 263
Kardelj, Edvard, 97, 98
Karmal, Babrak, 476, 480, 522–523,
  537, 556
Karski, Jan, 30

734

INDEX

Kasavubu, Joseph, 265
Kataev, Vitaly, 551
Kaunda, Kenneth, 441, 442
Kavtaradze, Sergei, 71
Ke Qingshi, 208
Keating, Kenneth, 303
Kellogg–Briand Pact (1928), 383
Kendall, Donald, 389
Kennan, George F.
  on arms control, 531–532
  Germany and, 102
  Long Telegram, 452
  on nuclear weapons, 75–76
  on opportunism of USSR, 439
  on Russia, 8
  on Stalin, 88, 107, 109, 593
Kennedy, Jacqueline, 284
Kennedy, John F.
  assassination of, 327, 390
  Bay of Pigs invasion and, 279–281
  Berlin Crisis and, 282–284, 288–289,
    292–293
  Chiang and, 307
  counterfactuals regarding, 425
  Cuban Missile Crisis and
    communications between Khrushchev
      and Kennedy during, 314–318
    ExComm debates, 304–306
    generally, 327
    Khrushchev and, 305–306, 314–318, 327
    quarantine of Cuba, 312–314
  election of, 270
  Gromyko and, 279
  Khrushchev and
    Bay of Pigs invasion, 279–281
    Berlin Crisis, 282–284, 288–289,
      292–293
    Cuban Missile Crisis, 305–306,
      314–318, 327
    generally, 12, 270–271, 595
  Laos and, 652
  PRC and, 309
  U-2 spy planes and, 303–304
  Vienna Summit and, 284–286
Kennedy, Robert F., 292, 304, 318–320, 373
Kennedy, Ted, 446, 578
Kerr, Archibald, 40, 43

Kershaw, Ian, 38
KGB
  Afghanistan and, 476, 490–492
  Iran and, 485–486, 488
  Middle East and, 397
  Novocherkassk riots, suppression of,
    300–301
  Olympic Games and, 540–541
  Pahlavi (Shah) and, 485–486
  Poland and, 511
  PRC and, 208
  Project RYaN, 529–530
  Reagan and, 521
  Yom Kippur War and, 418
Khaddam, Abdul Halim, 417
Kharlamov, Mikhail, 288
Khomeini, Ruhollah (Ayatollah)
  Afghanistan and, 495
  Brezhnev and, 487
  CIA and, 487–488
  imprisonment of, 484
  Iran Hostage Crisis and, 488, 691
  USSR and, 486–488
  Vinogradov and, 487
Khrushchev, Nikita
  accession to power, 145
  Afghanistan and, 475–476
  Africa and, 167–168
  Albania and, 262–264, 294
  Algeria and, 253
  arms control and, 238–239,
    268–269, 547
  Bay of Pigs invasion and, 279–281
  Beria and, 148–149
  Berlin Crisis and
    generally, 268
    Kennedy and, 282–284, 288–289,
      292–293
    Ulbricht and, 293
    ultimatum regarding, 230,
      236–237, 249
  Berlin Wall and, 290, 291, 293, 540
  Brezhnev compared, 382–383, 387, 597
  brinksmanship of, 212–213
  bureaucratic restructuring by, 207
  Burma and, 168
  Camp David Summit, 240–241

INDEX

Khrushchev, Nikita (cont.)

Castro and

Cuban Missile Crisis, 316, 319–322, 324–325

Cuban Revolution, 271–272

generally, 280, 284

at UN, 277–278

Chiang and, 219–220, 239

Cold War, role in, 268

Congo and, 264–265, 279

counterfactuals regarding, 425

Cuba and

Cuban Revolution, 271–272

fears regarding Cuba, 296–298, 324–325

generally, 279, 324–325, 595–596

importance of, 326

Soviet aid to, 277–278, 311–312

Cuban Missile Crisis and

American quarantine of Cuba, 312–314

backing down in, 319–320, 326, 327

"blinking first," portrayed as, 316, 327

brinksmanship, 314–320

Castro and, 316, 319, 324–325

communications between Khrushchev and Kennedy during, 314–318

Cuban reaction to, 320–322

generally, 596

Kennedy and, 305–306, 314–318, 327

PRC and, 402

Soviet missiles in Cuba, 305–306

on cult of personality, 177–179

de Gaulle and, 252–254, 258, 259, 273

decolonization and, 146, 252

Deng and, 259

denunciation of Stalin, 171–173, 175–176, 198

detente with West and, 251

dialogue with West, 249–250

domestic reforms and, 541

Dulles and, 151, 152, 212, 237, 288–289

East Germany and, 151

Eden and, 156

Egypt and, 146, 167, 168

Eisenhower and

animosity between, 270

brinksmanship, 212–213

Camp David Summit, 237–241, 248–249

diplomacy and, 273

four-power summit, 151–152, 259

generally, 12, 249–250, 264, 267, 373, 595

proposed summit with, 213–216, 219–220

foreign aid and, 243–244

foreign policy motivations of, 12

four-power summit and, 253, 258–259

France and, 252–253

Germany and, 150–151, 238

Gomułka and, 189, 190, 196–197, 232

Gorbachev compared, 540, 546

Harriman and, 235

Ho Chi Minh and, 235, 244, 263

Hoxha and, 262–263, 285–286

Hungary and, 192, 195–197, 361, 547

ideology as motivation of, 168

indecisiveness of, 197

India and, 168

Indonesia and, 167–168

international affairs and, 311

Iran and, 239

Iraq and, 167, 212, 217–218, 226, 228–229

Jinmen and Mazu islands and, 222, 224–227, 229

Kennedy and

Bay of Pigs invasion, 279–281

Berlin Crisis, 282–284, 288–289, 292–293

Cuban Missile Crisis, 305–306, 314–318, 327

generally, 12, 270–271, 595

Kim Il Sung and, 183–184, 187, 196–198

Kurile islands and, 151

Laos and, 279

legitimacy as motivation of, 168–169, 269, 559, 594–596

Liu and, 192–196, 198

Macmillan and, 212, 214, 258–259, 267, 273

Malenkov and, 200

Mao and

animosity between, 245, 247–249, 254, 261–262

claims to Soviet territory by, 334

736

INDEX

denunciation of Stalin and, 176–178, 180–181
generally, 12, 596
meetings with, 202
North Korea and, 187, 198
ouster of, 335
Port Arthur and, 151
rivalry between, 201, 203, 260
Soviet aid and, 158–159
Stalin compared, 334–335
"swimming pool" summit, 216–219, 221
third world and, 169
United States and, 208–209
Middle East and, 210
Mikoyan and, 118, 212, 294
militancy of, 287–288
military cuts by, 251–252
missiles in Cuba and, 298–301
Molotov and, 200
Moscow Conference and, 273–274
Nasser and
generally, 157, 160–162, 594
Iraq and, 211–212, 217–218
nuclear weapons and, 210
PRC and, 222
Suez Crisis, 164
at UN, 266
NATO and, 232
Nehru and, 157, 158, 247, 267, 594
Nixon and
generally, 248, 271, 288
"kitchen debate," 235–236, 373
suspicions of, 270
North Vietnam and, 355–356
nuclear tests and, 293, 653
nuclear weapons and, 145–146, 154–156, 170
Operation Anadyr and, 301–303
ouster of, 327–328, 335
overtaking US economy, goal of, 203–204
Pahlavi (Shah) and, 484, 485
peaceful coexistence and, 155–156, 170, 193–194, 254, 279, 291–292, 546, 558
Poland and, 189–190
at Polish Embassy, 215
Port Arthur and, 151

Potsdam Agreement, repudiation of, 232–233
PRC and, 170, 244, 261–262, 271, 294, 309, 595, 596
Putin compared, 599–601
quick fixes, propensity for, 294
recognition as motivation of, 168–169, 235, 269, 325–327, 393, 557, 594–596
release of American airmen, 270–271
Republic of China and, 12, 170
"rooster" speech, 249
Saudi Arabia and, 160
Second World War and, 1, 2, 289–290
security as motivation of, 167–168
sensitivity of, 240, 294
Shepilov and, 200
"shoe banging" incident, 266, 267, 649
Sino-Indian War and, 246–247, 306, 310–311, 317–318, 323, 326–327
Southeast Asia and, 332
Stalin, denunciation of, 171–173, 175–176, 198
as statesman versus revolutionary, 273
Sudan and, 160
Suez Crisis and, 146, 164–167
"swimming pool" summit, 216–219, 221
Syria and, 160, 167
Taiwan and, 247
third world and, 157–159, 167, 252, 594
Tito and, 160, 201–202
Turkey and, 296, 309, 654
U-2 spy planes and, 256–259
Ulbricht and, 232, 236–237, 243, 286–287
UN and, 264–267
United States and, 12, 203–204, 237–241, 595–596
Vienna Summit and, 284–286
West Germany and, 232
"widening cracks" in West and, 574
Yemen and, 160–161
Zhou and, 247, 292
Zhukov and, 200
Khrushchev, Sergei, 257
Khyber, Mir Akbar, 478
Kiesenger, Kurt Georg, 366

INDEX

Kim Il Sung
  Brezhnev and, 183
  criticism of, 184
  cult of personality, 182–184
  defiance of USSR by, 187
  on denunciation of Stalin, 183, 187
  establishment of North Korea and,
    134–135
  generally, 127, 583
  Khrushchev and, 183–184, 187, 196–198
  Korean War and, 111, 135–136, 138–139
  Mao and, 185–187, 288
  Mikoyan and, 185–187
  political power of, 181–182
  purges by, 181–182
Kirkpatrick, Jeane, 524
Kiryluk, Stanisław, 193
Kissinger, Henry
  on Agnew resignation, 401
  Angola and, 427, 443, 446–447, 450
  Brezhnev and
    CSCE, 436
    generally, 364, 433
    meetings with, 378–379
    Nixon, summit with, 353
    PRC and, 384
    Yom Kippur War and, 398, 410–412
  Brzezinski and, 458
  Carter and, 457
  Cyprus and, 428–430
  detente with West and, 403, 427–428, 501
  Dobrynin and
    Angola and, 446–447
    Brezhnev–Nixon summit and, 376, 377
    ceasefire efforts in Yom Kippur War,
      402, 403, 408, 409
    Cyprus, 429
    "deceit" in Yom Kippur War, 413–414
    direct Soviet involvement, in Yom
      Kippur War, danger of, 406–407
    generally, 450
    human rights, 455
    Soviet observers in Yom Kippur War,
      416–417
    spheres of influence, 500–501
    threats of other nations to enter Yom
      Kippur War and, 405

  Yom Kippur War and, 400, 402, 409,
    415, 422
  Ford and, 450–451
  generally, 421
  human rights and, 455
  Jackson, Henry "Scoop" and, 433
  Japan and, 434–435
  on legitimacy, 5
  Lend-Lease loans and, 381
  Mao and, 499
  Nixon and, 378, 410, 417
  peace talks and, 354
  PRC and, 349–350, 376, 384, 434–435
  prevention of nuclear war agreement
    and, 383
  Reagan and, 450–451
  realpolitik and, 499
  spheres of influence and, 500–501
  on status quo versus revolution, 594
  Vance and, 457
  Vietnam War and, 352, 354, 450
  Yom Kippur War and
    Brezhnev and, 398, 410–412
    ceasefire efforts, 402, 403, 408, 409
    direct Soviet involvement, danger of,
      406–407
    Dobrynin and, 400, 402, 409, 415, 422
    generally, 400–402
    Moscow negotiations, 409–412
    stalemate in, 407
    threats of other nations to enter, 405
  Zhou and, 499
"Kitchen debate," 235–236, 373
Kohl, Helmut
  German reunification and, 570–576
  Gorbachev and, 579, 582–583, 586, 587
  NATO and, 575, 576
Kojeve, Alexander, 3
Korea. *See also* North Korea; South Korea
  Eastern Cominform and, 120
  Japan and, 135
  Moscow Foreign Ministers Conference
    and, 65
  partition of, 134
  Republic of China and, 51
  Russian Empire and, 134
  Stalin and, 134

738

INDEX

Korean Air plane, downing of,
507–508, 534

Korean War
Chinese Eastern Railroad, negotiations
regarding, 141
generally, 111
Kim Il Sung and, 111, 135–136, 138–139
Mao and, 135, 136, 138, 139
Mikoyan and, 140
negotiations to end, 140–142
outcome of, 138–139
Port Arthur, negotiations regarding, 141
PRC and, 138–139, 146
Sino-Soviet relations, impact on, 139–140
Soviet intelligence intercepts and, 136–137
Stalin and, 135–136, 138–140
Truman and, 138–139
United States and, 138–139
Zhou and, 140

Kornienko, Georgy, 444
Kosovo, Tito and, 81, 82
Kostov, Traicho, 100
Kosygin, Aleksei
Brezhnev and, 352–353, 370
death of, 514
detente with West and, 356
domestic reforms and, 541, 545
Hungary and, 360
Johnson, Lyndon B. and, 362
Mengistu and, 469
ouster of Khrushchev and, 327–328
as prime minister, 335
Sadat and, 408–409, 412, 676
Siad Barre and, 469
Vietnam War and, 338–339, 344,
347–348
Yom Kippur War and, 408–409
Zhou and, 348, 362–363, 368

Kovács, Béla, 93
Kovalev, Ivan, 121, 129–132
Kozlov, Frol, 235, 237, 261, 300–301
Kozyrev, Andrei, 591
Krenz, Egon, 564, 573
Kroll, Hans, 283
Kryuchkov, Vladimir, 575
Kudryavtsev, Sergey, 280
Kukliński, Ryszard, 513–514

Kulikov, Viktor, 413
Kurchatov, Igor, 74, 138, 154
Kuter, Laurence S., 223–224
Kuznetsov, Vasily, 314–315, 402
Kvitsinsky, Yuly, 564
Kyle, Keith, 165

Laing, R.D., 6, 8
Lam, Hoang Xuan, 346–347
Laos
Communist revolution in, 449
Kennedy and, 652
Khrushchev and, 279
North Vietnam and, 347
PRC and, 481–482
US invasion of, 347
Vienna Summit and, 284
Larsen, Aksel, 173–175
Latvia
Gorbachev and, 582
independence of, 571, 582
in NATO, 591
Le Thanh Nghi, 340, 342
Lebanon
bombing of US Marine barracks in, 535
Israeli invasion of, 525
US intervention in, 210, 219, 220
Leebaert, Derek, 520–521
Leffler, Melvyn, 5
legitimacy
ambition, relation to, 3
Brezhnev, as motivation of, 328, 356, 559,
596–598
Cold War and, 169–170
decline of, 13–14
East Germany and, 231–232
Gorbachev, as motivation of, 542, 556,
559, 578–579
internal sources of, 6
justice and, 5
Khrushchev, as motivation of, 168–169,
269, 559, 594–596
Kissinger on, 5
legality and, 5
Mao, as motivation of, 142
Marxism-Leninism and, 6
as partner versus as adversary, 7

INDEX

legitimacy (cont.)
  Russia and, 592
  Soviet conception versus conception of
    others, 5–6
  Stalin, as motivation of, 65–66, 109, 110,
    592–594
Lenin, V.I., 126, 542
Lesur, Charles Louis, 452
Lewandowski, Janusz, 343
Lewis, Jeffrey, 37
Li Jishen, 114
Li Peng, 577
Li Zhisui, 202
Li Zongren, 114
Libya
  Cyrenaica, Litvinov and, 52
  Litvinov and, 52
  Molotov and, 49, 52
  Moscow Foreign Ministers Conference
    and, 65
  Stalin and, 49, 52, 67, 157
  Tripolitania
    London Conference and, 54–57
    Molotov and, 52
    Moscow Foreign Ministers Conference
      and, 65
    Stalin and, 52
Lie, Trygve, 77
Ligachev, Yegor, 556
Lightner, Alan, 292
Lin Biao, 383–384, 669
Lincoln, Abraham, 544–545
Lippe, Just, 174
Lippmann, Walter, 74, 318
Lithuania
  Gorbachev and, 571, 582
  independence of, 571, 582
  in NATO, 591
Litvinov, Maksim
  allies and, 19
  as Anglophile, 17–18, 21, 54
  Bulgaria and, 20
  Cyrenaica and, 52
  decolonization and, 49–50
  Dodecanese islands and, 51–52
  Eritrea and, 51
  former Italian colonies and, 51–53

France and, 20–21
Germany and, 19–20, 27
ideology and, 21–22
imperialism and, 21, 68
Italy and, 20–21
Libya and, 52
Molotov and, 19, 21
Palestine and, 51
Poland and, 20, 30
Romania and, 20
Roosevelt and, 19
Somalia and, 51
spheres of influence in Europe and, 18
Stalin and, 38
Turkey and, 20
UK and, 18
Yalta Conference and, 30–31
Liu Shaoqi
  on "bullying" of PRC, 309–310
  CCP and, 177
  Hungary and, 194–196
  Iraq and, 218
  Khrushchev and, 192–196, 198
  Mao and, 206
  Moscow Conference and, 274
  self-criticism and, 307, 308
  Stalin and, 124–125, 128, 180
Liu Xiao, 310, 311
Lloyd, Selwyn, 160–161, 234
London Conference of Foreign Ministers
    (1945)
  Bevin at, 54, 55, 59–62
  Bulgaria and, 57–59
  Byrnes at, 54–57, 60–63
  Dodecanese islands and, 57–58
  failure of, 57, 63, 104
  former Italian colonies and, 54–57
  "four-against-one" argument, 58–61, 67–68
  France, participation of, 59–61
  Germany and, 104
  Japan and, 61–63
  Molotov at, 39, 54–57, 59–61
  reparations against Italy and, 58
  Republic of China, participation of, 59–61
  Romania and, 57–59
  Tripolitania and, 54–57
Lozovsky, Solomon, 20, 101

740

INDEX

Lumumba, Patrice, 265, 279
Luong, Le Van, 347
Lüthi, Lorenz, 10–11

MacArthur, Douglas, 136–137
Macedonia, Tito and, 81
Macmillan, Harold
  generally, 263
  Khrushchev and, 212, 214, 258–259,
    267, 273
  Mikoyan and, 234
Main Intelligence Directorate (GRU), 47
Maisky, Ivan
  allies and, 19
  as Anglophile, 17–18
  Bulgaria and, 18
  decolonization and, 49–50
  generally, 25
  Germany and, 20
  Harriman and, 41–42
  Hungary and, 18
  ideology and, 21–22
  imperialism and, 21, 68
  Poland and, 18, 30
  on reparations from Germany, 45
  Romania and, 18
  Stalin and, 38
  Turkey and, 18
  UK and, 18
  United States and, 20
  Yalta Conference and, 30–31
Makarios III (Cyprus), 428–430
Maksimov, Aleksandr, 364
Malaysia, USSR and, 347–348
Malenkov, Georgy
  after death of Stalin, 145
  East Germany and, 147–148, 231, 631
  generally, 64
  Hungary and, 191
  Khrushchev and, 200
  Molotov and, 154–155
  nuclear weapons and, 153–155
  ouster of, 151
Malik, Yakov, 404
Malin, Vladimir, 297
Malinovsky, Rodion
  Cuban Missile Crisis and, 306, 313

  as minister of defense, 200
  Republic of China and, 64
  Soviet missiles in Cuba and, 295, 299, 301
  Zhou and, 335–336
Malta summit (1989), 564–565, 567–570
Malviya, Keshav Dev, 317–318
Malyshev, Vyacheslav, 154
Manchkha, Petr, 442–443
Mao Anying, 124
Mao Zedong
  Africa and, 441–442
  Algeria and, 254
  Brezhnev and, 13, 364
  Castro compared, 463
  Chiang and, 32, 35–36, 307
  Chinese Revolution and, 122
  in civil war, 113, 115
  claims to Soviet territory by, 334
  conciliatory position of, 274–275
  Cuba and, 254, 278–279
  Cultural Revolution and, 350
  Deng compared, 459–460, 471, 499–500
  detente with West and, 368
  Duan and, 274–275, 349, 355, 357
  Eastern Cominform and, 120
  economic development and, 177
  economics and, 205–206
  Eisenhower and, 169, 245, 260, 269
  generally, 171–172
  global leadership and, 227–228
  on "golden hoop," 176–177, 198
  "Great Harmony," vision of, 207–208
  Great Leap Forward and, 206, 207,
    241–242, 275
  Gromyko and, 218
  Guomindang and, 35, 117
  health of, 442
  Ho Chi Minh and, 274–275, 332, 344, 349
  Hoxha and, 263
  Hungary and, 194, 197–198
  ideology as motivation of, 433–434
  industrialization and, 199
  international affairs and, 311
  Iraq and, 217–218
  Jinmen and Mazu islands and, 221–223,
    225–227, 229, 249
  on joint navy with USSR, 215–217, 256

741

INDEX

Mao Zedong (cont.)
Khrushchev and
animosity between, 245, 247–249, 254, 261–262
claims to Soviet territory by, 334
denunciation of Stalin and, 176–178, 180–181
generally, 12, 596
meetings with, 202
North Korea and, 187, 198
ouster of, 335
Port Arthur and, 151
rivalry between, 201, 203, 260
Soviet aid and, 158–159
Stalin compared, 334–335
"swimming pool" summit, 216–219, 221
third world and, 169
United States and, 208–209
Kim Il Sung and, 185–187, 288
Kissinger and, 499
Korean War and, 135, 136, 138, 139
leadership in Communist movement, 202–203, 252, 260–261, 311–312, 338
legitimacy as motivation of, 142
Liu and, 206
Mikoyan and, 118–122, 215–216
Molotov and, 132, 201
Moscow Conference and, 274
Nasser and, 162
nationalism and, 334
nationalities question and, 119–120
Nixon and, 355, 377–378
North Vietnam and, 333
nuclear weapons and, 169
overtaking US and UK economies, goal of, 205, 206
peaceful coexistence and, 280–281, 338, 377
on "people's war," 344
Poland and, 193
recognition as motivation of, 142
security as motivation of, 308
self-criticism and, 307, 308
Sino-Soviet Treaty of Alliance (1945) and, 119
Sino-Soviet Treaty of Alliance (1950) and, 126–134
Southeast Asia and, 332

on Soviet chauvinism, 179–180, 193
Soviet criticism of, 253–254
on Soviet economic development model, 205, 206
Sputnik and, 100
Stalin and
animosity between, 201
civil war, during, 32, 35, 36, 64, 112–114
comparison, 261, 334–335
on denunciation of, 176–181
generally, 593
meetings with, 111
obedience and subordination to, 125
standing up to, 126
suspicions of, 123–124
as statesman versus revolutionary, 350
steel and, 207
as strategist for socialism, 193, 198, 201, 355, 595
Suslov and, 253–254
Taiwan and, 128, 138–139
technology and, 178
third world and, 158–159, 227–228
Tito compared, 121–122
UK and, 205
Ulbricht and, 286–287
UN and, 267
United States and, 120–121, 205, 227, 238
in USSR, 111
Vietnam War and, 336–339, 344, 355, 357
Yugoslavia and, 181, 201–202
Zhou and, 205–206, 275
Zhukov and, 201
Marrequin, Murilo, 227–228
Marshall, George
Chiang and, 89
Germany and, 104
Poland and, 43
Republic of China and, 114, 115
as secretary of state, 89
Stalin and, 89
Marshall Plan
Czechoslovakia and, 90, 94–95
Germany and, 104
Molotov and, 89–90
origins of, 89
Poland and, 90

742

INDEX

Stalin and, 89–90, 108–109, 593
Zhdanov and, 91
Marx, Karl, 368
Marxism-Leninism
decline of, 13–14
as driver of Soviet foreign policy, 3–4
legitimacy and, 6
Stalin and, 37, 38
Masaryk, Jan, 90, 95
Maslow, A.H., 8–9, 598
Matlock, Jack, 521, 565
Mayorov, Aleksandr, 522
Mazowiecki, Tadeusz, 561, 577
McCarthy, Joseph, 138
McCloy, John, 289
McNamara, Robert, 304, 341–342
Medvedev, Dmitry, 600
Meir, Golda, 407, 413–414, 422–423
Mel'nikov, L.I., 124
Mengistu Haile Mariam
Brezhnev and, 466
Castro and, 463–464
generally, 473
Kosygin and, 469
recognition and, 472
Siad Barre and, 463–464, 466
Somalia–Ethiopia War and, 470
Menon, K.P.S., 283
Michael (Romania), 40–41, 92–93
Middle East. *See also specific country*
Brezhnev and, 374–375, 392, 397–399, 423–424
Eisenhower and, 210
geopolitical interest of USSR in, 392
ideology and Soviet interest in, 392
KGB and, 397
Khrushchev and, 210
Nixon and, 396–399
recognition and Soviet interest in, 392–393
United States and, 396
Mielke, Erich, 518, 530
Mikołajczyk, Stanisław, 28–30, 40, 43, 66–67, 85–86, 92
Mikoyan, Anastas
Berlin Crisis and, 233–234, 284
Brezhnev and, 118
Castro and, 321–323

Cuba and, 277, 297
Cuban Missile Crisis and, 313, 657
on cult of personality, 177
Czechoslovakia and, 90, 118
Dulles and, 233–234
Eastern Cominform and, 120
Eisenhower and, 186, 234
generally, 64, 128
Gomułka and, 190
Guomindang and, 118–119
Harriman and, 235
Hungary and, 192, 194
Khrushchev and, 118, 212, 294
Kim Il Sung and, 185–187
Korean War and, 136–137, 140
Macmillan and, 234
Mao and, 118–122, 215–216
missiles in Cuba and, 298–299
nationalities question and, 119–120
Poland and, 190
Port Arthur and, 141
PRC and, 198
Republic of China, mission to, 118–122
Sino-Soviet Treaty of Alliance (1945) and, 119
U-2 spy planes and, 258
United States and, 120–121, 233–234
Zhou and, 119
Mikoyan, Sergo, 297
Miller, Chris, 543
Mitterrand, François, 570, 572–573, 583, 584
Mobutu, Joseph-Désiré, 265
Mobutu Sese Seko, 441, 442
Modrow, Hans, 573, 580
Mollet, Guy, 166
Molotov, Vyacheslav
after death of Stalin, 145
Bevin and, 58, 60–61
Bulgaria and, 57–59
Byrnes and, 60–61, 67, 78
Chinese Eastern Railroad and, 141
on collective security, 150
Dodecanese islands and, 57–58, 67
East Germany and, 147–149, 231
Finland and, 59
former Italian colonies and, 52, 54–57
Germany and, 104

743

INDEX

Molotov, Vyacheslav (cont.)
Greece and, 83
Harriman and, 41, 43
Hitler and, 19
Iran and, 78
Japan and, 61–63
Khrushchev and, 200
Libya and, 49, 52
life of, 54
Litvinov and, 19, 21
at London Conference, 39, 54–57, 59–61
Malenkov and, 154–155
Mao and, 132, 201
Marshall Plan and, 89–90
Moscow Foreign Ministers Conference
and, 64–65
NATO and, 150
nuclear weapons and, 47, 154–156
percentages agreement and, 23
Poland and, 40, 42, 43
on reparations against Italy, 58
Republic of China and, 112
Romania and, 41, 57–59
Sino-Soviet Treaty of Alliance (1950)
and, 133
Stalin and, 64
Tito and, 99
Tripolitania and, 52
Truman and, 42
Turkey and, 73
"two camps" and, 90–91
UK and, 93
UN and, 42
Molotov–Ribbentrop Pact, 19, 27
Mondale, Walter, 528
Mongolia
Chiang and, 120
generally, 10
Gorbachev and, 559
Soviet aid to, 244
Soviet influence in, 32–34
Monkey King, 176–177, 198
Montreux Convention (1936), 72, 73
Moorer, Thomas, 415
Morgan, Michael, 436
Morocco, Yom Kippur War and, 407
Mosaddegh, Mohammad, 146, 484

Moscow Conference (1960), 272–274
Moscow Conference of Foreign Ministers
(1945), 64–65
Moscow Conference of Foreign Ministers
(1947), 89, 104
Moscow Treaty (1970), 369–371
Mossadegh, Mohammad, 146, 487
Most Favored Nation (MFN) status, 381,
389, 428, 431–432
Mozambique, Gorbachev and, 559
Mubarak, Hosni, 583
Mukhitdinov, Nuridin, 417
Mulroney, Brian, 567
Munich Agreement (1938), 322
Murphy, Robert, 237, 644
Myanmar. *See* Burma

Nagasaki bombing, 47
Naguib, Mohammed, 159, 160
Nagy, Ferenc, 93
Nagy, Imre, 190–192, 194–196
Naim, Mohammad, 476–477
Naimark, Norman, 30, 66, 85
Najib, Mohammad, 556
Namibia
Castro and, 448
Cuba and, 448
Narożniak, Jan, 513
Nasser, Gamal Abdel
accession to power, 159
Aswan Dam and, 161–163
Bulganin and, 164
Eden and, 161, 163
Iraq and, 209, 211–212, 217–218, 228–229
Khrushchev and
generally, 157, 160–162, 594
Iraq and, 211–212, 217–218
nuclear weapons and, 210
PRC and, 222
Suez Crisis, 164
at UN, 266
Mao and, 162
Nehru and, 163
PRC and, 162, 222
Sadat and, 394
Shepilov and, 160–162
Six Day War and, 393

744

INDEX

Suez Canal, nationalization of, 163–164, 195
Suez Crisis and, 163–167, 195
Tito and, 163
Zhou and, 162
NATO. *See* North Atlantic Treaty
  Organization (NATO)
Nehru, Jawaharlal
  "bullying" by, 309–310
  Khrushchev and, 157, 158, 247, 267, 594
  Nasser and, 163
  nuclear tests and, 293
  PRC and, 246, 308–310
  Sino-Indian War and, 306–307, 310
  USSR and, 168
  Zhou and, 306–307
Nenni, Pietro, 88–89
Netherlands
  colonies of, 49–50
  Litvinov and, 18
  PRC and, 528–529
  Taiwan and, 528–529
Neto, Agostinho, 440, 444, 445, 447–449
New Economic Policy (NEP), 542
New Thinking, 13–14
Newsom, David, 479
Nguyen Van Vinh, 345
Nicaragua
  Bush, George H.W. and, 568–569
  Gorbachev and, 568–569
  revolutionary activity in, 276–277
Nicholas I (Russia), 274
Nixon, Richard
  Aleksandrov-Agentov and, 390
  Brezhnev and
    condominium concept and, 385–388
    detente with West, 420, 421
    generally, 13, 364, 388, 597–598
    Middle East, 397–399
    personal relationship, 428
    PRC and, 380, 386, 388, 597
    prevention of nuclear war agreement
      and, 383
    summit with, 352–354, 376, 378–382
    suspicions of, 345–346, 373, 378
    Vietnam War, 345–346, 350–351
    Yom Kippur War, 407–408, 419
  Cambodia and, 349–350

Churchill and, 422
counterfactuals regarding, 425
Cyprus and, 428–429
detente with West and, 403, 420, 421, 501
Dobrynin and, 362, 407, 416, 421
Dong, Pham Van and, 350
downfall of, 389–391
Khrushchev and
  generally, 248, 271, 288
  "kitchen debate," 235–236, 373
  suspicions of, 270
Kissinger and, 378, 410, 417
Mao and, 355, 377–378
Middle East and, 396–399
Pahlavi (Shah) and, 485
on perestroika, 565
PRC and
  Brezhnev and, 380, 386, 388, 597
  visit to, 268, 350–351, 376, 378, 499–500
Reagan compared, 507
Roosevelt and, 422
"Saturday Night Massacre," 409–410
Stalin and, 422
Tito and, 373
Vietnam War and, 345–347, 350–351, 378, 379
Watergate scandal and, 389–391, 401,
  409–410, 422
Yom Kippur War and, 403, 407–408, 412,
  416, 419
Zhou and, 350, 378
Noriega, Manuel, 568–569
North Atlantic Treaty Organization
  (NATO)
  Able Archer exercise, 535–536, 548
  after death of Stalin, 145
  Bush, George H.W. and, 576, 578
  Chernyaev and, 581–582
  Czech Republic in, 591
  de Gaulle and, 366
  eastward expansion of, 575–578, 591,
    600, 601
  Estonia in, 591
  Germany in, 560, 574–575, 584–587
  Gorbachev and
    Bush, George H.W. and, 581, 583, 587
    eastward expansion of, 575–582
    Germany, 581–586

745

INDEX

North Atlantic Treaty Organization (cont.)
  as political versus military pact, 566
  post-Cold War vision, 576–577
  Hungary in, 591
  Khrushchev and, 232
  Kohl and, 575, 576
  Latvia in, 591
  Lithuania in, 591
  Molotov and, 150
  Poland in, 591
  proposal for USSR to join, 150, 170
  Putin and, 600, 601
  signing of treaty, 110
  Turkey in, 146
  Ukraine and, 591
  West Germany in, 146, 150, 170
  Yeltsin and, 591
North Korea
  establishment of, 134–135
  food shortages in, 182–183
  generally, 10
  Hungary compared, 196–197
  Korean Workers' Party, 182
  living standards in, 182–183
  PRC and, 187, 198
North Vietnam
  Cambodia and, 347
  Czechoslovakia and, 361
  Khrushchev and, 355–356
  Laos and, 347
  Mao and, 333
  move away from PRC, 355
  PRC and
    drift toward, 332, 333
    generally, 198, 332, 333, 355
    move away from, 348–350, 355
  South Vietnam, attack on, 252
  Soviet military aid to, 339–341
  Thailand and, 347
  USSR and, 345–348
  Vietnamese Workers' Party, 346–347
Norway
  Litvinov and, 18
  Norwegian Communist Party, 174
  US bases in, 296
Nosek, Václav, 95
Novocherkassk riots, 300–301

Novotný, Antonín, 319, 359–360
nuclear weapons
  as backbone of Soviet power, 538
  Beria and, 47
  bluffing of Soviets regarding, 74–76
  Bulganin and, 155, 156
  Churchill and, 46–47
  in Cuba, 306
  Cuban Missile Crisis and, 306
  Egypt and, 418, 678
  false alarm, 534–535
  Gorbachev and, 533–534
  Gromyko and, 533–534
  Hiroshima bombing, 47
  hydrogen bomb, 155
  Jinmen and Mazu islands, threatened use
    in, 223–224
  Kennan on, 75–76
  Khrushchev and, 145–146, 154–156, 170
  Malenkov and, 153–155
  Mao and, 169
  military exercises relating to, 153–154
  Molotov and, 47, 154–156
  Nagasaki bombing, 47
  peaceful coexistence and, 155–156
  PRC and, 210–211, 229, 335
  security and, 8
  Soviet interest in, 47
  Soviet nuclear tests, 293, 653
  Stalin and, 46–47, 74–76, 152–153,
    156, 593
  threats by Castro to attack United States
    with, 320–321
  Truman and, 44, 46–47
  USSR acquiring, 136, 138, 153
  Zhukov and, 154, 155
Nye, Joseph, 553

Obama, Barack, 600–601
oil, 71, 76, 425
Olver, Stephen, 429
Olympic Games (1980), 474, 503, 540–541
On the Beach (Shute), 251
Operation Anadyr, 301–304
Orlov, Andrei (Terebin), 112–113,
  117, 120
Our Tasks in the Pacific (Maksimov), 364

INDEX

Pahlavi, Abdul Reza, 485
Pahlavi, Ashraf, 485
Pahlavi, Mohammad Reza (Shah)
  accession to power, 71, 146, 484
  Brezhnev and, 484, 485
  demonstrations against, 486
  flight of, 484
  generally, 285
  KGB and, 485–486
  Khrushchev and, 484, 485
  Nixon and, 485
  Soviet views of, 485
  Vinogradov and, 486
  "White Revolution" and, 484
Pak Chang-ok, 182, 184, 186
Pak Hon-yong, 135, 138, 182
Pak Il-u, 182
Pak Yon-bing, 182, 183
Pakistan
  Afghanistan and, 522–523
  PRC and, 499
  US bases in, 296
Palach, Jan, 561
Palazhchenko, Pavel, 584, 703, 709
Palestine Liberation Organization
     (PLO), 525
Palestine, Litvinov and, 51
Papandreou, Georgios, 82
Paraguay, revolutionary activity in, 276–277
Parkin, Ben, 93
Partial Nuclear Test Ban Treaty (1963), 327
peaceful coexistence
  Brezhnev and, 558
  Chernenko and, 536
  Chernyaev and, 558, 702
  Gorbachev and, 558
  Khrushchev and, 155–156, 170, 193–194,
     254, 279, 291–292, 546, 558
  Mao and, 280–281, 338, 377
  nuclear weapons and, 155–156
Peng Dehuai, 186–187, 221, 245
Peng Zhen, 261, 272, 274
People's Commissariat of Internal Affairs
     (NKVD), 32, 45, 47
"people's war," 344
PepsiCo, 389
percentages agreement, 22–25, 30–31, 501

perestroika
  Chinese economic reform compared,
     542–544
  foreign policy and, 545–547
  generally, 539, 553
  NEP compared, 542
  Nixon on, 565
  rapid pace of, 545
*Perestroika and New Thinking for Our Country
     and the World* (Gorbachev), 546, 589
Pershing-II missiles, 529–530, 533, 535,
     548, 550
Peter the Great (Russia), 452, 473
Petkov, Nikola, 92
Petrov, Apollon, 36
Petrovna, Nina, 284
Philippines
  Bush, George H.W. and, 568–569
  Gorbachev and, 568–569
Pimen, Patriarch, 388
Pipes, Richard, 520–521
Pishevari, Ja'far, 71–72, 77, 79
Plato, 3, 9
Pleshakov, Constantine, 4–5
Pliev, Issa, 301, 306, 313
Podgorny, Nikolai, 327–328, 353–354, 360
Poindexter, John, 551
Pol Pot, 481–482, 498
Poland
  Andropov and, 512–518
  Brezhnev and
     generally, 598
     martial law, 512–513
     nonintervention, 514–517
     political situation in, 509–512, 518
     Reagan and, 520
  Bush, George H.W. and, 706
  Carter and, 513–514
  Catholic Church in, 509
  Chernyaev and, 511–512, 516
  Churchill and, 27–30, 40
  Communism in, 188–189
  crackdowns on workers in, 508
  debt in, 560–561
  degree of independence from USSR, 197
  Eden and, 40
  electoral fraud in, 86, 92

INDEX

Poland (cont.)
  failure of socialism in, 508
  failure of Soviet policy in, 537
  fall of Communism in, 561
  food prices in, 508, 510
  Gdańsk Agreement, 510
  Gromyko and, 512–516, 520
  Haig and, 519, 521
  Hungary compared, 196–197
  IMF and, 509
  KGB and, 511
  Khrushchev and, 189–190
  lack of reform in, 561
  Lenin Shipyard, 510
  Litvinov and, 18, 20, 30
  "London Poles," 27–28
  Maisky and, 18, 30
  Mao and, 193
  Marshall and, 43
  Marshall Plan and, 90
  martial law in, 507, 512–518
  Mikoyan, 190
  Molotov and, 40, 42, 43
  in NATO, 591
  Polish Committee for National Liberation, 27–28
  Polish Peasant Party, 92
  Polish United Workers' Party (PUWP), 188–189, 510, 561
  Polish Workers' Party (PPR), 518
  Poznań uprising, 187–188
  PRC and, 192
  Reagan and, 524
  Roosevelt and, 27–30, 40
  Solidarity (Solidarność), 510, 511, 513–515, 517–518, 561
  Soviet aid to, 515
  Soviet hegemony in, 39–40, 69, 92
  Soviet nonintervention in, 513–517
  Soviet troops in, 189–190
  Stalin and, 27–31, 39–40, 43–44, 66, 85–86
  Stalin Metal Works, 187–188
  Suslov and, 511, 515, 517
  "Titoists" in, 100
  Truman and, 42–44
  UK and, 43

  United States and, 43, 599
  Ustinov and, 512–516, 520
  Warsaw Uprising, 27–28
  Workers' Defense Committee (KOR), 508–509
  Yalta Conference and, 27–31
Polyansky, Dmitry, 335
Pompidou, Georges, 368, 372, 387–388, 443, 673
Ponomarev, Boris
  Angola and, 444, 446–449
  Carter and, 455
  Cuba and, 276–277
  Somalia–Ethiopia War and, 467
Popović, Vlado, 96
Portugal
  Angola, uprising against Portuguese rule in, 440
  fall of regime in, 449
  Litvinov and, 18
postwar period
  generally, 17
  London Conference. See London Conference of Foreign Ministers (1947)
  percentages agreement, 22–25, 30–31, 501
  Potsdam Conference. See Potsdam Conference (1945)
  security as prime concern during, 22
  Yalta Conference. See Yalta Conference (1945)
Potsdam Conference (1945)
  Churchill at, 44–45
  Khrushchev, repudiation by, 232–233
  Molotov on, 46
  spheres of influence and, 45–46
  Stalin at, 44–46
  Truman at, 44
  Turkey and, 73
Powers, Francis Gary, 255, 270–271
PRC. See China (People's Republic of) (PRC)
prestige. See recognition
Primakov, Evgeny, 394, 679
proletarian internationalism, 423
Przhevalsky, Nikolai, 334
Pugachev, Emelian, 113

INDEX

Putin, Vladimir
accession to power, 599
Afghanistan and, 601
on American "exceptionalism," 599–601
Brezhnev compared, 599–601
Crimea, annexation of, 601–602
Gorbachev compared, 600–601
Iraq and, 601
Khrushchev compared, 599–601
NATO and, 600, 601
Obama and, 600–601
recognition as motivation of, 602–603
Russian "exceptionalism" and, 602
Stalin compared, 600–601
Syria and, 600, 602
Ukraine, invasion of, 602
United States and, 599–600
Puzanov, Aleksandr, 490–491

Qasim, ʿAbd al-Karim, 209, 217, 219, 226, 228, 229
Qavam al-Saltaneh, 76, 77, 79–80
al-Quwatli, Shukri, 165

R7 missiles, 295
R7A missiles, 295
R-12 missiles, 295, 299, 314
R-14 missiles, 295, 299, 314
Rădescu, Nicolae, 40–41
Radhakrishnan, Sarvepalli, 334–335
Rajk, László, 100
Rakhmanin, Oleg, 461, 526–527
Rákosi, Mátyás, 93, 147, 185, 190–192
Ramadier, Paul, 88
Raza, N.A.M., 309–310
Reagan, Ronald
Afghanistan and, 522, 554, 555
Andropov and, 530, 531
arms control and, 547
assassination attempt, 520
back-channel communications with, 520–521
Brezhnev and
animosity between, 526
first meeting, 518
Israel, 525
personal letters, 521

Poland, 520
SALT-II, 519
suspicions of, 503
Carter compared, 518–519
counterfactuals regarding, 425
Cuba and, 517
"Evil Empire" speech, 531
Ford and, 437, 450–451, 453
generally, 554
Gorbachev and, 548, 549, 557–558, 567
Gromyko and, 524
Helsinki Final Act and, 524
Israel and, 525
KGB and, 521
Kissinger and, 450–451
militancy of, 507, 519, 526
Nixon compared, 507
Poland and, 524
Reykjavik summit and, 549–552
sanctions against USSR, 524, 537
Taiwan and, 527–529
realpolitik, 499
recognition
ambition, relation to, 3, 5
Brezhnev, as motivation of, 328, 357, 387, 393, 557, 596–598
failures of USSR and, 538
Germany and, 592
Gorbachev, as motivation of, 557
in International Relations, 9–10
Khrushchev, as motivation of, 168–169, 235, 269, 325–327, 393, 557, 594–596
leader of international Communist movement, USSR as, 6–7
Mao, as motivation of, 142
Mengistu and, 472
Middle East, and Soviet interest in, 392–393
PRC and, 9
Putin, as motivation of, 602–603
Russia and, 13–14
security, relation to, 8–9
Siad Barre and, 472
Stalin, as motivation of, 65–66, 74, 592–594
superpower, USSR as, 6–7
third world, and Soviet interest in, 472

INDEX

Renault, 88, 367
Renshon, Jonathan, 9
Republic of China. *See* China (Republic of)
Reykjavik summit (1986), 549–552
Ri Ju-yon, 138
Rice, Condoleezza, 576
Richardson, Elliott, 409–410
Roberto, Holden, 440–442, 448–449
Roberts, Geoffrey, 24
Roca, Blas, 254
Rockefeller, David, 458
Rodriguez, Carlos Rafael, 324
Roh Tae-woo, 583
Rokossovsky, Konstantin, 189
Romania
   Byrnes and, 57
   degree of independence from USSR, 197
   electoral fraud in, 92–93
   fall of Communism in, 562
   Litvinov and, 18, 20
   London Conference and, 57–59
   Maisky and, 18
   Molotov and, 41, 57–59
   Moscow Foreign Ministers Conference
      and, 65
   National Peasants' Party (PNȚ), 92–93
   peace treaty with, 89
   percentages agreement and, 23
   renunciation of German interests in, 46
   Soviet hegemony in, 40–41, 69, 92–93
   in Soviet sphere of influence, 45
   Stalin and, 39, 58–59, 67, 85, 86
   United States and, 63, 599
Ronning, Chester A., 342–343
Roosevelt, Franklin D.
   Chiang and, 33
   death of, 41
   Germany and, 26
   Litvinov and, 19
   Nixon and, 422
   percentages agreement and, 23–24
   Poland and, 27–30, 40
   Republic of China and, 33
   on spheres of influence, 40
   Stalin and, 22, 379
   at Yalta Conference, 24, 26, 29–30
Roshchin, Nikolai, 112, 119, 130

Rostow, Walt, 341–342
Roussos, Petros, 82
Rozhdestvensky, S.E., 153
Ruckelshaus, William, 409–410
Rusk, Dean, 296, 304–305, 312–314
Russia
   Chechen war, 590–591
   Crimea, annexation of, 601–602
   economic problems in, 589–590
   Georgia, war with, 600
   Kennan on, 8
   legitimacy and, 592
   oligarchs in, 590
   political turmoil in, 590
   recognition and, 13–14
   survival of Cold War motivations in, 10
   Syria and, 600, 602
   Ukraine, invasion of, 602
Russian Empire
   Korea and, 134
   UK, rivalry regarding Iran with, 70–71
   United States, rivalry regarding Iran
      with, 71
Russian Revolution, 125–126, 487
Ryzhkov, Nikolai, 556

Sabri, Ali, 165–166, 394, 671
Sadat, Anwar
   Amin compared, 491–492
   Brezhnev and, 394–397, 417–418, 424
   Camp David Accords and, 424
   Carter and, 483
   generally, 478
   Kosygin and, 408–409, 412, 676
   life of, 394
   Nasser and, 394
   opportunism of, 424
   Soviet military aid and, 397
   unpredictability of, 395
   US and, 396
   Vinogradov and, 394, 399, 409, 411, 424
   Yom Kippur War and
      advance notice of, 400
      Brezhnev and, 402
      ceasefire efforts, 403–405
      Israeli advances in, 408–409,
         411, 414

INDEX

launching of, 399
uncertainty regarding, 402
Sadchikov, Ivan, 77, 79
al-Said, Nuri, 209
Sakharov, Andrei, 153, 454, 456, 553
Salinger, Pierre, 288
Samatar, Ali, 466–467
Samoilenko, Viktor, 522
Samoteikin, Evgeny, 495–497
Sapeło, Piotr, 513
Sarotte, Mary Elise, 591
Sarper, Selim, 73, 296
Saudi Arabia, Khrushchev and, 160
Savimbi, Jonas, 440–442, 448–449
Scali, John A., 317
Schabowski, Günter, 563
Schlesinger, James R., 437–438
Scowcroft, Brent, 409, 416, 565
Second "Bandung" Conference (1965), 441
The Second Hand Time (Alexievich), 590
Second World War
Brezhnev and, 1–2
collapse of Germany in, 24–25
France, destruction in, 86
Gorbachev and, 2
horrors of, 1–2
human casualties in, 2
Italy, destruction in, 86
Khrushchev and, 1, 2, 289–290
material losses in, 2
Stalin and, 8
security
Brzezinski and, 472
Cold War and, 169–170
Deng and, 472
as driver of Soviet foreign policy, 4–5
Gorbachev, as motivation of, 578–579
Khrushchev, as motivation of, 167–168
Mao, as motivation of, 308
nuclear weapons and, 8
postwar period, as prime concern
during, 22
recognition, relation to, 8–9
Sino-Indian War, as motivation for,
308–309
Stalin, as motivation of, 106–107, 110
third world, and Soviet interest in, 472

Serov, Aleksei, 297
Serov, Ivan, 190, 208, 298
Shafiq, Shahriar, 485
Shakhnazarov, Georgy, 543–544, 582
Sharaf, Sami, 394
Shebarshin, Leonid, 486, 584
Shehu, Mehmet, 263
Shen Jian, 311, 322–323
Shen Zhihua, 210
Sheng Shicai, 31–32
Shepilov, Dmitry
Khrushchev and, 200
Nasser and, 160–162
Suez Crisis and, 163–166
Shevardnadze, Eduard, 555, 556,
575, 578
Shi Zhe, 117, 126, 127, 130, 638
Shifrinson, Joshua, 575
Shultz, George, 530, 549
Shute, Neville, 251
Siad Barre, Mohamed
Brezhnev and, 465, 467, 470
Carter and, 469–470
Castro and, 463–464, 466
Dobrynin and, 469–470
Ethiopia and, 464
generally, 473
Gromyko and, 469
Kosygin and, 469
Mengistu and, 463–464, 466
recognition and, 472
Suslov and, 469
USSR and, 464–465
Sidorov, Ivan, 314
Sino-Indian War
Chiang and, 307
generally, 246–247
ideology as motivation for, 307–308
Khrushchev and, 246–247, 306, 310–311,
317–318, 323, 326–327
Nehru and, 306–307, 310
security as motivation for, 308–309
Zhou and, 246, 256, 259, 306–307
Sino-Soviet Treaty of Alliance (1945)
Mikoyan mission to Republic of China
and, 119
Stalin and, 124

INDEX

Sino-Soviet Treaty of Alliance (1950)
Chinese Eastern Railroad and, 133
generally, 111
Mao and, 126–134
Molotov and, 133
Port Arthur and, 128–129, 132–133
Stalin and, 126–134
Taiwan and, 128
UK, impact on, 127
United States, impact on, 127, 131
Zhou and, 127, 129, 132–134
Six Day War, 393
Slánský, Rudolf, 100
Snow, Edgar, 377
Solod, Daniil, 160
Solov'yov, Yury, 314
Somalia
Brezhnev and, 466–468
Brzezinski and, 469
Carter and, 469–470
Castro and, 468–469
Chernyaev and, 466
Dobrynin and, 469–470
Ethiopia, invasion of, 467–471
Litvinov and, 51
Ponomarev and, 467
PRC and, 465
Somalian Revolutionary Socialist Party, 465
Soviet interest in, 464–466
Sonnenfeldt, Helmut, 433
Soong, T.V. (Song Ziwen), 33–35, 112
South Africa, Angola and, 441, 443, 446, 448–449
South Korea
Chernyaev and, 583
Gorbachev and, 583
Korean Air plane, downing of, 507–508
South Vietnam
fall of Saigon, 354, 435
North Vietnamese attack on, 252
Tet Offensive in, 345, 357
Southeast Asia. *See also specific country*
Khrushchev and, 332
Mao and, 332
Soviet expansionism and, 453
Vietnam War, outlook for Southeast Asia and, 347–348

Soviet Union. *See specific topic*
"sovietization," 85–86
spheres of influence, 18, 40, 45–46, 500–501
Spiru, Nako, 96
Sputnik, 199–200, 222
SS-20 missiles, 519–520, 531, 547–548, 550, 553
SS-23 missiles, 553
Stalin, Joseph
Africa and, 39, 473
Albania and, 100
Austria and, 85
Berlin blockade and, 109, 110, 593
Bevin and, 73
Brezhnev compared, 387, 597
Bulgaria and, 58–59, 67, 85, 86
Byrnes and, 58, 60, 62, 67
CCP and, 32, 34–37, 64
Chiang and, 33–34, 112, 117, 123, 128
Chinese Eastern Railroad and, 141
Churchill and, 17, 22–24
coalitions and, 86–89, 108–110
Cold War, role in, 37–38, 70, 106
cult of personality, 177–178
Czechoslovakia and, 86
death of, 145
defenders of, 171–172
denunciation of by Khrushchev, 171–173, 175–176, 198
East Germany and, 101–106
elections and, 593
Finland and, 85
foreign policy motivations of, 11
former Italian colonies and, 52, 53, 55–57
Germany and, 25–27, 101–106
Gorbachev compared, 540
Greece and
civil war, 82–85, 98, 100–101
generally, 24, 594
withdrawal from, 109, 110
Guomindang and, 34, 35, 112, 116–118
Harriman and, 63–65
Hitler compared, 74
Ho Chi Minh and, 120
Hokkaido and, 47–49
Hoxha and, 84, 85, 96–97, 100

752

INDEX

Hungary and, 85, 86
ideology as motivation of, 107–108
imperialism as motivation of, 37, 108
impression of strength and, 68
Iran and, 73–74, 76–80, 109, 593, 594
Italy and, 109
Japan and, 32–33, 61–64, 67
Kennan on, 88, 107, 109, 593
Khrushchev, denunciation by, 171–173, 175–176, 198
Korea and, 134
Korean War and, 135–136, 138–140
Kurile islands and, 32–33, 47–48, 127
legitimacy as motivation of, 65–66, 109, 110, 592–594
Libya and, 49, 52, 67, 157
limitations of, 66
Litvinov and, 38
Liu and, 124–125, 128, 180
Maisky and, 38
Mao and
    animosity between, 201
    civil war, during, 32, 35, 36, 64, 112–114
    comparison, 261, 334–335
    on denunciation of, 176–181
    generally, 593
    meetings with, 111
    obedience and subordination to, 125
    standing up to, 126
    suspicions of, 123–124
Marshall and, 89
Marshall Plan and, 89–90, 108–109, 593
Marxism-Leninism and, 37, 38
Molotov and, 64
Nazism and, 103
Nixon and, 422
nuclear weapons and, 46–47, 74–76, 152–153, 156, 593
paranoia of, 64
on PCF, 88
percentages agreement and, 22–25, 501
Poland and, 27–31, 39–40, 43–44, 66, 85–86
Port Arthur and, 141
at Potsdam Conference, 44–46
psychological pressure and, 66–67
Putin compared, 600–601

as realist, 108
recognition as motivation of, 65–66, 74, 592–594
removal of body from Red Square Mausoleum, 291–292
Republic of China and, 31–37, 67, 593
Romania and, 39, 58–59, 67, 85, 86
Roosevelt and, 22, 379
Sakhalin island and, 32–33, 47–48, 127
Second World War and, 8
security as motivation of, 106–107, 110
Sino-Soviet Treaty of Alliance (1945) and, 124
Sino-Soviet Treaty of Alliance (1950) and, 126–134
"sovietization" and, 85–86
on spheres of influence, 40, 45–46
split with Tito, 95–101, 107–108
status quo versus revolution, 593–594
Taiwan and, 128
third world and, 156–158
Tito and, 82, 95–101, 107–108
Tripolitania and, 52
Truman and, 66–67, 594
Truman doctrine and, 85, 108–109
Turkey and, 72–73, 80, 593, 594
UK and, 93–94
"widening cracks" in West and, 574
at Yalta Conference, 24–31
Yugoslavia and, 85
Stassen, Harold, 50
State Defense Committee, 47
Statsenko, Igor, 302, 303, 313–314
status. *See* recognition
Stennis, John C., 409–410
Stettinius, Edward, 50, 53, 54, 56
Stevenson, Adlai, 220
Stimson, Henry, 42–43
Stoessel, Walter J., 389
Strategic Arms Limitation Treaty (SALT-I) (1972), 379–380
Strategic Arms Limitation Treaty (SALT-II) (proposed), 433, 435, 489–490, 502, 503, 519
Stuart, John Leighton, 114–116
Sudan, Khrushchev and, 160
Sudarikov, Nikolai, 462

753

INDEX

Suez Canal, 44, 163–164, 195. *See also* Suez Crisis (1956)
Suez Crisis (1956)
  Bulganin and, 166
  Dulles and, 165
  Eden and, 165, 166
  Eisenhower and, 165–167, 195
  France and, 164, 166–167, 195
  Israel and, 164, 166, 195
  Khrushchev and, 146, 164–167
  Nasser and, 163–167, 195
  nationalization of Suez Canal, 163–164
  Shepilov and, 163–166
  UK and, 164, 166–167, 195
  United States and, 166–167, 195
  Zhukov and, 165
Sukarno, 157, 594
Sukhodrev, Viktor, 384, 490
Sulzberger, C.L., 87
Sumulong, Lorenzo, 266
Suslov, Mikhail
  brinksmanship and, 213
  Castro and, 449–450
  Cuba and, 276–277
  Cuban Missile Crisis and, 313
  on cult of personality, 177
  on food shortages, 512
  generally, 514
  Hungary and, 192, 194
  on international situation, 449–450
  Mao and, 253–254
  Moscow Conference and, 272–274
  Poland and, 511, 515, 517
  PRC and, 253–254
  Siad Barre and, 469
  Vietnam War and, 344
  Yom Kippur War and, 413
Sweden, Litvinov and, 18
Syria
  Brezhnev and, 417
  Khrushchev and, 160, 167
  Putin and, 600, 602
  Russia and, 600, 602
  Soviet military aid to, 405
  USSR and, 424–425
  Yom Kippur War. *See* Yom Kippur War

Taiwan
  Deng and, 527–529
  Guomindang, 223
  Haig and, 527–528
  Jinmen and Mazu islands. *See* Jinmen and Mazu islands
  Khrushchev and, 247
  Mao and, 128, 138–139
  Netherlands and, 528–529
  PLA attack on, 128
  PRC and, 309
  Reagan and, 527–529
  Republic of China and, 51
  Sino-Soviet Treaty of Alliance (1950) and, 128
  Stalin and, 128
  Truman and, 131
  United States and, 131, 527–529
  Vienna Summit and, 284
Taraki, Nur Muhammad, 476, 478–481, 490–491, 502
Tarun, Sayed Daoud, 490–491
"Tashkent line," 526
Tătărescu, Gheorghe, 92–93
Taubman, William, 649
Taylor, Maxwell, 304–306
Tehran Conference (1943), 24, 498
Teltschik, Horst, 582–583
Thailand
  Duan and, 347
  North Vietnam and, 347
  PRC and, 498
  USSR and, 347–348
Thatcher, Margaret, 525, 540, 572
Thieu, Nguyen Van, 346
third world. *See also specific country*
  Communist movements downplayed in, 157–158
  Gorbachev and, 559
  ideology and Soviet interest in, 471–472
  Khrushchev and, 157–159, 167, 252, 594
  Kosygin and, 596
  Mao and, 158–159, 227–228
  recognition and Soviet interest in, 472
  security and Soviet interest in, 472
  Soviet opportunism in, 473
  Stalin and, 156–158

754

INDEX

Tho, Le Duc, 350, 354
Thompson, Llewellyn "Tommy," 215, 233, 257
Thorez, Maurice, 87–89, 91
Thucydides, 368
Tito, Josip Broz
  Albania and, 81–82, 96–97
  Brezhnev and, 373
  Bulgaria and, 81, 97–99
  Chinese criticism of, 124
  Churchill and, 80
  Cominform and, 92
  election of, 620
  generally, 69
  Greece and, 81
  Khrushchev and, 160, 201–202
  Kosovo and, 81, 82
  life of, 80
  Macedonia and, 81
  Mao compared, 121–122
  "mini-USSR," plans for creating, 81–82
  Molotov and, 99
  Nasser and, 163
  Nixon and, 373
  split with Stalin, 95–101, 107–108
  Stalin and, 82, 95–101, 107–108
  Zhdanov and, 96
Togliatti, Palmiro, 87
Tolubeev, Nikita, 448
Töre, Ali Khan, 31, 36–37
Treaty on Conventional Forces in Europe (1990), 600
Trilateral Commission, 458
Tripolitania
  London Conference and, 54–57
  Molotov and, 52
  Moscow Foreign Ministers Conference and, 65
  Stalin and, 52
Troyanovsky, Oleg, 257, 298–299
Truman, Harry S.
  accession to Presidency, 41
  Churchill and, 78
  former Italian colonies and, 53
  Greece and, 83–84
  Gromyko and, 41

  Harriman and, 41–42
  Hokkaido and, 47–49
  Iran and, 73–74
  Korean War and, 137–139
  Molotov and, 42
  NSC-68 and, 138
  nuclear weapons and, 44, 46–47
  Poland and, 42–44
  at Potsdam Conference, 44
  Republic of China and, 114
  Soviet–American relations and, 41–42
  Stalin and, 66–67, 594
  Taiwan and, 131
Truman doctrine, 83–85, 108–109
Tsaldaris, Konstantinos, 83
Tsedenbal, Yumjaagiin, 244
Tshombe, Moïse, 264–265
Turkey
  American bases in, 296, 318
  Bevin and, 73
  Castro and, 321
  coup in, 296
  Cuban Missile Crisis, linkage with, 304, 318–321, 326, 327
  Cyprus and, 428–430
  Khrushchev and, 296, 309, 654
  Litvinov and, 18, 20
  Maisky and, 18
  Molotov and, 73
  in NATO, 146
  Potsdam Conference and, 73
  Soviet setback in, 69, 80
  Stalin and, 72–73, 80, 593, 594
  straits, Soviet intentions regarding, 72–73
  UK and, 73
  United States and, 73
Turner, Stansfield, 692
Tuva, annexation of, 32
Twining, Nathan D., 223

U-2 spy planes, 255–259, 303–304
Ukraine
  coup in, 601
  Crimea, Russian annexation of, 601
  NATO and, 591
  Russian invasion of, 602

755

INDEX

Ulbricht, Walter
- Berlin Crisis and, 233, 281, 282, 293
- Berlin Wall and, 286, 290, 293
- economic situation in East Germany and, 231, 232
- generally, 234
- Khrushchev and, 232, 236–237, 243, 286–287
- Mao and, 286–287
- Soviet aid and, 243, 281
- as Stalinist, 147
- uprising in East Germany and, 149
- USSR and, 147, 148

Ulunian, Artiom, 84

United Kingdom
- colonies of, 49–50
- Cyprus and, 428–429
- Falklands War and, 525
- four-power summit and, 253
- Greece and, 84
- Iran, Russian rivalry with regarding, 70–71
- Jordan and, 210, 220
- "Keep Left" group, 93
- Labour Party, 86, 92, 93
- Litvinov and, 18
- Maisky and, 18
- Mao and, 205
- Molotov and, 93
- peace efforts in Chinese civil war, 115–116
- Poland and, 43
- PRC, diplomatic recognition of, 130, 131
- sanctions against USSR and, 524
- Sino-Soviet Treaty of Alliance (1950), impact of, 127
- Stalin and, 93–94
- Suez Crisis and, 164, 166–167, 195
- Turkey and, 73
- Yugoslavia and, 80

United Nations
- Chiang, expulsion of, 132
- Hungary and, 196
- Iran Hostage Crisis, sanctions proposal, 495–497
- Khrushchev and, 264–267
- Mao and, 267
- Molotov and, 42

"shoe banging" incident, 266, 267, 649
Yom Kippur War and, 404, 412–414, 419

United States
- Afghanistan and, 490, 492, 601
- Africa and, 472–473
- Amin and, 479
- Angola and, 441, 448–449
- bombing of US Marine barracks in Lebanon, 535
- Brezhnev and, 340, 375, 381
- Bulgaria and, 63, 599
- Cambodia, invasion of, 347, 349–350
- Castro and, 488–489
- Central Intelligence Agency (CIA)
  - Afghanistan and, 478, 554
  - Cuba and, 303
  - Iran and, 487–488
  - Khomeini and, 487–488
  - Yom Kippur War and, 397, 418, 420
- Chiang and, 119
- Chile, US-backed coup in, 487
- China Aid Act, 114
- Cold War, role in, 106
- Communist Party (CPUSA), 175
- Cuba and, 277, 488–489
- Cuban Missile Crisis and
  - airstrikes as possible response, 305–306
  - ExComm debates, 304–306
  - quarantine of Cuba, 312–314
  - Soviet missiles in Cuba, 303
  - U-2 spy planes and, 303–304
- Czech Republic and, 599
- Deng and, 459–460, 462, 483, 527
- four-power summit and, 253
- Germany and, 101
- grain embargo against USSR, 503, 521
- Greece and, 83–84
- Grenada, invasion of, 535
- Iran, Russian rivalry with regarding, 71
- Iran Hostage Crisis. *See* Iran Hostage Crisis
- Iraq and, 209, 601
- Italy, US bases in, 296
- Jackson–Vanik amendment, 432, 433
- Japan and, 146
- Jinmen and Mazu islands and, 223–224
- Khrushchev and, 12, 203–204, 237–241, 595–596

756

INDEX

Korean War and, 136–139
Laos, invasion of, 347
Lebanon and, 210, 219, 220, 535
Maisky and, 20
Mao and, 120–121, 205, 227, 238
Middle East and, 396
Mikoyan and, 120–121, 233–234
military power in Mediterranean, 405
missiles in Europe, 502, 507–508, 529–530, 533, 535, 548, 550
National Security Council, 131, 136, 138, 214, 523
Norway, US bases in, 296
NSC-48, 131, 136
NSC-68, 138
Olympic Games, boycott of, 503
Pakistan, US bases in, 296
peace efforts in Chinese civil war, 115–116
Poland and, 43, 599
PRC, relations with, 124–125, 458–459, 462, 471, 499–500
President's Foreign Intelligence Advisory Board (PFIAB), 536
Putin and, 599–600
quarantine of Cuba, 312–314
Republic of China, relations with, 114–115, 120–121
Romania and, 63, 599
Sadat and, 396
sanctions against USSR, 524, 537
Sino-Soviet Treaty of Alliance (1950), impact of, 127, 131
Soviet expansionism and, 66
Strategic Defense Initiative (SDI), 531, 549, 551, 552, 702–703
Suez Crisis and, 166–167, 195
Taiwan and, 131, 527–529
Taiwan Relations Act, 462, 528
troops in Republic of China, 116
Turkey and, 73
Vietnam War and
  authorization of, 333
  cessation of bombing, 346
  credibility as motivation for, 494
  defeat in, 449
  escalation of, 341–342
  losses in, 341, 347

  resumption of bombing, 351, 378, 379
  "Vietnamization," 347
  Watergate scandal, 389–391, 401, 409–410, 422
  Yom Kippur War and, 401–402, 415–416
USS Maddox, 333
USSR. *See specific topic*
Ustinov, Dmitry
  Afghanistan and, 490, 493, 522, 554
  arms control and, 531–533
  Carter and, 455
  Iran Hostage Crisis and, 496
  Poland and, 512–516, 520
  policy making by, 507

Vafeiadis, Markos, 84, 100–101
Vance, Cyrus
  Afghanistan and, 488
  Brezhnev and, 456
  Brezhnev–Carter summit and, 489
  Carter and, 489
  Chernyaev and, 457
  Dobrynin and, 455, 461, 488, 489
  Gromyko and, 457
  Kissinger and, 457
  PRC and, 458, 461
Varennikov, Valentin, 494
Vashugin, Nikolai, 289–292
Vienna Summit (1961), 284–286
Vietnam. *See also* North Vietnam; South Vietnam
  Cambodia, invasion of, 474, 481–482
  Carter and, 498
  Chinese invasion of, 474, 482–484
  Eastern Cominform and, 120
  Gorbachev and, 559
  PCF and, 88
  PRC and
    generally, 499
    invasion of, 474, 482–484
    Vietnam War, 331, 336–340, 343–345
  Soviet aid to, 358
  treaty with USSR, 482
Vietnam War
  Brezhnev and
    generally, 355–357, 374
    Nixon and, 345–346, 350–351

757

INDEX

Vietnam War (cont.)
   peace talks, 342–343
   PRC and, 340, 344
   Southeast Asia, outlook for, 347–348
   Soviet military aid, 338
  CCP and, 338
  Deng and, 343
  Dobrynin and, 346, 352
  Dong, Pham Van and, 342
  Easter Offensive, 350–351
  fall of Saigon, 354, 435
  Ho Chi Minh and, 343, 344
  human casualties in, 343
  Johnson, Lyndon B. and, 331, 341–343, 346
  Kissinger and, 352, 354, 450
  Kosygin and, 338–339, 344, 347–348
  Mao and, 336–339, 344, 355, 357
  Nixon and, 345–347, 350–351, 378, 379
  Operation "Rolling Thunder," 341, 351
  peace talks in, 342–346, 354
  as "people's war," 344
  PRC and, 331, 336–340, 343–345
  as Soviet victory, 331–332, 358
  Suslov and, 344
  Tet Offensive, 345, 357
  United States and
   authorization of, 333
   cessation of bombing, 346
   credibility as motivation for, 494
   defeat in, 449
   escalation of, 341–342
   losses in, 341, 347
   resumption of bombing, 351, 378, 379
   "Vietnamization," 347
  USSR, importance to, 331
  Viet Cong, 346–347
  Zhou and, 337–340, 343–344, 348
Vinogradov, Vladimir
  Afghanistan and, 495
  Iran Hostage Crisis and, 488
  Khomeini and, 487
  Pahlavi (Shah) and, 486
  Sadat and, 394, 399, 409, 411, 424
  Yom Kippur War and, 400, 414
Vorontsov, Yuly, 413–414
Voroshilov, Klement, 155, 212–213
Vyshinsky, Andrei, 40–42, 131–132

Wadsworth, James J., 266
Wałęsa, Lech, 510, 513, 518
Wallace, Henry, 41
Wang Bingnan, 307
Wang Jiaxiang, 179–180, 307, 308
Wang Ming, 245
Wang Shijie, 54
Warsaw Pact
  Albania in, 263, 290
  Czechoslovakia in, 360
  establishment of, 150
  Gorbachev and, 566, 584–585
  Hungary in, 196
  Prague Spring, crushing of, 361
Washington, George, 177
Watergate scandal, 389–391, 401, 409–410, 422
Watson, Thomas J., 459, 461
Weinberger, Caspar, 520–521, 524
West Germany
  Brezhnev and, 366–372, 387–388
  Bundesnachrichtendienst (BND), 303
  Chernyaev and, 371
  Cuban Missile Crisis and, 303
  establishment of, 105
  Gromyko and, 369
  Khrushchev and, 232
  in NATO, 146, 150, 170
  Ostpolitik, 366, 369–372, 388
  sanctions against USSR and, 524
  Social Democratic Party (SPD), 371,
    372, 667
  trade with USSR, 374
Westad, Odd Arne, 5, 439–440, 471–472,
    494, 501–502
Wettig, Gerhard, 105
"whataboutism," 7, 45, 455
Williams, William Appleman, 106
World Congress of Peace-loving Forces, 420
World Federation of Trade Unions, 260–261
Wu Xiuquan, 324

Xia Yafeng, 210
Xoxe, Koçi, 96, 100

Yakovlev, Aleksandr, 552, 574, 585
Yalta Conference (1945)
  Churchill at, 24, 26, 29–30

758

INDEX

generally, 37
Germany and, 25–27
Harriman and, 33, 40
importance of, 38
Litvinov and, 30–31
Maisky and, 30–31
Poland and, 27–31
Republic of China and, 31–37
Roosevelt at, 24, 26, 29–30
Stalin at, 24–31
Yanukovych, Viktor, 601
Yazdi, Ebrahim, 487–488
Yazov, Dmitry, 584
Ye Fei, 224
Yeltsin, Boris
attack on Parliament by, 590
as chairman of the Supreme Soviet, 583
Chechen war and, 590–591
Clinton and, 591–592
NATO and, 591
political power of, 588
reelection of, 589
resignation of, 599
Yemen
Khrushchev and, 160–161
Soviet aid to, 324
Soviet Navy and, 392
Yi Sang-jo, 184–185
Yom Kippur War
advance notice of, 400
Algeria and, 405, 406
Andropov and, 415, 418
Assad and, 399, 400
Brezhnev and
ceasefire efforts, 403, 406
DEFCOM 3 alert level, 416
evacuation of Soviet civilians, 400–401
generally, 401, 418
Israeli advances in, 413–414
Kissinger and, 398, 410–412
Nixon and, 407–408, 419
Sadat and, 402
Syria and, 417
ultimatum from, 414–415
ceasefire efforts, 403–405, 407–409
ceasefire in, 412, 419

Chernenko and, 415, 416, 418
Chernyaev and, 417–418, 423, 430
CIA and, 397, 418, 420
Cuban Missile Crisis compared, 420
DEFCOM 3 alert level, 415–416, 419, 421
detente with West and, 426
direct Soviet involvement, danger of, 406–407
Dobrynin and
ceasefire efforts, 402, 403, 408, 409
"deceit" in, 413–414
direct Soviet involvement, danger of, 406–407
generally, 400, 402
Kissinger and, 400, 402, 409, 415, 422
Nixon and, 416
Soviet observers and, 416–417
threats of other nations to enter, 405
Egyptian missiles in, 418
generally, 393
Gromyko and, 411, 413, 415, 416, 418
Haig and, 415, 421
Israeli advances in, 408–409, 411, 412–414
Jordan and, 405, 406
KGB and, 418
Kissinger and
Brezhnev and, 398, 410–412
ceasefire efforts, 402, 403, 408, 409
direct Soviet involvement, danger of, 406–407
Dobrynin and, 400, 402, 409, 415, 422
generally, 400–402
Moscow negotiations, 409–412
stalemate in, 407
threats of other nations to enter, 405
Kosygin and, 408–409
loss of weaponry in, 400–401
Morocco and, 407
Nixon and, 403, 407–408, 412, 416, 419
PRC and, 402–403
Sadat and
advance notice of, 400
Brezhnev and, 402
ceasefire efforts, 403–405

759

INDEX

Yom Kippur War (cont.)
    Israeli advances in, 408–409,
        411, 414
    launching of, 399
    uncertainty regarding, 402
  Soviet observers and, 416–417
  stalemate in, 407
  Suslov and, 413
  UN and, 404, 412–414, 419
  United States and, 401–402, 415–416
  Vinogradov and, 400, 414
Yudin, Pavel, 211, 215–217, 256
Yugoslavia
  Castro and, 276
  challenges from, 146
  in Cominform, 96, 100
  Mao and, 181, 201–202
  percentages agreement and, 23
  Soviet "loss" of, 69
  Stalin and, 85
  UK and, 80
  withdrawal of Soviet experts from, 262
Yun Kong-hum, 184

Zachariadis, Nikos, 84, 98, 100
Zahir Shah (Afghanistan), 476, 486
Zaire, Angola and, 441, 443, 446
Zakharov, Matvei, 299, 301
Zhang Wentian, 179–180
Zhao Ziyang, 565
Zhdanov, Andrei
  Cominform and, 96
  France and, 91–92
  Italy and, 91–92
  Marshall Plan and, 91
  on PCF, 88, 91
  Tito and, 96
  "two camps" and, 90–91
Zhirinovsky, Vladimir, 590
Zhivkov, Todor, 467–468, 516, 544, 562

Zhou Enlai
  Chinese Eastern Railroad and, 140, 141
  Cuba and, 278–279
  defense cooperation with USSR and, 211
  Dong, Pham Van and, 343–344
  Great Leap Forward and, 242
  international Communist movement and,
    242–243
  Jinmen and Mazu islands and, 224–225
  Khrushchev and, 247, 292
  Kissinger and, 499
  Korean War and, 140
  Kosygin and, 348, 362–363, 368
  Malinovsky and, 335–336
  Mao and, 205–206, 275
  Mikoyan and, 119
  Moscow Conference (1960) and, 274
  Nasser and, 162
  Nehru and, 306–307
  Nixon and, 350, 378
  Sino-Indian War and, 246, 256, 259,
    306–307
  Sino-Soviet Treaty of Alliance (1950) and,
    127, 129, 132–134
  technology and, 178
  Vietnam War and, 337–340, 343–344, 348
Zhu De, 176, 179, 636
Zhukov, Georgy
  Beria and, 148
  Eisenhower and, 155
  Hungary and, 195
  Khrushchev and, 200
  Mao and, 201
  nuclear weapons and, 154, 155
  Suez Crisis and, 165
Zhukov, Yury, 381
Zilliacus, Konni, 93
Zolotov, L.A., 172
Zubok, Vladislav, 4–5, 382, 584
Žujović, Sreten, 98–99